A LASTING CALM

Joy Esterby, Editor

THE INTERNATIONAL LIBRARY OF POETRY

A Lasting Calm

ISBN 1-57553-449-5

Printing and Binding by
BPC Wheatons Ltd, Exeter, UK

Editor's Note

One of the greatest strengths of poetry is its compact nature. Making this work of art concise is also one of the greatest challenges to the developing poet. One needs to know what information is extraneous and what is essential. The words and images a poet uses thus become powerful tools to be chosen carefully as each adds a different implication, tone or colour to the piece as a whole. A poet accomplishes much more with one word or phrase than simply furthering the literal level of his poem's meaning.

For instance, in Paul Hooper's poem "Long Sundays And Lonely Friends" (p. 314), the families are "cozy in candy coats". The word "candy" seems a rather peculiar description for coats; immediately readers derive connotations from their experience to connect with the word "candy". Candy can be thought of as sweet, sugary, bad for the teeth, an indulgence, artificial in colour and flavour. When the readers combine all these connotations, they discover that Hooper's description is an effective characterisation of the families.

In addition, the poet must supply a message for the poem, ensuring that all the words and images and their connotations work together cohesively towards accomplishing this theme. Paul Hooper's poem, as it states in its last line, is a commentary on "hypocrisy and its cost". To enhance this theme, Hooper uses words such as "tawdry", "smug", "supercilious" and "pompous", and images such as "papier-maché people", "suburbia [vomiting] life", "evergreen mums" and "sunny boys". The tone is cynical and sarcastic, and all is executed within a compact five-stanza, rhyming poem.

Many other poets within this anthology are deserving of special recognition for meeting the poet's challenge and creating exceptional works of art.

Derek Pluck's "Wilderness" (p. 309) is a riveting study into the state of our selves and our relationships when we grow old carelessly. Pluck uses the common picture of a middle-aged couple living in suburbia to warn the "average" readers about the way their lives can decay. The metaphor of vegetation, representing our lives, is consistently maintained throughout the poem so that we may easily follow where the poem leads. The poem effectively describes the transformation which has occurred in this ordinary couple's life:

> . . . [O]ur lives [have] grown so unkempt with empty
> Promises to each other and ourselves,
> That a hopeless wilderness has sprung up
> Between us - rampant with dry dead wood -
> Diseased from years of neglect.

The couple's "ordered suburb garden", a carefully tended source of pride for the couple, has become almost "absurd" because it is merely a facade for the disordered state of their life.

Pluck suggests that when they were young the couple was full of hopes and dreams and love; their lives bloomed with colourful flowers. Now, fear has replaced hope and the future is bleak. Pluck then instructs that some "judicious pruning" of their vegetation could have maintained the couple's emotional health:

> *For us, cosmetic thinning, rather than*
> *Green buds of new beginning; for years*
> *We've hedged our bets, uneasy that some*
> *Future Autumn will find us leafless of ideas.*

By concentrating on the "cosmetic" appearance of their lives and their relationship, the couple has avoided dealing with their individual and mutual problems. Thus, their lives have become stagnant and useless.

In his poem "The Kinsfolk" (p. 90), Robert Lindsay communicates a similar warning for the future using consistent religious imagery. In this situation, the characters' lives are mired in what is hinted to be religious conflict. The persona's mother has died, and her relatives have come to mourn her death:

> *We didn't send, they knew that she had died.*
> *And so they brought brown eggs, gifts from afar,*
> *They said the griddle bread, the butter churned today,*
> *Was as she knew it.*
> *I looked for a star.*

The kinsfolk are likened to the three wise men of the Christmas story; somehow they know to come without receiving the news directly and they bring three gifts, in this case, eggs, bread and butter. After speaking with the relatives the persona sees a revealing vision:

> *The mystic dream was born and she was there*
> *With clogs, in lamplight, on an earthen floor;*
> *The orphan donkey, standing near,*
> *And Christ not very far.*

The kinsfolk inspire within the persona an image of his mother as she must have looked when she lived in her country home. The image is serene and appropriately religious; the persona realises that beyond their "animosities" and "feuds", his mother and her kinsfolk really had much in common regarding their religious beliefs. Yet, Lindsay subtly suggests that the family conflict may continue, when the persona says, "Father forgive them now that mother's dead." Though he is willing to forgive, the persona is also indicating, perhaps unwittingly, that he believes the blame for the conflict lies with the kinsfolk. Lindsay is warning us to resolve our family conflicts before their effects are perpetuated.

Another fascinating piece dealing with the inner workings of the human mind is Anthony Smyth's "Intimations From A Witness" (p. 47). Smyth uses the movement of air in nature to describe a witness's complex relationship to truth. The persona has witnessed some event unknown to the reader and is now in a natural setting trying to decide upon the "truth" of what he saw. Nature seems to talk to him:

> Speak with a tranquil heart
>   or remain silent.
> Quiet voices rattle whispers
> Through ears of broad-leaved maize,
> And the busy tongues of leaves
> Cluster green conversations
> In the groves along a foot way.

At the same time, Nature seems to be withholding the truth from him. Smyth speaks of the "secret breath", the "quiet voices" and the "Hidden breath" found in nature and draws us to the conclusion that "All the touches of truth / are tentative". A witness's clear vision of the truth often seems to pass like the wind. The images within this poem are crisp and can easily be seen *and heard* in the reader's mind. Alliteration adds to these sounds. The result is a well-constructed, extraordinary work of art.

Another excellent display of craftsmanship is the grand prize winner of the competition associated with *A Lasting Calm*. Emeka Obiandu's "Justice And Power" won high honour for its powerfully concise and cogent depiction of the authentic traits of a good leader. Obiandu cautions us to be careful when searching for a leader; there are very few who are truly worthy:

> Among all men search still,
> For those few men of power,
> Battered and scarred in common fights,
> Yet whose biceps twitch and dilate,
> And from whose pores and wounds
> Ooze litres of brine and blood,
> As they fight for the powerless.

In short, the men Obiandu considers deserving of power are men who, in positions of power, have been tried in conflict and have worked hard, despite strong opposition, for what they believe is right. These are men whose very hearts and souls have fought and are fighting still for justice.

There are several other poems featured within this anthology which you will not want to miss: "The Sketcher At Lukov" (p. 527) by Gregory Jones, "Lieutenant Deathword" (p. 390) by Barry Mansfield, "Sonnet to November" (p. 115) by Doris M. H. Brownlee and Meriona Armstrong's "Becoming Me" (p. 345). In fact, there are too many excellent poems to name in the space I have. All poets whose work is contained within the pages of *A Lasting Calm* should be proud of their accomplishments.

Acknowledgements

I would like to say a special thanks to those who have made *A Lasting Calm* possible. The editors, assistant editors, judges, graphic designers, and customer service representatives have all brought their talents to bear on this project and I sincerely appreciate their assistance.

Joy L. Esterby
Editor

iv

Winners of the International Open Amateur Poetry Contest

Grand Prize Winner

Emeka Obiandu / London

Second Prize Winners

Meriona Armstrong / North Yorkshire

L. D. Hardman / Greater Manchester

Debra Hunston / North Wales

Graham Hunt / Suffolk

Gregory Jones / Oulu

Robert Lindsay / Belfast

Rosie Major / Hampshire

Barry Mansfield / Surrey

Derek J. Pluck / Lancashire

Anthony Smyth / Gwent

Third Prize Winners

Frederica Arulanandom / Greater Manchester

S. Ashford / Isle of Man

M. Atkinson / East Yorkshire

Elizabeth Beale / Bedfordshire

Graham R. Bell / Yorkshire

Thomas B. Besch / Sussex

Brian Blackwell / Leeds

Jessica Brown / Northamptonshire

Doris M. H. Brownlee / Gloucestershire

Rosaleen Clarke / Belfast

Maureen Cropley / Avon

Thomas Dade / West Yorkshire

Joyce M. Drackett-Case / Newtownabbey

Carolyn A. Drury / Nottinghamshire

Christopher Dunn / Nizonne

Derrick D. Dunn / Birmingham

Maurice Ebbage / Beverley

Chris Fell / Gloucestershire

Tess Good-O'Brien / Co. Waterford

Angela Gregory / Avon

Mary C. Hastie / Surrey

Kathryn Hodgkinson-Szommer / Tasmania

Karen V. Hodgson / Chorley

Andrew G. Homfray / Dorset

Paul Hooper / Kent

Viola Hughes / Co. Antrim

Karl Hulme / Dorset

J. Onslow Johnson / Gloucestershire

Owen D. Jones / Derbyshire

Christopher Kewell / Devon

G. B. Langley / Berkshire

Lynda A. Liddell / East Yorkshire

Maureen Love / Lanarkshire

Maria B. Lynch / London

Sheila Manley / Coventry

Michael J. McGlynn / Co. Offaly

James McHenry / Avon

G. McKeown / Fenfrewshire

Anne Melling / Leicestershire

Stephanie Metcalf / Berkshire

Pauline Palmer / Surrey

Alf Parry / Leicestershire

Dean Poland / London

R. J. Radley / London

Robert W. Reed / Kent

Oscar Guardiola Rivera / Aberdeenshire

Joanne Robins / Norfolk

Brian Rysdale / Gwent

Shiv Sharma / Cheshire

E. R. Skinner / London

N. Smith / Cornwall

John Stephenson / Tyne & Wear

Paul R. Taylor / Shropshire

Gregory P. Udeh / Surrey

Ann P. Vesey-FitzGerald / Hampshire

Dorothy White / Clydebank

Iris M. Willis / Middlesex

Craig M. Wood / Lancashire

G. A. Youldon-Hockey / South Glamorgan

Congratulations also to all semi-finalists.

Justice And Power

Say not of the untried,
Though tested in battle,
"Here's a man, a good man.
Encamped with the oppressed
He does injustice to none.
Had the world many like him."

Among all men search still,
For those few men of power,
Battered and scarred in common fights,
Yet whose biceps twitch and dilate,
And from whose pores and wounds
Ooze litres of brine and blood,
As they fight for the powerless.
Search for those
Whose roads are strewn
With the clean bones of injustice,
And whose corridors are littered
With the fresh bodies
Of nascent injustice.
To the world recommend these few.

Emeka Obiandu

One Summer's Day

Babbling, Sabbath afternoon,
Crazy wasps wrestling the breeze,
Mother's peeling back eye lids to search for pesky flies,
The warm milk swilling a wink as the early crocus dies.

Toy poodle boys thrashing the relaxed pond with sprints,
Diving at the blind depths from jagged, platform rocks,
Washed in mammoth fall that endless water weeps,
The mossy emerald velvet locks.

Come the fringe of circus day when sulks the fading sun to half,
Patios swept of paper plates and menthol cigarette filter tips,
Sister's gone to steal strawbs from the fridge, and heavenly junket,
Still to set, that wicked child, she sips.

And as the rotting potting shed stretches deep its earthly shadow,
As the coiled dog lies resting in his master's chair,
The blood-blister serenade of mewling toms and happy queens,
Twist cork screws in the evening air.

Fully pumped, the Jack Russel jumps, then scrats, then sniffs
At the crease of light sifting through the basement door,
While the wireless yawns some old, jazz tune,
By the light of Able's Hardware Store.

Thomas Dade

Bristol Blitz 1942

All vanished in a night. One flash
Of Empyrean flame, bright lit
By torch hell drawn of Lucifer,
And these the charred remains.

Fire-blackened men, haggard of cheek,
With dark rimmed bloodshot eyes,
Unconquered yet, probe silently and grim
Among an indeterminate rubbled mass
For something that might live.

And stretcher bearers now their formless loads
Raise in procession over widening cracks
To slide them on the shiny ordered racks
Of waiting vehicles, that swiftly move
Their battered cargo from the scene of death.
Come now the vultures—grey reconnaissance,
Gloat on the wreckage, on the dark stained soil
Of this our city's heart. Its pulse beats on,
And fresh renewed within its fecund veins,
The Bristol blood flows free. Its spirit, Phoenix crowned,
   Is rising yet.

Vera Baxter

Subject: Caring

Who cares for the old folk? You too, will become old
Do you not feel compassion, nor your arms yet enfold
Those sad and hurting, left alone with the strife
Having lost their partner, not wanting to carry on with life

Sometimes no daughters to help, nor sons to carry their name
Is there really a purpose, they feel, or is life a game?
The ones loved least, or sometimes not at all
Are the really old, forgetful, impatient, awaiting their "call"

No one to really care, whether they live, or tomorrow die
Yet they fought wars for our freedom, left all alone to sigh
What a waste! Their true tales the mind will surely thrill
Those taking time to know them, they're not "run of the mill"

The "old folk" taught us manners, values, often our prayers too
Is there someone you can reach out to? One day it will be you!
Old folk are wise, love to give advice, so caring as well
Knowledge lost, if not shared, when on earth they cease to dwell

Wake up your compassion, your love and your soul
Help today, our old folk, make this your goal
Love is a wonderful gift, which you must give away, not hide
God promises its return, many times, multiplied.

Julie Bryan

Poetry Is My Life

Poetry is my life, my dreams and aspirations,
My sadness and my joy, my soul and inspirations,
Life is meaningless without it,
I live to pick up my pen and write,
The emotions surge through me, like a river,
At the end of the tunnel poetry is light.
It stays with me through pain and sorrow,
Through joy and happiness,
Poetry is my dream and my ambitions, poetry is zest.
Poetry never leaves me,
It is the very air I breathe.
It was my special gift in life,
And it is all that I believe.
It is my friend when I am alone.
It is my teacher when I do not understand,
It is my emotion and my faults,
Poetry is my right hand.
Poetry is my strength and my weakness.
It is my love, and my pain.
It is my condemner and my saviour, and for it, I live in vain.

Elizabeth Ann Hobbs

Orphan

I live in a war zone
I am just seven years old
I should be out enjoying myself
Playing in the sun
But we have to hide in the cellar all day
As the shells rain all around
The noise is quite deafening
It's a wonder we can hear at all
I was out collecting water
When a shell fell upon our house
Now I have no Family
I am all alone
I cannot cry
The tears are all inside
What is to become of me
Now that I have no family

Imelda Graham

A Journey To Inner Space

The music exploded with one massive sound,
mounting up in the air, rumbling down and down,
bouncing on the floor from the left to the right,
waving and rocking from side to side.

It entered their bodies, penetrating each bone and
Like a cosmic rocket set them off to the twilight zone.
With long, easy strides they danced away in the space,
moving their hips around and curving their waists.

Jumping up and down, pirouetting on the heel,
they were slowly absorbed by an aerial whirl.
Touching the Moon, reached the climax of ecstasy,
which accomplish their journey to all night fantasy.

Margaret Carrick

Writing Poetry

Writing a poem words flow with ease
Choose subject wisely then it will please.
Flatter a friend or slag off a foe,
You don't have to show them - no one will know!

Write about daydreams - your hopes and your fears
Write about sad things - leave them in tears.
Make jokes and cause laughter and fun for them all.
Make love to the reader - then give him a call.

The words that you write - make secret or not.
They are mostly outpourings that hit the spot.
The best mental therapy that I've ever found
Are my outpourings on paper, keeping mind sound!

Pamela Duley

Arthritis

With her twisted limbs and aching joints,
I watch her shuffle past.
She lifts her stick and points.
I pray her suffering can't last.

Remission's due, I feel quite sure.
Her suffering for a while shall ease
No more pain, tomorrow to endure.
An answer to a prayer, please.

Yet never a complaint I hear.
No self pity and no tears.
She struggles through each day without fear,
Indeed she seldom shares her fears.

Perhaps soon a drug shall be found
That'll cure this terrible disease.
Or at lease make it easier to get around,
Reducing the pain in elbows, hips and knees.

Some days I struggle, unable to bear
The sight of her suffering, it is so great.
Sometimes I think it is so unfair,
And then, it is myself I hate.

William Frazer

My Doris

Without her here, I feel so alone
There are people around me
But there's no-one home.
I have no more days, only one long night
And I can't find my way
For I have lost my light.

I long to feel her warm embrace,
To hear her voice once more
Or see her smiling face.
Just to have a reason to carry on
Because my love for her burns
Even though she's gone.

As I begin my life alone, why does it hurt so?
Friends say "Time will heal"
But for me time passes slow.
Therefore, I must re-assure myself
She suffers no more pain
And that my deepest loss
Is now heaven's greatest gain.

C. A. Stapleton

Just You

It doesn't cost you anything
To smile and say 'Hello'
To listen for a minute
To another's tale of woe.

Or perhaps they're feeling happy
And have no-one else to tell
Have you thought they might be lonely
Withdrawn in their shell?

Perhaps they'd like a helping hand
But are too proud to ask
You too, can get such happiness
From such a little task.

Try to see the good - not bad
In others that you meet
Spread a little happiness
The whole world's at your feet.

You wake up tired - it's cold, it's wet
And you are feeling blue
Say "Thank you God, another day
I'll do my best for you".

A. M. Hoad

Aftermath For A Child

Waking up. School today, hooray! Getting dressed, breakfast, watch
TV. Walking, running, skipping. Hello friends. Here's my teacher.
PE. Great. Where's my bag? Here are my shoes. Everyone in the
gym. The world explodes. Noise, shouts, everyone crying. Gun.
Bang—is that the noise? Still. Everything quiet.

Noise again. People crying. Policeman. Ambulance man. Police lady
holding my hand. Doctors. Teachers. I want my Mummy. Daddy help
me. Where is my teddy? I hurt, don't touch me, what's happening?
People looking at me, doing things. I'm frightened. Where am I? Why
are they crying? What happened? I remember. I want my Mummy.

Hospital is fun. The boy makes me laugh. Everyone stops talking.
What did I do? Cameras, lights, people, it's exciting. Mummy wants
to hold my hand. Daddy isn't tickling me. Tell me a joke Daddy.
When can I go to school? Please talk to me, tell me what's happening
Here is a picture. I am draw. This is the man. He's got a gun.

Bang, my arm hurts. Where is he? Will he come again? These are my
friends. Where are they now? Did you see the blood? Was it real?
I like my teacher. Mummy says I will have a new teacher. Will she like me?

Can she tell stories? I don't want to go to sleep. I've got
pictures in my head. I can draw them. Talk to me. Tall me I'm
alright. Do you love me? Was I good? Will it happen again?

Helen Kenward

Dad's Green House

My Dad had a greenhouse, that he loved very much,
He spent a lot of time in it when he retired, growing flowers tomatoes and such.
He worked away in his greenhouse even when it was freezing cold,
which proved to be too much for him, as he grew old.
And when he died quite suddenly in December last year.
I could almost here him saying "please don't leave my greenhouse here."

So when the funeral was over, I thought what can I do,
Until the rest of the family said "take it home with you."

So we got a nice man with a van to transport it carefully,
And brought it home to our garden, where it was rebuilt so painstakingly,
And now we grow our own produce think of the money that we save,
And I am sure sometimes when I look out at it in
The garden dad gives me a little wave.

Maureen Arnold

Daylight Summer and Dark Sound

There is an intense silence in the wood
but for the cooing of doves and the chattering of pigeons
The watery mirror of the stream reflects the bright hot sun
When the Earth is at night asleep the singing of the birds will be far away
And the broken silence of the Summer's day
will by the hooting owl be in dark sound withstood
The flowers and moon-daisies are then, in time, of every flowery hour
Up until full-bloom measured in sequence by each closed
and opening and opened, growing and grown flower, leaf and bud.

David John Scott

The Wall

A dreamy maiden strolls my mind a thousand times a day
I've tried so hard to make her stop, I've tried to make her stay.
But she's as free as any breeze, she journeys through her dreams,
I'd never want to hold her down, I know how much it means.

If only we could be as one and share eternal pleasure;
that would be the time to die, that's something you can't measure.

Though love is not the right word, it seems much more than that,
For what we have is tigeresque, whilst love a pussycat.

Unless you cross the frontier and free your mind and soul,
You'll never find a meaning, you'll never find a goal.
Forget about the outer shell you have to climb inside,
And once you're there immerse yourself in every thing you find.

Seek ye all things beautiful and hold them in your mind,
For these are all your building blocks, to build the wall you climb.

Andy Barnes

Alone

A withering hand reaching,
towards that light of day
A power from within coercing with strength.
A mind fighting out against an estranged mankind.
Everyone looks,
although their eyes I cannot see.
Everyone laughs,
although a tear I can only taste.
A portrait of a beast, a voice unspoken, a sight unseen.
My beauty is within,
far beneath this strange exterior,
yet your eyes don't care to stretch that far.
For within my heart,
I feel the laughter, the crying, the humour, the heartaches.
Why am I different if I feel all your love and pain.
Don't push me aside,
don't push me away
I cannot bear to be alone,
for a friend is all I need,
let me grasp that light at the end of my day.

Lisa N. Charles

My Garden

The blackbird arrives in my garden each day,
Sitting on the fence it has a lot to say.
Looking at the window if there is no food,
Then looking away trying not to be rude.

Under a large bush his wife I do see,
Keeping an eye on a magpie in the tree.
Beneath this bush seems her favourite place,
It's there I put food that pleases her taste.

The magpie flies upon its mischievous way,
There is no hurry, he has all day.
A tiny bird in the roses I see,
Why, Dear Jenny Wren it happens to be.

Young sparrows in the bird bath do splash,
This peace in my garden I hope will last.
The birds seem happy to come here to feed,
I only hope that they get what they need.

Although I feed the birds every day,
They always repay me in their own way.
Green fly on my roses I have none,
The birds' good work on them is done.

Peter Brian Ford

The World Is My Oyster

The world is my oyster I do not want
With its cold frontiers I have to haunt
The world is my tomb I have no escape
With its walls and barriers and mental rape

The world is my oyster I cannot own
With its kingdoms and kings all on the same throne
The world is my grave I have to fear
With its utter complexity never feeling sincere

The world is my oyster it dictates my needs
With its bountiful harvest it lets me feed
The world is my fool I have to smile
With its joy and abandonment at every mile

The world is my oyster I cannot trust
With its pain and suffering my dreams are rust
The world is my slave that holds me down
With its arms of strength my life on the ground

The world is my oyster I no longer crave
With its endless curve I cannot save
The world is my hurt, can't escape if I try
With its earth and rock, I'm here till I die

Daryl Tomlinson

Memories

Memories are like a book, turn the pages, take a look,
See the sorrow and the tears, see the hopes and see the fears.
See the dreams that all came true, and the ones that faded too,
School and work and holidays, all revealed as back you gaze.
See the child at five years old, wrapped up warm against the cold,
A broken heart, so sad, so sore, soon isn't broken any more.
Turn the pages once again, see the laughter and the pain,
See the youngster in her teens, with ponytail and new blue jeans.
Now you see her as a bride, with her husband by her side,
See the babies at her knee, happy with her family.
So you turn the page once more, and they aren't babies anymore!
Soon the children all have flown, but even so you're not alone.
Memories will still be there, something that you both can share,
And you will open up the book again, to wander back down
Memory Lane!

D. Miller

The Show Has Begun

The stage has been set, bring on the clowns
  Make way for the laughter, get rid of the frowns
Voices are singing, join in with the throng
  Everyone's happy and bursting with song.

The dancers are waiting to open the show
  Everyone's nervous and rarin' to go
Strike up the band, let the melodies ring
  The audience waiting, is starting to sing.

The feeling of magic abounds in the air
  The tension is mounting from the edge of each chair
The dancers have started, the show has begun
  With the music and rhythm the tension has gone,

Each of the acts was supreme in its class
  The jugglers, the conjurers all quite unsurpassed
Comedians, singers and chorus girls too
  Have given their all in response to their cue.

And now it's all over, 'twas a matter of course
  So hands all together, for a standing applause
The clapping goes on expressing delight
  Bringing the end to a star-studded night.

D. Livingstone

My Dogs

For half my life I've been walking dogs,
Be it in Wellingtons, sandals or clogs.
Together we've covered many a mile,
And their antics would make me smile.
Now as Jacob and I go through our places,
Visiting all our favourite places,
Somehow I sense it won't be long,
Before I will be singing a sadder song.
We went everywhere, my dogs and I,
Our days were full, no time to cry.
Their baskets, bowls, brushes and comb
All remind me of when they were home.
And as we walked along the way,
I gave little thought of the sadness today.
Their leads hang limply on the rack,
Just in case God sends them back.

Hazel Grant

"Sweet Flower"

Heal that's faded to a wafting gentle breeze
Evening walk that's quietly taken at one's ease,
What's that smell? Nearer must I draw,
Scent to me delightful, has no flaw,
What did I experience of it first? Scent or colour?
Oh please sweet flower, let your being be not duller.
First taste indescribable to mind,
First sight more lovely than second look does find,
Left in its proper place, the flower waits on
for others, cheering up face and heart that lately have felt wan.

William C. E. Howe

5

The Painter

Paint splattered sheets shelter the world from
    heaven's decorator
God painted the universe star white
    Earth protected from stray paint drops.

Earth remains in a mirage of fumes
Dragon's breath hanging loosely
Around the Dorset Countryside

It is all a fragile wing loved plaited
In hair swinging with the rhythm of the sixties
Silk painters anonymous
Stomp in "Doctor Martin" boots through puddles of cerise
    acid rain

A Glastonburg gathering of tribes swop ideas surrounded by
    beast beats
like a heartbeat of the world's youth.

Fresh bridesmaids clutching posies of life
    in a dying world.
The potpourri libraries of knowledge
    merge into the melting pot
Making a soup of purity to feed to hungry souls
    clutching for guidance and
    Star white.

Rhiannon Jennings

When Spring Returns

Through the twinkling grace of the sun's reflection
the stream continues without cessation
its course meanders first left then right
past reeds and bushes it seemingly races
to reach its destination

Not long ago it appeared to stand still
under a coat of white it held the chill
of winter's sleep, but now along its bank
the crocus peep their cheery heads
spring finally arrives, to awaken the earth

Everywhere you look there's new growth, new birth,
daffodils nod in the gentle breeze, first buds appear on twiggy trees
new chicks follow mum to the water's edge
on their first attempts they shiver and splutter
but they seem to inherently know how to swim, to fish

Children's squeals of pure delight disturb the birds
who take off in fright,
but later return realizing they're in no danger
from chubby toes testing the water,
the sun's reflection hides the truth,
but they care not, in the excitement of youth, in the spring of life
their own rivers flow, but where it will take them no one can know.

Yvonne Wilson

'Fame'

Ambition burned with a brief consuming fire
Drawing me close to the vagrant flame
As if to seal my fate.
Applause defied this mind naive, ego soaring
Desirous of the poisoned bait - unheeding!

But, hands that grasped this naked flame
Now waver - unpractised to its heat
As pressure serves to falsify
This talent born of me.

What future this, of wealth, acclaim, false goals and self deceit?
The questions light and burn within
Will downfall be complete?
As my chameleon clings to drama's crutch
Will conscience seek my swift retreat?

Now safe away from footlights' glare
Discordant will take heed! The error of misguided zeal
Must surely cool this fire in me.
Fantasies reined, disguises shed - but still the spark remains
Now phantoms haunt my smouldering dreams
Stirring the ashes of that stardom scene.

Elizabeth Beale

As Blades Of Grass

Lord made us the blades of grass, which grow world wide in field.
Many millions yet to each great wonders he does reveal.
Each country has its special plants, own trees and water ways,
With people living through their lives in form to suit their days.
He varied each land's animals according to his will.
Hot lands have brilliantly coloured flowers, garnishing them still.
Cool big lakes, long rivers, hold fish life in every hue,
Other wonders high above held in his skies so blue.
Silver moon shining each night there in galaxy,
Millions of stars adding bright light there for all to see.
Sun his golden rays will spread, each day's fresh miracle,
Other planets spinning round, just as the earth does too.
each item on this world of God's, in its own special place
Is there because he made it, amongst them is no waste.
Each creature from huge elephant to tiny little flea,
has job to do within God's plan, just like you and me.
Because God gave us all free will we often muddle on,
Trying to solve our destiny, knowing we are wrong.
When we gain understanding, which takes time coming to pass,
Then we really are men, no longer as blades of grass.

Barbara Goode

Butterfly

Touch the warm, beautiful silk,
That is your love
And silently, whilst you sleep,
I caress you and say that I love you.
At night bare my soul to you and cry,
As I sing softly the sweet sound of what I feel inside.

Blowing gently on your hair,
I feel the comfort of your body next to mine.
Darkness and the cold night destroyed, by the touch of you.
Thinking of a thousand kisses, shared days and happy,
laughing memories,
Then another thousand kisses
And the deep, drowning passion of my love for you.

All my senses guided towards your silent, sleeping shape,
A light within a dark tunnel.
Sheltering inside and searching further
For the extra bond that holds me so close to you.
Forever I look at you as you sleep peacefully,
Forever I love you.
My choi-choi, my butterfly.

Bobby McPherson

Accident

If I were to die, and then hear sudden glad laughter
It would surely mean I'd joined you in the hereafter.

It was a moment accidental the day you died -
Denied by those who caused it, though I knew they had lied.

Their view that the world is a place of danger today,
Of the quick and the dead, it's for your soul I should pray,

Was obviously uncaring, and so negative
I became angry, found it much too hard to forgive -

For the shock was such that I was taken by surprise,
Condemning those who had caused your untimely demise,

Not willing to accept that a new life had begun
Without you for company, when we always had fun.

For we were so close we knew each other's every joke,
And could read each other's thoughts before we even spoke.

So I'm sure going to miss you, find it hard to adjust
To being without you, creating no further fuss -

You see we were both young, with the future still ahead
To look forward to, between us so much left unsaid -

But if I were to hear again sudden glad laughter
I would surely know I'd joined you in the hereafter.

Laura Edwards

The Invisible Tie

She hadn't seen me standing there
That breezy, sun-flecked day.
The Hills lent mystery to the scene,
The grass - the scent of hay.
Her hair a-tumble o'er her brow - the child intent on play.

In all what wonder I could sense
An air of sadness there
The child looked up - had he perceived
The presence of her care?
He plucked her skirt and nestled up to love and comfort her.

The fleeting shadow left her face,
She smiled and held him close -
So close I feared that he would break -
Were that embrace for me I'd trade the riches of the world
To worship at her knee.

But as she loosed him and he turned
Once more to childish play
The tears were glistening on her cheeks
And I quietly slipped away.

Frances Alder

"A Prayer For Peace"

Guns are blazing, Lord, all around—
Children hiding, Lord, underground.
Not enough food is there to go around—
Oh Lord, give them peace.

A frightened mother, she sheds a tear—
Santa Claus won't call this year.
In a war, no Christmas cheer—
Oh Lord, give them peace.

No more gardens, Lord—Nowhere to play—
A sea of mud to greet each day.
And who will take the guns away?—
Oh Lord, give them peace.

Night is falling, Lord—deep and dark—
Far to near, the cannons bark.
You can see the fuses spark—
Oh Lord, give them peace.

Children huddled on a mat—
Outside the guns go "boom" and "splat."
What kind of lullaby is that?—
Oh Lord give them peace.

Kate Brookes

Wishing For Tomorrow

All alone.
Watching the waves slide gently o'er the sands.
Sounds of the breeze are only to be heard.
The cold air presses against me as I sit staring out to sea.

On my own.
I know he's with me, still I feel his presence very near.
Somehow I hear him whispering my name.
I know he will be back.

Waiting.
Without him.
I feel his arms around me: only in my mind I know
I'm comforting myself dreaming it was him.

I think of his departure over and over,
Remembering his last wave before he left.

My heart aches knowing the pain he may be going through,
Hoping he will soon be home in his uniform of bravery.

Agonies of age have passed without letters of reply.
His promise of survival echoes in my mind.

Maybe tomorrow there will be sun.
I dream that God will be forgiving: I dream that love will never die.

Nicola Maclachlan

The Dance

Passion, drama, love, hate
Song of the dance of life
Beat of two hearts so fast together
You can hear the cry of passion in there
Blood as they move as one on the sea
They flow towards the sound of creation
They look into each other's eyes
They see each other as one forever.

Olive Irwin

To Someone Not Yet Born

Spirit, Yes you! From somewhere there, beyond this life of mine.
Hear me as I call to you, from somewhere back in time.
Are you just the same as me, with failings human still?
Or has our evolution taken your free will?
Do you hold the heart of one to whom you are most dear
Do you know of happiness? Do you still shed a tear?
Do you feel the wonder of your sweet child's embrace?
Do you feel the sun and wind, and rain upon your face?
Do you still grow old with time, lines etched on your brow?
Are you still a human mould? If not, what are you now?

Penniluck Nicolson

In The Wilderness

Who stands and scans this haunted desolation
And does not weep with pity for himself:
For all that passed before it came to being,
For what was his and which he never had?

What strange obsession led me to this desert
Seeking I knew not whom, and yet I knew,
Within such lost immensities of nothing
That veil such lost immensities of all?

Over these ruined walls, the silted harbour,
Upon deserted pathways, empty sea,
Only the hungry wind roams, ever seeking
The rose that blossoms in the wilderness.

Embittered are the stars, the moon has soured,
For who still stirs within these wastes beneath
Whose destiny remains for them to govern
Since they brought us together, you and me?

Come, let us hide, lest in their idle envy
They should conspire to sunder again,
Or, lest the wind should chance upon the rose-bloom
And strip the petals, leaving only thorns.

R. Ingrid Clapham

Bank Holidays

The loneliest times are Bank Holidays,
When there's no one who cares around,
The hours hang heavy and empty,
And my face wears the mask of a frown.

I daydream of romance and loving,
I fantasize that he's attentive and kind,
But alone on weekends and Bank Holidays,
The tears sting my eyes and I'm blind.

I long to be cherished and needed,
To find a soul mate to share in my life,
But alone on weekends and Bank Holidays,
I am nothing, not even a wife.

During the weeks I am working and busy,
My days are filled and I thrive,
But alone on weekends and Bank Holidays,
I feel I am barely alive.

It's easy to be cheerful in company,
To keep up the pretence and to act,
But alone on weekends and Bank Holidays,
Dreams fill the attention that I lack.

Sylvia Carraud

Sweet Relief

My plan is ready - I lock the door,
No one else knows what I've come here for,
I've found a way to relieve my woe,
A chance to bow out of this ailing show,
My veins are full, and calling out,
"Use your blade," I can hear them shout,
They're blue and dark, nice and clear,
My one last hope to escape from here,
I make a cut, it's smooth and deep,
The cost to keep living was way to steep,
Death is my answer, it holds the key,
It's the only real solution for me,
I watch in amazement at my open vein,
Feeling sweet relief, no hint of pain,
With a crimson tide running down my wrist,
I clench my fingers into a fist,
The blood pours out with increasing power,
Sprinkling the room with a scarlet shower,
I stumble, fall and hit the ground,
And soon I cannot hear a . . .

Martin Bowell

Untitled

There's beauty in a wrinkled face,
Goodness, heartbreak, sadness, grace,

Tired eyes that now are dimmed of light,
So many things put out of sight,

Look closer still and you will see,
The lips that once were kissed by me,

I knew her then long years ago,
I loved her then, I loved her so,

She nods her head for she is sleeping,
Soon she will be in safe keeping,

Wrinkles gone - no lines to trace,
Peace has come to take their place.

E. J. Owen

Advice For The Bride

You took the step, walked up the aisle,
A picture of elegance, and of style,
You've now become a loving wife.
Why should he be happy, all of his life.

You promised to love, honour and obey,
But, be sure to have the final say,
Be firm, determined, make a stand,
Obey him only if you like the command.

For richer or poorer, better or worse,
Make sure all the money goes into your purse,
If ever you argue, or he rocks the boat
Just warmly embrace him, by the throat.

Start your new life, as you mean to go on,
Nights out with his mates are all dead and gone,
now you have caught him, you'll change his life,
Why! He should be happy that you are his wife.

Annette Mercer

The Millionairess

I open my eyes and I'm surrounded by gold,
It's nice to feel warm and not freezing cold,
There's light all around me and I know sheer delight,
I gaze at beautiful colours, subtle yet bright,
I am very rich and have jewels by the score,
There are so many and yet I want more,
I can't get enough of this beautiful sight,
But don't think I'm greedy, because you wouldn't be right
For my gold is the sun, my jewels the flowers,
I still can't explain their mystical powers,
But aren't I lucky that I can see,
These wonderful gifts from God to me.

G. Chettle

Obsession

Was I innocent? Possibly. Shallow? Oh yes,
And that shallowness shattered a dream,
Were we ever in love? Well I was I guessed
When I asked 'Do you love me? Darling confess'
She said, 'That remains to be seen.'

I thought love would come, if I just gave her time,
So I bought her a ring with a diamond supreme,
I asked her to wear it, with verses in rhyme
I'd care for her gladly, her every wish mine,
Her reply, 'That remains to be seen.'

Her resolve eroded by my constant pleas,
In the end she consented, to my long desired scheme.
We married in spring-time, and I vowed on my knees
To the moon and the stars, to the flowers, the trees,
That never would I treat her mean.

And I meant it, at the time and for months from that day,
But the challenge once sated, soon lost its sheen,
Shame of rejection led her away
Alone with her pills and a note just to say,
She had left the remains to be seen.

E. Mills

Youth

How much I do yearn and am longing to see
You standing there, wishful, and waiting for me,

Wanting that which we both knew soon was to come,
When we were young, spirited, most highly strung.

Your voice was a melody, tuneful and clear,
Like the song of a lark on balmy spring air.
Your laughter came freely, delightful to hear.

All doubts were dissolved in ensuing sweet bliss
When our lips met in hungry eager first kiss.

In thrall to compelling impassioned desire,
Both lit by a flame, then consumed by a fire.

Your arms held me close in a warm ardent embrace
Affirming our loving, of restraint not a trace.

Now I seek day and night simply longing to find
Someone looking like you, of my dear one remind.

For the love aroused then I've since discovered
Is so steadfast and strong I've never recovered

My yearning for you brings only hunger and fasting,
My affection for you has endured, everlasting.

Laura Edwards

Can't Wait For Tomorrow

Will it be a big party mummy.
Will all my best friends come.
Will my cake be very big mummy
So my friends can have some.
Will there be candles.
Pretty coloured candles
Alight, shiny, and bright.
Oh! Mummy will there be lots of things to eat.
Like jelly, crisps and sweets.
Will we have games.
Will we have lots of games.
And the music too.
Will my friends bring me their presents
Like they always do.
Mummy I'm all excited.
I can't wait for tomorrow
When I'll be ten and older.
Well, it is my birthday
And I want it to be - "just so".

Jean Lloyd-Williams

Seasons

The bright green leaves are changing their colour
The perfumed flowers are closing their eyes
The warm summer breeze knows it's time to get cooler
The sun is low in the skies

The golden colours of autumn are glowing
Cool winds are beginning to blow
The sleeping meadows of winter are showing
That soon they'll be under the snow

But spring, with its new life will soon be arriving
The snowdrops and crocus beginning to show -
The meadows and flowers and trees are still thriving
And everything's starting to grow

So nature goes on from season to season
Living and dying and living anew
Giving us joy and hope and reason
For striving to live as we do

Barbara Scriven

I

I will be the darkness of the night,
    the shadow of the dancing tree.
I will be the flutter of the wing,
    the cry of the frightened gull.
I will be each day the rising dawn,
    and the glinting light upon the leaf.
I will be the thought that follows prayer,
    to pull the shade upon the restless mind.
I will be when time repeats and comes again,
    in the beginning and in the end
    I Will Be.

Thomas Norman McCarroll

Distinct Discretions

I thanked Death profusely.
A woman had passed,
yet I live for the present.
Mystery man's love will be mine
    very soon indeed.
    Her heart was weak,
    and I knew it!
Death prescribed acute anxieties.
I, enlightened, gave each dose
    with cautious confidence.
    She slowly faded, I slowly bloomed.
The process like irritated molasses
    continued.
After discreet decisions,
her Artist averted his attentions
and looked to me for inspiration.
    Cries pierced the morning air,
    but I hardly heard them.
Instead, I watched the departure of
Death's enchanted procession.

Kenia Nottage

Evening Reflections

The heat of the day is no more,
As the cooling breeze caresses the shore,
The palms sway gently to and fro,
Back and forth with nowhere to go,
Waves lap gently over the sand,
Lovers stroll by hand in hand,
The scent of exotic plants abound,
To grace the senses all around,
Sunset is a time to reflect,
Casting giant shadows, a magical effect,
The waters edge dances to a tune,
Mirrored in unison by the moon,
This tropical isle can live without end,
A place to enjoy, one I do recommend,
It's paradise lost and found all in one,
A treasure to behold basking under the sun.

Trevor Reeve

The Poet

Like a winding staircase I am ever in motion,
Occurs to me the notion that perhaps this well
Concocted "wordy" potion, does not quite
Require the intimate devotion that I like to
Think it needs. Yes indeed, miraculously ink
Spills from the pen and bleeds its way into
The paper. I only the words' curator not
in fact the verse dictator.

Still more time for rhyme and rhythm. I merely
The reflector, inspirations prism, but tainted
With my realism or should that not
Read cynicism, no doubt but words keep
coming out, free flowing, sentence sewing,
Shocking sometimes mocking no signs of
Stopping, elegantly interlocking. Invites you
To read and pleads that you find a meaning to
This literal screening.

I only the vessel. A steamship of words.

Paul Ferry

My Love

Love,
When I am with you, my love,
Your love surrounds me totally.
Like I'm lying on a bed of rose petals,
Like I'm floating naked on a soft breeze.
It's a dream.
For, my love, I know you would fight,
I know you would die,
Would give up your worldly possessions,
To love and to cherish,
To honour and obey.

The dream is real.
Your kisses are a soft breeze,
Your skin is made of rose petals.
You surround me totally
When I am with you,
My love.

Rebecca Tong

Thunder Of Love

Through the long crashing hours of a thundering night
Our bodies entwined well into daylight
And all through the passion of a candlelit room
'Tis true that from here you can see the moon
And never before with such burning desire
Was lovemaking such that we never tire
A man and a woman engaging in lust
'Twas here that they climbed their first steps of trust
And after the storm came the calm...
Like soft falling rain...
Afresh with red rose and a breakfast champagne.

Paula Marozzi

Bygone Days

How I long for those bygone days
Oh how the years just fly
When the children were young and beautiful
And so I thought was I
Cooking, Cleaning seemed just fine
Nappies blowing on the line
Days seemed always filled with fun
As up the school you would quickly run
To sit by an open fire and roast
Eat piles and piles of dripping toast
To walk to the park not far from home
When there never was fear to let children roam
Outing to the seaside, Buckets, Spades and food
Returning home at tea time in one happy mood
Little faces tired, but laughing all the while
Made your heart feel happy and brought a loving smile
It's nice to travel down memory lane
To relive those bygone days again

Maureen Cleak

Love

A man needs to be loved, I need you.
My life revolves around your every move.
I live, breathe and perpetually think of you.
My hopes and dreams totally embrace you.
Yesterday I loved you, today I still do.
Could you see what lies ahead,
You would have visions of a life,
Clad in joy, happiness and hopes.
You are my present, you are my future.
You are my lover, my wife, my life.

Robert H. Connor

Love In An English Garden

Across the shining river the hills still carry snow
The wind is blowing from the north, yet you would hardly know
That winter was still present, something you would not guess
When strolling warm and sheltered in the lovely grounds of Ness

Down in the peaceful valley spring flowers face the sun
Where can you match this blossom yet the year has scarce begun
Soon blackbird, yaffle, chaffinch each will their love profess
Love in an English garden, this Eden known as Ness

Known widely for its excellence of shrub of flower of tree
The finest teaching garden in the country it must be
Not only birds and insects their suit with fervour press
But many a maid when courted here has also answered yes!

Love in an English garden! What better place than here
Where sea and marsh and mountain at each viewpoint appear
Where perfume form and colour are perfect, nothing less
For love in an English garden the choice is surely Ness

F. J. Camenisch

My Prayer

Heavenly father, hear our plea
We, thy children, call to thee
Guide us, teach us, lovingly
So we may turn our hearts to thee

Show us all the one true road
So those following must surely see
That though the way be long and rough
It's the one true road that leads to thee

So dear father, do not fail us
In our trials give us strength
So that one day we may be rewarded
And see, at last, your smiling face

Margaret MacDonald

The Light

The light it shines, it beckons me.
Where does it come from?
I can see, but only dimly, for I am almost blinded
by the brilliance, brightness, beauty
of such an ethereal, eternal, enervating intrusion
into dismal, doubting darkness.

The light, the light,
It is becoming clearer; and yet,
Can I bear to have it shining, searching, seeking me so intensely?

In stillness; yes.
It beckons and illuminates and sustains my being.
After stillness; fear.

O Lord, Lord of light, you have found me.
I am yours completely, to be filled with your light and love.
There is no fear in light, overpowering light.
Dismal, doubting, darkness is dispelled.
Light does not come and go; it is always there at work,
Waiting, wanting to enrich, enhance, envelope my being eternally.
Fear is cast out. Faith has come in.
Hallelujah! Praise the Lord, the light.

Rita D. E. Holland

Our World

Our life on earth, is given to us
    To love, enjoy, and toil,
So people of our world unite,
    And bless, this sacred soil.

Teach your children, all that's good,
    Show them love, as parents should,
Tell them, we all have a duty,
    To respect, our world, and all its beauty.

Come together, one and all,
    Turn your backs, on hate, and war,
Summon all the meek, and mild,
    Teach love, and kindness, to every child.

All people of our world unite,
    Reach out and pour your love,
Give thanks to God, for giving us life,
    and pray, to heaven above.

Wendy Patrick

To A Child Prostitute Seen On Television

When I glimpsed your face
With its young sadness,
I wanted to help,
But your image passed.

Your lost expression
Longed for gladness;
Not the oppression
Of one outcast
With whores and beggars, and all accused
That I'd judged to be
Some lower race,
Not knowing how you had been used.

Now, each face,
I search in turn,
And when I love,
I find you there.
But if I fail
Such hatred grows.
Once your face fades
I feel despair.

Sara Negus

Teidi—Cool Lady Of Tenerife

Calm, aloof—she stands serene,
Quite effortless she steals the scene.

Countless numbers are her guests—
In jeans, or shorts—e'en tatty vests

She welcomes all with gentle smile,
Till—suddenly—the crowd seems vile!

Snow cap she dons, pulls down her veil,
Calls up the winds to blow their gale.

Her lovely face turns dark, and cold—
To visit then, few are so bold.

Yes—calm, aloof, she shows her pride,
True lady, she, with fire inside.

Anne Abbott

You?

You love me, you love me not.
You hate my guts, you like me a lot.
You say hello, you wave, you smile
Your name is written all over my file.

You're always friendly, you like to flirt.
It's not with me, it's another skirt!
I want to cry, I want to yell
I want to tell you to go to Hell.

All of this, I really cannot do,
because all I want to do is say
'I Love You'.

Sara Campbell

Life

Oh flow not, not away from me my deep blue waters
that lie so tranquil and so peaceful at my feet
Flow not oh not away with so much laughter
to meet the oceans so turbulent and deep
I feed you from the snow upon my head
and from the rain that beats against my breast
That runs down my lined and craggy face
and come to rest in you with loving gentle grace

Listen to the silence all around
until the birds wake up with so much sound
And twitter and cry as they roar
so high above the animals upon your shore
And listen to the insects and bees, that flutter in and out the trees
That line your banks, and give thanks
To you for all that you can give
to nourish and to help them all to live

So leave not my feet my deep blue water
But stay forever just as you are
Give food, give help, give life, to all who line your banks,
and who in return to you will give, their sincere and humblest thanks

John Gilliland

The Hollow Ache Of Loss

Fate's ugly arms were open wide
Anxious for you to step inside
Wandering blind in life's heavy smog
Your star was but my only guide
And when I sank into the depths of sleep
Memories of you haunted me
I saw your image standing tall

But in reality I was left to fall
You hide from me and my memories
Oblivious to the pain you left in me
But I've seen you in the sand and sea
And on the bed lying close to me
I've longed to be there by your side
But wrongly pondered on suicide

This ache inside I can barely abide
So float me away to your paradise
The secret place in which you hide
There I will find my wandering soul
And hollow I will be no more
Hollow I will be no more!

Lorna Reid

Death's Crime

Death lifted his scythe and knocked at the door.
Like he'd done so many times before.
The old lady smiled as she welcomed him in,
her body was bent, and withered, and thin.

I've been expecting you for a long time now
and with her hankie she wiped his brow,
the Lord he giveth and taketh away.
She knew it was her time to die today.

She felt no pain, nor sadness, nor grief
but only joy and long awaited relief,
For now her soul was free once more.
And the angels smiled for they saw

That death is not an awful thing,
For they know the harmony it can bring.
As she floated away, the angels they sang,
Harmoniously as only they can.

And death he watched, with a tear is his eye
as she became one with the heavens and sky,
then he turned away and continued his crime
that he's committed since the beginning of time.

Giselle Hoad

Moving On

In each book of life there are chapters
Pages we wish we could change
Others we yearn to recapture
Yet that we can never arrange
A new testament can only begin
By leaving the past behind
Believe in yourself and you will win
With faith in heart and hope in mind.
When our world's turned upside down
All our efforts seem fallen in vain
We should never stand still but keep walking
Then in time we will run again.
We can't retrieve the life that has gone
So as months turn into seasons
We learn again to laugh and sing,
To love life for different reasons.
So turn the page over - begin again.
The world has the paper but we hold the pen.

Valerie Reid

No Hope Service (A Geriatric Lament)

Past the 'sell-by' date?
Be-grudged 'room on the shelf'?
Then get a second opinion
After all - it's *you - your own self.*

Consultants leave the old 'uns' high and dry
Dole out the valium with a smile and a lie
Euthanasia's a blessing
They (privately) cry

More work for the grave diggers
More smoke to the pyres
Queue for the golden gates
Or descend to the fires

Too old at 40?
Maybe more than 40 to go?
The little white pills
Lure with a radiant glow

Suicide's dirty? Not on your life
First make sure there's enough for the wife
Musn't be selfish, both must rejoice
Toast each other with joy, You've made the right choice!

Bryn Bartlett

A Peaceful Mind

Oh for the taste of freedom,
Like that of the Hawk and Dove.
Away from the hassle of life below,
To the peace of the blue sky above.

A blue that is deep in contrast,
To the blue that we know down here.
To where there's a sense of peacefulness,
Compared to a sense of fear.

Away from the greed and needs of man,
And the troubles that walk alongside.
Away to a world of plentiness,
Where Muggers and thieves can't hide.

A place where there is no traffic,
And no sight of a bustling crowd.
Where if you choose, sit peacefully,
Upon the crest of a passing cloud.

If we could turn these worlds around,
Our Earth would be full of love.
And all the troubles of mankind,
Would be miles and miles above.

Dave Lewis

Epitaph For Sadie

Your picture looks down from the TV
You lovable faithful old hound
Why did you have to leave us
We just loved having you around

There are times I forget you aren't here
And boldly cry out your name
Expecting to see you come running
And look for you always in vain

You were the odd one in the litter
As a springer you didn't make the grade
Your teeth had an uneven number
Not for you cruft's show parade

Obedience wasn't your strong point
You always just went your own way
But faithful loving simply gorgeous
Our lives stopped when you died on that day . . .

Jill Howard

Memory, Time And The Kiss

Memory is water turned into wine
The net cast by the mind
Seeps into untroubled depths
The past caught after a long subsidence.
Memory is loss, unfettered and loose,
As free as the undulating waves, the terrible sea.

Silently the kiss restores life within its compass
It washes away misery
Finally the kiss announce the emptiness
That will reverse the moments preceding.

Time slips away so that life has lost
Self-consciousness
Time slips away and this means decay

Memory and time dance in tandem
And past and present entwine
Memory and the kiss reveal desertion
Until the past is past and the future slips away

Baret Magarian

If, Elise

Whisper my love upon my brow,
Sweet breeze within my hair,
Of fiery steeds to burn my eyes,
Of love, of passion's burning flame,
Like silken threads upon the morning rise.
To fall, caress, low upon the wake.

For your breath, softly,
Is like the sweetest hush,
An open touch upon my naked skin,
A gentle whisper of dim desire,
Like a dream, half waking sin,
Embers beneath its resting fire.

And your voice, it is
So deep within my heart,
As to draw the very tears from my patient soul,
Of wan despair bathed in light,
Of the very echoes of my distant life, to console,
Like the healing arms of an angel's wings, so you can, my love,
Keep my waking moments still.

I. A. Scott

Untitled

Only endless drizzle spot spreading calm sea
Lap of light wave over beach pebble
Silent slip past of small vessel
Freshly caught fish slithering
On disused pier wet wood
Anchored yacht slight mast sway
Slowly moving ship showing from mist
Red funnels glaring

G. McKeown

The Revival Of A Has Been

I used to think that my opinion mattered,
Now I have my doubts,
I'm too old for this,
Not skilled at that.
It seems the time has come,
Now that my hair is turning grey,
To sit and dream of what might have been.
    But
Then I remembered that little girl, a mother yet to be
Who hangs on every word I say.
There is a future still,
Wisdom of this age I may still impart
To those prepared to listen.
Whilst my story I unfold,
I glimpse of what the future holds and kick my chair away.

R. O. Playfoot

The Crutch

I am a crutch,
I am picked up when you're too weak to go.
I am a crutch,
Oh so much loved when strength in you is low.
I am a crutch
I get picked up when things are going wrong,
I'm leant on very heavily, I'm leant on for so long.
But when the power's back in you,
There's so much that you want to do,
And now this crutch that's made of wood,
Stops you from doing things you could
Without it, so it cannot stay,
And so you throw your crutch away.
I am a crutch,
Discarded now, I lie here truly broken.
I am a crutch,
Not needed now, no looks, no words are spoken.
When you were down the priceless value that you saw in me,
Is now forgotten, in the past, you're out, you're free, you're free!

Sharron Phillips

The Magic Of Dolphins

The moonlight glistens upon the sea,
a cool wind blows incessantly.
Waves gently breaking on the shore,
there's a sense of wonder I can't ignore.

The shimmering water suddenly gives way
to a most awe-inspiring, magical display.
Gracefully leaping in two's and three's,
jumping and swimming with so much ease.

The sight and sound of dolphins is magic,
helping the unfortunate whose lives are tragic.
Speechless children can learn to talk.
They also inspire a will to walk.

Watching them leaves me totally enraptured,
but we must prevent them from being captured.
These intelligent mammals deserve our respect.
The joy they have given, I will never forget.

Barbara Lettin

To Samuel, My Husband

In the lonely silence of the night
Soul reaches out to soul to seek its own
And somewhere through the swirling mists of time
A love immortal joins again as one

When in your deep despair did you not know
The one who loves you, knew you long ago
Stood by your side to cherish and amend
And echoing your prayers did comfort you

My love, my dearest love, you could not stay
The years swiftly passed, now you are gone
The music that we made will never end
Enchantment was the singers not the song

Monica Scarlett

Focus On This

Focus on this and dream me a dream
Let me burst from the ground
Like a fresh mountain stream
Let me dive the deep oceans
With speed on my side
And await my return on the turn of the tide.

Focus on this and inspire my mind
Let me warm like the sun
Let me shine on mankind
Let me paint you a rainbow
To colour the skies
And await my return when you open your eyes.

Focus on this and teach me to learn
Mould me and shape me
For knowledge I yearn,
Let me be wise
In this world of despair
And await my return on the breeze of repair.

Dawn Reed

The Animals' Carol

The beasts of earth had waited long
To sing anew Creation's song,
When in a little Eastern place
They sensed the movement of God's grace.

The cock was first, and loud did cry,
To show God's Son to earth was nigh.
His call arose above the rest;
He sounded, "Christus natus est!"

The beasts all wondered, "Where is He?"
And oxen lowing said "Ubi?"
The simple sheep - O good for them! -
Gave answer, bleating "Bethlehem!"

Come then, O men of human race,
Draw nigh and know th' eternal grace;
Come man, in God's own image made,
And see God's glory thus displayed.

There is no human show of might:
An Infant is the Holy Sight.
This simple, lowly sign of love,
Makes angels' anthems up above.

Arthur H. Kirkby

There Is No Colour In The Dark

In quiet hours of darkness
There I lie
Gazing around me,
Gown hanging on the door,
Curtains, bed, books, covers ink-dark,
All dark, no-colour dark.

But with the dawn
Colour steals in.

The sky is shot with gold and blue.
Pink-edged clouds mass slowly.
Russet roofs glow across the street.
In the garden
Green-yellows, blue-greens, green-whites shine.
Geraniums, roses, coral bells, peonies
Glow rich in reds.
   A girl in a blue dress,
   A field of yellow rape,
   And far away, a haze of poppy red
   Hangs on the horizon.

Oh, colour comes to life in the light.

Leila Pool

Ignorance Is Never Bliss

I see the suffering and the pain, I plead blind, for ignorance is Bliss
I see the poverty and the shame, I am unaware, for ignorance is Bliss
I see the crying and the tears, I walk on by, for ignorance is Bliss
I see the faces and the fear, I'm not the only one, for ignorance is Bliss
I see the crime and the dirt, I am innocent, for ignorance is Bliss
I see the victims and the hurt, I am not the judge, for ignorance is Bliss
I see fascism, persecution, discrimination, the people, the pain in all
the nations - I feel nothing, for ignorance is Bliss
I see the popular prejudice, the dire consequences, then the benefits
   of pleading blind
For I am caught up in a society which has hardened my heart, so much
It has infested my mind.
Alas! Not until my dying day will I realize what I have missed
As I look to the skies, then close my eyes and die knowing
   Ignorance is Never Bliss.

Cherylle Millard

Heroes Are They

The ghostly sound of marching men echoing down a lonely lane,
Their souls entwined leaving
Behind the blood red field of poppies in their wake,
For our sake all lost their day.
No monuments needed for heroes such as they
Their glory as they marched along the lonely road
Were the many kindnesses they bestowed.
Ordinary men from simple homes and work
And when duty called they didn't even shirk
But marched bravely on to war.
What debt we owe them all and never can repay
Except to remember they gave their tomorrows for our today.
And through the tears we see the poppies blossom where once they trod
Their honourable sacrifice is a lasting reminder of a living God.

M. Wiles

As I Sit By The Menin Gate In Ypres

Wipers they used to call it, those chaps who went through hell,
My old man was there at eighteen as he was so proud to tell.
But of those brave lions who fought there so few are left today
To remember their mates who perished in so many a horrid way.
World war I was the end of an era or so we are sadly told
By those who were the romantics when others had to be the bold.
But what of an era that thought man little better than cattle
And gloried when he trudged bravely forward into distant battle?
Can it have been so great and so full of proud hope and glory
or was it just transient like sun shining on a frost so hoary?
Thank God not for glorious victors when a million men have died
Just hope that their souls go on marching with sadness and pride.
I am sick of hate, the bullet, the bomb and ethnic cleansing,
Please God give us a peace that does not pass all understanding.

Denis Easterby

Lines on the Death of a Dear Friend

You came, a tiny pretty girl, on my doorstep my first sight of you,
You were so frightened, yet did not need to be,
You knew your name and 'out' and that was all.
I loved you then, I love you still,
You brought me happiness and joy and love.
Gradually you changed and learned to trust
And also understand the words I spoke,
We went for walks, I did not dare to let you off the lead
For fear you'd run if other dogs or traffic startled you.
This was your home and garden too,
You learned to play, though not with ball,
You came upstairs and followed me, my silent shadow,
Rushing by to get there first.
You suffered pain, we tried so hard to make you well, but could not,
So farewell my own sweet Cleo.
One last quick kiss from you I shall remember always.
You came, you stayed so short a time,
Just three short years, my darling,
One day I hope we'll meet again.

Joan M. Wood

Faulty Ladders

Trouser seat worn through the years.
A driving ambition he no longer steers.
Creases sketched 'round weary eyes
Depiction of his working life.

Social rings corrupt in time
Especially when you've reached your prime.
Stride too long to reach the top
Rivalry is burning hot.

From mid height he peers on down
At puerile skin and noble gowns.
Emeralds return the stare
Wishing they were half way there.

Dripping fear pecked from higher steps
His plausible role had overstretched.
A wad of notes. A limp handshake.
A whole life force burnt at the stake.

Trace of cotton ingrained in pew
Before invasion of recent coup.
Dormant files that bear his name
The only trace of his serving reign.

Karen Veronica Hodgson

Water Meadows

Gently the river meanders through the meadows
Somnolent now in the Hot Summer sun
Somewhere in the distance in muffled sonorous tones the
cathedral clock chimes the hours
And Jackdaws disturbed from their resting circle chattering,
In the long grass a cricket chirps and a bee drones drowsily
overhead

The watcher lies silent in the sweet meadow grasses
and his mind wanders free down the alley of the years
till the drone of the bee and the biplane are one
boyhood and a patrician future beckoning
no knowledge then of time's most awful reckoning
and still the river flows,
like the waters of Lethe, like the waters of no-more-pain

Some things at least do not change
Pleasant black water of pastoral peace and peaceful permanence
Only the chimes of the cathedral clock form the cloistered close
Only the cooing of pigeons in the sunrise
And the crowings of pheasant before dusk
to mark the passing of the hours,
only births and deaths, sowings and harvests
to mark the passage of the seasons and the passing of the years.

Maurice Hemmant

"Life"

I've got a disease that'll kill me,
And free me from trouble and strife,
But then I will go to a far better place
Where violence and hatred's not rife.

'Til then I'll get on with living,
Not worry about what might have been,
Like I've never been skiing at Christmas,
Or I've never had lunch with the Queen.

No, I'll just enjoy what God sends me,
Birds singing, the frogs in the pond,
Dogs' tails wagging, the laughter of children,
All the people of whom I am fond.

What I won't miss are extra-long bus queues,
Or the bills that come in the post,
But I will miss the sun in the summer,
And the love of the one I love most.

For I have a disease that'll kill me,
And release me from trouble and strife,
Yes, I have a disease that'll kill me,
A Terminal Illness called Life.

Mary Phillips

Autumn Thoughts

She shuffles trembling down the russet pathway,
And mutters, lest her errand be forgot.
For such as she, how long may seem the daytime,
And evening brings no respite to her lot.

Her fourscore years have wearied her in passing;
Her friends, and all her family are gone.
Yet see her smile, beholding autumn's glory,
Whilst joy lights up her features pale and wan.

The falling leaves in red and golden clamour
With yellow, green and purple intertwine;
And shadows lie across the russet pathway.
She marvels at the magical design.

Within a pool the colours are reflected.
A robin passes, foraging alone.
The sun peeps out to bless the russet pathway,
And cries, "Old age has beauty all its own."

Mary Pledge

The Magic Of Autumn

Falling leaves, early morning sun
Gathering of Harvest fruits one by one
Wheely bins outside the door
Gathering rubbish as never before

Silence as golden as we breathe
God is there for all who believe
That truth must always prevail
The paths of truth are very narrow

Wander and one gets out of depth
Sometimes water is more than shallow
We struggle out and pause for breath
When morning comes new hope is there

Difficulties disperse as we breathe fresh air
Starting a new day, with more hope not despair
Faith restored in our daily bread
Peace on earth we most desire

Loving our neighbours we all see
Is the only way to eternity

Mabel Smallpeice

The Message

"I've got too much to do."
"I'm going to be very busy."
"I can't plan anything yet."
"I don't know what I shall be doing."
"I may be going away."
"I don't have my diary with me."
"I'll let you know."
"I'll ring."
Any, or all of these, you could have said.
You never spoke!
The message though, was clear;
It said, "Goodbye"

Geraldine Squires

A Step Forward

T travellers along the same road,
H harmony helps sharing the load,
E everyone involved, should be the theme.

Y young people must be part of the team,
O older people, must the young, involve.
U unity, or community voice will dissolve.
N numerous talents we should explore,
G group involvement we cannot deplore.

A adolescence is no interlude,
D developing skills we must not preclude.
U unity, need not be uniformity.
L liaison is a must, though not conformity.
T trust is the binding factor!

J. H. Lightbody

Dad

Whether in the Garden
Or pottering in your shed
Watching all your war films
Or "resting your eyes" up in your bed
Tinkering with your models
Painting all things red
Talking to each one of us
Those words of wisdom to be said

Most times you'd make us happy
Or "debate" until we're sad
But your thoughts or "bloody-minded-ness"
With best intentions to make us glad
Now empty autumn, winter, summer
And spring will be so bad
We'll miss you not here beside us
Because you are forever, forever are our Dad

Paul Hanley

Goal Glory

He was running with a football
Past mid-fielders big and small
Running rings around them
With skill as bright as a gem
He was running around
Beating defenders with every leap and bound
He was 30 yards out
So he decided to give it a clout
Off the post it came
So I decided to do the same
When it came to me
I was as still as a tree
I had slipped in the mud
Which made me as black as soot
The ball hit the goalie and then hit my foot
By the end we were all very wet
I was pleased the ball had hit the net.

Patrick Challis

Unchained

I hated him!
Every night he would come home in a drunken stupor, filled
with rage
In a blind fury he would lash out hitting, punching, kicking me
because I was in the wrong place at the wrong time

My body wrecked from his abuse
To the limit of the pace being too much
I ran from his endless torture

I fled to the streets
Begging, pleading, hoping, to be given a new life
Suffering, starving because of him and his abuse
Security a cardboard box

Too much but no longer
Falling, fearless yet free
Away from the dreadful demon and dark depth I once hung in
Safely bound for the Isle of Tranquility.

Carri-Ann Daniels

Shadows

Shades of the night of deep purple-black tones,
Moving shadows sliding across the lawns,
Moving and flutt'ring in the silv'ry light
Of the lunar orb... lantern of the night;
Melting and reshaping the dark monster
Of one's subconscious, freeing the lodestar
And, thus, wand'ring amongst shadows of night,
Wailing and moaning its terrible plight.
And the moon looks on in ghostly splendour,
Tinging the shadows with hellish colour,
Casting cold silvery light far and near;
Stealthily it moves, bosom pal of fear.

Gwen Douglas

Inspiration

Inspiration is a rare gift given to few to atone,
In our destiny, we don't stand alone.

I understand fate differs
Many conclude this definition
"What's for us will not go by us"
Which to me is preposterous.

Can you grasp the vein?
It means perhaps you can do no wrong
The jigsaw will perhaps fall into place
Without attempting to solve the problem.

To predetermine the power of agency
Is not beyond human power or control
Spiritual guidance is specified.

One's lot or course of events
Is still to be transacted
Your destiny is in your own hands
What you make of it.

John Sneddon

Our Walk On Harrow Hill

The place where the late Lord Byron rests
The place where the Robin red-breast nests
We stand in bliss in each other's arms
Detached from all of man's quarrels and qualms.

A carpet of golden leaves at our feet
Cushion our footsteps as they line the street.
Like the hands of Jesus Christ that bled
The sunset paints the sky a shade of red.

The Church tower stands so proudly above
Like a symbol of our eternal love.
We stand amongst the souls which the graves house
We hold each other and exchange our vows.

The leaves fall down and settle on the grass
And they will feed the soil as time will pass
Creating new life at the start of spring
And a brand new beginning they will bring.

For our love each day is like a season
The day may end, but our love just keeps on
Like the fallen leaves, in much the same way
Our love grows stronger with every new day.

Harry Mavromatis

The Netherworld

You are trapped in the Netherworld,
it's completely different from your own.
With strange, weird beings
and fantastic structures made of bone.
To get back to your own world,
there is one thing you must do,
slay the demon killer,
and retrieve the forbidden ewe.
For those who live in the Netherworld
are not there by will,
they were failure of the task,
and who are living there still.
Sitting up in my bed,
thinking I must have been dreaming,
but it all seemed so real,
my mind must be deceiving.
But then all of a sudden I felt a sharp prick,
and a feeling of great sorrow,
blood dripped to the floor,
to leave the words see you again tomorrow.

Joanna Simpson

Autumn

I see the mist-blue wood smoke, drifting up the air
And the old man in his garden, sweeping leaves up there;
Whilst just beyond the beech hedge, along the golden lane
Lie puddle-pools of amber, from late September rain.

I see tall chrysanthemums lean against the wall
Ready for their cutting, to adorn the lofty hall.
I hear the russet-robin sing, his clear cut crystal tune
And the daisies of St. Michaelmas are in their perfect bloom.

I can see the orchard beyond the autumn mist
Where apples glow like lanterns, and children can't resist?
While just above vague rooftops, a misty moon hangs high
And little icy starlets, float across the sky.

I can smell damp leaf mould and hay from ancient barns
Sweet clover from the cows' field by the little farm.
So soon it will be harvest time, to reap what man has sown
And gather to the churches, all that man has grown.

Rosemary Diane Harding

Going Home

Derelict are the houses, it's a blue day.
Yet, the forest and woodland in springtime are free.
The buds of May and birds in flight need no looking glass.
Curiosity in Scotland is El Naturale, like summer flowers.
Feeling abandoned, that's a stormy day, no love.
Friends, like the ducks on the village pond, that's the big one.
At low tide, there is now blue orchid.
But there's a castle in the mist.
Look, a single butterfly and a boy fishing, that's a gift of flowers.
Remember the dunegol scene and the Ancient game, that's past.
Reach for the classic flowers and the french village,
There are no still ships.

Emily Burnett

The Beach By Night

The sun goes down across the beach,
The sea gulls are coming in.
Most of the land is deserted,
The light is very dim.
But jumping over the sand castles, chasing crabs away,
Playing with the seaweed and prowling along the bay,
Ready to catch a fish or two,
Hiding there so small,
Then pouncing on the black and red fish,
Becoming so big and tall,
Stands a beautiful black and white cat
So tall, so big, so proud.
He starts to roll on his back
And purr so very loud.
Then the beach is silent,
The sun begins to shine,
Wake up everybody,
It is morning time.

Elizabeth Simpson

Monoliths Of Doom

Up and up they soar,
Those faceless monoliths,
Silhouetted against a smog-filled firmament.
Gods in ancient Greece were ne'er so worshipped
As these modern monstrosities.

The once recognized line,
Where sky meets earth,
Has succumbed to those hideous idols
That blot out the light
With their symmetrical inscrutability.

So let us bow,
Pay homage to them,
We pre-programmed robots.
They are the masters, the deity of the doom,
We the architects of our own damnation.

Dave Simpson

Mirror Mirror

The sun reflects on a freckled brow
A wisp of hair rides on the wind
Pursed lips, deep hazel eyes
A glazed almost childlike smile
Blushered cheeks on a milk white canvas

A picture revealed for all to see
A fragile delicate shell
Reflecting hopes of past and future
Passion creates a radiant glow
That shelters the heavy burden of regret

A complex portrait paints a story
So apparent yet cunningly disguised
Images expose desires and dreams
Memories unite happiness and fear
Laughter and tears live as one

The sun reflections on a freckled brow
- The picture it reveals is me.

Deena Wilson

Tim

I pulled a hedging glove over his head
So he wouldn't bite the vet
Poor Tim had the last injection
He would ever get.
He had a tumour in his leg
For which there was no cure
But 'twas hard to see him go
As he slipped silently to the floor.
For years he'd helped with fetching cows
And kept intruders at bay
For hours and hours out in the yard
With his large black ball he'd play.

Now he's buried in the garden
With all the other pets
His photos in the album
Will keep his memory yet.

R. J. Moulton

Shortcut

If there was a spine that I could grab,
Find a pulse and measure it.
I should be like them.
Break a code (or shatter the enigma)
and find the secrets of the form.
There will be a link to them.
Rows of them over all the lands,
Endless corridors,
Infiltrating every home.
There's a silent humiliation as I try again
To discover the key to open a path for me.
Another failure and I will go back to
Studying the designs, the new formats;
The diction, the prose, imagery and themes.
Read them and weep or read them and pause,
Wondering,
But never breaking the code.

John-Paul Harold

The Bluebell Wood

Today I walked in a bluebell wood
Where the dappled sunlight danced upon the leaves
My thoughts flew back to by gone childhood days
When we acted out our games in woods like these
Where are they now, those friends of long ago
Whose voices echo still within my mind?
Do they still think of me, as I of them
And wonder where those carefree days have gone?
The years go rolling by and then I see
The humble bluebell carpeting the ground
I am a child again arms full of blooms
Years lost to me and yet, in nature, found.

Catherine Bridger

The Cuckoo

O lazy bird of Spring,
Seldom these days, do we
see thee on the wing.
We hear thee though.
At early dawn.
Thy mocking call, unique of all,
In thy feathered world.
Foul weather does not put you off.
Your journey northwards to our Isle.
Your calls to make,
A home to find, of some smaller bird,
Your will.
This unkind act of laziness, to dispossess.
No home to build to call your own.
Yet, your call to all, in that mocking tone,
Never fails to thrill.
If our Spring is early or cold and late.
We are assured that Spring is here,
When we hear you call cuckoo!
Lest we forget the date.

W. E. Speake

"Ziggy"

She leaps and prances up and down,
She bounces like a rubber ball.
She flings her pliant body
Here, now there,
With infinite grace—as light as air.

Luxuriant whiskers crown her brow,
Her coat is jet, her paws are white.
Each pad the palest pink—on each,
A spot of black,
How delicately fashioned in this cat.

Pale is her chin, her eyes are green,
At her tail end, a puff of snow,
Reaching for windblown leaves,
Imaginary foes,
She stands and dances on her toes.

She crouches in the grass, she springs,
She rolls upon her back with joy.
She climbs.
She stalks an hurrying ant until, dead beat,
Quite suddenly, she drops and falls asleep.

Leslie Grant

England The Land I Love

At dawn the light begins to glow,
The song of birds enthrals me so.
Both thrills one in early spring,
Then summer's onset pleasures bring,
Birds are nesting, flowers grow,
The starlit sky it sparkles so.
Midsummer comes, the moon does shine
And fills the land with light divine.
The summer sun with shimmering heat
Watches sea, and land - the small lambs bleat.
The cattle rest, the swans in pairs,
Pigs, sheep, and burrowers in their lairs.
Blessed are we who spend our lives in country dells
Away from cities, noisy traffic, crowds and smells
To listen to nature's sounds around
Gives one a feeling of peace profound.
Long may this be, before the builder's hand
Removes - trees, fields and wild life from our lovely land.
A daughter of England I am proud to be
This lovely land much bounded by the sea.

D. J. Fee Smith

Waiting In Vain

From the window, the days turn to nights
She stares in wonder, this can't be right

Waiting in pain, as the days pass her by
Her strength is weak, unable to cry

He said "One day I'll return my love"
Was this the truth as she looks to above

Oh God, I wish I could know
Was I right in letting him go

His love I've carried for so long
But his love for me—it must be gone

Maybe one day our paths will cross
But for me—it's oh such a loss

I waited on his return for so very long
The years passed me by and now they've all gone.

Breige Crilly

Confusion

Feelings,
Mixed and un-relenting
Grappling, fighting, taking over
One's whole being.
Changing
Like rippling sands on the tide,
One moment of elation
Certainty and assurance,
Then
Despair
Uncertainty and confusion.
Fleeting glances, smiles and friendly gestures,
Warm embraces, promises and love and
Loneliness, deep, un-explained and threatening.
Dark days
Confusion.

Ann Harrison

Everyone's

Everyone's stroking the hair of the one they choose,
but why aren't I? In love it seems I always lose.
Everyone's staring into the eyes of admiration,
I want to feel that stare filled with someone's passion.
Everyone's holding the hand they want to hold,
to experience this I would sell my soul.
Everyone's kissing their good night kiss,
Why must I be the one to miss out on this?
Tonight as I sleep everyone will be making love,
but before I sleep I will pray for love from up above.
One day I will stroke someone's hair,
into someone's eyes I will stare.
I will hold a hand and again the feeling I'll never miss,
soon I will kiss a good night kiss.
And like you do in heaven up above,
with someone I will make love.

Kim Douglass

The Windmills

I walked on alone through the milling crowd.
Past all the houses and pubs, shops and grills.
Then spied with shock, high on the hills, a proud
Far away group of war-like white windmills.
Running along the pale blue-grey sky-line
Manifesting the tawdry way they stray.
Uniform their tall, smooth, unapt outline
Reaching out to a far distant highway.
The grass soft beside their solid pathway
Its timeless green-peace colour contradicts
These new wind-fed humming towers so fey.
But, I realized, how my needs conflict

And stared, knowing I should give some support
For all the cheap electricity they brought.

Susan Holmes

That Stuff

I smell It on my hands
I smell It on my feet
I smell It in the house
Or when I'm walking in the street
What is It, that I smell
I don't really like to say
It's the stuff I put upon my back
To ease the pain away

When my day is done and it's time to go to bed
I put this stuff upon my back the smell goes to my head
When I want to sleep no matter how hard I try
That smell drifts, into my nose as It goes passing by

When we meet, in the street
You shake my hand
You smell a little smell
I'm sure you'll understand
I still put on that stuff
'Cos I know I really should
One day soon that terrible smell
Could be gone for good

Dennis N. Davies

A Small Creature

There is a small creature, who lives here in God's house
His name is Oscar, a little brown mouse,
He has a wife and a family of four.
He lives by the radiator, next to the door,
Don't come looking for him on a Monday night,
It's the family's night out, not a whisker in sight,
It's those bells in the belfry, what a noise they make,
Just make the whole church shiver and shake,
Just loves weddings and wedding rings.
But not very often he hears a choir sing.
He loves christingle with candles so bright.
With little faces beaming in a circle of light,
But, his favourite time throughout the years
Has been the harvest festivals, all those apples and pears,
What has happened, he wonders, to the harvest bread,
Was always a nice meal before going to bed,
So if you see Oscar here today,
Don't shoo him away, just let him stay,
This is his home, here in God's house,
He's one of God's creatures, this little brown mouse.

June Lucas

Sagacity

Winter abed with Autumn gold
Plucks the late fruit touched by first frost
And drinks a wine more subtle and divine
Than any tried in youth.

Revived, old winter drinks again
All season's kaleidoscope into one
And sage tranquillity attends his final hours.

Thelma Easterby

Sunflowers

A tiny seed falls to the ground
children cover it with a trowel
the seed cowers under a warm blanket of earth
through rain, snow, shine and wind
sleeping for ages, on and on
it wakes up
it feels the glorious sunshine
beaming down on the earth from heaven
it hears the children playing ball
it bursts through into the light
a fresh green shoot
after a year a tower of green
with a crown
a large sun-like flower
shining with power and light

Judy Louie Brown

To Be A Bird

O to be a bird upon the wing
in cloudless skies I'd hover and sing
as in-built instincts hasten me away
we may meet again one summer's day

My wings outstretched with effortless ease
on unseen thermals I follow the breeze
over hills and dales with meandering streams
there is just no end to my travels it seems

After thunderous storms and mountainous seas
I am glad it's changed to a gentle breeze
I have landed here I know not where
but there's hundreds of twitchers everywhere

The nest is built now we hatch the brood
it's time I went to catch the food
from early morn till late at night
until in turn they all take flight

The chorus has started it's early morn
to announce a new day is being born
I sit at the top of a sycamore tree
so that all the humans can listen to me.

Nick Holden

'Where The Sun Don't Shine'

So frequently I saw your face pictured in the mirror
of my affections
worn by richness
a fading cloud dispersing rain within my heart
as though an endless pit
I briefly came round
so you gathered all hope to manipulate my grace;

Your fatal dream to destroy a life so gracious
now taking shape
yet you trespass on untrodden ground
or lost sense of reality!

In day you wait for night to fall
in all its splendour where darkness surrounds
blackened except the rays of the moon
solitary hung like a picture in the midnight sky.
No nails to keep it there;

Yet with so much romance, comes so much lust
I saw it in your eyes
I look deeper but find no love or forgiveness
so I gave to you my undivided attention
for you to cloak it with hatred!

C. B. Lambourne

Boundless Love

When I stand upon the shore
And see the rolling sea
I think about the vastness
Of God's great love to me

His love is like the ocean
Whose depth no man can tell
Abundant, flowing freely
To save my soul from Hell

Love beyond all measure
Boundless as God's grace
Touching every country
Seeking every race

God's love has no equal
For He gave His Son
Who, on the cross of Calvary
Died for a world undone

To all who own the Saviour, as their Lord and King
Love in all its fullness, Jesus Christ will bring

Swelling and yet swelling, like the restless sea
Greater and yet greater, is His love to me

Horace Hartley

Morning Prayer

Thank you our Father, for the rising sun
That tells the world a new day has begun
The golden rays that sweep the bight away
And awaken us to face another day

E'er I begin to face my daily task
Keep me from sin Lord, this I humbly ask,
May something of thy character of love
Be shown through me to those amongst I move

Show me the path that Thou wouldst have me tread,
Keep me from falling, give me daily bread.
May all my thoughts and actions honour Thee
That others see something of Christ in me

I thank you for the privilege of prayer
At any hour, knowing Thou art there,
Unchanging God, for evermore the same
Our prayers are offered in our Saviour's name

When evening comes, and time has come for rest
When yonder sun sinks slowly in the West
Grant that my soul be at one with Thee
So that in peace my hours of sleep shall be

Horace Hartley

Elves And Fairies

One morning very early (after break of dawn),
I tiptoed down the stairs and looked out on the lawn;
There on the sparkling grass I saw a tiny elf
Dancing and singing, and laughing to himself!

Little legs a-flying he kicked his wee feet high
'til I thought his chestnut boots would surely touch the sky!
Blue cap a-bobbing he seemed to dance for hours -
Then crept exhausted to rest in the flowers.

Later in the morning (from my secret bower),
I saw a tiny fairy, bright like fairies are!
With a silver thimble and tiny golden spray
She was sprinkling each flower that came her way.

Her dress was heavenly blue; shoes, the palest pink,
Her shining crown and her wings, gossamer, I think.
And when she saw me watching her, she said 'good-day',
Spread her tiny wings and quickly flew away!

And later in the afternoon I looked up high,
And saw elves and fairies helping paint the sunset
On the sky. And in the evening (bed-time hours),
With their silver wands, helping light up the stars!

Jean Jane

Missing You

Do not stand looking for me on your way,
Sadly I am not here . . .
I am a thousand miles away from you.

Do not try to find my face,
In those of hurried people on the busy pavements.
Do not try to find me sitting on a deck chair in a park.

For a short while, I cannot be with you,
To share laughs as we usually do,
To share secrets on our way back home.

But . . .
I will be in the wind that blows,
In the rain that gently touches your window,
In the leaves falling with the coming of Autumn.
I will be with you in my thoughts,
In places we used to be together.

Sadly I am not here . . .
I am a thousand miles away from you,
Thinking about you . . . missing you.

Maria Lucia Da Costa

Permanent Patients

Draw a line, a dead straight line
Build a wall upon it to
Paint it black with Judas eyes
And have it rendered with your view

At its peak it's higher now
Much higher than before
With no access to your reasoning
Blind words become a bore

Each course you build is opposed to see
Where old bricks join the new
You can't suppress late primal scream
Jesus Christ had long hair too

Richard Gautier

Morning

The alarm clock awakens the house to life
And peace no longer reigns.
'Though it's warm and cosy here inside
There's frost on the window panes.

A clinking sound comes from the street
As the milkman makes his round.
The children scamper down the stairs
Oh! What an awful sound.

The smell of cooking fills the house
While the kettle cheerfully sings.
The newspaper pops through the letter box
I wonder what news it brings.

Every day it's the same routine
To start the morning right.
Then it's off to work and off to school
And I'm glad they're out of sight!

Mary Stanford-Mowat

The Basket Of Dreams

Fragrant Isles where palm trees lean
Emeralds in blue caribbean
a Spanish Galleon on the main
with creaking oar and shining chain
A noble sight for English eyes
For Drake himself a worthy prize

An Indian brave above the trail
who scans the distant waggons sail
What war whoops hear that pale face band
faint echoes where a city stands
no wigwams now, nor cedars high
Tall building 'gainst an evening sky.

With silken threads these pictures weave
On the satin cloth of make believe
Or a boy beside a woodland pool
with patched trousers truant from school
This embroidery basket on the chair
What coloured threads and dreams lie there.

Matt Murray

"For Sheila"

The years have passed yet all but seems
like yesterday
When first we met
Another time, another place.
And thro' those years my heart has found
Such peace of mind for me to say
that in my days, alone,
I found that peace when thinking of your face,
For it's the one I love,
And all the joy it gave to me
along the years when worlds apart were we—
Till now—to-gether here—residing in
Our Home of dreams,
I think once more how only yesterday
It seems.

J. Hinde

A Whisper In The Fields

Silence was the only sound
Before I opened my ears to listen,
But now there's a light, almost mellow swooshing
As the wind races to and fro.

I hear the sound of tweeting birds
As their wings flap within the clouds,
And crickets fiddling in the grass
Beneath trooping ants as they climb a settled bark.

Leaves rustling in trees up high
As the early signs of shower fall;
Tiny bombs of water exploding on a leaf,
Its crisp cracking echoing along the wind.

The more I listen, the more I hear,
'Till I can record sounds from afar:
A dog's low growl, an engine hum,
A whispering in the fields.
C. P. Clarke

The Gambler

Fixing the Normandy Invasion,
The cold winds blew with loneliness and hate,
He struggled on against an unknown fate,
His courage grew with each cold blast.
He knew he would make it at last!
A gambler born to fight the wrong.
That rang around him like a song.
The traitor stepped up into view.
Up went his gun and he shot true!
The traitor fell in mortal pain.
Shouting out the devil's name.
But true the gambler's luck ran out.
And in his ears he heard a far off shout!
"You've played a great game and won my son".
So come and join us in the sun,
His fading eyes they saw a sail,
Approaching fast like in a fairy-tale.
He saw his comrades from the past.
He smiled a smile of peace, on deck at last!
Gordon Paul (Epitaph)

"The Power of Prayer"

Those who believe in the power of prayer
Know you can pray just anywhere;
You can pray while dusting
Or walking the dog,
Riding in a bus
Or having a jog.

The Lord will answer in His good time;
His timing is perfect, you just have to wait,
So don't get yourself in a terrible state
Thinking the answer will be too late.
Don't be impatient as time goes by
Hang on to His promise and await His reply.
He may say "yes", "no" or "not just yet"
But He'll answer for sure -
He'll not forget.

Remember He loves you and knows all your needs -
You just have to ask,
And wait - and believe.
Peggy C. Crossley

Elvis Superstar

Gone from this world, but not from our hearts,
you were the king right from the start.
So young and good looking, a rebel at heart.
You sang 'Love Me Tender' and then 'Surrender'.
Swayed to 'Don't Be Cruel',
jiggled to 'All Shook Up'
and rocked to 'Blue Suede Shoes'.
'The Wonder of You' took the world by storm.
'I Just Can't Help Believin' 'How Great Thou Art'.
Helen Barrie

Red Nose Wars

Ten years on and the children, they're still hungry.
Hungry for your love, Hungry for your food,
But most of all they're hungry for what we can do.
We can feed them, cloth them, help them build.
Sisters and brothers are we,
Sisters and brothers are they.
Help our victory, Make theirs a special day.
Now the years have come and gone,
We will be the ones.
Feed the children, see them smile,
now to see it all worth while.
Feed the children, see them play,
their hunger at bay.
Ten years have come and gone,
and the children, they're still hungry.
Hungry for our Help.
Hungry for our Love, is it still there?
Maxine C. Parkinson

Margarite

Margarite my Margarite
    You are so fair.
Beautiful beyond compare.
    with sparkling eyes.
And smiling face.
    charm and grace to behold.

Yet all the time we are apart.
    I think of you with all my heart.
Each day my passion grows for you.
    You were my treasure from the start,

I bless the day we met
    You were the one.
That taught me to care.
    I will always remember.
The rose in your hair.

You're like a golden dream
    in my heart never ending
Through darkness of the night till morning light's splendour.

I shall never forget you with your smile so warm.
Passion like beauty and so full of charm.
Mel Bentley

Newborn Babies

Lying beneath the burning sun
Life for them has just begun
They are naked, they're in the nude
They don't care, they just want food
    Opening wide their starry eyes
All you hear are their cries
Holding on so very tight
Once their mothers are in sight
    Safely then they're cradled up
Gazed upon from their mother's look
Innocent they start their days
In so many different ways
    Newborn babies are a gift
All our hopes they shall lift
That as a seed, when nurtured flowers
So child will blossom in this world of ours
Joanne Kirkbride

"The Ocean Of Life"

The ocean waves smash and roar,
'Til trickling waters reach the shore,
and boats that glide upon the deep,
where fishes swim and dragons sleep.

So, tell me friend - where does it start?
But then again - where does it end?
Like life itself, we do not know,
We just go forth along the flow.
Madelaine Ratcliffe

Precious Moments

Moments so precious and rare,
Should be taken up within a glance.
Don't think of the tomorrows or yesterdays,
Only of today, this moment, here and now.
Live and experience it to the fullest,
In all extremities.
For life is short, and those hidden delicacies,
That come once in a lifetime must be swooped up,
Or will rush by like the wind.
They are there for the taking,
Only for a moment in time.
Take, receive whatever pleasures so come forthwith,
Allow yourself to be free.
Enter into the Kingdom of serene beauty,
For a door is held with open arms ready to embrace,
You alone possess the magical key to unlock the most deepest
desires that stir souls.
Envelope a cocoon around you,
Escape to this secret place,
Whenever life begins to take its toll.

Zarina Ramzan

Northern Trucker

Northern Trucker I'm watching thee
From indoor occupations flee
Like bird of song on wing so free
No bars or chains detaining thee

Northern Trucker, no fixed abode
Residence for you, the road
No responsibilities bestowed
Forever dodging life's overload.

Northern Trucker run away
Live hand to mouth come what may
No consequence to face today
But they'll all catch up with you one day.

Northern Trucker fight the fight
With trusty steed and armour bright
Point thyself north and give all full flight
For the Northern Trucker's home tonight.

Paul Hoffman

Time

Time is a clock that ticks on the wall
It ticks away our lives so sweet and so small

We grow up quick yet we don't realise the
time that is gone when we open our eyes

But time is a clock that ticks on the wall.
It ticks away our lives no matter how small

Majella O'Sullivan

Victory For Europe

Today I travelled fifty years,
Beside an army frail and spent,
I heard the sirens, saw the tears,
And talked of war that came and went.

Victorious soldiers cast aside,
Too late these furious flags that wave,
A nation's welcome long denied -
I smelled their musty, weeded graves.

Embedded in those furrowed brows,
Scenes and sights of savage carnage,
More vivid then; fast faded now,
Our freedom found; theirs long tarnished.

Fate forced the gamble - who'd survive
The piercing bursts from molten lead,
Stiff upper-lip of English pride
Outlived the war and raised the dead.

Philip Holden

Teardrops

From the corners of my eyes it creeps,
To the edges of my cheeks and then it leaps
Down my face, to splash elsewhere,
Releasing feelings I would not share.

I do not share these thoughts of mine,
That cause my eyes and cheeks to shine,
For in that moment of release,
Do I find sorrow or do I find peace?

If it be sorrow from this small flow,
Then I'm not sure I want to know
About such thoughts, up in my head
That churn my mind like molten lead.

But then again, if it be peace,
Could it be that pain will cease,
And show the way to happiness,
Oh, that would be a sweet caress,

So flow little pearls, from deep inside,
And open a path that's wet and wide,
Only then by what's been said,
Shall I know which path to tread.

David Turner

The Point Of No Return

And so too came the masses.
Their hunger and thirst for power overwhelming
And their followers misguided by the task in hand.
Destruction loomed.
Evil minds consumed with a passion for power,
Lusting after an unknown quantity.
Diverse in their knowledge,
Seeking a hidden entity.
A glut for something quite abominable in every aspect.

Then came the sudden eerie silence -
Almost a welcome relief following the raging storm.

Man stood back in horror and surveyed the destruction.
What carnage!
Had man stooped so low he could no longer ascend the realms
of humanity?

Oblivion reigns supreme.
What have we done?

Pat Stone

Vagrant R.I.P.

Smashed in the road the vagrant lay
Injured, expected to die,
Hit by a car on a foggy night.
And there's no-one to care or to cry.

Hanging on to life by a slender thread.
Helped by machines and drips
But no-one to sit beside him,
And moisten those poor, parched lips.

Death holds his hand now, and beckons to him,
To wander the roads no more,
And there's no-one who cares to detain him.
No-one whose heart is sore.

A last look back down the lonely life
Of a vagrant with-out a home,
Then he closes his eyes with a weary sigh,
Never again to roam.

There's no-one to claim that poor, broken man.
No-one to say him a prayer,
No-one to weep at his grave side
No-one to give it a care.

Greta E. Dye

Untitled

I weep for the wee ones.
The unborn packages so dear to all.
How can they enter this world?
The torrent of blood is thick and where lies escape, the
lifeline thrown to the drowning?

The waves are high.
I cannot swim. Help me!
So many cast a flimsy line, well meaning, good intentions.
The strength is not there.
They cannot pull alone.

A world put to rights.
It is too late.
We overstep the mark.
Point of no return.
Man cannot sink much lower in the blood of his fellow man.

I weep for the unborn child. But he will suffer no pain.

Pat Stone

My Wife

Often through the day
as I work away
I plan to get home early
with some flowers for my Girlie
kiss her hand, her lips, and say,
Have I told you lately
you look so lovely
Every time I see you, my heart melts away

When I think of all the girls
I could have been stuck with
I sure was in luck with the one I drew
Have I told you lately
how much your husband loves you

Brian Richards

Search Dog

Who would know? To see her stand, perhaps to stare...
Gingerly sniffing winter Lakeland night air,
She alone can sense where fragile life has lain,
Under flimsy floating fog, or mystic rain...

Who would know? If 'neath any icy bed of snow,
Hard-packed, where human rescuers' feet trudge slow,
A climber's heart may beat... or is it still?
Will Mother Nature's mountain claim another "kill"?

Who would know? Above all whispered prayers...
Frenzied digging... layer to deeper layers...
Striving... to set free the soul which makes no sound...
Canine instinct drives her deeper underground...

Who would know? Set deep in Winter's final cast...
Where to dig, now death white avalanche has past
She tugs an arm... 'shows' the climber... safe... below...
Barking to the Rescue Team... 'I told you so'...

Alexander Crawford

Bird Song

Oft wonder what the birds do say,
Clutching the branches as they slowly sway.
Soft silent light into the bedroom streams
As I awaken from my dreams;
New, wondrous day.

I wonder what the birds do say,
Chirping and trilling at the dawning day.
Pure glorious music, so to me it seems,
But oh! I wonder what it means?
Well, who can say?

What is it that the birds do say?
Every one in its own special way.
"All thanks be to God and the Seraphims,
And glory to the day that beams."
That's what they say.

Elwyn Williams

Village Churchyard

Where grey tombstones mark the place
Around the ancient little church
They sleep; the villages of old.
They sleep while chestnut's candles bloom
And air is filled with lime flower's scent
They sleep through summer's showers and drought
Through day breaks filled with songs of birds
And sunsets flaming in the west
They sleep while leaves begin to fall
Quietly or blown in droves
When Autumn storms rage through the trees.
They sleep beneath grey Winter skies
And when the snow's white blanket spreads
Sleep then, you villagers of old
At peace now in this quiet place
Which in life you can loved so well.

I. W. Newbury

To Sleep

Fast away he may well be,
Safe, amongst whatever he should care to see . . .
Here still supposed to naturally settle in,
And cast away the day like skin,
To wriggle under, lie alert,
Turn and wonder . . .
Must desert the habit of the thinking cogs,
But time and time forever jogs
The weary mind to cry 'eureka';
Tired theories, waking weaker,
Better then to sit and stare
Until in numbness unaware,
As quiet louder than a crowd
Releases its relieving shroud
Upon the room, where lying we,
Are silent with the breath of three.

Lindsey M. Holland

The New Road

They by-passed our village, which killed off the shop.
They've stolen the fields, where once rabbits hopped.

They've banned us from going where the motor car is king,
And told us, 'be silent' it's not a bad thing.

The noise and the dust when the tarmac was laid, hung over
the village like a cloak made from suede.

Our doors and our windows, we shut up tight,
Whilst inside the houses we cleaned up the blight.

The protests were many, but action less clear, and some of
the road men travelled in fear.

But the road went on through, with hardly a break.
To swallow the copse, the barns and the lake.

R. K. Jackson

To Cachel

Thank God for little boys like Cachel who scrape their knees,
And tumble to the ground with the greatest ease.
Laughing, giggling, little boys who tease
Their mummy with a wriggling worm.

Thank God for little boys with wide grins
Playing make believe games of who-dares-wins.
Innocent-looking little boys
Who break their toys

And say 'Mr. Nobody' did it.
Never mind, mummy will mend it.
Or daddy will buy you a new one -
Lovingly chosen for 'my only son'.

May he find Peace, Contentment and Love.
An innocent lad
With a face like his Dad
And the 'Imp' of his mother in him.

Gladys F. Herberts

It's Time

We have all the time in the World,
But we only have five minutes:
Your heartbeat is fading like an echo,
Running from me on the breeze:
I try to catch the air fragments
To make from scattered blossom your flower;
Every precious second I whisper to you must be kept -
The words you reply are branded in my eyes,
Bright sparks when I cannot let you see my tears.

The grip from your fingers dents my hand; falls limp:
That is when I cry aloud,
Uncaring what I need to say to retrieve you;
I scream but anger dissolves to silence:
It is time now....

Time to sail alone, let go of love's hand,
For he has put you on a path which
You must learn to follow;
Listen to the last murmur:
"You have all the time in the World -
Make every second precious."

Emma Wilson

Was It My Choice?

Was it my choice to be born on Planet Earth?
Was it I who chose my Human Form at birth?
Mundane contact made me think it can't be mine
As, on opening my eyes, I did scream and whine!

In the nuclear big-bang of my creation,
I emerged in an eye's twinkling duration;
I steered clear of miscarriage and abortion,
Thanks to my Bio-Mum's care and precaution.

I soon became an entity well defined,
In Physique, and Form, and Genes, and Frame of mind.
Hampered, I grew, sans silver 'spoon in my mouth',
Squeezing the nectar of life, the hard way out!

Biological organs are grown in Labs;
Transplants now made to humans from Pigs and Cats!
Even genii Medics, cannot life create,
That which only God Divine can procreate.

In time's fullness, whence I came, thither I'll go,
A smile beaming on my cadaver, aglow!
To the nebulous abyss—the shore sublime,
Eureka!, it is my Maker's choice—not mine.

Welch Jeyaraj Balasingam

Summer's Perfume

The sweet sweet smell of a summer's breeze,
Full of the fragrance of lavender and rose.
The lush green grass swaying gently with content,
The dew forming like crystals between each blade.

The sky is painted spring blue,
The sun shines bright, like a golden nugget.
The air is so dear, and so fresh,
The opening of summer's perfume.

The summers idol the sea, shines out its radical beauty
As the glistening sun dances on the waves.
The grains of gold sand reflected its openness
As it spreads for a mile of land.

The warm shadow in the shade of a forest,
Where the trees hide out the sun rays,
Cannot escape under the glorious cover,
As the blossoms pattern displays on the ground.

The heat of the summer brings happiness,
Wherever it happens to flow,
It cleans out bad feelings for others,
And gives warmth for friendships to grow.

Pollyanna Arnott

Problems

Kids in one street,
Huddling in street corners,
They've got no home,
No love,
No money,
what can we do to make this world a better place?
To have enough homes,
enough love,
and enough money,
for everybody in the world.
No fighting, just peace,
No pollution,
Just a perfect, picturesque place.
These are just some of the world's problems
Only we can make a difference,
For the sake of our children,
And our children's children,
It's up to us,
To stop it before it's too late.

S. E. Atkinson

Growing Old

Now youth has gone, the years have quickly sped,
Down memory lane, my thoughts have fondly fled
To the days of careless chatter,
When tomorrow didn't matter,
When each day was so inviting,
And the evenings so exciting,
When men were kind and very charming
How they've changed is quite alarming.
When my babies were so pretty
They're grown up now, it's such a pity.
These halcyon days fly far too fast,
If only one could make them last.
Now I live a life of ease
Doing mostly what I please.
Now my life is much more stable
I do the things that I am able.

G. E. Yates

The Swans

The white swans they are beautiful,
  How stately, large and how graceful
Upon the still river they glide
  Now singly or now side by side.

There are three types of white swans mute,
  Bewick and whooper, among loots,
They look majestic and so brave
  Shielding their cygnets they must save.

Not only on rivers they're seen.
  At slim bridges too, they steal the scene;
Among the ducks, geese and wildfowl
  They are forever on the prowl.

By the sea there's Abbotsbury
  Not far away, the swannery
Is found; the mute swans are seen there,
  Outnumbering ducks everywhere.

B. S. Mussellwhite

Through The Window

Looking through the window the day is grey.
The streets shiny with the morning acid rain.
The woman ambling down the litter-strewn streets.
The neon lights slowly knocking off, their night shift over.
The sun breaks the skyline and burns the morning smog.
The old fella is awake, it's time for work while kids play.
It's a new day, more bills to pay - with very little pay.
A pint and a smoke, home for thy grub.
A kiss in the night with the wife then good night.
Looking through the window the day is still grey.

P. Sutton

Memories Of Elvis

'The first time ever I saw your face'
I was hooked, by the way you sang and looked.
I was young and you were young then too,
isn't it funny how time slips away
You were the perfect 'U.S Male'
I just can't help believin' that like
a 'Bridge over troubled water' you've
helped us through our troubles and sorrow
I've lost you yes we've lost you, but
you're still our 'big hunk O' burning love.'
We've not 'lost that lovin' feelin' for you
because memories are pressed between
the pages of our minds.

Helen Barrie

Innocent

So innocent, yet still a victim,
No life, yet still a child
Laughing and smiling until some sick man went wild.
Everyone is so sorry and so very glum
But there is no excuse for what this madman has done.
So young and so pure, so silent and unharmed.
Never could you imagine in this small town could be such harm;
Going to school for a normal day
This terrible man ended their lives in a shocking way.
Tears are shed and flowers are spread,
To open their curtains people are scared.
In my opinion this man did not deserve a life,
They should have stabbed his heart, with a 10 inch knife.
To shoot himself was an easy way out.
Everyone would agree, I have no doubt.

Melissa Clark

My Everything

Like a star in the sky, you shine so bright;
To darkness you bring a splendour of light.

Like flowers, you are full of colours that gleam;
As the sun's rays upon the ground, you beam.

I will love you for life, that I want you to know;
The feelings I have for you will always grow.

Life will end one day although my love will never die;
For you it will last until my blood runs dry.

I wish you could see how much you mean to me;
And how much I hope and pray that it could be.

I'd give you the world if it were mine,
For you I would wait until the end of time.

Flowers will always grow, birds will always sing;
I will always see you as my everything.

C. Panayiotou

Somersal (1964)

Somersal's like a posy the children pick in May.
It's small and neat and fragrant,
And hidden quite away within fringe of
green leaves, far from prying eyes,
But like a children's posy, it's full of sweet surprise.
    The hawthorn froths its hedges,
    The wild flowers deck its feet,
    No discord mars its beauty,
    Only the merry feet of children and their
    Laughter disturbs this quiet retreat.

When I am back in the tumult and turmoil of the town.
I shall see again sweet Somersal
In her shimmering May day gown,
And hear the sounds of husbandry
And the children at their play,
And the quiet patient cattle
As they pass along the way.

R. Dawtry

Fatal Consequences

You've heard of the dangers, still give it a go,
"It won't happen to me, I'll be fine, I just know."
And that's what the girl said who took it last week,
that girl who's no longer with us here to speak.

You swallow the pill, and at first you feel great,
but later that night, get a feeling you hate.
You fall to the ground and your vision is black,
but the drug just won't stop and there's no turning back.

Then next comes the siren to take you away,
and you know it's not you, but your family who'll pay.
You hear people screaming, "she's dying" they shout,
for the sake of one drug it's your life that's in doubt.

You feel like you're drowning, you're gasping for air,
and to know that you're dying just doesn't seem fair.
But you will not awake to know what went wrong,
you're life has been short but your death shall be long.

You feel yourself slip, can't hold on anymore,
it's your brain that is dead, and your heartbeat is poor.
"We've lost her" they say, and you ask yourself why,
for the sake of 10 pounds was it worth it to die?

Jemma Ryan

The Blurred Love Statue

I fell in love with the statue of moon,
And saw its shadow glance at me and gloom.
Swift greyish tunes of coloured myths combined,
The lightest emotions in my hidden thoughts designed.

I rowed the boat in the lake of cold water - blue,
And thought myself being loved by him, too,
Then went on gliding, escorted by my water shadow,
And heard the whisper of unity twitter through the wood's sparrow.

And night showed its gold at evening time,
And made its choice incoherent, not considering mine;
So there I stood, with steps reversed,
As though the statue had me cursed -

Poor sorrowful tears, filled up with fears,
That tore my gracious shadow apart,
And tore the last bit of peace in my heart.

For then I knew, my destiny,
And thought myself to be till eternity free,
Now wanting to admit, the denial I had to commit,
That love had shown itself - that transparent light,
And shook its head, facing mine, leaving me with no delight.

Katerina Rayvazo

Stolen Dreams

Amble along this lonely path, as it staggers through the trees,
A feeling of warmth and calm envelops the breeze.
I behold a lazy cloud, as a stream passes by,
Washing away the tear stains, in a twinkling of an eye.
In the waters of reflection, my conscience is growing thin,
My soul free of guilt, when true guilt is held within.
These empty days slip away, like quicksand through my fingers,
I grapple free this dwelling pain, but the fear still lingers.
The candle of peace and hope is burning the way I feel,
In this ominous chapter of life, where animation becomes real.
Crimson sea of flames, lick their lips of desire,
Tossed a coin for my dreams, but the well just gets drier.
The raging storm vents its anger, towards the turning tide,
I twist and turn to escape, like the feelings deep inside.
On crumbling foundations, I still build brick by brick,
Torn thoughts of illusion, of a future now derelict.
This town's graveyard dust, blows through the wind of sorrow,
Glaring at this sad old joke, who's laughing at tomorrow.
I'm trapped under the wheels of love, with her behind the wheel,
See the sign of happiness buried upon the hill.

Andrew Wiltshire

Trust

It's the strength of personal amity
And the creator of national unity,
The betrayal of which
Will bring a great calamity.
  It's the pillar of stability
  And the preserver of tranquillity
  It has a great potentiality
  To bring us the sublimity.
It has a pervasive quality
It's own wonderful speciality
Which makes it a rare novelty
That creates and strengthens our understandability.
  It teaches us perseverance
  In whatever we want to do
  But, if we don't maintain our adherence
  We will then certainly rue.
When we abnegate trust
The humanity in us is just,
Depravity becomes a must
And then our name becomes dust.

K. S. Seehra

Dreams

Dreams are the silken threads of memory
Weaving a tapestry of uncertainty
Transporting me into realms of fantasy
An inner vision of unreality
Their vividness haunts my waking hours
The dread of uncontrollable powers
The Spider of the Night awaiting
Till sleep offers him my soul trembling
The watchers of the unknown spheres
My terrors and my troubled fears
Distorted images the agonizing cry
The sense of falling and the anguished sigh
Help me in my downward flight
And banish from my sleep the ghosts of night.

Daphne Day

The Magic Of Scotland

Skyline of fire like embers that glow
Mountain tops white when covered wi' snow
Deep are the shadows neath the darkness of pines
Scotland your magic so hauntingly mine

Sweet flows your music of rivers and burns
As they tumble o'er rocks and green leaves and ferns
Flower of my Hame'land colour of wine
My kinsfolk, their laughter I match now wi' mine

The blueness of loch's so still and so deep
Surrounded by hills like giant they sleep
Magic of my land you're always sae dear
Deep in my heart you'll always lie near.

Patricia Thoirs

Woman

Still, as the axis of a wheel
in the midst of her activities
raying out in all directions
from the central core
like spokes from the hub of a wheel
open to all points of the compass
distractions destroying the saint-like quality
cracking the hub of the wheel.

But no matter if the core remain
living in that inner grace
which translates itself into outward harmony
to find a balance 'twixt retreat and return
a swinging of the pendulum
between solitude and communion
achieving that stillness
not only for her own salvation
but perhaps even for our civilization.

Elizabeth Vardy

And So To Sleep

Those who claim that euthanasia is bad
Are probably the ones who've never had
To watch over a loved one, suffering the agonizing pain,
Of an incurable illness, enduring the strain.

Losing their battle, their dignity, their pride,
While those near and dear sit at their side,
Praying for each breath to be their last,
Trying hard to remember happier days past.

When quality of life is no longer there
And relatives and friends who deeply care
Are left feeling helpless, inadequate and despairing
Of the heartache each one of them is sharing.

When hope for the future is all but a dream,
Surely then, it must only seem
Kinder, less selfish and more humane
To put them to rest and remember them sane.

Why then, I ask, isn't it legal or right
To simply and painlessly end the plight
Of the sufferer, the carers, their families too?
Euthanasia holds the key for me and for you.

Amanda Couchman

The Close Of Day

The afternoon draws to its close as darkness fills the air,
the shadows creep along the walls and seep in everywhere,
a night owl hoots a lonely call; the bull frogs cease to croak,
and night descends upon the scene, a silent velvet cloak.

The smell upon the evening breeze reminds us autumn's near,
the bracken and the pine cones are strong this time of year,
the wood smoke from the bonfires that light the evening sky,
and the pungent smell of fungus on decaying trees nearby.

The sounds upon the evening air are muffled by the night,
the rumble of the distant storm the animals in flight,
a dried out branch that snaps so sharp, a stag that runs away,
the heavy tread of tired men who homeward wend their way.

The scudding clouds so full of rain engulf the pale night sky,
small creatures scuttle for their homes to places warm and dry,
and I am left alone it seems to watch the falling rain,
and ponder on the reasons why this scene gives me such pain.

When here at last as darkness falls upon this country scene,
It reminds me of the days long lost, of joys that might have been,
If only I had taken time; to see what passed my way,
perhaps there'd be a happier man, to watch the close of day.

Cyril Mepham

"My Friend"

A little boy was standing as if he couldn't care,
A dimple in his cheek and hair that was so fair
Down his face there rolled a tear from big and sad blue eyes,
There was no sunshine in his life—just dark and cloudy skies.

I said, "Oh little boy why do you stand and cry?"
He just looked up at me and gave a great big sigh.
"There must be something wrong which makes you oh so sad;
If you could talk things over I'm sure it's not so bad."

I seemed to gain his confidence he looked at me quite coy,
My heart went out to this ten year-old wee boy,
"You see", he said "Mister," at last he wants to talk,
"I used to have a friend and every day we'd walk.

Now I am left so lonely and always on my own,
Why did my friend have to go and leave me all alone?
One day we were playing and I was full of joy,
The next day I was so miserable—a sad, sad boy.

I went to bed last night and said a little prayer,
Because my friend took ill—and for her I did care,
I didn't want to lose my friend, I always called her Molly,
You see my friend, so faithful, was a little Border Collie."

Sheila Irvine Fraser Wann

Just The Same

Alone for the first time, knowing no-one,
Not knowing where to look or how to act.
Whispers from the corners,
Drift gently across the school yard.

Big eyes gazing,
Do they think I can't see?
The thing I'd like to know
Is why they treat me differently.

No one to talk to
No time to sigh
No one to confide in
Nowhere to curl up and cry.

I'm just as clever as they are
And I can read and write and draw
Pinch me and I feel the pain as others do
And red blood runs through my veins.

Sarah Gleeson

The Sunshine Flower

Where the quiet-coloured end of morning smiles
The sun does shine for miles and miles.
As the rays of heat do spread
My sunshine flower rises from her bed.
My sunshine flower is my spring
All my light and happiness does she bring.
She is my angel, my guide, my friend.
Her loving arms does she lend.
to hide, protect and to love
She's as pure as the snow white dove.
In flight and in grace
Forever the flower the sun embrace.
She's like a butterfly trying to break free
My flower holds the deepest part of me.
I know with her my love is true
Believe me Grandma, my sunshine flower is you.

Sara Baldwin

Untitled

The feeling got stronger each day
I felt as if two people were pulling me apart
one way then the other
the feeling was heavy and sad
For it was not light and happy
it was ugly
not beautiful
for this feeling is stabbing me.

Nicola Peeling

Happiness

A peak on the plain of content.
A moment of pure joy uplifting
Heart and spirit, focusing thought
On just the present time
Past forgotten and future ignored.
Such bliss is winged and swiftly flies
It cannot stay too long.
But when it slips away it may
Leave sweet content behind.
The memory of it lingers on
And gains more joy I find

Sometimes sorrow enters
When joy flies away
Bid it then a brave farewell
And think the sorrow sweet
For it is better than the pain
Of happiness denied
Where life has been a dreary plain
With no peaks of joy uplifting
When through life we're merely drifting.

I. W. Newbury

Shooting Days

Remember the day when Edgar's dog, put up the pheasant in the snow!
"Boom", "Boom", a left and then a right and folks would say, "That's Doctor
Joe" up and away the snipe would veer in zig-zag fashion across the bog
"Boom", "Boom", a left and then a right retrieving was up to Johnston's Dog

Bitter cold days, not long ago when Edgar would shout "Now Doctor Joe"
The dog would bark and excitement grew as rabbits bolted into view
O'er hill and dale and steep incline and Edgar would say "This one's
mine" then a flash and thunder sounded the dog went in, a "Yes, She's found it"

Aye, those were the days, not long ago when locals would say, "That's
Doctor Joe" the big car parked in some leafy glen and on the hill, the
shooting men yes I remember blanketnook when friends would say,
now that was a fluke came birds fell in the morning sun from the
smoking barrels of me father's gun!

Boy, that shooting stick, she was some brick little thought of
conscience or of morals and when she spoke and coughed up smoke she'd
hardly soil the barrels though these days she stays away no longer
does she boom her stock is strong and her beauty shines as she did in
those happy times. And I remember when Edgar's dog put up the
pheasant in the snow! "Boom", "Boom", a left and then a right
And folk would say, "That's Doctor Joe."

Paul Devlin

"The Ark of Compassion"

I beg of you, I plead with you, do not let them die;
The little calves, the little lambs - in a horrible! horrible! way.
Dragged by a leg to the slaughter house; hung by a leg - throat cut;
   blood pouring to the floor.
Helpless, innocent blood - still pouring - - - fear in the eyes; looking, crying - - -
Is there more!! It is a long, cruel, wicked, barbaric thing, this ending.

Baby calves stand in small crates; five months agony; liquid fed.
No solid food; cannot move or lie down, just barely able to move the head;
Travelled for miles - - - no food, water, or fun - - -
We cross the sea to another Hell! It is - - - a crucified one;
Mother; where is she, Oh! Is there no mercy! Not even for her - - -
What have we done to Man; waiting, wondering, not well now, still alone.

Compassion, compassion - - - was not found on the cross;
Forgive them; for they know not what they do - - -
Man does know what he does; he does what he does.
Compassion, compassion, for all kinds of Animals of the Ark.
It is in my dream, and held truly, deeply, in my heart.

Whatever those of you decide, on your conscience is blood forever spilt.
In this world of destruction, guilt and cruelty;
Man, all animals feel, fear, smell blood - - - give them back respect
and their dignity. Vanity they know not; they cannot speak, cry
help!! I care for them - - -
with freedom, and Mother Nature's wisdom.

Josephine Stewart

A Sumptuous Feast

I wish to say that long ago one summer's day I was so fascinated by
the strawberry field with mesmerizing hues of red and green. There
I felt I was in the garden of Eden. All its scarlet berries big and
small charmed me to forever hold me in thrall. Their overpowering
sweetness tantalized my nostrils, filled the air to create a blissfully
restful atmosphere. At the same time the glorious noonday sun
intensely bathed me so as to irresistibly whet my appetite. Finally
having treated myself to some sweet and succulent fruit I found my
life had never been so good. For so much happiness and joy
suddenly invaded my heart and soul. As it seemed to me I was
being entertained at a sumptuous feast fit for kings and queens.
What's more, I sensed that the strawberry juice while racing
through each vein, like God's nourishing nectar, made me feel
stronger every moment, in every possible way, able to conquer any
obstacle so to establish myself one day as the only master of my lot
and fate. Thus I had discovered that the strawberry field, with all its
magic delicacy, was the world of my dreams. No wonder today,
whenever I glance at a strawberry, I am instantly carried away
to that fabulous place, ready to relive that bliss and regale again
just to find myself, as before, so secure and content.

Lucy Carrington

The Lover

A broken heart that needs mending
A solution that's not impending
I go to sleep nervously awaiting my lover to visit me
The night is long, the bell fails to ring
The haunting memories begin.

A fool I have been to no avail
Unloved, unwanted, a long sad tale
I must recover the strength I once had
Separating the fool from the cad.

The journey forward must prevail
I need to walk that long hard trail
Heading forward to journey's end
I need a place to stay therein
To mend my heart that's been broken within.

I will move back to this place
And join once more the human race
The world out there being a joyous place
I feel a need to enter that race.

A great contester I will be, Red Rum having nothing on me
Starting off at 10-1, what's the bet I end up odds-on!

Lee Lowsley

Earth Woman

I'm the woman of the ground
my soul springs through mountains and rivers.

I don't belong anywhere, then, I belong somewhere;
but my voice has the sound of all hymns in harmony.

My song is elevating to infinity
where the sea and the sky are united forever.

The wind brings me back to the origin of time;
the sun's tenderness rests in my roots, and
I become alive again with the flowering of colours in the summer.

Hope grows up in my leaves, after, when autumn arrives
they're transformed into an ardent rainbow, flying at will
feeding our interminable hunger of the future.

The dew caresses my shapes, the fountain of new life;
my blood runs like rain
in the thirsty earth of my flesh;
my bones are rocks
drawn by the breeze and the dance of the waves
as they play flirtingly in my senses.

I hear, I see, I smell, I touch
the sweet salt of the hidden secret.

Carmen Lamas Waldron

Quo Vadis, Britain?

The future leaks bleak, even more so than the present!
Could it really be so, since what we need, we haven't?
When this government falls, will we turn to the left,
To save us the treasure of which we are being benefit?
 But what of the future? What have we in store
To take us forward without suffering still more?
Where are the true statesmen? Is there not one left
To lead us out of this jungle? One really left?
 Worry not, you people, you are in good hands!
Who dares to say that and set loose the bands
Which are stifling progress in all spheres of life -
Morally, spiritually - leading to strife?
 From the pent-house downwards is little but woe,
Not one clear way to show us where to go!
Will Europe save us from this slough of despond
Which sinks even deeper - a bottomless pond?
 Have we really lost faith, even in ourselves?
We must not behave like misguided elves!
We must not let mischief rule the day
And let the prince of this world have his way!

Claude A. Knight

Kingdom Of Mist

Misty morning
Conifers bathed in dew
Tall, majestic, emerald kings in a fairyland
Their shadows cast to mark supremacy
Wood pigeons call
Caretakers of the trees in royal chant
All is well
Flapping wings, like toy-land gunfire through the silence
From tree to tree, for sovereign and servant
Survival begins a new day
Gossamer cobwebs sprinkled with dewdrops
Diamonds glistening in the pale morning sun
As sun and mist fight for command
Silken drapes, designed by tiny creature architects
Guardians to the palace jewels
Enticing with deadly intent
Sun conquers mist
Magic fades
Emerald kings give up their crowns
To await the coming of another dawn

Patricia A. Maubec

A Little Balloon

A little balloon, on a dull dreary day
Turns on the magic, we love to play,
Puffing and blowing, it really is growing,
Babies' eyes widen, dear, will it frighten!
When big, puffing papa plays; 'Pop'!

Out in the street, two tiny feet
Merrily run, with the strings
Fast, floating, funny, magical thing.
It floats around, without a sound,
Cheering all it seems to meet.

Way, way up in the tree
Tied together, you will see
Boyhood pranks big bright balloons
All beaming back at me,
Set to go to the moon, maybe!

Summer fair, cylinders of air
Fly balloons high, into the sky,
The miles to chase, in the big balloon race,
My pleasure, my treasure,
Life's little balloon; My Ace!

Anne Oddie

Faith, Hope And Love

Have we lost all faith, even in ourselves?
Seemingly that is so, whenever one delves
Afraid to trust a brother, sister, father or mother,
And constantly betrayed by every body other.
Is money alone the root of all Evil
When secrecy erodes all life like a weevil?
Would more open honesty not be a boon
To the public in general and not too soon,
For though hope may spring eternal in the human breast,
Who can entertain the thought with any form of zest?
Governments are crooked, turning lives upside down
Leaders so inept, world wide not just our own
With no degree of constancy they chop and change around
Those good things which would help us keep our feet firmly
 on the ground.
Ever planning for the Future, ignore oft the present mess,
The world and our own Country's in, denied a loving caress!
Is it wilful blindness or incompetence and prejudice
Which makes men run aside from such obvious injustice
to the millions forever suffering, unloved, world wide?

Claude Augustus Knight

Greatest Gift Lost

Often we wonder as the years come and go,
what you would have been like, but we shall never know,
would your eyes have been of the deepest brown,
or a bright and vivid blue,
and your hair, as soft as down,
your skin so soft and silky too?
You would have been smart, like your dad.
and artistic, just like me,
and it makes us feel so sad,
that this will never be,
too perfect to live,
should that comfort and mend?
it's so hard to forgive,
when we can't comprehend!
we never got to see your face,
we'll never watch you grow,
but your memory can never be erased,
and we will always love you so.

Carol Wilson

Children Are Special

Children are special, their needs are the same.
The love that they have would put us to shame.
They are our future, be it happy or sad
What we put in is what we get back.

Armed with this knowledge let love be our guide
With hope and understanding we may turn the tide.
The world would be such a dull silent place
If the gift of God's children were ever erased.

Mary Shaw

"My Lad"

I wander o'er the heather with a heart that's full of joy
for soon I hope to meet the one who has filled my dreams,
my own darling boy.

We parted some time ago with vows that we would meet
each to fulfil our destiny, whatever that might be.

His has taken him across the lonely sea,
mine has been to wait and wonder endlessly.

Somewhere in the distance I see someone,
I wonder is it he, will he recognize me.

As he gets nearer I whisper, God please let it be
the same sweet lad who left two years ago today.

Mary Shaw

The Wandering Dove

There was a boy who in his young years
and without any fears,
left his home and travelled for many years.
From north to south and around about,
never seeming to shed any tears.

Over the water to places far and near, meeting new faces
and seemingly shedding old gear.
This boy became a man and shifted into any gear,
any type of work he seemed to be in the clear, or so he
thought.

Has this traveller wandered
far and near seemingly without a fear, deep within
feelings became clear and then with a little fear,
for this heart and soul wished for something so dear.

The one wonderful day
this man became a boy again
after visiting somewhere very dear,
and on his return after meeting
spirits and souls so grand
his heart had unfolded
and he had nothing to give but love so grand.

Michael J. Taylor

Sad Times

The cat and the bird went for a walk in the park.
And after a while light went to dark.
The moon popped up, the starts came out to play.
Then all of a sudden the cat had something to say.
'Why are we enemies and supposed to be foes?
For the fighting and killing the reason, who knows?'
The bird piped up after logical thought.
'Things to be sold and things to be bought
It all comes down to money, and what you can buy
The murder, the carnage that make all folk cry.
Greed and selfishness rule this earth
It has been the same since our birth.
There's no hope of saviour now it's too late
Destruction is inevitable and death is our fate
There is no solid answer to saving our race
Just don't worry and wear a smile on your face.'

Steven Laurie

All The Wars

We remember our dead with great respect
If they were to come back what would they expect,
A peaceful life for which they fought
And freedom of life with death and pain they bought,
but we still have wars that cause pain and strife,
for which all these young people gave their lives.

So what was it all for at the end of the day
No one is sure but with their lives still pay,
For the freedom of life they still fight every day
If we could all speak calmly together,
perhaps we could have peace forever
What a dream this is,
for the dead and maimed a kiss.

*June Saunders - (the above poem was mistakenly
published under an incorrect name in* Awaken to a Dream*)*

Tears

Tears of sorrow, tears of pain
  tears that fall like showers of rain.
Tears when nothing you do is right
  tears on your pillow, in the still of the night.

Tears to hold back, tears to be shed
  tears for the living, tears for the dead.
Tears so ready to fill our eyes
  when a child is born or a dear friend dies.

Tears for your children from deep in your heart
  tears that fall when you must part.
Tears of pride, when they have come good
  tears that say we knew you could.

Tears for feelings we can't express
  sometimes tears of happiness.
Tears of love are so bittersweet
  how many more tears must we weep?

Your tears must dry now, and fall not ever
  the ties that bind at last must sever.
The memories filling your heart must stay
  your legacy now, forever, every day.

Christine Farquhar

Happens To All

Life is a thing that happens to all,
From the child being born, to the flower send fall,
Where does it come from, where does it go,
These questions asked but we cannot know,
Life of a flower is one so short,
Gives us a smile with its beauty brought,
Insects so small are not what they seem,
Elusive butterfly once caterpillar green,
Birds and flies not forgetting the honey bee,
We all cherish our lives all creatures and thee,
Then one day return to our maker we must,
Back through the winds as our new form, dust.

Glenys Linda Reid

Emanon

Is there a place where nothing lies?
If so what would it look like?
A corner of an empty room; as it seems,
In fact not so empty or desolate; filled with life,
To which the meaning is unknown.

Would you be blind to this nothingness?
Would it render you powerless;
Choking for one last breath of air
Would you fall or fly, live or die.

Nobody knows the meaning of life,
The answer put at 42 or 90,
Seems like another puzzle to solve.

Maybe that's the meaning,
Everything is never ending,
A cycle going on forever,
How long is forever?

Infinite........

Does time end, did it ever begin?
What is time?
What is our purpose?

Lindsey Barker

Untitled

There is a lady by the name of Page
Not diamond kill, all fraught with rage
But a lovable soul, all gentile and kind
Whiskey galore, she is my kind.
She never alters in her looks with age
Always attractive, and one hundred percent vintage

C. J. Duncan

The Octogenarian

The old looking-glass
In simple wooden frame
Smiled reflectively
As if in curious game
A trick of light?
Maybe!
But was the image
Really he

He sought a silver mirror
Framed with filigree fine
And held her closely
To reflect each laughter line
Softly she responded in truth
Antiquity embraced his youth

A jewelled vanity-glass encrusted with gold
Entrusted respectfully an image to behold
Of sculptured age serene - sublime
Weathering sands of time

Anna MacDonald

Via Satellite

Even as telescopes aim at outer space
and humanity's satellite dishes are poised -
searching for intelligent beings in another place -
so your neighbour is ignored.

In the abyssal sky Poseidon's trident
flashes information to a cellular unit.
Jupiter's majestic presence commands wonderment
but wanes in the shadow of the television set.

Love through the Internet -
conservative, hygienic romance.
Son, fax me your school report,
and I'll e-mail my grievance.

Long-dead ghosts commune with higher ideals
while watching their children frolic
in mute fervour.

Catherine Maclay

A Last Farewell

I stood at the window, the night was dim
I heard the angels singing your favourite hymn
Your pain too great to bear, I know I saw but didn't know where.
The angels called come home to rest, for I know they only take the best.
To rest asleep Our Lord to keep, even though you know we will weep.
I stood at my window, the night was dim
I heard the angels singing a hymn, their voices sang so loud and clear
I remember you when in the choir, your voice was strong and bold
Better than silver and yet as pure as gold.
May you rest at peace of mind, leaving all your pain and troubles behind
For God above on high does see so much sorrow in you and me
The pain in our hearts we will keep, but still we all sit and weep.

Elizabeth A. Wilkinson

This World We Live In

I suppose those up in heaven shouldn't really cuss,
But if they do, their reasons are all because of us,
What an awful mess of things we're making here on earth,
We, who have it in our charge, have no earthly worth,
Daily too, it doesn't improve, in fact it just gets worse,
And we, the ones who people it, are its biggest curse,
Everywhere you care to turn, things which once were good,
Man has left his thumb print on, where he never should.
Our beautiful world, which once it was, truly was an Eden,
Until man with all his faults, chose to leave his seed on,
We are God's good creatures, the ones which he had made,
But when he watches what we do, he sees the price he paid,
No matter where you choose to look, the world's engaged in wars,
And when they've counted what they've won, all they'll find is sores,
Religion seems a reason for some to cause a fight,
And if we all were colour blind, we wouldn't know black from white,
What a world to live in, a world which could be good,
And but for man's great follies, it sure and truly would.

James Robinson

From The Heart

I wish this pain would go away, it never ending seems.
I'm drowning in such sadness, of how it could have been.
My son, Oh how I love him, was born for me to care.
With washing, dressing and feeding and not for others to stare.
Educational statements, fighting for his rights.
Stress and worry all the time, many sleepless nights.
Walking is a problem, special shoes on feet.
Tiredness and tears, he finds it hard to speak.
Lots of operations, and hospital appointments too.
Speech and physiotherapy, I have to cope, could you?
Medicines and physio, at home the norm to give.
He's my special boy, with the strongest will to live.
Heart disease and epilepsy, learning disability too.
Dyspraxia, asthma and blood disorder, what's a mum to do?
You learn to live, to carry on, to cope and say your prayers.
To be grateful for his love, and see through all the despair.
What he needs is lots of love, and confidence instored.
Encouragement, not criticism, nor overlooked, ignored!
The sun comes out, when I see him smile, and laughter fills the air.
I hope and pray for God's kind help, a friend who's always there.

Ruth Elizabeth Westhoff

A Husband's Lament

It is four o'clock in the morning, I cannot go to sleep
I am on my own and lonely, I miss my Dear Loved one,
and I weep and weep, and weep
The loneliness is unbearable, when you are no
longer here to stay
I wish the good Lord would take me, so that we
could be together, forever and aye.
We had been married for fifty golden years, my dearest
precious Love.
The Good Lord had taken you, to wait for me above.
I am grieving for you, my Darling, for you were my one and only love
God must have sent you from Moses, the Ark, the bird (the dove)

Thomas Duncan

Old Age

I hate the thought of growing old,
I have seen the problems that unfold.
Our dear one's characters seem to change,
The way they behave can become quite strange.
They cling to you as tho' they'd drown,
And don't seem to care if they drag you down.

Their demands on you get so great,
And you do your best not to turn to hate.
These thoughts you hope you do not convey
And feel the guilt for thinking this way.
To change, I am sure is not their intention.
How I wish there would be some prevention.
It makes me feel so very sad
When I think of the good life they have had.

I know everyone is not the same,
And to blame them all is my shame.
Many grow old, I'm sure, with grace,
I hope it'll be so in my case.
I don't want my family to wish me dead,
I want to stay their friend instead.

Gillian S. Roberts

Dying Child

'Jambo'. My greeting robust.
'Jambo'. Her response croaked.
'Habari'? Silly of me, to ask
'What news'? In hell.
'Mzuri'. Weaker croak.
'Good news'. Even in hell.
Swahili etiquette even in last rites.
'Maji, bwana'. Water, of course.
Plastic from First World.
Black claw clutches bottle
from white, podgy hand.

'Asante'. No need for 'thanks'. My privilege.

'The kids dying. Living have propriety'
from Blue Beret.

'Locals won't help. Wrong tribe.
The right to die in dignity. Surely, her priority?'

'I wouldn't do your job for a million dollars'

'Neither would I, Blue Beret'.
'Kwa Heri bwana'. 'Not good-bye. Oh no'.
White fingers smooth lids staring into sun.

W. R. Haines

On Countisbury Hill

On Countisbury Hill, where time stood still
When, as a child roaming free at will
And summer days went on and on
Imagination was conceived and born

Remembering one balmy summer's day
There, by the blackberry path I lay
The warmth of sun-drenched bracken pressed
Against my adolescent breast

The drone of bees as sipping nectar
Caressing breeze with gentle love, where
Jewels of iridescent hues, to view
In turquoise splashed sapphire blue

Moments captured, trapped, for when
Thoughts of then, I would think again
At future milestones on my way
Remembering one balmy summer's day

On Countisbury Hill
Where time stood still
And, where now other footprints fill
The blackberry path on Countisbury Hill

Patricia Maubec

Mersey Waterfront

Mother Mersey swelled with tide, molten lead 'neath winter sky.
What secrets keep you in your deep; how man unsung heroes sleep?

Ancient monks first crossed your wide, a barter for their ferry ride.
Waiting on the shifting tide, to take them 'cross to t'other side.

From my vantage point I scan, where once an overhead railway ran.
Seven miles of docks it spanned, from Dingle, north, to Blunde L Sand.

Cunard building, Albert Dock, Custom House and Liver Clock.
For me, no waterfront exists, to match this architectural kiss.

Majestic steeples, skyline scar, amidst the poverty they saw,
Religion to sustain the poor, their hungry bellies they'd ignore.

And here on lovely Wirral's side, once my playground, I would ride.
I'd Hoylakes leafy lanes aspire, far from smoky chimney spire.

From Seacombe to New Brighton's Pier alas! to say, no longer here.
Upon this shore as kids we played, happy were those summer days.

Tray of tea for Mum and Dad, images that make me sad.
For us, candy floss and lemonade, all ghosts of "Ham and Egg Parade".

Mother Mersey swelled with tide,
One of your sons views you with pride.
And though my visits new are few,
you're in my mind, my heart, my soul I'll miss you!

R. Evans

Realms Of Wonder

The composers of old could not compete to capture the music of the
stars, in realms of wonder, mozart, brahms and strauss, all tried to
capture the melody, elusive, as a music note of the stars in realms of wonder.

A rainbows glow of haunting lullabies, far above sing songs of true
love, soars high to the stars, songs love in realms of wonder the
stars sing their lullabies of love in realms of wonder,

In realms of wonder, the stars sing their songs of love in haunting
lullabies to a heart that's true, haunting melodies floating in the
air, for lovers everywhere, in distant enchantment to dreams yet
untold love stories unfold, in realms of wonder.

Be true to the one you love, the one you care for let your heart take
you to realms of wonder the music will take you, starlight will shine
Moonbeams glow, the aura's of enchantment surround you dance about you
There, dance to the music of the stars in realms of wonder.

Perfume will fill the air, stars dance about you there all the glow
of the moon and stars, come my love with me, to realms of wonder, let
the magic touch you as nothing, else would do. The music will take
you, to realms of true love bright starshine will shine for us two
moonglows dance with us our true love vow true love to one another in
realms of wonder.

Janet Middleton

Celebration Of The Cook

A wisp of hair awry, a smudge of flour on nose,
A nervous anxious sigh, for a cook there is no repose.
The ever advancing ticking clock, amongst the vegetables and dishes,
At her post she remains a rock, translating all her wishes.

She stands in splendid isolation, surrounded with steam and heat.
The family in eager anticipation, wait within their rooms so neat.
Shopping done some days before, planning carefully written lists,
Layout of table and much much more, hurriedly scans in kitchen mists,
The timing of the soup unsure, urgently consults a reference book,
"Isn't it ready yet?" calls a young voice,
Results in harassed frazzled look, (Was this really the best choice?)

The warming plates ready for their load,
Father the drink prepares for this muse,
The maestro in her cooking mode, the sizzling fizzing bubbling brews,
"It's ready? Come and get it!" cry, (Just watch the warming apple pie)

It does seem that within a trice
The plates have left the mats.
The ever hungry squeaking mice, become fat contented cats.

So the family now do muster, around the sink for washing up.
The many plates pans dishes cluster, we clean and dry to the last cup.

D. R. Sharpe

Innocence

When toys waited for the midnight hour
before springing to their feet,
and tiny garden fairies danced
in the hazy summer heat.
     When Jack Frost starched the window pane
and witches ruled October skies,
when dragons waited under beds
to take you by surprise.
     When Guy Fawlkes burned amid howls of glee
and seeding dandelions were clocks,
when hedgehogs wore pinnies and mop caps
and rabbits wore old fashioned frocks.
     When a goodnight kiss aided restful sleep
and a best friend held your hand.
When princes rescued maidens
with a shiny wedding band.
     It was then, reality held fantasy
and the future looked so good.
When daisy chains were priceless
in the eyes of my childhood.

Helen Long

"Is This The End?"

When someone dies, it hurts you,
Whether it be family or friend,
It scares you to think that their life,
Has suddenly come to an end.

You never got to say 'Goodbye',
It hurts to think this way,
But remember don't lost faith,
You'll see them soon someday.

At least you have the memories,
Shared their laughter, cried their tears,
Even if you lived in hope,
They'd still be here for years.

You knew inside that they were ill,
And soon they would be dying,
But never knew that it would be,
This soon that you'd be crying.

Now you know someone that's died,
You've formed a self protection,
And hope that you will be around,
To see their resurrection.

Maria Cracknell

Lonely-Ness

I am such a lovely person
     no one cares for me,
Being shy and introvert
     has caused me misery.

If only I could find a friend
     where my lonely life would cease,
Then this would be most wonderful
     my troubled heart might then find peace.

But being sort of tongue-tied
     and very taciturn,
That I tread this lonely path
     and friendships always spurn.

Yet deep within this heart of mine
     I know my character is good,
It is only with what nature gave
     I am never understood.

If a person would only come along
     and trust me as a friend,
Then this would give me happiness
     and my lonely life would end.

Lachlan Taylor

Rekindled Flame

As I drifted on life's ocean, in solitude, in space,
My lonely prayers were answered, when I beheld your face.
Up leapt the long-lost mem'ry of the time we first took 'flight.'
Our eyes gleamed bright with passion, switched on in wild delight.
Your kiss, sweet kisses swept me, to pleasure 'til-then 'unknown'
And now you're close and closer still, as love's deep roots are grown.
Your absence hurts when you're not here, a burden to be borne;
Though let's hope soon you'll be around, to love, to hold, to warm.

Bill Mitchell-Crinkley (Priory Bill)

The Sound

It's amazing in a prison how the news soon gets around
Where many a word is spoken though you seldom hear a sound
He was going mad, "well nuts", that's what the grapevine said
The making of the gallows was going to his head
The carpenter was hammering his wood was straight and strong
His busy saw with work did sing it won't it won't be long.
The prisoner in the condemned cell the floor did often pace
Although his mind seemed far away the sound kept up the chase
Don't you hear it? Don't you hear it? His voice was shrill and clear
But neither guard would answer him and louder grew his fear
Don't you hear it? Don't you hear it? He's screaming even yet
His mind is still so far away but the sound he can't forget
He hears it in a padded cell in a place for them that's "queer"
But the strangest part about it all, he's deaf and cannot hear

Matt Murray

Season's Symphony

Summer slips quietly into Autumn - melancholy days of gold and brown.
Rose hips and blackberries blanket the hedgerows.
Farmer's furrows have gouged the ground.
Morning mists on dew drenched meadows - cobwebs cling as filigree lace.
Owls screech their protest to silvery moonlight
Swallows fly southwards - ribbon in space.
Chill breezes rustle the leaves that have fallen from
trees standing sentinel, barren and bare.
Ghostly outlines against the horizon - grim and forbidding in the foggy air
Soon cruel winds over snow-swept carpets will herald
the winter with gusts of contempt.
Rivers lie captured in sullen silence - grey and still, their banks unkempt.
Feathery fingers of frost paint the windows,
snowflakes swirl wildly - confusing the mind
Icicles glisten in pale winter sunlight like cascading
crystals suspended in time.
The countryside slumbers in sweet anticipation as
over the crisp air church bells ring
God is preparing his never ending miracle.
Soon it will be Spring.

Elsie Francis

The Curse Of The Dreaded Zit. . .

Why do people suffer from spots, that's what I want to know?
They simply appear. Huge on your face, In a deep red glow.
You scrub your 'mug', every night with unperfumed soap.
Moisturizer and a mud pack, which makes you look like a dope!
The best brand names, Pat your skin dry, and not forgetting a regular 'steaming.'
Open up them clogging pores. All ready for the creaming.
But alas, to no avail the dreaded 'zit' has struck.
Right on the end of your nose. Total shame. You spent pounds, on all that 'muck.'
A massive, huge, yellow head, that you simply have to squeeze.
This you do will venom. Again and again. Even shouting "please."
You have a party to attend and this "bulbous Monster", is not invited
As if it knows. It would not burst. In fact its getting bigger, I believe its excited!
With your deformed snout, sticking out, full of blemish stick and foundation.
The party is a flop. You feel your a laughing stock. People staring,
as if your exhibiting this 'creation'. . .
Inevitably you leave early. Make your excuses and run.
Knowing no-one believes you. They'll all be laughing at your spot,
enjoying making fun...
Pimples go eventually, when they're ready, withering bit by bit.
Until the next time, you can almost hear them say...
The curse of the dreaded 'zit'!!!

Andrea Garvey

The Ego

What fragile beings our egos are
to bend or sway at each event,
that comes to give or take away,
each thief to bear some cruel torment.
Remember how you felt that day,
the tremulous, humiliating, hideousness,
and fear her own cruel part to play
in aiding egos quietus.

Remember then the learning of
and how it took such time to mend,
how slow to shake the armour off,
your ego to again ascend,
and with each breath had designed to grow,
a slow but steadied even keel,
your ego bare to shine thereof,
regaining what life dared to steal.

Anne Davison

When I Wer' A Lad

When I look back o'er the years, when I wer' a lad,
And lived wi' mi Mam, brothers and sisters, I didn't 'ave a Dad.
We were hungry, ragged and poorly shod,
And sometimes wondered, is there really a God?

I'd look at the better offs, those we called 'toffs',
Did they go to bed hungry at night,
Shiver under bed clothes, too thin and too light.

Did they go to school dinners, plates of greasy 'hash',
'Ave grown ups look at them as if they were 'trash'.
Did they stay off school when they'd no shoes to their feet,
Or did they turn up wi' shoes polished and neat,

Did they go hungry, wi' little food in their belly,
Or was it crumpets for tea, followed bi strawberry jelly.
Did they appreciate the good life they'd got,
Or would they 'ave swopped it for our little lot.

Did they go to church and pray for the poor,
Forgetting they'd got some near to their door,
Did they realize what riches they had,
Not to be born poor, when I wer' a lad.

Lade Henderson

Just Once More

Just once more let me see the leaves
upon the trees before they fall
just once more let me see the birds before they fly
away in the sky to places I don't know
just once more let me hear the breeze
fluttering through the trees as they follow the call
just once more let me watch the waves as the seas
lash against the caves in the cliffs far below
just once more as I prepare to leave this place
let me see the face of my beloved son
just once more before I close my eyes
tell me beloved you realize my time has come

E. Hemmings

The World Today

Tea dances on the moon, they say,
Are not so very far away.
And all around
The miracles of sight and sound
Now very common ground.
A Russian died for peace today,
We heard about it yesterday?
The hostage cries and pleads in vain;
His God forgives their God the pain
(won't stop them doing it again)
It seems the world is fine and bold
for those with lust for power or gold;
But—sick and tired, we need to find
More than words for all mankind.
Defend our rights—take action stations;
Forget the moon, United Nations!

Alan D. Smith

Summer And Rabbits

Long ears that turn towards a noise,
And eyes are bright with life.
What timid, sweet creatures run with poise.
The grass is rich in summer green
And rabbits leap with bounding grace,
Their homes of warmth and safety.
From young to old they are to be seen,
The colours of the meadow
With flowers in rich brightness.
Skies filled with white cloud.
Light winds that blow towards the willows.
All wondrous things seen on a beautiful day
As dusk comes falling from brilliant skies,
Shadows draw a final closeness.
Eyes shut with sleepiness and content.
The grass and willows slowly sigh,
Darkness engulfs this peaceful land.
Noises from the night bring stillness,
Till the morning light brings life afresh
And all of this at nature's hand.

Julie Airey

Rushing Rivers

Rushing rivers
Sparkle Sparkle Start
Like quivers sparkle sparkle coming
Out the earth about. Sparkle sparkle
Rushing past the cities the town, sparkle
Sparkle getting bigger all the way sparkle
Sparkle they go past the wood as they
Stray sparkle sparkle. They get bigger
as they move on their way. Sparkle
Sparkle. The nymphs in the trees shine
Right through sparkle sparkle.

Naama Rietti

Diana

Diana is a name that just rolls off the tongue,
She is rather pretty, and can be full of fun.
Her status in life can be only defined,
By the man she will marry, or has on her mind.

Rich girl, poor girl, or even roy-ale,
Her charm and beauty still seems to prevail.
Her smile also makes things around her bloom,
Which I feel quite certain is a must for her groom.

I feel sure you'll agree, Diana's a nice name,
It's a pity that some girls might put it to shame,
By shortening it to Di, and creating a feeling,
That leaves a man flat, or sends him reeling.

Of course, there's the more commonal living Di,
Who gets hitched to her spouse and is tempted to lie.
To these girls I say, "O.K." have your flings,
But don't be surprised if someone clips your wings.

Bill Rowsell

Daydreaming

As I lay sunbathing one summer's day
A dark cloud came across my way
It hid the sun out of sight
That a moment earlier was warm and bright
My mood is relaxed as I study the sky
A gentle breeze helps the clouds go by
They change shape when upwards I glance
Some appear to float and others to dance
I dream of drifting through the sky above
With my friend, partner, my only love
The gentle warmth from him I feel
Is the love that I will always need
Now when I look up there's no cloud in sight
The whole of the sky is a summery bright
Life and nature is a wondrous thing
As delicate and complicated as a butterfly wing

Margaret Sanders

Bejewelled Imprints Of The Mind

The candelabrum plumage of imperious oaks.
Glossy mahogany chestnuts that lie, and poke
Their indentations on the chocolate earth,
The bark of massive trees age shewn in their girth,
Sunshine sparkled rinds, on encrusted diamond waves,
That bathe the shore, erasing ripples, and plays
Around the sun-baked feet of weary men, who toil
With boats, and nets preparing for their day break shoal,

The panorama of the clouds depicting rose-tipped ranges,
Or great duvets of grey, black bruises, swiftly change
To clear the heavens for approaching night
As the angel's jewels of starry wonder emerge slowly into sight.
That sudden strain of music, uplifts, and reaffirms,
All beauty is around, if one only looks, and learns,
To see the furled filigree of ferns so heavenly green.
If only for a little while small imprints reign supreme.

Then down to earth, I must be dreaming,
It's back to juggling meals, and scheming,
But my lovely imprints of the mind,
Uplifts my soul, like vintage wine.

Freda Thompson

To Be A Mother

As each baby came my way
In awe I would quietly pray
Those precious hands and little feet
Would one day learn to play.
Those eyes of either brown or blue
And smiles so very sweet
Would one day learn to be good and true
Warmth and happiness to keep.

Growing up can be a strain
For parent and child a lot of pain
In times of stress or after a scene
I would remember five infants warm and clean.
Here I am in my later years
I think of their hopes and fears
And then I ponder down memory lane
Oh how I wish for those times again.

I look at eyes so grown up now
So wise in all they see
I loved them then, I love them now
And hope they still love me.

P. A. Murphy

Glances And Chances

Glasses contact lenses and bifocals
Spectacles sunglasses and coloured goggles
Pens rubbers and propeller pencils
Books crayons and all sorts of stencils
Bowler hats fezzes and umbrellas
Headmasters students and member fellows
Rushing around but all agree
It's a matter of opinion if they will get a degree

Geography History English or maths
Which road to take there are many paths
Bachelor of Science or Bachelor of Arts
Or will we just be "The Queen of Hearts"
Send a card to congratulations
From family friends and relations

Grants bursaries and social needs
Someone has to attend to all the good deeds
Some can't read and some can't count
But what we should do is help them out
We can't all be good at the same subject
So why should we feel like some old reject

Ann Copland

Grieving

I was asked today what do I miss,
In this part of my life called grieving.
Is it that early morning kiss?
That disappeared with your leaving.
A kiss that welcomed another new day,
In this life that we shared.
We were so full of plans, oh why couldn't you stay?
In this life you showed in so many ways
that you cared.
Is it the laughter that showed in your eyes,
Or the touch of your hand when you knew
I felt sad.
Nothing then seemed quite so bad.
Maybe it was just that you were always there
To laugh with me—cry with me—yes even be angry.
The one thing I miss in my life is your care.

Betty Brown

The Comforting Wind

In the summer she cools us, in the winter she chills,
The element that nobody sees,
You feel her, you hear her, she comforts our ills,
She hides in, and plays with the trees.

On a desolate hilltop alone with your woes,
She'll blow in a comforting way,
She'll hug you, and send you the scent of a rose,
For this friendship there's nothing to pay.

She doesn't ask question, she'll always be there,
But on still days her presence is weak,
So when life gets to much for you, too much to bare,
A breeze is what you should seek.

A walk in a gale can unmuddle your mind,
So strong you can hardly stand steady,
Despite all her power she is gentle and kind,
When you need a good friend, she'll be ready.

Steve Blackman

The Quiet Mind

Sometimes in the quiet hidden places of the mind
Things we think forgotten, spring unbidden we may find
All our hopes and joys, our sorrow and our tears
Because you see the heart remembers, through all the years

Memories are part of life's rich pattern as we know
We look back on youthful dreams as on life's path we go
In the looking glass of time we see mirrored there
Such a bright kaleidoscope of colours rich and rare

The golden moments of our life come readily to mind
The heartbreaks and the sorrows we would gladly leave behind
But we find them woven tightly and our hearts know well
We have so much of "heaven" we must have a little "hell"

So treasure all those happy moments as they come along
Then you can look back on them when everything goes wrong
Always look with hope a new towards each coming morn
For any day you may see a bright tomorrow dawn

J. M. Ball

New Girl, Black Girl

All eyes stared as the door creaked open
There was a shuffle and a whisper as she came into view
At the back of the room there was giggles and laughter
Everyone was silent no-one knew what to do
Most new kids would have hung their heads in shyness
She stood and hung her head in shame
She had been through it many times before
But when she was young it seemed like a game
But now she was older she had known what it meant
Those harsh racist words that the other kids had sent
She would never have children
Why put them through hell
But the heartache inside her to help others she will tell.

Lisa Brown

Their Last Mountain

Dear, Sweet, Alison Hargreaves and Julie Tullis,
Our thoughts are always with you,
Your lovely smiles, we sadly miss,
We wish you had not died on K2.

Your hearts were in the mountain,
As you climbed its rugged face,
Trying, desperately, its peak to attain,

As you neared the summit, far from base,
Cruel, icy blizzards, forced you to stay,
We searched, with heavy hearts, and cried,
When we discovered where you lay.
The bravest, loveliest, women, who almost reached the top
had died,

If only the weather had not changed,
You would be with us still,
But only God has re-arranged
That you should climb His highest hill

None will ever know,
Why the bravest and the best,
Feel called from far below,
To conquer K2 and Everest.

Betty Owen

To The Memory Of My Siamese

For nineteen long years you owned me,
    until it was time to rest.
Through all those years of companionship,
    how could I but love you the best.
You understood every word that was spoken,
    your miaow, your purr, I hear every day.
But you had to grow old and leave me,
    and in my heart you will always stay.

Christine Barton

Forever

We watched the years go rushing past
We knew our love was made to last.
Not for us "'Til death do us past"
Our love was deep within the heart.

We lived our life, the good, the bad,
Mostly happy, rarely sad.
Our love was deep when will or ill
And though you've gone, I love you still.

That love endured from age past
It will live on forever.
Until we meet again at last,
Our love will leave us never.

I could not wish you back with me,
To suffer all that pain
But love still binds us very close
Until we meet again.

Mary Jones

Life Is For Living

Life is for living, and love is for giving
To those near and dear, every day.
Friends are for caring, and keeping, and sharing
The pleasures which come o'er their way.
Our children grow up and leave the nest
Venture out in the world—a fearsome test,
They think of love and devotion which they have been shown
And try to live up to the memories of home.
Sometimes it's hard, but they hopefully learn
To do the right thing, while a living they earn.
We wish good luck to all couples in love
And hope that they find their love grows and improves
That their lives will be lived to the full, always,
And filled with the magic of wonderful days.

Gwen Ives

Ladder Of Lights

In life's winter the bright light shines.
In the summer of my life the darkness glows and takes sway,
Why, oh why do I let that winter's light slip away
Year in . . . year out.
That golden hand is offered without prejudice,
outstretched, impersonal;
waiting patiently for my homecoming year in . . . year out.

I see, I know,
Yet again my preoccupations delude me and carry me away
Summer is here again, darkness everywhere.
Oh, for that soothing light of winter.
That ladder of lights I will climb this time,
To the top will that golden hand lead me.
There I will remain, with all things bright.
That bright winter's light;
that summer's dark glow
forever there, while I am here now,
at home at last, with my past laid bare,
with my future assured, with my now just here.

G. C. Heath

Cliches Of An Up-And-Coming Writer

With the world at my feet,
I could make the grade,
I believe in calling
A spade a spade,

I met a fellow writer,
And said, "Hey, let's do lunch"
Even though it's purely platonic,
He's the creme de la creme
The pick of the bunch.

With several books in the pipeline,
It's time to knuckle down,
Put my nose to the grindstone,
Get earlier nights,
You can't burn the candle at both ends, now.

I just know that I'm going to make it,
If not, the public must be blind.
I'm sure to have them eating out of my hands....
Daddy's novels help, I find.

Lorna M. Irvine

The Voice Of The Dissentient

You know the greb, the crusty, bleeding heart and hippy
You know the freak, the greeny, anarchist and commie
Yes I'm the long haired yobbo, these labels I've been named
Oblivious to what I plead for all crimes am I blamed
The stereotypes you brand me with: A means to slam the door
This easy to dismiss the words your conscience does ignore
My only sin to fill your mould the clay your own hand shaped
Initiative to question what is wrong you did awake
Individuality, distinction from the pack
Voicing my beliefs is this the monster you attack?
Who redefined subversive to include what's plainly right
These, the values you instilled to which you turn from sight
But look I urge to future times, your legacy to be
Those unborn will curse those here but they shall not blame me!

Ian Sen

Second Childishness

Into the way we slip and slide
Strange beginnings side by side
Reach for the grave straight from the womb
Mad circles inside our life blood's tomb
Green fields now lie where once we ruled
Instinct survives beside tepid pools
Higher and higher into the sky
Like birds of a wing that dared to fly
Until a sleep that shrouds as night
Pulls fortune's chance free from sight
Laid to waste as time pretends
Fight off the chains, it's time, ascend.

I. S. Caddie

To The Night

I long for seduction into your unknown
As others endure their temporary deaths
One thing us mortals can't bear in your presence is to be alone

Conceal our concrete madness with your nothingness
As we reveal to you our primal fears
We have only each other to be scared of
A flaw that dates back a thousand years

Evil uses your blanket cover for its darkest crimes
All those myths and tales revolve around you
Are they just products of an overactive mind?

Everyone wants to lose you in their counterfeit sunshine
Whilst I find solace in your silent embrace
Your sensual darkness is what I'm drawn into
But still I find you a burden to face

Let me dance with the vampires, for I desire you as much as they
I slip into your garments and dissolve invisibly into your beauty
While my eyelids are pressed shut you are air-brushed away
But I know you'll return as it is your duty

Malcolm Carelse

Seasons

Little days, bright sunny mellow ways,
bundled sheaves, yellow brown leaves, misty morns
darkening afternoon, time to reflect by firelight
flicker moments of summer gone.

Breath on the air days, frosty cold finger ways,
winds that blow bare the trees, brown furrowed field
and lees, hurrying home days, warm soup and toast ways,
time to reflect by firelight flicker moments of autumn gone.

Shirley Mason

Horatio To Hamlet

O my dear Lord Hamlet whence received thou
Thy grounding in omniscience. The world itself
Has contracted into thy mind. Scorning drink
Yet art thou drunk with God. And like unto one
All the knowledge thou thought ne'er possessed
Have fashioned themselves into a single point
And are so totally available to thee
That thy mind runs free and thy vast consciousness
Is universal mind, feeling and knowing all things.
And why? Because thou art all things,
Good and bad, humble and proud, beggar and king.
Thy love is open to all without reserve.
Thou art as honest and as true a man
As child, fool, drunkard, madman, sage and saint,
As Christ thy master or the dead themselves.

Paul Frame

Have You Ever Paused To Wonder

Have you ever paused to wonder at the world
At a magnificent pink tropical dawn
Or looked at the first snow as yet untouched
Did you glimpse a fresh rainbow arc across the sky.

Have you ever paused to wonder at new life
The gift of a child when just born
What a miraculous transformation
From womb cocoon to naked light.

Have you paused to wonder at family strife
Why conflicts come between a man and his wife
Have we become so selfish
Is "I want" the ever-present theme.

Have you ever paused to wonder at wars
Why two opposing sides will fight
Death and devastation
Each believing they are right.

Have you ever paused to wonder
How perfect it would be
If each person loved every other
In a unique, selfless harmony.

Jenny Lai

Bienn Bhreagh (Beautiful Mountain)

Out of the cold clear ocean she stands
the constant ebb and flow wash her sands.
She stood alone years before
and she'll be standing here for many more.
Her hillside covered with a virgin-violet face
which smiles in my memories of this place.

Spring has no greater beauty than here
silver streams of melted ice flow fast and clear.
Violets blossom in purple, blue and white.
Birds dance across her sky in effortless flight.
When spring sleeps on her bright blue seas,
summer sparks in her warm salty breeze.

Autumn sweeps a brown blanket of deadened leaves.
The violets are gone, leaving only bare trees,
but the violets aren't dead, they will come again
as does the sunshine and the pouring rain
Bienn Bhreagh lives on even through winter's ivory snow
her immortal beauty untouched by mortal hands. Better so!

Patrick Rennie

The Earth's Complaint

As I hang here doing nothing,
I watch myself being destroyed.
People putting holes in my o-zone layer,
As more holes appear I feel naked.
I think to myself -
Would they like it?

Pollution, pollution, pollution
Although it chokes me I eat it up,
I have to!
More and more cars, lorries and vans are made,
Do they think it's good for them - for me?

Wars, fights, deaths,
They blow holes in each other and me,
Why?
Do they think it's fun?
I don't
It's painful for everyone!
My message is - leave me alone, stop this bullying.

Sherlene Shevlin

Out All Night

Where do you go to, when you're out all night?
Are you painting the town red, till the early morning light?
You sleepily walk in through the door, just like you've often
    done before
You go straight to the kitchen for something to eat
And while I prepare it, you go and take a seat
Then you disappear - there's no sound, not a peep
I discover where you've gone to, right off to sleep!
After you've rested, we have some time to play
Then after more food, you're up and away
It goes full circle, my little tom cat!
But nobody is as special as you, when you're curled up on my mat.

Sheryl Williamson

Pain

My darling, I came to see you today,
I cannot leave you this way,
O know I wish I could stay,
If only I could create wings - so strong,
That would carry us off the same day.

When I saw you lying there,
With your head held high towards the sky,
My love for you will never die,
How can I empty my soul of sighs.

To ease my pain I stroked the hair upon your head,
Kissed your face,
Then closed my eyes and made a wish that
I would rise up and beyond the distant skies.
Away from my cries.

Constance May Tolley

My Grandson

My grandson is so warm and round
As he plays in his soapy bath,
With tails of ghost ships sailing by,
Fish chasing him, an early snack.

As I dry him snugly in the warm towel,
He chatters away sleepily.
It won't be long before he's off
On another kind of dream, far away.

He talks to me on the telephone,
Telling me of his adventures of the day,
Asking me if I've bought him a present.
He knows I spoil him that way.

We stroll along to the station,
Watching the trains go by.
I would love to see into his imagination,
Find the mystery behind those green eyes.

Children have so much fun.
Love and mischief they share,
Giving themselves to everyone.
But this time I'm the one there.

Hazel E. Henshaw

My Quest

I have a quest, a life long dream,
Achieving something not yet foreseen.
I pursue most things a woman should,
Helping others, doing good,
Having children, being married,
Holding a job, many if I tallied,
Working and keeping house.
Decorating and gardening is a must.
But then I have to do knitting and sewing,
Catering for the daughter's wedding,
Train spotting with great zeal,
Eating out, please no jellied eels,
Playing darts and pool and cards.
Bingo, bandits, and raffles I take part.
Pottery I've yet to try. Stamps and antiques I buy.
But most of all I write free style.
Poetry is my passionate wile.
I've freedom of words I long to share,
Singing in my head as I prepare.
Please listen to my verse and rhyme,
While I entertain you for a little while.

Hazel E. Henshaw

Wilt Thou......?

Wilt thou as by thy fireside warm
Remember those so cold in wind and storm

Wilt thou as in thy bed all soft and deep
Spare thought for those on concrete hard that sleep

Wilt thou with shoes and clothes so grand
Share glove with someone cool of hand

Wilt thou so full and satisfied with wine
Invite some poor and lonely wretch to dine

Wilt thou with mansion servants wealth
Greet the poor and drink their health

Wilt thou with greatest strength and might
Assist the frail and weak in plight

Wilt thou with happy mind contentment blessed
Comfort those with heart and soul distressed

Wilt thou the adolescents face
And raise them free from all disgrace

Wilt thou with conscience face thy faults
Be fair with all and share their thoughts

Wilt thou who know there is no end
With others fruitful life ascend

Nicholas Bryans

Untitled

On happy happy V. E. day,
When all our cares were thrown away,
The bells rang out loud and clear,
And the people's hearts were filled with cheer,
On that happy happy day,
50 years away.

Now the final battle had to be won,
To let us live in peace with everyone,
So the lads got to grips,
To end the war with the nips,
And made it possible for us to say,
Hooray hooray for V.J. day.

Now let us not forget the two wars they have won,
To let us live in peace with everyone,
Don't let it be all in vain,
That they lost their lives without any gain,
So the answer must always be,
Peace and hope continuously.

M. V. C. Grant

Summer's Promise

Lonely but not alone, my heart has yet to find a home.
One where loving, caring and sharing becomes so natural
and you feel as one.
   Life drifts by with its seasons of change.
I change too, but the pain remains.
   Echoes of the past invade my thoughts,
my mind, life's serenade.
   Lessons I have learnt, my heart beats once more for a
light has appeared through the crack of a door, soft
whispers and caresses all, heal me now at last spring has
come now; it's time to grow.
   Ever strong, ever loving this heavenly glow,
the flower bud opens the petals show stronger
and stronger the earth awaits for
   Summer's promise when all awakes.

Deirdre French

The Lonely Chair

Each day I pass this window I stop and have to stare,
For in the corner of the room sits a lonely chair,
Once upon a happy time many graced its seat,
Now it sits alone, so sad, on hand carved legs and feet,
The further to my asking I find it's up for sale,
And on its back was written this funny little tale,
"Rest your weary body, let me take the strain,
For I am here to serve you, to ease your aches and pains,
Take my seat, rest for a while in times of good or bad,
I will try to make you happy and stop you feeling sad".
It tickled me immensely, those words I thought were fun,
So I bought it from the owner for my garden in the sun,
You might find this rather silly but when I sit on that chair,
I never have a worry for my cares just disappear,
And that chair sure ain't lonely anymore.

Joseph Walker

Our Treasure

Sapphire in the sky at night
Ruby of glorious dawn
Topaz on the aqua seas
Garnet hills and emerald lawn
Diamonds in the space of time
The golden circled sun
Tall and rustic shaded trees
Where the songs of the breeze were sung
Opal horizons silver moon
Turquoise and coral beds
Golden sands and clouds of pearly white
Agate bloodstone rocks more still, than dead
What more is there to look upon
And all for nought, thy pleasure
With these riches all around
Our world is full of treasure.

Agnes Lawson

The Brave And The Bold

He wasn't very big
And he wasn't very strong,
But he fought for his country
Be it right or wrong,
Little more than a child
As he handled a gun,
And his parents prayed
For their only son,
Over the country the battle raged on
And his parents prayed
For their only son,
They longed to take him by the hand
Away from that horrible, war-torn land.
Although he was wounded
He fought on still
The shots rang out over valley and hill.
But his comrades found him
Stiff and cold,
The bullet-scarred body
Of the brave and the bold.

Nora Kathleen Cooper

A Cry For Help

They say the voices in the head
are madness of a kind.
Yet I think they are wrong
it's the pressures to the mind.

This life is like a long dark tunnel
weaving in, and out,
the thoughts that make me wonder
what it is all about.

Now the needle is coming
it's like a viper's bite,
for weeks life is normal,
but not quite.

Now you with healthy bodies, and minds,
trying to poison them
with drugs of every kind,

Why will you not be satisfied with life
when you are well?

Not suffering with illness,
in this dark mental hell.

Iris Tennent

Relationships

'Is it a girl?' I said
As my firstborn showed his head
Four years on, more joy
But again it was a boy

After time I felt it was heaven
Washing strip for the ghastly eleven
Why had I yearned for girls?
With their flounces and poutings and twirls

And then there appeared on the scene
My daughter-in-law called Jean
I so longed to be her mother
But she had one and wanted no other

Excitement, my granddaughter came!
But much to my ultimate shame
I rushed down the ward to the cot
The presence of Jean I forgot

Whilst her own mother went to her side
And held Jean's hand with pride
She gasped 'I'm in a whirl'
'Well done, my lovely girl'

Sheila Beatrice King

Tara's Lament

Tara here, and I wish I state
I now know my lot - my fate
My forever forever is not far away
My forever could be - just one day
Remember - arms entwined walks along the deserted beach
Wishing for material things - way out of our reach
I quoted: Forever forever I will love thee forever forever will you
love me sadly- my forever forever is not far away
    my forever could be just one day

How can my head handle what I know
My ailing body shivers it's as cold as snow
I could become hysterical-scream and shout
I could stay calm say my goodbyes - and take the easy way out
I could be serene and surrender to God's (your time is up) call
and walk to meet my saviour with my hero - St. Paul
I could fight - refuse to be hauled over death's very high wall

Decision time decisions to be made before in my silk lined coffin
I'm laid leave the end to nature - why break the law -
How brave she was, they'll say as my coffin glides thro the
    crematorium's door
Alas my forever forever will then be no more

M. A. Teece

Flying Dreams

Have you flown on a sunny day, high above the clouds, in the bright
blue sky spread below a world of snow-capped mountains, frozen
glaziers and icy valleys

Do you see Roald Amundson at the South Pole placing his flag
Scot of Antarctica exhausted, hauling his sleigh, the final camp,
inside the tent hear his last words defeated he retreats forevermore
in the howling blinding blizzard

The icebergs, the screams, still steaming, the Titanic sliding to a
watery grave the polar bear catching his prey, the arctic hare
escaping to live another day the penguins, the seals, the whales
spouting in the bay

Amid the blue sky the otter weaves through the evening dusk
Touching down at base camp, among the canvas and wooden huts
The husky dogs, the skiers and caterpillar tractors churn up the frost

Below now, the clouds abate, the fields and houses come into sight
Slowly descending nearer the ground, with a bump the plane touches
down yesterdays dreams and adventures are passed, tomorrow a new
journey will start

S. J. Adkins

Flying Fish

Flying Fish! - You are the Jewels of the Seas!
Your sapphire brilliance lights the less
Of ships who pass your way;
Their gleaming keels, with graceful bows, cut through the foaming spray
Once rowed by slaves, they cleaved the waves where tidal oceans meet
You lead their way - now, as before - when steam replaced the sheet...
Your faithfulness to mariners of ancient times,
Is written into history with their rhymes
How, with all the dangers of the roguish deep,
Like flashing stars your leadership you keep!

You are the Angels of the fleet! A guide to all in sun or sleet
And today, as ships still yaw, you are the same as Nelson saw!
You use no wiles to Death's cruel door, as do exalted 'Men-of-War'
Those jelly-fish, whose membrane hooves, to sail the oceans and the coves,
Beguilingly, with shades of pinks and white, azure blues and mauves,
They float like fallen petals on the waves
But we must beware! For they are Sirens' knaves,
Guilty of iniquities - whose evil embrace leads to graves...
But Flying Fish! You are, each one of you - a sailor's star —!
Stay forever true! Diamond bright and blue! Talismen for all who sail afar!

D. R. Payn Le Sueur

Ring-A-Ring Of Roses

Through the enigma of this nursery rhyme,
Through all the never-never nonsense
I think I see
A sought-for vision
Of some kind of surety.

Through the simpleness of sad refrains,
Through the rock-a-bye reposes
Under apple boughs,
The frail blossoms of a beauty
Shimmer through this surety
And fade,

So the form is not quite formed,
The vision not quite verified;
And on along
This path of half-real fantasies
With halting hop-scotch progress
I follow still that stone
Thrown hopefully in years and moments past
After the shadow of a solid form.

Barbara Jean Jones

The Elephant's Tears

The elephant herd ambles by, head to tail
The matriarch leading, she knows the trail
As the midday sun beats down from the cloudless sky
They're looking for water in this land so dry.

Into the river, Oh! It's so cool
"Children first, you all know the rule"
Mother muses as her son wallows in slime
Proud of this young bull, "He's all mine".

Suddenly alert, a new noise in the air
A dragonfly on the horizon, drawing near
Panic sets into the now restless herd
Mother tries to guide but they're all running scared.

The huge insect now hovering above
Humans appear from this thing no one could love
A crack sounds loud as the young bull drops
Screams from her offspring but the slaughter won't stop.

Deep in the shadows, she's somehow been missed
Helicopter gone now, all culled on the list
Dusk falls quickly and the scavengers appear on stage
Crazy cackling of hyena as they feast on the carnage

Mother returns at dawn to the killing field
Silence now as her tears start to yield
Her family gone, her earthly bliss
How can she survive in a world such as this?

Eric L. Bailey

The Silence Of The Snow

How gently falls the snow at night
And, how precise each snowflake finds its bough,
Like Myriads of Heaven sent messengers, trite
Invisible to our Earthly peering eyes like angels white,
Blown about in total darkness, so cold, but yet still regal.
Perfect individual and superior by far than airborne kite or Eagle.
Each unique snowflake ends its cold unerring downward flight,
Then, and only perhaps by the silent voice of God above,
Which allows all the snowflakes as one giant white dove,
To change all earth below to a new wonderful sight.
Beautiful uniform scenes unfold, as dawn's early light
Now shows church, spire and cottages, all gleaming, pure white.
Children awaken surprisingly early, alas! Parents are treated
   now rather unfairly,
(And, Parental advice now it's not well respected)
For breakfasts (well cooked), are now utterly rejected
Outside, it's all Magic, as children by the score,
Go up hill and down dale and sledge across t'moor,
Meanwhile, as Robins etc, fight hard to survive,
Hope springs eternal, in all things alive.

Thomas Maher

A Test For God

Never a perfect union be worship and faith,
And thousands the Church-goers without Christ.
The zeal to pray and the chanting a ruse.
Shadrach, Meshach, Abednego the rarest faith deliverance;
Daniel kept a date with a lion and death,
Triumphed over both by prayer and faith.
And so the 'pastor' his Bible he firmly held,
A Zoo he climbed, unpermitted, unseen;
To robe or bell the lion a riddle still being,
For there the University of Ibadan kept a lion.
   A thud and a fright, the lion went into hiding.
Courage revived, the animal fiercely charging,
And into threads the 'pastor' and his dress.
   The strange happening a crowd hurried to witness,
But for the Bible undefiled and cleanly
What creature encountered the lion a mystery simply,
And his name on the Bible, the puzzle solved.
   'A voice charming the Lion' a worker testified:
An unprovoked attack it was, and for God a test.
And now the 'pastor' in heaven or hell, all the guess.

J. Ayo Aderibigbe

Desert Flower

Piecing together like a puzzle
Until the whole is reached,
But are the joints sturdy?
The web so intricately woven,
Series of relationships and love.

But to see her eyes turn cold and her smile fade,
To feel her body slip away from mine.
To see her eyes shine and her smile blossom,
Her body moulded against mine,
That security and love;

The web so delicately woven,
So easily taken away,
Springing up like flowers in the desert,
With the coming of the rains,
And yet to wither and die:

The beauty and splendour,
That was fresh and innocent,
Thorns against itself and leaving scars,
The web so intricately woven is torn,
And hangs limply - vulnerable!

Henry King

A Bridge Too Far

A bridge too far our country's tears bled,
Obey, ordered, and demanded, my country by Tory government led.
Cursed by, to erect a bridge. Spanning Scottish water.
One we didn't want, wish or desire.
Persuaded, already planned and arranged
The government said "We oughter
To traverse across the water. Above to the magical misty isle."
A monstrous constructions of concrete over the sea at Kyle.
Designed sadly seen erected built.
Our Scottish beauty to spoil and mar.
Now landscaped routed for future foreign travelling tourist car.
No more from mainland by ferry crossing
Waiting, crossing to arrive and depart.
Rendered robbed of romance stolen from my crying heart.
Forgotten ignored. The begging plea to take to Scottish poll.
Alas!! Now built. The bridge of high ransom toll.
All I ask for someone, heroic and bold
Before I leave this historic world of old.
Knock down or dislodge the bridge
Now standing on sad lone Scottish ridge.

Yvonne Fraser

Time

The days roll past, the years as well.
But we my darling, could never tell
If age was creeping up or no.
We have a love that keeps us warm.
Safe, secure in knowledge firm
That we, to each other do affirm
Undying loyalty, love and care,
That takes us through from year to year.
Never worrying, not a care.
Just as if the world's not there,
Just you and I, a perfect pair.

Ron Stuart

Guide

The silence breaks with the hoot of an owl
And the unseen shadow falls against the stone wall.
I hear his scratch, his leap and growl
And whistle, but silence repulses my call.

He was the light that flickered in my dark
And jolted my memories back into the past
And removed my fear with his unusual bark.
He cut through my gloom and solitude
My Prince and guide of a true cast
There of the uncertain step that we both did share.

His shining coat as black as mine
An empty chair, no wagging tail
His silky ears, so smooth and fine
No friend to enter my darkened jail.
The screech of brakes, the harsh of a thud
I hear his scream! I hear his cry!
The vision and visit of a knowing truth
And wince with pain as I see him die

Leslie Edwards

Thoughts Are Easy, Action Works

As we think so we are
how fortunate it's not so far
We can redirect our thought
when fear intrudes, best forgot

Relief from worry if we live the axiom
let go, let God live life to the maximum
See what happens with fascist powers
be thankful for a days worth of hours

A little strip over the abyss
feeling giddy, one of life's tricks
It need not detour us from positive action
the part we play, merely a fraction

Imagine your good fortune today
keep it simple live that way
A gratitude list for the good in your life
Helping greatly when there is strife....

Jean Tennent Mitchell

My Dream

I had a dream and it came true
I dreamed I'd spend my life with you
When I reflect, confused I get
Since at that time we hadn't met
I'd searched for love throughout my life
A trusted friend and devoted wife
I treasured visions in my mind
Of the kind of girl I hoped to find
It began to look as time passed on
That hopes of true love had now gone
Our paths didn't cross and we didn't meet
My heart with serious doubts did fleet,
Then life took on a different hue,
As you appeared, from out the blue,
From that day on and our first kiss
We've revelled in a kind of bliss
We've loved forever or so it seems
Marlene, darling, girl of my dreams.

Robert H. Connor

My Mum

She carried me for nine months, with sickness and with pain,
but the joy she felt inside her was well worth all the strain,
she gave me life, she gave me her love,
as she held me in her arms,
and I knew I felt protected from any kind of harm.

She raised me as a boy, and taught me right from wrong,
and often eased my nightmares,
with her smile as sweet as song.
Her heart is as big as the sky, and warmer than the sun,
and I am so proud that I can call her mum.

As I live from day to day, with all its trouble and its strife,
she is always there to help me,
throughout my daily life.
So thanks for everything, I hope that this verse will be
a tribute to your kindness,
for you mean the world to me.

Michael J. O'Rourke

Assessment

When I stand before the judgment seat
to thank our just and loving God
for the blessings of each day He gave
I'll thank you God for every day
the mystery of joy and pain
for parents to guide with love my early days
the friends and idealism of youth
a wife, life's greatest joy
our children each and all
they taught me in so many different ways
Your love
and in the evening of that life
the shining little stars
grand babies from whose lisping lips to learn
love's wisdom
Through life's lessons they taught
love which transcends me
to my loving Father God.

B. J. Bramwell

Because You Loved Me

You are my strength you are my destiny
Because you only saw the best in me
I am everything I am
Because you loved me

When I was weak and couldn't go on
You were that strength that helped me on
You gave me courage to face the world
Your smile, your hand and I was strong

You helped me up, I stood so tall
Your love was there if I should fall
I am everything I am
Because you loved me

Iride Cerbelli

Milk Eyes

I don't see evil doers begin to hack.
I don't see pain or hear the lies.
I don't see the knife in his back
because I'm looking through milk eyes.

I don't see the blood on your face
I don't see the hate or hear children's cries.
I don't see anarchy nothing's out of place.
because I'm looking through milk eyes.

I don't see the sky turn black.
I don't see people in hunger or hear their sighs.
I don't see you taking crack.
Because I'm looking through milk eyes.

I don't see the colours fade away
I don't see the look of fear as he dies.
I don't see the night turn into day
because I'm looking through milk eyes.

M. A. Sajid

Retail Trade

I have a shop, in Gateshead town,
The trade has dropped,
And getting me down,
People are so hard, and tight,
A shop in Newcastle, I would be
Alright.

People there are a different breed,
Gateshead folk, it's just pure greed,
Owt for nowt, and tuppence change,
Red carpet treatment, top of the
Range.

John Hall made it, so why can't I,
If trade doesn't pick up,
I will turn gazza, and cry.

High rents, and rates, bare-faced cheek,
Moans and groans, every week,
Don't get me wrong, there is some canny
Folk, but business in Gateshead, is no
Joke.

June Cameron

Changing Ways

The changing of the beginning
As of many disruptions in the world of sinning
Has upset ways of living
It's time to lend helping hand of giving

In helping the folk to get around
It's doing what is true and sound
Why not help the lame ones up
With every care and keep the door shut

What little help do they get this day
Volunteers are far and few in a way
As the young live a life of their own
While the old folk are left all alone

We can't perish the thought
It's often in our minds of a sought
We feel responsible in a way
So with regret we must not delay

But little help is seldom offered
To the lame, some can't be bothered
As life gets tedious all the same
Once again who is to blame

Lyn McGurk

The Elephant Man

The elephant man, disgusting and vile,
See this beast and you'll run a mile.
Should be kept in a steel cage,
He is Mother Nature in a deadly rage.

This monster will give you an unforgettable fright,
Who can stand this hideous sight?
An enormous head with fungus-like skin,
But is he a figure of evil within?

Despite the difference from ordinary folk,
Under all the layers of flesh is a human bloke,
But instead of joy, just endless fears,
And a deep, deep river of bitter tears.

A life of humiliation, a life of strife,
Impossible to lead a normal life.
Despite being textured like an old oak tree,
He is a human being trying to break free.

So you see, my friends, he is a lot like us,
Despite being as wide as a London bus.
He wants to live regularly but I doubt that he can,
He is John Merrick... the Elephant Man.

Qaiser Talib

If I Owned The World

If all the world belonged to me, the sun, the moon, the stars, the sea
I'd have a righteous policy, if all the world belonged to me

Instead of turmoil and unrest, abounding joy and happiness
And there would be sweet harmony, and absolute security

I'd give the poor a whole lot more, for them I'd build a treasure store
I'd take the yoke from off their necks, and issue them with empty cheques

I'd give according to their need, and make the rich pay for their greed
I'd gather up the wealth of earth, and tot up what the lot is worth

I'd weigh it on an even scale, in equity I'd never fail
I'd share the world's resources out, and hoarders I would surely rout

I'd prosper every O.A.P, who's had to go on bended knee
To fat and wealthy city cats, for scraps of this and scraps of that

I'd change their lot enormously, if all the world belonged to me
I'd give them all free holidays, and theirs would all be jolly days

No child would starve in my domain, or suffer cruelty and pain
I'd not allow a thing so crude, as mounds and mounds of surplus food

Despots I'd banish to outer space, weapons would vanish without a
trace. Fighting would cease, I'd insist upon peace

This is my philosophy, I'd snap my fingers, one, two, three
If only the world belonged to me

Mary G. Kane

All For Love

The slightest hint, the merest trace of a half forgotten scent
Announces your arrival, louder than words ever could
Oblivious of your effect, you enter with the grace of angels
Your presence fills the evening air, in ways you'll never know

The trill of your voice, as you call my name, sets my heart racing
A quality of sound that shames the sweetest of nightingales
With love bordering on adoration, I hang on your every word
And marvel, that of all the people you have met, you chose me

Long raven tresses fall softly, gently around your shoulders
To frame the face of beauty that haunts my dearest dreams
Concentrate, I must concentrate, to listen to your words
To formulate replies, to distract you before you see the love I feel

My heart yearns as my hand moves towards your hand
I watch your lips and hear the words but little registers
I long to hold you, tightly, in my arms tonight and forever
And achingly, I pull back before you notice or all will be lost

But it seems that no matter how close you are, we are far apart
Never meant to be together, in love or as lovers, evermore
And so the time comes, again, to part with many things unsaid
And with all the goodbyes that pass between us, another part of me dies

Dave Skeaping

Deprived Innocence

I can hear the sound, of your feet on the ground
And my heart is racing like crazy;
You are renown to be wild, but I am still a child,
My mind is now all hazy.
The fog is so dense, my fear is immense,
No one will see a thing.
You now grab my hand, with a force, as you stand,
Ahead, as if you were king,
Now you face me so bold, with the power that you hold,
The word in my mind is "escape"
Why am I here? To you it seems clear
The thought in your mind is "rape"
The tears are now streaming, and a loud sound of screaming,
These actions I cannot control.
You hold me down tight, in the dead of the night,
All my youth and my innocence, stole,
With your malicious grin, and detestable sin
You stand then just walk away
But you were so wrong, because now I am strong
As for you, all I can do, is pray.

Carol Dobbins

Life Time

Life being the luck of the draw not to be scorned
Is cycled from the moment you're born
Treasure it for as long as you live
In expectations such as this

You say how can we live this life
Be true to form well up to your rights
We wonder what is there to be had
So count our blessing and be glad

Welcome true friends of nature
In to the class of our dear saviour
With our recorded prayer every where
From our hearts, for all to share

Let not nature fall into decline
As after life we have to resign
Nothing is sure any more
So what have we left to reign for

Well now it takes all sorts to rule the world
Which is our nature as of old
So we leave the next of kin to reign
The job is tough which is the same

Lyn McGurk

Sorrow

The constant motion of life around him
seems unreal, and the long moment of his
suffering rushes around and around in
circles; making each day akin to its
brother, and as his pain engulfs him;
he does not seek from within it, sympathy,
condolence or understanding.
    He is doomed to be solitary, but because
of it has no bitterness against the world,
from which he seeks only simple but great
things. The sea, trees, flowers, brother wind,
sister rain and the golden rays of the sun,
for he has left behind the encumbrance
of endless repetition. No longer is he a
Philistine in a mad, conceited and rushing
world. A place of pitiless greed and course
brutality, and as a mere spectator of life,
looks upon the broken heart of the world,
as from his sorrow comes love. Which to him
is the only truth.

Martinella Brooks

Early One Morning

The Minister rose. As he put on his socks
    He eye fell upon his red baronet box.
His coming ordeal in the Radio Car,
    He feared still his overnight studies would mar.

And as he combed carefully through his grey locks
    He thought, "Now it seems they have brought back the stocks
But strangely the emphasis has quite reversed
    The wise and the learned are now the accursed."

He thought of an answer the might 'save his life'
    If asked if he had stopped beating his wife.
He'd say "no, at tennis I still have the edge
    At Scrabble she's better or so they allege."

He smelt fresh hot toast through a door left ajar
    "Perhaps they'll serve tea in the Radio Car
Just who will be asking the questions today?
    And will I resemble an old stag at bay?

"My answers I'll give in three words or four
    And then filibuster without saying more
And when the Scots terriers have barked through their brief
    The House I'll re-enter with joy and relief."

Eric G. Curling

Snow

The calm fields rest, covered in fragile white beneath a
hanging moon,
Feathery flakes float gently downwards,
Brushing my face like tiny damp cloths,
A touch of morning freshness in the late evening light.

Yet these delicate flakes,
Which singly, harm not a butterfly,
Together, do crush men and villages to powder,
And fill the air with thunder.

Thus do kindly men and women,
Who nod and smile on meeting one to one,
When gathered in a nation's millions, kill,
As no creatures ever killed, in all earth's tragic past.

Kindness lies in the world like lamb's wool, but beware, my friend,
For the soft mingles with the hard, and the hard with the soft.
Pale moonlight gleams on gentle snow, frozen in time,
Yet from this soft white carpet shine a million needle points.

Stuart McEwen

Marriage

Marriage is like a rock and it can corrode and
When it begins to crumble many stumble.
Desires are like electric wires, a current
Which flows then that voltage becomes high and
It overloads and explodes.
Rot is the worst when it is within and in time
It can be treated and much patience is needed.

Love is energy which is disbursed it can die
And be buried beneath the earth.
Along comes that rain and the seed of love is
Watered again it begins to grow and buds into
A rose and the fragrance each one of us know.
Life together can be sweet and with love
It is complete.

Valerie Barton

Separated Love

It is quiet. - The room is dark and still.
Not so my heart.
My heart is alight with love,
The memory of those precious hours together.
The joy of meeting eases the pain of parting,
Now over.
The nights together, wrapped in each other's arms.
The kisses,
The joy of love refound - now deepened by the parting.
Soon to be parted again, the borrowed hours,
The heart crying out against cruel time, who runs so fast.
But hope is there.
The parting is not so long - time will not stop,
And soon the waiting ends.
Once more the joy of reunion,
Those few precious hours again.

Sue Lord

The Dream

Last night I dreamt that all was still
    The world had ceased to be,
Yet countless people of all creeds,
    Were there in harmony
Mistrust had gone, all hate had gone.
    All fears now, hold no sway,
The evils of the world we knew
    Had all been blown away.
Death, hunger, and disease had gone.
    They; no longer played their parts,
That; caused the hatred, that once they knew,
    In other people's hearts.
Mankind lived in peace; whilst children played,
    And colour had no fear,
A better world, I dreamt last night;
    A better world; By far.

F. Truscott

41

Four Legged Transport

A horse is an animal, quite loving and sincere,
There are brown ones, grey ones, and dapples too I hear.
You can ride them, you can guide them, race them, chase them.
They'll do what you ask them, as long as you're kind.
Have you ever watched a pony, romping and prancing?
Just like a lady, singing and dancing,
Kicking its feet up, shaking its mane,
Not a care for the wind, the hail or the rain,
Loving each moment as it has a game.
Or the old work-horse of shire or the like,
Pulling a dray full of bottles and barrels,
Up hill or on cobbles, never a murmur,
Huge muscles moving with power and stamina.
Through sowing, or reaping, through most anything,
He does not have breakdowns, or power cuts, or other such things,
He works like a puppet, when you pull the strings.
You can ride on his back on a saddle or bare,
For work or for pleasure, there's nothing to beat,
The smell of hot leather as you take to your seat,
On the back of a jumper, the time clock to beat.

Janet McKinney

A Love That Wilt Not Let Me Go

Darling, you were my whole world,
Now, that world is torn apart,
The legacy you left me, a tired and broken heart.
I think of you each day, and in the nighttime too,
I miss your arms around me,
The way you used to do.
Maybe I was selfish, because I loved you so,
I knew you were in great pain,
Yet I was still willing you to live.
I could not bear to let you go.
God created Adam, he also gave him Eve.
But he has left me here alone,
All by myself to grieve.
I take out my book of memories,
Each page a fragrant flower.
I feel that I am close to you.
This is my favourite hour.
When this world is through with me
And I enter your domain,
Please be there with open arms, and love me, once again.

N. Butterfield

The Meaning Of Xmas Is Love

There's a-stirring afoot - many folk are about.
Shop windows have toys, for all children no doubt.
There are gifts for giving, and for giving it's true,
Is on everyone's lips. May love and joy come to you.
'Though there's many days ere Christmas we shout.

The tree is a-glitter, bearing gifts from afar,
Like the three wise man, love shines from their star.
Christmas puddings we've made, we've stirred while we wish
And silver coins, for luck, we've put in the dish.
Christmas is coming, heaven's door is ajar.

The wind blows cold, black darkness our nights,
Our toes and our fingers are numb with frost-bite.
The turkey we've ordered, the bells are a-ringing.
There's love, laughter and joy. Children's voices are singing.
Tomorrow is Christmas and our world is alright.

It's the birthday of Christ, every minute we'll treasure.
Goodwill to all men. Let's ponder at leisure.
Families are gathered, Christmas stockings are filled
Carols are echoing from the dales to the hills.
Christmas day is today. Love knows no measure.

Merrily, merrily, onwards and above.
Let every day be like Christmas, its symbol the dove.
Throughout the whole year and always and ever.
Let us shout from the roof tops in every endeavour.
That the true meaning of Christmas is love.

Kathleen Aldridge

"I Will Be Here When You Awake"

Maybe I could find the words to say
if loving you is wrong I will never be right.
When you fell into a deep sleep I too became tired,
don't expect me to walk away
because you cannot, that I could never do.
You gave me your heart and asked
me to take care of it forever,
I said, "It would be my pleasure"
Now that you can no longer dance in my arms
the way you used to,
I would rather not hear any more music play,
without you hearing it too.
God made you for me and he said,
I have moulded your lady the way she should be,
love her with all your heart deeply
but most of all tenderly,
don't ever let the sun go down
without your arms around her secure,
and remember to tell her,
"I will be here when you awake and of that you can be
assured."

Jennifer B. Small

Ode To The Sylvie Lydie

I stand by the harbour
On the threshold of a world unknown
To me, yet I
Enthralled by the mystery and wonder
Of these elusive seas
Contemplate the multi-coloured fishing boats
Aloof and proud having carried man and fish to land but
Task yet incomplete eagerly await
Another trip to sea

Full of hope and gaily bright
They gracefully depart to
Face the raging cold green seas
With a splash of colour, light in heart
Under the clouds and atop the waves
Go brave toward horizon yonder
When this present work is done
The harbour once more to adorn.

Rosaleen Mulcaire

The Ocean Of Time

If I ever go adrift on the ocean of time,
don't worry about me because I'll be fine.
And if which year is which slips from my mind,
please understand, child, do try to be kind.

J. D. Bailey

Poling Station

I beat him before, and I'd beat him now,
He bettered my vault, but I'd show him how.
I looked at Czalor, young, accomplished Slovak,
And a frisson of fear found its way down my back.

The sweat came in beads, and I glanced at the bar.
I started to jog. The vault didn't seem far.
Breath came in sharp gasps; I was nearing the jump.
My leg muscles tightened. My heart gave a thump.

A swing of the wrist and the pole stuck tight;
My body jerked upwards and put me in flight.
The ground spun below . . . I was reaching the bar,
Then—I heard way beyond me a shout from afar.

My foot caught on something; I jerked round and fell.
To my disappointment, the bar came as well . . .
I lay on the ground, as salt tears filled my eyes.
One moment's distraction, ambition's demise.

'There goes my medal.' These words sprang to mind,
As the victor, Czalor, approached from behind.
I scowled at the man, features creased by the sun,
Then . . . I shook his hand, for I'd lost, and he'd won.

Gary Bingley

Being Homeless

No one to love me, no one to care, I watch the people who just stop and stare.
I've got no belongings, no family or friends, no money or shelter, only clothes that I rend.
Hungry and cold, left out in the rain, no hospital treatment - I suffer in pain,
An old shop doorway is home for tonight, tomorrow - uncertain, alone in my plight.

No job to go to, only money I find, on the floor with the rubbish, I'm sure they don't mind.
Rushing to work with their money and car, if only they'd give me even one chocolate bar.
My hair is dirty and so are my clothes, I'm starving and lonely, "How far have I roamed?"
"The world is your oyster," the rich people say, "Get out and work," is another old phrase.

If only they tried it - living like this, they'd soon miss their lives, which were pleasant and bliss.
But I have no belongings - no car or t.v., what I wouldn't give, just to drink some warm tea.
One kind person who stopped and smiled, offered their hand and drove me some miles.
They gave me a drink, some food and a bed, some clothes and a job, "Good Luck" they said.

I'm now one of you and so happy, you see, I look back at someone who used to be me.
Now when I look at someone alone, with no luck, I offer my hand and pick them back up.
It doesn't take much time or effort from you, it would mean such a lot, and you'd feel happy, too.
That you'd given someone homeless a much needed chance, and not just walked past,
but made a difference at last.

Carol Spurway

Ma Ain Wee Sister

A Bairn has come awa' tae stay in Ma Mither's hoose, if ye please
She says the weans her pride an' joy, she's a lassie an' I'm a boy
Wee lassies arna as steerin' so they say, wait 'til she gets big
an' I'll show her the way
I'll mak' her climb an' fight wi' stanes, she'll no hae a frien' amon' the weans
I'll mak' her run awa frae school, I'll teach her hoo tae tangle wool
'Cause I hate the teacher when she gies me knitten an' makes me try it on for fitten
I'm knitten a hat wi' a hole in the croon whit's the sense when the rain cams doon

Me wee sister could hae that hat, if I knitted on an' did a' that....
Maybe she'd help me dae me sums, maybe she'd help me fight ma chums
It's no a bad idea at a' tae a sister on your side o' the law
Oh I wish tae goodness she'd get big, we could hae a smashin' game o' tig
We could run the errands yin by yin — an' share the blame when we'd return
'Cos we'd likely bring the wrang thing hame an' mither would call us by anither name
Oh I wish tae goodness she wis five — 'av a' these years tae wait 'til she thrives
It's an afu' lang time when ye think o' it no but she's an' ma ain, no wish it was you?

Elinor Evans

September Song

There's a chill in the air as I walk thru the park, early in the day
And as the sun rises to break up the clouds, I love every golden ray.
The shining wet leaves, the dew on the grass. The spider's web in the
bush all herald the coming of Autumn but in the park, there's a hush!
Holiday's over. Back to school. The place is so quiet now.
Easy to hear the Autumn sounds, as the apple falls from the bough.
The fruit on the trees is almost ready. Time to start making jam.
Apples, pears and plums so juicy. There are blackberries down by the dam.
The summer was lovely. The days on the river - the horse with the barge on tow.
The sea, the sand, the day at the zoo but it all seems so long ago.
The trees are so pretty. The colour of the leaves turns the landscape from green to gold.
As the days get shorter, the nights get longer. Soon it will be quite cold.
Then the chimneys will smoke from fires being lit - comforting warm, glowing ember
And the earth will change her summer for the beauty of September.

Joy Wingrove

An Affair Of Conscience

Night falls, the curtains draped, blackness fills the room.
I lay awake listening to the wind, calling, telling all untruths.
Tightening my eyes, squeezing my face, I lay not moving, too scared to make a sound.
Counting sheep, can't concentrate, frightened and guilty of deceit.

I lay wanting, willing myself to sleep, no words or actions can be heard or seen.
Thoughts rush through my head, questions, answers, not wanting to be told or said.
The ticking of the clock, the creaking of the floor, something blowing in the wind.
Silence is so dense, yet so fragile.

My body tired, weak and frail, my conscience alive and burning.
My head aching ready to explode, willing a thought to light the fuse to enable me to sleep.
Why only I can tell, but no one is to be answered.
The secret shall remain!

Patrick Anthony Williamson

43

My Dream

Windsurfing can be lots of fun
Especially when you're on your home run
Jumping waves and getting splashed
Laughing at those who've already crashed.

As the sun glistens on the sea
I wish those cheers and claps were for me
Although I still have a lot to learn
I'll win the championship, if I wait my turn.

Then in the mags I will appear
As the mega-stars do disappear
And in the end, they'll all be new faces
Winning and entering all of the races.

But the stars from now will never be forgot
As they are admired an awful lot
And their reputations will live on
For a long time after they have gone.

Amanda Davison

The Life And Death Of A Cigarette

If you smoke forty cigarettes a day,
You won't feel life ebb away.
But slow and sure the signs are there,
Brittle nails and greying hair,
Don't make out you do not care,
Whether it's right, or whether it's fair.

The wrinkles, sallow looks of age
Which grow, quickly for a weekly wage.
Your lungs in pieces, rotted away,
The pain, the hurt, and the decay.

All this to be a macho fan,
Looking good, but feeling wan.
Then you're dead, here no more,
Rotten to the inner core.

Too late to tell then what they've done.
You have lost.
The cigarettes have won.

Margaret Baker

Age

An old man sat upon a chair
   Fingers twisting his pure white hair
Suddenly, he gets up throwing down his
   coffee cup.
Age he thinks is so unjust.
   With youth and vigour all gone bust.
But carry on he knows he must.
   Forget his pain and not be fussed.
Then turning up the fire high,
   A chill, it filled his being,
Drifting into dreaminess,
   Is this a vision he is seeing.
Then he lay down upon his bed,
   With thoughts of childhood in his head,
And calmly, gently, all serene, passed away.
   His slate wiped clean.

Margaret Baker

Wife's Lament

A dancing man I am.
Wife, shoes, an owd van.
We danced on nearly every floor.
Now she's gone to dance no more.
Her ashes scattered up in't heather.
Now she dances in all weather.
I see her dancing in the clouds.
Her dress just silvered shrouds.
I'll search the dance halls for another.
To dance?
Like our kids' mother.

Bill Mitton

Going For A Song

A woman leaned against a lamp and lighted up a fag,
The cold of night enfolded her, she searched within her bag
To find no coppers for some tea. She walked towards a pub
And hoped that she would see a likely fool to pay the bill
For good and something hot to drink.
For she was cold and tired of life,
Just tottering on the brink of suicide.
The crowd was dense and men were there, propped up against a bar,
The place was warm, she faintly smiled, and viewed them from afar
As though she were not there.
The younger women all engrossed with chatting up their males,
She had no signs of interest shown, but thought,
If all that fails, I won't give up!,
There's got to be just one who will fancy me!
The pianist thumped the music out. She wandered to his side,
She saw a glass of spirit set, already for his break,
And forgetting all her pride, began to hum the tune he played.
"Have you a voice?", he asked, surprised. She smiled.
It had been so long since she had faced an audience.
He grinned, pushed the drink across, saying, "That's going for a song!"

Freda G. Tester-Ellis

Emotions

Please-help-me, I am burning, and I feel, like-I'm, on fire.
Please-help-me, I-am-burning-up, with-both-love, and desire.
There's-a-warm-glow, that-surrounds-me, and a feeling, so divine.
And-I-thank-the-Lord, up-above, for making you, all mine.
My-darling, I-love-you-so-much, I have this longing, within-my-heart.
And-it-feels, so-much-deeper-now, than-it-did, right-at, the start.
Without-you, the-days-of-the-week, feel like ten, and not, seven.
But-when-you-return, I-feel-like-I've-died, and I-have-gone, up to Heaven.
When-you're-not-there, and-all-I-see, is-this-big, empty, space.
I-just-feel-the-tears, in abundance, roll down, my face.
Can-you-imagine, what-it-is-like, to stand, and stare?
And-when-you-open, your arms, there-is-no-one, there.
It-is-just, sheer-hell, when-you-go, away.
It's-like-losing, the-sun, on a summer's day.
When the sun, in-its-heavens, touches-the-horizon, on the sea.
It-reflects, the-intimacy, that-is-felt, between-you, and me.
What-wonderful, love-hearts, rain-down, on my head.
When-I'm-missing-you, desperately, I-just-grab-my-pillow, instead.
If-this-is, being-crucified, with-true-love, and desire.
Then-turn, off-all-water, and-never-put-out, this fire.

Linda George

The Therapist

I'd like to scream and rant and rage, and pour expletives on the page
I'd like to swear and curse and shout,
Grab hold of anger and shove it out so where does it come from?
Where can it go? Is it something you're able to show?
What will he think if I explode in fire?
Plastering the room like a blown out car tyre
"Calm down, Relax, Breathe deeply" he'd say
So I'd bottle my feelings for another day,
He'd probably come over and give me a hug,
As I squeezed my emotions back under the rug
"It's just not done to behave like a child."
But anger's amoral, it's hungry and wild, temper unkindled,
Energy Depleted, I'd return to myself feeling strongly defeated
"It'll lessen with time, but it can't be suppressed,
That's a sure fire way of becoming depressed"
He slimes the smile of the smugly sane "you'll feel better soon,
do come again" eyebrows arched I snort in contempt,
His eyes look up quickly to see what I meant
"Now that's called projection, you're transferring to me,
it's you who is angry, with yourself, do you see?"

Sarah Morris

Eve

It was the eve of the eve of Christmas eve and I said to Eve that eve,
Let's go out this eve the eve of Christmas eve I said to Eve that eve,
And Eve said to me that eve the eve of Christmas eve let's wait till
New Year's eve said Eve that eve the eve of Christmas eve Eve said.

Edward Travers

Autumn

Red and yellow, golden and brown,
The leaves of summer lie on the ground.
Trees that were once majestically adorned,
Now look naked, dull and forlorned.

The moon's silvery shadow at six o'clock shines,
Denoting the coming of wintry times.
Dark nights followed by dark mornings,
A sure sign that winter soon will be calling.

Winds from the North begin their cold blow,
The icy rain falling whispers, snow, snow, snow.
Geese in formation start their long flight,
Hedgehogs and small mammals settle to sleep a long night.

Gone is the chorus of morning bird song,
Gone are the short nights and days that are long.
Gone are the fields awash with pure gold,
Gone is the dormouse that once ventured so bold.

The Earth is a cooling, getting brittle and hard,
Old Father Winter is leaving his card.
But all is not lost, for soon we shall see,
The new year bringing the majesty back to the tree.

C. Popkin

A House Into A Home

A house is built of bricks and mortar:
Foundations and a shell:
To which we fill it with possessions
Dependent on finance and personal choice
Don't be too materialistic or make money a God: but
Work hard at making your house of bricks and mortar
Into a happy loving home...

Fill your house with plants and flowers
your garden too: then you will see the beauty of creation
As they begin to grow:
Fill your house each day with love and laughter:
Friendship and good humour:
Share this with your partner - also with your friends:
Then you will have the beginning of a happy loving home:

To keep your house in good repair
It needs some of your loving care
For if it's left to its own devices it will depreciate
Give these ideas a bit of thought and
Put them into practice: then
Your house of bricks and mortar will be a happy loving home

Ann Lewis

Step Ladders

Stepping under the step ladder,
My daddy painting above me,
Getting in the way as young kids sometimes do.

And one of time's superstitions says:
"Do not walk under a ladder,"
But I was just there watching how my daddy would paint;
I was there at the wrong place,
A boy getting in the way of adult's work.

The tin of paint slipped and spilt over and I was soaked,
Covered white in waterfalls of dripping paint.
With water and turps, what a clean-up job that was!

And now a days I always avoid walking under ladders,
As I remember me as a young curious boy
Watching my father paint; a boy under a wooden triangle,
Covered white in waterfalls of dripping paint.

And like the wall being covered and renewed
I think of the ladders I want to climb
Of the things I want to leave behind,
As I remember me, my daddy's son,
Covered white in waterfalls of dripping paint.

Anthony Thomas McKeown

Rejection

A faint light shines down
Through the rain, through the window.
The silent room
Containing her wedding gown
Laid out, perfect,
As pure as an angel;
Blemished only by the absence of wings.
A small teardrop falls on the ivory satin.
Another falls and another and another.
On the third ring the ansaphone begins:
"Name, number,
After the tone."
The voice gives a subdued reply:
"I'm sorry". It says,
"I'm sorry, I'm sorry, I'm sorry".

E. Boyd

Love Is An Open Book

Our hearts are like an open book
Our love the pages in between.
The cherished memories and
feelings fill every page.

Our story begins with the first
sparks of what would become,
Our undying love.
Then as the pages unfold,
you see our love grow day by day.
Our hopes, dreams and desires
become reality, as our hearts
and souls become one.

There is no end to this book,
as our life together is a never-ending story.
The pages being written day by day,
our love growing stronger in every way.

Andrew Cooper

Akhet

O waters rise, come flood this land,
Great Sobek bring us life;
Our soil is dust and sun dried sand
And famine will be rife.

Our life-sustaining seeds await
Renewal of the floods.
Above our world, Orion late
Foretold: Disaster broods.

Make offerings and libation
To feed our deity;
Land receiving inundation
Under sycamore tree.

Now temples flooded, dykes break down,
The waters won't subside.
Amenemhat, a solemn crown,
His hungry people cried.

The Nomarchs sell their land for grain;
The palace wins control;
Long may this caring Pharaoh reign;
Our Black Land is made whole.

Suzanne J. Price

Untitled

'Twixt earth and heaven, a silken thread,
Held close by spirits, their vigil keeping,
And so as we rest our weary head,
Does the soul for knowledge go seeking?
Travelling amid the astral worlds,
Where awesome, ethereal aspects are taught,
And gossamer shadows of truths are unfurled,
Bringing nuance, to each waking thought . . .

Lesley Erna Hamer

I Saw The Angels

I had a dream on Battle's Eve,
And saw on some forgotten plain,
A host, an army gathered there,
The ghosts of long dead Englishmen.

I heard the Saxon wild war-cry,
And odin, howling across the shields,
Three lions passing fluttered by,
And lorded o'er those phantom fields.

I saw the white horse banner there,
And Harold's fighting man, of Kent.
With Artos, Kay, and Bedeviere,
Beneath the blood rich flag of Gwent.

Harrowed ranks in russet green,
With staves of Yew, perceived I clear,
Whilst Ironsides, of Cromwell's fame,
Rode knee to knee with Cavalier

It seemed a voice called strong and firm,
'Tis you who carry these banners on,
Then woke I calm and unafraid,
To face the dawn, that day, at Mons.

Jess Thompson-Hughes

A Thousand Journeys

Through forest, woods, fields and dreams
Our minds meander and worlds are seen
By air or foot on those or thought
For real or a journey through imagination.

Magical cities, towns or village
We perceive the beauty or mindless ruin
Are our streets paved with gold
I know they can relate stories of old.

Seas, rivers, streams and brooks
relentlessly flow without intervention
Where do they start, where do they end.
Travel the world, chasing the moon.

A thousand journeys. Yes my friend
We all take them to a dreams end
Grasp your dreams and believe
Let them take you. Your journey has begun.

J. R. Baker

Inamorato

When I feel like a baby, he is
always there with lullabies - my very own fairy tales.
There to share jokes with me - my funny clown.

When I feel like a little girl, he is
always there to hug me - my incurable cuddler.
There to mother me - my father figure.

When I feel like I am changing, he is
always there to talk with me - my very own best friend.
There to dream with me - my handsome prince.

When I feel like I'm a woman, he is
always there with tenderness - my considerate lover.
There to share his life with me - my special guy.

My handsome prince, he is
A wonderful man, he is
My inspiration.

Lynda M. Korimboccus

Bitter Wind

Silent is the air, you will never know
The secrets of my heart, the pain, the woe;
So pure that you could not see it if you'd will
But so strong and powerful it can kill.
And it hath almost killed me;
Blew me side on 'gainst a thornéd tree
Were in it have pierced and torn me apart
Laughed in my face, ravished only my heart.

Jennifer Flood

Thoughts Of An Evacuee

I don't know where I'm going, I'm sent off without knowing
Bye Mum, Bye Dad, children crying, mad
Me and my brother without our mother
Sitting on that train we say "bye, bye" once again,
There's a feeling I can't control, somewhere in my soul,
The whistle blows, my mother goes, the doors close,
The sound of feet behind our seat
My brother starts to cry, I'm still wondering, why?
Why do we have to go, "I'm sorry, I don't know"
That's what I told my brother when he wanted our mother,
That feelings still there, it's not fair,
Half an hour has gone we still travel on,
My brother's asleep, this feeling's deep,
Oh no, I'm starting to cry, tears drop from my eye,
Then suddenly the train stops!

Anne-Marie Bulpitt

A Day In The Life Of

Lounging, lazily, listless in the sun.
No worries, no cares, nothing to do.
Lackadaisical, in largo, languishing 'til it comes,
it is very hot. It warms right through.
Loitering, lingering in and out sleep.
Birds and butterflies are unperturbed too.

Arouse it's getting cooler,
the breeze is on its way.
The sun has lost its brightness,
dusk is on its way.
The sky is growing darker,
night is on its way.

Moving in the moon-light in a mechanical way.
Hungry now. Plenty to do.
Macabre, machiavellian and menacing to its prey.
Don't mind if it's mouse, vole or shrew.
Maim, massacre and mangle, ignore the affray.
Claw, paw and feast with zest anew.

The satisfaction of repletion, a wash to keep neat.
Settle down, tired now. Time for sleep.

Ros Robinson

Opulence

I have been at tables set with silver,
Waterford crystal, gold candelabra.
Bone china laced with minuscule ivy,
centre piece, mignonette.
A pewter jug or two to dull the opulence,
A rose to stain the linen cloth.

I have dined on Prawns Maison, Avocados,
sometimes Lobster Thermidor.
Smoked salmon with all the trimmings,
occasionally Russian Caviar.

Tonight I spied the rainbow trout in
its glass coffin,
Its one liquid eye stared into mine.
Tomorrow I dine on water-melon.

Rosaleen Clarke

Mourning

Drained by now of all feeling she curled up into a small tight ball
And slept on into the morning,
Missing the waking of the birds and the yawning of the sun,
Unaware that in the huge brass bed she lay alone.

Brought abruptly to waking by an unheard disturbance.
A few moments without feeling, numbed and drained.
Then, memory seeping through her whole body in a wave,
Overflowing and escaping through sad, sad eyes.

Lying alone revisiting each detail of their last hours,
As if this was but her first day of mourning.
And she questioned, an until lately unfamiliar god
About when it would all end?

Wendy H. Taylor

What Price Peace?

What have we done to this planet earth,
This sphere in space, the place of our birth.
What drives us to become a beast
On other people's lives to feast?

Machines man-made to kill mankind,
Are the workings of an evil mind
As clouds of smoke engulf the sky,
Someone's life has passed them by.

God, creator of the human race,
Can see the sad and tear-stained face,
As lines of broken families flee...
Only grief and despair for the refugee.

Encaged in camps like a human zoo,
Bewildered, not knowing what to do.
Sunken eyes gaze from skeletal frames,
Pawns in the enemies' criminal games.

As one war ends another begins,
Armies guilty of a thousand sins,
Some will live and some will die,
What a price to pay for you and I.

Peter Houghton

Lost Life

You thought it was right to leave your life
Now you know it was wrong
You can't remember your family and friends
Because it has been so long

I'm thinking of you, are you thinking of me
When the cold nights set in
Don't worry now because I'm on my way
When I arrive will I be let in

There you were in the middle of nowhere
Sitting with your life in your hands
I looked behind your eyes and inside your mind
Trying to understand

Your eyes reach out and say
You don't want to be hurt again
Because all you can do
Is feel the pain of the deadly rain

I pick you up and carry you home
To a land that's far away
And as you look behind us
All you can remember is the hurt of yesterday.

Sean Pile

Is It Because She's A Woman?

She's Mrs. Jekyll, she's Mrs. Hyde.
She's Mrs. Nice, she's Mrs. Dread.
She's Mary Mary quiet contrary.
The girl with the curl in the middle of her forehead.

One minute she's good, very very good,
Next minute nasty and abrupt
It's like living with a rumbling volcano,
That is waiting to erupt.

She's tense, as tense as a coiled-up spring,
A spring that's waiting for release.
Then she'll let fly with the venom of a viper,
And as quick, turns back into the dove of peace.

Both the villain, and the heroine.
Like an actress playing both the parts,
One minute she's Alice in wonderland,
Then off with their heads, she's the nasty Queen of Hearts

Now is it because she's a woman
Or does she have a split personality?
A pseudo schizophrenic,
Or is it just because she's married to me?

Stevie Dore

Together

Awake. Alert. Alone in thought.
I listen to the murmured purr of sleep
evaporating in tufts
from his tongue.

He encrusts the night with himself
and carves a worshipped figure

imagination.
Emerald eyes blind the horizon.
Endless, soulless feet
meander the stony walk.
I listen as the chastising glass approaches,
a bubble for my head, heart and toes.
They proceed in satined worry
through my air
exhaling solemn kisses;
bitter mouth.

He awakes to discover, remembered,
a thousand careers of pain.

I lie awake to remind him
and satisfy the knife.

Nici Hunt

History And I

A moment...lapse. Enough!
'Neath transient sky of sombre ray, distorted shadows probe
among cool embers from this dying day.

The half moon weeps, as though
enlisted to illumine all. From scene of twisted steel,
and shattered screen. In mercy night shall fall.

Who will observe, and mourn?
Hosts gather unseen to reclaim, through whom their master now
commands to rise amidst the smoke and flame.

History 'tends. 'Tis done!
New owners reap this 'passing by'. Bedfellows cloned in time;
Unwilling partners...History and I.

A second...two, no more;
Microbes from waters rushing on. For what would be, became;
The spectre due, is here, then quickly gone!

Must it be so? Can I...
re-live, erase the dreadful scene? What harm if years I yield,
in lieu of fleeting seconds once have been?

This night...oblivion woo'd the slain; The innocent enshrined
in History, and I alone remain.

David Watts

Intimations From A Witness

Speak with a tranquil heart
  or remain silent.
Quiet voices rattle whispers
Through ears of broad-leaved maize,
And the busy tongues of leaves
Cluster green conversations
In the groves along a foot way.
Airs, warm from the south,
And warm on the mouth,
Draw cool across the skin.
Brushed bird-wing vibrations
And a secret breath, together dip and spin
Peace out of the sky.
No speaking thing deserts tranquillity.
The Hidden breath, the blue humidity,
Condenses the whole essence of processional presences,
And devastates the senses
  with a perfumed prayer.
All the touches of truth
  are tentative.

Anthony Smyth

Understanding A Loss

Life, love and walking wounded.
    There comes a time when these will meet!
A life of love, that ends in sadness,
    The future ahead so full of grief;
A love of life that keeps one living,
    Living the days that are so brief,
I understand! They cry quite softly,
    I understand, I really do!
He and she and they together,
    All understand the way you feel?
But true understanding
    Comes only in losing,
This sadness is not meant for all;
    Perhaps someday they will stop saying,
    I understand - it all!

Carole A. Ruben

To She

In agony I drowned in my own torment,
Head falling backwards,
Too weary to hold such heavy thoughts.
I used to bang my hands on concrete walls
To block out my mental pain;
A memory too sad to want to recollect.

In my own world I would smile for everyone,
Never once for myself.
Who was 'she', the mirror image
I turned away from in disgust,
The weak, tired, silly fool; full of mistrust?

I tried so hard to ignore her,
But, she killed the dying child
That wanted so desperately to grow;
An old tree's tiny, courageous little blossom that died,
While slowly 'she' in turn did deservedly bloom.

Debbie Mortimer

To Mam

We've had some laughs
We've had some tears
Still you've looked after
me over the years.
You've taught me everything
right from the start
As I have listened
from the middle of my heart.

When I've needed help
you have always been there
And when I've been ill
you would always care.
To you a thank you I'd like to send
for being my mother and my friend.

I know you love me, you don't have to say
You may not think it but I love you more
and more each day. That's why
I'd like to say thank you for all you have done,
for giving me a life under the sun.
Happy 50th birthday

Jane Whinham

Blessed Angels

The angels come from the heaven above,
To care for us, and give us love,
They guide us through our life from birth,
That we may spend some time on earth.

They watch us through our busy lives,
Taking the hardships in our stride,
Watching happiness appear,
Often shedding many a tear.

They see our families slowly grow,
And watch us aging, and they know,
They'll care for us, when it's time to go.

Barbara Mears

The Only Straight Road To Happiness

Happiness is gained when to others you do good
And to treat them as your equal you always should.
For all are descendants of Adam and Eve—
Whether you like it or not, it's a fact you should believe.

Why should you be separated by class or creed—
The world would be in peace, if from this you could be freed.
In heaven you all shall be treated as one;
Between rich and poor, distinction there'll be none.

Why claim you are of superior birth
When in death all you'll inherit is six feet of dirt.
Being humble is the only true way to make friends—
Do it now before it's too late to make amends.

To happiness in this world there is but one way
And it will never be gained if you go astray—
The only straight road to happiness lies
Is for you to heed the following advice:

Do to others as you wish them do to you—
Follow this principle and you'll never be blue.
Never be proud, 'cause pride shall one day have a fall
And the few friends you have, you will lose them all.

Thomas Herbert Fernandes

Outreach

Victim of terrorism, poverty and sin -
Some three years old: bewildered, lost and sad,
Alone and frightened - hungry, and in pain,
The boy had been bereft of all he had.

No mother, father, family or friends
When that great ball of fire consumed the shed
That once had been his home. He was outside -
He ran - but in the home the rest lay dead.

Sleep, for a while, had given him some ease -
But he awoke: no family in sight;
And, in the bush, he cried, and cried, and cried;
Would no one come? Would no one see his plight?

A rustle in the trees: a friendly face -
His rescuer had travelled many a mile
To ease suffering in countries torn by war -
The boy looked up. He gave a timid smile.

He asked a childlike question: "Are you God?"
"No, God has sent me. You may come with me."
The frightened child held out a tiny hand:
"Then God has sent you to look after me!"

Barbara Green

Nuclear War

I never knew until I was there in hell or hell to be
Heaven seemed a million miles away but my eyes revealed the truth

Beams of light destroyed by death, murder of the worst kind
Hell fires entice lives, innocent people damned to the hell war

Burnt faces rise up above my head
Who was next to go, would it be me?
My unconscious mind has taken over
Explosion is screaming through my head

The war continues as I look from above
People suffering from their own making
Who is responsible for this hell war?
As the smoke clears, it reveals . . .

Something unknown to most men
A faint glow looming out of the darkness
Then a silence, a long, lingering silence
Survivors waiting for something . . . anything?

A sudden flash, so blinding, so terrifying
Like a giant bolt of lightning filling the whole sky
The intense heat no human can bear
Then nothing . . . silence, a destructed planet.

Sarah J. Paling

Memories

Your face is so clear when my eyes close,
Like the smile of a sunset,
I see your bright sunshine hair,
I feel the breath of a new beginning,
I wish I could still be there.

Those distant memories are still very clear,
Shall I call?
Shall I write?
It's your voice I long to hear.

If only I could bottle my love,
And send it to you,
So you could understand how I feel,
My love is so true.

As my eyes gently open,
I see the old sun setting,
In the cold western skies,
The birds seem to have stopped singing,
As I wipe another tear from my eyes.

Kevin Yates

Untitled

I travelled the world for I knew not what,
I searched high and low for this and that,
I could not ease my ceaseless rage,
until I met a wise old sage.
Go home! Go home! He said to me.
help other people, and you will see,
rewards a-plenty of every kind,
contentment comes with peace of mind.

Agnieska Norris

Sunset

Endless mystery,
Immortal through history,
Still the course is set.
Winding solidly,
Glorious in solemnity,
We gaze with some regret.
Trees tremble at the sight,
Bow majestically to the light.
Now the hue deepens to richest red,
Fills our eyes, our hearts, our head.
The day is passing into night,
Darkness creeps from left to right.
Sadness as this time departs,
Yet hope for tomorrow floods our hearts.

This is perfection, this is creation,
This is peace, free to every nation.
This is the hope for the time to come,
This is the love from God through the Son.

Sue Sowden

Hurt

Until you have someone special tear you apart,
You couldn't have experienced a broken heart,
The amount of pain you feel,
Is so unreal.
It's although the world around you,
Is finally dividing in two.
All the tears you will weep,
for those happy memories you shall always keep.
Why all these complications to life?
I sometimes want to end them with a knife.
People may disagree and say that's not the way,
But how do they know when things aren't o.k.?
I just want to put aside all dealings,
As it's hard to cope with these feelings.

Michelle Warner

The Kitten Of War

The crying kitten in the corner meek, in part;
Showed me the lie of the land. Our church
pointing with unheeded finger, to heaven.
Men formed a circle, round me, the evening
shadows gathered. In the twilight, I recited
a suitable verse; in the utter stillness, I cried.
Held with a strange fascination, stood in the gloom:
War-stricken. The crucifixion, not the ascension?
Left and standing, God is love;

Our town centre lay, scattered about (debris)
Roofs battered in, by violence. Home is always
in one's thoughts, officer or civilian, behave alike.
Their devotion to the dying; their courage and
self denial are jewels that shine out like stars
and make us almost love, black night, of war:
A hole within the kitten, of human nobleness...

Wee Gerard Reid

You

You're there in all that I see,
In all I try to be.
In all my sorrow, in all my pain,
You're there in all that's insane.
You're there in all that I do,
Each page I turn the story reads you.
You're there in the air that I breathe
You're the pain in my heart and the tears that I weep.
You're there in each word that I write,
And when I can't see you are my sight.
You're there to fill in my emptiness,
With magnetic charm and fatal unrest.
You're there where my wounds bleed, and my flowers die,
You're there in all that I need,
Making it wrong or making it right.
You're there in all your puzzlement,
Enchanting, yet disturbing, desipient
When I see heaven breathe my last breath,
You'll be there in all of my death,
Where the road ends . . . I see you there.

Angie Blank

The Other Man's Grass

Why do we strive for the other side,
in a land that is greener than ours.
Why do we fight, never get it quite right,
for a land that is greener than ours.
Why do we care what they have there,
on a land that is greener than ours.

When last did we look to see what we had,
in our land that is greener than theirs.
When last did we say, "Thanks for my day"
on the land that is greener than theirs.
When last did we share all that we have,
from our land that is greener than theirs.

If we want what they have, and they want ours
then the grass it cannot be greener.
If they like ours better, and we prefer theirs,
then the grass it cannot be greener.
If everyone swapped it would be just the same.
Then the grass it cannot be greener.

Christine Webb

Loneliness

A silent hum in your ear,
A distant voice in your mind.
A slight ache inside your heart,
A empty space in your soul.

A lonely tear down your cheek,
A fearful gleam within your eyes.
A laziness in your body,
A invisible scream from your hidden happiness.

N. Carter

Distress Call, A Little Tragedy Of The Roads

I'd smashed a moorhen but I had not killed it;
I'd smashed a moorhen but it was not dead;
I saw it writhe on the wet Fenland roadside;
I'd caused its pain but was powerless to end it—
Then, out of the fog a cyclist appeared.
Over the wet road I ran to him weeping
"Please, please can you do it?" I asked and he did.
Seconds later, "All over" he called and had vanished.
Thankful and thoughtful I drove on my way.

An angel perhaps? "What a silly suggestion!"
Many would scoff, but I still ask the question.
Who <u>knows</u> the answer? None but He
Who once created the moorhen and me.

Wendy McQuillin

The Moon

Have you watched the enchanted light?
Tripping o'er the fields at night,
Stretching out her ray-light charms,
like my mother's open arms.

Have you tried to trace her rays?
Through a branch which swoops and sways,
wondered if she's there to please,
or if she's really made of cheese.

Nothing can escape her rays,
She gives the sun, rest from her days,
I hope that I can visit soon,
And meet the life upon the moon.

She's everything I want to be,
The stars around her dance with glee,
The clouds they pass across her face,
As if they're jealous of her grace.

So every night you're feeling low,
To the window you should go,
She'll shine down on you way up high,
And brighten up your deepest sigh.

Patricia Britton

D-Day

Pushing, shoving, crammed together like sardines in a tin.
We stopped, the engines silent and still.
Swish went the nets over the side.

"Down you go, men!"

Frozen, sodden, aching arms, rifles high.
Land at last.

"On your bellies, men!"

Quick, slither, slide, up the beach.
What's happening?
Where are we?
Darkness all around.

"Forward, men!"

Shouting, screaming, banging, sobbing.

D-day.

Gill Denyer

The Girl In The Corner

The girl in the corner, she feels so alone.
Her heart feels like a piece of hard stone.
The tone in her eyes is so unalive.
With a fake smile she dances with fame.
By hurting her friend she wallows with shame.
Around and around in a misty black room.
She dances with devils, with the feeling of gloom.
In the center of the room lies a huge mirror.
Into the reflection the only thing she can see is
.......me

Vanessa Schjelderup

Our Homeless

I often think when snow and ice or frost lies on the ground,
of people in a cardboard box, no home for them is found,
on city streets they sleep at night, in bags to keep them warm,
in wet and windy weather they lie in huddled form.

A doorway or an alleyway is very often best,
they give them some protection and let them get some rest,
but as the dawn breaks overhead, their bed they fold away
and mingle with the city crowds to start another day

Their breakfast is a mug of tea, perhaps a piece of bread,
a soup kitchen, or hostel meal, at lunch time may be fed,
but scrounging in the back streets bins is often seen to be,
the only source of daily food these people ever see

In summer time it's not too bad, the nights stay longer light,
but still these homeless people stay on the streets at night.
They vary in their age groups, some are in their teens,
whilst others are the elderly without support or means.

So when the nights get darker and the autumn winds do blow,
and we are in our lighted homes with fires all aglow,
our thoughts must be for the homeless, so cold upon the streets
as we snuggle in our soft warm beneath the clean bed sheets.

S. Brooke

The Car Is God

The Car is God to some,
Praying to a halo of petrol drizzle:
Grandma gasping in her rocking-chair;
(Rah... rah... rah... rah).
Our car... this car... that car... his car...
Her car... any car... the old car...
Grandma's car... take the car...
Mend the car...
Take a spanner and the jump leads.
(The blind mechanic from Flashdance spoke).
There's a spark!
There can't be...
Willow and weeds steering upholstery,
In Austin Seven... Nineteen Thirty-Four-Thirty-Five...
Grandma's car... Granddad drove...
She never drove, in years of respiration purgatory;
Inhaler and balsam antagonizing
The verandah of senility.
Terminal.

Norman MacDonald

Carpet Ride

Let me take you an a carpet ride,
High above in the star-filled skies,
Let me show you the heavens above,
Let me show you a world of love.

We shall float by on white fluffy clouds,
And see all the shuffling crowds,
Of people far down below us,
Racing about, all making a fuss.

We shall glide across the dark night sky,
Where all our worries pass us by,
No need for money or material possessions,
We will reach high to the highest heavens.

All around us will be a silence,
No weapons or violence,
Where nobody is killed,
Every person and creature is protective from a heavenly shield.

Let me take you on a carpet ride,
High above in the star-filled skies,
Let me show you the heavens above.
Let me show you a world of love.

Rebecca Blake

Life

Life is for living, not pondering
  on what might have been or what might be,
Life is for making dreams become reality
Life is for taking one moment in time
  and being aware of that moment as now -
Without your mind wandering into the future
  or the past
A 'still' moment; at one with your thoughts

Life should not be squandered on how things should be,
  but spent on how things are or could be

Life in all its magical glory -
  Let's learn to see the magic in order to appreciate -
  Life

Jane Deborah Burke

Would Things Have Been Different?

The streets are full of people in the day-time
It's funny how things seem better when the sun shines
But at night it can be lonely if you have no-one there
Can't bear to be alone but we hide away our fear

The world can be a lonesome place if none of us stop to think
Just how sad the world's become when some of us turn to drink
But it's not the answer, that's why we feel so sad
Escape in a world of our own
The kind of life most of us have

Walking the streets at night just to get away
Would things have been different than they are today
I guess we'll never know as the days go by
We live for another day with a tear in our eye

Been waiting over an hour for that special date
It's funny how things change from love to hate
But tomorrow is a new day and the sun will shine
You're no longer alone to face another night-time

Angela Shaw

Vengeance

Enclosed by hate he stands alone.
Head hung low. Another blow.
Pain.
An oozing puddle at his feet,
Red as a cherry, not nearly as sweet.
A familiar fist finds unblemished flesh.
Thump. Throb.
Spiteful sniggers swell
And swamp the hopeless moaning.
A heavy boot meets his shin with a crack.
Fear.
  Smack.
    Terror.
A swarm of scarred limbs circle him;
Scars which once he had been proud of
Now wanted their revenge.

Helen Donnelly

Empty Upstairs Room

Pipe cleaner legs gape from underneath
grubby, glaring multi-coloured shorts,
which only parade the colours missing
from their empty grey lives.
Thick Lancashire accents accentuate
every dull vowel and consonant clearly.
They sing and laugh like the fortunate
tots they will never be.
"Don't yer think we're lucky?" they cry,
offering thanks to a God grown blind
to the suffering of innocents.
Cheap clothes, cheap shoes and short haircuts
are the burden of the beggared.
Yet they still sing happily
to an empty upstairs room.

S. J. Murphy

Those Were The Days

When asked for a list of my favourite things,
I found it quite hard in truth,
For most of the things which I seem to like best
Are dredged from my carefree youth.

When aeroplanes looked and sounded like 'planes -
Not monstrous darts screeching by -
I loved the sound of their lazy drone
In a cloudless summer sky.

The donkey rides along silver sands,
Licorice, and apples candied,
Those huge minty sticks of seaside rock,
Leaving fingers and mouths pinkly branded.

The lavish musicals - Hollywood style -
They certainly couldn't be missed.
Any movie with Cagney, although I admit
"Yankee Doodle" is top of my list.

In future years will the kids of today,
When asked to think about it,
Recall with pleasure such simple things?
Sadly, somehow I very much doubt it.

Dorothy White

Live

The sun has set,
The tide is high.
A once golden sea
Reflects the silver night sky.

The ripples of the waves distort
The image of the moon.
This beauty is the last I'll see,
For I am leaving soon.

A single plunge is all it takes,
To wash away our worries and mistakes.
The ice-cold water stings my skin,
One smothered gasp and light brings me in.

Now all is silent, all is still.
I got my way, I made my will.
No more depression, no more pain,
I rejoice, life is in me once again.

Below, a blossom grows upon my head,
My grave has become a flower bed.
Those who mourn and weep and bow,
Never stopped to think until now.

Jane Collins

Reflections

Uniform in size, clean of skin, not too many eyes
So I picked my seed put them in trays to sprout,
Christmas had just barely gone with all its festive joys
Thinking forward to an early crop, no time to laze about.

I pictured one in spring of Eighteen Forty-Five
Steadily with shining spade he set out his lazy-bed,
Totally dependent on the potato merely to survive
Always when planting he gave of everything he had.

Then relief and modest satisfaction when the job was done
And a simple faith that time would do the rest,
He knew that after planting the battle was half won
And they would be rewarded who had done their best.

But demon blight struck a fatal blow in the autumn of the year
When healthy growth was turned to a putrid mass,
Faith too was thwarted, quickly it succumbed to fear
No one could understand such destruction come to pass.

Still thinking of the horrors our forebears had to endure
And what the great famine was all about,
Then I see another little bud, there to reassure
Again in trust I leave my seed to sprout.

Arthur McQuade

In Remembrance V. J. Day

We remembered the role you had to play,
We remembered dear dad today,
We watched them march, so tall, so proud,
You were there too, I cried out loud.
Looking down, watching too.

Yes Dad we are remembering you.
You were with us a few years only,
We were left empty and lonely.
What's that, will we ever learn,
As we think of those who did not return.

Yes Dad our thoughts are with you this day.
As down on our knees we pray.
In a perfect world, there would be peace hereafter,
There would be no tears, only laughter.

Pat Cannon

A Summer Day In The Garden

In the shade of the trees in the garden
I sit and ponder, at peace with the world
The old cat on the lawn lazily blinking
at the flowers' dazzling beauty, unfurled.
Butterflies as gentle ballerinas
Dance by in this world so bright.
On their stage for one brief moment
They seem thrilled with the sun's golden light.
The happy twitter of birds in hiding
And bees dart from bloom to bloom
Among pink roses and yellow hypericum
Surely an enchanting 'outdoors' room
an oasis of peace is a garden
Wealth of colour and such comfort here too
Thank God for the flowers and the garden
He made them for me and for you

Kathleen Woods

To A Prison Visitor

Whilst walls do not a prison make
And only thought can cage,
The dull round unrelieved by break
Seems much more of an age.

Small talk looms large when rarely heard,
As gold is repartee,
An adult, understanding word
Sets mind, thus matter, free.

Time, fleet or slow must needs be spent
And none can bank or hoard,
It can be given, never lent,
By those who will afford.

When precious freedom, golden time,
Are held at whim and will,
What is the reason or the rhyme
But love, them both to spill?

D. P. Downes

Friendship The Sinking Ship

Sweet angels float down on love's lost light
now nothing's right.
Never to be, can't you see it's not for me.
Friends should be there for you but do they
really care for you.
They say that they do but is it true?
Still I feel blue, but nothing's new.
Love or lust it was never a must, now memories
fade to dust.
Friendship a love that cannot be denied, so
why do I feel I have to hide.
I gave you a shoulder to cry on, someone to
rely on but you were never all that, and that's a fact.
Right from the start you dissed me but now
you're never to be missed.
A friend it had to end, a lie so I'll say goodbye.

Amanda Jayne Biro

Nature's Way

Life so precious, so futile.
Let me linger on awhile.
What to do, I search in vain,
confused by the mixture of love, and pain.
Yet search I must, although it's dark,
in desperation for that kindling spark.
That might show the reason why,
I go through life, just to die.
But sorrow, I'll not placate,
nor dwell upon my lowly state.
Best look forward to the morning sun.
The grass, and trees, there for everyone.
A smile on the face of an innocent child.
The song of the birds so free and wild.
Surely, these are the things.
That make it all worthwhile.

W. T. Davies

The Volcano

First came the thunder deafening our ears
Then came the lightening confirming our fears
The sun blotted out and the world turned black

We waited for the dawn with anxious longing
Would there be an another dawn?
Eighteen hours of darkness,
Not unlike the pit of hell,
Would we see the light of day?

A dawn there was, and welcome as it was,
It revealed a sight of utter desolation.
Streets covered with dark ash,
Roofs which had collapsed.
Everywhere devastation.

Trees hung as if in total despair,
Weighed down by the Volcanic ash,
Which had fallen like snow, but the colour
Was a menacing grey, not white.

People walked about aimlessly,
Stunned by the events of the night.

Catherine S. Gillibrand

Face

I saw a little old man the other day,
He looked so sad I thought I should say...
But then he turned his head away.

I didn't speak, neither did he,
I wish I had; his sad face haunts me.

He must have been hurt by something, somehow,
Wish I had spoken; we both might feel better now.

But I didn't know him, maybe that's how he looks,
Although that kind of sadness is mostly in books.
You never can tell from faces you see,
Was he unhappy or was it just me?

Eileen Tomlinson

The Heaven Which Lies Beyond Heaven

I dreamt I've been to heaven, I heard the
sweet sound of the door which opened to let me in.
I saw a creature with eyes as large as the
light of a motor car, and glaring the colour of amber.
I saw the preacher sweating, wiping his face
with an handkerchief, then exclaimed,
"Revelation chapter 21: I'm sweating!"
The scene changes, I was looking at the blue
sky of heaven, I was about to be taken up
into the heaven which lies beyond heaven.
I was afraid, so I knew I wasn't ready.
I never enter into that other heaven.
Then I awoke out of my sleep.

S. Freckleton

Streets

Sitting in the porch way
With only a sign
Saying Help, Lost, Cold, and Alone.

Not sure where I am
Not sure where to go
The clothes on my back
Are grey and worn.

Nights are the worst
My heart pounds faster than ever before
I cry myself to sleep
Not sure if I should slumber
I may never wake, I may never return.

People walk by without a care in the world
Not a penny to spare
Not a kind word to say.

Children snigger
Adults look away
It's no joke
Parents split up
I ran away.

Helen Clewes

Trapped In A Bubble

Call it civil, yet how can that be?
Cities littered with families of three,
Daddy out fighting? Lying bloody and still?
How can government call it civil?

"Bang! Blast!"—another life lost,
What does it matter, it's part of the cost,
Not fighting for reason, someone's belief,
Young innocent men, ill with the grief.

Whilst out fighting loved ones despair,
Give these men peace, not a medal to wear,
The end of the war brings no first place,
(excluding, death, pain, no conclusion to face)

Freedom these people pray for night long,
Is freedom to shake with those who do wrong,
A freedom deprived by those above,
Trap. A bubble with no means to burst.

Elaine Disbury

Love

If I should plant a tiny seed of "Love" in the garden of your Heart,
Treasure it my dear Friend and never let it part.
Look after this beautiful garden to the very End,
With care, attention, affection and Love to tend.
If that seed should "Bloom" into a beautiful flower,
You and I have come to reach the Final hour.
Treasure it, my Dear Friend, look after it to the End.
This is the "Harvest of my Love."

Tamara Zerman

Suicide

I think about how it's going to end,
Death seems to be my only friend.

The noose is hanging waiting for my head,
From which my body will hang limp and dead.

I scream for help but no one hears,
They're too concerned with their own fears.

In depression I've sunk deep,
I no longer want to eat or sleep.

I hurt myself but feel no pain,
I long to slit my wrists and bleed like rain.

How many pills, ten or twenty,
It doesn't matter so long as I take plenty.

Lisa Benjamin

The Conflict

The war broke out in '69.
On the streets civil rights
Were found.
Our excuse to the world
Was church and state.
If only we had known then
What was our fate

For twenty-seven years
We have struggled with war
Everyone living in dread and fear.
The pain and the grief
That we have suffered from loss
Headstones already gathering moss

As we lay our dead side by side
We keep asking the same question
In God's name why have they died
If only the key to the conflict be found
Perhaps our Leaders would all
Sit round and bring this land so torn apart
Back to the Peace we knew at the start.

Muriel Magee

What Do They Bring?

They might bring you pleasure they might bring you sins.
If they bring you pleasure you might get a grin.
But if it brings you sins you feel like curling up in a great big bin.
With all of your sins and forgetting the rest of the world
"Within"

Alana Burgess

A Special Love

The love between a mother and son
As everyone knows is a special one
Love from a mum you don't have to earn
She asks for nothing in return
With his first breath there comes a tie
That they will both keep until they die
When he is small she protects him so
She will find it so hard to let him go
But if she is wise she will let him move on
And that special bond will linger on
When the time comes for him to take a wife
Sometimes she resents this part of his life
Although happy for him she still hurts inside
Knowing she comes second to his bride
But it's all worthwhile when he shows her his son
And says thanks for everything I love you mum.

Valerie Cookson

Untitled

Summer light, late at night
Bright blue shadows
Emerald green leaves
Evening sun, yellow breeze.

The window's not big
There's not much to see
The leaves remind me of the days
Of Adam and Eve.

The summer night
Casts strange weary shadows
The colours of rainbows
In Picasso styles.

From my mundane room
Where women previously died
Full of sorrows
I still hear their cries.

I wonder if they
Ever saw the beauty that may have been cast
Outside of the mundane room
Where I live.

Sara Keats

Night

Aching pains from a hard day's work wash over me.
They seep through my veins.
Outside the crisp evening air is cooler.
To some an ominous cloud drapes over the empty and
deserted streets.
To others a welcome velvet blanket of black unfolds itself
across
the
landscape.
A time comes for rest throughout the world.
My energy drains away, my eyelids droop.
I am lost in my mind.
Small sharp streaks of colour dart around my brain.
They are interpreted as dreams.
Night

Jack Shenker

Morning Walk

The sea, smooth as silk, lapped the shore,
The sand cool and firm 'neath my toes.
The sun still veiled by strips of cloud
As I walked on the beach in the morning.

I felt strong and healthy and free,
Blessed by the peace of the morn,
But as I turned to retrace my steps,
I was suddenly aware you were gone.

Where shall I go, what shall I do
In all the years ahead?
For whom shall I care, with whom shall I share
Now you are no longer there?

God will show me another way.
Be patient my soul,
For He has promised to make me
Strong and steadfast and whole.

Val Davies

The Quotidian Nightmare

Dreams, dreams, fantastic dreams:
The possible avenues led to screams.
This way, that way, where's the lead?
A puzzling minefield to succeed.

Individual identity subtly abused
in a society spawning ideological views.
Chapel of birth, kitchen table, endless quests
doomed disable.

The subconscious passivity of the human subject
ironically influencing this invisible conflict.
Internal external incorporating hope,
The notion of achievement's drifting afloat.

The haunting conditioning in Post-modern culture
seemingly resulting in a one dimensional future.

James Williams

Summer Afternoon

The grass is bleached by the heat of the sun,
Crickets chirp and bumble bees hum,
Ivy climbs high protecting the trees,
Summer smells float in the breeze.

Laughter is heard from a long way away,
All children have fun on this hot summer's day,
Blossom lies white like snow on a hedge,
Butterflies flutter high overhead.

The sun shines down on a running stream,
It made it look golden, or that's what it seems,
As the sun goes down I'm drifting away,
Dreaming of that hot summer's day.

Beverly Sedge

End?

A time is here—a time
of longing—a time for crying.
It is almost here—the end time is now.
We have seen many wonders:
In the heavens and on the earth,
A time for good—a time for evil;
Almost here . . . Time . . .
to make a choice.
The heavens will be split
A dark side . . . A light side!
Oh the time to is coming.
It is time to chose . . .
Black as a crow or white as snow;
Alpha was the birth . . .
Omega is the death;
End of the time is Now.
When the Lord will come anew
those who were longing
will rejoice—those who were crying . . .
Black or White—it's up to you.

Sheila Hannigan

Reckless

Waifs and strays, spend many days,
Looking for new paths and ways,
To find an anchorage in life's crowded harbour,
Or fall prey to some Sweeney Todd, the demon barber.
A roll of fortune's dice often determines, clothed in rags or
draped with ermine.
A paper carrier to a leather briefcase, as a handful of comics
to the gilded tomes of Hopkins,
These references are a parody of fate,
As all war's victims, born too soon, find out too late!
Surviving, the Nomads, wander parched sands,
Hot soup from Sally Anne's kitchen, thaws frozen hands,
The gentry in the mansion, would not stoop to pick up,
A cardboard box outside the shop,
Home for some, trash for others,
But true lovers don't need silk sheets for covers,
The Rake then shows from his progression,
Appearances cannot decide a profession,
Then be sure of your aims, and beyond them don't cast,
Unlike cotton in the hot wash, life is not colour-fast.

Susan Fox

Wars Of War

A dead woman's son to his mother said,
Oh, mummy, oh mummy, why are you dead?!
No answer was heard in the little boy's ear
he clutched to his mother, all alone and in fear.
As he lay there, mind distorted and in shock
another bomb fell, on a house, in his block,
he looked up, tears blinding him to the sky
and said, What did my mother do! To deserve to die.
To find safety he got up and ran down the street
how did he know it was death he was to meet.
A wall of a house, at the corner fell upon him
and the suffering he was suffering was no longer.
Two months later his father came home
from a war he had won.
To find he'd no house, no wife, no son.

John McGinlay

The Cave

All dark and gloomy into the cave,
Splash on the rocks came a gigantic wave,
Something horrid gave me a fright,
And now I wish it wasn't at night,
Bats, dead wood and ancient bones,
Crunchy as I walk among the stones,
There's light coming through at the other end,
I've just got to turn a tiny bend,
I'm here and safe,
And out of the cave,
And away from the creeping, gigantic wave.

Annette Mooney

The Thesaurus

My wife and I, without a care,
Were sitting, each in easy chair,
When our son appeared before us
Asking, "What is a Thesaurus?"
His mother blanched. (It seems absurd
She thought it was a dirty word!)
She shook her head and looked at me
Mine the responsibility!

I remember how at school they'd bore us
With names of various kinds of - aurus;
Thought I'd better remember pronto.
Let's see, there was Ichthyo-, Bronto-,
Plesi-, Ptero-, Mega-, Dino-,
But of The - there was no sign. "Oh,"
Cried I, "try the Museum
There you're almost sure to see 'em
I know to which family I'd ascribe it
But just can't find words to describe it!"

B. T. George

Mother

A Mother is full of Love and Cheer,
She fills her child's thirst for knowledge year after year,
Her tender touch and smile from ear to ear,
Makes life easier for all who are near.

A Mother is full of pride and hope,
Pride that keeps growing day after day,
Hope that her child will turn out just right.

A Mother has love that does not rest in lips or eyes but
remains
deep
inside,
Such love is shown through kisses and caress,
That love I know is gentleness.

A Mother and Child share a bond that is much deeper than
any pond,
How do I know this I hear you ask,
This is but a simple task,
You see I have a mother that loves me!
A Mother and child, two people yes,
two lasting friends with love that always mends.

Kerry Heaney

Tempest

Cold is the night and eerie the wind gnaws at my face
Overhead a storm is brewing, I hasten up my pace
The track is dark and lonely, no moon to guide the way
This short-cut home seems different in the clear light of day.

Familiar landmarks hidden now by shadows of the night
The sturdy rock on which I climb has vanished from my sight,
I see no white-washed cottage, home of Dan McKay
Nor the ruined farmhouse where I often play.

The storm by now is angry, the wind chills every bone
Why ever did I venture to come this way alone?
My mother will be worried for the hour is very late
And I can just imagine her waiting by the gate.

As I battle onwards through the gale and pouring rain
Somewhere in the darkness I thought I heard my name,
Was it my imagination, or could it really be
That in the bleakness of the night somebody calls to me?

I stand still for a moment and then I realize—
That the voice I hear upon the wind is one I recognize,
There's only one who cares so much, no doubt there is no other
She's braved the storm to help me home, the lady is my mother.

Janet Griffiths

The Dark And Dingy Pub Kitchen

A dim light shone in the kitchen,
On a hot and dusty night,
A small fan stood on the work surface,
Out front there was a fight.

Sweat hung from the faces
Of the workers with the fags,
While making chicken sandwiches,
While taking bigger drags.

There was mildew on the cooker,
And flies stuck to the grease,
While the landlord appeared in the doorway,
Shouting "Those bloody dirty beasts!"

Or - shouting "I forgot to pay the lease!"

Sophie Trenear

Friendship

Friendship is an eternity of sorts
Valueless, unlike money,
A true friendship never aborts his friend
Friendship is stronger than steel
Steel will break in the end
But what better bond than an true friend?
Friendship is, entirely, utterly selfless
Helps you straighten out when you are in a mess
What more to say?
Friendship isn't words it's feeling
Sharing, caring, understanding and believing!

Ian Alexander

Memories

My memories I will always treasure.
Some of sadness, many of pleasure.
Of the love that I had from my father and mother.
The happy times spent with my sisters and brother.
Those childhood days filled with laughter and fun.
The holidays on the beach, in the sun.
Speech days, the thrill when I won a prize
And came from the platform with tears in my eyes.
The fifth of November, the bonfire, the fireworks.
What cheering and shouting, when burning old Guy Fawkes.
The magic of Christmas, the happiness, the joy
As we opened our presents, and gazed at each toy.
Prayers and rejoicing at each family wedding.
The organ, the choir, and the church bells ringing.
The sadness and grief to lose Mother, then Dad,
But what memories they left of the great times we all had.
Our dear nephew and nieces affection they have shown.
Good neighbours, great friends we are proud to have known.
Happy years we have shared as husband and wife.
Yes, I'll treasure my memories for all of my life.

Moira Wheeler

Results Day

The results, the result when they, it came,
Chances of riches, nonentity of fame,
The chance to work, shirk or shy,
Diligence, practicality, to try and try.

From amoeba, to the symphony of thoughts,
Come to friction or come to naught,
To play the game, and put on a good show,
If the result be good then to know.

To those on a high, to those on a low,
To read, retain, think and grow,
Will help you, and they in turn,
The benefit of knowledge you will learn.

Whatever the result, good or bad,
The richness is there to be had,
Time to feel, time to say,
Good morning, good morning happy day.

John Aubrey

Man Made

'Twas the night of a thousand shadows
When the wind like a prairie dog howled,
With a sky that was barren of moonlight
That the monster of misery prowled.

All doors were locked and bolted,
All windows shuttered and barred,
Not a cat to be seen in an alley,
Or a dog to be heard in a yard.

Every grown-up and child lay awaiting
Not a word, not a sound passed their mouth,
For the monster was surely coming,
From the North, West, East, and the South.

It can be noisy it can be silent but always deadly,
It can take a millions and millions, and still yet more,
It is the monster of all monsters of misery, it is the monster
man created,
We call it war.

Norma Cartwright

The Seeds Of Steel

I have a seeds of steel
And planted it in the battlefield
It grows high a full grown cannon
With a scope sight that reach to the moon

With its branches a machine gun
That point its barrel to everyone
I haven't gone to a war even once
And sweat myself against the sun

That ripen its fruit a grenade in hand
I counted them all a hundred and one
It fell to the ground and exploded around
Peace until now cannot be found.

Lorieto V. Acman

Memories Of Love In Health

In heaven in this beautiful sky.
I see you saying I wonder why.
 Don't weep for me.
I see you do this.
I blow you a very big kiss.
I'm waiting here for you in this beautiful land.
I'll open my arms and take you by the hand
But on earth in your land of glory.
Don't rush, take your time,
 enjoy your life
There isn't much strife
 Have a wonderful life.
I see you in the day.
 I see you in the night
And I'll see you all one day.
When you see that mystic sight.
 It is so bright and beautiful.
  like a sunbeam in the sky"
So don't I "But" or wonder why.
 Because here is where I lie.

Ann Lush

Hair

Little girls with pig tails look quite sweet,
Pony tails and hair bands keep it neat,
My little girl wants hair down to her feet.

Brushing and combing get rid of the knots,
Look out for screaming from the tiny tots.
There are buns and plaits to have in the heat
But wearing a wig it's a bit of a cheat.

Hair spray and mousse will hold your hair
This could come in handy if your off to the fair.
Shampoo and conditioner will make it shine
A hair dryer comes in handy when you haven't got much time.
Ribbons and bows look very pretty
Oh you've just had your hair cut what a pity.

Teresa Barnes

The Nine Fruits

What are the fruits of the spirit she wondered?
Quietly by the window she sat and pondered.
Turning the page she began to read.

Love, agape is principled love and applies to us all,
Joy comes with having this love for both great and small.
Peace is for those who hold dear to love and joy,
Long-suffering towards the sinfulness we employ,
Kindness and long suffering are hand in hand,
our imperfections to understand,
Goodness ministered generously in every way,
Faith in prayer to Jehovah God each day
Mildness under the yoke Jesus is keeping
Self-control binds together the fruits we are reaping
Tending with love souls mourning and weeping.

K. D. Collier

Looking Back

I stand on the high ground,
The battlefield laid out before me,
So peaceful now, ploughed fields and bird song,
But not so, yesterday.

Then it was ugly, a hell,
The mud filled trenches like a scar,
On land made desolate by stark wire fronds,
And death lay heavy in the air.

In the deafening roar of battle,
Shouts, whistling shells, the booming of guns,
Screams echoed, as blood flowed from a thousand wounds,
And stained the hungry soil.

Afterward, the stillness,
The ground strewn with obscene reminders
Of men, brave with thoughts of victory,
Their dreams forever silenced.

And now, as I linger here,
In this haunted place of memories,
I weep for those lost young British men,
Who died in the battle of the Somme.

Angela Gash

Out Of This World

As you destroy we collect
From out of this world we the select
Chosen to rid, purify and right
With stealth and thrift by day and by night

Saviours to a makers ailing creation
Taking away for a new formation
With 'magic' we preserve, nurture, love,
Carrying out the plan from above.

Mark Harrison

Seasons

Spring arrives young and fresh
And everything is new
From the bright new leaves to the daffodils
And the early morning dew
Summer's here, life's full of joy
And everyone's heart is aglow
God looks down from his heavenly seat
To the sunshine and flowers below
Autumn comes with its many colours
As the leaves turn red and gold
They fall to the ground like coloured rain
As winter starts to unfold
Winter creeps in with its ice and snow
And drives us all insane
So we sit in our cosy homes and wait
For spring to appear again

Patricia White

Autumn Treasure

Mist, like silver filigrees,
And the golden glow of the sun,
Make saintly haloes round the trees,
As an autumn dawn is begun.

Come another day, another dawn,
There'll be crystal from frosty rime
With tinsel dusting on the lawn,
And opal dandelion clocks, on time.

Such treasures mere mortals cannot match,
And, as winter comes, and autumn goes,
We'll sit by the fireside and watch
The sunsets rich red ruby glows.

Colleen Ashworth

There are days

There are days
  I get so tired of being me
There are days
  I just can't face reality
And dealing with people
  I just don't wanna see
Gets me thinking
  about you and me

In my mind I dream
  of how I wanna be
It's not the only way
  I keep my sanity

There are days I just can't find the energy
It seems so hard to find a little harmony
I don't have to question the things you do
There's never been doubt
  in my mind about you
You're the choice I made in my life
  I'm so satisfied
Heaven must have sent you to me.

A. D. Nielsen

Untitled

The sound of a gurgle, breaking into a laugh
with smiling eyes and waving hands
a step or two to fall down and crawl,
was that a new word or had I misheard,
the playing, the sleeping, the waking, the eating
forget all the bad things you've ever been told
these precious moments
of a 1 year old.

R. Roberts

The Circle

The winter wind, it whistles, across the snowbound plain
It blows white clouds of winter snow against the window pane.
Inside the log fire crackles and keeps the cold away
The warmth is greatest by the hearth this fearsome winter's day.

The ice and snow they deaden, and life it seems to cease
And frosty days and frosty nights preserve the winter peace.
But spring is drawing nearer and soon the time will come
When birds and bees and animals will rise to greet the sun.

The spring is here, the showery spring, and things begin to grow
Gone are the days of icy blasts of chills and mistletoe
The sun is here, the watery sun to warm us with its rays
To bring us back to life again and joy into our days.

The summer comes, it brings the heat that lulls us half to sleep
We all grow fat on this and that and watch the ripening wheat.
The cattle move so slowly as in the fields they graze
And families go from here to there to spend their holidays.

The autumn trees stand proudly, their heads of red and gold
But soon they come to realize their leaves are growing old.
The wind is getting cooler as it blows across the plain
And falling leaves ask in despair... must winter come again?

Don Hargreaves

Star

What keeps you there, what keeps you bright,
What makes you shine all through the night.
Why are you only very small,
It's as though you're not there at all.
For the moon doth glow so far away,
And the sun comes up to light the day.
Where do you go, where do you hide,
Why can't you shine and always guide.
For each night when I look above,
You're always there to watch and love.
You're a tiny light that shines so bright,
Look on the world from your great height.
Keep watch on me as I watch you.
And twinkle as you always do.
For when you die you fade away,
Just like a person everyday.
Yet in some place just like the sky,
There is a life we'll watch go by.

Adele Williams

Seasons

Spring - In the Spring the birds will sing
the trees will blossom the flowers look awesome
the wind will blow a cooling breeze
that passes through the tops of trees
the sweet smelling grass, just fresh cut
flowers give a scented input.

Summer - In the Summer have a picnic in the park
with the buzzing bee and the chirpy lark
Summer holidays, days off school
water fights how really cool
the air is hot it's stuffy and humid
the sky at night can almost play cupid.

Autumn - In the Autumn conker matches begin
you never know who will win, now the trees discard their leaves
at Halloween you'll laugh and tease, the costumes are so very fun
eat all the treats when the scaring is done.

Winter - In the Winter the snow starts to fall
can't wait to open presents large or small
everyone is happy when Christmas is here
right the way through to happy new year.

Nora Ward

Me

I look in the mirror and what do I see?
An actress? A model? No it's just me.
I may not be pretty or gifted or funny.
I may not be rich with pot loads of money.
But I know I'm special in my own little way.
And who knows, I may even be famous one day.
But for now I'm content being just me.
Quite frankly there's no one else I'd rather be.

Stephanie O'Neill

You Drive Your Car - And I'll Drive Mine

Don't shake your fist like that, man,
Your nasty temper shows.
It can't improve your driving,
To feel like raining blows.

Don't flash your lights like that, man,
For everybody knows,
It's not a legal signal,
For aiding traffic flows.

Don't sound your horn like that, man,
To keep me on my toes.
I don't need any showing,
That your ruddy horn goes.

Just pass me when it's safe, man,
Accepting that I choose,
The speed at which I travel,
It's my affair - God knows!

S. R. Ramsden

Prayer Of An Abused Child

God, are you there, can you hear me?
Please, take me home, I don't want to be here anymore,
I don't belong here.

God, why do I hurt so bad inside?
Why do I have to stay,
Why can't I come with you?
I want to go away.

My dollies are no longer fun,
My friends, I no longer play.
Why do I hurt so bad inside
I want to go away.

Why am I so bad Dear Lord,
I really don't want to be,
If I could just go home with you, so perfect I would be.

Please hold my hand and walk with me,
Take me far away so I can laugh and run and play,
No longer feel this way.
Suzette V. Wynder

Armchair Diva

My friends, twenty, here by my side
Church sounds quenching my thirst.
30's America a sign of hope,
Rolls Royce, Bentley or hearse?
2 in 1, I wash but don't go
A rug that fills no space
Good Morning Britain, Good Night Britain
Lemon is such a sweet taste.
Bonfire of leaflets
Pizza twenty four minutes away
Yours sincerely Mr. Milkman
Thank you for visiting today.
Andrew Lynch

Soft Bombs

Here are all the seas, breathing,
In our soft bombs, imploding
Swelling melons to bellows,
(Reddened greens, blueing yellows);

Which long talons, etched metal,
On hands that span islands,
Ravish with slashing, rip, to new sutures,
When, grey, laser-eyed, surgeons

Reassemble, by plunder, wonderful skies:
Which a flit, striptease, lightning,
Sears, with hot, dry, white, neon,
When lenses tic, stutter, on the blind,

Staring, shutters, of those graph-maddened cameras,
Which mimic numb, limbless, dancers,
Who twitch, deaf, to mute music, dumb:
Yet, flute moons remembered, our soft bombs,

Hot, throbbing, glow, glow, beyond gold,
In the kiss, of our sun!
Richard Westall

For Better Or For Worse

The volcano erupts before the villagers can escape,
Through the eyes of the archaeologist who has discovered a fake,
The excitement ignites inside him and explodes in his face;

I share my happiness with those who receive my grief,
When the avalanche begins as the climb ends as a mistake;

So I read into the future a month too late,
Now let's be optimistic about which blade to take;

I kiss her rose as it cuts my finger,
My hand clutches hers as she inserts the knife;
For better or for worse?
James Hollerbach

Sharing

A sacred grove,
with oak trees tall,
the ground turns brown,
as the dead leaves fall.
The woodcutter whistles his chirpy song,
as he saws at wood all day long.
The waterfall rocks,
in the sunlight shine,
as the caterpillar crawls
up the twisted vine.
Our world was made for us to share,
with everybody.   Everywhere.
Nicola Stubbington

Tapestry Of Strangers

Every swish of velvet
Heavy as it falls
Begins to mark the point
When all that we have done
Is fading in the memories of strangers

Every new horizon
Bleak as it arrives
Is marking the beginning
Of yet more love and lies
But gradually our friends form out of strangers

Every time an era
Descends into a close
We do not recognize it
'Til the moment it has gone
And time can turn the best friends into strangers

Every day eroding
The framework of our lives
Re-building and re-shaping
Then soon we realize
That we were born, (and always shall be) strangers
Leah Potter

A Storm

Clouds come down burying their heads in mountain's bosom
Steaming up any vision of sun
Rain does creative art on the window panes
A choir of winds strain to crescendo
The sky adjusts its garments causing static electricity
Whose resultant sounds cause terror in the hearts of many
Floods tear their way down laddering the hill sides
Nature's heart pumps overtime through veins of rivers
Storm once more asserting its supremacy
Space the mother of all planets
Watches carefully over its child
Keeping it safe in its protective gravity
Knowing the conflict will soon be over
And the child will emerge unscathed once again
Annie Doherty

Nature's Pattern

Look at that sky
The depth of the blue
White, where the sun beats down
Onto the ground so dry.

Feel for the plants
Their heads drooping low
Desperate for strength
Shrivelling, in pain

Look at that sky
Clouds darkening and grey
Blowing and billowing
Causing a stir

Feel the fresh rainfall
Smell the wet air
Look at the plants, the trees and the grass
Life springs anew.
Eunice Birch

Friends

Friends who stays forever will always stick together
And always be there for one another
Where ever you are neither near or far
We will always be there whenever you need our care
Friends are there when you need someone
They are people who you can depend on
Whenever you need to talk there is always someone you trust
Who will not make you blush but help you in a different way
When there's a crisis they will always be there
And all the fun times you will share
When you are depressed friends are the best
When you become teary they will always make you cheery
Friends are there through good and bad
A friend is someone who cannot stay mad
Friends come in every shape, size and race
They'll always show you a happy face
They lift your spirits up high and never ever lie
The world would be full of hate
If there were never any mates!

Eileen Chung

The Ring

A ring is a symbol of undying love,
A symbol as old as the stars up above.
A ring worth a ransom
A ring worth a pound,
A ring made to measure
A ring that's been found,
A ring with a diamond
That's worth such a lot,
Given and wearing
Shows the love that you've got.
A love that you hope will go on forever
A bond oh so strong that nothing can sever.

Briallen Richards

The Pilot

Up, up, and away.
The sky is clear, a perfect day.
Hangar doors open wide. A small plane waits eagerly inside.
Switches on, prop turns, engine throbs and purrs.
Chocks away, Taxi down to the runway. Final checks.
All clear, take off and leave the ground.
Free from dull earth, the pressures and ties that bind.
All cares just fall away, Pilots live for just such a day
Bank and turn away from the field.
The horizon's clear, it's looking good.
A steady climb into the box, a picture of sky dancing to
fill its frame.
Small turbulence will tip the wing, but a good tail wind as
we ride the air and hear the sound of our engine sing.
No crowds below see our display, only powder puff clouds
that blow away.
Mere mortals walk with feet firmly planted on the ground.
The kings of the air are of a special breed, who need to be
free, to view the world through different eyes, in the
timeless magic that is in the skies. They stay forever young.

Rita Roberts

The Eye Of The Whale

Eye that has wisdom, eye that has breath
Eye that is watching, eye that sees death
Eye all encompassing, eye that is catholic
Eye that is watching, eye that is biopic
Eye that is knowing, eye that mourns the world
Eye that is watching, eye of oracle foretold.
Eye that is harmony, eye of life enhanced
Eye that is watching, eye that sings balance
Eye that begs council, eye that fears drift net
Eye that is watching, eye that sighs kismet
Eye that is weeping, eye of eternal fable
Eye that is watching, eye that is Abel
Eye turn and look at me, eye see my deadly fame
Eye that is watching, I am your brother... Cain

Kathleen Sunter

Internal Reflections

The sun's rays should be golden and warming,
But instead they're annoying and dull.
Is this a vision of the real world?
Or just a picture from inside of my skull?

The mountains seem dank, uninviting,
Instead of all pleasant and green.
Is this how the world really is?
Or just my insides releasing a scream?

The rivers look murky and lifeless,
Not sparkling and not full of trout.
Is this a view of the future?
Or just my feelings all flowing out?

The sky is no longer clear blue,
But smothered and covered with grey.
Is this truly an insight?
Or just my emotions shouting "Hey?"

But one thing I know for certain,
The only thing about which I am sure,
If we always analyze everything,
We will never progress anymore.

Jenny Taylor

Memoir Of The Hunter

Trudging along the forest track.
Flicking compasses at studied maps
living in an unending cycle of scarcities and excesses
mind filled with great anticipation
contemplating the foolishness or wiseness
in lies of their whereabouts to their mothers.

Treasure hunters are always sworn to secrecy
Never to let their wives in to their goals
Always between delusion and illusions
Never content with the fruit of their native land
Applauding lies but hates the truth
lies being the ever presence treasure

With their success comes the prospect for lies
To scare away prospective adventurers
tales of armed skeleton defending golds bags
death of inexplicable source and agony
saving up the rest for their late years
in truthful lies account called m-e-m-o-i-r
Sitting back with an air of satisfaction
To witness the sure harvest of gold.

Gbolade Adegbesan

Painful Chase!

As I run on through the field, the wind whistles in my ears.
Breathing heavily with a pain in my throat,
I leap over the tufts of grass that have grown through the years.
The ghosts of dead leaves dance around my feet.
Gusts of strong winds force my hair to strike my face,
leaving scars on my cheeks.
My feet grow sore, suddenly I stumble,
my face hits the ground...
Slowly, covered in mud, I crawl to my scarred knees
and stumble to my feet.
I start running into a gallop, pulling my sore knee behind.
I push my hair away from my face to resume my sight.
My house comes into view.
I take a quick glance behind - still there!
I close my eyes and run faster and faster.
As I reopen my eyes, I find I'm there,
I open the door and fall inside.
"There, there," says a voice, "You're safe home now!"
I try to speak but it comes out in a whisper "Where are they?"....

Pippa Goodwin Self

The World's Best Mum

She's been there for me from the date of my birth,
Through good times as well as through bad.
It's blasé to say she's the salt of the earth,
- she's the best mum a girl ever had.
She protected me throughout my childhood,
She guided my teenager years,
She provided support when I first went to work,
and helped calm my nerves and my fears.
She was all that I had when my dad passed away,
our closeness developed and grew.
She's supported the times, though she's not understood,
when I've wandered down pathways anew.
She loves my four children completely,
not seeing them makes her feel sad.
I know I can't thank her for all that she's done, but
she's the best mum a girl ever had.

Sharon Whitehead

Irrelevance

The apple that impinged Sir Isaac's sconce
And gave his mind on gravity a grippin'
Was it a cooker or an eater once?
A Bramley or a Cox's Orange Pippin?

And Raleigh's cloak so prodigally laid
To shield the royal shoe from mud's embrace,
What coloured cloth, on what loom was it made
How cleaned without today's detergents' grace?

And that stout Cortes of the questing yen
With eagle eye and vision of a vulture,
Who puffed his way up peak in Darien
To raised to greater height the Spanish culture?

When Larwood bowling roused the Aussie anger
And menaced ties of trade and commonweal,
Was his recall another F.O. clanger
Among so many that archives conceal?

Will there be show, of much-needed aplomb
If lifted into limbo's outer spaces
Upon the broomstick of the nuclear bomb,
We prove irrelevance of human races?

Henry D. Jones

Sitting Next To Henry

Doves call soulfully in the afternoon sunshine,
a soft breeze causes the trees to laugh,
though autumn is still far away.
Gently nettles sway, proud of their claimed positions
awaiting the unsuspecting with the softest of barbs.
Some will not forget this visit.

Ivy clings, wandering the contours of Henry's companions
They lean toward one another as if deep in conversation,
Two heads are better than one.
Only the wild rose blooms for them here
no-one tends her aged thorn
She grows old gracefully for the men of this parish

Ancient stone looks down upon Henry
weathered and worn but with presence still
crafted by the hands of masons long ago,
did they dream their labour would still be standing?
Or do they lay close at hand?
And witness the passing of seasons...

Graham Hunt

Love, Friendship And A Piece Of Fruit

Sometimes friendship and love don't mix at all,
When you're in love your life can fall,
Love can be bad as well as good,
Love is like a piece of fruit,
The fruit would be ripe or so it seems,
But it could be bad inside,
And the things you planned to do with it might not work,
Love is like a piece of fruit.

Keri Young

First Night

I was married this morning, at six fifty-five,
in a full skirted dress, of Victorian times.
With thirteen bridesmaids, perfectly matched,
watched by a camera and crew, odd you might think,
but when you're a princess, you have no choice.
When the King points his finger and raises his voice,
you drop to your knees, and offer a prayer
that your true love might be spared.
The groom of course is a prince of the realm,
his father had ordered the match,
for the sake of his country, this must be.
His love had crossed the sea.
But we were born, to do what we should,
so now we must face, what we will,
what must be must be, our loves had gone.
And tonight is our night, as darkness falls,
with five-hundred looking on, we must face our fate.
As the lights go down, the curtain up,
the film of the year we shall see.
Our first opening night is here.

Audrey Allen

The Spider

Is it your eight legs that seem so imposing,
filling me with a misplaced loathing?

Is it your eight eyes that are all seeing,
making me recoil but wonder at your being?

Is it your habit of tracking my fear,
making me think that you are always so near?

What is it about you that I find so frightening,
yet at the same time peculiarly enlightening?

You build your home without invitation,
with a skill and complexity, a marvellous creation.

You prey on the insects that feed off my blood
without ever knowing you are doing me good.

You remind me to clean in all of the corners,
making me feel guilty for destroying your labours.

I have come to admire you but still I am uneasy,
an irrational fear, not hysterical or queasy.

We shall cohabit until I'm on my death bed,
so really I should get over this pathetic dread.

And start to appreciate my good friend the spider,
but somehow I just can't bring myself to abide her.

David Paul Cooper

Love Song

Let's meet in the middle, dear,
It's not such a long way to go;
Please try and let go of your fear,
It's the only way we'll know
If you and I, for all eternity,
Together, dear, we'll live through it all;
It says in the stars it was meant to be;
Trust me, dear, I shall never let you fall.
Let me be your rock and your haven,
In my life, you can be the light
Of your heart, I'll be the custodian;
In your eyes I'll find the strength to fight.
And so, with laughter and serenity
We shall walk side by side;
And with a smile fulfil our destiny
and never let our love subside.
Stay beside me, don't say goodbye,
You know in your heart as well as I
How our love is deep and strong.
It will last longer than this song.

Anne-Marie Peyron

Free Billy

I know this may sound silly,
But when I met a man named Billy
I wished that I was he.
His hair was greasy, his eyes were squiffy,
And his aroma could only be described as whiffy,
But he was as happy as can be.
He gave me a smile, he gave me a wink,
And was not concerned about his stink.
He was so at peace with life.
So I asked, "Can you tell me please,
Dear Bill to what do you owe such ease?"
And Bill replied "Eeeh I 'ave no wife.

Marlene Parmenter

The Cupboard's Bare

Stare into silence and see what's there,
You may find it's empty and bare.
On the other hand, you may find despair.

Travel via the soul to a height above
No other, is it the clouds and sun you see
Or is it lightning on ice that you feel?

But to be in silence in different than to see,
No other knows, whatever it may be.
On the other hand, you are what 'I see'.

And so onto you, what I see - you become,
That silence I spoke of, to you it lives.
Whether it's bare or despair, I forced

Onto you - a nightmare. To feel
Lonely or be encompassed with hatred
From that moment of 'drift', you'll stay there.

It's there I found you first of all,
Looking through and beyond your soul.
And travelling to it, no longer becomes

Part of it - 'it's part of you'!

Aisling Kelly

Seatless And Cynical

Present day woman strap hanging again.
How times have changed since I travelled by train.
Thirty years past it was considered the norm
To give up your seat to the female form.

Politeness and charm have left us alone,
To strap hang and suffer and loudly to moan.
Sometimes we happen to meet a real gent,
Who gives up his seat, he's heavenly sent.

Let's blame ourselves entirely, what else can we expect,
We've burned our bras regardless, to very great effect.
We're dashing off now, to attend our menfolk,
Female liberation... Huh, what a joke.

I. J. Price

Our Family

The baby who is the whole world to us
looks up wondering, what's all the fuss?

The child is getting very tall
still our hands go out lest he should fall

The adult may think we aren't so bright
but we do know enough not to fight!

They meet their partners we're so glad
and maybe they don't think we're so bad!

Now the grandchildren are here and
it all starts again - lots of pleasures, lots of pain

But they give us the greatest pleasure
and how we all enjoy our leisure
They are now our pride and joy
whether it's a girl or boy!

God Bless us every one!

J. I. Wells

Epitaph Of The Sink Spider

Was it something I did, certainly not what I said
That sent her off screaming—upstairs to her bed.
Is it the way I moved, or my manner of dress
With good looks I know I have not been blessed.

Eight long hairy legs and a big ugly torso
Us spiders need pity—and me all the more so.
Frightening to look at, but I'm not to blame
A victim of nature. Oh, what a shame!

It was certainly not my purpose, as I had no intention
To shock you so and cause such contention.
Just a mistake you see, so easy to make
I was on my way home, when the wrong route I did take.

Cold water! They're trying to wash me away
For them I suppose it's better this way.
Down the plug hole I go. I'm trying to hold on
If I'm lucky at all, they may think that I've gone.

It's so dark down here, I much prefer the light
Shall I venture again upwards? I well think I might.
But wait, what's this? More cold water, coffee and tea
Oh no! Boiling water! Alas, the end of me . . .

Beverly Tallbot

Man The Creator

Two abortions, children of permissive age,
Is all he has to his credit
So far as creation goes.
A naked woman, stranger until that evening,
Lies in his loveless bed, dead with flesh fatigue.
Slumped in the caved-in belly of a chair
He sits alone in a dark room,
His mind lit up like a dusty lamp,
And he thinks of poetry,
Playing with words as though they were toys.

Shiv Sharma

David

Oh David I love you, love you I do,
but you don't realize all you put me through.
You've teased and even made me cry,
but when I asked you to own my heart
you found my price too high.
When I think of love I think of me and you,
when I think of happiness I think of us two.
So I hope that one day you'll understand.
And once again it will be us two.
With a love that's real and love that's true.
So David I'm awaiting your reply
shall we go back to one another
and have an other try
or just seal it with a last goodbye.

C. A. Morley

Summer Skies

I sit and stare at the stars at night,
Shining out so beaming bright,
Up there it is so dark without those stars,
Close my eyes and dream of being on Mars,
A wishing star do I find,
Now what wish do I have in mind,
I also see the moon so very round,
Wish I could touch it here from the ground,
When morning starts to come around,
The moon changes its shape until it's gone,
It really doesn't take that long.
Soon the sky turns from black to blue
Sometimes clouds come along to,
All fluffy and white like cotton wool,
Different shapes you can make,
Out comes the sun so nice and warm,
Stays out sometimes until nearly dawn,
Sometimes I wish I could fly like a dove,
As it's so peaceful in the summer sky above.

Christine Kowalkowski

The Existence Of Our Soul And Creator

Our soul is our true everlasting self.
If nonexistent then neither would anybody have insight,
    That human races exist upon earth.
Men would be robots with brains of remarkable gadgets.
    A universal creator of all?
To create one who thinks there first had to be one who thought.
    Many think that if God made mankind,
We could not from an evolutionary means generate.
    God may use methods beyond belief.
Do we underestimate the skills of our creator?
    Now within modern technology,
With computer programmers perhaps we start to see light.
    God is a designer, engineer,
Computer programmer too, greater than wisest experts.
    God created mechanical seeds,
With memory banks to follow a form to his edict,
    In the shape of all things, including;
O bright stars, the whole earth, all living nature and salute!
    To bring forth man in his image!
In these timeless zones one day and a thousand years equate.

Louis Don Barrow

Bestfriend

Nothing can describe my true feelings towards you,
Nothing can replace what we share,
No one can untie our emotional knots, no matter what they do,
No one can separate us, no one will dare.

You and I share something very special,
Something that will stand the test of time,
If it were a competition, you and I would win a medal,
Knowing you, I'm sure you know the subject of this rhyme.

Distance may stand between you and I,
But I know our hearts will go on beating together,
Always till the day we die,
That is because you and I are the best of friends,
Always and forever.

Hana Haziem

Compassion

The sheets are clean. Free from germs.
Time to think. What are the terms?
To sleep, a pill. Will it distort my thoughts?
Was I wrong when I wished to kill?
Only a rabbit. Hold on! How did it feel
racing through fields, with predators close by.
Was it afraid of death, as both you and I?
Compassion! Just a word. What does it mean?
Perhaps the nurse will know
when she comes to wash me clean.

Mary Cutler

Life In This World

Gone were the days when life was a book of simplicity
No longer does it hold good for us
Bearing in mind what the end may be
God only knows that more is there to see
The Past is History and gone forever
The present is here to live however
Leaving the future is not for us to see.
He gave us the Winter, the Summer, the Spring and Fall
He gave us the brain and the brawn.
From strength to strength had mankind gone
And in their stride misused them all
Leaving this good earth in a pitiful pall.
It is, therefore, time for us to repent
Just in case the worst we resent
When it's too late to make amends
To God our only Friend.
So be ready to face the blunt of it all
In order to save us from the deep fall
And end this long-lasting turmoil
Into a peaceful and sweet-smelling soil.

Zena Heppolette

The Lark

Dedicated to my late wife Edna

I look up in the heavenly sky
this bright and sunny day
and a little black dot I do espy
up in that cloudless sky on high
ah the lark, its wings
fluttering like rotor blades in the sky.

then as it breaks into song I stand enthralled
it's like nectar to my soul
these little things God's gift to us we must enjoy
to calm our angry souls.

And then it swiftly descends to its earthly
home to tend her little chicks
and then food to them gives
God made all creatures great and small
but the lark my favourite of them all.

And as I go through my earthly life
I listen to my little black dot in the sky.

The sweetest song by far like a twinkling star
in the sky, and ere I leave this earthly fold
to hear the lark again would satisfy my soul.

Harold Jones

My First Love

When we first met we were just good friends
Soon we became lovers but what happens then
We entered into a world of our own
Where nothing mattered much
We planned on making our lives together
We had no worries as such.

You promised me we would never part
This you said from the very start
Our culture and customs did play a part
Hence we are so far apart
I know you loved me and you did care a lot
But our customs and culture did play their part.

Now that I am so far away I think of you often
And our gone past
The time we spent together being hardly apart
Nothing matters much now that it is all over
Good memories still lingers on
And it will go on forever.

Mani Bhuthadia

First Day Blues

The day has arrived, awoke bright and early.
Get the hair done, make it nice and curly.
Dress is looked out, washed and pressed.
Had a quick bath, now to get dressed.

No time for breakfast, couldn't eat it any way.
Dash to the station, my train, 1/2 hour delay.
Just my luck, I'll go get the bus.
I refused dad's car, didn't want a fuss.

Seats all taken, I'll just have to stand.
Holding on tightly with my free hand.
Handbag in other bursting at seams.
With my packed lunch and custard creams.

Got to the door with five minutes to spare.
Into my new office and sat on my chair.
I've finally made it, after four long years,
Nights of endless study and plenty tears.

My new busy life begins right here.
My first real job, a new career.
I'll do just fine, the future looks sunny.
The work starts here now, to earn the money.

Elizabeth Broadley

Springtime In The Meadows

It's springtime in the meadows,
the flowers are out in bloom,
the sun is shining in the clear blue sky,
and birds softly sing in tune.

The grass is growing tall and green,
the trees are no longer bare,
and bees collect their honey,
as joyous rapture fills the air.

And gentle breezes blow
across the pastures green,
and robin redbreasts sing their songs
to welcome in the spring.

The meadows are alive at last,
the winter it is gone,
and faces smile with happiness,
that once were so forlorn.

And high above us in the trees,
the fledglings prepare for their first flight,
they soar across the meadows,
it's such a wondrous sight.

J. McDonald

Going Home

I'm sitting on the train, and yet,
I cannot smile, I can't forget,
The days we've sheared, the things we've seen,
The places where we two have been.

I wave until you're out of sight,
Holding back the tear and fright,
But tell myself that I'm alright,
But you know as well as we, I'll love you for eternity.

The 125 it speeds on by,
The little town that gently lie
Between the valleys, green and lush,
Oh, this train stopped behind a bush, we moving now, let's rush,
rush
  rush.

You sit and talk to a train fiend,
For an hour, or till the end
Of your journey that will not fly.
And all I want to do is cry.

My journeys end and I am home,
I'll soon be on the telephone,
To say "Hello, I'm home alright,"
"I love you with all my might".

J. G. Danks

Snowdrops

I like the way you defy
The Winter's frosts
And snow, the ice-cold winds.
Like cats' eyes you pierce

The darkness of dank seasons,
Leap out at expectant observers,
Wield your stark and simple beauty.
You penetrate the rotting leaves

Of Autumn's fall and seek an early
Sun, ignore deft foragers, exploit
The drabness, laugh in the face
Of austerity and bleakness.

You show a bold front with your
Pristine whiteness, brandishing each petal
Like a scimitar against the sullen clouds
And squalid litter: You are the meteors

Of each galaxy of Spring.

Brian Blackwell

Stairway

The stairway to heaven I had to climb
And leave my loved ones, far behind
The steps are very very steep.
Made harder for me when you weep
So please, I beg of you stop your crying
Don't think there's something sad in dying
For death is but one short sleep
An appointment we all must keep
So now I'm gone remember do.
I love you all, and wait for you.
Listen to the breeze at play
And know I'm near you every day
The sun on your face, the wind in your hair
All tell you I am very near.
So please smile and stop your crying
There's nothing sad in so called dying.

J. Marks

By The Sea

Wet pebbles rounded by tossing waves, some wild, some gentle
Carrying the breeze holding the mysteries of the deep
Back and forth, back and forth.
Tiny white bubbles balance on top of the waves
Then roll over collapsing on the damp golden sand.

Time for tea I stretch and pass the salmon paste butties
Slices of tomatoes flecked with grit, a flask of tea and
Eyes close, eyes close
Beckoned by the mysterious deep
There I am beneath the green, drifting, drifting down
Passing burnished shells and velvety weed

Gentle fins brush my face
So calm, so gentle,
Floating timeless.

A sudden shriek brings me back and opening my eyes
To the sun dancing on water I see
Babies shrieking with glee, the water creeping up
Teasing little fat toes.

Lesley Styles

Achievement

Now I must take my steps along a certain road.
I am more sure now.
I know where I can stand and not feel the rocks shift under my feet.
I am as one crossing an ancient ford.
The river rushes, stones are slippery and round
With the algal growth of generations.
But like a traveller in a new land, I feel my way.
Each stone crossed is a new achievement.
I wish only to get close to the other side,
For I still fear success as well.
But like the traveller in the ford,
With the deep and rushing water behind me,
When I see the far shore close at hand,
When the water purls gently against the sandy bank,
And I am no more knocked by shifting stones,
Then I may skip like a lamb
Lightly onto the shore
And scarcely imprint the gravel as I pass.

Josephine McLaughlin

Frail Creatures

Eyes are little windows that scan all that's around,
Ears are little trumpets which gather every sound.
A nose has two nostrils which reaps in nature's scent
A brain so very active augurs good or ill intent
The hands that gather berries, fruits and veg of varying kinds
Oh so very active yet leaving some behind
The feet that travel miles and miles to take you to new grounds
The heart that works at top rate yet makes so little sound
To every living creature these are gifts endowed at birth
These help to make for laughter, sorrow and for mirth
So oft abused, becoming means of grave intent,
Yet could have been so wonderful, just as God had meant.

Claude Faull

The Knoll

On a country road, to I know not where,
  The car stalled and came to rest,
Near a field of corn, tall and spare,
  I left it there to acquire some zest.

Across the road, hedgerow and bracken,
  Through which I clambered with steps quicken,
Beyond - a knoll, gently sloped, but with what splendour,
Beneath, soft grass, above, azure sky and small puffed clouds,
sublime.

All caught in mid-moment, I broke with time,
  A scene or scent of paradise perhaps,
And at once, I felt what - free!
  Glad and wholesome at such a lapse.

With the start of time again,
  I returned down from the knoll,
I turned the key to the car's engine refrain
  And back to a world of apt recall.

Could I, would I, return to the scene,
  And moment too,
To the knoll,
  Once more to view.
    Patrick J. Harrison

Listen My Son

Listen my son to what I say,
Listen to the noises as you play,
Feel the sun on you warm and bright,
Listen my son, let your ears be your sight.

Listen to the soft wind in the trees,
To the gentle rustling of floating leaves,
To the kitten chasing them with all his might,
Listen my son, let your ears be your sight.

Listen to the rain as it thunders down,
Listen, it's stopping, it's quite gentle now,
The earth needs water, for without it, it dies,
Listen my son, let your ears be your eyes.

Listen as I get on with my work in the house,
Listen at night when it's quiet as a mouse,
I'm always here, there is no need for fright,
Listen my son, let your ears be your sight.

While you are still young, listen hard and learn,
So that when you grow up, there will be no need for concern,
But for now, use my eyes and together we'll fight,
So listen my son, let your ears and my voice be your sight.
    Frances A. Lewis

Bitter Sweet Love

I look across the table
And I see the flickering shadow of the
Empty wine bottle in the
Candle light,
I glance across the room
And see her in a drunken slumber.

I reflect on the past few hours.
Laughter, tears, love and hate.
Finally the room is still
And the crackle of the fire now
Holds the peace.

How I dreaded the sound
Of her stirring,
Her sobs and pain for a lost loved one,
Now this is her way of
Escape.

Reality hurts, believing they will
No longer be there,
But life goes on
And those around you will never stop caring.
    Lesley Thornton

My Robin

On the high bare branch of the sycamore tree
The 'Robinson Robin' sings happily
With cold blue sky above his head
He looks down on me, eyes bright, breast red,
Then swiftly down to the line he flies
Where I'm hanging the washing,
My fingers like ice.
And off he goes to the bush beyond,
Of my Robinson Robin, I've grown quite fond.
Christmas came, and we went away,
On our return, there, heaped on the mat,
Was a pile of feathers, the culprit, our cat.
I couldn't find a sign of red,
So hope Robinson Robin was safe in his bed.

I saw my Robin this morning,
He flew down, to show me he's here,
I've been a bit worried about him,
So I wished him a Happy New Year.
    D. H. Robinson

The South Downs

When as a lad I strolled the downs
where grassy tufts the summit crowns
a pebble kicked as along I walk
the paths in places mud and chalk

From Jack and Jill to Ditchling Beacon
the windmill sails keep turning on
the choice is now to stop and have an ice
or on to Lewes for tea would be nice

Now with age I travel by car
the new roads cut, that cause a scar
the gentle hills I love and know
that used to carry my toboggan in the snow

My parents told of long ago
a train to Devils Dyke would go
a few pence took you there and back
alas from Brighton now there is no track

As I rest upon this stile
my face lights up with a smile
I hear the children excited talk
a new generation in love with this grassy chalk.
    R. B. Fellingham

Stolen Time

Enter the world, scared and alone,
He holds you close as you are one of his own.

As you succeed, he beams with pride,
If you falter, he is there to guide.

He may not always agree, but never criticize,
The only clue is the look in his eyes.

Do we appreciate the time we share?
A bond between two people, often so rare.

As we grow older, we understand,
Life doesn't always work out as we planned.

I thought he would be the one to give me away,
Never imagined he would not live to see the day.

Signs are not good, we pray with all might,
But he can't hold on and looses the fight.

When we hold his hand, it feels so cold,
How guilty we feel of the love untold.

Do not despair, for I am sure he knows,
Even now, the love still grows.
    Michelle Caley

Salute To Our Existence

When in time to come, we look back
We shall salute our very existence.

We have marched with rubber boots
We have marched with steel boots.
Now we march with fur boots.

Praises, oh praises, we held on till the time
That time, that appeared unreachable,
That time, that was covered in dark clouds
That time, when darkness ruled our visibility.

But we held on, every step taken was enshrouded in uncertainty
Bitter pains anger and melancholy
But we held on, searching the heavens for a glimpse of hope.

Now the price for patience has been paid for fruitfully
Hold back the joyous tears and merry with me.

Sylva Ike Nwaohai

The Last Summer

It was a happy summer when you came to stay
My life was changed in every way
You brought joy and love there was no sorrow
You'd listen to my troubles of today and tomorrow
Our hearts were as one we worshipped each other
I loved you so much just like a mother
Time passed by the years quickly went
To see you grow old
Your years soon spent
I knew these would be your last summer days
You said your goodbyes in a loving gaze
Your short life had ended
Mine only half through
How could I carry on without you
I wanted to join you so we could be together
But that would be wrong suicide never
So wait for me loved one until my life is done
Enjoy yourself in heaven, please have fun
I look forward to the day when I can give you a hug
My dear dear dear Pug

Jean Toy

Time

If we only had time, to sit and dream.
Your hand in mine, for a moment it seems.
Years have come, and gone with time.
If only we could sit and dream, of
Things that could and might have been.

If only we had time to sit and glare,
At our children playing there,
Growing up oh, so fast.
If only we could make it last.
You went away. Before your time.
So young at heart, always kind.

Time stands still, is what they say,
In our promise land, so far away,
I still love you more each day,
So near yet so far a way,
If only we had time to sit and dream
Off things that could, and might have been.

Pauline Hunter

The Mysterious Jungle

In this mysterious land everything is green
Only plants and creatures are to be seen
Slithering snakes slide up the trees
While down beneath lie crunched up leaves
The monkeys screech up in the trees
As the wind blows its soft cool breeze
The dim light shines from cracks above
And creatures glide ones that I love.
The colours of leaves are so bright
In this dark mysterious jungle light.

Yvonne Probert

Questions??? Questions???

Where did time begin?, and where will it all end?
These questions I am posing, intellectuals to offend,
Life discovered among the stars on the planet Mars
Send the sceptics and theologians scamper to the bars,
Universe after universe the unlimited edition,
Help us extol this conservative tradition
Believe what you are told, biggest egos on hold
Still not be afraid, fortune favours those who're bold,
Suppression and secrecy governors do misuse their power
Hide and withhold, but the tree of knowledge yet will flower
And on and on and on and on not allow the moment wasted,
Until in full knowledge the truth we all have tasted,
The world is flat we once were said,
Those believing are all now dead,
Fear never must prevail, irrespective of our human frail,
Confining the weak to a self-made purpose-built jail,
Soldier-on, questions? Questions? Questions? Make us think,
Uncover, unearth, disclose, expose, bare-out all the stink,
From ever indulgent bullies, corrupt and living in disguise
Open our senses to see far and war beyond limitless skies.

James L. Henry

Betrayed

I feel so betrayed, as if there's no one to trust.
I'm filled with deepening hatred which I don't want
to conceal but I know that I must.
Behold the day I took my secrets away, never to be
whispered again.
The watching eyes have seen all the sickening cries
of pain through which I have been.
They wish to take away the pain to regain the
sparkling of my eyes and the red rose colour of my lips.
But with huge sighs and saddening cries their
dreams suddenly vanish only to be replaced by the
grey gloominess of my face.
And how can I subside the hatred which lies inside
when my only friend has betrayed me?

Tracy Skinner

To Fly

If I could only fly, as fly I might.
To fly above the clouds, like some majestic kite.
In aerobatic splendour, diving, twisting like the eagle.
To settle as the Peregrine, on minaret or steeple.
To skim above the surf, white horses of the sea.
To fly like Icarus towards the sun, but not as close as he.
To drift upon the thermal's rising towards the sky so clear.
O would that I could fly and see the earth, as God would see it.
To watch its changing face through the seasons and the climes.
To soar above the valleys and villages of England.
To watch the children playing and hear the church-bells chime.
All this I'd love to do, before my time on earth must cease.
But most of all the thing I want, is a world that is at peace.

J. D. Trainor

It Happens To Us All . . .

I hate the thought of growing old
The bedroom now seems awfully cold
There's no one there to bring me tea
Or even make a fuss of me

I hate the thought of growing old
Where once I used to be so bold
And always had a girlfriend near
To cuddle up and call me 'dear'

I hate the thought of growing old.
With no more work inside the fold
And nor more dreary nine to five
Just 'trying to keep the firm alive'

I hate the thought of growing old
And always doing what I'm told.
Just getting up now when I like
Not bothering about the transport strike
I love the thought of growing old . . .

Brian Goodman

Marmalade - School Cat

Champion high jumper,
Child boxer and fighter.
Suns himself on any high wall,
Falls to earth like a rubber ball.
He thinks it nice to catch mice.

Climbs the school trees,
Scratches angrily for fleas.
Milk bottle tipper
Casual "day-tripper",
Bird table watcher and pebble hopscotcher.

When content his natural bent
Is to purr his 'violin' to such an extent
That sir, complains of the din.
Pays no regard to his kith and kin.
Marmalade,
You saucy blade,
Seldom haughty
Always naughty
Skit-scat, fabulous cat.

Rhys Thomas

Nightlife

From pockets in his head the dreamer takes
A shining sphere too brilliant to behold.
Bright mirror of the mind what do you hide
What secrets dwell within you yet untold.

Running through a dense green undergrowth
Heart pounding, a strange beast's close behind,
Vast chasms, yawning, empty lie before you.
Such can be the tortures of the mind.

Sharp visions, mist clouded memories,
All will take the dreamer by surprise.
Deep wells of misery, bright shouts of joy.
Sunny days and deadly dangerous lies.

Balmy sunshine warms a sandy beach,
Laughter and a lover close at hand.
Life's riches spread out, all for you to keep
Wealth and fulfilment just as you had planned

Will his rest bring happiness or terror?
Each night he slumbers facing friend or foe.
Will he wake to find a new day dawning?
The truth remains, the dreamer does not know!

Kate Benson

So Much Of You

You were a little singing stream
of anecdotes and rhyme,
now swallowed by a cruel sea,
remiss of tidal time.
Rays of sun, shine through a mist,
and slowly, now I see,
the joys of life and laughter,
that once you gave to me.
In the trees, I see, the birds you loved,
and at home, your canine friends,
the butterflies, and wild-life,
and all that you'd commend.
So much of you, is here around,
oh, your face, I long to see,
but the stream no longer seems as clear
as once it used to be.
How rich, and good, the sea must feel,
now fortified, and strong,
once cruel, and dark, and restless,
now lulled by your sweet song.

Pauline Palmer

Brook Fields

The brook fields days and summer nights, harvest moons
were shining and the grass was high, buttercup meadows
and summer rain, these are the memories of the brook fields way.

Damming up streams so we could swim and finding a bird's nest
in the reeds within, then following the stream on its winding
way, it was under a willow tree we fell in love that day, but
what a far cry from my life just now for its high rise flats
in a rainy town.

Hollows in the meadows where the floods from the brook remained
these were the places we stayed to swim again, and hidden
cornfields where we used to lie looking up at a summer-blessed sky,
but what a distant dream from my life today for it's a broken
heart on the docklands way.

So now I'm dreaming only dreaming, I'll always yearn but without
her gentle loving looks there's no reason to return because
the brook fields with its moods in early May, with the violets
in her hand she quietly passed away, so now it's my reality
on the docklands way of high rise flats on a rainy day.

Kenneth Harris

Ten Days In India

A pungent smell, unbearable noise and heat, always heat
A young girl given her income, begging with a broken leg
A dead dog lies in the road, unloved, undignified, unnoticed
Hardened rickshaw drivers tout for business at New Delhi station
Old men pick their bellies in the gutters, passing time
Overworked horses decorated with brightly coloured tinsel like sad
    old Christmas trees
And sacred cows wander through the streets, the dusty streets
And then to Goa with its long golden beaches, the stench of dead
    fish in the early morning sun
But the cool blue sea is an escape for the backpackers
Where is the escape for the Indian children with their broken limbs
    and begging bowls?

Alison S. J. Taylor

Game Of Life

We could have played a passionate game of cards.
Your gleaming sequence needing the diamond queen and I embracing the
solitary heart for my rummy hand.

We could have let our emotions aim for maximum points across the board.
You spelling 'Yes I will' horizontally and I 'Marry me' vertically.

We could have cherished an adventure.
Feel the flow of adrenaline, climb rung for rung, dare our tongues to
the frustrated constrictors then gallop courageously on the white and
black knights and perhaps bypass jail for the rendezvous of mayfair.

We could have matched instead of fallen like dominoes.
Your delicate left hand, so warm and sincere, positioning your double
one to symbolize twins but your tender nostrils behaving like a bull
with flaring eyes and a right hand of stone that would ripen my cheek
because of lying down double six...
So I guess we could never play games.

Derrick D. Dunn

Who Am I?

Who am I? It seems a simple question, but the answer I wish I knew!
For years I have wondered and wondered and searched for a clue.
A wife? A mother? A grandmother? Friend and so on
I am beginning to wonder if my sanity has gone!
The answer I haven't yet found and my curiosity still grows
I cook, sew, wash and iron and I'm nearly always on my toes!
I'm at the beck and call of everyone who enquires . . .
and I just can't stop myself satisfying their desires.
I am relatively happy and satisfied with life
and to be quite honest I've not had much struggle and strife.
I've always worked hard and now that I have retired
it would be nice to know the answer before my days are expired.
Perhaps I should be content and thank God for what I've got
for compared to millions of others my blessings add up to a lot.

Doris Gordon

Love

Love, what is love.....?
Hate, what is hate.....?
Like, what is like.....?
Ask yourself!

Death, what is death.....?
To dream, but what is a dream.....?
To trust but what does that mean? These
days!
I don't know, ask yourself!

To kiss, but is it for real?
To kill, but do you feel the pain?
Endangered species..... but are they so
rare?
Ask yourself!

(The truth is out there)

Emma Collins

Where Were My Friends?

Where were my friends?
When I stood in the playground with the
two bullies stood at my side.

Where were my friends?
When I was scared and frightened and
wanted to go and hide.

Where were my friends?
When they took my lunch money and threw
my bag in the mud.

Where were my friends?
When they dragged me along by my hood.

Where were my friends?
When I was scared and frightened and small.

Where were my friends?
They were nowhere to be seen at all.

Kirsty Hawksworth

What Is Magic?

What is Magic?
Is it the art of illusion?
Does it lie in the mystique of hypnosis?
Could it be black and forbidding?
The Earth, The Sun, The Stars,
Our very existence,
Do they lie in the umbra of magic?
Can the computerised, technical wizards,
Calculate,
Itemise,
Logically explain,
And lift the veil of intricate mystery?
What is magic?
Does it lie in the lover's kiss?
A touch of hands?
The awareness of each other's presence?
The ecstasy of two bodies in a lover's embrace?
A fulfilment that defies description,
Surely,
That is magic.

C. H. Walker

Dreams

If only you could come home once more
I'd have your slippers waiting by the door
Your favourite chair, a cup of tea
Your happiness for all to see

But it is just a lovely dream
And dreams are never what they seem
And in the morning they fade away
But I can still dream another day

D. A. White

Have We Been Here Before

Have we been here before, in this world of ours, walked this way and
that through minutes, seconds and hours? Have we seen it all before,
the mess, pollution and strife, the heartache and troubles that we call
life? The destruction cruelty starvation and war, is this the second
time around? Have we been here before

The Seven Wonders of the world are such as we've never seen, yet hide
from us the answers, on how they could have been. A miracle of long
past growth, of science and mathematics, we cannot match their
ingenuity. They must have been fanatics, and yet, where is the rest,
where did it go? Was there a war? Is this the second time around?
Have we been here before

It's hard to imagine, many answers still untold, surely if we think
hard about it, the truth would unfold. With stories in the Bible of
seasons being one, of man destroying his images. Of Christ giving
up his Son. These things are happening over again. Will there be
a war? Is this the second time around? Have we been here before?

I hope that if this is the case, then we can get it right. Not be an
end to what we have and ever more take flight. Nor see our rivers
and our land destroyed beyond repair, or lose the beauty of all beasts
and creatures living here. We must hold on to what we have. We must
not have a war. If this is the second time around let's keep it evermore.

Christine Webb

The Savage Poem

Let vengeance be unconstrained. May hatred's moulds issue faultless
casts, lest benevolence better them. Fall upon the many numbered
kindly souls whose inner hearts feel not what faces show, just woe
and tribulations, blow by blow. Pure heart stand out bright white,
uncut, untainted by maturations flow. Take one act that slices
flesh to and fro. One act that batters feelings of they that are
not foe. And yea, our eyes shall wince all at once them calm to
think of future gain. To plot and weave our haters' pain. So
twilight of the mind what conjures thee? Good cogitations that will
please? Hear now such masters as attentive be. Simple slayings
shall not please. To fast despatch them to death's ease. No wrack
and torment know these knaves! No! No!, I say such cunning
stratagems we must lay.
No flesh must bleed, no bruise be bourne. No hammers
brought upon their bones. It is what they feel that we must
stamp on. Their hearts of gold laid ope' before the world. Bring
them into your trust good master. Get thee behind the mask. Learn
such confidences as will serve thee well. Wound with what thou
knowest. Would with all thy will. Wound such that no treachery
shall thy lane stray again. And thence sir, freedom.

Roy Hollinshead

A Memory Of Summer

Though autumn, crisp and clear, advances quickly day by day,
A memory of summer I wrapped and set away.
When in a summer bower, on a summer day lay I
And watched marshmallow clouds on a loganberry sky;
Felt the golden sunshine as it played upon the grass
And heard the golden bees quietly humming as they passed.

The warmth of summer mornings, the pinkly mottled dawn,
The birds that sing the world awake, the green dew-speckled lawn,
The heat of summer afternoons, the solace of the trees,
The summer fruits, forbidden jewels, within their guarding leaves,
The silent summer evenings, beneath a benign sun
We dreamed a summer dream of all the days that had now gone

You taught me much this summer, the languid summer nights,
The smell of honeysuckle sweet, the myriad of lights,
The paint box sunset with a hundred thousand shades of red,
Your voice when you had left me singing songs within my head.
A memory of summer, of one becoming two,
A memory of summer, of me entwined with you.

Let autumn, winter, stumble past and chill the hearts of men,
Just let me hold my sun-splashed thoughts till summer comes again.

Sarah Jackson

The Pit

The young men never questioned the role that they
would play, so they followed dad and granddad down
the pit, they had no say.

They descended into darkness, it was cold, a fearsome
place, and lay upon their backs as they attacked
the black coal face.

They grew older and they married and led contented lives
but now they worry for the future of their children
and their wives.

Their jobs are being taken, cheaper coal is coming in,
"What to do", they say, no work about,
these men just cannot win.

Their livelihoods are threatened and they look ahead
with fear, as they ascend from darkness to a
future of despair.

Our mines should be kept open, 'British Coal' the
people shout, don't dismiss the men who've toiled
so long to bring this feat about.

S. V. Jacques

The Fox Hunt

I saw a fox hunt today
It was the most evil thing I've seen
As I watched the fox run in terror
Hounds following where it had been.

As it hid behind the bushes
I knew it would soon be found
And torn apart by the evil jaws
Of an eager murdering hound.

I feel it's not the hounds' fault though
They were trained to hunt and kill,
It's the heartless beings upon their horses
That let it happen still.

The feeling of absolute powerlessness
Just tears me up inside,
As I watch the hounds rush in for a piece
The fox has finally died.

I can't believe these savagery chases
Still go on in this day and age,
Please don't forget my message to you
When you've finished and turned the page.

Alexandra Brown

Roy

There was a boy called Roy,
A very naughty boy I know,
It all started one sunny day,
When we went to the beach to fish and play,

We got in a boat and sailed out to sea,
It was very quiet,
Roy was looking at me,
It was a very strange look,
That I had never seen before.
He got up and stamped on the floor.

The boat started to move about,
I knew right then that I'd fall out,
I grabbed a float and out I fell,
That naughty boy Roy, I'd send him to hell!

But then I saw a horrible sight,
A shark was coming for us,
Oh what a fright,

It came right for me,
Right for my head.
But then it turned and ate Roy instead.

Serena Wilson, age 12

The Man Who Never Knew About Death

The man who never knew about death,
Thought vicars and funeral directors were such pests.

Vitamins and exercise did not excite a man with no demise.

In the dictionary mortality did not click with a man who
never felt sick.

Fish, chips and mushy peas would not bring this man to his
knees.

Imagine the money he could save, if he thought he'd never
hit the grave.

Insurances, wills, and hospital fees would not affect
this man's allowances.

Many women he would mate only to see his children reach
their miserable fate.

Death which he would never see, as long as there is a
thing called eternity.

Lynn Maxwell

White

Walls white - a prison.
No bars at the window,
but someone carries the key
to my being here.
Coats white - whisper
in my solitary cell,
instigating my sentence.
Smothering me.
Faces white - urgent.
Blood flows. Life dies.
The Sacrificial Lamb.
My freedom.
Hearts white - bled dry
of all emotion.
No pumping, throbbing life
lives within.

There are times when freedom becomes its own prison.

S. A. Smithard

Kashgar

Vibrant streets of dust and dirt
Crumbling walls of dark limestone
Incessant tinkle of clattering bicycles
and the jingle-jangle of donkey-drawn carts.

Goaty-bearded Uighurs, slow and wizened
Brown-veiled wives, brief and evasive
Mao-suited and cloth-capped,
Insistent whispers of 'change money'.

Shish-kebabs sizzling and mutton fat broiling
Twisted noodles bubbling and flat bread baking
Bowls of rice steaming and fried vegetables hissing
and sliced watermelons dripping in the midday sun.

Bustling bazaars, mosques and muezzin
Sunday's market, chaos and colour
Travellers tales, sickness and siestas
An oasis on the ancient route of silk!

Chris Fell

Wonder Of The World

Drifting on a memory way out to the sea,
feeling waves of love that should be here
with me,
In the curly swirly sea of green,
You're a wonder of the world that's never
to be seen,
How I long to hold you once again,
Oh my baby boy release the pain,
I know eventually everything will fade away,
But I'll miss you forever... and a day!

Hazel McDonald

The Passing Of A Day

I wake in the early hours, the night-time slipping by,
I peer through the darkened window
and see the clouds hanging in the sky.
Another day is dawning the minutes ticking past
I'm chasing around to get ready and having to move fast.
at last I'm out and on my way,
the rabbits and hedgehogs keep well at bay.
Trees and hedges go flashing by
but the clouds still hang there in the sky.
The day is long and strenuous, no windows to look outside.
Everything is happening out there, but we are having to hide.
I've done my day I'm as free as a bird
The day has gone this is absurd.
I'm now driving home slowly, to understand why,
the same clouds are still hanging there in the sky
The day is done the day has gone
This is just classed as another one.

T. J. McCowen

When Convenient For You

You say you love me, but I don't know.
You say you need me, how should I know?
You're never there when I need you,
you're always off with someone new.
Time flies by without a word,
then all of a sudden "why haven't I heard"?
You ring me up, you want to see me,
something to tell me loud and clearly.
First one and now another,
I already have a mother.
This time next week you'll not want me,
you'll have your own new family.
It's always the same, the pattern's true,
I'm only your daughter when convenient for you.

Melodie Thyer

A Dream Come True

I waited for nine months
The longest nine months ever
My first baby was on the way
I couldn't wait for the big day
Those nine months were the most exciting
I couldn't wait to see
The tiny little person we'd created
Then the day came
Panic, excitement, emotion rolled into one
I can't describe how I felt
When the midwife said you've got a girl
There she was—Katie Laura
Which was once just a name, was now a dream come true
My husband was there all the time
I couldn't have done it without him
The love I felt for him was indescribable
And she was absolutely adorable

Yvonne Kathleen Hill

The Altar

Your eyes are torn open by the pain of a new day.
Your mind and body are much colder than the grave,
and the voices in your head begin the tortured chant
that taunts you and drives you like a slave.

Whispering, the voices impart secrets of the Earth,
the kind of secrets only wicked children know.
In panic, you rush to find your altar undisturbed,
and only then does your heart begin to slow.

You pray to a wild God that you will never satisfy,
while the slaughtered lamb sleeps without her dreams.
The blood of her sacrifice has left its perfect stain
on the furred and feathered bones of distant screams.

Your hate is all consuming, like an acid in the bone,
but your special hate is for the innocent;
Because the ashes of your childhood smoulder with abuse
your twisted logic will not allow you to relent.

M. Rollins

Without Her

I lived for you and loved you so,
My memory will not let go,
You've gone from me, but you're still here,
Inside my head to shed a tear,
I miss your smile and tender touch,
Your lovely face I miss so much,
Those luscious lips so soft to kiss,
Those Spanish eyes I surely miss,
Your soft caress was heaven sent,
But since you've gone I'm in lament,
Why did you change cold heart of stone?
Destroyed my life, now on my own,
These endless days so empty now,
Without your love, a worthless vow,
The sleepless nights, you on my mind
You're in my heart our souls entwined
I'm dead inside, a robot void
Programmed to live yet soul-destroyed.
Now destiny calls I'll be no more,
To see you then at heaven's door.

Robert McGregor

Seasons Of Life

Softly, softly, as wind through the trees
Caressing the branches and stirring the leaves,
Rain crawls gently on a window pane
As tears on the cheeks resemble the same.

Fall changes to Winter, as the seasons must turn,
To deal with the pain, is what we must learn,
To cope with the loss, of someone we love,
As they begin their journey, to the land above.

It is not the loss of the life that we mourn,
But the loss to ourselves and fear of new dawn.
We selfishly go through life believing,
That those whom we love will never be leaving.

The void that we feel, as time marches on,
Is the space that new feelings must build upon,
We must try to cultivate with the fullness of time,
From grief to memories of the heart and mind.

As you travel this journey of changing seasons,
Don't analyze feelings or attempt to find reasons,
Allow time and space to comfort your heart,
And prepare yourself, as new life starts.

Jo Myhill

The Audacity Of Man

Audacious are the deeds of man,
Audacious! - It is true!
Below, I tell you what he's done,
And what he hopes to do!

He's sailed the seas, explored the deep,
And burrowed underground,
He's stood upon earth's highest peak,
And flown through air as fast as sound!

He's bred a thousand different breeds,
That were never known before;
He's analyzed the sand and rocks,
And diagnosed earth's inmost core!

He measures time as well as space,
And plans to reach the moon!
He makes his plans at such a pace,
It may be very soon!

But when the statesman's minds corrupt,
And threaten the world with war,
'Tis then the good work's all undone,
'Tis then his world may be no more.

H. Leslie Devey

Sail Into Daylight

The clouds reach down to touch the sea,
The sun's about to rise,
A glow is seen for miles around,
Like lasers cross the skies.
A swirling mist quite high above,
Casting shadows on the breeze,
Out on her wing a pure white dove,
In flight above the trees.
The darkness slowly disappears
As daylight comes along,
The chorus from a flock of birds,
Their morning welcome song.
The night time leaves now without trace,
The view, a lovely sight,
Although how near the journey's end,
To sail into daylight.

Julie Haig

The Swallow

The swallow though it doesn't sing
is very graceful on the wing.
It's also very very sleek
is so strong yet looks so weak.

It glides through the air with infinite ease
across the meadows and over the trees.
They twist and turn while in mid-flight
oh they are a beautiful sight.

They soar upward as if to touch the sky
They swoop back down to catch a fly
in the meadows they can be found
flying inches above the ground.

They fly around the old church spire
and sometimes settle on a wire
Although they look quite black in flight
They're blue and white when caught in height.

Edwin Campbell

A Soldier's War

A soldier, fighting in the war.
To fight and die for his country, he swore
He must obey the given command
Someone must die by his hand.

Must men seek to destroy one another
In war that takes a son from his mother
Fighting and killing in rain and mud
Who will be next to shed his blood.

He does not choose to lose his life
To leave his children and his wife
He tries to understand the war
The reason it was created for
Bombs and bullets, death galore
Just for the sake of settling a score
Is war really worth it, what is it for
Who on this earth, really wants war?

C. Jack

Life Time

The main adventure is not lost,
It starts right here, there is no cost,
Although your past may be wracked with strife
Only now can you live your life.

Seize the moment, catch the day
Look not back, nor far away
Learn the lessons of your past
But have no regrets, have a laugh.

Yesterday has been and gone
Tomorrow's time has not yet come,
Only now can we be free
And what is meant, is meant to be.

Philip Maddison

Our Planet

In the beginning God made mankind, made them in his image, but gave
then human signs, of weakness, frailty and intelligence guides.
Each he made different in colour in face and called us his children,
the now human race.

He found us a planet and called it the earth, with beautiful forests
seas, sand and earth. A blue sky above, with a sun and a moon, to
help us with light and for warmth to grow food. Next he put other
creatures to dwell at our side, and said "Now you earthlings had
better be kind. I'm trusting you, to look after all things,
reptiles, animals, birds, mammals fish. All whose intelligence
doesn't have your scan, I want you to be good to beast and to man."

But man's greed soon surfaced, he desired all things, so warred and
enslaved and hunted all things over the centuries we've never learnt,
power and avarice is what comes first. The animals God gave into our
loving care, are nearly extinct, for tusks, skin, fins, fur. Humans
are starving, torture still reigns, even our poor earth is dying the
same, forests are dying, so are the seas, from sewage waste, oil and
nuclears, rivers, and lakes, earth, ice caps too, acid rain falling,
earthquakes abound, hurricanes, volcanoes, cracked earth and
landslides abound. How in God's name can our planet survive, with
holes in the ozone, and vile pesticides soon it will die? And then
it will be, goodbye lovely earth. Goodbye you and me.

Stella W. J. Sobieralski

And Then Life Terminates

I'm safe, secure, protected. No needs or fears or worries.
My kingdom lined with warmth grows with me day by day,
And even though it's very small just try and turn me out.
But wait a minute! I feel a mild disturbance travelling towards me,
Trespassing in my territory, dismantling my privacy.
Alert to change in atmosphere, impending danger now I fear.
What's happening my conscience asks? Aliens with claws!
Infiltrating my delicate defences, as bailiffs out to evict me.
I'm frightened, frenzied, in a daze, my body has turned cold.
I've no weapons to do battle, no chance to air my point of view.
No one witnessing my silent screams, no place to hide or run away to.
Intimidated into retreat, as the cavalry they charge.
With no indication of emotion!
Their ferocious jaws - they capture me, suppress and overthrow me.
Rip and penetrate my skin and then destroy my tacit limbs.
Echoed cries sound out my doom as blood flows freely from my wounds,
And then life terminates.
Without leaving its station.

Michael Harden

Only Words

My dear friend, my true friend, are only words - it's true
but deep within these words so much warmth is held for you.
For someone with your caring heart how better to convey,
the wishes, hopes, I have for you today and every day.

The memories captured here within are moments sweet and rare,
to ponder and to savour when life presents its cares.
But in between the words there lies a special magic glow
born from feelings only you could sense and know.

So when some day you're feeling down, your confidence is low,
ponder once again my words, seek out the magic glow.
The glow which from your saddened lips a slow smile gently teases,
warms your heart with happy thoughts until your tension eases.

Until at last the pain has gone, your spirits start to lift,
and words have triumphed once again, released their precious gift.
The gift of love between true friends can never fade away,
it nestles here within the words, just waiting for your next low day.

Remember then my dearest friend, that words are only words it's true.
but deep within these words so much warmth is held for you.
Warmth born of the magic of friendship firm and true,
reflecting back the magic born in me, instilled by You.

Breda Nicholls

A Child's View!!!!

The slaves are working hard
perspiring in the sweltering heat,
weakening day by day hour by hour minute by minute.
Some collapsing on the fine sand
for lack of water, being beaten for
something they cannot help
Just for having different skin colour
religion and opinions
How man can be so hurtful and unkind?
I watched in wonder as a child.
I might look white act white but black in
soul, soul's what makes a person
I am older now, wiser too, I've seen
the stages of their lives the growing trace.
I look back I saw their potential
they had something a white man
could never possess: courage dreams
that were only a generation away
The slaves are sleeping and yet
I wonder if they're not planning their future here and now.

Tania Dean

My World

My world is nothing to be desired for
It's dangerous, polluted and what's more
You cannot do your own free will
People shout and cry over an unpaid bill

Fishes swim in chemically filled waters
The sun breaks through and causes cancers
Of the skin and of the lung
But still heavenly praises are sung

My home is but bare and happy
But others are not you see
In the darkness of the streets
There are people who need to beg to eat

We need people to fight for our justice
But their ignorance and greed results in tears
Taxes go up and wages fall down
Both corruption and dispute begins to tear all towns

While the rich live in luxury
And the poor live for another day
My world is nothing more but a hole in another galaxy

Katherine Elizabeth Younger

Hello Tomorrow

I am alone, and time stands still.
No rush, no bustle, no love.
He is gone now, so here I wait until
A stranger comes. Another chance at love.

The pain will almost disappear then
As it has done in past affairs.
I will recall sweet memories again,
But thoughts of you will bring the tears.

Parting should not cause such pain.
To hold on would hurt much more.
Release him. His loss is my gain.
I swim on to another shore.

I'm browsing in the record shop.
The boy beside me looks quite nice.
He turns and asks me what I've bought?
'John Lennon' - Great! But what a price.

We've hit it off. He seems o.k.
The stranger's come into my heart.
He's made me smile. He's made my day.
He gives me hope for a new start.

Beth Beauley

The Dream That Died

The dream of Euro 96 has finally died
when Moller scored that penalty I broke down and cried
to come so near, and yet so far, was all too much to take
and it was all down to one player poor Gareth Southgate.

The pain is doubled due to one undeniable fact
it's the second time the Germans have beaten us like that
in Italia 90 Pearce and Waddle were to blame
and now it's Gareth Southgate who must hang his head in shame

So there's to be no repeat of 1966
Garza and Darren Anderton just failed to do the trick
when the drama was all over I've never felt so low.
Oh why, oh why, oh why, couldn't we score a golden goal

Germany are the champions as they always seem to be
they rode their luck, came bouncing back to lift the trophy
as Furgen Klinsmann was presented with the European
Championship cup
my mind was playing havoc
if only Southgate hadn't mucked it up.

Mark Pitter

Am I Allowed To Try?

Am I allowed to cry... am I?
Is it ok not to run away; to hide, inside, deep deep down...
What if I die... what if I drown engulfed by the sea of
emotion that has been held back for Oh... so long..
'They' have implied I must be strong... they all have needs you see!
Will they feel abandoned if I relinquish this Image that is Me?
How I abhor the charade I feel I must parade ...
Am I allowed to sigh... am I?
It may reach ten on the richer scale... like a colossal whale
excuse me! Won't that mean Fail?
I've spent all this time beside it; underneath and going round.
My constant companion like an unwelcome guest, silent and
within me; held so closely to my breast.
If I don't hold myself together; you say that, "I won't fall apart"?
Can I allow the tornado to rip right through my heart?
Am I allowed to try? ... I am?

Joan Crimp

Dream

A dream is a delusion, a mistaken identity
To believe in it would be a total fantasy
Imagination unrestricted by reality,
it's just a hallucination the alleged
perception of an object when no object
is present.
Reverie fanciful visionary notion
Vagaryan erratic action
All of it is a mental activity,
an image of events occurring in my sleep
Please let them come true and to stay
in reality.

Natalie Watkins

A Vision

I looked round the corner
And what did I see . . .
I saw a man looking straight at me,
He looked so happy and so kind,
Then a thought came into my mind.
I had seen this man somewhere before.
He was the man who had been knocking at my door.
I had opened the door, and let him in,
His face was old, and he was in pain.
He stood at the table and started to pray,
I just watched him, not knowing what to say.
I closed my eyes wondering what I had done,
When I opened them again, this man was gone.
I never saw him again until today,
Even then I didn't know what to say.
Then all of a sudden, he was gone.
I realize now, he was just a vision.

E. Hinton

Be Positive

Be positive, don't give in,
With determined thought you are sure to win.

The summit you aim for need not be high,
With positive thought you can reach for the sky.

Some days you feel weary and terribly sad,
You look back on memories when times weren't so bad.

But with positive thought the sun will shine through,
And there is no limit to the things you can do.

Try not to be sad and let things get you down,
Wear a smile in place of a frown.

Love, laugh and be happy everyday,
For nothing can take those feelings away.

Stand firm to your goal, don't be swayed.
And in time the darkness will begin to fade.

So say to yourself "It's time to live",
Be Happy . . . Be joyful . . .
Be Positive!!!

Sarah Anne

A Great Big Hoax

We've had dinosaurs and falling stars
Flying saucers straight from Mars
But the greatest thing that we possess
Is this big monster in Loch Ness

Tourists come from far out places
People of all different races
Is it real or just an illusion
It's caused the world a lot of confusion

It has stalks on its head and a twenty-foot body
Is that what becomes of drinking Scotch toddy
No doubt we'll hear a few more jokes
But keep on wondering if Nessy is really A Great Big Hoax.

Agnes Donaghey

The Destroyer Of Worlds

I am the destroyer of worlds
I make tears fall like rain
I bring death wherever I go
I am the spreader of pain

Some call me prejudice, others hate
But one thing I know for sure
While they still fear what they don't understand
I will go on and they will perish evermore

Abigail Phipps

Depression

I have been sitting here all week
in so much agony
Wondering for the life of me
However could it be,
that my son, my darling son
whom I have loved so and adored
could be so far away from me
as though he were abroad.
I have watched him in his loneliness
I have watched him in despair,
watched him prowling about the house
thinking we do not care.
Life to him it seems, has not been very kind,
everything around him has been jumbled in his mind.
The stress of work and studying has made him very sad,
add to this the pressures of life, he thinks he's going mad,
why my darling son, when you felt you couldn't cope,
didn't you come to me for some comfort and some hope
Life has a sunny side, as one day you will find,
if only you will trust me to help to clear your mind.

Christine Goodchild

A Shared Glance

A glance, a knowing, a touch of shared joy, a hidden
ripple of breathlessness.
Soft caress of hair on skin, dance electric on dreams to be.
Exploration on points of light, a soft, joyous, painful, waking
into colour that gently explodes consciousness.

A pause, a silence behind words, a silence felt and
enjoyed in simplicity.
Soft sight screams out quietness.
Words, seen barriers to touch, writhe between
in sensuality.
Feed with lips, fill the soul's emptiness-walled places.

A softness touch, a wing's breath, a feather's kiss
upon a shy dwelling of electric tingle.
Breathe in upon bared senses, fan the awakening
knowledge, lost amid the dark, deep forest
of emotions maze.

Silent longing for oneness, barrierless, to walk between spaces.
To touch, to feel, to inhale your soul's breath deep within.
To slowly sink and drown in deep mind's joining.

Gerry Kane

"Memories"

Speak to me softly, whisper in my ear
those magical words, I love to hear.
Tales of a journey across the sea
a wonderful place, where I yearn to be
walking on beaches strewn with shells
listening to churches' far away bells.
Under the grape vines, cool and inviting
bunches of grapes, just ready for biting
fresh green figs, and olives abound
a horse and trap to take us around.
Hot Summer Days! a welcome siesta
in the evenings, a Grande Fiesta
People dressed in colours so bright
happily dancing away the night
friends sitting at tables, tastefully spread
with pasta, and vino, and homemade bread
hams and cheeses, fish freshly caught
scenes like these can never be bought
Etched into memories, held very dear
And spoken so gently in my ear.

Erica D. Martina

The Nature Of Poetry

I sit and write my poetry
Under the shade of the big oak tree
I purvey the scene that is all around
And watch a robin on the ground.

I listen to birds chirping in the trees
And amid flowers, the hum of honey bees.
I sit and ponder what to write
With the beauty of nature in my sight.

Blues skies freckled with fluffy clouds
It's lovely to be away from the crowds
Letting time slowly pass me by
Whilst fluttering by is a butterfly.

Still thinking of a poetry theme
I rest my head and start to dream.
Fairies and elves come out to play
And whisper in my ear what to say.

When I awake I start my rhyme
About nature and the passing of time.
Now this poem is almost done
Just as I watch the setting sun.

Gaye Torney

Untitled

Quietly, she sits on the bench and listens
to words that wash over me
passing by with the bread and wine.
Her hands move loosely on the page
and I stare into these gestures
caught in the testimony of time.

I remember other days—the worshipping sun,
the young girl standing in her love
across a lane, smiling.
I watch a dress glide softly,
bright with life's imitations,
grey with the loss of innocence, yet
content to touch a face and
turn towards the pulpit, persuading.

The flowered dress squats cleanly on the bench,
bleached, fading in the wind.
Shoes scraped and old.
Eyes glitter as she stirs tentatively towards the cross.
I pull my coat tighter, watching
her light amongst the shadows.

Ann Marie Jamieson

Grief Appeased

For you, my love, my heart doth grieve,
Your warmth, the trembling of your parts
So close entwined, no thought to leave,
The knot so tightly woven bound our hearts.

The cold awareness that you are gone,
Yet now, and then, I feel your breath,
The greater urge to live doth heal the wound
Deep, sore, caused by your death.

Still, the firmness of your mouth on mine,
Your nearness, the gentle warmth your presence doth exude,
Your pleasure still enfolds me as to grape the vine,
No matter the day, the wind how rude.

Drawn to the garden where to seek solace,
'Tis here, 'tis where I romp the lonely field.
I see you now beneath the drooping ash,
The beauty of your blush not yet revealed.

So shaded by this frothing powder puff,
Your scent doth reach me though I am not near,
Screech now thou wily wind and rough,
Our spirits here dance, ne'er more to fear.

Diana Grant

For Bella

Our Bella, wailing. Bent and anguished with pain
What sedation or comfort can I bring?
Skin stretched over your bones
Gnarled fingers that once wore a ring
Do not put your eyes onto my eyes
You who played with my hair
For I will fetch you some flowers today
And place them on your sill
Do not place your hand, pleading on my face
For your tears will tempt me to kill

I am glad they straightened your bones while I slept
Glad it was not me who pushed in the packs
Gentle lady, good mother, strong wife
Was I enough Bell, not too professional, removed or too young?
I hope you could feel that I cared
While you struggled to meet your end
We did not choose each other
I shall open the window above where you used to sleep
So that you can now fly away
This last task, from me, your last friend.

L. D. Hardman

Where Did I Lose Me?

No more are memories rosy,
Only images of darkness haunt me.
No longer does love taste sweet,
The scent of blood fills my nostrils.
Where did I lose me?
No more do I ache to be touched,
My heart cries tears of pain.
No longer do my dreams exist,
Only crumbling-fragments of once upon a time.
Where did I lose me?
I exist to serve and obey.
I have no opinions or thoughts.
Terror and fear are always close,
To wrap me in cloaks of darkness.
Where did I lose me?
My once beautiful dreams laugh at me.
Nightmares are all I have.
For you I would once have died.
Now it seems I will.
Please tell me, where did I lose me?

Michelle Ward

The Dregs Of War

I am just an onlooker,
At this savage scene of crime.
The anguish and the tears
Of a hundred thousand ruined lives.
The people here are downtrodden,
Dying with the rain.
Their graves, the blood-covered, bitter ground,
But at least they escape from the pain.
They have no place to return to,
So they wander round alone,
Following the wind in its futile path
As at death's door it moans.
The slaughter they are awaiting,
Tiptoes nearer every day,
Watching their fragile hearts,
Slowly seeping away.
Their faces like stone statues,
Their hearts almost standing still,
The tender thought of freedom
Is the only substantial meal.

Helen Tapson

Little Red Teddy Bear

Little red teddy bear sitting in the corner,
Little red teddy bear so soft and so nice,
Little red teddy bear was given some dope,
Now little red teddy bear just mopes with no hope,

Little red teddy bear was given some more,
Little red teddy bear was brought into a lure,
Little red teddy bear got busted and broke,
Now little red teddy bear is left hanging on a rope.

Joann Drake

Swift Summer

Summer shimmers on seductively;
Sunlight and soft showers spice and scent
Evergreen fields and flowers.
Though sultry sunsets hint of mortality,
Swifts and swallows soar skywards,
Then come dipping by with gleeful exuberance,
Finding freedom in airy flight.
The eternal summer swoops by softly.

So summer wings its way onwards to southern poles,
Swifter than any swift or swallow.
Gently it steals away in light breezes
And fluttering leaves that fall silently,
Swooning earthwards in coloured cascades
Leaving a golden light as summer fades.

Christine Robinson

Johnny

I know, I thought, I'll write a poem,
Just for Johnny, from the heart,
I'll put emotion down on paper,
Beginning is the hardest part.

I'm happy when we are together,
I miss you so when we're apart,
Come hold my hand, and sit beside me,
Say you care, now that's a start.

I never felt this way before,
I just don't understand,
I only want to be with you,
And share the life we planned.

Let us not wait until the day,
The day that we are parted,
To realize the value of
The one we took for granted.

Well that's my poem, I hope you like it,
If you don't, that's tough.
Just remember that I love you,
Goodnight Johnny, I've said enough.

Lynn Bell

The Wise Man's Words

In lands of old,
New stories told,
Of dreams and love and faith behold,
All was love and hope and grace,
From heaven to this innocent place,
At first all love did rule this land,
Until the fool laid down his hand,
He turned the rest to saddened souls,
They forgot the love the soul beholds,
Hate and prejudice were then planted,
"Turn to kindness", their lost hearts chanted,
'Twas faith in God that then did falter,
Marriages failed at the altar,
Lovers turned away from love,
Angels wept on high above,
And now they wonder as if all dead,
Rejecting love, but fear instead,
I pray they listen, before it's too late,
Or sadness and pain will be their fate.

It is but the past, that brings forth our future.....

Esther C. Donaldson

Grandmother's House

I tapped on the door and turned away,
The door creaked open.
Her icy cold hand touched my shoulder,
I turned and saw her wrinkled face,
It was the face of my gran.

She greeted me and showed me to my room,
No light did it show.
My bed was as big as a room,
And my room as big as a house.
There was an ugly old chair standing beside my bed,
It was embroidered and extremely dull,
Next to the chair was a dressing table, it shone at
  me with its emptiness.

There was no stove in the kitchen,
Nothing but a very weak fire, in the fireplace.
We sat on the chairs around it and ate,
The food had gone off and it tasted foul.
I will never forget the day I visited
  'Grandmother's house'.

Anila Vekaria

Untitled

Your eyes light up the sacred night,
Your beautiful colours burning bright,
A flame of fire amongst the trees,
Your sacred soul in the evening breeze.

Your body graceful with all its length,
A creature created with all its strength,
Each one of you special, individually designed,
A message to us all, a scent in our mind.

You're powerful and respected straight from birth,
The king of the Jungle,
The king of the Earth.
There is just one thing that stands above all,
And that is the human so terribly cruel.

I dread the night and I dread the day
Your beautiful spirit floats away,
And when your soul drifts apart,
I know that it will break my heart.

For you're the most wonderful animal around,
You are the tiger,
But soon ash in the ground.

Deborah Fletcher

To Know Right

When you have lain awake at night
to sort out in your mind what's right
then have to face an angry throng,
and tell them firmly "you are wrong."

If you can stand tall as a steeple
and face a nameless mass of people,
saying to them "I have no proof,
but sincerely believe I speak the truth".

If, on all sides you meet abuse,
and still, to hide in lies, refuse,
But shout aloud with a voice firm and strong.
"I know I'm right - I am not wrong."

If indeed, you have searched your heart,
and though it hurts, cannot depart
from the only path you see ahead
and by your conscience must be led.

When you know you've come to the end
and from that path you cannot bend,
and truth is your might,
Then this is right.

Betty Louise Patching

Lost Love

The first time I saw you I knew I would love you
I knelt down before you and offered my heart
Your eyes were divine in the moonlight above you
You said you'd be mine and that we'd never part
But now you are gone and my heart has gone with you
Come back to me darling, come back to my arms
My heart's far away and my thoughts are all of you
How lonely each day now that we are apart.

Barbara Willoughby

Occupation of Elegance

Your presence is enough to turn all heads
You walk through the door and wake the dead,
The power you have in your look
You hold the mystery of a closed book.

Your charm is placed on everyone you meet
The number of men who would gladly give you their seat,
You surround yourself with beauty and elegance
No one could mistake your self felt evidence.

To touch you must be like touching perfection
You give off the high of a narcotic injection,
How many people have fallen for your grace
And how many fantasies reveal your face.

Kim Cobair

His Life

The life of one lies in my hands
A tiny being seeking for love
So small and fragile but holding my heart

The sun shines bright like his soul
Beaming on faces making smiles appear
Giving life and something to live for

Light fades, a curtain is closed
Illness possesses this tiny creature
All is quiet but his heart still beats

His life drags on and pain grows stronger
A heavy weight only death can lift
Blackness shades expressionless faces

Barriers now built, protecting emotions
Shielding hearts so they don't crack
Walls break down, pretence is shattered

The sun goes down, stays down forever
My heart the cage, a home left desolate

The hands which held the life now tremble
The dam has burst and tears flood out

Love has drowned... never to return.

Wendy Robertson

The Barn Owl

Stealthy hunter in the night,
Swift but silent is thy flight,
Rapier sharpness of thy sight
Pinpoints prey in dimmest light.

Nocturnal rodent in search of food.
Ne'er aware the danger in shadowed wood,
Thy clenching claw cannot elude,
Now rustling leaf where once it stood.

Merciful death, no tortured sound,
Captured quarry 'tis swept from ground,
Secluded niche then hastily found,
Where few impeding predators abound

There to feast from thy lifeless prize,
Head rotating with ever watchful eyes,
Hastening this morsel whence to realize,
Darkness succumbs to light of morning skies

Majestic span as waving wings divide,
Whilst homeward to thy barn perch doth glide,
There to preen thy feather with tempered pride,
Thence to slumber in ignorance of all outside.

D. S. Laing

Hiraeth (The Longing)

There is a longing deep in my heart, for a place
of my yesteryear
It is where I spent my childhood days, a place I hold
so dear
I hear still the mournful cry of the colliery hooter
The miners' pit boots in the street.
And in the distance the throb of the winding engine
'Twas ever the Rhondda's heartbeat
Oh again to roam on my beloved mountains
To feel the grass, touch the fern, see the sheep
I shut out the scars on the landscape, of
The accursed mine owners slag heap
And I know that this aching in my heart for my
Rhondda home
Will burn ever bright inside me, no matter where
I roam
And the flame will be unquenchable deep within
my breast
And will only be extinguished when they lay
me down to rest.

D. R. Noblett

Caliban - Journey To Another Home

Before us lies a mystery; behind, our memories
Of flowers, sounds and creatures, gold and amber trees.
Around us rumble waves that ripple, tip and churn,
And in us smoulder fires of broken hearts that burn.
Above us flutters Ariel - a gull whose eerie screech
Travels on ahead of us to find our destined beach.
Below us creak the planks of the salt corroded deck,
And past us drifts the debris of Neptune's last ship wreck.
Through us cuts the wind that chills the marrow of our bones,
And from us stench and misery all mingle with our moans.
Around me there's a blanket, enclosed and locked, I am
In this lonely corner as weak as any lamb.
Up and down I'm rocking; this my cradle, how I'm weak!
My lips are blistered, flaming; no words can I now speak.
Through me shivers tingle; though up - Ariel still flies.
From me trickle tears that blur my weary eyes.
In me; through me; round me, shoot the pains whilst waters blue
Gargle temptingly at our ever-thirsty crew.
Before me lies a tunnel where the darkness starts to cease.
And to me comes a time once more to rest, and feel at peace.

Jane Stanton

Thank You Lord

Thank you Lord for the roof above my head
The walls around me and a comfortable bed

Food to eat and clothes to wear
And loving friends always there

Eyes to see beauty all around
And ears to hear every lovely sound

A nose to smell the sweetness of flowers
I thank you Lord for many happy hours

Above all thank you for those gone before
Who taught me to pray and you adore

And when dear Lord I am sad and in despair
My comfort is to know you are always there

Virginia A. Johnson

The Tree Of Life

My teacher always said 'reach for the sky'
Don't despair, you must always try
Look, learn, and listen, think big!
Climb the tree of life, twig by twig
Slowly and surely if you have a go
Climbing your tree, you'll see the stars glow
Beckoning you upwards, showing you the way
It may not be easy, you can always pray
As you climb your tree of life, the twigs may snap
Don't be put off by the first mishap
The boughs may bend, giving you a fright
Learn to dig in, hold on tight!
Some find their tree of life, an easy nut to crack
Others find it harder with each setback
But the view at the top is something to treasure
Your teacher's 'well done' will give you much pleasure

Amy F. Childs

The Almighty

I am indestructible
Above man and beast and power strive I
I am sheer supremacy of the Order Most High
Neither by weapon, nor witchcraft, nor sorcery do I blemish
I am the Invincible, the Stronghold, the Bold
I am the eternal concentration of might
I am the victor in every satanic fight
The immortal impenetrable shield am I
No entity, no revolution renders my force corrupt
Like Vesuvius, Hiroshima, my plight is to erupt
My mission, to conquer the universe
My aim to banish the evil curse,
In the elements, the lashing wave, the roaring wind lies my source
I will forever survive
For I am indestructible

Emma Gainsford

An Evening Stroll

The sinking sun reflects its rays
On rock flowers, a beautiful haze
Of purples, golds and richest reds
Some growing on the cliff's very edge

The wind has dropped and the sea is quiet
A gentle swish swish as the tide goes out
An early moon can be seen arising
as a golden sun begins departing.

It's twilight now, peaceful and still
Sea gulls have gone to find fish in the swell
Bobbing lights can be seen in the distance
As the fishing boats work, without resistance.

I climbed the footpath to find my way home
And I saw the lighthouse with its silver dome
The light was flashing, warning of reefs
So that ships of the night won't come to grief

The darkening sky reveals one star
Winking and shimmering, aloft and afar
A lingering scent comes from the heather
And I saw two owls flying together.

Dorothy Smith

In Memorium

I wish I could tell you how much I love you,
but I can't - because you don't love me too.
Every waking hour you are in my heart and mind.
Oh love, why do you burn within me? Why are you so unkind?
It didn't really hit me until you went away.
Now all I do is - look forward to the day,
when once more I shall see your lovely face,
and perhaps for just a second, hold you in a sweet embrace.
Too soon you'll go away and my heart will yearn,
for the sometime in the future - when perhaps you may return.

Roy J. T. Smith

Dog's Life

Life is a bonus, 'cos I haven't known death yet
But! I might change my mind, when I see this vet
A nice drive up, in the back of a car
Hey! It's really bumpy, I'm glad it's not far
To think that I was just going home
Running, and growling, all alone
Dodging about, where the street lamps glow
In, and then out of them, to and fro
Then came this car, so really neat
It hit me, it knocked me off my feet
There were people around me, some just laughed
I also heard a mention of Jack Russell skin graph
But! Oh no, here's that needle, just a little prick
Relax boy, lay down he sez, have a little kip
Oh look! A black bin liner, I wonder what that's for
He's left it here beside me, beside me on the floor
Life is a bonus, 'cos I haven't known death yet
But, I think I'll know death, now I've met this vet.

G. J. McIntosh

Party

Blind we sat, with squarish friends,
Who drank in moderation,
And bemoaned the public transport system,
Putting forward plans for renovation.
And as we sat we smoked,
Because our fidgeting would otherwise betray our lack of interest,
Stifled by their voices, choked,
By monotones that put our tired patience to the test.
Glasses clinked and muted laughter
Rattled, and we swore that never after
This would we accept
Those invitations that, politely offered and unthinkingly
replied to,
Bear witness to a promise never kept.

Lucy Warburton

Eyes!

Eyes to see with,
Eyes to open, to see the light!
Eyes to close to see darkness!
Shadows flicker in the twi-light! Casting shapes,
Objects! Forming pictures of true formations,
Distance lights glimmer in the dark,
Shadows dancing in the flicker of glimmering lights!
Mystery of feelings penetrate the inner-self!
Shadows dancing in the twilight! Objects moving.
Shaping pictures here, and there.
Jumping dancing, twisting! Twirling!
Glowing lights! Dazzling! Diamonds,
Sparks from flames, of glowing torches
Haunts! The beholder of the eyes.
To a triumph of exultation!
To a stirring of lifting ego,
To a calming rapture, of soothing bliss!
To behold the light of mystery of eyes!

Mary Ashmore

Moodiness

It descends slowly,
Like a light mist,
But before you know it
A thick blanket of smog
Embroils you, embitters you, envelops you
With a dislike of everything and everyone
Who comes within your reach.
You punish and alienate them,
Your tongue lashing and whipping like a viper
As your prey you try to corner,
Like a fox running for its lair
While the dogs are everywhere.
The speed of the mounts
As they splash through the wood
No answer to the desperation
Felt by the hounded
Of the one with the black mood.

Jacqueline D. Rhodes

Daddy Why?

Dear Daddy,
Why did I have to leave and not say goodbye?
Why did you depart and not wait for me?
Why I regret not knowing you more?
Why I miss and love you so much?
Why I can't bring myself to say goodbye,
As your memory lives on inside me?
  Forever Love,
    From your daughter Anh.

Anh Tao

The Staircase

As you fumbled along
Up the steps
Ahead of me,
You must have thought
I was not behind you,
Just because I was
Not able to comfort you,
Or because I was not crying at your story
Does not mean I was
Not there, with you,
I was there,
Crying,
The tears could not stop
Although I cried no tears at all,
I couldn't stop holding you,
Although I never touched you,
I couldn't leave your side
Although I was never near you,
I was always there,
Just a couple of steps behind you.

Jane Charles

Greener Grass

Average at school, despite trying hard.
Used to manual slavery for a moderate living.
Learning which friends to trust, and which really care.
Weeding out those that take without giving.

I feel reach with love for my family,
And angry when snooty folk put them down,
With comments like 'dressed up? In those rags!'
Or fire demeaning looks that would cause them to frown.

We work hard to provide for our youngsters,
But all we can give are the basic provisions.
It is upsetting to think they will end up like us,
Struggling and surviving on the wrong side of class divisions.

The struggle for existence will continue a lifetime,
It's hard to clamber up life's slippery bevel.
There will come a time when the less fortunate become equal,
When six feet of earth puts us all at the same level.

Heather Davies

Feelings And Emotions

Feelings are so real, and so hard to explain.
It seems a much deeper emotion
For us to try and describe
Without showing pain.

Thoughts are much crazier;
Though exciting and challenging too,
Leaving us all in puzzle, dawning over us all,
Bringing out the good side in you.

These are natural signs
Which only you will understand.
These have been going on
Since the first day of Man.

Christina Thompson

VE-Day Feelings Of An Evacuee

It's VE-Day,
I'm an evacuee
I've got to go back to my parents now
I'm full of glee.
I've got to leave my guardians now,
They've been so good to me.
I'm happy yet sad that the war is over.
Feelings and emotions are spinning in my mind,
I'm so confused.
I'm so proud that my country has won.
There is peace at last.
There are lots of street parties
People put on a happy face, but I know they are still upset.

Lisa Costanza

Rhossili Bay

I gazed across the ocean, as it shimmered
in the heat.
    The pounding waves of foaming surf,
that swirled around my feet.
    Shoals of tiny silver fish, darting
to and fro,
    A crab that scuttled on the bed,
not knowing where to go.

I turned my gaze towards the Cliffs,
that reached out to the sky.
    The purple heather clad the walls.
The breeze that seemed to sigh
    at Mother Nature's wondrous work,
of blue, and green, and gold.
    The mountain sheep that scaled the face,
and never lost their hold.

A far cry from my city home, of pollution, noise, and crime,
I was here on Holiday, the next two weeks were mine,
    To gaze across the landscape, ever changing, day by day,
And once again I was a child, back in Rhossili Bay.

Greta Kinnear-Williams

A Love To Treasure, Together Or Apart

I sit here remembering your smile and touch
only I know what I miss and how much.
No one can tell me to forget the past
because you're part of my life, and our love will last.
I can still see your face, as you were taken away
I can still here my voice, pleading with you to stay.
It was not your fault, I know that is true,
Distance can not take away the love I feel for you.
You said you loved me, and then left my side.
I had a million tears that I tried to hide
Maybe we were not born to be together
Or maybe our love was not to last forever
but underneath all the heartache and pain
one day soon I will come and see you again
I hear your voice on the telephone, and it breaks my heart in two
for no one knows the real depth of the love I have for you.

Tracy Williams

Thoughts Of Yesterday

As I stare through the day beside myself
Pictures of you, and nobody else
Soft heavenly eyes gaze upon me
And rendered so still, no words for the world to see
Only once in a lifetime, love rushes the heart
floods the mind's thoughts, of never to be apart
As dawn's ribbon of light rushes you with the tide
And it flashes through the dark, wakening you inside
Your beauty spreads a rush through my eyes
And the tears that I hold say their final goodbyes
Tonight I'm crumbling down, sinking in the memories
Shadows of you keep washing over me, bring me to my knees
The goodbye was bliss in your warm embrace
And my life soon sank without a trace
Every now and then I drown in thoughts of yesterday
When your picture slowly swept me up and carried me away

Matthew Nixon

The Circle Line

I would be lonely if not for my
subterranean friends.
I cannot see them, their averted gazes,
their impassive looks.
Each minute brings another party,
but a sombre party of strange companions
in my dark loneliness.
This one brings a spent collection of
moths, powdered like butterflies,
wearing a chaotic uniform of bacardi and roses.
I cannot see them. Each arrival is the same,
in the carriages rumbling through my mind's dark tunnels.
Grey men, clothed from a forgotten wardrobe.
Ghosts, who come and go. No-one said farewell
as they boarded my thoughts,
and no-one will say hello when they arrive
at an impossible destination.

Graham R. Bell

Life

Awakening destroys the simplicity of life
Life is simple because we are asleep
Not knowing of the world and its events.
People are people
Unbeknownst to themselves of the adventures surrounding them.
When will they realize this fact?

The conscious mind is the creator of difficulty
They believe they are alive when really dead
The galaxy is a deep dark hole
And we are falling.

Self-knowledge is the creator of doubt
Yet doubt is self-knowledge's parent
The universe of the self
Excludes the universe of the world
Yet both create the universe of the whole

Dave Mallick

The Problems With School

The thing we all hate about school,
Is having to obey every rule,
Don't talk in the classrooms don't run in the hall,
Concentrate on your work and don't stare at the wall,
Here is your essay it was handed in late,
Your spelling's atrocious your writing a state,
You got a D now go see the head,
He is the person that all pupils dread,
He sits in his office at the corridor end,
To him naughty pupils the teachers all send,
You go into his office and stare at the floor,
While he hands out detentions and such by the score,
Then the bell rings for the end of the lesson,
You have to go out for another games session,
You shiver outside in your T-shirt and shorts,
Cursing the fact that you have to do sports,
As you stand playing games in the rain,
There is only one thought that keeps you sane,
And that one thought it is true to say,
Is the school bell that rings for the end of the day.

Emma Ormond

The Drunken Driver

While standing at the bar that night
he never stopped to think
that before the night was over
he'd have too much to drink

When he went outside the bar room
his eyes could hardly see
but searching in his pocket
he found his old car key

He got behind the driver's seat
and started up the engine
but the death that was to come that night
was not his full intention

The kids were walking home that night
they had been to see their gran
the little boy was Jimmy the little girl was Anne

He didn't see them coming his mind was in a trance
the car was doing ninety they didn't stand a chance

He spent some time in prison but it didn't kill the pain
he swore when he got outside he would never drink again

He knows if he'd been sober the kids would be alive
so he's asking every motorist please don't drink and drive

Rosemary Morris

Love To Share

Life without love is nothing.
We can strive but if it is for us alone
Life is empty.
We can wish and be disappointed
When our dreams do not come true
If the wish is for another and they succeed,
Life is full.

Happiness can be complete
When shared with those you love.
A touch, a smile, a loving glance,
Life is full
Thinking not of oneself alone
But how to please the ones who care,
You're not alone.

Life with love is everything.
The fullness of the life we share
Encompassing the world
Knits us closer together.
Life and love for everyone
Is everything.

Georgina Oakes

A Quizzical Poem

Watching the cats, Minstrel and Sophie
Who are watching something
Infinitesimal - a microscopic insect
Seen only by the blue eyes of Siamese Minstrel
And the yellow eyes of Burmese Sophie;
Watching movement or non-movement,
Knowing that this alien exists, they watch.
Time is of no consequence;
Waiting.
Why are they waiting?
In the presence of a superior being?
From another age?
Another place?
Another planet?
Perhaps an ancestral cat
Who served Bathsheba
Or the Queen - Cleopatra;
But now, in this time -
A microcosm,
Not seen by my human eye.

Nita D. Spac

Slavery

The sore and blistered hands,
Twisted round the plant
His dark, lifeless eyes
Are lifted towards the scorching sun.

The tired, cut feet,
Pattered on the floor,
Her aching arms carrying
The heavy basket of clothes.

The greedy plantation owner
Sits basking in the sun
Sipping his ice-cold drink,
Watching his slaves at work.

The frightened slaves cowering
On the hard and dusty floor.
The harsh cruel laugh of their owner splits the air,
His whip still red with blood.

The plantation owner smiles,
Safe and warm inside his house,
Showing no remorse for what he's done
While his slaves lie bleeding in the barn.

Kathryn Steenson

Life Begins At Fifty-One

Life Begins At Fifty-One, it certainly was true for me,
I looked at life in a different way and could more clearly see
So much more in every way, my understanding just grew,
Things that bewildered in the past suddenly I just knew.

My mind seemed to stretch to a larger expanse
That demanded knowledge - I had been given another chance,
School was a pain and I couldn't wait to leave,
But later I realized that only myself did I deceive.

So much to learn, so much to do,
My brain clicked into gear - and my heart too,
They worked together well, life was such fun
To start to learn was really to live At The Age Of Fifty-One.

My energy and enthusiasm came in frequent bursts,
That all joined together - like winning many firsts,
Fifty-One! What a wonderful age for life to start anew,
How many others share this with me, I really hope quite a few.

The reason for the happiness now I am ready to tell,
I discovered a way to help others and believed I could do it well,
Now I study and practice the best that ever I can
Filled with the joy of knowing - I can help my fellow man.

Celia Young

Treasured Love

When love comes calling on the wind
In spring's eternal murmurings
You to me mean everything
You've always been with me old flame.

When love is here in a blissful way
I know that in my heart you'll stay
And life's been good I'm happy to say
Treasured memories are kept in a special way.

If we could make our happiness last
And dwell on shared childhood's past
But we must keep up with the times
But remember the star that always shines.

If I could have just one wish
It would be to tell you this
That all my love has not been in vain
I'll save enough for another day.

When birds sing on a summer's day
Some enchanted evening you'll pass my way
And you will come to me gently
And our love will be forever free.

Neil Gilley

Sharing

No more joy-rides, crashing gears
In stolen cars for pleasure
On Christmas day I'm sixteen years
An age that I will treasure!

Orphaned when my parents died
When I was only seven
My birthday's swamped by Christmastide
For some guy down from Heaven?

Why should He have all the fun
And see beneath the tree
Lovely presents by the ton?
No single one for me!

But now I've learned of Christ who shared
The same day of my birth
And when His suffering I compared
With my own life on Earth

I knew it would be all in vain
If I did not repent
I wished I could have shared His pain
I would be then, content.

Ronald Chantry

The Final Dawn

Alone I stand looking down on sandy tombs
Alone but in my thoughts we live
As soft winds gather thought into memories

You look from your life and smile at me,
We who wanted so much happiness, love,
You who are so much like we were

Kings and Queens no more, only the fox and a crow remain
To remind me of what we once were,
As golden days with showers of light vision shimmered,
But desire took us to where only intentions remain
Leaving life with questions never to resolve
For we have gone forever, now merely in memory alone

But from the dust we arise like the phoenix
Again to guide but not to lead so our journey must be brief
Like the flash of light that laid us down

Down to your destiny to live in a world where seas of sand
Meet the sea of hope and live eternally in eternity,
Now shimmering visions take us to the river source
Where all futures must be
For boundless and endless endures eternity.

Paul Robertson

Wanderlust

To see the world, that's what I'd love.
Golden sands beneath the feet, waving palms above,
Balmy breezes, drifting over surf-kissed shores.
All of this to see, and more,
I'd like to visit all those lands of history,
Of ruins, legends, steeped in mystery.
Fairy tale castles, with maybe, musical fountains.
I want to be there, in the forests, the valleys, the mountains.
Oh!, to descend from snowcapped peaks glistening and white
Please?, to be aboard that liner, gliding out of port at night.
Tiny villages with friendly people to meet
National dress to see, traditional food to eat,
Sadly, midst all this wonderland, there creeps a shade of grey,
Where sorrow seems to deepen day by day,
War, famine, lands of disease, and race against races.
People with poverty, pain, and hurt worried faces,
True, an ideal world would be perfection to roam.
Returning always of course, to that special place, home.

C. M. Morgan

Child Memoirs

Young, what is young, nothing more than a word.
Something people compare you to young.
You may be young, but young is just a word,
Nothing more or less, just an adjective.

People are there pulling faces and speaking weird
'Isn't she cute, looks just like her mother'
Mother, what is mother, just a word or noun.
No mother loves, mother cares, mother knows best.

Bright lights and songs but once a year.
Birthdays, what are birthdays?
Time to give, share or receive, does it matter?
It only comes once a year.

Like a word, you're born, you live, you die.
You come into the world one way, go out another,
Some say you come back a tree, a bird or an insect
The choice isn't yours.

Louisa Lloyd

What Will There Be

What will the future be
for descendants of me
Will the sea be free of oil
Will the snake always uncoil

Will dolphins be alive and free
To happily dive in the sea
Will there be such a thing as pure clean air
Or a rabbit or a hare
What will there be for descendants of me

Sarah Appleby

All Alone

I am all alone now, my parents have gone away.
They've gone to a far and distant land,
I know they're there to stay.
In their memory a statue I have made
but no more they're here protect me. I am so afraid...
What shall I do? Where shall I go?
I have all these questions, and answers I do not know.
When I was at the funeral, all my friends were there.
It was most annoying, it was at me they seemed to stare.
As the flower hit the coffin, it gave the slightest tap
but that slight tap to me seemed like the loudest rap
I had ever heard before.
I really miss my parents, my feelings I can't explain.
The only way I try is by saying "I'm in Pain".
I know I can't bring them back;
If I could, God knows I'd try.
But that's the way life goes,
So I'll have to say goodbye.

Patricia Rooney

Remembering

Closing my eyes I drift far away.
To passing days of lingering May.
The smells, the sounds of memories last,
have gone to rest for future's past.
Echoing voices of people gone by,
Mother, father, little Joe Boy.
I open my eyes to dampen the tears,
O' God how I wish my dears were so near.
Shadowing the distance I grasp a faint smile,
O' look everyone. It's little Joe Boy.
I've gone to the world,
with the beautiful light.
Homeward rest, I'll say good night.

Geraldine Fenton

Bend The Knee

Scent of incense on the air, swirling shafts of light,
Fiery cross upon the wall, piercing eyes so bright.

Calming coolness, marble chill, bend the knee and bend the will;
Supplication heaven bound,
Silent statues sanction sound.
Footfalls echo, whispers shout, countless souls are here about;
Hear their spirits conversation,
Smell the flesh degeneration.
Threads of music mist the altar, soaring angel voices falter,
Faith and adoration calling,
Fearful of a hellish falling.
Bend the knee and bend the will, God's right hand is with you still,
Offer up your supplication,
Spirits lone repatriation.
See how stone has worn away, hear how quietly men have lay,
Touch the coffin's polished wood,
Here I lie as soon you should.

B. Roberts

Heart And Mind

In the heart's domain, the human feelings are revealed,
While in the head's domain incessant thoughts are there concealed.
Both guide us in our deeds through active will,
Which, being the flywheel of our daily life, controls us still.

These three then are servants of the human being,
Continually they mould our life without us seeing;
And, if we will it so, all three are subject to our higher part;
Which, with consent, a form of guidance will impart.

Roland Store

One Troubled Stormy Day

A troubled girl sat bored in her room,
With her music playing lyrics of boom.
She sat writing, pen to paper,
When thunder sounded she did caper.
When thunder finished, lightening struck,
Oh this troubled girl's breath it took.
Earlier that day she had fought with her folks,
She sat and wondered why do women need blokes.
As it was herself she did fear,
But she knew deep down her folks loved her and were always near.
Yet she sat there frightened, trying to stay calm,
And deep down she knew thunder and lightening
would do her no harm.
The lights did flicker, now and again,
And pitter patter on the window did sound the rain.
She turned off the radio and put in a tape,
Then she pressed play, she was trying to escape.
A diff voice (But what was she trying to escape from)

She needed to break, she had to get away
From the sounds of thunder and lightening
    on this troubled stormy day.

Danielle Louise Bagley

Drought

The faded sky backs dark flocks,
Birds that hunger assemble early.
New clouds pan south
Dripping bones and feathers.

The scarecrow, bucket head,
Boldly, stand stinks,
Guards his blank, brown cards.

Even the worms remain in their underworld
Navigating the nest's battlefield.

The wind blows dry, dry,
Throwing the leaves ashes,
Husks spilling want seed.

The sun tracks the heavens
Flaunting his flaming corona edges.
Here earthly name rakes
Turn whorled-seed faces upwards in the heat's haze.
Silent cable, bare on show,
Stumble old hoop-holes to the streams dank trickle

Over-burnt, rank hedges,
The evening guests spiral a rain-dance.

S. D. Lewis

The Sea

The sea is a mystery,
Filled with unknown parts ,
From all aspects of the world,
Messages in bottles,
Floating on wayward waves,
of blue and green.
Seagulls dive bomb, around the sea,
Like fighter planes,
Swarming onto their targets.
The sea crawls up the golden moist sand
And covers it like a blanket.
Then, after a time,
Comes back down the beach
And releases the sand from its sleep
And lets the sun shine, to glisten on the top of the sand,
Like a sprinkling of sugar on a cake.
The sea is wonderful,
The sea is ruthless,
Breathing life and sometimes, taking it—
The sea.

Ed Finnegan

Society 1995

There's assault and rape of young and old,
and "do-gooders" who think we should only scold.
The police radar can see through the ground,
to find murder victims who there abound.

Boy racers kill with their stolen cars,
the public copy them after visiting "bars."
Have they conscience or is it subliminal,
should we not treat them all like criminals.

We build our houses on piles of waste,
put chemicals in food to enhance the taste.
Whilst some ministers live in "ivory towers",
and spend their time misusing their powers.

The soldiers with guns told guard our borders,
get put in prison for shooting marauders.
But just next door there is civil war,
among the extremists who are crazy for more.

The whole of society is damned for sure,
unless governments take action we do implore.
They'll condemn our children to a living hell,
before they toll the planet's death knell.

John M. Franks

Lost Love

Tears flow freely, show the pain
How long before I smile again
To see a place we used to go
Recognize a face we both would know
Memories stay, though love has gone
Racking my mind, where did we go wrong
Get a new life, must be right
Meeting new friends is not such a plight
How to start again when we had it all
Why ever did we let it fall
Like autumn leaves upon a tree
A united couple, just you and me
Began to crumble, fall apart
Split into two, a now broken heart
One must go on, just has to survive
Join a new group, start coming alive
Very easy to say, not easy to do
When the heartbreak has not happened to you
Time will heal, the tears will dry
One day common-sense will tell me why.

Jean Charles-Mumford

The Shape Of Love

The love of God goes round and round
Like an ever-growing circle.
Its limits knows no earthly bounds
For God's love is a miracle.

The love of God is like a square
Encompassing all safely within:
A free gift, most precious and rare,
Never-ending, bringing us back to Him.

The love of God is like a triangle,
Reaching out to us from every angle,
Showing the awkward and unlovely
To be equal with the good and holy.

The love of God is like a straight line
That goes on and on forever.
It can be yours. It can be mine,
If the line we do not sever.

The love of God is like a cross,
Pointing us onwards to the Heaven,
But with arms outstretched: the cost of love,
So that we may all be The Forgiven.

S. J. Wilson

Moon, Stars, Sun

The moon, it shines, oh so bright,
Within the darkness of the night,
A beautiful, glowing silver sphere,
Waxing and waning throughout the year,
Shining nightly for all it's worth,
As it orbits around the earth.

The stars, some glitter burning white,
Such a truly glorious sight,
Others red, orange and blue,
Twinkling dots, the whole night through,
Millions of light years away,
They disappear with light of day.

The sun, a fiery yellow ball,
The mightiest star of them all,
Its rays of ultra violet hue,
Bringing warmth to me and you,
Then setting daily in the west,
Having given us its best.

Nicola Cooke

Haunted (The Room)

The emptiness of this silence is demanding,
a silence to be reckoned with, waiting its due.
Not one for sitting in quiet reflection, but a sickening demand
something is overdue and won't wait much longer.

The rug stairs back at me knowing my uneasiness,
Its pattern somehow large and surreal.
The past has eaten the future, too many needs clambering for now,
something must do without, one existence overlapping another.

Who will say stop, it's over, they have all gone, this is just an
insane echo, the air stagnant with greed and good intentions.
The room cares not for explanations, it clicks, it fingers impatiently
and asks—Have you come to pay?!

Does anyone listen to the room?!
Each day the insane babble goes on, thick and incongruous, hard
against soft, rough against smooth, the endless thumping of insanity
and plain ignorance.
The room is sick, needs time to heal.
The night isn't long enough to bring results, only a cowering
respite for the daily onslaught.
The TV sits in abeyance held back by the switch,
the room creaks and moans its distorted form tries to sleep whilst standing.
There is something trapped that must be freed—give it back sometime.

Barbara Brandolani

Oh, Blessed Day

Summer in all her splendour ebbing on the tide of time, cooler breezes
whispering their little songs amongst tree branches green and roses
vibrant, sharing beauty for all to see. Yellow and green ivy with
fingers spread, climbs up your wall ever onward on house so tall.
Blue skies with fluffy white clouds skipping across the heavens.
Large and small trees, bushes huddled in long rows holding hands
tightly giving strength and withholding the cooler, sharper feel,
protecting bird's nest amidst the vine. Pretty green fields hiding
their secrets from us, homes for creatures small, seldom seen by
human invaders passing by with thunderous tread, sheltering, awaiting
silence and safety before they peep and venture out into their busy
life this day. My window and thoughts unveiled for me to see the
wonders of nature, with humility. I cross boundaries beyond compare
confined thus upon settee, swathed in plaster from big toe to knee!
The joys and enraptured beauty do fill my heart, sun shining for all,
bringing God's love of creation forever imprinted upon my heart.
There is no time or conclusion to nature's pattern, this painting
God's brush brought for all to see brings contentment, radiance,
peace, love and tranquillity. This late summer day, beauty and
splendour reach out to me, and at God's request I shut my eyes and lay
me down to rest in bliss. His colourful beams of light have my day blessed.

Barbara Mary Sheffield

What Lies Ahead?

Can we really know the truth of what lies ahead?
Will things really improve in the way it has been said?
Or will we destroy each other, before we understand the reasons why?
We have to stop this fighting, at least we have to try

All around us so much suffering, destruction, disease
People filled with fear, anger and unease
Parents cry in disbelief, their children cry in pain
We've tried before to stop this, but we have to try again

We are all the same inside, why can't people understand?
Why are we aiming weapons? When we should be shaking hands?
It is possible to stop these wars, in which so many have been killed?
We can all pull together and start a programme to rebuild

I am looking to the future, through eyes of yesterday
I can see a place of safety, where my children they can play
I am looking at a time when peace has been achieved
Can this be reality, or will it only ever be a dream?

M. A. Gardner

Untitled

The snow falls
It touches her heart and melts
The child who longs to play
Is an adult

She cries and her tears turn to ice
She forgot to care
She lost so much
And yet felt so little

The snow falls
Paints a picture of her youth
The memory of emotions
She wants to care but doesn't know how

Time goes by
She misses the warmth of her mother
And the protection of her father
If she falls there is no one to catch her

She mourns the passing of her childhood
And the disintegration of her dream
She no longer believes in fairy tales
And dreams only when she sleeps

M. Neal

Mother's Day!

I wish there was no such thing as
Mother's Day
"Why"?
Because if you're forgotten
It makes you feel Rotten
"Rotten"?
Yes. It makes your guts Ache
and you Cry
that's why.

The millions of chocolates and flowers
and cards...
But none

I'm not a bad Mum and I am all alone.
He's been busy. I'm sure that he's tried
After all
I'm his Mum every single day
of the year
Hang on! Hold the Cat!
That's the phone??

Diana Matches

Not Just Neighbours

What is a neighbour you may ask
When no one helps you with a task
The ones who lived next door to you
Once were so kind and helpful too

If you or them left for a break
Your homes were guarded for each one's sake
You could enjoy your holiday
For your homes were safe both night and day.

If you were seen by someone limping
Your neighbours rushed to do your shopping.
You had no need to ask for helpers
There was a rush of willing workers

Who heard of chains fixed to each door?
Except in prisons, and rightfully so
But now the boot is on the other foot
We are like prisoners, no one cares a hoot.

It's time we recognized our plight
It's time to stand for our own right
Let's hasten back to the good old days
Let's help each other, and mend our ways.

Islwyn Davies

Ashes To Ashes

This tobacco industry is sure one Hell of a racket,
Long even before the days, when woodbines cost seven pence per packet.
In those days of course we didn't fully appreciate the danger,
We saw Big John Wayne rolling up, a law-enforcing Texas Ranger.
There was no such thing then as government - health - warning,
First thing after tea, we'd light up the early morning.
Big John smoked sixty a day, as he swaggered around town.
A hero to one and all, that is until John Player shot him down.
On the screen we watch the gangsters, it was puff after puff,
We soon followed suit, just because we thought we were tough.
Doctors say cigars are safe, very hard to comprehend,
Where was Churchill when he smoked his first one? Right there at the end.
Nicotine is a deadly poison, like strychnine, or cocaine,
Yet we disregard the warnings, all of them going in vain.
Half of men's pay-packets may well end up in dust,
While on the kitchen-table, there may not even be a single crust.
Take a look at your fingertips, all burned a chestnut brown,
Imagine what your breath is like? Enough to knock one down.
It's time to call a halt friend, before your time here is curtailed,
As the priest says "Ashes to Ashes" and your last breath you've exhaled.

Sean McDermott

Guidance From Spirit

My father with his strong hand had already guided me through
the ups and downs of life's path. I imagined him being there forever
but I recently held his hand as he passed over to spirit.

So, I search for meaning now, at thirty four, my eyes and mind
probe far into the sky, like a child needing an explanation.

I feel I might see him within the clouds, hand lifted to wave
goodbye to me, his youngest child, I wave at times in response
to my imaginings, just in case; I feel so alone and sad.

I can't see my father at all now, it's hard to accept,
though I can feel his spirit at times around me, mainly
when I'm low and need encouragement, motivating and comforting.

I shed tears for his physical presence although deep
inside I do acknowledge his guidance still ever present in my life.

I wish his life hadn't ended for my own selfish reasons,
I miss him so much, my base has gone and so feel
rather adrift. For him though I'm certain he's loving
every moment of the adventures on the spirit plain as
much as he loved his physical life and his family.
So Dad, keep on eye on me as you've always done and
I'll keep looking out for you in those clouds.

Katrina Thomas

Full Circle

The saddest thing I ever saw was genius with a fatal flaw
Who broke the rules then broke the law in pure frustrated rage.

Whose inner strife too often sucked the skill to play, dictate, conduct
And drove him on to self destruct on such a public stage.

His self-set standards with the ball have been sublime and thrilled us all
Such heights to hit—such depths to fall, our roller coaster star.

The final straw that raised this shroud ? Just one more moron in the crowd
Wrong place, wrong time, wrong words too loud, wrong ego pushed too far.

This time there'll be no place to hide, he must dig deep beneath that pride
And quell the beast that lurks inside, his hardest match of all.

So come what may, I'll treasure still those cameos of perfect skill
The vision, the power, the pace, the thrill when Eric had the ball.

But two years on the tongues are stilled, the double double dream fulfilled
Both fans and critics simply thrilled as Selhurst's ghosts are laid.

The King is back, his skills admired, with self control—not temper fired
By fifty thousand fans inspired, their loyalty repaid.

Chris Godfrey

Going Home

It beckoned me with open arms, like a jewel shining in a distant crown.
As I drew nearer the jewel disappeared and all I saw was a dingy town.
As people rushed by me I looked for a sign of recognition, or maybe more.
In despair I found none and began to feel like I watched from a far off shore.
Had I belonged here? Was this my home? The thought of this was so strong.
I had wanted to come back. Perhaps I'd been foolish, perhaps I'd been wrong.
I walked on to the house I'd come to see. The paint was all peeling, the lawns overgrown.
I'd caused so much heartache. The fear welled inside me, would I still be known.
He answered my knock, he'd grown weary and old since I'd started to roam.
Suddenly eyes smiled at me, arms opened wide. I'm forgiven at last, now I'm home.

Sylvia Watt

What Country Means To Me

A country song is all I long for, one with country in mind. A
haunting lullaby of days gone by, of right and wrong, keeping on the
right trail, these modern day songs don't the heart at all an old
fashioned country song can beat those heartache blues only in a country song.

A country story of loves lost and won. The lives the people of times past,
Long ago in the west, cowboys cowgirls too, country towns along the trail
The stories, of a country's past the heroes the heroines,
live again in a country song, can beat those heartache blues only in a country song.

Beautiful thoughts pictures, of imagination, captured in a beautiful song
Coloured with stories of a country people, country ways can cure those heartache blues,
How I love those country songs of days gone by
stories of a country's past, old glory days filled with a heart of
country pride can live again in a country song, it's a cure for those
heartache blues only in a country song.

A heart filled with country pride in yourself, the meaning of what
Country stands for, right against wrong love before hate friendship
is what country means to me, I will always be a country girl at heart
with the values of those past forgotten days, gone by is what country means to me.
Country ways country days, in a country song can beat
those heartache blues, only in a country song.

Janet Middleton

Matrimonial Thanks

There is a reason why I'm so glad that you were chosen as my mom and dad.
You both stand out from all the crowd, and always try to make me proud.

I thought that on my Wedding Day would be the perfect time to say:
All my thanks I offer you, for everything you say and do.

As my father you walk me down the aisle, beside me with a confident smile.
They say that on your wedding day, the father gives his daughter away.
This is not true, you won't lose me, your little girl I'll always be.

Our special day is finally here, I owe a lot to mother dear.
You advised me on my Wedding dress, and helped me cope with all the stress.
I don't know what I would have done if you were not there to be my mum.

You guided me through my trouble and strife, and set me along the path of life.
I will not say goodbye to you, but still you'll shed a tear or two.
You don't have anything to fear, for my parents I'm always close and near.

Nicola Taylor

My Lonely Star

Dangling fingers in the dim waters of a long forgotten dream,
I could not grasp the slippery essence of the greeny-ghostlike bream-
Wavering below the rippling surface, as I sought and sought for shapes
To lead me down that happy pathway once again. Cool willow drapes
Curtained the banks where I lay in quiet reverie, - and I wept
With them, as the dream through jagged rocks and tumbling waters swept.

And slowly the darkness descended and wrapped me all around.
The sky was one with earth, with trees' soft sighing sound
Above the tumbling waters. Cold and disbelieving, I rose to see
One lonely star, a symbol of eternity, a sign to guide the free.
And stumbling here and there upon the unlit path, caught by cruel stone,
Knowing the fault was largely mine, the pathways that I chose alone.

Dark and lonely was the night, - no rest or comfort to be found until
The dawn. A lightening towards the East made me pause, - my soul stood still -
For all around my lonely star, a crowd of stars in Glory sung.
A beauty I had missed, so bowed my head, so full of pity wrung.
I fell upon my knees once more, but not to search for dreams, -
For knowing I was not alone, - could swim - not dangle, in those streams.

A. L. Taylor-Kent

The Princess

She sat on her throne a-holding court;
　A vision of beauty and grace.
Her flowing robes a joy to behold
　For her subjects who flocked to that place.

They offered their homage, their heads bowed low
　Save some who peeped a mite;
Knowing she saw but would forego
　A transgression so harmless and trite.

She lifted her gaze to the fields beyond.
　She claimed all she could behold.
Then lowered it down to the treasures below;
　Silks and diamonds and gold.

Soon all of these wonders would fade away
　And innocence youth and play.
And life may be harsh or tender or plain
　And never be good as this day.

No real princess had a reign like this,
　Or subjects ever finer.
Among the rags and the plastic bags
　And the jewels made of broken china.
　　Bill Sisk

Nothing Leads To Shelter

Cry softly, as not to wake the wolves,
For if their dreams are then disturbed
Their anger shall unite,
They'll see you there in your despair
and think not of your woe,
But leap to cease your mind and heart,
And then digest your soul.

Take heed my friend and ache in silence,
For pity, as their hearts, is cold,
Turn around and down the hillside soon
Before the night is old.

They wake in fright, their eyes delight
To see your timid frame,
You start to move with unsure step
Whilst fear consumes your brain,
They start to circle, with mouths so wet,
Their hunger now insane,
With pain removed, your death is quick,
Your anguish all in vain.
　　Fiona Roache

Roadside Flowers

Oh call us not weeds
We are flowers of the verge.
Dandelion, buttercup, thistle and spurge.
Don't plough us, don't spray us
Just leave us to be
So all folks around
Our bright colours will see.
　　Sheila Turner

The Pharaoh

Caught in the tomb-embalmer's wax he lies,
Snared, and ground-tied.
No rushes whisper him to sleep,
Nor does he wake more, open-eyed,
To gaze on Egypt's wonders.

Dead in the hot pyramid's core he dreams,
Dreams not; bound fast.
A captive in his self-styled cell,
He feels not heat, nor icy blast
Of night winds on the desert.

Wrapped deep in scents of centuries long gone,
He lies, a shell.
A Pharaoh aged, untouched by age;
And after him, his Egypt fell,
Like hot sand in a dust-storm.
　　Anne Rolfe Brooker

On The Death Of A Beloved Husband

You are gone,
And I am left alone to carry on.
We loved each other for so many years
It is so hard to hide the tears
Now you are gone.

You are gone,
And I know that I must carry on,
You would not want me to be sad and sigh,
So I try to laugh, but inside I cry
Because you are gone.

You are gone.
And I know that I will carry on.
One day we will meet again
And laugh and hold hands again.
But you are gone.
　　Barbara J. Pagett

A Baby's Dream

I wonder if I'll like it when the time comes to be born,
to leave this watery sanctuary—where it's beautiful and warm.

I wonder if I'll like it when it's time to learn to talk,
and if I'll ever get the hang of learning how to walk.

I wonder if I'll like it when it's time to go to school,
to work and play with others and not to feel a fool.

I wonder if I'll like it when I have to seek employment.
It could be somewhat difficult and not give much enjoyment.

I wonder if I'll like it when it's time to settle down,
with a partner for some company, in Country or in Town.

I wonder if I'll like it when my family is all grown,
with my bones all getting weary and the future so unknown.

I wonder if I'll like it when my days are nearly through,
and the years are all behind me, and I'm always feeling blue.

I wonder if I'll like it when the time comes for me to die,
to travel to an unknown place, some say beyond the sky.

I wonder if my soul will rise and look down upon the earth,
and gaze on future mothers who will soon be giving birth.
I wonder!!!
　　Doreen Massey

Foreign

Tokyo and smitten stunned in Bangkok, your being
Stirs a long dormant passion.

Again at Chiang Mai emotions collide, but when
Can one tell love that is true?

Third time, or fifth month?
What clock determines our fate?
Butterflies live just three weeks.

How will we learn how hot cool the water?
One sage said to taste is to know.

And when I had lost myself deep down those eyes
Perhaps it was just wistful thinking
But wasn't that you gazing back?

Two orphans huddle trembling in a corridor, grasping
And whispering to the night
Bumping heads into hearts.

And I said August in Ireland but why not Shanghai in the Spring?
Or to go for a stroll out along the Great Wall
To sea from within and out over the bridge
Best yet come to Cork where I am 92% certain

Gulp Gasp And Wow!
　　David G. McAuliffe

My Life, My Spirit

On horse back I ride,
Through the cold night air I glide,
Alongside my honour and pride.
I am not afraid,
For I have my shield to protect me.
To save me from horrors and doom.
From all nastiness and gloom.
I proudly ride on,
Like a knight in shining armour.
Charging into battle.
The sun rises, my fearful worries melt.
At last I've found what I've been looking for,
My delusion, dream stood before me.
I reached out and touched the bright, golden flames,
I caught it,
To bring the spirit of the flame into my soul.
For that is where the spirit lies,
Beyond that golden gates of the fire,
Waiting for me to give it freedom and life....
My life, my spirit.

Rebecca Council

He Remembers...........

When the Light of the World was with men but unseen,
and angels could fly through his tree boughs of green.

He felt mother's embrace and sang carols tender,
amidst howling snowstorms came warmth from the fender.

Memories and ghosts, and stories so tall,
fixed a child's gaze through his window, would icicles fall?

The school is remembered, the yard filled with laughter,
and snowballs he threw flown high to the rafter.

Girls' giggles, boys' shrieks, friends' hearts full with glee,
he remembers what Christmas time, it used to be.

The hope of surprises and promise to come,
vanquished with look on small face when day's done.

With sadness and heartache and longing for more,
but contented with memories, his heart it would store.

So the ice, it was melting, and sun winked between trees,
in the clearing a figure had sank to its knees.

And coal that had stared out forlorn, as an eye,
the snowman he knew that his passing was nigh.

Couldn't alter the seasons, halt sure march of time,
as the joys of that Christmas became memories mine.....

Paul L. Cowell

The Wall Of Silence

If I reached through the silence,
    would that I find her there;
So forlorn a figure: victim of
    an earlier time
And its legacy of pain that
    does not go away
For brute force was used on her
    and fear remains today.

Her silence is a safety-net, it
    protects and cannot harm;
Nothing can penetrate it, it
    offers a kind of balm
But like an umbrella, used as
    a shield too long
It forms a barrier that blocks the radiance of the sun.

If I reached through the silence and pulled her gently forth
What would be her reaction?
Would she interpret it as force?
For amidst the silence I hear a plea
To end the pain and set her free.

Carol M. Judd

My Childhood Hedgerows

People speak of days gone by
The things they did, which they recall
Of hedgerow blooms, the feathered plumes
Of birds among the trees so tall
When I reach back to childhood days
The things I did when I was small
My hedgerows were the crumbling ruins
Or terraced slums and bombed, scarred walls
On disused land we'd make a world
Of make believe as children do
No feathered plume, or hedgerow bloom
Could e'er outshine the magic hue
Of treasure found, midst broken stones
With dirty hands we searched for dreams
Buttons, beer tops long discarded
Shone to us like soft moonbeams
With broken glass, (called 'Banny Mugs')
A treasured find, like flowers rare
We'd sell for gold just old cracked mugs
We'd found amongst our hedgerows there

Lilian Glanister

The Direction

Can you really know what love is?
The way your heart burns and fills with layers of
unexplained passion,
But what if that passion and burning desire is
swept away,
Emptiness, the feeling is hollow,
Emotions mixed up and confused all echoing around my soul,

That is love, one minute it is there then you never
know the direction or flow your love shall go . . .

Diane Raines

The Six Weeks School Holiday

If I could only have a minute of myself,
This six week school holiday is driving me to mental health.
Wherever I seem to go, I can rely on the children to always show.
When I'm relaxing in the bath, the three of them walk in,
just for the laugh.
There's laughing and giggling when I'm on the phone,
Oh! Come on kids, leave me alone.
'Where's my place gone in my bed,'
That's not my husband, it's those kids instead.
I'm tidying their clothes, picking up their litter,
My bloody temper's getting bitter and bitter
The six weeks school holiday has been and now ended,
My furniture looks nice again, now it's mended.
Blimey why is it, it has to be?
The kids are back at school, but I'm wishing
they were home with me!

Susan Barnett

Shattered Dreams

Whatever I cared about I was deprived of,
Whatever mattered to me I lost,
Even your love slowly faded away,
And I was left all alone.

Now that you've deserted me so meanly,
Who'll care about me when I'm lonely and sad.
Who'll hold me in the dark cold winter days of sadness,
Who will I be able to love?

You're the only one I ever truly cared for,
you've let me care, you've even let me love,
And then you decided it's time to move on,
and leave me and my feelings behind.

But where in the world does this leave me.
It leaves my feelings shattered and my body deprived,
And as I watch the sunshine settle, behind the darkened hills,
I feel my morale slip away, far away, nowhere to be found.

Sanja Soldat

Untitled

Willingly offer to provide the light
Remove the opaque shroud
See them not as tasks to endure
But freely offer thyself

Enter the world beneath the surface
Hear the tales told in faith
Trusting arms wrap tightly
Soothing whispers rock gently
Erase the silhouetted memories that harbour doubt

Discover the strength
Explore this abandoned realm
Ride the white water created by emotions
Entwining souls bathe in fragrance sweet
Nurture this purity

P. A. Heppinstall

Love

Love is oh so blind
It's all in your mind
The man of your dreams,
Is not all he seems.
You think you've found the right one
But sooner or later he has gone.
It's hard to think you could love another
For once you wished you'd listened to mother
Men treat love as if it's a game
All in all have no shame
Why should we sit and grieve
When there's better things to achieve?

Victoria Redford

Growing Old

Now youth has gone, the years have quickly sped,
Down memory lane, my thoughts have fondly fled
To the days of careless chatter,
When tomorrow didn't matter,
When each day was so inviting,
And the evenings so exciting,
When men were kind and very charming
How they've changed is quite alarming.
When my babies were so pretty
They're grown up now, it's such a pity.
These halcyon days fly far too fast,
If only one could make them last.
Now I live a life of ease
Doing mostly what I please.
Now my life is much more stable
I do the things that I am able.

G. E. Yates

Summer

Hot days and humid nights
a sense of summer
The smell of hops across the river
The beer gardens
The late nights
Long days at the beach
Pointless days in vocation
Children eating ice cream on the way to school
Every chance we get going to the pool
Bus stops and short sleeve shirts
Tennis on the TV
masses of people invade the sea
Summer nights
Summer nights long and fresh
Walk thru town baring flesh
Convertible cars
Alfresco bars
Life goes slow, never fast
Enjoy yourself, have a blast.

Lee McCabe

Glueminous The Dragon

Glueminous the dragon was such a sorry sight
He tried to practice flame-throwing in the middle of the night
No matter how he tried, the flames just wouldn't come.
And all that Glueminous managed to do, was to go and burn his bum
Poor, poor Glueminous, he couldn't raise a spark,
Not even a smoke cloud, or a sparkle in the dark.
He tried to light a candle to see the flickering glow.
But all he got from that as the wax began to flow,
Was a sticky, smelly blob for all the world to see.
What a failure poor Glueminous could be.

Oh to breath fire, was Glueminous's dream.
So with a mighty puff, he gave a tremendous scream.
At first there was a flicker, and then a hint of smoke,
And then a little flame appeared, which made old Glueminous choke.
He got so excited and jumped around with glee.
"I can now breathe fire' oh lucky, lucky, me".
Now old Glueminous was happy.
As all good dragons should be.

Valerie Johnston

If Only

If only, I was born in a different time,
A different place, a different world,
My life would be my own.

Instead, what am I?

A mother, a wife, a cleaner, a cook,
Someone to turn to
When answers cannot be found in a book.

Instead, I am expected,

To be cheerful all the time,
Ready to listen and offer advice,
Solve their problems,
But, who will solve mine?

If only, I was born in a different time,
A different place, a different world,
My life would be my own.

What am I doing? What is the use?
Of reflecting on, if only?
It's not so bad, it's not so sad,
At least in my dreams
I can be me

Kashmir Randhawa

A Winsome Lass

O lovely maid whose gentle breast,
Of many endearing charms possessed,
With eyes of purest ray serene,
Of azure blue soft touched with green.
Rustic brown like gossamer her hair
And roseate cheeks not lined with care.
Full bowed her lips of rubious hue,
Moist blushed like early morning dew.
Swan-like the neck with skin of daisy white,
Soft lobed her ears part hid from sight.
Her shoulders stooped, but not in servile mood,
The sculptured frame from hallowed nature hewed
So shapely limbed with lithesome figure,
Toil worn, but still brim full of vigour.
Pale, slender hands with long-fingered skill
Cool and smooth to touch, yet tiny still.
A nymphal body with health of gladsome ray;
Her welcome presence to gild each happy day.
May perpetual joys around her always spring
With rapturous blessings each new year bring.

Bryan Colman Bird

Imprisoned Land

For years this land was left
Almost lay to transform
To a more natural state

Spared the suffocation
Of multinational grow faster chemicals
And incarceration from stainless steel
Prison walls

Animals mingled freely
With little to impair their way.
Even the fox had a name
and a place to eat.

But now that landlord has gone.
A more commercially viable
And financially aware warden
Has taken over.

The stainless steel glistens in the summer sun
The work has begun on a one way system
To renovate barns and farmhouse condos

As he rides past on his four wheeled bike
It's easy to tell if any inmates have escaped
Just read the numbers spray painted on their fleece

Sean Higgins

A Mind Of My Own

A pink dress? Bright pink?
I'd rather wear the kitchen sink!
Visions of terror filled my head,
I was trying to figure out what would be said.
An important party, an important day,
People would tell me just to go away.
They'd feel embarrassed, and so would I,
I might as well just die.

I thought I could fight against her, it would be a cinch.
But now I must be dreaming, someone give me a pinch.
I can feel that she's winning, the dress is coming near.
But wait! An idea begins to appear.

Fight back against her, I'm thirteen now,
I've got to be independent, but how?
'Mad' I said aloud, 'You must be mad.'
'Your fashion sense is really sad!'
An expression of shock came across her face,
When she realized how hard I was pleading my case.
'Okay you win....' Yes independent at last!
But will life be as good as it was in the past?

Claire Blaymire

Capricious Sea

I've watched you playing idly, sea,
Your wavelets tease the sun-drenched beach,
Chuckling pebbles join your glee
Whilst o'erhead mocking sea birds screech.

I've watched you, too, on starlit night,
Phosphorous currents ebb and flow,
Moon-stitched sequins twinkling bright
Add final touches to the show.

Then, in that self-same night, I've seen
Dark storm clouds build where stars had been,
Whetted winds your billows thrash,
'Gainst trembling cliffs huge breakers crash.

The sea birds, now no longer flying,
No longer mock you with their crying,
But cringe, deep under ruffled wings,
Helpless, battered, frightened things.

I've watched your moods, majestic sea,
Your fury, your tranquillity.
I've watched you, and I've seen the sign
Of God's great hand in your design.

Terry Lewis

Depression

The darkness takes me down to that lonely place.
Beneath its hood I know there is no smiling face.
In that awful blackness I can taste the sour breath
Of whispering nightmares that only sweeten death.

Nearby the screaming damned rage at time that's past
And wring their hands at fate, and their life chances lost.
While far in the distance the forgotten souls lie;
Alone they are waiting for time to pass them by.

These are the tomb-cold cells of hopeless despair:
The prison in my mind that's waiting for me, where
Only the loving and those who would love could bear
To want to seek me out, and listen to me there.

William Mann

Fireworks

It was a dark night.
Everyone was waiting . . . waiting . . .
Waiting . . .
Then the fuse was lit on that dark night.

Crackle, fizzz
And off it went
Up and up and up it went.

Then, on that dark night, a second's silence fell

Whooosh zip
Then . . . Bang
Showers of stars
Pink, blue, green, yellow floating down on us.

Then nothing.

It was all quiet on that dark night.
The people stood waiting . . . waiting . . .
Waiting . . .

Kirsten Murray-Borbjerg

It Was Such A Cold November's Night

It was such a cold November's night,
You kissed my lips and held me tight.
Your eyes met mine this winter's night,
My heart went bang oh what a night.

Those memories kept deep in my heart,
Are special songs you sing sweetheart,
For my heart keeps growing more each day,
As I think about you night and day.

For I miss those twinkling eyes you see,
And wish you could be oh so close to me.
And though I may be married that's true,
My heart is yours stuck together like glue.
And though you are so long far gone,
I know one day we will be one.

Elizabeth Cotterill

My Village

Astwood bank lay
Dust enshrouded
Ghostly in the ridge way glooming
As dawn is breaking
We hear the birds
Singing so loudly as if to burst
If the day is clear you can see the hills
Which are the malverns so proud and still
Sometimes the tops look white with snow
Or is it the clouds that are very low
We are so lucky living in Astwood Bank
With beautiful views
And Gorsey Banks
It was a small place
But is now expanding
With shops and school
And a lovely church
People so understanding

S. B. Bird

Thoughts Of Pleasant Weather

Dewdrops glisten so sweetly upon the blades of grass,
Where distant rolls of thunder and bright lightning flash
Illuminate the darkness of a black blanket sky,
With the soft patter of raindrops - as heaven starts to cry,
Flickering beams of moonlight, like lanterns out at sea
Rise and fall across the ground, reaching out for me,
The tide is slowly turning, drowning out my speech
As I get taken down by eddy, spiralling out of reach.

The whispering wind comes wandering, along its wayward way,
Rippling ripening ears of corn and fluffy swaths of hay,
Rampant swirling whirlwinds - may bow to let it by,
Whilst gathering up our Lord's repast, to take home to the sky,
Poised - a kingfisher watches, expecting to catch the breeze,
Stickleback seem a better catch, lurking beneath the trees,
Cloaked in darkest shadow, the fish so hard to find
Our fisherman now leaves his perch to fly home with the wind.

Charles J. M. Ball

Wedding Bells

He had to forsake the sport of kings
To attend the wedding of friends
Tho' he never complained, he would have preferred
To be dealing in dividends

Lacking the thrill of the race track
He soon began to doze
Until he succumbed completely
Into a figure of "Sweet" repose

The church was hushed for this solemn affair
There wasn't even a cough
Until the communion bell was rung
And he stood and shouted: "They're Off!!!"

Trish Joyce

Loneliness

Three score years and ten have passed
And I am all alone
I don't walk very steadily
I ache in every bone

My life has been a happy one
With tears and laughter too
But gone are the sounds I used to hear
And friends I have but few

I am sitting by my fireside
With no-one here to care
My life is such an empty one
And sometimes hard to bear

The nights are dark and long drawn out
I silently shed a tear
Oh! To have some company
My last few years to share

I do not even own a pet to love and care for now
Nor loving hands of my family to stroke my wrinkled brow

With feeble hands I wind my clock for I must go to bed
With heavy heart and troubled mind to rest my weary head

Esther McCaig

The Enemy

An enemy have I, as thro' this life I roam.
In waking, working, or at rest, he leaves me not alone,
'Tis just as though he waits, upon my soul to prey.
And such is life I fear, he'll have his wish one day.
Waste not one breath will I, one second any hour,
Or sure as night meets day, that waste he will devour.
Into his coffers kept: Redeemable by none,
Goes time both waste, and spent until
My share is gone.
So as through life I go, unfettered seeming free,
To him I'm bound I know, my end, his victory.

T. Sempers

Fast Bends

Dirt spurts, mud flies, engine roars, then dies.
Tyres go round, crunch on gravel, steam pours
from red hot radiator

Steering wheel jerked, brake pushed in
Clutch, next gear, accelerate, accelerate
Too much fast bends

Hot inside helmet, gloves make hand itch
sweat tickles back, teeth gritted
last lap, sudden death, neck and neck
Go! Go! Go!

Faster! Faster!
landscape waves goodbye!
Crowd gasp fire behind
rival crashed.
Squeal of brakes, amazed crowd
runs to wreck, pulls out survivor
wreck explodes.
Loud bang! Cheers! - lost race
but saved life, hero, real sportsman,
Too many fast bends.

Stuart A. Herkes

Warp And Weft

From the dark recesses of an ageing mind
flows a dewy fresh dawn of innocence,
wafted by breezes over summer warm air,
just three frilly daises could she find.
Never enough for a necklace chain,
better one buttercupped chin - the kind
of thrill to lift childish joy - yet make no sense
when worldly worries are of pounds and pence.

Away fly the hours to squat and stare
as inky-penned studies took their rightful place
fast leading to commerce and grown up garb,
where skipping and fun were replaced by a barb,
till her intellect grew to challenge more space.

Career changed to house and house changed to chores,
Two into four - and scant time for leisure,
though start once again with the daisy chain lark
such was the substance of priceless pearl pleasure
to be found in her ageless dreamy filled park.
Is it still there? With poppies so red and sparrows to feed.
Yes! all you have read lives on in her head - memories of
Argents Mead.

Jose Dorothy Johnson

My Father

I see you sitting in your usual comfy, crumpled, chair
half-opened book falling from your padded lap with
your head lolling in a dream-filled sleep, hopefully
bringing lucid, untroubled memories to your aching mind
which your waking does not.

I remember the father who showed me the world, chasing
every wonder with magical energy
answering Mastermind questions with aplomb and
laughing at the beginning of each fresh day,
marvelling at life's miracles.

Where have you gone?

I find you trapped in silent stillness, begging with your eyes
to be the man you were before
some evil hand just took you and closed all escape.....
gently I will lead you, as a child, by the hand to bed
settling you peacefully with kiss upon your cheek
as once you settled me.

And then, I think, I'll weep.

Jane Thursby

Self-Loathing As Murder Weapon

A man died
Because
I was too shy
To give him
Mouth
    to
      Mouth.
I didn't want to be a hero
Being a model citizen wasn't up to me
Picked on at school
For being "Courteous" and "Studious"
The last thing I wanted
Was for people to look at me...

Life-saving skills were often covered on television
But I didn't have a certificate or anything
Was never known
For a steady hand, or precision
And besides, he was wearing
A wedding ring.

Dulmini Wimalasekera

Families

A closeness of indescribable measure
Without the sex a feeling of intense pleasure
You are alone, but always together
a mistake is made but forgiveness forever

The roots of your past are deeply embedded
Others will follow the path you have treaded
The green leaves of life and of what is to follow
The memories gone by encased deep in its hollow

For each it is different but for mine all the same
No scores ever taken for those in this game
The feeling of security, worth and of trust
The silver maybe tarnished though I know will never rust

Between one and many a hurt may be healed
Between one and all a memory sealed
Treasure what you have before it is lost
Hold on to it tightly whatever the cost

Shelley Poulter

A Fatal Life Sentence

You were at the point of no return
Trapped in the stare of a thousand eyes
Nowhere to turn
Swept on the wave of exposure
Of prying, grabbing hostility
Reaching, snatching for a memory
To capture that moment in time
You were seized, thrust into a light too bright
Incessantly harvested by indefinable greed
Never alone, even in deepest solitude
All barriers of seclusion devoured
By unknown friends
Condemned before you were truly known
A fatal life sentence.

G. C. Fanthom

To Paul

Give me your hand
and I shall weave a rainbow road for you to walk,
with colours bright.
Where sounds unheard are known to you.
And you shall be a little knight
sure of step, for there are dragons to be slain.
And victor in the battles done
will be the boy
that is the man
who knows the way along the path of colours bright,
and sounds unheard
and dragons gone.

Linda Liggett

Cynthia Cardui

I saw her again this morning
As she flitted through the trees,
She came with never a warning
To dine with the humming bees.

Taking nectar from the flowers,
Sipping water from the leaves,
I will stay and watch for hours
As her magic spell she weaves...

She took me by the hand and showed me
The sweetest flowers, the lightest kiss,
Each one tasted, savoured, lovingly
Held in a moment of utter bliss.

Alas, the summer now is done,
And I am left alone again,
Oh Cynthia, where have you gone,
Lonely, I search for you in vain.

Did she really come to see me,
Or was it all a dream,
My beautiful painted lady,
In orange, black and cream.

Jean Thorn

For Eternity

When at night I lie awake
Thinking of you,
My heartbeat quickens and
My pulse does shake
And I know that for the rest of my days
I want only you.

When during the day
I see your face - your eyes that gleam
To be beside you - in your space
Is my deepest dream.

And in the autumn of our life
My hope remains that we shall see
Our daughter settled in her life
For as long as and peaceful as you and me
and on the day I fall asleep
I give to you my heart to keep.
And if and when you crash and burn,
I hope to me you shall return
for eternity.

V. F. Thompson

Untitled

The little old man sat by the fire,
in the little white cottage in Lancashire.
Toasting his toes upon the hearth,
now lay discarded his cap and scarf.

Smells wafted in and under his nose,
was it his supper or his strawberry toes?
"What's yer doin' in there lass", says he,
"Is it me socks or yer burnin' me tea?"

No sound could be heard of her reply,
for the pots and pans through the air did fly.
"I've darned your socks, an' I've made t'bed,
seen t'burns an kept 'em fed,
av washed your shirts an' av made a cake,
an' av scrubbed until me fingers ache."

The fire crackled, and he lay his legs down,
his face shone, gone was his frown.
"Ee lass you've done me proud",
then he laughed strong and loud.
"Ers y'tea, no need t'fret,
I'll not forget ya birthday pet."

Maria Maguire

Shadow Of Vesuvius

Eruption, silence.
Sudden panic,
Crowds form...attempting to escape the volcano's fury.
Ashes falling,
Silently floating, down onto the city.
Choking, muffling...cease the screaming.
Terror
Asphyxiation, deep slumber.
Taking death in its stride, concealing all signs of life;
Beneath the layers...

Archaeologists; brushing away dirt from long ago.
Uncovering history...1st hand sources.
Metres away, a couple entwined...lost and forgotten,
Now to be unearthed.
"2nd chance"
Still today,
People thriving...living...waking...dreaming,
In the threatening;
Shadow of Vesuvius.

Victoria Lee

Greatest Gran

I write this poem to the world's "Greatest Gran",
From the pen of your number one fan,
All my life you were like a second mother,
From this day on I know there will never be another,
I know you have gone to a much better place,
Where you will be walking about with your beautiful face,
You will be with your friends who have gone before,
It cheers me up that much I know,
I just wrote this, so you will know how much I did care,
About my "Gran" with the beautiful white hair,
So my poem ends from my own pen,
You sure have been the WORLD'S GREATEST GRAN!

Peter Anthony Batty

Twilight

Keep warm your heart;
Let not your crystal tears fall upon the ground
Thought now unseen,
Still, I am with you every precious moment

Listen close to the wind
And in it hear the gentle caress of my voice;
Words left unsaid
Now whisper softly by your side

Feel the strength of my embrace
It engulfs your very being,
The warmest of touches
So tender in its essence

For here amidst the twilight
My love to this time reaches you
Eternally, an echo in your mind
Whenever you wish me near....

Stuart C. Robb

Famous!

Performing a play upon the stage,
I hope someday I'll make front page,
I want to be famous
I want to be rich
Not stuck on the streets
Or in a ditch.
Looking up at the stars at night
I wish I were one of those twinkling bright,
Walking down the streets of Hollywood,
Just like every star should.
Seeing your name engraved in stone,
Spending all day chatting on the phone,
But performing a play upon the stage
I hope someday I'll make front page.

Sara McNicholas

The Kinsfolk

The day she died
My mother's brethren came,
With suitable solemnity in their country eyes;
We didn't send, they knew that she had died.
And so they brought brown eggs, gifts from afar,
They said the griddle bread, the butter churned today,
Was as she knew it.
I looked for a star.
Their rich Fermanagh voices so consumed
Our city home, the room in which she lay,
That we forgot the animosities, feuds there had been,
And when they spoke of places we had seen
Mentioned on Bible flyleaves Mother had;
Aghadrumsee, Tully, Salaghy and Kilmore,
The mystic dream was born and she was there
With clogs, in lamplight, on an earthen floor;
The orphan donkey, standing near,
And Christ not very far.
When they were gone I kissed her cheek and said,
Father forgive them now that mother's dead.

Robert Lindsay

A Moment In Time

With the lengthening of the shadows,
    and the earlier setting sun.
Falling brown and amber leaves
    the autumn has begun.

The planted grain in springtime,
    summer harvest gathered in.
Long dark hours, and cosy fires,
    the winter will begin.

Frost and snow may follow
    Then light refreshing rain,
With sun to wake the daffodils
    and spring is here again.

The time is passing quickly,
    Doesn't wait for you or me.
For time rolls by through endless space,
    To everlasting eternity.

Madge Roberts

Precious Thoughts

As I weep for my loved one in the day time
And I weep all day all alone
Not someone to remind me of my loved one
Only the things we once shared and once owned
So precious are thoughts and reminders
Of days and nights that we shared
Not to be anymore till I meet him again
In that world above all in a word
So until my time comes I shall live for today
As I know he'd have wanted me to
But my thoughts of him will remain with me
In everything and all that I do.

Patricia J. Bell

This Hour

Let not this hour so sweetly filled,
End in our memories, nor be stilled.
Its fragrance strengthens all our hopes,
Ne'er let it flicker nor be killed.

'Tis but a short endearing hour,
Blooming fresh, like springtime flower.
Spoil not its bloom, nor nip its bud,
But let its leaves spread full in power.

Sweet like the honey from the bee,
Blessed to all eternity,
This hour enriched with beauteous love,
This tender hour you share with me.

Roy Muir

The Cycle Of Life

Take a grain of sand upon the shore,
It's hardly ever noticed,
And life's the same, we carry on,
For one is never noticed,
Unless he's great, or proud, or big,
Or owns some big estate,
The commoner plays a mundane part,
And when he's gone, it's true,
They will be upset for a little while,
But soon carry on anew,
For life in cycles travels round,
As if spinning on a sphere,
For all grow old, however bold,
The trumpet blows like a clarion call,
And for those who can discern it,
Take up their robes and spread their wings,
For surely they have earned it.

John Nundy

Caledonia

Morning dew, starlit sky,
Are we to ponder, for reasons why?
Take my hand, will you walk with me?
As we sing our songs, and long to be free.

They shackle us, with chains of guilt,
And we hide behind these walls we've built,
But so bright is the light that shines from you,
By man nor beast will it be subdued.

As across the valleys, and over the glens,
You call once more to your loyal men,
To come to arms, and fight the fight,
And put an ancient score to rights.

For the time is now, the moment ripe,
Swiftly, powerfully, we must strike,
Bury the union, a thing of the past,
Caledonia, a free land at last!

Kenneth Mortimer

The Eventful Day

I thank thee, Lord for this lovely day,
For all the beauty You have placed my way.
The rolling banks, the grassy hills.
The deep blue sea, the air so still.
The birds, the gulls, as they dip their wing.
All of these things, make my heart sing.
Dear Lord, all of this I hear and see.
Because all of this You have given to me.
Mile after mile, we have walked today.
With all this beauty stretched far away.
It cost us nothing as we walked.
It cost us nothing as we talked.
As I looked up to the sky
and
Down to the sea . . .
My heart full of thanks,
Dear Lord to Thee . . .

Hildred Frances William

My Morning, Noon And Night

You are my morning star, and when you fade
Against the rising sun, all that you are
Is metamorphosed, for you're set to run
Through my world's day—truly the eye of heaven.
My sun, my warmth, the giver of all life to me,
My dear, sweet wife, without you it is night,
Darkness forever. Th'eternal void of death.
Never deflect your sorcery from me:
Use the in-born magic that is you,
And let me bathe unhindered in the love
You've shown me in days past and never let it die.

Harold S. Hillyard

Orange Turkey

Broken screw-driver handle stirs the jam.
He said 'You know you vomit like an angel'.
Whilst I dried my amber tear-drops away.
He picked me a posy of white violets,
Death with my scarlet pimpernel eyes.
Cut me a slice of his Simnel cake,
And cleaned my boots with windowlene.
I watched through inflated eyelids
The delicate fingers I'd felt so hard.
Didn't dream the broken whiskey bottle at seventeen years old,
Didn't dream the surreal seconds as his fist flew to my eye.
Another little broken angel dispels dreams as she hits the floor,
Sipping her tea while her iced tears melt.
Big city yawns and stretches while inside she's died a death.
Scarlet, Scarlet Pimpernel wants to pack up her bags and leave
But Pimpernel's partner don't want her to go
He likes to sit and watch me falling. So I can't go.
I sit and watch them on the T.V.: the ugly girls always win,
But we're here in hard knock high-rise:
They go burning your walls 'til the oven's rusty,
I see the Orange Turkey when I close my eyes.

Melanie Elmer

Two Worlds

I wander lazily through the trees
Warmed by the sun and cooled by the breeze
Surrounded by bluebells, foxgloves and fern
Wildlife around me at every turn.

Yet while this rural life abounds
I think of man in his surrounds
Building empires of bricks and steel
Forcing lesser mortals to kneel

Men at war killing each other
Sometimes unknowingly killing a brother
People dying of hunger and thirst
People dying with each shell burst

People cheating, killing and stealing
And yet not given to remorseful feeling
Avarice, anger, hate and greed,
All a part of our daily creed

Yet as I wander through the trees
Warmed by the sun and cooled by the breeze
I'm grateful that momentarily I'm free
The creatures and flowers belong to me

J. C. Morrow

A White Paper For Mum's

I know we get 'Mother's Day',
with breakfast in bed on a tray,
Chocolates and hankies, cards galore,
who could ask for anything more?

But one day out of three hundred and sixty five,
does not a mother revive!
Doesn't everybody agree, don't you think we ought'a,
get a week every quarter.

Let's have no more fooling,
bring out a brand new ruling.
Pass a bill in parliament,
"Up The Mother" heaven-sent.

We deserve a better life,
being your mother, sister, wife.
So take a turn with the kids for a week,
help us get back the zest that we seek.

After a week, we'd be ready to go,
all our new-found strength and verve on show.
So full of life, vigour, pep and vim,
ready to serve your every whim.

Phyllis Richardson

Sad Eyes

Oh let me see your sad eyes smile,
And wipe away that dark despair,
And then I'll see your true bright light,
In all its wonder sparkling there.

Oh let me hear your smooth lips laugh
And send a ripple through the air
And then I'll hear your own dear voice
In all its softness dancing there.

Then let me find my life again
Unite our hearts in joy so rare.
Away from me for such a while
Though still in body you are there.

Then let us sing our song again
What melodies will fill the air!
Together we will love again
But oh my darling when and where?

Dorothy Hall

Reflection Of You

Look within the mirrored glass
refrain from the reflected facade
pursue with your natural self
concealed below a labyrinth of confusion
a global allegiance to conformity.

Segregate each mortal
with peripheral prominence
Beauty, Wealth, Power, Status
with satirical savagery
each one condemned
would You consider yourself blessed to possess one?

Yet, would the lucid wonderland
disintegrate to dissatisfaction?
A lustful desire for the unobtainable
devouring your spirit in wanton greed
becoming possessed by your possessions.

Aldene Thomas

The Waves of the Sea

Waves can be so calm lapping the sand,
like a tight fitting coat,
or moderately rolling in,
with soft white horses on the crest of the waves.

The high tide's bright huge rollers coasters,
dashing the rocks and sea walls,
often wild like a cape swirling over your head
when the wind has lifted it over your shoulders.

Whatever the size of the waves,
they make beautiful scenes of nature,
sometimes cruel,
the waves of the sea

D. M. E. Harrison

Nocturne Of The Wild

Winds whisper and sigh and stir softly abroad
And rattle the boughs of some gnarled forest lord,
and hustle the leaves as they scurry and run
To tell jungle folk that the night has begun.

A warbling frog leads the others in song
And soon millions croak from the bank of a chaung,
The cry of a jackal comes harshly down wind
With the wails and yaps of the pack close behind.

The moonlight sonata fades into the night,
With insects still singing to show their delight
At the moonbeams glinting on silvery leaves,
That rustle and wave in the dark sombre trees.

The moon steers its course o'er the heavens so wide,
Past a few rippled clouds like sands at low tide,
And shines on the fairy-like land that's been born -
Which fantasies pass with the coming of dawn.

D. A. G. Dockar-Drysdale

On Bare Feet

Walking the universe
because the world's too small.
Walking alone
because man's so bad.
Walking in rage
because things run wrong.
Walking in agony
because everything hurts.

I'll find perfect harmony,
don't hold back my wish to meet
the responsible One I want to see,
I'm coming on bare feet.

Cannot find Him—leaving the universe.
There's no answer—coping with bad man again.
There's even no question anymore—returning to all the wrong things.
Arrival in agony—because now everything hurts more and more.

The world I'm living in is a hard one
but I stand unbearable treat,
it is my life that I will carry on
even on bare feet.

Mandy Zahn

Celebration Of Christmas The Holy Birth

C is to celebrate, the birth of a king
his name would be "Jesus" the angel did sing

H is for holy and hallowed his head
born in a stable, no crib for a bed

R for redeemer, God sent from above
to spread the word of his great love

I for incarnate, king of all kings
born to forgive us, for all of our sins

S for the saviour of all mankind
no greater love could we ever find

T for three wise men, who came from afar
to guide them along, they followed the star

M is for Mary the mother "Divine"
worshipped forever this lady sublime

A for angelic his countenance show
a promise of heaven from his face did flow

S for salvation for you and for me
This baby was born to set us free

Sarah Millar

The Perfect World

I would like to know why, in this beautiful place
so many men hunger for war?
Do they thrill at the pulse of the trigger?
Do they revel in other men's pain?
Or is it a game, just to kill, hurt or maim,
'the winner' the higher the score.

Aren't the loved ones of people so riddled with hate,
much more important by far?
Is their anger through lack of emotion?
Is their evil the devil within?
Or are they just blind, intent on slaying mankind,
the more bloodshed the prouder they are.

Our hopes for solution are fading away
unless we all join hand in hand,
from this moment all fighting and hatred would cease
whatever your colour or creed,
then it would be fair to imply, that our future may lie,
in an eternal and wonderful land.

Catherine Dulson

For Kirsty, The Girl With The Happy Eyes

I hold your hands, you look at me
My daughter's face is full of glee,
At seven months, your life is full
Of laughter, love and happiness.

From soft collie hair to rough stone walls
And sprinkles of rain to tickle your face
Your zest for discovery boundless.

You "ooh" and "aah" and shriek out loud
Excitement too strong to contain.
You captivate strangers, they fascinate you
As you share the hum of your day.

You wake up smiling and never stop
Even in sleep, you grin.
You give so much for one so young
Some say you've been here before.

All I know is that, I must tell you now,
You're the rainbow of my skies.
You're my daughter, my smiler, the one that I love
You're the girl with the happy eyes.

R. Donaldson

The Painter's Pallet

Her pallid complexion,
against the glare of the politically correct mirror,
reflecting but thoughts upon a screen,
her skin cold in that reflected stance,
vulnerability dressed upon her shoulders.

She wares no clothes
in this underground world,
lying naked against the blackness
of the people's critical, but creative eyes.

By this water's edge she sits,
with the wind rustling her moonlit hair,
she flickers with the current's breeze,
and disappears with the storm.

Clear spring in a crystal glass ripples,
as salty tears drop,
the surface clears, the image reappears,
the same as before.

The tears stop and blind to see
is the water's edge beside the old oak tree
for all that is left, is the figure of nudity.

Joanne Lorraine Collins

Alone?

I feel so empty and so alone
I could die and nobody would know!
When he left me I thought I knew
That I could live without feeling so blue!

I decided to go to a park
Where I sat, sobbed and thought 'till dark!
He came along and sat next to me
We looked like Tweedle Dum and Tweedle Dee!

We kissed and caressed from dawn 'till dusk
We were friends, then sweethearts, now more!
It was sure to me we were weds to be
When he asked the question on bended knee!

I was feeling so empty and so alone
Now I feel like I am on the throne!
He looks after me and treats me well
He has managed to ring my heart's bell!

What made me feel so alone so long ago
Has made me realise that life's a glow!
As when I was alone I was not really
It was purely down to being needy!

Charlene Bishop

Again

It's way after Midnight and I should be sleeping
but I can't because you're not here.
Private thoughts in my head I am keeping
and in my solitude I shed a silent tear.
Never knew before I could feel this way,
never knew love could cause such pain.
I miss the man, the voice, the smile,
and want to hold him in my arms again, again and again.
I remember the first time I saw you,
your eyes looked right into my soul.
You smiled at me, you said hello
and gently my heart you stole.
I never even felt you take it,
never missed it when I was with you,
but now without reason you're silent and invisible
and my heart can't find its way home.
It's way after Midnight and I should be sleeping
but I can't because you're not here.
I miss the man, the voice, the smile
and want to hold him in my arms again, again and again.

Gez Larkin

Morning Glory

Still is the night just before the dawn
Creatures great and small awake with a yawn
A curtain of mist o'er the lake doth lay
Feathered friends announce a bright new day.

Gracious is the birch, silver and tall
Bowing her head over one and all
The fauna take sips from the cold morning dew
As the flora unfurl a new leaf or two.

Magical rings on the lake appear
The angler waits, the fish are near
The majestic lom in black, white and grey
Glides slowly silently on his way.

The sun appears and scatters her light
Of glittering diamonds on the water bright
Dancing fairies ride the waves to the shore
But—with a blink—they're gone—no more.

These memories for all time to treasure
Of beautiful things that all give pleasure
And thoughts of feelings of a special kind
Forever to keep in heart and mind.

Wendy A. Howell

Faded Words

Tomorrow's promises remained in yesterday
Faded words he once meant yet not enough to stay
Affectionate gestures soon turned on to another
Treasured times with him I never will recover.

A misplaced fondness, a misplaced trust
Days of happiness now turned to dust
How many more times until I learn
That flame of passion can so often burn

He traced such feelings I thought I'd lost
Melted my hard image encased in frost
Said he hadn't felt this way in years
Now his change of heart brings me to tears.

The hours they go by but he's still there
He's in my thoughts, he's everywhere
He's locked up in my head or some unattainable dream
Running deep into my soul on a sentimental stream

He's crushed my confidence and left me sad
The emptiness inside, it hurts so bad
I try to forget about him, say goodbye
But he's one of those memories that just won't lie.

Paula Weston

Thoughts

Thoughts and memories will always remain
As you think of loved ones again and again
But life must go on that's what memories are for
So think of tomorrow as well as of yore.

Evil thoughts they bring you low
So think nice thoughts as on you go.
A little child at Christmas time
Laughs and smiles at pantomime.

Loved ones who live far away
Are thinking of you day by day.
I'll think nice thoughts that's what I'll do.
What shall I think of? Why, only you.

Ernie Bolton

Dead End

Whales in their home, in the sea,
passing the day, not like you and me.
They run and they hide away
from their fear,
because they know the ships are near
They swim faster and faster away from that place,
because they know next what to face.
The harpoon, the guns in their backs,
Just to be used as candle wax.
Screams and cries from their souls,
As the harpoons are sliced
Out and leave nothing but holes.
The knives are in and cutting around,
As the last bit of whales
Skin falls to the ground.
But they're still alive through all that pain.
But the people don't care they've had their game.

Claire M. Hutchison

Forever Green

Green carpet, lush Green, soaking up the yellow sun,
feeling its warm caress—
Allow my soul to feel your Green.
Let me lie on your bed of softness, on the moist Mother Earth.
And open my mind to your wonder.
Let me feel your beauty, feel your strength above the moist earth
Pushing life toward the skies—
Making its journey, making its circle, for Eternity.
I will share my Eternity with the Green—
Soak up its purity, gather its strength,
My soul will be surrounded by forever Green.

Maxine Lock

Do We Care About The World

Do we care about the world and all it brings,
The happiness and joy, the beautiful things,
Animals, flowers, land and trees,
All surrounded by beautiful seas.

Children and parent torn apart,
People nursing a broken heart.

A girl crying in the corner, not knowing where to turn,
Children chanting, call her names, bullies, they will never learn.
Slapped around the face and pinned to the floor,
Shouting, screaming, the slam of a door.

The weeps of sorrow as they say goodbye,
Truly missed, but all things die.
Stabbed with a knife, the screech of a car,
Hearings in court, a life behind bars.

There are happy times, but only a few,
I wish we could start a world oh so new.

All of the world, when will it end?
A hole in the ozone, some things we Can mend.

Vicky Smith

Growing Pains

I weeded and I seeded and I tended it with care,
I hoed and I ploughed, I fussed and I fretted, and I
Just could not settle. Then up from the ground
Game a large stinging nettle, I didn't give
Up, I started digging, and raking in sunshine and showers.

I'd sing while I worked, and just like the dwarfs I'd
Whistle a tune then up in the air grew a gigantic thistle,
This time I bothered no more, my muscles
Were aching, my blisters were sore, but nature
Took over, and through the ground, wee carrots were growing.

And also me lattice, and two wee swedes.
I gathered my harvest ache, it didn't take
Long, and I read all the instruction
To see where I'd gone wrong, next year I've
Decided between April showers I'll
Forget about produce, and instead,
I'll plant a few pretty flowers.

M. Copland

I Am...

I am the song amidst the breeze,
But don't cry, my dear, I'll never leave.
I am the pebbles beneath a stream,
I am the anger behind your scream.
I am the darkness in the midnight hour,
I am the brightness in a blooming flower.
I am the glint in your soft, blue eyes,
But don't utter, my dear, those bitter goodbyes.
I am the sunset behind the clouds,
I am the storm in a veil of black shrouds.
I am the olive branch in the beak of a dove,
But you, my dear, are my everlasting love.

Emma Garrick

Winter's End

The North winds bring snow on a Winter's day
And all the girls and boys go out to play
The ice as solid as a rock on the pond
Where ducks as they land skid awkwardly along
The snowflakes on cobwebs sparkling in the midday sun
And the weary worker's footsteps in the white walking his way home
The icicles hang like pyramids short, fat and tall
And the poor old snowman melts on the frozen lawn
Yes all these things Winter brings
Until it goes and turns to Spring.

D. Naylor

Pets Galore

Over the years we've had many pets
All loved by the children and by the vets
An assortment of fur, of colour and breed
All with strange names extra mouths to feed.

Guinea pigs our favourites and budgies in cages
Goldfish and tropical, all lived for ages
But by far the most popular were the cats and the dogs
Who sat on our laps or needed plenty of jogs.

Benjie and Penny two young dogs who wandered
Caused us much worry until they were cornered
No problems with Mitzi, Sue, Tammy and Timmy
Until we discovered Tammy was a Tommy.

Since then the cats have had interesting labels
Gismo and Splodge even Shana, but no Mabels
They all had a place in our family life
Sharing our best times, even our strife

We hope that these pets enjoyed their lives too
Even though our house was sometimes a zoo
We will always remember them but I often recall
That none of my family now have pets at all.

Corinne Smither

Fleeing Mediocrity

Fleeing mediocrity
Gentle, you smile
And giving seems no more like giving
Just living
Is there a better way, or are all paths only different?
While alive, I can only learn about life and observe death.
Yet there seems to be a noble dignity
In the clumsy strivings of youth leaving youth
When new is no longer new.
Delight in pain, delight in pleasure,
Paralyzed speech
Do we ever reach?
Or is all expression just an unfinished journey to another soul
Rolling thoughts of endless flow.
When actions reflect what is within
Translucent being can be seen
Emptying self of self
Until there is nothing left
No shell to harbour emptiness

Maria B. Lynch

Looking Within

Why so sad my heart? you lay so heavy in my breast,
And only sleep subdues and lets my sorrow rest.
Morning dawns and I must face another day,
Put on a smile, that mask I need to help me on my way.

How many people in this troubled world,
Walk in darkness, fake false cheer?
And no one knows or sees their fear.

One day, my heart, you'll be healed of this pain,
For I will have found my way again.
Where my destiny leads I must follow,
Today I exist, but who knows what tomorrow will bring.

At the end my heart, when you cease to beat,
And my Spirit soars free to its final retreat,
What will the world say of me? It matters not,
There is one alone, who will know my heart
When I return home.

Maureen Jones

The Country Man

The ploughman's furrow straight and prim
The horse's pace was slow
His work was always pride to him
'Twas straight where'er we go.

The blacksmith makes his anvil ring
As horseshoes he is making
The sweat pours from his wrinkled brow
The sweatshop now forsaken.

The tractor now has taken o'er
With power and speed invented
The horse not wanted any more
He's left to graze contented.

The carpenter a gate to make
With rails so straight and true
'Twas made just for the farmer's sake
To let the bovines through.

Whate'er your work or dealing
Do earn an honest dime
For it's here we leave our footprints
Bedded in the sands of time.

Reginald M. Williams

Why O Why?

Why o why do trees get chopped down?
And why o why does the world go round?
Why o why are animals killed for their skin?
When the only ones who care is their next of kin.
Sometimes this isn't the case,
When people are destroying the human race.

Hayley Funnell

A Trapped Soul

A trapped soul in a free spirit
My mind wondering across thoughts untrue
A true identity one unknown comes to life

Unknown love comes to mind in a world
Unexperienced that passes by
One taste of ecstasy drives a mind insane

So pure but so unruly
A situation with no solution
Anger when together desire when apart
A body yearning for a caressing touch

A story with no ending
A life with no meaning
A cold mind with a warm heart
Overtakes a mixed-up world

Emily Clark

Hidden

No one can see me,
They don't know how I feel.
I am hidden underneath a field of flowers.
These flowers make me feel free,
From these flowers my emotions are expressed.
Beneath I walk with my feet in the sea.
Life's worries can get washed up in there.
I go wherever the wind takes me.
  But still,
No one can see me.

Inderdeep Kaur Shambi

Lover's Song

How can I tell you what you've done to me,
The way in which you've overturned my life?
You are my waking thought, my sleeping dream;
I see your face—I'm twisted by a knife.

I kiss your lips—the memory of them still
Stirs up in me an unresolved fire,
Your arms around me bring a sweet content,
My body longs for you; my heart's desire
Is just to be with you, to know your love
Is all around, wherever I may go.
How drags the time whenever we're apart!
I love you—that is all you need to know.

I'll say no more than this 'til next we meet,
Then—give ten thousand kisses, oh so sweet!

Hilary A. Jarratt

Lifetime Of Darkness

Lifetime of darkness
Strangers are friends
Friends are strangers
As I tread wearily
Along the worn, dusty path
That those before followed.

My rage no longer lies there,
In my torn, broken heart.
Instead, a hopeless frustration and anxiety
Curses my people, my friends

Will it be like this from now on?
Do I need a higher knowledge,
To take me in, to nurture me,
To replenish my betrayed soul?

Throughout my sorrow
The questions are unanswered by all.
Strange, how my heart continues to pine
For all that I've lost.
I want to give up, but I'm the protector,
I can't.

Katherine Lapsley

Summer Day Begins In Heaven

Oh how beautiful it is today
There are flowers everywhere
Along the water river front
I run along with care.

A gentle kiss upon my cheek
A gentle breeze swifting by
A flock of birds across the sky
A luscious green field the truth no lie.

The mating season has begun
Animals eating from the trees
Animals eating from the seas
Animals eating on their knees.

If only you could see this place
Along the view point site
Beautiful rainbows in the sky
There's a beautiful ray of light.

Tralee Greggs

Inside

It's lonely here locked inside.
Visitors come but inside I hide,
Afraid to come out and just see,
Frightened no-one will like the real me.

Voices inside say, "What's there to lose?
It's lonely here but you must choose".
Doors open up within my mind,
I begin to realize people are kind.

Day by day my strength just grows.
I'm happier now and it shows.
Slowly the world takes on a new shape,
I see the love, not just the hate.

I have at last found the key,
Accepting myself and just being me.
I laugh a lot and do not hide.
There are no empty rooms left inside.

Hazel V. Evans

Dawn

At break of day I walk along the shore
Where surging seas rush on and then retreat
No sound is there that's heard above the roar
Of waves that on the shore forever beat.

There on the hill the grass is wet with dew,
The quiet sheep lie drowsy, full of sleep.
Upwards I climb to see the distant view
Across the bay, far o'er the ocean deep.

And now a light breaks in the eastern sky.
There, pearly pink the clouds embrace the sun.
The lark his drowsy mate calls from on high.
The night has flown and morning has begun.

And so, refreshed, I homeward wend my way
Grateful for every dawn and each new day.

Joyce M. Hewett

Attic Solitude

'The world is still, woven into silence,
Only the throbbing of my heart disturbs,
I am trapped in a cocoon of indifference.
Body unmoving, afraid to break the quiet.
In memories I wander through time;
A ghostly figure amongst the real,
Hearing nothing, but witness to all they do.
I am invisible to them, imprisoned somewhere within.
A vacuum of thought is sucked
From me as I return to their world,
The silence slowly unravelling,
Shattering my cocoon, like crystal
To the wooden floor'.

Natalie Clarke

Just Our Luck

"That's just our luck" you'll hear "Him" say when things start to go Wrong
But in our lives it needed luck to help us get along
Lucky in that we both could work to change our living style,
From pokey room to roomy house I know it's taken a while.
Three great kids, two girls, one boy, such a loving family,
Who care about one another, that means so much to me.
As they left home it broke our hearts, but luck was on our side.
Two went to "Uni", one found work, our hearts were filled with pride.
Now "He's" retired, I still work, our luck goes on and on.
Lucky to have good neighbours and good friends to call upon.
Yes luck, you've helped us plenty, kept us fed and in good health
Never too much of a good thing and never lots of wealth.
Just enough to keep us going, a push along the way,
I thank you and God for giving me all I have today.

Audrey Parry

The Raindrop

A tiny raindrop falls upon the pond, and is as if an angel
waves her magic wand.
Ripples spread far and wide, making patterns as they ride
across the once smooth surface.
The sun comes from behind a cloud, a golden light shining
strong and proud upon those tiny wavelets.
Diamonds, stars in a million colours dance and follow one
another. Magic is as seen by the eye, as in a dream.
Thoughts race through the human mind, oh, what mysteries do
they find. A dancing year, a falling tear, wedding bells to ring out clear.
Miles and miles of far beyond, those ripples stretch from land to land.
One could go on for evermore, linking up from shore to shore
the magic created by one tiny drop of rain.

Clarence Gascoigne

The Perfumed Garden

The seasons come - the seasons go.
My garden awaits the time to show its beauty to the world.
All in their turn, the flowers and weeds will supersede each other.
They have their day, and who will say one is better than another.

The rose stands tall - loved by all
in my perfumed garden.

Bees at work, they never shirk their duty to perform.
From flower to shrub and back across the lawn.

Butterflies abound without a sound.
They flit about, wings spread out coloured magic to behold.
Their life is short and they will fall like petals on the ground
but nature will prevail again and promise more untold.

Work intense but no laments
to keep my perfumed garden.

The night is still, no sound is heard and fragrance fills the air,
I walk content at peace with man and know my soul is there.

V. J. Hall

In the Absence of Humanity

The winds sing an eerie tune to me,
The night brings with it a comforting feel.
My dead friends I can no longer see.
I hear their dying voices being drawn into the abyss.
I want to sleep but that's a pleasure I dare not risk
In my heart my sweetheart never leaves my side.
Are we grabbing the lantern of peace or just allowing destiny to decide?
As the bombs start to scream overhead
I know I shall never see another sunrise.
Yet fear is no stranger to me or the endless blood which is shed.
But I still dream of home and all the memories and fun.
The charge begins, no thoughts in mind just waiting for the end to come
A shot fired by a man whose name I shall never know.
A bullet from the enemy.
The only escape death, this seems to be the only remedy.
My ragged, twisted body lays among the dead.
My last breath is taken in the field which runs red,
Terrified of dying I am not...terrified of facing the devil's gaze!
No!...just betrayal knowing that this war will be one day swiftly erased.

S. McLeod

Remembering My Love

I remember the first day we met
my heart was so full of joy, I didn't
think we would be together, because we
where so far apart.

Now I begin to wonder whether this
was really fate. We had our fun
and laughter too, now there's nothing left,
but a broken heart and sorrow too.

I still sit down and day dream about our
love, all it seems was a fantasy, with our
white doves.

One day I hope I'll see you again, and
recapture our every moment. Maybe it
was me that was to blame, for our dying
love. But my heart still feels the same,
Without a doubt and without any shame.

Filiz Kizrak

Missing Place

As a child if ever there was a hero,
It had to be you, it just had to be you,
from a child growing woman, moving on now,
I feel so proud to have been part of you.
I never saw the pale stranger as he waited
that day, in the shadows of your life,
did you see him, did you know,
were you frightened?
Heroes never die, did you know?
Searching back through my childhood, I'm running
running scared that I'll miss you at the gate,
It's not that you won't come, you always did;
It's just this time I know I'm too late.
There is no sleep through emotional nightmares,
I feel anger, I'm frightened and sad,
for I will carry your missing place
Always,
I've lost a great friend,
My Hero
My dad.

Maria Bloomfield

Disquietude In Love

It doth seem strange to endeavour
to take upon the task which is so personal;
and yet, each one of us is affected by love
its power, so strange, enigmatic and universal.
Sometimes it is not an easy concept to grasp:
It can bring joy, laughter, or be extremely hurtful.

People meet, fall in love, as a course of nature.
Though many are lucky, more fortunate than others
if it happens as mentioned, there's life-long love:
If not dissatisfaction, and then other lovers.
Oh! Of only were as simple as movies depict it
and singers sing it; love would then be a bed of feathers
or a floating cloud. Do we blame you love,
or each other? Perhaps it's easier to love our mothers.

Rachel Burton

Blue

Blue is
A carpet of bluebells in a springtime wood.
The summer sky.
The sapphires in a lover's ring.
Forget-me-nots.
A kingfisher's iridescent wings.
A Wedgwood vase.
Our planet viewed from distant stars.
His faded denim jacket, draped across a chair.
The way I feel when I'm away from him.
Our new born baby's eyes.
Picasso's painting - (Life) - 'La Vie'.

Wendy Frost

Reflections

The Old Man sits in isolation in the slowly darkening room,
He nods his head and smiles at some remembered dream
The red rays of the setting Sun frame the picture on the wall
Of a dark haired lass reclining with small dog at her feet
Whilst time itself stands still for them as man as wife once more
Are reunited in those happy days of love and understanding;
'Twas not for them the passions of which romantics rave
But the growing strength of love and trust
Maturing with the years as time fled by
His pulse rate quickens as he recalls when first she caught his eye,
All images of others fled like leaves before a growing wind,
The Old Man smiles at thoughts of just how hard she was to woo
For he has no Lothario, his platitudes were few
But still she came to Love him though the road was sometimes hard,
Together they surmounted each pitfall as it came;
Then fate dealt him a cruel blow by snatching her away;
Once more that fateful day returns, he wipes away a tear
Then smiles again for though she's gone
He know's she's always Near.

E. G. Gray

Unfolding Spirit

In the stillness of his look
I reached out and touched him,

There was no movement between us,
no words exchanged,

Just a look,
and so many, many images, flickered through my mind,

Can't share them all,
Can't define them all,
Can't even list them all,

I can say,
I felt warm, safe, at peace.
A feeling of oneness, not so much with him
but with myself, how strange.

This feeling was strong, yet delicate,
Was caring, yet uncaring

For a fraction of a second I flipped over like a fish in water,
Letting this feeling bathe through me,
and with a smile,
I turned my glance to the Skinny Bridge,
Knowing I could always return to his gaze.

V. E. Knibbs-Hughes

Genealogy

Across the miles of land and sea,
The echo of a distant voice is calling me,
Calling me home to my place of birth.

A place of memories, tall tales and true,
Of history, love, work, old and the new,
Hand reaching for hand.

Granddad B was a hard working man,
Big, quiet, providing in the hard times as best as can,
Living a long, hard country life.

Granddad W even though I knew him not,
A resourceful man in his life and vegetable plot,
Gave all he had to those he loved.

The women in their lives poles apart
Yet worked for the families that they loved from the heart,
Even if for some it's only now they realize.

These bloodlines came together to provide me with life,
When a son of one took on the daughter as wife,
And in the fullness of time came me.

I hear them speak my name in quiet moment,
I feel their love around me - family.

Alison Clifton

Attraction

I go funny when I hear your voice
Get these sort of butterflies in my belly
And those eyes are completely scrum
That sometimes I just want to run!

I want to feel the world about my attraction
As I feel that I'm the only one
So I've wrote this poem
Because...

I go funny when I hear your voice
Get these sort of butterflies in my belly
And those eyes are completely scrum
That this time I've no need to run

I sit and look and look and stare
I stare behind those eyes of yours
And realize that I'm not alone
As you too have an attraction
Now isn't that just scrum

Tonya Bishop

Parting

Outside, the trees bend in the cold November wind
and rain falls, as helplessly as my tears
and floods the earth.
No sweet birdsong now, only a distant flutter of wings
dancing upon a pale winter sky.

I shall not look in the direction of your meadows,
lest the sight of you steals away another piece
of my fragile heart.

Nor shall I listen for the sweet echo of your love song
in the deepest hour of midnight,
lest we still sing in tune . . .

Carol Ann Bowers

My Dream

To me, my dream is the best place ever,
But now this place ain't coming, never.
Tell me now where this place has gone,
just like a star, when it's dawn.
There's never been a place so amazingly still,
There could have been a place like this until.
Man invented cars which polluted the air,
Now in life people think I don't care.
Truth be known my heart is filled,
With anger, fear and things I willed.
We should have stopped it,
but, now we've copped it.
All I ask is for clean air,
I never did it, it isn't fair.
Please let me breathe in air that's clean,
stop it now, you're being mean.
Torturing me like this just isn't nice,
it's like making an eskimo eat the hottest spice.
That may sound funny weird or blue,
but to me, it's heartache all the way through.

Sindy Bangham

Freedom

She wrapped me in chains as too did he,
how huge the yearning to break free.

Children are always demanding,
my inner self reprimanding.
Suddenly it all began to ease,
I felt some relief,
deep inside I saw new belief
that I am Me.

Now, I am free to create all I desire,
the future's goals grow higher and higher,
no longer suppressed by a constant liar.

I Am Free.
I Am Me.

Sharon Ince

Distance Never Separates Two Hearts That Really Care

Although you may be far away
I still think of you every single day
Your friendship will never be forgotten
For distance never separates two hearts that really care.

We might not see each other very often
However your face is one I'll never forget
You bring a smile to my face even when I'm sad
For distance never separates two hearts that really care

Days, months and years pass by
This special bond we share will never die
No other friend could be as wonderful as you
For distance never separates two hearts that really care.

No one treats me as kind as you did
You're the one person I really, really miss
You've touched my heart time and time again
For distance never separates two hearts that really care.

Charmaine Peters

A Smile

A smile is a beautiful treasure to share
A smile will halve all your troubles and cares
To greet people happy with a smile on your face
You'll lighten the hearts in many a place
Just carry on smiling, and you'll find you will save
You'll have twice your smiles back, for each one you gave

Barbara Flamson

A Tree Of Golden Dreams

As long as I can see a tree, with its leaves of golden dreams,
And a bird singing sweetly to me,
Then the world is still beautiful to me

The rays of the sun still glow down on me,
and the flowers continue to give a profusion of colour,
Silky, slender, petals of colour,
As delicate as the spiders web it carries,
Delicate beauty, and yet all powerful to me.

We threaten our world with the stale breath of industry,
With its acid rain, its gripping pain,
But as long as I can see a tree with its leaves of golden dreams,
And a bird singing sweetly to me,
Then the world is still beautiful to me.

So proceed to destroy if you dare.
God's creation, he made for us all to share,
But as long as there is yet one tree,
With its leaves of golden dreams
Though sad of the solitude of this tree,
The world is still beautiful to me.

Gillian Cromie

Falling Tears

I was in the corridor, sitting on the floor,
Waiting for the teacher to come through the door,
"What's wrong?", I said, when I saw a girl weeping,
"Charlie's gone, never to wake from his sleeping".
When I heard the news, I felt like falling,
Crystal rain drops calling, calling,
My eyes were dreaming far, far, away,
"Come on" I heard the teacher say.
My friend was sitting next to me,
Weeping soft tears for thee,
"Charlie has died?", she said under her breath,
The classroom was silent when the teacher had left.
Everyone's eyes were misty with tears,
People's hearts were filled with fears,
"Did he leave to hurt our lives so?",
"Did he really have to go?"
He will never be with us, come tomorrow,
We will live with his memories and the sorrow,
Those memories we have and always will,
And hope to feel his love around us still.

Kasha Dunne

Untitled

A knock on the door,
A vow of silence,
An hysterical wind chime,
The obscenity of violence,
Poisonous scream that falls to the floor,
Direction so misguided,
A hit so hard to ignore.
Love so used, never provided.
Like a broken promise,
Or a field of unfulfilled dreams.
As the cherry blossom breaks,
A new day wakes,
The black circle spins,
One day she'll win.
When the crow learns to fly,
The fish learn to swim,
What comes so naturally,
Will never come to him.

Susanna Henson

What Part Am I?

What part am I in the infinity of space?
What part am I in the eternity of time?

Each smile, each thought, each word,
in less than measurable space
lands on the compost heap of the past
from which today has grown.

The future floods the present.
Can all the egos guide the flood?
In guiding can the 'I' be separate
from the formless mass
which to posterity will be history?

What is the 'I'
but spirit out of space and time?
A cosmic communal spirit
lighting the way,
inspiring the world's descendants?
A personal spirit of the earth bound
offering hope?
Personal and cosmic are lost and held
in time's eternity, the infinity of space.

Mary Baldwin

The Attainable

The road unwinds in the dark abyss of my mind.
It stretches unendingly swerving neither to left or right,
There seems to be no relief, no lightness beyond
Will I ever reach the end of this road?
I chide myself at this thought,
A certain perversity will see me through.
So I wait for peace of mind
A new hope, a reawakening, a rejuvenation,
If you like.
A realization that one has at last
Reached one's journey's end.
Where there is hope and light
Where one is no stranger
And there is a welcome for everyone
No matter what race, creed or colour,
So I console myself
For I am content and at rest.
At last

Amrita P. Mohamed

A Special Christmas

One Christmas thousands of years ago a baby boy was born,
But this mother did not know for him that she would mourn.
She laid him in a manger bed softly padded out with hay,
He slept not to wake again until another day.
She named the baby Jesus Christ the saviour of mankind,
He cured the sick, he healed the lame, he even helped the blind.
He died on the cross to set us free to take our sins away,
But to the Virgin Mary he's a baby in the hay.

Rose Anne de-Leuw

Ash Vale

I've told you the story
of the Ash Vale crash, how I was crippled
in a roadway smash, robbed of a marriage
the man I loved. War, oh war,
four years later, at a limbless centre
I met a soldier, a prisoner of war,
who came from Australia,
a fractured spine and bunions on his feet,
he'd been blown up off the isle of Crete,
in Stalag 3 and 3 he'd spent four years
in that war,
We married at Christmas, had children six
and for the next thirty years, I loved him to bits
if war has a purpose
I ask myself why
now fifty years on,
Men still have to die.

Margaret Vinall-Burnett

Winston Churchill

There was an M.P., from Oxford he came,
He resigned from the Cavalry, which seemed a shame.
He supported the disastrous Gallipoli Campaign,
So a battalion commander in France he became.
Soon he became more involved in law,
He was Minister of Munitions, Secretary of War.
For the Tories he then became Chancellor of the Exchequer,
And he certainly changed things for the better.
His opinions soon were approved by all,
He picked up the country and gave them a call.
In 1940 Prime Minister he was,
And everyone said there was a good cause -
For him to say, "We shall meet them on the beaches."
This was one of his many rousing speeches.
After five years of working extremely hard,
Hitler's hopes of winning were barred.
At election though, Labour won,
And Churchill's time had sadly gone.
Everyone knew he had been tremendously mighty,
But in 1965 he died, aged ninety.

Claire Burgess

Untitled

Windswept and grey are the hills of Northumberland
sheep on the hill side the curlew o' head
Rocky and grim are the hills of Northumberland
scared by rough season in the days that are gone
Smiling and green are the vales of Northumberland
watered by rivers like the Tweed and the Tyne
Many fair counties has England our mother
none can compare with this Northumberland of mine

C. L. Bolam

A Posy Of Flowers...

Weave me a picture of primroses and flowers,
The finish of winter,
The cherry blossoms bowers,
Soft green for moss to soothe the day,
A handful of Forget-me-nots,
Would be here to stay.

I would like Delphiniums so passive and blue,
Don't forget the Hollyhocks, I love them too.
It could be arranged in a posy of flowers,
I would delight in their colours,
For hours and hours.

Add a few butterflies to mix with delight,
A nectar of wishes weaved in the night,
As I watch it develop, as it springs into life,
It will have plenty of promises,
When finished it will be right.

A few pink roses to enrich this circle today,
Amidst the wild flowers would be a beautiful array.

June Maxwell

Spike

Our Spike, he was a funny cat,
With white whiskers and paws, and the rest of him black,
He liked to be stroked and tickled sometimes,
He'd roll on his back and give tickle me signs.
He'd go out for hours, and then he'd come back,
Guess he got hungry, so he'd have a quick snack,
But one night he left,
And he never came back,
We miss our old Spike,
Our lovely black cat.

V. Smith

The Forecast Of My Heart

A see has fallen upon barren ground.
Hath sprouted its roots and begun its reign,
Calmly conquering without a sound,
Sweet yet tough like sugar cane.

Spring shower of hope begin to fall,
Opening new doors to unknown experiences,
The seed hath grown into a tall tree,
Each strong branch full of assurances.

Suddenly lightning flashes, full of warning,
Thunder strikes with an ominous growl,
The strong tree shakes with a cry of mourning,
And then falls with a defeated howl.

The atmosphere is filled with defeat,
The wreck of the tree can be seen on the ground,
The sky and clouds with grief meet,
Unfulfilled dreams lying in a mound.

Fatima Hussain

Love

Twas the light of love I saw
Shining so far away,
But so close, close to my heart
And distant from my body,
As I felt the love shining nearer
I saw your face glowing in the light,
I could feel the love surrounding my heart,
And your presence, so close
I'm sure I could have reached you,
As I felt my soul rising from my body
Into your world of happiness,
Of white clouds undisturbed,
As you took my hand your love led me away,
Away towards a new light
Of happiness and joy.

Natalie Forrester

Daughter University Bound

Sadly I waved her goodbye
With tears of joy in my eye.
To Uni she was going
So I decided to write a poem.
I felt so proud of my little lass,
Thrilled to bits that she had a good pass.
She is hoping (please hope) for a degree
As she wants to be a teacher in PE.
The house is so quiet now she has gone,
No one to say, 'Do you like this new song?'
How tidy her room is, not a thing on the floor,
No 'studying' sign hanging on the door.
The phone is so quiet (no one will ring).
It's always been ringing with a ting-a-ling-ling.
Just lately she's been busy packing her bags
(Writing her name and tying on tags).
I've washed up my pots (I really am blue).
Not so much washing and ironing to do,
So I think I'll enrol and be a teacher too!

Daphne McDonald

The Past

You shook a hand to make a deal,
It was not questioned, like a seal;
You raised your hat to bid good day,
Respect was found in every way.

You knocked the door to enter in,
You asked if you might borrow pin;
You dressed your best on Easter Day,
You entered Church to listen and pray.

At School you sat in desks upright,
You did your work with lips sealed tight;
You raised your hand when question asked,
You learnt your tables, read to class.

Through war you covered windows black,
Warden screamed if light through crack;
Exchange of food was used by many,
This comradeship cost not a penny.

The blackouts gone and lights shone free,
The roads got busy with traffic spree;
The rationing ended and freedom broke out,
Folk wandered and wondered what war was about.

John Paulley

Brother In Memories

A frail and tragic child lies in a
Tiny glass coffin, an incubator.
My baby brother, whose sweet smile and
Piercing cry kept me contented.
How could I understand? How?
He was barely one month, still an
Embryo in my eyes.
A small child's death is always the worst.
A whole life ahead of them, and then deprived.
So cold and sad, his pale white face
Like snow and this body as cold as stone!

And now all that's left
Is a small grave and a memory of a child I didn't know.
Should I feel sad? Why don't I?
I feel ashamed at not having any feelings.
I know him only from pictures in my mind.
One month . . . And a few days.
I have so few memories, none of any significance.
Goodbye my baby brother.
My Adam.

Sarah Cartwright

Anger

Anger is when someone might cry.
Someone might tell a lie and if they do
You might cry then you will need a hanky but why.

Anger is when you might go mad
And your mum might say you are bad.
If you are don't run up the wall or you might even fall.

Anger is what people don't like.
They stamp their feet and walk
Down the street to their house.
Sometimes that's what they do.

Anger is when you don't like someone
And they might not like you.
You could close your eyes and count to ten then
You might feel better.

Anger is when you can shake hands.
Then you might be friends, and if
You are you will probably be happy
You are lucky that you are not sad.

Anger is nuisances when you get into trouble
But when you've got a friend it's nice.

Tamsin Clemence

Poem Of Racism

I was walking through the gate,
I could sense all of their hate.
They could not hurt me, not here.
But I could not help release that strangled tear.

"Go Back You Don't Belong!"
I could not say it but I knew they were wrong.
Even though here I was born,
They want possible friendship torn.

My bloody nose and bruised arm.
I got that and I have not done any harm.
I am different but that's me.
Oh why can't they let my colour be?

Sarah Dockery

Content?

Trapped
Left here to struggle relentlessly
Against elements which dare not reveal themselves
Fear grew from the conjecture awareness will birth sight
Leaving dangers unmasked
Inevitably cure, prevention, destruction will dawn,

Tormented
Left here to struggle a mentality non belief
Cast fled left for an experience of the new sedated mannerisms
Acquainted with ease.

Freedom
Left here to struggle with guilt, pain, misery, loss and waste
The grass by no stretch greener, only taller with as many
tangles and bugs
if not more.

Left here trapped by freedom, reeling in torment.

Kris Thurbin

Seasonal Conclusions

Now the sun and moon have set
And time's long debt is paid
It's time for us to start again
And rebuild the nests we've made
For eternity of lust has caused
Man to have delusions
But yet his strife has still to bring
Unambiguous humane solutions.

Remember the past with thoughts of love
And how with visions of grandeur
We caused the earth to sing its song
And with arrogance: failed to hear her
The universe with its antiquity
Must now rotate its field
And hope that future life will bring
A more grateful, successful yield.

Richard N. Smith

Little Bird

Little bird on roof top
What have you seen to make you hop
Such energy for one so small
In such a long winter
It's a wonder you survived at all.

God gave you feathers to keep you warm
You don't have to worry if your jacket gets torn
Or have to buy shoes
When others get worn.

You have been given wings
For you to fly
We humans would like to try
Must be lovely up there so high
First I did see you, now I cannot
Maybe you are keeping warm
Behind the chimney pot.

Eve Wyatt

Night Creatures

Moonlight shimmers through the trees
Leaves whisper softly in the cool night breeze
Old owl sits on a branch out of sight
Look out mouse, you're his supper tonight
Down on the ground little creatures at play
Fox slinks by looking for his prey
Rabbits playing, darting here and there
Better watch out for the poacher's snare
Brock the badger comes out of his set
Wondering what sort of nice tit-bit he'll get
Down in the farmyard the hens squawk with fear
They all know the fox is quite near
The farmer comes out and fires his gun
So foxy turns tail and starts to run
Back in the wood they all hear the sound
It sends them all running across the ground
Each in their own little holes they scoot
Old owl on high gives a nervous hoot
Then all is silent in the evening air
And no one would have known they had ever been there.

J. Linacre

My Darling Wife

To Commemorate Our "Golden Wedding"
21st September 1996

For over fifty years I have loved you,
I know I always will.
Every time I hold and love you
Everything stops still.
I cannot live without you
It's much more than I can stand
You make my heart flutter
Just to hold your hand.
When we are not together it's
    terribly hard to bear
So long as you will always love me
Then, I just don't care.
If you think and love me, as I do of you
Then my love forever will always be for you.

K. Goodman

The Dark Is But An Ally...

The dark is but an ally, in this war that controls us,
The morning brings but sorrows, and the light is all but dimmed.
The evening dusk that gathers, whips tendrils round my head.
And the little boy that dances, weave needles in his hair.

The dark is but an ally, in the comfort of the dim,
The morning brings but troubles, and the daylight spoilt by sin.
The evening dusk that gathers, plays gently with my hair,
And the little boy that dances, weeps needles in his tears.

The dark is but an ally, in the prospect of a 'peace',
The morning brings but horrors, the glory outshone by malign.
The evening dusk that gathers, teaches me to fear,
And the little boy that dances, dies from a needle in his throat.

T. Maja

The North In Pain And Beauty

The swans glide gracefully down over the
undisturbed lough,
The trees and grass move ever so slightly in
the gentle breeze.
People greet others with pleasant smiles,
Friends group together -
All happy with the freedom they have gained.
But now...
The water slashes violently as the helicopters
pass overhead,
People keep their heads buried in their chests
looking at no one.
Lives are pierced by the enemy's bullet,
Hearts are broken and destroyed
Forever.

Eimear Carron

Visions

I wonder why is the sky so blue,
When below the grass is green.
The earth with many shades of brown,
Grow flowers for man to see.
Their blooms of pink, red, orange and white,
Really must look a most wonderful sight.
The golden leaves sway to and fro,
When through the branches I hear the wind blow.
Silver stars shine in the night sky.
Streams, where clear Crystal waters swiftly flow by.
The Rainbow showing its colours bright,
Reflected in the rays of misty sunlight.
Purple heather, on snow capped mountain sides,
Woodlands, and forests where small violets hide.
These colours, what do they mean.
For none of them have I seen.
There's only one colour in this world for me,
Just close your eyes, and you will see.

Irene E. Bailey

Stranded

Alone and worried
We don't know what to do
look at my watch, it's dead, the teachers too.
As I scream and shout,
I just get a clout
but still don't know what to do
My friends are crying,
They think they're dying
but still don't know what to do
Then help comes along,
we all sing a song
and now I know what to do.

Holly Scotson

Mirror

As I watched the tear drop from her eye;
     That no-one else will see,
I saw the pain she felt inside,
     For what will never be.

I watched her think of what to do;
     To occupy her mind,
To wipe away thoughts of him;
     That she must leave behind,
To start afresh, to start a new:
     To venture forth alone,
To avoid that thing they call love;
     To be happy on her own.

As I watched the tear drop from her eye;
     That no-one else will see,
I saw the pain,
I saw the mirror,
I knew that girl was me.

Caroline Gibbens

Jeffy

There's a black and white cat who lives next door to me.
His name is Jeffy and he's as playful as can be.
He runs around the garden and climbs up all the trees,
He chase all the birds away and all the bumble bees.

Sometimes when it's sunny he likes to sleep on the lawn,
but when it's cold and windy he stays indoors to keep warm.
He's a friendly little pussy and when his owner goes away,
I go and feed him every day.
Sometimes he has chicken, sometimes he has fish and then a
drink of milk in his little blue dish.

Jeffy was feeling lonely until just recently when a new cat
moved in to keep him company.
The two cats play together and get on very, very well.
Oh! I nearly forgot to tell you her name
  It's Tinkerbell.

Sylvia Hardie

The Bull-Fight

Hello, can you see me? It's dark down here.
Is anybody there? I'm lonely down here.
I feel I'm in a box and I can't see,
I'm hot, I'm tired and there's no air to breathe.

I can hear the running of feet above,
I can hear the cheers of the people above,
They shout, they groan, they laugh . . . but don't cry.
It'll be my turn soon as their cheers grow high.

My back feels lame loaded with sacks,
My horns feel blunt, lame like my back.
My eyes feel like jelly, they're blurred, they're sore.
I feel like death, I can't take any more!

Is this entertainment? Maybe for them.
I don't understand it, locked in this pen.
They don't realize it's not a fair fight.
They don't know how we're tortured before sent to the light.

I look down from heaven as the slaughter goes on.
Many bulls are killed, soon there will be none.
This barbaric torture by awful man,
that still tortures me, when will it be banned?

Rebecca Lee

Old Age

The years pass by and we grow old,
There's not many stories left untold.
We've raised our families, told them all,
How life can be such a ball.

Folds upon folds, the wrinkles appear,
People say "Oh! What a sweet dear"
We could do with a filler to hide them away,
Not a day over forty, then people would say.

Grey hairs come, take over our heads,
It's caused by worry it has been said.
We go to the shop for colours and dyes,
Get rid of the grey with a satisfied sigh.

Then our bodies start to go,
Everything we do is done so slow.
The hill we used to climb is now steeper than ever,
Puffing and panting, it must be the weather.

Our spines gradually decide to bend,
A walking stick we have to lend.
Tottering here and tottering there,
Old age! It doesn't seem fair.

Joyce Thomas Mulligan

As I Gaze Out Of My Window

As I gaze out of my window
on a cold wet windy night.

I see people going to and fro
Guided by the street lights.

And with a sigh my thoughts went
back to summer and the sea.

The wonderful exciting holiday
My parents had planned for me.

The day of my departure came
It filled me with delight

I was off to Paris to see
the wonderful, wonderful sights.

My holiday soon over
and summertime had gone

The fire was so inviting
as I closed the curtains tight, on a cold, wet windy night.

Grace Bushell

Eyes

Our eyes are but an instrument
Controlled from within
The pictures processed in our minds
Depend on the mood we're in

For when we're feeling happy
Everything looks bright
But when we're feeling really down
The brightest day looks like the dead of night

The beauty of growing flowers
Their magnificent display
So appreciated when we're happy
Yet when we're sad
Turn into a bed of impending decay

For we always see
What we want to see
No matter what's before our eyes
If what we see
Isn't what we want
Our brain tells little lies

David Arthur

Desert in Flames

At wars end, a cloud of burning noxious oil,
Great billows to a sunless sky,
Until the day became as night,
To sear our hopes of things to come
That this could be a wondrous world,
For all to live alongside
Hills and tress and bubbling streams.
Or will this become a memory
Of halcyon days long gone
Of soil now soaked in oil.
Or can we say "Here we planted trees
In this so troubled age" and thus
A century on, will our children see
Re-birth of forests green
To swathe their future world,
And heal the scars of this so ugly age.
And dare we, as this millennium ends
Hope to see, a cleaner, saner, purer,
Peaceful world, and children comprehensive
Of their duty to maintain.

Roy Valette

The True Yourself

You say
Lots of strange things to my simple mind.
You act
Like you've never been a child.
You mock
At what others say.
You stop
When they even cannot start.
You pretend
To understand what is beyond
You seem
To predict the future from the past.
You behave
Like a pompous fool.
You talk
Like a wise man of the world.
You love though you deem it cheap.
You live
But you act as if you should deserve more.
Nothing times ten equals still nothing then.

Pawel Osuch

From South Wales To Harrogate

'Twas mid July in early Morning dew
A coach Collected quite a few, of folk with one intent
On holiday they were all bent in a good hotel they were going to stay
At harrowgate for more than one day
Five days in fact, with nights just four
It had all been quite well arranged before

Along the motorway we moved, and in perfect comfort as it proved,
There was no fear or nervous tension,
Because our coach moved on pneumatic suspension
A few hours ride came to a temporary end,
As all disembarked a 'penny to spend'

Onwards we sped past the Midlands to make, at a motorway station a
luncheon beak, we reboarded the bus a motley crew, quite happy because
we knew, the rest of the journey was nor far We just had to pass Leeds
to get to Harrowgate Spar

On this sunny afternoon we were in mood quite joyful, to see the
Imperial Hotel looking majestic behind, the splendour of gardens most
beautiful eventually we entered the foyer so lofty and airy, to
gather in chattering groups at the reception area, to be given the
keys to our sleeping places, and a porter to help with our bags and cases.

Stan Strawbridge

Insurance Claims

I'm really frustrated - I'm in such a state
Call it what you will - perhaps it's fate.
I've put in two claims for which I'm due
Just be patient - that's the Insurance Co's point of view!!!

My son had an accident and broke the glass in an interior door
I wasn't going to leave it - and that was for sure...
Could General Accident pay - "Oh, of course", is what they say -

I also had an accident whilst on a ramble on a stile
And the mess on my hand was ghastly and Vile.
Again I must patiently wait my turn for my Pay Out
It's turning me grey with worry - Of that there is No Doubt!!

That's why I wrote those poem - I mustn't be deterred but try in vain
I mustn't give up - but I'm trying to stay sane...
I also worked for an Employment Agency who said they sent a cheque
    direct to my home
It never arrived - So I definitely cannot afford 'A Holiday of a
    Lifetime in Rome'.

I wrote this poem to try and get rich
And hope from now on things will go 'Without a Hitch".

Caroline Hyer

Alone

Confused, alone, where are the people?
Desolation faces me, invades my future,
Cold, barren, vast expanse before me,
Self inflicted, destruction, nothing living.
Twisted metal, ugly, cruel to see,
Dust blowing, burning my throat, so thirsty.

Senses of my mind envelope me, smothering reality
Hope submerged, despair converged with misery

How did I survive? I wish I had not
My eyes had to witness the end of existence
The charred blackened bodies, there laughing at me.

Shuffling my feet, I'm feeling so weak
Not long now to admitting defeat
No food, no water, no love, no one
Lay down my head, doesn't matter where,
No-one to see me, no one to care.

If only they could see what they have done: burnt the earth, wiped
out everyone. Scalding tears run down my face, I cry for me, for the
human race. Global warfare brought on by man's greed, annihilation
in one manic deed.

Tessa Grandi

103

Adam

Come bide awhile with me on yonder hill beside the stile.
We'll talk of nonsense past and yet to come,
then soon we'll see him o'er on yonder hill.
A shy young lad no more than ten,
he'll be by soon though I'll never know the when.
Then down the hill he'll race as if the very devil's at his heels,
and with his every stride my heart he steals.
He'll ford the stream by swinging 'neath the bough,
but why he never tumbles in I'll never know the how.
Then up towards us wends his way,
not by the well worn path,
but through the rain soaked hay.
He'll spot us soon then pick up flagging speed,
his bright blue eyes will break a smile as if to fill my need.
And as he gaits the last few measured strides,
he'll say the words I'll never tire to hear,
Hello dad, what are you doing here?

Graham Wragg

Now And Then

There was a time, when we were young
When all we thought was, life had begun
Where did it go, what happened, when?
Where are we now, where were we then?

We cast our minds back to long ago
To how we felt, what did we know?
We really knew nothing, in the balance we hung
Our life was yet a song unsung

This world now shows us our fears were right
Those niggling thoughts in dark of night
Aspirations gone with a brave new world
Emotions bared and fully unfurled

What does the future have in store?
Love, sadness, pain, who knows the score?
With all we suffer, with all we endure
Oh, if life could again be so pure!

Julie K. Priddice

Death

Death comes first, grief comes after.
Sadness and sobbing fills the days that follow.
Salt tears trickle down grey faces.
Everywhere you go, you remember.
Everything you do, you remember death.
Because death takes and never gives back.
Death can never give back.
Death is so greedy, it takes and takes.
Leaving the living with holes in their hearts.
Stranded and lonely they feel for a long time.
Passing the days, with only thoughts of their loss.

April Kent

Of Space Sky, Mind And Dream . . .

Where time evades all illusion
When swirling starts fill my eyes.
Where imagination is the truth, and like children we feel
pure magic white and good.
Where the cascading rainbow casts her light,
and star sparkling coloured cosmic diamond dust,
showers and flaws the dark jewel of infinite night.
When worlds begin and life is born,
and dawns shimmer, with the brilliant new morn.
Who liquid star light floods the heavens
and yearning souls
call their nightsong of dreams up at those skies
as such mystical wonder streaks across
their eyes.
Faraway and outward bound, a flight of thought
beyond chasms of space,
the timeless unvanquished deep jade eye,
that forever shall engulf such dreaming
night sky . . .

Paul Holland

The Big Four O.

Time has ticked by much faster than I thought,
And yesterdays dreams are nowhere to be sought.
Old familiar places, too many to recall
So many faces, I have forgotten them all.
Now here I am at middle age,
Just another story, on another page.

So if this is the time for my life to begin,
Well it could always start with a lottery win!
With no longer a care for poverty and strife
Looking only to the finer things of life.
A Mediterranean villa or two in the sun,
Spending my days sipping champagne, having fun.

But then I think of all the misfits I would come to know,
Who want to be your friend, but it's all for show.
So if it's money you need to make it with the best,
How many millionaires would like to put it to the test?
Who would give up their wealth, for a life of less?
In the hope of finding happiness not stress.
But I have wandered away from the purpose of my rhyme,
Which is I'm 40 now, and about bloody time!

Sandra Wright

My Music

Music has always been close to me,
When I look into music there is a lot I can see.
Something deep down tells me to play,
Something I have never been able to say
Different styles come and go,
Each one has a meaning so very low.
Listening and playing are two different things,
so are the ladies and gentlemen who sing.
When listening to music there are many things I hear,
which some are meant to seem so dear.
When playing my own music I play with meaning so much,
Which others may not understand but I do such.

Laura-Jo Dowbiggin

Untitled

Night sky slips drearily into
Overcast morning gray and brown
Veined and mottles leaves
Empty from stark trees, whispering
Mottled grasses droop and withered
Butterfly lies broken on wet tarmac.
End of Indian summer, suddenly
Rites of winter, sing on a skein of wings.

Morag MacKenzie

Trooping The Colour

The Guardsmen on The Mall are stood at ease,
As still as statues, 'spite the stiff June breeze.
A stirring picture, framed by waving trees.

We're waiting for the bands to come, you know!
They lead the men in red, row after row.
They're London's pride, a truly splendid show!

Now! Hark a sec! Is that a drum we hear?
Yes, here they come, let's give the Guards a cheer!
Welsh, Scots, and Irish, Coldstream, Grenadier.

The drums, the flutes, the pipes, the sound of brass,
The crunch of marching boots as columns pass,
Band after band - but they'll return en masse!

Now from the palace comes a mighty cheer.
The Queen and yet another band appear.
This band's on horseback - they must play and steer!

They're on the square now, marching round and round.
The best part's yet to come, though, we have found.
Yes - massed bands on The Mall! 'Jove! What a sound!

Ron Roberts

Lost And Alone

My life feels non-existent
and I feel so alone
sometimes I feel like
killing myself
then maybe I won't be alone
but although I think these thoughts
I know I love you all
and that's what keeps me from
the burning black hall.

May be one day I'll go
and say good-bye to you all
then I will be facing
the burning black hall.

I'll be gone forever
and you won't care at all
but I know that someday you'll
be following me down that hall.

I'll be waiting for you and
hope that you say someday
I really did love you and everything will be o.k.

Rachael Emily Fleming

Evil Innocence

The yawning feeling kidnapped my lips,
my hands hung loosely around my hips.
It possessed my body and caressed my soul,
now I'm limp and floppy like an old rag doll.
My breathing is long, deep and slow,
my heartbeat faint and peaceful low.
The reassuring dark smog creeps in,
it's an evil night, a night for sin.
I'm asleep but awake and wander around,
I tip-toe gently not making a sound.
The knife reflects the shining full moon,
my revenge is growing, breathing soon.
It smoothly slices the sleepy victim,
I love him still, but still I hate him.
I settle down on the blood-stained bed,
The horror of the deed repeats in my head.
The blood is thick and dark as night,
regret clasps my throat and squeezes tight.
My dreams are dark and gruesome still,
I am not a murderer, I could never kill.

Mandy Rosemary Coulson

A Change In Seasons

As I look around with a frown
I see the leaves of the trees falling down.
Autumn is here, winter is near,
Summer is over, dear oh dear.
In this season the wind does blow,
There is always the chance of some snow.
If you're not careful you may pay the price,
By slipping up on the ice.
The sea is sometimes rough,
For sailors it can be very tough.
In this season it's rare to see a flower,
And the clocks change by one hour.
You need to wrap up to keep yourself warm.
You could get caught in a storm.
The weather sometimes can be a pain,
With lots and lots of heavy rain.
There are days when it is clear,
It will not rain, so have no fear.
These are the times to have some fun,
When you are out in the sun.

David Renshaw

The Big 40 Enigma

Oh dear, is this it, have I lost my get up and go,
I see a different person in the mirror, I can't believe it's so.
I need someone to tell me, I still have a teenage physique.
Although deep down I realize some reactions are getting weak.
I imagine everyone is looking I'm sure they can see the signs,
The greying hair, the slowing down, and the inevitable face lines.
No longer do I spring out of bed. I need to take extra care,
It's only to be expected, I'm not twenty-one I need to be aware.
So when I come to terms with all of this, it doesn't seem so bad,
I begin to notice those with walking sticks and zimmer frames, then I almost feel glad.
At least I can get about reasonably well, although age is beginning to show,
I don't want to join those ranks quite yet, there's still a way to go.
I'd start to get depressed, and then I meet a friend who's seventy five,
He's worked hard and now he's writing poetry, he says it's great to be alive.
Age is no criteria, he says, he's going for the "ton",
So what is life about, I feel ashamed, I'll forget age from now on.

Reg Morris

Wishful Thinking

I wish I could sit on the grass and feel the wind through my fur.
Taste the dew in the morning, enjoy the warmth of the sun.
I would like to nibble some fresh greens instead of limp, dry weeds,
picked by someone in a hurry, thrown at the end of the cage.
Will I ever be able to race downhill, run and leap in the air,
sit up and look into the distance and see other creatures there?
For now I press my nose to the wire, I watch the children at play,
and hope that they will remember it was for them I was shut in here.

Jeanne Bexley

Holiday Happy - Scotland

The shrill family gather, brushdown and go
singing 'Summertime' up the moss muffled stone stairs.
Clumsy bees can now be heard carousing in the lavender
Pollenpissed, they careen towards me; veer off chuckling at nose level.

And the whisky tastes like burnt honey: caramel searing the throat
The view, refracted, has a haze - late afternoon and best blended
product of Scotland

Another family tousle the tranquillity in a timer release photograph.
Progeny (Male) howl "Biker mice!" at camera
Pinned, screaming, for posterity against a hill of transcendental
green. And I sip straight from the bottle
Holiday happy in a swirling tide of clans and their kindred.

A small fleshly girl, pale sausage in pink gingham, appears;
Solemnly sees my summertime sun, Scotch and crisp apple orgy
turns and panting runs back to the angry castle.

"Why?" - Sound grows, mutating then muffled in mother's ample
arm wails infant in yellow at the foot of the stone stairs
And I know, in a holiday happy hazy way; that makes me lazy smile,
exactly what she means.

Katheryn Thal

Embers

What are you writing? Lost love asked me. Sad things, I replied.
My loss of you brought this to me, I am now in awe of my destiny.
It was not meant to be you know. You and I. Why? I do not know.
I am not wise or very bright, but despite the pain of loss, the
Constant fight, the battle deep within me the core of life; I do
Not regret that I was to have you for the shortest time. A second
Of my life in which I was to have loved and lost. Unjust it may be,
But it was my destiny, my fate to cross your path, to touch your life;
briefly like a kiss, a caress. Destiny bore me to you. Collision,
hurt, anger, frustration. Off course. The embers that once were
flame; bright as the brightest sun did not die, can't die, won't
give up the ghost. Forever a shadow upon my life, my soul. But
I was glad to stop, to care, to share. Some gift I am certain is
born from destiny on behalf of each one of us. Each to pass on
to the other; often hidden not found; not realized for a long, long
time. I know not what gift I gave to you apart from my love; myself.
If it was of any value only you can comprehend; understand, accept
in time. Perhaps never.

Martinella Brooks

Grandad

We laid the brown man in the browner earth.
The Essex clay so like his smooth brown cheek,
His ninety-four years past belying,
The elms let fall their golden tears,
But ours were dry: - His life a burden had become
Saddening his joyous nature by so many years.

I never heard him mention God.
His gods the sun, the earth, the feeding rain
His cross the shears, his book the changing skies
His staff the hoe, his creed the seasons' sure refrain.

"Get back to bed", they told him, "It's the
    morn - so light you think it's time to rise."
He laughed, and went back to his room.
But she <u>had</u> come, and softly took his hand
    and let his gentle spirit on.

J. R. Dawes

Friendship

In life people come and go
Some hold value, while others cause woe
Never quite sure who it's safe to trust
Will they weather the storm, or be gone in a gust?

You cannot spend your life in hiding
With no gentle hand caring and guiding
Solitude is used to harm and torture
Destroying any hope of a brighter future

Sometimes it feels all hatred and betrayal
But that's all I see from beneath my black veil
You have to take a risk and let someone close
You may find they will be there when you need them most

Think of the emptiness of a friendless world
Lonely, desolate, no experiences to unfold
No one to share your happiness and achievements
No one to share your anguish and bereavements

When you do find someone who is loving and caring
Believe that they are there for confiding and sharing
And whatever you do, do not let it end
For there is nothing in the world like a genuine friend

Sarah E. Dorkings

Roses

Roses sway silently in the garden
Obedient children no longer guard them
Swift their movements to and fro
As the wind gently blows
As spring flows merrily in the air
For this the children dearly care
Meaning they can easily share
The sweet scents and sights
Of the swaying roses
But now it's gone they do not care
If the rose is trampled till it's bare
So roses sway silently in the garden
Waiting for feet to carelessly harm them.

Leanne Cripps

Call Of The Wild

If I were a blackbird I would sing the day long—
Of the beauty we had, but is now almost gone.
If I were a skylark I'd soar high above—
To see desecration of this planet we love.
And if I were a dolphin patrolling the deep—
The filthy pollution would make my heart weep.
The butterflies too—and the beautiful bees—
All under threat—and carnage of trees.
What is being done to halt the despair?
And save planet Earth, which was once so fair.

Valerie Melnyk

Nature's Prism

Cherish your life every waking hour
Absorb its beauty, colours devour
Skies so blue, the warm sun so bright
Contrasting to darkness and the cool of the night

Fields so green after April rain
Awakening bulbs, seed and grain
To bring forth colours fresh, anew
Pansy, primrose under skies so blue

Rapeseed fields, a mass of yellow
Waving in the breeze so calm, so mellow
Corn rising up, shining gold in daylight
Apple trees enticing bees with blossoms pink and white

Purples and reds of the setting sun
Grey of clouds and seas as day is done
Colours of a rainbow say it all
Leaves crisp and brown in Autumn Fall

So pure and white winter snow drifts down
Covering our Earth with an innocent crown
In the blackness of the night, look up and see
Silver stars glistening down on you and me

Rosalinda Whalley

Garden Seasons

In a garden four seasons bring:
Daffodils, tulips and crocuses
From bulbs, it's spring.

In summer brings the swallow, larkspur,
Bluetit, butterflies that follow.
Flowers standing, some so tall
In the garden, children playing with their ball.

Now the harvest from crops they reap.
As autumn rich coloured leaves fall into a heap.

Cold winds, rain and sleet
Bring bought of cold feet.
The bare boughs of the trees
"Look out", here comes the winter freeze.

Carol Anne Risdale

My Love

I cannot show you, the love that wells
up inside me,
I'd love to let you know how much you
mean in my life.
I try to show you in the things I do, and
throw out my love in what I say.
Each day you mean more to me, more
than any other things on earth.
If I lost everything else but you my
life would still be full of love,
when I'm not alone—you are carried in my heart.
If you ever get upset and down
remember you are part of me, without
you I am not whole.

Brice Angilley

Nearly Christmas

When needles shiver on the old pine tree
And wild grey geese fly over the sea
When meadow grass is white frost rimed
We know it's nearly Christmas time.

When bells ring out with joyful sound
And carol singers make their round
When a special star shines sparkle bright
We know it's nearly Christmas night.

When angels sang and shepherds gazed
And in a stable Mary prayed
When Jesus slept in cradled hay
We know it's really Christmas Day.

Meryl Champion

Perfection

'Perfection' really is a peculiar term
With absolute meaning to many minds
From which we have so much to learn
Today, tomorrow and all other times.

And yet, 'perfection' can mean so much
So little too, in all its forms
Is it kindness, intelligence, or friendship as such?
Or achieved when, on us, eternal light dawns.

Can you name a single 'perfect' man?
One who makes no fault and does no wrong
Never causing or caused a single qualm
But a man who's 'good' his whole life long?

Perfection's in each of us - old and young
To be seen in the loved, ignored in the bad
There is no-one without it - not a single one
To realize that would make everyone glad.

It's unique, individual, cannot be described
We're the ones to decide when we've reached our goal
We get there by many adventures through lives
That will teach, mature and enhance our soul

Vicky Burley

Tree Of Endless Vision

Today I put aside my fear of mankind:
I had a visitor, a little girl.
With adventure in her eyes and
Music dancing in her heart,
She sat beneath my bough and we talked.

Many a time she came.
We sat watching the bright lights of the city below.
She'd stay to watch the sun go down,
Then disappear.

She'd disappear into the wilderness,
Where I cannot venture, into the suburbs of the city.

Now a grandmother, the child,
We look together across my beautiful city:
Seeded skyscrapers, sprout high,
Earth-destroying pollution turns
Black, the once blue sky.

My branches once beautiful, are now limp and frail.

Time stands still for no one:
Mortality takes its course.
Listen to the dead silence.....

Sharon Elizabeth Webster

Dedicated To The Falkland's War RIP
You Need Fight No More

And as they marched,
So brave in hearts,
Walking towards the wall of wire,
I watched as they started to fall.

The screams of pain,
The moans of the dying.
To this day I remember,
And tears fill my eyes.

These brave knights in white satin,
Giving all,
To uphold what they think right.
But all of them destined to fall.

To hell with the government,
To hell with fighting.
This pain I can take no more.
I'm turning away and closing the door.
I'm going to solitude,
And fighting alone, for what those men died for.
God bless them all.

John Hughes

The Sea

Look at the sea . . . so vast, and so deep,
A promise to man . . . its secrets to keep.

Cool and refreshing . . . like a light summer breeze,
Hard and relentless . . . bringing men to their knees.

Gentle . . . like the baby who grabs at the air,
Playful . . . like a toddler, with long flowing hair.

Ranting and raving . . . like a teenager's thirst,
Wanting all that they see . . . wanting it first,

A watery grave . . . of histories past,
Of galleons, pirates, its treasures are vast.

No man is it master, no mistress its love,
Only time its companion . . . like the stars up above.

What of the creatures that swim in the sea,
These are its children . . . not you . . . and not me!

Ageless in beauty . . . it laps at your feet.
Caressing . . . as it whispers, to the sand on the beach.

It can roar like a lion, coo like a dove,
The sea . . . is tempestuous . . . like a woman in love

Sylvia Connor

The Monster Under Your Stairs

I know a man who has two races
He can only walk two places
He also was three heads and three beds
He is the one who hides under your stairs
Fingers like snakes and spiders in his hair.
He thinks he is really funny but he
Is just a real dumb dummy.

Stephen O'Hare

I Can't Hear The Silence Anymore

The 5.15 from Croydon to Victoria
Rampages over the bridge.
People busy with gossip and small talk
Avoid what's really being said.
Rush hour traffic clogs the roads, horns blown.
Abuse hurled at drivers jumping the green men
By irate pedestrians with screaming toddlers in buggies
Trying to get to the other side.
At home, the radio and the television
Cancel each other out.
At the charismatic meeting
Everyone speaks in tongues louder than thou.
I can't hear the silence anymore.

W. Morfey

Kismet

An anguished howl.
The infant's corpse.
A smell so foul.
Tears, like ripened apples, fall.
The citizens of death call.

Smiling faces of celebration.
One hundred candles,
Create a pool of illumination.
A wrinkled face, eyes that no longer see the page.
Yet a soul blessed with the gift of age.

Blood-bleached feet.
She stumbles on,
Determination battling the heat.
The children alone, a worried mind.
She never stops, food she must find.

The speech finished,
The party began.
Arguments on either side diminished.
Behold! A banquet of fish, fruit, blood red meat.
Oh my! What shall I eat?

Kate Williams

Seaweed

Slimy
and pretty grimy
Crabs and fish.
Yuck Yuck Yuck!!!

When I am in the water
creepy things crawl around me
things like fish and crabs splash around me.
Then I hear a little splash splash splash
and I am out like a flash.
I hate seaweed!

Elsbeth McStay

A New Leaf

Today is just a beginning
Soon you'll feel like singing

Beginning the new life you want
Instead of saying I can't

Be positive in things you do
In the past you were always foo

Days went past in a blur
Your words turned in to a slur

People stopped looking at you with pity
Shunned by all in the city

Dirty, haggard and old
Furniture and sundry all sold

But forget all about this
Because drink you won't miss

Enjoy life again and be sober
As a new leaf has just turned over.

Shiela Mavin

In The Dark

I always look under my bed
for monsters that would bite off my head.
But one dark, spooky night
I got one heck of a fright
There was something under there!
I screamed myself right out of my hair
But it turned out to be the cat
in my Los Angeles baseball cap.

Tom Bannister

Untitled

Here we are almost through summer
it will no doubt, soon be December.
Where has time gone, so fast this year
then you came along, and held me so near.

Passing glances across the room
wanting to touch, but dare not, too soon.
The yearning for passion strong and sure
physical contact the only cure.

Oh for the day we could be together
loving embrace you and me forever.
I struggle along each day at a time
wishing and hoping you will be mine.

Soon that day will come along
When you and I can be alone
Hearts will be racing, bodies quivering
passion and lust the inevitable feelings.

Can we afford this moment in time
I just don't know till you are mine.
And so this year will have gone by fast
Do you think that we will last?

Gloria L. Carr

The Dancer And The Dance

Oh, I have lived and loved and played and danced the dance of life,
Soared to heights of happiness, plunged down to bitter strife;
Laughter I've known abundantly and tears beyond belief;
Have drunk of life's euphoria and supped the gruel of grief;
Walked hand in hand with loneliness, embraced old devil despair,
Regrets I've had, remorse I've felt and guilt beyond compare.
I've scaled the heights of ecstasy, lived with agony and doubt;
Have been rejected, spurned, put down, abandoned and thrown out.
Compassion felt, and tenderness, I've been cared for and adored.
Lived every moment passionately, never been bored,
For life is an exciting stage on which I've played my part
With zeal and zest, the worst, the best, I've danced with all my heart
And when upon the wall my death the moving finger writes,
Before the falling of the curtain, the dimming of the lights,
Before I make the final curtsey and I know there's no encore
One last request in earnestness 'ere I leave the back stage door;
To those I love who loved me well - oh, can you understand
About the pulsing surging music and the urging beat of the band?
For I'll be dancing the last tango till the fading of my breath
And finally, excitedly, I'll dance the dance of death

Christine Stirling

Fear

Mothers of existence your tools of creation cease to function, nothing
goes on the canvas of who and what we are, and our toys of self
destruction continue to haunt our memory clouding the canvas of life.

Mothers of existence your fear prevents us from seeing the future as
it can be, your fear does not allows us to see clearly that the
cleansing rain has stopped and the tears of pain have dried up from
lack of attention.

Mothers of existence reach deep inside and regain control denied you
for so many life times, you have the insight and the tools, help us
end the destruction.

Allow our minds and eyes to see the world from your special place, our
very survival will depend on you and your strength, yes we ask much.

Face your fears so the memories of our children will not stop, and
they will not stop, and they will be safe, and they will understand
the reason for their existence.

I fear the fathers of existence lack the emotions and insight so long
denied them to see the future through your eyes, I fear they lack
the strength to be gentle, I fear.

Mothers of existence show us now the gentle, the healthy way, the
future is in your hands, use that time wisely as it is the future
of the fathers of existence and our children of tomorrow.

It is the reason for our being, let your insight end the foolishness
of having no purpose, because we really know, yes we know.

Terry Ducheane

Smite Hard The Steeple

They're pulling half the old town down, destroying our yesterday
Replacing fine old art with grey cement, grotesque in every way.
Modern architects, short sighted, think of cost, they think of space
How many buildings to the plot, not beauty, style, or grace.

A heavy ball on steel-linked chain, swings from crane arm high above
Smiting hard the old church steeple, built by men with skill and love.
The sculptured cross, the weather vane, with heart-breaking tearing sound
Collapse on walls of Gothic stone, to lie shattered on the ground.

Walls and carvings sculpt with pride, figured windows in leaded glass
The rage of swinging ball do meet, to join steeple on the grass.
Terraced houses where people lived, who in the church did congregate
Wait, with shattered windows, to be demolished by ball of fate.

Then when their task completed, and site fit for reclamation
Work-men pack their ball and crane, leaving total devastation.
And now where church and homes stood, with local shops and friendly pub
A dull concrete jungle there abides, with ring-road at its hub.

Multi storey blocks of flats, and supermarkets by the score
High-rise office suites, built close, shopping malls, neon signs galore.
But just one brick church, built round, and plain, dome-shaped roof in toughened glass
No church steeple, carvings, cross or vane, no bells to herald mass.

Frank Ravenscroft

Summer Fragrance

The beauty of a summer rose
Where a butterfly rests for sweet repose
The scented stock - a fragrance rare
All is tended with love and care.

The hydrangea in its pure array
Is just perfect on a summer's day
So indeed is the potentilla
And the blazing star - a majestic fella!

The montbretia in its delicacy
Looks lovely underneath a tree
The Copper Beech - a joy indeed
Adds contrast to the garden weed!

The carnation - which is a gentle flower
Gives lustre to the heavenly bower
The hedgerow thick with foliage
Is a delight in this day and age.

It is God's garden here upon earth
For us to sow and reap its worth
For only when the work is done
Can achievement be reached - and the prize won.

Gillian Morgan

Our Daughter's Wedding

Our daughter's getting married in Scotland today
The months' careful planning have drifted away.
We've helped her to dress and her make-up's in place
And I can't help but gaze at her beautiful face.

Where's that little girl we brought into the world
Her eyes brightly sparkling and golden her curls.
A beautiful woman now standing alone
Entering a union and making a home.

Peter enters the room with the bride on his arm
Gives our daughter to Lee and remains very calm.
Tom hands over the rings places them on the book
Rachel looks at Lee with a meaningful look.

Michael the vicar begins then his prayers
Calls on Rachel and Lee their love to declare
Love, loyalty, trust as long as you both shall live
A true lifelong union give all you can give.

They're joined now in marriage their union complete
We pray that their future is happy and sweet.
Good health and happiness is what we all wish
And the bride and the groom seal it all with a kiss.

Mrs. Christine Baxter

More Than A Dream

I walked along a narrow path, the sun shone warm and bright,
I came across a meadow—Huge, no words describe the sight.
Imagine fields of bounteous flowers, sharp in colours,
different shades.
Can you imagine endless beauty, even in the forest glades?

The brook beside me, full of life, was dancing in the sun,
And music came from all around, and people—full of fun,
Can you imagine music, from the ripples of a stream,
The dulcet sounds of water flows, are notes, high in esteem.

Singing is around me still, and colour music dawns,
Just like a rainbow in the sky, the notes create a form;
Further on, an edifice, built up of sapphires—true;
It shone like diamonds, pure and clear, yes: jewels—white
and blue.

It wasn't long before I heard a bell ring loud and long,
'Twas my alarm clock, ringing sharp, to welcome in the dawn,
I sat in wonder on my bed, of where I had just been,
A dream, I thought—No—it was more, than just a dream I'd seen.

Ruby Flavell

Scarlet Ribbons

The birds sang a chorus, the bees hummed a tune.
"My love's on the ocean, he'll be with me soon.
He'll bring back my ribbons when homeward he sails;
Home to the river, the hills and the dales,
To the family who'll greet him, and friends cheering wild".
Then she slept on the warm grass - heavy with child.

Weary from war - as he crossed the wide ocean.
He stood on the deck, felt the ship's gentle motion.
Deep in his pocket, scarlet ribbons were there -
The ones that she'd worn in her dark flowing hair.
This longing to hold her was so hard to bear.

The sudden explosion! Smoke and flames everywhere!
None could survive. Precious lives had all gone:
If love can transcend, could the soul linger on?

Stirring from slumber, confused by the mist:
Drawn to the water - she could not resist.
The mist it was rising as a boat drifted by
With a shadowy figure - arm held high.
Transfixed, she stared as it reached the shore:
On the seat scarlet ribbons were all that she saw.

Toby S. Endlar

What Has Happened To Lulu? The Mother's Reply

Oh Lulu, I love you,
I hope you're not far.
I'm not happy when you're not here,
Like a night with no stars.

I am sorry if I hurt your feelings,
I just want you home.
We'll start from the beginning,
We'll go with the flow.

If I could turn back the clock,
Believe me I would.
Life would be different,
Just like it should.

We have to go on,
What's done is done.
I know you're feeling down,
But we'll rise like the sun.

Since you have gone, the house has stood still.
No sounds of laughter, no stories or thrills.

The house is in darkness all the flowers are dying.
There is nothing left, just tears and crying.

Siobhan Moran

Mrs. Ebrahim

Our teacher is orange
She is a bright sunset on a summer night
In a rose garden
She is a sunny day
She is a bright flowery dress
She is a sunbed
She is Susan of Neighbours
She is a surprise cake.

Jemma Kiernan

The Port

As I walk along this windswept shore,
Where many people have come before,
Surrounded by a landscape lush and green,
Unlike anything I have ever seen,
Listening to the gentle sounds,
As they gather all around,
Takes me on a journey back,
Trying to imagine how life had been,
When my father was young and keen.

Eamonn James McGrath

The Garden I First Knew

How well I remember the garden I first knew
In childhood's memory there I oft return
To gaze at flowers of a glorious hue
And leave my heart in gentle sweet sojourn

How well I remember the winding paths and bowers
The pear tree upon the garden wall
The heavy fragrance over summer evening hours
The sweet peas - the arum lilies tall!

How well I remember - how 'ere can I forget
The heart and hands that shaped such beauty there
For they live on within my memory yet
To fill my soul with thoughts of yesteryear.

Joan R. Osborne

My Dear Friend

I am made of stone in the form of a statue.
An excellent work of a sculptor.
Credit goes to its creator.
People look at my erotic figure,
They appreciate its artistic beauty.
But I have my own feelings,
That nobody wants to know.
I am free, a young girl, spending time with flowers.
Birds and rabbits are my friends.
I cannot stand the noise of the people.
They are not my type.
That's why I like to be on my own,
And wander in the green garden.
Accidentally, I bumped into a statue,
was startled to see it looking at me.
I exclaimed - what a beautiful creature you are!
My dear friend.

Sati Sen

Let's Go Hunting

Let's go hunting a boy said one day.
There are rabbits and hares in the fields of hay.
We will hunt far and wide until the noon-day.
But the good hunting ground was far, far away.

So we walked through the woods where we met Farmer Jones.
With a pick and, a fork and his jodhpurs on.
He gave us a hint then he showed us the way.
Yet the good hunting ground was far, far away.

Then at last as we came to an old oak tree.
We saw signs of good hunting for more than us three.
So we set our traps and snares in the hay.
And the good hunting ground was there to stay.

So we hunted at length from day to day.
Woth rabbits and hares for our prey.
When we return home we were happy and gay.
Far, far from the hunting ground over the way.

W. W. A. Joseph

War

Darkness,
Trapped,
Alone,
Frightened,
Misery in the cheerfulness of places,
Pain in the unhurt,
Crying in the thousands,
Death in the millions,
The innocent dying, the guilty living on,
We pay for the government's mistakes, their choices,
We have no choices, but we get the pain
Grief
And death
After they started it, government v. Government,
But us the innocent bystanders get dragged in,
Called to fight, to die for our country,
But,
how does our country repay the dead!

Katie Smith

Love Thy Neighbour

We sensed at once, our homes were hutches:
no amount of pastel paint or wallpaper
could cover up the cracks of truth.

For the first seven years of marriage
Our foundations proved unworthy-
If I recall, your house sunk first!

We sat up philosophizing in your kitchen
Shivering as the fire turned to ash-
at times, we hit the nail on the head....

We found nuggets of wisdom in a river of tears
Shifting through our real or imagined misery:
Closed ranks on the men who made us cry

We sought advice and gave counsel-
growing wiser than our husbands could handle
We rocked the boat, dyed our hair- red!

Wore clothes and colours that gave us strength
Knocked down walls by ourselves,
suffered the consequence, choked on dust.

Noelle Vial

Money

Money is evil in the wrong hands
It has been the downfall of many lands
It is stolen, borrowed and taken on demand
Yes, and even used as contraband.

Amusement arcades and fruit machines
Gobble it up and sweep the board clean
Standing charges are robbery in disguise
Helping to fill the pockets of monopoly guys

The decimal coin was a very big con
It replaced the penny with the Queens head on
Now there is talk of a new coin too
May I introduce the European Ecu

So where do we stand in this money-grabbing land
With opportunist and contraband
The Ecu will never take the place
Of our sterling coins with the Royal Monarch's face.

Sylvia Spicer

Business

Sitting in the station thinking
Thinking in his Bowler hat
Bowler hat covering a wrinkled brow
A wrinkled brow from stress
Stress in a pin-striped suit, smoking a pipe
A pipe blowing out Hamlet clouds
Clouds of unknown thought
Thought clouds thinking of interest
Interest in money?
Money and the exchange
Exchanging thoughts between businessmen
Businessmen and women
Women for dating, or marrying?
Marrying Women and businessmen
Businessmen sat in a station
Station full of stress in suits.

Abi Roper

Love

Is to be on top of the world
To be enveloped in your lover's arms

Is to know true peace
To laugh and play with someone special in your life

Be it a child or adult
Is to let your inner child out to play

Try to learn to enjoy your love and question it not

For just to have had the experience
Is more than some ever have

Sammy

The Last Tomorrow

He left me a world full of places that he and I have seen;
a heaven full of wishes that he and I have dreamed.
He left the poetry and songs of love, the words for us alone;
the magic and the mystery of all the wonders we've known.
He left the laughter and the sunshine; the passion and the pain,
of days and nights and moments that will never come again.
He left me a heart full of memories to last my lifetime through.
He left me no tomorrows -
he took them back, for you

He left me the ochre sunsets and the rainbows we might have shared,
to find castles nestling in the clouds - knowing he'll see them there.
He left me misty vermilion dawns, oceans of gold meshed foam,
and the everlasting promise that my heart remains his home.
He left to me that never land where dreams can all come true,
where he will forever be waiting, dreaming my dreams too.
He left me the solace of starshire, the rivers running with tears.
He left me no tomorrows -
to give you back the years

Rona Clark

For Bill

Born in 1931—that makes me old I suppose.
No one knows, except a few of necessity.
A gleam on my hair, a rinse to take care
of the grey—but discreetly.
A dress sense that hides little bulges inside,
drifting elegance and simplicity.
Colours that sing of seasons
Pastels of blush, creations of fragrance,
Scents of intriguing serenity.

An ode to self? Oh yes, but more,
To stay the same as I was
Before when Bill was here.
To keep the glow alive, our togetherness to survive
the numbing rubbing out time makes
of memories scintillating.
Not wild and hedonistic ways but sweet and happy days
of buttercups clinging to our shoes
on rainy walks and serious important talks on everything.

The tears will pass for love is endless and will outlast
my grieving—and hug me close as I go on—deceiving.

Margaret Mitchell

Nature's Decorations

A swirling white landscape, sculptured in white.
Snow bright, blanketed ground glistening.
Trees hung with ice clear crystals.
Brown branches shining with glittering highlights.

Lakes glazed glassily over and dully gleaming.
Horizons fused, grey to white, blurred.
Spiders webs hang, stiffly suspended.
Frosted fern patterns on window panes.

Once cascading waterfalls are still, petrified in ice.
Sounds are muffled, no echoes resounding.
Snowdrops, their heads bent, herald the spring.
Mirror-like, the scene reflects moonlight.

Silvery white diamonds seem to glitter everywhere.
The holly tree berries, glowing like rubies.
The wind howls its lonely message.
Owls sit hungry, blinking, prey spared tonight.

The moon looms in a dark sky, mercurial and bright.
The night is silent, it could be another time.
The only movement, drifting snowflakes gliding silently down.
Nature's decorations, beautiful, richer than any jewels.

Rosalind Lee

The Astronauts

Grey and foreboding, the astronauts said,
Of the moon whose silvery light
Shines far on the world below.
What did they expect, these modern men?
Who probe the world outside our own?
No more for them can the moon hold romance,
No sound here on this planet, just silence.
Men exploring a world far from earth,
Held a different image in their minds,
As they gazed on the world far below.
So out of the capsule they had stepped,
Beneath their feet a grey powdery surface,
Around no sign of the sun's reflected beams.
Now seeing the moon so cold and grey,
Shattering their dreams of magic and mystery.
When the astronauts return to Earth,
And they see the moon smiling down,
For them the magic could not return,
But the wonder of God's creation
Will live forever in their memories.

Barbara King

My Collier '36

An enigmatic face my collier, neither young nor old
Ageless on black damp canvas, indelible in sunlit gold
Flamboyant shades of a braggart, a gambler, and a card
Wrestling with death for a living, in the devil's own backyard
A ready quip upon his lips, strong beer to slake his thirst
To a mate entombed in hell, the siren brought him first
A philosopher on haunches, playing the cards fate dealt
His belly lean with hunger, bitter pride drawing tight his belt
Laughter coloured his dust-rimmed eyes, music filled his soul
His heartbeat strong with courage, his life the price-tag on coal
The pithead a stark monument etched on a blood red sky
Poignant on the widowed wind, stoic tears, a bairn's cry
Fifty years, five hundred, memory will past and present mix
Time nor distance never erase my brave collier '36
Now with his lamp among the stars, no plaster saint, no sham
But as he was, just as he was, standing tall as any man.

Lily Duncan

Loving Thoughts

An old man stood in his garden thinking of years gone by.
When with his wife and partner they worked side by side.

Now alone and aged. No one to help him along.
He watches the flowers fading.
As the light from his life has gone.

But as his life grows shorter he knows he will meet
her some day.

In that heavenly garden of flowers never to part again.

Lydia Lee

Beauty And The Beast

A smoke ring dissipates as dies noble ambition in
breezes of apathy. Cobwebs occupy cornerstones of
principle that lie within, but remain unchallenged.
Where belongs constancy, that surely resides not
'midst such unchosen vacillation.

Would that a gentle wave might bestow its gift upon
me, knowing no other cause even unto demise on
its mattress. It falters not in winds that seek to
divert. It finds no shame in predictable course.

Can a diadem be other than itself, or a snake upon
the earth? Is there falsehood to be found in truth,
or blood within a stone? Nay, 'tis mischief, for
intrinsic description utters unshakeable destiny.

But of me, there is intemperate paradox. My path
to tread, oft veiled with idle robes, leads me not
up mountains, but into valleys of broken dreams.

I find that many others journey there also.

Trevor E. Gear

2 (Two)

2 pots of tea, 2 heads of steam
2 gardens green, 2 flowers cream
2 children still, 2 lives to fill
2 spaces vast, 2 heads of glass.

2 streams do flow, beneath thy brow;
2 hearts equate, as heads deflate.

Where will they go?
What will they miss?
2 paths to take, 2 lives to make.

He chose them both; he lost her close.

If he is happy let him be
If he is not well, wait and see.

2 stubborn souls are best apart,
Too much anger to depart.
To you I am the happy smile
The shadow of your former style
A memory clear
A wish so dear
That you will fear...
4 ever

Nicole Curnow

The Seed

Out of the packet it looked so small
  but I was promised, "It will grow tall."
So I made a hole in the ground
  and the seed went in without a sound.

Out of the blue the seed starts to grow
  it must have now been two weeks or so.
To an insect it must have looked so tall
  to me it looked so feeble and small.

The shoot was strong enough to form the bud
  as if the shoot was making love.
The two born together now are one
  pointing upwards towards the sun.

Then as the flower came into bloom
  with petals all neatly groomed.
Its colour was so powerful and strong
  and a scent that we all longed.

It took so long to grow
  but the flower was beautiful you know.
The pleasure the flower gives to me
  is as rewarding as nectar is to the bee.

Sharon Irwin

Life's Stormy Sea

Life can be like the stormy sea
An inner searching yearning to be free
Back and forth and to and fro
In and out the sea must flow

Upon life's shore the breakers roar
Sadness and gloom knock on our door
Life continues on like the endless sea
Calm and tempting this life can be

Beware my friend of the changing sea
The tide and current are also free
Seek and find the depth you choose
In this way you can never lose

Deep in the dark below the sea
A ray of light, just look, you'll see
Life may be dark like the evening dusk
'Tis then my friend that you must trust

God made the heaven, earth and the sea
For each one's part of life's great tree
So live and learn you'll soon be free
And don't you ever be lost at sea

Bruce Hadden

Heaven, And Hell, On Earth

Instead of enjoying the heaven around us all the time,
it seems to be only the hell we seek to find.

Heaven to see the sun, and feel its warmth, Hell is a fire raging.
Heaven is raindrops against a window, Hell is bullet's ricochet off a wall.
Heaven to see clouds of rain, Hell to see clouds of smoke.
Heaven to hear the wind howl, Hell to hear a bomb explode.
Heaven to breathe the fresh air, Hell to inhale toxic fumes.

I'd rather tremble with cold than with pain and fear.
I'd rather hear a baby laugh with joy than hear a child cry with hunger.
I'd rather step in a puddle of water than a puddle of blood.
I'd rather walk in a field of clover than a battle field of death.
I'd rather take shelter in a forest than an underground bunker.
I'd feel safer from a thunder storm than an atomic bomb.

Heaven to see the birds fly, Hell to see bombers use up their space in the sky.
Heaven to hear them sing their tunes, Hell to hear words of war.
Heaven to see the moon and stars, Hell to see rockets and missiles.

I'd rather touch the branch of a tree than a barrel of a gun.
I'd rather feel its leaves fall on my head than feel tears roll down my face.

Heaven when a chick leaves its nest, Hell when a young man leaves for war.
Heaven is the nature Mother Earth gives us, Hell is when we tear it down.

Cornelius McGurgan

Pictures In The Sky

Aurora hues of flamingos as dawn comes up from watery bed,
Amidst the pink and purple glows they stand serene, or drift and dredge.
Then, as the sun comes into view and meets the sky in radiant shine
Tall ships come sailing on the blue, with wind in sails they move in line.

The sun has climbed up from the dawn, bright shafts are drawing water up
To make black caves and dragons strong, with fiery tongues and languid lope.
A tiger rests, haunched, by a tree and wispy feathers make a bird
Fly up and up and quickly flee beyond fine castles, dark and weird.

When course of sunlit day has passed and sinks down through magenta veils
Come roseate swans, adrift, amassed as silvery moon lights up the dales.
And peaks of mountains, sharp and cragged, tower over landscapes pale and cold,
As stars peep through like jewels splashed on velvet trimmed with precious gold.

Anne White

My Wise Old Friend

Her body is old and frail,
Yet her heart is young and strong,
Her mind a galaxy of memories, has yet to fail,
As her eyes glistens when she recalls thoughts forgotten for so long.

I can tell her of my day, my work, my play, my romance,
She listens with her eyes closed, her usual way,
Then she opens them and looks at me with a knowing glance.

She remembers the complexities of youth,
She is the only person who understands me,
I tell her no lie only the truth,
About the factors to my anxiety.

She has seen the problems of the world over her seventy-five years,
I have seen them only over my sixteen,
That is why I listen to her advice, which banishes my fears,
She arouses encouragement in me to look for positive aspects on life I had not seen.

Who is she you might ask, this woman with wisdom compared to no other,
She is a woman with a goal in life to carry out a special task,
Which is to be, a friend and most of all to be the very best grandmother.

Wayne Hanley

Foolishness Of Farewell

To say goodbye to you is mockery; You never leave me.
In bidding me farewell you travesty; You but deceive me
To thinking when I turn from you, you've gone. My sense belies it;
That when I walk away, I am alone. My heart denies it.
I press your hand, I turn, I feel my loss. Amazed - I start!
For lo! You're nearer than before; You speak from my own heart.
And then, days passing, you remain with me, at times scarce known;
Sometimes so keenly close, I stare to see myself alone.
I think, my love, that then more near we press;
Welded in an invisible caress.

Mary M. Gillespie

The Power Of Prayer

When we feel all hope has gone, and we slip into despair,
A good friend may remind us, there is the power of prayer
Life has no further meaning; we have no wish to carry on,
Distraught has taken over our loved ones, dead and gone.

At the time we may feel angry, and say "Lord it is not fair"
Then we get the inner feeling there is the power of prayer.
In the past we may not realize what the power of prayer can do,
Until we face the crosses that saddens me and you.

Each and everyone of us have borne misery and tears.
The power of prayer is always there to heal our hidden fears.
A loved one may have left us, for a reason we don't know.
Only prayer can help us, the progress can be slow.

It's said that prayer moves mountains; we believe it very true.
If that belief is strong enough, peace will come to me and you.
When the trials of life catch up on us, and we find it hard to bear,
Don't despair! Help is there! It is the power of prayer.

The time may be delayed, but the answer is sure to come,
The feeling of an inner peace is felt when day is done,
With our troubles all behind us; all the hurts we couldn't bear,
All our peace of mind returned — through the power of prayer.

Agnes O'Donnell-Hakesley

I Wish I'd Walked My Dog

The rain came down incessantly - as if 'twas filled with hate.
While you sat waiting patiently beside the garden gate
Your wait went unrewarded - your patience was in vain
I'd other, better, things to do
Than walking in the rain!

I always took you for a walk about that time of day
To romp and play among the dunes - across from Findhorn Bay.
I lit the fire and sat there wondering if ever we'd get a break
From rain! Rain! Rain!
And have some decent weather.

The next I knew I heard a shot - and then I heard another
An icy hand clutched round my heart
And I cried out "Oh! Mother"
I ran outside, across the dunes, calling out your name
"Josie, Josie, please come back" I cried - you never came.

I wandered over to the fields as if I was dazed by sleep
And then I saw you lying there among the flock of sheep.
My mind goes blank, my heart stands still, my eyes begin to fog
When I recall that rainy day
How I wish I'd walked my dog.

Aileen Gass

No Greater Love

I remember her face that had gracefully aged,
And the sweet smile she always shared.
The soft honest eyes, that never showed rage,
But much expression of compassion and passion so rare.

Her delicate frame she would carry so well,
Attempting difficult tasks when stubbornness prevailed.
Her time on the earth you never could tell,
Succeeding in her world my grandmother never failed.

The love that she showed me was endless no doubt,
There could be no greater love.
Her hugs that gave security, she was never without,
I miss what we would share, while she sleeps in heaven above.

Sometimes my world feels empty, when I drift away in thought,
A sense of sadness and loneliness sets inside.
I wished she was here, many tears I have fought,
My best friend I lost, and yet pain will not subside.

I remember the day and the last smile she shared,
The last kiss I gave, a return smile was strained.
That day she left my life, a fight she lost so rare,
One day I'll see those smiling eyes, when our worlds will meet again.

Helen Riddell McDougall

Me?

It's always there, somewhere inside, when I go to sleep
  and wake up.
I can never quite find it, no matter how hard I look.
Just when I think I have, it slithers away deep into my body.
I don't know what it is, maybe I'll find it someday,
My real self.

A false smile, a concerned face, when all I want to do is laugh.
I've dived into a big bowl of insecurity and cannot get out.
I'm drowning . . . drowning in myself.
My confidence and happiness pushed under the surface,
And I can't save them as I can't swim.

I'm trying to find the real me, but can't reach it
Perhaps I don't want to, scared of what I might find
Of what evil, ugly object might crawl out from inside,
Like a worm under a rock in the garden.
I mighty regret what I uncover when I lift the rock from myself.

I just want to escape, throw off this heavy lead weight which
  hangs on my mind.
I don't know how to do it, I'm not strong enough.
The best I can do is to move it piece by piece,
Chipping away, and perhaps someday I'll be free
  of this sadness.

Alison McCall

Moving On

Lashing waves of harsh bright colours
Vanish from my life
Everything I breathed for, cut me like a knife

I struggled to continue
So bleak my future looked

Why does the pain carve my soul?
How can I achieve the ultimate goal?
All my feelings just disappeared
The out look for us just needed cleared

Young, naive and helpless
Our lives drift far apart
Under rocks of heavy fear, scratching out our hearts

My eyes fill up with stinging tears
And love spans over many years
Keeping ourselves generally sane
Even though we don't see through the rain

I walk through life staring fast
The worst part is - love never lasts.

Pam Nelson

Holidays!

We get up late to start a long and luxurious day,
they seem sunny bright and extended; it's funny how
nothing is quite as it was in the time before heat wave relaxation.

The days are long and blend; as one day leads late
and early to the next through repetitive task and
interesting boredom, the passing of time sitting
impatiently doing nothing, awaiting the return of
work, which, somehow, is less interesting than nothing.

The enjoyment of time spent freely, taking time to do
whatever is needed, this is all a novelty to those
soon-to-be pensioners, who have little time left to play,
this holiday or of their lifetimes.

They hunt around urgently and nervously, looking for
things to amuse in-operative minds; for things to
occupy empty but busy days; until the return of
discipline and frustration, they struggle to find
interest, something unusual to a usual state of mind,
to impress the routine calm and tedious, and to destroy doing nothing.

And so the day arrives one fateful, unwanted,
yet eagerly awaited day, when there's 10 minutes more boredom,
and 10 minutes left of the same!

Clare L. Wigley

113

Midnight

Oh Midnight, how soft your smile seems
through moonstruck glimpses and dancing
stars that wink silent secrets, your gentle
breeze whispers essence of another being.

Oh Midnight, your tranquillity transcends any
peace perceived by mere mortals, and how
your deep blue sphere soothes even troubled
souls, as mingled thoughts you untangle!

Oh Midnight, you surpass any serenity found
in day; you walk beside restless hearts and,
like fragile spirits, you cradled them to calmer
corners in their mind.

O' midnight! How I love your mystique
beauty thrust in an alluring angelic
enchantment!

Amanda Reason

A Dream Into Death

Lying on the bed, encircled with silence
Not a word being said, just hoping.

Caving in and enveloped into a dream
Seeing nothing but wisps of white
As if all walls of existence ceased to survive.
Travelling on a track, to a destination unknown
Observing the route of "Eternity."

Eyes like pendulums swaying from side to side
As curtains unfold memories, memories of the past.

A whistle blew, proceeding with the journey
Winding through this immortal land, seeing the light ahead.

Approaching a platform; a halt
The opening of a door, entitled "Heaven"
A hand reaching out for his
A voice calling, "Come child, come."
It was only a matter of time before he lost this race.

He still lay on the bed, though pallor pale
With relatives mourning the loved one.....dead.

Navkirn Randhawa

In Spirit

I'm thinking of you night and day,
and there is something, I need to say,
you're a good person, with a gold heart,
you've been there for us, from the start,
you don't deserve, what you've been through,
good people like you, never do.
Please remember we're all here for you,
there isn't anything, we wouldn't do.
I will treasure their memories in my heart,
I then know, we'll never ever part.
To me, you know, they'll always be here,
when I'm alone, I feel them near.
They were loved in every way,
and it grows stronger everyday.
Now they're at peace, but still with you,
in everywhere you go, and all that you do.

Carolyn Langridge

Untitled

I crawl through clouds of reality
Like my father and his father before him
Who thrashed the wheat with palms of poverty.

The dry skin of labour all to be forgotten.
We float through life, but in the unconscious world
We climb like ants carrying our rewards from past to present.

The golden cup of life rests on an invisible pedestal
Like Jesus on his cross.
We reach and pray for it but it lies naked with legs of stone.

Sam Davies

It's A River's Life

Trickling, splurting into a little stream
Rushing downhill spluttering everywhere
Bubbling just like a mini waterfall;
Thinking if it should make a river yet
Echoes are surrounding the noisy alps
I am hoping it will get quieter
The little streams are now a big river
Quiet and peaceful there is not a sound
The noise of washed up pebbles just around.
Now it is big and wide and very long
Everywhere you look water surrounds you
Flowing gently not a sound to be heard
About one mile is the rough sea
Now it's gone, gone in the wide
deep blue sea.

Christina Dickinson

The Rustic Bridge

Time stood still when I was in that place
When I wandered through gates honeysuckle entwined,
where winding paths led to scenes of pure delight,
garlands abundant draped softly like the morning dew.
Trees stood resplendent in their Autumn glow
transformed to ice sculptures, in the winters fall,
old timers gnarled and bent had a beauty of their own.

I was content, no other place for me would do
there was that special rustic bridge,
many hours were spent just leaning on its rails,
my heart would leap with joy - I was entranced
and joined the choir in their harmonious song.

It's where waters in gentle motion flow
enticing all to this safe haven for a while,
it's where I felt the warm caressing breeze
where tantalizing perfumes waft on the winds,
where pleasure for my dogs to share.
And where gentle slumber beckons - in final repose
who needs to go to heaven, it's already here!,

Helen J. Lewis

Faith, Hope And Charity

This world of ours could be a happy place
For everyone in the human race,
Let's give a helping hand to everyone
Then the battle for peace will be won,
Treat each other like sister and brother
Let's all try to understand each other.

You have got to have faith, hope and charity
To help you to reach reality,
So let's all pray for all our worth
Then we shall have peace on earth.

There is always faith behind a smile
If you take a look once in a while,
At the people you meet along the street
Instead of passing them by, just turn and greet,
There is always hope in every heart
If each of us has a greeting to impart.

Kathleen Knott

Divine Dedication

As the sun sinks low on the landscaped site
And shadows advance on the lush green slope
And the church on the hill bathed in golden light
Evoking in mood an aura of hope.

Endowed with the gift of eloquent speech
For forty years he kept alive
The faith of those now out of reach
And all of them who still survive.

And now the sun has set at last
On all his labours for the Lord
Now let him reap from the shadow he cast
May peace and joy be his just reward!

John Nicholson

The Bully

Hey you, get aff that swing and leave ma wean.
Jist leave him. Ma son disnae deserve that,
aye and stop punching him,
or you'll be singing your last hymn.
Whit? You dare to answer me back?
I'll take a stick to you, hit you were it hurts.
You're the school Bully so they say,
kids can't even enjoy their play, they can't speak for fear of you.
Now, I'll call your bluff! I've had enough!
Trying to peddle your drugs eh? Well listen to me.
I'm going to set your arse on fire you little liar,
I'll make you sad, make you feel really bad.
On your way, get your kicks elsewhere.
No more drug dealing here, no more living in fear,
so get right out, with your hash for cash,
and your wacky bacci, you Bully.

Catherine Kane

The Butterfly Tree

If a gentle-colourful side of nature you would wish to see,
Come with me—I will take you to view our butterfly tree.
As you approach a sweet aroma fills the air
It is much heavier: now—oh—we are there
The tree is in full summer bloom
Covered in flowers—long purple plumes
Butterflies flit around you as you approach
As the boundaries of butterfly kingdom you encroach
A host of butterflies are feeding on the flowers
They are really beautiful—of various colours
Some butterflies gather together and dance about the tree
  in gentle flight
This display is on view all the day—from morn till night
Gardener's call it a buddleia—tree—that maybe
A beautiful picture presented by nature and it is all free.

J. Authbert

Outcast

I am the spark, that leaves the fire,
of turbulent society.
The outcast, the spark that is slowly
fading and soon will die.
I live in a world of cruel darkness,
I a prisoner of sorrow.
My life a perfect graveyard of buried hopes.
How I wish, how I long just to feel warm inside.
But no, I am excluded, treated like a leper,
viewed as a fugitive trying to escape.
The flames lick towards the sky with
colours so bright.
The pressure mounts, I feel my blood boil.
Just as the rocket surges towards the
heavens, then coldly bursts.
So year by year my fear of living
grows too great to bear.
No splendid display for me
but sadly I fall back to earth spent and dead.

Naomi Penfold

My Love Is Gone

My love is gone. No bird should sing
  or build its eager nest.
No flower should wreathe its petals wide
  for pollened feet to rest.
The sunbeams should not pierce the trees
  to sleve the shadowed vale.
The butterflies should still their wings
  and cease their nectared trail,
The evening gnats not weave their dance
  upon the steps of space.
He is not here to see and smile,
  nor may I watch his face.
How can they dance and sing and play
  as if it were still yesterday?

Muriel Chapman

Dance With Me

The angels sing on Heaven's streets
Of days when lonely hearts would beat
In time with those who keep them strong.
So why do angels sing sad songs
That tell the dreams of every man?
They'll cheer for joy, and shout with peace,
Or happiness at most, or least.

Come Happiness, and dance with me.
Come home and stay so we can be
Forever just as lovers should.
They day will come, through bad or good,
When the angels will sing just for us;
And then this world we know will cease
In happiness, for us at least.

C. E. Robinson

Sonnet To November

The curtains are drawn close, the fire burns bright,
Idly my thoughts down questing pathways stray,
Till scene and scent and sound call forth to light
The warp and woof of a November day.
The lace of rookeries against a sky
All saffron-barred; gilt froth of ivy's flower;
Guy's baubles bold through tawny haze that fly,
'Mid children's mirth and mud; remembrance hour
Whose alchemy to radiance can transmute
Each redly-falling petal; spindle; leaf-dank wine
Of amber pools; spindle, a robin's flute
Spilling thin sweetness; haloed saints ashine
At holy All Saints' tide. When all is told
November's tapestry is wrought in gold.

Doris M. H. Brownlee

Summer Storm

The sky was blue, awhile ago
Now white clouds turn to grey,
I hear a clap of thunder
A distant rumble, far away.
Flash of lightning, there's a spot of rain
Another, and another, on the window pain
Fast and furious the rain came gushing,
We can hear the thunder crashing,
Sweeping past us like a stream,
Looking at us very mean
As we watched the rain descending
And thought it was never ending
The rain is now peaceful and calm
The heavens open up their arms
To see the sunshine, and blue skies
And everything has beau'tified.

J. Walster

The Lady And The Fag

Complacent you stare at the cigarette.
Is it yours? Your last one?
You won't tell me, a silent beauty.
It should be smoked by now
an immortal fag I s'pose.
No yellow stain to bare testimony to this habit,
your hands are well manicured
and the ring? Are you married?
Your "low-cut" dress says no
but you keep staring . . .
Hate to break the news, but
you smoke a fag with your mouth
not your eyes, honey.
The dress, the choker, the eyelashes—black.
Who died? But you
and that perfect fag
still stare at one another,
both burning.

Lisa Feeney

Tiffany

Twilight's tranquil shimmer catches your eyes,
Illuminating them like the gossamer wings of a butterfly.
Fireflies dance to the melody of an Autumn song,
Flitting on the velvet mist to the laughter of dusk,
Angels chorus in harmony to life's lullaby.
Nimbly like the caress of champagne blossom, silent
Yet echoing in the depths of my heart.

Imps and fawns leap to the mellow murmur of your voice.

Like silver droplets of crystallized whispers,
Orchestras of doves play on the willow white snow,
Violet against dawn's cold blanket.
Eagles soar in the shadow of your beauty.

Yielding golden flashes across the wavy dark oceans of your smile,
Oracles of light rainbow through the softness of your hair, leaving
Unending spirals of colour, breathing in a world short of air.

David King

Solipsism

Age takes its toll, the limbs are stiff and weary;
The body must assume a different rôle.
The thirst to know can tire eyes grown bleary;
Should one decide to seek a different goal?
When Beethoven and Milton faced their problems:
How to make music with one's hearing gone;
Or, blind, to write of freedom, verse and prose,
These creatures from the wicked fallen race
Dared to defy the worst that fate could offer
And threw their life's achievements in his face.
We lesser mortals, pygmies without talent,
With walk-on part on an inferior stage,
Seeking rôle models for a way of life,
May find a useful moral in their story.
As was declared by Milton's fallen angel:
"The mind is its own place, and of itself
Can make a hell of heaven, a heaven of hell".

Maurice Ebbage

My Dream

I would like to fly into the sky
And through the clouds which are so high
They look so soft and fluffy to touch
It is only a dream, I dream so much
My dream one day nearly came true
As off to Portugal I flew
We flew so high up in the sky
The clouds that I dream about, passing by
The clouds alas, I couldn't touch
So it remains my dream
As I dream so much.

Thelma Hill

How Can It Feel This Wrong?

When I try to reflect I feel nothing,
I can't find my way anymore in this once simple life,
My soul is like a empty chasm and the person
I once knew is forever out of reach,
My spirit has vanished, found its way to a good place,
My body knows loss with steady failure it weakens,
What is it that has made me feel so numb?

I've lost all my emotions, they disappeared in the fog,
The inner emptiness has made its home,
Should I surrender to its power?
I'm chasing dreams I've never seen,
Please come and share in my loneliness,
There's room enough for two or three.

I'm guilty of blackness robbed of the light
Nobody knows me to hate me but can I forget?
Can't anybody see that it's all for nothing?
The frustration that drills its own well,
Maybe I should forget it, release my lost resources,
Lie down and lie still.

Sarah Findlay

The Mean Years

Middle aged and feeling frumpy,
Sylph like figure now looks lumpy,
Waking nights with copious sweating,
Spend the days with endless fretting,
Time to get a hold on things,
Change your image, spread your wings,
Get yourself a brand new hairdo,
Ageing image that will ne'er do,
Change your wardrobe, change your style,
Greet each daybreak with a smile,
Convince yourself you're not off balance,
Search yourself for long lost talents,
Overhaul the body's system,
Convince the brain it's full of wisdom,
Go and get some HRT -
A wonder drug or could it be -
You took the test and now you've passed,
Emerging a butterfly at last,
And after several years at pupa stage,
You're looking splendid for your age.

Carole Clark

Bees

There were bees on the heather
In the garden, in the sun.
Buzzing away happily
Before summer had begun.

There were bees in the pear trees,
There were bees on the plum,
Buzzing round the daffodils
Saying, "Summer will soon come".

There were bees around the bee hive,
Basking in the rays
Of the bright, warm sunshine,
Of the lovely spring days.

There were bees out on the Broad Beans,
And on the apple trees,
Telling everyone how happy
They were, for warm days like these.

M. M. Sellick

Satisfaction

...And the world turned and man
went forth to conquer.
He built great ships and aeroplanes
and rockets to the moon.
He raised great armies,
he crossed great seas of wrath
and man made his mark on the world
but he wasn't satisfied....

....And man strove onward and upward
his ingenuity knew no bounds
when the frontiers of this world were crossed
Man reached for the heavens.
But mortality made him stop and think
how can death be overcome?
And God had made his mark on man
and was very satisfied....

Eric A. Caldwell

Glimpse Of The Fairy

She drifted across the rhododendrons like an ice skater on ice,
Her sleekly white dress gleamed in the evening sun so nice,
Reflecting the beaming sun off her mirror-like wings,
So smooth, so glassy, so fragile are these things,
Her hair so long swayed with every move,
Only for a glimpse I saw her and to this day I could never prove,
In a split second she had gone.
Where did she go? Why did she leave? I sing
My little miniature dwarf with wings.

Shirley A. Ceri

Things To Remember

As I lie upon my bed,
I think of a nurse, and
what she once said.

This happens to people like
you, who keep working away,
something changes in their
life, and then they have to pay.

If you must work so hard, have
a rest before you get tired, because if
you don't problems will start
then you begin to fall apart.

Now I have learnt to write poems
to relax, while lying here resting my back.

Having a peep at the time, must
go to sleep, and rest my mind
so I close my eyes, to ease the strain
and in the morning, I will start again.

Thinking of what I have been told
I must think in the future as I get old.

Peter R. Beard

Search

Where to find this special place—therein to dwell!
Holds riches more than words can tell,
No day—or date—in which to start!
It comes from deep within the heart.

There is no place, no time, no season there,
One cannot buy this precious fare,
This seed was sown so long ago,
With love and care it did gently grow.

It comes! Quite soft as morning light,
Like winged bird—in trembling flight,
Expanding down the winds of time,
The thought gains speed—without decline.

The warmth begins—it comes anew!
In mellow gold and sceptered hue,
It gives it all—has never lied,
In truth—beyond the mortal glide.

Oh! Joy of joy—still waters deep!
Transcend my being—so long to keep,
This beauty bind and never cease!
Deep bond within—thy name is peace.

Sylvia E. Findlay

Everything

Everything you are I miss so much,
All through my life, I knew that sweet loving touch,
Re-birth of the pain the loss still brings,
When I think of so many wondrous things.

Be still! My heart, I feel your presence — there,
Just beyond my reach, yet it will forever bring,
The warmest glow to rise and ascend,
So deep this love its power transcends.

A mirrored image to see deep within my mind,
That thought to hold, always to find,
The wealth in reaches on a greater plain,
A place not of earth in man's domain.

To trust and hope we shall meet again,
To believe in this and in truth proclaim,
Love never endeth it is written thus
A greater 'being' loves us all so much.

To meet once more as we did so oft,
All sense of time and space so soon forgot,
That step beyond not too far away,
To reach the Kingdom on that eternal day.

Sylvia E. Findlay

Questions And Answer

Where am I going? Where have I been?
What am I doing? What have I seen?
So many questions when life's span is nearly done
who will remember me when I'm gone?
My family of course will remember my name
but I haven't done any great deeds of fame
I haven't climbed mountains or yet tramped the earth
just package holidays for what that is worth
I know what I'll do, I will write me a rhyme
perhaps get it published in 'A Passage in Time'
A beautiful book for my grandchildren's room
and maybe one day a family heirloom.

E. Fisher

Confusion

Amongst the pieces of a shattered life, he sits.
Watching, Restless. Every breath is filled with mourning.
Love wrestles with death.
All glimmers of hope become faded, but still he sits.
Helpless. Night and day mean nothing now,
only images of the past surround her.
The child like behaviour confuses him.
Angrily watching, guilty. So much life unlived,
but now only a blank faced smile remains.
Tormented pictures crowd his mind,
for some only emptiness exists.
Torn memories become too painful as he watches her.
Silently he grieves the loss,
unable to shake the vicious thoughts from circling his mind.
Contented, she sits watching.
Cruel bones age her body.
Peering into the hazy scenery, he wonders what she's thinking.
Soon she will be sleeping. Condemning her new life,
he walks away, awaiting the peaceful end.
Silence enhances the deathly smell. Who is he, who is she?

Christopher J. Taylor

The Year

Spring is here and the primrose is showing
Down in the wood where the windflowers are blowing
The buds on the trees are turning to green
And the earth's re-awakening all around can be seen

Now here comes summer - spring must give way
The flowers all bloom in their finest array
Long lingering twilights to close each day
And the farmers are busy making the hay

Russet and Gold tell us Autumn is here
The days grow shorter now I fear
But the beauty of autumn is there to behold
Try not to think that the year's growing old

Icy fingers grip the earth
Cold winds blow for all they're worth
Mankind shivers now Winter is here
But spring will come - as it does each year.

E. Fisher

Lawrence Of Arabia

In a shady field they've laid him,
The man who was the Arabs' King:
His remembrance is an emblem
To win the hearts of other men.

His wish was not for rank or fame;
He did not want an honoured name,
His aim was not for war and strife,
Although he had a gallant life.

His name will live, though him we mourn,
The Arab clothes that he has worn
Will leave their mystery far behind
Around the life they intertwined.

Edith M. Veitch

The Old Man

The old man sits and smiles at me
His kindly eyes warming me
His years of living, knowing me
Loving and understanding me

He knows what I say, though he doesn't hear
He sees my dreams, but not with his eyes
This man who knows so much
Has seen, has done, and wants to show me

I remember a man, younger in years
Full of laughter, jokes and fun
Hours of stories of dragons and dreams
Of scarlet ribbons in my hair

The years drift by like a boat on a stream
Like the dying autumn leaves
Fading away... almost gone

A pear tree, a wood shed, an old musky coat
Remind me of an old man
Who sits and reads
And looks up and smiles at me

Amanda Mead

Our Cat

She got up every morning and saw me off to work
she saw it as her duty and this she did not shirk,
and after I had gone through door to earn my daily bread,
she toddled back up our stairs and she went back to bed.

We'd play a game with a ping pong ball, we'd roll it to each other
and when she got fed up with that, it was back on the lap of mother
she used to climb upon my knee and she would claw my sweater
she purred so softly in my ear, I couldn't help but let her.

She was so full of love for us she had her moods I know
little did we realize that so soon she'd have to go,
It broke our hearts to see her leave the grief we could not mend
we thought the world of our little cat,
our cuddly furry friend.

George Vail

Sharing

When in my arms they placed you,
so helpless, so sweet, so small,
in my arms I cradled you,
you were mine, my all.

And as I watched you growing,
in my mind I knew
the day would come when
I must let go of you.

The day has come much sooner than I had in mind;
to let you go my darling is to be kind.
So, go my darling dearest for your life's your own,
for me the day has come for sharing
the dearest gem I own.

So, go my darling dearest,
and may God always watch over you,
for now the day has come for sharing,
and I must let go and let another have their share of you.

Anna Guida Romero

Trapped

Notice me, notice me!
Can't they see
in this uniform I'm not really me?
So quiet and very shy am I,
to be bold and strong makes me cry.
Words are important to see us through life;
they are used so cruelly
and hurt more than a knife.
I want to escape, and let everyone see,
in this uniform I'm not really me.

Lisa Halls

Ghosts

There are Ghosts in the Garden of our house beside the sea,
Ghosts of little children and one of them is me.

When I walk the dog at night and go out on the cliff
And gaze towards the Isle of Wight, it often seems as if
I'm not alone, but all around are those who've been before,
Who've all played here, beside the sea or down upon the shore.

My Granny N, who built this house, I wonder if she's here
To guard her precious roses with a cry of "Careful, dear!"
As my Brother and my cousins all played here with me;
We dared not shout but ran about absolutely free.

Twenty-five years later my four children too
Discovered the same pleasures and saw the island view
And now their many children have it all again,
Which gives me so much pleasure and just a little pain!

So many happy memories, while sixty years went by,
Are bound to leave an aura, which, I suppose, is why
There are Ghosts within the garden of our house beside the sea—
Ghosts of little children—and one of them is me!

Patrick Davies

Investigations In Hospital

One goes into hospital - something's wrong
One suffers indignities all day long
The trolley arrives, and with it the needle
Not well on arrival, each day one's more feeble.
"Can you tell me yet nurse what's wrong with me"?
The answer comes back "Just wait and see".
The usual "thing" they think I'm a cabbage
I'm not, nor so much useless garbage.
Into hospital I go, with so much hope
But need they treat me as if I'm a dope?
Like a cod on a slab, or am I a spook?
Stripped of all pride, whilst all take a look.
I know sometimes it's best not to know
If there's no future, or where I shall go!
Investigations, when they have ceased
Shall I be a person - or just a deceased?

Helen Smyth Thomson

To The Bride To Be

May your day be just fine, you'll be walking on air
You'll be looking divine, and be almost aware
That your dreams have come true, don't look back down the aisle
With the blessing quite through, for the camera then smile
The reception and speeches may be slightly dull
But soon you'll away in the midst of a lull
Then behind be the wedding, into song you may rally
For that honeymoon you're heading, to Falmouth don't dally
The groom we all envy, his bride is a dream
If we could accompany, we'd walk so supreme
Alas, it's not to be, we really wish you well
Fond memories of your special day, you'll tell
And wondrous times, in future years to recall
With nursery rhymes, and grandchildren, almost two feet tall

G. E. Portnall

From The Start (My Grandad)

Now he is no longer here,
there seems no end to the tears.
He was so special to me,
even from childhood when I
sat on his knee.
I know he couldn't carry on,
yet it's impossible to believe
he's really gone.
I feel so very empty inside,
I keep running, but where can I hide?
I remember all the things he said,
it's all just memories now he's dead.
He'll always have a special place in my heart,
the same place he's had
right from the very start!

Naomi Jane Pelling

The Clyde

The river Clyde is "oh" so silent
No work to do for the river pilot
No more loading and unloading
It's as if the city's gone into mourning
When one recalls in bygone days
It used to resemble one giant maze
Pleasure steamers going "doon the watter"
All the buzz of the "glesga patter"
The Tenement families whose great delight
Was to board the steamers fair Friday night
Two weeks in Rothsey or perhaps Dunoon
Nobody left in old "Glasgow Toon"
I for one although only a nipper
used to mix with those happy trippers
remember the days of fun and strife
when the river Clyde was full of life

M. M. Cameron

Just Between Sisters

Sister you are very dear to me,
I love you very much, and this shall always be,
You'll always have a place in my heart,
Although maybe now, you might be drifting apart.

You've always shared my joys and tears,
I know you really because I know your fears,
Life has many turns and this may just be one,
But this true friendship can never be undone.

Although unconditional love is hard to find,
Together we've been one of a kind.
Your dear to me Sis, and you must see,
Without you just where would I be?

Majida Khaliq

Tranquillity

Inside my head (or could it be my heart?)
There is a place, a plane set quite apart.
No one but me can ever come to know,
Those secret things and thoughts which come and go.

For here, within this silent lonely place,
The spirit softly reaches out for grace.
And grace does come like breath upon the sand
And soothes my spirit like some calming hand.

There, in some restful corner of the mind,
Perhaps from other lifetimes left behind
Did nature plant some long maturing seed
To flower when I should recognize the need?

Or does some cosmic force to me unknown
Come unto me at times when I'm alone
And help to bring that calmness of the mind
Which is the greatest lack of all mankind.

W. J. Dack

The Rainbow

What is a rainbow?
So high in the sky
colours so wonderful and bold
I wish I could fly
clouds grey and dark, then
a huge thunderstorm
then beautiful sunshine,
a rainbow is formed
how majestic a wonder to see
God's power and wisdom holds the secret key
I always find a rainbow such a delight
of all the colours the red and
orange seem like candle light
such a sheer joy and pleasure
to watch its formation, it's like
finding hidden treasure
then gracefully it fades away
O well, perhaps there will be
another tomorrow or the next day.

Lynda E. Schoepp

Unrequited Love

Burning aching desire
Love has no boundaries
Like the mosquito bite, quick, painless,
Sensuous in its quenching,
Lingering for an eternity
How powerful, how futile
Now is the dawning of our dreams and desires.
Flesh upon flesh dream upon dream.
What is truth and what is a distant cloud
A sunset for all the world to see
But not for any human touch
No matter how calm how devout
Love is but a myth a legend
A melancholy ache
Never to desire is never to have been so alive.

B. M. Chatterton

Forever Yours

Dearest, I am so fortunate to have met you,
I was beginning to think that my life was through,
that I had done what was intended of me
but now I'm not so sure, and must wait and see.
I sit by the phone waiting for you to call,
you really must know I'd give you my all.
I don't care what you have or have not,
I'm not a materialistic person and don't give a jot,
you are fun to be with, considerate and kind
I consider myself very lucky having made such a find.
Life can make us deviate from our true way,
so let's think of us without too much delay.
My children are grown, out doing their own thing,
I sit in at night, play music and sing.
I wish to have a companion for the rest of my life,
so I can be the loving, caring, dutiful wife.
This is something I have been cheated of in the past,
and I really need to know, deep down, that we will last.

Miriam Elizabeth Langley

"The Night Before Christmas"

On Christmas eve I dared to peep,
to see if all the world was fast asleep,
the night had come with glistening snow,
to prepare the way for Santa you know.

The trees all glisten, they seem to say,
Hurrah! hurrah! Here comes Christmas Day,
so pop back to your warm bed and sleep,
then before you know it, Santa will keep.

The promise he does every year,
so a lovely surprise will awaken you dear
with lots of presents for you all to share,
in fun and laughter without a care.
So "Merry Christmas" to one and all
"Santa" is on his way to pay "his call."

Agnes E. Wood

The Magical Glow-Worm Dell

The twisty windy path followed the white rail into
a secluded copse.
Where trees and bushes mingled quietly,
their branches and leaves silhouetted in the moonlight
against the black of night.
A necklace of luminous white teardrops shone out
of the darkness,
their glow seemed to ebb and flow like the tide.

The light of glow-worms,
Their piercing luminosity shone like Christmas
lights.
And now I was surrounded everywhere by these
dancing bright fairy lights.
I beheld a grotto of fantasy and slipped back
into my childhood where I dreamt of living
amongst elves and fairies in a quiet dell.

J. A. Cutting

119

The Dolphin

So shapely, so graceful, each tells a story.
So wise and so bubbly, joyfully playing,
dancing between waves such dominant life forms
possibly the best of nature's creations,
flowing so naturally, still a mystery.
So much to discover, so much to gain,
they've kissed the earth, touched every dream.
Such wondrous beauty, such perfect perfection.
Why create this pain we hill the willingly
They lose, we gain, the agony there
Why destroy our world, this greed, this pain,
and it's all in vain; they've done no wrong,
hurt no soul, the perfect creation,
their hearts pure gold creating such joy.
Such curious creatures, the mysteries unfold,
they've thrived for centuries: let them live on
belonging to no one, these timid life forms
each to their own. The fact remains
perfectly plain: have we no shame—
too much to discover, too much to explain?

Donna Williamson

To The One I Love

I've never before had what I have with you,
you're always with me in everything I do.
You're my definition of love and I keep you in my heart,
it's as if we're together whenever we're apart.
If we ever end which I hope we shall not,
I will love you forever no matter what.
Our love is caring and our love is kind,
and the love I have with you I will never leave behind.

Jennifer Magallona

Places, Please

Did anyone ever point out point A to point B?
No, I didn't think so.
The insurmountable task of living is overshadowed
by an obvious conclusion.
You must fail at A in order to reach B.
Those that say you can reverse the process have time to ponder,
the rest are locked in the pursuit of things,
objects, trappings, coffee table magazines.
Changing the ambitions of humankind leads to alienation.
We must all choose, but some don't know we can.
Theirs is the quiet life, so quiet it extinguishes the flames of
passion, a passion that celebrates the wonder of being.
If human kindness is a sweet and sticky milk then,
human hate is the acrid and burning sap of envy.
Wanting and taking in rapid succession, we are slow to give.
To give is to lose and that in turn is failure.
We close off our world to a unit of one,
self contained, self reliant, self, self, self.
If angels do indeed weep for us,
then our only concern is how to own the tears.

Maria Ralph

Bereavement And Friendship

Fortunate am I to have you as a friend
Your home has always been an open door for me
A place wherein I am myself with no need to pretend.
Would that I could take away your pain
Ease your sorrow, help you bear the grief
With something more than words we speak in vain.
'Time will heal' are those most often used
But when the wound is raw, how meaningless
When you feel so disordered and confused.
A hand to hold and memories to share
Time to talk and listen when you feel the need
Is all that I can promise to show you that I care,
So in your fragile moments remember I am here
With undemanding friendship to offer when you call
To give you strength and comfort with affection most sincere.

Eleanor West

Towards A Zen Metaphysical Verse

Standing at the edge of human perception:
And everything was unresolved,
in a timeless scenario,
where all beyond stood dissolved and shifting,
and all objects had acquired a sentient being.

The question was asked, and the room declared
it was a room: Space often needs to be told it is space.
The ceiling disputed the floor,
and the door didn't care either way.

There was a zen simplicity to everything.
Light on emptiness had revealed much;
but not as much as steaming vegetables
and singing canary:

For when we reach into sublimity
we can never leave the every day.

Thomas Taylor

Untitled

Simple can be the thought,
only too soon the tears flow,
loving may be a dream,
woken by a silent scream,
clustered are the emotions,
that struggle to break free,
raindrops that never fall
leaves the heart full of woe,
but the always present tear,
never hesitate . . . to stain the dry cheek.

Meera Umachandran

Dawn

The break of dawn is here at last
the sun is bright and warm.
The grass is damp from the morning dew
the casting shadows are a magnificent sight.
At last the birds have started their song.
Starlings, sparrows and blue tits call.
Mixed tweats and squires are slowly drowned.
Although it has stopped there's nothing wrong.
Cars and lorries start the rush hour.
People going to work so fast.
The call of birds has now stopped.
People start their day with will power.
The dusk is here.
The day has gone.
It has gone so fast.
Another dawn is near.

Karen Pratt

The Magic Of The Garden

The mystic boughs of winter burst
into green serene with abundant thirst.
The garden's spell has just been cast,
buds and blooms unfurl at last.

Pergolas blessed with an English rose
of which variety no one knows.
Fragrant pathways to stroll along,
summer bees and thrush's song.

Summerhouses donned with green
gingham curtains lace the scene.
Cucumber squares for afternoon tea,
strawberries and fairy cakes for me.

Tartan picnics in the wooded glade
abandoned tools, fork and spade.
Rippling water, stones and bamboo,
statues watching and on guard too.

A magical enchantment to take at leisure
something so free can give much pleasure.
What better bliss than this can there be,
perfection's choice, peace and tranquillity.

Marilyn J. De'Ath

Dinner By Candlelight

We ate heartily, drank lustily, spoke rapturously.
The candle waxed its shimmering gleam;
Soft, sweet music gently fused the mind with body.

We were of one mind, one accord, one feeling.
The candle spluttered, flared and died
And dimmed our senses deep into oblivion.

We were unaware of time, of place, of people.
The inner dream of life was now reality;
The mind become subdued into soliloquy.

We arose gently, spoke softly, left silently.
The world outside was still, unruffled;
The night air balmy with indifference.

We walked slowly, embraced tenderly, parted sadly.
The stillness of the night now echoed all my feelings;
I felt alone, unloved, unwanted.

Conal M. Finegan

The Non-Conformists: Burns, Keats And Shelly

This gift we left you, is yours to take.
It came from the soul, that life cannot break
So moved with emotion and passion were we
That an early death came to all three;
Like a suckling child at a mother's breast,
We put our destiny to the test.

Mortal men in ourselves we could not see;
For poets, romantics and lovers were we.
Rebelling against convention, unable to conform,
So the seeds of our poetry, and satires were sown.

Read into our souls, be our heart;
We can beat as one, never to part.
Our lives were as short as a blade in the grass.
It's amazing how things come to pass.
For famous people we appear to be;
Keats, Shelly and Me.

Margaret McAneny

Retribution At Eighth And Fifty Second

A nodding ghost that once breathed crystal air,
Resents the city noise with futile stomp,
And as it slumbers in Columbus Square,
Still dreams of summer pastures in Vermont.

I sat in Central Park and heard the jeers,
A horse and Puerto Rican in a dance,
Some Spanish oaths to raise the silken ears,
And vicious kicks to wake it from its trance.

But even as I moved to interfere,
I sensed the bridled anger from its past,
And knew that cruelty had sparked resolve
To fight this evil tyranny at last.

All traffic on its way to Central Park
Has slowed at eighth and fifty second street
An upturned carriage, now a splintered wreck
Is strewn around the driver's lifeless feet.

Tethered loosely to a kerbside rail,
The rescued mare, untroubled, crops her hay,
A yellow cab has rammed the offside wheel,
And nemesis, the goddess, has her day.

Thomas Bernard Besch

Hurting

Sitting here lonely as yesterday,
Today, and tomorrow, am I able to pray.
That the hurt and fear that suddenly came.
Will soon be gone and not leave me lame.

My memories are spoilt and the past far away.
My marriage a stranger, the future I cannot say.
I'll live for my child, the one shining light.
My love must be buried to continue the fight.

Diane Howarth

Stranger In The Family

You stand between me and the doorway
Block the escape because you know me well
See, I'm listening for once today
I feel I've done wrong and you can tell

Me, the stranger in the family
Me, the cut against the grain
Me, the alien in disguise
Me, the gap in the chain

But you do love me, really love me
Doing this for my own good
I won't stop you when you touch me
You know I never could

Me, the stranger in the family
Me, the cut against the grain
Me, the alien in disguise
Hanging on to the chain

J. W. Tooze

Alzheimer's

She sits in a chair with eyes that can see,
but she knows not what.
She can hear, but can't understand.
Her body only is there, for her mind has gone to some faraway land.

Ghostly images haunt this land,
people, places, milestones of a lifetime.
But the people have no names,
and the places hold no meaning.

Suddenly, she stands and slowly walks around the room.
Is she going to meet her first love?
Or is it her wedding day?
Perhaps she's playing with her children,
or visiting a friend.

She turns and goes back to sit in her chair,
the memories have gone now and left her alone there.
A prisoner in a land no one can visit,
a land she cannot leave,
condemned to a silent death.

Elaine Margaret Wilkinson

Last Day Of Winter

As the snow falls softly on the ground,
And the smooth breeze passes slowly by,
I think of the time I spend,
Watching each day go silently by.

The soft ticks of the clock on the wall,
The smell of the warmth inside,
Lost and alone again,
This time there's no place to hide.

It's not very long now,
Hot and cold feelings inside,
Deep deep sleep is coming soon,
And God will be by my side.

Sabiha Sheikh

On My Own

I want to walk alone, along the deep blue sea
where the sea gulls fly and the waves crash
against the sand, I want to walk alone,
along the deep blue sea where you can hear
the sea through a seashell, I want to walk
along the breakwater and see from miles
around, I want to walk alone, along the
deep blue sea at night when all you can see
is the reflection of the big white moon and
the shiny little stars, I want to walk alone,
along the deep blue sea and think of all
the happy times we used to have and now
my friend has moved, moved far far away,
I hope that one day she will read
this poem I have read to you.

Annette Murphy

Knowledge

Question existence;
And look beyond man's realm of reality
To perceive the inner world
Where truth reveals itself
Slow and unfocused
In suspicious shards of confusion.

Know, life
That offers such beauty and every answer
Pieces together man's mottled dreams
And beneath the sheath of ephemeral happiness
Casts light on every shadowy doubt
Created by the human mind.

The cry of the new born
Heralds the death of its mother
Like laughter,
Bubbling from a spring of sorrow;
Understanding that time does not exist
Is the essence of knowledge in man.

Shaista Tayabali

Sacred Companion

A painted pony running wild
I chase to claim a horse, a friend,
For days and nights it seems I search
I'm lost, alone, forsaken, and then just as
The sun goes down I hear a distant thunder.
Is it from my brother sky or of the hooves
Of horses racing.

As darkness falls I find the place
To wait until the morning,
As water is the spring of life,
My own and his survival.

At break of day he comes to water,
Wades in deep to quench his thirst,
I leap onto his back and stick just as a leech,
He rides in temper, then in fright,
Then with exhaustion falters.

For the next few days we are as one,
We eat we drink together,
Then slowly grows the friendship of
Brave and painted pony.

Susan Hadden

Colours Of Sunrise

Soft the whispers of the night.
Ever on towards the light,
Searching for a promised dawn,
That's now but shadow on the lawn.

Lazy mist becomes the dew
As pictures turn from black to hue.
Night creatures scurry to the earth,
To await, again, the quiet rebirth.

Comes from the slowly lightening skies,
The mornings sparkling, bright, new dyes,
A sun to fight the night time grey.
A golden crown for each new day.

Julie-Ann Kirton

The Moon

In the sky at night,
A great ball of light
Glistening and gleaming down on us,
Still letting the dimness be,
Gives us light for us to see.

Raindrops glitter as they fall,
The river gleaming silver streaks of light,
Making the river very bright,
Cats' whiskers sparkle as they run,
This makes the night lots of fun.

Nicola Spittal

Our Son

Our son Paul he is autistic, he plays in his own way. His world
is such a lonely place every night and day, we give him hugs and
kisses and try to find a way to make him understand we love
and we adore him and thank the Lord each day as he brightens
up our lives in his very special way, his cheeky face and big blue
eyes could melt your heart for sure, a ninety-nine carrot diamond
that's our little Paul, if you were to see him I'm sure that you
would see why we love him very much a love that will not die,
we'll care for him and hope some day he'll say two very special
words that we both long to hear just mum and dad that's all we
need to make our lives complete.

Andrew & Renee McAlpine

I Can't Fight On My Own

If only I could understand the way I really feel
My life would be more simple, I could finally break the seal

I want to struggle through this, but I can't fight on my own
I want to go back to myself, the one I've always known

I need a shoulder to cry on, someone to understand
Someone I know that I can trust to be there to hold my hand

Someone who knows what it's like, to be doubted for so long
And who's been through everything, to tell me I'm not wrong

I don't want to feel like I do now, I don't want you seeing me cry,
Why can't my feelings go away, just leave and say 'goodbye?'

Do you understand me or are my feelings wrong?
I'm trying really hard to fight, but I'm just not that strong

Can I really trust you not to leave me on my own?
I need to know who's there for me, to know I'm not alone

Rosaline Basile

The World's Child

I am the child from all of the worlds.
I am the innocent in the womb.
My brother is Ethiopian, my sister Somalian, I am Romanian.
I have this numbing stomach twisting nothingness within the depths
of my being.
  I am hungry, Father,
  Feed me.

Softly whisper hope to me, sing me lullabies of dreams.
Familiarize love to me, cleanse my face with your warm tears.
Gently rock away my anxieties.
  I am lonely Mother.
  Miss me.

What "I" have is "yours". I have Syphilis, I have Aids, I have Leprosy.
I am a Beautiful Innocent Baby.

What you have is mine. Medicate me, warm me, respect me.
  Love me.

I am their child, I am her child, I am your child.
Embrace me friend. Help me heal my life.
  Kiss me.

Catherine Mountain

From A Distance

From a distance, the world appears peaceful.
Though not, the strong words dull to a medley of whispers on the air.
The ground takes on a new form.
The coloured fields pieced together, like the design of a contemporary linoleum,
or more simply a bizarre patchwork quilt.
The ruler straight line of a canal slashes its way across the pattern.
And the metallic sash of a river gleams below the dark canopy of the wood.
Towards the ocean the mud flats appear a deluge of brown and yellow.
Swiftly being repossessed by the advancing tide.
Of which the surface holds a sheen of moire silk.
From further, the clouds rag and shred from thickness into smoky trails.
The green of the land and blue of sea.
They contrast and compliment each other.
Such like two fabric skeins side by side.
What beauty the birds must see.

Matthew Baptist

The Mission

I met a homeless youngster who had nowhere else to go
Said to me, can I come down yours, my parents don't want to know
Of course my boy, come down mine, I'll feed you twice a day
I'll even take you fishing and throw in lots of play
I took that youngster fishing and gave him lots of pleasure
In the end he turned his back, gave me nothing that I treasure
As you journey through your life, let me give you this advice
Remember that a helping hand will never help you twice
It takes a man to apologize, a child seldom can
But then it's up to us to teach them how to be a man
The moral to this story is never trust a living soul
The ones you help the most are the ones who play most foul
If you find these words quite hurtful, they are meant to be
For I won't even let a dog leg up against my tree.

Leonard J. Rayner

Precious...

I am a very special and beautiful stone.
A precious jewel.
I can shine like gold. Twinkling stars.
I could be chocolate
or toffee.
My smooth sides catch the light like a mirror.
You can roll me. Catch me. Hold me.
Run with me. Lie with me.
Always old and always new.
I come from a land out of time.
I can follow the lines
or run in circles.
At home in the hand of a child
or grace the neck of a Queen.
If I fall I may roll away
or lie eagerly waiting for a heart that will cherish me.
In the hands of unbelievers I am dead.
But to those who have wings and can fly
I Live...

Elizabeth Nicholls

Mother Said There Would Be Days Like This

Mother said there would be days like this when I was Seven.
Sister said I would never go to heaven
But burn in hell
And the doomly knell disturbed my rest.

Mother said there would be days like this when I was older.
A friend's smile turning colder
Granting favour
To another, much braver, when I failed the test.

Mother said there would be days like this when I sat by the phone.
Came home from the dance alone
A weary wallflower
Lacking the power of curves in hip and breast.

Mother said there would be days like this, and she was right.
Days when all the good dreams take fright
And flap away
Leaving in the dust of the day, could-be joy suppressed

There are bound to be days like this.

M. J. Lawrence

Alone

Here I sit in the lonesome night,
The shadows giving me quite a fright.
I've got nothing to do I feel so bare,
I just sit by my window and I stare.
I know I won't be able to get to sleep,
The darkness really gives me the creeps.
Outside I see it has started to rain,
I watch the water rush down the drain.
I can hear the sounds of the floorboards creaking,
As I look up I see the ceiling leaking.
I feel like I am in a world of my own,
It's so horrible being alone.

Mandeep Sohal

Love's Bitter Kiss

It was love, but it shall be no more.
It died like the last flower
this world could bear.
The feelings still live,
but deep inside.
A place which I wish never to find.
With thoughts of you shattered.
And it was true of which the foreseers uttered.
Of you and I together, but not forever.
Oh such dreams have I dreamt
and such wishes I have wished.
But it has ended.
With love's most bitter kiss,
the one of death,
through my heart and soul.
But I must go on ahead
always remembering you
and wishing I could say
all the things I never said to you.

Toyin Odusanwo

Resigned

There's not much danger felt
Here inside this humble frame
That once did greatly need, and sought, your love;
But no love came to it your way, so day by day
The cards were played as dealt.

Alexander Russell

A Living Wonder

If miracles be then one is me,
My body is a wonder!
I have two eyes with glee to see,
Two ears that hear the faintest thunder;
I praise my lungs that breathe with ease,
A constant heart that never slumbers.

I can talk have legs that walk,
My arms will lift or cuddle
With hands that hold a knife and fork;
A brain that's sane avoiding muddle,
It has a mind for all good thoughts,
Steering clear of evil troubles.

I smell nice things I feel what stings,
Amazing are these natural skills,
As when I sigh, even cry and then from laughter sing;
Once fed it's bed to sleep at will,
A welcomed time that living brings,
Where in this lair I do share the body's sacred thrill!

Ronald S. D'Ark

The Complexity Of The Mind

If the operation of the mind were likened to a clock
Then the clock would have hands that were unable to stop
So intricate in its design, so clever in its construction
That its potential is staggering as it works upon instruction

Just wonder at its complexity as you ponder its formation
The duties carried out are simply too numerous to mention
Thoughts, feelings, emotions, beliefs and inclinations
All form a personality with special considerations

Deliberations, cogitations, speculation and persuasion
All go to make that person different from any other creation
To discern, to distinguish, to observe - all qualities unique to man
So complicated in its purpose that no scientist can understand

How clever the mind is made, matchless in every human being
It gives the motivation to life, love, care and fellow feeling
How compact in that head of yours, have you ever thought of this
How often must you remember that both eyes you need to blink?

To contemplate these things surely heightens our appreciation
The way in which we are made - a perfect marvel of creation
No computer could ever equal it, no invention could you find
Which would even come near to matching, the complexity of the mind.

G. P. Baker

They Are

Needed, trustworthy, always there.
No one is alone, ever
support and chatter they provide, everyday
but always in times of despair.

Separated by age, character, colour,
sex and mind. Each is individual.
Yet inevitable bonding occurs
between them. So different yet so alike.
True friends is what they are.

Claire Kerin Sullivan

Now Don't You Cry My Little Boy

Come here little boy and talk to me,
Tell me, what is wrong?
There is no need to be nervous,
I will never harm you.
Are those children laughing at you again?
You are so very upset,
Little boy there is nothing to fear,
I will stay close to you.
Now don't you cry my little boy,
And I will tell you why,
You are nicer than the rest,
And you are very special.
They may think you are ugly,
But, let me tell you this,
The ugly duckling became a beautiful swan,
And you will become beautiful too.
Now don't you cry my little boy,
One day you'll spread your wings,
And you will become beautiful,
And the others won't bully you again

L. A. O'Hare

Ecstasy Is For End

No-one knew what you had done,
But you we're only having fun.
But we knew that you were ill,
You had tried that fatal pill.
In such a short time you had no control,
It took you over body and soul,
As doctors and nurses run and shout.
You didn't know what it was all about.
Others cried and felt so sad,
Be it brothers, sisters, mum or dad.
Please don't die, don't convulse,
Doctors, nurses, feel his pulse.
Take the wires off, God let him live,
For he has so much to give
They pump his heart to make it beat.
Please, please, let us win it can't be defeat.
You were so vulnerable,
And after all it wasn't such a ball.
God wake him from this dreadful trance.
Please give the lad another chance.

Carol Whitnall

Untitled

"I drink your health", he said
    And held the wine glass high.
"In blood and sweat and tears"
    She thought, and smiling, gave reply.
"My Dear beloved, I drink yours
    In dark and ruby brew"
She drained the goblet silver deep
    And gently, placing it aside, silently withdrew.

We little know what each we mean,
So sparsely do our words convey,
But hark the spaces in between
As they mean what we really say.

Gene Perret

Nothing ever happens in Macondo

After eons dreaming of ice
the land of my father awoke to find itself an immense plantation.
The yellow train of the United Fruit Company pulled in, rolling over the li(n)es
coughing telegraph poles and post offices,
new streets with pool rooms and brothels
all those wonderful things of God's new creation
which would make all men, it was thought in those days, like brothers.

Campesinos came by thousands
one for sorrow, two for joy, three for four, four of them
forming furious waves which crashed upon the shore
of Santa Marta, Aracataca and Fundación
where the father of my father still wanders as a ghost
of those four hundred cut-down by the lightning of Changó
as machine guns and rifles emptied upon the childhood of my father
one forgotten day in 1928

I've been wondering all these years why my father left paradise
just as those who, like him, once left their homelands empty:
West indians, chinese, black africans
who took the yellow train to sell themselves as merchandise
in the capital of the empire
even though they knew well such was not their desire

It wasn't poverty, now I know.
Escaping death, they were pursuing secret hopes yet unborn
The unspoken words of their children yet to come.

Oscar Guardiola Rivera

Simply - God Within

Have you ever thanked God, each day, that you can move?
To fill your lungs with air, to see, to hear - be finely tuned.
The trees, so beautiful, shelter birds, whoever seeks to rest.
They lift their branches skywards, as if it were to bless.
Their Creator, their Source of life, upon which they depend.
And so, we too, as every creature knows, deep down, the pull of
that great Love, comprehends!
The intangible, that links us, when so long ago ordained, to be
part of God's plan, in this age.
To follow His example, to be an instrument of grace, to love when
it's not easy,
to overcome our weakness, our frailties.
To have that mantle, which means to turn the other cheek.
To hold our tongue, to be very silent and not to speak!
This means, that central to us is the cross - but no shadow cast
but a great light and love and joy and peace!
And so, this renewing, this turning right around
Ensures a balance and no confusion but a mind that is sound.
With these thoughts, our days can then begin.
No stress, no imbalance but simply God within!

Mary Comley

Alzheimer's—Thief In The Night

Like a thief in the night you came, silently, slowly, taking your time
Surveying at first, just exploring what you could take from this mother of mine
Over the months you then grew bolder, "Why wait until she grows older?
No, her family have had her time and now I'm going to make her mine"
Like a thief in the night your grip took hold of someone once so sharp and bright
Robbing her of the life she knew, of faces, friends and family
Of organizing holidays, Sunday lunches, shopping sprees...
Greedily devouring day by day, hour by hour, minute by minute
Her mind, her heart and the love held in it
You've stolen a wife, a mother, a friend,
A gran, a sister—does your greed have no end?
And yet finally, when you want her no more
Like a thief you'll retreat through a silent back door
You've spat out the bits you couldn't digest
You've taken the best - we're left with the rest:
A wife who doesn't know him, a mum who doesn't want us,
A gran who isn't even aware that her longed for grandchildren are finally there
But we are, we're here and we'll continue to show
Our love for someone we no longer know
Yet someone who was once my mum.

Anne Burgan

A Walk In The Snow

"It's Snowing" I would say
And rush outside to the dazzling snowflakes.
I would slide around on the frosty ice.
Softly I walk to hear the crisp
Crunch of the snow beneath my feet.
The further I walked up the bank the
deeper it was and I nearly sank.
The sight of the snow is like cotton
wool laid on the ground.
The icicles around the gutter are melting away.
The snow makes me feel cold and
happy all mixed in one.
The silver coloured snow glitters
And sparkles upon the ground
On the powdery smooth and frosty
Snow there are footprints of man and animals.

Richard Anthony Screen

My Home

I live in the country, in a beautiful place
'Midst trees and fields, where there's plenty of space,
Where the small fish swim, and the eagles soar,
And we're far away from the traffic's roar.
And I watch the sheep, and I watch the cows
As they chew the cud as the wild deer browse;
I watch the hills whence the white swans fly
With a rustle of wings as they go by.
Then the heron passes on his lumbering flight
To fish in the marshes; and I love the sight
Or an orchid flower or the wild dog rose,
And the summer skies, or the winter snows;
The song of a stream, or the curlew's cry
Are the sounds I love, and as years go by
I can't help but look at the hills and space
So glad that I live in this beautiful place.

Margaret Clarke

Loneliness

The house was silent,
She was alone.
As she wondered aimlessly from room to room
Her footsteps echoed, bounced from wall to wall.
The kettle was filled with water as cold as her
Heart seemed. Yet effortlessly it was warmed.
If only she had been given some understanding,
Some love.
The bedroom was desolate, cold and empty.
Her tears of despair sank away into her pillow
Though her frown of sorrow never altered.
For many years her life was the same.
Many felt she could not, would not love.
She felt rejected and began to act,
The same act, the same person.
And so the vicious cycle of loneliness was formed
And no-one ever intercepted,
No-one seemed to care.

Sarah Holt

Menofearthereaper?

This conformity controls my consciousness,
Moulding my very being in the stencil of its likeness;
I try Hard to break free of its crushing grasp.

My demons overwhelm us and this

Emptiness
Leaves me helpless, holding on to (you) what?

Memories of you pick like vultures at this decaying carcass,
This chilling corpse, this Hollow shell once upon a time called me,
Now the victim of its own inadequacy.

This compliance consumes my character,
Rotting my individuality and self-esteem.
I am (not) nothing.

Laurence Andrews

A Pirate's Fall

What once was a shelter as storms arose
Waves crashing and tumbling around,
Men fighting the fury of whistling gales
Hanging on as the rain beat down.

The thunder is angry, the lightning strikes
A direct hit to the mast and hull,
The sea comes with power to tear down the sides
As water pours in through the holes.

All is alight in a blazing glory
Men jump and abandon the wreck,
The darkness still looming all around
No life left upon this deck.

As she goes down in terrible shame
Slowly followed by crew and all,
Their voices scream 'til, no more to be heard
Murky depths their lives do fall.

With oceans deep and oceans wide
Stolen jewels now lifeless as stone,
They hold no meaning, they hold no joy
To be left, undisturbed down below.

Teresa Cooper

Where Were You?

Alone in my species, yet surrounded by a thousand
fearless giants.
Alone, I thought, not knowing of all the others who
failed to stand defiant.

Where were you when a million hands grabbed my
helpless body?
Where were you when my sadistors pushed me to
the ground?
Were you acting hero elsewhere?
Did you hear a muffled sound, a crack of bone, a
Whispered moan when you first heard me as a lively one?
Did you ever believe I would change so?

You thought my frolicking would never fall that
Low, but I trusted and depended for a few
Happy weeks when the snow fell and no one
could tell.
Was I really worth the birth when a piercing
death was my destiny?
Did life really stand a chance against a fate
like that.....?

Neidra Le Gear

Just For You

Soft rememberings of a gentle affinity, trembling
close to you,
like a warm bath on a damp day,
golden forests settling the mist,
children's laughter in Autumnal fall,
a burst of happiness on a cold crisp Christmas.

You're the anticipation of a smile,
a rush of oxygen,
a heady liqueur.
A becoming.

Insisting within me, a secret whisper, a longing to share
our gentle gifts.
A voice from beyond, a calling,
begging the future to be together.

All my life I've been searching for someone
to travel with.
When our centres touch I feel like I've found the way,
like I'm whole again.

Ian Foster

Cottage Garden

A few minutes to sit, relax, and allow my mind to wonder
At the sight, before me, while sitting on the veranda,
The delights of many flowers large and small, colours abundant.
Flowering teasel, bees going round and round each prickly shaped dome,
Buddleia acting hostess to many peacock and red admiral butterflies truly at home,
The small pond decorated with heathers and shells, containing one fish, that's really grown
There's the tall grasses, water lilies, and stately bullrush,
Here and there a miniature horse chestnut, elm or conifer bush
Not forgetting the baskets of petunias, busy lizzies with trailing Lobelia.
And the assorted tubs and pots with geraniums and begonias in full regalia,
The aviary with twittering parakeets and budgies, also has plants hanging on the frame,
And the greenhouse with the fruity tomatoes turning colour from green to flame
What a sight, the lovely scents and vivid colours a joy to all,
Even the tingling of wind chimes and the kidney beans growing up the wall,
The birds, bees, flowers, trees, a heavenly scene; no, definitely not a dream.

Colleen Pearson

The Old Man

"What do you think of, old man?" I asked, as he sat there in the sun.
His eyes were misted and his stare was blank,
"I think of when I was young."
"What do you see with those aging eyes that look through me standing here?"
"The streams and woodlands of home." He said, and wiped away a tear.
"And what of the sounds that fill your mind, for my voice must pass you by?"
"I hear the sound of laughter sweet and of birds that fill the sky
And I smell the scent of roses and of loved ones near to me."
His voice dropped to a whisper as he sank in reverie,
"I think and see and feel and hear sweet moments from my life,
The laughter of my children...the sharing with my wife.
All these things are memories that no one can take away.
That's what I see and feel, young man, as I sit here today
But go your way...your time will come and then you'll be like me,
You'll maybe sit in this same spot and recall this memory."

Evan Keith Freeman

Unhappy Love

Oft' lately, have I seen you low, as in dull and grim black winter.
You, on whose fair complexion, spring's fairest did bestow, and summer's graces did adorn.
Now, fearsome thunder-clouds of this bleak season is worn.
How long must I despair at your despairing and curse my heavy heart at your distress.
Confound this cruel world, its lack of caring and all human folly my darkest thoughts redress.

Begun! Let not your ill-continuance plague me, nor plead with eyes of pain, your piteous state.
How can I look on you and still see, when my sanity threatens catastrophic state?
To o'erwhelm in abjection my mind's churnings at the evil that your situation wrought
On which I beheld a tender beauty, though, beauteous still, so painfully distraught.

Think not that I am harsh or beyond caring, I care so much I cannot bear to see.
All the pain and needless suffering that is tearing, a gentle kindly heart, that means so much to me.
How I yearn to see your mournful season over, replaced by happier summers' graces we both knew.
I pray earnestly to God, the one prime mover, to return spring's attributes to you
That you may blossom once again in all your beauty.
Bring happiness and joy and lasting peace.
Watch your rose-bud life bloom in gentle laughter.
See you smiling once again and never cease.

Terry Elloway

The Power Of Love!

It is the reconciling love, the reconciling love - of the Cross!
It is the grace that we speak, the life that we speak to those we reach out to and love.
It is the contented of heart, the gentle of heart, enriching all that we see and touch.
The purity of heart, cleanness of hands, delivering, healing - Jesus - His life in us.
Such power in His words, in His path all wisdom. His glory will surely abound.
The will of God, divine and eternal - heart peace; standing on holy ground!
The awesome love of God beckons to us - child know My thoughts and My mind.
My compassions and mercies never fade - knowing the holy bring understanding, you'll find.
Apprehended for now - created for holiness, infilled with My spirit of grace.
Your highest good - My perfect plan - daily I set in its place.
My glory cloud and fire, indwell in you - awesome glory - you have yet to see.
But - all is on time, all is established - all surrendered to Me.
And then, will such worship echo the heavens, such glories bathed in great light.
The glories of heaven, you cannot imagine, the Father's love, His children's delight.
Beholding My Son, you too will become, overcoming children, by grace in My name
Transformed by the holy, My character showing - you surely are never the same!
And so, as you stand, daily forgiving establishing My Great Love
I will be watching, tenderly caring, assuring My welcome "Well Done"!!

Mary Comley

126

A Little Girl's Prayer

Sweet Anna-Marie climbed on a chair
To gaze in the mirror at her pretty hair
She wishes her hair could be long and fair
But it was dark brown—so this was her prayer

She knelt by her bed, her eyes shut tight
And said, "Please Jesus, listen tonight,
Could you change the colour of my hair?
I don't want it brown, I would like it fair."

She climbed into bed feeling satisfied
Her request had been made of whom she relied
When morning came, she sprang out of bed
Making straight for the mirror to look at her head

She didn't understand—her hair was still brown!
In search of her Mum she hurried down.
"Mummy, why didn't Jesus answer my prayer?"
"He did", she said "Now you have beautiful hair".

Shirley Travis

Young Hedgehog

Little hedgehog, you're too small
To hibernate this year;
Your body will not stand the cold,
Your weight's too low, I fear.
So we shall keep you snug and warm.
Away from winter's spite—
Safe from all the perils of an icy, frosty night.
When the spring comes, warmer days will herald
Your release:
Once taught to forage for your food, your need
For us will cease.
And then you will be free to roam, to do what
Hedgehogs do,
Our work is done; now we must hope that life
Is kind to you.

Mary Lawrence

Our Planet Earth

Our planet earth is a wonderful place,
With every creed and every race.
With all the colours you could ever see
With the blue of the sky, and our wonderful sea
All the bird's both large and small
To greet you as the morning dawn
The butterflies flying from place to place.
Showing all their beauty, and all their grace.
Bee's buzzing around every flower
Never stopping for hours and hours
With our four seasons of sun and snow,
Spring and autumn makes our planet glow
So be pleased we live on our wonderful earth
With all its beauty we all share.

C. Clarke

A Bird Singing

Awakened early by a bird singing
A blackbird—singing his heart out
Heralding the new day with his happy burst of song
Happy to be alive
A new day
Like a new page in a book,
Waiting for words, thoughts, ideas, plans to be written
All new
A new life,
New hopes and dreams for the future
Anything—everything possible
Joy and happiness—precious things, look to the future
Turn the page of the book and leave the past behind
To be thought of occasionally—with joy, with sorrow
The future, still to be lived, with hope in heart
The present—to listen to the bird singing,
Singing with joy and happiness glad to be alive.

Jean Hands

My Bedroom Alive

I went up the stairs to my bedroom one night
The first thing I did was to switch on the light

Right in the corner was a box full of toys
Some were for girls and some were for boys

I opened the lid and to my surprise
The toys came alive with wide open eyes.

The monkey was swinging and having a lark
Lassie and Spot began to bark

Batman and Robin went off in their car
Looking for Joker who wasn't that far

Tiny tears and Tim cried for a feed
Then a nappy change was in need

The cars were whizzing around the track
Whoops there was nearly one up my back

Sindy went swimming in her pool
Then there was water all over the room

The ducks were quacking all over the place
Happy to be in that very wet space

With all the excitement I lay on my bed
Had more pleasant dreams as my pillow touched my head.

Clare Borthwick

Matrimonial Blues

I sometimes wonder who my husband will be;
Whether he'll be handsome
and how much he'll love me.

Just in what way is he going to propose?
What will be his height
and the shape of his nose?

Will he be blonde or perhaps dark?
Is he gonna be a gentle kind
or dangerous shark?

Above all I'm curious, how long will it last?
Forever and ever
or will the end be fast?

But whoever my other half might be,
I don't want him to arrive just yet;
for now I prefer a mystery.

Still, Mr Husband, don't take too long!
You wouldn't want to miss the chance
to be where you belong.

Sara Krajina

The Way

The path we tread is paved with trials -
We seek the way and walk the miles.
God has a plan for you and me.
This is not always plain to see.

We wander here, we wander there.
We should leave time to sit and stare;
To stare at what God has provided,
And seek to mend our souls divided.

Forgive the wrongs folk do to you.
Enjoy your days, however few.
Help those in need, when you pass by -
True happiness will with you fly.

Take up your cross and fight the fight
To do God's will, and what is right,
If the road is rough, and the days are long.
Just grit your teeth and sing a song.

Enjoy the wonders to be found
In nature's beauty all around,
Relax and pray, rejoice each day;
The way you'll find and joy will stay!

Priscilla Langridge

I Wish I

I wish I could hold you close to me,
And feel the magic of your charms.
But this is impossible,
Because I do not have any arms.

I wish I could run to see you,
That would give you a surprise.
But this is also impossible,
I have not got legs or eyes.

I wish I had a mouth to speak with,
So I could say hello and pardon.
But I am just a vegetable,
That is growing in your garden.

Jason Foulkes

My Inflatable Psychoanalyst

My inflatable psychoanalyst
Is a handsome man I can't resist.
He fixes me with a glassy stare
As I recline in the patient's chair.
As I pour out my hopes and fears
He flushes pink about the ears;
He's worried now as I list my sins
Clutching tight my box of pins.
As I jab them in with great delight
I'm pleased to see he's taken fright:
A pop, a gasp, a hiss of air,
Hooray, I'm cured and he's not there.

Pam Baker

Drawstring Purse

I loved you to the bottom,
of my drawstring purse
You loved me to the bottom,
of your beer glass thirst
I see now,
conversations made fake
You held me at arm's length,
for all that followed in your wake
Endless innuendoes in friends songs
Deny that I ever felt your shake
You left me standing,
standing on my threadbare carpet
My drawstring purse,
My drawstring thirst.

Victoria Vigurs

Water

Do you drink water every day
Have a swim and wash each day
Water garden, have cups of tea?

Are you glad you're not me
Living here in a drought?

No one hears me cry or shout
won't someone hear and
help me out.

You could help to stop
this drought.

B. M. Fuller

Untitled

Whose hand brushes the sleeping
        sky
bringing the first wisp of colour to
        my eye?
It is the great artist of the dawn,
Jehovah, paints the night and light
        is born.
I get up quickly so that I can see,
do raise your eyes and look at it
        with me.

S. Hine

Evacuation Day

It's evacuation day
I don't know what to say
I'll miss my mum and dad
My brother too I feel so sad.
I'm moving to the country
A place so strange and new
Moving in with someone I don't know.
I'm feeling so blue
Waiting on the platform, saying
My last goodbye.
I'll never see my parents
Again, if they're going to die.

Emma Flynn

My Sister

When we were young
and lived in Devon
Life was not so near to Heaven
We were poor, knew no other.
Mary Bob and older Brother.

Loving parents Mum and Dad.
Glebeland's didn't seem so bad.
Roses growing round the door
oil skins on the toilet floor.

Life passes we are older
no longer crying on each shoulder
getting married pastures new
getting fatter, feeling blue.

Now my sister, you have flown
across the ocean
—not on your own
But I miss you, we both do.
Good luck and love to both of you

Barbara Hartshorn

4 June 1996 Commitment

I am here today
Could be gone tomorrow
Would you give a damn?
Would you drown in your sorrow?

I could be so happy
And then be so sad
Would you notice me gone?
Would you think I'd gone mad?

I could drown in the water
As I swam in the sea
Would you send out a boat?
Or let me sail free?

I could fall off the edge
And crash on the rocks
Would you pick up the pieces?
Or leave me to rot?

Louise Sullivan

God's Gifts

The sea and the sand
And the sun in the sky
Are all God's creation
And come from on nigh
The moon and the stars
And the rain and the snow
Will always be with us
Wherever we go
The trees in the forest
The flowers in the field
They give us such pleasure
And help us to yield
Our praises to God
And the angels above
To thank them again
For their wondrous love

Walter James Sermaine

Why

The sun has been blocked
Right out of my life
Since I lost you dearest
you were my precious wife

Darkness now fills me
There's no room for light
The sunshine we once shared
Has gone out of sight

The crying fun and laughter,
We shared together
The Lord has taken from us
There'll be no more ever

Why is it that the Lord
only chooses the best
and decides in His wisdom
to lay them to rest

When there are bad ones out there
Who live a life in clover
and do wrong things to others
But their lives are not over

J. E. Hill

Dandelion Clock

Wonder on the face of a child
Dandelion seeds are blowing wild
Though they do not say tick tock
Time is told with a dandelion clock

Little whispers from the mouth
Blow the seeds north and south
Magic reflected in their eyes
As the fairy flies up to the skies

Watch the parachutes float away
To settle and grow another day
Another child will get lost in time
With pursed lips repeat this rhyme.

B. Eyre

The Power House

Oh man! you're very clever -
You've accomplished many things,
You've aped the birds and given us
Mechanically driven wings;
You've linked us all by radio,
Telephone and telly screen,
So now the world's diminished
In circumference, it seems.
You speed along your motorways
In your super powered cars,
You've reached the moon
And have ambitions for the stars;
But as you're hurtling onward
Into the mysteries of space,
It's really worth considering
What drives the human race.
Try not to feel too clever
In your scientific tower,
Remember only God can give
To life, the needed power.

Jean Love

The Guardian Angel

Is there a guardian Angel
For everyone who prays?
Does God allow His Messenger
To help the one who strays?
I know I must believe this,
I'm sure it must be true,
For the unexpected meeting
With the one who helped me through
Times of stress and trouble
I give my thanks to You.

Elsie Downes

Summer

Spring is here and winter
gone
Summer once again
reborn.

Fields are filled with
tiny feet
Little lambs they skip and
bleat.

Trees, hedges, flowers
and plants
Sing the resurrection
chant.

From every tree the
music sweet
The feathered choir
in rehearsal meet.

See the shimmering
shadows dance
On every tree and
every branch.

Hewri Termonia

Sanctuary

Rabbits
Stood on wasteland
Knee deep in broken glass
No-one could offer
Sanctuary.

Poised
One fur paw
Waited to avoid noisy thunder
Vibrating the glass
Shards.

Fear
Made fur stink
As dirt trickled out slowly
From little white
Tails.

Alone
On middle ground
The pair leapt forward together
Into the unknown
Sanctuary?

Linda McPherson

Spring Returns

Spring has returned once more
Too the sound of birds galore
Each pair raising their young
Only to hear the bang of a gun

The farmer doesn't seem to care
Shooting at things so rare
Rabbits running wild and free
While a squirrel scampers up a tree

Flowers blooming here and there
Their lovely perfumes fill the air
And as each day passes by
Only to be covered in green fly

Young love is truly here
With boys and girls everywhere
Not a rain cloud, to be found
Just a happy, joyous sound

Today there's a lovely blue sky
And a butterfly gently flutters by
For all this, and more
I sit here and adore.

Maureen Hyam

The Garden Ornament

That little stone boy in the garden
Upon his little stone mound
That little stone boy in the garden
Unable to murmur a sound
That little stone boy in the corner
Sitting there day after day
That little stone boy in the corner
Has no troubles coming his way
That little stone boy in the garden
Beside that old rose tree
That little stone boy in the garden
I wonder, can he see?
That little stone boy in the corner
Could he be thinking the same as me?
That little stone boy in the corner
Could he be wishing that I were he?

Dave Lewis

Untitled

Why am I taken by surprise
To find that I am in this guise?
Gradually we all succumb to age
After sixty years I am at this stage.
Have I ignored the warning signs
Things other than facial lines?
Costing gallons from price per litre
How many feet in those metres?
Indications of one's mind track
Being calibrated way back.
Other preferences have their way
Favourite film star, Doris Day
Sinatra too in my set plan
I knew him as a younger man.
So many things I could mention
But, get with it man, accept the pension

D. G. Thompson

Back To Wittering, West Sussex

We lost all count of time
In the lee of the old timber groyne,
Mesmerized by the sound of the sea
The soft warm breeze and sun.

The pebbles seemed quite smooth
As they moulded to our thighs
Our backs to the oaken baulks
Under heavenly blue skies.

A precious day and rare
So happy to be there
Thro' maze of mind and mime
The surging seas recall that time.

Wilfred Purton

Merrie The Cherry

You are a catch of my eye
You flirt before me and you fly.
You are a star in the sky
The beauty I really love to try
I crawl over you is a wish
Shawl of your beauty is so rich
Can't speak and I tell you this
You prevail over me but can't kiss
You are the one who hail me
Arresting in your thoughts you jail me
All my attentions quick as you take
Tensions in my mind so you make
The love alarm in me you raise
You disturb my peace and bring craze
In my motions you come and go
You are a great chum and so
Without you my world is so gone
I am lost and I am torn
Times you part me with a sigh
Times you come alive before my eye

Sarwan S. Deol

The Wildness In Me

My wild spirit
my wild spirit
riding on a wave
into the abyss of
passion the soft moans
of my voice and the
wild moans of my
lover and knight in one
sends my wild spirit
to heaven and hell and
back to the silent and
rhyme of his heart beat
we share as one.

Olive Irwin

Li + Kr + Es + Ra = ? (Mk II)

Something binding
Don't know what,
Keeping us together,
Two little dots.

Atom plus atom,
Please hold tight,
Keep things forever,
We'll always have the night.

Now squeeze me,
Tell me I'm dreaming,
The keeper and the soothsayer,
Will aid my believing.

Jonathan Simms

As Time Goes By

How could it have happened
Where did it all go
All the friends, the partying
I used to love it so
All the letters and the phone calls
The things they used to say
Hurry, get your glad rags on
We'll have some fun today
So off we'd go and sure enough
We'd dance the night away
We giggled and we flirted
And we really had a ball

Now suddenly it's disappeared
There's nothing left at all

V. Ray

Forget Me Not

Forget-me-nots bloom every year,
And with them bring us
Summer cheer.

Their tiny, your tiny bright
colourful faces,
Blow gently in God's warming winds.

When I see all those tiny
delicate flowers,
To each and every one of your
missed faces
- I'll forget you not.

My heart will remember all
the braveness and courage
you must have shown
- I'll forget you not.

My own children are so
precious to me,
with each year they grow older
-I'll forget you not.
God bless you all.

Wendy Clark

Wheel

I watched them, the giant machine
and prepare it for its flight
and as I looked I marvelled
at man and all his might.

I watched them walk across the drone
the laughing youthful crew
I gave a thought to their folks at home
as if I already knew

Within a second so it seemed
the plane and crew were lost
swallowed up in flame and smoke
all seven at their post.

They went before their allotted span
to their home beyond the sky
these men whose country called them
and taught them how to fly.

W. Ragan

Bardsey Sound

Drugged peace hides
anxieties, intrusions, hopes;
even dreams
recede like dismissed impulses
tappable
concurrently there being lost.

Glimpses, - sounds
of the sea bashing Lleyn Headland
takes away
grosser particles - human kind.
Bardsey Sound
light reflecting on its surface,

hides currents
which can peacefully disturb, in
this tiny aspect of world distilled
calm brings God's only
peace. Glimmering it surfaces.

Robert Shooter

Memories

Precious memories in the mind
As the years go rolling on,
Memories we store as gold
Relive them one by one.

Treasures come and treasures go
As all our lives will change,
Day by day old time moves on
But memories backwards range.

Old familiar friends we knew
And some who have passed on,
As long as we are living still
Can they be truly gone?

Keep storing in the memory bank
Things beautiful and good,
Someday when the health is gone
Recapture the happy mood.

Gladys Thompson

Ode To Anthony

Full of life and full of zest.
Anthony was the very best
of youth today.
Mum and Dad and Sister too,
Will miss him so—well wouldn't you!
What will they do without the boy,
Who was their very pride and joy.
They'll think of all those happy years,
And then they'll wipe away their tears.
For Anthony was loved by all,
But God loved him the most of all.

Madeline C. Burden

Wonderful Words!

A b c d e f g
H i j k l m
Words are so exciting
Each a potential gem.

Certain words once spoken
Seem to live on and on,
Will my words be golden
Someday, when I've gone?

Like drops of silver finery
Etched in finest tracery?
Some silver and gold I possess
Words bring greater happiness.

To help maybe the ill and infirm
A worthy place may I so earn
As we travel along life's lane,
Then my living will not be in vain.

Gladys Thompson

Our Cat

With agile bound
And purring sound
By fire is found;
And when unwound
This furry mound
With outline round
Is fat!

Brian J. Dunn

Lace Curtains

Every day I passed this house with its
lace curtains dirty, blowing in the
breeze through broken window panes.
Someone, sometime had made those
curtains clean for all to see
through sparkling window panes.
Who had worked, played, slept in
that now derelict house with its
doors wide open for all to see
the dirty lino and the old settee?
Someone, sometime had shouted
"Close that door" had cleaned the
lino and the floor, washed the
curtains and window panes.
Then scrubbed the front step after
polishing the door at number 24.

B. J. Tomkinson

The Fox

You cunning, sly and handsome beast
One shot from me your life has ceased;
You wonder why my hand is stayed,
No debt I owe, no pact was made.

Are you the wild pup that I freed
Into the trees, and did you breed,
My thoughts as then might save you now,
Fine feelings friend I still allow.

Red tinged coat of silken fur
What wild and wondrous scheming cur,
Grand bushy tail of fluffy rouge,
Sharp featured face with eyes aroused.

What prey espies your beady eye,
What weak frail life you hope will die;
Your skinny gut demands some filling,
What offguard creature is so willing.

Don't stare me out, don't eyeball me,
Though beautiful you seem and free;
We've shared these seconds and I'm glad
Your free spirit, one glimpse I've had.

John F. McCartney

Childhood Days

Country walks and bike rides,
Whichever to our delight,
Climbing trees, hide and seek,
Even camping out all night.

Those days were called our fun days,
And plenty for us to do,
Always doing as we were told
Helping old folk to.

Our parents never worried
How far away we strayed,
For green spacious common land
Was the ground on which we played.

To look back over yesteryears,
How different it is now,
Our own beloved offspring
Seem insecure somehow.

And yet, that lovely common land
On which we used to play,
Has never changed, but out of reach,
We moved too far away.

I. A. Chivers

Why?

I see a mother weeping
A child lies at her feet
His belly is all swollen
Still nothing for them to eat.

I see a mother weeping
a child's eyes growing dim
He rolls around in agony
No food to give him

I see a mother weeping
Her child lies in a heap
No longer is he breathing
There was no food to eat

I see a mother weeping
her child still at her feet
Too weak to even bury him
Still no food to eat

I sit in front of my TV
It's now my turn to weep
How can we let them die
From lack of food to eat?

Lesley Baker

The Silent Goodbye

It's time for me to say goodbye
I hope I don't break down and cry
Although I know our paths must part
You'll still remain deep in my heart

I've known that we could never be
The day would come when you'd leave me
Our worlds could never be the same
You need to play a different game

I have to let you go away
And it must be done today
Whilst I'm strong and you can't see
Just how much this is hurting me

Walk away and don't look back
I don't think I could handle that
I cannot let you see my pain
In case you feel you must remain

My wish for you is a great life
Free from trouble and from strife
All I ask for me is this
Please just give me one last kiss

Lesley Baker

The Stream

Life is a stream, a rushing stream
Born free upon the heights,
In rills and rivulets it starts
There while the rain alights.

Lightly it tumbles wandering
Down every channel bright,
In youthful voice a thundering
Full-blooded for the fight.

Sprays as it dashed o'er the rocks,
Foams through the pebbly strand,
Lingers awhile in crystal pools
Pondering the wayward land.

Now slows the current in its course,
Strong in its even flow;
Broader and deeper are the banks
And the music low.

'Til in the roar of ocean might
To liquid depths it glides;
Mingling its substance in the night,
Serving eternal tides.

Martin Knebel

But For Now . . .

I saw death the other day.
 Its eyes were glazed,
  and moved slowly.
 Its mouth was open,
  a little.
 Its head moved slowly,
  a little.
Then with a flick of a hair,
 it was still.
 The mouth is open,
  a little.
Of death in a small bundle,
 Outside they have sold the medicine,
  which would have opened my eyes.
My mouth would have moved,
 in a cry.
 But for now,
  let me die.

Mohan Bahra

Blood On Snow

Great wings outstretched, eyes ablazing
Death swoops down to seek its prey
Twisting, driving, running, hiding
Her victim cannot get away
Talons strike, ever tightening
The searing pain and it is done
Ripping, tearing, shredding, sharing
The hunter home, she feeds her young
All is silent, all is still
Nature is cruel, was always so
Listen to the deathly silence
See the blood upon the snow

Monica Scarlett

Sheer Khan-Age

Tiger Tiger burning bright
With an iridescent light
Tiger Tiger burning bright
Is that a slightly dimmer light

Tiger Tiger glowing slight
Heading into total night
Tiger Tiger if we fight
Can we keep you in our sight

Tiger Tiger where's your light
Medicinal bones caused your plight
Tiger Tiger you lost your fight
Out of mind and out of sight.

Stephen Wiles

Who Knows

If the way
We,
As civilized beings
And intelligent animals
Treat
Other innocent life forms
The way
We do at present
We,
As well
Deserve such treatment.

We expect
To escape
Such behaviour in life.
In time,
Time will catch up
With us
And the goodness of life knows
What will happen to us.

Farid Finzi

My Window

I have a special window
Where each season can be seen.
Through the leaded patterns
I watch nature's changing scene.

I have a special window
Where spring and summer come to life.
The country lane I've walked my son,
The fields I've walked my wife.

I have a special window.
Autumn spreads her morning mist.
I see frost upon the countryside
Where once was summer bliss.

I have a special window.
The winter sun breaks feebly through
Warming winter's snowscape
And glistening on the dew.

I see through my window
What my life is all about.
For it is through my church window
I am looking out.

Frederick Seymour

The Perfect Kitten

I saw a little kitten,
A little ball of fluff on legs,
It was playing with a ping-pong ball,
Then it started on the pegs.

I saw a little kitten,
It was so tiny and wee,
It scampered around the shiny floor,
And then it came to me.

I saw a little kitten,
It was so round and fat,
I found it hard to imagine,
That it could ever become a cat.

I saw a little kitten,
It was very, very playful,
It was stripy like a tiger,
I thought it was beautiful.

I saw a little kitten,
It started to nod its head,
It fell asleep in front of the fire,
Curled up in its little bed.

Rebecca Homer

Peace

Peace is here,
Peace is there,
Peace should be
Everywhere.

Peace is great,
Peace is loving,
Peace is a new
Sign of budding.

Peace is harmless,
Peace is fun,
Peace is there,
For everyone.

Power and money,
We all want more,
But peace in the world
Is better than war.

Donna Browne

Please

My son has sent a cheque to me,
To order a book from you.
To own that book, my greatest wish,
In his heart he knew.

I'm choked up with emotion,
And in my heart such joy.
The only time I felt like this,
Was when the nurse said "It's a boy."

So please I beg you order,
"Awaken to a Dream."
If I don't get a copy,
I'm sure that I shall scream.

You made my day when you sent to me,
A letter with good news.
For everything I ever wrote,
Was to air my inner views.

M. Muirhead

Love

A broken heart
A shattered dream
A yearning for what might have been
The pain begins tearing churning
A part of me felled like a tree
Left to die in misery
Completely devastated...

Christine Mountney

Love Is Forever

He always sat by me,
His hand in mine,
His eyes always gleaming,
Reflecting in mine.

He'd say he'll always love me,
That love is always by,
But that night he fell,
My heart fell as well.

When I see his picture,
I always seem to cry,
But I do stop eventually,
Because I know he's somewhere by.

I remember the hugs he gave me,
I feel his presence come over me,
His love starts to appear now,
For, the one last time.

As our hands come apart,
I know you have to go,
I know we can't be together,
But our love, will be forever.

Sabrina Shanker

Dream Of Peace

There is a castle in the sky.
So clear, so calm, so far, so high.
There is a fairyland we see
Of knights and maids in harmony.

A land where people still do keep
A peaceful harvest, and who reap
Not war and blood and grief and woe,
But peace and joy where'er they go.

They do not seek with greed as we
To take from others land and sea.
For all is shared and all is free.
And that is how we too should be.

If all would give instead of take,
Then we too so soon would make
A land as happy and as free
As those lands in the sky we see.
Joan Hills

The Aftermath

When there's gun-fire and blasts,
Lives wrecked in a mad-man's task,
In the hurt and the grief,
Many children believe,
We have a cure.

There's illness and sorrows,
Lives wrecked, no tomorrows,
In the hurt and the grief,
Many children believe,
We have a cure.

Politicians and their policies,
Lives wrecked, nations politics,
In the hurt and the grief,
Many children believe,
We have a cure.

Parents toil and strife,
Suffering other pitfalls of life,
In the hurt and the grief,
Many children believe,
We have a cure.
Angela Henderson

Spring Poem

"Oh" spring you have come back again
My garden's turning green.

The little flowers are pushing up,
Its beauty to be seen.

The days are getting longer,
Birds now sing at last.

It's good to look and walk around,
Now winter it has passed.
Peter Williamson

When Love Is Lost

Who is she, this woman I call me.
Am I real,
Do I really live and feel.
Am I a woman buried alive.
Day by day trying to survive.
Was I really born to bleed,
Will no-one ever sense my need.
Will it always be this way,
Must I live in silence day by day.
I shout and scream on an empty stage,
My audience is this empty stage,
Of which I write of my need to live,
Is there anyone still listening . . .
Will anyone give.
Lynne Harris

Awareness

We must make time to stand and stare,
   We must make time to be aware
Of the beauty that is around
   And of the creatures that abound
But how long will they be around
   If no solution can be found
To man's inhuman acts of murder
   Both to creatures and much further
Man feels superior but what's he worth
   When he can't see the future's bleak
Because the World is getting weak
   Through atom blasts and acid rain
And creatures never seen again
   We must take time to stand and stare
And make them see and be aware
   That what we have upon this Earth
Is precious and has boundless worth
   Maybe if we strive to preserve it
We can feel that we do deserve it.
J. D. Holmes

Storm

Every time the lightning flashes
a new star is made.

Every time the thunder crashes
the whales come out to play.

Every time a raindrop falls
the streams begin to flow.

Every time the sun comes out
a baby flower grows.

At the end a rainbow appears
all its colours shining.

See it's not so bad
After all
now the sun is shining.
Katie Lamb

Dawn

With the dawn comes a serenade
so sweet,
As a blackbird answers a
robin's cheep,
And the thrush lifts its beautiful
slender throat,
And trills forth a song...
such perfect notes.

'Tis a joy, indeed, to wake
with the dawn,
And know a new day has just
been born.
To lift up our hearts in
a joyful prayer
Of thanks for a chorus,
so splendid to hear.
Winifred Davis

Autumn Leaves

The wind is in a hurry,
As it rushes through the trees,
And leaves of brown and yellow
Are dancing in the breeze.

They whirl and twirl and pirouette.
And gently settle on the ground
To make a magic carpet
Of green and gold and brown

This russet autumn carpet
Which whispers 'neath our feet
And like an autumn sunset
Transforms our world to gold.
Emma Hunt

Reach Out And Touch My Hand

Reach out and touch me
Reach out and touch my hand
Reach out and touch me
I hope you'll understand

That I'm going to a better place
No one has ever seen
And I'm going in darkness
Just like in a dream

Don't cry don't shed a tear now
There ain't no sense no how
Because you knew as well as I did
I had to go somehow

Don't fret don't worry now
The Lord He will be there
To show me how to carry on
Without you all there

And if at last we meet again
Beyond the great divide
I will walk through eternity
With you by my side
Russell David Gill

VIGILANT BREAKFAST

QUIVERING
tinybody on twiglegs;
As myeyes
FREEZE
birdprofile,
SURGING
surgicalbeak
PLUCKS
proteinminutiae from breadrock;
Watchful sidewiseeyes
PERCEIVE
th'imperceptible! Trigger's
SQUEEZED!
Hypertimid bomb
EXPLODES!
Wingblur
ELEVATES
Diminutive to
th'invisible...
Graham M. Norris

Friends

Anger has taken over
Everyone must run
If she sees you looking
You will soon be done

Red is in front of her eyes
Blood is being shed
She thought they had feelings
But none instead

The sea speaks to her
Telling her to be calm
But she has the devil in her
Soon they'll all be gone

The devil's voice takes over
They never did care
Saying yes to many things
But never to be shared

She's ready now to kill at ease
But inside a sweet voice
Begs her not to, please.
Meadhbh Murphy

A Whisper on the Breeze

A whisper on the breeze calls to me
Amidst England's majestic scenery
Gifted by our ancestors
for generations to come
the glory of their sacrifice
for which our freedom was won
The serenity of a village church
Gathering on the green
A pretty oak beamed pub
To complete this tranquil scene
Where else on earth would you find
Pleasure of a more rewarding kind
gifted by those who paid the price
With the final sacrifice
for the land you and I now know
Where peace and love may grow

Sheila Burke

Drunkard

Staggering, swaggering
Struggling to stay on his feet
He suffered two broken teeth
When he fell, lips starting to swell
I helped him up
I came to the conclusion he was drunk
He stunk of alcohol and cigarette
I could smell it on his breath
He cursed and swore
Swung punches galore
Got into a brawl
To cap it all
Someone called the police
They took him away in a van
Poor man

Leslie King

Helping Hands

When we bear each other's burdens,
It's all action sweet and rare.
A special kind of goodness
That is quite beyond compare.
Everyone needs help, sometimes,
A'travelling on life's way.
And when it comes with special love,
We don't know what to say.
For the giving and the caring
Is blessed, so we're told,
Believing that the love we've shared
Is treasure more than gold.
If only we would live our lives
Well guided by God's hand.
By trusting Him, whate'er betide
Then we might understand,
To make a heaven here, on earth,
All men upright and true.
And so to do Our Father's will
As He would want us to.

Enid Rathbone

Hero, Traitor, Or Cynic

Why do rebels defy their breed
perhaps the place are born.
For if awoke in other climes
would be Judas on another side.

O liberty in chains
or anarchy O no:
not yet open-minded
to weigh calm mature views

though with we so loyal
warlike the other body's sway

depends upon the soil
first found beneath the feet.

Herbert Wilson

Untitled

Our son was born
Tenth February 95
We were ecstatic, I felt
so alive
We were excited as we'd
Waited eight years
My husband was overjoyed
In his eyes he had tears
Kyle weighed 6lb 15oz when
He was born
Thank goodness I didn't
Get torn
Every 3 hours he wanted
To be fed
It wasn't long before
It was 8 o'clock bed.
But now he's two, he's
All over the place
He looks at me cheekily
With his bonny face.

Deborah Thomas

I'm Sorry If I Hurt You

I'm sorry if I hurt you
If you thought I didn't care
But in my heart I loved you
Even though I wasn't there
Now you're gone I miss you
More than any words can say

The pain I feel inside for you

Won't ever go away
I'm glad for the time we had together
The love we shared
No other love in the World
Can ever be compared

Carol Tuckett

Butterfly

Butterfly, butterfly,
Hopping, fluttering, colours
Why won't you stay for a while?
You look so pretty
sitting still in the
bright sunshine
foliage green, wings bright.
Stay oh! Stay!
My pretty butterfly.
Be my friend for a
moment longer
than a moment.

Sally Davis

Our Baby

Babies are our pride and joy
It may be a girl or boy
Whether they are dull or bright
They are still the parents' delight

When it gives its first cry
The mother gives such a sigh
Then when she sees the little mite
It is the proudest moment of her life

The father is not far away
For this too is his first day
He rubs its nose and its chin
And says what a lovely thing

As they sit and ponder
At this their tiny wonder
They know it is a part of each other
And its life is their tomorrow.

Anna Lilian Locker

The Privilege

Eyes most precious to behold
Although they now are growing old
Beauty only, wish to see
Ugliness discomforts me

To witness colours all around
Cowslips, violets, on the ground
Bud-caressing trees nearby
Blue-birds flying in the sky

Shimmering lakes where I have been
Wild geese complement the scene
Inflicted noise corrodes the day
Leading tranquil souls astray

Twilight years do compensate
In my heart a great debate
Choice is mine, therefore decide
Look solely on the country side

Maureen M. Weitman

Blossom

The May blossom lies on the grass,
below the trees now green,
Like snowflakes in winter passed,
A carpet of blossom is seen.

The birds tiptoe over the carpet,
Picking up morsels there,
Like little nymphs among the blossoms,
Flitting everywhere,

I love the summer in bloom,
Even in wet days,
For each day holds magic,
I never stop being amazed,

Hazel E. Henshaw

Why?

Why does it seem, when things go wrong,
The world is at an end
Or when you've finished a good book
That you have lost a friend;
Why does a problem seem less big
When shared with someone close,
Why does sad music from a film
Make people feel morose;
Why does the snow fall silently
To make a perfect world
But then is spoiled immediately
By rubbish that is hurled;
Why do so many people die
From illnesses they've caught,
Why were the children of Dunblane
Wiped out without a thought;
Most people have a cross to bear,
A problem in their life,
Why can't we wave a magic wand
And banish all the strife?

Brenda E. Jones

A Purple Place

Purple birds in the trees
Purple life, purple breeze
Purple oceans and the streams
Purple thoughts, purple dream
Purple streets, purple cars
Purple movies and their stars
Purple cafes and purple bars
Purple rain, purple spas
Purple laws, purple rules
Purple crime and abuse
Purple screams and purple pain
Purple wars, no one gains
Purple sights, purple gaze
Purple time, purple days
Purple people, a purple place.

Craig Shuttleworth

Be Mine

A leaf falls lightly,
From an autumn tree,
Swaying slowly, side to side,
'Til it lands right next to me.
It seems the tree feels no pain,
It doesn't seem to care,
But then they all begin to fall
And the tree looks cold and bare.
Maybe you should think about this
About how I look and feel,
When I say I love you, look deeper
Then you'll see that I'm for real.
Sooner or later,
My last leaf will fall,
Then you'll see I'm all truth
And nothing else will matter at all.
I hate hassling you
All of the time.
I need you
Please be mine.

Nell Brigham

Bob-the-Collie (Holiday Time)

I've never been to the seaside
I've never even seen the sea.
The nearest I've been to the seaside.
Is this pool that's in front of me,
My mistress will take me one day,
of this there is no doubt
It will be when the heavens cloud over.
And there's all that fog about,
No I don't fancy going to the seaside.
I'd rather stay at home,
Stretched out on this nice warm carpet
And tucking into a nice juicy bone.

J. Chadwick

Untitled

Eggshell of the moon.
In the moonbeams scattered
'round me
I can see your face reflected
and your spirit comes to
haunt me
In the daydreams you've
perfected

I can feel your heart beat
near me
and it all seems so persuasive
then I wake in realization
just to find you more
evasive

Emily Eastwood

Spaces

Spaces between words
The notes of a song.

Space between trees
The leaves on the bough.

Space between table sofa and chair
Space between pictures
That hang on the wall.

Space between months
The days of the week.

Space between minutes
Second of time.

Space in the universe
Spacing the stars.

Space in my life
That I may know
Love.

Jackie Draysey

Life On Earth

Acid rain falls, trees expire,
The bomb a silent threat but dire.
Hatred burns like a furnace fire,
Is this life on earth?

Silent they lie, their battles fought;
Victims of wars they had not sought.
Lost to sight but not to thought,
Is this life on earth?

Shrunken frames, stricken cries,
Hunger stares from pleading eyes.
Bodies covered by skin and flies,
Is this life on earth?

Workers once, for dole they queue,
Giro not pay slip now their due.
Staring at a blank wall view,
Is this life on earth?

Treasure all life, the earth restore,
Share what there is, loot no more.
People and planet revere and adore,
This Is Life On Earth.

Warwick Steels

The Clouds At Night

The clouds at night are sleeping,
Resting till the dawn,
The sky at night is bleeding,
Ripped apart and torn.

Somewhere in the distance,
The poorest city cries,
While in the midst of mayhem,
Rich business deals in lies.

Confusion rules the chaos,
The desperate turn to dread,
As money lays foundations,
We pray for daily bread.

The clouds at night are sleeping,
Another child is born,
The sky at night is bleeding,
Ripped apart and torn.

Ian Deal

Salvation

I was so lost, my head hung low,
There seemed no hope, nowhere to go,
Then Jesus called, held out His hand,
said "Follow me, I understand".

He led me down a brand new road,
and took away my heavy load.
He gave me all He had to give,
And restored my will to live.

And He can be your Saviour too,
He wants to share His life with you.
Ask His forgiveness for your sin,
Open your heart and let Him in.

Audrey Coe

Untitled

When you're in love with someone
It's like being born anew
Everything seems so lovely
Even on a dull rainy day
The raindrops seem to whisper
Sweet nothings in your ear
Then when you see the rainbow
High up in the sky
You turn around and see her
The one that you adore
Then at last you can say
I've found my pot of gold

Henry Brown

Life

We live one day to the next
not knowing what's in store.
We say we're happy as we are
yet we're always seeking more.

We strive to make things better
but not for us alone
We give to other people's needs
when we need it for our own.

They say it's the way we are
so why are we not the same
there are people in this world
that put the Human Race to shame

Amanda Winn

Waiting: War And Life, 1939-1941

When you left me that day
On account of the war,
I tried so hard to be brave,
I said goodbye so sadly,
With tears in my eyes and heart,
Trusting that you would come
"To no harm",
With your new son in my arms.

Four long weary years,
Full of hope and fears,
If we could ever be really
happy again without tears,
To be together once again,
To begin life anew,
To live with hope also
Without all our fears.

The after years were hard to bear,
Three children we had in fact,
We had to survive all that,
But you came through that fight,
With God's help we did survive,
That is the meaning of 'War and Life'.

V. M. Moore

Ay, I Heard The Lips That Kissed

Grow in silence beautiful
Ever scare me with your tears
Make me tremble,

Ay, I heard the lips that kissed
I lay and ever

Whisper wild and sweet,
Yet hold me, (n)ever hold me.

Monika Hutchinson-Traub

It Came

Munching moon,
Ate the stars,
Blew the clouds,
Swallowed the snow,

Kissed heaven gracefully,
Licked the sun red,
Stroked the sky with blue birds,
Breathed heavy satisfaction,

Rolled the world round and round,
Admired the ground,
Spoke commanding communion,
And covered it every half time,

Then it came,
The rain,
Things grew—
Old,
Inhale, exhale life.

Lyn Byrne

The Meeting Place

Hello, it's you, of course it is
you haven't changed a bit
Great to meet you in the park like this
Have you got time to sit

Please tell me you remember me
And all the fun we had
Through school and university
Aren't you really glad

We helped each other all the time
We even fell in love
He looked at me, held out his hand
And touched me with his glove

It's such a pity there is no time
To reminisce some more
You really are still beautiful
More beautiful than before

I looked into his deep brown eyes
A smile upon my face
For a moment we were young again
In the park, at our old meeting place

Anne Sim Logan

Our Savage World

Into this savage world we are thrown
Vulnerable...
Like an abandoned seal pup
Amidst the extremes of the North Pole

Dazed and confused
Into this mad world, we are to expect
Laughter, Joy and extreme pain
Mentally, physically we endure
In the depths of our soul

Continuing to hide behind our screen
Who's to listen anymore in
Our selfish world, who's to care
I'm number one, says the Great Master

Into oblivion he lets scream
The beast, the king of the jungle
Man's greed will befall us all
Like stars falling from the sky

Who'll listen to us now
Amongst the ashes
Is our fate....

Irene Eastwood

The Angel Boy

It was last autumn
I took to my bed
with flue and as I
    opened my eyes there

Was a small boy and a
    cat at my bedside
The skeleton of the cat
    was distinct and in the
    dim light

The word was mother
in large letters
They stayed a while till
I felt better
It was a visit from heaven

The angel boy and the cat
    The cat was Tabetha my cat
    fancy that

B. A. Linney

I'm Just Jam

Here I am, there you are,
I'm just jam in an airtight jar
You're the bread, I'm the jam
We go together like potatoes and lamb.
On the outside you're so free
I'm sticky jam for someone's tea,
You get cut nice and straight
Then put on a nice clean plate
Without me you taste so dry
You need me so stick close by,
Look out - here they come!
Soon you will be just a crumb,
People push and poke at me
With that great big knife you see
Very soon I'll be gone
And it looks like it won't be long,
Here I am, there you are
I'm just jam in an airtight jar.

Linda Roberts

Motherhood

Mother screams,
Push once more,
Suddenly amidst the panting,
A baby's cry
Tears of joy and happiness
It's a boy!
Now the troubles start
Early learning
Mother swells with pride
School!
Tears on both sides
High school comes,
Time flew by.
Sorrows begin, shouting arise
Police at the door
Bad news to follow.
Oh, how short it was,
To the morning in bed,
Cradling the newborn child
Eighteen years ago.

Sheila Dougall

The Snowstorm

Snowflakes snowflakes falling fast
I just wonder will they last
They are so thick I think they will
Now they've reached our windowsill
I cannot see our lawn at all
And that is after just one fall
The trees look lovely dressed in white
They really are a wondrous sight
Without their leaves they look so bare
In wintertime this is not rare
But in a month or two we know
Again they all will start to grow
We must enjoy it whilst it's here
It might not come again next year
We hope it will but not as much
'Cos when it melts it turns to slutch
This makes it hard to walk upon
Then we are glad when it has gone

N. Minett

Untitled

I cherished the days
you came my way
You brightened up each lonely day
I longed for you to hold me
To tell me that you care.
But hope is all I can do
Now you're not there!

Lynn Jones

"Father God"

How tender are your mercies
How loving are your caresses
How thoughtful and kind
You are with me in mind

I deserve nothing
Yet you give everything
Through your son Jesus, eternal life
So that we need not strive

For your company, your time
There you are waiting
Smiling, with loving arms outstretched
On your palms my name is etched

With heaven's angels celebrating
Watching your daughter love you back
For with you truly there is no lack
Of love, of life, of joy, of abundance

What can I say?
But thank you, thank you, Father God
For each new day
Living with you is the best way.

Sharon McLafferty

Colour The Clown

Colour
The clown looked up.
What colour?

Distract.
The mirror stared back.
No answer.

Decision darlings . . .
Let them gaze and be dazzled.
Mild laughter.

Confess . . . admit . . .
Did anybody see the clown?

Answer.
Laughter.
Clown?
Colour?
What?
No.
No longer.

Ian Hiscock

I Live Without Life

I offer myself in darkness
    for light is none but an enemy,
I give blood choice
    for blood is all that matters.
Evil is the power in this world
    The power we need to rule.

Your heart is in darkness
    and in yours eyes is cold hunger,
Rock me with your power
    rule me within your might,
Come feed on me in coldness,
Kill me you cannot
    for I am already dead.

I ask you to lift my soul
    give me pain,
Remove all warmth,
Let evil take over,
Do not resist your thirst for blood,
Live in the night,
Live without life.

Leanna Skinner

Memories Of Love

Melodies fill the silent air,
Recalling how you used to care,
Once more plays that sad refrain,
Of hopes that were to die in vain.

Days of laughter, nights of love,
Stars like jewels in heaven above,
Now gentle raindrops fill the sky
And mingle with the tears I cry.

Promises so quickly made,
Only then to be betrayed.
I sit alone and contemplate,
Blind delusion, or just fate.

Let numbness overtake me now,
Too easy to recall our vow,
The rosy dreams in misted eyes
They could not see that love was lies.

Anne Wilson

Cover Girl

Lips pout
  Ribs jut out
Hair sleek
  Sunken cheek
Provocative pose, freckle nose.
Seductive eye, heels high,
Pale skin, arms thin.
Undeveloped
  Uncovered
Adolescent
  Pubescent
Anorexic
  Bulimic.
Exfoliated
  Exhibited
    Exploited.
Fill out
  Grow up
    Cover up
Cover Girl.

Cathy LeFeuvre

Love Me

I wish I could float in the clouds
And fly with the birds up so high
I wish I could just make you love me
And say hello instead of goodbye.

I wish I could dive in the ocean
Without even taking a breath
I wish I could just make you love me
I'd even swim out of my depth.

I wish I could ride a wild stallion
And control him without any reins
I wish I could just make you love me
And rid of this heartache and pain.

I'm glad that we both can be happy
I'm glad now that everything's right
I love you and I know that you love me
When we kiss and you hold me so tight.

Helen Webster

War Game

The Nazi's planes are overhead
Their noisy drones we hear though
we lay calmly in our beds, though
Danger's drawing near, the Ack Ack Boys
will give them it.
  So children don't you fear, just let
your mum tuck you into bed and
dream that dawn is near.

Robert Oliver Stevenson

The Snake

The snake
slides slyly
through the
scented grass.
His cold, scaly
skin is
velvety soft.
The leaves sigh
as he slithers through
them silently
and all is calm...

Amy Higgins

The Sea Empress

Wonderful, golden beaches
Miles of glistening sand
Waves of crystal clear water,
lapping on treasured land.

Nothing was quite as peaceful
as my favourite place in the night.
Barefooted, thoughtful and happy,
before that tanker took flight

Now tears of oil and anger
fill the tainted air.
The dark and deadly voyage
has caused these towns despair.

Cries of anguish from sea gulls
will it ever be the same?
So many bitter and tearful,
the beauty has turned to pain.

Elizabeth Jones

Dedicated To Mothers
On Mothers' Day

This day is when our love is shown
To those we think have always known
Just how much they mean to us
Without our making too much fuss.

We shrink from saying important words
Afraid of sounding false when heard
But sometimes deep inside we dare
And want to know how much we care.

Today is such a special day
To let you know in every way
Just how much you mean to me
And that my love will always be.

A great big hug and kiss is sent
With words that are so truly meant
It means so much that you are there
And that we have so much to share.

S. H. Townsend

Coming Closer

Slowly slowly
Laying down
Resting her sleepy head
The blunders of her past
Made sure she didn't rest
She knew her time was ending
Her life drifting away
She knew she had to fight it
Not to end the day this way
But fighting was so hard now
Death was coming near
She had to prove her worthiness
To live her life just here
But death was already upon her
Life gone out of sight
Too late to put a fight up
Death was proud of her catch tonight.

Victoria Rhodes

Truth

Truth seems rarely simple.
Complex and ill-defined,
It beguiles the best of people,
And confounds the rational mind.

At times a contradiction,
At others incomplete,
An illusory delusion,
A will-o-the-wisp, a cheat.

All analysis is impotent,
Logic falls on barren ground,
Attempts to seek significance,
Fail long before it's found.

Yet truth is but a paradox,
Intuition knows this well.
Which relative, which ultimate,
Only the wise can tell.

Amanda Leighton

Brigitte

Back here in her native France
the stone is too cool, too unfair.
I detest the year passed.
Could her laughter rend the granite
her eyes might shine with warmth,
tho' she was gentler still;
a kiss seems too harsh,
or lips brushing cheek.
Softer yet, a smile,
now still, now gone.
Peace is hers, not mine,
I ceased to be, yet am here, still,
our turbulent despair now mine.
A thought, softer than a smile,
which leads to the ache of love
torn, broken,
unending

Stephen Young

A Mother's Love

It's always there, a feeling
Never ending, never faltering.
At times comforting,
At times suffocating but always there.

Who can explain the power it has
At times it can be tested,
at times it can be strained,
But it never has to be explained.

We feed off it,
we thrive on it,
and some can take advantage,
but we all need it,

A mother's love.

Louise Robertson

The Mason

Board on crate he placed
Mortar mixed and ready.
Stones to sort, and some to number,
Grey, precise, and cornered, heavy.
First course backbreaking lowness,
Better as the sides grow.
Open centre, passage through,
Stone on stone, much higher now.
The tricky part is just beginning,
Template put in place.
Each stone in perfect harmony
Curving over central space.
The arch has taken shape,
The church porch is complete.
The opening now is ready,
For many tramping, reverent, feet.

Fred Magan

You And I

How blessed we were you and I,
Giving to her who gave us life
Our love, our care;
Watching her aged smile;
Hearing her simple prayer
Wafting into a rainbow
Through clouds of anguish and pain.

How blessed we were, my sister,
Through the darkest nights,
Our hands enclasped,
Listening to her whispered lullaby
Of a cross that moves all suffering.

How blessed we are, you and I
This still summer's morn
As we remove her golden band
And robe her in a silken shroud,
At peace with God.

Sydney Davies

Home

I see the familiar hillside
its purple, ash and oak
reflect its weary struggles
with war and time and hope

Yet who may comprehend
that chaos now surrounds
its beauty and its spirit
sapping underground

When first I missed his presence
I couldn't understand
Why I was being so sentimental
for this piece of land

But years of strange eyes
now sealed in my ungrateful being
make it hard to recognize
just how clear my seeing

Sabine Laudan

The Light Of Life

Life is like a candle,
A match lit,
A light of life is born,
The glow in the darkness,
A face in the darkness all alone,
The light of life works itself,
Standing tall and radiant,
Burning its brightest,
Trying its hardest.
Certain experiences ware it down,
By the end of life the light is low,
The flame gets smaller,
The will to wither get stronger,
Residue remains,
Memories held by others,
The light of life is gone.

Susan Kelly

The Shadow

I lay in bed at night.
Over in the corner lays a shadow,
Nothing is there.
I lay and wonder,
What could it be?
A ghost, a monster,
I don't know,
I'm just scared.
I want to know what it is
So I can sleep
I want to sleep
I fall asleep . . .

Tracey Greensmith

A Tribute To Ch. Eladrew's Polly Flinders

At eight months Polly came to me,
she settled from the start,
to bed she went with me that night,
and really won my heart.

Off we went to her first show,
head and tail held high,
Two firsts and best of breed she won,
I was floating to the sky.

Two tickets away from champion,
she kept us all on cinders,
but what a cheer the crowd sent up,
for champion Polly Flinders.

Two months passed by,
we still had fun,
she went to the shows,
and won and won.

A treasure I wasn't meant to keep
God closed her eyes.
And let her sleep.

E. Lucas

What's The Difference

So what if someone's different
If they're not like you or me.
Does that mean they're wrong
And should loose their dignity.

So what if someone's different
If their skin's not white.
They are classed as outcasts
Surely, that's not right.

So what if someone's different
If it's different how they walk.
Does this mean they're weirdos
Who are we to talk?

So what if someone's different
If it's different how they dress.
What gives us the right
To make them feel depressed?

So what if someone's different
If they don't look like you do.
This does not mean they're wrong
The wrong one could be you.

Joanne Joyner

The Stray

A dog was walking along a path,
In hastened eagerness to pass
The milling crowd, who's footsteps trod
Upon this unbeguiling dog.

The journey of this dog pursued
To different corners of the mews,
But still the pace, it did not slack
To fray the hackles on his back.

That night was heard his sad retort.
As kindly words were all he sort.
His legs had grown so tired and thin
And tears slid down his bearded chin.

So alley ways he took to hide.
As life was ebbing, like the tide,
Skinless bodied bones he bared
Searching eyes for one who cared.

Next day he lay amongst the grime,
With loneliness his only crime.
Disillusioned and dogged out
Nothing left to care about.

Brenda Dawson

Untitled

It ambles aimlessly
In its own domains
And it curses
With every inch of ground it gains.

It clings to shadows
As if they were dreams,
Because every action
Is not what it seems.

It chooses to crawl
When it could walk.
It chooses to grunt
When it could talk.

This obscure creature
Wanders within my home,
Among so many people
And yet alone.

I wish I could speak to it
And pull it out of its misery
But it is hard
When this creature is me.

Stephanie F. Galliano

Slave

Is the night cold?
All through the long day hours,
I have toiled,
I'm weary and sleepy,
Working hard,
So the white man will keep me.

A bit of broth,
A piece of bread,
The cold, cold wind,
Sears through my head.

The direct slap from
The whip,
The heartache and the suffering,
How have I sinned?

The free stars in the sky
Stare down at me, blinking,
These are the thoughts of a
Black slave just thinking.

Hayley Hughes

Wales

Wales the land of legend,
The place where I belong,
Land of true tradition,
Land of stirring song,
Land of many mountains,
Valleys, lakes and streams,
If ever I should leave you,
You'd still be in my dreams.

Your legends tell of my many things,
Of fairy tales of love, and kings,
Of brave King Arthur's knights of old,
When every knight was brave and bold,
Of towering castles, cottage small,
Of fiery dragons feared by all,
I love to hear these stories told,
I'll tell them too when I am old.

Beryl Bright

Freedom

Your crying eyes no-one would wipe,
Your starving mouth no-one would feed,
Your screaming lungs no-one would hear,
Your tortured body no-one would save,
You suffered when your blood was split,
But now your soul is free.

Tara Elizabeth Brooker

Dream

Soft were his lips,
as they pressed against mine.
Hot was his breath,
on the nape of my neck,
Gentle were his caresses
along the white of my skin.
Tight were his arms,
as I lay close to him.

Bright! was the day,
as I opened my eyes.
Cold and empty was the bed,
where I lay.
Warm inside was the
feeling I felt.
Vivid and real was the
dream that I dreamt.

Sarah Louise John

The Pond

The hole is dug
the levels right
the men are in attendance
the diggers gone
the seed is sown
grass grows in abundance
the liners laid
with greatest care
the water now is pumped in
it rises slowly to the rim
I'm tempted just to jump in
No no, I jest, for this is not
the object of your brain child
I hope it will be a favourite spot
for Muscovy duck and all things wild.

Cathryn Summerland

Creature Of The Mist

Dark faced, bad tempered and gaunt,
He moves and prowls thro' the night,
Haunting the dark misty moors,
Using all his might.

Deep gruff voice and stuttering words,
Mumbling and moaning curses,
His voice echoing around,
Singing weird verses.

With the dragging of an leg,
A shuffle and limp by,
Spreading fear upon the wind,
Moon glints the evil eye.

Dread and coldness in the air,
Punching the fog with his fist,
Is he really there? Or a
Creature of the mist?

Becky Lockett

Don't Let Life...

Get you down
remember to always smile,
remember not to worry.
Don't let life get you down,
don't let life get you sad,
don't let life get you angry,
life is for living to the best
of your ability,
life is for living superbly,
remember to lift your head up high.
Remember to always smile,
remember not to worry.
Don't let life get you feeling
so blue, let life make your
pleasures come true.

Mariam Ibin-Ibrahim

Nowhere

Nowhere I lay outward,
  I cannot found
  A destiny abound.
Nowhere a place to hide
  I cannot deny
  Where was I.
A place of dream, a journey.
  Cannot be seen - there is vision
  No one seems to follow; take notice,
Nowhere a voice, not a whisper
  Nor a rains fall - they heed.
Nowhere I stand a place
  A quest ahead.
Nowhere a sight of light
  Lighten my way.
Nowhere an unspoken word
  Of my heart ... be heard.

Monien G. Pagtanac

Bleed into me

Bleed into me
I have time for the flood
to turn to flow and ebb

Breathe out to me
exhale the stale despair
suspended long inside

Give in to me
let me absorb the bile
corroding you within

Reach out to me
your trust is my reward
—exchange is always fair

Nicky Blumfield

Motherhood

I'm dying for a cup of tea
or just the chance to do a wee
but neither can be done, you see
because I've got a young baby!
My husband thinks I am lazy
truth is I'm busy as a bee:
bouncing the baby on my knee
Whilst looking for the lost car key
cooking dinner for an extra three
... Dreaming of a shopping spree!

Amanda Edward

Untitled

I gave you my heart
Gift-wrapped with love,
Labelled "Fragile: Handle with Care"
But still you broke it.

Brenda Molyneux

Innocence Is No Protection

Pig Pig squealed and squirmed
as fingers fondled pink flesh.
Its frilled bonnet billowed
like hoisted sails over erect ears.
Soft tones, her lullaby
eased a labouring heart,
they understood one another.
Pig Pig sucked on offered teat,
the warm sweet milk his reward.

The fire roared and crackled,
spat hot cinders at all who neared.
Soon hungry flame licked and lapped
at suckling flesh.
Searing, sizzling then sealing.
Pig pig hung, impaled and hollow.
Mouths drooled as Pig Pig burned.

Marlene-Ann Tica

I See You There

I see you there, you stand alone.
I long to reach out to you,
know you, see you.
Why is it so hard?
Why so wrong?
Do I scare you?
Are you scared of others?
And what they may think?

You ignore me, avoid me, tease me,
torture me with your dancing smile,
and your lingering eyes.
You are my everything.
My life, my love, my obsession.
You didn't know how much you hurt me,
do you even know I exist?

If I was not so scared of rejection,
scared of you, your laugh,
I might just say a word,
one word to break this icy box.
But instead I stand alone and watch.

Danielle Aryaman

Untitled

Intimacy of goldplate or pulpy
captive Aphrodite and embers
waiting and feigning of a prey
panting and gambling of death

Alain Lacouchie

Looking Through My Window

Looking through my window,
into the garden
I can see
two patches lower than the other grass
What happened here?
We covered our ponds up so my
brother would not fall in.
Looking through my window,
into the garden
I can see
A big apple tree
How did it get there?
It was there when we moved in.
Looking through my window,
into the garden
I can see
Some pretty flowers
Who grew them?
My mum.

Kiranjeet Rahi

Ode To A Mammogram

Today I had to visit,
The hospital you know.
To face that dreaded mammogram,
No one would gladly go.

You arrive there in the x-ray room,
knowing what comes next.
They tell you to remove your clothes,
and put on a fancy vest
With "hospital property",
written across your chest.

Now you face it,
filled with gloom.
That dreaded machine,
machine of doom.
It flattens you,
and squeezes tight.
Until your bosom,
fits in right.

Carolyn Herbert

Petty Coat

I notice you
do not notice me
so I walk over
and introduce myself

As we talk
I bang my knee
on the table

And you pull on
your Freudian slip
as if it needs
to be tighter
than it already is

James A. Rowlands

Life

Life, a funny word
With so many definitions
Life, a cunning word
Itself, epitome of contradictions
Life, not easily understood
Leaves you in a different mood
Life, a place of pleasures
Man made it difficult with measures
I have thoughts of what to become
It's destiny duty to choose the form
What is in the future?
I wish I can be sure
Having not seen life fully
I wish for a success
I am committed to it wholly
I won't find myself in a mess.

Ena Oyoma Barovbe

Awaiting Daylight

At night awaiting daylight,
I abscond from thoughts
that we live in a world
falling apart,
but do little
for course to avert.
The masters
of our planet,
life number and value,
not more
than cigarette cinder.
Thoughts wish I could erase
by closing my eyes,
and be awakened at morning
by water cascading crystals
under the sun blistering rays.
I know it's an haze,
a cowardly haze,
dictated by human
for riches never ending race.

Luigi Migliaccio

My Country Dominions

My country, my inspiring tree
You, like God made me
or a rib; that's how I feel;
the apple was up
in your sky creed,
and I, doomed creature of temptation
and greed
stretched out my hand, touched its
self-sustained shape
and began to eat.
This happened once,
and its effects propagated
to infinity.
I've felt for you
my country, the banished one from me.

Corina Catuti

Lycanthrope

Quivering with the note
Scenting crisp, glittering snow,
Watching the night stalk in
With her weird nocturnal show.
Now, the fever burns the soul
As each fibre cracks and grows,
The evening is a hunting ground
As thought begins to slow.

View the world through feral eyes
And taste her spirit's freedom,
Relax content in lunar guise
Of bestial, predatory nature,
Comfortable with power and size
While padding the twilight woods,
You throw Hecate's the killer cries
On returning to a daylight coat.

Cerne

If Only

If only I could see
What the future holds for me
Would I live today
In a very special way

If only I could say
Fond words that went away
It might have let you know
Before I let you go

If only you were here
The one I hold so dear
Again to hear you say...
Too late - you went away

If only time could be replayed
To right mistakes that I have made
But time is here and then it's gone
Sealing all that's said and done

If only I could see
What the future holds for me
I'd live this precious day to last
Making happy memories of the past

Josephine Western

Bazel

Small, black and tan,
I'm his greatest fan.
Running every hour of the day,
Getting in everybody's way.
He tugs at your clothes,
How he keeps you on your toes.
Round and round, he chases his tail,
Trying to catch it, watch him fail.
Squeaking his favourite toy,
Boy, how he does annoy.
Tickle his tummy,
Watch him wriggle all funny.
With food splashed on the floor,
Up the wall and around the door.
He climbs into his little box,
God bless his little cotton socks.

Julie Sankey

The Moon

The moon is so bright
it's like a bright light.
take someone there
there's love in the air,
so when you're in
bed and you're all alone
when there's a bright light,
don't worry, the moon
is in sight.

Samantha Jayne Weir

Blue underground

Dawn congeals
about the drowsing city,
sprawls across the rooftops
like a mangy cat.
Invasively, the soundtrack builds;
the clink and drone of urban morning.
Radiovoices murmur
in a thousand dreary kitchenettes.
Elsewhere, perhaps
rain falls softly on distant highways;
people starve;
orphaned children play
in bombed cathedrals;
but here,
we buy our papers from the stand,
glance up at the sky and glide
into the smooth,
blue underground.

Chris Drewe

Deserted Island
(To The Emigrant Islanders)

(translated from Croatian by Maria Matas)

You have gone
There is desert here now.

There are traces of you
In our feelings and our bodies

Which are old
Worn out.

Outside the houses
Ivy weeps
In the fields
There are weeds and thorns.

Through the long waiting
In your
And our eyes
Hope has frozen.

Ana Ivelja

Untitled

The hand of fate touches all of us,
and the mission of justice,
judges us all.

Charlotte Hole

Fondest Memories

Fond memories of long ago
Still linger in my mind
Forgotten roads, I walked along
When I was just a child,
And I still hear the church bells ring
As on Thanksgiving Day,
Of all that's treasured I'll not bring
Remember me today.
Remember me, O' fields of green
And leafy woodland glade,
Many an hour, when I was young
Within you I had played.
The magic that you held for me
Time cannot take away,
No matter what the future held,
I knew I could not stay.
As now the years are passing
It's very sad but true,
Where have I gone, I've wandered on,
But I'll not forget you.

Elizabeth Anne Tonkin

Out Of Reach

Oh please, will someone tell me why
The Library books are placed so high
All those wonders there for me
Just out of reach, how can that be?

Maybe I should have grown some more
But too late now, of that I'm sure
I've been this height now for so long
And Library designers can't be wrong!

There's a world of wonder there for me
If only I could reach and see
Or maybe - it's designed that way
To tantalize my thoughts and sway
Me to use the Library more
'Cause maybe one day near the floor
Will be the books I cannot reach
And I will find the books that teach
Of wonders, prose and poetry
So, please dear Library, think of me
When you decide to place so high
The books I want, up in the sky.

Jennifer Williams

Simply Blind

All I see is darkness
I can't see a thing
I just can't wait for Heaven
Where I'll hear the angels sing
Tell me what are colours?
What's rain that falls from sky?
Who are Asians and who are Welsh?
and who are you and I?
Tell me what are branches?
What is red and green?
You lot are so lucky
for these colours you have seen.
Tell me what's the matter
With these eyes that are so wrong?
I know that I can't see you
but my hearing is so strong
Friend, thanks you have listened
you've been so extra kind
but I know why I see darkness
it's because I'm simply blind.

Louise Rodgers

Reflections Of Time

Who was that little bundle
Laid into my arms
It was my baby daughter
I believed my life was charmed

Who was the young teenager
Walking down my path
It was my little girl
Don't they grow up fast

Who was this young woman
Walking down the aisle
It was my beautiful daughter
Through my tears I smile

Who was that little bundle
Laid into my arms
It was my baby grandson
Believe me I was charmed

Who is this young teenager
Running down my path
It is my dear grandson
Don't they grow up fast.

Jean Brown

In The Midst Of Darkness

Eerie shadows in each corner
The ticking of mantle clock
Whispers from the gentle breeze
Are all the sounds I can hear

Now the darkness all surrounds me
Solitude is all I have
Everything is still and quiet
Not a sound to be heard

Breathing slowly restful mind
Quiet thoughts surround my head
Calmly glancing around the room
As I lay upon my bed

I rest my head against my pillow
My heart beats like a gentle drum
Curtains sway by the open window
As the darkness lingers on

E. M. Gibson

The Conflict

I cover up my fears
By never shedding tears
The bellows, the shrieks
The voices grow weak
It's only peace I seek
I don't understand
Why it can't all be canned
The bangs and crashes
The china and glass cause more
smashes
Here I am cowering
From the earth-shattering war
Life's just an illusion
Full of confusion
My head starts spinning
My heart jumps a beat
I'm sweltering in the heat
Each and every night
It's the same old fight
Will it always be this way?

Clare Connerty

Me

At times I feel like giving up
I'm really not that strong
To have those foods that I would like
I know that they are wrong

A chocolate bar, a fresh cream cake
Scrummy through and through
Instead I have to count my sins
And have my two for you

But then I think of my weight loss
I'm happy as can be
I will be slim
I'll stay in trim
I'm doing this - for me.

Heather Poole

Paradise Beach

The warm summer sun sets,
leaving a trail of flaming crimson
drifting on the far horizon.
Palm trees silhouettes gently sway
in front of the darkening sky.
The sea glistens as it slithers
along the soft white sand.
The salty aroma of the sea
blends with that of the coconut tree.
Tranquillity reigns until dawn,
when the birds' perfect song
unites with the sound
of the gently breaking waves.

Lisa Caprai

Dreams

There's a man selling dreams
in the market place down town,
he's standing there with robes on
preaching to a crowd.
"Come in the waters lovely
when you swim the sea of life,
your world may become ugly
when you allow unwelcome strife."
Bright and happy faces
start to mirror signs of fear,
wondering if what could be
would eclipse what's already here.
The preacher engulfs the many
that want more, but dare not to say,
and catches the spirit of young folk
who live their lives from day to day.
"Fill your souls with offerings,
let all others feel your glee,
come in the waters lovely
let your hopes set your mind free."

Emma Charville

Life Can Be Compared . . .

It's true life can be compared
To a winter's evening.
One moment everything can be calm,
And running along just fine.
Then just like a winter's evening
Everything can blow up in your face.

No matter how good we are,
We can never seem to tell what will
Happen next.
And again when we feel cold and lonely
That's just what you will see
When you look out the window

When we listen to the howling wind
We sometimes feel like joining in.
And again like the wind,
We all have a rocky point in our life.

Margaret Campbell

Two Of A Kind

Python,
you muscle-clasp me;
no crushing
but caging and crooning,
nuzzling and cupping
where you can,
where I am,

Cobra;
half-coiled,
and when you do not hold me down
my head rears and sways
away.

I long for the day
when we slither off together.

Pamela Turner

Premature Spirit

The minute I was born
my heart went to sleep
it was as if I climbed a mountain
that was so steep
But then I fell
tumbled down
into hell.
A baby was I
who was born too early
and decided to die
because the minute I was born
my heart went to sleep

Angela Hancock

Swimming

Town centre swimming,
Through the crowds, diving down,
Feeling free.
Met the girl, not a word,
Not a sign, but you know
Your luck's in.
And you laugh, and you kiss,
She drags you down
To the depths, lost your breath.
Panic!
You break away,
She doesn't know,
Feels betrayed.
Swimming up,
Grasp a breath,
Gulping air,
You're alive.
She breaks the waves, you explain,
Deep embrace, loving face . . .

Andrew M. Boylan

My Treasure

I looked in the mirror
The other day,
I saw not a boy
But a man old and grey.

There, on the top of my head
Is a big bald patch,
Where once I had
Such a glorious thatch.

My teeth have gone
They've all dropped out,
And in my big toe
I've a touch of gout.

When I look at myself
I'm not very well,
For you see
My co-ordination is all to hell.

But it's not all bad
I still enjoy life,
For I do have treasure
And she is my wife

William A. Stowe

A Frozen Mass

A frozen mass
  over which to move
Of holds and grooves—
  to overcome the void

A frozen sea
  of immobility
on the edge of improbability
  But of potential possibility

A vertical dance
Linked by an umbilical cord
  perchance to fall
  a lonely glide

A mathematical problem
an in depth game of chess
of human frailty
But superior intellect.

To overcome the fear
to surmount the problem
  and yet
also, sometimes to fail.

K. W. Birkett

A Child's First Snowfall

Wet flurries,
We hurry through time and place.
Your fresh young face
Beaming,
Seeming as if to burst with vitality.
Reality is but one step away.

We clutch at passing snowflakes,
Catch and cradle.
The moment melts
And slips through the fingers
Of an outstretched hand.

Sketch this scene,
Crystallize and set.
Some things we don't forget.
I try to understand
And carve your name
On this limestone land.

Larry Roe

A Field Of Dreams

The air rose up high
as my feet left the ground,
I was light as a breeze
with that beautiful sound.

I could neither speak
nor utter a word,
but the music that played
was all my ears heard.

As I walked through the fields
my thoughts they all merged,
and the birds flew above
and my heart how it surged.

The depression of life
had been left far behind,
and all that was left
were the thoughts of mankind.

Siobhan Torlop

I Know

I love to see the trees,
  The flowers and the birds,
I love to hear the breeze,
I can't describe by words,
  The wonder of the day,
  The night that comes and goes,
  The blossom trees in May,
  The sea bed and its bay,
What nature brings and birds in flight
When robins sing when snow's all white
  This earthly mass
  The green, green grass,
The sun, the rain, the snow,
  It's wonderful, I know

Christine Bell

Moments

Lovers and yet good friends
Secrets never to be shared
A moment here, a moment there
Please stay as I really care
A cuddle, a kiss, a touch
Please don't leave, I couldn't bear
As I love you so much
They don't understand
They never will
Good friends and yet lovers too
It will carry on, it must do
We see each other every day
Mustn't touch, mustn't say
You go back, and I must, too
I don't really want to, but say I do.

Susan A. De La Mare

The Sky

All above there is a sky
it often catches my little eye
so much so I shall tell
you why.

Darkest black, contrasting blue,
simmers into a reddish hue.
When clouds are forming they
make you think, steely grey,
then white, then pink.

Style dictating all the way
changing the night into the day.
The sky exhibits great wonders
to view, the planets, the stars,
the moon, and of course the
big sun too!

Oh sky! Oh sky!
I love you
why?
you guard mysteriously
my Creator's eye!

Margaret R. Harrison

Spring Daffodils

The daffodils come out in spring,
They grow in different places,
As the birds around them sing,
They light up children's faces.

They like to sway about a lot
In the nice cool breeze
The sun shines down so hot
And around them fly the bee's

Their colour is so nice
Yellow like the sun that shines our way
You don't have to pay a price
To watch them swing and sway

The daffodils move about
All the time they swing
The children all run and shout
This is the start of spring

Emma Louise Laird

Window Scene

When she looks through the window,
something tells her
of the life and times of all those
who had become a part of her.

When she gazes so intensely,
something traps her
of the mind and acts of all those
who had harshly lied to her.

When she closes her eyes softly,
something warms her
of the smile and hearts of all those
who had shown love to her.

When she throws her head backwards,
something reminds her
of the days and months of all those
who had tied thoughts to her.

When she looks through the window,
something tells her
of the life and times of all those
who had become a scene for her.

Lorraine White

Untitled

Is it the mist, or my mind!
Why! Oh why! Are things hard to find.
When we were young, it was simple,
Clear to see, healthy and nimble
Must be November, or December
If only I could remember

The days being short, soon it is dark,
Yet I hear children, out in the park
Lights switched on, only a glimmer
Eyes getting hazy, and dimmer
Life has been humorously happy,
Since mother left off my nappy.

To infants, years didn't matter,
Enjoying ourselves, having a natter.
Looking back, as the days did unfold,
Things I could have done, now too old.
Sitting here, no good being sad,
But reminisce in the past, feeling glad.

Henry Coates

Suicide

Yesterday I saw a sad face
Today she's gone away
Once she had the gift of life
Now she's thrown that gift away

Gone tomorrow, still here today
Look in deep, beneath her eyes
She doesn't think she's anyone
Because you didn't have the time

And now she's left the living world
is there any sound
Or is her soul and body
Buried together underground

Or is she in the promised land
The reward of better things
The paradise place in the sky
The land of angels with wings

She died and then her loved ones
Grieved until eventually
Another generation was born
Now she's no longer even a memory.

Paul Churchward

Our Sunrise

I love to watch the sunrise
Casting spectacular colours,
I love to watch the sunrise,
Alone with my lifelong lover.

I love to watch the sunrise,
Bringing with it another life,
I love to watch the sunrise,
Romance cutting deep like a knife.

I love to watch the sunrise,
Knowing not what the day will bring,
I love to watch the sunrise,
Closer than we have ever been.

I love to watch the sunrise,
Real life feels many miles away,
I love to watch the sunrise,
For such beauty we need not pay.

I love to watch the sunrise,
Though it does not last forever,
I love to watch the sunrise,
We'll share many more together.

Trudy Greenwood

We Two

As I look back across the years
Remember the laughs the tears
My mind goes back to a certain day
When we were happy in every way
The family around the table sat
To eat a meal and have a chat

Then one by one a place was bare
Somebody missing from that chair
Till one day we were on our own
All the little birds had flown
Leaving home for pastures new
And now we dine alone, we two.

Mary Dunne

Hedgehog

A hedgehog is a little thing,
But if you go too close,
It curls up beneath its spikes,
From tail to tip of nose.

Some folk are like hedgehogs,
To them you cannot get near,
Like spikes, put up a barrier,
And others they seem to fear.

Perhaps they have a problem,
That only themselves know,
So they are hard to understand,
Make every friend a foe.

Only God can help them,
And bring their fears to an end,
And if they will accept Him,
He'll always be a friend.

Katy Heeks

Maybe Tomorrow

I don't know if I'll see tomorrow
As I leave the safety of my burrow
It all looks still no one around
My ears prick up was that a sound
The farmer sees me as a pest
My heart beats fast inside my chest
I can beat the farmer's gun
With speed and cunning I will run
What's that noise I heard a bark
Should I go back and wait till dark
In and out a job well done
I've beat the farmer and his gun
Even though the danger's past
I can't slow down until at last
I'm with my family safe and sound
Inside my burrow underground

Patricia White

Heat Of Love

Warmth soothes your skin,
Eases your worries.
Strong light,
Closing your eyes.
God's hand
Touches your face
And mind,
Relieving.
Pause to absorb
The tranquil
And peacefulness
From the strong ray.
Sharing the secret greetings
Between you and God,
Who's always there
When the sun shines
Everywhere.

Maria J. Buckley

Love

It starts at the beginning
Love surrounds us everywhere,
Parents and relations show us
Just how much they care.

It soon becomes impossible
to live without emotion,
we feed on love and share it out
Until there's deep devotion.

If by chance we lose it
Our lives can fall apart,
We cannot be without it
It can even break our heart.

Give it out and you'll receive it
Hold it back and you will be
So empty and so miserable,
It's fantastic and it's free.

When you have love, hold onto it
Don't throw it all away,
Remember it is special
Here forever and a day.

V. Darling

Russian Roulette

Dancing with death,
With every breath,
Russian Roulette with fate.
And your own epitaph's dare.

Dancing with the devil,
On the edge you revel,
Waltzing with your destiny.

Dancing with your life,
You tango with fates dice,
Playing Russian Roulette,
With your life as the bet.

Beverley Scholey

Gentle Persuasion

Come on now
Why take your time
I've watched over you
You're doing fine
Pink is your colour
With tinge of red
Come on now
Don't hang your head
Our time is limited
As you know
Come on now
We'll miss the show
Because of your beauty
It's you I chose
Come on now
My perfect baby rose.

J. V. O'Connell

Waiting

I study the catkins,
Sunlight on each new bud
Symbolising new life, birth,
Resurrection, Easter.
And I yearn for the resurrection
Of my life with yours.
Yet as I gaze
New buds remain tight,
Silent
Waiting for the onslaught of birth.
And I realise that we
Are in the Good Friday of our love.

Angela Excell

Beggar Man

People passing all around
But they don't see
You upon the Ground
They passed in silence
No whisper or sound

I watched the heartless pass you by
As I passed you, I turned around
And I thought to myself (heartless)
But so am I
Why did I pass you, why didn't I stop
I wonder why?

Is it because we're too proud to stop
For reasons of our indented ways?
Or because we're too proud to give
That you may live a few more days?

Louis Massiah

This Night

Gently as I sleep O Lord,
refresh my soul this night,
take away my rage O Lord,
and fill my soul with right.

Softly as I lie here Lord,
make my mind to calm,
take away all hatred Lord,
use your love as balm.

Quietly as I slumber Lord,
give me the strength anew,
this life to live for you, dear Lord
the fight to fight for you.

V. K. Copley

Homeless

Walking down the street at night
Looking for somewhere to stay
My feet are sore and tired
Because I've walked all day

My clothes are really dirty
And as tatty as can be
No wonder all the people
Just stand and stare at me

So now I keep on walking
Just walking down this street
God knows where I'm going
God knows who I'll meet

And now I keep on standing
Just standing by this lamp
Who cares or thinks about you
When you're a dirty tramp.

Pauline Iris Browne

Night Angling On The Stone Pier At Harwich

I saw the sun tonight,
setting,
a roseate, molten orb,
slipping down
seemingly beyond recall.

And then towards the East
I turned
and there the harvest moon
spawned, like Venus,
from the living womb of sea.

To trace with halo'd head
a score
across the arc of night, before,
like dreaming,
it fades into tomorrow's dawn.

J. N. Dixey

"Unfair to Mum"

I find it really quite unfair
    That when we Mums get ill,
No one really wants to know
    Or seems to care - until...

Their social life's affected
    A friend can't come to tea,
Or someone can't be taken
    To the cinema by me.

It almost seems that if ignored
    The problems go away
Life must go on as usual -
    Must not disrupt their day.

They will learn in time I hope
    To care and to be kind,
And spend more time in thinking
    Of others, and will find...

That when they reach an older age
    With children of their own,
They will, I think, appreciate
    What they were taught and shown.

Karen Snell

It's Your Hen Night . . .

It's your hen night,
Be on your guard,
It'll be a night to remember,
You have been warned,

We could get you a stripper,
Ooh! Wouldn't that be fun,
All those bulging muscles,
And just look at that bum!

How about something simple,
Yet, sophisticated and chic,
A shiny black bin liner,
Would go down a treat,

Now for the finishing touches,
An 'L' plate or two,
A few brightly coloured condoms,
And a big bow for each shoe,

The party's got going,
We're all feeling jolly,
It'll be a good night,
When we arrive at Tivoli . . .

Michelle Wilson

Forever Diamonds

I suppose I love my husband,
I've been with him sixty years.
Would have gone and left him long ago,
had it not been for my fears.

But he's always there to lend a hand,
hard working, and so keen.
Just let there be a problem,
and he's first one of the scene.

It's really just amazing,
what a marriage can survive.
All the fears and tears and misery,
when it takes a deep nose-dive.

Just remember, often marriage,
is no different to another.
Enduring and enjoying,
can't have one without the other.

Now I'm glad I didn't leave him,
when I needed desperately to go.
These days it's all too easy
so I guess they'll never know.

Barbara Ann Gummerson

A Working Woman

She stands upon the curbside
Skirt way above the knee.
He draws up right beside her.
This is punter number three.

Business transaction over
She climbs out of the car.
Puts the money in her pocket.
It's not over, not by far.

She still needs lots of money.
Six months should just suffice.
She wants an education.
A decent living would be nice.

This lifestyle isn't easy.
It's not what she wants to be.
She's got it all mapped out.
Degree, career then family.

People judge her by profession.
Pigeon hole like all the rest.
But she's going to bloody show them.
She'll soon be at her best.

Amanda Sherwin

Ocean Depths

I'm a vast expansion
Of clear blue sea,
Deep, like the waters,
are the thoughts that fill me.

And endless, like the motion
of continuous streams,
are the nightmares that scare me,
or fruitless dreams.

And as the water flows,
it could be my tears,
And as it evanesces,
it could take with it my fears.

And in places it is shallow,
like the obscure view,
of those who witness it,
but don't have a clue...

As to its depths or
the secrets that lie,
just under the surface
is where you'll find I.

Ayshea Hameeduddin

Beauty And The Beast

In our English Country Gardens
From Inland down to the coast
Why do we name things of beauty
After things we hate the most

We most always have some fleabane
With daisy flowers pink and bright
And as a focal point of interest
A Locust tree is a splendid sight

And what about polygonum
Or snakeweed as it's commonly known
Coupled with some vipers bugloss
It's a bed well left alone

We sweep our homes of cobwebs
For those six legs make us cower
Then we go into our gardens
And we plant a spider flower

We buy bugbane and snapdragons
Why do we do this every year
And I've come up with the answer
It's the morbid thrill of 'Fear'

Maria Unwin

143

Sapphire Eyes

The colour that comes through
the clearness and strength
And another look at you
my assumptions are met.

The blueness of your colour
there will never be another
Of beauty and glamour
with intriguing content.

I would call it amazing
As I am gazing
at your blazing eyes upon me
Falling shadows and emotions
as my actions are turned into motions.

The excitement and thrill
as I finally come near
My passions overfill
As I watch you disappear.

Milton Kilgour

Destiny Or A Messy Sestina

One beds and weds by accident
Much more than by design.
How is it then, my dearest love
That in the course of time
We cleave to forge twin destinies,
Two souls that intertwine?

Age cleaves and clings, my darling
To what it has denied
Or where would be the purpose
And what would be implied?
The past must seem predestined
At the final, great divide.

The past must seem predestined
When we reach the last divide
Or what would be the purpose
And what would be implied?
We bed and wed by accident
Much more than by design.

Martin Hocke

Tears

You turn away,
You look straight past.
The love I thought would always last.
The time has come to walk away,
Not thinking about another day.

It's at an end,
Time to say
Maybe friends,
We can stay.

Kim Richards

First Love

I shared a love once, long ago,
Until it broke in two,
I thought my tears could mend it,
But it shattered, through and through;
I picked each precious fragment up,
And laid them in a box,
Then tied a satin ribbon round;
A bright, white, shining lock.

With love within, and life without,
They say that time heals all,
But time has yet to ease this pain,
My love I still recall;
Years cannot tarnish memories,
Though ribbons age and fray,
Young love shines ever silver,
While white satin fades to grey.

Linda J. Pitman

Burnt Offerings

Here is my cadenza.
A personal enigma;
An epitaph.

Ashes from the crucible
offered to the winds,
An evocation of suburban drudgery.

The sky opened,
Split wide for all to see -
subtle plagiarism.

This work is not yet finished.
I have lost the key.
If it is found,
it shall be put to rest.

Its head in the north,
Its feet in the south.

Craig Martin Wood

Unicorn

You dance among the bluebells,
and chase the silver rain,
You see the crystal waterfall,
and gently shake your mane.
You roam your land with majesty,
your princely head held high,
your beauty and nobility
we never should deny.

Oh! Gentle creature, wild and free,
as pure as driven snow,
your magic and your beauty,
the world shall never know.
For men in all their ignorance,
deny that you were born,
You're magical, you're mystical,
My wondrous unicorn.

Sheila Bishop

Fight For Freedom

Governments making our decisions,
Our destiny carved in stone.
We never try to change things,
The people, we just moan.

Watch the news late at night.
Another struggle, yet another fight,
We see our people crying,
And watch civilization dying.

We must try and take a stand,
To save this green and worthy land,
Watch the great powers begin to fall,
Now our people are standing tall.

Governments not making decisions,
Our destiny new and bold,
We managed to change a way of life,
Now the story, it must be told.

Sam Lismore

To My Beloved

In the moonlight,
My shadow stands alone,
Waiting for you.
Independence is my hallmark,
But right now I am lost.
Wandering in a maze of adulation,
of which accumulates for your return.
My body yearns for your tender touch,
while my arms caress your space.
But time is not a problem,
For my love for you is eternal.

Tracy Anne Evans

Shades Of Sarah

I stand within a Rose Garden,
And look for Sarah there,
It's hard to tell which one is she,
The pastel shades compare.

Blue pools of deep expression,
the mirrors of her mind,
The answer to my questions,
Through her eyes I find.

Change of mood, no reason why,
Little girl of seven years,
Study and play in each other's way,
One minute smiling, the next in tears.

A small child with so much love,
Dancing through her days,
Making our lives richer,
In a thousand different ways.

I stand amid the roses,
Rain and sun made grow,
As Sarah's smiles and teardrops,
Create her own rainbow.

Jean R. Morrall

Impressions

I'm not impressed by roses,
It doesn't mean you care,
I really hate you posing,
And pretending I'm not there.

I'm not impressed by flirting,
Or playing hard to get,
Don't treat me like I'm dirty,
Or ignore me for a bet.

I'm not impressed by romance,
It doesn't make me high,
It doesn't put me in a trance,
Or make me want to fly.

I'm not impressed by groping,
My body is my own,
There's no point in moping,
I'm in a modern zone.

I'm impressed by love and sharing,
Telling everyone I'm nice,
I love boys who are caring,
who are made of sugar and spice.

Nadine A. Mills

A Song Of Praise

What man is there
That can compare
With mine - so fair,
A God so rare?

A manner fine,
A brown divine,
Two eyes that shine
Like sparkling wine.

Straight as a wand
I see him stand,
Gentle of hand
And golden tanned.

With hair that curls
And teeth like pearls
He dances and whirls
With all the girls

But mine is he,
He'll ne'er be free,
While he has me,
Then, mine he'll be.

Eleanor Jones

The Snake

Slithering through the soft sand
The long snake slides,
Hissing at its predators
Behind a rock it hides.

Smelling with its tongue,
Looking sharply through its eyes,
Coiling up like a snail's shell
Changing its size.

With a flick of its neck
And a jab of its fangs,
Blood seeping out of its body
The dead prey hangs

Sliding down its throat
Devouring its food,
The snake moves onwards
Until its next killing mood.

Julie Denby

Don't Do That!

When I was young I used to sit
Upon the fence and show my legs.
Mother hurrying in from shopping
Calls out "Don't do that!"

I'm growing tall and along the hall
I swing from the bannister rails.
Mother horrified takes a look
Shouts out "Don't do that!"

I'm twenty-one now, nails all red
My eyes are black as night.
Mother sees this startling vision
Whispers "Don't do that!"

I'm married now with children five,
My daughter is biting her nails.
I hear my voice like mother's
Saying "Don't do that!"

My granddaughter has come to stay,
I thought she was out playing.
She sees me with my wine and cakes
"Oh Grandma... don't do that!"

Margaret M. Leather

Natural Restorer

The rhythm of the waves
Which man cannot alter
Absorbs the whole being.
Attuning the psyche
To the sea's healing influence.
As a child to its mother.

Alwyn Jolley

Reflections

These are cool waters;
Here strong cattle
In the shadowed shallows
Sip dark leaves,
There is no sigh,
Mad summer has molested
And is gone,
As autumn slips
Into high stretching branches
October's child is born.
There is no fret or fever,
No fear of pain,
Your glance prevails,
And rushes from the sky
To where the river
Lingers on your sighs;
The horseflies flicker
And the foal is gone,
As stained glass windows
Gather in your eyes.

Robert Lindsay

Dawn

There's a noose around my heart, love,
There's a dagger in my side.
My pride burns as I realize,
My face splits as I cry.

I sense her in your spirit, love,
You bring her to our bed.
Pardon my shell splintering,
Your guilt is made of lead.

You lived another life today,
I died another death.
You spend another dawn away,
I take another breath.

I've turned the other cheek again,
Your secret's in my glove.
Into triangular matrimony,
She buries me, my love.

Alia Brahimi

Red As A Flame

I start off as a tiny seed,
so small,
Will I ever grow
into a beautiful flower
And not a weed?
Stretching out
Tossing and turning
weaving in and out
with a long deep root,
Making my way
Up to the surface.
Blind.
Not knowing which to turn,
Pushing up hard
I'm popping out at the top.
A speck of light.
I stretch up tall.
I'm a beautiful poppy
Red as flame.

Natalie Sagar

Mothers

M-others love us all,
O-verreact some times.
T-hink about us all day long,
H-elp us when things go wrong,
E-njoy peace and quiet not very long.
R-eally know us well.

Paula Lufflum

In Stereo

It sits on my shelf,
makes no demands.
Satisfaction gained
from a flick of the hand.

Numerous buttons,
one volume control,
a graphic equalizer,
has it got a soul?

Or blues of some kind
as the beat pumps away.
From nine inch speakers,
compact, I like it that way.

No visual picture
intruding my mind.
Just CD tape and Radio
through an ariel line.

The faithful stereo
girl's best friend.
The musical trip,
I can't stand it to end.

Joanne Duckles

Strong

No one seemed to care for me,
I was trapped.
Then you came along.
You plucked me from the wreckage,
And now my heart's grown strong.

No one seemed to love me,
I was lost.
Then you came along.
You dragged me from the cliff side,
And now my heart's grown strong.

No one seemed to want me,
I was bewitched.
Then you came along.
You helped me build my life again,
And now my heart's grown strong.

No one seemed to need me,
I was confused.
Then you came along.
You saved me from despair,
And now my heart's grown strong.

Emily Hunter

Atmosphere

There's a strange mist upon us
Its fragile lustre shows
Beyond man's recognition
Who sees, who cares, who knows?
We'll move along awhile
Before any major effect
Are we ozone friendly?
Do we have any respect?
Is nature closing in on us?
We don't have recognition
Or kiss the earth goodbye.

Hazel Forrest

The Rainbow

The colours of a rainbow
Are reflected from the sea,
Arranged around the heaven,
To please both you and me.

From sun that's followed by the rain,
Its lovely form is made,
Then in just a little while
The coloured arch will fade.

There's supposed to be a pot of gold
Where its arches end,
But the gold is in the rainbow,
And in the gaze you rend.

June Jakeman

A Single Tear

A single tear ran down your cheek
I pretended not to see it
For in that tear there was a river
That bled into a sea of pain.

And into that sea there was a place
Where only you could go
And I could only sit and wait
On some unknown shore.

I saw the tear, wanted to kiss it dry
But I pretended not to see it—
For in that tear there was a heart
Broken, not wanting to show it.

A single tear, ran down my cheek
I didn't let you see it.
I turned my face, then held you close
Hoping that time would heal all this.

Cilla Ashburner

145

Devil In Disguise

Slowly, my eyes widen,
As the realization sinks in,
This crazy, cruel murderer,
Is living in sin.

He's a mad, human killer,
Who takes innocent lives,
He's an insane, crazed man,
Who enjoys to play with knives.

My heartbeat slows down,
Everything pauses in slow motion,
I glance up to his face,
In his eyes flicks an evil potion.

As I stare straight at his mouth,
A crooked smile begins to spread,
He's hungry for blood,
And he can't wait to be fed.

His fingers curl around the handle,
He draws back with a start,
My world begins to shatter,
As he's plunging through my heart.

Zoë Hoddle

I Wish That I Was Young Again

If I was young I'd run and race.
And feel the wind upon my face.
I'd scale a tree and make a den
I wish that I was young again.
If I was young I'd cycle far.
And make a wish upon a star.
For in the land of make believe,
Dreams and wishes I receive . . .
In that land there is no pain,
All things bad come right again
Now my bones are old and frail,
I am on the downward trail
But in my mind I still can see,
How my childhood use to be.

Rosemary Churchill

An Autumn Breeze

Red and golden are the leaves
That fall so silent from the trees
In the soft autumn breeze.

The autumn sunshine's on the leaves
That have fallen from the trees
In the soft autumn breeze.

Autumn's here and summer's gone
Along with all the summer sun
Along with all the autumn leaves
That have fallen from the trees.

Louise Duncan

The Garden

God made us a garden
And filled it with flowers,
He planted in trees
And refreshed them with showers,
And then He made man.
And put him in it too
But man wasn't satisfied
What did he do?
He upset God's garden
And planted instead
Things he'd created
Like greed, hatred and dread.
And so this garden,
That God made for man.
Is becoming a hell
Where a heaven began.

Audrey Briggs

Never

Never was a life so fair
Nor a heart so wildly free,
Never bathed in such a glare
As when I first set eyes on thee.

Never was the air so clear
Nor the sky so deeply blue,
Never felt heaven so near
As when I felt the warmth of you.

Ne'er did birds sing so divinely
Nor the flowers smell as sweet,
Never felt love so sublimely
As when your eyes and mine would meet.

Never where the days so splendid
Nor the nights e'er look the same,
Never were two hearts so blended
Since I first soft-breathed your name.

Never was my heart so gladdened
As when our bond no soul could sever,
Never was my heart so saddened
As when you left my life forever.

Robert G. Baker

Mum

Mum, it's sometimes hard for us
to show just how much we care,
for everything you've done for us,
and the love you've always spared.
You always help us freely,
and don't expect things in return,
just a simple smile and a thank you,
to show it has not gone unobserved,
it's because of these reasons,
although there are many more,
for loving you today,
and forevermore.

Belinda Varney

Contrasts

Noise, heat, rush,
Machine crash,
Brain crash,
No clear view,
Confusion.

Calm,
Cool breeze,
Time to think,
Time to reflect,
Time mastered.

Stark contrasts,
Work and holidays,
Justified, perhaps,
In touching the limits,
Of the gift of life.

Douglas E. J. Ashpole

Do I Love You?

Do I love you?
'Yes' of course I do,
But do I really love?
Romeo and Juliet loved,
They loved to death,
So can I love you?
Can love exist without death?

I think I love you,
But can't be sure,
Where is love like theirs?
Can it exist now, without death
How do we know where love is?
What love is?
We don't.

Stephanie A. Clay

Life Itself

We all start exactly the same,
As a baby with nothing at all.
Then gradually we become a person,
Which way will the line of fate fall?

School? It was magic or a chore
But the years of schooling just fade,
As we rush to become a grown-up,
Never thinking of the troubles we made.

As we grow older and wiser
As we look back on this - our life
Is it any wonder that we ponder
We, who were husband or wife.

It is hard to remember everything
But we can pick out of memory's store,
The happy days that were spent
together
With the loved ones we have no more.

So how lovely it is to be able
To awake to another new day.
To recall every one of those memories
That can never be taken away.

Betty Singleton

Reverie

Still quiet sky, L'heure bleu,
Warm air wafting around my head.
Thoughts reach out to sweet times past
With you and words unsaid.
Now you are gone
And I am here alone and sad
With only my dreams for comfort
In the long hot nights of summer.

Jennifer McLarens

Loveless

I'm seeing without sight
I'm feeling without touch
I'm screaming without sound
I'm dreaming without sleep
I'm wishing without hope
I'm hurting without bruises
I'm bleeding without blood
I'm crying without tears
I'm living without life
I'm loving without love.

Joanne McLaughlin

In The Late Streets

The cries of drunken youth
In the late streets,
A motley crew -
Unpredictable, menacing,
Caring not a jot
For anyone;
Mauling each other
In spiteful mood,
Rude to the passer-by
Who, by stealth
And with a heartfelt sigh
Escapes the bubbling brew.

Swaying brainlessly along
They wend their feckless away
Excitement craving
To release their pent-up ire
Ere jumping into bed
Bloodshot of eye,
Fiery of head,
Raving.

Haward Clarke

A Child's Imagination

As I was sitting playing with my ball;
I saw an enormous kitten,
My guess was five feet tall.

He looked like a tiger
As he jumped down from the wall;
He opened his mouth much wider
Was it for me or for the ball!

He then sat down a purring
Looking all around;
He saw the windmill turning
And heard the church bell sound.

I wondered if he had lost his way
Or escaped from a zoo;
But by the way that he did lay
I had not a clue.

Suddenly, my mother shouted to me
This proved that he was tame;
He got up stretched his legs
And went from whence he came.

John A. Phillips

My World

At the age of eight,
My world fell apart.
My parents split up.
It broke my heart.

The hardest thing of all
Was leaving one to see the other.
There was the hurting pain inside,
Seeing Father, seeing Mother...

Would they ever get back together?
Or would my world stay in two?
I kept wishing and wishing,
But there was nothing I could do.

After some amount of years,
They both found someone new.
I was happy for them,
But sad for me too.

Michelle Baugh

Small View

As she sits on her rags,
In the middle of the streets,
She cries out for help,
To all the people she meets,
Some are too busy,
Some watch, but that's all,
Some bustle right past her,
Some don't care at all.

Her jar is a waiting,
But there is nothing within,
Sharp tears take her over,
And gather in her eyes,
There seems to be no future,
But all she can do is cry.

Hannah Ireson

Untitled

Goodbye to pain,
Sorrow and grief.
I welcome the smile
That greets the relief.

My heart is blessed,
With all that surrounds.
No more will I weep,
No more will I frown.

Josephine Wilson

Shoppers Nightmare

I'm waiting at the check-out,
there's a queue and I'm the last,
we don't appear to have moved that far,
but already ten minutes have passed.

There's a trainee on the till,
young and spotty faced,
He's going slower than a tortoise,
and they don't have much pace.

Should I move to another,
I can't stand here much more,
A can of coke and a packet of crisps,
That's all that I'm waiting for.

Where did that old lady come from?
She wasn't there before,
That's it, I've had enough,
I'll go and try the shop next door.

John G. Willard

Dumbstruck

To me you're a big word
'Cos I'm so small
I once grasped you
With your deep meaning
But now I'm left crumbling
Looking over my shoulder
Picking over the pieces
Of half-finished statements
like bits of stale bread,
Which you once force-fed me
Stomach churning I couldn't eat
And the words were too large
But now you're away
I'm eating them all in large chunks
And you're making me
Fat . . .

Lorraine Priest

The River Wye

I'm a cat in a fight,
As I undergo the rapids,
Pulling and pushing,
Twisting and turning.

I'm a scuttling mouse,
When the weather's bright,
Quick and quiet,
fast and unnoticed.

I'm like a snake,
When the water's shallow,
Slithering and sliding,
As I wind round the rocks.

Tracey Read

Love Is A Disease

Love is a disease,
that eats at your heart.

Love is a disease,
that blinds you
from all badness.

Love is a disease,
that takes over
your thoughts.

Love is a disease
best shared.

Love is a disease,
for which there is
no cure!

Fiona Flaherty

You're Still My Dad!

As soon as we said are last
Good bye,
My heart had shattered into a
hundred pieces,
I really do wish you'd hold me
tight, and never let go even at
night, you've stabbed me silently
right through the heart,
And awakened my fears,
into light and to dark.
Please forgive me for I was not
there, to tell you how much I
really do care,
even now we're far, far apart
you know I'll still love you
for now you're a star,
And "Dad" you'll always be
deep in my heart!

Claire Appleton

To A Black Cat

Now, sleeping alone,
it is your absence
that bothers me more than his.
Perhaps because your annoyances
are like my own:
made tragic by a rainy Tuesday
and forgotten in a moth on the window.

S. Scott

A Walk In Queen's Park

Easy wandering steps
I take and loosen
In the gracious English green,
Thrill to the limbs and senses,
Soothing path and landscape,
Oasis of vibrant calm.

Stately silhouettes around,
Festive feathers on the ground
And swans displaying in the pond -
I enjoy - and birdies
Taking to a kind soul mate
And figures lying for a sunkiss.

I share contentment
With a child and a playful pet,
A breeze with trembling leaves,
A breath with crisp petals,
Reliving moments of love;
And restored, cross the bridge.

Giovanni D'Attoma

Seasons

Shorter days
November haze
Frosty glaze
Winter entrees

Lighter nights
Prancing kites
Flowers bright
Spring delights

Welcoming heat
Burning street
Picnic treat
Summer meet

Corn sheaves
Cool nights relieve
Squirrels thieve
Autumn leaves

Allen Jessop

What Is Love

Your hair may be white
And your teeth a bit brown
On your smokers cough I'll
try not to frown
you may need glasses to read
the small print
But at push you could still do
a sprint

We've had lots of laughter
We've shed a few tears
We've shared so much through the years.
But I think you'll agree we've
Got something special you and me.

Joyce Green

Nan

You walked the one way street of life,
You chose which doors to open,
You walked forwards never backwards,
Carried on regardless,
You collected titles along the way,
Daughter, sister, wife and mother
Auntie, friend, nan and great nan,
Spreading love around you.
And now you've closed your final door,
The time is right to say good night,
You will be missed,
But not forgotten.

Heather Valerie Dean

Claire

Kind,
Considerate
My tower of strength,
The tree that supports me,
Cradles my pain.
Bears the fruit of friendship,
To fulfil my hunger.
Provides water for my thirst.
Tall,
And wise beyond years.
Suffers in silence.
My tree I protect you,
From evils of pain,
My tree I cry with you again.
Time passes, you blossom with age.
Together we stand,
My tree and I.

Alison Jeanne Spowart

Suffer No More

It was a cold dark alley
from which I followed a cry
trying hard to ignore
the noise from the pub nearby.

It came from a small child
who sat in her tears
and as I knelt beside her
she told me her fears.

She said her parents had died
that she was now all alone
and the place where she once lived
was no longer her home.

I watched as this weak girl
curled up and died
no one could say
that she'd never tried.

I touched the body's cold shoulder
then got off of the floor
now at least I know
the girl will suffer no more.

Niki Heath

The March Wind

I watched him start his capers
As he hurled across the sky.
He battered at the tree tops
With a wild unearthly cry.
Then he flung himself beside me
Like a panting, waiting train,
Rested for a moment,
Then started up again.
He tore across the meadow
In a frantic, flurrying swirl
And ended up in nothing
But a wandering whispering whirl.

Julia Harlow

In A World Without

Without your lips
There would be no kiss.
Without the time you share
Many moments missed.

Without your touch
There'd be nothing to feel.
Without you in my dreams
Nothing would be real.

Without your voice
There'd be nothing to hear.
Without your embrace
Nothing to hold dear.

Without your smile
There would be no sun.
Without the promise of you
There's nowhere to run.

Without your understanding
What would anything mean?
Without you in my world
A king has no queen.

David Marsh

The Dark

I'm so afraid of being in the dark
People think it's such a lark
When I go to bed at night
I always get a massive fright
When the light goes out
I always shout
Don't turn the light out Dad
It drives me mad.

Sarah Carroll

Moments

If I could only
Hold the moments when,
The light first tiptoed in
Across your primrose lawn,
To touch upon your sleeping cheek
And awaken
The morning first seen;
Just in case
A lost tear should form,
To spoil the opening view.

To call the early breeze
To move upon and keep,
Your golden dream as if it were
The first opening crocus of spring,
To be held in cupped and caring hands
For all time;
And to hold the moments
Like the delicate petals,
Without the cruel crush
Of final parting.

Norman Royal

A Place To Die

If I could choose a place to die,
it would be in your embrace
in a magical place,
in a castle veiled in grace, lost
within vagrant violets and licentious lilies.
Lay me upon a bed of lace,
let me wipe the tears from your face.
Hold me, tenderly touch me.
A momentary breath of mystical
moon rays capture elegant
loveliness and my still hopeful
rosy lips would beg for one
last kiss, and the tear that
you weep did fall upon
my cheek.

Taran Cameron MacDonald

Searching

I've searched my brains
I've searched my heart
To find the three words
Which are always on my mind
It wasn't in my heart
I found it in my brain
Surrounded with courage
Just to say...
...It's all over

Berna Mustafa

Gallop Through The Fields

The wind in my face as I'm moving
With the pace of my galloping horse
So big and bright enough to give
anyone
small a fright.

As we slow down to canter
my horse starts to panta

I give her a pat as we slow down
to trot.
Home we come with a mighty rear
everyone in their gardens looks round
to see her.

So big and frightening she may be

Lots of gracefulness for people to see

Katy Eyre

Fly Away

To the golden gates my cousin rides,
On a horse he takes to the sky,
And flies and flies.

My heart is shattered,
Bit by bit,
Away, away,
Now gone,
Flown away.

My heart is empty,
Full of woe,
But I knew one day he would have to go.

His bed is bare
He had fair hair,
I can still remember,
As if he were there,
Watching me.

I feel his breath over me,
At night when I sleep,
I dream that he comes back to me,
But now I guess his soul is free.

Hayley McNulty

Prescription Love

For me to love you completely
Totally and utterly true,
I need to feel wanted
And loved and special too.
I need for you to talk to me
And in your secrets share,
To think about me constantly
And promise to always be there.
You have a special place
Locked inside my heart,
And no matter how far away you are
We will never be apart.
For love is the most special feeling
That can ever be prescribed,
Between two very special people
Who care deep down inside.

Louisa Dwight

Untitled

A storm blows up inside my mind
From every direction I find
A barrier made out of motion
Coupled together, a serious potion

Bringing forth a memory
For all its being not clear to me
For my conscience I substitute
Myriad thoughts of ill repute

Back and forth flows my grit
I am beaten without knowing it
So, futile is my every action
But in losing I see the attraction

To retain my inner calm
I hold here in my palm
A tiny shined of innocence
Obtained by recompense.

And like a shock I see the past
The life that slipped from my grasp.
All too clear is the message
Dictated without presage.

Change my ways before it's too late
The winds of change invigorate
As placid as I can be
Will this be how you remember me?

P. M. Clegg

A Window Of Hope

I look through my window,
For the things I cannot see,
For the times that have passed us by,
For the things that cannot be.

The sky is full of poison,
The ground's like toxic lead,
We think that we can't help it,
Of course, we'll all one day be dead.

The church clock strikes six,
A raven flies above,
But can we change that raven,
To a soft and downy dove?

Time's deadly essence,
Scents the air perfectly,
And I look through my window,
For the things I cannot see.

Yes, I look through my window,
For the things I cannot see.
For the times that have passed us by,
For the things that cannot be.

Helen F. Johnson

Realization

The brother who does not know me
passed me in the street,
greetings falling
redundantly into words
of illusion - the company of ghosts
endlessly reinventing themselves
for the larger ambiguities
of our old expectations.

Once, the unexamined lie
stayed us,
a tonsure of vague recollections
but; now
our circle of stern insistence
has wrapped itself
into clipped, broken shapes
that have nowhere to return.

G. A. Youldon-Hockey

Beaches

The view is blue,
The waves crashing on the rocks,
Admired by people like you,
No sight of an animal or fox,

The sound of people splashing,
Along go the boats,
The waves crashing,
While people take off their coats,

The hot sunny weather,
When the sun goes down,
The wind lighter than a feather,
When the kids leave your
Sure to see a frown.

Hayley Bartlett

Affair

His head was pounding
as he thought of it all,
the wife he had . . .
she was beautiful.
Content with just the simple things,
like sharing their home
and her love with him.
What game had he played?
By risking it all.
Like Russian Roulette
had he been such a fool?
His affair had been
so addictive and sleazy
The habit of lying
so casual and easy.
Game now over—what was the score?
He'd lost everything,
and what was it for . . .

Jillian Dennis

Sand Dunes

Break off a piece of heaven,
And hold it in your hand,
Catch the falling shadows,
And bury them in the sand,
Nobody knows where they have to go,
And nobody knows where they've been,
Break off a piece of heaven,
And light up a piece of their hearts.
Right along the flowing stream,
I built myself a bridge,
Where the river meets the sea,
I thought I heard the raven scream,
I left my home to come here,
But I'll go back again someday,
As they tried to chain me to the floor,
I walked, towards the door.

Rachel Lane

I See Him

I watch the eagle fly
have I ever seen anything
    so strong, so independent

I've seen it on the top
    of a cliff
Have I ever seen anything
    so alone

I admire him
Strong and free
    flying above us all

It takes a course, speeds up
    and strikes
He gets what he wants

And once again
I see the eagle on the top
    of a cliff

Milla Kauhanen

Foreigner

A new country
Different culture
Strange language
Feeling like you don't belong.

Listening, learning
Making new friends
Adapting
Starting all over again.

Missing things...
Family
Friends
Things you would never imagine.

Loneliness
Confusion
New experiences
It's all up and down.

Moved away
I've changed
Unrecognizable to myself
I'm a foreigner now!

Jayne Moran

Hamburgers

Big, fat,
Cheesy, yummy, juicy,
Hot to eat,
Hamburgers.

Kathryn Husband

Home

The key turns in the lock
I enter the room.
All I can see is the
light coming from the windows.
Shining a long light.
I turn on the light, drop
my bag and put the music on.
Go in the kitchen put a pizza
in the oven,
Cheese and tomato (nice)
After a long evening all a
girl wants to do is lay down
and put her feet up and
watch a film, something like
"The Cable Guy".
After that go up to bed
and write in my diary and
go to sleep.

Chantelle Patterson

Feeling Alone

Why am I always the one,
Who misses out on all the fun?
Who feels alone and sad inside,
Who changes moods with the tide?

I always, always seem to be
So down in the dumps, full of misery.
Why can't I be happy for just one day?
Why can't everything be okay?

Why does everything seem so wrong?
How come I never seem to belong?
Where are all my childhood friends?
These hopeless feelings never end.

I just want to fit in,
I want a happy time to begin.
I want to sleep for just one night
Without waking up in fright.

Feeling alone is a terrible thing,
Sadness is the only thing it brings.
Maybe the future will be bright —
I hope, I really hope I'm right.

Aine Bonner

Roses

Small, perfumed,
red, growing, prickly,
they grow on bushes,
Roses.

Hamish Hepburn

The Little Cloud

A little cloud sat in the sky
    With nothing much to do
He had no friends to play with
    And felt so very blue

He cried and cried throughout the day
    And made his eyes quite sore
But down below the little plants said
    Please won't you cry some more

We like it when you cry a lot
    And make the ground quite wet
Because we need the moisture
    To help our flowers set

So keep on crying little cloud
    Don't let the soil go dry
For in conditions such as that
    Our flowers would surely die.

Now don't you worry little ones
    Just hold your heads up high
And I will send you gentle showers
    To help you by and by

Sheila M. Shipley

Madame Fancy

She seems to think
that her soul is free.
Her mind is yearning
to be tampered.
She spent those nights
locked within those
young men's minds.
Freeing their souls
of passion,
discouraging their
blood from entering
that vicious soul,
from the madame
who rules the insanity
of falling in love.

Claire Stimpson

Contentment

I enjoyed being young,
But now that I'm older
The things I can do,
I'm really much bolder,
I wear what I like
Not minis of course,
I don't ride by bike
Nor a car or a horse,
I walk now for miles
And enjoy all the views,
I chat to all folk
Don't mind P's and Q's,
Just being myself
Releases all tension,
I've time to have hobbies
I paint! Did I mention?
In fact I feel great
So as I grow older
I'm looking for friends
Like me who are bolder.

Olga Thomas

Untitled

So sad, the eyes that cannot see
Devoid of colour, shape or form
So sad, the life that cannot be
Denied the joy of being born
So sad, the mouth that cannot talk
Expressing feeling, fear and thought
So sad, the limbs that cannot walk
Bereft of movement, ever taut
So sad, that fate has dealt the blow
To see, to speak, to be, to move
The greatest tragedy to know
So sad—
The heart that cannot love.

Christine Halstead

Regarding Love

I fall in love so rarely
it is really quite a shock
to suddenly realize
my heart is no longer mine
but, has been taken by some other
selfish swine.

A cynic I may be but,
emotions I can feel
just go ahead and pinch me
I'll scream, really I am real.

This disease called love,
I find
is really hard to know.
Some people make a lot of it
I think it's all for show.

Jane Stewart

Untitled

The two halves shall join
on the day that fate
has chosen, but the
two halves are one
existing to those who see
their love for each other, that
shall never be able to part but
no one shall be able to
break this strength
between two which shall
grow stronger with the
commitment of life, forever,
till death do thee part.

Yvonne Longueira

Drugs

In a dusky darkened room
Music's frantic deafening boom
Cigarettes glowing in the gloom
Were these creatures born of a womb

Greasy hair and dirty faces
Tired eyes and hunger traces
Movements jerky, voices slow
Taking a trip on powdered snow

Tattooed arms and twice pierced ear
Tatty clothes and worn out gear
Make-up over make-up plied
Clean skin only where she cried

Unwashed bodies, insect ridden
in their secret places hidden
Erotic fantasy set free
Among this drug crazed lunacy

Happiness and thrills are great
but have to come alone
Those that come at needlepoint
bring misery to atone.

Anne Clark

Daisies

Pretty, white, small,
bright, wild,
they grow in my garden,
daisies.

Alison Colvin

Plaiting Tears

I am weaving tears into
this silken braid;
my complex network of
thoughts and concepts.
This hair is yellow
and soft, and long,
its beauty is but
heightened by my sorrow.
Drops fall and darken
the blondness,
and the hair becomes longer
as I bury myself.
And the hair leaps
from my grasp,
(and tears)
and I am left with empty void
for comfort.

Amanda Laffan

Spring

When sea gulls whirl
throat-stretched
on salt-stained sea breezes
and a swim warm sea
calls with a slip-slap
on a warming shore,

When dog-deserted dunes
shake themselves free
and hair-flat dune grass
colours itself,

When the crisp hard overcoats,
give way to summer colours
and winter turns its shoulder
to rest a while,

We can gasp for warm breath
as the blood-cold dark months
gather dust
like old men on park benches.

S. Quigley

Spring Dawning

The March winds have now abated,
as spring now does approach
The winter cold it as been sated
And jack frost no longer gloats!
The days they grow longer
And the sun is in the sky
The snows have now all melted
And the larks are flying by
My heart it grows lighter
With thoughts of days to come
To be walking with my loved ones
In the warmth of the noon-day sun!
The flowers in the meadow
They now begin to grow,
The farmers in their fields.
Their crops they start to sow.
So step forward into springtime
And let your heart begin to sing
For now you realize
This is the start of spring?

James Barnes

Hamsters

My hamster,
furry, fat,
Soft, noisy, cuddly,
Move their beds to different places.

Susan Nicoll

Christmas Fever

Greenest of trees the Christmas now
Is hung with presents on the bough,
And stands beside the fireside
Tinsel decked for Christmastide.

Now all my cards are safely sent,
Last week all the parcels went
But what a shame that Mrs. Bore
Should send a card to me once more

I took her off my list last year,
She must be aging fast I fear,
But never mind I have some spares,
It's really no use splitting hairs.

The cake is made, the mince pies too,
Yes a Happy Christmas too to you..
How the callers keep on flocking
The price of sherry, now it's shocking

It's no use looking at the clocks,
Postman's here for his Christmas box,
Oh find my purse and money do,
Yes a Happy Christmas too to you.

Margaret J. Smith

Balance Of Nature

To look upon the distant rock,
I cast an eye upon its wroth
For it to fall I dare not move,
Perhaps because this will prove
an object of infinity that can destroy
and destruct, could become the object
effecting the balance of touch.

Life is but a game of chess,
Each one of us a player
Fragile as crystal rock
Shattered by a fatal drop.

I've looked upon that distant rock
I've seen its fatal blow
Shattered by a fatal drop,
The balance of nature froze.

Janet Munro

Autumn Poem

'frond of shame, unfurl yourself...'

Soon
You curl yourself up
like a dry Autumn leaf
And sift, asleep
Across sandpaper paths

    Shed your skin
sweet, rusting Autumn leaf
Return shell to earth
Drift loose-souled
skyward

Angela Gregory

Cats

Cute, cuddly,
Clever, timid, furry,
Purr when they are happy.
Cats.

Thomas Davies

Animals

Bees humming
Sparrows singing
Hedgehogs sniffing
Song thrushes calling

    Rabbits thumping
    Dogs barking
    Cats purring
    Mice squeaking

Cows mooing
Pigs grunting
Sheep bleating
Horses neighing

    Bears growling
    Elephants running
    Lions roaring
    Leopards leaping

Anne Miller

My Rabbit

Dozy is my fluffy friend
I play with him to the very end
I feed him and pat him every day
Then of course I stop to play
We let him run around the grass
He really is very fast.
Dozy is my fluffy friend
I play with him to the very end.

Eleanor Cushnie

My Piano

At one time, my piano played,
So merry in its tune.
But no-one plays my piano now,
It stands shrouded in its gloom.

My fingers were the last it knew,
They danced upon its keys.
But now the daylight and morning dew,
My piano never sees.

Upon the lid, red roses stood.
They made my piano glow.
But those red roses are now mud,
Or in the wind do blow.

My piano's notes are out of tune.
That bothers me no more.
For, I will be very soon
Strolling to death's door.

Alex Proffitt

The Biker's Song

For me it is the biker's life,
No time for home, or babes, or wife.
To come and go just as I please
To ride my bike o'er hills and leas.
I work all day, and sometimes night,
Thinking, "Is the bike alright?"
Come rest days, be it sun or rain.
I'm off out on my bike again.
I have no girl, I have no home
I'm free to choose where I can roam.
Enjoying working night after night
Making sure my bike's alright...
Nuts and bolts and piston rings
Carburetor, cranks and springs
The smell of engines, oil and grease
Bring to me a sense of peace.
Suzukis, Hondas and Triumphs too
Names to conjure with - that's true.
My bike is my life, my life is my bike
It's freedom.

B. V. Scotney

Message From Me To You

A Christmas message from Scott
to Maria.
I'm sure you realise now that
I will always be here.

A special wish from me to you
is that all your dreams from summer
have been unwrapped and suddenly
come true.

Excitement on your face was
for all to see.
That you my love were
meant for me.

Now we're engaged I know it was
the right thing to do.
From now on I hope it is just
me and you.

Scott Magee

Poodles

Furry, noisy,
pretty, big, clean.
The perfect dog for me
Poodles.

Daisy Radford

They Were Going Home

"Are you going home dear,
Are you going home?"
"No not today my love,
Don't want to go alone.
Loved each other, long and true,
Together we were maimed.
Don't cry for us when we're gone,
For that would be a shame,
That car, it crushed us both, you see.
They were going just like mad.
But as long as we're together
It will not be so bad.
We'll cross Jordan together,
Into the pleasant land,
We'll see a far horizon
And there will be a band
Of helpers to receive us.
So we'll not be afraid,
The light of God will go before,
And all earth's griefs will fade.

D. I. Day

Untitled

Autumn leaves are falling
red and gold and brown.
Up the street, down the street
all around the town.

Lawns are completely covered
trees are almost bare,
winter's coming, snow is due,
and green is very rare.

The birds have all migrated,
every one has flown.
Gone to warmer climates
until green buds are grown.

Spring is round the corner
leaves have started to grow,
the birds are all back nesting,
till again it starts to snow.

Pam Denham

Untitled

They command me to apologize
But I decline.
They take everything
But I won't let them take
What's mine.

They tell me to give up my place
But I say no.
They steal it from me
But I try not to let the hurt
To show.

They insist I die
But refuse I do.
They kill me promptly
But there is as much life inside me
As there is - in you.

My dignity lives on,
I was not born in vain.
My life was worth it.
People shall not sneer,
As they speak - my name.

Julia L. Buxton

The Joy Of Love

While all the world is sleeping
I see the darkened night
The stars watch over lovers
The moon they use for light
a moment that is magic
the beginning of their love
To them the world is theirs alone
A blessing from above

Lorraine Jones

Dusk To Dark

Blue,
Deep, empty, blue
All around;
As I think of you.

So empty, so alone:
No star
To guide me in my search,
For you tonight.

Deepening blue:
Still no sign of you returning;
I begin to drift
Into a solitary sleep.

You're out there,
Somewhere: I'm comforted to know;
We share the same
Now midnight blue

Fiona Taylor

Clouds

The dark clouds came again tonight
Not in the sky but in my mind
Memories past and memories present
Refusing to go away

The time of rest and peace is here
Of slumberness and pleasant dreams
But still the dark clouds linger
Refusing to go away

They used to be such happy clouds
Dancing in the sun
Until the dark descending clouds
Came blocking out the light

But times are slowly changing
The happy clouds still there
Trying hard to pass on through
Throwing the dark clouds away

Until then the dark clouds stay
Jostling in my mind
Memories past and memories present
Refusing to go away

Jeanette Wilson

Looking From My Window

When I look out of my window
all I see is pain
The woman sleeping on the bench
trying to hide her shame
she gets woken by the sound of
laughing boys and girls
she opens her eyes and sits up
then she cracks the seal
for thirty years she's lived like this
sad and all alone
maybe someone will someday look past
her appearance that's first shown.

Kerri Harris

God Cares

I held a stone within my palm
So ugly, cold and grey
And just as I was going
To throw it far away
I felt a gentle thudding
Like a tiny little heart
And realized with wonder
Of creation this was part
A rose it has great beauty
A canary sweetly sings
But the stone is a reminder
God cares for humble things.

Linda O'Dwyer

Just For Me

I wish to start my life again
The Lord has given me a chance
Only this time without such pain
I can see more clearly at a glance

I don't feel bitter but warm inside
Knowing I can make it on my own
With friends who truly love me
Then I will never walk alone

My one big pleasure in this world
Music is my one true love
My world will be brighter so I'm told.
A gift to me from up above

Never knowing what hurt could be
That dark cloud that came over me
My heart is lighter and I'm free
To begin again but just for me

Norma Ann Clark

Clumsy Pudsey Bear

When Pudsey Bear went out one day,
He fell upon a stack of hay.
He got a fright and ran away,
To stay away until it was May.
He came to a field where the winter
flowers grow,
And he fell into a puddle of snow.
He was all wet and soggy too
And so was his hat and his scarf and
his shoe.
One day when he was fast asleep,
He heard a noise just like a sheep.
He tumbled out of his own bed,
And had to let the sheep be fed.

Marie-Christine Bottger

Pointless Youth

Come yonder ye peasants
And look at the pheasants
So grand and aloof
So strong in their youth

They strut and they wander
Through strife, here and yonder
To please peasant's master
For they are the faster

Then fly up in chorus
And here as a bonus
The master docs show us
That death does not know us

The pheasants they fall
To drop all in all
Like stones thrown into the air
They pile up in pairs

The sport is now done
The peasants quietly go home
The master serves large banquets
The pheasants become feather blankets

Tom Cairns

Pastures And Dreams

Pastures, meadows, mountains, streams.
Loving pictures invade our dreams,
upon waking - reality.
Pictures of darkness
are what we see.

Pastures and meadows,
green velvet grass.
Peace and contentment
a few pleasant hours.
Horror of horrors!
the real world invades.

God has created
a world for us to share.
It should be full of happiness
instead, we have despair.

Marcella De-Santis

Dreaming

Last night as I lay sleeping.
I started dreaming

Fairies dancing in their silver and
white dresses glittering

Oh what a beautiful sight with
singing and music softly playing
all night.

How they danced on tip toe lightly
and sang so sweetly

I woke up so happy, radiant.
Glowing even singing.

J. M. Lauricella

Rain In August

The drowsy clouds have wakened
And rain falls on the fields
Where rape and wheat will ripen
And multiply their yields.

The rain falls hard, obliquely,
It purrs and thuds and sings
And magpies in a cornfield
Fly out with dripping wings.

The parched full trees are grateful,
The rain has soothed their thirst;
A sun-stretched cat is startled
As if the world had burst.

Rain storms are short and sudden
When summer days are old,
They douse the land and turn it
Into fields of harvest gold.

Patrick Redmond

Sunrise

Effortlessly
Elements shift,
There's a drift
Not a beginning.
Switched-off lights
Merge with a
Switched on
Adrenalin
Kick-start
Dawn.
Bells ring in
A cockerel chorus,
Dogs bark for food
Still light years away.
Your face looks softer
Then a velvet petal—
If only petals
Didn't fall.

Peter Ronson

Sleepy Head

I watch you as you sleep
Curled up snugly,
Breathing softly,
Spidery lashes
Resting in slumber
On your flushed face.

I smile as you stir
In your world of dreams
The stillness of night
Rests on your tired head.

You look so peaceful lying there.

Emma Ordish

Fifty Years On

A nation stood in silence
To honour those who died
While waging war upon a man
Who clearly had no pride

The main intention of this man
To obliterate the jew
To force upon all others
His nasty point of view

It took six years of fighting
To stem his fearful tide
Now a nation stands as one
to salute all those who died

They stood to show their gratitude
For the freedom that was earned
So silent was the multitude
Not a single voice was heard

Brian Wassell

Soliloquy

I'm feeling nice and warm and snug,
All wrapped up in my bed,
All cosy, safe, and comfortable,
Soft pillows for my head.
A lovely coal fire in the grate,
With flames of orange and gold,
Makes dancing pictures on the walls,
Such magic to behold!
While outside - in all the darkness,
A silent fall of snow,
Has covered all the world in white,
As off to sleep I go.
Then my cat steals in beside me,
And purrs softly in my ear.
The fire's still burning brightly,
And my little friend is here,
So whatever happens outside
On this cold and wintry night,
We'll snuggle down together,
And wish you all goodnight!

Charmaine S. Dawson

The Fire

There it was spitting at me,
You could see the reflection in my eye,
Burning all my furniture,
But nobody knew why.
I opened all the windows,
I opened all the doors.
But when I walked back in the room,
The fire had arose.
The house inside you could not see,
As it was full of smoke.
I ran outside the front,
Just before I nearly choked.
The blues came round the corner quick,
While I was on my hands and knees.
My neighbours reassured me,
While my brother came to tease.

Donna Webbe

Believe

I can't believe it's true,
'Coz it's just me and you,
I'm only feeling happy,
When I'm lying next to you.

My feelings are rushing,
Flowing round in my head.
I want to be with you,
Until I am dead.

You shower me with kisses,
You shower me with pride.
And if you ask me right,
You know I'll be your bride.

I'll love you always and forever,
I'll love you now and then,
I'll love you 'till I'm dead,
And I'll even love you then.

Lisa B. Jenkins

"Memories"

Memories no-one can take away,
forever here they will stay.

Locked inside the heart and mind,
"the key" that only you can find.

No clearer picture could one paint,
however distant, however faint.

They are now a part
of our History,
Like "the passage through time,"
"a mystery."

J. R. Marsh

Butterfly Love

Like the wispy butterfly
We drift from leaf to leaf
Skim the surface of others' lives
And cause each other grief

Are you afraid my friend
To touch another's heart?
To take their hand in yours
And make a brand new start?

The summer of our lives is sweet
Though painfully too short,
A commodity so fragile
Don't let it come to nought

Let's cast away our winter fears
No time now for remorse
Let joys abound aplenty
As nature takes its course

Come rest a while sweet butterfly
Touch my life a little longer
With love and understanding
We may grow a little stronger.

S. A. Milner

Rain

My love for him is pouring down
Upon my head
Upon my frown.
It doesn't stop
It keeps on showering
Drop to drop
It never stops.
No one knows
It doesn't show
No one can guess
The love I share
If they did I shouldn't care.
I love him like
A rose in bloom
Enchanting the garden
In the midst of June.
I adore him so dearly
I can't really see
If it was truly meant to be.

Susie Lindsay

God's Gift

Have you seen the glory of the morning,
And sunset at day's end -
Have you marvelled at this beauty
Each and every day will send?

Have you ever watched the sun rise
Like fire from the sea -
To burst forth in its glory
And fiery majesty?

Have you smelled the scent of roses
Heavy laden with the dew?
Did you walk upon a beach
And taste your salty lips - did you?

Do you marvel at the beauty
All around you everywhere -
Have you caught your breath with wonder
And known for certain God is there?

Do you know - just like I do
that inside you he resides -
Helpful - ever watchful -
He is there and sure to guide.

Vivienne Greenwood

P. R.

You are a protected species
When I smile,
You look the other way.
When I speak,
You do not listen.
When I touch,
You turn away.
When I express my mind,
You close yours.

Your ignorance protects you,
But for how long?

One day, you will -
Smile,
Speak,
Touch and
Express your mind,
And others will be
The protected species.

Bill Philip

My Sadness

My sadness is like no other's,
Out of everyone I know,
As I stand in the doorway,
As all my friends go.
My sadness is like a rose,
Once brightly blooming.
Now the petals are all withered,
Now they are grey and gloomy.
Is there not one spark left,
To light my white wax candle?
The wick is dark and burnt,
I see, as I hold it by the handle.
As all my friends leave,
My small yet humble home.
I sit for all eternity,
Silent and alone.

Sarah Harries

Getting Old

When you get old
Your hair will fall out
And bit by bit you'll find
It hard to get about

Your muscles may weaken
And you'll start to get drowsy
Your hearing may fail
And sometimes you'll feel lousy
You'll sit all day with nothing to do
But you'll find there's friends and
family to help you through.

Elizabeth Abbott

Your Love

Your love is like a blanket
On a lonely winter's night
It wraps itself around me
And keeps me warm inside

Your love is like the summer sun
Shining through the rain
Because no matter what goes wrong
I know you'll ease the pain

Your love is like the first snow
So fresh, so clean and pure
Our love is everlasting
Of this I can be sure

Your love to me means everything
It warms me through and through
And I will love you all my life
Because your love for me is true

Suzanne L. Ross

Summer Smiles

A field of flowers, a daisy chain,
And falling from a tree,
A garden wall, I recall,
And Summer smiled at me.

A fishing line held off the pier,
And paddling in the sea,
A bouncing ball, I recall,
And Summer smiled at me.

A walk along a country lane,
And sunlight through a tree,
A lover's call, I recall,
And Summer smiled at me.

Happy days as man and wife,
For all the world to see,
Life's golden ball I recall,
And Summer smiled at me.

My body holds me captive now,
But I am ever free,
As sunbeams fall I recall
When Summer smiled at me.

Mary Ellis

How Strong The Steel?

So tear our bonds of steel apart,
Stab to death this useless heart,
Amputate these clasping limbs,
The hand on which I wear the ring;
Help me keep the vow I swore -
That I'd be vulnerable no more.

Drain the tears from either eye,
For I've no time nor need to cry.
Free and clever; life is mine -
To stand back, laugh as others pine!
Extract this fragile human core,
That I be vulnerable no more.

You began this - end it well!
Leave me hollow like a shell,
Then after all the pain I bore -
I'll be vulnerable no more?

Karen A. Harris

Death

Death is love and
Love is death
So hold hands and
Take a deep breath
Give a kiss
To numb the mind
Drift away
Arms entwined
Together you soar
Together you fly
Together you sink
Together you die

Stacey Hayes

On Armistice Day

All but gone, that generation,
Honour bound to march away,
At duty's call, to Armageddon.

One or two may yet, perhaps,
Entangled in the sweat-soaked saps
Of nightmare memory, live it still.

The very last? Maybe their sons,
Enforced by fate to face the guns
A second time. But after that?

In peace, in paradox, it seems,
All innocence is left to dreams
And cenotaphs in Flanders field.

C. P. Baker

Untitled

I see you standing there,
smiling at me,
staring at me.
How awful I feel!
I smile back.
Do you know what I'm thinking?
You think I feel the same as you,
I know you do... but I don't.
I feel nothing for you anymore.
I destroyed what I felt for you,
and you helped me destroy it.
I betrayed myself.
We were friends,
then lovers,
that was our mistake.
I loved you once,
but now?
You are still smiling at me.

Oriana Moran

Drugs

Life has just started,
  I did it for fun,
    My life ended,
      And a new one begun.

I found a bottle,
  I started to drink,
    I got so drunk,
      I just could not think.

I took the syringe,
  Now it is too late,
    A drug addict,
      Now this is my fate.

I died for the drugs,
  Cannabis and speed,
    A bit of smack,
      That's all I would need.

I would not believe,
  It could not be true,
    So think before
      It happens to you.

Kristan Louise Barraclough

Seasons

The trees are bare
Autumn is there in the air
The leaves have all fallen
Down to the ground
A carpet beneath our feet
Winter is round the corner
Then we shall have snow
Our feet and fingers will glow
But children will always greet
Spring will not be far behind
Then buds peep through the snow
The birds will sing
The world awakes
What joys there are to know
Then summer is here
And children play
The days are long and sunny
Flowers bloom
The trees are green
And bees are making honey

E. Bedford

Dreaming

Dreaming in a world of reality,
Where dreams don't even exist.
Dreaming of the future,
That will never be in reality.

Fareen Akram

Robert's Love

You stood at my bedside
The day I bore your daughter
And your eyes were filled with pride
When into this world I brought her.

The joy that only we could share
Our union of love was no mean feat
Now we were three, no longer a pair
A family at last our happiness complete

Together we will remember
The meaning of our love
When an evening in September
Was blessed by God above.

Fay Westwater

Silence

Listen, can you hear it,
There's not a single sound,
Just the peace of stillness
Settled all around.
Listen, birds are singing,
Hear their cheery song,
The breeze is whispering in the trees
As you stroll along,
Far away from traffic
And the bustling town,
You can find a peaceful spot
And lay your burden down,
Take time for silence
Let your troubles float away
For a few precious moments
In your busy day.

Josephine O'Neill

'I Feel Used'

I feel used,
I feel sad,
that horrible man
done something bad.
I couldn't scream,
I couldn't kick,
the things that happened,
happened so quick.
I am scared,
I am upset,
I should of done something,
that's my regret.
I can't forget,
I can only cry,
I didn't do nothing,
I don't know why.

Tanya Freeman

Continuation

Death is but a gateway
To a new dimension,
It is not the end of life
But a new beginning.
What would be the purpose
Of our earthly life,
If after such a struggle
There was nothing.
As we are born
So we must make this transition
called death,
Just stop and think what is life
but a school of learning.
To attain knowledge.
Death is but a continuation
Another experience,
A furtherance of knowledge
into the unknown
Something beyond our comprehension.

Medina Nicholls

Oh! Great Thy Father Of Mine

Oh great thy father of mine
How as a child I missed your
Caress, tender loving care,
You chose not to care and flare . . .
While we stood and stare.
Still visibly comes back
The time said not to call you dad
Ain't it sad dad?!
We loved and worshipped you,
Were forced to live without you.
How time flies...
By blood you are still mine
Now all alone you are
By all means I am still yours.
This is not my style
For the love of being your daughter
I forgive and still love you.

Helene Michelle Amblavaney

A Sense Of Humour

I have tried to write a poem
With wit, and charm, and zest
I truly did try and try
To be the very best.

I tried to write a poem
On birds and bees and such
But the words that came to mind
Just didn't amount to much

I tried to write a poem
On memories of the past
The trouble with getting old
My memory won't last

I tried to write a poem
I sat up from morn till night
It really didn't help at all
That I have failing eyesight

Well I really tried to write a poem
It is my life long ambition you see
To open a book on poetry
And find one written by me

Audrey Brooks

Cats

Cute, gentle,
cuddly, soft, playful,
knocking over plant pots
Cats.

Rachel McIntyre

The Greatest Pain Of All

It hurts when you
lean on crutches
in the rain,
and no-one holds an umbrella
over you

It hurts, the daily toil,
lifting and carrying,
climbing the steps

It hurts when voices in white
say it's only nerves,
when they hand you
a piece of paper
and say next please

It hurts, the medicine,
which turns you into a robot,
taking away your power
to question,
bringing you to silence

But the greatest pain of all
is not to be believed

Sandy Lunoe

A Mission All Its Own

I saw it one day,
Like for the first time in my life,
It glowed most spectacular
And oh so very bright,
I watched it pass,
Though it took all day,
I even questioned its brilliance,
But my mind's eye never strayed,
It moved with such patience,
It had a mission all its own,
Like a dream moving forward,
Never stalling or overthrown,
It left me that evening,
I felt envy and disbelief,
For it was so beautiful,
It almost gave me grief,
But I know it will come tomorrow,
To start a new day,
And therefore, I am grateful,
To have seen it pass away

Samantha Hancock

New Life

I know how it feels
To lose a loved one,
That you didn't even know.
On the outside, you're quiet,
But inside, you're breaking in two.
For a while you are numb,
And then you are fragile.
But all these seem to be natural.
It is just the feeling,
Of losing something, like an eye,
That is important to you,
But not vital to life.
That is what hurts the most.
You wonder if there was
Something you could have done.
But you shouldn't blame yourself.
It was the kindest way,
That Mother Nature could say,
"It just was not meant to be."

Sian Pickering

Depression

A dark shadow deep within us all.
A cold and empty world,
A life in total darkness.
A distorted picture of colour,
A life of disbelief and fear.
A shadowed dream,
A never-ending nightmare.
A defense against pressure,
A constant flow of meandering tears.
A long road to no where,
A killer of too many.
A fading body,
A confused and misunderstood mind.
A lonely soul.
A cry for help!

Priscilla Dawn Dolloway

Tin Roof

Wild harmattan winds whip you
    but still you stay.
They spit dust all over your gleam
and twist your sharp cutting edges.
The rains come zinging mud
with their own tapping music;
    yet you remain
- my pride -
my very own tin roof.

Nii Parkes

155

Wonder

Amazing emotions wonder brings,
From all the weird and wondrous things,
Happy thrills of admiration,
Surprising gleams of fascination,
Shouts of laughter, squeals of fun,
These words of wonder have just begun.

Wonder rises from the sky,
Different people wonder why,?
Unusual happenings going on,
Cheerful smiles shining on,
Gleaming faces, sparkling eyes,
Wonder brings this from the skies.

Wonder fills the heart with joy,
Wonder cheers each girl and boy,
Wonder does these wondrous things,
And what happiness it brings,
Wonder brings joy to the eye,
Wonder is bold and never shy.

Claire Cannon

Merlin The Black Cat

He came one day,
Not intending to stay?
A streak of Black across the lawn,
What's that! Not another cat.
He came one day,
and decided to stay.
Amidst protests "He'll be a pest."
A loaner chased by other cats
No good at catching mice or rats!!!
He came one day
and stayed, and stayed
He's won our hearts
A proper creep!
Now we are feeding him best meat.
He came to stay!!!

Elizabeth Yarwood

The Magic Of Music

The magic of the music,
Pulsates through my body;
It stirs the soul,
And opens the heart,
Racing through my veins
reaching every part,
It possesses, turns and tortures,
Full of strength and guidance,
It fades, it's gone, it's vanished,
Back to deafening silence.

Sharon Hall

The Future

The future cold and harsh
As through eyes our children see it
But alas our race is fading fast
so to be we will join the dodo
just a mere name on a dust-covered book
But life goes on for all in the city
a city far underground
no town hall or civic centres
But as the last piece of dust falls
The last lamp turned off
The last clock strikes the hour
The last man ever gets out
They say a city never sleeps
But this one sleeps
Not one soul will move again
It is the hour of the storm
The time of darkness
A flash off light
The sun explodes

Paul Byrne

Papa

I once had a dear old Papa,
Who was very kind to me.
And when I was in trouble
He sat me on his knee.

One night as I lay sleeping
upon a feather bed,
An angel came from heaven
and told me he was dead.

I woke up in the morning
to see if it was true.
Yes, papa had gone to heaven
upon the sky so blue.

So children, obey your Grandparents,
and do as you are told.
For if you lose your Papa,
you lose a heart of gold.

Amanda Murphy

Bears

Dangerous, fierce,
furry, soft, fast,
live in a cave,
Bears.

Gareth Samson

Sweet Dreams

As darkness falls
across the land
You reach out
and touch my hand.

You caress my
soul and heart.
Protecting me as
night time starts.

As sleep consumes
my walking mind.
Thoughts of you
are all I find.

Feeling your love flow,
holding me near.
Although it's a dream,
it seems so clear.

Happiness at long last.
I've found my soul mate.
True love from above,
given us by fate...

Michelle Knopf

Memories

Childhood memories oh so sweet
of joyous laughter dancing feet
long happy days filled with love
birds and flowers blue skies above
no clouds to darken any morrow
with never any thoughts of sorrow
blow, oh blow, sweet gentle breeze
moving so softly amongst the trees
may all my hopes and dreams come true
I will always love and remember you

I stand here now, time has gone
since the days of childish song
wisdom may have come with years
But I cannot stem the tears
for the girl of long years past
time sweet time has gone so fast
blow, oh blow, sweet gentle breeze
moving so softly amongst the trees
remember the girl of long ago
gently, so gently, let her go.

Rosamund Hudson

Summer Holidays

Playing splashing in the sun
I'm going to the beach to have some fun
Eat ice creams.
Eat ice lollies.
Lying in the sun and getting a tan.

It's time to go back to school now.
Better go to bed early.
Coming in early too.
Lots of hard work and tests too.
I wish I were still on holiday.

Joanne Myles

Tammy

Where are you Tammy, my love.
My eyes are searching to see.
Running across the meadow.
Rushing to greet me.

Her lovely sparkling eyes.
Her soft silky coat.
Her long bushy tail.
And a white bib at her throat.

She was my child, my little girl.
She was my life, my whole world.
As tears fall from my eyes.
It's so plain to see, she's there.
Among the stars, waiting for me.

Daphne Jean Aldridge

A Poem To A Summer's Day

How still the air, how sweet the scent,
The lilac hanging heavy.
The busy hum of passing bees,
Petals lifted ready.

Trees towering high far o' head,
The grass so green below...
How small I feel just standing here
How little yet I know.

Thank you, God, for giving me
The power, the eyes to see
The Beauty of a Summer's Day
It brings me near to thee.

Sarah Williams

Watery Reflections

Yards away beyond the fence
leafy trees, foliage dense
River Garnock, quiet, unseen
runs through banks of grass so green.
Remembered floods, the river high,
worried folk in homes nearby,
wondering if the banks will hold,
everlasting rain so cold.
Come the dawn, the rain had stopped
each passing hour the water dropped.
Nature playing tricks again
hopes of sunny days in vain,
birds are back, magpie alone
lost his mate? Now on his own,
time for hope, spring in the air
nature kind, the weather fair,
time to leave, it's hard to go,
I shall return, this I know.

Ann Odger

Selfish Man

Selfish, selfish man,
doing things only you can,
doing what you want, every day,
not caring who or what is in
your way.

Natalie Wilkinson

On The Street

Once I was at home warm and dry
Now I'm out with the winter's sky,
How I got here I really don't know
What shall I do with nowhere to go?

I should be at home with my family
Instead I am here without any tea,
Life on the streets is really rough
I have no friends but I must be tough.

I ran away without thinking it out
Now I forget what it's all about,
I'm getting really cold I feel all numb
What shall I do I need my mum?

I'm dying here in the frozen street
With nothing to do and nothing to eat,
No one will notice no one will care
Why should they I'm not even there?

Here I came
And here I will stay,
I'm dying here
But first let me pray.

Anna Gough

Eyes Of A Child

A child stands in the corner
Trying to hide
His heart beats like a drum
Eyes open wide.
His mouth moves to speak
But not a sound is heard
He knows what to say
But can't find the words.

A scream goes right through him
Loud and dying
His mother on the floor
Crumpled and crying
His father standing over her
Tears down his face
Saying how he's sorry
Standing in disgrace.

The child sees it all
Could think it's all a game
Will he grow up, get married?
Will he do the same?

S. Tingey

Pollution

Oil slithering on the sea
Kills all the fish you will agree
People coming as a team
With equipment to wipe it clean
Everybody arguing;
Time to call the green group in
Pollution coming from everywhere
Do you call that torture fair?

Mark Chambers

Amanda

The one who bears the sweetest name,
who is always with me,
through trouble and pain.
Who sheds tears when happy,
and consoles when sad,
the most beautiful girl,
in all the land.
All my life I'll spend with her,
for there truly is no other,
that could ever take the place,
of my dear Amanda.

G. Zanre

The Old Woman

She sits alone, so
  motionless and still
Her mind adrift, in long
  begotten memories
of life, unknown today.
The dear wrinkled brow,
The hair like shimmering tinsel
around frail shoulders lies,
Conceals their secrets from
other probing minds.

Thelma Duggan

My Floral Tribute

Flowers of beauty, enriched with colour
bedeck my meagre garden
They sway together peacefully
as if experiencing the harmony of love
Their offerings of pleasure
seem in return for my caring touch
Some stand majestically
as if proud of their position
Others huddle together, whispering
secrets of their magic
Perfume fills the evening air
filling my senses with affection
A breeze passes by
transforming my meagre garden
into an ocean of dancing waves

J. E. Ward

Perennial

Summer's fading once again
Autumn starts to fall
Flowers in the garden fade
Now there are none at all

Winter is here, cold and damp
Then white for all to see
As we watch, the trees are bare
Everything set free

Again we feel a warmer strength
And life begins once again
The buds just peep above the earth
If softly falling rain

What a lovely feeling now
Spring is here to tame
Flowers for a summer grow
A new year in the frame

P. Cotterell

My Grandfather

I looked into his big grey eyes,
He wore a smile on
His old wrinkled face.
He loved sitting by the fire
But only in his own place.

As I sat by his bedside,
Held his hand in mine,
I felt his pain rising up in me
As his eyelids shut tight.

My heart, now breaking in two
As my Grandfather leaves my life.
I thought he'd open his eyes again
But that was an awful bad night.

O, how I'm going to miss you.
I will think about you every day.
I will always remember the good times
That both of us had
In our own special way.

Dona Smith

The Scarecrow

There was a worsel gumage,
Jon Pertwee was his name,
And on TV he found fame,
Watched by children of all age.

He was a partner with a rag doll,
Aunt Sally was her name,
She thought him rather dirty,
And told him so, just the same.

I am made from a wooden stake,
Finished a very important place I take,
Old clothes I have stuffed with straw,
Much interest I do seem to draw.

My head is a turnip really fat,
Adorned with an old trilby hat,
They stand me in a ploughed field,
Seeds and corn I must shield.

It is very boring I have to say,
Standing here day by day,
But when I see the corn come through,
A job well done is oh so true.

E. R. Shepherd

Rabbits

Fury, soft,
Pretty, colourful, cute,
Clever, cuddly,
Rabbits.

Susannah Stark

What's Worse?

Ghouls and a ghost
take blackened toast
heebie-jeebies
scrape it clean
imaginations running large
spread a little softer marg.

Creepy noises do not fade
and lots of lovely marmalade.
A spine-chilling feeling
it tastes like it's off the ceiling
things that move
as you eat burnt toast.

Scaring even the brave
self cooking's not a rave
it was here, not there
as the flavour raises your hair
what else could go wrong
as you eat burnt toast?

Dave Cobb

War

Watch out!
Bomb!
Crash!
Destruction!
People panicking.
People screaming.
People shouting.
People crying.
People hurt.
People alone.
People terrified.
People stuck.
People in dark.
People no food.
People dying
People dead
Watch out!
Another one!
People, why us?

Karen Aim

Riding The Waves

Jumping on a surfboard
makes you feel so cool,
a rush of Adrenaline
Swirls round inside.

Riding the waves
makes you feel sexy,
forget your problems
and the body you hate.

For those few minutes,
precious minutes,
you feel so good,
then when you stop
you return to earth.

Alice Watts

Let Go

Don't cry nor be afraid
Be happy as life ends for one
It begins for yet another
They watch with their upset faces
Longing to touch you
Longing to make you happy
Their heavenly wings are paralysed
As tears are shed
Stop those tears, let them go
spread their wings, help them fly.
Forever Love

Katrina Patton

Untitled

The clown is a funny man
   everyone knows
He dresses in bright clothes
   and puts on a nose
He always is happy
   and never is sad
To be a clown
   can't be bad
when I'm bigger,
   think I'll be a clown
I'll move the big circus
   into the town
Play all my tricks in a very
   funny way
Then leave the circus alone
   to go off and play

Susan Spratt

To Live, To Love

Our past is now a lesson in life
Our future is noting but dreams
Our present is a combination of both
Will we find out what life means

Our life is like a candle
Burning through its time
Are there guides to guide us
Or do we always look for a sign

To be what we want to be
To go where we want to go
To be always searching for knowledge
Or do we simply want to know

Life is full of love and hate
Is a soul mate something we create
Within the person we hope to meet
Will they make our life complete

To give my life, my heart, my breath
To give my love until my death
For this commitment in life to be
Is the ultimate lesson I want for me

S. Church

Untitled

To a very special couple
On your silver wedding day
Our love and thoughts are with you
Much more than words can say
We wish you health and happiness
May your hopes and dreams come true
For there is no one in the world
Deserves it more than you.
As you travel down life's highway
With its joys, its sorrows and tears
May the love you have for each other
Be with you through all the years.

E. Hallam

Tomorrow's Doom

Brittle dreams without rivets
Vacuous stare of forlorn children
Like a fish on dry dust
Bitter thoughts to swallow
That home is on fire

Ignoble sights to behold
Hordes of hapless images
Foraging in garbage dumps
Like the swarm on a beehive
And the flies not a match

Hauled through dark paths
Tortuous trek on strange streets
A frantic flight from home
Running from deadly tunes
That unsettles native peace

In the gloom of lonely depths
Drenched in misery rain
Grousing in righteous rage
Mourning tomorrow's denials.

Cosmas C. Okolo

Sisters

Sisters old sisters young,
playing with your hair,
borrowing your things,
and bossing you about!
Calling you sweet names.
O what a shame!

Ain't you glad you got such nice
sisters!

Rebecca Rainbow

The Swallows

On a lovely April day
Sitting near the shed
Two swallow flew low
Over my head into the shed

They worked very hard
With mud and straw
The nest was ready
And eggs were laid

No time at all
The chicks arrive
Softly they fly in and out
Feeding the young.

Five little ones come out
Afraid to fly they rest
On the wire across the shed,
October is here and
All swallows are gone for another year.

Breda Hand

The Ostrich

I read that when an Ostrich
From danger tries to hide,
He puts his head into the sand,
But leaves the rest outside.

Because the danger he can't see,
He thinks he's hid from sight,
And will not heed your warning,
Though you shout with all your might.

Many men are like the Ostrich,
When from women they try to hide,
They think they're always perfect,
But to woman it's the opposite!

The Ostriches don't take the warning,
Or take the strength to run,
They just go on believing
That in sand they're fully covered.

Deborah Coffey

A Spacious Place

Holy the land, that spacious place
Whereof so many tales are told.
Tales of king and palace,
Of fortress and slave.
Tales of war and peace,
Of love and hate.
Tales of joy and sadness,
Of humility and grace.
Tales of angels and shepherds,
Of a birth like no other birth.
Tales of mounts and miracles,
Of sea and storm.
Tales of a cross,
Of betrayal and forgiveness.
Holy the land, that spacious place
Whereof so many tales are told,
Tales of humanity and holiness -
Of a love like no other love.

Thelma Norrish

The Horse

Head up
tail down
legs moving
looking proud.

Reins tight
shoulders straight
you've lost
it's too late.

Walking, sitting, trot
looking good
looking hot
looking proud
big crowd
that's it, you've won again.

Leah Jordan Nedahl

Love's First Kiss

Gently the tender flesh
Unites,
Sealing the passion
Of their emotions.

Surging through both
Body and soul,
Are blood, love, and
Life itself.

For an instant the two
Become one,
Both mentally and physically,
Held together by
Love's first kiss.

Marjida Sabir

For Expansion Or Greed

After the white man
wasted its land
it moved to the West
and the dark years began.

People came and people went
didn't ask to lend the land
or barter for rent.

They used it, abused it,
then threw it away.
But not until the Nations
had dwindled away.

Look now, reflect back,
think of how it must have been,
where you always lived
white men are moving in.

It couldn't have been easy,
It must have been hard,
imagine some unknown heathen
moving onto your back yard

M. D. Hinchcliffe

Counterpoint

We stopped below the standing rock;
The earth was still.

A lark,
rising invisible,
proclaimed in song
  - All life is joy, all joy is free -
A grateful Alleluia.

We started forth towards the edge,
serenely calm
with gentle tread.

The stopped lark recalled us.
The earth was still.

Far below in the spreading dale,
never suspected,
a tinkling water limpid lay,
an azure counterpoint,
in canon with the sky.

And turning back our hearts were full,
joyful,
and at peace.

John P. H. Coath

Grease Paint

An actor is the thing to be
upon the stage for all to see
learning lines and dressing up
drinking from a silver cup.

Waiting, shaking in the wings
not much room for props and things
cue line coming up at last
take it easy - not too fast.

You're on the stage so do your bit
just like a jigsaw make it fit
the scene is set for your first line
this magic feeling is your sign.

Your nerves are gone - you are a star
forgetting who or where you are
the pause is good, now play the part
the words are coming from your heart.

End of show - successful run
drinks all round and having fun.
Director beaming over there
no greater feeling - anywhere!

Sylvia Iveson

Little Snowflakes

Little snowflakes in the air,
carry me up there.
Above the tree tops,
over the clouds,
to the place up there.
I heard up there,
there is Peace,
not War.
Somewhere up there,
is a place for me.
To Dream,
to Think,
to be whatever I want to be,
up there is the place for me.
O' little snowflake,
take me there,
please take me there.

Katherine Herne

Secret

A whisper
Caressing, touching
More than any flesh could touch

A web, spun
Of the finest silk
Beautiful, but easily broken

A gem
Shining bright, if only
It could be brought into the light

A weapon
Atomic words
Mushrooming to cover a bright day
Then, fallout

Nigel Bangert

Romantic Intrigue

It's a dream,
It can't be reality,
He looks at me with just a glance,
And I can see he loves me.
His eyes,
O his eyes they're bluer than the sea.
With such a face,
How can it be that he likes me.
It's from the heart you know,
And where feelings flow.
Love is born,
Like a flame on a candle,
And the warmer it gets,
The closer you get,
Love is all around you.

Hannah Clarke

A Backward Glance

I walked beside the water
How familiar, deja vu.
This path I trod many times
I strolled along with you.

A farewell kiss upon my brow,
The action is reversed.
So many times I did just this
But oh, where are you now?

The waving hand, the shining smile,
To me it is just the same.
The bond between parent and child
So precious, history repeated again.

You passed away a long time ago
But still I know your face.
For beside the water I stroll again
I find you in this place.

A. Rudkin

Untitled

But you were there, your time not ours
sometimes a stare for hours and hours
I sit and watch you, life and death
the footsteps wake me and my breath
will not survive alone for long
although my voice will fight for song
unheard to you a distant cry
the whispered words of how and why
they will be hidden in the spaces
behind the masks of frightened faces.

Beyond the clouds in tearless skies
the whispered words of how and why
so soon to come and then to go
away some day though bound to know
that time in life so slow to stay
in what you think will be the day
of spaces filled and voices loud
where I will roam above that cloud
and will arrive with footsteps bold
in time to see the masks unfold.

Sarah Cartwright

Bereavement

Oh, I have lost my gentle man
To nature's cruel way.
Ill health it sapped his manly strength
and stole his breath away.

All through the night I held his hand,
and longed for him to stay,
But he had lost his mortal fight
before the break of day.

I closed his eyes and kissed his brow.
How could I live without him now?

But, wherever spirits wander through
The great expanse above.
I know that we are ever bound,
by a silver thread of love.

V. L. F. Wilson

Dreaming

Oh, dreaming is
such a wonderful thing
Oh, and so often
do I forget it . . .
But, maybe . . . and, only, maybe
Tonight I'll dream
Purple clouds, green sky . . .

And, maybe tonight
it won't be a dream
Maybe, I'll stay inside it
After all, who knows
What is reality
And what is a dream!!!

Dragana Ivanovic

Goodbye Dear Heart

In that quiet moment
There was only you and I.
The world tilting in sharp sunlight,
Dappled shadows, rustling leaves,
Vibrant bird song.
Crystal clear, in slow motion
We tore apart.
A great cocoon of numbness
Drawing the skin from our faces
The silent screams from our mouths
We parted.
Me, trapped beneath the blue, blue sky,
You, up and onwards into eternity.
Goodbye Dear Heart, we cried.

Helena M. Ball

Queen Of The Snow Kingdom

The Snow Queen with her creatures
walking round her feet,
sees the wondrous mountains
and the Valkyries vast fleet.

She transports to her castle
with pennants flying high,
and nods to Heaven's host
in the dark vaults of the sky.

Her wisdom is all-knowing,
her robe's a perfect blue,
and the whiteness of the snow
gilds the clouds with ghostly hue.

This woman is not mortal,
she's not made of flesh and blood,
she is true ethereal beauty
like a rose that's just in bud.

Daf Richards

Bleakness

A windswept moor, bracken dry
Sky above me, will you cry.
I long to feel your sorrow fall
My dying limbs, rejoicing call

Once I was ferny, green and blue,
And gambolled o'er by all of you.
My ugly brown has turned away
The footprints in my iron clay

But natures cycle soon will turn
No longer will I parch and burn
With spring will come my savour, rain
And I will learn to live again.

Teresa Burnett

Oh, Daddy!

I love you Daddy, I really do
But I just can't get close to you
I try to please, I do what's right
But somehow we will always fight.

Why do I feel I must impress?
Will you love me any less?
Why do I strive for your affection?
When all you give me is rejection.

No one's perfect—I can't be
So will you love me, just for me?

Ann Gravells

Accident Prone

To My Husband Richard

I know you want to help me
And I know you think I moan
But when it comes to mending things
You should leave well alone.

Remember the immersion heater
You'd fix no trouble at all
But turned the mains full on, not off,
And flooded the landing and hall.

Attaching the kitchen towel rail.
You nearly met your doom
You pierced the electric cable
And were flung across the room.

Then came Auntie's pelmet.
Looked good without a doubt.
But when she pulled her curtains
It fell and knocked her out.

You even lost the dog last week.
That was the final straw.
You hadn't even missed her.
Please, don't help me any more.

Christine Ash-Smith

Untitled

That feather in the wind
I glimpsed
or rather sensed
I know now
was a touch of angel wing
with subtle guidance
merest breathed intent
working
to show the way
more surely
than rationale alone
or any considered argument.

Francesca Greene

The Moon Dance

We had a special place
No one else knew about it
Being free from society
The moon was our shelter
You would dance under the moon
Laughing, saying everything was great
I loved spending time with you
You listened to me, took my side
Everyone thought I was crazy
I knew I wasn't crazy, just happy
I miss you so much
People say I should get over you
I wish I could, but it's not that easy
I know you're not dead
It's just that I've grown up
And I have real friends now,
But they never dance under the moon
Or laugh or say everything is great.

Joanne Frances Nugent

I Wonder

I wonder about nature
And how it came to be
The budding of the bushes
The setting of a tree

The hills and dales and waterfalls
The deep blue sea
The birds and bees and animals
They're wonderful to me.

The sun in the sky shines so bright
The clouds go rolling by
The moon and stars come out at night
I wonder why.

P. Robinson

Friendship

Friendship is a great thing,
It's always there for you.
When you have problems,
Friends will pull you through.
Some can come and go,
Some are old and new.
But no matter what happens,
A friend is always true.
When you feel life's hard,
And it's a struggle to go on.
A friend will stand by you,
Giving the hand to be strong.
The light at the end of a tunnel,
A bond that will never break.
As long as you understand each other,
It's all about give and take.
Having fun and laughing,
For confiding in late at night.
When you face endless trials,
Friends are there to make it alright.

Laura Cation

On Call

Just waiting
     Just hoping
          Will it?
               Won't it?
                    Will I?
                         Can't I?

It's happened!
     Can I?
          Hands shake
               Heart pounds
                    Hard swallow
                         I'll try

It's done!
     Any good?
          They're alive!
               They're breathing!
                    They're something!
                         Am I?

J. Francombe

Music

When my working day is through
And pressures seem to block the light
I turn to music to calm my mind
And lead me through the night.
I hear the sounds, I feel the mood
It helps to set the scene.
I close my eyes and leave the room
And wake up in a dream.
The drums, the strings, the voices too
Yes lyrics mean the most.
Words are all the world to me
They help to lay the ghosts.
The past and future are in the songs
And thoughts go spinning round
But the only way to escape the world
Is to sink into the sounds.

Chris Rigg

The Spider's Web

There's a spider's web in my garden
It stretches along my wall
The builder is patiently waiting
For insects to make a call

But if they land upon his web
They'll struggle for liberty
And he'll just sit there smiling
For tonight they are his tea.

Graham Peter Dennis

Let Me Be Free

That lonesome feeling
Is always there
Even when socializing
Amongst friendly people
As movement in a wheelchair
Makes it impossible to move
Without causing disruption
To the furnishings in the room
But to enjoy oneself
Eyes must be kept closed to the
People that gaze and try
To sympathize and understand
The problems that have to be
Overcome so that you can mingle
In the hope you meet
Someone who will
Replace that lonely feeling.

Pauline Finkleman

Forgiveness

Mistakes are made time and again,
And we always pay the price.
But lessons can be learnt from them,
We don't attempt them twice.

We are usually forgiven
For the things that we do wrong,
But if we're constantly reminded
How can we possibly move on?

At times I think of things I've done,
Mistakes that I have made.
Or points and stories I've ignored,
And warnings disobeyed.

So, in conclusion to this poem,
No deeper will I delve:
To be forgiven for our mistakes
We must first forgive ourselves.

Leeanne Graham

Dinosaurs

Big, dangerous,
tall, scary, fierce,
eat each other,
Dinosaurs.

Jennifer Strachan

The Window

I can see as far as
I can see,
The way of the land
Into infinity,
The dark greens,
The light greens,
The violets and the blues,
There is to my vision
Such a heaven
In the colours of the skies,
So if you ever want
To look at a view
Through my window,
Just stand next to me,
I will take you on
A guided tour
Of my wondrous infinity.

C. Hush

The Poor

As I sit in the dark,
On a cold winters night,
I look up to the sky,
And I shiver with fright.

The morning awakes me,
It's time to get up,
Looking for breakfast,
In the old rubbish tubs.

I find some cold chips,
And a core of an apple,
An empty old can
And an old sweet wrapper.

I have not a cent,
Not a penny to spare,
As I walk through the town,
People gave me a glare.

It's night time again,
Sleeping on the street,
I'm poor and I'm hungry,
I just want something to eat.

Gwen Jones

My Granddaughter

Julie
Unruly
A mischief at heart
Always a winner
Quick as a dart.

Julie
So loving
Soft arms twining tight
A kiss and a cuddle
Then off like a light.

Julie
So pretty
Bright eyes, rosy cheeks
Her love for her gran
I do not have to seek.

Julie
Is growing
Her visits now short
As she studies and works
But I'm oft in her thoughts

Barbara Reeves

Just You And I

I walk alone in mellow glow
Of moonbeams on the shore.
The hungry surf with constant flow
Sets deep my heart and lower.

These thoughts of thee take up my time
With dreams of what could be,
If you would send me just one line
Of words to set us free.

An ocean's span and continent
Divide between us both.
It adds much to my discontent
And angry words flow forth.

Why is it so distressing me?
Why can't I hold you near?
With you it is I long to be,
'Tis you I hold so dear.

I love with passioned heat and flame,
My heart and soul enriched,
Just thinking of you once again.
I surely am bewitched.

Thomas Eccleston

Fifty Years On

Men, grey-haired and upright
March along with pride
Do I detect a little tear
They try so hard to hide?

Their thoughts go back to yesteryear
Was it fifty years ago?
Left behind in a foreign field
Our Bert and Ted and dear old Joe.

They remember well the "few"
Who streaked across the sky
So young, so brave and carefree
Who'd barely learned to fly.

These lads all did their bit
To keep this country free,
In desert, Burma, sea and air
And a beach in Normandy.

If doubters say "I wonder why?"
When these veterans come their way,
Tell them of those who gave their all
That we could live as we do today.

K. G. Wood

Do You Care

Are you thinking of me right now
Am I in your heart somewhere
Do you want me in your world
If I vanished, Would you care?

How important is my love to you
Is it ordinary or something rare
Would you fight to keep me yours
If you lost me, Would you care?

Do you know what you want from me
Do you know, are you aware
That I could love you all my life
Do you know this, Do you care?

Should I put all fears aside
Should I give all, could I dare
If I gave up everything for you
Would it matter, Would you care?

I sit and ask myself these questions
While your life goes on elsewhere
I tell myself one thing is certain
That I love you and I care...

Jacqueline Smith

The Loveless State

Each locked in a compartment
Rigidly contained
Bound about with prejudice
Identified and labelled
All journeying on the same train
It makes no sense.

Trapped in awful silence
Fearful of echoes
Inner noise clamouring
With passionate entreaty
All journeying on the same train
Yet all are mute.

Mere shadows without substance
Missing the mark
Doors dead-locked from the inside
Self-imprisoned, self-constrained
All journeying on the same train.
The key is love.

Joyce M. Drackett-Case

Bereavement

We question God.
The reason why!
Our life's partner
Has to die?

We don't get answers.
It must be planned!
Friends say "I know
I understand".

But! No, they don't,
And they can't see,
It happened, not to them
But just to me!

Until this happens
In your life,
Whether loving husband, loving wife

You don't know
The dire stress
Caused by the
Dreadful lonesomeness.

Flora Passant

THE FALL

On that day

when I heard the voice of God
deep in my consciousness
a guilt stung me like a snakebite
I felt the unexplainable shame
of my nakedness
and saw the dark side of my soul

in the horrifying moment
of utter loneliness
when the animals abandoned me
and the nature recognised me
as its enemy

I fled The Paradise.

Anja Clarke

Kittens

Small, soft,
Furry, playful, nice,
Run and never stop,
Kittens

Jade Nielson

The Old Cove

I walk under deformed trees
Bent double, ankles nettle-stung,
To the old cove where the sticks
And stones of childhood lie bare.

Spat-out Jonah sitting safe
Amongst the driftwood, I feel
My gnarled knots untwist like a
Foetus forming digits and

Recall my novice strokes,
The bubbling convulsions, secret,
Silent confessions. Washed up,
I was marked by the high-tide.

It seems so small now, the cove:
I can almost touch, with arms
Outstretched, both sides of the cliffs
That once dwarfed my water-fights.

Ross Pitcairn

Dinosaurs

Ferocious, different,
Fast, big, carnivorous,
interesting to read about
Dinosaurs.

Iain Adamson

Expatriate

Once a week as I sip gin
Comes the man to take the bin
Through the shamba to the bush
Where he gives one mighty push
So the contents all lie bare,
Chicken bones and underwear.

Later, he returns in stealth
To exploit the latent wealth:
Polish-tins for pots and pans,
Roofing from Jeyes fluid cans,
Soured milk to feed the goats,
Worn-out shorts for children's coats.

What the jackals leave alone
Now is brought in triumph home,
Ready for a second start;
Stranger, when you see my heart
Shattered on the iron ground,
Leave in peace what you have found.

John Bishop

The Lonely Valley

Here I stand alone in this lonely valley, far, far away from the rems of time. I listen to the secret stretching way down in the deep as they dine. What joy it brings come to think of it, the valley has peace, and it will never cease.

Oh, timeless valley, how I love thee so much, for the fruit of your origins seems never was touched, such sweetness, and silence, such showers of love when the night shadow falls this valley still glorious, and how I love thee and all.

I hear the sweet voices of the valley as it calls so I listen as it echoes through the airing of time, look around you as it whispers so sweet, see the dawn over yonder from the hillside as it passes, I cast my eyes to the glorious sky where the crimson sun shines out of the blue, one gazes again one long last gaze and shouts aloud, oh, valley how I love thee, you are everything to me.

I hear the roaring of the great valley, as it moves around in harmony, I listen to the distance "music" as its sounds seem echoed from far and wide, well, I am here in the midst of this never ending beauty where I will never have to worry, neither will I hurry for in this lovely place, you can just relax.

R. Wright

You Have Discovered An Angel

You have discovered an Angel peace be beyond you into me I'm here before you my love in my shadow of the trees offering you the helping hand when I can, some of us live for reality some in the shadow of dreams looking all before us it seems some of us wanting to stay others not knowing where to go, some of us live in torment, others wondering of it seems but take a look at me I work it out it seems I'm here for you angel of mine living in the shadow of dreams maybe afraid to wake fearing to face the world, life and all it takes but then I smile for you angel of mine treasuring precious moments together our secret, thoughts memories to come let me lead you to the path, of the fountain to the overflow trickling down with love, yes, I smile dearest angel picturing your happy smiling face loving every move you make so peace be beyond you it's me I'm here before you my love in the shadow of the trees come take my hand to guide you along to help and protect you through this lonely path sharing happy times we had a good laugh those geese followed us up the road, the bull chased us in the field, we slipped and fell down a hole those were the frightening moments but we came through together a lot has happened since then so, cheer up dearest angel of mine let me bring you peace beyond you, to ease your troubled mind if you are happy I am, if you are sad I am, so you have discovered an angel peace be beyond you it's me, for now I am here for you always in all eternity

M. Jackson

"A Mother's Memories"

When I think of my "son" I have oft times cried, a finer "son" would be hard to find.

For 19 years our pride and joy, a happy, smiling, very kind boy. As a policeman always did his best, and gained commendation with the rest.

This was for bravery, and I'm so proud "Peter" stood out from the usual crowd. Six feet tall, a handsome lad, platinum hair, blue eyes, like his dad.

Duke of Edinburgh's silver and gold he achieved, "Peter" could always take the lead. Then fate stepped in, and took him away. We can't find a reason to this day.

And yet another bitter blow, fate took his Dad, 'cos he needed him so. Now I think of the blessings I have and see, a wonderful daughter

Kind to me; "Jill" misses Peter, but doesn't say and spends her time to brighten my day; she phones a lot, and takes me out.

Her children keep me happy, there's no doubt. Grandchildren and great grandchildren are such a treasure,

And all I need to give me pleasure. When they're around I smile once more, and find I need them, more at my door.

So I think of my "Peter" so dear to my heart, and I smile again, as my memories start.

Jean Margaret Walker

The Lost Ones.....

We are the shadows that shade out the sun
  We are the new lives that had hardly begun
We are the thoughts that you see in your mind
  We are the ones that were never unkind

We are the stars that come out at night
  We are the snowdrops, a blanket of white
We are the forest where trees all grow high
  We are the lost ones, you never knew why

Our tears are the moisture you see after the rain
  We are the ones who want to ease all your pain
We are the seeds that could not grow
  The reason why we do not know

We are the waves that move with the sea
  We are the wings on the birds that are free
We are the ones who did not survive
  Who had no heartbeat, who could not thrive

We had gone too soon, we could not be born
  We have just our spirits for you to mourn
We are the babies conceived in love
  Who were taken away to Him above
    Lannette Lusk

Trust!

Trusting a person,
Through and through out,
Is going to be hard, Make there no doubt.

Telling your secrets,
From deep in your heart.
The secrets that matter,
The ones that are a part.

To confide all your feelings,
To one other being,
Is a great way of letting
Your trust to start freeing.

Also make sure you know
from deep down inside,
That this person can trust you,
Like an incoming tide.

And Then.....

When the trust between two people,
Becomes so very strong,
It's something to cherish,
For your whole life long.
    Lisa Claire Shipton

For Simon: Transplant Journey
Through Someone Else's Eyes

Switch,
Blade—glided along the soft skin of him,
Half—I am but a tourist in my native land.
I wish to know more than of him—will I get the chance?
They speak of numbers—but what are numbers,
They are only something to count with!
Sporadic burning—why doesn't this water sort it out?

He is etherized—will it stretch to the horizon?
There is an end point, there must be!
But he shines,
Glowing he smiles—he is an angel
He is here to show you and me.
Can I see his soft face without expression?
Innocence—but it's blinding,
This dark light; I cannot see,
Put on your glasses stupid—there!
Whrrr, Whrrr, Whrrr,
Go on, draw it—I love you
—Alive

    Dawn Harris

Impostor Inside Me

There are confused feelings inside me
Emotions totally different
Mixed together almost eternally,
Crying, Laughing, Shouting, Smiling.
What are these feelings meant to be?
Who's this impostor inside me?

There are delicate frustrations inside me
Screaming in my mind
Telling me what I'm meant to be,
Hesitations, Imaginations, Obligations.
What are these feelings meant to be?
Who's this impostor inside me?

There are outbursts of happiness inside me
Showing themselves through impossible places
I have to do what others do,
Wish, Love, Hope, Think.
What are these feelings meant to be?
Who's this impostor inside me?
    Sebastiana Alexandra Moncada

Depression Of Love

Love is the colour of heart-warming red
But when it goes all wrong, it tastes like lead
with the smell of depression in the air,
you feel like your life is not to share.
With the look on your face as it lets you down,
in the quiet, still room, there is no sound.
You feel like your life has all gone wrong,
but really it's just hard and long.
    Yvonne Costello

Good

A boy gives love, another gives hate.
First boy is early,
Second boy is late.
One boy likes reading,
Two boy to fight.
Which boy is wrong?
Is the other boy right?

Good boy has parents, bad boy has none.
Good boy hates gambling
Bad boy's just won.
Good boy is crying,
Bad boy will not.
Which boy to heaven?
Is the other boy to rot?

Dead boy is leaving,
Which will it be?
Good boy deserves it. Can you not see?
For the world is a place,
For the bad boy to be.
The good boy is in heaven, where else would he be?
    Ian Cook

Colours

Drops of water falling from a waterfall,
Like sparkling diamonds in the sun,
Smashing as they hit the lake at the bottom,
Forming a rainbow which reaches high into the sky,
With blinding colours such as bright reds, oranges,
blues and greens,
Which blend together to make a cascade of colours,
Soon they disappear as the sun fades,
Leaving nothing but darkness,
Then the stars start dancing around the moon,
Glistening with happiness.
The moon sends down its rays of light,
Which light up the whole city,
But soon the sun reappears, and brings back
the bright colours of day.
    Emma Milton

Blue

An eye that strikes revenge is blue with rage,
Sky in a cage of pollution is blue,
My crayon is blue, I colour without any disturbance,
My hair has blue streaks of dye down the middle.

Verse 2
Blue is the colour of my cat
Strange it sounds!
But no that's the way it was found,
Blue is the colour of the
Poisonous rain,
Blending in with the wind.

Lesley Tuplin

Kiss In Time

He looked down into my eyes,
And whispered those words,
That sounded like the heavenly song of the morning birds
His touch was so warm,
His embrace gentle yet tight,
I let him hold me, I did not fight.

I wanted time to stop,
The moment to last forever.
I didn't want him to leave my arms, never.
The kiss was sweet and soft,
Full of feeling;
I knew with what emotions I was dealing.

Then the kiss ended
But we still held into each other.
He held me like the baby in the arms of its Mother.
As we held each other's gaze
And my heart began to soar,
I knew right then we were destined for more!

Taryn Norman

The Third Planet

A wind that only blows a wisp of breath a tragic
feel of bewilderment, the earth is stopped to
make the scene of beauty lost, forever dreamed.

Birds no longer fly above its crest to sing
their songs of wonder, no heaven on this
earth shall be found as man's footprints have
stamped it out.

As the heartbeat truly gone, the passion left it
sighs, to create that once promised paradise,
or should it give in to let the darkness win.

A rolling ball of blackness comes, threatening
to engulf a tired but once proud globe.
"Oh if only", it whispers in the bitter breeze,
a flicker of light, it might have justified, if
only man had left it dream a while.

"Could this have been too much to ask", too late,
for now it takes the chosen path, all memories
faded lost and gone forever, as it explodes
beneath its sun . . .

Gertrude Beacham

Time!

The twisting hills of time have gone,
the disappearing earth could soon be no more.
Please stop destruction, it hurts the world so much,
poverty, death and war.

Throw away your life,
if you don't really want it.
But for once, think of the people that have to,
because the end of their path of life, is not lit.

Past, present, future,
history, now and after.
Each one of these needs sorting out,
so then we can get back to a life of joy and laughter.

Rebecca Coulton

The Earth

This is a poem of another time.
It's going to be hard to make it rhyme.

It begins before monkey developed to man
And even before the dinosaur ran.
It begins at the beginning when things started to grow.
Not a soul on the earth had begun to show.

First came the sun and the moon to make day.
Then later the sea and the land came to stay.
But the thing we like best, the best of it all,
Was when the weather was made and the rain came to fall.

The rain on the land made little green shoots.
These shot to the sky and made underground roots.
Some of the plants stayed small near the land.
These plants could grow anywhere, some even in sand.

But then came the really great things on the earth.
These were the living and started from birth.
They were the animals, none exactly the same.
Different types with a different name.

They didn't live peacefully together for long,
Because when people were made it all went wrong.

Lindsey Hobson

Dream World

The wild wind blowing in the never-ending sky,
The flowers moving with a twinkle in the eye.
The whispering water flowing in the clear blue stream,
Like a shimmering mirror, with a natural gleam.

A spirit that soars,
My imagination emerges higher above,
For no-one can capture the bird of life and dreams,
As it flies high, with the prospect of love.

The innocence and truth of the dreamer's dream
Shall forever dwell in thy heart.
For that world, so much different than this,
Can never be torn savagely apart.

This world has no wars, no fight for money or power,
It is constituted of truth, justice, and peace.
Its horses and deer all run wild,
Not afraid of the human race.

There is no anger, hatred or jealousy,
But love, hope, and charity.
This is my dream world, of which I dream about.
I only wish it was a reality.

Onjali Bodrul

My Girls

I sit in my cottage on a hill,
Tears are forming, threatening to spill.
What I would give to see my girls.
Instead the tears fall like pearls.

Thinking of the laughing ways, in which
My Steffi played and strayed,
Vanda so lovely, small and dark,
with devilish eyes, so warm they spark.

I miss those loving faces that are mine,
now vague memories, like mulled red wine.
But wait, there's also Janie's giggle!
as on my knee she used to wiggle.

All my girls, all three are great,
But off went two, to emigrate.
The other followed like a sheep.
leaving me here to brood and weep.

I close my eyes and see their faces,
just one thought and my heart races.
Please come back and be with me,
You funny, loving, happy three.

Janina Boyce

164

Out In The Storm

The howling rain had soaked my cold, wet feet
But now I warm them by the fire, basking in the heat.

The swirling wind threw the leaves and chilled me to the bone,
But there was just nowhere to hide - out in the storm, alone.

Lightning cracked across the sky - a hundred forks of light,
And all the fires in the world couldn't glare so bright.

Thunder rumbled through the air just like an orchestra sounding,
Or almost like the panicked sound of a thousand hearts pounding.

And so I was out in the storm on that cold, wet night
But now I'm finally back at home, safe within the light.

Gregory Tate

Another Mother's Son

The scales of illusion have fallen from my eyes
I see things as they are now and suddenly, I rise
I cross now to the window where a man is lying dead
His brains are on the floor and there's a bullet through his head.
He came here tonight to kill me, in a typical vengeful way
To make me another victim of the bloody IRA
But I was warned about his coming and bought myself a gun
Now here he lies - dead, alone - just another mother's son.

Did he see himself as glorious, in his maniacal way?
Furthering the cause for 'good' that maims and kills today?
Did 'they' tell him it was duty to rob me of my life?
When killings are so common here and brutality is rife?
I must flee now back to England and begin my life again
Where the accent is not Irish and crime is so more sane
As for him? His life is over, before it had begun
And here he lies - dead, alone - just another mother's son.

Susan Jane

The Land Called Nod

Go to sleep—close your eyes, drift away—fantasize.
The fairies will be there—to hold your hand,
They'll take you to Nod—the sleepy land.
Where clouds of marshmallow—are all soft and light,
And curious music—plays all through the night.
Where pastel colours—are floating around,
And all pretty bubbles—glide down to the ground.
Then you see rivers—all sparkling and blue,
There's no-one else here—just the fairies and you.
There's a sweet smell of strawberries—wherever you go,
The temperatures lovely—and there's no wind to blow.
You try to hold on—as it all slips away,
But then you wake up and find that it's day.

Rebecca Forsyth

The Tales Of An Average Man

"It was gloriously fought", is easy to say
The unmerciful battles, from day to day
And through all this fighting, on air, sea
    and land
There comes the story of an average man.
One, average man, on one average day
Started a game He knew not how to play
But like every soldier, Brave and proud
"Let's fight for our country", they would
    shout out loud
But whilst underground, in meter deep
    trenches
In his hand, a photo he clenches
He longs to be home, by his cosy warm fire
Away from the mud, the blood and the mire
The wife he left, the kids lay so small
He picks up his feet, and leaves it all
He runs over the trench, into no man's land
He screams to the world, as he makes his last stand.

Andrew S. Knox

Sweet Dream

Sing little sweet bird, Sing a song for me,
Tweet little sweet bird, Tweet a song for me,
Spread them wings and fly so high, Touch the heaven in the sky.
Come here little sweet bird, let me hold your wings,
Take me with you, let me feel the breeze.
I'll hold your tail, and you flap your wings,
Away we go on an adventurous dream.

Oh look little sweet bird there's an eagle over there,
Oh come little sweet bird, let's see its nest of eggs,
Spread them wings and fly so high, and meet the eagle in the sky.
Flying through the breeze with so much ease,
Tranquillity has been achieved.

See little sweet bird, the trees down there,
See little sweet bird, the different coloured earth,
Spread them wings and fly down low, find a place and I'll let go.
Thanks little sweet bird, for the loan of your wings,
And the greatest dream of any dreams.

George Tokkallos

Just Stop

Every time I'm on a high,
Something goes quite wrong,
I look in the mirror and say to myself,
"This has been happening for far too long".

My parents split when I was five,
My sister was just one,
For children who were as young as us,
Divorce is not much fun.

It's not much fun at any age,
But I could not understood,
Why my Daddy had left me all alone,
With no one to hold my hand.

As I grew up I understand,
Why my Daddy had to go,
Life would have been bad if he hadn't have gone,
And that we all now know.

I just want things to get better now,
And lead a normal life.
I want to stop this aching feeling,
That in my back is a knife.

Verity Holloway

Zoo

On a visit to the local zoo
Impression from the animal's point of view

The Ocelot gets cross a lot
So does the thick skinned Rhinoceros
All the Camels have the hump
The Kangaroos refuse to jump
The Hyena hasn't laughed in years
A Crocodile cries real tears
A Chimpanzee with tight clenched fist
Sees a Gorilla dream of far off mist
A Leopard sees spots before its eyes
Or are they burnt out Fireflies?
The Eagle can no longer soar
The Lion has no need to roar
Storks and Cranes seem in a flap
Sea lions no longer clap
Flamingos don't feel in the pink
A Skunk thinks he'll kick up a stink
And was the taming of the Shrew
A necessary thing to do?

Michael Rowe

Cornwall

I am the Shore. I am the Wind
That lifts the sea gulls' wings.
I am the Sea. That Light far out
Beyond the shore is me.

I am the sinking sun at Mullion Cove,
Streaking in blood and gold.
I am the Afterglow. I am
The ebb and flow of the Eternal Sea.

The warm earth rests upon my stony heart,
The bones that pierce my skin are iron made.
I fly the storm that bends the oak,
Those granite teeth am I.

I am the Rage between the Land and Sea.
The sea that beat upon my ancient rocks
Saw Earth emerging from Infinity -
Each fleeting wave a second out of time,
Each year, another thousand years to be.

Patricia Pope

The Lonely Place

My heart is my lonely place,
Where rushing corpuscles run
over lumps and bumps.
The thump thumping of drums.

This is the best place on Earth,
Nobody knows how to get there.
Peaceful and quiet,
My own secret place.

I have always dreamt of a place like this,
were there's always sunrise,
Always red.
A fire burning

Rosie Bufton

The Mind

The mind is a weird and wonderful thing
Storing the problems that life will bring
Keeping those thoughts at the back of your head.
Reminding you of all you've done and said
Sometimes you wish they would just go away
Start with a clear head every day
But that thought arises again and again
It will go away, the question is when?
When another worry starts to gnaw at your brain
Another attempt to drive you insane.

Sharon McConville

Breaking Up

Both you and I knew that it was great
It's not like to say that one year was fate.
We have a lot of good memories that can keep
   this relationship going,
We get along so well the river will keep on flowing.
I loved you a lot but I don't think you knew
If I hadn't spoken to you,
My day would be blue.
You used to make me feel so good
Every time we were together,
I really wanted us to be together forever.
I know I will always love you
And I know one day you'll find someone right
You think it's me,
But I know we'll forever fight.
Hopefully one day we'll give it another go
We'll both be mature and older, and our feelings
   will always show.
I'll be thinking of you even when we depart
I love you so much,
I wish we had another start!

Xhola McKoy

Spring's Here—No Need To Fear

Lambs are born,
So fluffy and white,
They're jumping about,
So lively and bright.
Tulip, daffodils growing strong.
Listen to the birds,
Listen to the song.
Can you hear the song of spring,
And the bright colours it brings.
Folded buds and blossom on trees
Hooray! We've got rid of the winter freeze.
It comes once a year,
Now it is near,
Winter is no longer here,
So there's no need to fear.

Rachel Copeland

Ralph's Cross: North York Moors

Through the canopy of cloud
filter fine drizzle cools a warm cheek
and glistens the dull tarmac.

Tomb-like grey mists
form into clinging shrouds
hushing the rising wind
which wails like a quartet of haunted flutes.

Sheep meekly cluster,
like pump oatmeal dumplings
whilst a canvas of Autumn shades
seek to embellish
the hard nakedness of the horizon.

Sacred Ralph's Cross
weeps forgiveness to the vandal.

Lynda A. Liddell

The River Wild

The Wild River runs wild
With the blood of us, it breathes
The air from the bowl of fire
Of hatred and greed.

Just like a hungry wolf
It pounds upon
The World's goodness and truth,
Gulping it down to all its need.

Splashing, dashing, gushing, thrashing,
Coming your way now in a speed.
Beware! Beware! It's a wild, wild river.
Wild as a river can be!

Shumaila Ali

The Antique

The very fact that you are old,
Heightens your value, in my eyes
Rounded corners, smooth to touch, solid,
Representing permanency in this
Uncertain world.

If only you could tell
Your absorbed experiences,
Received alongside polishings,
The good times, the bad.

Yet, you have weathered all.
Silent, sure proof of past,
Speaking only in evidence
With your very presence.

Possessing you, I am possessed
With senses of security.
Your creator, long gone, I respect,
Preserve you, for posterity.

Pauline Boncey

The End

A blackened cloud engulfs me I cannot see the light.
My hands and feet are bound with grief
I have no strength to fight.
Sorrow wrapped around me no warmth within its hold.
Just darkness where the light should be
and loneliness and cold.

Thoughts for other people, or myself are meaningless,
purity devoured I only want to rest.
Memories of happiness are many miles away,
to those I love I leave behind, it would be wrong to stay.

I hold the blade before me recall that I've done wrong.
I ask God to forgive me then I realize that he's gone.

Relief at last engulfs me, I close my weary eyes,
but still I see before me, the woman, as she dies.

Lindsay Mason

A Lover Dreams Of His Hopes For Love

Love is a gift, not a word
Lightly given and thrown around
Hoping 'twill alight, who knows where,
On some unwitting soul who crushes it to ground.

Loving is a vital living dream,
Delicate as a flower petal
That once was but a seed
Planted by nature and flowering at natures need.

Love grows strongly in the heart
But cannot there remain, having no purpose,
For true love needs the warmth of another's kiss
And the sweet soft touch of celestial bliss.

When love is truly proffered, press it gently to your breast
For true love grows from heart to heart,
And growing, ends doubt and troubled rest.

Take this love I offer dearest one,
Freely given and ever hoping that sometime, maybe,
You in your turn will speak the words I long to hear,
For trust and faith go hand in hand with love,
Allows no doubt and binds two hearts in sweet surrender.

Edgar Wall

Polo Fields

I'll tell you who I am
When bleak English wind creeps under my skin
Claiming ownership
claiming to tell truths

When turgid throes of thought rush into my brain
Begging to fester
Claiming epitome

When impartial veils of the vain
Flower beneath the heat
Boasting usurped genes
Shrilling blood
          life
          love
When simple unassuming lives
settled by the park
Hesitate to request importance

I'll tell you who I am
Of sweetened milky teas
Of loving flies gathered
Flattened sands
Of Polo fields
breads
quiet nights
And the solitude of neighings

Layla Dasmal

Red Squirrels In The Park

Red squirrel in the park
Where do you lay your head after dark
Is it in the branch or in the dray
Oft I have wondered where you lay
You flit from tree to tree
Collecting food for Winter's chill
when days are short and food is nil
Heaven sends us your presence full of glee
When Spring arrives your babies are free
Chasing up and down the tree
I hope the day will never be
When red squirrels aren't around
For us to see

Ellen Oakley

Living In Hope

Johnny sits on street corners
From morning until dusk
He's tried and failed for legitimate work
So now he has to busk

His life is hard, he's sleeping rough
Through no fault of his own
All he has is his old guitar
But you never her him moan

Brought up in poverty, he struggles on
He knows no other life
But he wants to change and find a job
And maybe one day, a wife

But no one will take the time to look
At the man inside this shell
His scruffy clothes make folk shy away
So he lives in his quiet hell

But he'll carry on as best he can
Although it maybe in vain
He's a decent man under this disguise
But will he ever live again?

Susan Prescott

War!

War is unfair, victims are killed without a care.
A bullet whizzes passed your head
And ends up in someone's bed.
Can't they just agree on a peace treaty
Crawling through the mud drenched
with sweat, tears, and blood.
Hate is in the air; no smiles on faces just glares.
What have they to gain except pain.
Peace is what we need.
Give us peace, please!

Kerry-Anne Moulder

The Heart Of The Matter

I'd loved you when we left for moments few
Controlled, and hidden secret glances, brew
Of passion warmth, enough to give no game away.

I'd lost you some weeks, to test
By separated, feeling fantasy's haze,
Or was it real this mind-engulfing craze?

And seeing you again we knew that something sweet
Happened, brown eyes met and what was said
Was not the message left nor lasting laid.

I cannot hope, nor let me further go
I suffocate my need for you and pleasure throw
For others need us too so much you know.

In early time youth's years I would have
Worshipped, courted, moved to get to know
And far too late, time's shifted love too slow!

Mike Morrison

Letting Go

The girl sits on the rocks,
And stares down at her reflection in the pool.
Plain hair, pale face,
Her eyes filled with tears.

Her eyes filled with tears,
She allows to fall.

The girl sits on the rocks,
And listens to the seagulls' raucous cries.
Calling and screaming,
Teased by the wind.

Teased by the wind,
She watches them fly.

The girl sits on the rocks,
Her head filled with thoughts of the family she knew.
She smiles for their mem'ry,
But weeps for her loss.

She weeps for her loss,
But that love remains true.

Hannah Fitz-Gibbon

Don't Go To War

As soon as the news 'bout the War had come,
I was there: Helping to fight the Hun!
What glory, what honour did I think I would gain
In being in that hell, in Satan's domain?

The people they said "Yes, we'll come and fight!"
But the ones branded cowards were the ones that were right.
I was young, I was foolish, but I thought I was grand
Now I lie in this barren and accursed land.
War is immoral - war is insane. I shall never fight again.
I think it's a devil - I know it's a fraud.
The generals give medals, the people applaud.
But what's in it for me, now I'm alone,
Just lying in earth, just dreaming of home?

I tell you young soldiers, young bravehearts you all.
Don't go to war. Don't fight no more.
Don't think of the glory - just think of the pain
And all the things you won't see again.

I used to be a soldier,
But now I float in mist.
A bullet through my head, a peace-note in my fist.

Brenda E. Hole

Patterns Of Life

Life starts with sunshine, light and love
It grows and grows and touches our soul.
The pain and laughter, tears and sorrow,
Are part of the patterns of life

Sweet smell of flowers, the taste of wine
The erotic touch of tenderness to the skin
A kiss, a tear on a woman's cheek
Are part of the patterns of life

Growing tall, staying small feeling cruel.
Break the rules fall in love, hurt your heart
Talk in riddles or make sense tell the truth
Are part of the patterns of life

Learn to listen, know when to talk
Take your first steps, go the wrong way, start to walk
Hold back your feelings keep them hidden
Are part of the patterns of life

Feel love and heartache, laughter and pain
Show your feelings to each other again and again
Hold out your hands, take what life throws out
Are part of the patterns of life.

Diane Hall

Beach Tears

Beach tears muffled by the sound of waves,
Splashing and crashing against the cliffs,
Where the eagle sits,
Waiting, maybe watching,
As water laps the shore.

Wet sand stings the cuts,
And the tears get louder.
Dark clouds overhead
Beckon a storm,
The eagle watches on.

As the lightening bolts,
And dashes,
The eagle flies, leaving her nest,
Her home... her place...
To shelter in a crack.

A crack, just slight,
And out of sight,
But sheltered,
Sheltered from the sound,
The sound of death.

Eva Christy

Destiny

As you stood there
The wind running blissfully through your golden hair
Gazing into the beautiful sunset
All alone and still
I imagined my destiny
My love for you and only you
And I wonder if there is still a space left in your heart
for me
But as our lips met for the first time
I realized it was to be
Yes my love for thee.

Fergus Dunne

Silence

It waits to claim me,
Stealthy, caressing,
Beating through the barriers of my drums
With feather pulses of strength.
Once inside,
The dull roar and shrill scream
Drench the fibrous interior
Of my skull
And chill roots embed in the walls
Of my consciousness.

Lucia Rae

Why He Chose Me, Why He Chose You

He chose me to bear a child who could not hear
At times this seemed too much to bear
Bad news to come, much more to unfold
'His brain is damaged', I was told.

There was more pain I must endure
The Healer sought 'Please find a cure'
I loved the child, there was no doubt
'It is not fair', I used to shout.

Years passed by, the child a man
Has found too that now he can
Encourage others to help and care
For many like him and to share.

My nagging pain was clear to You
You took my hand and led me through.
The young who care for him now ask
'How did you face such an awful task?'

I say to them 'Just look and you will find
A wisdom to see beyond the crippled mind
And answers clear will shine right through
Why He chose me. Why He chose you.'

Eileen St. John Crees

The Bird

Waiting. Peaceful. In search of prey.
  Looking for a new dawn, to come its way.
    Stands tall, with confidence, patience in mind,
      all the new wonders it could someday find.
        Never to learn, yet always to know,
          Never to have been, yet always will go.
            Never to fly, yet swift like the wind
              Trapped in a prison and always within.
                Many a visitor,
                 but none to meet,
                Many a family
                  Yet not to greet,
                Trapped in a prison and always within,
              Never to fly, yet swift like the wind
            Powerless and yet sharp like a knife . . .
          Never knowing the freedom of life
        All the new wonders it could someday achieve
  no family, no friends, no visitors, to believe.
Waiting. Peaceful. In search of prey,
looking for a new dawn, to come its way.

Gemma Hewitt

Prayer Of Any Wife

Lord, let his heart incline to mine, and make
Him true for Love - and not for Pity's Sake;
And if his fancies ever start to roam,
(As men's thoughts will), let him remember Home!

Not as four walls where Duty bids him stay,
But as a haven at the close of day;
Let not the circle of his wedding ring,
A sense of shackles or of bondage bring.

As years creep on, and we are growing old,
And youth is like a tale that has been told;
May he, in little sons and daughters, see
Some likeness of that girl I used to be!

And in the features of each precious face,
Find what he loved in me of grace and charm;
And last of all, dear Lord, till this life ends,
Let us walk, hand in hand, the truest friends!

Katie Darrah Pundole

Ode To Hell

Pulsating feelings, emotions collide,
Wanton valleys where shadows hide.
Demons and devils collect at the end
Of the ravenous pit where you will descend.

Fear of frustration, jealousy and greed,
On these emotions, evil does breed.
Nothing but evil exists in this land,
The fear in your eye as death takes your hand.

Suffering in silence, so it seems,
Listen to the atmosphere engulfed in screams.
Pain and torture, the demons desire,
Shadows contort profusely in fire.

Crime and violence await you here,
Confront the Devil and your fear.
Then question your victory, have you really won?
Your eternal life in hell has finally begun.

Diana Elizabeth Keen

The Traced Heart

As we drove home, along the Dead End road,
the cold iced up the van.
With the hand that wasn't attached to his
I drew a heart.
Within that Heart I placed Initials,
mine tenderly with his.
As the van heated up, the heart was erased.
Our love would not be erased as we had lived, we had loved,
We had loved each other.

Amy Watts

Places

There are places I have been to,
and filled my wildest dreams,
I've been to see Niagara Falls
also the Taj Mahal.
I've also seen the pyramids, and climbed Mount Everest,
I've scuba dived and swum with Dolphins by my side
I've been to visit Africa and seen animals all free,
I've gone down to Hawaii and eaten coconuts all day
And lain beneath the palm trees and watched the palm leaves sway,

I've even been a flyer and gone up in a balloon,
and watched a lovely sunset.
And sat beneath the moon.
I've rode a big black horse in a rodeo
and skied down a mountain side.
And watched a wild west show.
I've ridden on a camel
And sailed the seas with Captain Hook.
and all this have I done,
within the pages of a book.

Hazel Webb

Brixham

I stand on the cliff admiring the view stretched out before me.

The sea is calm, quietly calm;
Only the silent lap of the waves on the pebbles.
I feel no breeze, breaking the tranquillity.
The air is melting on the horizon in a distant haze.
The sun, though, is as an elf dancing on my back,
Its pointed toes, prickling the nylon of my swimming costume,
The heat radiates pleasantly through my body,
Sparking off my outer senses.

A salty reminiscence, tastes in the air.
And the clamour of sea gulls, the wingbeat of fury, plays
above my head.

Glancing across to the beach, it is half-empty
Too early for the common society.
Only the peaceful swimmers, gliding through the quiescent water,
Forming patterns in the diamond-streaked surface,
Not wanting to come back, from their refreshing
Other world, away from noise and trauma.

A ferry roams across the backdrop of blue, its destination
certain, and undisturbed.

As I stand on the cliff, admiring the view stretched out before me,
No-one can pull me apart from my Brixham.

Emma Tatnall

Meeting Of Forbidden Lovers

My princess breaks our embrace
As dawn finds us once more,
Its unmissed, vagabond sun
Then ogles at her gentle curves
Through the soft white negligee
That sways around her like a splendid flag,
And as she scrambles away to her formal residence
Across our meadow bed
Mingling with its roused incense
And receding sheets of mist
Becoming ghost-like,
Death stirs in me,
For Mind or not
I must now mingle with unworldly souls
And for hellish long hours Alas!
Till this new day's end
When alone in her chamber
And free from the nagging of her court,
The night of life
May escort her back to me.

Stewart Gemmill

Autumn

Autumn time is here again
The leaves are falling fast
Summer days are at an end
The sun shines in the past

Squirrels hunt for nuts and seeds
As they tumble to the ground
The leaves on trees which once were green
Have turned to shades of brown

Yes summer days are over now
Autumn time is here
Leaves are changing everyday
My favourite time of year

Lisa Stow

Friendship

I walked with him to help him start his journey home,
He preferring company of sky and tree,
To diesel fumes and apathy.

We didn't say a lot, didn't need to speak at all;
Our minds were quiet sufficiency, a union of sentiment
And love, fused long ago in plenary communion and reverie.

So at the bend I stood and watched his loneliness recede;
Leaving mine to sour and spoil;
I saw the hesitation, then his arm upraised in salutation,
His Au Revoir held in silhouette against the winter sky;

And thought . . .
Dear God, if he should go now; if he should die,
If he should die . . .

This final canvas will display forever in the gallery of my mind,
An etching from a point in time recurring,
A broken stylus scratching endlessly . . .

If he should die—if he should die . . . ,
He would stand forever painted in the sky,
A small sad figure in the dusk, held for all eternity . . .
And I could stare, and cry, and cry . . .

Frank Dickinson

Death

Death, no-one knows,
no one knows what is, or isn't,
I sit here sometimes wondering whether it's all
worth it,
faith in one hand, doubt in the other,
what do I do,
no other way out;
happy and free at last.

M. Mateer

Dreams

Each night in my dreams we share all our love.
I think you've been sent from heaven above.
We run though the sand
By the sparkling blue sea.
In all my dreams it's just you and me.
Face to face. It feels so good.
you have been sent from heaven above.
You and I are meant to be.
It will happen one day my dream will come true.
So I hope soon you will notice me please.
We'll be together forever and ever.
Until then I must keep dreaming my dreams.
Then I wake up in the early morn.
It was a dream, you are not by my side.
We no longer kiss to the sound of the tide.
I need to hold you to kiss you all night.
And when we get together I know our love will be right.
So come on and notice me soon.
My dreams are meant to be lived,
And not to stay dreams.

Michelle Edwards

A Living Tree

My eyes are homes for squirrels, owls and insects too.
My hair is luscious, fresh and green, a huge, huge canopy.
My hands hold many wonders like bee-hives and birds.
Fungi grow up my neck, to them I'm their home.
Animals of all sorts live in my hair.
Squirrels live inside just like loads of bugs.
Ants crawl up and down carrying all they need.
Insects nibble at my hair eating all they want.
Smaller plants grow in my ears and up my nose.
Why should people cut me down?

Andrew R. Pond

The Agéd Mariner

He sits beside the gently-murmuring sea
Across the Bay his wistful eyes are cast
As turning o'er the leaves of memory
He muses on those scenes forever past.
No more for him the circuit of the seas
Nor distant lands where dusky tribes reside.
Old age constrains him to a life of ease
Content in narrow confines to abide
Moored to his Island home, no more to wage
A truceless warfare with the truculent flood,
Now in the twilight of life's pilgrimage
He calmly waits the summons of his God,
Till death's dark cruiser berths along the stage
And the Grand Pilot signals him aboard!

William Teare

Let Me Be Me

Love has been, love has gone,
Sadness took its place.
No matter what I do,
Love never stays for long.

Is it me or is it them?
I have asked so many times,
Trying hard to be
What other people want.

Many years I fault myself,
It started as a child,
Why can't you be like? Why can't you be like?
Was always the plaintive cry.

God made me as I am, I love to be helpful and kind,
Yet no matter what I do,
I never receive the love I crave,
Love me as I am please!
I am tired of trying to be
Another human being,
That isn't really me.

Monica Phelan

Magic

The magical smile of your own first born, so innocent and
pure, perfect and sure,
That in your arms, his safety is held, while your hearts bond
together with that invisible weld.
He'll test your aggression to see if it's real, he'll test out your
patience with the mischief he deals.
He'll break your heart harshly, then mend it with a hug, he'll
cherish all your loving, at your heart strings he'll tug.
Your wisdom is boring, so often it's not right, throughout all
His childhood you're square, out of sight.
You don't understand him, you don't want to care, you never tried
To help him, you were never really there.
Ungrateful and selfish, 'til they grow older too, when they
realize the hurt that they put you through.
But they'll pay back with interest, the love, the sweat and the
care, and then they'll remember the times that you shared.
He'll go on to love another, to stay with to the end, and
cherish his first born, for whom he can tend, with a smile
Just like magic so innocent and pure, of this there's no
guessing, of this I am sure.

Martin Horsefield

The Dung Heap

I was looking for a dung heap,
To cool my fevered brow.
But I looked to God when the going got steep
And now life ain't such a cow.

I went looking for a Saviour,
All clothed in shining white,
But I found a baby in a manger
And above him bright star light.

I came, I knelt, I wept, he smiled
At me, at ox, and ass, and ewe
He touched, though I was so defiled,
And my soul trembled - it was true.

I was looking for everything bad,
Bitching and biting, fallen from grace
I was weary, and worn, and sad,
But I found love in a Saviour's face.

Daphne W. Canning

James' Dragon

There was a boy called James,
He had a dragon with a name,
His dragon was called Ivor.

The dragon was a green dragon,
But had a bad temper, and roared,
If the dragon didn't come when called, little James bawled.

He (the dragon) flew like a rocket,
Then he choked on a sprocket,
And flew into a wall in Nantucket.

G. Lane

Pernicious End

Deeper and deeper
His evil lust and impurity
thrills him
His name IS Putrid
And how he loves to smirk.

She feels numb
But still she can summon a scream
He is motivated
by her pure fear
And how it makes him chuckle.

She peers down - SHE is scared
He *stares* down - he is thrilled
as she pours the 'claret' from her chest
The contrast is complete.

How he loves his 'odd' fortune
But how she hates her barren end.

Jessica Brown

Autumn Beach

Deserted now, and left for winter to enjoy,
With savage wind, all trace of Humans to destroy.

Different now, when cars no longer queue the mile,
Migrating Man has sought his winter domicile.

How silent now, the mournful seagull makes his cry,
No other voice, just winter's stormy lullaby.

Sun weakens now, reluctantly it loses power,
The days grow cold, and nights grow longer by the hour.

So distant now, to mariners' eyes a misty line,
Hard to recall, the golden sand and summer fine.

So hostile now, the sea is grey and rough and mean,
So strange the change, to what in summer days had been.

So empty now, the shuttered chalets watch the sea,
The season's passed, and all that's left is memory.

W. G. Prince

Wasted Life

The streets are very long and noisy,
With children running wild,
As they wickedly stare at you.
There is no one there for them,
No Mothers, no Fathers to look up to.
Trashing the bins just for fun,
Oh what a shame.
What innocence has gone to waste.
What tragedy, who's to blame?

Wasted Life.
Society has given up on them.
People see them as nothing but trouble.
From a seed came a stem, from that stem came branches.
Without love and care they will simply fade away and die.
Give them a chance, let them grow.
Show them the way and they will follow.

Kelvin Abraham

Broken Glass

Now I know exactly where I belong,
I'm not proud that I was wrong,
The truth is hard to take,
I always thought that our relationship could never break,
I tried to hold on to you forever,
I tried taking it slow and tough,
Even when you got rough,
You just might regret it one day,
But then you'll be the past of my life, and to you I'll have
nothing to say,
All the dreams I ever had,
Have all faded away like footprints in the sand,
It's hard for me to see a cheerful tomorrow,
As so far I've lived my life in sorrow,
It ended with a simple stroke of pen,
Oh, it ended with a simple stroke of pen.

A. Bains

Summer Holiday

I like the summer holidays
I like going out to play
In the lovely weather
And when it starts to get dark
I have to go inside
When it turns to morning
Another new day starts

And then it's time to go back to school
The summer holidays passed so quickly
But I get to see my friend again.

Simon Evans

What Love!

What kind of fruit is this, that I have eaten from?
What kind of love is this, that just goes on and on?
Growing and astounding me more each day
With a beauty that transcends all other,
Yet—it pierces my heart more sharply than a sword?
I cry out! Not knowing why.
There's pain and pleasure,
Bound inextricably together,
In a joy that rises from a source so deep within
Yet beyond the farthest recesses of my mind.
I cannot understand it,
The core of my desire,
This all-consuming fire,
And the remains of what I once held dear, lie there before me,
Turned to ash:-
I stretch my hand,
I reach to touch the flame
Drawn magnetically by its brilliance.
Oh! How it burns
And yet—I cannot now draw back!

Di Rogers

Sunset

The golden sun is sinking in the West,
This day with warmth and beauty has been blessed
A burnished path emblazoned on the sea,
Way of the viking, when his soul was free.

Earths's rim stands out against the sinking beams,
Now all has gone, 'tis if I had but dreamed,
I look above, the sky is dark and deep,
The night is here, it's time for all to sleep.

The darkness wraps me in its cold embrace,
The sun has gone, yet still is in its place.
The World goes round, yet Earth and I are one,
We're on our way to meet the shining Sun.

J. Jenkin

The Next Millennium

In the next millennium I woke up
It wasn't nineteen ninety-six anymore
Everything was destroyed by war
They had been burnt
Robot soldiers roam the city
On little buzzing buggies

There isn't much in the next millennium
Just destruction, war and fighting
Everywhere you look there's something bad happening
I don't like it much in the next millennium

In the next millennium there are no humans there
Just robots destroying everywhere
In the next millennium destruction's in the air
In the next millennium no one gives a care

Michael Francis

Life Force

She rises each morning from the East,
like a giant fire-breathing beast,
and sets each night majestically in the West,
In a kaleidoscope of colours is by far the best.

Warmth and heat she exudes each day,
bringing warmth to the people and life to the hay,
the very North she shines only slightly,
but in the South burns far more brightly.

Only one celestial ball she works with well,
the other spheres she treats like hell,
and turns her back on others showing no warmth at all.

Her daily routine lasts million of years,
bringing joy to some hearts but to others brings tears,
at night she lights the stars like candles high,
in daylight hours stands proud in the sky.

Without her we would not be here,
but like a beautiful beast she must not get too near
She watches us all and is worshipped by some
full of fire and mystery that's the secret of our sun.

Carl Scaife

The Dream Catcher

Made to hang above our beds
A net of brightly coloured threads
Adorned with beads and cast off feathers
To this our nightly dreams are tethered
Set within a birch twig frame
It has but only one real name
The Dream Catcher

Most souls dream and then forget
Or recall only parts, frustratingly, yet
To remember the who, or the where, or the when
Would give satisfaction, relief even then
But to find the way? To unlock the door?
The key is in Red Indian lore
To bring back those dreams that go round in your head
Just hang a dream catcher over your bed

J. M. Young

A Lesson Too Late

As the rain drenched the pavement around him,
The man with no coat shook his head.
What ill luck, he mused, of a truth I've been used.
A man so rich mere months ago
Must now beg bread from friends and foe.
Why did he believe her, he dared to think,
Her love came, and his money went in less than a wink.
Her friends warned him off,
But he preferred to scoff.
A man who made policies in his time
Now finds himself without a dime.
But experience is without doubt a great teacher,
A fact he discerned just after he lost her.
He looked up to heaven, and back down to earth,
Thinking to himself, just what is man worth?
If such frailties will destroy a man thus,
Can we say without doubt that life is just?
But his fate's his own making and no favour he's asking.
He knows for a fact, his cross he must bear,
All part of the plan of life's wear and tear.

A. Casim Andrews

Our Son

We adored you the moment we saw you
A love so strong and so pure,
We held you with such admiration
Goodbye to the way that we were.

The pain when you were unhappy,
Was our pain and our joy when you weren't
We guided and taught you the right ways,
We were joyful and proud if you learnt.

Your future was lying before you
Like a white sheet of driven snow,
We warned you to watch how you tread it
For every step would surely show.

Though sometimes you never would heed us,
We grew angry and cross and felt hurt.
We forgave you for each misdemeanour
And prayed it would turn out alright.

Though hearts have ached over the years dear,
Immense feelings of love always won
Each milestone we've mastered whatever
We will love you forever, our son.

Judith Tye

Divided..... No Divide

Divided by the River Mersey,
A road bridge spans the two towns easy,

Widnes is Northside, born in Lancashire,
Runcorn South, since olden times of Cheshire,

The River is not the only Divide,
Why we all differ, no one can decide,

But... one cold winter night;
With not a star in sight;

Families came from far and near;
Young, old, with good cheer;

Bands played, folk danced, roads closed in each direction,
Police and everyone, all, with lots of affection,

Traffic stopped; Road Bridge cleared; all lights out,
Oh!... Fireworks, Laiser Lights, what a sight,

Once again utter darkness;
Suddenly after brightness;

His Worship the Mayor then pressed a switch,
"Our Bridge", floodlit, all without a hitch,

We all felt so happy, warm, with goodness inside,
In that wonderful moment, there was... no Divide.

Eunice Davies

Absent Friend

Although the birds sing and the night is turning to day.
Sleep will offer no kind release, not however long I lay.
Your beautiful face and laughing eyes are all I see
And I say a quiet prayer that you are happy wherever you may be.
The crushing pain of knowing you are far away,
Will be with me throughout yet another day.
How I miss your kind words and tender touch.
Not hearing your happy voice is just too much.
You made me laugh, forgetting the serious me.
You made me feel more alive than I thought I could ever be:
You are such a special person my life was kissed,
And your kind friendship will be sorely missed

J. M. Smith

Trevor

I am not going to be morbid,
I don't wish to be blue
Just to tell you a few home truths
Trevor Davey is the love of my life
Whatever went wrong, he always put right
He was kind, thoughtful and true,
Trevor, my darling, I will never find another like you.
A father, a granddad, friend and mate we all knew,
He told me to tell you, be happy not blue
friends of my husband please try to do this
Then Trevor will sleep in his heavenly bliss
God bless you my darling in heaven above
You know when you left us, you went with my blessing and love.
Sleep well, Trevor Davey you're always in my heart,
The memory of you, I will never part,
Till we meet again in God's house above
We are thinking of you in thoughts and in love.
God bless you my darling Trevor Davey.
Rest in peace, Your Loving Wife, Anne, and family.

Anne Davey

Remembering A Dream. At The Age Of Fourteen

As I slowly walked by I saw two distant figures,
Motionless with each other in a tranquil embrace,
I knew I had seen them somewhere before,
Unexpectedly my heart began to race.

They stood out like coloured peacocks,
Prominent from a dull crowd for all to see,
Wearing nothing but admiration and splendour,
Oh how I wished that was me.

Walking away my heart felt desperation,
From my glazed eyes fell hopeful tears,
Before feeling curiosity of whom the figures are,
My dreams had erased confused fears.

My head turned for a fleeting moment,
Once more to gaze upon this silence before I leave,
The figures were of hope and creation,
They were of course Adam and Eve.

Feeling contented in another world,
My heart did fill with wonder of this dream,
My mind with peace amidst moments of sleep,
At this tender age of fourteen.

Rachel Liveley

Heavens The Place

Oh Grandma, oh Grandma
I love you so dearly and wish you were here
really, really, really.
But now you're out of the human race
I hear you say heaven's the place.
You made up poems sweet and sad
They were good and never bad
Although my visits were not always of great length
You made me think you gave me strength
but we now meet here today to say goodbye in no usual way
Grandma we'll always love you so
And although not here, we think you know

Claire Derry

Paradise Lost

Nobody listens as I call,
Nobody comes running,
Am I invisible?
Or do they give me a filthy look?
I cry and cry
But the feeling never disperses.
I've lost every real friend I dreamed of
Whilst growing up all my talents are
Drifting slowly into the wilderness.
Why do we lose everything we love
And keep the things that don't mean so much?
So life enters into the why
For the question why is stronger than man
It powers over us and sometimes makes us dull.

I am sad, are you?
Sometimes it makes you dream of floating into paradise
Without care life is peculiar, can you figure it out?
Life is just a mystery without a tale to tell.
Could this be the end or the beginning?
This life that we all live?

Claire Zalman

Dunblane

Twenty-eight children off to school,
No one can stop them it's a rule.
Man in hall, four guns in hand,
Shoots all the children down to the ground.
Sixteen dead children, twelve badly hurt,
One dead teacher wearing a blood-stained shirt.
Mothers crying, children too,
At the thought of it happening to me or you.
At nine thirty, a minute of silence,
And a thought of a world without any violence.
Helpless little children dead Why Them?
If guns aren't banned it will happen again.

Alison Francis

My Life

What can I say about my life?
Nothing much unless you include:
Bad relationships with boys, friends and family,
My sister's boyfriend, who I despise,
Listening to people's problems,
But they don't hear my cries,
Parents divorce, I was only four,
But memories remain of my father's force,
Whilst I sat and watched, unable to defend my mother, of course.
New friends every month, I'm trying to find the one
Who I can confide all my problems in,
But they still haven't come.
So I guess I'll keep all emotions inside,
Until arguments with my friends collide.
Then I'm back to the beginning again,
Building up every emotion,
With everyone giving their little contribution.
But I guess it will stay this way, never changing gears,
Until that one comes along, then I shall let out all my tears.

Katie R. Dearn

Andreas

If only I could see you just once and hold you tight
I'd give you all my love, I'd love with all my might
I'd ask you why you did it? Why did you go?
But that will never happen and I will never know
I really do love you, I know I should have said
But when I wanted to tell you I found out you were dead
I've still got all the letters, the photos and the cards
The memories we shared, the jokes and all the laughs.
I still come to see you and lay a rose by your head
Tell you that I need you and I wish you weren't dead
I know I shall see you up in heaven in the sky
But for now Andreas my love I can only say goodbye.

Lisa Frost

173

In The Depth Of Despair
(A Tribute To The Tiger Trust)

In the quiet stillness of the wilderness,
The antelopes eat unaware
Of the beautiful orange tigress,
As she seeks her prey with care,
The silky markings on her coat
Hiding her from view.

An antelope lifts its head,
Looks this way and that,
The tigress sees her chance and pounces,
Running across the land so flat.
Mother Nature casts her spell,
Man wins; he shoots it dead.

The orphaned tiger cubs watch forlorn,
As their only hope for survival
Is taken from them by man's evil hand,
And man's heart so cruel,
For he takes their lives too,
And much more than we'll ever know.

Natalie Jordan

Land Of The Dead

Far away is the land of the dead
Where mortal hope are ripped to shreds
Youth is dead, there is no fun
No shelter to hide, no place to run
When deathly sheeves have got their grip
A sea of loneliness, without a ship
Death sings its grim lullaby
The twisted words make weak men die
The ironic thing about the land of the dead
It is only found in a bitter man's head.

Allison Aldridge

Life Eternal

I lie not here beneath this stone.
I do not leave you all alone.
Take with you now, this peace on earth.
And celebrate my life, my birth.
I am the quiet, silent sound.
Hear my footprint on the ground.
Listen to the whispering breeze,
See dancing light on glistening trees,
A snowflake in a chilly night.
Hung poised, I watch you all, mid-flight.
Touch me, I'm the breath of spring.
A memory now in everything.
I lie not here beneath this earth.
This is my soul, my love, rebirth.

J. C. Dove

It's No Good Asking

I live in a silent world.
No one! Is interested in what I say
Empty words.
Meaningless—like a sun-drenched day.

I ask for help
A request for an ear
To listen to some problem or two
No one's there, no human form
Can help me as you do.

I'll say no more
My thoughts are my own
I'll not share them easily again
I have no fear, no inward threat
You'll never cause me pain

You just don't know how to give to me
Just support me just one time
No! You're wrapped up in your own embrace
For you! That must be fine.

Adrienne Jenkin

When Autumn Comes Christmas Comes To

When Autumn comes, the wind comes too, bringing the rain with it,
The leaves come down and whirl around, all around the ground.
Now winter's moving in, nights are getting dimmer,
The snow comes shortly afterwards, and suddenly turns to ice.
The traffic slows down as the wind blows harshly.

As fires come on, lights appear, glowing around the town,
The glistening window displays are changed from autumn to winter.
Now Christmas is becoming clearer to the eye,
Large trees are appearing everywhere with multi coloured decorations hung on.
The tinsel glitters in the doorways of the shops in town.

More people are coming into the towns shopping around for gifts,
Christmas lists are appearing round the homes.
Children run around with large smiles on their faces,
Mum's hands piled high with boxes.
Inside the different shaped boxes hide amazing gifts for the family.

A doll for her daughter, a train for her son, pop out on Christmas morning,
The turkey smell grows greater to the stomachs of the children.
Christmas carols are heard all around the village,
But now Christmas has to come to an end.
And the new year is slowly drifting in.

Emily Kirby and Laura Ryczanowski

More Than A Bad Influence

Flashing lights filter through the haze
of indifference, mingling with curiosity.
Self. Hidden by the obscurity
of appearing to be more than what we want to be seen as, but
revealed by our instinctive, pressing search for unity
in a world where rejection is expected and conflict, a game.
A world of contrasts deeper than understanding,
Functioning on a subconscious level, driven to danger as a release from...What?

This is what we cannot register in our minds:
That the need we feel to be here is more than just desire or
adrenaline, more than youth culture and its orders to rebel
More than escapism and more than amusement.
For here we find the atmospheric aphrodisiac, the
Culmination of all that we are supposed to be denied, for our own good!
Soon, however, this crawl though danger will not be enough, and
Desperation for a greater forbidden element will only take us back
To animal instinct, regression to the pre-civilization
And the circle that begins again.

Youth ideology is a powerful tool.
Be careful how you are used by it.

Georgina Joy Heath

Gypsies

They are woven in our rural scene, these nomadic travelling bands,
For many centuries they have been, a fact within our lands.

So many folk who know them not, think them to be one crew,
And as one type do class the lot, but this is far from true.

There are some of ancient Romany breed, who travel from pure joy,
And rules of countryside do heed, unlike the dirty diddycoy.

They camp where'er their vans may rest, on lay-by, verge or lane,
They're scarcely tolerable at best, 'til driven off again.

They are suspect of every crime, committed in their wake,
Sometime 'tis true but many a time, 'tis others blame they take.

But in this modern motor age, they danger and nuisance cause,
For permanent sites the pundits rage, where they may safely pause.

Now in principle we all agree, against no voice prevails,
But while we all agree these sites should be, they should be
Somewhere
    Else.

Bob Roberts

Legacy Of Grey

The environment we live in could one day cease to be,
a green and lasting heritage, no more for all to see.
If we ignore the warning signs, that global warming now defines,
the trees will all disintegrate, and violent storms would not abate.
Live for today, forget tomorrow, time is of plenty, for us to borrow.
But what of the legacy we might leave for our future mankind,
who are left to grieve?
And why are we helping to pave the way for an earth that is
covered with shades of grey?
Never to see the sunlight as it flickers through the trees,
Dappling tiny diamonds over the rich green leaves.
The earth would be a chasm of all that's dull and dark.
No more to hear the flapping wings, or the singing of the lark.
Our future generations would not thank us for that day.
Or for having gone and left them
with a Legacy of Grey.

O. L. Mokes

Thoughts

Thoughts are secrets in patchwork minds,
    inner voices whispering in rhymes.
They have no colour, neither black nor white,
    invisible spirits that haunt at night.

Thoughts can be useful, creative and fun,
    or drive you insane with their constant hum,
Sometimes memories, things that have passed,
    maybe a dream you wish could last.

Thoughts can be complex, things you dread,
    they go swirling round inside your head,
Ideas and notions, plans and schemes,
    they keep on forming in endless streams.

Thoughts are silent, yet invasive and loud,
    like a screaming mob, a crushing crowd,
They never pause to let you sleep,
    but they're yours alone to share or keep.

L. E. Hemmings

Loneliness

I know what it means to be lonely,
In the midst of a multitude,
And to feel the depths of loneliness,
In a noisy solitude.

I know what it means to be lonely,
In a gay and thoughtless crowd;
When the lone heart cries for fellowship,
And no fellowship's allowed.

I know what it means to be lonely,
When words their meaning have lost;
When the speech of a friend is prattle
The heart's stopped counting the cost.

I know what it means to be lonely
The heart lives in solitude,
With silence vast as the blue above
Naught can that silence intrude.

D. K. Dunster

What Love Is

Love is special, for it comes from one's heart.
Love is true, like how parents love their children.
Love is giving, like how friends love each other.
Love is pure, like a baby which is just born.
Love is kind and gentle, like a little lamb.
Love is worth more than money, for it is the key
to one's heart.
Love is beautiful, like a world without pollution.
Love is full of joy and happiness, like a couple which
are just married.
Love is a symbol which represents God.

Jennifer Patel

Memories

The days would go slow,
Agony on the people's faces would show.
Guns are fired, bodies lying on the floor,
People praying that there would be no more.
Hiding in shelters, children would weep,
Staying awake all night and couldn't sleep.
Food and drink was getting so low,
As shops and homes came to a blow
Wounded people, with blood all around,
Bits and pieces all over the ground.
Not knowing where your families or friends are,
They could be in hiding or lying somewhere afar.
I say to myself, when will it end,
So we can live again and make amends.
All I want is peaceful places,
With no enemies or wars, just smiling faces.
Please God, make this war end.

Maria Seager

Spring Will Be A Little Late...

Father had died, friend and counsellor had passed on.
    I remained to live in that Spring which came too late.
In my heart, an empty space; he would forever be
    A beloved memory.
Sadly tearfully, I turned the pages of memory:
    Remembering childhood days, in his dear company.
Music shared and understood: A violin in its case of wood.
    The ghost of a favourite melody - lingered on - always would...
The sadness of his sweet smile, after travelling many miles
    I came at last to his side.

The frailty of his gentle face, now lined with age
    And marked by pain, would never be the same.
With tears in my heart - kissing the gentle brow
    hearing the softly spoken words "Spring is a little late!"...

Came at last, the final parting: we both knew it had to be,
    with a gentle smile, a frail hand lifted to wave.
Blinded with unshed tears - I turned and fled.
    Later Father died, peacefully he passed into his
    "Eternal Spring"

Olive-Joyce Noble

Gifts

On our wedding day
I hear you say

That you want me as your wife
That you need me all your life

I gave you my heart
Right back at the start

I give you my hand
to wear your band

Tonight I'll give you my special flower in darkness
And love will grow in our likeness.

Louise Lavorel

The World's Just Like A Jamboree

The world's just like a jamboree
The houses that are up for sale
Enough to make the people wail
The murders, rapes
Also jail breaks
The olden days were far the best
At least we went to bed to rest
The birds will soon be unable to fly
Because of pollution in the sky.
What's this lovely world come to?
My heart wants to cry.
Sometimes I feel I could lie down and die
I wonder if some people in this world will change
I know I'd just love
To re-arrange

Caroline Smith

To An Absent Inspiration

I think of you, a memory stirs,
An image drifts across my mind,
The way you were, the things you said,
The shadowed dream you left behind

I saw you walk this way each day,
Softly, with a ghost - like grace,
So near, yet strangely far away,
A wistful look upon your face.

Hard times when you saw so much pain,
Of empty hopes and silent sighs,
Are bravely masked but still remain,
In your tired smile and troubled eyes

Your quiet, poised determinations
Your independence, strong and free,
Your acceptance of all gained profound admiration.
In you I saw all that I wanted to be.

It's hard to hold on as the memory fades
Time leaves an aching, changes what you believe,
But I still see you turn, watch you walking away,
Leaving your tired eyes and sad smiles with me.

Louise Singh

The Teardrop

A little boy with a badly grazed knee
A sad little face gazing up at me
A warm little body pressed close to mine
Willing that I make everything fine.

And as I looked down I saw trembling there
On a curly eyelash that matched his hair
The most perfect teardrop I ever did see
Which even as I watched was gone from me.

Like a first snowflake full of beauty profound
Only to vanish as it touches the ground
So the teardrop rolled down his rosy face
Just like snowflake to vanish without race.

If only it were possible for me to imprison
This perfect teardrop in a little glass prism
There for all time for me to see
To awake a memory of a little cut knee.

When you too are grown and gone away
I could keep it to gaze at every day
Part of your childhood then gone from me
Part of the child that was given to me.

Dorothy N. Davies

Everyone Is Important!

Everyone is important.
No matter who they are
No matter what they have or haven't
Dripping on toast, or caviar.

It's not what we own that makes a person
It's what we are inside
And how we treat other people
with a clear and healthy mind.

Don't clutter up the hates
The anger and such like
Tell the grudges and the jealousy
To go and take a hike

Life is so important
And we let it pass us by
We clutter up possessions
And leave them when we die.

So make the very best of life
And enjoy every minute
And make it a better world
For all the people in it.

I. McCoy

If Only . . .

In England a little girl
Prays for what she'd like.
She wants another doll
And perhaps another bike.
She looks around her bedroom;
It's not as full as she'd wish.
She wants a little china dog
And maybe a small goldfish.
She looks up at the sky with a tear in her eye,
And sighs deeply.

In Africa a little girl
Gets on her knees to pray.
She asks that her family
Won't go hungry that day.
She looks all around her
And gets onto her feet,
She sees a black hard ground
Which won't grow anything to eat.
She looks up at the sky with a tear in her eye,
And sighs deeply.

Gemma Dixon

The Dance

When at the dance I sat a while
And watched the people and checked their style.
With a sigh of relief I looked to see
Many were aged the same as me.
No-one asked me to dance that day,
So relaxed from side to side I'd sway.
All by myself on the dance floor
I'd turn and wind 'till I could no more.

Oh music of sentiment so fine,
Didn't you hit me with rhythm and rhyme.
Didn't you make all my senses flow,
Like a warm river with nowhere to go.
Didn't the sun reflect and glisten.
Didn't birds sing and didn't I listen.

When at the dance that summer's eve,
No real partner did I need.
In the midnight heat, in the early morn,
I knew no badness, no devil's scorn
I'd sip my drink and watch the pace
Of others dancing in every space.

Elaine Bangura

A Poem Of Dreams

In a world of confusion I seldom ask much,
I wish for the guarded to reach out and touch,
To break down the barriers when walls stand so bold,
To feel the warm inside when outside it's so cold.

To have someone mend me when my heart is broken,
To know someone hears me tho' words are not spoken,
To feel I'm worth millions when I've only pence,
To be understood when I'm not making sense.

To give to the world when I've nothing to offer,
To know that the victims of violence won't suffer,
To reach to the dying and help them to breathe,
To have something sacred in which to believe.

To find self-esteem when my confidence is battered,
To live out the dream when my dreams have been shattered,
To feel I've not lost when you've already won,
To rest not in darkness when all light has gone.

In a world without answers confusion is all,
That I have to keep sanity contained in these walls.

Natalie Wood

A Time To Remember

Free to walk the country lane
Miles from nowhere, I'll not complain
Sad and alone, but memories remain
My thoughts return when first I came.
'Twas September the third '39 I remember
When the course of our lives was changed forever
The war was upon us and survive we must
Accepting the hardships, for the struggle was just

Looking back, I often think
The choice we had to swim or sink
Remained for each of us to decide
Do all we can, and hope to survive

Ruth Lelyveld

A Child's Obsession

My head is filled with illusions, my sleep is plagued with dreams
My Nightmares are more vivid and louder are my screams
My tears fall more often, upon my carpet floor
As I think I hear your footsteps approach my open door

I'll never forget that night, when you did disregard my age
And even though I protested, you stamped my empty page
So I lost my prized possession, because my sanity had flown
Because of a child's obsession, my virginity now you own

And now I feel ugly, unloved, unwanted and used
As my manner kind and flirty, you simply just abused
And now you have gone, you left me on my own
Listening for your voice, and waiting by the phone

I know that I love you, I guess I always will
But trying to regain my feelings, is to climb a vertical hill
So I pray that you'll come back, that one day you'll return
But until that sun is risen, my heart is left to burn

Janine Ayres

Perception - Journey Eternity

The twinkle of stars in their ebony bed,
The glisten of dew on a gossamer thread.

The sensation of feeling a velvety kiss,
the taste of salt tears upon quivering lips.

The odour of rain from the earth which it dose,
the rich, extravagant aroma of an elegant rose.

The crashing of waves as they pummel the rocks and
the echo of time pounded out by a clock.

But touch, Daddy dear, is the best sense of all,
you touched us with love and your heart and your soul.

Your earthly body is gone but your spirit is near,
now I know you are waiting death holds no fear.

But how I wish I could see you, feel you, smell you, hear
you, touch you. I've never known such pain.
Someday, Daddy, I'll be with you again.

Thank you for giving me life and love.

Lynne Chapple-Crees

The Horror Of The Somme (WWI)

Man against man in a blood thirsty war,
All classes rich and poor.
Another bombardment to end our lives,
Man after man, he sleeps, he dies.
Mothers, Fathers they wait for news,
But what they hear just concludes,
The end of a life, their son, their boy,
That very same one who brought such joy.
Now they grieve sad and alone,
All because kaiser wants top of the throne.
What I am in for, what have I done,
I thought this war would be nothing but fun.
But all I've encountered is anguish and death,
Surely soon I shall take my last breath.

Debbie Young

The Question

What does it feel like to be old?
The young man asked of me.
How do I tell him; what do I say?
I am still the child of yesterday,
Living each day as it comes, to the full.
Days of difficulty, trouble and love.
Long days of working - working - bone tired despairing,
Laughing when all else has failed.
Each day endless - when a smile was more than gold.
Learning, always learning, discovering I was wrong.
The years slipped by uncounted - unnoticed;
But I am still the same child - still feeling;
Still loving, living each day to the full.
My friends and family are passing now,
I too will pass ere long, life so short
There is no time to be old.

M. Hanson

Emma's Chicken Soup

Standing at the oven, dinner's nearly done.
In come some of my family, children at a run.
Emma my granddaughter smiling sweetly up at me,
Said "oh please Granny, may we stay for tea?"
"Yes of course you can my sweet",
Wondering how I'd stretch the meat.
"Granny that does smell good.
Are we having Yorkshire pud?"
"Yes and meat, potatoes, carrots and peas."
"May I have lots please?"
Another hour there I stand.
Cooking for five more than I'd planned.
At last I'm putting their dinner on their plate,
Worrying because it's rather late.
"Now Emma what is it you want for your tea?"
"Thank you Granny, just a tin of chicken soup
for me."

Audrey F. Pearson

The Leaves

I wish I were clear
but my nature is cloudy.
I'm a little Oriental
like a bleeding medusa
at the corner of the sky.
Hidden in Plato's thought,
we're all dreaming to gather round life.
Someday maybe
I'll be forgetful.
The lovers are dying,
there's a sense of guilt
and they're dying
they're dying away.

Eleonora Bagarotti

There's Been Days

There's been days when I've felt like smiling,
and others when dreams have come true.
But today there's a part of me dying,
'cause I never can live life with you.

I don't think you've noticed me crying,
Or begging for you to stay,
There's part of me missing when you're not there,
but you don't care anyway.

You don't know just how much I love you.
You don't care how I'm feeling inside,
and no matter just how hard I'm trying
from you, my feelings I can't hide.

There's been days when I've felt like smiling,
and others when dreams have come true,
But there's days when my life's not worth living,
and that doesn't matter to you.

Lindsey Cross

Fading Away

I feel so tired, I know I look ill
My weight is dropping, I'm losing still
My stomach is crying out for food
But my mind is in a different mood.

I know I need help but I don't know from where
And my family has such a burden to bare
The laxatives I take make me ill
But at least my weight is dropping still.

I'm sorry for all the trouble I've been
And the things I've done you haven't seen
I eat my food and then I'm ill
But at least my weight is dropping still.

If only I could eat from day to day
To stop from dying this painful way
I know I have not long to go
My mind and body feel so low.

The life has drained away from me
And now I know it has to be
As I lay here and await God's call
I just want to die and end it all.

L. J. Chesters

My Children

My children are so precious,
They bring me so much joy,
They mean the world to me,
My three girls and one boy.

I love them all so dearly,
I won't ever let them down,
And if ever they're in trouble,
I'll always be around.

I'd never be without them,
because they mean so much to me,
So God, don't let me lose them,
I beg you'll hear this plea.

When they grow up and leave,
Please don't let them stray.
I hope they'll come to see me,
If it's only for the day.

One day they'll have children of their own,
I hope they'll feel no pain,
Then I'll be a grandmother,
And experience the joy once again.

Maureen Bayliss

A Daughter's Choice

Before I was born my Lord said to me,
"If you could choose a mother
Just how would she be"?

It took me a moment,
A second or two,
And there in my mind,
Was a picture of you.

"Well Lord" I replied,
"My mother would be
A person who'd always
Take good care of me,
With a face of an angel
Who would make me feel safe
And a heart full of love
No one could replace".

And now that I'm here
And reflect on my dream,
I know that God really does care,
For He not only gave me all of the above
But He totally exceeded my prayer.

Susan Rose Stratford

Pure

If nothing exists without another,
If pain without happiness or joy without sadness
Nor laugh without a cry, nor a scream without some cheer
Is there ever pure happiness or pure sadness, undiluted, unexposed,
Pure and clear from a young mountain spring?
Can one laugh a laugh of ecstatic joy and cry in complete despair?
Or is everything good and bad?

Would we even notice if it did happen?
Just once, for a split minute of a second,
everyone felt completely happy, as if they had felt it all the time.
And we laughed off pain until our sides ached.
Men and women with heavy guns stretched across borders and
hugged their patriotic enemies.
Then, just for the tiniest, minute second, we felt an utter and
Complete despair,
Our lives were a miserable sham of hailstone pelting rocks and we
Were crushed by the pain.

Would we even notice, though?
Would we miss those two tiny minute seconds of our lives when we
Have so much more time to laugh and cry and grow???...

Clare Daly

Heaven Is A Garden

Heaven is a garden, where scented promises jostle
amongst the echoes of seasons past.
Velvet carpets of dewy moss on ancient walls
hide a secret corner that offers hidden treasure,
germinating at the warmth of a lover's caress,
matured from innocence to reveal its beauty in the fullness of time.
Stately oaks bear centuries of witness to each rite of passage of the
generations as they toil to leave an impact on their microcosm of Mother Earth.
A sapling sets root, mirror to the delicate beginnings of life that,
with care, survives the dangerous droughts and turbulent storms of youth.
Marriage becomes a rose; perfect in bud, awesome in fullness,
masking its antithesis in the thorn.
Loneliness is banished on rediscovering the tender touch of a
departed loved one in a clematis and ivy entwined.
Surprised anew with pain at the memory of lives so joined
the suffering is fleeting, giving way to a tear-filled smile
for the beauty that so constantly brings peace.
Tempest and tranquillity, the vibrancy of life in its wholeness
awakens in profusion, as sweetness after rain; restoring the soul with a
profound certainty that in all things, there is a purpose.

Caroline W. Haines

The Old Salt

He lived in a tiny cottage upon a pebble shore
Remembering so well the tales he told through its forty years or more.
He sat outside his cottage door smoking his pipe made of clay,
No one ever walking by failed to pass the time of day.

The young, like me would always stop to listen to seafaring tales,
Of his adventures around the world in ships with tall white sails,
He would tell of tropical islands, with sands bleached white as snow,
Where primitive hostile natives lived, where no white man dared go.

How once while anchored off their shores the natives crept aboard
The captain and crew repelled them, with their bayonets and their swords,
How once the ship becalmed through lack of wind and tide,
In scorching heat, no water left they had but almost died.
The good Lord saw it fit to send a violent storm,
So water we had aplenty, but a ship all battered and torn.

The bronzed lined face I still can see, with eyes a faded blue,
His knurled old hands outstretched to greet the many friends he knew.
I visited him again this year, but could not see his face.
Gone was the cottage where he lived; he had sailed to a better place.
There was only one epitaph I could say—,
A sailor sailed home, the good Lord's way.

Christina Clinch

Love And Life

Love is for life,
And life is for love,
It's sent as a blessing,
From heaven above,
When we're together,
You make me see,
Love's not just for life,
It's for you and me.

Life is for love,
And love is for life,
Whether between boyfriend and girlfriend
Or husband and wife;
Whether they've been together
For two months, or two years,
If one is unfaithful,
It will all end in tears

Sarah H. Smith

Ode To My Golden Girl

Outside my window stands a tree
So large indeed that all can see
Its mighty branches standing high
Majestic there towards the sky
Slowly a bough to path descends
This isn't real (it's just pretend)
The leaves now part, I alone perceive
A tiny dog runs down through the leaves
And comes to me
'Twas just a thought, it cannot be
Because my Topsy has gone from me.

When the sun is shining on the sea
My companion in memory comes to me
She loved it there upon the sands
She would race about when I clapped my hands
Our tears for each other have filled the ocean
I know this really is only a notion
But a fact I know, when I'm by the sea
Is that I loved Topsy and she loved me.

Jean M. Riches

Christmas 1987

A trouble is halved when it is shared,
With a friend who showed they really cared.
But don't forget the good news too,
As all too often we tend to do
Remember families are always there,
But friends need rather special care.

Carol Robins

Little Innocent

I hold you so close
That you become part of me.
My blood flows from my heart
Into and through yours.
Around your tiny scared but radiant body.

Oh, sweet angel of mine,
After all we have been through,
All the pain, worry and breath of death,
So many times I have cried for you.
So many times have you been cut and hurt,
As I stood by your crib in fear.

Yet you're still here in my arms,
Even now as you cry still in fear,
In sleep, of doctors and scalpels.
I pray you shall never remember all,
And I pray you shall remember me
When I am gone.

Love cannot account for what is between us.
For what can truly describe the bond
Between a sister and her baby brother.

Donna Moore

The Year 3000

In the year 3000 life will be cool.
There will be no work, there will be no school,
Everyone will just lie around in the air and on the ground.
Yes, that's right, we'll be able to fly,
There will be theme parks and buildings in the sky.
Now, you see, there will be lots of space
And lots of room for the human race.
Everyone will wear silver trousers,
There will be silver shops and silver houses,
There will be silver cats and silver dogs,
Silver toads and silver frogs, silver kitchens and silver sinks,
So bright and shiny they'll make you blink.
The ozone layer will be protected,
'Cause all the pollution will be corrected,
No smoke, no gases, no poisonous acids.
To stop car pollution we will go around,
On bikes that can lift right off the ground,
You may ask what happened to gravity that stops us being able to fly,
We will use wings to make us go high. With all the best things,
life will be full, Yes, in the year 3000, life will be cool.

Amelia Lane

The Commandments We've Forgotten

The world today is on a downward slope, slippery, unsteady, and insecure,
Things happen which we cannot comprehend,
   Because, we put our trust in God no more...

Yet, God sits there and watches all our failings and our sins,
And, I guess he smiles and shakes his head,
   Perhaps just sits there and grins...

Because after all he is in charge of our every breathing minute,
And when he decides to intervene there'll be no question in it...

He is changing even the power of the sun, we call it Global warming...
But God knows best and he decides, but he never gives a warning...

The skies he rents with lightning and, terrible drums of thunder,
How can we mere mortals doubt His power, His love, His wonder..?

Until we acknowledge all our faults our sins and all our failings,
The world will continue to fall apart, and He'll not heed our wailings

We will have to go back to the very beginning
   Yes, start at the very bottom,
And do as our forbears did,
   Re-learn The Commandments We've Forgotten...

Eileen Greenwood-Sadler

Forever Intense Enacting Fantasy

La jeunefille doyen of dance and ecstasy
She, my darling beloved, is sheer exquisitry.
Bewitching bloom of thoroughbred pedigree
The perfume of her flower, a delicious pungency.
My houris in shadow and silhouette robed curvaceous,
Frivolous emerald-sapphirine tinted garb, fragrant, luscious
Conjuroress of heliotrope, gerbera, ruby and moonstone clear.
No blossoming orchard grove, or garden festive-fruited
Ever could boast the like, our love is deepest rooted.
The resolution; to cultivate with my flower.
Nurturing my frenzy-focused berserk power
To yield our fruit, the bounty of love between us.
The nativity of seed, our plant a plus, of us.
Arched bodies blissful coupled, night, day and night lovemaking.
Love fabulous limitless glorious masterful lovemaking.
Lavishly royal rejuvenating ululating affection. Kermartinir.
Incomparable; these ecstatic experiences, ultimate, entrancingly exciting.
Delectably transported by absolute passion tireless each in each desiring
KaM orgiastic, majestic flame, kin royal with regal kin.
I have worship of that ecstasy and love of that kin.

Martin Snasdell

The Beginning

My father and brother were keen photographic men
and encouraged my interest from when I was ten,
I wasn't very lucky with photo equipment
some that I handled got decidedly bent.
The family box brownie some damage did sustain
when I left it out one night in the rain,
being made of pressed cardboard it went sort of floppy
not so my father, he got a bit stroppy.

I next dropped his big Kodak, his joy and his pride
he took out his anger on my backside.
A few weeks later to my surprise and delight
gave me a 620 Brownie one Saturday night,
a prize for showing that I wasn't a complete fool
by winning a scholarship to the grammar school.

I was chuffed with that gift and I'm happy to say
I've held onto that camera, still have it today.
It started me recording the laughter and tears
and a hobby I've enjoyed for 60 odd years.

Eric Gregory

Eden

Beneath the stars we'll camp tonight
Light a fire so warm and bright,
The summer leaves flutter overhead
With the scented air so cool and fresh.
Clouds are floating high up above
The cool evening breeze gives them a shove
And the sparkling droplets of the rain
Are sent to replenish the stream again.
The stream rolls gently on its way
And the rain now ceases to remain,
We look to see the crimson sunset
A sight before I have never met.
It gave the sky a mighty glow
Which will remain with me, that I know,
The peace and tranquillity of the night
Is disturbed briefly as a bird takes flight.
Everything is so natural and clear
From the rustling trees, to the trickling stream,
Untouched by man's cruel and greedy hands
Eden is truly a green and pleasant land.

R. Notley

Autumn

The wind is telling its woes to the eaves,
As the trees sway in mourning for their leaves
Scattered like ashes around their roots
Their dirge being sung by the key hole flutes.
But the sun pokes its fingers through the clouds
Warming the feathers of the gathering crowds
And above the annual autumn funeral
The starlings rejoice in their constant carnival.

Lisa Clark

The Toys' Secret

At night when it's dark and you can't hear a sound,
The toys that you love are up and around,
Asleep in your bed you would really never know,
What they get up to as it never shows.

As soon as the lights are out they think we're asleep,
Up they all get and to the playroom they creep,
Big Ted and little Ted all the dolls too,
They all must be careful not to leave any clues.

Out comes the train set it's surprising we don't hear,
As it chugs round the track and they all start to cheer,
Soon they get hungry and search for our crumbs,
Asleep in the corner Tiny Tears sucks her thumb.

When the sun rises they all pack away,
Ready for the next time that you want to play,
All the toys go creeping past at quite a speed in case,
You wake to spoil their secret as they rush back to their place.

Lisa J. Brake

For The Life I Know Not Of

Happiness comes and goes like rain showers
In the desert: Long sad days and nights fill
My dreams and wakened hours. The fear I hold
inside tears my heart and shadows my life.
Nothing can be as it was before.
All changes and will never be the same. Ever.

Looking forward, not behind is unknown to me.
My past has more of a future
than my present. Fading memories and
lost dreams slant my view of life. For me, the
only thing worth staying for is what is
not yet here. But that will change tomorrow.

I think of change. There is nothing else to
think of. New beginnings are close and I
fear for what I know not of. New life, old
dreams - no longer something to shelter my
days. This beautiful new life will take mine
and know not what it is doing. Ever.

Paula Roach

Sympathy Of Our Love

We all love you very much.
So don't be afraid to keep in touch.
We will be here, when you shed a tear,
We will be here when you're ready to appear.
We will all do our very best to get you through
So be strong forever so long.
Your children will look after you so take care and
remember that we all love you.

Emma Bartholomew

Untitled

Self infliction, once again
Lethargic, there seems to be no end
Watch my desires, my wishes crumble,
    as time ticks by and my soul slowly dies
Dramatic I am being
Look at my reflection
    dark circles now
Permanent around my eyes
    Pale and ugly I do feel
Weight attained from gorges to try and cease
    infinite boredom
I cannot go on like this
Pride and sorrow at my father
    for surviving so long
Wish to make my life full
    so as to somehow also save him
Selfish yes. But I do not know how
    to take this normality
Please I plead
    but who must I plead to?

Karie Tamar Soehardi

Sad Dad

Dad's a ready steady machine that makes money every day.
He pays for schools and holidays and keeps the wolves at bay.
He's expected to provide all your avaricious needs.
And be present just to glorify your egotistic deeds.

Don't worry if he's tired or been hammered by the boss.
He's supposed to be unstinting and hardly ever cross.
Society says a macho man must never ever cry.
He is your Dad and you demand his image to comply.

Dad has to prove his valour, he's much stronger than the rest.
You couldn't bear a Dad who you perceive was not the best.
So rain or shine he marches on, he wants to make you proud.
He knows that you demand of him, to stand out from the crowd.

One day he feels the pressure, so he hides himself in drink.
He can't admit he's weakened, what would his children think?
When times get worse he runs away and finds a woman's arms.
She'll start the roundabout again, seducing him with charms -
Sad Dad.

Allan F. Munn

Untitled

I've driven a Lorry all my life,
Long periods away from family and wife,
Summers, winters, autumns and springs,
So now I reflect on all these things

Big lorries, little lorries and them that wouldn't go
Supercharged turbo's and them that went real slow
Full loads, half loads, some, no load at all,
But no regrets on this road of life, in fact, I've had a ball

Highways, carriage ways, by ways and motor ways,
Outbacks, dirt racks and car ferries too,
Overheating, snowstorms, thick fog and heavy rain,
But I must admit to you my friends
I'd do it all again!

Customs and excise, police, wardens and the boss,
I've met them all along the way
Sometimes with fingers crossed!
So hand brake on, ignition off, it's time to end this lark,
And as I'm 65 today, it's time for me to Park!

D. W. Coupland

Anticipation

I walk through a tunnel so dark,
Alone scared always afraid of hurt and pain that remained,
Now I see an end I have such a good friend,
A lover I suppose you could say,
He makes me feel good just like he should,
No longer am I afraid,
He holds me tight fills me with delight,
Puts me on a pedestal higher than a kite,
I cannot show my feelings just yet,
I hope I will soon and have no regrets,
He's kind, he's good, he would give me all he could,
All I ask is to be loved.
I've been hurt I think he knows,
Swallowed pride I won't lie,
He's given me back what I thought I'd always lack,
My confidence and pride no longer will it hide.
I hope that this won't shatter with one hell of a clatter,
Or will it?

Stephanie Haldenby

The Midnight Sun

The hungry cold consumes my warmth,
Our star, glowing like a furnace,
Yet still the looming chill remains,
I'm blinded by the sun's gleaming rays.

Reflecting brightness on deep ice pools,
A fire blazing beneath water surface,
My footsteps now imbedded in snow,
Frozen forever, concealed by ice.

The witching hour heaves a heavy sigh,
As she leaps from night to day,
The sky never left silhouettes to haunt,
The midnight sun shines over all!

Helen Moverley

The Offering

Don't cast aside love's mantle
For to do so is to spurn God's gift
Look inside your heart's temple
And see that love's needs must be nourished
Give all of yourself
And tender your love with care
So it may grow and flourish
Wear love's mantle as your armour for the hard times ahead
And wield your devotion in the face of uncommon sacrifice
Let your passion run unchecked
And yield to love's full splendour
For it is life's most precious offering
And God's most sacred gift

Carole Langhorn-Hoolihan

1945-1995 Fifty Years Hence

Oh why! Oh why! The ultimate price this soldier had to pay
Let his bravery ever shine light among the stormy way
Son of a minister prepared to die so others remain - survival
of the fittest - pittance to the weak
That was the reality he had to meet.
The banner raised he answered the call
worshipped by platoon - Welsh and all
Refrained all onslaught to the front go
Leader of men to the core.

To all nations let it be known - who wants war?
Not this gallant officer - did not want to go
Served his country deservedly so.
Hell let loose the Reichswald Forest was his fate
Fought like a tiger - did not flee - died in pain
His Ardennes award repaid in full
others saved that was the aim.

In life did not want earthly gains
But honours shared
A minister's son to the end
"Better death than shame".

T. W. Edwards

Forever

The lonely road has many faults,
I fear the distant past.
Filled with happiness masked by the fields of maize.
The four figures in the sun.
On the bridge we'd hear the trees, watch the sun and feel the breeze.
Waiting then for the sun to set,
Watching time and every step.
Four figures in the moon, six months they grew
    close, they knew the why's and the reasons for the doing
Watching time and grasping but only waiting,
    knowing it couldn't last.
But one had gone not forever, just apart,
Taking mind and soul but leaving his heart.
The friendship's there forever.
One last time the burning ball will rise again but never fall.
The water and the time had broken heart
    until the tears could come no more.
Lying in the moon, it's just the start.
The wet on my cheek just falls apart, these are not the tears
    from my eyes but the tears from my heart.

Claire Wilkinson

Water Colour

A Turner tree
the leaves in hornet clumps, free
standing, near a spire
the others sporting bird song aerial choir
below - the cultured lawn
where the rustic yokel has shed spawn
sporting his freedom with a lass
speckled and mottled by the light of leaf
he holds his lover like the reaper holds a sheaf.

Should they dare to turn their gaze
from the azure sky and the sun's rays
staring back across the fell,
is a wooded hillock shaped like a bell
a sportive spinney—an oasis of repose
bounded by a rivulet that glows.

Is this their Eden—abandoned in the evening light
for the dusky baseness of a carnal rite
or wisdom on a landscape of Arcadian repose
where Adam and Eve disport in evening clothes
and tread the fields and paths of innocence abroad
freed from the terror of a primitive God?

Francis Scallan

The Lakes Of Keswick

The rolling hills and mountains green
Breathtaking views of God's great scene
Shimmering lakes, so still and calm
Golden sun, on my skin to embalm

Serene and peaceful here at the lakes
Life all around, takes a much slower pace
Nature in its splendid glory
Every creature, has its own story

Vibrant colours locked in flowers
Fragrance of earth, emitted from showers
Poets inspired to write great verse
Of this beautiful land, here on earth.

Patricia Johnson

Ode To Autumn

Oh trees you look so lovely.
You're gold, yellow, wine and green.
How we loathe to see your leaves fall.
Even though the brown earth takes on
    the colour that your dear moving branches offer down -
Your leaves; as if a sacrifice to earth.
The wind has robbed you of your glory.
The earth that so greedily takes the
    rain, now glows with your 'beauty'.
Soon the frost and snow will steal
the colour from your fallen leaves.
Another season has begun. -
Time heals all pain and we must wait.
It won't be long till buds burst forth;
And branches moving in the breeze
Will once again 'Dance' to the music of Spring
Dressed in shades of softest green.
Oh trees that bring such pleasure;
Sleep awhile your day is done.
'Tis winter now, God's will be done.

Elsie Morris

News

News is on at any time
For example: Six and nine.
It could be either bad or good,
But, they tell it as they should.
Some people are naughty by breaking the law,
For example starting a war.
People go missing everyday,
Sometimes found far away.
Murders are happening all the time,
And that is how I'll end this rhyme.

L. A. Umpleby

The Bridge To Your Soul

As I'm walking down the long road of life,
I wonder if I can end the monotony with a knife.
"Life is not for questioning", so they say,
I too must play the deceitful game.

But what about love, surely it exists?
I once tried to grab it with a desperate fist,
Just when I was sure it was finally clasped in my palm,
time weakened my fingers to unravel a broken heart.

The unshakable shadow of fear and insecurity,
clouded my vision while I acted foolishly.
Yet still I wandered as blind as ever,
As my subconscious planted the seeds of anger.

'Twas bitterness that forced me to pause,
I had to stop to search for the wound's cause.
Easier it is proceeding with the blindfold.
Yet the bumps on the journey slipped it off.

The road is the bridge to my heart and soul,
Suddenly it all seems so worthwhile and whole.
They who don't dare question must realize,
Being true to yourself wins that deceitful game.

Arezoo Saboohi

There Are No Rules

There are no rules
Just go along and get what you want
There should be all one-way streets
But instead people come in all directions

No traffic lights or cross roads
The cars are made of metal
And very hard to steer
Although no lessons are required
And no driving test to pass

All sorts of drivers come to this place
Some are slow, careful and
Watch where they go
Road map in hand
Others are fast and know
Exactly the direction to take

At the end is a place to unload the items
Collected and accumulated along the way
You then have to pay a toll to get out
Some have to pay more than others
Depending on how many goods you have

J. Odell

Paradise (Queensland)

"Ever dreamt of Paradise", the thoughts of how it could be,
Close your eyes and fly away to the land
of the coconut tree.
Breathe out and absorb the warm sweet air.
Running from your toes to the tips of your hair,
No fears, no worries, simply melt away.
Words can't express what you wanted to say,
The blue crystal waters, the warm golden sands
the rich coloured fish that kiss your sweet hands.

God's little creatures, so unusual to see,
the pink gecko lizard, up a melalouca tree
The different coloured birds that fly freely and sing
Unaware of their beauty and enjoyment they bring.
Never found Paradise, well now you can see
Close your eyes tightly and come follow me
To the beautiful land of the coconut tree.

Sandy Moore

The Valour And The Honour

Young and proud soldiers, so willing to give
Urged by their government hoping they'll live . . .
Live through the valour and horror of war
But soon they will come through the hospital door

The troops were outnumbered by 50 to 1
Marched to their death, it didn't take long
Battered comrades in hospital, together as one
Outside, the battle raged on and on

The bones of the murdered, in rivers were herded
While nurses were raped and the dying were tortured
By enemy soldiers, closing in on the scared
No-one could help them, no-one had dared

Now all those still living would have to surrender
Relinquishing with honour, the role of defender
To prisoner of war camps, they were forcibly led
And soon they would come to envy the dead.

Shirley Bailey

Do Remember This

Make the most of those you love, while they are by your side,
Let them feel the warmth of the affection - you might hide.
Have no regrets - live every day of every year
As though each one may be the last you share.
For time so quickly passes by - and life is short.
Make every moment precious - keep love in your heart....

Marjorie Cookson

God Loves Us All

God loves us all that we all do know
No one was ever given everyone was lent
Down from heaven sent
So give a helping hand to others
And also a great big smile

So when you return to heaven you
Will know your life on earth was worthwhile

And when we are tired and weary
God frees us from all our pain

He opens up His loving arms
And takes us back again

You cannot buy your way to heaven
No matter how rich you are

So be kind and loving to each other
Then I know you will all go there

Tressie Rose M. Kislingbury

Reflections

A man awakes
Alone in the dark 'The Wife' by his side.
Stumbles to the dreaded bathroom
Where unfulfilled dreams
And frightened inabilities await.
Reflections of wasted talents
Side by side with frustrated "if only's"
But should the *inner* mirror crack
And the fearful man with fearful eyes
Looks . . . in
Bye-bye!

Eugene Stretton

For Chloe

We waited and waited, when would the day come
When we would finally see our bundle of fun
But when the day came it all seemed so near
That shock and bewilderment followed by fear
I tried to be strong, I tried to be brave
My mum always told me I had to behave
But nobody told me how hard it would be
I had to dig deep, it was all down to me
I pushed and I cried, it went on for hours
But my mother was there, I felt all her powers

And then there she was, my daughter was born
A bright new beginning, a wonderful dawn
The daughter I wanted to share all our dreams
Of family devotions and of course the ice creams
The love and the wisdom I learnt from my nan
I'm sure she will learn from her worldly wise gran
From daughter to daughter it's passed down the tree
Just like it was passed from my mother to me

Paula A. Watson

Life's Seasons

A warm caress through breeze and sound,
Is the mark of the season's change profound.
At least in the fashion of summer's theory,
A natural relief of winter's weary.

The landscape's residents all in full bloom,
For time is the essence as winter comes soon,
Bright, beautiful, complimentary together,
The end of a chapter once and forever.

The rule's exception is a regular one,
As for many there's no comfort nor fun,
For when the cold vale of darkness falls,
Some hear only the Devil's calls.

With hindsight the jewel, the effort must be,
Keep thought and memory clean and carefree,
Always keep movement positive and concise,
For the passage of time will not happen twice.

Nick J. M. Geddes

Split In Two

One and two makes three
But duality divides me.
People inexorably pass me by
Without a second thought of why
I am like I am.
Anonymity and invisibility go hand in hand
When people bury their heads in the sand.
I do not live but instead exist
And the beating of my heart persists.
My saviour is detachment, my love is self.
Two pens writing on two pieces of paper
A short valediction.
A crying man, sitting in the park
With a gun in his hand, takes aim and shoots.
There's total oblivion
When people bury their heads in the sand.
Every day and every night, I continue with my fight
Against my conscience, which divides my thoughts.
One side in opposition to the other,
Duality does my mind smother.

J. Moore

Pain of Mine

The pain that I've gone through, the tears I've wept when cried
The things that I've been through, then gone on home to hide.
　The names that hurt more than violence, not seen.
　I thought they were friends, how could they be mean?
The torment in lessons, at break times and lunch.
It hurts more than a beat-up, abuse from a bunch.
　The days that went by, not a smile on my face
　The time, the school hours, went by such slow pace.
My stomach would tighten, as school came into view.
I'd get home feeling terrible, I said I had the flu.
　The Christmas weeks were joyful, but soon the time had come
　To school the place I hated, Dad noticed and my mum.
More days went by so slowly, feeling worse and worse each day
Abuse was written on my books, "Bitch, Bitch" it would say.
　I got home cried my heart out, till my eyes were red and sore
　all I kept on saying was "not again, no more no more."
Her phone rang, she got told everything, from the first day till the
Last I had to let it out for once, from the suffering in the past.
　It's now getting sorted, and I feel a bit more pleased
　I'm here alone in a little room, no lessons, I feel at ease.

Janine Down

Intergalactic Rings

Circles of times evolving, revolving,
I may encounter you upon the way,
Tomorrow will become yesterday, yesterday
Our transient spirits fragile and eternally fey.

We may collide in another century, entity,
With all the dearly beloved ghosts
Replaying the same tragic manifestos, scenarios.
Scenarios, manifestos, not manifestos, scenarios
You could be the receiver and I the host.

Numbers and letters foretelling, portending
Their intricate coincidental pattern,
You are J.P. I am JP we are J.P's JP's.
Forever linked in time, the eternal turn.

We may become another letter, number, asunder,
On the galaxies wheels of lotteries,
A happy accident exploding, revoking,
A quantum leap of love, the charis.

Why? Does cancer defy it all, beit all,
A single cell, the answer to fabulous man,
The glories, Anno Dommini, magnificence, significance,
Of music, nature, endless cycles that ran.

Jennifer Porteous

Terrible Tiger Trauma

Don't harm the tigers, they don't hurt you,
Only when you hurt them, will they do anything to you?
Don't buy tiger skin rugs, or medicine from China,
Don't buy tiger for tea, or even from a diner.

Don't harm the tigers, they don't hurt you,
They are beautiful creatures, better looking than you,
No-one wants the tooth of a tiger, hanging round their neck,
If they do they are as bad as you, a total hypocrite.

Don't harm the tigers, don't put them in a zoo.
People just stare and jeer, would you want that done to you?
It's bad enough being shot at, but put in prison too,
Come on give them a chance, the tiger is not as bad as you.

If I were a tiger I would run and hide,
Because most men are out to fight you,
Just for your skin and your insides.
Just leave them alone and let them get on,
In this terrible tiger trauma.

Stephen Popple

Heaven Sent

You were a part of me for months
Everywhere I went, I felt you so near.
I felt so happy "I shed a tear".
When at last "The great surprise was here,"
The pain and fear seemed to disappear.
A darling daughter "so beautiful", so very sweet.
You made my life, my heart complete.
The moment I held you in my arms
Will always be cherished with all your charms
Your little tiny fingers, and ten toes
Right down to your shiny button nose.
Your sweet little face, and eyes full of mystery
My darling child, you were heaven sent to me.
So gentle, so meek and mild
That was my baby child

Janet M. Harding

Childhood

Fifteen years ago I was born in Wales
And I remember many childhood things:
Red uniforms; the coast and ships with sails;
Ballet and friends; playing in the park on swings.

When I was five we moved to PNG:
Houses on stilts; coral and crocodiles;
Blazing sun; malaria; sand and sea;
Green uniforms; open classes and childhood smiles.

We moved to Scotland later still:
Rain and snow and the River Clyde;
Blue uniforms and gym; riding horses up on the hill;
School blowing up, on fire, and watching open-eyed.

Five years more and down south we came;
New house; new school; new friends to make;
Green uniforms; boys and the changing game;
Growing older, growing up; new decisions to take.

Viki Allen

The Waif

Her eyes were grey and sad,
  She had a lost look that was pathetic,
    Her small body was thin and hunched
      As though from many beatings.

Her clothes were like rags on her body,
  And she shivered miserably with cold and hunger,
    Her fair hair hung like string upon her shoulders.
      And her feet were bare with cracks and blisters.

Sometimes when I am out walking and I see her,
  Or I think of her in the warmth and comfort of my home,
    I feel my heart will break.

Olive Ray Tumbull

Angel Face

You walked into my life with such ease
  like a dove circling on a breeze.
My immense feelings and emotions
  came out of the blue - and flew straight into you.

You made me see love, thank you, my gift from above.
We lay under the dotted sky drifting away
  as gently the water began to sway.
We vowed I was yours and you were mine
and imagined we were in another place and time.
The dawn breaking pronounced our unspoken fears.
Circles forming on the water surface, no rain, just tears.
You managed a smile, our bodies wound tight.
Parting was so wrong for a love so right.

My days so long, my nights so sad,
gone is the happiness I once had.
I'm crying inside, my world is tumbling down.
But my tower of strength is nowhere to be found.
Inside me such an overwhelming pain
that I will never see my Angel Face again.

Rebecca Hennessy

Eternal Youth

Without a form I caress my loved one
who has no knowledge of my being.
Vulnerable now to the winds from the
North, South, East and West which carry
my helpless spirit over sea and ocean,
Hill and valley.

As I travel along with this invisible
force I see people laden with sorrow,
overwhelmed with joy and destroyed by
guilt, death being one man's enemy and
another man's escape. The fear inside stirs
my conscience and I am awake . . .
Realizing that it is not I who is dead
But . . . but you, my friend in my mind
you will never grow old.

Brian McDonald

A Prayer

Although I cannot see or hear you
I will know you understand,
With your loving hand; Guide me in everything I do and say,
Help me through the nights ahead, listen to me when I pray,
Teach me please the kind of living that I know should be done,
Make me understand more clearly, my fellow beings every one.
Show me the way to loving and giving,
That I may love and give more dearly
Make this life of mine worth living
Walk with me when I want to run.
Chase away my fears and sorrow
Watch over me while I sleep
Keep me on the straight and narrow
Though the path be long and steep
Lend me your strength and courage, that I may give to others, too,
Catch me when I reach out oh Lord, my failing hands to you.

Doreen Scott

For What Reason?

The changing of society is such a hectic pace,
You see it right across our globe, those standards set to face,
But is it right to think success, when all you have is greed,
To satisfy a changing world, an ignorant selfish breed.

Money is the driving force, the fuel behind the fire,
Let's fell the trees to reap the cash, fulfilling our desire,
An oil slick is nothing, when it comes to being wealthy,
A sporty car, four bedroom house, a bank balance that's healthy.

Beware to all establishments, the people in the know,
For nature will see through you, and defences she will grow,
And perhaps without you knowing, she'll counter your attack,
Infections without cures is her way of fighting back.

Lisa Ward

I Need A Ripe Fruit

Patience is my lover;
Our love has not yet brought forth
The tempting fruit.
I wish that my lover and I loved
As other men do;
Rushing around,
Between one and the next.
I want to feel strong,
Speak bold and true
Yet something holds me back;
My resolve crumbles,
My spirit quivers,
I stand before her,
Unarmed,
Bare to the bone.
Then patience is there pulling at my arm
Despite what else she does
She always keeps me free
From harm.

Saul Grant

Untitled

Oh! Santa Claus! There's something I must ask,
How you accomplish such a dreadful task
As coming down our chimneys which are black
While every trace of sootiness you lack.
With all you do for us might have feared
There'd be a spot of dirt upon your beard
But ne'er a smear or smudge can e'er be seen.
How do you keep your whiskers white and clean?

Alex J. Gooch

Sally

Sally and I had been friends forever,
We vowed to be pals till the end,
A friendship that nothing could sever,
And if severed it always would mend.

But then one dark weekday morning,
Sally broke down and began to cry,
Because, as the bright sun was dawning,
Sally was told she was going to die.

Her health deteriorated so quickly,
For Sally, just living was a strain,
It broke my heart to see her so sickly,
To see her suffering such pain.

Two months later Sally died,
And my heart was filled with such grief,
But I know Sally would not have cried,
As, for her, death was a relief.

Nina Louise Ryder

Untitled

She's weeping and wailing but nobody hears.
she's weeping, and wailing but nobody cares.
She cries and cries for the love she has lost,
for the feelings of safety that now were gone.
She wants help but doesn't ask.
She needs help but has no one to ask.
A knife in her hand she does hold and
still her tears are running cold.
Please somebody, anybody wake up and see
She needs help, oh why don't you see.

The sun still shines and the wind still blows
and nobody knows why she did go.
Nobody helped her and nobody cared
and now she is lying on her bed.
Her tears have stopped and her wailing
No more, the knife she was holding
now on the floor.

Shannon Lurie

When We Change The Clocks

The winter nights are long and cold
'Specially when you're gettin' old.
Such a joy to see the sun, good old faithful current bun.
Flowers abound just every where,
All around spring's in the air,
The time to change the clocks has come.
Backwards? Forwards? Oh! What fun!
There is one thing that God forgot,
To put a switch upon my bott.
Then at each change, what? Twice a year?
I'd have no problem - just click my rear.
Of course my 'Sam' should have one too
Not forgetting poor ole 'Boo',
They must think it very strange
When routine makes a sudden change.
Their morning walks were in the light
And now it's back to being night.
Slowly though we do adjust, the T.V. Programs say we must,
It's not too bad I must admit,
'Thought four days late, we've at last got it.

Angela E. Jones

Free!

She walks briskly to the cliff's edge,
Through the fields where the wild flower grows,
Feeling alone within herself once again.

The wind blowing through her golden hair,
Sprays of water touching her silk-like skin,
as she stands there gazing at the waves flowing in.

On the edge of what she may think a cliff,
Or is it really her life to begin.

The cool brisk breeze freezing her tears.
Tears of what use to be joy and happiness,
But now they are only of pain and sadness.

As she gazes at the ocean,
Through pools which flood her beautiful eyes,
Brightly lit by the sun which shines,
Memories appear.

Peace, joy and happiness once again,
No more tears and no more pain,
All of her sadness has now been erased,
Her life about to begin.

Giulia A. Tomlin

Mother

In this life, you can have a thousand girlfriends
In this life, you can have a wife or two,
In this life, you can have a score of children
But there's only one mother for you.

You've only one mother, you can't have another
Look after your mother, I'm telling you brother
There's only one mother, for you.

The years roll by, and I look with a sigh.
At the heartaches she must have gone through
When times they were hard, she pulled us along
I remember, 'cause we had to do,

You've only one mother, you can't have another
Look after your mother, I'm telling you sister.
There's only one mother, for you,

So, remember your mother, you can't have another
Of that, I'm sure it is true.
Remember your mother, dear sister and brother
And I'll remember her too.

Michael Meade

Faith

The sound is loud on the stone walls
The door slams
My head is bowed, guilt hangs

I move and start to feel better
Start to believe again, the guilt lifts
And I am left alone standing
With the sun streaming in

The altar stands proud
An iron cross
A picture of the Lord

I, breathe heavily, outside not a hint of life
I touch, cold and empty I touch, and laugh

Pictures dance before my eyes
Weddings mourned, funerals celebrated
A new life added to the flock

The flock of mindless faithful
The blind, the ignorant the oblivious the rich

And through this my own faith shines
Clear and believable
Faith in my own life, and my own inevitable end.

Samuel Scholefield

Alone

I am alone, I wish I wasn't
I wish someone was here.
I am scared of the future yet to come,
Why is life like this?
Life is so strange, so dull, so unfulfilled,
I need someone to love,
And someone to love me back.
I am so alone. I sit and wonder
What is love? What is life?
What is laughter?
I am scared to live.
I am scared to die.
I don't know where I am.
Don't know if I'm here or there.
Wherever I am. I don't know where.
All I really know is I'm alone.
I don't know life, I'm unhappy and scared.
Life is strange, so unaware.
Nobody wants me, I'm all alone,
In a world by myself.

Lisa-Belinda Eberhardt

Rock

There is a piece of rock born to a shooting star
That bears upon its back - a scar
Of life from worlds and times afar.

But what of that other rock? Theologians may insist
The Rock of Faith proclaims just this
That God and Man alone exist.

This rock of ages looks quite small - dissected by the few
The Truth is sliced by scientists alas to prove anew
That Man does not live by bread alone but by what they say is true.

Still, the point is clear - we are not alone down here
It is an article of Faith of fear the unexpected and the queer

While we accommodate the current view
We still hold this to be true...
Salvation comes but for the few

So I write a little rhyme in the terror of the new:

You men of future shock
You Guardians of the clock
Whose tick beats faster by the hour
At night inside the tower I can hear you lock
The doors of sanity on all humanity and all the ages rock

Colin Barron

Ain't Life A Bitch

Work is for the workers and living's for the rich
The trouble is with working, it gives a certain itch
To make a lot of money, so's you can be up there with the posh
Or maybe win the lottery, with lots and lots of dosh

We try it with the scratch cards, and with the football pools
but we are just working dreamers, poor deluded fools
If one day my ship comes in, I know I'll feel alive
Only with my luck just lately, it'll sink before it'll arrive
So I suppose I'll keep on working, at good old honest toil
And when I see those rich folk, it'll keep me on the boil

I wonder if they're happy, those rich folk, or if they're ever sad
I suppose just being a working man, ain't so very bad
I'm strong, I'm fit and healthy, I have a bit of a flutter
And I haven't got it all to lose, to end up in the gutter

My dream is still to make it, and get there some sweet day
Then I'll meet some rich old conman, who'll take it all away
So dreaming's for the dreamers, and living's for the rich
but as my old man used to say, "Ain't life a piggin' bitch"

R. J. Newman

Growing Pains

Look inside a child's heart and see,
No secrets to behold, no conscience be.
So why when we are grown do we hide
All those deepest feelings locked inside?

So innocent we play when we are new,
No prejudice, no spite, just being you,
So why as we grow older do we gain
All those hatred feelings that cause pain?

Maybe we should take a while to wonder,
Why we are so better when we're younger,
Trace back the steps to reach inside and find,
All of that special person left behind.

Lisa Ward

Working Man's Week

Dawn crack waking sees the working man
In out street, shed his sleep, don his boots,
Sup hot sugary tea, drag his fag,
Flat on his cap, and climb his bike.
Discipled he follows this route six days a week,
To tannery, river and canal, the chemical works and the morgue.
Just about making the lung coughing journey home,
He chews greedily, slumps in his armchair,
And dozes a fire fume sleep.
If he makes it through the week,
His Sunday morning hangover brings him downstairs,
In time for a sullen family dinner,
Children at table - ghosts from a Victorian era,
Seen, but definitely not to be heard.

Ed Thompson

The Window Dummy

Behind this window of the large store I stand,
Most elegantly attired in the latest mode.
'Exclusive' displayed upon my outstretched hand,
Workmen are drilling a hole in the road.
Passing traffic increasing the volley of noise,
Alarms the invisible girl; silent and cold,
Representing a world of gentility and poise.
Sporting in summer the briefest bikini so bold,
In winter, garments for warmth rather than charm.
No dignity remains save the stance so proud,
A cheeky lad has seen them unscrewing my arm,
Prompting levity from vulgar men in the crowd.
Now a public spectacle, brutally undressed,
Steadily appraised by those two searching eyes,
He clings to the window with nose moistly pressed.
Throw over white calico cover isolates my sighs,
The world is ever changing as hello becomes goodbye,
Yet I know it never changes as many times as I!

B. M. Hover

A Prisoner

The nights are lonely when I am all alone,
My heart pounds loudly, for a loving touch.
At times my tears roll gentle down my cheeks
Seeking love, warmth and comfort
From those who care.

Then as the morning breaks its dawn,
I look around, and all hope is gone,
Gone because it's just the same day as any other
Filled with heartaches that goes on forever.

I look around the corridors of despair
I looked on the many faces filled with fear.
Wondering when the sun will shine on them
Wondering when we will see; our loved ones again

What can I do where can I go.
Father dear father God, are You there?
Please forgive me of all my many sins.
I'll open my heart Father for You,
Please come right in.

The nights won't be lonely, if You are here
I will, now pray, that I will have no more fear.

E. Junor

Don't Be Sad

You think I've left you and gone away
All your troubles to cope with, alone each day
I haven't you know, and this is true
My love and strength, I will always give to you

I'm now in a world that you can only try and comprehend
A world where life never comes to an end
A place of beauty, love and calm
And unlike earth nobody here would do harm

As you grow weary and your body grows old
Your purpose on this earth will begin to unfold
And when your time comes as it surely will
I'll be here to meet you, the turbulent waters to still

Your cheeks should be dry, not wet with tears
Remember the good times we have shared over the years
Your heart should be filled with happiness and you should be glad
For it grieve me, and others around me that you are so sad

You must keep laughing, your days filled with joy
To achieve this, I ask you, to really try
I promise you I'll be here, when your passing comes along
And until that moment, please be happy and strong

Roy Lockwood

Love's Rewards

Since I became entwined in love so deep,
And raised my head like rose to summer's sun,
I feel a kind of warmth and happy glow inside,
Contentment knowing my inner being love has won.

Like tulips, daffodil and crocus hands stretching out,
To grasp that voice from whence comes life,
As nature arms itself with leafy growth,
I glory in my find of deep emotions; love so rife.

Could I liken her to sun or moon or orchid rare,
Or pluck from the grassy field so green,
I would not know my soul to do—but wilt,
Ne'er in the past nor future such love by me be seen.

Of all the wonders of the world we see in awe,
And magic shapes and colours making hearts a-beat,
None other could my mind embrace so strong,
Than that which once upon a time I did meet.

There could be no other being warms me so,
And sweet contentment calm my inner part,
There are so few things that I could compare,
With my dear love who once so gently stole my heart.

A. N. Jenkinson

Behold My Dreams

Let the essence of life be satisfied with happiness
Like the energy of the sun action flows
Illuminating my heart with rays of love

Dreams of love, dreams of joy, can it be true
Glitters with hope for warmth in abundance
Just show me it's true

Dancing winds accompanied with love
Blows the kisses gifted from your soul
Sending messages of love and affection

Dreams of love, dreams of joy, can it be true
Or are we separated when we awake
Only uniting in the light of night

Mind so strong like the spirit of a warrior
The heart shines out like the stars at night
Action and adventure that never dies

Dreams of love, dreams of joy, can it be real
So joyful is the wholeness here inside
Were true happiness is fulfilled

R. Watts

Fairy Tale

Be gone, be gone, to float and sing,
In the place that's peaceful, where bells gently ring,
A place where, there is no pain and sorrow
Where people don't worry what will happen tomorrow
A place full of trees and rivers and hills
With water gently flowing past ponds and mills
Where there is no smoke belching out into the sky
Where no lorry's on motor ways pass you by
Where roads and cars don't even exist
A place where the sunset creeps out of the mist
But where is this place your soul does cry
It's something I only see in my mind's eye

Sarah Wyatt

Does A Butterfly Get People In Its Tummy?

We talk about the animals every single day
We use them in examples in everything we say
So I wrote this little poem just to let you see
How it would sound if animals could talk of you and me.

Is it raining "men and women" when it pours on cats and dogs?
Is a "person in the throat" very common among frogs?
Do snakes play "men and ladders" when they tire of snap and rummy?
Does a butterfly get "people" in its tummy?

When a toad sits down to dinner does it have "person in the hole"?
Does a stork spread "man" or butter on its tasty morning roll?
Do crickets play at "person" when the days are warm and sunny?
Does a butterfly get "people" in its tummy?

So when the dog lies down to sleep "boy-tired" upon the floor
And the horse gets on his "high man" and slams the stable door.
Don't call them just dumb animals or scream and make a fuss
Remember, what we say of them, they maybe say of us.

Susan Wilson

What Is

What is the purpose of the head except to ache
What is the purpose of the heart except to break

What is the purpose of the eyes except to cry
What is the purpose of the mouth except to sigh

What is the purpose of the legs except to lapse
What is the purpose of the lungs except to collapse

What is the purpose of the mind except to vex
What is the purpose of the hands except to protect

What is the purpose of the feet except to run from danger
What is the purpose of the back except to feel the whip of a stranger

What is the purpose of the ears except to hear a lie
What is the purpose of life except to die

Kate Richardson

Dead End

Black.
Not pink.
What about the stink?
The stink of addiction.
In my own head
Relatively dead.
Wanting to give up
Wanting more. Full of bull;
A what's in store
Demonstrator purchasing a packet in
Spite of.
Will power crumbling towards a dead
End. Endless butts. Defeatist
Shadowy grey: Reaching for
Another before the last, unlit
Detestation I crushed beneath a boot sole
Is blown away with
The wind.
Sitting out of breath, contemplating
weakness.

J. Michael O'Donnell

My Yellow Friends

The dancing has stopped, and
the heads are now hanging,
The yellow has gone and the
necks are left dangling,
How colourless and limp, look the daffodils today,
When only a few days ago, they laughed as they swayed,
But wait till next Spring,
When they start to unfold,
Their bright sunny heads, what a joy to behold.
Then the dancing will start, as it does every year,
And their spirits will soar, as they step into gear,
What a wonderful sight, such a treat to my eyes,
The gaiety, the dancing, right through to the night,
It should never, never end, but continue all year,
Still, bye, bye, my sweet daffodils, I'll be waiting right here.

Val Turatti

For Peace In Eternity

Let not her spirit unquiet be,
But rest in calm tranquillity,
Resolving fears, and earthly tears,
Oh may her soul reside in peace,
and restless wanderings find their ease.
Dear Lord of Heaven, on earth and sea,
Show her the way, that she should go.
Direct her thoughts,
and guide her feet,
Lead her, to Eternity.

Patricia Whiteley

Oh! To Be In Love With A Teddy Boy!

He looks a bit mean, but I'm sure he's slick,
Just look at those side burns, and that lovely quiff
Wouldn't I be glad to be his chick!
Drain pipe trousers, boot lace tie,
"Come on now, this is no time to be shy!"
Adjust your ponytail, and your flared skirt,
Make sure my seams are straight in my stockings
"Look at his lime green socks, aren't they shocking."
He's got size 11 bopping shoes,
Hurry up, no time to lose!
I have size 3 black high heels,
Let me just see how he feels.
With a wink of his eye and a nod from his head
This is it, I'm going ahead.
Hold his hand and turn around
It's oh! So good to jive to the sound
of rock and roll, well I'll be bound!
He likes me too, what have we found?

Patricia Dawson

The Silent Crying

I used to be a boy, then I was a man; what am I now?
You let them take from me all I might have been; who am I now?
There was no reason for it all, each season can recall my loss,
Yet still I kneel before thee to give thee thy glory on your cross.

I called your name a thousand times or more,
You said you'd hear but tell me, are you sure?
You didn't even answer me, a child I was, what sanctuary?
But I am not that child anymore.

You promised me you'd be there for all time,
And if I followed you the sun would shine,
But that's not how it was to be, tormented I was guiltily
Left all alone to find the real me.

Why did you let it happen, a young boy all alone
And still the scars are carried though now I'm grown.
I spent my lifetime silently crying
And now I'm spending this time silently dying.

You will not hear me call your name again,
The way I feel can never be the same;
I've learnt to live with all the pain, I know now I was not to blame,
But couldn't you have told me way back then.

Michael Bolwell

If Only...

If only you could tell it to my heart
Tell me I'm the only one
Is this really love
Or just a game
If only...

If only you could open your heart to me
Cause baby I hold the lock and you hold the key
When chains are unlocked then
Love would be free
If only...

We have talked and met at last
Everything just went so fast
If only the days and nights were longer
My love for you would have grown stronger
If only...

If only there was no more sadness
When I kissed you goodbye
The sun was bursting right out of the sky
I searched the whole world for someone like you
If only...

Zehra I. Malik

For A Restless Spirit,
Or One Who Is Searching Blessed Arousal

Gripped by fear in death's dark night,
Lost to faith in morning light.
Drowned in sorrow's deep despair,
Lost to hope of answered prayer.
Awakened by the spirit's breath,
The soul is roused by love's caress.

The sunrise in the valley deep,
A searchlight for the straying sheep.
A love that bathes away the night,
As shadows yielding to the light,
-Converge in rainbow beauty bright.
Morning star in diamond radiance glows,
Within a sapphire sky ablaze with rose.

Reverence and passion in loving embrace,
Spiritual advent, dawn of grace.
Soul merging in the tenderness,
Enraptured in a lovers bliss,
Dissolves within the sacred breast,
Conceives a life that's heaven blest.
Deo Gratias.

Brenda Chung

Oceanic Obstruction

The waves forcefully crashed,
Against the jagged rocks,
It seemed as though it was real life,
An argument between the two,
The sky a miserable grey in colour,
Threatened to whip the rocks below,
A spray of sea water from the aggressive waves,
Came towering high into the angry sky,
The small innocent fishing boat,
Was muddled up in this quarrel
Whichever way it tried to turn,
The disagreement seemed to follow,
The sea gulls began to shriek boisterously,
As the wind buffeted against the
deteriorated rocks below,
And the salt from the sea gave off a nauseating odour,
Intimidating all of the living creatures nearby.

Victoria Lowes

The Mighty Sea

The mighty sea rushes to the shore,
Only to be driven back once more,
By a force that she cannot comprehend.
What is that force, that twice a day,
Rushes to the shore, then ebbs away?
Is the sea in love with the earth
That she rushes forwards
To meet the home of her re-birth?
Is she seeking out the rivers, lakes and streams,
The forgotten places of her dreams?
But in times of quiet contemplation,
As her waves caress the shore,
Her dreams are still unfathomed,
As she awakes to our world once more.

Lena Maureen Raine

My Sentinel

Sentinel of mine, Invisible immortal stand.
Life forever entwined, protecting stature so grand.
Twinkle of my mould, sentinel of my fate.
Star of my soul, mortal thoughts you abate.
Soft caress of tortured minds, shrouded in encasing arms.
Whispers of wrong and right it finds, pulsating light from
guiding palms.
Guardian of day and night, bathed in Holy glow.
One sentinel, one light, so many minds fail to know.
Shrouded by a special one, from beginning ways.
Be it daughter or son, until the end of days.
Plough of life, wrapped in its wings.
Overseer of strife, protector of my being.
Listening to my fright, my sorrow, no one to share.
Turning to your light, only you to care.
Sentinel of my Euphoria, angel of my delights.
Guardian of my Pilopia, sentinel of my days and nights.

R. A. A. E. Johnson

This England

This England, our glorious heritage.
   Beloved by old and young,
In verse, in prose, in music
   Her praises have been sung—
And mightily has she fought to keep
   Her sea-girt coast secure,
So thus from age to age
   Her ramparts shall endure—

Through all her winding lanes and flower-starred meadows,
   By stately mansions or by shepherd's cot
On windswept hilltops or by sleepy rivers,
   From landscaped gardens or by humble plot . . .
The glory of her heritage stands triumphant,
   Though lesser dynasties may rise and fall,
The glory that is England will forever
   Overshadow and arise above them all.

Joan Andrews

Another Granddaughter

Will you be gran's frilly wee girl
Lover of jewels, amethyst, pearl?
Not denim nor suede, but velvet and silk,
Satin and lace, some even handmade.

Not clumping thick shoes but soft strappy sandals
To go with full skirts
And long flowing scarves,
Just to be pretty, never to flirt.

Then you will meet a rugged athlete
Who wants you to share his world of the track,
Then trainers and tracksuits, sweatshirts and towels,
Become more important than anything else.

But you'll still remember your love of fine things,
When the occasion arises you'll dress up again,
Perhaps as a bride, with a long flowing train
Flowery tiara and soft silky veil.

Whatever you wear be a happy wee girl
Smooth satiny hair, perhaps a soft curl.
Tailored suits, casual slacks, chunky sweater or little T-shirt
Dress to be happy wherever you are.

Barbara M. Reeves

Angel Of Love

She fell from the sky, and there she was
An absence so serene, so loving, so beautiful.
I wrapped my arms around her, engulfed her in my love,
It was so divine. My heart expanded to trap her within.

No book of knowledge can unravel the dark mystery of my soul.

The light shone bright, the cloud lifted and there I stood
Naked as the day I was born.
"Welcome little one, welcome to reality
You are me I am you, we are all one."

The tears fell
The love so great, the experience so beautiful
Engulfing all of me—Body and soul
My heart expanded to take all that was given.
"Don't be afraid little one, you are loved so complete
We are with you always—Don't ever forget
We will survive all of us, the beauty and love is all
All is one, one is all.
You will feel lost at times
We are here, surrounding you with a love so divine
No anger, no pain, no hurt."

Rosemary Reader

Trapped

Trapped in a minor cell of destruction.
There is a barrier between me and the outside world.
There is a door for me in which I can escape
But I have no key.

I'm isolated in the room
with no other companion but myself.
I'm trapped, no air, no oxygen
except for the cracks in the wall
bitten away by the rat's hunting,
desperate for its pray

I often wonder what the people outside are doing.
My friends and everyone else I know.
No communications I can use.
I wish I can tell people how trapped I am,
how lonely I am sad how sad I feel.
But no one will listen they are too busy getting on with their lives.
What about me?

Everyday the walls of the cell grow closer together.
I wonder if God will have the will to free me of my isolation
Before I fall to pieces and suffocate.

Melissa Forbes

Farewell

The last time that I saw her, the clouds were open wide
And the rain was swiftly falling, as we hurried, side by side,
To a shelter by the bus-stop, where we had to say good-bye,
For that night I was sailing beneath the storm filled sky.

From the dark and stormy heavens the drops fell thick and fast,
And though the moon was waxed and waned, and quick the
    time had passed
My Darling as you stood there, so sweet and full of charms,
I wished that I forever could hold you in my arms.

I remember as we waited your eyes were sad; it rained
A great deal harder and the skies were black and stained;
We knew what we would suffer while we were miles apart,
Oh lovely, day, when once again, I hold you to my heart.

The parting seemed much harder, my leave had been cut short;
I hope the time will quickly pass 'till I reach my home port;
The farewell kiss you gave me I'll hold in memory
Until those same lips greet me on returning from the sea.

I loved you then, My Darling, I love you much more now,
But just how deep my love is, I doubt you'll ever know;
A sailor's life is lonely while he is far away,
But when he holds his girl again, then it's a wondrous day.

Brian E. Bewley

A Cat's Life?

The sleepy blink of the ginger cat,
The sunbeams on the doormat.
The engine noise of a happy purr,
The delicious warmth of his soft clean fur.

A twitching ear records some sound,
A stretched out paw rests on the ground.
A small pink tongue on a small pink nose,
As dreamily he hunts his foes.

Now he wakes and wants to go,
Now a stretch from head to toe.
Now a yawn with all his might,
Another stretch, left leg and right.

Alert at once his eyes are bright,
His muscles ripple with delight.
He smells his food, it's time to eat,
He lithely walks on padded feet.

A full and happy cat once more,
Returns to sit by the sunlit door.
He licks his paws and licks his face,
Then slumbers down in his favourite place.

Rose Turvey

Tender Loving Care

I'm writing this poem about our working years,
Taking care of geriatrics, understanding their fears.
We wash and undress them and put them to bed,
Making sure the soft pillows are under their head.
They sometimes fall over and get a bit bruised,
We try to console them when they are confused.
We chat while we're working and sing them a song,
And tell them to call out if something is wrong.
Although we're kept busy, we linger a while,
Their eyes search for kindness, patience and a smile.
We try not to hurry, but listen instead
To the stories they tell, while we tuck them in bed.
They have no idea we've heard all that before,
Are the milk bottles out nurse, have you locked the back door
The ones that get anxious, their worries we share,
They're old and arthritic and left in our care.
One day we'll take their place, so hope that we find
The people that care for us are gentle and kind.
So please don't get cross when we wander or fall,
Old age is a certainty that reaches us all.

Margaret Lozowski

Watching

I can see them sitting upon their chairs,
I call them, but nobody hears.
The old mantle clock is ticking away,
I want to cry, to turn back the years.
I watch them playing their video games,
In my time these things weren't around.
Their father is sitting there swinging back beer,
The mother sleeps quiet and sound.
If only they knew me, knew I was here first,
It's my house they live in,
life's so cruel and perverse.
They sit in their blindness, their own little world,
They don't know I'm here,
If they did, would they fear?
My life it is over, theirs wonders on,
Oh I wish I could live again, wish I'd not gone.
So I just stand here watching,
as the years tick away,
I don't mind these people, I don't mind if they stay.
For without them life's lonely, stuck here day after day.

Lesley Mager

The Garden Gate

Wonderful memories of when I was young
Of paths we trod and songs we sung
Weekends of freedom and sheer content
Warm Sundays fishing and nights in a tent

A gang of seven, sometimes eight
Our mothers watching at the garden gate
Sweet sunny days, not a care in our head
Our only disappointment, being put to bed

Swimming togs rolled in a towel
Sharing the river with the water fowl
Bread and jam and a bottle of pop
Wrapped in paper, for a picnic stop

Autumn came, with new pleasures to find
Bright shiny conkers were then on our mind
Large chestnuts, loaded with a wealth of treasure
Their fate to be tied on laces of leather

Now, like my mother I stand and stare, recalling my youth if I dare
Was it yesterday? A dream, or a lifetime ago
The children pass and I know their fate
It is to take my place here, at the garden gate.

M. W. Eccles

BELSSEN!

Bergen-Belsen—Bloody-Belsen!
Spiked cages forged for fearful throng:
Bergen-Belsen—Bloody-Belsen!
Brave barbed-choir sang their souls' last song!

Bergen-Belsen—Bloody-Belsen!
Dread deranged discordant rhapsody begotten:
Bergen-Belsen—Bloody-Belsen!
Obscene lost cause of man gone rotten!

Bergen-Belsen—Bloody-Belsen!
Hatred's Holocaust Hell from beyond belief:
Bergen-Belsen—Bloody-Belsen!
Mad Satan smiles with golden teeth!

Bergen-Belsen—Bloody-Belsen!
Base delusion's surreal dark nightmare scene:
Bergen-Belsen—Bloody-Belsen!
The whole world's sick sad silent scream!

Bergen-Belsen—Bloody-Belsen!
From such heinous hating genocide derives
And yet, God damn you Bloody-Belsen!
The indomitable spirit of mankind

Survives!

Michael Caswell

Untitled

Springtime.
The grey veil of darkness
That is winter
Lifts, and I feel anew.
They come and sit down,
Laughing,
Enjoying each other.
Summer.
I watch them,
As they bask in the sun's golden warmth,
Before finding shade
Under me, on the cool grass.
Autumn.
A colour change
That will inevitably lead
To my being bare.
Winter.
It feels so cold
As I stand alone
Naked.

Josephine O'Leary

Birth

Oh such pain, the loneliness of it all.
The waiting, the duration to speak,
The closeness, yet so far to fall,
The longness, just over a week.

Then it finally reminds us the time is near.
Stopping, starting, the continuity.
The highness, the excitement, the fear.
Oh, for the minute, my eyes will see.

The time has come,
The joy, the shock, the love.
The labour of life, then fun.
Time has flown like a dove.

You are mine, you are my own.
Tears of sadness depart, then fun.
The seed is sown,
You are my son.

Sharon Tracey Williamson

A Few Lines Follow A Question

How can the inhuman be so cruel?
So without any care?
Just harm in their objective
To earn their fare?
God is ignored by them.
As God will have no harm
To creatures or humans
Made to live in strife
In what should be a contented life.
Thank goodness for when the change comes,
It's nearing all the while
When cruelty, greed and lust
Is not any longer considered just.

Rosemary L. Postlethwaite

Autumn

A silken net the spider weaves
Reds and gold adorn the trees.
Bees grow drowsy. Hover round
Shorter days are quite profound
Summertime now has gone
Another season has begun
It's autumn with its lovely hues
Misty mornings till the sun breaks through
Enjoy them all. These simple things
A different season always brings

Marjorie Davis

Again

Dedicated to Malcolm

Everything had died deep inside, an emptiness I had thought.
Withered to dried dust, from years of endless painful rejection,
The cold disregard of my love, buried it deep in agony of death.
Thought too late to feel again the passions of my womanliness.
Past such depth of feelings, unable to love anymore, life passing.
Life over, never to experience that sweetness of loving again.

I didn't want to feel anymore, didn't want to open up for pain.
You found your way behind my strong defense, to stir the soul,
And stole this being with a kiss, now it won't leave my dreams.
The heart feels so much it overwhelms me to the very fingertips
Just the memory of you turns this body fluid white hot, and light.
Never thought I would experience the exquisite pain of loving again.

I fear the dragging hurt of not seeing you or hearing you ever.
Weeks go without a word, think you have lost me from your head.
Feel alone, sad, heavy, rejection expected again, raw damage.
At times my whole being aches with longing beyond earthly bounds.
Keep in touch, you said, I know not where you are, when you're back.
Why do I have this emotion they call love, all that sweet pain again.

Joy Best

Flowers

In the warmth and brightness of the spring sunshine
The bud is tightly closed like a clenched fist
It is quietly sleeping, sleeping awaiting its birth.
Its elaborate and delicate features are being protected within its cocoon
In a world of solitude and darkness. The flower
Begins to awaken, the sun acting as an alarm clock.
It is time for life, for its short life to begin.
The flower blooms like a burst of sunshine
The petals are rays shooting in all directions
As an umbrella opening slowly, very slowly.
The petals' deep red blood colouring glistens like precious stones,
The air gently caressing its heart-shaped petals
Making it feel secure and relaxed.
Its silky skin is perfumed, the fragrance drifting aimlessly in the breeze.
The flower's pollen is gold dust to the endless visits of bees,
Gently hovering among its petals.
Its purpose has been served, now weakening in the cold air
The flower's skin wrinkles and sheds, falling gently to the ground.
Its short life is now over as death, a slow death, looms closely.
With the help of nature, its clones will emerge to carry on its task

Claire Nunn

What Is War?

War - is it honour and glory for the victors?
A dent in their pride for the losers?
No - war is unbearable conditions and gruesome reality.
War is agony, torment - watching helplessly as your friends die
lingering deaths.
War is poor food and dirty, cramped conditions,
Constant stress and anguish - death and illness.
War is innocent men losing their lives slowly and torturously -
Lingering death and helplessness.
War is weapons made to kill; kill in the most fiendish and agonizing
ways - weapons made to inflict death, destruction and torment on
fellow human beings.
War is bone weary tiredness, constant stress and emotional anguish -
ruining your lives, your health, your everything.
War is heartbroken relatives left with shattered hearts and minds;
left with the huge gap of a lost son, husband, brother, friend.
War is mass destruction for seemingly pointless reasons.
War is your worst nightmares and fears.
War is finality - the end...

Shara Benney

Changing Waters

Hissing waters shabbily trimmed with white rippling
along the jagged shoreline,
Flushing gently against statuesque rocks,
Golden sands glistening, soaking up the flowing tidal waters.
With such depth, no-one knows what lies in this sea bed,
For violently the tables now turn,
Forgotten are the early peaceful waters and murky sands appear,
As the nighttime sky darkens, the sea and sand's shade too.

Linda Kenna

The Mid-Summer Ball

Now is the night of the mid-summer ball
the fairies and elves are there in the hall
the palace ablaze with twinkling light
The costumes and gowns a splendid sight.

A hush falls on the crowded scene
as the Heralds announce the Fairy Queen,
The fairies curtsey and elves bow low
and the Queen appears - her court in tow.

The minstrels are ready - the music to play
but the Queen looks cross and is heard to say
"The Jester's not here - where can he be?
he's dancing the very first dance with me
I should not have broken the Royal Rule
and promised to dance with the silly fool"

Now according to ancient fairy rite
the Jester is king for mid-summer night
The Queen found the Jester sitting there
acting the King in the Royal chair.

"Just for tonight you may have your way"
said the Queen with haughty glance
"but remember tomorrow's another day
so get up from my throne and dance"

Joan B. Galpin

Who Am I?

Born in a world without status,
Born in a world without care.
I question why I am here,
And wonder will it be fair?

Born in a place without comfort,
A place where I am who I am.
A place that will always keep turning,
A place where I'll be on the run.

I hope I find a purpose and a place to rest my inner-self,
Before I find I'm slipping down a path of right or wrong.

Contentment is a way of life,
That serves a purpose if you're right.
But for the discontented a place must be found,
Where the unconscious mind can wallow and roam in ecstasy.

Who am I?
Where do I belong?
I hope I find my resting place,
I hope I find my soul . . .

Heather-Jay G. Jones

Joy Of Living

Swift hooves race through the grass, manes whip in the wind,
With shining eyes, the herd wheels and flies
Back on its tracks.
Beautiful swift horses,
Coats gleaming, muscles moving
In harmony of movement and thrill of speed,
Rejoice in the strength they can feel
Blaze high in their bodies.
Their shadows fly behind,
Moving, tied to their feet,
A flick of quick darkness over the day-bright grass
As it bows in the breeze of their running.

J. M. Perrot

Paradise

Drenched in saffron light paradise beckoned,
With fertile hopes and a blaze of tranquillity
Set against the still greenery of the Laurel gateway
And the sombre darkness of the garden beyond
That lay subdued in the shadows of the night.

And in silhouette, framed in the archway by her aura,
A girl stood, statuesque like Hamlet's Ophelia,
Drowning in the darkness, bathing in colour
Breathing in the heady scents of the future.
Yet not a hesitant step to the light was seen
Only a tear splashed against a translucent cheek
As she turned from the light to remember darkness
And tomorrow waited in paradise . . .

J. A. Thatcher

Forbidden Love

My darling, my dearest, I love you so much,
But I cannot have you, and I must not touch,
You belong to another for better or worse,
My heart aches, my darling, I yearn and I thirst.

I wish I could hold you for a moment or two
Just wrapped in my arms with tender loving care,
For a moment of pleasure I'd gladly share,
But that cannot happen for it would not stop there.
We'd want more time together to love and to spare.
Instead I'll adore you, from the window I stare,
Just to catch a glimpse of you passing or just standing there.

I'll love you forever, I promise I will,
Even though you're not far away, I'll never have a chill.
I yearn to be close, I yearn to touch,
I yearn to be near you, I love you so much.

Patricia McNulty

If I Had A Dream

A refugee from civilisation
A life alone, my only destination
The only outcasts are the ones I've left behind
Who've decided their lives in a way so blind.

Deserted my friends, through no choice of my own
Feeling a loneliness I've never known
Taking steps, distance ever increasing
Never to find a destination, so pleasing
As the sweet sensation of being where I belong
Instead, I sit here singing my sad song.

If I had a dream, it would be this
To return, back to the place I miss
Don't believe in superstition
So I'll trust my intuition
That some day
I'll find a way
To be happy as I was before
Give me this, and I won't ask for more.

Steve Beattie

Sadness And Joy

It's been a long time
but seems like a short one
there one minute, and not the next.
My first thought is why
Why did you leave, why not stay
the only thing you left was memories
but the sound of your voice is still inside.
Some say people are taken
because they are too good for us.
All the time I think what will you be doing now
I don't know, who does.
You left the ones that love you,
to find the ones you love who left.
Wherever you are, whatever you do
be happy.

Sarah Bain

Emotional Electricity

Just when I reconciled myself to another evening
Reflecting on the wayward-way I'd been lifetime-living;
So alone in the folk-dancing, cocktail-laughing crowd,
Outcast, forever waiting in the lost and found;

You caught my eye;
Made me smile,

Your impish humour
Transformed this war-weary loser

Into a little boy having fun
And thus, a battle was won.

You: so sweetly shy
With baby-blue eyes,

Queen of poise and grace
And yet a little girl's face.

But could all this just be me
Or is it two-way electricity?

William Greig

Battle Cry!

"Pick up thy sword!
And behind me, let us march unto the battlefield.
How dare he,
That last man, turn his head and run,
When those before him
Have laid theirs to the soil.
For King and Country we shall fight.
I shall lead thee,
And bestow in each man
An honour so strong,
And fill him so with pride,
That he could fight on this alone.
Our strength is our cause,
And our cause is so great,
That we shall fight to the last man if need be.
Let me see not the back of a coward,
But the faces of dignified men!"

Guy R. F. Thomas

Tomorrow

She'd done it again, she knew the score
Knew what was coming before her head hit the floor
No steak on the table, her hair not right
No glamorous vision to come home to at night
All her fault the kids were a mess
Running noses and sick down her dress
Not his fault he wasn't really bad
An argument in the pub, he'd come home mad
Explosive pain as his fist hit her nose
Steel capped boots crushing her toes
His temper high after his walk in the rain
Hadn't he promised never to hurt her again?
A foggy haze, a child's whimpering cry.
Daddy, please stop. Mummy, don't die.
A darkening shadow, his figure at the door
This had to stop, she couldn't take anymore
The knife in her hand, a stab to the heart
Tomorrow a new day, time for a fresh start.

Jane Leonard

Tidal Waves

Tidal waves lapping the seashore,
Forward, and backward, as ever before,
Washing pebbles with foaming waves
Searching into smugglers' caves.

Waves sweeping over the golden sand,
Where once buried deep, hidden contraband.
The ebb tide recedes, leaving echoes to last
of bygone deeds, long gone past.

L. McKee

Rain

Life's companions, cloud and rain
Persistent drizzle, muted sounds
Rhythmic richness of the downpour
Icy needles pierce and stun
Pale northern skin
now angry pink and shades of red

Creaking bones and aching joints
Foul-smelling boots
obstruct dank passages
Pulled-up collars on hunched passers-by
Intent on shelter from slate-grey skies

Meditative music, suppression of spirit
Rain-filled clouds enfold tall steeples
Invading hearts and crushing hope,
Slowing momentum with mud-logged feet
Rain, inescapable rain
Life's companion.

Kay Phelan

The Scheme Of Life

Oh, where in the scheme of life am I meant to be,
I keep on wondering, and yet I can not see,

Sometimes it feels like a lot of dreams,
Yet to escape is harder than it seems,

Perhaps at night when it's dark and quiet,
Could be asleep, but your mind runs riot,

The wish, to awake and it would all be clear,
If this happened, I would raise a cheer,

I'm tired of sorting and sifting all the time,
Someone please tell me the end of the rhyme,

It's certain that we all have a place in life,
But what is mine is the present strife,

So for now I will live from day to day,
Drifting, yet hoping I'll find my way,

There has to be more to life than this,
'Cause a sad way of life I seem to exist,

Oh, where in the scheme of life am I meant to be,
Soon things will change and then I will see.

J. Ruth Hewett

This Too Shall Pass Away

This too shall pass away
Words a famous man did say
Not just true for the "USA"
Just as true here, in "UK"

True to the world of yesteryear
And today, when all the world's more near
Sometimes these words, a comfort be
Some times, cause pain, for you and me

First day at school, so long ago
So much to learn we did not know
We worried, if laughed at, by the "class"
Not knowing, how forgotten, it would pass

Adult life came with the struggle to work
Duty to parents, we must not shirk!
Would we find love, and a partner in life?
Years passed, with long forgotten strife

So many modern devices, to acquire
Age, can no longer set the world on "fire"
Baffled by our ancient ways, youth is sure to have a perfect day!
To find this too, shall pass away.

Mary Armstrong

Aerial Ballet

High above the watermark
Where pinioned mortals dare not go,
Intrepid seagulls plummet down
And skim the wavelets far below.

Snowy wingtips dip and turn,
Confident in graceful flight.
Swiftly borne on thermal currents,
They plunge into the fading light.

Roosting on the salt-sprayed cliffs,
They watch the rhythmic tidal flow
Where seasharp shingle sidles in
And seethes beneath the undertow.

Across the sustained westward sky
A cabaret is offered free;
A tumbling aerial ballet blown
Across a backdrop of the sea.

Marion Jones

These Joyful Simple Things

Yes! The simple things of life are fine
For they are the one's that are sublime,
And to have the feeling that I once knew
A damsel so sweet, and ever so true,
These things make up the joy of bliss
And if only to remember, one's first kiss.

A kiss so gentle and lips so soft
I knew at once that I was lost
To such beauty and charm that's beyond compare
A love so rich and ever so rare,
Yes! A pretty maiden from the lovely countryside
From this land of ours, so far and wide.

To stroll hand in hand through pastures green
And with the most beautiful girl I'd ever seen,
Just to see her smile and talk to me
It filled my heart, with joy and glee,
For she was my first and only love
Now I trust and hope, she's up above.

Gerry J. Stubbs

Predator

He moves with stealth through the moonlight and shadows.
He makes no sound, only the dry grass whispers as he passes by.
A night jay perched upon a bough spreads her wings,
But did not fly or give her usual warning cry.

On the open plains he raised his nose toward the stars.
Searching the perfumed breeze for the scent of prey.
Finding it he coughs softly and swiftly makes his way.
Where impala browse on sapling tree and sweet grass.

Crouching low he watches them, eyes glistening bright.
The jay sends her raucous notes echoing across the land,
Alerting the peacefully grazing beasts, that danger is at hand.
Heeding the warning, they turn as one and bound into the night.

The hunter follows at greater speed and swiftly outruns
The youngest and the weakest beast, whose tired legs give way.
Beneath the leopard's weight she falls, beneath his paws she lay.
No more to browse upon the plains, or frolic in tomorrow's sun.

R. A. Walmsley

A Tale of Two Tails

Once upon a time lived a little brown mouse
All by himself in a little brown house.
He didn't like cheese and he didn't like pie,
But he didn't say much so I don't know why!

This little brown mouse met a little grey mouse,
So he asked her, "Will you marry me and keep my little house?"
She pricked her pretty whiskers and twitched her lovely tail,
But she must have said "No" because the house is up for sale.

Margret Lavinia Bray

You Know Me Not

Look not surprised nor mystified
When kindred meet and do not speak,
What do you see, you know not me
A stranger am I as I walk on by,

Think not of the past in which we were cast
Of times of yore that are no more,
You that were mine way back in time
Though I begot, you know me not,

Why try to speak, what do you seek?
Is peace of mind that hard to find,
You cast me out of that no doubt
So shed no tears whate'er your fears,

Ties have I none a family gone
Like autumn leaves blown in the breeze,
No kith or kin, no feeling within,
No memories left, all thoughts bereft,

A stranger you see not known to thee,
What once was he, you do not see,
You know me not, so do not stop,
Just walk on by, don't speak don't cry.

J. E. S. Stokes

The Moon

You see her sailing through the night
On silent wings she passes by
Her silver glow so fresh and bright
Her velvet gown, the darkened sky
Jewels she wears exquisite starlight
They glisten and shine on high
The wind will sigh of her gentle flight
That will only cease when morning is nigh
She can lift the hearts on those below
The feelings she stirs are deep
The touch of a hand, a sweet hello
But her mystery she'll keep
Sometimes on cloudy skies she'll ride
As we look above at her face
Her beauty she can never hide
Or that gentle lovely grace
On some dark nights she isn't there
Her flight is free and high
But as you search, do not despair
She will always be there, for you and I.

Joan Walker

Fantasy Foetus

Would you be small and fair like me?
Would you wear dresses and short flowery socks?
Would you play games with your Sindy and Barbie
Kept neatly inside their box?

When I heaved you out, glancing at
Splashing red in that grey egg box bed pan,
They would not let me see you - it wasn't nice.
Covering you over with green paper towel
They took you and your contents away
To flush you down the sluice, still warm.

Would you be Alice or Jennifer?
Would you come shopping and help me choose?
Would you play in a Wendy house?
Would you demand black patent shoes?

Only a foetus. Only a bunch of cells and blood.
Bad luck. Just nature being wasteful.
I was sorry I couldn't grow you.
Inside I was angry. Perhaps I could only grow boys.
Nine years on and still creating this foolish female fantasy.
Still asking for you, still receiving no reply. Even now I am asking.

Juliet Sargent

The Devil's Vineyard

With nimble hands tutored in brazen guile,
The infamous sower struts with his watering can,
Dousing the blooming growths shielded with briers of vile;
Tending the tares that will profane the land.

Veins frothing with hate; branches bent with poisoned fruits;
Vicious roots that mark the earth with cracks ruinous:
Loud testimonies of the master brute's
Silent fingers at work - ravaging, deadly and furious.

The land, now desolate, with all its flowers gone,
Turns a devil's vineyard and a veritable loom,
Where threads of life's perverted dramas are spun,
To weave labyrinths laced with tearless gloom.

Labyrinths littered with debris of wasted generations.
Rudderless progenies now awaiting social regeneration.

Gregory Patrick Udeh

Sonnet To Snow

By coming on the morning unaware,
And blotting out the colour of the tree,
And causing chaos, feet to give a care
On road and path already slippery,
Oh winter's trav'ler why come here at all,
So rare a visit, unexpected too;
Yet silent footed snow for Christmas call
We'd hand extended welcome given you,
But now the busy life cannot enjoy
Your beauty, magic, or your silence. No,
To clear away like rubbish, make you go.
Now take to heart, and come at proper time,
'Tis not now Christmas, but St. Valentine.

E. Jane Seagroatt

Simply Words?

Writing another pros, words to share with you
Simply put throughout, children read too.
Line restriction twenty-two - title, signed.
Thoughts, write them down - may cause some to frown.
Others split sides laughing, life's happier side.
Words of wisdom try to write, brings tears
Life in papers read, crude, sordid other styles
Thinking too hard, mind boggles - afraid
Why are we here on earth like other species?
We are not wonderful creations
All we cause is contamination and rot.
Look around - ugly towns and urban sites,
Concrete, fumes in overcrowded cities.
Crime, murder, poverty, diseases, increase
Few rule our lives - why do we vote them?
They cannot manage their own lives with all their wealth
Yet we let them destroy everything?
Create happiness with a little of your time
Give a smile, wave, few kind words true and
paradise you'll know free, you and I found.

B. L. Fenn

What Is A Book?

A book can be a source of joy,
A book can be a children's toy,
As you turn each brand new page
A story can be told for any age.
A source of comfort for the lonely.
A source of learning for students only.
A book that is read to a child in bed
Can soothe his fears for the night ahead.
A book that is given as a gift
Can give a heavy heart a great uplift.
A book can teach a foreign tongue,
A book can teach songs to be sung,
A book can bring you many friends.
A book can bring you many different ends.
My favourite book you must agree
Is the book that taught me my ABC.

R. Tucker

Untitled

A shaft of sunlight pierced
the hungry air.
A myriad insects quickly gathered there.
It lit a path among the woodland trees,
And there remained, unruffled,
whilst the breeze
Played with the branches waving overhead,
And, swiftly as it came -
the bright shaft fled.

Nora M. Kirienko

Soul Searching

She stands all forlorn looking out to the sea
In a daze she is pondering of what is to be
The peace and the quiet help her thoughts to express
Her feelings of fear and of dark emptiness
Of what will become of her life from hereon
And if she has strength to continue as one
The pain that is felt is too great to endure
The blue of the sea is so totally pure
To end it all now would be simple and sweet
Knowing forever that her life's incomplete
But suddenly there on the horizon afar
In the dusk of the night there appears a bright star
It twinkles and shines on the waves of the deep
And makes her heart flutter and wanting to weep
She realizes then that life has its pleasure
And there are many things left to want and to treasure
With a sprint in her walk she turns from the shore
And hurries on home to start life once more

Leila Caryll

Pure Maths

E - MC2
If energy is mass at light speed squared,
    Then mass is energy - does this mean ought?
By this equation is the mystery bared?
    Or revelation to the spirit brought?
By intellect unaided can we find
    A key to open the doors in the arcana?
Can written symbols the great scroll unwind?
    Or mathematics probe the font of pain?

Pure mathematics is to abstract thought
    As stick to a blind man, it gives him aid,
But cannot give him sight. Its symbols fraught
    With meaning only prove that truth essayed
By intellect alone is recondite -
    'Tis intuition gives the spirit sight.

Henry Harding Rogers

Thank You

Everything that's bright and beautiful
all creatures great and small
we thank the God who sent his Son
who died to save us all

Thank God for the life that is given us
and the days and happy hours
the fruits of the trees, the song of the birds
and for the beauty of the flowers

We thank our God for the things we see
or are able to be heard
the sun above the ones we love
and the goodness of His word

To find the light for which we search
seek a peaceful place to pray
there in that sacred personal church
he can listen to what we say

For all the blessings that we have
the good Lord made them all
for everything that's bright and beautiful
and the creatures great and small

Bob Dalton

The Ballad Of A Working Man

He asked for nothing and that's what he got,
up at the crack of dawn, sharp on the dot
To do the job, he was lucky enough to hold,
Mostly, a strong chap, robust and bold.
His work was a grind, that he laboured at indeed,
For more often than not,
There was an extra mouth to feed.
Then at the week-end, when he got his pay,
It was little more than pittance I'm sorry to say.

Nearly all of it he gave to his wife,
For she was the one who had to struggle and strive
To make ends meet, as best she would,
To feed her family, as only she could -
While he for his labours, got little enough,
Just a small glass of beer,
    And, five Woodbines to puff.
Then to sweeten his pleasures, which were but few,
a trip to a local football match,
with old pals that he knew;
But, - would he ever make it to Wembley to see the 'cup'?
Well, - he was an optimistic bloke, who never gave up.

Irene Hurd

February Moon

As though a bonfire some long time lit
A shaft of pale sunlight, soft glinting,
Sending weak wisps of smoke
Amidst bare branches,
    With tips of Spring just hinting.

Elegant arms of Winter prunus
Boughs dredged with cruel frost's hoary rime,
Tracery of sparkling icy crispness
As if aglow with fine white blossom,
    Long before it's time.

Plump blackbird, its feathers all a-fluffed
Motionless on a twig in perfect trance,
Whilst far below, an eager squirrel scampers
On crunchy leaves of brown and gold,
    In wild exuberant dance.

Trembling spear of grass, bejewelled by the dew
Waiting in frozen silence for the warmth to bless
And time so short, merely a breath
Before the golden orb melts all,
    With the softest of caress.

Margaret Callow

Take A Moment

Take a moment and think of those far away
Who dread and suffer each living day
For fear of withering into the breeze
In the quick, brisk second of a sneeze

Take a moment, open wide your eyes
At those innocent faces, covered in flies
Those sunken, hollow stomachs left without
This is a crime, there is no doubt

Think of those children, so frail and thin
With their small wrinkled hands and permanent grin
Legs that can no longer support the frame
Oh! It is such a crying shame

These lives, filled daily with hope and despair
Waiting for a heart that will truly care
So take a moment and whisper a prayer
Because it's just not right and it doesn't seem fair

When young I used to wish upon a shining star
but now I bend my head and ask of Allah
To protect and save them from their misery
To set their minds, souls and bodies free

Clayre Bennett

Mature Love With Friends

There is nothing to touch it
Yes everyone knows
A love that is mature
A love that just grows
Old wines and whiskies mature with old age
But love makes one wiser, as wise as a sage
To grow old together can be pure delight
A kiss and a cuddle makes life seem so right

The present can never compare to the past
For we love each other more as the years hurry past
It is so nice that we two are life's longest friends
We are lovers and sweethearts and will be to the end
Good companions and mentors
The list has no end
Remember that old wines mature much better with the years
The same as a couple through all sadness and tears
They are there for each other right up to the end
As lovers, as sweethearts, as loving good friends.

Eleanor Dunn

Bygone Days

I lay in bed the other night, my mind was in a whirl
Trying to think of all the things I did as a little girl
I had to clean the knives and forks and I played a little too
Then I dusted and I polished till you saw your face shine through

I'd get up in the morning and before I went to school
Take the barrow to the ice house for a block of ice to keep
    the fish all cool
We had a fish and chip-shop, there were lots of things to do
I had to help to peel the spuds and then to chip them too

I've helped to make the batter and I've took the orders out
If I was gone a long time my mum and dad would shout.
Come on and eat your dinner now or you'll be late for school
Hurry up, do all things well, that was the golden rule

Jean Skitrall

Wonders

The wonders that lie around us are things we fail to see
We take them all for granted except for two or three
The wonders of a snow storm the flakes that dance with ease
The changes of the scenery snow blown upon the breeze
The flowers bravely waiting for the right time to appear
The warming in the daytime, the night sky so very clear
The sky that's clouded over, the rains that gently fall
I see them all and wonder how God can paint them all
The sheep that graze so peaceful, their lambs that stay close by
The trees with so much blossom are visited by bee and butterfly
The air with fragrance laden by perfume on the breeze
The blossom like confetti is blown from off the trees
For those who through the winter did rest
Now rush around doing their best
And all the birds you hear do sing
Hooray, wake up, for now it's spring

Elizabeth White

When you are old...

When you are old, you hear things like,
"Past it", "Over the hill",
"Golden oldie", "The pension",
"Bus pass", "Aged", "The home".

When you are old, you hear people talk about
"The nursing home", "We have to do it",
"She can't cope on her own", "He can't live on his own",
"She's old, you know", "He's 65 now of course".

When you are old, they never hear you say things like,
"Let me be", "I can do it",
"I can still see", "I can walk you know", "I can still do that".

Because you're old, it doesn't mean you're not young,
You're just a young old person not an old old person.

"Old is a state of mind, young is a state of mind".

Jeffrey Griffin

Last Words On Babel

Imagine if the chosen spoken word of the 'New World'
Had not been English.
Those familiar 'movie' lines would not have been known.
Whether dislike or relish.

Imagine a cowboy brawl without 'okay wise guy, make your bid!'
Or the John Wayne Drawl 'go grab for yer gun!'
Or Bogart's 'here's looking at you kid'
And 'play it Sam' (Casablanca's jab at the hun.)

Imagine 'Tom and Jerry' with English sub-titles.
Or 'Gone With The Wind' without Gable's ending
'Frankly, my dear, I don't give a damn!'
With this in mind take it a tread more. No moon phrases

Such as 'One small step for man, one giant leap for mankind!
Come to think of it, would the world wars
Have turned out differently if the two powers
Had not been unified by the common tongue of English?

R. Peter Smith

The Wild One

If there be Gods above whose care they are,
The primitive, the fallen and the maimed,
Grant him a gentle death, his pride intact,
His independence haltingly maintained.

Aggressive, yes, and beautiful he was,
With feline arrogance he ranged alone,
Scorning or alien ways, he yielded not,
Nor offered up his ego for a home.

Except for sustenance when nature failed,
Disdaining all our gifts - we proffered much,
Repulsing, cruelly too, if we should seek
To breach his citadel with friendly touch.

Now that he falters, do not humble him,
Or force him, nearing death, to ask for aid,
Grant him a quiet passage, curling round
In solitude, unconquered, unafraid.

Winifred A. Thorn

Leicester Square

Communal; waiting point; meeting point; greeting point:
"Haven't you changed your hair? Oh" - nervous hug and go;
Hurry through scurry. Panic then relief, and vice versa.
"She's half an hour late, did you tell her the right place?"
Hopeful trepidation, nervous self-awareness, side by side.
"I don't believe it...since graduation?" "Fancy a curry?"
"I thought we said seven." "You know 'convent' Gardens?"
"You could have gone to the football, I never stopped -"
"You waiting for someone? Oh" "There's a nice Italian?"
Endless people river. Hustle. I have a Big Issue.
Mobile phones. Impatient moans. Shirts that groan. Drone.
"We thought you weren't coming. No, no we were early."
Strangers stand silent. Lovers stood up. Drunks fall down.
"I didn't look 'round the corner" "Why do we meet here?"
Made plans. Met Love. Lost tourists. Now where do we all go?

Nicola Murphy

THE EMPTY CHAIR

Vipers burn my devilled brain a
Mind in torment whip my writhing threshing body————side agape
Yearning to be filled by you on sight which longs......
Ribs that bind the seeping bloody wound its panacea retreat to
Sweet imagination memory transposed of you at bedside
Sitting   Patiently   A Prayer   Quietly
Slowly   Turning   Pages over parent's frame
You watch at peace I lay
And sleep..... you sit at vigil and we are one
Nurse me through until......
You end my hope.......... or..........
Realize my pretence in Truth and Love
When I will be fulfilled by touch and Life!

Joan D. Nicholl

Autumn

The leaves have turned to golden brown,
And like a snow shower flutter down,
Leaving the trees to creak, and sigh,
Like skeletons against the sky.

Pine needles cling to the frosty ground,
And foot-falls make a crackling sound,
The evergreens, now number one;
Shimmer in the Autumn sun.

Migrating birds have flown away,
Our native ones, so bravely stay,
The sun lies low in the West,
The days grow short, and nature rests.

Patricia Ena Price

For The Children Of Ireland

Families love each other
and standing hand-in-hand
they link with other families
right around the land.

Skin colour doesn't matter
nor race, nor even creed.
One God created all of us
He sent a child to lead.

He taught us all compassion,
kind laughter, helpful ways...
to see the good in everyone
and brighten up their days.

We must learn to value people
...each person great and small...
teach PEACE in homes and families,
then LOVE will reach us all.

The soul would have no rainbow had the heart no tears.

Margaret R. O'Brien

The Cenotaph

Majestic I stand, no feelings, no tears,
A memorial to death, throughout the years,
I'm clothed all in white, my feet planted firm,
The hearts of a nation, encased in me yearn.

Honoured decorated, for all to see,
A tribute to life, given so free,
Memories sacred, the living file past,
Souls of men marching, time's frozen fast.

The eleventh hour approaches, in silence behest,
Remembering loved ones, comrades, at rest,
Eternity stops, the past takes its place,
The tears of the dead on the Cenotaph's face.

For Queen and for Country, they've given their all,
We Will Remember Them, standing tall,
For freedom they died, to give us today,
A pathway to peace, a debt to repay.

Philip Tittensor

Breaking Up Love

When all the feelings you gave are lost,
a numb is cast over future thoughts.
Natural time becomes delayed,
tomorrow's love grounded by shade.
The hurt you feel is all in the mind,
but in the soul it stays for all time.
In weeks to come you'll wonder why
the reason it finished, the excuse a lie?
You get too attached too quickly, thinking the best
a mistake which slowly gains a quest.
The phone will go; the heart will stop,
believing it's her, realizing it's not.
The incurable disease which fastens tight,
the last thought by most who bid you goodnight...
Love.

James McClymont

197

My Precious Child

I said to the Lord with tears in my eyes
And a tear upon my cheek,
Lord why do you hurt and punish me so?
By taking the one I love dear.
The Lord replied,
My precious, precious child,
I love you and would never hurt you
For I love you so.
Your loved one's task is over.
He has proved he was as good as gold
He was picked to bloom in the heavens
Because I needed him so,
Now when you have done your duties
And your task is over and done
He will be waiting for you
In the years to come.
Till then just be patient,
I'll help you day by day.
I'll let the sun shine on you
To help you on your way.

Janet Clift

The Gates Of Heaven

Open the gates of Heaven Lord,
My life on earth is done.
Open the gates of Heaven Lord,
And welcome this prodigal son.
I've done my time in purgatory,
So open the gates and let me in.
Open the gate of Heaven Lord,
And forgive me for my sin.
I've tried to live a Christian life,
I've tried to follow the holy book,
But as I travelled life's highway Lord,
Some wrong turnings I have took.
So please open the gates of Heaven Lord,
Don't refuse me, don't say no.
Don't send me down to Lucifer Lord
Please don't send me down below.
So please let me into Heaven Lord,
So I can atone for all my sins.
Let me become an angel Lord,
Let me earn my halo and my wings.

George Warren

The Silent Ones

They stood there cold - unmoving
Looking with unseeing eyes
With cold white - expressionless faces
Just standing around looking so cool
In the "Walker Art Gallery" in Liverpool
These sculptured stone cold marble people
Not one heartbeat between them
They hold hands, dance a minuet
Even sit, think, and read books
Push a pram, walk with their children
All these ordinary everyday things
Done by these silent sculptured people
That should be cold but are not
I feel the glow of warmth from them
Because the artists have left the heat
Of their red hot hammering chisels
No longer now silent works of art
But moving, living, beautiful people
Speaking volumes to all on-lookers
No longer now the silent ones.

Mary Agnes Pitt

Untitled

Please tell me who I am because I don't know at all,
What is this world that I live in, can I survive it all?
Can I tell them how I feel, please don't let me fall.

I've found a room, which I can run to,
But I know in the end, it will lead to my doom,
But for now I feel safe, I've not learnt of a place to which I feel
safe, into which I could stand my place.

If I was allowed only one memory it would have to be the sky,
With all its different shades of blue, and stars that twinkle so high.
If you stare at it, you'll become lost, it'll seduce your every thought,
You'll never experience tears or pain its beauty is your reward.

If I was a bird, I would fly forever upon the clouds over the rivers,
but if I saw a person just like me I would fly down and set them free.
I would not let them go, I would guard them against their fears,
I would show them love, I would dry their tears,
I would show them who they are, and that they would come to no harm.

Elisa Smith

Night Mare

Silver white, pale, sleek and proud.
Strikingly clear against the shadows.
Stepping daintily onto the black clouds of night.
Night mare.

Luminous against the night, unwilling to blend with shadow.
The night mare, sleek and silvery, pale and ghostly.
A pale silhouette against the moon, half-hidden in dark, shadowing clouds.
Night mare.

Gliding like silk on her golden wings, winging her way through your dreams.
Dancing upon charcoal fires, gracefully fluttering through blackness,
    stillness and fear.
Smoke enveloping her, though never blocking out the agile movement.
Night mare.

The night mare.
Sliding down on a silvery moondust path into the golden new sunrise...
To vanish with the rising of the sun in a new day.
And you open your eyes, contented, slept well.

Anna Seenivasagam

Freedom

I have not known the horror of wartime fire and hell,
And yet I feel deep gratitude to all of those who fell,
Far beyond the sea, they lay, in dark and muddy tomb,
While still I was protected within my mother's womb.
But still, despair she passed to me, for those who died on land and sea,
For those in far off foreign grave, their lives the sacrifice they gave
That my life may be free!

J. A. Hogben

Homecoming 1926

Kettle singing on the hob is there to make the brew;
Milk is poured into the cups and pot is warming through;
A bowl of sugar passed around is for anyone to take;
With bread and butter, cheese or jam, and scrumptious lardy-cake.

Everyone has had their fill, the young ones put to bed;
Older bairns have settled down with books before them spread;
The set of questions written down by teacher, when in class;
Must all be answered properly if tests they want to pass.

Lesson books are put away, and children go upstairs;
Have a wash and clean their teeth, then kneel to say their prayers;
Mother comes to tuck them in and wish them all, 'Goodnight!'
When you have finished chattering, please turn off the light!'

She goes into the sitting-room and draws the curtains close;
Then bends and picks her knitting up to count the many rows;
Father sits with open book, his story nearly read;
Whilst there upon the sheepskin rug their ginger tom lies spread.

The clocks are chiming half-past-ten, 'It's time we thought of bed,
Shall I make the fire up, dear?' our Father yawning, said;
'Yes please! The night is very cold; it helps to warm the house!'
Then turning to the cat, she said, 'Make sure you catch that mouse!'

Celia Stringer

The Organist

A figure in the church-yard stood!
By a headstone cold and bare;
He stood alone in the silence,
To offer up a prayer.

Bells tolled in the belfry a message of the day,
A welcome to all people, gathered here to pray.
The preacher in the pulpit, before the lesson said,
We have no organist today, could someone play instead?

An old man staggered up the aisle
His raiment old and worn.
A sad sight for folk to see
In church this Sunday morn.

But as he touched the organ keys,
Without a single word,
The music that did echo
Was the sweetest ever heard!

The sun shone o'er the altar steps.
And the hymns were sung that day.
To the music of the organist
Who volunteered to play.

Douglas Neale

Tides And Changes

They were taken from the fields,
Calm, smiling and innocent,
They, too, were young as you are now,
Soon their shoulders would be heavy-laden,
Their once smooth skin ploughed in furrows.

Laughter which lately echoed through the house
Would be remembered by those left behind;
Home, to those who were forced to leave
Would became a shrine to the past,
Though they didn't realize it then.

There was no last goodbye, spoken softly,
Just some high-spirited gesture of patriotism,
Almost theatrical, full of hope and glory.
I waved goodbye to the boy forever, yet he returned,
But a man, a stranger, walked in his shoes.

Youth did not materialize, so it was never lost,
But as we celebrated with smiles and tears,
He stood in reflective silence, alone.
There had been words, though only a few,
For his eyes looked out at strangers, too.

Rosalind Armstead

The Spring Of Life

The beauty of those distant hills
Their wooded slopes and rocky steeps do show
A spring of life pours from the crevices it fills
Falling headlong down its rocky path below

Force and fury calms to a peaceful river stream
Babbling through the shallows into its deeps
With reedy banks and pastures green
Meandering on, a flow that never sleeps.

Its habitat and wildlife busy about their quest
Whilst the rising trout take the stricken flies
Gathering storm clouds roll in from the west
Turning a trickle to a torrent from the heavy skies

Urged on by the rising force
The flood removes the torpor in the tide
With foul ditching that inflowed its course
To restore the splendour and its pride.

Activity it does provide, bringing oars to the hand,
Spread of sail and barque of many kinds,
The spring of life so vital to the land
Converging with the sea it so readily combines.

Kenneth C. Burditt

The Fairs In Town

Merry go rounds and candy floss,
Proudly riding on a white horse.
The fair is in town, it's lovely to see.
The fortune tellers one, two, three.
The bearded lady, side shows galore.
Jolly clowns tumbling across the floor.
The bumper cars are drawing the crowds.
Fathers and sons shouting aloud.
The big wheel has stopped, crowds begin to run.
Hurry mum, the children all shout.
It's filling up. We'll be left out.
They have waited a year to welcome the fair.
They'll enjoy every minute of the time it is there.
It's over so quickly, this annual event.
When it has gone, and the money all spent,
The pleasure it brings, no longer there.
Leaves a very flat feeling, an air of despair.
This year it's over, the excitement's died down.
But there's always next year, twelve months to the day,
They'll be cheering and shouting, "Here's the fair, Hoo-Ray."

Daisy Rodgers

To My Brother

I had a dear brother Frank,
And for his birth the Lord I thank.
Every day he did good deeds,
And for his family he met their needs.
In school he taught for many years,
Both boys and girls were full of tears
When it was time to end
His life-long work, which helped to send
Them on their way to a new career,
which gave them hope and mums a cheer.
But all those children did not forget
That man who patiently set
Them tasks both hard and tedious
And never showed how much he needed us.
His family loved him very much
And every day he wished to be in touch,
With all his friends so good and true
Their voices brought him strength anew.
But as his breath began to cease
He went to God to rest in peace.

Kathleen M. Kyriacon

Peril Of The Deep

Beneath the rugged cliffs patched in browns and greens
White horses dance on the wild and raging seas
The super tanker wallows on the heavy swell
Her future is uncertain, no one can foretell

Fast aground holed beneath the water line
With decks awash oil gushes forth into the brine
The slick grows longer as far as the eye can reach
Turn of the tide brings disaster to many a cove and beach

Miles of coastline this dark hell does secrete
Lifeless seabirds blackened from the peril of the deep
Guillemots and many other gulls in a sorry state
So prone, so helpless, awaiting their fate

Colonies of seabirds now sparse on the wing
Survival so hard for all living things
Their habitats so bleak, barren and bare
May the miracle of nature steadfastly share

The greed of the greedy to fuel their needs
In enormous proportions a folly of dreams
Another disaster has now been unfurled
A peril to nature and life in this world.

K. C. Burditt

199

Compliance

Forgotten are emotions I used to know,
Those nurtured by hope; the wish rules my mind
Not to survive here on earth over long
Until no one living recognizes me.
Every day a cripple totters past
Outside; I watch him struggling to make it seem
The pain has eased; although he is younger
Than I, death must be preferable to that;
Hedonists condemn this verdict as wrong
Before they learn how briefly pleasures last;
Thus I have become less reluctant to go
To the world without instinctive male hunger
For a woman born truly loving and kind
Who, when met, offers more than sympathy,
Since that, for me, remains a frustrated dream;
The silent void is now my true habitat.

Robert H. Hanworth

Please

There's a magic little world
That works wonders when it's heard.
Although it sometimes seems to lose itself with ease.
But there's such a charm about it
That we cannot do without it
And that magic little word is only "please".

Derek Burgan

Farming

A hard life, a tiring life, working in the fields,
Starting well before the dawn to keep up those milk yields.
A hard life, a tiring life, working in the pens,
Staying there, well after dusk, bedding down the stock and hens.

A hard life, a tiring life, working in noonday sun,
Making hay for winter feed is never that much fun.
A hard life, a tiring life, plodding through the storm,
Making sure each animal is safe and warm.

A hard life, a tiring life, working through the chill,
Ploughing fields for new spring growth on and over the hill.
A hard life, a tiring life, scattering seed for corn,
This should feed those animals not yet born.

A hard life, a tiring life, to work through day by day.
You need to love the life, toiling hard that way.
A hard life, a tiring life, but benefits for one's heart.
As witnessing the miracles of life is one's part.

A hard life, a tiring life, a life of love of giving
To benefit the life that benefits your living.
A hard life, a tiring life where work never ceases.
A drudgery no, as love of life releases.

Zoe Ryle

The Call Of The East

The magic and mystery of the East have always beckoned me
To visit those exotic lands so far across the sea.

One year I flew to Bangkok - city of many charms -
And sailed in a speed boat down a river fringed with palms.

The beauty of the temples in shimmering blue and gold
With their encrusted jewelry is wondrous to behold.

In the crowded city I used to paused a while
To speak to the friendly people with their ready smile.

The traffic in the evening is not so much fun.
One felt one just wanted to alight and run!

But the traditional dancing in the concert hall
With its grace and beauty has not changed at all.

So Thailand with her traditions embedded in the past
Has forged in my mind fond memories that will last.

Beatrice Hann

Country Crafts

If you take a walk around the village green
here are some country crafts that can be seen,
To the right of the Chapel-of-the-Blessed
the Thatcher repairs the roof of the Pilgrims Rest,
Over the bridge and along the lane,
the Dry Stone Waller rebuilds the wall again,
past the church where you can hear the choir
nearby the Blacksmith's forge, horseshoes red hot in the fire.
Outside the house of the Lacemaker,
the Saddler smiles in conversation with the Basketmaker,
close by the Inn "The Evergreen Hop",
the Candlemaker is busy in his shop.
Here is a man with a magic feel, the Potter toils at his wheel,
barrels and casks from the Coopers roll,
at his loom the Weaver replaces a shuttle pole.
Checking that the wheel is true and round,
the Wheelwrights hammer makes a clicking sound,
as you complete your walk and leave the green,
call in the dairy and collect some cream
try to remember what you did see, head for home in time for tea.

Chris J. Brown

So Damn Easy . . .

Desolate surface of my carcass so thin
The voice I speak echoes hollow hope within
A scream of a million Munch painted it so well
A cry of the lonely without souls to sell
Vulnerability despair all upon an epic scale
So alone I fear my body's conquest to fail
Get rid of the used and used I have been
If anyone's truly worthy remains to be seen
Self-worth devoured in a binge of skinny ideals
Purity just a word it has no body with which to feel
Within life's womb my miscarriage is awaiting
Snares around my pit of horrid procrastinating
So false are the smiles which cover their hate
So fake is the sanctuary that is always too late
I'm a widow to myself as part of me has died
From the years of torment and grief deep inside
Standing naked before a cracked mirror I see
A helpless victim of heredity
In the radiance of bright shining death
In the name of God please take my last breath.

Clinton J. Evenden

A Poem Of The Fruits Of The Spirit

The fruits of the spirit (very special) have come;
The fruits of the spirit we gladly welcome!
If you believe in the Lord Jesus, you know they're all true,
In each loved child, in each of me and each of you.

Love is what you get from your Mums, Nans, and Dads,
Joy is something very special each one of us now has.
Peace, gentleness like gerbils, are all quiet and all soft;
If frightened, gerbils sometimes creep up in the loft.

A lot of lovely people don't have all these things;
But God made us like birds so we could spread our wings.
The spirit shares out patience, goodness, faithfulness;
Some have strong self control, sweet kindness, thankfulness

Come fill us Holy Spirit, to enjoy God with delight;
To glorify him forever and keep walking in the light.

Angela McGreal

A Smile

To live our life with a smile
Makes life's Journey more worthwhile
A smile is the sun on a dull day.
A cheery word to pave the way
We all have our troubles so keep smiling through.

You can always find some one much
worse off than you.

Joan Anne Gurley

Rule Of Line

The rule of God. Once held sway.
Over men of wisdom. In bygone day.
But academics. Thought the rule of line.
Held more power. Than laws divine.

And sad to say. By minds like those.
The world grew darker. In new found prose.
No eye for eye. No tooth for tooth.
And lost forever. Wisdom's truth.

As men grew further. From God on high.
They became more blinded. The reason why.
There is no faith. In human creed or kind.
For man grows empty. Without a mind.

So kiss the man who kills. And then.
Set him loose. To kill again.
And give the thief. Another chance to do.
All those things. You don't want him to.

And those who offend. The weaker flesh.
Treat them kindly. And let them e'mesh.
Other lives. In hell's design and mire.
And let madness touch. Our earth to fire.

Alfred Campbell

In Sheringham Woods

I sat and I listened I heard the birds sing
In Sheringham woods it was early morning
My friends they had taken the dogs for a run
I saw little spiders their silvery webs spun.

The squirrels were swinging way up in the trees
The warm sun was playing a game with the leaves
It was all very quiet there was not much ado
Then out in the distance the joyful cuckoo.

There's wild flowers of every colour and hue
There's ragwort and campion ragged robin too
Bonnie blue bells with their heads hanging low
And hundreds of others that I do not know.

There's fern and there's bracken and leaves yearly shed
And mosses that feel like a brown and green bed
There's tall trees and some that lean on their neighbours
All shaped by the Hand of God in His labours.

There's moths and there's butterflies wasps and there's bees
Small creepies crawlies and lots that don't please
I sat and I listened I heard the birds sing
In Sheringham woods it was early morning.

William Arthur Littleford

Beyond The Aldwinkle Road

The sky has lost its brassy hue
as the sun dips slowly in the west.
No traffic now is passing through,
the lovely land's at last at rest.

Soon golden bands across the sky,
soft flushed with pink and creamy hue,
will tint the night in glorious dye
for gone the day-time's azure blue.

All too soon the colours fade
as the sun sinks slowly out of sight,
the twinkling stars their presence bade
the earth to sleep through moonlit night.

Only the bats are now astir,
and ghostly moths upon the wing,
a gentle breeze disturbs the air,
and darkened shapes the shadows fling.

When dawn awakes the sleeping world,
and sun's first flush lights up the sky,
the glowing colours now revealed
are spread over Heaven's panoply.

Mary Ward Hunt

A Prayer For Anna Xmas '95

'Tis a lonely Christmas time I'm having here
No-one to kiss under the mistletoe, no season's cheer
Just me alone, so alone with me
But still even though my Christmas is lonely
I myself am not for I am not alone
Angels come, singing songs making a sweet sound
And the angels I refer to are thoughts
Beautiful thoughts which are brought
To help me make it through the night
They descend from above and make light
The burden of isolation, not having you here
For you're so far away all the way there
And I'm thinking and hoping and praying
That come the day when we no more shall go a-roving
I pray that angels shall come to you
As beautiful thoughts that will make come true
Consolation when none nowhere is to be found
And silence becomes the loudest sound
I pray you will find a peace of mind
as I, in this lonely Christmas time

Vivian Anglin

Puppy, Love

I awake in the morning with a wet nose on my cheek,
And get out of bed, or a puddle she will leak,
I must have been mad to choose Peggy Sue,
She's eaten all my plants and hidden my shoe.

She's long and she's gangly and falls over her ears,
She is so trusting and without any fears,
I feel very sad when I leave her alone,
But she is always pleased to see me when I arrive home.

She yapped the loudest whilst in the pound,
She was in the Department of the lost and the found,
She brings me great joy she is my best friend,
She gets into mischief that she doesn't intend.

She asks for very little just a walk in the park,
But it has to be early as she is unsure of the dark,
I teach her new tricks which she is eager to learn,
I throw her a ball which she will always return.

When I am sad or shed a tear,
She will snuggle up and stay near,
Peggy Sue, is here to stay,
I am so happy I saw her that day.

Kathleen Hainesborough

Crime And Imprisonment

High wrought-iron gates, with padlocks on,
Not swinging open, freedom is gone.

Security cameras, mounted on the wall,
Sensitive lights, and that is not all.

Windows barred, and bolted shut,
That also goes, for any outside hut.

Doors that take, half an hour to open,
Peep holes to look through, out at the men.

Are the criminals now, safely in prison?
Are we now free, has all fear gone?

It isn't the criminals, that I am talking about,
They are all on the streets, walking about.

They haven't got anything, to fear,
Nobody will touch them, they dare not go near.

It is the victims, that are all behind bars,
Cringing in fear, locked in their cars.

Locked in their houses, paying for protection,
With all the latest gadgets, for detection.

Who says, that crime doesn't pay,
The victims are paying, in every way.

Eunice Bolton

Miracles

'Do you believe in miracles?' she said.
I answered 'Yes', for in her garden there
I saw a rose, its petals starred with dew,
A miracle indeed, for all to share.

And then I thought - what other hand than God's
Could clothe a song in feathers, and toss it to the sky,
Or make such wonder of the leaves in spring,
Or paint them with such glory as they die?

And then I thought - the greatest miracle
Is not Creation, marvellous though it be,
But that the Lord of all created things
Comes down Himself to dwell with you and me.

Believe in miracles? Oh yes I will,
While ever flowers bloom and song-birds sing,
While ever God is near me on my way
I live with miracles from day to day.

Mary Schofield

Such Misery

I don't see you anymore
Such misery
If only I could feel your kiss
And how it used to be
If you could give me one more chance
I'm sure you'd care
And all the love that disappeared
Would still be there
Think of the days we were together
And the hours we used to spend
Who would have thought these precious moments
Would ever come to such an end
I don't see you anymore
And nothing's left
Except the memories of love
And love bereft.

Odette Short

In My Imagination

My England as it might always be
A lovely jewel set in the sea
Around her shores, valleys and hills
Rivers and tiny streams clear and still
A lush village green, a cricket team
The whack of Ball on Bat
And chaps looking fit and lean
With ladies getting tea in the Pavilion there.

How peaceful the church and little pond
To the stranger passing their soul responds
Tall majestic trees, old and strong
With birds singing in their leaves like lace
And children safely playing with happy face
No more evil, but all of the same mind
To give a thought to each other's needs
With no more hunger and disease.

Alice Dickinson

Sonnet

I think of you less often-Time's broad hand
Has blurred the furrows in my scarred heart
And since I flowered for you no other hand
Has touched a light to every trembling part -
No other hand so much as stirs the shroud
That lies atop the child who danced for you.
He sleeps more still than a mole in winter, ploughed
Down earth's dark corridors - to wake anew.
My friends approve this fine and fancy free
Deportment, say my judgement's clear at last.
And now, my dear, I see things logically:
A youthful love affair. What's done is past.
Ah, heaven knows I wearied of that pain,
And yet I wish my misery back again.

J. M. Nixon

Wondering

I wonder as the years fly swiftly by
When I am alone and still trudging on
Life's chequered way cheered sometimes by its joys
And oft times troubled by its countless griefs
I wonder if unseen, unheard, unknown
It may be mine to whisper thoughts of strength
Some inspiration from a higher plane
That I may be permitted to convey
Raising your courage, lifting up your heart

Not in the heights above the sky
Those many mansions need we seek
Of joys surpassing human thought
Of which no mortal man can speak
Around us hidden from the wise
The Home of our wondrous desire lies

Our eyes are dimmed, we cannot see
The angel presence close at hand
Our ears are dull we cannot hear
A voice we fail to understand grant us the blessing to receive
Of such as see nor hear yet still believe

R. D. Hiscoke

You Make It So Hard To Believe

If there is a God in the sky,
Then why oh why did those little children die?
They had barely time to know their name,
Life to them was one big game.

They went to school, the school bell rang,
Days in assembly all the children sang,
But now there is a silent calm,
Caused by a man with his firearm.

How or why we shall never know,
Those children, the families to suffer so,
There cannot be justice it must be true,
Suffer young children to come to you!

Not in this way, it is not fair,
Those young ones did not have a care,
They were their parents' joy and delight,
They could not even put up a fight.

I wish in my heart that I could do more,
But we must not think to settle the score,
In our prayers, our hearts they should remain,
Those children taken from us, at that school in Dunblane.

A. J. Ferguson

Ruined Abbey

In breathes view beyond the wood,
The Abbey's calm serenity
Fragmented both by time and man,
Still holds tranquillity and peace.

Each perfect arch devout by curves
Like pilgrim bowed all Altar steps;
One complete pillar yet remains,
One broken flag of Cloister walk.

And in a coign of sheltered calm,
A golden bloom finds sanctuary
From pitiless pursuing winds.

Think not the Abbey weeps and mourns,
But rather it devoutly prays,
And spreads its incense of the past . . .

Then in the glow of setting sun,
Shading thus the mellow stones,
A tinkling bell deceives the ears.

The silence holds a mystic calm.
Ah . . . Savour it with sublime care.
There is a reverence in the air . . .

Fred Alston

Hurting

I am not worthy of your esteem, love.
I cannot be what you would have me be.
I look upon the future, filled with panic,
That there lies only loneliness for me.
I long to be confident like those around me,
Who seem to find the world so safe and free;
But paralysing fear in all surrounds me.
And saps my strength and all my energy.
Your will is strong and mine is weak and feeble.
I'm fearful that my spirit you would break;
Force me to mould myself into a pattern,
That God never intended me to take.
I wish that I could tell you all my worries,
That I could find the words to explain best
Why I can never reach the heights you set me,
Why I should fail in every single test.
You've problems of your own, enough without mine,
And so I keep them bottled in myself;
But most of all I fear that I might hurt you
And in so doing, hurt much more myself.

Patricia A. Stretch

You

Why do you hold me hostage to your smile
Why do your tears fall heavy on my heart
Why do your triumphs give reason to my life
Why are your failures my despair

Memories live in my mind's eye
Of days untravelled with care
With life's sweet promises held before me
Which to choose; time stretching lazily by

But then there was you
All else became as nothing
How little did I know of life
How much more it is I am learning

E. F. Ansell

The Enigma Of Life

How can I be halved when I don't yet feel whole?
The world is not ready for her; the flowers cannot hold her
but my arms ache with longing, my breasts full of milk.
I push and push to find myself and make myself and make
another. I am not who I am until the day she comes,
but the gift of life we must wait for.
We are more together now in the promise of the future
Thought is free and we are one,
    We cannot be divided when we are not yet begun.

Madeleine Bennett

Meandering

What time is spent—a wondering why?
Question, reason, so quote I—
The ever-changing world respects
Each change of reason, to inject!

Now time a-flying, years' increase
Our worldly knowledge, eagerness.
The time of yore will never cease
Centuries pass, 'ere we do sleep.—!

Each day a challenge, flowing by,
With rivulets that 'catch the eye'—
Questions yes questions, so to understand,
We await times' fate, o'er each and every land!

Many things a-happening,
Distress and conflicts bearing,
So we must take our stand, to reason.
Yet nature remains—the 'change of season'!

To listen, not to speak, we rent,
our every optimism is spent—
From day to day, each day a bonus given,

we try to extend our love, 'forgiving for, giving . . . '

Gloria J. Tinkler

An Angel From Anlaby

There is magic in the air
With just the whisper of a stir
Arising from the tragic
The lowest one might feel
Then - as if from a page - comes this hush of magic
The pages unfold; many tales are told

With it there is much of ebb and flow
Many tears and woe.
But with the character of Jenny
Comes a new sixth sense (or seven)
A feeling from heaven

With the tangle joy of angels
Entangled with the phone
There is the general chit chat
And then perhaps a moan
But overall there is the magic
The magic of an Angel
At Anlaby on the phone.

Dan Brown

Granddaughter Samantha Jane

Samantha Jane is the name she was given.
Born on earth, but created in heaven.
She's a beautiful girl in every sense of the word
But when she's annoyed, she makes sure she's heard
In her life she has suffered great pain
But now thank God she is alright again.
She tries to do well at work and in play
And makes the most out of every day
Her mother's pride, her father's joy
This tale could not have been told
    Had she been born a boy.

Josephine Madlin

Oh, I Feel A Poem Coming On

The trouble with writing poems, is that when I get an idea;
I have to write it down at once, or else it's gone I fear.

The ideas come all of a sudden, and can catch me anywhere.
in the most unlikely places. But there's always paper there.

I'll leap up from the table, saying "I feel a poem coming on.
I'll have to write it down right away, before the ideas gone."

I'll be sat in front of the telly, watching Match of the Day.
But I'm not really concentrating. My mind is far away.

Many's the time I'll leap out of bed to write an idea down.
Sat there freezing, for I hadn't time to don my dressing gown.

Once I was even sat in the bath, and shouted for a pen,
Which my wife brought me with paper, saying "Oh no, not agen."

But now it's time to leave you. I'll say ta-ra and so-long,
'Cos I've got a funny feeling. I think it's a poem coming on.

K. Rayner

A Nation's Folly

A country's leader strong and true
It's not I, it could be you
Starting a war the people cheer
Onward to victory we've nothing to fear.

They fight for patriotism and a belief
No one wins, only tragic grief
Letters to mothers regarding their sons
There's always more to face the guns

Soldiers of fortune arrogant and vain
Into battle fighting for monitory gain
Death and destruction it's a crime of shame
The countries responsible they're to blame.

He had the power remember his name
His poor nation was never the same
The politician he had no remorse
After the trial they hung him of coarse.

Ronald J. Baird

Renascence

When walking in a field of green,
A wondrous miracle was seen.
The mid-October setting sun -
In seventy-three - it turned and spun.

Where glistening gossamer streamed before,
Like water by a green-lapped shore.
A sparkling, dew-bright, flowing light...
Each raindrop prism clear and bright.

It seemed the sun on water shone
And, as it did, it slowly spun!
To comprehend this sight sublime
Required a distancing of time.

The message giv'n each church once knew,
But mists of time hid it from view.
For Christian Celtic mysteries
Recount the dead to life will rise!

It resurrection first doth show...
Rebirth then given to earth below.
Through Love and joy all wars then cease...
At last the whole earth knows God's peace.

G. J. V. Hutnik

Going Home

When I went home to Coniston, I remembered I was there
And as I knelt in silent prayer, all alone
I looked, I saw, what I had known, all along
That I belonged.

'Brantwood' seemed to speak to me and wrap me in humility
For in my deepest memory, I could see reality.
Immortality is found
In feet that walk on solid ground.

Am I your Rose or just a thorn?
Did I die and was I born
Again? I love you, John
I'm so at home in Coniston.

In tranquil peace, now I see, you live within my memory
And as I pray for you, my dear, please pray for me.
Is this the truth? I hardly dare believe it
Am I Rose La Touche?

If truth be told, I do not know, but I was there
And as I knelt in silent prayer, all alone
I looked, I saw, what I had known, all along
That I belonged: I left my heart in Coniston.

Mary Ellen Connelly

The Burial Of Muriel

She died at a quarter to ten a.m.
Though some said a quarter to two.
They said she had died of a heartache
But some said it looked like the flu
She was pale at the time of her passing
Though some said green suited her well.
They said she had taken the tablets
But the others said Beer, you could tell.
She was wearing a black and white costume
On the day that she came to her death.
But some said she wore simply nothing
And they whispered it under their breath.
How stout she had seemed very lately
But some said how thin she'd become
She was laid out in all of her beauty
In a box, no, a basket said some.
They carried her into a carriage
But some said a horse and a cart.
They said that she'd had a good marriage
But other's had called her a tart,
They buried her in an old churchyard
Which some say she probably hated
The others said it was pure nonsense
Because the old tart was cremated.

D. S. Higgins

A Hollow Life

An insult, a yell,
I fell,
And then again, a hurt, a pain,
My self-esteem got kicked,
and soon my confidence was bruised,
until I noticed the hollow eyes, the tears,
the years all taken their toll, and stole,
a life, a smile, a friendly word and left
a scar, a scowl, a furrowed brow, a curse,
I stooped and stumbled,
and fell a little further down.
Got up dusted off
and fell again in pain.
No more first aid, standing unsteadily alone,
A stranger now abides inside, where once a human being lurked,
Jerked into reality and propped against the tide,
bobbing freely in and out, no doubt or thought or deed.
Just flowing with ease along the river of this hollow life

Julie Mills

Halcyon Days

Sounds of summer fill the day
on country walks so far away.
The bumble bee, the curlew,
a rabbit, stoat or weasel
all make their sounds to mingle
with the painter at his easel.
I scarce dare breathe for fear I break
this magic that I feel,
nor tread too hard upon the ground
of Mother Nature's wheel.

I breathe in deep, then walk away
Continuing my stroll today.
My step is light, my heart is gay
As woodland creatures resume their play.
Oh halcyon days like these are few
enough to savour them while I can
for life on earth is a brief span.

Elizabeth Crabtree

Stogumber

A steep hill winding through the village
Stogumber its strange sounding name
Set in the heart of Somerset
During a holiday one day I came
Thatched cottages, church and very old inn
My ancestors once lived there as farmers
With an unusual surname called Pinn
I had seen a picture on Granny's wall
With some of my family, I could recall
I felt at peace and warm inside
That lovely old village filled me with pride
I had found my roots on that warm summer's day
Said a fond farewell and went on my way.

Brenda M. Hadley

Loneliness

We walked together on the sand
Planning what to do when we grew old,
Now the beach is empty and the sky is grey
And the wind unmerciful and cold.

We sat together by the fire
Talking of the years that would be ours,
Now the hearth is dirty and the ashes dead
And the clock ticks off the lonely hours.

We lay together in a warm embrace
Confident our love would last the years.
Now your place is empty and the bed is cold
And the dreams have faded with my tears.

It isn't the beach or the room or the bed,
Just the long grey corridor stretching ahead.

Mavis King

The Old Oak

He had seen many a year come and go
Warm sunny days and winter snow
The leaves on his branches have all been spent
Now he is old and his back is bent.

He remembers the days when upright he stood
With other young trees safe deep in the wood
Small birds built their nests way up in his leaves
In autumn the squirrels on acorns would feed.
Flowing nearby was a clear small stream
Into it bright rays of sunshine would beam
Many's the time autumn winds blew around
Then gently his leaves would float down to the ground.

Once happy birdsong filled the air
Young fox cubs played just outside their lair
Nothing disturbed this peaceful place
Life went on at a gentle pace.
Then times changed in the tranquil wood
A pathway was built where the trees once stood.
So now all of this seems a long time ago
The old tree stands alone, at the side of a road.

Dawn Parsons

Freedom

Whither away, my soul, my soul, whither away my soul,
Away in the tents of the world, my soul,
or some more distant goal?
Break loose the chains, unfetter me now
Give me the chance to be free.
Whither my soul, does it matter now.
  If I can be truly me.

Who am I then, my soul, my soul, who am I then, my soul?
A fluttering cry, a subconscious dream,
Some essence of a scheme,
The real in the unreal, or the unreal in the real?

Whither away my soul, my soul, whither away my soul,
Away in the world of nothing my soul
Or some more worthwhile role.
But I must go, regardless of where,
My soul demands to be free
To seek, to find, to lose, but not share,
  then can I be truly me.

Betty Simpson

A Meaningful Sky

I look up and what do I see,
A mackerel sky that's looking down on me.
Those puffball clouds all merging as one.

I see grayness of anger, coming in from the west
A meaning that says, gardeners take a rest.
Soon the still that was will be gone, the wind
will blow and the rain will come.

Birds fly for shelter, and man runs for home,
the summer is over, and the winter has come.
The beauty is breathtaking, leaves falling all
around, colours so brilliant, so marvellous to
be found.

The clouds now parted, blue skies have returned.
Yet tonight, particles of frost shall scatter the
ground, a picture of cleanliness abounds.

The first snow of winter, now heading our way,
let's pray it won't stay.
The gardeners are restless, they want to work their
ground, the weeds are there just waiting to be found.

Lesley Barber

Spring

When days were short and nights were long
we yearned for days with birds in song,
with trees that come to life again,
an end to cold, the snow and rain.
The sun now shines and days are bright
and nature again has won its fight
with colours bold in every hue,
it's all out there for me and you!!
Our hearts can lighten and now can sing,
it's the season for love, yes — spring.
But make the most of every day,
while the world seems brighter in every way.
Time doesn't stop for anything,
love and passions come and go,
then fade away like melting snow
now spring and summer pass behind
and on those dark and endless nights
we remember the world so colourful and bright.
  Just think of love and passions too,
and all that spring now means to you.

R. M. Jarvis

A Brutal But Honest Confession

Guilty smiles as your shame is on display for me to see
Before I knew I held you in great store, but now I am no longer sure
As my feelings of affection have all but disappeared

You dismiss out of sight the fact that you could ever fall in
love with someone with a disability

When I show surprise at your honest confession, you try to
explain your position that you now find yourself to be in,
perhaps you should have studied your words more carefully
before speaking

Your true colours are now on display for me to see
It's sad but true because I've lost total respect for you
on this night of your honest but brutal confession.

Mark R. Hostler

Destiny

Terror strikes with unseen hands,
an unsuspecting world.
Darkness spreads its awesome wings
the tempestuous atmosphere.

Tortured souls cry out in vain,
amidst the fear and desolation.
Diminished in a silent void;
Forever God's creations.

Devastation reigns supreme,
the angered answers, never to be named,
tormented elements consume the last remains
Of man's inane destruction.

Angela Vonranken

Attraction/Reaction

Although we were born in different lands
And grew up guided by different hands,
Different cultures, different learning
Different lives and different yearnings,
You with the warmth of your Island race
And me with my colder English face,
We've met and felt such a friendship grow
And something has cast a golden glow.
You are the radiant sun,
The glow of the fire.
You are the red of the blood,
The heat of desire.
I am the chill of the wind,
The coolness of rain.
I am the ice on the pond,
The frozen hand's pain
But - when your passion meets my frosty heart
I melt, and the volcano erupts.

Christine Archer

Day Dreams

Endless days of childhood dreams
That never seem to fade.
To close your eyes and bring them forth,
In sunlight and in shade,
The pony standing by the gate,
His nose was soft to touch,
His breath a warm breeze on my face,
I loved him oh so much.
A summer stretched in time and space,
Strands of hair, blown, around my face,
The turbulence of all our lives,
That follow through the years,
Stirs in our minds, and takes us back,
In laughter and in tears.
Restored, we rise, go forth renewed,
There is still so much to do.
Maturing dreams that lie ahead,
They really could come true.

Rosemary Lake

Nature's Way

Rain lashes down. Thunder crashes above.
And the wind howls in a desperate frenzy.
It is cold, dark and miserable.
Nature's way of releasing her anger,
Inflicting her wrath on the helpless earth.

Night gives way to day. A new calm dawns.
The sun rises, stretching out its golden rays.
The air is warm and still. The earth glows.
Nature is content, wearing a happy smile,
She becomes a gentle giant.

A short time span. A stark contrast.
This makes the world so special.
Unpredictable by never assuming a constant state.
Perpetually changing to reveal her various moods,
Nature's way of always being in charge.

Douglas J. Spinks

Untitled

My stories they say are so too clean
My characters are like they wish to have been
But they don't know some such people do exist
More much more than just a short list
These characters to some seem rare
But just look around and you will see a pair
Look at their faces, look into their eyes
Clean and bright, like the stars in the sky
Life is too short, for such as some write
Why not make it clean and bright
It is not fantasy but fact
And if you look back
These stories that still and always will be
A wonder and thrill, that will live through eternity
Like a precious gem
You will read over and over again
Such words such saying
These old masters the art this is true what I am saying
Up there in the life beyond
In the halls of knowledge where they belong

E. M. Mitchell

Heavenly Bliss

There is a lovely golden stair, that reaches to the stars,
You climb among the gold dust, up to Jupiter and Mars.
The cobwebs are of gossamer, and glow worms light your way
And with the brightness of the moon, turns darkness into day.
The evening star will carry you, on a journey into space.
Where tiny starlet lanterns hang, so small, but full of grace
A magic carpet takes you, right to the Milky Way.
And falling stars delight you, as round Saturn's rings they play.
But when you have to go back home, straight down that golden stair,
Just look back and remember - God made our heaven up there.

Mollie Sage

The Past

The shadows and cobwebs of bygone days,
Little urchins, living their ways,
Their faces all grubby, eyes full of tears,
They looked much older than their years.

Living in the dirt and dark,
Nowhere to play, not even a Park.
No green fields, or buttercups too,
We are more fortunate, me and you.

Scruffy clothes, and a dirty scarf,
Hands outstretched, and with a sad laugh,
They would plead, for just a small crumb,
Walk the Streets, until they were numb.

Nobody cared about their plight,
As they wandered through the endless night.
Helpless and homeless, burdened with sorrow,
Praying there would be a new tomorrow.

So my Poem came from the Past.
I hope they are happy now at last,
These poor Souls, from the dark of night,
Into the arms of Eternal Light.

W. Booth

Secret

And one morning the transformation occurred
(When nothing very special was happening at all)
Against a sheet of crisp cold air
The veins of the cherry blossom seemed to spring to the fore

At once! Branches taut and nondescript
Had they almost given in to the coarseness of life?
Exhausted, fatigued from long winters past
Suddenly, what a truly majestic sight!

Before my eyes the foliage had unfurled,
Dead wood erupted into illuminated flower
With canopies of confetti weighing down the boughs
Buds appeared from nowhere and grew by the hour.

Twirling ballerinas with a translucent air were
Fragile flowerets with a grasp made of steel
Dropped onto gnarled fingers of an old woman's hand
As winds whistled through with that April feel.

Like a paintbrush dipped into Nature's pool
And swirled repeatedly over the canvas of life
As the seasons change, so colours contrast
And combine, to reveal such evocative sights.

Emma L. Peacock

She Is My Mother

She was the one my Dad called his lady
And brought into the world a beautiful baby.
She was the one who nursed me when I was young,
And rocked me to sleep with a nursery song.
She was the one who pushed me around,
And picked me up off the ground.
She was the one who I insulted,
by the first words I ever uttered.
She was the one who kept me clean,
And dressed me up so I would be seen.
She was the one who took me to school,
And cried when she said, "Don't be a fool."
She is the one I honour and respect,
for the things she taught me I will never forget.
After all is said and done,
In my eyes she's never wrong.

Because she's my mother and I love her,
and she means the world to me.
She is the one I can turn to when I'm in need of company.
I thank her for the love she gave, for she's always there to hold.
You will always see me arm in arm with the best mum in the world.

Victor Maynard

There Can Be No Death Without Life

At random, the colours of Spring
splash, stimulate and saturate each cell
of visions perceived by the brain
and nerve fibres - like searching fingers - bring
a message of softness well
understood by skin and rain.

A restlessness of breezes sweep
atoms over the cosmic stippled sands
and up into the void of sky,
where patterns of undiscovered worlds seep
dust from aliens' severed hands
and among the stars there fly.

Man-made seconds watch the hours
trying to understand the universe
time-fed by a galactic spoon:
the elixir of life it devours,
swallowed by thoughts which disperse
and are digested too soon.

Etelka Marcel

The Bachelors On Parade

Well dec and con we certainly
  "believe" in you,
With a heart that's completely true,
Pip and I "wouldn't trade you for the world,"
So, when I see you again I promise
  to have my hair curled;
Sitting "In the chapel in the moonlight,"
There you were, what a pretty sight,
How we love you both day and night,
And to hear you sing, gives us great delight,
Thanks for the hits you made,
In fine attire you were arrayed,
On beautiful instruments you have played,
So work hard now for the grand parade.

Lynne Charlton

Last Moment

I sat with you in my arms,
Your head lay in my lap.
We watched the dawn break,
And lay the world before us like a map.

The sun rose slowly in the sky,
And touched us with his golden glow.
I knew that I would have to say goodbye.
I knew you had to go.

I had watched you grow so pale.
I had watched you grow so weak.
Day by day your body died,
But no stronger love I could seek.

Your spirit is always with me.
You're in everything I do.
I hear your voice in the wind,
As it whispers, I love you.

Louise Jane Holmes

The Sighting

Bright light streaks across the sky,
Spectacular speed - climbing high,
Sudden stop! Gasps from the crowd.
What could it be? No shape, no sound!
A vision of the future or of the past?
Will we ever know? Universe so vast.
Men in black appear, ask, probe and tease,
All information gathered, collected, seized
Why the secrecy? What do they know?
Are they visits of friendship or foe?
What of the technology, intelligence, race?
Such glorious mystery - outer space!

Richard Turner

Lost Meadow

I walked in the meadow in the early hours where only nature stirs,
Where novice fledglings practised flight midst oaks, elms and firs,
I saw dew on frosted grasses, droplets flowing and wild,
The pearly glistening of each sphere innocent as the tears of a child.

The strengthening sun brought butterflies, their colours greet the day,
Blossoms opened to visiting bees, splendour in array,
Animated by the breeze wild flowers did sway and nod,
Their roots stretching to the new warmth forming in the sod.

The creatures of the night retreated to a secret hideaway.
Rabbits leaped and frolicked in their own peculiar way,
The water in the pond reflected the sky of clearest blue,
All this was free to everyone on every morning new.

And little did I know, my friend, whilst walking through this scene,
I'd come across a predator - a trundling huge machine,
With surging oil as blood and an engine for a heart,
Within that place of life and beauty it surely had no part.

Despair I felt as the menace moved, its iron jaws poised to bite,
All living things before it had run away in fright,
Farewell my happy meadow, in my memory you will stay,
No crime had you committed - but your executioner was on his way.

Phil Broadbent

Life Is Like A Mountain Climb

Life is like a mountain climb, as we travel on life's way;
We face the unknown hazards, on our journey day by day.
For a while the paths seem fair, then we reach a hidden bend;
The grass is slippy - the stones are loose, and it feels like journey's end.

But if we are lucky, we have a friend, who gives a helping hand,
And so we go on, and try again, with one who can understand.
Then as we go on, we begin to tire, we fall, and lie in pain,
So, we offer a silent prayer to God, to give us strength to go on again.

Then, one day, when we reach the top, and we know it's been hard to do;
We look around in bewilderment, as the mist obscures our view!
So, with a heavy heart we go down again; and with sadness and dismay,
We rest awhile, and plan again, and make up for the short delay.

With determined hope we climb again, without a backward glance,
To overcome the obstacles, and give ourselves a second chance.
We avoid the rough and hazardous path, and aim for the safer trail,
Then ask God's help when we falter, as His guidance will not fail.

So, when at last we reach our journey's end; we have strived, and overcome
All life's hidden dangers, and God will smile, and say, Well Done!

Josephine M. Quinton

Reflections

I have no fear of death now, I have nothing left to lose,
I did not ask for very much, I did not ask for abuse,
You pulled the punches, you also threw a few,
Now I fear nothing, least of all you.
You said that you loved me, and I believed your lies,
But you flirted and flaunted while I watched with downcast eyes.
I do not want your pity, I do not need the shame,
I know now inside me things can never be the same.
It's hard to face people, it's my fault they say,
How could they know what was going on, as you went your own way.
I've weathered the storms now even 'though the going was tough,
I've learned a lot since last year, now I have had enough.
Even now you tell me that you still care,
but where were you when I needed you? You were not there.
I sought affection in another's arms,
He makes me feel all woman without any false charms.
Now it's my turn to be the strong one, don't think that you've won,
You will never know the pain or the damage that you've done,
My nights of crying are over, I'll laugh again one day,
I hope you're there to see me happy and smiling, going MY OWN WAY.

Doreen Scott

Summer

Come, my beloved, let us trace
The golden tessellations of long summer days,
When dawn's blush merges slowly into noon's bright haze,
Among the fragrant roses,
　　Until the shadows lengthen,
And jewelled stars adorn the evening sky.

At sunrise. We will crush the cool, green grass
Beneath our feet,
　　Then cross the dewy meadow
To distant sand dunes.
　　There we will listen
To the softly murmuring sea,
　　And run across the rippled sand
To plunge into the waves.
　　There we will lie
With face up-turned to summer's azure sky,
Then rocking, gently rocking
　　In our sea cradle,
We'll trace the golden hours,
　　As they drift slowly by.

　　S. Cassidy

The Fir Tree

Little fir tree in the forest, how proud you must be
As each new Christmas day you represent 'He'
Who came to this earth so humble in birth
And was laid on the corn that first Christmas morn
In that faraway stable 'He' wasn't able to fend for Himself.
Just like you now in that forestry belt
Soon you'll be fetched from your humble pine home
A 'living' story of Christ's glorious throne
A star will be placed on your pointed head
And 'presents' around your eagle feet spread
In the glitter of glory 'round your fir cones brightly spilled
Is the angel heralding 'His' coming
To the shepherds on the hill
A 'symbol' little tree you always will be
To each and every family
As your thorny pines next tell of His calvary
How He died and relived again setting us free
So it will be, each new year we
Will see His 'love story'
In that little fir tree.

　　Eileen Wilson

Man's Inheritance

Large fields sweep to horizon's edge in shades of green and gold,
Encompassed by close-chopped hedges, bare soil beneath.
Some say there has been progress on the land,
But where have the wild creatures gone?

No birds' nests because thick hedges do not rise,
Animals have no cover under which to build their homes,
Without wild flowers, butterflies and bees do not come.
These are some of the casualties of progress.

Rain forests have been plundered for nothing else but gain.
Acid rain has belched forth from chimneys by the hundred.
C.F.C.s have helped to rend the ozone layer;
Below drifts a pall of carbon dioxide.

Waters stretch out endlessly with hazards in their depths;
Nuclear waste is dumped therein and toxins seep from the land.
Sea creatures are poisoned, and lost oil ebbs with the tide
As tankers thrust on to win trade's fortune.

Mankind has seldom learned from history's mistakes and mess
That through greed and thoughtlessness catastrophe is earned.
How shall we be viewed as years march on through time?
As spoilers of the earth or its guardians?

　　Joan Knight

A Summer Night

Roses, reckless, throw the day's last scent
madly upon the night's forgiving air;
and all, of summer's heat, have had their fill,
their weary stems in heavy silence bent. And all is still.

And as the God of light, its work complete
snuggles down under horizon edge,
it gives a gentle touch of sunset red
as if to ask redemption for its heat. But some are dead.

Bled dry amid the fury of its glare
and withered, brown. The others bow their heads
in terrified respect, their green-ness weak,
too fragile to stand straight, even if they dare. And all are meek.

The dry grass sizzles, cracks like brittle bones
upon the living graveyard of the earth;
the air shimmers as if to burst in song,
such sweet despair to melt the very stones. Yet some are strong -

Look. Under streaks of cloud in coolest blue
like fingernails scratched across the sky,
they slowly raise their heads, against their will,
and feverishly wait for morning dew. And all is still.

　　Jennifer Churches

A Country Observation

I walked my dog at the start of today,
And I noticed that Autumn is now on the way.
The sun sat much lower as he greeted the morn,
Surrounded by mist, in a hazy cool dawn.

The corn has been cut in the field down the lane,
It will be nearly a year before it ripens again.
The tractors that pulled the heavy old plough
Are standing so still and so silently now.

There are cobwebs of dew laying on blades of grass,
They shimmer and shine, as my feet gently pass.
The trees are changing to pillars of gold
And the garden annuals have begun to look old.

The wildlife has noticed a much shorter day
And the farms have great stacks made out of hay.
Birds are still singing, there is a change in their song,
They will be leaving their nests before long.

Though during the day the sun still sits so high,
At morn and at eve it is low in the sky.
How sad that the summer will soon go away.
I saw all these things, with my dog just today.

　　Muriel Grace Colebrook

Wishes, And Dreams

If wishes, and Dreams - could all come true
I'd change this world, for something new
Restore compassion - in every heart
Give love, and caring, a real kick start

Check all in power - with views insane
Abolish the greed, of material gain
Condemn to death - throughout our sphere
Dealers in drugs, both far and near

Dispel the myth - that crime does pay
Unless! You mean, in the legal way
Open the eyes - that refuse to see
Policies! That cause, crime to run free

A job! Is a job - beyond comprehension
Of leaders, with brains - in a saline suspension
Born into power - by various means
Often! Resulting, from dubious schemes

If wishes, and dreams - could all come true
A pale shade of red, would replace the blue
The blue, now fading - to a dismal grey
It's time for change - They! Have lost their way.

　　Ernie Martin

Children Of God Dunblane

Our little Darlings, we all loved you so,
Why did God take you, we'll never know,
God loves little children, so we are told,
Perhaps He needs more to love in His fold.

Know if you look up to the clear sky at night,
There brand new stars are shining bright,
These are the souls of our babies fair,
Winging their way back to God up there.

God's Angels will guide them as they fly on their way,
To a Paradise land where God holds sway,
Where only true love reigns supreme,
The Kingdom of God is not just a dream.

So all you dear parents hold tight to the end,
The Angels of God are there to befriend,
Your beautiful babies have not said goodbye,
They'll wait for you lovingly up in the sky.

Vivian A. Smith

The Little Seed

I'm a little seed blown by the wind.
Away from my mother I'm free.
When I land I'll put down roots,
And grow into a big tree.
The warm spring rain will make me grow,
And my boughs will spread.
My buds will open, and turn into leaves,
And in autumn they will all turn red.
I feel so cold when my leaves fall,
Winter is here again, but I have grown.
What's this falling on me soft, and cold?
It's covering me white, it's snow falling down.
Years have passed, and children have played here.
But now I am in the way.
I watched those children grow with me.
Now they come to watch my agony,
What's that noise? It cuts like a knife.
Is it today the chainsaw takes my life.

Jeanette Bunn

Heavenly Refrain

I'm wide awake - 'tis barely dawn,
   I listen to the blackbird's song
And marvel how such little throats
   Can sing those truly perfect notes.

His aria is long and sweet,
   Often there's a full repeat.
With trills he hadn't tried before
   That really make the spirit soar.

Emotions are high - eyes are moist.
   My heart is full - how I rejoiced
To hear that little golden voice
   Privileged to share in his musical choice.

Betty Adams-Mailey

Sorrow

Heartache and pain, torment and grief,
wherever I go there is no relief.
To live like this on all days that pass,
must surely be a ridiculous farce.
I can only hope with spring and summer to come,
that I shall end up feeling totally numb.
With no sense of feeling and unable to cry,
this would be bliss indeed that money can't buy.
To learn again what life is for
the pain removed, like some festering sore.
To partake again from life's varied dish,
this would be happiness indeed - my most fervent wish.
The pain and the torment at last effaced,
again a member of the human race!!

A. Blake

The Figurine

While walking round the shops one day,
I saw a figurine on display.
So gracefully dressed in her finery,
No one in my home would think so but me.

She looked so elegant standing there,
In her beautiful gown and her auburn hair.
Most men don't have a taste for art,
But something about her touched my heart.

I would love to have bought her there and then,
But I live in a house and my family are men.
They wouldn't appreciate such delicacy,
They would rather have something tasty for tea.

But maybe someday she will be mine,
I'll just be patient until that time.
To own her would give me a great deal of pleasure,
A real work of art, a trophy to treasure.

P.S. The figurine is now in my possession,
She is one of the Royal Doulton collection.
Mothers day, birthday gift rolled into one,
She was bought for me by my eldest son.

Ina Higginson

Tea And Tears

The lush green lawn sloped down to the River
The boy at the door had a telegram to deliver
We all sat in the sunshine with Mother at three
Best china, sparkling silver, for afternoon tea.

We rushed to her side, my brother and I
She told us so bravely, with a tear in her eye
"Oh my dears", she proclaimed, "the news that I dread.
The man from the War Office says Father's 'presumed dead'".

As the years passed, many friends came and went
My brother and I helped Mother frequent
Stations and Halls, wherever soldiers would be
To serve them with rolls and afternoon tea.

Mother would weep silent tears now and then
As young soldiers returned but had now become men
Never once did she give up the hope that one day
Her heart full of happiness once more would display.

It happened as she said it would, one sunny afternoon
We were laughing at my brother, behaving like a goon
When this pale, tall man, smiling tearfully, joined we three
Mother kissed him gently, sat him down and served afternoon tea.

Celia Ann Phillips

The Seasons Of The Country Roads

I love to walk in springtime, along the country roads.
To listen to the birds and bees, and the chorus of croaking toads,
To walk and see, fat, and leafy buds awakening,
To warm the trees, their grotesque and scraggy limbs a'quaking,
But now, when winter's wind is gone, green and fleshy leaves adorn,
The bare and a'ged limbs, of grotesque and scraggy form,
To walk beneath a myriad, of dancing sunny lights,
A beauty rarely seen, by man's unseeing sight,
To walk beneath a canopy of rustling emerald green,
Where gnarled and swaying branches on each other lean,
When cooler blows, the breeze, that tells you autumn's nigh,
To listen to bird songs, carried, on each whispering sigh,
To walk where winds-hustle and bustle through the trees.
Their summer dresses - now a shower of golden leaves.
Beautiful leaves, so soft, and thick, and golden laid,
To walk where footsteps tread, unbeholden unafraid,
To see bare branches, their crumpled twigs entwined.
Clasping each other in frenzy, throughout winter's time,
To walk again, where grotesque and scraggy forms a quaking,
Stand wrapped in snow - the country roads forsaken.

G. G. Tully

My Mum

June twenty fourth is a special date,
For us all to celebrate,
Ninety years of age are you,
To reach it, are, but very few.

You have not had the best of health,
Neither had a lot of wealth,
I never, ever, hear you complain,
When you're suffering and in pain.

No other mum will I ever find,
Who is so loving and so kind,
Happy days we've spent together,
These treasured memories will last forever.

The day will come when we have to say goodbye,
It is not for us to question why,
Tears and heartaches we will feel,
Given time, we hope to heal.

Enjoy your special day today,
To celebrate, in, your special way,
Friends and neighbours they have come,
To wish Happy Birthday to my Dear Mum.

Beryl Marjorie Ramsay

M. S.

Solitary, searching, serene and still,
Losing my soul against my will,
Blank and staring, lost in thought,
The trap was set, I was snared and caught.

My lair was raided, I shied away,
Defences diminished, easy prey.
I couldn't run, I couldn't hide,
I'd lost my courage, lost my pride.

Piercing deep, my senses cease,
My body overtaken, piece by piece.
My thoughts were stolen, I held no claim,
This demon disease was warping my brain.

I sat there helpless, all alone,
Eyes a weapon, wheelchair a throne.
My body was dying while I was alive,
My will power gone, would I survive?

Solitary, searching, serene and still,
I lost my soul against my will,
Blank and staring, lost in thought,
The trap was set, I was snared and caught.

Emma Kate Smith

A Lifetime

Some things only come with age
When you know you're turning
Your last page,
Of a life so precious
You took for granted
Looking back, at the things you've mantled,
The things you've put off until tomorrow
While handling the happiness
The love and the sorrow,
Before you know it
The years have flown
You're getting old
Your kids are up and grown,
Where's time gone?
What's it all been for?
Is this our only life?
Or is there more?
Thoughts remain inside of me
we only live once,
Or do we???

Joan Farlow

The Man In White

Alone he stood on the beach while his thoughts danced in his head
The thunder roared once more as if in answer to his turmoil
His white suit a sharp contrast to the dark sky and crashing waves
To stay true to one meant betrayal to another and again the thunder roared
The sky turned darker still and his thoughts were of his friends
His decisions he knew would change forever the life he had known before.
Lightning flashed splitting the sky
At last the answer, a welcome thought, came to him
And as if in reflection of a choice well made
The sky cleared and the sea was still.
The man in white knew what he had to do.

Anne-Marie Pratt

Thoughts Composed Upon Your Thirty-Eighth Birthday

At the age of thirty-eight four hundred moons have crossed your paths
To see your fears, your hopes, your dreams, your laughs
A billion stars advised you from their eternal bed
A thousand times you made it up but more than once it was fate that led

Through the adventures of thy past, from there to here
Most of which - that's for sure - have to do with me
This year there are some important roads to go
First the grinder has designed for you a professional bow

Hidden worlds beyond the one you know will come true
To make you cheer to make you see to make you feel that man is poor
If all his strength'n enterprise lead to nowhere but to solitude in life
All your expectations shall fulfil if to unexpected shores you dive

Sometime do turn round, look back and remember me!
For me there's nothing left but to say that I love thee!

Klaus Grevelding

The Seasons

What is nicer than the springtime when the cold, dark winter's past,
When all of Nature's bounty comes back to life at last?
The dormant buds unfold to show the green leaves hidden there -
And daffodils nod in the breeze, where before the earth was bare.

Then spring gives way to summer, colours bolder, brighter, true,
Gardens decked with blazing colour, lacy clouds in skies of blue,
Children playing on the sea-shore, bodies brown and daubed with sand,
And the cuckoo shouts his greeting right across this fertile land.

Autumn comes with misty mornings, hazy sunshine, chilly air,
Shining cobwebs hung with jewels on the frosty hedges there,
Glowing leaves and burnished conkers make a carpet on the ground,
While the pungent smell of bonfires in the breezes all around.

Now once again it's winter, short cold days and long black nights,
Cosy teas beside the fire, Christmas trees and fairy lights.
So the year has come full circle - and we wait again to see
Spring once more wave her magic wand over bird, and flower and tree

F. Rogers

The Nature Of Art

Poetry. Painting. Music. What else could they be but Art.
And what else could Art be but Magic. To enhance the human heart.
Poetry to take for just one instance. Has a magic of its own.
It plays on words. Imagines things. Thinks of things unknown.
No other creature has this gift. For no other creature can.
Look into the future and forward looking plan.
For how could Man achieve such things as aeroplanes or cars.
Unless he first used mind and words and put things down on Scroll.
Painted lovely Pictures. Or let great Music flow.
Without an Artistic Nature. The ability to plan.
Technical achievement could not have come to Man.
Like the other creatures round him he would just have lived and died.
Leaving not a sign of passing upon Life's passing tide.
Instead. This Gift unique. This ability to plan.
Lets him look into the future to pave fresh new ways for man.
And though others take advantage and build upon his dreams.
With Practical Technology and design all sorts of clever schemes.
When they boast of such achievement. Let them look into their heart.
For in the end. No matter what. They owe it all to Art.

J. S. Reid

To Be Whole

When we are small and the world is so big
We feel whole
We know that it's safe with those we love
Even though it's a scary place outside
But that's our goal

As we grow, the world gets small
Then we feel empty
Looking for the safety of love's gift
To feel comfy and whole inside
But who can see?

As we age and the world fills up
Then we feel alone
We lose love's gift and fill with shame
That we again find it a scary place
And all we want
   is to be whole

Debbie A. Howell

The Wind

Hear the wind
Feel the wind
But you can't see the wind
Only when the plants and trees move.

What is wind
Wind can be light
Wind can be strong
Wind can cause damage as it goes on, on.

Where does it come from
Where does it go
These are the questions
We'd like to know.

Leeanne Shires

The Wonders Of The Hedgerow

A soft breeze makes the trees sway,
Back and forth and every way.

The birds are singing while flying high,
And glide across the light blue sky.

The butterflies' wings are so bright,
Their wings are such a dazzling sight.

The brambles prick, the cleavers strangle,
And all the plants get in a tangle.

The branches look like witches' hands,
They hold the leaves and there they stand.

No two leaves are the same,
And neither is their precious name.

The gnats are flying round and round,
They fly up high and to the ground.

Emma Skinner

Moelfre Beach

The roar of the Speedboat passed us,
The Dachshunds all barked passing by,
A red sailed Yacht bobbed on the water.
While fisherman sat silently by.

Casting their nets out to the stream,
Where all the seven pounders pass by,
While the birds screech on Pelican Island,
A young couple on bikes pass us by.

This is our favourite past time,
When we visit our wild pebble beach,
Where little boys, throw them out madly,
To see how far they can reach.

The Mamas lie next to their trolleys,
The little boys round the rock pools,
The dogs swim out after pebbles,
While big jellyfish, wait for the fools.

Edith Freeman

Mother Heaven How I Love You So

I wish to spend the rest of my life building on our unique closeness,
Cherishing the heavenly qualities you possess that bonded us together;
From the beginning you sheltered me from evil and kept me safe.

For nine months you nurtured and cultivated me in that dark mystique;
Oh wondrous world! Forever evolving and creating life in thy blessed womb;
That mechanism of creativity; the sanctuary of every developing child.

I had all I needed to survive, which made me strong, intelligent and kind.
Naturally I was contented, growing in that wondrous world I called home.
And I just want to let you know how much I appreciate that fact.
I was born and raised in heaven, and heaven's house turns out to be you.

May the fruit of thy womb be blessed! Strong in principles and morality.
Dear mother, there is no counsellor as great or prominent in truth as you.
You taught me that I can be whatever I choose to be, as long as I believe in me.

I remember you saying when you educate a woman, you educate a nation.
And the hand that rocks the cradle rules the nation and its future destiny.
Mother heaven, you truly are my heroine, and no other could take your place.
For you made me a warrior of truth, in spirit, mind, body and soul.

Teaching self awareness with consciousness and a purpose of being free
Dear mother heaven, truly I thank you so.

Jonathan Hanley

Day Break

The shadows flee to shimmering heights,
Silver to yellow from darkness awake,
Infinite awakening to a perfect new light,
A new dawn is born for us all to take,
Darkened clouds now pushed well aside
These gates of life are opened wide,
It's here to greet us just for a while,
Beckoning us all to step inside,

Heaven above, give us a golden array. Opens its arms to prepare this
new day; purple, yellow and white to golden blue pathway circling
blending, but not to stay; small fiery stars glitter from this massive
dome; a pale moon broken weakens out of sight; winds, through a pine
tree softly moan. The dawn pair of doves softly take flight.

Light from the east with powered might, rainbow colours now changed to
deep red; from the earth's horizon the sun now takes flight, tumultuous
upheaval after the stars have fled. Please? Let's not waste this
precious new day, blended, created as canvas and oil. Very soon this
creation will quickly pass away as the sun journeys back to the earthly soil.

Percy Reginald Willson

Childish Misconception

   He sits upon his grandma's knee, eyes shining all aglow,
"Oh Grandmama, please Grandmama, tell me stories of long ago".
   The dear old lady was happy too, because as she reflected,
audiences were far a few, and not to be expected.

   Though looking through a haze of time, her eyes could clearly see,
visions and memories, painfully clear, of a youth that used to be.

   Sirens, families huddled in shelters, happy babies, weeping
babies in cot, waiting for their nourishment, and unable to
understand why not.

So what's to do about it, what's to do?
For wasn't her secret dream-man, Thomas, a rear-gunner in Air Force
Blue, never knowing of a sweet girl's love, forever strong and true.

There must be some work really worthwhile, for a true Anglophile was she.
So she drilled and riveted Cabins and Wingtips, plus anything
else that was needed; and so the Lancaster glided through the Hangar,
looking magnificent and free, with smiling semi-child, in quiet
observation, never realizing sacrifices to be.

And later, not much later... Oh God! Dear God! I beg you please
help me! Oh Thomas, dearest love Thomas, you never knew of my hopes to be.

I loved you then, I love you now and for all eternity...

So, am I here? or am I there?... Then stark reality. A four-year-
old child is urgently pleading, "Grandmama, please Grandmama, will
you please make a bomber for me".

Elizabeth Pemberton-Ward

211

Darkness

Standing in darkness all alone
Looking for a heart I no longer own
It once was mine but is now irreclaimable, gone forever
Snapped in half, not able to get back together
Dissipated on a person that was not worth the torment, adversity
The whole situation got out of hand and now nothing is left but me,
Without a heart that was once full of love and kindness
Just left with a black hole that takes up the place it must
For without a heart a person is nasty
He or she depresses in their own acts of barbarity
A heart is the most precious thing on earth
It has reasons for being where it is and is not an object to hurt
From an experience just to let you know
You need your heart so don't ever let go.

Jasveena Heer

The Holiday

Out of the dirt and dust and grime,
We wandered away one holiday time,
Just Jack and me, and Berel and John,
With a magic carpet, we rode upon.
Through the new forest midst the
trees and the flowers.
With the queen of the fairies, we
wandered for hours.
And sat down with the ponies so
happy to have us,
We felt we'd come home, with no one to
nag us.
Then we picked up our carpet and rode
on for miles.
Then there was dear mother all waiting
with smiles.
To welcome us fondly to her dear
little cottage.
With home baked bread and roses and sausage.

Jessie Cherry

Beauties Of Nature

Out on the fells what do I see?
The beauty of God is all around me,
I see the bracken and the fern,
And more of God's plan for nature I learn.

I see low hills and a woodland view,
Blackberry bushes and other fruit too,
Then down in the valley I catch a gleam
Of the sun-dappled ripples of a slow-moving stream.

Rabbits are jumping, and so is a hare,
Playing as though no human was there,
Flowers are blooming, all different sorts,
These beauties of nature impress on my thoughts.

I look, and I try to resolve His plan,
His works of nature in relation to man,
Of one thing I'm sure, it's certain to be,
If God loves His nature, then God loves me.

W. C. Niel

The Penguin

Slithering through the icy waters of the Arctic sea,
Hunting with their friends for soft squids,
Their wings not been able to fly but every so often flapping,
Walking with their clumsy but comical walk,
Looking like dolphins from a distance,
As they jump under the water and then pop back up with a splash.

Then blizzard comes all the penguins huddle
together shoulder to shoulder,
Their blubbery skin under the black and colourful feathers,
They are water proof like an umbrella and so warm,
Penguins sliding along slippery slopes, skidding
and slipping on their stomachs.

Rachel Seymour

The Golden Days

Walking through the park today
There was a cold, cold breeze blowing my way.
Through the rustling trees it blew
Watching the golden leaves that fall fluttering down
to the green and golden ground.

Walking through the park today
I watched my feet disappear into nature's golden array.
Feeling quiet fresh and alive
I watched a robin, the excitable sparrows and the
sea gulls from afar
Crying their sad winter song.

Yes—it is a bright, sunny, cold autumn day
with the sun twinkling and sparkling through the trees
golden as far as my eyes could see.
I stopped and stared and uttered to myself
what a wonderful world this is
with its cold, cold winds blowing its beautiful
golden trees,
and the fluttering, rustling leaves, down
to the green and golden ground.

Alice Jackson

Love Less

In my mind I'm running,
far away from the darkness.
In my dream I'm drifting,
far away from the loveless heart.

In my laughter I'm blowing,
against the tears into the wind.
In my desires I'm flowing,
against the pain into the ocean.

In my heaven I'm dreaming,
far away from the fears and the screaming.
In my reality I'm lying,
against my hunger and my dream.

Thandar-Khin Do

The Patient

The hard clamping of heels,
The loud squeaking of trainers on the wood tiled floor,
You know exactly where to go,
Because you've been there before,
The ward large and bustling with nurses,
Patients sleeping,
Talking quietly with family,
Some relatives crying after they hear the news,
A loved one is dying.
You sit there by the bedside wondering why,
Then you hope she is not in too much pain,
You tell her you love her,
And you'll see her again some day.

Lauren Norris

Sweet Dreams Kind Thoughts

My ritual, each and every night, is something to behold,
When all things that are dear to me shall readily unfold.
I say my prayers with meaning, then rest my weary head,
So all kind thoughts come to me, as I'm lying in my bed.
I think of all the animals, of each and every bird,
I think about their freedom, of things they may have heard.
And what of all the fishes swimming in the sea,
Might they, also, be thinking the same kind thoughts as me?
My thoughts then turn to children who are less fortunate,
Who have no-one to love them, but still they show no hate.
My thoughts turn to the countries, the ones that cannot cope,
Food shortage, death, starvation, yet they never give up hope.
I then think of dear mother, with a joyous little sigh.
When dad comes into my sweet dreams, it's time to say goodbye,
For, by that time, my weary head just wants to lie and rest,
To gather up these kindly thoughts, the thoughts with which
I'm blessed.

Neil MacTaggart

New Eyes To See

Look straight ahead into the light;
Look left, look right, with all your might!
Look here, look there, or not at all;
Read this, read that, upon the wall.
Zap the firefly vanishing light!
Flashing randomly in the night.
Doctor Willby! Doctor Willby!
Shall give to me new eyes to see?

Anaesthetize one pair of eyes,
With painless limpness, no surprise.
Transform the cloudy, hazy night
Into the daylight, clear and bright.
Doctor Willby! Doctor Willby
Who gave to me now eyes to see.

Antoine L. Berry

War And Faith

The skylark soared—higher and higher
into the blue of a summer sky
He lay a-wounded, by shrapnel flying
And dreamily wondered, as he espied
the skylark—so free, alas, here I lie
Why can't I in the sky hide?
But no, as battle raged, the pain and fear
Noise and terror, a wound so deep
A prayer to God—please, please hear
My cry of anguish—then oblivion and sleep.

He dreamed of a skylark, soaring high
He dreamed of a an English village green
He dreamed of roast beef and apple pie
And then—he awoke, in a hospital bed
No pain—no fear—where have I been?
His shattered leg and bandaged head
Conveyed to him he wasn't dead
His prayer to God, his faith in life
His duty done amidst the strife.

Dennis R. Rowe

Nature By Night

I lay my stare across a star studded land,
I see the trees sway in the light wind
That ripples across the lake.
The skylark breaks the silence
With its high pitched scream.
A light thud upon the ground sends
The rabbits scurrying into their burrows
As the deer roam overhead.
The light mist is momentarily broken,
By a salmon, jumping with delight
Of the freedom of the lake.
Here I am with nature in pure bliss.

Linda Sammon

Winter's Phase

I listen to the angry breeze
Rushing through the beautiful trees.
The sun has pierced its way through clouds
Casting shadows beneath the boughs.
Snow is falling all around
Covering the earth in a ghostly shroud.
Delicate snowdrops now appear
Defiant above the shroud they spear.
People walk warily along the streets
The ice is thick beneath their feet.
Children on their way to school
Throw snowballs as they laugh and fool.
The birds have ventured out to seek
A tasty morsel as a treat.
I watch them as they fight to gain.
A share of what there now remains.
They then move on and hope to find
Someone, somewhere will be so kind,
To bear a feathered friend in mind.

Grace Pengelly

Whales, What Were They

Swimming with my baby in the deep blue sea, out there free my
baby and me, the salt air fills our lungs with every breath, the
sea washes us and keeps us alive.

Alive we are alive and free to wander these great open seas,
not to harm nor to kill, only to live and to feed. On the horizon
something appears, something grey, something dark. That dark grey
object closer and closer to baby and me, swimming peacefully in the
deep blue sea. Something has ripped through my body into my soul,
I struggle and fight to get free but I grow weaker and see red, red in the sea.

Mummy, what is wrong, why are you lying on your side, one eye in
the sea the other towards the sky. I watch my mummy going away,
I cry out to her but she does not hear. The sea is empty now and
I grow weaker with every day that passes, no food have I had, no
mother's milk. I cannot go on, I am too weak, I must lie
here a while and have a sleep.

John Davidson Scott

Destiny

Sweet yellow bird - on wire he sits, presents his song of joy
As we observe - the vine he quits. His flirting - just a ploy
Distracts our eyes from time and place, commands attention now
Takes flight to send our thoughts through space, fulfil an ancient vow
To where the Douro winds its way through vineyard covered hills
Casal de Loivos spends its day, the stony earth it tills

Of heavy toil it knows so much yet when carillon plays
A lady is revered as such. All dream of better days
When fruit is ripe, grapes plump and dark, and harvest time is near
They will arise with voice of lark and hope for Vintage year
Whilst underneath each sombre mask their dark eyes watch and wait
For yellow bird in sun to bask, resume affairs of state

Sampayo weaves a magic spell, entrancing all who hear
Brave hearts risked all and then they fell. Were not afraid of fear
They suffered for their destiny, a vision they held high
Of God, proud land, King and Country. Republicans? Defy!
The yellow bird shall rise again but will Braganza see?
There could be yet another name fulfil a destiny.

Marilyn K. Hambly

Futility

I am not here on earth today, for I was never born to yield
And massacred my father lay upon a foreign field

Some might call it destiny and God alone knows why
My present, past and future gone, my father left alone to die
for King and Country so it's said and millions of others at his side
Leaving those they loved and cherished. The ignorance I can't abide.

But who am I?... a spectre who took my father's hand
willing him to survive so I could walk upon the land.

As he looked into my presence, alas he had to come and pass my way
knowing then my chance had gone I'd never see the light of day

If I'd been born I would shed my tears and swell the waters of the Somme
But I was never born or lived I was not there I could not come!

W. Stephenson

Eureka!

After thirty-two years of playing the game, albeit by trial and error.
I've at last discovered the secret of Golf, and becoming a "Fairway Terror."
All of that time, when striking the ball, it has gone from left to right.
Unintentional, must also add, be it a huge slice, or a fade, so slight.
No tuition, never had a golf lesson, all my faults, I admit, are self-taught.
I set-up as the instruction books say, a swing-change I never have sought.
But now, just like the professionals, that little ball, is, at last, under control.
And really all that I now require, is R&A, *please* increase size of the hole.
But to stand relaxed and balanced, with this renewed confidence on the tee.
Knowing that I can play it straight, or right or left, really does thrill me.
But just what is this amendment, that I have inadvertently stumbled upon?
I do not think that I can it disclose, if I do, then my secret has gone.
Just a little clue, it involves the angle of club, correlated to the stance.
After three decades, you may also it find, since it is really a matter of chance.

Arthur J. Tickle

213

Take A Look At Me

Not so long ago people took a look at me
And saw a girl alone.
Laughter and fun when in a crowd
But behind closed doors there were tears,
For solitude just did not suit.
Partners appeared just to disappear
And the emptiness returned.
Then the corner was turned.

People took a look at me and saw a girl in love,
Besotted with her man
Only to be told it won't last.

Now people take a look at me and see a girl complete,
With everything she needs and desires
A girl secure that the bubble won't burst.
A girl with so much love in her heart and sparkle in her eyes
That no one can deny they were wrong.

Now people take a look at me
And all they can see
Is how happy you make me
Michelle Baker

Burning Candle

Surrounded by darkness, you're hidden in the core,
You stand prominent, but little I notice you,
Among no logic, but you are there.

You glow stronger with each breath you take,
And burn smaller with each heartbeat,
The loss of stamina, pushes your flame somewhere new.

You last long, with all potential,
But soon you burn beyond your speak,
And nothing is left to thrive from,
You smoulder your way out of existence,
And there was nothing you could do,
But you glowed the best, better than any other,
And gave my darkness your pleasure.

It returns to blackness, and now I realize you have gone.
And I remember that once you did exist,
Now it's too late, you lit up my darkness,
And gave warmth to my coldness.

You fulfilled all meaning, all logic, all aim,
The glimpse of hope,
You were everything . . .
Emma Louise Kingsmill

Octogenarian Reminiscences (or ramblings!)

The scents and sounds of yesteryear
Come creeping back to nose and ear.
The sights I saw with glad surprise
Come flashing back before my eyes:
Fresh coffee roasting in the cafe,
The boisterous sing-songs in the NAAFI,
The sudden seascape from the mountain,
The changing lights of Bournemouth's fountain.

The wonderment of simple things
That every fleeting memory brings.
The coal-fire pictures burning bright,
Our babies crying in the night,
Reminding us this old, old earth
Renews itself with every birth.

Churchillian growls that gave us hope,
All part of life's kaleidoscope,
With rich new patterns yet to form,
Fresh sights and sounds our hearts to warm,
For, thankfully, I'm not yet dead:
Maybe the best is just ahead . . .

Ken Waite

Flats

This is no place for a child to be
Stuck in a flat constantly
Their eyes grow dim, their laughter stops
They must feel like they're in a box

There is no garden, there are no flowers
They just sit indoors for hours and hours
The nearest that they get to the sun
Is through a window or on a shopping run

There's no fresh air, there are no trees
They don't see the sun or feel the breeze
They grow very pale and are never well
Poor little things, they must think this is hell

This is no place for a child in a flat
This is no place for a child, that's a fact
Give them trees and flowers and grass
This isn't much, is it, for a child to ask
Louise Muir

Untitled

Time has really flown by,
and now it's time we said goodbye.
I never meant a thing to you,
I wish you told me that before.
You hid a secret deep inside,
And always kept me far aside.

You never really understood me,
And never thought your troubles I'd ever care to see.
I always thought my love you'd feel,
And make it easy not to seal.
I often thought you saw my deeds,
And that always fulfilled your needs.

We probably weren't made for each other,
But now it really doesn't matter.
We never tried to find the way
And now our meant-to-be-"Love" fades away.
For love is not an easy game.
Niray Shah

Alone

I feel adrift in the sea of life,
abandoned in an ocean of trouble.
The only way to survive is to hold on
and hope someone will find me.
I hear a weak, feeble cry in the
distance only to find it was an echo
of myself in turbulent times.
A snivelling wreck approaching, unravelling,
into a pathetic failure, bewildered by it all.
Drifting further into solitude with its
intensity wrapping itself around me.
Still there is hope someone will find
me and release me from my loneliness.
Maria Boore

A Light At The End Of The Tunnel

You walked into my life
as clear as the sun that shines in the sky
you gave me the world
then taught me how to cry,

Gold, silver and diamonds were just some of the things I could
have given you,
but freedom was just more precious to you....
Those memories will always stay
and the songs we shared won't fade away,
the cigarette butts still remain in that same ashtray
it's just like the hurt inside that won't go away.

The days went on, months and years too...
Then the magazines, nightclubs and parties all become the
thing to do
but suddenly it happened way out of the blue
along came someone as wonderful as you....
Rosa Rocha

214

Ballinruan

Walking in the country side,
  upon a bog I came,
all around was deserted.
I shut my eyes, took deep breaths,
  the air it was so clear.

Ghost of Irish people,
surrounded me, I swear.
Men were digging way down deep,
  peat was everywhere.
Irish folk were singing,
  laughter in their eyes.
Opening my eyes again,
Only birds' songs filled the air.

Walking away from the bog, that day.
  I had to look back and stare,
sure enough I did see, people waving to me,
Irish ghosts, their arms in the air,
Imagination you may say,
but I'll say to this day,
magic was everywhere.
  Carole Waters

If Only

If only I could have my life all over again,
What would I do to change the life I have today?
Would I be Prime Minister, or in the House of Lords,
Be a clown in a circus, be the hostess with the mostest,
Be a TV presenter, a doctor, a dentist, or even fly a plane;
Or a ballerina or even a lady-in-waiting to the Queen?

Now what could I have been, I wonder, to differ the life I have today?
Would I change a thing, I wonder, would I go for more,
Or be content with what I've got with the life I've had so far?
Have I not a lovely husband, and two precious little ones?
Now would I change a thing I ask you, would I go for more?
I tell you chump, not I!
  Anna Wylie

Death Of A Tree

Straight and tall it stood
Surveying the world.
We can but dream of the changes it's seen
Down the years.

The birds found refuge in its branches
Now, it seems, only I shed tears for the beautiful sentinel of
  our avenue.
It was a sign of all that was strong and brave.
Now its branches lie broken on the grass - a lonely grave.

It was too tall, they said, a danger, they said, to our houses
  in time of storm.
I say we need these fine, strong trees.
Their very being gives us a good, safe feeling - warm.

Maybe they'll plant another,
Its branches again a welcoming place.
No, more likely, a small, safe bush
Where once grew our friend - now, no trace.
  Alfreda J. Stephenson

Lonely

Captured in a mist of silver,
Looking down the winding stairs;
feeling tired, depressed and lonely
In a world where nobody cares.

All alone, stepping down
The cold and dark spiral ladder,
Looking for someone to hear your cries,
Wanting to be healed of your pain.

Cries from the heart are echoing loudly,
Beating on the cold stone walls,
Vibrating silently to the sound of nothing,
Will anyone ever hear the silent calls?
  Melinda Armitage

Goodbye

As you walked through the doorway I thought "it's time, this is it"
I said "Sorry it's over" and you threw a fit.
"What do you mean?" you shouted hard
"It's because I'm sick of being bullied, punched scarred."
"I'll change" you said over and over again
but I couldn't trust you, all men are the same.
They say one thing and do exactly the other
I'd get on better staying with my mother.

As we carried on arguing we both got uptight
I wanted you to leave before it turned to a fight.
You muttered "look forgive me" I sighed "get out mate;
apologies are no good, you've done it, it's too late."

You stormed outside, you didn't see the car,
you walked out on the road a little too far.
I heard the Siran zooming down the lane,
I held you gently and said "I'm sorry, wake up Cain."

You struggled but managed to open your eye
and spoke your last words "I love you, goodbye."
  Rebecca Simmonds

Despair

Me? What do I care? With a cardboard box as my easy chair,
the Daily Mail to keep off the rain and having to sleep on the
  kerb again.
Weary? Yes! And sad am I. Tired of sleeping under the sky.
There is no warmth, no love for me. Life is as bare as a
  Winter's tree.

Christmas time is here again. I press my nose to the window pane.
The news is on the shop TV - and I see? Despair!

"Just move along" I'm always told.
No matter that I'm tired and cold
But - where to?

I once had hopes and good dreams too.
For many reasons they fell through.
I shuffle through the fallen leaves and I dwell on the past
But no family grieves - for me.

Please - give me hope - a friendly hand, a smile, that's all I ask.
A pillow on which to lay my head and a mundane, daily task.

Give me back my self-respect, tell me of work to do.
Treat me - not as a 'down and out' - I am a man - like you.
  Anne Cooper

Life

As child I played is Wood and Dale
Oh sands by sea I took my pail

In youth I walked those Woods and Dales
My sweetheart with me without fail.

We later brought up children three
in our cottage by the sea

As middle age crept onto us
The children left our nest for good

And then my love took leave of me
Oh grim that day by cruel sea

I now just sit there all alone
it seems life as full circle come

But yesterday I rose at dawn
and Woods and Dales once more I roamed

I watch the sun there rise once more
The birds did sing the world did live

And though this life seemed nearly done
I know now that it's just begun

The tide has turned I must be gone
To what there waits beyond that sun
  P. Lawson

Biker

Foetally young, his face
Like a debauched choir boy.

Twenty years ago I would have wanted him.
(we didn't say fancied then.)
Now I looked on that seraphic evil
With something approaching horror,
Thankful that he was not my son.

I watched him pull a bird,
Settle her on the back of his monster from hell
And roar away into oblivion.

I thought of his mother. Did she care?
I thought of the girl. Would she survive?
Physically perhaps—but emotionally?

I thanked God that I was mature and sensible.
And then I wished that I had been that girl.

Shirley Bragg

Fortune Favours The Brave

Fortune favours the brave,
Not the poor forgotten social slave.
He wonders why they do not think of him,
In the evenings as the light grows dim.
They think of me because I did not
Leave myself vulnerable to the social rot.
Helpless convention found no foot hole
To carry it forward and take my soul.

Looking back I could have drowned,
Being so adamant and standing my ground.
Will it be him that man of my truth
Who gives me the total believable proof?
When I die will they think of me,
The one who wouldn't be what they wanted me to be?

Charlotte Stevens

Ultimatum

Oh tinted leaves why do you droop and weep?
Is it for men who fought once, now asleep
After their toil and dangers night and day,
Resting so peaceful now in freshly turned clay.
Forget not that the spring must come again
And hope return of peace and end of pain
Once more the earth her bright fresh garments wear
With swallows wheeling in the crystal air
God from his highest heaven will look down
And from his forehead deep will pass the frown
Caused by the wilful savagery of man
To mutilate His mighty timeless plan
Time must elapse before this state ideal
To man eventually make world-wide appeal
A warning to those who with war would toy
Without a doubt they must the world destroy

John Frederick Brook

English Seasons

Spring, you give new life, new hope,
That which seemed so dead is new again.
Fresh green leaves, bright blossoms,
Early flowers, after gentle rain.

Summer, how we welcome your long, light night;
Time for pleasures and sport.
Warm sunshine, happy birds,
Gardens with all the flowers so bright.

Autumn, your splendour is in the trees,
Beautiful days, following the mist of morning tide,
Precious to us are days, such as these.

Winter, with your frosty world of white,
Your winds, your sharpness, snow flakes too.
Evenings for crafts, skills and warm fires;
'Though God gave Christmas, best gift of all
Winter, to you!

Barbara Ashmall

Untitled

There's no other person in this world that's as good as you,
You're good and pure and Holy, through and through and through,
You look upon your children when they are doing wrong,
You open up their joyful hearts and put inside a song,

And when their heart is open,
The Lord can enter in,
Just to touch their heart with love,
And throw away the sin,

So whenever anyone of us
Thinks of doing wrong,
Just ask the Lord to put into your heart,
An ever loving song.

Jessica Wright

Angels

With the innocence in their eyes,
They were so much alive,
Full of laughter, full of fun,
Someone's daughter, someone's son.

They went to school that fateful day,
Playing merrily on their way.
When in the gym a madman came,
Those little children to kill and maim.

As we weep, and as we mourn,
For those who have lost, and are so forlorn.
For little children no more to wake,
We ask did our God Dunblane forsake.

If you didn't, oh Lord above,
Can you tell us how your love,
Could leave a nation to sob and cry
Could let sixteen little angels die?

Susan Hurst

Untitled

When all around you seems black, and everywhere is plagued with darkness
And no matter how hard you try you cannot find the light.
Not a star to guide you home, or a candle to show the way.
Not a voice in the distance—just echoes of silence and shadows of night.
Not one figure of realness, just spaces of imagination.
No shreds of reality, only fields of empty memories
When all hope is gone and victory seems unreachable.
When defeat seems the only option and you seem to be trapped by death, misery and hopelessness.
Look further, deeper—search wider for the comfort
And feel, desperately, for the solidness of normality.
Walk past ignorance;
Fight the hate, jealousy and envy and reach out for the end.
Never give up—believe beyond belief
And you will succeed.

Carly Jones

The Presence Of God

I feel your presence but cannot see you,
I know you are not too far away,
You are all things that are beautiful,
The brightness of a star, the light of day.
The fragrance of a flower upon the grass.
The warmth of sunshine too,
The gentle breeze upon my face
Fresh as the morning dew.
The coolness of a shower on summer nights,
The gentle fall of rain,
A snow flake on a frosty lake,
A bird singing on the plain.
You are my strength in weakness,
The courage in my strife,
My hope in tribulation,
My happiness and life.

Veronica Tangri

90's Summertime

A poem for the summertime, the best time of the Year,
We laze around, we barbecue, as bluer skies appear.
It's mad dogs and the Englishmen who brave the midday sun,
But would we be as British though if someone stopped the fun?

Some head straight for the local pub, great beer bellies to show,
Some drive 10 miles to take a walk, some watch the garden grow.
Some dare the coast, a cooler breeze, but children love the sea,
Sand sandwiches and warm ice-cream, then fish and chips for tea.

We lose out on an evening though, as temperatures are falling,
At seven on the continent, no warmer clothes are calling.
But we often need this chilling time, one's skin is now on fire,
We stroll around in lobster red, this colour some admire.

The summer ain't so bad here, I guess it's now the norm,
My highlight of these middle months has got to be a storm.
It rains and clouds for three weeks long, then roasting hot the last,
Then faces are at windows until flash and bang has passed.

Schools are now on holiday, work has a two week break,
The stress is gone, the sun is out, enjoyment is at stake.
But just think twice in future years before stepping on the plane,
It might be hot and sunny there, but mosquitos are a pain!

Catherine Brougham

Spirit Of Love

There is no pain, there is no fright,
There is no darkness, only light,
There is no bed of thorns today.
Only dreams in which we lay.
It's been so long, so hard.
With a thousand tears along the way.

It's getting stronger every day,
As our emotions come into play
The power of darkness put to flight.
Feeling so real, feelings so right.
Now there's no song, no words,
To compare with the sounds from the light.

Getting over, bringing out.
From the anger, from the start,
Freedoms feelings rise again,
No dark shadows can remain.
From the head, from the start,
Freedoms feelings rise again.
No dark shadows can remain, from the head, from the heart.
Spirit of love, can never contain.

Philip H. Buckley

Untitled

A world conjured of all emotions that you feel,
Ones that are unrealistic and ones that are real,
My hatred of regrets, of weakness and inability,
Ones so subnormal and some of pure senility.

Barricades are strong, a force not to be broken,
A world of different spectrums, words hushed unspoken,
Fortresses guarded securely, tightly under a spell,
To hide the constant fear of which no-one wants to tell.

Inside's another realm, a paradise wanting to be found,
Warm and tender yet still gentle and profound,
It is this land that needs to be discovered,
A chapter of passing time over which a sheet's been covered.

Where once love used to roam so free,
A place of peace, a discrete eternity.
But then came sin a contagious disease,
To destroy a people who loved with ease.

Give me back my youth, my days of innocence,
Where anything I did was not at my expense,
Now I am still young but too old to be free,
Secrets and dark whispers is now all I see.

Michaela Hastings

Dark Night

The noon day sun is dark,
Music is discordant,
When the heart is low.
It is hard to understand why
Shadows loom today,
While under the same conditions yesterday
All was aglow.
I must pull down the iron curtain
On these gloomy thoughts,
And be on my way
To earn my bread.
When Jesus withdrew to Gethsemane
He asked his friends to accompany him part of the way.
It is hard to reveal the darkness of the soul
To trusted friends.
It is as if you need them in the background
But you have to face the darkness alone.

Mary Quinn

A Poem Called - Me

I unlock the secret door that's deep inside of me.
I look inside and wonder, who am I meant to be.
I'm unfulfilled inside my heart, my soul cries
out for more.
What am I all about, says I, there should be
more to me, what is inside my secret self
that cries out to be free.
I have not left a single mark that makes the
World remember me, so I despair and wonder,
Who am I meant to be.
To understand the mystery is all I'm asking for.
I look inside that secret door and still don't know
Me
Who am I meant to be?

Sheila O'Gorman

Intensity

With the blood from my heart, I'll write your name.
With my soul, I feel this intensity forevermore in my heart.
For you, I would fill a bottomless well with my tears.
For you, I would use myself as a shield to
protect you from any harm.
What I am experiencing with you is something new to me.
Something exciting and unique.
What I feel for you is not love, it's beyond.
It's a feeling that's rare to the world.
An emotion not possible to justify.
I gave to you my flesh, in fact I gave to you my all.
Though do you know why? Do you understand why?
Do you take advantage of this naive little girl,
or do you love her intensely too?

Joanna Yianni

Ambush

A discovered cache of weapons hidden well from view.
Alone they were quite useless we need the gunmen too.
So pretend you haven't seen them and they don't exist.
Then sneak back there at nightfall like spirits in the mist.
Lying quiet in the shadows keeping ever still.
Takes all your concentration you need an iron will.
Time goes by so slowly each hour seems a day.
Waiting for your victims to come along that way.
To stay alert and listen as the hours go.
The cold and damp discomfort drag your spirits low.
Day turns into nighttime then nighttime into day.
You wish it was all over and you didn't, have to stay.
Four long days of waiting then suddenly they are there.
You grip your weapon tightly your body to prepare.
Then everyone is shooting and time is flashing by.
And through the haze of gunsmoke you see the gunmen die.
Your body wracked with fever struggling to survive.
Now it is all over you're thankful you're alive.
You think of the waiting, the time you had to spend.
It was over in ten seconds from first shot to the end.

W. Bond

Dream House

It carries me back to the place it was then,
A disjointed jig-saw of women and men.
Feelings and faces forgotten with time
Invade my dreams when my mind's not all mine.
Echoes of my past conjuring familiar strange places,
Fond remembered voices with half hidden faces.
Loved ones and places not forgotten over the years,
They enter my unconscious,
Why exaggerate my fears?
Memories of all my yesterdays mingle in my dreams.
Dream house holds my childhood joy and my adult screams.
Can a house hold our history,
Can it tell of our past?
Could a stranger discover?
No it's in my Dream house they will last.

Jonathan Lloyd Harries

Sleeping Beauty

Eyes shut,
Sense of activity kaput,
Sighs of sleep,
Not even a peep.
Legs afling,
In him there is no spring.
'Tis possible to shake beauty's hand,
To stroke his tummy and,
Though beauty is asleep and has no cares,
Beauty's loved ones stand around him as guarding bears.

Anna Orchard

Perception

On bus nine this morning I was deliberately told
"Go sit in the back" by a voice so cold
A voice from a man with ivory teeth
boiling with hatred in his heart underneath
"No I will sit in the front", I declared
blacks in the back wondering how I had dared
Dead silence swept over, sealing all sound
my fears disappeared and words I found
"Let your ears be your eyes and listen to me
Judge me on my words and not what you see
Give me a chance to tell you my story,
being a black on bus nine is never a glory"
Astonishment appeared in the white man's eyes
eyebrows rose, pupils increased in size
Never had it happened that a black man disagreed,
the white man so surprised with an ego to feed
"Now if you don't mind, move out of my way"
the pale white man thought of nothing to say
The white man nodded, I sat down appeased
from that day the problems on bus nine were ceased.

Vanessa Åsell

The Visitation

Marie was sad, her mother lying there so pale and so still.
Her once rosy cheeks so wizened and white.
Were to haunt Marie as she tried so hard to sleep each night.
When her mother passed away, it was a blessed relief,
As her pain and suffering were gone.
But for the ones left behind, the grief still lingers on.

Marie was in a fitful sleep one night.
When she awoke to see a soft beam of light.
She was afraid at first and just gazed in awe!
It was a vision of her mother as she was before
Fear disappeared as she stretched out a hand
To touch her as you will understand!
"Oh, you cannot do that", she gently said,
   Then she just drifted away.

The nightmares vanished from that time on,
Who is to explain this phenomenon?
Maybe it is not for us to try,
The only time when perhaps we'll know
   Is when at last we die?

Dorothy Mezaks

Drink Driving Night

Stood right next to my bed,
Stands a man who says he's dead,
He has no name, he has no face,
Been rejected from every place,
Talks to me about how he died,
He wished he'd never took that ride,
A drunk, a drunk who did not think,
About how much he had to drink,
He does not know where we are,
He thinks we're sitting in his car,
It must have been where he died,
The place his soul has chosen to hide,
He gave his life to save a child,
A child who had already died,
The man is young and smartly dressed,
With a gate post poking through his chest,
His eyes are red, his hair is white,
The result of a drink driving night.

Richard John Parry

Cruelty

Cruelty, who wants it?
Just now while you sit,
It's going on
Animals are being cut up,
Something like a seal pup
There's testing of lipstick on rabbits,
A harmless pet for you and me
Then you see bath foam is set on another,
Oh Brother!
In other countries there's
Killing of elephants for ivory
Rhinos killed for horns,
Export of birds in cages
I could write pages and pages,
Do something about it - say no!
I hate it all!

Kelly Davidson

Revelations: The Empire Of Steel

I did walk through the streets of a catatonic age; Empire of Steel.
The towers of steel were erected around me as they met the
sky with silvery glare.
The sun was struck; struck down by thy awesome presence,
it left me there.

Empire of Steel; the sun blessed them all,
until the girders of steel began to fall;
thundersome, almost, the sun chose to cower;
suburban terrain, not the flowers of ages being,
the metal began to fall.
It left me there. I was one of the few who chose to stay.
A shout, a curse, as the metal hit the earth and chose to dig in:
ha! The show was one to bring upon extensive curses.
The showerfall fell;
and that was when my own world fell too
Empire of Steel.

Peter Belton

Untitled

The mighty beech tree.
Alone and peacefully.
The other trees it is schooling.
It stands proud and ruling.

Now so grand in root.
From all those years, when it was just a shoot.
The scars from its battles, you can tell
On that hardened, solid outer shell.

In its wisdom it shows.
Long great stretching boughs
It is king in its small corner of the woods.
King over all the other trees, plants, fauna and buds.

L. M. Pearson

218

Fighting In Action

Bombs and bullets from every direction
That is what it is like when you fight in action
Fighting people you don't even know
Your name is called and you have to go
You fight all the time just trying to survive
And crawling on your bellies trying to stay alive
It is an awful experience to have to go through
Not knowing where to go or knowing what to do
Living on orders every bit of the time
Scared to run in case you stand on a land mine
So in dug out muddy holes we are told to stay
That is where we fight, eat, sleep and even pray
Dirt all over our bodies and on our face
When you get your order to run there are dead boys
    all over the place
Some of them are friends but some are from the other side
You get a sick frightening feeling that is impossible to hide
Thousands of innocent people die in a world war
And they go to their deaths not really knowing what they
    were fighting for.

Diane S. Manning

Romeo And Juliet

Over the crowd, across the room,
Over her head, a halo does loom,
Beauty of an angel, queen of the sky,
A dove without wings, unable to fly.
I fear to behold her, so pure so divine,
I've fallen in love, how I wish she were mine,
Every movement, performed with such grace,
The gentle and tenderness of her embrace,
I steal a kiss, she steals my heart,
Together, forever, and never apart.
So brief an encounter, with the love of my life,
Such holy words spoken, she shall be my wife.

Christy Marns

The Magic Toy Shop

Advent, snow cold, the air, small girl in toy shop stare.
Pure fantasy, like her, I were, dreaming of a bear.
Herself proclaim, frost scribble on the pane, she wrote her name.
The longed-for toy, the joy repeat her pain.
Holds out soft paws, if only yours, could be, to share a nursery tea.
And best of all when last prayer said, tucked into bed.
His furry face and growl endear
Next morning sick with fear, to find he isn't there.
He's lost no bear, who sat beside Jack-in-the-Box.
Scrape pane frost free to better see,
good fairy top the tree, grant wish for me.
Your light did lead Three Kings.
Your wand does wondrous things,
it silver angel wings, glow golden rings.
Guide Santa's eyes and lift the slay to rise.
One ray to stop, the deer before the shop.
The bear bring back, join toys within his sack.
Light candle flame, watch girl who write her name
Gleam in the frost, ne'er let her wish be lost.

A. E. Doney

For Someone

Of sand of sea of sound
A precious find, I found
As one is lost, too late to see
Yet thoughts abound familiar—yet unique
A broken shell—no voice to speak.

One's heart of many changes be
Tightly held in fingers cold
As they look on, the weight is lead
But eyes, they look, onwards, instead
Now are shut and secrets told.

That find I found, there was no key
The find was you, the keeper, me.

Belinda Pearce

Warwickshire

The leafy lanes of Warwickshire
A picture springs to mind
Carpets of bluebells in the woods
Wild flowers of every kind
Violets, primroses, celandine too
Foxgloves and cowslips to name but a few
Morris dancers on the village green
Children fishing in the stream
Sunday morning church bells ring
Listen! Hear the choirs sing
Raising their voices in joyful praise
Praying for peaceful and happy days
Thatched cottages in country lanes
With gleaming latticed window panes
Later watch the cricket teams
How serene everything in the village seems
Leaving this idyllic scene
We travel home to sit and dream
Of the future, when maybe we
Can return to such tranquillity.

Frances Mary West

Time Burns

Sitting in the waiting room of time
Waiting for the passing of my life
I looked around and in the faces I could see
Sad people who didn't get what they wanted to be
Hell, that ain't gonna happen to me
I'm gonna make time burn for me
Yeah you just wait and see
I've got the fire burning deep in me
Yeah you just wait and see
I'm gonna unlock the door now I've found the key
Time's gonna burn, burn for me
Time is time and time is life
Just like the fire it fades and dies
With a spark the flame will grow
The fire grows out of control
Time burns your heart, time burns your soul
Use the fire before time takes it all
Time burns for me, time burns for you
Do what you really wanna do!

Dave Cherrett

Family

What a precious thing family is
You always know you'll get a kiss
When dearest friends may go amiss
What a precious thing family is.

They cradle you through the wonder years
Make you smile and wipe your tears
They build your heart, and calm your fears
What a precious thing family is

Robert Dyer

Words

Words can sometimes mean everything, or nothing at all
Words can plunge you into deep despair or with joy enthral
Words can instill within a feeling of immense power
Or create a pleasant scene, a fragrant bloom, a flower.

Words can often be used by skilful orators to mask
Unwholesome truths about themselves or deeds when put to task
But words can also be used by others to soothe and heal
Then perhaps the truth from sufferers they're to conceal.

The skilful use of some words can often conceal a lie
White's not white and black's not black and however hard you try
You sometimes cannot read between the clever lines to see
That some words do not mean what they say, it's a mystery.

Words can and do however create pictures in the mind
All kinds of acts and scenes can appear, even to the blind
Words can win you friendship, love and help of every kind
Words have to be looked for but if you seek them hard, you'll find.

Roderick Fitzroy

When Love Takes Hold....

When life is good but wanting it better
Reading his words over in an unexpected letter
Walking through life at a brisk steady pace
Stopping abruptly upon seeing his face

Sun shining through the clouds, but clouds spoiling the heat
The tune of love has played before but never skipped a beat
Walking through abandoned fields, in the pouring rain
Not realizing the bitter cold - thinking of him again

Snow on the ground, so white, so new
Wanting to lie down and feel the warmth of you
Willing the burning passions never to grow cold
Fighting to stay free, yet hoping to be caught,
  When love takes hold....

A. J. Davey

Trip

Don yer leathers, git on yer bikes
Kick 'em! Over, we're travelling nights

Along the roads and over the hills
Smoking grass and poppin' pills

Stop for gas I can't stand still
I gotta catch that rovin' hill,

Along the roads and over the hills
Smoking grass and poppin' pills

Corner comin' my luck can't last
Shiftin' down but I'm going too fast
Rubber burning, tyres squealing.
Road's hard, but my wounds are healing.

Never again will I go too fast
'Cos this fine trip has been my last

Richard A. J. Andrews

Untitled

As lads we roamed the friendly hills
Running, jumping, having spills
Failed to see with artist's eye
The trees, the colours, the open sky
But we as men, no time to spare
To walk or wander anywhere
Sense beauty, scents and creatures' noise
We sadly missed when we were boys
But mem'ries stored in inner mind
Bears fruit, years later, and we're inclined
By prose, or verse or painted scene
To prove, by sight, where we have been
To peoples, right throughout all nations
That we'd not missed our God's creations

Gordon James

Tomorrow

Tomorrow comes too soon.
Lying awake, drifting in tranquillity
Shadows form, but still I cannot see
Or find the person I should like to be.

Tomorrow comes too soon.
I wonder, will I waste another day,
Let my life just drift away
By how I live, and in the things I say?

Tomorrow comes too soon.
And so will age, but will I then know more
Be a better person than I was before
Or just become an even greater bore?

Tomorrow comes too soon.
Lying awake, I wish it were not so.
I need more time to learn and forward go,
Look towards new horizons, but I know,

Tomorrow comes too soon.
Inside the shadow of the person I am now.....

Berit H. Stutt

Widow's Bereft

On my bedroom wall at the foot of my bed hangs a picture
of a sailing sloop with her white sails all billowed and spread
when sleep evades me, sweet dreams come, we sail aboard it
both me and my love, gentle the sea and soft breezes too
There is no land, just horizon to view
My love was a sailor, his eyes deep blue
All I ever wanted was to be in his crew,
Then one day a cold wind blew, it took from me my dear love true
Sad though it is, for a while I must stay
Aboard the boat I sailed with him
Keeping the decks clean and its sails trim
Once again, who knows that boat I will crew
The children we had have abandoned me
They have left me alone to finish the trip
Though the sea blows rough or still and calm
Though my heart aches, I wish them no harm.

B. T. Sharp

To 'Ear Or Not To Hear

This is the story of Grandma Esther
She couldn't hear a word ye said to 'er.
For many long years,
With a few private tears.
Those oft-missed quiet words
Or the whistling of the garden birds.

With great courage she sought,
After a great deal of thought,
The help of her quack
To stop the gossip behind her back.

The doctor a good lad she knew
Loudly proclaimed "This is what we'll do.
We'll take some skin off your bum
(Polite people refer to their rear)
And from it form a new ear drum
Which will fix your deafened ear."

Christine Hinchliff

First Love

My heart stops beating,
The love we shared is lost.
Never again will I hold him in my arms,
His sweet words will never again,
Send exciting shivers down my spine.

He is still there, his taste is on my lips,
His smell in my room and in my hair.
He will always be
With me in my mind.

I will never forget the love we shared,
The dreams, the secrets and the visions.
It's all over now, it's truly the end.
But I shall not grieve,
For my love for him is still true,
Burning deep in my heart and soul.

Kathryn Paley

The Mirror

She stood there one morning smiling at me,
I frowned and I wondered just who could she be?
With faded brown eyes and grey in her hair,
A face that was lined but once had been fair.

She looked so familiar but I could not recall
Just where I had met her, was it when I was small?
Her face told of sorrow in her life she had known.
Her smile held a sadness, little love she'd been shown.

My heart ached for her as I held out my arms
To comfort this woman and keep her from harm,
But I stopped in mid air, with a shock I did see
This woman in the mirror was no other than me!

Marie Adams

A Little Magic

Julie, today's your Birthday, I remember it quite well,
For you came in quite a hurry, now there's a tale to tell,
But enough of reminiscing, about that fateful day,
It's this weekend we must think about to help you get away,
You're going off to Paris, on a holiday for two
You know! My darling daughter, that simply will not do
for you've reached the age of thirty, it's time to settle down,
Not to fly across the channel, to that strange enchanted town,
For people who have visited, often have a distant stare
Even though they're back in England, there mind is over there,
I don't know what's the secret, of that city on the Seine
but I hope "a little magic" will work for you again!

John Hatfield

The Old Grey Owl

As the golden moon rises slowly behind the hill
The timid mice scamper over rafters in the mill
An old grey owl sits in an ivy covered belfry
Lonely and cold. Silent and ghostly
Looking over a moor dark and still
Where sometimes the Owl has found his kill
His hoot is such a weird and harrowing cry
As silently he flits across the starry sky
And what a sight to see him at night
When he sees a wondering mouse in sight
Then suddenly, with a swoop he pounces,
Then towers away with a mousse, to his lonely house
And eats hiss meal upon the silvery beams
Where the Old bell, now silent in the moonlight gleams
Then he goes to sleep all day, until
It's night-time again.

Kaye Yeomans

Untitled

A person! There!
Or you don't see what I see?
When I say, - "Right!"
You'll scream out, - "This is wrong!"

I say that this goes to the right side,
You'll take it to the left.
We have a lot in common,
And you shall not regret!

Your heart is full of hate,
And mine is full of love,
A little hug, a smile now,
And this is what we have;

A person! There, you see it!
It's right couldn't be wrong!
Go, bring it to the right side,
We are a common world!

Anna-Marija Nacvalovaite

Grandad Lewis

Shooting, soaring, flying high
Grandad Lewis was dreaming
Asleep in his rocking chair
He dreamt he was floating through space

The stars shining bright
The planets aglow
Grandad Lewis holding on tight
His eyes were wide
His jaw was dropped
So he told me when he woke!

I shot past Pluto
Took a bite out of Mars
I went swimming through the Milky-way
He'd tell me again and again

After lunch
(What he called brunch because he slept until midday)
He would go to his beloved place
And dream for the rest of the day.

Julia Newton-Mercer

The World We Live In

Such beautiful scenery
We have round the world
Mountains and rocks
Sea and the fields.

Photographs are taken
Art pictures are drawn,
That's all we have left
Of this beautiful world.

What's happened to nature
Most wild animals extinct,
Bombs being dropped
Our children, so lonely, poor little things.

Nobody notices
Nobody cares
Just carry on fighting
Putting on dares.

If only fighting
Could be so rare,
We would not have to live
In a terrible nightmare.

Jacqueline Staples

Cold Comfort

It's sad, this silence -
Lonely as the tomb,
But not as lasting.
The odd sea gull's wail,
A wave breaking
On an unseen shore,
Shrouded in mist.
The dampness of the morning,
Grey-ghost clouds
Above the chiselled rocks,
Giant cliffs like tombstones.
The sea's a pool of tears,
Dropped from a mourning gull,
Salting the air,
And washing the tiny stones.
They sigh deeply in grief.
It is a sad, sea-cold morning,
With cold comfort
From the trembling marram grass:
"The world may weep, but sorrow has to end".

Rosalie Pike

Cry Baby

I've held you and fed you,
    You can't eat much more
I've cleaned you and changed you,
    Your bottom's not sore.

I've walked you and rocked you,
    I've left you to lie,
I've turned up the heating
    Oh why do you cry?

I leave you in silence...
    Then turn up the sound,
It's an endless cycle
    Around and around...

...Oh how can a baby wield so much power?
    6 until 7 - the arsenic hour.

And finally sleep comes
    But someone's at the door!!!
I don't want to be
    A mother no more!!!

Sara Levison

Political Asylum

The contents have gone, the bottle is empty
Smashed glass, the bottle has broken.
The emotion is sickly, it eats at the brain
Dissolving solitude, but not the pain.
This cannot over run, I cannot allow it
What I need to express, I just want to show it.
But red wine stains the carpet
That flies through the sky
Left with one option
And that is to die.
Death to my past, to my present, my future
As I watch the dregs flow away;
The contents have gone, the bottle is empty
Broken glass, last entry.
I want to kill a politician, I want to kill them all
But I'm not sure of my reasoning
And that won't do at all.
Maybe I should go, maybe I should stay
I don't really know
Whose decision is it anyway?

Robert Barlow

Final Hour

Too far for echo, secret on the hilltop -
The fated castle, further than wrath or music,
First lodge to strangeness and to dreams' beginning;
And must we go as far as that far castle?

And must we find it, too, a witless ruin,
Walled-in and brooding, in a nightmare sleep?
Delicate dreams still haunt this outpost building,
Gable and garden still some quiet keep;

Or do we haunt it, at the lintle standing
With image conjured from that distant vision,
Awakened by its presence, and foreboding
That we have leagues to journey ere we slumber,

Leagues there are yet to travel without number,
And we must on our way - and leave this brooding
    House on the edge of day...

Elsa Ivor

Cleopatra's Kiss (So Close To Babylon)

The wild jackal squeals into the moonlight.
A blessing of rain tumbles into the cloud of belief
I needed into the past
The door to Babylon, only with my next breath
Her eyes opened and eloped me
The cautious cat is now the lion

If the tail of the lion is in retreat
Then we can take a step forward
Golden promises want me still
How will I retrieve
The passion of the wish
Cleopatra's kiss
So close to Babylon.

Paul Avon

The Autumn Glades

Through his Iron Glades,
Comes silent autumn,
Swishing his long burgundy tail,
Looking with his pale crimson face,
As silent autumn appears,
Colours fade to their doom,
Mahogany, mist and grey.
He does not stop to speak but nods,
Leaves melt quietly away.
Under his feet, through his dull honey eyes,
All living start to die, wearily falling to their graves.
The sky turns to russet, burnt amber and red,
The fiery flame of autumnal acid,
A sunburnt sunset, ruby wine,
As silent autumn comes on his way.

Angela Goody

The Road Of Regret

I am alone, alone to face this black path of pain which I have chosen.
I encountered the crossroads someway
back along this forsaken path, and I choose wrong.

I chose the path that looked rich and happy,
The one that was not overgrown and difficult to pass through.
The other bore briars and thorns higher than the eye could see,
They were thick and would have taken time to get past.

I was led by cheerful voices, and the sound of mellow music.
But oh! How false that image was, it was only to lure me into
    this isolation.
But I, I followed, like all the rest of those foolish sheep,
I was weak, and selfish, I was indolent.

At those crossroads, I left behind all that was important to me
    in life
Everything, including my sanity.
If only I could have seen through this illusion I wouldn't be here
Standing in a pool of regret.

I turn back now in this blackness and try to find my way,
But alas the journey is slow and difficult.
But if my faith is stronger than the dark, I will make it,
and I know I will make it, in time,
In time the pain and sorrow will turn into tranquillity again.

Aisling Fraser

Aristocratic Hedonism

Presidents and ministers live in another world,
In State Houses where honey flows.
They float in the mire of milk and sugar,
At the expense of the common man, the tax-payer!
Yet their slogans do not stop. I look for wax to seal my ears!

Allocations of milk, sugar and relief-aid all go to henchmen!
Relatives and friends, depriving the least of their basic needs.
Corruption is rampant, misallocation of public funds at all levels.
Cost, demand and hyper-inflation are the order of the day!
Tax increments followed by budget cuts in all spheres.

Yet the common man feeds on left-overs after VIPs have feasted!
We get drunk because of fermented food and sleep all day.
Votes of no confidence? Why not kick the fat toads out of office?
But without the gun, you don't have the guts!
A charge of treason for those who dare in vain,
Then hanging or firing squad execution.

And the poor, hungry man in his shovels can only grumble.
"No, this is African Politics!" they say.
Democracy is good for the West and bad for us!
Let's wait for the next elections!

Charles Lwanga Ssenkungu

Down And Out

Hungry, helpless, desperate souls,
Skinny dogs and begging bowls,
Matted blankets, woollen hats,
Cardboard boxes, grubby mats.

Fingerless gloves, shoes with no laces,
Oversized coats and haggard faces,
Under bridges, bitter cold,
Some too young and some too old.

There are no glowing streets of gold,
No fortunes waiting to unfold,
The hopeful dreams that once were uttered,
Now lie tormented, dashed and gutted.

And what of conscience and compassion?
That pass us by in some strange fashion,
Are we prepared to share the blame
For treating them so inhumane?

Excuses fly from deep inside,
We shy away this helpless tide,
Of homeless lives that haunt each city,
No more procure the slightest pity.

Jan Gleaves

If

If thou were a flower, a sweet smelling blossom
A honey so sweet I would make from thine eyes.
If thou were a bird, a magnificent bird
A melody so enchanting I would make from thine song.
If though were a princess, a proud beautiful queen
A million stars I would steal to make thy crown.
If thou were a portrait, an enigmatic masterpiece
A rainbow so glorious I would make from thine colours.
If thou art none of these, just pure and simple
I beseech you to forgive.
For I know not how to make all those things. However,
If thou were mine, a legend of our love would others make.

Shailesh Sharma

My Heaven

A night can be perfect,
   When you're with that which has a precious clasp on your soul;
Within a world of any girl's dream.
   It is a perfection in its self.
A clear warm night, twinkling jewels in the sky.
   The sparkling moonlight radiates into my heart off the clear lake.
The hand embraces mine,
   The warmth spreads through my body.
What affair can conquer this graceful love that we do possess.
   Not on this earth.
How I wish not the night to end,
   For to me it is ecstasy.
My Heaven.
   But unlike that of the Godly father this does conclude,
In a farewell kiss of divine beauty and love.
   Walking away across the air,
My heart longs to hold that which is now forbidden,
   'Till the next night.

Sian Davies

Like The Night Stars

Like the night stars that fade into darkness,
And the dawn that is soon finished,
And the storm that is followed by calmness,
When turmoil has not fled or vanished.

Like the prayer that has no answer,
And the sleep that cannot be got,
And the thunder that rolls ever after,
In the ear of the soul who rots.

As the dreams that must be shattered,
And the hands that are twisted and bound,
And the body which lies down battered,
When last hope cannot be found.

So the poison must burn inside,
The shadows must shed no light,
For to accept the way things should be,
Is to dwell in eternal night.

Najla Al-Riyami

The Grim Reaper

The sun is shining, the birds are singing
And the spring breezes are blowing
The church bells peel out their ringing
Telling all farmers it's time to start sowing.

Now Joe Jack and Jim prepare to begin.
The tractor, the tiller, the roller, the ridger
Between them created a terrible din
And the newly tilled fields seemed much bigger

Warm summer sunshine started the seed to grow.
Soon fresh green growth waved to and fro
Then later the golden corn stood still
And heard the reaper across the hill.

My ankles are cut, my knees are tied
My head is bashed from side to side
My heart is forced from behind my back
And out through a pipe I fall into a sack.

Olive Newman

The Fairs In Town

Merry go rounds and candy floss,
Proudly riding on a white horse.
The fair is in town, it's lovely to see.
The fortune tellers one, two, three.
The bearded lady, side shows galore.
Jolly clowns tumbling across the floor.
The bumper cars are drawing the crowds.
Fathers and sons shouting aloud.
The big wheel has stopped, crowds begin to run.
Hurry mum, the children all shout.
It's filling up. We'll be left out.
They have waited a year to welcome the fair.
They'll enjoy every minute of the time it is there.
It's over so quickly, this annual event.
When it has gone, and the money all spent,
The pleasure it brings, no longer there.
Leaves a very flat feeling, an air of despair.
This year it's over, the excitement's died down.
But there's always next year, twelve months to the day,
They'll be cheering and shouting, "Here's the fair, Hoo-Ray."

Daisy Rodgers

Doll's Wood

Softly we wandered, afraid to disturb the air,
Peaceful harmony clasped in our hearts.
Fearful of harming this sanctuary we moved with trepidation,
And darest barely breathe.
The sunlight filtered through a canopy of ardent young leaves,
Sprinkling dancing green shadows on the woody floor.
The leaves crunched beneath our feet and seemed to echo endlessly,
Betraying our presence.
Suddenly before us we glimpsed the purest of colours,
And came across a carpet of bluebells,
So delightful,
Full of tiny heads playing a silent symphony of sound,
Curtsying and nodding as we gently brush past.
A fragrance so sweet drifted by causing us to swoon,
I imagined falling there and lying amongst nature,
While time passed by,
This placed mesmerised us,
And I wanted to be a part of this picture forever.

Amanda J. Cornish

Heavens

There are signs in the heavens astrologers say,
That tell me my future, they map out my days.
I know the reasons they tear at my heart
To find and release them means making fresh starts.
The fear of rejection, failure and pain,
Should offer a challenge, a path that is plain.
But oh, how easily one can be led,
By easy roads chosen by others instead.
To choose at each crossroads takes courage to act.
Something astrologers' signposts may lack.

Damien Aked

Seasons Of Your Family Tree

The spring of life is when you are young,
And looking back, it's not so long,
Then marriage, a home, and children to rear,
You know all too soon that summer is here,

The summer of life with its ups and downs,
Its laughter, tears, smiles and frowns,
Then autumn so calm, more free of care,
When children have married and moved elsewhere,

The grandchildren, clumsy, noisy, but sweet,
They visit and become your Sunday treat,
Your love and your care are still needed the same.
But you know at this age, you can't start again,

The years fly by, and in a while,
Your face, though happy, wears a wintry smile,
Though you feel less agile, you know you're now free,
For there are off-spring to carry on, your family tree.

Annice Webster

223

Crack The Drug

There is "Speed and Marijuana, Heroin and Crack"
And any of these you fancy will put you on your back
They lift you high and you feel good
For "two hours, three or four"
But when the highlight passes
They will find you on the floor.
Your brain's immersed in water
Your words won't come together
You feel that you are dying
You're finished with it forever
But then your friends are happy
Speed is lifting them off their back
They shout "Come on it's great! Let's try a little crack"
It's fun, it lifts you higher
But there is another snag
For drugs there is a long hard cure
But from crack (there is no coming back).

Norma Playle

Rich

If you are rich, then you have jewelry and money,
and the working class are poor but funny.

When you are rich, then you have glamour and style,
and the working class are dirty and vile.

If you are rich, then you have investments and homes,
and the working class have debts and loans.

When you are rich, then you are happy and content,
and the working class are miserable and spent.

When you are rich, you are watched and admired,
and the working class are pushed and fired.

Now you are rich, you are one of a few,
but remember, the working class gave it to you.

Now you are rich, you should be bright and clever,
But The Working Class With Money? Never!!!

T. Page

Loneliness

I stood on the cliff at Atlantic Bay,
Staring wistfully at the calm clear sea.
Sky painted grey; end of one more long day.

A cloud of misery is stifling me,
No one to turn to, no one on my side.
I never imagined how it would be

To be so alone but nowhere to hide.
Hoping my tears will wash away the pain,
Just like sand is washed away by the tide.

Search for ray of hope, but always in vain;
Nothing will penetrate my cloud of gloom.
Thinking thoughts that lead down memory lane.

Listen to birds: they sing of hope, not doom.
I listen, hoping that this will end soon.

Marie McGinley

To My Wife

As sunlight from the east young flowers
To life once more awakes, or sparkling dew
Sweet grassy glades and shady bowers
Th' enchantment of fresh being brings anew,
So dawns the secret smile that doth entrance
My very soul, filling with subtle grace
And tender meaning each long loving glance.
There is a look of glory on your face.
You felt a tremble of the life within
And beauty born in innocence shone
Through star strewn eyes: a wondrous vision then
From other worlds I glimpsed, ere it was gone.
This perfect joy is sent us from above:
A child to us is given to crown our love.

Ernest N. H. Lack

The Wind Around The Tower

The wind around the tower
Blows strong and wild
Beating on the stonework, like some mischievous child.
The wind around the tower
Blows and blows all day
Blows cold and icy, will not go away
The tower, empty and desolate
Run down, in a state of ruin
Yet still a place to shelter, when there's a storm a brewing,
Standing lonely on the hill, standing all alone
To the birds and field mice a place they can call home
Soaked by the rain, burnt by the sun
Frozen by the snow and ice, a meeting place for some
A haven for young lovers, to, in secret meet
Far from the madding crowd
Where they can be discreet
The wind around the tower
Blows strong and wild
Beating on the stonework, like some mischievous child.

James Molineaux Starr

The Taste Of Honey In A Nuclear Age

Where have you been, my long lost friend.
Amongst the rubble ain't that a shame.
Scratching a living in this nuclear age,
In rocks of fusion we sign our names.
Where have you been, my long lost friend.
On the front line or on the flying stage.
Your signature blows out this time.
Forever changing mega crimes.
Where have you been and can you see
The pavement of society.
They crumble, crushed beneath our feet.
This night we cannot see to bleed.

Outside the neon fades to naught
And so the multitude they hope
To cry and die in peace; but show.
That they don't know which way to go.

Where have you been last lonely man.
Who's lost his passions, loves and home fields of mystery unknown -
Mega waste split energy. The taste of wine lies heavy on your mind,
A taste of honey will be forever mine.

Peregrine Saint John

Aaron William

He never felt the warm spring sun
shine upon his face

He never felt the soft raindrops
dance on his baby head

He never heard the cheerful birds
singing in the sky

He never ran through soft green meadows
or stooped to pick a flower

But he did feel the love of a mother's arms
and a gentle mother's kiss

He did hear a father's loving words
and saw his tearful eyes

He died at twenty minutes old
frail and weak and helpless

Now he hears and sees and feels
more things we can only dream of

He's happy with the angels now
still we miss you Aaron William.

Roisin Gornall

Another Day

As I open my eyes to another day,
Lift my thoughts to spirit and say,
"Let it be a wonderful day."
Filled with the gifts of love, and life,
Not another day of grief, and strife.

Oh to lay on my bed in the still quiet morn,
Listening to the world come alive with the dawn,
The sound of the earth as she stirs and she sighs,
Knowing that mother nature is wonderfully nigh.

Listen carefully, hear the sound of the air,
Whispering gently, "Are you there?,
Open your window take deep of me,
Smell the fresh wind and the salt of the sea."

To feel the warmth of the sun on my face,
To know that man must fall in disgrace,
For man is forever sowing the seed,
Of total destruction, morals, and greed.

Jacquelyne Thorne

Daniela's Ashes

I follow your trajectory to the diaphanous sky
an unplottable line that deceives me.
Your friends are open like books
but I can't read a word

I think of your smile, while grasping the land
I think of the rituals, while opening my hand

Music whispers you away
and finds a path through your ashes,
your lightness is touching
the surface of our skin.

I talk to you, just something plain
I talk to myself, you're laughing again

Luca Pelli

Death Is Nothing

When somebody you love passes away,
Don't bottle up what you need to say,
Try very hard not to lose your way,
And never forget to talk and pray.

That person has gone to a better place,
A place that doesn't worry about sex or race,
That person will always be there,
When you feel it's time to say a prayer.

So remember that person is still there,
Beside you ready to listen and care,
Always loving and never unfair,
Waiting for you to say that prayer.

Huw Loxton

Him

He sings of our life through his eyes,
He sings of his dreams in our lives,
He prays for better things to come,
He prays for the truth to be won.

With his song he reaches our souls,
With his song he warms the cold,
The love he shares becomes a part of us,
And burns inside frozen hearts.

Our word to him is never kept,
His faith in us is never met,
The pains he goes through we'll never know,
For his burdens are greater than he'll ever show.

When he is gone and all is left,
Is an empty space, will we forget?
He chased away our greatest fears,
And behind his smiles lay tears.

Esha Dasgupta

Napoleonic Sea Scene Of Pride And Fear

The wind was fair off Scilly, as we beat down for Ushant. We knew
that England stood alone, and Boney did scream and rant. At noon
that day, beneath low cloud, Nell's fleet did break to view.
Beneath reefed sails we all stood too, Boney's bill was almost due.

With weather foul the seas ran high, but our spirits never
quenched. Our hearts and minds were mortified, our willing bodies
drenched. From ship to ship the message flew, our wait was not in
vain. The morn will bring us to our goal, the might of France
and Spain. A watery sun and heavy swell, did greet the morning watch,
the helmsman calling 'Full and Bye' and the Master cut a match. With
rum and song we braced ourselves to face the holocaust that day.
'Twas October 21st year 1805, and the drums begun to play.

No rattens end was needed to move old England's sons, the ports
they slowly opened to the staccato roll of drums. Like Leviathans
afloat, and signals flying clear, the wooden walls of England, took
us where sane men fear. The commons roared, and grape shot flew.
The maimed, the dead, the dying, and us, the lucky few.

Patrick Myers

Seasons Come And Go (And So Will I)

Beneath a violet sky and scudding fiscus clouds
Below the land lies comatose
Awaiting the first hint of a summer sun
And the fresh bloom of the rose
Children anxiously wait with bated breath
Hoping for their pool side fun
Trees grow bolder, me ever older
As each season brings in turn
My gradual demise
It will come as no surprise
When I die.

A. C. Jones

Count Your Blessings

B - Be ever grateful for our blessings, we can always find someone
worse off than us
L - Love - hate, good health - sickness, happiness - sorrow, riches -
poverty, there is always opposites to every gift God gives, and thus
E - Every time life strikes a blow our heart breaks, but there is a
rainbow around the corner, so we pick up the pieces and smile
S - Sunshine always follows the rain, so, be determined to carry on.
After all, isn't life really worthwhile.
S - So, no matter what is around the corner, have faith and God will
see you through
I - Into each life some rain must fall, but the good times outweigh
the bad
N - No one can take away our memories - the happy times and
sometimes sad
G - Gather your thoughts and remember, life must go on, and say
S - Sharing, caring, loving our neighbours, will fill our hearts with
happiness every single day.

E. Cawdery

Out Of Body Experience

We walked across the hills together we didn't care about the weather
The wind was cold, the sun was bright, over the hills and out of sight
Onto youth we held so tight, no day went by without a fight
Years passed by when hope did fail, the light went out when I was pale

The Lord was good, he came along, he lit the light and sang a song
He sang a hymn I once knew, every word is really true
When in life I climbed so high, please O' Lord don't let me die
I love the Valley of my youth, yes O' Lord I tell the truth

I pass this on to a friend of mine, for him I hope the sun will shine
I never thought I'd tell this tale, for you I hope it will not fail
My love for you will never die, I hope I do not make you cry
It's hard to say these words just now, I love you more than ever now

The day I died I thought of you, I hovered there just over you
I tried to speak but all in vain, I found it hard to stand the strain
I took a knock upon the head, now I thought that I was dead
Everything I say it true, now I know I still love you
I'll think of you till the day I die, please remember to say good-bye.

Pat Clarke

Worry

Worry looms, then zooms to try our souls
For courage, strength and humanity
But why, to our poor mortal roles
Does God address adversity?

Himself, He came and took the glove
Which His heavenly Father decreed He should
But without help from Him above,
Could He, then mortal, opt for wood?

Our steps we hasten, to outrun
Those crosses bleak which He bestows,
But, though so swift we may become,
We'll ne'er escape such dogged foes.

Yes, we poor humans, would hesitate
To permit an unkind act of fate
Trespass into our Utopian state,
He says, "Admit," we unlock the gate.

So worry, ere you set your course,
Ensure your visit's imperative,
Lest that which you may then enforce
Should challenge mere man's will to live.

Moya Byron

Return From A Dreamland

The magical views are dispersing,
The radiant energy is dying,
The whisper in the wind is cursing,
As the child starts crying.

Her soft tears, one by one, are falling,
As the flame, tear by tear, is burning,
Her quivering voice begins calling,
As her world starts turning.

The precious memories are blurring.
The essence of her life is aching.
Vibrant colours are occurring,
As the child begins awaking.

Who is this intervening?
Bringing her back to this place.
Is there a hidden meaning,
Behind the cause of this sullen face?

As she lay down her head weeping,
So unable was she to discern.
She longed for the world of sleeping,
So to that place she could return.

Jennifer Jazwinski

For Sale

The cottage nestled snugly near the stream
I gazed at it, had I seen it in a dream
A roof that curved out of the thatch
Not another one near that it could match

Oh peace, tranquillity, it did foretell
As it nestled there in the dell
On to its walls the honeysuckle clung
I knew my journey had just begun

But I wanted to stay there oh so much
A longing, a yearning, at my heart did clutch
Feeling as if I had just reached home
Yet knowing I hadn't, I felt so alone

Whose little house must this be
Somebody must live here, you could see
An open door, a contented cat
'Twas cleaning its paws on the mat

And then I saw the sign right there
'For Sale' and then without a care
I knew I had come home at last
Hurrying towards that door, so fast

Barbara E. Steadman

No Matter

No matter what I say
No matter what time does
No matter what a poem says
No matter what a song's lyric does
No matter what the world thinks
No matter if anything holds you back
No matter what the boys say or want me for

No matter what the sun, moon and stars say
No matter what my eyes say
No matter what the desert's mystery states
No matter how high the mountains are, I'll find a way to get you closer.
No matter if you don't see the way things really are
No matter if you look in the mirror and take a final look at your
face and think once your hands held the world

No matter what others say about how the oceans and how the world works
No matter if you find your own way.

Nasrin Ramzan

Poem

My beloved mother

You are a form of beauty
With your natural face no make up on.
    Your heart is full of love and kindness.
You have most degree of all mothers
You are sweet like honey with strong personality and faith.

My beloved mother.

You are not short not tall but a perfect height to me.
    Your intelligence makes you the leader of the house and them all.

Yes you are beautiful beyond belief
The lady of the writer respectable man full of talent (Mr Awl).
then the daughter of Jama the honourable grand.

Oh beloved mother.

You have the gold colour of skin browned by light within like when
morning sunlight shines.

Oh beloved mother.

You have a trustworthy cheerful face which makes you innocent like a baby.
    The words you say seem some part of poems.

They are not song, then you add your beautiful smile
    oh thanks to God who makes me her lucky daughter Ayan.

Ayan Farah Mohammed

My Welsh Boarder Collie

My lovely boarder Collie dog, is so cute, though she doesn't beg,
I've had her 9 years, soon be 10, she answers to Meg,
She's black and white with spots on legs and feet,
Now and again she likes a Bonio for a treat;

She had one puppy, which was not planned,
A lovely dog Sam, grew like a donkey, and got out of hand,
We feed them well, but they like to bite,
Neighbours, friends and family, don't let them out of sight.

We take them to South Wales nearly every year,
To farm land where their brothers and sisters live near.
Take them to see sheep, which they don't understand,
After a day or two they settle down, which is really grand.

Life without a dog seems an awful thing,
Because so much happiness they seem to bring;
They make a mistake, a puddle or two for you to remove,
Then you're cross and shout, ears go flat, they know you disapprove,

By and large a dog's a good friend and guards you well,
If able to talk they would have a good tale to tell,
Sue, Jim, Meg no. 1, 2 and our Sam are some of the names of our Dogs;
Most have gone to heaven, and will be entered in St. Peter's Logs!

M. Harrott

Untitled

Pain is an experience that we all feel,
Healing is something some people can give,
Humans are vulnerable to emotions so real
Let's care for each other so we can live.

I remember him with dress very neat.
What about the church with tapered spire to caress?
His ashes are scattered in the peat
He's transformed my smile to look of distress

Yet, while I'm resting the bluebirds are nesting and fine.
The moon rises up, when my spirits are deep
Then the sun comes out and everything is sublime.
But, our lives are stolen away by sleep
For waiting for the dawning day is a crime
Because will we wake-up again and be able to pray?
And just as important watch the children at their play.

Julia James

Illusion

Life goes on
memories lost and gone
people come, people go
but I still don't know
how life goes on
promises made; slashed with a blade
feelings hurt; heart covered with dirt
but I still don't know
how life goes on
never should love one; future is made one
education, marriage, kids
filled with slits of time and foe
but I still don't know
how life goes on
should've been warned
skip the time I mourned
I realize to let life be -
it will take its own way, I have no say
from the day I was born
life goes on

Maya Lakhiani

To Live Again

Dedicated to my mother and father
Mr.R. Brownless and Miss S. Thompson

So frail yet so lonely
gripping his pain with his heart
only wanting his love to bloom again
to share the obstacles and happiness of life with yet another
and to feel the passions and desires we all share inside
having the freshness of laughter and joy around him
to let his body and soul live once again
Only he can dream of pastures green, the sun within
it's beautiful moments
for he will never become the king of his castle
for his queen was once found then was lost.

T. Brownless

So Little Time

We start out as nothing, a glint in the eye,
Two cells struggling to join but not knowing why.
We split, we divide and yet we stay joined,
Repeating the patterns, forming our mind.
We're surrounded by liquid cushioning our fall,
And the dark reddish glow of our surrounding wall.
There's a pulsating beat penetrating my brain,
We split, we divide, a never-ending chain,
Form into a shape, we're becoming one.
I'm beginning to realize what I've become.
Then in one sudden movement I'm thrown from my world,
There's light and there's sound and my screams can be heard.
My world has been stolen and I'm trapped outside,
There's so much to learn and so little time.

Wendy Smith

The Soldier

He joined with his mates, yes soldiers they would be,
To fight the war for freedom to save our liberty,
It was great to be in uniform, he could not get home
quick enough to show his dad and mum,
Then after two weeks he was gone, to wait orders to go
overseas, he did not know what he was in for,
it was no life of ease, as he soon found out.
Very little training was given to him
all men were needed at the front
to fight with every ounce of strength they had.
He remembered his dad telling him that it was
the same when he was a lad,
as he sat in a dugout more than a little scared.
He heard a shattering sound overhead;
he thought he was home again.
Hello Dad, hi mum, then he fell flat.
This brave young lad was dead.

Jessie Williams

The Sky Painter

The Sky Painter waits until the morn,
To paint the sky all the colours of dawn.
When he is done, he looks and sees
The beauty of what he has done to please.

He will sit all the day in his house of clouds,
Until the dark of night becomes the world's shroud.
He will paint the night sky and has painted the evening.
He said farewell to the sun as it was leaving.

If sometimes a storm we should see,
He will paint the sky as black as can be.
He may paint a rainbow with its seven lovely shades,
Then sit and wait some more until the colours of it fade.

The Sky Painter's friends are the fairies dear
Who keep the colour on Earth all through the year,
But the sky painter himself, he paints just the sky
All through the nighttime until morning is nigh.

Leonie Cole

Memories Of Twilight

And there were willows, dancing in their magical expectancy,
Dipping their graceful arms in the mirror's silence.
The grasses swayed gently in the cooling breeze,
Whispering softly to the nymphs and fairies.
The murmuring water lapped in solitude
At the reassuring firmness of the encircling bank,
And the sun was born.

In the Forests of the Night the pine trees shivered,
Keeping their sinister watch in the murky twilight.
The bracken cowered on its bed of needles,
Trembling in the fear-tinted air.
On its lone branch the Owl itself was silent,
Waiting for neither day nor night,
And the sun died.

Katherine Desborough

In Bloom?

Daisy dee, daisy doo,
Today you look not white but blue?
Has the harsh wind painted you a new colour?
Did it decide these bruises would make you look fuller?
Maybe the grass will hide your disease;
Not attractive anymore to the wasps or the bees,
Maybe like me someone will pluck you from the roots
and replant you far away;
Till the healing is done and the scars are all that
remain some day,
But now, my sweet daisy, you not only have to
live with the pain, inside,
But with those other daisies gaping at you,
And wondering how someone could paint
you black and blue!

Jacqueline McNamara

The Things I Love

Snowflakes dancing over my head,
The warming smell of freshly baked bread,
Watching the sun come up at dawn,
Jack Frost's patterns on a cold winter's morn,
The red sky of the sun set,
Dew drops making all things wet,
A full moon in the sky above,
All these things I love to love.

Stars twinkling in the sky at night,
The way your blood races when you've just had a fright,
Peanuts that go crunch when you munch,
Eating grapes by the bunch,
Driving through the countryside,
Standing on a beach to watch the tide,
No moon in the sky above,
All these things I love to love.

Cheryl Joanne Prescott

Our Own Worst Enemy

We were given this planet to love and enjoy,
but all we seem to know now is how to destroy.
The pollution we're causing when driving our cars,
now the sky is showing all of the scars.
Trees we are felling once gave us fresh air,
we're fishing the sea until it's almost bare.
There's violence, hunger, politicians and war,
people are dying by the score.
The pain and suffering bound with sad memories,
we really are our own worst enemies.

Roslyn J. Heather

Washington Cathedral

Though not my city, I love it well.
For there I found a jewel, a precious gem
Built with love, by skill of men.
A house of jewels rare.
A temple of beauty, for all to share.
Proud am I, that a piece of ancient Britain
dwells within.
And queenly hands have worked with
thread and pin.
Dear Lord, how pleased you must be,
In this age of desecration, to see
your house growing in sacred trust,
youth of Washington, love it well.
Your heritage this majestic sentinel,
Built by loving hands to live
Three thousand years or more.
Spires reach out to an evening sun.
God's gift and man's in unison.

E. M. Norbury

It's Good Tae Talk

Come on Al, be a pal,
Pick up the phone and gee's a cal,
I know you'll say "Ah take a walk"
But all I want is you tae talk,
About our holiday at the end o' this year
So hurry up and buy the beer.

We're all excited about the date
12 weeks today, we'll no be late,
The kids are chatting and on a high,
"What's it like up in the sky.

Passports, visas we're nearly there,
All we need now is tae pay the fare.
All this working and being stressed,
But we ken this Christmas will be the best.

Cuddly Koalas and Kangaroos
Possums, lizards and dingo's too.
Platapus, wombats all tae see.
Sunny Australia's the place to be.

Liz Manson

Snowflakes

The snow swirled lightly in a strange pattern.
It twirled and circled, went up and round.
But it never seemed to reach the ground.

Once in a while, a flake would settle on the window.
And I would press my finger against it through the glass.
Each tiny flake was pieces joined together.
Until they melted.

The wind blew the snow up and round,
Mischievously stopping it from touching the ground.
Upwards it swirled, then falling it twirled.
Until it reached the end and melted.

I watched, as people battled on through the biting cold and
falling snow,
Determined to complete an impossible task,
Noses turned red and fingers turned blue,
Feet trod on the soft lying flakes
And they melted.

Joanna Salmon

Lonely Planet Pluto

Lonely planet pluto,
far far away, in the depths of the universe
is where you always stay.
You have no neighbouring planets to keep you company.
Oh lonely planet pluto, what is your destiny?
You are the ruler of scorpio,
You are the planet of death.
You are the darkness that covers light,
the cold, the sadness.
Even though you are a planet of destruction,
The planet of an end,
To an end there is a beginning
which we must all begin again.

Antonia G. Hart

My Love Is Gone

When you left me, what was left to me?
The kiss of a languid wind, whenever I go for a walk,
bringing to me your memories from every corner.

A shy, nostalgic song filling my empty room,
making me sleep to the sound of your melodic voice.

A tree, seen through the window, where precious fragments
of our love nest hang in every branch.

A flower, from where a butterfly has brought to me
the scent of your body.

An empty swing where both of us, like two acrobats,
tried to coordinate the complexity of our feelings.

Those words you told me, the words I told you,
and one or two pictures to remind me that
I still love you.

Jorge de Sousa

A Perfect Earth

A perfect earth, that would be great,
There'd be no fighting 'cos there'd be no hate.
Every person would be a friend,
All the times of enemies and hatred would end.
All living creatures in love with each other,
Your ex-enemy will become your brother.
No hunger to be found anywhere at all,
Your friends will be there incase you should fall.
Animals and people will walk paws in hands,
Happiness will spread throughout the lands.
Peace and tranquillity, no hostility around,
No people who aren't needed anywhere to be found.
If all this were true and we lived for each other,
Life would be special living sister for brother.

This would be a perfect earth,
Which would be given the credit it's worth.

Kerry-Ann Deane

Friends at Heart

The sky was blue but rain came down
The street was cold but sun shone strong
Their faces were happy but held a frown
Their love was right but the time was wrong.

His heart was pure his mind full of spite
Outside it was day, inside it was night
Her face was a cover beneath she cried
Her feelings were true but her words they lied.

They both felt something but never said
Their feelings seemed free but locked in their heads
They rode together and fell apart
Two loves in their mind but friends at heart.

Jenna Trolley

Stan

So tall I thought,
As I looked and of what he'd bought.
Arms so full with more to come,
Of beautiful things so pink and blue,
He exclaimed "they're all for you"
Oh so kind happy so help full
His forward way he'd show me where to plant them,
He'd slam the gate, he hated cats
Though soon opened it for a friendly chat
He loved the children we loved him
But compared to Joan our love was dim
His beloved garden his pride and joy'
So beautiful flamboyant not at all coy
He worked so hard beautiful flowers to please
And every year purple pink sweet-peas.
A perfect place a perfect man
So gracefully loved forever "Stan".

Patricia McKenzie

Have I Seen You?

Have I seen you
Projected upon my soul?
I know not, I know nothing.
Who are you that invades?
Topples the walls of Jericho
That cradles my inner sanctum,
Denying all alien, all unknown.

You...me...us
We are one.
The unknown divides,
Enigma enchants.
You resurrect me from transience.
We are eternal,
Yet thou hath no vision for mortal eyes.

My spirit calls me to follow a sign,
The mortal resists the unseen divine.

Christopher Chapman

The Despairs Of Motherhood

Out of love, there comes anguish, sadness and despair
for a mother in her caring work
she thinks of everyone but herself
and is never thought of as needing help
when weariness sets in, she doesn't have time to sit
The family needs looking after
for everyone relies on her
but won't admit it 'till they're older
after all the years of hard work
the rewards are finally clear
all those years of love and affection
make them give her a grand cheer
now finally her children have stepped in her shoes
they now have children too
so God bless, they're mothers
who have it all to come now too.

Nicola Manton

Labour Camp Of The Mind

My warm tongue runs over my mouth,
Giving temporary relief to my cracked lips.
Paled by the dust,
Yet reddened by my own anaemic blood.
I can't even tell if I'm in pain.
I am a slave.
Exposable, exploitable, unsavable.
This is the identity they have given me.
Funny thing though,
I can barely remember who I used to be.
An image comes to my mind;
I am lying in my bed with the sheets tousled all around me,
The warmth of the mid-morning sun illuminating the
cosiness of my bedroom,
And my beloved girlfriend who is sleeping peacefully in my arms,
Am I remembering or dreaming?
Or is this present moment a nightmare from which I will
eventually waken?
Odd, it seems so real.

Susan Naraysingh

The Addict

The addict in his numb, bewildered state
Stumbles blindly to his tragic self-made fate,
Caring not for anyone, man or beast,
Not knowing that already he's deceased.

When he slid away from simple things well told,
He didn't dream of maybe growing old.
He never thought he'd have to look for shelter
Or if his plight ought fetch an eager helper!

Was it not best to look around and measure,
In which direction was perhaps his treasure?
If any! Surely in some book and not in the foolish void
between two stools.

He shied away from bells and surplice white.
To go in his direction was his right!
His arguments and talk could justify.
But beneath the cloak of drugs he sought to fly.

But I mustn't smirk and say "the stupid fool",
It's easy to be a prude and play it cool.
Perhaps he wasn't made to take the strain,
Of the stupid cut and thrust for money gain.

Dermot O'Grady

The Death Of St. Valentine

Scarlet ribbons of blood were flowing out,
Tinging the February frost pink.
My bruised face stared blankly now.
The knife cold in my hand, dropped to the ground.

The stench of his whiskey hovered in the air
My feet crunched on broken glass and china
As I walked to the sink.
Strange, how even the cold water felt warm.

Too tired to move him—I slept, soundly,
Peacefully at last.
Waking up a new day, a new time had dawned
February 15th seemed warm; the winter cold and dead

Cleaning up the mess, I cut my hand.
Droplet of blood fell to the carpet,
Some blurring the writing on the Valentine's card.
Sucking my fingers and blood—I smiled.

Bending over, my back ached from rhythmic punching
I picked up the withered roses,
Petal by petal, the flowers died a slow death
whispering softly, he loves me, he loves me not.

Fiona Burns

The Same 1941

The same moon shines on you my love,
That's shining on me now,
The same stars wink at you to-night,
The pole star and the plough.

The same sunshine's on us today,
Though thousand miles apart,
The same breeze kisses your sweet face,
And that thought cheers my heart.

The same sky o'er us both is spread,
Each breathes the self-same air,
And what are miles, but man made things,
That lead just here and there.

The God who made the sun and moon,
The breeze, the twinkling star,
I know will reunite us soon,
Though now you seem so far.

And then my love again we'll meet,
Though parted now by war,
And together we'll thank God above,
And live, and love, once more.

Holland Garside Hague

Untitled

A day to live and no one knows,
they don't feel my pain
or understand my loss.

A day to live
my days of agony soon forgotten.
As I grow weaker, my dreams fade.
Who cares . . . ?
Who cares . . .?

A day to live
24 hours with more of life's torture.
I dream of all I'll never be,
insecurity is all that lies in me.

Underneath the stars I'll lie,
forgotten and not missed.
My life is over,
what have I achieved?

Don't believe that's all there was to me.
Don't believe that's all there was to see.

You don't know what I wanted
You'll never know the real me.

Jane Lazic

I Have An Illness

I have an illness
I told them so
But they just didn't want to know

I went to the doctor
Yes, what can I do
I have an illness, no it's not yuppie flu.

I have an illness, what can it be
Doctor, please just listen to me

I'm sick and tired, I ache you see
I'm so fatigued, no energy.

But you're the doctor, I'm sure you'll agree
I have no symptoms that you can see
But I suppose you'll say to me,

Go home, my dear, have a cup of tea
I have no illness, well that's what you said.

I'm sorry to tell you it's all in your head
So if one day you're ill
Like me, don't ask your doctor for sympathy

Just help yourself to get well
And let your doctor go to hell.

Isobel Wilson

The Parting

Now the time has come for parting and I lose my hold at last,
I remember you so differently over all the years that have past.
Your smiles and tears of babyhood, the fears that childhood brings,
When boys took your affections I remember all these things.
You're now a breath of springtime that only youth can give,
I'll keep this memory with me for as long as I may live.
This parting has come sooner and the distance far too wide,
Your freedom gives me heartache and these tears I cannot hide.
As I wrap my arms around you and hold you close to me
Know my love is going with you and I hope that you can see . . .
'Though you roam this wide world over, as you fly both wild and free
From this father, to you daughter, please come home safe to me.

Anne Pugh

An Ode To Reg

For all of your life you have created sin,
From the affairs of your heart to your business within.
Your family around you, you cower behind.
Your strength is no more and your love it is blind.
The respect you once held has faded away.
Your body is old but your mind it is sharp.
You have manoeuvred and manipulated right from the start.
Now nobody cares and nobody sees the little old man down on his knees.
Just for one moment you thought you had lost,
But your sharp little mind outwitted them all and then once again
they all came to call,
To plump up your feathers and to say you were right.
Just remember old man in the dead of the night, when you lie in your
bed and you're rigid with fright,
With that hurt in your heart and that pain in your eyes, that life
is too short to be so unkind.
For no-one will care when you're buried and gone and the unhappiness
you started will not carry on.
For always out there, kindness will win.
Remember these words as you knock at the gate.
"Let me in, let me in, I just hope it's not too late".

Julie Sawdon

The Death Coach

Awaiting night, dreading slumbers loss of consciousness,
for deep in mind, I'm knowing the death coach is making progress,
sleek ebony horses, black plumes waving they rush through the night,
their hooves clatter on non-existent cobbles, features distorted, mere
   presence instilling fright.
The faceless hooded coachman yells 'onward', whilst whipping of his team,
slumber overcomes me, unconscious now, can anyone hear my scream?
This coachman knows to take my soul, my life, take whatever man I am,
still the coach presses on, myself I can't awaken, alone in mind I wonder
   does anyone give a damn?
Outside death's coach arrives, the coachman beckons life and soul to proceed,
boarding, my will to live cannot gain strength, so to the death coach
   I must concede,
door slams!, I cannot see, nothing stirs inside but mist that swirls
   and smothers as if hideous and alive,
day dawn's, but no one shall awaken life this morning, for last
   night the death coach did arrive.

Brian Burns

The Golden Years

Thank you for the Golden years,
years of love and of peace.
Thank you for your kindness, tolerance, your time
I would not have had these very happy years were it not for you,
you are so very thoughtful, in everything you do.
A warm human being, a friend, so caring, so innocent, so loyal, so true.
All these things are precious, they came with your soul.
Do not change, stay the same always for others will always envy
these treasures that God has entrusted to your care, knowing that
you will always tend them lovingly,
just as you tended me, in my time of need . . .

John Anderson

Playing The Game

I sit home at nights, I scheme and I plan,
You know I won't rest 'til I've done all I can.
You build up those walls and you think you're protected,
But a crack in the painting has gone undetected.
Like a master chess player I've discovered your tack.
I'll move discreetly and cover my tracks.
You won't see my shadow, nor trace a line crossed,
Your walls are like Jericho, tumbled, you've lost.
You've played your game well, that I admit,
But a good player knows it's now time to quit.
A few mistakes made, an unintentional foul,
But the seconds are in so throw in the towel.
You think you are cool but I can be cunning,
So give it up now, put a stop to your running.
I know you've been hurt, this game can be hard,
But the odds were never better, so lay down your guard.
I've seen your scars and I can hear you cry,
But you'll gain no more points if you let your love die.
Just hold out your hands, make this a good catch,
We're both winners now, game, set and match.

Louise Fisher

Time For Bed

As the sun goes down behind the trees,
The remaining sun and moon do tease.
When the sky is a mixture of yellow and red,
You know it is really time for bed.
The sunset is truly beautiful,
And for most people the feeling's mutual.
A dark blanket descends over the sky,
With thousands of sparkling stars up high.
And when you're snuggled up in bed,
The moon is surely overhead.

Catherine Woodley

Crying Acid Tears

I am crying acid tears,
Acid tears, full of fears,
So full of fears are my acid tears
Acid fears so true.

They burn my heart,
They burn my mind,
They burn my life, all the time
They burn so hard they make me cry.

And then, it starts to hurt inside,
I cry for a need,
I cry for a love,
A love I'll never find.

And then the love I need so much,
It makes me cry and it hurts my mind,
I can't stop crying, it hurts so much,
I need it far, far, far too much,
Why will it just not come to me and dry the acid
tears?

Roberta C. Wagstaffe

Music

Music is a great subject
It gives me the musical affect

Music makes me dance around
I dance on the table, chairs and on the ground

Music, music, all around my ears
something pop pop in front of me appears

Music makes me dance up and down
music makes me dance so much I even
start dancing in my town

Music is in my mind wherever I go
this secret is between me and you
so I don't want anyone to know!

Kirandeep Flora

When Darkness Falls

From dark distant pastures mist drifted in,
A ghostly mass of grey
Moving always onward through fading light,
To where the valley lay.
A farmer returned from work on the land
His dog was by his side
To reach his house he had walked through the wood,
The moon his watchful guide.
Before him was a golden sea of corn,
Which swayed from side to side,
Each stem moving in the wake of the breeze
Like waves at evening tide.
He stared at the lights of the distant town,
Heedless of passing time
Above the sound of the wind in the trees,
He heard the church bells chime
Leaving the trees he walked slowly away,
With a wandering mind
When his form became as one with the fields,
Darkness closed in behind.

Wayne Adams

Tears

Every time a tear falls from my eye it rains
Every time a day goes by I miss you even more
Every second every hour
When you are near me I am blessed with power
The power of the love you give me, the love I need
I can hear the rain
Or is it just me crying
Crying over you
I love you, I really do
It would break my heart if we had to split
In two
I love you
I really do.

Caroline Anne Yates

Precious Things

Looking for something that's precious to me,
Looking on land and over the sea,
I wonder where it could be,
That something that's precious to me.

I'm looking for it everywhere,
Even in my favourite teddy bear,
I wonder if it could be there,
While I look people glare.

I wonder if it don't want to be found,
But here I am looking around and around,
In the distance I hear a dog hound,
Apart from that I hear no sound.

I will never forget that precious thing,
Now it wasn't a necklace or a ring,
It was something not even fit for a king,
Cause it's my own precious thing.

Trudi Chew

A Little Tear

I have so much to tell you, yet in truth I cannot speak
I feel happy and excited, yet a tear torments my cheek
If to me it would listen, this is what I'd say
Little tear, I know you glisten, but please don't run away
I know you're always running, this way, that way, to and fro
But little tear, stop to think, you have no place to go.
Sometimes with joy you are laughing, sometimes you just pretend
But little tear you can't fool me with endless streams of friends
You say you're never tired, never resting for a while
Yet I've seen you playing in the corner of a smile
Are you really happy when you distort a smiling face?
When there's no-one there to catch you, do you vanish into space?
I don't know where you come from, for I've never seen you start
Why don't you do something useful, try to mend a broken heart

Walter T. Griffiths

Poor Boy

You've had nothing but trouble all your life
All you seem to see is all that strife
Your parents see you as a threat
Of your birth they regret
Since then you have received beatings
And to much of all this teasing

If only they could love you it would be great
All they can show is hate
This time they've caught you off guard
They've gone and beaten you too hard
Lying on the floor black and blue
This time you look through

They've taken you away and put you in care.
If only your parents had learnt to love and share
This is the only life you know
Kind feelings you cannot show
Cannot trust a single soul
Life is a pain on the whole

We all wish you luck
But you've been stuck

L. A. Foulger

Untitled

How long must I wait
When will I know
Where is my destiny
The start of the show

Where must I search
How far must I look
Where is my beginning
The start of my book

Will it be shallow forbidden of love
Shall my fingers be mittened
And never have gloves

Will it be joyous, colourful and bright
Where I can now have the apple
I've been longing to bite

Where are the dreams I see in my head
Where is the adonis I seek for my bed
Maybe it's fiction, fallacies and lies
If this is the truth I may as well die

But how will I cope if I were to die
When I have not solved the problem of who am I?

John Gillies

The Pencil

The pencil is sharp and the pencil is round,
The pencil originates from out of the ground.
It came from the wood of a tree that was tall,
A tree that was looking right over my wall

I remember it well as it stood so straight,
I used to admire it from my garden gate,
I would sit on its roots on a warm summer's day,
And dream my dreams of time far away.

Then came the day of the terrible storm,
It rained and it thundered from evening till morn,
I looked through my window and where was my tree?
Nowhere but nowhere my tree could I see.

Next came the men with their saw and their axe,
They cut up my tree and put some in their sacks,
The heavy trunk was loaded on a really long lorry,
I was told furniture would be made like a tea trolley.

One man said as he saw tears in my eyes,
"I'll get to the factory so please don't cry,
And ask them to make you a special present see,
Of a lovely pencil that came from your tree.

Vivien Winter

Departure

The twinkling lights upon the shore, diminish, you are gone,
I stand here watching at the rail, dry eyed,
A thousand feelings flutter through my mind, I'm here alone,
Where has it gone? The passion, love, just died?

How brave we were so long ago, love will conquer all
We thought, with innocence and youth and blinded eye
The passion that consumed us, burnt us, let us fall
And the lasting love was only a disguise.

The silver ribbons of the wake stretch endless back to you
My heart cries out to touch you just once more.
The night comes down and cloaks the world with midnight blue
And my straining eyes can't see the distant shore.

The sea gulls wheel and cry, becoming fainter, then are gone
And the wet spray, flying, blinds my aching eyes
And my heart is cold and heavy, dragging like a stone
Down below the depths where Neptune lies.

But suddenly a feeling surges through my heart
I can see beloved outlines through the gloom
I see your face and feel your kiss, and know we're not apart
As I slowly, gently, sink to meet my doom.

Pamela J. Loftus

The Stillest Night

'Twas the stillest night that no man slept
Locked in futile combat did they lie
No wind no rain but silence all about
Waiting ever waiting but to die

Yards apart but wilderness between
Not a word of German nor of French
The chatter of teeth was a salvoed magazine
That broke the still of a disenchanted trench

A million stars like hearts in battle slain
Burned in the cloudless vacuum of above
And deep into these souls of haunted pain
Was writ on Heaven's scroll a tale of love

Though these fields were white and red and green
A full moon bleached the colour from all eyes
What tragedy that Man had never seen
What honour could be earned at such a price?

And longer did they lie and longer still
Waiting ever waiting but to die
Thy kingdom come this night upon the hill
'Twas the stillest night that no man slept nor I

Andrew J. Smith

The Other Side

The other side of the horizon was where I once resided,
Scheming and dreaming with absolute meaning
To find the unknown and bring her home,
For the childlike soul to evolve and mould
Into the rhythm and prism of a bustling world.

Jumping over the horizon I would take my leave in water deep.
Dipping and slipping and finally sipping
The song that would throng
Through every part of my joyous heart
Sowing and growing in a bustling world.

The other side of the horizon is where I realize,
Caught between the waves that push and pull
Sometimes on top but occasionally fall,
Becoming a reel on a wheel
Of a song written wrong in a bustling world.

On the other side of the horizon there's another horizon
Biding and awaiting with absolute trust,
To find and discover her I must.
For the childlike soul to evolve and mould
Into the rhythm and prism of a bustling world.

Katie Webber

Moments

Many times have I passed this way,
This is the street—where I used to live and play.
Hopscotch games chalked along the floor,
Every house had on open door.
Memories I recall of things said and done,
Some are sad, but most were fun.
Each moment I remember with a word or song,
My thoughts of days, now forever gone.
Brothers and sisters, father and mother,
The moments we shared, I would change with no other.

Dorrien Thomas

Where Are You?

Round was the fruit, a perfect sphere
And it shone in the midday sun.
Its scent set the fountains of the taste buds flowing
As it begged her to come near.

"Eat me, and you will never die,"
Came the voice from... she knew not where.
The thought set the longing of a proud heart growing,
And she took it though she knew not why.

Then, to her husband, across the lawn
She ran in the setting sun,
Their love sent the memory of God's words running,
And they ate as the sun went down.

Great was the shame as they stood there naked
In the light of the terrible deed.
Fear set the beat of their bare hearts pounding
So they hid in the trees, in the bushes, in the shadows,
In the darkness...

They hid from the light.
From the voice of God as He said,

"Where are you?"

Pauline S. Huntington

My Own Self

On my way to Thy Abode, my Lord, I came out alone
Lost in thy thoughts, repeating thy name, enjoying my walk
And hoping to reach my destination before the dawn of day
But who was this that followed me in the silent dark?
He raised the dust beneath my feet and made a harrowing noise
Many a time he dragged me into the grip of desire
Hungry for thy love I sought to escape from worldly appetite
All my efforts to elude his presence always ended in naught
He pursued me as a shadow pursues a walker in the sun
Then I discovered, Lord, it was myself that I could not throw off
Escaping him might I have thus attained thee, Lord, my love and
Destination?

J. L. Datta

Solitude

The sun sets with an orange glow
Across the mackerel sky,
The colours sharpen behind silhouettes
As time ticks by.
Now everyone has gone home
To their comfort and something to eat,
All but one shabby figure
Walking along the street.
It's a tramp, with his belongings,
Looking for somewhere to sleep the night,
So off down to the old bridge
In the shadows from the street light.
Huddled up in his little corner
No company for him to share,
He has probably eaten from begging
Surely he would find someone to care.
To wake up refreshed in the morning
Arising to the beauty of the early sun,
No direction, or stress, and thanking God
For this new day which has just begun.

Rose M. Rawlings

The White Nymph

She came to rest quiet near my knee, for my skin
Not six inches from my shin,
And there her hairy legs, they tickled me,
Her wings they flapped for all to see.
Her little head, so black, it twitched and brushed,
The long antenna quickly rushed,
And with my leg I swayed the giant wings,
To watch the patterns that this brings.
On bending close I saw her fine black hairs,
While all around I gathered stares,
So I twitched my leg and made her fly,
The crowd went up with one big sigh.
And as she flew far out of sight,
I knew I'd seen a strange delight.

T. V. Lattimore

The Perfect Moment

The perfect moment,
it never came,
nothing ever happened
it all stays the same,
people come and people go
my heart beats slow.
You don't exist, I never knew you,
you won't be missed
and I won't feel blue.

But if I never care I'll never find out,
what life and love are all about.
I'm a free spirit,
I can roam the air.
Free, confined, empty and full,
all I want to do is care.
Perfect moments never come my way
but a perfect heart will discover mine someday.

Laura Dempsey

The Pain Of Waiting

Today I stand at the door of your heart as a beggar
Yesterday I did the same.
Tomorrow...
My thoughts lead to hope and desire as tomorrow dances
through my mind.
I wonder will I stand at the door as I do now?
Or, maybe, somehow, that door shall open
I look at you
And I love you.
I see your pain and your hurt
But I see that space within you
That silently calls my name.
Sadly, you don't hear it
Your mind is far, far away.
My heart cries tears of anguish
As you go your own lonely way.
So, all I can do is love you,
From this space outside your heart,
I have to wait until you hear me.
Someday it will happen,
it will be the start.

Laura Dempsey

Remembering

The memory of your love, still surrounds me now,
The shadow of your smile, I still can see.
Although you've gone away, I still remember you,
For love's the strongest bond there'll ever be.
Your lovely face,
So full of grace,
You'll always be not far from me.
So as each day goes by, I will remember you,
Remembering all the things that we once shared,
I know one day that you and I will meet again,
Till then, your treasured memories will be there.

Linda Trohear

Birth

From your cosy world
How we wanted to hold you,
Only through your kicks and stirs
Did we get to know you,
You came for a purpose
To fulfil our dreams.

At last you arrived
In the middle of the night.
The pain was worth it,
Across a span of muscle
You fought your way through
A bundle of joy stained with blood
You came to our world.

Holding our breath we waited for your cry
Which echoed through the summer night.
Since you came,
Suddenly everything is bright and beautiful.

Siona Marcella Chohan

Eyes

The eyes are the windows of a person,
The gateway to the soul,
The door into the depths of the strongest heart,
The exit through which secrets are told,

The eyes are the means of getting in;
Sliding past other defences,
A way into the deepest, most locked-away fears,
And the pain suffered by princes,

The eyes are the means of searching inside,
The fears and the pains you feel,
The eyes are the way of telling on yourself,
So protect them if your secrets are real.

Sarah Braime

Creation

I have often listened to the rhythm of the waves
As they rush onto the sandy shore it's strange how they behave
It reminds me of a driving force that no naked eye can see
But deep down in its mystery, there is tranquillity.

I've watched the wheat at harvest bend in the wind with ease
It looks so long and fragile, as it wavers in the breeze.
But try and pull a blade of it and you very soon will know
Underneath its fragile looks, is a toughness there to grow.

I've marvelled at the mountains so majestic, standing tall
Looking down on all the world, at the beauty great and small
For hidden in this beauty are living vibrant streams
Nestled in their mossy glens where the sunlight sheds its beams.

Maybe we can learn from this, that beauty can unfold
in unexpected places, prepared by heaven's mould
So why not take a moment, and have a look around
Creation in its truest form, provided for mankind

Hilary Margaret Spencer

The Inspiration

I love you, so in the depths of your shining eyes
I planted the sees of an endless love,
So whenever you look deep within my eyes
And see this love shine back to you,
It will be an inspiration for all you say and all you do.

I love you, so in the light of the moon
I imagined happiness as divine as love,
So whenever I lose myself in its brightness
And only find things brighter still,
It urges all the unloving to love and do whatever they will.

I love you, so in the heaven of our entwined hearts
I wrote our love across the night sky in stars,
So whenever you glance up at the enclosing darkness
And see tiny glimmers of light break through,
It will declare to all that you love me and that I love you.

Michelle Emery

Feelin' Good

All is silence, not a peep,
Like cat voyeurs we watch them sleep.
Dreaming away the hours
Of prowlings amongst spring flowers.

The butterflies you chase after,
Your cuteness and our laughter.
As curious little noses
Sneezed at the pollinated roses.

And such innocence doth enchant,
As a newborn nephew to his aunt.
Tranquil as a red sunset,
Calm as a storm unmet.

As they sleepily awaken from their doze,
A yawning purr and a lick of the nose.
A stretch of claws, and how they mewed,
A hungry demand, a cry for food.

Oh cats, what a beautiful pair,
As you lie upon the pillowed chair.
What strange thoughts pass through your heads,
As angels dance, and lovers wed?

Jeremy Charles Willliam Bloomfield

Hopes And Dreams

What a wonderful world this would be
If it were filled with Love, Peace and Tranquillity.
No more war, no more Hate,
Life for us would be so great.

Lots of giving, lots of sharing,
Lots of loving, lots of caring.
No more dread, no more fear,
Life for us would be full of cheer.

Full of peace and tranquillity
Also love and harmony.
Happiness and contentment
There would be no need for resentment.

Far more patience and understanding
Would make our lives far less demanding.
Far more thought and consideration
Would make this a wonderful generation.

Whatever it takes, it would be worth it,
If only life could be this perfect.
However impossible this may seem,
We can but live with hopes and dreams.

Janet Warren

The Journey

Every sign post
passing,
faster,
I tried to grab them.

Every car
Individual,
familiar,
but I am still lost.

Feeling compression
spinning,
loosing,
was this my choosing?

My destination
numb,
silent,
everything seems detached.

Trying not to be seen,
past,
regret.
The roadside generator—looked like a guillotine!

Lisa Natalie Jones

The Essence Of Time

Time on your hands to sit and reflect
You ask yourself what now to expect
Days gone by, good and bad
Love given freely, love you have had
Times to remember, times to forget
All part of life but I wonder yet
Laughter, tears or joy to behold
What lies ahead of hopes untold
If there is happiness awaiting somewhere
Let it come soon whilst there's time to spare
Family feuds are a thing of sorrow
Best sorted today, as there's no tomorrow
Tomorrow never comes they say
So try to think clearly and find a way
To solve the problem without condemnation
With brother, sister or close relation
Resentment is like a thorn in your heart
Festering away and tearing you apart
Love is a gift anyone can give
So why not share it, live and let live

J. Wood

Where Are You?

Where are you, child?
I am here.
Sailing down the Spanish Main,
My pirate ship driven by the winds of my imagination.

Where are you, woman?
I am here.
Here with the one I have chosen.
Together we build our lives, brick by brick.

Where are you, mother?
I am here.
Here with my child.
Holding him gently and marvelling at his warm sweetness.

Where are you, my friend?
I don't know.
I'm lost in the memories of what I once was.
Swirled away by dreams of what I might yet become.

Where are you?
I am gone.
I was taken away and returned to what I used to be.
Now you'll never know where I am.

Sarah Johnstone

A Day, My Way

I rise at five
Trying to stay alive,
A cup of tea and a fag
If I let it my life could be a drag,
My disability is a sword pointed at my heart
After the paper, the post, what has to be done? I must make a start,
I water and feed my plants, they are so healthy
All the time, listening to the groups on the radio, who are so wealthy,
But my love is my life I lead, and my wife
Who tends and cares for me without too much strife,
After helping with the groceries, I have my lunch
All that in one morning, makes me tired as punch,
When my letters are written and my chores done
I sit down to watch a comedy video which can be so much fun,
A game of scrabble and the afternoon has gone
My wife and I watch television, which is on,
We switch channels then watch a tape
Before I know it the time has past, it is getting late,
　It is the end of another day
　Which I try to live, my way.

Philip M. Gant

War Memorial

Between large, boney-armed trees
Windswept, desolate,
Engulfed by nature's dark hand
Lies unattended; cracked, crumbling, sadly concealed,
A lonely, grey marbled cross-shaped stone,
Covered by a living blanket of moss-green fungi,
Mingled with strands of stringy spider's web,
Kept in, kept away,
By rusting green iron bars, placed around,
Merging with dew-covered grass underfoot,
Name, after name, after another,
Journeying downward, downwards towards earth
Death lingers around; no sound, no smell, no feeling.
Light expelled by grey shadows of dark wood,
Letting only rain
Explore and read these forgotten names.

Steven McCombe

Reflection

I light a candle
And watch the flame
And think of you.

I watch the candle
And concentrate . . .
And think of you.

I concentrate on the candle
I feel close to you
And know you think of me.

The reflection of the candle symbolizes the other part of me
We are one and the same.
I don't exist without you.
Once the flame dies, so does the reflection.

Hazel Harrop

Dearest Nan

It's been a year and every day I shed a tear,
The pain never seems to heal,
Is this how I'm supposed to feel?
Whilst you lay in your bed,
You squeezed my hand as I kissed your head,
There were no goodbyes as you shut your eyes.
Down came my tears as it was my worst fears,
And I know one day it will be a treat,
When we finally gather together to meet,
When you got to heaven on the 10th of May,
All the angels gathered that day,
And showed you to the pearly gates,
As that is where the family awaits,
With open arms you stepped in and now your new life will begin,
Tonight, and every night, I promise to pray,
And look forward to meeting you again one day.
Goodnight Nan, love you always, Donna

Donna Rispoli

Barbwire Child

The grim walls of the prison rear up,
And through its tangled crown the wind whispers.
It tells tales of suffering and pain,
And the despair of human kind;
It sighs, 'People die within these walls,
But no, do not grieve for them—
Not now their souls are free.'
Outside beneath the prison walls
A homeless woman strains,
In pain of labour she cannot listen,
Only sorrow for the babe.
Now, as she brings the new born to her breast
He opens his innocent eyes,
His first sight: a stone cliff,
Man-made and topped with metal thorns;
And though he knows not how,
He understands deep within his newborn heart
That he will never be free.

Kyrsti A. Bonham-Noyle

Fright Night

The slightest noise within the night
Keeps me from sleeping though I put up a fight
I toss I turn I'm almost there
I envy the relative who dreams without care
That snore I deplore it escapes through her door
The smoothest car engine appears with sound
Doors open, voices echo as a foot hits the ground
Nearing footsteps magnify then fade in the distance
I wish I was dreaming
The clock rattled I glanced alarmingly at the time
Twit twoo haunted an ever-alert night bird
The black cats unlucky as its mate is a witch
At which point I felt a twitch
"Boo hoo, I'm gonna get you" said a low voice
I looked up without choice
I found this thing had no smiling face
I could see no hiding place
I jumped because of fright into the returned daylight.

John Beals

Love

Love is a beautiful thing
'Oh' how much joy it can bring
You can see tragedies and experience despair
And that makes you think 'is this always fair?'
Some people say it's destiny, they say it's meant to be
Others search to discover, 'why did God give this to me?'
They never find a definite response
But only the belief, 'God will give me another chance'
Only true faith can restore love in your heart
And give your life another start
Love is the act of giving
Which helps you taste the sweetness of living
May you always live
To love and be loved
And to taste
The eternal sweetness
Of life.

Dina Benzaquen

The Wait

He stands aloof, an equestrian Adonis
His fluid muscles aflow
I often wonder what's in his head
Deep down he knows, I know

Those soulful eyes, his searching muzzle
So velvet to the touch
Enquiring what I've brought for him
I love him oh so much

He puzzles why I have to go
He tries to come along
Resentful for just one split second
In five minutes I'll be gone

And then he'll wait with ears pricked forward
Then back and fore again
Until I spend a bit more time
Explaining where I've been.

Erica Stanton Powell

Special Friend

I'm overjoyed to be your special friend,
I long for your voice and hope this happiness
will never end,
We will walk and talk in the sunlight hand in hand,
Over hilltops meadows by the seashore,
push our toes in the sand.
I hope it will bloom and grow like a flower,
Week in week out, hour by hour
Open your heart and be sure to see,
That my darling you're so good for me.

John Follett

The Pathway To Paradise

The water gushes between barrier rocks,
Gurgling like a baby as it pounds the surface and
Breaks into a virgin foam.
As the high summer's sun beats down on the glass surface,
A golden sprinkle of magic is cast.

The smooth-pebbled bed forms a natural habitat,
Each creature oblivious to their surroundings.
The world using the brook as a looking glass
To admire the overwhelming beauty.
Reflecting a harmonic environment.

In each direction of the brook,
The end is never in sight.
To the East lies the vast coloured ocean,
While to the West the brook winds ever upwards,
To the mountaintop origin.

It is true to say that the brook is the essence of life;
A microcosm within the wide spread of colours and sounds.
You can never be lost while the waters flow ever on,
guiding you to a place of pure beauty,
Guiding you to paradise.

Dale Mitchell

Only Time

Bouncing off the walls and landing on your feet,
It's a trick you ought to learn,
As the skyline turns a thousand shades of red,
Does the silence start to burn?

Cornered in a conversation you can't win,
Talk yourself into the night,
Back to back then face to face and cheek to cheek,
Hope she's worth it in the light.

And I'll tell you now it's only time that holds you down,
But it's always yours to spend,
And I'll tell you things that up till now I've kept within,
But I know it's only time, it's only time.

Settling down again to find your sense of purpose,
Climb a mountain, reach the top,
Taste the victory now, and as you take the tape,
All that's left is how to stop.

Go beyond the eyes to catch up with the past,
Trawl the aisles and choose a book,
Just the usual stuff, a quick flick through and that's enough,
Read a chapter, know it all.

M. Brooker

The Vampire

Holy water, garlic and crucifixes
By the side of your bed
wind outside
A cold night
Just about to get colder still

Pale face at the window
Looking in on a virginal girl
A blur of velvet, satin and lace
He vampire has now begun his hunt
the hunt for a virgin's sweet ruby red blood

He paralyses you with his eyes
that glare, you know what's next
as razor sharp teeth plunge and bite your neck
you thrash in bed
but the battle is soon over, he drains you of your blood

He gets what he desires
you were just his life source
he flies off towards the moon
The Vampire
The Hunter!

Rosamunde F. Gage

People

All different people,
all different places,
so many colours,
so many faces.

God made us all,
equal and even
yet so many times,
it all ends with grieving.

Politics, religion, creed and colour,
the love in the world could be so much fuller,
war, hatred, envy and rage,
so many differences—all on one page.

Death and destruction,
all over the place,
caused by only,
the colour of a face.

All different people,
all different places,
Why can't we just love
all of our faces?

Sean Kavanagh

Seasons Of Life

Where were you, Lord, when I was born
Did you stand by my mother's side
Yes, my child, I was with her then
And my love I could not hide

Where were you, Lord, when I was belted and bled
Were you there when I stubbornly stood
Yes, my child, I was with you then
And the stripes I would take if I could

Where were you, Lord, when I left the fold
And went on my rebellious way
I was with you, child, in the distance I stood
Knowing you would be back to stay

Where are you, Lord, when doubt and fear
Take their toll on a weary life
I am there, my child, to comfort and guide
I am there to give peace through the night

Where are you, Lord, as the doubts creep in
And I stumble and fall on the way
I am with you, my child, my word is true
And I am with you still today.

Gwenda Coleman

Secret Love

You're there, always. In my heart, in my sight.
I can't get you out of my head.
You don't know, you don't care.

My heart aches for you.
My heart yearns for you.

I dream about you, I imagine you.
I talk to you, but you don't answer.
We are together, in my head.

I see you now, you come closer.
Real, you're so real

You pass, I try to call out,
You're gone, too late.
Always the same, I'm too scared.
My hearts beats faster, I begin to perspire.
I missed you.

Back to square one. Just the same.
The dreaming, the imagining.
Until you pass by again.

Katie Hall

Why Is He Late?

He went out saying 'Be back by nine,'
He seems to go out all of the time,
I sit and wait - it's now ten fifteen,
Where oh where can he have been?

Time is passing - it's now half past ten,
When is he coming, when - when - when?
My stomach is getting tied in a knot
I'll make myself a drink that's hot.

Eleven now, oh, what is he doing?
Perhaps the railway crossings queuing.
Shall I ring the Police Station yet?
He'll walk in, just as I do, I bet.

Now I'm getting really tensed up,
Who shall I ring if he doesn't turn up?
Here comes a car - oh no it's gone past.
Here's another - Great, it's him at last.

Now eleven thirty, thank God he is here,
Why do I worry, I wish I didn't care,
I want to hug him with relief - instead I scream
Where the bloody hell have you been!!

Avril Lowdon

Love's Last Stand

Affectionate blades sever the Pain
That walks hand in hand with Grief
And waters the lover's eye
To be consumed in the depths of remembrance

The all self contained Destruction
Purposeful in its attempts to pull apart
With petty jealousies and explosive confrontations
The kindred souls of opposing spirits
While Love looked on with pitiful gaze
Upon its failure and fled the war

Remnants of memories discarded and forgotten
The repressed feelings reinforced with
Concentrated Hatred and without Love's touch
Open wounds which bleed into the mind
And tears the beating heart to unleash
The scream of Agony which drowns
The taboo of "I Love You" silenced by silent lips

Emptiness fills Love's absence and Time allows the recollection in
preparation for self confession of what was blind unacceptance
"Love had loved me once", "And I had lost that love"

Sean Fisher

The Song Of Nancy

I sit in the darkness of the room,
amongst the quiet dead of night,
just waiting for my Bill to come,
drunk and ready to fight.

I can hear his tuneless drone,
flowing through the house,
I can't bear for him to find me,
so I'm as quiet as a mouse.

As he hammers me with his stick,
I can feel myself going cold,
I know I must stand up for myself,
be strong, be bold.

And then there has to be old Fagin,
tall, and ugly, and grim,
why should I bow, down to beg,
forgiveness from him?

His ambition to rule our city,
to be the whole of London's king,
because of my life I do and will always,
the song of Nancy sing.

Louisa Handley

The Swan

The day is over, the sun has gone down
She lays alone on a cold damp ground
Her limbs are numb, and her body so weak
She knows she is dying but the memories she keeps
She thinks of her friends and what life will bring
To see them once more would make her heart sing

Does man realize the mistakes that they make
They are killing all life on this beautiful lake
They pollute, they destroy, they kill all God's things
Do they not see the beauty that all of it brings

Oh! To feel the cool waters and the sun on her back
To be free of man and the compassion they lack
Is there someone out there who will stand up and fight
Who will undo the wrong and take up her plight

She looks to the stars as her life ebbs away
Man has killed again at the end of the day.

Josephine Causley

Firefly Summer

The blazing August sun sets itself to rest
As the day makes way for the darkness yet to come.
In the evening's dusky haze, the flowers
Gently bow their heads in homage to the Summer's end.

The young girls revel in the twilight's warmth
As they stand amongst the swaying grasses that brush
Against their legs. They appear oblivious to the onset
Of darkness with their firefly lanterns aglow.

And all too soon the night will fall and their lanterns
Will slowly burn to an end. Weary from the
Day's excitement, they shall traipse their
Way home, hand in hand, to the sanctuary of their beds.

Katy Cash

Heroes

Oceans once blue, churn deep in red
As yesterday's heroes, lay dying, or dead,
Like a shoal of fish washed ashore,
Hundreds, thousands, countless more.

Skies once clear, plume with smoke
As targets are mapped, pinpointed to scope
The burning of flesh, a rancid smell,
This is where death, and evil dwell.

Soldiers of fortune are those with their lives,
Today, maybe luck, but tomorrow, is a prize.
With rifles a lance, as bayonets are drawn,
For king, and country, his life, he has sworn.

For this is to be, a final stand,
His body, pierced, as bullets land,
Leaving the barrel, to find new host,
As the bugle plays, a soldier's last post.

David Johnathan Daniels

My Life

I look through my window,
In the evening of my life,
And think of when I was a child
With all the trouble and strife.

Then I think of my first and only love,
And my life was all aglow,
But then came my babies
Then life was one big wow'.

And now my babies have all gone
To see what life's in store.
I sit and think of my one and only love,
Who died one November morn.

Now I thank my sweet Lord up above
For all of my dear grandchildren,
The most precious gifts of love.

L. Thompson

Cry Of The Unborn

Predestination ruled that I should live.
Had this not been good cause, bereft of other
Companionship of sister or fond brother?
In dust here must I lie,
While up above me fly
Exulting in their freedom, birds together?

Whose is the choice to slay me in the womb,
My bones and body to a certain end
So intricately formed? Do comprehend,
O mother! Let me live -
Then I might also give
My life for brother, sister, country, friend!

Pray, who'll preserve my body and my soul;
Provide the panacea for my plight?
No libertine, no fraud, no proselyte:
But one who fears the Lord,
Assimilates His word
And bears His laws and liberties to light.

Christine MacLeod

Wonderful

Thick oozing layers of dull grey clouds,
Trying their best to hold in the icy rain.
They lose it, water starts to shred.
It gets heavier and bursts out.
Hailstones crash land on the
poor beaten-up window.
I'm munching away on a
cook breakfast, fried with fat.
Half asleep, my eyes look bubbly and
candy floss soft,
Opening and closing like shutters.
I'm lounging around, in my
Powder blue towelling dressing gown.
My lungs are sticky like honey.
Nicotine is in the air, clinging onto
the already mustard-stained walls.
Sitting here, stroking my dog with my feet.
I like this life,
For now, it's at its best.

Denise Norman

The Habit

Nobody needs them, nobody cares,
They don't see what I see.
Lives at expense. Expense.
"Cold bonfire smoke over hot tarmacked roads", she said.
Nervousness.
I don't feel what they feel.
Should I be worried?
No. Not me... them.
Regret.

Amy Claire Taylor

Homeless

Curtains close early to keep in the light
Of the hundred watt bulb that's unnaturally bright.
Double glazed windows that hold in the heat
Keep out the cold and the damp of the street.
Between the glass layers is a neutral place
Not one thing or another just empty space.
Central heating pumps up the temperature
Everything sweats from the walls to the furniture.
Manufactured comfort keeps most souls indoors
With glowing gas fires and carpeted floors.
Outside in a world of biting winter cold
A very different tale is being told.
Shivering near death exposed to this weather
Homeless and hungry they huddle together.
Doorways and dormitories, derelict and damp
Beneath plastic, paper and cardboard they camp.
Perhaps they may dream to be peacefully lazing
Between the layers of our double glazing.

Nigel D. Luton

A Winter's Walk

Walking just walking with nowhere to go,
taking big steps, underfoot is deep snow.
How quiet it is, everywhere is all white,
what a wonderful day, such a beautiful sight.
The snow gently falling I just stop and stand,
little snowflakes melt in my hand.
The snow like a carpet so new and not worn,
covering pathways and everyone's lawn.
Cars driving slowly being careful not to slide,
a cat gingerly walking, its eyes opened wide,
as I turn a corner a robin catches my eye,
it's on top of a roof, having flown from the sky.
I carry on walking but now I feel chilly, I slip,
lose my balance. I feel awfully silly,
I hope no one's seen me as I struggle to my feet,
but some children are giggling, their faces so
sweet. So I giggle right back and they do the
same as they carry on playing their building
game, building the snow into a huge dome,
I turn very slowly and make my way home.

P. E. House

Nan

A warm creature, full of joy,
Her heart aching, yet filled with love,
Her personality, very coy,
Yet physically, elegant like a turtle dove.

On the inside, her heart does wither,
Sadness, sorrow and pain,
Her soul temperamental, gentle, soft as feather,
Unselfish in her aura, nothing done for her own gain,

Her family meant the world to her,
Productive she once was,
Children is what she had for sure,
Her offspring were her sanctuary, just because . . .

Her life once dull, torn apart,
Until her babies came along,
Then grew ill and fell apart,
When left home and all were gone.

Love to thee, oh blessed one,
You're always in our hearts,
Now lay to rest, wonderful woman,
And let your next journey start.

Wendy Bain

An Echo Of Beauty

An unchallenged beauty patterns our horizon.
Guarding us all by towering on high.
Elegantly swaying backwards and forwards
Gracefully fanning the moody blue sky.

It stands permanent and proud.
Standing in the path of progress
It is severed from its roots
With its skeleton branches ripped off
Then cast aside.

Who cared that this elegant beauty dressed the earth?
Fashioning it with succulent leaves of velvet green.
Who respected its wealth or its infinite knowledge?
Proudly holding its arms to umbrella the world.

Silently-screaming, with its tears falling
It died from deep wounds.
Its long history shattered in a mighty blow.
Now an emptiness stands where its beauty should grow.

But its echo will forevermore haunt our souls.

Kathleen Wood

The Playground Of Life

She stands in the playground her eyes wet with tears
And shudders inside at the thought of her fears
Her school days would be happy, so her Mother had said
So why does she faces each day with more dread?

The big children come to laugh, tease and scold
Is it because she is only five-years old?
She vows that when she has grown
She will not tease, but will leave the small ones alone.

She stands in the playground her eyes wet with tears
For children don't change much in their young, older, years
The big come to tease and the little crouch low
Yet it was the same for the big kids not so long ago.

The moral of this ode has yet to be defined
For human nature comes in many a different kind
The strong to succeed? The weak to fail?
Yet it's not only boats that can be made to sail!

Carol Topliss

Dreamland

I lie in my bed and dream away
I open my mind and float away
I levitate climbing higher and higher
Being greeted by space admirers

Something to overcome the madness
Something to override the mind
Something to rise above mankind

Surrounded by layers and layers of dense fog
Lifting me up into a cylindrical pod.
Amazed and frantic my mind has flipped

There moving into my mind of darkness
my mind of doubt
my mind to please let all the bad things out

Telepathic users don't drain my head
telepathic users please levitate me back to bed
telepathic users communicating with me
Communicating through peacefulness and tranquillity
I open my mind and float away
I lie in my bed and dream away

Robert Rice

Inside A Girl's Head

A world that turns all day long
The birds that sing the same old song
People get up and go to work
While the hungry and homeless just 'lurk'
Ignorant people with selfish minds
To the poor they just close their blinds

A world with no meaning or challenge ahead
Just a dull routine, you could say it was almost dead
There is a time to laugh a time to cry
A time to live and a time to die
Forbidden thoughts are to be kept inside once they get out
People laugh, become cruel and start to shout

Some live in wealth, some to fulfil
Some thrive on health while others are ill
Some are born feeble and in need of care
Some are born moaning about their hair!
I was born to be happy and grateful for what I have

Will someone please tell me why the world is so unfair,
why am I sad when I should be glad?

Sally Carr

Untitled

How could we have known the feelings we would have
When the call came to say "It's me, I'm a dad".
A granddaughter to be proud of, to love to hold
God's way of compensating us for growing old.

The questions we asked, how much did she weigh?
What colour is her hair? Is mum o.k.?
The relief of knowing that all is well.
We did not mind if it was a boy or a girl.

Who does she look like? What shape is her nose?
Can't wait to see her and tickle her toes.
The months of waiting are now at an end
We have telephoned the family and a few close friends.

Sometimes when we feel that life is unkind
We will think of this moment and bring to mind
The joy we will have as we watch her growing.
What her future will bring, we have no way of knowing.
One thing is for certain, come what may,
We will always remember this special day.

Jennifer Turner

Getting Old

When I was in my prime.
I was a lady at that time.
So pity me, if you must,
But please, don't look at me in disgust.

I've work to do, how can I rest,
"Sit down" they keep saying, "you're a pest"
They don't understand I've a family at home,
Who will look after them? They're all alone.

"This is your home" she says with a scream,
I've got my own home, what does she mean?
My dinner's put out for me to eat.
Oh my goodness, they've forgotten my teeth.

Oh my God, this is a nightmare,
I want the toilet but I'm put back in my chair.
"You nasty madam, why didn't you ask?
I've enough work to do, without this task."

Try to understand, with a kind word, a gentle hand,
Try to be more patient, this wasn't planned,
I'm sorry, you'll all have to get resigned,
For we all will get slow, in body and in mind.

May Tromans

Ending

Struck dumb by the words tripping in a torrent
from your mouth.

Pain reached out and held me close,
burying its fangs deep in my heart.

It itched to touch you and hold our love fast
But it flew in a stream between my fingers.

Betrayal—my anguish left me mute
I shake—not us—we were inviolate.

Our joining, witnessed by the stars
Pulled asunder by your weakness.

Wicked torment, daily I visualise the worst
My soul bound and trapped in anguished images.

Tears—I never knew there could be so many
Sorrow, I ache, I am incomplete.

The best of me is dead and gone
Wake me—the nightmare must end.

I grieve—unending torture.

Henrietta Lilley

A World Of Change

Whenever I switch on the news,
I hear about the world which we abuse.
There always has to be a cause,
for racism, famine, deaths and wars.

Dead people all over the place,
what are we doing to the entire human race?
People are dropping like innocent flies,
it's time to face reality and no more lies!

People separate the blacks and the whites,
but who do they think they are, they have no rights!
All different nationalities should come together,
to create worldwide peace that'll last forever.

In the third world people have nothing to eat,
we can't ignore them it's time to face the heat!
People are dying, children and babies too,
what can we do to help, please give us a clue.

Lets change the state of the world, and make it its best,
where all of us can be happy, and live in rest!

Laura Dowdie

I Love Thee

I love thee
When dew silvers each blade and flower,
And sweet birds awake and sing this hour.
In my heart, I love thee.

When shy the violet lifts its shining face,
Then sweet spring will surely take its place.
In my heart, I love thee.

When the haze of summer's golden heat
In each thing the pulse of life doth beat.
In my heart, I love thee.

When golden corn is ripe and high,
For long-gone summers the breezes sigh.
Still, in my heart, I love thee.

When winter's frost seeks hard to hold,
And even time seems locked, bare and cold.
Warm, in my heart, I love thee.

I love thee
When blessed soft night creeps, sleeps to bring,
Eternal stars in heaven do sing.
Forever in my heart, I love thee.

Joan Hardy

My Soul And The Sea

Let's go to the sea again to fight tumultuous waves.
Let's get bare feet on deck rubbers, I'll have none.
Let's open our mouths out wide and take in the ocean's spray.
Let's spit it out again and shout Hooray Hooray.
Let's climb up the rigging to nearly touch the sky.

And at night on deck

Do not touch me then my friend just let me lie
and in my mind's eye
all alone I'll be engulfed in the night sky
floating in the blackness with just the twinkling stars.
Looking down to the sea again.
I know I must return from my reverie in the night sky
to the ship and the stern.
If one rough and stormy night my ship in peril is doomed
my body tossed upon savage waves, strength I'll have none.
And when the sea has finished me and my body is no more.
Matter it will be as it is swept towards the shore.
Forever it will be "My Soul and the Sea."

Peggy J. Elwood

Night Light

On that night, like many times before
The dog and I, we walked the moor
But this time I had such a fright
As I was bathed in brilliant light
And I would take an oath to swear
That I was lifted in the air
Small beings with strange eyes did probe
My body wrapped in just a robe
Then suddenly, without a sound
There I was, back on the ground

I dare not tell my friends or neighbours
For they would think I'd got the vapours
So at night now, as I lie in bed
I say such thoughts are just in my head
But then a car comes up the hill
Headlights beam above my windowsill
The dog beside me grows quite tense
And then I know it makes good sense
That we no longer walk the moor
But stay inside, and bolt the door!

S. M. Fuller

Our Staircase

Kisses on the staircase,
It is Sarah, going to bed.
Kneel slap step, climbing one board each time,
She turns, sends kisses to dad.

Mother's standing close behind,
Dad's caring each step she makes.
"Goodnight little poppet", 'n' charms her,
"See you morning," her little hand shakes.

She turns again - may this happiness ball,
Bounce and dance to the end.
My concern and love remain,
'Til the staircase is climbed past the bend.

Tom Whitby

Life

Life is a special thing from God,
Which can't be bargained down or bought,
It can't be used as sacrifice,
Or labelled by the highest price,

Life is just your every breath,
Which will stay with you until your death,
It is your hunger for survival
From the day of your arrival.

But sometimes a life from us is taken,
And we feel as if our hearts are breakin',
But for this life which has passed away,
We must be strong for it and pray.

Don't grieve for them because they're dead!
Be happy that they've gone ahead,
Ahead to a new brighter place,
A world where they cannot be traced.

And so when of death we get our share,
They'll come back and take us there.

Sinead McAnoy

Beaches

I walk along the ocean, looking afar,
My sunshine curls, flying about,
My sky-blue eyes, twinkling like stars,
The water lapping around my feet,
The sand between my toes,

Children are laughing and playing,
Building sand castles and chasing gulls,
While crabs hide in sea crevices,
One of nature's splendours, and it would be perfect
If there were nobody else in the world.

Shelley Morrison

Sickle-Cell Anaemia

The white world doesn't know me the African and Caribbean
world knows me well
I came with a mixed blessing my story I shall tell.

Born and raised to fight malaria in my blood lay my defence
So to change my disc to sickle seemed to make some of sense.

Through the centuries to my descendants my defences I passed
We defeated killer malaria the natural way possible at last

Alas, although once your saviour your newly discovered illness point to me
Your researchers have found a problem I am not the hero you thought me to be.

I deprive your blood of oxygen, they say
The result is you need constant care everyday.

What have I done? Where did I go wrong?
Researchers must find out, is there a solution about.

My people must be advised how best to lead their lives
Provide them with hope and facilities to cope

Although the white world doesn't know we the African and Caribbean
World knows me well,
But as the races intermingle I, the sickle become
A common problem.

I live in hope that one day a story shall be told
Of how I was once sacrificed so that blood can be whole again.

Catherine Kainja

Snowdrops

Little snowdrops no frail and no fair
You come when we must need you, when gardens are night bare,
You face the cold world oft snow lying around,
You do not wait for the sunshine you come through the cold ground
Maybe I should leave you where you are, but I long to caress you.
To inhale your sweet smell, so I'll pick just a few
I'll hold you gently in my hand for you are so small,
I'll find a wee vase to hold you for you are not tall.

Little snowdrops you remind me of our Creator, our Father above
He has sent you to remind me of his eternal love.
After long dark days of winter of snow and rain I've grown tired
Then to see your little white heads I know spring has arrived.

Soon my garden will be ablaze with colour,
Daffodils, tulips and other flowers too,
But little snowdrops, you will not be forgotten
I will remember you.

M. E. M. Schlette

Modern Youth

Damien's a trendy lad, in trendy gear you'll see him clad;
His modern cut and colours mad would make you sigh.

A 1990's trendy creep - his trendy air would make you weep;
He follows fashion like a sheep - this trendy guy.

His trendy shirt is open necked, with hoops and pins his ears bedecked;
His trendy glasses - colour checked - blot out his eyes.

His trendy hair is wildly messed, his torn jeans are never pressed;
And 'twixt two hairs upon his chest, a locket lies.

He visits trendy bars at night, with trendy drugs and flashing lights;
And as he watches trendy fights he'll stand and mime;

Knocking drink back like his chum, his mouth stuffed full of trendy gum;
And to the beat, his trendy bum gyrates in time.

His colours scream a trendy song, as trendily he walks along;
His brain as agile as King Kong - this trendy guy;

A trendy girlfriend at his feet, a trendy clone - but very sweet;
The trendy image now complete -
Let's pass him by.

John S. Mercer

The Maypole

Life is like a maypole
Destiny in the pole
Throwing out its many ribbons
For us to catch and hold
There are many coloured ribbons
Which one have you caught?
Is it red, blue, yellow, white
Hold on with all your might
These ribbons weave a pattern
Now which way shall we go?
Which coloured path, is it high or is it low?
Where shall we go, who shall we meet
Is it destiny that moves our feet?
Is there some mighty power
Controlling the many strands
What happens if, the ribbon slips from our hands?
Do we choose another colour
Weaving in and out
Who or what determines life's many coloured strands
Life is like a maypole!

Mavis Dickinson

Untitled

Oh oh lottery
The odd's so great
It takes only fate to get the numbers right
And if by chance you get them right
It could put you in a spin
The spin could be so great
It could change your fate
And leave you in luxury
The answer lies within yourself
To see how strong you'll be.
Oh oh lottery
What a wonderful thought to think it could come true
And leave you in luxury
So every time you try
Think of the spin you might be in
The dream may one day come true
Take hope you have strength
To do what is right
The day it may come true.

K. H. Pittard

Destruction Of The Soul

I'm not sure if you'll ever know
the hurt you caused me,
after all you separated not to hurt,
but hurt me more than you could tell.

Maybe someday you'll realize
you should have answered all the questions
you left unanswered at the time.
The hurt would have been less - I guarantee,
for living in the unknown, is what really destroyed me!

Sonia Golt

Is This Love Cooking?

A warm oven to bake the goods,
No hurrying the lady fair.
No micro-wave to slam its heat
To cook through, but oh so ugly!
You the gas, all flare and whoosh
slightly odorous, so easy to turn on and off
here or gone.

I, the much slower of the two
Electric elements slowly burning red.
Once there I give a constant heat
Reliable, effective and sure
But once switched off
I am very slow to glow again
So be warned!

Jill K. Alexandrou

Only Dreaming

I have a dream when I am not asleep,
A dream which usually makes me weep.

In my dream people love and care—
For one another without fear.

There is no spite and jealousy.
There is no strive and lunacy.

There are no pains, no tears, no worry,
From people always in a hurry.

I float along like I'm on air,
With everyone so very near.

I laugh and love and feel serene,
In fact, I feel just like a Queen.

A Queen of feelings not of crowns.
A Queen of laughter and of clowns.

Then I fall down from my weightless height,
And find that life is not so right.

My tears come rolling down my cheeks,
Because I dreamed whilst not asleep.

Eva

Why

You asked me why, in your eyes and your words,
but no reply could break the silent world

The word so simple, so short, so dead,
fell upon my heart
like loaded lead

No answers are given,
there are none to give,
we are but pawns on a check-mate grid

The word we would scream in the still of the night,
but our strength couldn't break that one word's might

No utterance more foul,
no heartbreak more complete,
than the one word on earth
that can make me weep

Why is so simple,
so short, so true,
so why should it kill me when I think of you?

Alice Fee

On The Brink Of Emptiness

The crying got closer, the nearer the emptiness got,
A shell of withering emotion, devoid of numbness and rot.
Lonely, endless years past by, my heart had shattered,
The missing ingredient, boredom no!
Nothing really mattered,
Lousy, that's a feeling; at least one,
Dimness, I could describe but everything had gone.
Life seemed pointless, death seemed in vain
No feelings of emotions, it was driving me insane
Up and down long long days, nights further still.
Repeated depths of misery, fathoms of
lifeless-ness and will.
I closed my eyes, hoping this would go away.
But on 'waking' I recalled everything,
The emptiness was here to stay.
The cheerless chores that are bound to fall
Neatly on my knee.
But no-matter what you try to change
What will be! Will be!

Julie McGreevy

The Pool

The sky-blue face of heaven shining bright
upon the placid stillness gives the promise blest
of warm and everlasting sheens of light
gleaming in clear tranquillity and rest.

A breath of air, no more, within a trice
scatters the magic glass to scores of green
and glittering chips of brittle ice
which melt as if they had not been.

But soon dark lowering clouds appear
with lashing rain and roaring gales
which shriek and scream as if in fear
that hell itself with evil rails.

So can the changing elements within
cause love or hate its progress to begin.

Frank Inman

Riding The Stallion

Ride on the stallion into the moon
Gallop so fast, let it be soon.

Chase the stardust fluttering down
Into deep seas, never to drown,

One soft word and soul is bewitched
Falling then flying all is just fixed,

From this Universe we continue to dash
Out of the Cosmos in one blinding flash,

We rode the white stallion into the moon
And landed on Earth rather too soon.

Michael A. Geraghty

Timescale

Life is but a single drop.
Moving ominously away from the mainstream crop.
Falling aimlessly through the dark hole of time.
Thrashing wildly, striving to conquer the river of time.

Passing through the mirror of life.
Images passing looking on by.
Shadows reflecting time gone by.
History forming moving on by.

Living the cycle, swimming the time.
Grasping the cycle, slowing it down.
Dreams reflecting reversing the clock.
Time is relentless reversing there's not.

Suffocated by the motion of time.
Victim of life . . . once passed by.
Reaping the harvest, stacking the crop.
It's back to the start . . . the single drop.

J. P. Bell

A Student Under A Northern Sky

At four o'clock I looked up at northern skies,
The wind, blowing unanswered sighs,
The clouds gliding like an eerie death,
My misery entwined within its breath.

The city breathes a floating smog,
Streets deserted like an abandoned dog,
The hills rise like a female chest,
A commuter returns home for rest.

The clouds rush away like they've seen enough,
The snarling wind blows a silent puff,
Office lights highlight the sky,
 . . . In my lonely room they pry.

A corporate building manipulates the skyline,
Thunder raging as if inclined,
Rushing air and shrieking cries,
The day I glared at northern skies.

Heath Jay Kirk

The Place Where Nobody Talks And Nobody Walks

I know a girl called Lucy
In my eyes she's a nutter
In my eyes she's a hippy
I met her through an ad
She wouldn't leave me alone
Always writing, ringing the phone saying;
We're going to a place where nobody talks
And nobody walks anytime of day
So if you're listening please take me away
Away to the land where nobody talks
And nobody walks anytime of day

So I took a walk down by the river
One fine one cold
One sunny winter's day
And I saw a sight
To make you quiver
Down by the river
Yes down by the river
The land where nobody talks
And nobody walks anytime of day

Ian Hall

Thoughts From The Quay

In front of me
Four harbour fish
Form a formation,
Swim through the murk,
They smirk,
Their bellies a creamy blue,
But speckled like a pebble I once found.
Each scale a golden coin
Borrowed from the eyes of a shed sailor.

Michael Jones

Woman Child

I'm feeling like a lost child...
Vulnerable, insecure, confused
I want to cry for my mother
to wrap me in cotton wool

I want to tug at my dress, make a mess
I want to kick and scream
I want my dream, even just to hold it
for a few moments

Like a lost child
Lost in the forest of life
Sinking in its swamps
Someday hear me

I want to run, as far and as fast as I can
Maybe my new shoes will help me
One, two, buckle my shoe

I need to cry and say no
I want to play in the snow
I want to go naked and show my scars
I want to fly to Mars

When I grow up, I want to be me.

Margaret Mitchell

The Birds In The Sky

The birds in the sky and all things that fly,
but for how long will they keep on flying?
In the past they were large,
now they're all so much smaller.
In the future will they shrink to nothing or die?
Or fly round with gas masks tied to their heads?
So that they can breath through the toxic fumes.
And then when all the birds are gone we might stop and think
will it start to happen to us too?
Maybe none of this will happen,
maybe they'll get bigger again and cast a shadow wherever they fly,
but what if any of these did happen and why?

Alan N. Bundock

The Mallard Duck

From river bank to Trafalgar Square,
You'll find the Mallard swimming there.
From coast to coast on pond and lake,
You'll find this multi-coloured drake.

His mate may look a second best,
But she can blend onto the nest.
Protects the eggs and keeps them warm,
Till all the baby ducks are born.

Then mother takes them straight away,
To water where they feed and play.
And when it's time for them to rest,
She guards them back onto the nest.

Chests fill out and change to red,
Yellow bill and blue-green head.
Orange webbed feet that make a good paddle,
On land they cause the duck to waddle.

Deborah Johnson

Untitled

Hear the sound of the earth's shrill cry,
The sound of a world soon to die,
Vicious cuts begin to bleed,
Celestial host to a parasite's greed.

A petrified world that's hurting
Praying for its wounds to heal,
Waiting for a race to care,
Depending on people to feel.

Some try to heal, others mock,
Tiny minds refuse to understand,
Self-inflicted deafness prevails,
Therefore all the healing effort fails.

Time for the human race to all work together,
A world-wide joining of the healing hand,
A desperate gathering merging of forces,
To ensure our earth will further withstand.

Morgan Wynn

Away From It All

Up in the mountains high, there's a place I know
Waiting for me, where the wild winds blow.
Away from cares of the world affairs.
Up in the mountains high, I'll watch as clouds roll by

Up in the mountains high, to the snow-topped peak,
I long to fly for the peace I seek.
'Neath skies above, there's a place I love.
Up in the mountains high, I'll watch as clouds roll by.

'Ever see a mountain that you had to climb
'Ever see a tumbling waterfall.
'Ever stand and look across a briny sea
And tried to get away from it all

Up in the mountains high, where the white clouds play
I long to lie, 'neath the golden ray.
'Neath scented pine, where the world is mine
Up in the mountains high, I'll watch as clouds roll by.

John Harvey

My Love

My love has left me all behind
And gone to look for peace divine
To leave behind the aches and pains
That this poor body they gave a name
Gone was that sprightly upright lad
An in its place a poor old man
Still to me he's the one I love
I gave my heart an the marriage was done
Not all was easy but that is life
Shared in this world as man and wife.

P. E. Hales

Sisterly Love

When they first told me about you, I ran away with fear
I longed to be the only one as I had been for many years
I wondered why? Do they not love me? Do they not care?
Was I not enough? I thought to myself over and over again

Time soon passed and the birth was near
I felt so alone; they smile, I cry
What is wrong with me? Am I selfish or just human?
There was something inside me acting like a devil
Why? I ask myself, do I feel so much hatred?
My friends adapted so why can't I?
I gazed out of my window
My friends were playing with their young ones
When all at once the thing inside me
The devil maybe? Seemed to go Just vanish into thin air!
I walked down the stairs and took a look at our mum's tummy
It was like an open window I could see you!
I turned to my mother and smiled
My evil thoughts on you had gone
It seemed as if the devil had been replaced
By an angel!

Leanne Baxendale

The Seasons Of Life

Spring arrives and everything awakens.
Tiny buds peep out of the soil; baby lambs are leaping and
springing in the fields.
And you and I are born.
Childhood is the beginning of the rest of our lives
Fate will decide what our futures will hold,
and the paths we take.

As we grow older we reflect on our childhood.
We were so innocent then,
no worries or fears to stand in our way.
We may wonder at our destiny
We cannot control our fate.

And - just as Summer turns to Autumn -
So does childhood change to maturity.
Age creeps upon us - unawares -
Slowly... at first; and then,
quickening its pace; or so it seems.

Growing old, like the winter, we cannot stop.
Our memories are good and bad.
Happy and sad - ...we are no longer afraid of dying.

Christine Elizabeth Watkins

My Jewel

Dedicated to Michael Jackson

Once I saw a child as special as all,
He could hear his heart as it whispered its call.
A voice, a motion was inside him he knew,
He told me, "it is hiding inside of you."
    Touring the pages, listening to his words sing,
    I know I too can do anything.
    It's like stepping into a river, joining the flow.
    What if I fall? Where will I go?
Beautiful soul as the child grew strong,
At twenty-two he carried me along.
People drag him down, that cannot be,
He said, "I am standing 'though you're kicking me."
    Don't you all see good, only bad,
    This man is our voice which we never had.
    I heard him singing I listened.
    A mysterious force touching me on my back.
Harmless person, only human by far,
I kept the faith now I have an 'A' star.
Helping always when I am feeling a fool,
To me he is needed like a ring missing—My Jewel.

Victoria L. Haunch

Written Off

Taken ill, there seemed no chance;
Hospital and ambulance
Rushed her off, oh what a blow.
Sudden illness can be grim,
When the lights are growing dim
And the battery's running low.

Sands are ebbing, like a sieve,
Sorry, Sir, she will not live.
They all seem so very sure.
Doctors; Nurses; write her off,
Tell me that she's had enough,
Will be coming home no more.

Well done, sweetheart, that's the stuff,
Show them that you're rather tough.
Dodge the ever-widening net,
Don't give in at any cost,
Sometimes all's not really lost,
Whilst there's life, on you I'll bet.

Brian Humphreys

Death Of Flight

I never knew better,
thought beauty was to keep,
I thought that I could feel your freedom,
through the colours of your sleep.
I never knew my net could kill,
the passion in your flight.
I thought your beauty was there alone,
for the pleasure of my sight.
In tangled bushes where I sat,
and stroked your silver frame,
I took away your glowing freedom,
my innocence was your blame.
Your silver presence in the sky,
was precious as the clouds,
Now lying in a withered heap,
your eyes were a deathly shroud.
I'll never forget the heat of my shame
as I took your sky away,
No longer to swim in the brilliant blue,
which paved your silver way.

Charli Day

Life

Life is very important,
You must not forget that.
Because if there was no life
The universe would be flat.

And if there was no universe—
There would be emptiness all around.
And no matter where God looks
Nothing would ever be found.

Without nothing there would never be anything.
What kind of a life would that be?
No people no animals, no anything,
No land no sky no sea.

Kirsty Sykes

Plants

People need drink like a tulip that's pink,
People need food and plants do too,
People need air and plants need care,
People need love, laughter and fun,
Plants need warmth and plenty of sun,
People grow lots and lots,
But all plants need are their own flower pots,
So leave them to grow flower, and bloom,
And they will look lovely in your front room.

Hayley Louise Vasey

Final Farewell

When death comes my thoughts turn to the simple things of life,
Cricket, holidays with the boys and the tender love of my wife.
This is not a letter from a boy who fears death, but one who is resigned to it,
And when the moment comes I hope the time, the place and the irony all fit.
You were both Mother and Father to me as you raised me on your own,
I love you as dearly as your every stitch of cloth was sewn.
Your careful upbringing prepared me for this beautiful World,
You moulded me like a sculptor moulds his statues and combed my curls.
I would have spent all my life in pursuit of Beauty, Truth and Goodness,
And yet, in the Shadow of Death, I have found true happiness.
The rest of the crew were a fine lot of boys, remember them too darling,
And think of their families when our final hymn you sing.
Don't let people forget us when the war is over and peace reigns,
The way we died was easy, it will be difficult for those who remain.
Tell survivors the responsibility for the World is in their hands,
This must be told to everyone and spread to every land.
I hope I grew into the kind of son you wanted me to be,
Please don't weep because by the time you receive this I'll be free.

Linda V. Rogan

Meditation

Our day to day existence so often seems a bore
And lacks the sparkle we once knew, how often do we stop and think
Of the million things we see and hear, oh so few!

We all have taken and still do so much for granted all our lives,
The selfish streak rears up its head
And remains with us until we are dead.

To see and watch someone who's blind,
Brings stinging tears to my watchful eyes,
To hear them tap their way along, never seeing the skies beyond.

The guide dog such a faithful friend becomes its owner's eyes,
To watch the marvel of this canine's work
To the very end, he never lies.

Can you imagine a silent world
No sound of birds or music or even idle chatter,
To go about one's daily chores without a noise,
Not even able to listen perhaps to neighbours natter.

It is often said if we lose a sense the remainder becomes more acute,
This maybe so, but how do we know lest we ourselves are mute.

The world is full of sickness and pain for many their days are numbered,
Healthy bodies and minds take heed, lest they become encumbered.

Eileen M. Holmes

Days Of Sunshine

Silver clouds and silver linings, make me think of my little darlings.

So much joy and laughter, now it's me they look after,
Those smiling faces of young innocence, bring back so many
memories of years gone by.
But to them their love will never die.

I remember so clearly those days in Walney Park,
it was always sunshine and never dark,

Playing on the swings and slide,
they were always by my side.

I remember as they came running up to me, so I could pick them up
and twirl them around
until we were dizzy and fell to the ground.

With those silly impish giggles,
and the odd niggle,

All in all they were so sweet,
As we sat hand in hand on the park seat.

William Anton Frankowski

Street Walking

Combing the streets,
Dodging sparks of deadly disaster,
Dusky shadows floating in the abyss of reality,
Twilight whispers drifting into alleyways,
The savage nectar of illusions,
Cringing behind forbidden walls,
A vivid flame of purity,
Soiled by the vile essence of lust,
The carnal call of cruising cars,
Running on instincts, drugged by the torturous hour,
The raw desire of a woman stirs,
The blazing core of masculinity awakes,
Flesh pressed close against flesh,
Merge into one,
As ghostly smiles,
Emerge from quivering lips.

Frederica Arulanandom

Cruel, Cruel World

Down the street, round the corner
A young boy sits crying
Hugging his teddy bear
With no shoes on his feet
Through the door go inside
The sight will make you cry
Rooms have been torn apart
Nothing but fragments where children slept

Look outside through broken windows
Soldiers hide in doorways
Sound of guns, smell of fear
There is nowhere left to run
Lying down scared to move
Innocent people say prayers
For an end to all this bloodshed
And a life that can be free of war

Robin Grigsby

Scott

He's a good friend
a real person who I can depend
when upset or in trouble
I know I can pick up the phone
and laugh, cry or moan.

We can talk for hours and hours
through the sun, rain or light showers
keeping in touch is what we do best
whether it's a few days, weeks or months
we make it through better than the rest.

We moved around the same month
splitting us, like grapes from a bunch
one end to another
but with people in the middle
to now and then help us recover.

Krista Micaela Brocklehurst

Lost But Now Found...

In this world I was once lost,
With someone who basically didn't give a toss.
His hands he used to beat my skin,
No-one knew the hurt within.

I don't want it to be like before,
The hurt, the pain, I am sure,
The love I feel now I try to ignore,
Because he may go and decide to withdraw.

The time will come when he will go,
Miles away with coldness and snow.
I want to tell him what he should know,
Is that my love for him can only grow.
He may come back and try to find
The girl whose love he left behind.

Joanne Prescott

The Rock Of Ages

In my Grandmother's house
   when I was small,
A picture hung there, upon the wall.
At this picture I would stand and stare,
To me it was wonderful and very rare.
I loved that picture upon the wall.
Rock of ages it was named-
Old and worn, and badly framed
But it was hung with pride and much acclaimed.
"What is it child?" my Gran would ask;
Is it such a difficult task for you
   to understand at all?"
"The Ocean is the sea of Life,
The Hands outstretched are full of Strife
They are pleading with Christ upon the Cross
To save their souls, for they are lost"

Many years have passed, since I was three
and I sat upon my Grandma's knee
She would hug me tight - in case I'd fall
But I will always remember that Picture on the wall.

Patricia Gent

Love

When you speak to me about love
You're talking a language I just don't understand
A foreign country I've flown over
And crashed into several times
I've never had a smooth landing
And a quick departure has been known
But in all of my travels, adventures and dreams
It's the only place
I want to go.

Sidonie

To My Abuser

Why do you do me such wrong and treat me this way
Hurt me and abuse me whatever I say
Whatever I do, I don't understand
I anger you badly and I suffer at your hand,
Where did I go wrong I hear myself say
Did I deserve to be treated in such a tortuous way
In another life I must have been bad,
To be expected to live now all broken and sad.
The bitterness and hatred that flows through your veins
The poison and anger that causes me pain
I see nothing of what I liked just a stranger with me
I want us to part but I'm frightened you see
I know deep in my heart that I mustn't blame myself
That there is something quite wrong with your state of mental health
That you would abuse a woman in this terrible way
I see myself cower in fear every day
of what is to come I do not know
The end is near I feel it, but I can't let it show
How will this end will I be in peace at last
Will I have space for me and time to heal this past

Julia Hale

Petal

Oh what a joy to be alive this season
Walking through the world, seeing you in full bloom
Delicate and yet so strong, what is your reason?
To bring happiness, where once there was sullen gloom.

Your subtle fragrance hangs lightly in the air
Captivating the beholder, there can be no escape
Small and perfectly formed, skin so soft and fair
Pure and luminescent, evocative in shape.

Unique in structure, yet so common on a flower
Dear, sweet petal, content with your lot
Poor young man, lost in love, only you have the answer
She loves me, she loves me not.

Jonathan Winship

Untitled

It was nearly noon
When the front doorbell rang
To say come here soon
I opened the door
And what did I see
Two ladies standing in front of me
It was sister Jean and a friend
Whoever she might be
We will come inside, said she
And then let us go round your garden
It quite fascinates me.
They saw the bare patches on the lawn
Which the black-decker scratcher
Had cleared the moss for me
They saw the potato tops turned brown
By frost - but they soon recover, said she.
I pointed to the pretty white flowers
Gazing up at me, but they could not name them for me.
Back indoors Jean came with two plates
All set out ready to eat you see.

D. Robertson

Saintly Disgrace

Tears fell from angelic eyes
Small silver droplets running down,
Those red wet eyes full of frustration
Those red wet eyes showing their emotion
Red wet eyes closing in recognition.
Clasping her cross tightly in her hand
She slowly floated above the ground
Rising up, to meet the clouds
Gently rising up to greet the Lord.

She had tried so hard to give us some sort of indication
But we were too ignorant, too stupid, too openly stubborn
Could we possibly believe in a world of peace and tranquillity
With no more depravity or hostility,
The thought occurred, but was no more than absurd probability.

So now mankind is left alone to survive
With nothing more left than her holy shrine.

With one last tearful look she can only but stare
At another war at some far off distant shore,
There are no more tears running down her face,
We are left alone in her saintly disgrace.

David Blasby

Separation

The Island is a barren place
Far beyond the ruined bridge,
No moving shadow on the shore,
No light upon the ridge.

Where long ago there used to be
A presence and a peace.
When all that slumbered in the dark,
Was held by sure release.

There was a graceful harmony
That lingered for a while,
That graced with shelter from the storm,
This lonely sceptered isle.

But now the sea and wind bear down,
With cold relentless hand.
The images of bygone years
Are traced upon the sand.

The echoes of those former days,
Still murmur now and then.
Can you hear them when they whisper,
Who will build that bridge again?

B. G. Whitby

Untitled

I dream alone at night sometimes
and imagine the life that I once had.
And slowly drifting off to sleep
Remember the good times clashed with bad.

I can't imagine how it could be
If I hadn't moved away.
And left behind the subtle haze
that begged for me to stay.

But then my mind returns to now
and a smile heals the hurt
as my son glances across at me
I remember my life's true worth.

Clare Hastie

A Stranger?

There is beauty in his face,
Unshaven, sickly and pale,
But beneath it, the strength and character
That lies in heart and soul.
I know it's there.
I've seen, felt it, wanted it.
But reaching out, fingers stretched and aching.
Hopelessness prevails.
Both our minds hold secrets;
Precious secrets, never to be unfolded;
Not even to be known to each other.
There is love and passion that can never be.
Only thoughts can help it live,
But thoughts breed pain and it dies.

Linda Lewis

The Ultimate Vanity

Dusk, the beauty and the rest, the
sun has gone to serve elsewhere.
The glimpse of fading lights draws
attraction to the silhouettes. The
darkness seemingly causing clarity, and
yet, the realization that less is known.

The wonder and the attraction and
yet, at times the intimidation.
Not dark, not light, in limbo, a reflection
of life itself, still not knowing yet
theorizing on a day that will soon be.

Darkness falls, the silhouettes turn
to more assumptions of what is a
vain knowledge, that at next light
all will be as it was before.

Daylight arrives, refreshed, refreshing,
reassuring, the appreciation caused by
the absence. Soon it will leave again
but the hope of a return becomes
knowledge, yet still remaining a hope.

Daniel Moore

Loss

The day you left me all alone.
I had no-one but myself with me.
The muffles of the outside world goes on.
The seconds, the minutes, the long hard hours,
go tick tick ticking on.
Which fell into those bitter years.
The pain for me is still unchanged.
Like the photos of you and me, on my bedside wall.
I still sit and tell myself I will come and visit you.
This is just one of many ways
dealing with the loss of you.
Nothing feels the way it use to do.
Christmas birthdays and everyday.
Now is all cold unfeeling and bare
good night sleep tight.
I will see you again tonight,
When my eyes are shut quite tight.

Paula Fox

Never-Ending Circle

When starlight is swept aside by the brightness of the sun
Mankind, temporarily, may forget its existence,
But, the dawn of yesterday will rise again as the night come
And tomorrow shall intertwine the present with persistence.

Today shall greet yesterday reluctantly, in a brief encounter
For life is a vicious circle, coiling towards eternity,
When daybreak and twilight finally come together
The joining of the circle shall bring forth the dawn of our destiny.

Bright sunshine shall thaw the cold frostiness of the night
Forgotten, will be the chilling memories of pain and sorrow,
Warmth shall encircle a loving soul, who never lost sight
Of what must be . . . shall be . . . will be . . . tomorrow . . .

Rosemaria Lucas-Foster

The Opinions Of One

Etched denials, stained on souls.
In turmoil, self destruct mode.
Frail remorse, life is on course.
A bitter pill, so sweet to swallow.
In gland esteem and yet so hollow.
Split the atom, no tomorrow.
Epitomize tears, shed for years.
Impulsive sneers, repulsive jeers.
Racked in doubt, in fear of peers.
And how weak, yet strong, beliefs not wrong.
Time well spent, much do resent,
Collective, corrective, bemused and rejected.
Patriotic, hypnotic, a gift we've all got it.
Repent, heavenly sent, many angers to vent,
In a snare as one stares at the darkness out there.
That sparkles and flickers, as life starts, stops and jitters.
To new beginnings and sorry ends of many endless foes and friends.
Conflicting stories of many passed glories, the mimic,
The mocking, the onslaught non-stopping.
Peace so serene is ideal it would seem.

Michael Berry

Tears Of Sorrow

She feels the pain that others feel
She swallows their hurt so they can heal
She cry's inside where there's no where to hide
As she sits and cry's by the fireside
The tears find their way some how or some way
I think by the trails that the teardrops had made
She came into your world alone
Now you've left her all on her own
She sobs so much it echo's
Now she's left with her sorrows
For longer then tomorrow
She sobs till she can't swallow
She cry's till her insides are hollow
I wonder will she survive until tomorrow
She needs to hear your voice
For you to say hello
As she feels up with new tears
Ready for tomorrow
Then I often wonder
Who's tears has she borrowed.

Julie Richardson

That's Life

As I walk down the path of life, my destiny to find,
I look forward to the future, forget what went behind.
Much time has passed, much more will come, before my
    day will end.
And when that day approaches I'll look back and
    comprehend.
I'll look back on all the good times, I'll look back on all
    the bad,
I'll look back on all the loving and the loving never had.
And when my life begins to fade away, I'll know it's no
    mistake.
For God created living and life is his to take.

Darren Phillips

The Day Of The Animals

The animal kingdom is shaking with dread,
If things don't improve they will soon all be dead.
We are killing the foxes and hunting the deer,
And the rabbits breed well, but they still disappear.

We club little seals that are only just born,
And the rhino is slaughtered because of his horn.
There are young baby elephants dying of grief,
While their mother is slain by an ivory thief.

Badgers no longer are safe in their set.
We train dogs to fight to fulfil someone's bet.
Chemicals kill all that live in the soil,
And the fish and the birds are polluted with oil.

Cats have had fireworks tied to their tail,
The dolphin is dying and so is the whale.
Donkeys are tortured and left to their fate,
And monkeys transported packed tight in a crate.

Perhaps it is time that we started to think
If we don't change our ways they will all be extinct.
Or, perhaps they will rise and decide on a plan,
To conquer the world, and their enemy, man.

Rene McDermott

Child In The Chapel

For Del with love

The soft candle soothes my darkness,
As warm tears flow gently off my cheeks,
And from the corner of my eye I see...
A child in the chapel, a reflection... of me?
What did mammy pray for, that time we went to chapel
What thoughts were running round in her silent drooped head?

The child is smiling and singing and moving around now,
But never moving far from her mother's side,
Did my childhood song ever have such a happy tune
Was my childhood voice ever as sweet or innocent as hers

Where's her Daddy? I hope he never hurts her...
Maybe he's working or in the pub, or maybe he left
Maybe they're better off - that way.

The mother stops praying and looks at the child, the little girl
takes her mammy's hand and they light a candle of happiness
in my heart
When the little girl asks...
Can we go home now? I want to see Daddy, I love my daddy.

They join hands and walk together into the light of day,
and as I watch them I can see.....
The child in the chapel I wanted to be silently walking away.

Katie Lee

Untitled

Whilst we are apart knowing our time together
will be far and wide deep down in our heart
knowing we could never part
the wanting and the needing growing stronger
sitting by the phone hoping it will ring
the deep pain that grows inside of you
hour after hour day after day.

Before our day is over before my life is done
there is one thing I would like to do
to set the world on fire with our great love and desire
to show the world how things should be
with a love as strong as you and me

You are the one great love of my life
you make it worth going on
when I am down you pick me up
filling my life with a great warmth
for better or worst you have bound me to you
with a thread so strong no man can undo
so keep on loving me for my lifetime
and I will keep on loving you . . .

Jane Fergusson

Remember Them

I struggled and strived but to no avail,
To waken my master from that blood soaked, trenched trail.

I fought on through the smoke, the guns, and the fire.
We horses at flanders knew we musn't tire

We were the silent anchor and crew
We didn't need orders to know what to do
Our love for our homeland was keeping us going
For God knows, there was no way of knowing
Now I've done my share, my life ebbs away
I've got no regrets to be dying this day
There calls my master it's time to be gone
To God's glory home where the battle is done.

Kathleen Parsons

Brokenhearted

I am Broken-hearted my kind Brother
You came from London to be with me
We both loved our music
But now I shall miss you
With your Al-Johnson and begin the Begee,
We sang at Colwyn Bay
The old Cockney Sang Lambith Walk
And won a Prize for Singing
I am broken-hearted my kind brother
I will still have my music
    and memories of you
Your flowers will be here
So God Bless You, my kind brother

Doris G. Parry

Vale Of Daffodils

Wild orchid crocus, thistle down
Like diamonds sparkling in a crown
Translucent pearls of early dew
Expose a scene of silver hue
Pale zephyr fondled dewdrops thrive
Where cowslips and frail violets strive
Neath beech and oak and sycamore
For freedom on the forest floor
Emerging spring the valley fills
With hordes of golden daffodils.

Unchecked, unfiltered, pure and free
An Eden of tranquillity
Wandering streams and crystal pools
Adorn the landscape like rare jewels
An alternating graphic scene
Of copper, jade and emerald green
Enchantment, peace, serenity
Contentment for eternity
Soft breezes blowing from gorse lined hills
Caress this vale of daffodils.

Billy Hoare

Cold

Not from the weather, but from the inside.
This chill spreads outwards
Like ripples in a too still pond.
A frozen tear falls, languidly but inexorably
Into the glacial beyond - unnumbered, unseen.
This growing numbness invades all parts;
A crack appears, and, with each glittering tear,
Widens to an unbridgeable chasm
Irreparably damaging the fragile structure
Which could, with a single breath,
Shatter into a myriad shimmering fragments.
But the sun God smiles - softening, thawing, melting, fusing
His fingers leaving a trail of fire;
His lips igniting where they touch;
His warmth all encompassing, golden red and fiery.
His magnificence awakens an answering blush;
A forgotten glow; an unforgettable desire.
Oh sun God, smile on, for me.

Heather Mulligan

The Beggar

Tattered and torn, a beggar was he,
Strolling along as one could see,
Hands in the pockets, eyes on the floor,
Rattling on somebody's door.

Sitting on the doorstep,
Grumbling at himself,
Haven't I got anything,
To feed upon myself.

A baker rode by,
Out fell his bread,
He saw the beggar sitting by,
Who said, "Please give me a crust of bread."

"OH, no!" said the baker,
"No, not for you,
You're not a worker,
So no bread for you."

So off went the beggar,
Grumbling upon himself
Why is this world so tough
For a poor man as myself?

Margaret Murphy

A Diary Of A Puppy

December 23rd—Pet shop, doing well,
Puppies going, selling well.

December 24th—Puppy put in a box,
Ribbon tied, puppy cried.

December 25th—Box brought in,
Ribbon torn, lid thrown off,
Puppy passed—from hand to hand,
Hugged and loved—or so it thought.

January 2nd—Puppy put out on street,
Left to die, doesn't know why.

For days it wandered helplessly,
Becoming more scrawny and thin,
For days it walked the streets,
Hungry and all alone.

Until one day, two weeks later, a cold frost set in
Puppy cried, tried to hide, as the cruel north wind blew

Two days later, the puppy is found, a pile of shaking bones.
Taken to a rescue centre, but nothing can be done.

January 18th—Puppy dies, no-one cries.

Alice Williamson

Our Little Miracle

I have seen a vision of your face.
It is a beautiful face - the most beautiful face,
Smiling with the knowledge of being so wanted, so loved,
With the unconditional love of a mother to her child.

I have seen the furious beating of your tiny heart
Which consumes me with wonder and awe at the miracle of life.
The knowledge that you are here within and amongst us
Gives me the greatest joy I have ever known, and with this joy,
Great love, fulfilment and contentment.

I have no fear of what is to come or the changes you will bring,
Just the longing to give you my wisdom, affection, devotion
and care which are infinite.

You are so very special -
it was time for you to bless us with your presence;
with a message of need and of love.
I just hope I'll be the mother you deserve
and await your arrival more than you'll ever know,
But am patient as I know that you are worth waiting for
My - our - little bundle of joy, so wanted;
to be so welcomed in time - in the time of your choosing.

Colleen Jonsen

Escape From Reality

If only I could escape from this nightmare I'm living in and
live in the world of my dreams;
in the world where people listen to what is written deep down
in the depths of my heart instead of letting it all bottle up
inside me until I can take it no more but still have to
suffer pain in the world which has no end except death.
If only I could fly like the birds in the sky instead of
marching along the lonely road; alone.
If only I could break away from these vines of life which are
pulling me further and further down this hill I have to climb.
If only I could free myself from this body which stops me
enjoying things I long to enjoy.
If only I could escape from reality and live in the world of
my dreams.

Charlotte Morris

Thorns

Thrown against a thorn bush he lies upon the ground,
grasping the grass with his fist his face is
contorted with agony,
his naked body struggling with the earth is shedding blood,
with every drop that oozes from his wounds they
are being sucked by the thirsty earth.

He cries out in despair! There is no one to hear him;
    His cry echoes, but his voice gradually fades away;
    it is dark, desolate and silent.

At random, thoughts run through his mind
    of past love and brotherhood
    but then of the future to be met with vengeance.

Alas, the severity of the pain numbs his body and mind;
    He falls into a deep sleep,
    he is neither to be healed nor awakened,
    he being the Human Conscience.

Muhammed Jakir Ahmed Jabbar

Both Ends Of The Tail

"Oh fish!" I cried out as I sat on the bank
And ruefully gazed at my prey.
"Oh Fish, you're a scheming and slippery rogue
You have wilfully ruined my day.
For an hour now, or more, I have played at your game
Oh the patience and skill I have used,
Just to have all my hopes flicked away with your tail
And my sportsmanship sadly abused.
You have taunted and teased and flaunted your prowess
At swimming and biting the bait,
And now you have the effrontery
To come up and gloat o'er my fate.
Oh Fish", I then said as I grabbed at my rod,
"'Twas indeed a most dastardly prank.
Oh Fish", I looked down as I stretched out my arm.
"Oh Hell!" said the fish . . . and sank.

Catherine Clough

Hiding My Tears

Walking home in the moonlight
I feel you by my side
You lift my chin but I look away
For my tears I try to hide

You place a hand on my shoulder
And gently turn me to face you
A single tear trickles down your cheek
For you know what you must do

Our love has balanced on a very fine line
And I have been hanging on the threads
But now I have to let you go
My heart I feel in shreds

Maybe we will fall in love again
Our future no one can see
But if you decide you would like to try
You know where I will be

Lorraine Marshall

The Fairy Ring

A circle of toadstools hidden in the grass,
Goes un-noticed by most of the people who pass,
But those with a mystical, whimsical mind
See gath'rings and parties of fantasy kind.

Pixies and fairies with gossamer wings,
Titania she sleeps as the fairies they sing,
On awak'ning poor Oberon she'd then deceive,
(Or so The Bard would have us believe!)

Light fairy voices like tinkling of bells,
The skipping and dancing of pixies and elves,
Perhaps it's a wedding or some celebrations
Enjoyed by all fairy-folk friends and relations.

Fallen petals of roses make delicate clothes,
Their perfume entrancing the sensitive nose,
Open flowers in hedgerows make miniature beds,
Where fairies of all kinds lay their tired heads.

We mortals are never permitted to see,
The meetings of fairies beneath yonder tree,
But if we sneak carefully one moon shiny night,
And luck is on our side - then maybe we might.

Cheryl Warrillow

My Death

Please let me die with dignity.
Don't let me die alone.
Please comfort me and my loved ones.
Please let me die at home

Please laugh and cry about me
When my life has gone.
Please talk about the things I did.
Please sing my favourite song.

Please share the joy and sorrow
My dying may have brought,
Please let my loved ones mourn for me
In whatever way they want.

Please help my loved ones cope
With all that's to be done.
Please tell them that you're there for them
'Cos they'll never cope alone.

Please don't rush the process
That it takes for them to mourn,
Please let them take the time they need
To grasp that I have gone.

Yvonne M. Fox

Happiness Cures All

Having a state of mind that brings out the sunshine
Appearing to others around that everything is fine
Projecting that image that daily chores don't bind
Prompts a little happiness, not just a state of mind

Injecting a ray of sunshine into other daily lives
Nurtures friendships in our world, busy like beehives
Every day we have the time to lend a helping hand
Surefooted as we walk to guide others in quicksand

Secure in the knowledge that happiness can bring
Comfort to the lonely hearts or with no words to sing
Under pressure from the boss or just can't find the key
Results can be profoundly good with help from you or me

Everyday we have the time to lend a helping hand
Surefooted as we walk to guide others in quicksand
All the way to happiness, friendships and good health
Lots more than pots of money, happiness is wealth

Lots of happiness all around brings the sunshine out
Children sing, skip and play, laugh and dance about
Parents watch the merry throng in the streets of home
Wondering why must it stop,
HAPPINESS HAS WON!

Dave Horner

The Gulf Bird

To fish and fly along the shore
This is my role, nothing more,
A mundane life now silent fear
The war machine will not shed a tear,
My domain and existence ebbs to and fro
Will ever again the morning glow,
Life blood of war is all I can see
As this vile blackness creeps over me,
How can we hope to raise mankind
To a plane of thought not war aligned,
If we will not see how life should be
With the existence of a bird alive and free

James Connolly

Piper Alpha Tragedy

This simple tribute is from the men on the Forties field
To remind us all of the "Piper and our workmates whose lives were to
yield and how much they sacrificed and how much they gave
As deep alone they lie inside their watery grave
So on this day, on their death, afar in places high.
Please don't be sad and please do not cry.
For you, our workmates, we will always have you near
As we continue working. Yes, sometimes even in fear
Our hearts are with you and your loved ones. You'll never be alone
We will not forget you, you'll never be on your own
On each 6th July we will remember we will stop and pause
And think of the "Piper" and pray there was a cause
For you the lads, now no pain no worry or no strife,
We all hope and pray you have all gone to a better life.

R. Magee

Waiting For A Bus

Strolling to the bus stop
Together,
Malleable darts flew from the Alien's lips.

Overtaken by numbness long before he left me
Waiting,
Alone.

Stood-up by the bus I began the trek home,
Blind.
Perhaps my heart would catch the next one . . .

Zena Briggs

Unemployment

That's it love you have a lie in,
Nought to get up for, except emptying dustbin.
Eee what a lad, a sometimes wonder if he won't go mad.
Anyway dole day today, cheer him up abit,
The great big dolloping twit.
Well John Major, you have got a lot to answer for,
Mind you, you could always start another war.

Janet Lord

Golden Wedding

A golden time, a life of love,
A marriage blessed from God above,
A lifetime of sharing, loving and giving,
A family you gave, the great gift of living.

Time has flown by, your family all grown,
All settled and happy, with kids of our own,
But with each generation, of Parker's descent,
We'll know what the love, of our parents has meant.

We've all had our problems and given you grief,
Headaches and heartaches, longstanding and brief,
To hold us and love us and show how you care,
With each little problem, we know you're both there.

So dear Mum and Dad, for all you've been through,
We'd just like to say, how much we love you,
So here's looking forward and when this day's done,
We'll all look to celebrate, Anniversary fifty-one.

Tracey Wells

Sleep

As darkness claims the sky for night
The sun bows in surrender
Sliding down behind the earth
From whence next morn he'll rise in splendour
Up glides the moon to take her place
Amidst a galaxy of stars
She'll ride the sea of midnight blue
Aligned with Jupiter and Mars
The land is hushed, night's blanket falls
To wrap the earth in dreams night deep
Then gently slows all living breath
And falls as prisoner of sleep

Elizabeth Zurinskas

Free Spirit

I want to fly around the moon, applauding
The stars twinkling bright.
Soaring effortlessly across the cosmos and into the night.
To travel the galaxy's rim, no thought
Of where to go, like a spaceship under
Mind control; not seen by a living soul
    To be free of bodily restraints, to fly
so far from earth my thoughts, if lights, would be so faint.
Spreading faster than ever perceived
I'd visit other worlds never revealed.
Zooming over their surfaces, drinking in their
splendour. Locking them in memories, to open
sometime for a little reminder.
    Like an arrow I would shoot fast and true into the hearts of
nebulas for a magnificent view. Once that was done
I'd head on until the morning to the nearest
sun. Taking a hard right I'd blast into the
deepest space racing as fast as light, close to the night's dreams.
    To the barriers of time, sound and light,
hope you are broken so I can visit other places out of earth's sight.

Ciaran Rafferty

I'm Leaving Home

I'm sorry to say this is my last Christmas here
No, don't get upset, not one single tear
I'm not going far, just across the town
You can come and visit, I've got the address written down
I will miss you both so very, very much
So, of course, by all means - we'll keep in touch
I'll be coming home at least once a week
When the cupboards are bare and when things look bleak
We knew the day would, of course, arrive
Yes, in the Christmas of '95
I'm leaving home - yep - fleeing the nest
I just want to say, living with you was the best
Anyway, just a big thank-you for looking after me
In case anything goes wrong - I'll keep my key!

Debbie Arnold

April Diary

Come gardener, dig out that compost heap,
Dig it out and spread it deep,
And sow broad beans in a double row,
Between each crop you see your hoe
To kill off all those seedling weeds,
And cultivate your early seeds.

And in your greenhouse there you grow
Tomatoes for an early show,
and peppers red and aubergine,
Marrows, sweet peas and runner bean,
And if there's time to cut the lawn,
Make sure that it is lightly shorn.

Set carrot, beet and garden swede,
And all the bedding plants you need,
And if the soil is not too wet,
Chitted potatoes can now be set.
But do not heed those aches and pains
To get work done before it rains.

Walter Howarth

The Departure

The sky clouds over, like the shadow surrounding my heart,
The sun ceases to shine, as I stand and watch you depart,
As the rain descends, I feel the tears stinging my eyes,
And the daylight gradually fades, along with my strength,
  as we say our last goodbyes,
The moisture is penetrating deep into my soul,
Memories flash though my mind, of all the kisses from you
  I stole,
I cry out, into the darkness, my voice echoes all around,
But you do not return, and I slowly sink towards the ground,
I am lost and cold, like a ship wrecked by the raging sea,
A lifeless body, for you have taken every part of me.

Wendy Elaine Parkes

The World's Past, Present And Future

Yesterday's world was happy,
People were not so snappy,
The sun would shine and shine,
And everything would be just fine,
The grass would be fresh green,
And people were not so mean,
Everybody would laugh,
And nobody would really starve,
But today's world is not as good,
Nobody would smile as much as they could,
People would argue, people would fight,
It's a much more unpleasant sight,
Jobs are more insecure,
Which made people more unsure,
People would laugh but only on the people who starve,
But tomorrow it shall be,
Kids going to school, redundant men playing pool,
Thugs and gangs on the street, posh people they will beat,
Trust and faith, the world will lack.
If only the time could tick back.

Susan Tong

Mum

Where did you go on that cold night,
Why didn't you put up a fight,
You left us all behind,
The love we had was so hard to find,
I've been so mad over the years,
I find it hard to keep back the tears,
Why did you die,
Why is life a lie,
You were so pretty and so young,
you were always full of sun,
I'd like you here once again,
Just for a cuddle or something,
I feel so insecure since you went away,
I always thought you'd be back that day,
Just to see you for a moment or two,
So I could say good-bye and I still love you.

Donna Mills

Dove Love

You're a dove me love, so my mother said,
Go into the world, find a crust of bread,
Find a house with a person who's soft in the head,
Who'll respond to your 'coo' and get out of bed,

Just stand on your perch,
Look 'em straight in the eye,
Please leave a crust out for me or I'll die,
Without a doubt, for you they'll feel sad,
To starve such a poor little dove would be bad.

So turn on your charm,
You'll come to no harm,
They'll open their hearts up to you,
They'll go in the house, as quiet as a mouse,
And return saying 'One crust or two?'

Judith Smith

The Wilting Rose

Into the darkest night
The silhouettes are fading fast
Once as bright as dawn - misty eyes they cast
Ne'er tell another lie my sweet rose; for
I gave it to another so many times before

Mask forever, sorrow deep
Wilting - 'tis for the rose that I weep;
Take no more, I ask of thee, misty eyes
Brushed its thorn a time or two - bled inside
Yearning never; seeds forever budding new...

Patricia M. Wilkinson

Fair Weather Friends

Once you were here, then you were gone,
My fair - weather friends
Did you decide that you didn't belong
My fair - weather friends?
Perhaps my face was too honest,
or my smile was too real,
For my fair - weather friends.
Could you not control, how I made you feel
My fair - weather friends?
So you chose to move on and
forget that we met
My fair weather friends,
Even now that you're gone,
I won't ever forget
My fair-weather friends.

Tania Hague

A Day At The Beach

I come from England to this place,
where palm trees are all green.
The place where I am is a sandy space
where no one has ever been.

In this world it's humid and hot
with a gentle refreshing breeze.
It feels like you're sizzling in a pot,
and sometimes the breeze waves the trees.

I jump into the warm sea
the waves crash down on the shore,
the water splashes all over me
I think it's fun, I want more.

There's yellow sand everywhere
and it tickles my feet.
But I don't really care,
I care about my skin in the heat.

Abigail Stevens

The Big Black Bull

When I was out walking
Crossing a field one day,
A big black bull
Was standing, barring my way.
I demanded of him,
Trying not to show fear,
For what was the reason
Of him standing out here.
After a little snorting
He got his message through,
And if I did not heed his warning
He would toss me in the blue.
It seemed he had not been fed that day
And this made him rather mad
But when he had his stomach full
He was not really bad.
I reached into my pocket, to see what I had got
A penny, an apple, and a string tied in a knot.
He said he would settle for the apple and that would do as pay
But if I should want to cross his field again, to bring a bag of hay.

James Haigh

To A Harmonious Friend

My life would not be the same without you.
You bring me pleasure but also tears
You remind me of the good times but also the bad
And sometimes situations best forgotten.
You provoke reactions which only you can do
You soothe me when I am stressed
And pick me up when I am down.
I close my eyes and escape into another world
Sometimes one of peace
Sometimes one of adventure
And sometimes one of fantasy
Wishing I was something I can never be.
In a silent world
You are a friend that I would surely miss.
You are a part of my life
Past, present and hopefully the future.

Helenna Davies

The Dance Of The Earth

As the unforgiving torrent of pure, fresh rain cascades down
Onto the weak flowers that begin to blossom . . .
Each fragile petal gracefully uncurling and rising up,
Waiting, waiting for more strength,
A different kind of strength.
It comes, shining like the holographic echo of life that it is,
Descending through the cotton-wool clouds,
And beating down on the pulse of the earth.

The flowers worship it and begin to conquer one another
In the hope of another beautiful ray splashing down
And fully healing their colour and fragrance.
The rain has silently moved on, uncomplimented and unseen,
But still content in the knowledge that far away,
Someone, somewhere will need it,
And praise it for eternity.

Samantha Callaghan

Alone

The grip on his bent spoon tightens,
his pale skin stretching to reveal the knotted bone beneath.
Eyes fixed on the soup as it shivers,
awaiting its arrival to his mouth.
He rises from the chair, gripping the table in agony.
Facing the mirror, he looks into the eyes of a stranger
to see a bleeding heart sigh.
His eyes lower, attempting to hinder heavy tears.
His head jerks as he remembers . . .
Happy memories still haunt him.
Placing his hand to his quivering lip
he stares into the empty room.
His ears burn as he listens to the thundering silence.
Head low, a tear trickles to his chin
as he realizes his only companion is loneliness.

Shabnam Mujaver

Love Lives On

Slowly the shadows are lifting, as hope replaces despair,
You can almost sense a feeling, an awareness they are there,
So when the dark clouds gather and your tears they fall as rain,
You know in time the storm will pass and the sun will shine again

So don't be in a hurry and live life day by day,
And as the sun shines brighter, it will help to light your way,
Your life may change direction, the signs may not be clear,
But love will help you conquer take away your fear.

The power of love is endless, these feelings will remain,
To help and give you comfort, and let you smile again,
For love is like a candle burning brightly out of sight,
That helps you through the long days and longer lonely nights.

In time your pain will lessen, you'll learn to laugh again,
Your path it may have altered and life won't be the same,
But life is still worth living, there's still so much to share,
For love is never ending, and they are always there.

V. Holmes

Lost Love

I had a love a long time ago,
Where it went I do not know.
I often think way back to then,
And know I will never get it again.

It was a once in a life time love,
Pure and special like a white-winged dove.
That only a few will find,
And keep buried deep in their mind.

So if you find a love like this,
And everything in life is bliss.
Hold on to it or you could miss,
The greatest love of your life.

Yvonne Fowler

Leaves

Leaves as green as the green green grass,
Leaves as brown as shadows cast,
Leaves as yellows as the burning sun,
Leaves as red as poppy's come.
Conkers dangling on a string,
Oh what fun the Autumn will bring.

Amy Elaine Griffiths

Memories Of Africa

Africa, oh Africa, keeps calling out to me.
How I long to be in Africa, so that once more I could see
The wonders that are many, the wild beast of the plain,
I would love to be in Africa my homeland once again.

Young warriors chant their tribal songs, their bodies painted bright.
Their camp fires lighting up the sky in the darkness of the night,
The proud tribes wander o'er the land, possessions on their back.
We think they haven't anything but nothing do they lack.

They have the freedom we all yearn, no worries, cares or woe,
Always happy always smiling wherever they may go,
Such strange but friendly people, they quickly won my heart,
As did their land called Africa from which I had to part.

The sunsets are outstanding, the night birds fill the skies,
As I sit on my veranda, tears flow gently from my eyes.
The memories come flooding back of times we spent together,
In that dear land called Africa, I will remember it forever.

And as the days roll slowly by, I pray to God above,
That he will send me home again, to the Africa I love.

M. Willis

Benevolence Welfare Providing

In quiet stillness sitting there with sight dimmed eyes
  and silver hair,
The old man fashioned flowers, Red, then hand upon his
  breast he said,
"They shall grow not old——
  Dear Lord help us".

Standing bright eyed, eager, waiting, fast beating heart
  upon the station,
"Home is my soldier boy" she cried, and holding him
  to her breast she sighed,
"As we that are left—— Dear Lord help us".

Silently weeping, so deep the pain, a boy will ne'er
  come home again.
The sun shone bright when he went away, she sheds her
  tears with the rain to say
"At the going down of the sun—— Dear Lord help us".

There's a meeting at the Club tonight, to hear the wrongs
  and put them right.
There could be no better reason for The Royal British Legion
We will remember them Dear Lord help us.

Reg Greaves

Dearest Dad

The pearly gates were opening, in heaven, way up high,
as God was calling you away, all we could do was cry.

We often sit and wonder, why did you go that day?
And would you've had to suffer, if God had let you stay.

And now it's five years later, our hearts still crushed and sore,
the pain is never-ending, we love you more and more.

Well there are new additions, to the family you once knew,
one being Aidan, I called him after you, and then there's baby Grace,
such a cutie, what a joy, and so you have two grandchildren,
one a girl, and one a boy.

And oh we wish you'd met them, they'd love you as we do,
all we can do is tell them, of special times with you.

We bring them to your grave side, yes, they say prayers for you,
we teach them of the wonderful things about our dad so true.

So now you've entered heaven, you've gone to eternal rest,
we just want our dad to know, you are the very best.

   Maria Carr

Why?

Why is there a world at all?
Why the heartache, the misery, the terrible gall
Of physical pain and mental stress
When our being seems such a hopeless mess?
From where do we find the strength to carry on?
To whom do we turn when all seems to have gone?
From somewhere does a light begin to show?
Do we regain fight enough to conquer our foe?
To face up to reality, make good out of strife
And rebuild the foundations, start a new life?
I think we must, or how would we survive,
To smile again, and thank the Lord... to be alive?

   Hilary E. Thomas

Dad

You've been gone a while dad, but still the pain is there,
The little things you used to say, the way you used to care.

I miss your laughter and your smile, our family's not the same,
But I have special memories, these help to ease my pain.

I think back to the happy times, and smile as I recall,
The trips, the treats and outings, when you were with us all.

When all the sky is clear at night, I find your special star,
I like to think you're watching us and know that you're not far.

If I could have just one more day, I'd spend that time with you
I'd remember every moment, I'm sure that you would too.

You were so very special, there for me all the way,
I'll miss you for a lifetime, forever and a day.

Wherever you may be, Dad, even though we are apart,
My love for you will never end, you're always in my heart.

   Tania Ede

Terrible Things

The terrible things that happen today
Make you want to kneel and pray.

In the press and on the news,
Either one, there's nothing to choose.

Murder, rape, terrorists too,
This is to name, only a few.

Our children aren't safe going to school
Even old ladies, are conned by the fool.

It would be nice to have a day.
With everything bright, a happier day.

The pictures we see of suffering and pain,
The whole world over, without any gain.

   E. Woods

There's No Place Like Home

Too many exotic countries, I have travelled
At so much beauty, I really have marvelled.
But as far, as I myself, has been concerned
the truth of which, I very quickly learned.
To me, there's no place like home!

Each and every country holds its own magic spell
Especially to the people, who within its precincts dwell
Tho' enjoyed the times, that I spent there
That something was missing, I was certainly aware
To me, there's no place like home!

It was nice seeing new places, making new friends
Enjoying their life style, their different trends
How the others half lives, was a constant thrill
Their various cultures show great skill
To me, there's no place like home!

Yes, visiting other countries, stimulates the mind
Adventures, unlimited, away from the daily grind
But no matter, the pleasures, I really must confess
In spite of it all, tho' wonderful nevertheless
To me there's no place like home!

   Jane Osborne Clachrie

The Hawthorn Tree

White fairy flowers in sunlit hours
   hang from the old May tree.

When I am old and life turns cold,
   I will remember thee.

Haw berries red are overhead,
   I smell fall in the air.

Trying to hold back summer days
   as white weaves through my hair.

Sweet fairy boughs, gnarled magic boughs,
   they whisper with the breeze.

Secrets of life, and time, and age
   are blowing through the trees.

Soon winter will undress the boughs
   with fingers icy cold.

Pray snow like benediction falls,
   to clothe them white as spring,
      while I grow old.

   S. Ashford

Wings

They stand upon the tarmac grey,
side by side in neat array.
Their tanks are full, their engines checked,
like giant birds upon a deck
Silent, waiting for the sound, of hurried feet upon the ground.

The bombs are loaded, engines whine,
as each great aircraft leaves the line,
Down the flight path fast they fly,
and rise into the starlit sky.

Bombers on their lonely flight,
go onward through the silent night,
The crew are calm, they know the task ahead,
of opposition, fire, and bursting shell,
A target to reach amidst a living hell,
and beams of searching light.

So with the dawn, these heroes of the sky,
return once more, until another duty call,
They seek no worship, claim no prize.
Their home, and country to defend
Until its great victorious end.

   Morwenna Bateson

For Emma

Clouds swirling in the morning dew,
as they clear I see a vision of you,
your face so pale, like winter snow,
your eyes cool green, with a frosty glow,
I feel so lost, alone inside,
my eyes so red from where I'd cried.
But you are wearing a calming smile,
which lifts my spirits for a while,
I remember your vibrance when you were here,
happiness and love when you were near.
Alas the vision fades away,
I awake, it is another day,
but you are deep within my heart,
even though death keeps us far apart.
I still love you and you me
see you again when I dream.

Tracy George

Darkness

Why are you afraid, of a world without light?
Why do things look, so mysterious at night?
Even with the stars, that cover the sky,
That's not much, for us to see by.
You wander on slowly through woods, and by streams,
Controlling your heart you think of your dreams.
As the night grows darker and the stars go in,
You begin to wonder what you're doing.
Under the cover of darkness, the trees come to play,
They claw at you, grab you, and you think that they say . . .
Stay away, Stay way, Run away, Run away.
You're running now, you trip and fall,
You lay there and cry, you try to call
But no one can here you your voice is too small.
You fall into a dark and restless sleep,
Curled up into a tight little heap.
All the things that belong to the night,
Please be gone with the dawning of light.

Andrea Lane

Lunch Time

I met a girl today,
dying next to a Ford Cortina,
sleepy from valium,
sluggish from alcohol and
swollen with bruises.
She'd just sat down on the pavement
and fallen asleep,
her head resting on the passenger door.
I asked if she needed help,
but I couldn't help her.

She told me she was an alcoholic,
She combed her hair in the street,
my mum used to say "nice girls don't do that"
Her name was Pauline and she was twenty-eight,
same age as me.

Sarah Wilson

The Drunken Father

Quietness, clocks ticking, fear.
Mamma awaits for the key in the door.
The sound of heavy footsteps, a cough
then a roar.
Pain. A cry from Mamma as she falls to the floor.
A laugh from him as he boots her once more.
Furniture flies across the room, ornaments
break as they crash to the floor.
Vulgar language spits from his mouth.
A crying child appears in the hall.
He stops then no noise at all.
Eyes meet. Fear to shame.
Then Mamma yelps out in pain.
Child embraces her with love and pity.
A door bangs closed.
Safe once more.

Michelle Marie Surgenor

To Ionica - My Son

"Don't waste the time!" I have been told,
"Don't waste the time!" I tell you now.
Perhaps repeat that time is gold
Must keep an eye, to spend it, how.

You have to count how long you chat,
Or stay not doing proper things,
You must be happy when you act,
And feel like having magic wings.

To do something, means to create,
To add, to build, to conquer.
For great action dedicate
Whole life, you, poor caller.

Don't waste the time is my advice,
Please, do create something.
My words are true, not a caprice,
I simple want you working.

Rodica Victoria Steriu

Sunday Crosswords

I think that word's "coffee", no, maybe it's "toffee"
It could be "banoffee". Oh! Not enough space.
Laos in Asia? Don't be a clown. P'raps you are right though
I'll just write it down. What word do we know that begins with JT'.
Leave that for a moment, we'll just wait and see.
Wish you'd give me a chance to read through the clue
No, I don't want the answer. I think that I know.
Where on earth did you get that silly word from?
Well, why write it down if you know that it's wrong!
Are you sure that word's right? I suppose it will do
Well, it will if we alter the gist of the clue.
The reference books are all there on the chair
"Go on, look it up. Are you sure it's not there?
As each clue is answered, an inquest is held, the wrangling gets
fiercer, near riots are quelled, why on earth do we do it, these
crosswords on Sunday, the last minute dash to get posted by
Monday? Is it the challenge? The test of ability or is it - in my
case - to ward off senility? Whatever it is, it's with us to stay
and one day, who knows, it might even pay!

Brenda Fehrenbach

Imagine

Imagine a day without the sun,
Imagine a river with nowhere to run,
Imagine a mountain without its cap of snow,
Imagine a sailing ship with no wind to blow;

Imagine no stars in the night sky,
Imagine a bird with nowhere to fly,
Imagine the sea, and a beach without a single shell,
Imagine a world with no colour, sound or smell;

This is how empty my life would be,
If I was without you, my wonderful Tracey,
You are my breath, my strength, my reason to live,
I love you and thank you for the love that you give.

Roger Michael Hewitt

Walk The Sleepless Night

Oh I walk the sleepless nights
wake up and think I am free
well we are all prisoners of
other people's nightmares everything is
wrong and nothing is right
The trees whistle and the wind blows
and the clocks tick tock, tick
clowns are here and everywhere
they know it is but they don't grow
just shadows you know grow taller
shadows. But people don't really know enough
life's a cruel game win or lose
it is a game lost for some and
others run to the sun.

Steven Knight

Conversations With Self

"Hello, hello, is there anybody there?"
"What's that, you've fallen into total despair?
A draw full of bills, various ills and pills,
No time for dreams, only paying the rent, Doctor being sent..."

"Hello, hello, are you still on the line...?"
"What's that, you can't get to sleep on time,
Wake up before dawn, nightmares till morn,
No time for vanity, only holding on to sanity, with all my might...."

I look to my bookcase and scan the array
Of writers I know who will never decay,
Goethe and Shakespeare, Byron et al,
Inspirational thoughts from infinity's old pal,
They dared to listen to their inner sage,
Like a magical fountain, words poured onto a page,
Each tender moment celebrated and loved
not negated, suffocated, walled-up or gloved,
The mysterious language of the human heart,
connected to life, compassion and art.

"Hello, hello, is there anybody there?"
"At last, connection, I'm here, I'm here".

Sheila Wilson

The Family

Kids fighting over what's on TV,
mum trips over dog, and spills her tea!
The eldest daughter wants to go out,
this raises a row without a doubt!

The eldest son is still on the phone,
he notices a change in mother's tone!
Dad arrives home from a hard day's work,
three-year-old son spills juice on his shirt.

Mum remembers dog hasn't been fed,
and tries to send all the kids to bed.
Eldest son still on the dog and bone!
"Son it's bed time, get off the phone!"

The eldest daughter puts up a fight,
mum wonders if this will last all night!
Dad puts his food upon the table,
while the house looks like a horse's stable!

Eventually kids all go to sleep, and the dog gets something to eat.
So quiet, you could hear a pin drop,
everything's so still, you'd think it stopped.
But mum is still full of sorrow,
'Cos this will all happen again tomorrow!

Dean J. Wing

Destined Paradise

Dedicated to Steve McManaman of Liverpool F.C. and England

I look in your eyes and what do I see,
A picture of paradise for just you and me.
The water runs blue, the soft golden sand,
Us in the moonlight, strolling along hand in hand.
Could it be possible to become lost in your dream,
Should it happen to you, you'll know what I mean.
I know you're not near me, but you're close to my heart,
There's so much I could tell you, but where would I start.
Maybe if we met, you'd feel the same way,
It won't be tomorrow, but who knows one day.
Each time I see you, I'm flushed by the heat,
And at times I feel my heart missing a beat.
There are times in this world when we need our own space,
And what would I give to be held in your warm embrace.
To be on our island, on a paradise beach,
Represents me and you, far from each other's reach.
But the way that I see it, my love for you is true,
For I feel the pain of my heart breaking in two.
So look into the future, what do I see,
Some destined paradise for just you and me.

Tonia Pritchard

Made For Each Other

As the night follows day,
As the sun follows rain,
As death follows birth,
As positive follows negative,
As black follows white,
As summer follows autumn,
And autumn follows winter,
And winter follows spring.
All these have one thing in common,
Which is that they were made for each other
Just like I was made for you,
And you were made for me.

Davinder Reehal

Let Me Be Yours

Let me be your pen or pencil so you can hold me when you write,
Let me be your electric fan so I can cool you down at night,
Let me be your jumper so I can warm you up,
I'm not asking much, I just want you to
let me be yours.

Let me be your tape player so I can play our songs of love,
Let me be your light so I can turn as white as a dove,
Let me be your bag so I can hold all your things,
I'm not asking much, I just want you to
let me be yours.

Let me be your car so I can take you far,
Let me be your stallion riding you away,
Let me be your band-aid healing all your broken wounds,
Let me be your keys letting you in every time,
I'm not asking much, I just want you to
Let me be yours.

Delphine Simmons

Spring

Winter has cast off her white shimmering gown of frost and snow
    Weary of the fading season she has no illusions, it's time to go.
Spring bursts in, a young bride beautiful in her creation,
    Radiant with anticipation.
Stunning and very becoming in many ways, she sets out her
    garden with a glorious display.
Crocus, daffodils, tulips are all on view
    Of the many species of flowers these are just a few.
There is an awakening of the senses to warm breezes in the air.
    Fragrant blossoms are beginning to bloom everywhere
I feast my eyes on the beauty that surrounds me and smell
    the heady nectar of the flowers.
Their sustained growth brought on by sunshine and showers.
    How I marvel at their strength and resilience
When they bend and sway in the wind, battling against—
    nature's elements
    Birds twittering their early morning chorus
Building their nest in the hedges and trees around us.
I have watched and waited all winter for spring to arrive
    To lighten the darkness as I walk my dog through the countryside

Margaret Davenport

Reflections

There was a time when all the World seemed green,
Not just the trees and grass but everything,
Save the bright wild flowers and the sheen of a blackbird's wing.
I can still recall the scent of the wild dog rose,
And the smell of honeysuckle pleasant to the nose,
Then friends' faces looked so clear and smooth,
Movements were so easy and flowing like a dance,
And thoughts came easy too—sharp as any lance.

Now my reflections take a different form,
A bent grey head and wrinkled face the norm,
My friends grow less with every passing year,
The World is changing fast and soon I fear
Will go on without me, yet, it still seems gay and bright,
But only when I close my eyes and dream at night.

Tom Page

Thoughts

The bleak wind whistles through the branches
Bending the leaves until they fall
Into the flowing ice cold water
Reflecting the bare proud trees so tall.

My thoughts are like the bubbling whirlpool
Moving, swirling in search of what.
Why can't I stop to count my blessings
And be content with what I've got.

Have I done the best I can do
Is my life worth much at all
Will I leave something behind me
For the others to recall.

Like the streams and rivers ending
As they flow into the sea
Perhaps these questions will be answered
When I come at last to thee.

Pauline Brookes

The Driving Force

Money is the fiend that drives the soul,
That pushes the body to reach the goal,
That burdens the mind and weakens our will,
That makes us slaves upon the treadmill.

Work is the tool, to it we are bound,
Where values are worthless on common ground,
Where egos abound and greed is vast,
Where the stage is set to which we are cast.

At the end of our time, when we've fought for the first place,
Overlooked and ignored he who now we must face,
Our wealth in this life for him has no meaning,
He cares and looks only for spiritual breading.

So look not through your day for "Opportunities" great,
But for ways to become a person of better state,
Develop that soul and will you've been given,
And let not yourself by money be driven.

Wendy Makepeace

Homeless

It is cold, the wind breaks a chill,
I shiver,
All I have is a cardboard box as a home.
You have warmth.
Scrumptious food and a family.
I have nothing,
I have a thin old blanket to keep me warm,
I have leftovers from the trash.
A dog rummaged through that,
Animals urinate in that,
I Eat That!
I am homeless,
My mind is not my own
It's yours, it's his, it's hers.
Why me?
Why do I have to sleep here on the street?
Why do I have to live in a cardboard box?
Why do I have to eat food which is diseased?
Why am I homeless?

Phillippa Chilvers

A Walk At Dawn

A shimmering dawn of dusty pink and ochre, stains the
winter morning's sky.
Clouds of cotton drift lazily on, like wisps of dreams gone by.
Beads of dew like sparkling gems haunt the lush green grass.
Softly blowing like trembling hands as the chilling wind cuts past.

Sleepy mist shrouds the scene like bandages around a wound.
The sun-warmed hills lit by streams of gold from heaven
comes so soon.
Delicate trees of velvet green quiver in the chilly morn'.
Two inquisitive eyes drink it all in, on an early walk at dawn.

G. M. Quarterman

Bondage of the Soul

O! That I am the soul of Man captive in this body
Imprisoned in a cage of sinews, bones and flesh

I yearn to be free of these shackles, chains and fetters
I am a droplet longing to merge with the surging ocean

A grain of sand in the vastness of the empty desert
The body will shrivel and shrink and decay one day

Like a falcon I will soar high in space
I touch the stars, the sun, the moon and planets,
  which I disdain

For they are nothing but slaves of an orbital system
Forever, in perpetual motion like a millstone

I seek the great soul Whose Word I am
To lose myself in Him

I have no isms, no country, no homeland
I wish to be one with Him in his great realm

There will be no toil, no sweat, no tears, no stress, no strain
Where His Will is my will, His wish is my wish

Peace, harmony, serenity and tranquillity reign supreme
In this Kingdom of Heaven, I am free of all bondage

Sajjad H. Shamsi

Footsteps

Raspberry ice lolly stains on the sole,
childlike decoration and mould.
Tell tale signs of Mum,
slithering chaotic, belly full of rum.

A distinguished pair they might say,
sharp, clean cut,
a man of today.
Strangers hold out their hands,
but what do they know of this man?

Size 4, size 6, size 10 who didn't walk out again?

Angela Haygarth

One Man's Fight

From voice of mind, from heart of soul,
there is a story that's never told,
of one man's fight to be but one,
though his fight for humanity has
just begun . . .
. . . From the day he is born to the
day he dies, accepted for what he is,
what he was, and what he will be,

Though still his fight has not yet passed by.

Dawn Bradshaw

History

The ancient castles remain high
And untouched by the ephemeral clocks.
They rise, their atrocious yellow-brick walls
Still surround the dead lives inside.
Their founders, releasing the power of vanity,
Forever subside in my memory.
The chambers of these citadels
Hide the secrets of mortality,
Now bottled up in the
Glass menageries of history.
The lavanter runs through their vanes,
Gently evaporating,
Leaving a trail of unforsaken sin.
The lament of the night,
Endlessly reflects on the chamber windows,
Through the dust of time, roads never taken.
Realize me in the drop of the morning;
The sun of gold, the tears of rain.
Someday I will find oblivion
In your burning emotion.

Tijana Vukadin

Everlasting Friendship

Friends may come, friends may go
But with you I'll always know.
Know how much you're there for me
Hence I give my love to thee.

Come now, let us share
How much we really care.
Care for each other in a way
Friends do every single day.

The sun will shine upon our hearts
That gave us friendship right from the start.
The start of feelings yet to be explored
Something that should never be ignored.

The precious moments we have together
Will enhance this love forever.
Forever the peace within our souls
Set no limitations toward our goals.

The friendship we have will be there
For you and I, and everyone to share.
To share this emotion keeps me sustained
Throughout my life this love is retained.

Donna Lee Allen

Twins

When I look in the mirror
this is what I see
myself looking straight
back at me.

When I go to college
this is what I see
that same image
looking back at me.

I feel like a shadow
when I'm with her
because she's so good at everything
so I'm always behind her.

I never mean to hurt her
in whatever I do
but when I see her cry
I have to cry too.

Even though it's like being a whole one
even though we are a half
it's good to know you
have somebody close to your heart.

Karen Lesley Hazeldine

Melancholia

As I grow old and still live on,
I wonder where my life has gone.
No more words, no smiles, no songs.
No future to reflect upon.

So many answers I need to know.
When did it happen? Why did they go?
My only crime, to love them so.

I've been alone now three full years,
Yet at night in dreams they still appear.
I run, but cannot beat the fears
And wake to darkness, cold and tears.

The brightest sun will never find
The strength to penetrate soul or mind.
My life remains in a distant time.
The gift of memory so unkind.

My only solace in darkest thought,
At night when escape from life is sought,
Is that peace of mind for which I've fought
Will finally be mine.

Kate Partner

A Mum's Memories

I hear the key in the door, and look to see your face once more.
I hear your voice speak my name, nothing takes away the pain.
Friends rally round and talk to me. I sometimes think 'oh, can't
you see, life can never be the same for me'.

The day's so long the night time too, all I do is think of you.
They tell me time will heal the pain, till we meet once again.
I go to your room and touch your things, nothing can take the
memories, the little things we used to do.
I hear your laughter in the air this takes away some of my despair.

I know you won't want me to grieve too long, so I listen to your favourite songs.
I feel your presence in the room, hear your voice sing out of tune,
I know that you're not far away. This helps me through another day.
And at night as I try to sleep, often ending in a weep,
'oh God, why did this have to be?'
She was loved so much you see. And I wonder why not me?'
Life for her had just began, she was so full of fun.
They always say the good die young.

But I must put away my sorrow and try to make a new tomorrow,
helping those who need me too,
but this won't stop me thinking of you,
goodbye my darling, and God bless you.

Pauline Tilbury

Fallen But Not Forgotten

The old man standing in the Memorial Gardens, his body revealing
his age, chest thrust forward and erect in proud memory of the wars
he had to wage. Dreaming of past glories and the friends he lost
too, to save this country we all love... Freedom for me and you.

With his head held high, tears of sadness he can't disguise,
as the last post sounds he remembers the eire battle cries.
The good friends he had... The good friends now lost,
never to the forgotten...bravely killed in action, never mind the cost.

Regimental flags flying proudly albeit at half mast,
for the first young man who fought and lost until the very last.
Shimmering medals and ribbons the old man has draped across his
chest, a constant reminder of battles won and how he stood the test.

With the memory of war fading slowly from his ageing brain,
his facial expression acts as a reminder of the horror, torment and
strain. The stench of rotting corpses of the dead and dying too
fill his nostrils as his terrible memories come flooding back through.

On this cold and damp November morning... somewhat overcast and grey,
the old man stands still for a minute's silence, salutes and walks away.
What can I hope for as I observe the old man and his glorious past,
that the war his friends fought and died in... will be the last.

S. M. Parry

Cardboard House Of Life

Life is like a cardboard house with walls built of illusion,
it's shaped within a blink of time, then gone is our intrusion.
Unknowing we will point our feet towards a hidden destiny,
across the stones of love and hate, success and great adversity.
Contract your house of life with care and thought for all creation
not hemmed in by walls of antique law and roofed by ostentation.
Avoid those false foundations where meaning dare not enter,
let wisdom grow as you mature and place it at its centre.
If delusion of grandeur blind your eye, gaze up at the wondrous
sky, where some of nature's gifts reside, like wind and rain, the sun's bright eye.
Cast your mind upon a tree, enduring aeons patiently,
from the soil below it feeds, then gives its bounty to birds and bees.
To learn from this that we were born, not to amass and fortune own.
When the sharpened blade of scythe cuts your silken thread to life,
the shaper of all destiny then your final judge will be,
time holds its breath while he decides whether you brought worth to
life perhaps he'll set your spirit free, yet it may be...that
...frail and alone, your soul might once again be born.

W. Hinterlang

Autumn Gold

Autumn gold,
    Worth its weight in harvest,
Young children rush
    Following fathers in big machines
Up, up the shallow slope
    Rolling down the gentle hill
Plunging to the copse
    Buried deep in fresh fallen leaves.
Kicking up a flurry,
    A stray red leaf caught by the wind
Stirred higher,
    Clipping others now fluttering down,
Up, up, vanishing from sight
    Lost in the gaze of the rich yellow sun.

The squirrels watch the children
    Who look up at twigs and branches:
Revealed again, older than before,
    Summer still green in their minds
And now to face the cold winter chill
    Warmed by the fire and the ginger nut biscuit.

Christopher M. Binsted

Someone

I was alone in that room yet someone held my hand,
Someone wiped my tears away and helped me understand,
Someone gave me courage when the darkness fell on me,
Someone hid my eyes from what I did not want to see.
Someone gave me comfort when I had no place to lie,
Someone was my friend when my friends had passed me by.
Someone lay there bleeding from a wound inside of me,
Someone tried to take my pain, tried to set me free.
Someone held me tightly but with no arms around,
Someone talked for hours yet did not make a sound.
Someone lay me down so finally I'd sleep,
Someone kissed my forehead and told me not to weep.
Someone lay beside me, someone did not leave,
Someone was the air around me, someone helped me breathe.
Someone took the nightmares, someone gave me dreams,
There I lay without a sound, yet someone heard my screams.
I know somebody held my hand in that room there on my own,
Although I wake up lonely, I'll never be alone,
With memories of you with me I'm never far from home.

Eleanor Meadows

At The Altar

As he stands nervously at the altar
waiting for his bride to be
his knees trembling, waiting impatiently

As she arrives, the doors open slowly
as she walks down the aisle
he looks and gives her a smile

As they stand together at the altar
both saying their vows and "I do"
and with a kiss the ceremony is over
as they hold hands and leave the altar

Rachel Wake

The Fight

I hate you with all my heart. Why? You ask,
because of everything you've done in the past.
You have no friends, this fact you try to mask.
I think you will find that I was the last.
I know that this hate is quite upsetting,
and I know that it is making you sad.
But there is no other way of letting
you know that you've made me really quite mad.

This hate I have may make me feel red hot,
and everyone has hate, but some are worse
than others. But some may have a large knot
in their stomach. Others just want to curse.
And walls of silence may build between two,
where it soon becomes time to start anew.

Sharon Carter

The Stranger Inside

Stealthy as a cheetah, he stalks my nights of doubt.
He lurks at the corners of my unsuspecting mind -
he pounces upon my heart and I fear his power -
but his paws are soft and gentle upon my breast
and his eyes hold a longing for my trust.

He thrusts into my life with ice-cold blades
and twists through my heart with a searing edge.
When he is done, he waits quietly by -
spent by his wounding, impotent and limp
until I can cleanse him with forgiveness.

He is fire - he burns my would-be temples
and I stand amidst his spiral of destruction
searching through the ashes with hurting hands
until I find an ember he forgot
and tenderly nurture it with flames of love.

Ruth McMullen

My Bunny, Flups

Lazy as a lion.
Floppy like a mop.
Friendly as a wood-louse.
Loving, never stops.

When I wake up in the morning.
Flups is always there.
Nose in her food bowl.
She's shaped like a pear.

Sometimes when she runs around, in the entrance hall.
She digs up the carpet, and mum goes up the wall!

Pretty as a butterfly.
Cuddly as a pup.
She wants attention all the time.
That's my Flups!

Laura Adams

Untitled

Into the river of my dreams
I've cried a million tears
Wondering how the youthful days
Turned into passing years
Across the pastures oh so green
Was a lovely sight to be seen
All the animals used to roam
Waiting for the farmer to call them home
So now I am growing old
The rest of my days will be
Confined to my home

K. D. Walker

Tension

Frustration is building
Something must give
prepared to be alive
But not prepared to live.
Tears of emotion can't tell the whole story.
Dwelling on the past
Reflecting on former glory.

Can see the light
but it does not shine.
Can see the train
but it's not on the line.
Can see the sky
but what does it mean?
Always stood up
but now must lean.

Is it imagined?
is it pure fear?
Don't want to go
Don't want to be here.

Gareth Jones

Woman To Woman

Just a few words, woman to woman.
Sometimes wise yet foolhardy,
strong, but with too much sexuality for him to
comprehend.
Compassion and tenderness are also our virtues.
Obsequious in how he likes us, and in this role
we excel,
always wanting to please when two become one, but
how soon they forget our youth and all the softly
spoken words on the pillow of life.
Patiently we wait for the dawn of his life, when
man's exuberance starts to fade and his mind
becomes the avenue and his eyes the tools of his
desire.

Loretta Worthington

Wolf

Enter though your life's at risk
Many nights come to this
Sounds around you loud and clear
Chilling, worried, complete with fear.

The moon shines down through shady cloud
And no-one knows that howling sound
A four legged creature with fur on back
that howling sound means
Attack! Attack! Attack!

Lying here bleeding, life source slipping by
Going to that peaceful place
Heaven in the sky.

Juliette Zillah Shepley

Rejection

He stands alone, and watches them,
The laughter, the hugs, the kisses.
The sense of belonging -
That is what he really misses.
There is love, so much love here,
Surely a little could be spared for him?
People are giving presents,
People are happy.
He receives nothing -
He is unhappy.
The people are receiving each other,
Yet he is rejected.
Why?
  A child is innocent,
  So why is he rejected?

Neelam Zahir

Darkness's Delight And Despair

The day's sun falls to the horizon,
And darkened clouds create streamline banks
Between which the river skies flow.
The blood-rose, ruby-red sky gives the day away
To darkness's delight and the pre-night twilight
That reigns in its display. Birds give song as they settle down
For the coming hours in which they'll rest for a new day.
Darkness falls, night-time calls, the silver slick moon shines bright,
Millions of stars on drawn curtains of black,
How I love this sight.

Cool, still air breathes on my skin, that I have exposed
To night and the moon so bright; this delight everyone can know.
As night draws on and the hour grows late
Houses fall dark everywhere.
People sleep, night creeps, the hours tick on to darkness's despair.
But night is still young, and nights creatures are awake,
The four-legged prowl, the winged ones fly,
Each has its own things to do. On each other they prey.
But everything dies,
And so will the night-time too.

M. E. Powell

Young At Heart

With walking boots and woolly hat
My life has changed its pattern
Retired from work with time to spare
Things now begin to happen

Hiking 'round the countryside
Seeing sights I've never seen
The lakes, the dales and beautiful peaks
All places I've never been

There's a freedom in the open countryside
That cannot be explained, no traffic or fumes and a steady pace
Just sun, fresh air and maybe rain

The hostel in sight at the end of the day
At hot shower and a hearty meal
A place to rest your tired feet, how good it makes you feel

There's a local nearby, so we go for a drink
And perhaps a game of darts
Some can play and others can't but everyone takes part

Back to the hostel, already for bed, which bunk is going to be mine
Some like the top and some like the bottom
So everything turns out fine

A. Haggarty

Breath Of Goodbye

Dedicated to Father George West who died of leukemia, age 44 yrs

Snow pilfered the black night stars outside the window,
the room alight with the soft glow of snow,
the wind resonance a cheery hello on the pane,
bringing an air of necessary jest into a room in vain,
a room full of unforeseen sorrow.

Intrinsic decor of magnolia paint, furniture sparse,
machines of colour, shine lights of red and green into shadows harsh,
tubes of indispensable clear juice going straight to the heart,
keeping alive the body and all body parts,
not a room of palace royal but terminal departure class.

Six months this has been my home, my lair,
my body wilted, blood lacking cells, no immunity, void of hair,
no point on introspection, my thoughts are but a fleet,
my questions go unanswered, with this incursion of misdeed,
my pain won't subdue, my body fritters away.

My breathing becomes more shallow, my life seems but a sham,
rushing before me like the tracks of a city tram,
rapacious and fading into the distance of the forlorn night,
my soul searching, as the loss of word, of sight,
the last breath of goodbye.

Donna West

My Secret Hiding Place

The waves pulled in crushing against the
seafront like a tempestuous tiger.
Footmarks lay across the dark grain brisky sand.
In the distance fading bodies disappeared amidst
the forgotten clouds.
The only sound of life echoed the sea gulls facing the wind.
For this time of year silence ruled the day.
Peace and tranquillity sought through people's minds
as one by one they come here with ease.
One could walk for miles and miles just to distance
themselves from the world at large.
It was like a hiding place, or to coin a better phrase a secret
mission, a mission that would capture one's heart to infinity.
It was like an unforgotten world which had
taken its time to be discovered.
I preferred to call it simply my secret hiding place.
It looked particularly pictorial especially at night when the sun
settled and the waves calmly laid to rest.
The vivid scenery looked charmingly quaint
and was pleasing to the eye.
A sudden thought came to my mind as someone once said
to me: a ship that sails backwards never sees the sunrise!

June Williamson

Thoughts

In this life, do I want to share
Misery beyond compare
I think not, life's one big struggle
All I need is a little cuddle.

I'd like to touch and reach the sky
But I will have to learn to fly
Like a bird that's full of grace and woe
I still will have nowhere to go.

When I am called to God's domain
I know I'll be at peace again
Until then, I must get on with life
And carry on with all the strife.

Be very happy, jolly and gay
There will always be another day
Time very quickly passes by
When our time's up, we'll be ready to die.

But alas, life isn't all that bad
We mustn't be so very sad
So take a little tip from me
You needn't be a misery.

Jean Grace

That's My Friend

With long brown hair
and the eye of brown
with white little teeth
as white as snow
with a smile up to
her ears which means
kind, nice and friendly,
with hands waiting to help.
That's my friend.

With her long nose
breathing the clean air.
Running around trying to make the team win.
Running around making us
happy and trying to
show the teacher that
she could do better,
that's my friend.
I will never find a friend like her.

Sandra Matika

Help The Aged

Give a thought to all the aged,
Specially those who live alone.
Lets make it our priority,
Don't leave them on their own.

It must be such a lonely life,
In a flat, or Bungalow.
Just a visit from the Warden,
Who calls to say Hallo.

If someone living near you,
Is aged, or infirm.
With goodwill, pay them a visit,
Let them know of your concern.

Should they need some shopping fetching,
Or a hand to make their fire.
Maybe a little bit of gardening,
It's your help that they require.

One day you'll reach "Old Age" yourself,
So bearing that in mind.
That as you treat your fellow man,
God will pay you back in kind.

W. G. Hyde

My Aunty Sheila

Visiting to me was such a bind, war stories, cake and tea,
I was bored and wanted to go home now, why didn't my parents see?
There was one however I didn't mind, in fact I looked forward to seeing
She was different from all the others, the only human being!

My Aunty Sheila was her name, she talked and laughed with me,
She was the one I looked up to, the one I dreamt to be.
She always wore a friendly smile throughout the night and day,
Her family too was just the same, her boys and I did play.

I never expected the day to come when she did pass away,
It's a shame to all, I miss her much, and wished that she could stay.
My birthday was the day she left, the tears swelled in my eye,
I could no longer fight them back and I began to cry.

I believe she went to heaven, that place high in the sky,
But still it seems unfair to me, I couldn't say "Goodbye."
No photos do I have of her, just this poem to remember her by,
It's been a year, but still it hurts. Why did she have to die?

S. Jones

Demons

Demons of the dark await, to dance within your mind
Their sticky fingers poke around to see what they can find,
They know just how to make you squirm, to scream a silent scream
You pray to God that you awake you pray that it's a dream..

While in your sleep there's no control, no secrets can you keep
The demons find out everything so many nightmares buried deep,
Such horrors leave you feeling cold, you feel you've been abused
You hope someday you'll sleep in peace instead you feel confused..

What reason do these demons have, to claw inside your brain
What purpose are they serving why do they still remain,
Perhaps there is a reason, these horrors bother you
Maybe the time has come at last to sort out problems overdue....

Maureen Lewis

Empty Lives

And I wonder in the end, just who this sacrifice will mend
Or make the world a better place
The moon and stars, sea and sand change face
And finally the pain forsake, when all too soon God's calling take

And whose destructive right by pressure brought our ending
That in the flush of youth, turned stubborn and unbending
Will remember later yet, in sadder thoughts unmended

As years unfold with tests and trials
The longing for our unborn child
By now the culprits long forgot the reasons for their treacherous plots
And yet upon their selfish whims, wreaked havoc to our dearest dreams
And lightly take the pain they caused,
For righteous deed and noble cause
And settle back in easy guise, content their changing of our lives
And never even realize, the ever present pain disguised
of two hearts living empty lives.

S. Talbot

False Dreams And Future Hopes

Looking back upon the sixties when I was just a lad,
I recall sourly complaining about the daily chores I had,
Up at four to herd the cows in for the morning milking,
How soon could I escape, seemed to be what I was thinking.

An address at school by a military man extolling the virtues of the force,
I thought after all those early mornings the army couldn't be much worse,
His words they would not leave me as I wandered round the town,
I walked into the recruiting office and swore to serve the crown.

At fifteen years I left my home to train in the art of war,
I was taught how to handle firearms and what soldiers used them for,
After long days on the training field and the lads had gone to bed,
I got to thinking about my dad and the harsh words we both had said.

Now twenty-five years later having seen what I have seen,
Ireland tours, Desert Storm, the battle for Goose Green,
Now my time is served, I've settled with a family of my own,
Having told them of my service days, I hope they stay close to home.

Peter Barber

Pretty

I'm sorry to say
I don't feel pretty today.
You will have to forgive me
For the way that I look,
But I don't feel pretty today.

Despite what I say,
Despite what I do,
It doesn't reflect what I think of you.

It's just that today
I don't feel right.
I don't want to pretty myself up
Just so that someone can look at me and judge me.

Today I am going to be me.
And,
I don't feel pretty today.

Avril White

Not My Time

You came to me, one winter's night
You were standing by a golden gate
Your aura glittered, in Christmas lights
I saw freesias, that smelt of garden fetes
You beckoned me, with open arms
I heard your voice, you called my name
The sky was filled with angels singing
I danced to their music until I was near
You were one side, I the other
With out stretched hand, you welcomed me
I could not go, at least not yet
It was not my time, on that winter's night
To pass through the golden gates

C. Abbott

Silhouette Soul

Slowly dripping upon a bitter dream,
my shadow of life altogether lost.
Surrounded by the wall of my own scream.
I'm seeking fulfilment, but at what cost?
A massing of fears, a parade of tears,
a lonely traveller in desolation;
and in the soul are shadows that can pierce
a segmented heart during creation.
In total abandon, love is stolen
by God's ignorant, glacial cold, heaven.
A resourceful man will believe, toil and
eventually die; debts with God, even.
    Every man needs a goal to guide his life
    but God will steal love, leaving only strife.

Lee M. Horsted

The Lost Child

In the dark stillness of the night,
subconscious thoughts alight,
the child from within ventures out to play,
enacting the fantasies not allowed
as an adult by day.

In the safe secrecy of the mind,
adventurously searching to find,
the child that never was, why?
Always comes the answer because.

Along flower-filled meadows
and streams flowing free,
skipping and hopping, laughing with glee,
this is how it should be.

Consciousness is on the verge,
just as another fantasy is about to emerge,
the child with a smile retreats once more,
knowing this subconscious friend
has many more delights in store.

Michelle Bromley-Davies

Broken Memories

The sun, the moon, the stars that shine,
the hearts of love that flicker in time.
But the memories of hatred, battered our souls
replaced by the laughter, the love and the joy.

The summer, the winter, the autumn and spring
they're the seasons to remember, throughout eternity.
The leaves that fall, the sun that shines,
the wetness of rain, the coldness of wind,
these feelings they quiver the love that's inside
to remember you always towards the back of my mind.

The sea a deep blue, the clouds of pure white,
the silence of darkness, the love that's confessed,
where together our souls, together as two,
with no evil to split us, no fear to harm us,
just the love from one another
so battered but new!

Samantha Downs

Lands End - The Last Labyrinth

Months have passed and I return again
to this place of mystery and enchantment.
The Sunken City calls out to me,
Shark Fin Rock and lapping waves
had swallowed all my memories.

Yet as I stand and gaze afar,
the warm breeze swirls around my face.
I wish I could have lived in the days of
King Arthur and his faithful followers.
It's hard to imagine the sea so wild,
why, oh why, erode away such beauty.

I will return and take my pose,
if only to imagine the laughter,
the cries and the pain.
Something stops me from reaching out
to solve the mystery of the storm
on a dark winter's night!

Sandra Bromley

Runaway

I am a runaway
I have nowhere to hide
Someone is out there hunting me down
I cry, I cry for food and money
But there is never any money to spare
I am a runaway, running from trouble
I have been homeless for almost a year
Just sleeping rough, winter's on its way
The bus shelter welcomes me home again
As elderly lady walks my way
With food and blankets to brighten this cold winter's day
The people who walk by, take a look at my face,
They turn and walk on with looks of disgrace
They see a dirty young girl
But it's not me that they see
For I am a spirit that longs to be free

Kerry Read

Go, Fly With The Winged Ones

Go fly with the winged ones, away from heartless gravity,
fly with the winged ones, now thou can be so free,
go fly o'er the oceans, above every sea,
soar o'er all the mountains, lose this terrible reality.

Go fly with the winged ones, thy words once heavy as lead,
now all tongues are still, all blood has been bled,
go fly into eternity, away this tortured second,
fly as with a winged ones, as from this earthly prison abscond.

Go fly with the winged ones, and dream with the angels,
fly with the winged ones, sleep with the gods,
go fly with the thoughtless, no more strife, hopes forlorn,
fly at peace, dear peace with the martyrs,
and the heroes who are waiting to be born.

Terry Goodman

Homage To Rene

He walked silently down the aisle
Lightly touching each pew as he passed
In tacit acknowledgement of their solidity
In the midst of his own unreality.

No black clothes,
No flowers, she had said
But his soul cried out for sackcloth and ashes
And a flower to take her place.

Just so had he waited for her as a bridegroom.
It had rained
But the radiance of the day had been all around.
Now he waited for her, alone,
And the sun shone on her stark coffin.

Irene Lewis

Winter Love

Oh this cold Winter's morn,
Jack's fingers bite deep
The countryside silent, a shroud, complete.
The polo sun, rides its high peak,
Hardly touching gaunt trees around.
Friend Robin she flutters, from branch to branch,
Cars splutter past with cold.
For a long time now my heart's been still
Silent, as the stream, its state turned to ice
But now -
The sun has shone,
The ice melted,
The river runs fast,
Trees whisper softly encouraging words
Love is bound once more.

Georgina Rook

He Cares For Us

God cares for us, it's wonderful. He really loves us all.
If only we would take time off and listen to His call
The flowers, birds, and butterflies, all radiant and gay
The corn, the veg, the beast and fish, to feed us day by day
But none of this could e'er exist without sunshine, snow or rain
So all we do without His help would sadly be in vain
Our duty so we understand's to help all folk in poorer lands
So fellowship we need to share to really show Him that we care
Our mission is to share our wealth
Help sad and sick folk back to health
All He asks of us is this
Love your neighbour as yourself
For others we must learn to pray
For all is freely given if we respond and do His will
Our reward will be in Heaven

Kathleen Heyden Dale

Feeling Is Believing

A thick blanket above my head
Three hours or so until I lie in bed.
A deep blue sea up there miles away from the eye.
Nothing but a lonely starless sky.
Clouds cover what distance reveals.
Time lingers on but nothing heals.
Pain burns inside my chest.
For the first time I put a loved one to rest.
I said my prayers and hoped all was well.
When I see him next only time will tell.
I said goodbye on that cold rainy day
I heard myself speak what I thought I'd never say.
I felt the tears slowly run down my face.
How I needed that warm embrace,
For someone to tell me it was all a bad dream.
I'd wake up in a minute, that's what it did seem.
When I'd wake up I'd let out an almighty sigh
Instead of always wondering and asking "Why?"

Tina Rosemary Abbott

Childhood Memories

I think back to when I was young,
Of happy days, and lots of sun.
Of holidays beside the sea,
Harvest time, then home for tea.
Paddling in water, ever so deep,
Bursting tar bubbles with our bare feet.
School days, and chewing gum,
Puzzling over very hard sums.
Special days, and happy hours,
Memories that will always be ours.
Now that we are adults grown,
How the years seem to have flown.
So children who are out at play,
They are your memories for another day.
It is so soon you will be a man,
Enjoy the time now while you can.
Time goes so fast, come what may,
Oh! Childhood, those halcyon days.

Isabella Muir Ward

The Boy Of My Dreams

Loving me, loving you
Good times, bad times, the whole day through
Thinking you're my number one
But now I can see how I was wrong
Oh how embarrassed and stupid I feel
To think our love was oh so real
Now I wish the heartache would go away
The pain I feel every day
As my confidence began to die
My friends comforted me, I began to cry
Remembering all the pain I'd been through
Just wondering what to do
But though we're forever apart
I'll always know you'll be in my heart . . .

Katy Holdway

The Stray

I am only a dog and I have no home
nowhere to go, only the streets to room
It is terribly cold and wet outside.
But here is a church with doors open wide.
Oh it is lovely and warm and nice in here
And today our Saviour's birthday is here
He would not leave me to lie in the snow
And I am sure he would find me somewhere to go
He would love me with my doggie charms
And I know he would gather me up as his arms
I am only a dog but this I know
If Jesus had only been my boss
I would have followed him right to the cross

Iris Lloyd

Sister - Don't Go

How can I concentrate on my work
While you in foreign parts do shirk
Treading the decks of unsafe ferry
Drinking the wine and making merry

If tragedy occurs, in the water you tip
Hang on to the captain, go down with the ship
Both arms round his neck as you make your last wishes
Float gently away as food for the fishes

Will you bring a rich frenchman back home for me
With a hint of strong garlic and whiff of the sea
An enormous yacht with a sunbathing deck
And string of french onions hung round his neck

Do you ever give your sister a second thought
As you fill your trolley with good things bought,
Pate, brie, croissants for you and your hubby
Do you realize these things will just make you tubby
I have perhaps been a bit over zealous
But the truth is, I confess I am jealous

Kay Kidd

Mum's Birthday

Dear Mother listen to what I say
I know I hurt you in the past
And I wish you all the best on your birthday
I know now, life goes so fast
You always had life so hard
Now it's time for the laughter
But never let down your guard
That's why I love you dear Mother
As my crimes got worse and worse
You kept your head held high
You never showed me any remorse
Not even when I said goodbye
I will always be your son
No matter how far we are apart
Now this is your time for fun
And you will always be in my heart

Andrew Ian Marshall

My Number One

There's lots of teddies everywhere.
Some have patches, some have no hair.
But one is missing, where has he gone
He's my favourite, my number one.
Last time I looked he was there
Sitting in his favourite chair.
I've looked in the cupboard and under the bed
I wished he'd told me, I wished he'd said.
It's very lonely without him here.
He's such a lovely little bear
With nice soft fur, and cuddly too
Oh! Number one I do miss you.
What shall I do at the end of the day?
Why? Dear teddy did you go away?
What shall I do when I go to bed
And you're not on the pillow next to my head?
But listen! What's that, did I hear someone call?
Yes it's teddy, he's not lost at all.
He's been helping mommy make the tea
Now we're back together again, just him and me.

Iris Taylor

Since You Left

Since you left,
Such a longed for peace pervades
These now neat rooms.
And where your music blazed
About the halls
The strident bells have ceased
Their day-long wrangling in my brain.
And stereophonic bedlam sleeps,
Silent under plastic domes.
Why then this ill-content -
Wishing you near?
You should be here.
Blasting these walls again with your music -
Causing a chaos in the rooms.

Amelia Graves

More Or Less

Houses stand empty—yet people have none,
We're deep in recession, the good times have gone,
Factories silent, machines stand and rust,
Once clamouring iron—now cobwebs and dust,
Shop doorways—night dwellings for souls nurtured weak,
The great dream has vanished—a future so bleak,
Visions of Eden lie fallow and staid,
The spirit endures though all hope starts to fade,
People go hungry while food goes to waste,
Excuse the unfortunates, save for those graced,
Suffer those meekly in these times of need,
While the prosperous and soulless rake in all their greed
Armageddon looms closer, Noah waits to return,
All's equal in Heaven, all want in Hell burn.

Russell Duncan Johnson

My Soul Cries Out To Thee

My soul cries out to thee
For succour in this hour of need
I see the pale shades drift
In the grayness
Of the wasteland.
And Sorrow
Fills my heart.
Pain stirs in my soul.
And I feel their loneliness
Their sadness, their sorrow.
They wander down the dusty paths
Meandering through the dark
Roaming in the maze
Of long dingy alleys.
And Sorrow
Fills my heart.
Pain stirs in my soul.
Their darkened eyes are glazed
Looking for the way with unseeing gaze
Moving with the hopelessness of the lost.

Linda Morgan

For Being Nearly There

Everything and nothing, all in one go
Isolated, desolate, with little to show
Mind ill at ease, no laughter, no pain
So confused, so alone, yet totally sane.

On the outside looking in, the eyes cannot see
A soul at the doorway, so totally free
Wings spread outwards, to the arms open wide
Nobody noticing that soul as he hides

How bad would they feel, with their guilt and their fear
That shell gone forever, "but we wanted him here"
Too late to say, too late to pray
The target shot down, that contest won
For the winners your prize...for I have none

The scales of life tilting to and fro
Ever harder they swing, they just won't let go
'Til that fateful day the balance tips
Kiss the soul goodbye upon his lips.

Paul Davis

Summer Rain

Summer rain—Like translucent mist falling upon your face—
  Like a fleeting kiss
  So soft, so gentle, it caresses the blossoms, the grass and
  freshens the air.
  Inducing aromatic fragrance that you did not know was there.

Summer rain—Lifting your spirits with its wispy spray
  Some magic in its silent sound
  Seeping in to the gasping ground.

Summer rain—Making the world green again!

Barbara Hill

Somewhere To Stay

We live out our lives on the streets everyday,
  It wasn't always like this, times were good, we just lost our way.
We've nowhere to go, we're homeless you see,
  We go to the mission where the meals are free.
These people keep us together in body and soul,
  Unfortunately we're not eligible for the dole.
I'd like to sleep in a bed again,
  But my plot's out in the wind and rain.
We carry our things and they weigh us down,
  But nobody cares, we're not known in this town.
Winter is coming and the days grow short,
  My health is ailing, and my nerves are fraught.
All I want is a job with pay,
  But there's a catch, to get a job, I need somewhere to stay.

J. K. Raynor

Euthanasia Please!

I've really had enough of life and all this pain!
I'd never want to go through it all again!
It's time, I think, to call a halt, - call it a day,
And find a way to drawn the thoughts - wash tears away.
And who could say my way is wrong or judge my acts
When I'm the one who feels the hurt and knows the facts?
And why should I, who's hardly known a minute's peace,
Go on and on in living hell when there's release?

So, I'll decide the time, the place and do the deed,
And, just this once, I'll listen to my inner heed.
For peace is all, and nothingness is my desire,
A welcome rest and no more pain of which I tire.
And who would, in the end, feel any loss?
For life goes on, a lighter weight with one less cross
And one less beating heart, - the burden lifts
While sounds of time continue on tide's endless shifts.

The sun will rise and set, the seasons change
And life and death are never far out or our range;
Despair is always there, upon life's cruel shore
And I would lay it down forevermore!

Wendy P. Frost

In Pensive Mood

When evening falls and stars emerge
From out the misty clouds,
I slowly amble to my couch
Where solitude descends.

Alone in peace, whilst silence falls
And night is now subdued,
There with my thoughts I lie awake -
Till morn comes crawling through -
And slowly leaves my other world
Which held my thoughts of you.

So now comes dawn - then also fact
So bitter, oh so cruel!
And I once more find you are gone
And then appears my act!

Oh sweet pretence, oh solitude!
A mixture so immense, no one knows the torrent
Which leaves me cold and tense.

So take advice from one who's learned - from one who didn't know,
Appreciate what one has known -
For you may find as time may go that you are quite alone.

Ann W. Wilson

Michael

There is laughter; there is fun;
But where is the calmed-worth-sea on the sand-drift shore?

Without you Toujours:
Je ne fais que travailler, courir.

As a mirage; others feel the Romantic-toss,
... my thoughts are as snow-flakes on the streams.

Blue skies; blue moons; blue roses blown-too-soon.
What is a brown diamond? What is a Pear?
Your aura over me; days silver tinted;
Gold is your lair.

The wandering-web of the Snake round the Cat;
Who cannot resist the iridescent;
Drossed rain-drops-in-mist . . . Lovers entanglement.

Let the squirrel forage in his Autumn-leafed-days,
Sleep-sweet until the Spring's canopied-aviary

This gift where the winged-birds fly,
Reflection in deep pools and sigh.

Follow the molluscan-spin; plus and minus magnetism,;
Six and one nucleus makes Magic-seven;
Therein my Love and your interrestial intuition.

Constance Noy

Looking To The Stars

The Stars, so countless in their number.
Hundreds of millions.
Like points of light.
Travelling through space and time.
All in a vast dance of galaxies and super novas.
So I sit and look at the night sky.
And begin to wonder.
Is there anybody doing the same?
Is there anybody thinking the same?
Just imagine, for one moment.
Imagine the possibly that there is something other than us.
Looking out at the night sky and thinking.
What would it be like, to be confronted with the other?
Face to face, with something unbelievably alien.
Something that is completely divorced from our world....
I look up at the night sky.
There look! A shooting star.
I make a wish.

Richard Norman Craig

You

You are my compass on a misty heath.
You are my rainbow's crock of gold.
You are the shelter I stand beneath.
You are the coat to keep out the cold.

You are my left and you are my right
My north, south, east, and west.
You take my dull days - and make them bright.
You take the worst of me - and make it best.

You are my last thought when the day is old,
My first thought at the morning's light.
You are my wrong and right - my hot, my cold.
You are my morning, noon and night.

You are my future and you are my past,
My summer, winter, autumn, spring,
You are the first things and the last.
You are my all - you are my everything.

Dorothy Dobbins

Eternal Faith

As I walked along life's lonely road,
A life of emptiness I foretold,
When suddenly, my hand was touched,
And saw the Lord, and gladly clutched,
"Do not despair", the Lord did say!
He cares for all, each passing day,
Whilst on this earth, we must do our best,
To earn everlasting eternal rest
Now I awake with gladness in my heart,
As His love for us will never depart.

E. J. Cranfield

To Nature

Tarry awhile, be still, there's time enough
For all the plots and schemes, the plans.
For now, be still, give to the heart its own
Quietude, peace, love, and look beyond
The hustle of the day to Nature: God's great gift
To all; wherein the pastures green,
The waters still, hills, valleys, plains,
Sheep calmly grazing, lambs at play,
Their shepherd watching by. Be still, and gaze.
And in this quiet place of hallowed peace,
Let the spirit soar, the heart rejoice,
That there is still, amid life's frenzied rush,
A place, a country spot, where we can go
And bide awhile, amid God's simple naturalness,
And feel His very presence in our souls.
Time enough for rushing headlong to the grave!
Then make of this precious hour a time
For contemplating nature, and, in so doing,
For being close to God . . . for He is there.

Elizabeth Marshall

Autumn Leaves In The City

Each year in spring buds lift their eyes,
Awakening leaves to the open skies,
From shining green they slowly go
To the golden glints of an autumn show.

Russet, gold and tawny brown,
The autumn leaves come tumbling down
To decorate the city street,
Walked upon by countless feet

Unheeding eyes just pass them by,
Allowed for weeks thereon to lie,
Their colour dimmed by mud and slime,
A coating of the city's grime.

Above them reaching to the skies
The stark bare arms of trees arise,
Each with a beauty of its own,
Outlined against the heavenly dome.

The winter's come, 'tis time to rest,
Ignore the city's endless quest,
Sleep and dream of next year's glory,
Repeating nature's endless story.

Eva Dickson

My Thoughts Of Spring

The summer is fading fast
we always know it can't even last
It's winter we must learn to bear
Nothing can stop it, it's always here

Now if you can forget winter days
And think of spring in its many ways
If you do this during winter I'm sure
Spring will bring pleasure more and more

Now that spring is here again
Flowers are blooming even in rain
Snowdrops are showing their pretty heads
Bulbs are coming up in their beds

Other things happen to our delight
The sun shines more the nights are bright
So forget about winter and all its trials
And remember the things which bring out smiles

Spring is a time of year of hope for some
Who thought—by now their time was done
But when the flowers spring up again
Me think we also can not be living in vain

Kay Taylor

Monet's Garden In Springtime

Monet's garden in Springtime
   Is prettiness beyond compare,
As apple-blossom feathers the air,
   And colours splash everywhere.

It is hard to paint in words,
   Images of this jewel-place,
Where a fine man and God together,
   Through hard work have left their trace.

The pink and turquoise farmhouse
   Stands safely nestled and secure,
Framed by joyous, bright-coloured borders
   As each visitor makes his tour.

Caressing waiting water's edge,
   Weeping willows drop golden tears,
Beckoning beside silent sedge,
   The first, fresh lilies to appear.

Waiting till with Summer air,
   Lily-pads on water so clear,
Cradle within their lush, leafy palms,
   Those radiant blush-pink spears.

Sylvia Sherriff

Christmas Behold

Christmas time is of one wish.
Look at the faces of joy which behold it.
Giving is a gift and so is the opening of it.
Remember the birth and think of the new.
Look to the past, remember the old.
A star is a sparkling on a tree
Look ahead, what do we see?
Angel of heaven shines over thee.
With wings of prayers behold thee.
One dove brings us peace, remember
Those and give them a wish forever
And for now.
Family is strong and will always be
Caring for you and me.

M. Jackson

A Fishy Tale

One night I had a dream
I dreamt I saw a light
a light so bright it was on my mind
if only I could follow; what would I find?
twinkle, shining it was so far
now I know it must be a star,
I wanted to fly, oh my, oh my
up up so high, high in the sky.
But then again if I could fly
I would ask myself "why"?
because I was not meant to be
you see; I'm a fish and live in the sea.

R. Maskill

Midnight Sun At Tromso

The view atop of Tromso
Is headier far than wine:
This peak, the goal of travellers,
Is the pinnacle of desire.

The Sami in their chilly tent
Sleep oblivious of the scene -
Houses scattered like ladybirds
On a water lily leaf.

Then down in the city's silent streets
Uncurtained the houses stand,
And the lone nightworker pedals home -
Is it really all a trance?

And now from the plane we marvel
At the dazzling glare of the sun
On the snow and the cliffs and the waters,
Something never to be outshone.

Jane Flatley

Dream Of The Ancient Astronaut

You alone I long to meet
Flying down the moon-filled street
Of cold white memory.
Your voice alone I long to hear
Calling me and drawing near
From out eternity.

With anguish in my failing heart
I pushed the windless night apart
To search among the stars,
But there I found no whisperings stray,
No message from the Milky Way
Nor word of you from Mars.

I launched you free from Earth's constraint
To beat a trail and navigate
The timeless space above.
Please call me clear and tell me true
Are others there as well as you
My Satellite, my love.

Pamela Tulk-Hart

If Only We Could

If we could think of others as we would wish them to think of us,
What a happier place this world would be, for each and all of us.
If we could smile or nod our heads as down the street we go,
Then this old world would be filled with sunshine,
come rain or sleet or snow.
If we could see people as they are instead of their race or creed,
we would find this world a happy place.
If only we could indeed.

Gwen Iles

Words Of A Sardonic Nomad

As spiders settle on my face
I return to an empty place
I scratch my eyes to make them bleed
I search for the hunger that I need
I turn and watch the sparrows fly
I sit and watch the day pass by
And as the night returns again
I know I'll never be insane
They think they love but they just breed
Their art is blinded with their greed
I know the river never flowed
I was king and then it showed
I know there's money in my purse
I have to steal 'cause it's a curse
I fought for things I don't believe
And as I think my shoulders heave
With the weight inside my head
I comfort the empty dead
And then I leave.

Carolyn Salter

Perfection

Do you look for perfection, in every thing you do?
And expect other folk to feel the same as you
It's great to set your standards high
You've tried so hard and strived
Against injustice in the world
That in your mind survive
People are all different, that's how God made us all
So don't give up, when you look around
And see, how their standards fall!
You may grieve and worry, over things you cannot change
But who are we, to try someone's life to re-arrange
So when you feel that people, you held high in your esteem
Have let you down so badly, think of it as a dream
For dreams can be so pleasant, or frightening or sad
And people are the same, though in different cloaks we clad
Then when the cloaks are cast aside, disappointed then are we!
To see them not as we would like, but as they wish to be
So set your standards high, but remember one thing do
You cannot change the world alone, however you may try to!

Rosina Davidson

The Spectre

From the darkness of the night
The pale dawn broke with baleful light
and by my bed
I saw with fearful gaze
A spectre through the misty rays
and in his hand a book
bound with red and gold
Inscribed across in words of black
God's inventory of the old
tremulously haltingly with words of dread
I spoke, Grey Phantom whence have you come and why?
The answer swift, all men must die
In this tome God's will be done
And whom God loves he now wants back
The ghostly fingers took my hand
Leading me gently, softly from this land.
One last look I turned my head
to see calm peaceful as asleep
my earthly shell upon the bed.

Ron Challoner

The Office

Monday through Friday all day long
The phones and the fax keep on and on.
Brokers, solicitors and applicants too
Together with branches, scream 'What can you do?'
Chase up the reference, we must have an offer.
Completion is set for the day after tomorrow.
Pink files are stacked from floor to the ceiling,
Everyone 'Urgent' it sends our heads reeling.
We spend so much time just trying to placate,
There isn't a chance for 'Notepad' to up-date.
so please, lend a hand and phone after one.
Give us a chance to get some work done.
Now, if it's urgent and the fax won't suffice
Then give us a call, but remember, 'BE NICE'.

J. A. Stacey

The Barn Owl

In the corner of a cornfield, neglect to years of time and strife,
Stands a barn, steeped in history, a monument to bygone life.
Rotting timbers, twisted iron, as time its ugly head does rear,
Silhouetted on the horizon, at dusk as through the haze appears.
From the barn, a ghostly canopy floats through the ink-blue skies,
Silently with outstretched talons, as it a small vole spies,
Somersaulting falls to earth, its barbed feathered wings out wide,
Showing off soft downy feathers, with them his victim hide,
Silently as it landed, back into the starlit night,
Passes its catch from claw to beak, as in a flash of light,
Along the hedge-line of a field, pausing on a gate nearby,
Back into the secluded retreat, on rotting timbers up high,
Skilfully with amazing accuracy, in the pitch-dark dusty roof,
Returns the barn-owl complete with catch, sits proudly and aloof.

Veronica Tilbury

The Carousel

Spinning round the carousel goes, horses
and swans move in the light, Boats that are
rocking to and fro, people laughing with delight,
Swings of garish gold and red, with tassels of a
golden thread, You hold on tight and pull the cord,
and swing through the night of your own accord.

The helter skelter's busy too, mats gliding to the
ground, Lights and music blazing out, shouts and
laughter all around, Dodgem cars that bump and
spark, weaving to and fro, The Big Dipper and the
Whip, everyone wants "a go."

Girls in their best dresses, all having lots of fun, Sticky
sticks of candy floss, toffee apples or a bun, The Big
Wheel is so full of lights of various coloured hue, Seats full
of courting couples, while other's wait in a queue.

It only comes but once a year, bringing the magic to
our town, With side-shows and the Carousel, once
gone, no magic around.

C. Snowden

A Timeless Beauty

In nineteen hundred and seventeen when you were born
A lovely babe soft and warm
A chosen child, a wanted daughter
A wonderful mother no one could falter
Amidst the hardships of life you came
But still you loved life all the same
Many tears have left your sad eyes
Of loved ones and friends when they've said their goodbyes
Eight children you bore to love, to cherish
Forever in your heart, yet never to perish
God joined you in marriage, till death do us part
And when our dad left us, it broke your sad heart
But through all the pains of life's ups and downs
You've come through it all, happy as a clown
But now you have gone, my heart it is aching
To turn back the clock is not in the making
So for now, for me, this is just a short break
For I know in my heart we'll meet at heaven's gate.

Patricia Ann Norfleet

The Farmhand's Daughter 1952

My childhood meant to me,
Sitting on my daddy's knee
When he could spare the time.

A farmhand dad who played piano on a sabbath night
whilst neighbours came and sang by warm fire and
flickering glow of pale gas-light.
Aunt May got out the rubbing board and Jill
could play the spoons,
Mum's saucepan lids and comb "kazoos" accompanied the tunes.
Stone-flagged scrubbed farmhouse kitchen floor
Dad's ex-army great coat on the back of the old stairs door,
Scrubbed white farmhouse table on oak legs carved and black
Standing boldly astride our worn out coconut mat.
Billy Paver and Alan Quinn sang, mostly as duet,
Oh those happy Sunday nights I never will forget.
Then dad would play that same sad melody
in the evening glow.
I'd cry, with a mouthful of home-baked scone,
and off to bed I'd go.

C. D. House

Painting By Numbers

And God said, "Let there be light".
Then on earth's canvas He painted it white.
The patchwork of fields, running corduroy brown,
Pale green of spring, ripe corn's golden crown.
Skies stretching forever, of celestial blue,
Silver rain, then God's promise arched, in rainbow hue.
Pale pink of blossom, and sunsets a-flame,
Snowdrops and crocus the New Year proclaim.
The paleness of morning, the dusk before night,
Sunshine's glowing orange, the spark of starlight.
Then seven days after the work God began,
He finished the canvas, and painted in — Man.

J. A. Meering

Crash Course In Brain Surgery

Open up your mind
to see what you can find
I found a dream
a dream unseen
trapped in the realms of my brain
a dream that pours on me like rain

I can't feel, it's not me
I take two sugars in my tea
it shows someone I love, it's you
maybe you could love me too

I don't know if this can be
I lost my head and I can't see
pelican crossings are all that we need
all our dreams need to cross and be freed
the eye is our sin
please close your eyes and let me in

Kriss Fotheringham

Romance

Last night we danced—an ancient tribal ritual
Of innocence and comedy—and my eyes were enraptured
With the varying closeness of your smile;
It was beaming real vitality, and the silence of ourselves
Pealed forth in muffled pounding sounds
Surrounding us, serenading the stars, through
The secret shining cracks in the bridge above our heads.
And the stars tried hard to match the brightness
Of your eyes—something life endowed and only love allowed.
Gallant, victorious, you touched me briefly
With an urgent whisper, elevating me as it tingled
And rang in my reddened ears. The performance
Of piercing adoration (common sense in the icy air)
Was hidden. Careless, I smiled at our perfect isolation,
And wallowed in the molten warmth of waves
Of laughter, and romance.

Roslyn J. Nisbet

Expectations

I was strolling along the road one day,
When I met a stranger, going my way,
His features contorted, but handsome too,
Was he from my world or the planet Q?

We chatted together as we went along,
Stopped in at a bar, for a drink and a song,
I admired him, as his thoughts matched mine,
And before we knew, it was well past nine.

He invited me back to his home pad,
But should I go? Was he, 'a bit of a lad?'
He pressed his watch dial, and right on cue,
The space car was outside, - front of the queue!

We were whisked away at the speed of light,
Then beamed up into the spaceship, white,
Welcomed on board, then entered his pad,
Want to know more? - well, you've been had!!

Evelyne A. McMaster

Lioness

Lioness crouched, eyes on prey,
on her silky belly, lay.
A tiny movement with the end of her tail,
and then a swish, a swish a flail.

Slowly raising sandy-hackles,
Dead, dry, grass beneath her crackles.
A tiny motion and ready to spring,
all of a sudden she starts to run
stops in the air.
    The crack of a gun.

Verity Mackenzie

Why I Love My Dog!

When she was a pup it was her eyes that caught me,
now she's grown up its her eyes that taunt me.
She's naughty, devious, calculating and bad,
but equally loveable, cuddly and mad.
She's there when I need her, circling around my feet,
waiting for my command to 'go' or 'retreat'.
She plays in the mud and jumps in the stream,
but when it comes to bath time she's not so keen.
She barks, whines, howls and growls,
and when she's wet she soaks all my towels.
At night she lays with her head on my knee,
waiting and watching for one word from me.
She loves her bones, sweets and toys,
which she spreads around the house making a mess and a noise.
She gets on my nerves when she barks in my ears,
but if anything happened to her there would certainly be tears.
But at the end of the day, what makes it all worthwhile,
is her unconditional love for me that I receive with a smile.
    That's why I love my dog!

Andée Strickland

Hands

Backs against an upright couch,
Side by side we gaze ahead,
Eyes fastened to the opposing wall,
Fingers imperceptibly moving closer,
The feeling of almost but not quite touching.

His fingers inched endlessly towards mine.
Mine stretched and reached longingly yet
Hoping this would never end.
Anticipation postponing fulfilment.

Flesh on flesh, his hand slid into mine,
For one glorious moment, it was enough.
Faces turned, lips seeking,
Soft lip against soft lip,
Straining closer, eyes unfocused.
No need now to see further than the tip of one's nose!

Lorraine Doyle

268

The Better Side Of Life

Why do people of today
React to things in a twisted way
Life is so short it passes fast
Let's all make peace so it may last.

Look at ourselves and try to see
How other people find you and me
Are we a saint, a leading light
Or do we cause trouble in everyone's sight?

Look at ourselves and what do we find
A person of love, gentle and kind
Look at ourselves lest we forget
We all have done something we often regret.

Why not sit back, look and see
What nature does for you and me
We sow the seeds, we reap the corn
So we can have bread for every morn.

Look at ourselves, let's start a new life
It won't come easy we'll all have to strive
To make a better future, let us all try
To bring peace on earth before we must die.

Robert J. Fleming

Summer Joys

Fresh spring days now have gone
Summer's here at last.
Bright new mornings, days are long
And shadows now are cast.

There are poppyheads amongst the corn,
Where pheasants seek their food.
The sun is high, the days are warm
And flowers their scent exude.

The farmer waters, prays for rain
To speed the growth of crops.
But, children on the beach again
Hope the sun will never stop.

Those holidays you hope will never end,
When all your worries disappear.
Children's games of 'Let's Pretend'.
The memories that last all year.

Then it's time to cut the corn.
The birds will soon migrate.
Another season soon will dawn
When for warmer days our hearts will ache.

Gwen Hare

The Sea Shore

White horses ride on the sea so blue
As the waves roll over the sands anew.
Fishing boats sail along for a catch
As the gulls glide along after a snack.

The sun shines brightly from skies clear
There's shoals of fish in the waters near.
Pebbles glisten in the sun
They are round and smooth to sit upon.

The cliffs stand so proud and tall
With wonderful colours we look at with awe.
The white clouds go drifting along
The skylarks are singing their song.

The lifeboat skims along the sea
It's out of practice and nice to see,
As the divers prepare to go into the depths
The lifeguards are watching from the steps.

Children are playing and flying their kites
Water skiers are now in sight.
It's great to see the world go by
Thank God for nature and the reason why.

Aves Swanson

The Eyes Of Inhumanity

I stare at piercing eyes; suffused, soul seeped, pervaded by
an infiltrating gaze of sadness to the infinite of despair.
While twisted and distorted limbs reach out for some small sign of
indicated comfort and affection, silent words conveyed by shaking
movement, churn my stomach through invasion of disturbed emotion.

Little one, I cradle you and grasp your tiny wasted hand.
Your feeble grip conveys the absence of vitality and long gone
sense of any hope, yet eyes bring forth a new-born ray, that
pleads the value of compassion and all veritable deliverances.
Discomforted am I to think that Mankind could do so much more
to heal your suffering, and prevent its evil preface.

Innocent children, victims of man's strange eternal conflict, would that
I could fade beside you, thereby helping to atone for evil blindness.
How despite your torment, and life's breath ebbing slowly away,
can you still smile? As if to say, 'Far better to live on to fight
the replication of all needless suffering'

Therefore this I pledge my little one - God bless, now close your lovely
sad blue eyes, and go to where you're sure to find that cruelty and
pain will be no more the elements of daily bread, and rest
your tiny broken head upon the sweet soft bed of God's discharge.

Graham Jenkins

A Prince Among Men

A little boy waited patiently among the V.I.P.'s
For his parents to return from their "Royal Tour" overseas
There was no kiss or hug for him, after his long wait.
His parents smiled as they passed by to greet Ministers of State

I watched this little boy grow up throughout the following years
The way he smiled to hide his hurt when people joked about his ears
From his birth he'd been told that he'd be king one day
And he was constantly tutored for the part that he must play.

He always put his duty first, as he'd been told he should,
He didn't enjoy the freedom that the poorest of us could
And when he came to manhood he was told he ought to wed
And think of fathering children, to rule in the years ahead.

Eventually he got married to a virgin, fair and shy,
The people were delighted and raved about "Princess Di,"
But I always had misgivings that she wasn't "shy" but "sly"
As she glanced sideways through her lashes, never eye-to-eye.

I admit she was good with children, and in a short space of time,
She provided two new princes to carry on the line.
But now the marriage is over we should remember just one thing.
After years of training from his birth, Charles should be a GREAT King.

Marjorie M. McCafferty

The Last Cut

Rain Forest, cut it down to the nape, forget the red tape.
Would it not be better left to Nature,
Than to scatter the tree, that's there for free.

The birds flying to save their lives matter not, in the weather hot.
It's a task for cash. It's cool for the fool who chops, and hope to
Cut down the Roots of the next. It's in his text to leave nothing to
Swing in. It's the 'In thing'.

They're gonna waste. They have the taste, stealing lives. That's how
Their business thrives. What makes them drive to their Chopping
Crimes? Trees, do they matter if they drop? There are plenty more to
Crop. In the past the jungle was vast. What does it matter - we'll
Scatter some more. There's more money to take on the next Rake.

Is it natural to pain the forest? It's a mad fever, to gain instead
Of maintain. Better left to the Beaver? Chopping's more fun, why
Worry what the Sun will do? They're on the take. Forget the snake.
Forget the bird. They have the herd to wipe all out, without a doubt.
Forget the Plantation. Forget the Wild life. They have the drive to
Wipe out all that's about. Because, pound for Pound, it's the only
Sound to be heard in the Forest.

Ignore the human races. Forget the places. They have to make new Traces.

K. Gharu

269

Dreams

I am young in my dreams,
In my dreams, I am often there,
Country of my birth place,
Vivid, as if it were only yesterday.

I run, through vast ripe cornfields,
Moving, shimmering,
Under haze of sun,
Like sea of melting gold.

I touch the kernels of corn there,
Red poppies, that bloom among,
And cornflowers of deep blue,
With my unplaited hair.

Short, but vivid my dreams are,
On awakening, I lie quite still, then,
I touch my hair to find red poppies,
And cornflowers of blue I have left behind.

Maria Shaw

Inspiration

An interior desire, that has been unleashed.
A notion conceived only by the individual.
An integral sensation of contentment, yet
The inner request to inspect the perception
To the depth of personal appease.
The path lit up, that has lain dormant
In darkness, like a flash of lightning revealing
A splendid scene, through the bleakness.
The confidence to break the chains, and
To have the freedom of expression.

Zara Hayes

Forbidden Reality

You cannot hide from me
We did the deed with a price to pay
You knew the glory with no escape
No use pretending you no longer care
I can see in your eyes you enjoyed the pain
Pleasure can hurt at times
I know because I wrote the book
On how to untangle emotions
From a rotting soul back to reality
The reality of me and you and twenty-four hours

Remember how you cried out my name
Not hers, but mine—*I* am the adored
Damp unison as the clock hit three
I dare you to stare and mock
Unable to meet my shining eyes
Go on, deny everything we created
Hell-bent conscience is disposable
Can you sleep tonight alone, alone
In the emotional hole and hiding place
Where pain was exquisite only yesterday?

Jo Mercer

King Coal

From earth's dark strata one bright vein,
Helped make Great Britain great again,
Salute our forbears, for they found,
Vast stores of wealth, deep in the ground.

In thirty nine, the Nazi threat
Gave coal its sternest trial yet,
The challenge met, coal reigned supreme,
Dispelling Hitler's sordid dream.

When twilights chill, creeps o'er the land,
Finds curtains drawn with careful hand,
With coal-fires charm, we'll never tire
Just watching pictures in the fire.

There's been a price, with miner's fears
With pitheads stark, and widows tears;
Without brave hearts and purpose though
Coal would have stayed way down below.

W. Ledger

The Mermaid's Purse

The night was cruel and hard, no moonlight blessed the bay.
The foaming sea cried Evil songs and stole a man away.
A fisherman frae Doolie Ness, a married man wi'four.
He paid his debt tae death chilled sea and evened up the score.

For, weeks ago, as casting nets, a sea nymph he did catch
And, breaking laws as old as time, her treasures did he snatch.
The mermaid swore an oath of truth, a curse to carry home.
Before the fourth full moon in May the sea would be his tomb.

He garred her tae bite back the charm and leave his soul tae fate,
She shook her head, he knifed her dead, used waist tae tail as bait.
As sunrise gleamed a brand new day he rowed his boat ashore,
And sold his catch in Market square then hid the jewels he bore.

The homestead's door was open wide when he returned tae wife.
He showed her pearls and gems and all and blood upon his knife.
She cried a wail of sorrow then and knew her man was cursed,
For all should know what comes of men who steal the mermaid's purse.

They planned tae leave the village and find themselves a farm,
For in amung the dreels o'muck the curse could do no harm.
Then husband vowed 'just one more tide, I'll swap my nets for plough',
But the sea took him, gems and all, how precious were they now?

C. C. Wilkie

Free

The long shape quivered as from a troubled dream
From which she wakened to a distant sound
Deep within the forest, the call of the wild,
Instantly alert, tail swishing slowly
Body low on the ground.

She knew he was calling her, he of the awesome mane
King of the forest, she his queen.
She had slept long, tardy crossing the plain
Now padding swiftly to their chosen lair
Yet never seeming to lessen the miles between.

She crashed through the forest not heeding those who trembled in her wake
Nor stayed to slake her thirst.
She heard again the roar that called her,
Louder and louder, but the way was long;
Perhaps he would reach her first.

She felt him nuzzle her head, sensed the softness of his tawny mane
As she slept.
The keeper gently stroked her, she who now lay still,
Then quietly left the cage,
"You're free now, old girl," he said, and wept.

Kathleen Hilton-Foord

Regret

She treads the boards, so silently, so quietly and cold
She'd been a famous actress, before she got too old.

Men threw themselves before her, it was a common thing
She had the choice of many, she skipped from whim to whim.

Her acting was perfection, so honest and so true
But the pain that sat within her was known to no more than a few.

Her parents hadn't wanted her, at least that's what she's been told
And because of that she's been reserved, some say, severely cold.

Many men had wanted her and many asked for her hand
But she'd been in no immediate hurry to put on some golden band.

She told herself her life was full, that she needed nothing more
Dismissing many offers as having heard it all before.

Suddenly she was older and her looks had fallen from grace
Old father time had finally crept along and won the important race.

She couldn't stand the loneliness and her eyes often filled with tears
Should she have changed her life, then, back more than 60 years.

And now she treads the boards again, as she used to do before
But as a lonely spirit, who had missed heaven's open door.

Jean Nesbitt

Absent Without Leave

I'd pushed him so far he'd hurled his dentures
they lay broken in two by the dog bowl
He picked them up, sat at the kitchen table
pushing the pieces together
trying to stick them with glue
even then I wouldn't, couldn't, back off
I pushed him still until she stepped between us
and then he left
I skulked before the window, waiting, brooding,
a numb blonde kid close to tears, buck teeth, bony elbows,
what did I know about anything?

All his life he'd chanced, made no enemies,
wasn't interested in gain, made people laugh.
When he was seventeen he decided to enlist, the army.
He begged, pleaded, until his father signed
Posted to Germany he learnt to drive on the Autobahn
had to join up the dots to see; he wasn't suited.
He'd a life, a family of his own, all he wanted.
He wasn't timid - he'd headed for home
Just like that!

Mark Renney

Taken Away

I spy you dawn, chilling and grey,
go away! Don't want to start this day

A day full of mourning, where was the warning?
When he was taken away.

A handsome man, now forever young,
this is for you, my brother, your song to be sung.

A day full of sadness, oh this is madness
he was taken away.

Birthdays and Christmases are hard times ahead,
your niece and nephews, you won't see them wed.

A day full of tears as I long for those years,
he was taken away.

Oh, brother, he was, much more than a friend,
my tears on his chest at the very end.

A sad day for me, did it have to be, him?
That was taken away.

I miss you today as I will tomorrow
I'll remember my love, but not my sorrow.

There was no other like my brother, I like it that way
so come on dusk, if you must. The end of another day.

P. W. Silk

The Eyes Of Alex James

O winter, 'tis season of the darkest nights,
And 'May' often comes with the brightest sights.
I say: "Both will never . . . ever unite . . . ",
But both did: Into the eyes of "Alex James".

Whenever I see stars sparkling in the sky,
And the sun shines early so high . . .
I wonder . . . "Both will never . . . ever be together . . . ",
But they are: Into the eyes of "Alex James".

Sharp are the swords, and are made to fight
Every guilty . . . to defend someone's right.
I wonder: "They never kill if kept into scabbards",
But they do: Into the eye-brows of "Alex James".

Since the Creation begun, man invented legends,
Nymphs . . . Griffins . . . witches amuse and disappear in
seconds.
I say: "Legends are no more existed in this world".
But all are: Into the eyes of "Alex James".

The eyes saw thousands and thousands of eyes,
Each with a story into deep lies.
For all the hard riddles I solved before,
I lost my way . . . into the eyes of "Alex James".

Lina M. El-Hadidi

Black Roses

Dark as the night it rests on my heart,
These feelings of mine are difficult to part,
The happiness I felt with you has gone,
There are plenty men of e.g. Matthew, Mark, Luke and John,
But none do I love, as I love you,
So who wants me? Not you!

I remain in the blackest of moods,
I do not want any kinds of sympathy foods,
I just want your true love,
So white and pure just as heaven above,
Why do you push me away?
When you call me back the very next day.

When you're sorry do not send me a gift,
This is not just a lovers tiff,
It would not be right that's all,
Do not even call,
Although I am willing to sacrifice, just as Moses,
Whatever you do don't send me...
Black Roses

Tanya Amaral

Feelings

I feel like a cat that's been given no milk,
I feel like a chair that has only three legs,
I feel like a star all alone in the night,
Or the only soldier left after the fight.

Not 'till I'm home will the cat get its milk,
Not 'till I'm home will the chair get its leg,
Not 'till I'm home will the stars fill the night,
As for the soldier, he'll be alright.

David Miller

Wooded Vale

As dawn breaks and the sky begins to pale
The sweet tones of the song thrush float down the vale
Chirping Sparrows interrupt the Larks melodic trill
The vale is awash with natures musical thrill
Sycamores on the hillside stand proud and tall
Are filled with the Magpies chattering call
Many shades of green fill the vales expanse
But in the breeze bluebells and buttercups like fairies dance
Mother rabbit ears pricked sniffs the air
Her young at play know it's safe while she's there
The stream leaps and laughs like it were alive
Flowers and insects along its edge thrive
Its surface breaks a trout leaps high
Taking full advantage of a careless Mayfly
The sky grows dark as night time falls
A new song caresses the air as the nightingale calls
A goodnight to all is the message it sends
As in the wooded vale another day ends.

T. M. Oldroyd

An Ode To Us

You are getting old my dear
Yes you are getting old
But gracefully my dear
And nice to behold
Don't begrudge the passing years
For lost youth shed no tears
I too am growing old
The waist is gone, and I am going bald
But as we walk hand in hand
On life's path look behind
To joys and sorrows, hopes and fears
To our beloved children
And their little dears
Our path is short now
Nearing the "Gates"
Theirs in green meadows each to our fates
Yes we are getting old, but thankful to God
For each year He gave us
To have and to hold

N. Wilson

And So It Had To Be

The day had dawned,
And I had felt anxiety,
And before I knew,
He had passed away to eternity,
It was very sudden and I could not cry,
But I prayed beside his body and wished that I could
Die,
The priest with worldly wisdom,
His arms out-stretched to me,
Explained that God had called him,
And so it had to be,
I murmured to myself, why God should this happen to me,
We had been married for so many years, and this is
where he should be,
But silence was the aftermath,
And as I kissed my love,
I realized from now and on,
It was only going to be me,
For the Heavenly Father had called him,
And so it had to be.

Dagmar W. Meyer

Untitled

Shadows form across the sky
Never fade in the Devil's eyes
Darkness falls across the sun
Makes sure the Devil's having fun.
As he rises into the dark
The leaves fall from the trees in the park
As his laugh rings through the peace
The evening fun begins to cease.
The priests say their prayers before going to bed
but even in sleep his footsteps they dread
All this may be a dream
but how real to some it may seem.

Wendy Skilton

Friendship

Friendship is a priceless gift
That cannot be brought or sold
But its value is far greater
Than mountains made out of gold
For gold is cold and lifeless
It can neither see nor hear
And in time of trouble
Its powerless to give us cheer
It has no ears to listen
No heart to understand
It cannot bring you comfort
Or reach out a helping hand
Cannot solve a problem
Or even understand
You don't need diamonds pearls or rubies
No matter what we send
There is nothing stronger
Than a true friend

K. Dean

An Observer

As Protestants and Catholics we look the same
You'd never really guess the game
It's dog eat dog and the hunger grows
Where it'll end only heaven knows

King Billy and the Pope play a part in it all
The originals are dead but
There's murals on the wall
They're secured so fast, never to fall

Time passes by, time goes on
We should remember these people
With a poem or a song.
Secure in the knowledge we are as one.

Ann Kennedy

Recorders

The sparrows chirp from wall and bough
stories of their own, unknown to us, yet how
do they know they will be understood
by their young who are very good?

Messengers of Heaven - if only they could talk
they would translate into English and how we would gawk
to hear of their daily vision from far above our heads.
Of their nearness to their Maker who gives them daily breads.
They'd tell us tales of channels and ships from afar.
They'd tell us of the dawn and the morning and evening star.
They'd tell us of our airways, and of their form of travel
and many tales of other things we might not easily unravel,
They'd tell us of the bright blue sky, and of the morning sun,
They'd tell us how old they were when Life was first begun.
They'd make us theirs and that is true to think quite hard, me and you.
And what do they think we wonder of humans like ourselves
Who chatter wherever we are, and disturb the very elves.
For fairy folk are faithful friends of every bird and mite
And with these thoughts of parting we wish you all
"Goodnight!"

Barbara Fox

A Mother's Love

She was a mother through and through.
She had four children and knew what to do.
She brought them up with love and care.
The best she knew how. But they didn't care.
She worked so hard to help with the home
  But now she's left all alone

Her children don't care, they don't give a damn,
They don't care if their Mum's in a jam.
She did all she could to keep them together.
Her children she loves and always will.
They should remember their Mum for what she did.

She misses them so and feels so sad.
She's the only Mum they'll ever have.
They're all she's got now and forever.
But cheer up, Mum, it's not the end of never.
Think of the good times and not the bad.

Your life's just beginning again at last.
So enjoy what you've got and make it last.
And think of the future and forget the past.
Let the sun shine in your heart, then your life will begin to start.

Margaret Grostate

Untitled

Once more alone, yet without a sigh,
I ponder love, for love once passed me by.
Time, how can I speak of this -
when, with one last kiss
all but memories passed.

And how I love her, yes with all my heart,
for death itself my love could not impart -
this wonder born of life, yes this!
For her in death I still would miss
as life has taught me how.

Could I be happy in such a place,
where I would not see the smile upon her face?
This could not heaven be -
in spite of mountain grandeur, moor or sea,
I should long for other where.

Yes! I would rather have her love
than peace offered from above,
for happiness I have found
in lesser heights, on earth's bleak ground,
with love to keep me there.

Stephen Clark

The Curse Of A.I.D.S.

A.I.D.S., a fatal disease for which there is no cure,
Spreading rapidly throughout the world until man exists no more
As sex is on the screen depicted,
The virus savagely kills the afflicted.
Men boast and brag how many they've done,
But if only they knew what has just begun.
They think it's from Africa, that's all hearsay,
When in reality we're doomed whether we're straight or we're gay.

Our jobs are in jeopardy because of this dilemma,
When all we wanted was some innocent sexual pleasure.
But injecting those drugs proves fatal "No Lie",
They die and get buried can you tell me why?
Has he got it? Has she? Don't they look thin?
They've contracted the virus that kills from within,
He forewarned and told us pestilence would come true,
He sits and he waits there for me and for you.

Celebrities and the like, they're not unique
For them as for us the future looks bleak.
So be cautious, gallant, faithful and true,
And you may prevent this curse coming to you.

Byron Anthony Clarke

Seashore Memories Of A Child By A Parent

Pebbles rolling—waves foaming,
Settling with an effervescent fizz no longer roaming.

Stones of differing colour and shape,
Left stranded by the wave's wake.
Where were they a wave ago? Now in new patterns
Colours, hues of glistening indigo.

Staring unforgivingly—eyes now shining like the
Pebbles before, nestling happily on the seashore.

A void of thought—senses a joy with the noise of
God's motion, smells of salt—nostrils have caught.

Pebbles clicking—in time to a music never written,
Collections of vision forever spitting, splashing across souls
emission

To see, hear and even feel this child of mine,
Is insignificant to the joy of souls combined.

This is now what I see in the pattern,
Of pebbles, glistening wet with God's sweat,
A picture a beautiful picture of you and me.

Michael John Goldsworthy

Wishes

I wish I was not alone on my chair
Saying to myself where are my friends
    I wish they would care
I know I am slow I even dream
But things are not always what they seem

I wish I could be clever like others
My friends my sisters and my brothers
They try to help me but it's all in vain
Their patience with me starts to wane.

I wish I could paint a picture I do try
But when I have thought about it the paint has all gone dry
I wish I could sing in the choir
But I just sing all the wrong notes
It makes the people turn and look at me
So I end up hiding in the coats.

But what are these wishes I say to myself
As I sit and gaze at the books on the shelf.
I can't be as clever as Sally or Brad
Oh dear I must not be sad then as I drift into a trance
Something tells me I do stand a chance.

Margaret Ann Clark

A Pattern Of Life

As I look out beyond the trees
I gaze on fields of bobbing grasses
And in the distance, walkers ease
Their way along the winding passes
Up into the hills I love
To rest awhile on rocks above
Refreshing themselves with food and drink
Maybe giving themselves some time to think
How strange it seems that they're really the same
As the moving specks—distant 'pawns' in a game
Being played below, all around me now
My neighbours seem to be having a row!
While others languish in summer sun
Their efforts at gardening barely begun
Friends meet, and pause to chat awhile
The antics of children making them smile.
Someone is running to catch a bus
A dog running loose is creating a fuss
Leisure and pleasure, trouble and strife
All of us weaving a pattern of life.

Maureen Holland

Untitled

Screaming and shouting will do no good
for it is a torture dwelling within that is tearing you apart.
You have to make it stop though,
You have to make it stop.
I know that this desolate, sunless prison doesn't help,
this humus filled gas shall packed with hungry scavengers
trying to suck and drain the last drop of biotic
energy out of the withering mass of atoms—
I know what it feels like—forever trapped inside yourself
I know the pain, the rushing torrents and whirlpools of emotion.
But somehow you'll find a way out, a way to save yourself.
Until then, my friend, never walk into the sunset
Brightness has always failed me.
I am the Empress of the moon and will seek forever myself and you.

Nvala Graham

The Cathedral

Each step you take has been trod before,
Someone has stood within the door,
Someone's knelt in peace to pray,
Maybe troubled? Who can say,
The history seeping all around
The peace, the quiet, is that a sound?
To visit and be within those walls
Distant dreams, memory recalls,
A monument that's there for all
Sandstone splendour, stained glass tall,
A Cathedral! There long when we're dust,
Recalling history, part of earth's crust.

Lilian Summers

The Cuckoo Clock Salesman

You stood before me with death's garden behind,
Under the peeling plane trees,
Shaded from blistering sun.
Cool breezes swaying our bodies.
Pushing hands. Eyes closed.
But I couldn't discard the self which the world had made;
Couldn't get back to the seed of self-knowledge.
I was trying too hard . . . too hard to let go.
And the accurséd "sorry" slipped out.
I knew not your name.
You knew not mine.
No preconceptions of trivial knowledge.
Let it be. Let it be.
If it is a start, then so be it.
If it is the end, amen.
For the delight and fright
Of that August day
Is forever mine.
Historical isolation belongs to the past.

Mary E. Upson

273

A Plea For Forgiveness

The glow of the early rising sun, through the grey and misty hue,
When crocuses raise up their heads, from the damp sweet morning dew,
Spider webs lying. Like fine silky yarn, The wise owl flying, going back to his barn,
His night's work is over, His feasting is done.
Now it's his turn for sleeping. A new day has begun,
The silence is broken with a cry from the sky, The beating of wings
from a swan flying by.
Somewhere in the distance a cockerel crows, A rabbit hops from
his burrow and sniffs with his nose.
At the sweet smells of nature, A scene to enjoy,
of peace and tranquillity, that man is set to destroy,
What right has man to spoil this earth, to rape and pillage this land,
It was after all, created by, a much more heavenly hand.
A look around us, we need to take, to see what can be done.
If only for our children's sake, now we have had our fun,
In a world of beauty, we have lived, if it changes we are to blame,
Surely our children must have the right, to experience the same.
One Day the world could be a barren place, with no wildlife left to kill,
This may all be done by human hand, and yet may be God's will!

R. L. Sheffield

"Nightflight"

I had a dream last night so real but true you won't believe me but what's new
Two spirits came took me out of sight they said it was time for my nightflight

They showed me death but don't be blue these words of wisdom I say to you
The feelings that I had were of such elation I don't want to go back to the devastation
The peace and happiness was so real a feeling which we'll never feel
Until our time has come to go to the nightflight starlight show
Joy and happiness all around it really made me feel spellbound

So don't feel sad and don't feel blue these words of wisdom I say to you
When your time has come to go to the nightflight starlight show
They brought me back without delay and said sorry it wasn't my time or day
So when you go to sleep tonight please don't be scared of the real "nightflight."

Juliette Pearson

Sunday

Sunday sat in the window, oh what a place to sit
He watched the birds in the hedgerow, sparrows, blackbirds, and bluetits
He wondered in anticipation, just how they would taste
So, down he jumped from the window, and out the back door in great haste

He crept along the pavement, until he reached the bend
He licked his lips with excitement, his body twitched from end to end
He flicked his tail quite madly, the blackbird he could see
You'll do me just right thought Sunday, you will make a lovely tea

The birds they sat there singing, oblivious to what was about
Sunday was ready to spring, when he heard his mistress shout
What are you doing, Sunday, you know you don't catch birds
You are supposed to be a mouser, but that would be absurd

Sunday jumped back up in the window, but he did not wish to sit
To watch the birds in the hedgerow, sparrows, blackbirds and bluetits
Instead he lay in the window, happy to sleep and dream
Of fish, meat and biscuits, and possibly some cream.

Rita Parfitt

Thoughts On Leominster Priory

Seen against the sky, and gently rolling hills,
Presiding over all, stands the great Priory Church of St. Peter and St. Paul.
In the year of Our Lord, six hundred and sixty, Merewahl, an Anglo-Saxon King,
    founded it here, to bring the Christian message.
Until eleven twenty-three, those earlier centuries seem wrapped in mystery.

Nowadays, from far and near, people will come along to see a page in England's history.
Some have an interest in three architectural eras, others to decorated capitals are drawn.
A medieval font, pre-reformation chalice, a Ducking Stool - all have their devotees.
Yet, in sixteen ninety-nine a disastrous fire might well have swept away the well loved
    Priory, as it is to-day.
Saved by Leominster's loyal and generous people, in the South Aisle a tribute
    stands to them, and to their benefactors, Earl Leofric and Prince Kenelm.

After a long and chequered story, an aura of rare tranquillity abides.
Perhaps it is that thirteen centuries of prayer are in the walls, and in the air.
And sometimes, within these graceful naves, it seems that time itself stands
    still, to pay due homage to the King of Kings.

Helen A. B. Bradley

'Coming Home'

In the darkness of the night, a light shines brightly through the mist.
Shimmering and glimmering, flickering and fading, now shining bright again.
As I get nearer, the light shines brightly through the windows of the house.
A warm glow illuminates the building, an aura of anticipation envelopes all.
I open the door and step inside.
Warmth, and smells, and welcome hit me all at once, softly, gently, caressingly.
In the fireplace a log fire burns, hissing and spitting, making
shapes to invite imagination.
A wooden table surrounded by chairs claims the centre of the room.
On that table stands a bowl of steaming stew, a cob of bread, a rich
brown mug of tea and a large deep spoon.
I sit down unhurriedly, basking in the warmth, and the soundless welcome.
I lift the spoon and take the first taste of stew, rolling it around
the taste buds of my soul.
The tea is sweet and strong, the bread is crisp and soft.
There is silence, there is peace, there is no other creature here, no one but me.
And yet I feel the presence of concern and care and love.
Whose hands made the fire, the meal, and the tea, left the welcome,
left the warmth in which I glow?
I am breathless with expectation, I know! I know!
I feel your presence, you are here, I am home! I am home!

Thomas Larvin

Untitled

Men must do what they think is right, and so they go to war and fight
Leaving us here to weep and mourn, and see the sorrow this has borne

Here the grass is quiet and green, depicted in a summer scene
For it no cloak of crimson red, to show where men have fought and bled

Yet our fields have had their day, when men on their pastures lay
While women wept and saw no cause, for power gained by senseless wars

The campaigning politicians cry, of peace, is just an empty lie
For country, rights, religion, creed, one small excuse is all they need

In the end the crave for power, will surely bring our final hour
The bombers up, the ships away, no man will see another day

The button pressed, the danger done, the losers this time, everyone
For people see and yet ignore, the utter hopelessness of war

June Walden

High Time

Times and traditions are passing us by,
and kids of today want a newer high.
Cigarettes and alcohol have become a bore,
young adolescents are searching for more.
Anything explored for a longer lasting thrill,
innocent adventures that eventually kill

Today going out to find the crack has different meaning than it did way back.
Gone are the values of yesteryear, morals and ethics held together by fear.
I wouldn't trade places even if I knew how, for teenage dilemmas as they are now.

Smoking a joint or taking an E, just temporary escape from reality.
Unemployment is high, no jobs to be found,
emotions and dreams crushed into the ground.
Each aspiring to be the best, survival being the ultimate test.
What is the future for the human race, if only the fittest can withstand the pace?

Have we no pity for the feeble and weak,
who comfort themselves with the drugs that they seek?
So many ambitions unjustly shattered, when all these young lives should've mattered.
It's high time society acknowledged the price, protect our young from this deadly vice.

Pearl Martin

Renaissance?

I sometimes sit and contemplate, as the day draws to its close,
What fate has wrought upon me; what might it, yet, impose?
When down memory lane I wander, nostalgic thoughts ever stray,
To much happier days, of my childhood, when life meant just pleasure all day.

Soon, thoughts of my future intrigued me; I would scheme out what I would be
When launched all alone on the merciless waves of a cruel commercial sea.
With what mixed emotions I lived through each phase,
'til my interest flagged with the passing of days;
When all I had strived for seemed done but for nought,
And my ship for success, in dire distress, had berthed; but at the wrong port!

If I took the wrong paths on life's journey, should I lay the blame to fate?
Or to my own miscalculations; to my own lethargic state?
But it's useless to bathe in self pity; to attempt to clutch at a straw,
For, I know, in my past there's no glory, so why dwell on what's gone before?

There's a moral to every story and equally so to this one:
For, it's not where I failed that's important, so much as what's yet to be done!

R. E. Wakefield

Cold Winds

Darkened waters, pearls of blackness
foaming ripples, green with hate.
Birds are sheltering in the hedgerows
from the winds with arctic bite.

Green fields, scattered, different colours,
dark green, light green, gray and dead
gone the wheat and gone the barley,
now they're ploughed and newly fed.

Howling winds and breaking branches,
leaves that make a frightening sound
in the morning, winds abated
scattered debris all around.

Fallen trees, dead and dying
gone to earth by nature's might,
next year, new growth from windblown seed,
warm themselves from newfound light.

John J. Axon

You're Mine

You're my sun, my moon, my stars and sky
my hands, my feet, my laugh and cry
You're my stream, my river, my ocean and sea,
my seed, my stem, my flower and tree

You're my north, my west, my east and south,
my eyes, my ears, my nose, and mouth
You're my good, my bad, my right and wrong,
my mind, my thoughts, my words and song.

You're my second, my minute, my hour and day,
my month, my year, my work and play,
You're my summer, my Autumn
my winter and spring,
My dawn to dusk, my everything

Kirsty McCann

Hamish The Hedgehog

One morning my mate Hamish
Went to cross the road,
His friends were on the other side,
Old Badger, Fox and Toad.

He took a brave step forward,
Then another two or three,
His friends were saying 'Come On Hamish!'
But, Oh No, he didn't see...

That a car was coming for him,
And a lorry after that,
So Hamish, being a hedgehog,
Curled up, and then went Splat.

His friends, they went towards him,
Fox broke down crying, and Toad,
It really is a pity
That he didn't make it across the road.

Kathy Feltham

Sadness

She looked at me, but through me
I saw her pain and felt my own
Her pain became my pain
Sharp . . . like a knife . . . removing
Breath . . . head spinning . . . stomach
Churning . . . setting nerves on edge
I wanted to look away . . . to block
My ears . . . to remove myself . . . but yet
I did not want to look away or block my ears
Or remove myself
To-day she knew . . . so sensible
Yet without sense
No words could comfort or amuse
No actions could console or sway
No amount of love could help
Sometimes we need more than love

Rosemary Hughes

Across The Fields To Alverthorpe

"Let's cross the fields to Alverthorpe"
    my father used to say,
To fish for tiddlers in the dam
    and pick flowers along the way.
So, with net made from a stocking top
    fixed to a length of cane,
We set off in the evening sun
    down the quiet country lane.

Wild flowers in profusion grew
    on those Yorkshire leas,
That lay beside a silver stream
    lined with willow trees.
A little taste of paradise -
    'though we did not know it then,
That fleeting glimpse of heaven on earth
    may not be seen again.
Now, half a century has passed
    and I look back with joy,
To my childhood walks with father
    where he trod as a boy.

Stephanie Newton

Maimed

My heart grows heavy with the ache of injustice,
As people walk by in the streets,
Piteous words on their lips,
Sad looks in their eyes,
I need no pity,
I need acceptance.

Children walk by with frightened expressions
Thinking I'll gobble them up in the night
Unthinking parents shuffle closer
Protecting their children from me, ME!

Whatever did I do to the world
Did I kill the dogs, the cats, the people, the fish or the trees

No,
Not I,
I stayed behind helping people,
Until the day people turned on me.

Accept a criminal with looks on his side,
Reject me, a good man, but maimed,

Forever Maimed

Rachel Martin

Empty Chairs

Empty places empty chairs
Did no one hear the fervent prayers
Out there in the stormy water
Where death stalked amid the slaughter
Where ships were sunk and sailors died
And boys were men and survivors cried
Was it ever a game of trick or treat
And whichever we chose we knew we were beat
Or was it a game of truth and dares
Are they still remembered in their empty chairs

Empty places empty chairs
Did no one hear our desperate prayers
Was God out there in our hour of need
When time would remember this happy breed
Time when we needed Him most of all
As we cornered the Devil in his fiery stall
And the man at the gate now standing so tall
Wrote in the sky in a fleecy white scrawl
The way to Heaven is up the stairs
To the empty places and the empty chairs

F. W. S. Greenway

Ode To My Grandmother

A beautiful woman sat in the sun
The shafts of light broke through the trees
And defined the smooth angels of her calm face,
In her aura the world was at peace

When she looked down at herself I saw the
    pain in her eyes
She would never accept the beauty I had always
    seen in her
I want to tell her now.

Being part of her, does that mean that I too will
Capture her amazing quality in one face?
If so, to me now, time is not the enemy
I hope she understands her beauty.

If everyone could be like her
We would need no healthy body
And even if she can't move
I know she'll walk with me forever.

Kate Ford

Solution

Engulfed by tears which reflect change, deception and pain,
Human nature betrays love and I am falling.
Separated by the vacuum between myself and destiny,
Caught by an anchor which holds me still for a moment
A single moment of hope . . . But I have nothing left.
A wave of unhappiness is destroying me.
No longer forbidden to forget my sorrows
Darkness kills the truth in my life.
I am unable to hear the intake of breath
A barrier of unbearable anguish is pushing me down
And I am falling . . .
My thoughts and dreams are fading.
Time stands still for an eternity.
My eyes are blind to the light, but my mind is opening . . .
Reality dies.

Louise Perry

Our Endangered Elephants

Elephants never forget
We should always be in their debt
For all the suffering and pain
Caused by the human gain

Elephants are gentle giants
Who will became extinct
If we don't buck our ideas up
And stop and think

If we gave a little and save the sights
This will help
To save the elephants plight

So join together and lend a hand
Save these elephants
From a far off land

To cap it all
One lost moan
Please leave the world's elephants alone!

Danielle Henke

My Teapot

Oh my teapot, my teapot, where would I be,
Without you on the table, brewing my tea.
You're always a warm and friendly sight,
First thing in the morning, noon or at night.
Your lid, it does rattle, when you're full up to the top,
When pouring my tea, you don't spill a drop.
If you weren't there to sustain me all thru' the day,
My life would be so dull, at work or at play.
There's no substitute for you, dear teapot, you see,
What's the alternative? - Oh! No! - not coffee.

Jenny Newman

Special Friends

It's oh so good to have dear friends,
Who make the darkness light,
Who offer comfort, with a listening ear,
And say just what seems right.

To know they're there when one needs help,
In times when all seems lost,
They give one hope to carry on,
They give help, that has no cost.

They do not know they mean so much,
It is their natural way,
But to those they have befriended,
They mean more than words can say.

Elizabeth Hardy

Through The Seasons

The autumn is a changing scene
Of red golden and brown
A multi coloured shower of
Leaves falling to the ground

In winter it's the berry bright
While the crocus hugs the ground
Most beauty still lies in wait
For spring to come around

In spring there are blossoms everywhere
Daffodils soon appear
Flowers continually then will grow
To the ending of the year

Summer brings a different view
And the green grass quickly grows
Yet of it all my joy is with
The first bud of the rose

Adela Llewellyn

The Stream

Drip that dreary waiting room, drip,
Home on a rainy afternoon, drip,
Eternal hours in hospital gloom, drip.
Trickle friendly chatting after work, trickle,
Lying outside in a warm, sunny nook, trickle,
Occasional glances over the edge of a book, trickle,
Wading through a cool and bubbly brook, trickle.
Whoosh organizing a yearly vacation, whoosh,
Fun and party animation, whoosh.
Drip taking notes and paying attention, drip,
Interminable dissension, drip,
Monday morning "redemption," drip,
Everlasting fourth dimension!

Irene Dun

The Tramp

What demons could have etched into his face
    such tales of plunder through the passing years?
His eyes, like windows of an empty house,
    are made opaque against the joys or tears
that somewhere back along the road were lost
and he no longer cares about the cost.

The world goes by and he goes by the world,
    tho' some may make enquiry of his health,
but all too well he knows he will be left
    to scavenge in the dustbins for his wealth.
And as he stumbles through this day's charade,
he dimly wonders at decisions made.

There, in the void that once had been a soul,
    so empty that it cannot feel despair,
is it so cold that not one warming spark
    or gleam of light, can find an entry there?
And can there be for that abysmal tomb
a shred of living hope to pierce the gloom?

J. Onslow Johnson

Roses

Beautiful in colour, yet extremely vicious
If held wrong.
They grow, feed, reproduce,
But, don't feel.
"If you don't feel, you can't get hurt!"
Just walked over.

"Look but don't touch!" springs to mind,
Yet, there is always someone,
Someone who knows how to hold you,
And you're cut.
You struggle to survive - then,
Water!
Life to all, but you need more.
"What you need and what you get are two different things!"
So you whither and die in front of your,
Your Axeman.

"Back to the Earth from whence you came."
Not to grow; feed; reproduce;
Just to get trodden on
And to let others feed off you - still.

Allyson Jones

Love After Summer

On this Thursday autumn day
Watching the breeze make the tree branches play
The golden leaves that fall
I hear echo your name
Whistling their shiny dance
Around this lane
Hearing those echoes
Until I get home
Still in my head
When I'm sat alone
But you are everything
That only spring and summer shows
To me you are the prettiest rose
Like a new colour
That nobody else has seen
The most beautiful flower
There has ever been
And your petals hang from you so well
Bringing me love's most sweetest smell.

David Miller

Haunted

The face of a young lad sleeping in a doorway now haunts me.
Travelling home feeling cold after the warmth of the coach,
    I reached the station and was chilled through.
I thought of the lad sleeping in the doorway - I bet he's cold.
I got on the tube, nice and warm and remembered the lad in
    the doorway.
Eventually I reached home - sat round the fire with hot drink
    and toast - I remembered the lad in the doorway.
As I lay in my bed all cosy and snug I remembered the lad in
    the doorway.
Every time I feel warm I think of his face - it haunts me.
Should I have stopped - I had luggage and wanted to get home.
He has no home.
Should I go back and find him - give him money for a coffee
    is that enough, he is one of many.
But his face haunts me.

D. C. Knowler

Why?

Old man,
Did you need to speak to my child of death
Or tell her dancing feet will gradually slow?
Why did you tell her the stars will shine less bright
Or the road stretch out longer than she will want to go?
Old man she could tell from your rheumy eyes
And your clomping stick as you go your solitary way
That you are old, but why tell her that she will bend
With the weight of years, as she dances through her day?

Norah Harding-Owles

One Grey Morning

These feelings are trying to surface
I cannot let them
Their intensity will serve no purpose.

My heart must remain my own
For now and forever
My wish to love makes me feel so alone.

Although abandoned, I will still go on
Effervescing my willingness
With sadness and solitude, let the present be gone.

Helen Kirby

Trust In Love

Your road is long, as is the walk,
You'd cry at night, if not for talk.
For talk you must, and secrets share,
And in the truth, you'll find love there.

A love that shows trust from within,
Does help survive the winter's hymn.
But trust without a love that shines,
Stays within friendship's confines.

Your love does glow, in broad daylight,
And in your heart, it sings at night.
But pain does show, on rocky ground,
Before you start, your heart's decrowned.

Through pain comes love, as such is yours,
And dreams of love such pain does cause.
But such as yours have turned out right,
A handsome day, a beautiful night.

Andrew Rodgers

Lashing Out

Don't smile at me
I'm brittle, ice,
fractured
like old bones piled in an open grave.

Don't caress me
I'm sharp, blades,
rusted
like dead nails pushing into fresh veins.

Don't hold me
I'm poison, acid,
corrosive
like radioactive waste, sick and silent.

Don't love me
I'm anger, war
destroying
like grief-stricken children, lashing out.

Don't know me
I'm lost, madness
bleeding
like animals hunted, surrendering to the blade.

Jackie Gleeson

That Loving Feeling

Love is such a beautiful thing it can bring such
happiness and joy, and when you're in love you
must treasure it for love is not a toy.
It can bring such wonderful pleasure yet at the
same time it may bring pain, though if you try to
measure your love, your love will not remain.
So when you're with your special love just tell
them how you feel, and together you can work
upon your dream of true love coming real.
You see deep down is where true love comes from,
from deep within your heart and you'll know that
if your love is true it will last
when you're near or apart.

Sarah Gilhooly

The Things To Me That Are Beautiful

The things to me that are beautiful
Are God's gifts to us that are free
Like the colour of flowers in the sunshine
And the sound of the open sea
Leaves smouldering in the autumn
And the smell of the earth after rain
The song of the blackbird, the thrush and the lark
The singing of swallows and house martins until dark
A skein of geese crossing the sky
The wind in the trees that are ever so high
And on cold winter evenings the warm fire that glows
A cosy chair and my thoughts of all those.
Mona Tindale

Living

Life goes on, it's never still, there's always something new
sometimes 'tis happy, may even be sad
it might happen to me or to you
some people are laughing - some just moan
others could be crying
a new life is given - a baby is born
and somewhere there's somebody dying!

A child in pain, a woman in love
a man full of hate and remorse
a couple just married to start a new life
a couple just had a divorce!

Yes life is strange, it's hard to survive
to succeed you have got to fight
to be what you are and say what you think
from morning until night!

The days fly by - the years come and go
and so many things we go through -
perhaps one day we will find out why
we live the lives we do?
Janet E. Long

Season's End

He saw nuisance of cold drifting snow
Wished that each winter would hurry and go
Loathed summer sun, the bird song of spring
And the dank rotting leaves that autumn brings

She saw a world that filled her with awe
The rolling surf as it broke on the shore
Blossoming trees of a thousand kinds
And the promise of change as each season unwinds

He needed no one, his goal clearly plain
Reaching and striving for power and gain
Friendships were lost in his bid to succeed
His family resigned to his hunger and greed

She needed 'round her the ones she adored
Each one embraced as they walked through her door
Hopes and dreams shared brought a peaceful content
Memories were cherished of each moment spent

Now he lies neglected, his resting place bare
No one to mourn him and no one to care
And she lies beside him surrounded in love
Covered in flowers by those grieving above
Marjorie Blyth

Reflections

There's a dreary muddy puddle at the bottom of the hill.
The dog laps lustily—the puddle is an oasis of wetness
after a long run.
The children splash life into the puddle—they dare its
depth against their wellies
I watch the drops expand in a myriad of circles
Reflections of trees and sky shudder, stirred
The puddle is a masterpiece of beauty.
Patricia Marshall

Making Mistakes

I've made mistakes in my time
And looking back I must have been blind

At the time you think things will never go right
That the only solution is to stand up and fight

You try hard to discuss it, resolve it with speed
Let me explain I'm sorry, you plead

You're a liar you hear from a so-called friend
Now on acquaintances' words you have to depend

As she calms down and tries to relax
She tends to listen, and collect the facts

The situation calms down and you sigh with relief
The solution is simple and luckily brief

You decide to shake hands and go your own way
Thank God it's over, until the next day

In time realize mistakes make you learn
The key to the answer is stand up and be firm
Diane Casey

Water

Graceful swans swim in the river
Their beauty will be there forever and ever
How peaceful the water and glistening the stream
I've never seen such a beautiful scene.

I like to watch the water rippling on a pool
In a nice gentle breeze on a cool winter's day.

When a steam of water is very near
You can see the plants as the water's so clear.

Better to swim in a gentle pool
Currents and rapids are fit for a fool.

We wouldn't be alive if it wasn't for water, without water
   nothing would matter
So we do need water, the dolphins and us, and water
   plays its part
but someone who's willing to pollute it
Mustn't have a heart

The seas are made for the lovable dolphins
and their friends
And there they stay till everything ends.
D. Sutherland

Saying Goodbye

When you love someone very much
It's hard to say goodbye
The kind of goodbye that's forever
And said when their soul reaches God's sky

For memories will live forever
And great ones fill your mind
These memories you will always cherish
And remember deep down inside

When your days of life on earth are gone
This you will know when you hear God's call
We will all experience this special call
The greatest call of all

We will all feel the warmth of the hands of God
As he takes us under his wing
While our loved ones left kneeling at our graveside below
Songs for our souls they sing

For death is nothing to worry about
It's a reunion of the ones gone before
We will all meet again in heaven one day
When God leads us through the magic door
Evelyn Griffin

Mirror

There is a child in the corner, playing
Laughing, exploring without any worries,
It sits there quietly knowing only joy

There's a child in a playground, running
Running as free as the wind that is blowing,
That is the freedom it knows, and loves

I see a child stumble and fall,
It feels pain so it cries,
Then eventually it stops and smiles again,
But wonders why there had been pain

I see a child crying, weeping and shaking,
There is no one to hold it,
There is no-one to soothe its pain,
It sits there and cries alone in the rain

I look in the mirror,
And it dawns on me,
That the child I see is me

Komal Purwaha

"Strange"

Have you ever wondered what it is about?
I have often, often what? Did you say?
Wondered of course, what else,
Explain I should, if I may.

It is all around us, did you know?
Makes you want to shout,
Shout what? Please yourself,
The time is near for it to show.

Nearer it creeps from left to right,
What? Why? Who cares,
The end is near, what a sight,
Look out, don't fight it, it's hopeless,

It is unbelievable you must agree,
Search your mind if it's still intact,
Will it? Won't it? Why ask me?

Jean Marsden

To My Children

On the morning sun I write your name
As my mind sees your smiling face
And as I work I think of you
Always to me as fresh as dew
And when I reach my lonely bed
Sometimes I write it in tears instead.

But each morning brings re-surging hope
A letter will come to help me cope
What marvel that the purest love
Can be conveyed in an envelope.

Tom Ellis

School's Out

It was near summertime,
an evening calm but cool
about 50 happy girls
come running out of school
some ran and some leapt
like fish in a pool

Away they run with games on their minds
and souls not yet touched by sin

Like sportive deer they walk about
their hats are off and coats undone
as they run, Lord how they shout
and catch the blessed breeze

Leaf after leaf they turn it o'er
not even glanced aside
for peace and soul they read that book
in the golden eventide.

Rebecca Pouncey

Freedom

When I was 15, to me freedom was;

to be able to scribble all over an exam paper,
to be able to burn all the massive thick text books, or
to be able to smash all the bottles of chemicals and watch the lab
blow to smithereens.

Being 25, to me freedom is;

to be able to park my car on a double yellow line,
to trample on a garden full of prized marrows,
to wear a miniskirt to a synagogue,
to abolish any instrument that tells the time,
to have a mind which is isolated and not under others' influence,
to stand on a part of the world where no one cares about my appearance,
to exchange goods for love and not for money,
to rid myself of the desire to gain power and energy at the
expense of other organisms
to release the past and forgive everyone,
to approve, accept and love myself,
to recognize the magnificence of my being,
to acknowledge that every cell in my body has divine intelligence.

When everyone is free, the word 'freedom' will be no more - yet I know
that when I am 25 I will still write about the word 'freedom.'

Rekha Vara

Dreaming

The other night in dreamland I tripped down memory lane,
Went errands to the corner shop, attended school again,
With all my pals around me took part in children's games,
Recalled again excitedly those long forgotten names.

I glimpsed again through childish eyes my dad and doting mam.
My little brother lay peacefully sleeping in his pram,
A blazing fire in the grate, our puppy on the mat,
The farmyard dog barked furiously whilst chasing next-door's cat.

After school with other boys played football on the green,
But very soon the local bobby came upon the scene.
He didn't really mind the game, just couldn't stand the din.
"Shove off you little tykes" he yelled, "You'll have them windows in."

So with lots of muttering we scampered down the street
To have a game of kicky tin, another child's treat.
Then mother's call came from our door, "It's bath time now, you boys.
Remember now the bairn's in bed so don't make too much noise."

A slice of cake, a glass of milk, and up the golden stairs.
My mam was at the bedside insisting on my prayers,
And here I left my dreamland, awaking with a shock,
To find that I had overslept. I hadn't heard the clock.

Maurice Pinkney

Seeking Of A Dream

Strolling through the mists of time, seeking the dreams
that we hope, and pray we all may find.
The dreams, no, not the wants or greed, that we could all so easily seek.
But the true needs of life, and creation, an understanding, for
the freedom that each and everyone feels an equal need.
Caring for the each other, yes, even the simple things,
like the comforting and wiping away of a tear from a lost child's
cheek. It can, and does make a difference.
No one is an island, neither the strong nor the meek.
Dreams and faith are the needs of everyone, because
without them, onto what would we all grasp?
There must be a faith in the future of life's basic needs,
the architectural foundations on which all life depends.
Not just to be surrounded by the riches and trappings of wealth.
The riches we seek within our dreams should be equally
shared by the strong and the meek.
The love of our neighbour, the kindness, the thought,
and the hope for the future that all these can bring.
Are not these the dreams for which all nations' people have sought.

Barry Scott Crisp

Life!

Life is so valuable when it's about to be taken.
A man's soul snatched for want.
So much pain felt, it's put away.
You never know how much you love and need
someone until they're gone.
Why? It's not simple enough to answer.

Life is too short for some,
but way too long for others.
Some people live for the next day,
that might never come.
Some just live for what they have.

Power is a very dangerous thing.
But who knows how we would live without it.
There are so many questions to be answered in life.
I guess we'll have to just wait and see.
Or maybe it's not our place to know.
The pain in a true man's face, is the true pain in his heart!

Sula Graham

Dans Le Jardin

When I was a child
(life full of promises and expectations)
I thought and did what a little child ought to do
but yet I wondered about this thing "grown up"
I studied and copied things of the matured
in anticipation of that grand old title "an adult."

Now I am old
(world full of corruption and deceit)
I try to do what is expected of an adult, but yet
I wonder how it feels to be a child again
life full of promises and expectations
blissfully ignorant of the tales of dolour
escaping into a simplistic existence
eyes wide with innocence and a ready smile
where everything and everyone is
enamoured by me.

Esther Umude

One Magical Night

It was Christmas Eve as I crept up to bed,
Stories of Christmas and Santa filled my head,
Snow piled on the ground all fluffy and light,
To me this is one magical night.

As almost falling asleep, something caught my eye,
A sleigh and some reindeer soared through the sky,
I smiled, he waved and was gone out of sight,
To me this is one magical night.

That night I learned how to believe,
Thanks to the night before Christmas, Christmas Eve,
And when I woke the next morning early and bright,
I knew it had been a magical night.

Stephanie Brown

Fatherless Thoughts

It didn't sink in when I was first told,
now my heart is slashed from the pain I hold,
caused from the news that you had died,
gone from this world without a kiss goodbye.
Mixed up emotions swell in my brain,
and all my happiness begins to drain,
sorrow and emptiness fill me instead,
and escape into the tears I shed.
Torrents of hot tears flow free,
easing the hurt inside of me,
the pain will never go as people will say,
the coping just gets easier day by day.
Looking at your photo it's definite to see,
that parts of you has made what is me,
because, as your daughter, I will always have pain,
until the day when I see you again.

Andrea Hart

Last Request

Please plant a rose-bush on my grave
My love, and do not weep, be brave.
I do not crave a marble stone
A stone is cold and I am all alone.

A rosebush full of summer flowers
Exuding scent in rainy showers.
How like my life in sun and rain
Brimful of gladness and of pain.

So full of sadness and despair
And yet what joys so deep and rare.
Your love and laughter, what delight!
And friends to make my whole life bright.

Your hand in mine - love does not die
It forms an everlasting tie
From you to me, from man to wife
It does not even end with life.

Please plant a rosebush, not a stone
That I may never feel alone
Where summer birds will gaily sing
Of courtship and eternal spring.

Gertrude Black

Candle Of Death

I wonder, if I'll ever see
This land, of fight and bitterness free.
Sweet smelling sounds of life and praise
Through leaded rain and smoky haze.
History dictates that the future should be,
To search within, for them and me.
A way to bridge this useless divide
What man or woman can not hide.
So much alike, yet world's apart
We hear with tradition, not with our heart,
A time to unite or maybe oppose
Damned hatred brings a lasting repose.
Walls come down to march around
Beat bigger drum to silent sound
Time won't stop to save and heal
Discard the past, the future feel.
Life out there in heavens blest
Upon this land, your outstretched hand rest,
Feel my anxiety, heal my lungs with your saving breath
Blow bright the furnace of light, blow out this candle of death

Sean Wright

The Last Farewell

The air was damp, and raw, and chill,
The sky was dull, and grey,
I hunched my shoulders, as I walked,
It was a dreadful day.
I didn't really want to go,
I didn't feel prepared,
To take the strain of someone's pain,
And feel their black despair.
I knew the time was drawing near,
When we two friends must part,
I wondered if this was the day.
A chill fear gripped my heart.
Though near to death, with kindly smile,
She talked of happy times we'd shared,
She seemed her old self, for a while,
I hope she knew how much I cared.
I struggled hard to find the words,
To bid goodbye to this dear friend,
But all I said, was just, "Adieu",
No more was needed, in the end.

J. Edwards

Spring - Cleaning Day

The objects are worthless, their owners long gone,
but the joy that they gave to us all linger on.

Old-fashioned toys; discarded "things"
but oh! The memories each of them brings!

A rubbery doll, with fingers all bitten.
A long-ago story, only half written.

A thread bare Teddy with only one eye.
Ted brought so much comfort, whenever you'd cry.
A bright knitted toy, moth eaten but jolly
and you love him still that battered old "Golly"

Holey old socks and rings that won't fit;
a collection of stamps, and a thre' penny bit.

An old-fashioned engine; a kite that won't fly.
They all bring back mem'ries of days now gone by.

their owners have gone - but the memories stay,
in the things I've discovered on Spring-cleaning day!

Valerie Warner

Sea Stroke

To Laurie Dearest. Father. Friend.
Daily driving beside the sea,
observing it, observing thee,
I saw reflected in your mien
the self same struggle spent with pain.
Oh! Piscean soul, whose pulse and strength...
(your Tempest passed, receding fast),
gained domination of the stroke at length,
Look now, to the reflection of your soul.
The sea's soft susurration held at bay,
and smoothly hovered beach laid bare,
your shallow breaths skimming over pain.
Yesterday all the greys swelling, drowning
downwards, depression, whorling, imprisoning.
Today micro-wavelets simmering, I shall find you
vulnerable, emotions spiking, surfacing through.
And a tomorrow soon. I'll bring you away
to the trees and the hills.
Gentled, rested, strengthened then from all your ills
you will return home again, near the sea.

Pamela M. Peacock

In The Shadows

I was standing in the shadows watching from afar
only the moon with the clouds scurrying past
knew that I was there
I saw your silhouette outlined in the dark
you had stopped to kiss the girl in your arms
I had followed you as I'd wanted to see you
for just once more
to know for myself to get rid of pretence
that you weren't alone.

Now as I stand here in the shadows
feeling empty from inside, hot tears
running down my face bereft of any pride
only a numbness remains of how
I'd been completely taken in by all those lies.

I slipped quietly out of the shadows
shivering in the cold night air
dragging my weary feet behind me
lost in the depths of my despair

The clock in the distance struck the hour as to home I made my way
leaving those memories forgotten for yet another day.

V. Thompson

R.E.M.

I awake in relief as the dream subsides
But the hollow feeling is clawing inside
Sharp as I realize the dream is true,
I remember that I have lost you.

Sleep is a mantle which covers the pain,
short-lived as reality hits you again
and you cannot escape wherever you turn
the blinding light of truth will burn.

I wonder, do you ever feel regret?
Perhaps I am something you would rather forget.
Remember me before I let you down.
Swirling memories, let them drown.

I'll be there when your ship comes in
I'll break the bottle and cut my skin.
Love can give but love can take
So now I will sleep but never wake.

Julie Wright

Winter Is Over

Brave little Snowdrop who raises her head
to push up through the snow,
to face the cold and winter winds
and tell the snow to go,

Colourful Crocus who follows next
to lay a carpet for spring,
then quietly stands aside to let the
Bluebells sing,

Primroses and Daffs in their yellow gowns
make way for Tulips with their
brilliant crowns,
Peonies, Lupins and all the rest
following on in their Sunday best,
Dahlias, Chrysanths and others too
come to remind us the year's nearly through.

Joyce Humphreys

Life

A kiss so simple yet means so much,
What is shared together when two people touch,
You draw me in and I let go,
Then you put me and my feelings on show.
You change in the glint of an eye,
This just isn't what I wanted.
Can't we give it one more try.

A shattered heart with deepest cuts,
A wound that will never heal up,
Time may take away the pain,
But memories bring it back again.

Sarah Dent

Love

Love is a feeling you cannot describe
Or maybe it's that beautiful sick feeling deep down inside
It starts in the tips of your fingers
And goes down to the ends of your toes
Love is the feeling in each other's touch
By day or night it can mean so much
Love is a kiss love as a smile
Love is laughter all the while
Love can take you up in the air
Or into the depths of deep despair
Love can make you laugh or cry
Love is the most precious thing if you're willing to try
Love is caring in sickness and health
Love is growing old together and sharing in each other wealth
Love and faith are the best medicine around
For my love for you knows no bounds
By now you must know just how I feel
For my love for you is more than real
Love is the gift that has been given to us both
Love is everything we'll need together with all our hopes

Jennifer Hirst

Seasons

The buds are breaking on bare branches of trees,
Crocus flowers are standing erect, in their bright new uniforms.
Delicate snowdrops hang like dew drops on slender stems,
It's spring and the feeling of new life fills the air.
The summer sun now warms the green turf,
The air is heavy with the scent of roses.
Houses are adorned with hanging baskets filled with fuchsias,
Dancing ballerinas in flounced skirts.
The days grow longer and so do the shadows,
The once green leaves are now glorious shades of copper and gold
They flutter to the ground, making a crunchy carpet to kick
    and run through.
The wind whispers it's autumn,
The birds wing their way to warmer lands.
The snow brings a stillness to the air,
Animals sleep and life seems to stand still.
As the white blanket melts, the word is passed,
Wake up world! Spring is with us at last.

Jeanette Toms

Secret Garden Of My Mind

I wander though the secret garden of my mind.
Imaginary adventures to find,
to meet my secret love,
and together we'll escape.
On the winged horse called love,
towards the sweet pink moon of desire.
Blowing away the winds of suspicion.
Let's toast each other with champagne
drunk from a glass slipper.
And slip away on clouds of dreams.
In the secret garden of my mind.
Together pick forbidden flowers of passion.
Let's walk along by banks of the river of love
and dive in the cool water.
together consummate our love in a sweet embrace
in the secret Garden of my mind

Debbie Evans

My Dream

Warm and cosy snug in my bed
Wonderful thoughts drift through my head
With you my love, our arms entwining
Together, so close a bond so binding
Never to part or our paths divide
For many long years ever side by side
Loving and giving as we grow old
This is the dream my heart doth enfold

Eileen Pickford

The Queen Of The Night

The Queen of the night
"What makes you leave your home and house,
Up and down the streets all night out,
Seemingly dressed to kill like a buxom barmaid,
Searching for a false lover's face?"

All these hues and cries against AIDS
The dreadful disease that slowly kills to disgrace
Through indiscriminate sex mostly it drains
Daily scaring mankind without aid
"Ooo!" All seem blur and deaf to your ears' frames

All that glitters is not gold 'O'
The wealth you're hustling and bustling to own
Worth not more than a wedded lady
That sings in her bridegroom's home daily
"Oh what can I do for you, sir, my darling?"

The Queen of the night
With flabby hips bubbling - wobbling up and down,
Sweet succulent breasts jutting out inside a shaky gown
Like the ripe mango fruit which tastes so good,
Why not get hitched to bear your kind so bloom?

John Asiedu Sarpong

Poppies!

I remember them a field of dancing pixies wearing red velvet gowns.
Kicking their dainty green legs and humming like clowns.
I watched them gently move to the command of the wind.
As the powerful wind fell silent the gay humming dimmed.
The figures then stood silent and they gently bowed their heads.
They looked like they were sleeping in a field of tiny beds.
All was silent, darkness fell.
Maybe I should go and rest as well.
I went to see the pixies many, many times.
The dancing dainty fellows singing pixie rhymes.
The days went on, the pixies grew old.
The trees turned bare, the weather grew cold.
Why are their dresses so ragged and brown?
Why can't their gay singing be heard throughout town?
The pixies grew tired, they all fell asleep.
They will never awake as their dreams are too deep.
Dreaming their dreams, dreaming of the day.
When they will all reunite and become one once again.
Until that day the field will be bare.
With no merry pixies dancing there.

Kelly Gray

On The Sudden Death Of My Sister

When she died she stole some part of me,
Her dying unshaped my sense of self;
The space she left
Layers a grey blanket over my bed at night
And in the morning sun
The edge of my shadow is blurred.
Grief stirs at the unexpected footstep,
A stranger's laugh, a familiar tune.
My tears mirror raindrops on the window,
Washing pain in rivulets to a timeless sea,
Till warm memories trickle through crevices,
Breach the wall of numbness,
Gather in murmuring streams,
Flow unchecked between the twin dams
Of guilt and anger,
Surge in diminishing waves towards the shore of loss,
Withdrawing with a sigh,
Before spreading a soothing web of balmy foam.

Margaret Eddershaw

September Reflections

How hazy and calm this warm September day
A fugitive from troubled summer
That has quietly slipped away.
I remember a day in September too
When high above the famous spitfires flew,
A dance macabre but earnest and deadly
High in the sky a frenetic medley.
Now long in the past and dim memories grow
But September so calm with its autumnal glow
Its mists and its flowers last radiance to be,
Will always be so special to me.

Violet Smith

Anything

Your eyes are as bright and clear as the sky
as blue as a clear blue sea,
I won't forget you till the day that I die
I just want you to love me.

I'd love to be with you just now
for you to hold me tight,
my friends all said that I was wrong
but I know I was right.

I hope that maybe someday
we'll meet somehow, somewhere,
if you'd just name the place and day
I'd quickly be right there.

Kathleen McKendrick

Cliff Top View

I see you standing ghostly white
against the salty waves at night
high above and far beyond blue seas
whispering around the windswept trees
all your friends are hung in the sky
where sea gulls live and die
gazing out on troubled water below
watching the ocean ebb and flow
washing your rocks with a salty lick
crashing waves wear you away quick

The sea stained air blows you grassy mounds
here on your hill my little heart pounds
to my eyes the shadows appear
and sleepy grey they fall
I hear the eerie cry of a sea gull call
darkness hanging like a shroud
not even a hint of cloud
wind catches my breath
I love to remember this view
where I lost my love to death.

Shelley Barry

Our Holiday

We had a great holiday, me and my wife,
Was one of the best in our whole married life.
We sat on the sand for hours, what a sight!
Getting brown as two berries in blazing sunlight.

They had girls on the beach who wore nearly nuffin'!
I thought that their mums 'ud be uffin' and puffin'
Till I saw an old lady with hair like white cotton
And her top 'alf was bare as a new baby's bottom!

One morning we went for a short camel ride;
We bumped up and down and swayed side to side
On smelly old things that snorted, and worse...
And a bloke right behind - he didn't 'alf curse!

On one lovely day we hired a motor
And drove up an 'ill to take a nice photor,
But me missus got stung in a place I can't mention
'Cos it only is me as can give it attention.

Now me forehead's gone red though me ankles is white,
And me tattoos have faded in all that bright light,
And the chips were all sodden and the beer tasted rotten,
So perhaps those two weeks had best be forgotten!

Arnold Marks

We Still Remember Them

Young boys went to war all saying things
like, 'We fight for country and for King;'
but as those tortuous years passed by
weary men thought of home and wondered, "Why
did we ever join this war?
We can never be as we were before..."

But fight that bloody war they did,
and lived through four long years amid
the din, disease and the dead,
until those dreaded words were said:
'Over the top boys, off you go;'
then like a river blood did flow.

Many nations of the World fought with the French;
in no-man's land and in the trench,
from the Somme to Gallipoli,
in order to let you and I
live today, people free:
A priceless result, as was the fee.

Fifty million souls were lost back then;
of course we must remember them.

Alan J. Greer

Rain

A distant swirl of repetitive mist,
Like the unknown all in one place,
A moaning voice that won't leave me alone
But the voice just hasn't a face,
Yet something wet is touching my face,
It's creeping up through the mist,
There's more of it now getting harder and harder
Attacking my legs, my arms, my fist.
Slowly and gradually I see no more,
My red hands turn to ice,
The evil drip gets more and more urgent
Like a constant poltergeist
Why won't the wet things leave me alone
My blind eyes see once more?
Why can't I leave this horrible world
Go through another door?
Through the door to paradise
From December to the month of May,
One pull at the little hopeful door,
To a bright and sunny day.

Emma Davis

The Orchard

The orchard is gone now; but the birds still sing.
From neighbouring trees their songs pour down
On piled up rubble, trees, bushes, old stone
All levelled, and mixed with grass and weeds.
Amber sunlight replaced by dull grey.
Maturity built up over generations
Dispersed in one half hour.

The orchard was planned well, neat paths, small box hedges,
The apples trees serried with sunlight flickering through,
Bramleys, Russets and Pippins, Cox and Orange.
Each tree known, important,
And the earth was fragrant with windfalls.
At apple picking time, plenty to share with birds and insects,
Hard work to keep the weeds down, the hedges trimmed.

Careless piled up rubble dots our mindscapes too,
Our certainties uprooted and beliefs grown wild—
When the bulldozer arrived, I wept for a hurt child.

Moira Collins

Hogging It

Apple-hopping hedgehog
Skittering through brown veined leaves,
Did divisive dinosaurs expel your prickly humps.
Who decided porcupines and hedgehogs should be plated
When our domestic porkers have nothing but pink fluff.

If all the quills we need to use are those that write our letters,
May they be as sharp as yours to pulverize our fetters.
Setting children from the paths in apple orchards, scratching
To twist their quills and learn to give
As good as they are getting.

Hazel Heasley

Seventeen Deaths

The television tells us
What happened that day in a small Scottish town.
I dare not cry with my family around.
Instead I go to bed, my eyes heavy with unshed tears.

No feelings: a cold hand has
squeezed my sponge-heart
And all emotion has dripped out of me
Tear by tear.

I cannot excite anger or hate;
Just a lump of dread eating my stomach
Telling me it was real, it did occur,
Lives were lost.

And now I can cry because
I've realised that
It could have been stopped.

Kathryn Jarvis

Will I Live

As he shouts 'go over the top.'
My arms shake and my heart stops.
Will I live another day.
To hear my officer say,
'Move on men and do your best.'
Again my courage is put to the test.
At home my wife sits and prays.
That I'll live to see another day.
The food I eat is hard as steel.
But as it's so cold I cannot feel.
Feel it get stuck as I take another bite.
Soon again I know I will fight.

The land is full of men so scared.
Because they know they're not prepared.
For the sight they'll see, hear and smell,
Am I tough or will I fail.

Fight with strength and heart of gold.
Succeed you must forget the cold.
Britain's people soon will say.
The men who fought gave us our today.

Fiona Crouch

The Night

Midnight has come.
Lying still.
Afraid to move.
There's nothing there.
The curtains are drawn together,
Blocking off the outside world-
Except for the street light,
Shining through a gap.
Casting strange shadows.
A light breeze across your face.
Then, a noise.
Growing louder and louder,
Nearer and nearer.
Moving, gradually, along the road.
It passes your window.
Then, the disturbance becomes quieter.
Until, it is a distant sound.
The night becomes quiet once more,
Until another car heading for home passes.

Davinia Johnston

Rivington Moor Is A Special Place

I go there to escape.
The peace and stillness and beauty
of scenes, are just like being in a dream.

I can drift all day from
dawn till dusk.
I never tire of the beautiful day,
raining, hail, sun I stay,
time to rest and think awhile,
let my memories wonder,
I've been up here with Dad a lot
he's given this to me,
a love of life, of space
and air, it's free to breathe
and laugh and stare,
I just don't give a care,
it lifts me up and sets me free,
the wind blowing so silent,
lets go home now Dad,
we are happy again in not sad.

A. A. O'Malley

Free

Likeness of a bird who flies so high
Freedom of a prisoner who prays to die
The life of a rich man who lost the will
Poorness of a pauper who is suffering still
The health of a sick man who now is strong
The love of a good man who makes you belong

Carole O'Neill

Waiting

Love of my life, where are you
never to see me again.
Love of my life, where are you
help me nurse this pain.
My years have gone, I'm youth no more,
but my heart remains the same.
Forever yearning, forever burning for you.

Love of my life, remember me
when your days draw to an end.
Just speak my name; I'll hear you, then my heart will begin to mend.
Just to hear your voice once more my love
will see me through I know, we'll meet again after all this pain
then our love will continue to grow.

Heaven will be blue and fluffy white, you will be there to hold me
tight, we'll make up for love's lost time, eternally will be yours and mine.

Love of my life, where are you, never to see me again,
love of my life, where are you, help me soothe this pain.
My years have gone, I'm youth no more, but my heart remains the same.
Forever yearning. Forever burning. Forever loving you.

Pauline Gregory

Hyrath

Tyde immigrated from North Wales and went to live upstate New York.
When I was just a little girl, mother told me he had sung
before the King of England.
I could see him in my child's eye, standing solitary at the throne
all five feet, eight inches tall,
likely scared,
but proudly singing.

He was called the Lark of Curig. "Eos Curig" on his gravestone.
Far away from Snowden and the A5 that came later.
He had breathed too much of coal dust,
He was dead at forty-seven.
I never knew him.

But I come back to Britain to live and make it my home
a full one hundred life years later.
Now, I know it was a male choir standing there upon the small stage
when the King came to Caernarfon.
And my Tyde was one of many,
many men who stood together
tall as mountains, tall as Snowden.
Likely scared,
But proudly singing.

Lee Nordberg

Grandma

Saving pennies for a rainy day - my grandma used to say,
For pennies soon turn into pounds and help you pay your way.

A lady always wears clean shoes - my grandma used to say,
You can tell a persons breeding if the scuffs are kept at bay.

Leave a little food upon your plate - my grandma used to say,
But choosing just which bit to leave would cause me such dismay.

Remember to use elbow grease - my grandma used to say,
And her tone quite clearly signalled it was wiser to obey.

Make sure your underwear is clean - my grandma used to say,
You know how neighbours talk if they see knickers that are grey.

She's mutton dressed to look like lamb - my grandma used to say,
But I rather liked the feathered hat worn by Aunty Vi that day.

Best make hay whilst the sun shines - my grandma used to say,
But it's wet and cold and windy and I can't go out to play.

God helps those that help themselves - my grandma used to say,
As we walked to church in our Sunday best and together we would pray.

Oh! How I miss my grandma, miss her cuddles, miss her smile,
Miss her funny eccentricities, her elegance, her style.

I use her same expressions now I've children of my own,
And through her love and guidance, know I'll never walk alone.

Beverly Ann Barton

Love Of A Human

I want to tell you every day
my heart yearns for you to stay
close beside my side as I sleep,
my feelings for you are deeper than deep.
Some people really get hurt by love
and it makes me thank the Lord above
that you understand my love for you
is stronger than the deepest blue.
You are more beautiful than the brightest sea
who knows just how to look after me.
You make me feel safe within your arms
and keep me away from danger and harm.
I love you more than a bear loves his honey.
I love you more than Scrooge loves his money.
I hope you feel the same for me,
because I think this love is to be.

Joanna Thorn

Untitled

What do you do when all you love is gone,
Do you cry, laugh, hide away.
What do you think,
Is it me, is it them?
The whole world is against you
Closing in on top of your once perfect life
How do you carry on,
In joy, in pain?
What do you do next,
Live on, or die?

What do others think
You don't care, you're strong.
Confusion, anger,
Will they ever go away?
Will they taunt you forever?
Happiness, joy,
Will you ever see them again.
Only you have the answers.

Michelle Fraher

Satisfaction

You kiss me wanting her - I know you do.
'Tis in your mood; the longing. Not for me
I swear! Duty is all I'm granted. So!
If it my duty be to bear the agony of loving true
I will love you...
Unfaithful? Yes! Yes!
To leave me seeking her. Don't try denial.
'Tis in your step the eagerness.
Excitement lights your eyes - but lit in me?
All hell's resentment burning!
How I despise this agony of loving true -
And still I do - I do!
Waiting? Of course! For what must surely be.
Don't plead! I know. I know!
'Tis in your touch; remorse. But not for me!
You fear you've lost her. So!
Sweet guilt I greedily devour
Knowing my pleasure now will be
To share your agony of loving true -
And comfort you...

Peggy Scott

In Mourning

At the cemetery I stood head bowed, with faceless people.
Grief hung like a cloud, I could not look them in the eye.
The mind reflected upon the life of my good friend, Harry.
Behind tinted glasses my eyes moistened, I began to cry.
Thinking of Harry and the good times, it made me so sad.
I told my wife. How I'd not recognized any of the mourners,
Come to think of it, I did not even see his mom or dad.
I described how I'd stood there shedding tears and thinking.
The mourners stared at me. And I shared in their sorrow.
Later my wife tried to cheer me up, recalling happier times.
Then she said, 'By the way, Harry's Funeral is tomorrow.'

Terence J. Bradley

Living With Change

What is change?
Venturing into new and different things.
The turn of a page,
A new life awaits yet the old still clings.

What is change?
A new environment, and different faces
The change of age,
Adjusting to people and places.

What is change?
A new set of rules, for a different start of life.
Over with pretence,
In with strictness as harsh as a knife.

What is change?
A new aloneness and a different confusion.
The switch of a button,
Taking daylight into utter emersion.

Change is fear.
It can happen without you realizing
Or it can happen and give you a vision clear
Whatever way—life is always changing.

Mandi Manota

Vigilant Soulmate

Spider on the pane, blackbird peeking in at me;
Nature cannot restrain, the power of your entity.

The zephyr touched my face, as if it was something more.
I feel you, every place, from the forest to the shore.

Gentle calls of the morning dove I anticipate each day;
Bring back memories of love and keep my heart at bay.

Different twists of fate, prevented my life from end.
With those I equate, one who I still depend.

Destiny I have come to know - the way the road turned;
Finally have begun to show, teachings I have learned.

Never a day comes I forget, throughout my remaining years.
While many a day regret, endures within my tears.

In everything, you reside, I'll not doubt that belief.
Still, a fragment of my soul has died, and you - its thief.

Your abandon, not in vain! It is merely my spirit spent.
As this heart shall wane, and thoughts provide repent.

Time it truly does restore, and forces one to see.
Altering the course before, a meaningful degree.

Shelene Skillings-Caldwell

What Age Is Antique

You might think I am antique but
I don't I know I am only at my peak
There's many a long year yet before I take a back seat,

Would you like to see me sat in the
Corner, well I have no intention yet
Of making a day out for the mourner.
You are my son and daughter and I want
To stay your friend you know the rule
That I like you to follow but that
Rule you both bend

When I pick you up from the disco it's
Because I love you and worry but I know
You think I am spying and you end up
Embarrassed or even crying
But no matter what you say I will always
Be there for you even though you think I am praying

So think on, I am your mother and would
Not dream of hurting you or harming a
Hair or you head. I do say three o'clock
In the morning you should be home and in your bed.

Rose Morley

Hope

As each new day unfolds like the petals of a flower,
Realizing we are small at the side of infinite power.
Losing a loved one into God's warm embrace,
Remembering the peaceful look upon their face.
The sun keeps on shining and the stars don't fall down,
Winds whisper and blow as tears melt from a frown.
Try not to be sad, but cling to memories dear,
Faith and hope will sustain us because God is near.
In every clean heart, beats the truth, finds the words,
To express innermost feelings like the songs of the birds.
If I could share my contentment and gently touch another,
This day will not pass in vain like the pain of a Mother.
Never to feel the hug of such sincere love again.
Yet finding a blessing within death's dark shame.
Being released to heaven, asleep in the clouds of time,
As the dew drops evaporate in the sun's rays that shine.
I can only imagine walking within a dream by a river,
Peace and tranquillity, waiting for the holy spirit to deliver.
We can only strive to do good in this mere mortal life's fight,
And hope to be remembered with love pure as light.

Carol Rashid

Frog Watch

We couldn't see them, hidden in the pool
but, sometimes, in the cool of evening
we'd hear a splash and know they were around.
And then on closer scrutiny, we'd see
a pair of eyes above the water's edge,
and find that we were scrutinized instead!

We loved our frogs who spent their days with us,
and saddened at their going from the pool
to hide in secret places damp and cool
and winter in the compost heap.
But they'll be back when Winter turns to Spring
and, once again, we'll hear the croaking in the night
and, in the morning, find another generation is in sight!

Margaret Willoughby

To Our Disabled

Long years ago in our forefathers' day,
a disabled person had to fall by the way
with no hope of work and less hope of pay.
What an awful life they must have led
Having to stay at home and in bed
with no one but family to help them get fed.

But through the years what a change there's been
with our welfare state, and helpers keen.
They are taught to work and helped to play,
to live useful lives from day to day.
There is nothing they cannot do,
from making a table to mending a shoe.

St. George's, Dame Hannah's and Remploy do
employ these people and help them too.
They have socials and outings and lots of fun.
A good time is had by everyone.
So enjoy yourself with zeal and zest,
the helpers are doing their very best.

Rose C. Mahoney

My Son

My first born son,
My pride and joy,
Was taken from me when just a boy,
My heart was broken, I wanted to die,
I lifted my head up to the sky,
I prayed to God to hear my cry,
I looked around and what did I see,
Three small sad faces looking at me,
I lost my son,
They lost their brother,
All they had now was each other,
God gave me strength and at last,
I became the mother they had in the past.

Irene Dodds

Birds Of A Feather

Just watch any bird in its flight,
With wings outspread to gain more height,
From Spring to Winter, all seasons long,
It preens its feathers, and sings a song,
To keep alive, from day to day,
They go in search for easy prey,
As time goes by they want a mate,
Can build a nest at fantastic rate,
Somewhere sheltered, away from harm,
They lay their eggs, and all is calm,
Taking turns until they hatch
With more mouths to feed, and little 'catch'
Care and devotion, they will thrive,
Teach them to fly, and stay alive.

J. J. Gunn

Sunrise

How grey the morning lies,
Awaiting the light to filter through the skies,
And o'er the path, grassy and sometimes bare and worn
Gently rise the misty vapours of the morn;
And along the path one's walk may go
Gathering moisture on the shoe,
And on each leafy blade of green
Sparkling gems of beauty can be seen;
Till we come to the woodland path bare and dry
There the ever rising sun is glimpsed through branches up on high,
Spreading her light wide and far away
Lighting all that once was grey.

C. P. Baker

Summer Album

So many camera stills,
Remnants of a sparkling summer
When so much was ours,
When everything succumbed to
Spontaneity and passion.
Musee, metro, la tour et cetera:
A truth of time cannot be disguised,
The moments speed by, only memories meander.
Even tremendous todays and tomorrows
Tremble at these yesterdays of celebration.

Must keep moving on though,
Surpassing early summer's pleasure,
Building, building, building from beginnings,
Recalling the simple five foreign nights
That sped station to station like so many outbound trains.
Building this love.
Somehow it will always be real,
If slightly blurred, but not a teasing dream,
Or empty frame. Thank you for the heart and caring
That pulse through my life, making everything summer.

Robin Kirby

The Wind

What a terrible trouble the wind causes us,
In a frenzy it swirls and blows, dust in a gust,
It blows down the fences, rips up the flowers,
Its force is terrific and a formidable power,
It scatters leaves everywhere, making a mess
The devastation is alarming and causes such stress
But what is better than a gentle breeze,
That whispers sweet nothings amongst the trees

I'm sure it can talk, you can hear it sigh,
But what it says I can only surmise,
It caresses your face - hold it up to be kissed,
So cool and gentle it is really quite bliss,
Now the wind we will forgive in all its ferocity,
Its formidable power and alarming atrocities,
If only it leaves us the gentle breeze,
That whispers and sighs amongst the trees.

C. Petchey

A Secret Wish

Mummy says she loves me, anyway.
But she never looks at me except to say
There is something she does not like to see, in me,
That reminds her of Daddy, who works at sea.
It is not from her family, for sure.
There's no reason she can see, to be that way.
What will people think of me? What will they say?
Wherever will it lead me, in life's hard way?
I think of things to please her, at least to try.
If I could be like my brothers, pigs would fly.
I'm a little girl, whose hair won't curl,
And I bite my nails.
I like to sit astride my chair, and tell such tales.
If Daddy is like me, he'll know I need him every day
To be with me, and show me I'm O.K.,
Or I'll grow up in a muddle and go astray.
I'll end up like the queerest fish you ever knew.
Mummy's love is special, Daddy writes. I know it is untrue.
And it makes me feel unfinished, like a soleless shoe.
Have you ever wished she'd love you too?

Mona Drion

The Tree

It stood there in magnificent splendour
The tree so strong and yet so tender
Beneath its sheltering arms grayed
Folk have planned and Cupid played
Through rain and shine it's proudly stood
God's creation made of wood
But us poor mortals, could we create
Such wondrous beauty
So regal and sedate?
I fear no for we have not his power
That we can make wood that e'er also flower
I only know God's gift to man
Ever since this world began
The tree in all its grandeur has stood
God's creation that's made of wood

V. Cambridge

Nothing I Can Do

I sit in this cage crammed all day,
I fantasize of eating fresh lettuce and hay,
I feel so hungry, tired and ill,
How many more of us are they going to kill,
My eyes are covered with shampoo,
But there's nothing I can do,
My fur has turned as hard as a rock,
And I've forgotten what it feels like to walk,
I've got perfume on my ears so they're really sore,
I don't know if I can survive anymore,
The animal tested products that people are buying,
Are responsible for us animals crying and dying.

Amalie Grant, age 13

The Young Warrior

Don't touch love unless you can cry
Nor raise a gun unless prepared to die.

The lacerated arm rests on the gun's wheel
His rifle now too ponderous to lift
The pain gone, only emptiness to feel
Clutching the photo his lover's gift.
The helmet fallen from the bloody head
Only waiting now to enrol with the dead.

What use the orders, the martial songs
His life such value to him alone
The propaganda of the enemies' wrongs
The boyish pranks, the love he had known
The experiences of times past
Ebbing through a mist so fast

He raised his gun unprepared to die.
Now his family left to mourn and cry.

Richard Keller

Stitching The Wounds

My wounds are healing, the memories are fading fast
I'm looking to the future, I'm letting go of the past
I will learn to love again one day
Open up my heart and soul I may.

It's easy to drift, it's easy to dwell,
But fate is unknown, you can never tell,
Trusting, caring, more careful this time,
Rivers to swim and mountains to climb.
Laughing, singing happy times ahead,
As well as crying with pain whilst lying in bed.

Some lessons can never be learnt,
No matter how many times my fingers get burnt.
Who would I be if I never loved or shared,
What kind of coward would I be if I never dared,
Not knowing the future it's better that way,
Taking life as it comes, taking day by day.

My wounds are healing, my memories are fading at last,
I'm looking to the future, I've let go of the past.

Sally Duguid

Remember Me?

I am the beast of the Jungle that you kill and maim
Destroying my land for your selfish gain
Remember me?

I am the creature beneath the ocean, once so clear and bright
I cannot swim with the pollution and waste you blight
Remember me?

I am the bird who soars so high
When you ravage my forest, I will die
Remember me?

I am the old and infirm who has given much, but what do you care
If I am suffering and have to live on a pittance you deem fair
Remember me?

I am the disabled, deaf and blind who do not cause a fuss
When "cut backs" have to be made you always start with us
Remember me?

I am the Child of the Future, full of Faith and Hope
In a world spoilt by men's greed I will have to cope
Cruelty, poverty and famine, with no ray of light
Without love or pity, you have stolen my birthright
Have you forgotten me?

Bez Clarke

Love Never Dies

Show me the place where we parted and whisper to me
that we're there
Without any words can I hear you
Without any touch am I near you
I try to recall all my feelings but all I can reach for is night
If you want to share my confusion
Then you'll always be touched by illusion
I would always close my eyes to all the things which healed me
My darkest dreams were borne inside
My kindest place I had to hide
In ever-lonely waves I wept and drowned the tides away
Did I ever ask more than my right
Would the figures now fly from my sight
   Shining by my precious bride
   The softest skin was held in pride
   And they with all their bitter games
   Could never cast her flame aside
   Tomorrow never knows its way
   Or seeks the path from yesterday
   But only plays the truth that is
   Love never dies - just fades to grey

Kevin Davies

The Willow

He casts a shadow upon the ground,
to protect young lovers on whom others frown.
He covets them as if his own,
his branches for comfort they have flown,
to cover from the staring eyes
which cast a doubt from cloudy skies.
He stands proud and yet holds his arms out wide
to gather his children to his side.
He braves the scorn of wiser men,
for he was once young just like them.
A virgin trunk with tiny shoots.
A new bed for which his youthful roots
did plant their trembling feet into.
The solid ground from which he grew,
to nurture those beneath him now
He stoops a little—neigh a bow.
He weeps for lovers lost below
their love alive in his shadow.
A million hearts for safe keeping.
How aptly named—the willows weeping!!

Kathryn E. Murdoch

Commentary On Christmas

Who brings the presents, let's face the facts
A Xmas the legend of Santa is taxed
Between you and me and Walter, now seven,
This is an enquiry into a child's heaven.

I have a message from Santa, for he is real
I know, I've seen him, so here's his deal

That all boys and girls who do believe
Will shout with joy round Xmas eve
But any child who has a doubt
May sadly have to do without.

Walter Neilson

The Snow

Gently, softly fall the flakes, swaying to and fro,
Crystals all in assorted shapes,
Reflecting the lamp light's glow,
Sparkling stars of a million fold,
To dazzle through our windowpane,
A creation of designs unfold,
Which memories will bear again,
Of far-off days, of years gone by,
When we were all so young,
When we would sit by our windowpane,
To watch the flakes far flung,
We could not pick a single one,
To watch where it would lie,
We watched them change from grey to white,
While falling from the sky,
And all the world to us would change,
From grey, red, brown and green, to white, that covered all our range,
A sight I ne'er before had seen, and now, with many years gone by,
And water 'neath the bridge did flow,
I'll forever sit with bated eye, to watch the falling snow.

David D. Brodie

Gun Down A Jigger Law...

Torched night; darkness ablaze, a light fettered haze,
The Law a hole in the dark surrounds where privacy abounds.
Public the flicker aglow for truth to show.
Light! Let there be light to chase the dark of night
So flay secrecy at play and light a Public way.
For Laws to be just their honesty's a must
That of them who devise words when justice applies
Let them refer to heart and soul and leave not a loophole
That curs might hoops leap for gains which Fat-cats reap.
Let a tailored fit, as of the sun which true since time begun,
Chase the elusive darkness so become chaste unto fitness.
Torch! Torch the night and let blaze true the light.

Let not the dark overcome the light lest we fear again the night;
The dark darker side of man - a flea bitten Law none can withstand

Lloyd Carley-West

After The Genocide: Bangladesh

Amateur Freud
look deep within these twin muddy pools and declaim
watch my greed's tentacles burgeon like fireflies
over foetid swamps,
eddying
yet abidingly stoic in purpose
this lucid plethora signals messages
to my engrossed entirety:
Twentieth century miracle - man
with your blueprint of my brain
is this the ultimate analysis of my psyche?
Dismembered I have ploughed the field
tethered the oxen strewn the paddy
slaved the sweat of my armpits, sold my birthright
for the husk, the chaff, the bowl of meal,
peddled my sister for a song
now, dare and rend asunder
my neuroses from my fetish
this leprous soul a begging bowl
for my hunger

Lita Samad Chowdhury

It Is Time

The future of our world lies in the hands of our young,
The situation as it is, with great changes to come.
It is a time of great growth and evolution,
Time to stop decline, and all pollution.

It is time we taught our young from good example,
It is time we gave the guidance they deserve,
It's a time of great growth and revolution,
Time, to draw on all of our reserves.

It is in the simplicity of life that you advance,
Appreciate the true values of life.
Don't ignore, or deny, your duty,
Or abdicate any of your responsibilities.
It is time, it is time, now is the time.

For the future of our world lies in the hands of our young,
It's a time of great growth and it's already begun.
Teach them well, and you will see,
That they will fulfil their destiny
It is time, it is time, now is the time.

Penny Maine

Lookback

In retrospect I do reflect on the deeds that I did wrong,
some by mistake some by design, I was sometimes a bit-of-a-swine
all the fault of course was mine.

In retrospect I do recall
the times when not to be there at all,
would be the best place to have been
but then just what would I recall?

In reflection then as oft I am, I seek the benefits I had want to
cause, and the positive action I forsook and I weigh the balance
to score in my book of honesty.

In retrospect I weigh the fact, and as if in some horrendous pact,
when measures have been calculate
I find myself on the collecting plate, of wanting.

I seek the reason for my negative act
and lo and behold it is a fact
that I am a being human,

My inner story then is told
but I am not so bold at prolonged oratory,
so on my little machine I'll relate my sordid dream
and to give my tongue a needed rest, I print it out in poetry.

Norman Lowe

No Quarter

Time and tide, relentless, no respite
Have worn away her pride
She lies, held fast by shifting sands.
Rotting timbers, tattered rope
Desolate, no quarter asked
She slowly died without hope.

Only the seas remember and the winds
That once billowed out her mighty sails,
Her men beneath the mast held her fast
In calm waters or tempestuous Gales.

The song of the wind mourns the past
Her bows breaking every wave
A Proud Ship, her beauty unsurpassed
The seven seas her willing slave.

Now her anchor is embedded deep
Her hull in death's last sleep
Sea gulls rest upon her, cry loud their requiem
At tide's approaching wave across her grave

The Wreck, No quarter did She give, none ever taken
A proud Ship once, now forsaken.

Emma Hood

Behind The Old Green Door

The frost was glistening on its dusty pane,
A tree branch tapped; stirred by the wind and rain,
Against the old green door;
Which creaked gently to and fro.
Crumbling walls dripped plaster on squeaking boards,
A winding staircase stood, where frightening hoards
Of shadows, flitted round!
Yet an eerie stillness,
Quiet as the restless moon,
Pervaded the musty gloom:

A ghostly place! Where phantoms seemed to rest!
Although the moon and stars at their behest,
Lit up the fields around,
Into a magic wonderland!
A happy place where timid creatures played;
Which scurried to their homes, when break of day
Sent sunbeamed streaks of light,
To chase away the dark.
These banished fears once more,
Behind the old green door

Barbara Saum

A Voice From Heaven

God came to me, and as He took my hand
He said "Come with me to a better land"
Where there is no evil, hurt or pain
And you'll never be afraid again
So I went with the man with the kindly face
And He took me to a beautiful place
A lovely home in heaven above
To live in everlasting love
When we got there, the doors opened wide
And I felt a great warmth, as I stepped inside
I met many people, some strangers, some I knew
They said "Welcome dear friend, we've been waiting for you.
And I felt a great peace, in that heaven above
As they welcomed me, to the kingdom of love
So be happy for me, please don't be sad.
Remember the good times that you and I had.
Go on loving me still, because I'll always be near
Though you can't see my face, speak to me and I'll hear
And then one day, when your earth life is through
With arms open wide, I'll be waiting for you.

Margaret McNeish

The Path Of Life

Weep not for me as I grow old,
For I have seen life's path unfold
And shown to me the way to go
Along the path with friend and foe.

Live your lives with love and laughter,
Without envy, greed or malice.
Be proud and happy my sons and daughters
Raise up and drink from life's Chalice.

With my love of many years
We've very close to journey's end.
We've passed along the path of life.
She is my life, my love, my friend.

W. E. Clements

Memories

Just remember the good things
They will outnumber the bad,
Little things that you forgot
Come back and make you glad.

There are things which make you sad
The things you can't forget,
They bring back precious memories
There is no time for regret.

There are memories which make you laugh
And some that make you cry,
But the saddest memory of all
Is when we have to say goodbye.

R. Thew

The Highwayman's Vigil

A clear dark night as the moon shines down
Across a snow-kissed land
The wood lies silent still and calm
Dressed in its winter's gown
Amongst the trees like sentries
By this old and well worn track
A horse of grey stands patiently
Her master on her back
The pair have never moved a hair
For over an hour or more
The rider pulls his cloak in tight
The air it chills the bone
But his gaze stays fixed upon the road
For now he sees his goal
With pistol primed and ready, black mask upon his face
He moves the horse from cover as the carriage gathers pace
"Stand fast now and deliver!" The rider he does yell
"Throw down your gold and silver or I'll send you off to hell!"
With bags of coins a singing, strapped hard across his back
Rider and horse soon vanish into that night so black

Peter Routledge

This Is It

Well, um, this seems to be it.
Although of course, you probably don't look at it that way.
The thought's always been there
But, well, you know..........

Don't forget me will you.
You see, we've still got the memories,
Remember, I mean November, had all the good times.

I hope you won't venture too far from here.
Because Bridgwater is a nice place really,
It is really, it is most of the time.
Some things are bad, but well.....
it's a very, very nice place really,
I mean you do belong here.
I mean you were born here.
I mean your family lives here.
I mean, I mean,
I mean, I'm here.

Laura Costello

Soldiers Of Spring Are Slain

On my way to work each day
I pass the flower beds that display
The wonderful and cheerful sight
That Spring is here with all its might
And majesty, and colour divine
A perfect, pleasurable sign
That vandals, youths and those we slay
Have not taken their vengeful way;
To damage nature's works of earth
That make this enhancement a creative worth
But now to my distaste and anger
These Soldiers of Spring have lost their splendour
Crushed and dashed and even slayed
And all for what, "I am dismayed"
Why should we stand by, not to care
While this our town, becomes a Fair
Ground, and round, and laid to rest
These glorious flowers of ours, are best
Kept, and nurtured, and allowed to shine
Along our roads and pavement line.

Nigel L. Maltby

The Mountains

O'er the mountain tops spreads a golden glow
From the light of the rising sun;
Then it turns to dazzling whiteness
As the hours pass one by one.

On the mountain tops there's a silver sheen
'Neath a moonlit winter sky;
A vision of matchless splendour
As the cold, still night goes by.

Oh, rosy red are the mountain tops
In the sunset's crimson glow;
And the dusky valley is brightened
Where it stretches out below.

In purple cloaks are the mountains clad
In the haze of an autumn sun;
Oh the mountains are all beauty
That shall last 'till time is done.

John Clancey

Cornwall

Through a haze of purple tamarisk,
In a mist of salt seaspray,
In a burst of bloom and cascade of broom
In a glory round each bay,
Here lies the Cornwall few folk know,
'tis the inner, hidden heart
Of a land so private, secret, fey,
That to know it is to chart
A journey mystical and bright,
By pebbled strands and magic lands
To Lyonesse, the place of light.

Marian Cull

Music That Soothes

Those melodies which penetrate, deep within your being,
Your innermost thoughts, they seem to be freeing,
Of peace and love, and an inner contentment,
To neutralize the negative, you feel you should vent,
How you wish this feelings, could always be so,
Instead of the turmoil, of the to and fro,
The feeling of calm, and an inner resolve,
That never again, thoughts of hate you'll involve,
Sweeping aside, those negative thoughts,
Which in your mind, quite often haunts,
So listen to that music, that seems to inspire,
And of which you never, seem to tire,
Perhaps one day, you will be free,
They say times a healer, just wait and see.

Antony L. Toon

An Ugly Whisper About America

Every zone in Bosnia is Serbian mate,
They're armed with rage with hundred atoms of late,
No heart shall beat any more, only sorrow fills,
Which shall make the silence across Bosnian hills.

Fifty years, Serbs' soul to God, with Tito You shred,
Until the Country's Fathers and Brothers are dead,
Your staged curtain thus will fall in the tragic joy,
Like the souls of men to God You helped to destroy.

Serbs wish to see America the Mother of Earth,
The dignity of all people may You protect,
And hold up the righteousness that gave You the mirth,
Truly and thoughtfully, the Deeds, You could inspect.

And stop exploit division amongst the Brothers,
The Country was created by their great forefathers,
With true love of understanding and self-control,
With the natural-kindness for the Good of all.

Make the illumination, that mankind could spread,
Let each man brighten the path, his family tread,
Switch on all knowledge of people's Righteousness,
So that the hearts are not filled with the bitterness.

Milan Trubarac

The Final Curtain

Dreaming of nights of loud and frenzied applause
and taking those constant demanded curtain calls.
I felt a gentle presence in the darkening room.
A familiar voice spoke from out the dusky gloom.

An offer from my faithful old agent Fred.
Good heavens! I really thought him dead.
A local performance to play the hero's lead,
the part was really mine, no need to plead.

The perfect part for one so frail and old,
No lines or speeches to learn, so I am told.
Lying very flat throughout the final scene,
Playing centre stage, an ageing actor's dream.

Prostrate and as quiet as any little mouse,
Not a laugh or dry eye throughout the house.
The final curtain closes with a whisper, tight.
I take my exit, unseen, slowly to the right.

No great applause or bellows of riotous mirth.
Past critics gathered speak only of my worth.
My sombre audience leaves with heads bowed down,
to see my ashes reverently scattered on the ground.

Len Stevens

Untitled

I travelled back to the old house today.
A derelict state now,
but still the home to our childhood dreams.

Broken windows stained with years of neglect,
and the front door clings to the frame,
its hinges rusted away.

Inside, the overpowering smell of dampness prevails,
to remind my senses of how the years have elapsed.
A gentle tepid breeze blows through empty rooms.
Only the flutter of cobwebs,
acknowledges its presence and keeps the house alive.

Through the pouring rain,
I thought I saw your ghost at play in our garden.
Your laughter fading into the patter of rain
against the window.

The old wise oak still holds the etched message,
we made together so long ago.
A fitting epitaph for an undying love,
untarnished by time and absence.

Ian Shaw

Renaissance

I once sat surrounded by four walls in a foetal room
Here I sit again (or at least I'd like to)
Every page of every leaf was different then
Now every leaf I read is the same as the first
Why should it happen that our vision becomes cursed?

I once sat surrounded by four walls in a foetal room.
After nine months I was forced out (into an amazing yet confusing world).
The trees independent lexicons soon mingled and became one.
I wish the lexicon never became known.
And my wonder and awe was not just on loan.

Here I sit surrounded by four walls in a foetal room.
I know nothing of nature's gothic playwright (at least I believe I don't).
I know not what to expect when I leave and the irascible tension will not go away.
I'm going to leave my foetal room and rediscover the lexicon of a tree.
If I leave my foetal room I may rediscover the independent lexicon of me.

I no longer sit surrounded by four walls in a foetal room.
As I open the seventh page of an acorn it never ceases to differ from the previous page.
Nature engulfs me as an independent entity.
I left my foetal room and rediscovered the lexicon of a tree.
In leaving my foetal room I rediscovered the individual entity. Me.

Amanda Jane Kerry

Remember Me

A child is born - a joysome thing - so warm, so small and sweet
His mother's love will nurture him and keep him clean and neat.
His faintest cry will soon be heard, for mother loves her son
And ne'er the thought goes through his mind - will any remember me when I'm gone?

So safe within his childhood home, so sure of love and care,
So treasured by his family - such happy days they share.
Whatever he may need is brought and showered upon this precious one,
And never comes the chilling thought - will any remember me when I'm gone?

He grows and plays and learns each day with friends on every hand,
They swing and slide and run and jump, build castles in the sand.
The youth at school, one of the gang, is never on his own
From morn 'til night he's with the boys - he only sleeps alone.

The man, at work, at war, at play has little time to spare,
He makes small marks in earth's vain dust while earth marks him with toil and care.
To those within his special clan he's the important one
Who never thinks, as he rules the roost - will they remember me when I'm gone?

He sits now in his lonely room with idle hands at last
And ponders in the gathering gloom on all his life that's passed.
And younger hands are busy now - of leisure there is none.
At last he wonders - all alone - who will remember me when I'm gone?

Miriam Galway

Mother's Ruin

My, my what a tangled web she weaves
When practising to relieve herself of responsibility
Cycling in tandem, ever onward to the moment of conception

A new life, how precious to begin
Necessary bonding, the fight for love to win
Oh why embark on a facade of selflessness only to
weaken at that crucial moment

Illness gives way to illness, the sickness of adultery
The lovelessness of a half neglected life
Abandonment cutting like a knife... through shredded fibres
Given to sway with any overpowering gust of wind
Without shield, empty presence, hollow shells, white canes and dark glasses
Hearing but cannot, nor see death in life, adult reflection child retention
To cross this awesome gap with unchartered map, Help! we cry... nothing heard,
Not alone able to unpick the second-hand garment
We weave anew, caution, walk again, talk, trust, dare we?
Help! we cry... a faint voice heard
could it be perhaps the voice of understanding
Hope not fleeting, a permanent hand, hope, do we dare?

Gin..... that it were.

Carol Rose

292

A Thousand Words In A Smile

A flicker of wonder, a sentence of many, as I regarded a man with a smile.

Instant recognition, his lips spoke of a wild abandonment without a word.

With shining eyes, a wicked glint, a never will know.

Happy already, with each of our lovers, but our minds had first thought the same.

Another smile, another face, a different melody.

A melancholy look, a tell-tale dart, a crying tearing grin.

I question this with beads of kind and a woven care.
It a lie of cheer, to hide the multiplicity of the pain.

A whispering smile, caught in pleasure, with the sight of a new born child.

Or an echoing of a splendid love, right from the heart of a source.

A deceiving, sly, cripple of a smirk.
Written is intent, a cunning craftiness.
A ready, to strip naked, to gnaw a flesh wound deep.

The smile is a written book, with a constant character of change.

It bridges creeds and cults, it webs the world wide.
So watch every face for a smile, and hear all a thousand words clear.

J. Cross

The Day After

Accomplish your Sorrow, Laugh, Cry and Sleep,
You'll somehow make the leap to Safety, from your Deepest Heartfelt naivety.
From your own dying flair, in times of age old despair, in
ultimatums of Misery, death seeming pretty to you and me.
Don't forget me. That was then, this could be now,
Hold abandoned fate at bay, it will soon seem like yesterday.

When there's only pills, your life marked in nills.
A height only to fall from, only a guide rope to an ending,
Nothing left to say or do, an unnerving, rising blue.
To straddle the high bridge, a primitive ridge,
Standing to suicide, bailing out from social's betterside,
or to sit in your chair and pull the coffin's trigger.
To feel such a way, off the grounds of a general love course,
left hanging in mid-air, feeling sorrowful remorse, through love's
deadly insane force, out of the friendly lair,
waiting to be released and fall, back and forth reasons do excel, your
shadow a target..... and nobody can tell you your blood is too thick.
This torment does vent, it was all meant to check your relief, none
are responsible. So get out of the grave unstable, back to the green light above stable.
The sky, the sun, the ground, the air... beautiful....

James Bell

Words Scratched on Paper at 9.20 pm on Tuesday
5th Sept 1995 in Darkness.

i can think of nothing nicer right now
than to die some kind of dispassionate death...right here...right now...
to escape the phantoms which haunt me day to day and every day -
about who i am, what i am and what people demand from me...
and what they command from me...set me tasks and i rush on
to fulfil them - obliterating me - ...for what am i really?

i am a small tight ball about to burst open and
inside would be found decay and death where once memories
and imagination bloomed and grew.
and i am sick. i am dead. i am nothing.
but a speck waiting to be cleared up and taken away
an empty piece of paper waiting to be scrawled upon by some
madman with his sickly yellow pen.

i can float - indeed - i have floated in the past - been known for it even -
won an award for my achievements in that area - I stayed there for days
bobbing upon the surface tackling the big waves with the mucus
building up all around me. i felt drop-dead drunk as i distorted the
truth - took it away and disguised it - made it tangible and questionable
and chaotic -   - i had lived once -
upon that watery page on which i mutated myself.

Julie Eggbeer

Nature's Comfort

I only know when flowers bloom
and waft their scent around my room,
My loneliness seems to depart
And joy takes over in my heart.

I know as I walk by the stream
The ripples say -'tis but a dream.
The sadness in my heart today
And all my tears are washed away.

I know as I walk through a wood
And lift my eyes up as I should,
I see the blue sky high above
And then I know that God is love.

I know as I walk down the street
And a neighbour at her gate I meet,
A cheery word and a loving smile
Just makes me feel that life's worth while.

I know now on returning home
There is no need to feel alone,
Tomorrow I'll make another start
Hope springs eternal in my heart.

Eunice Dance

Being Friends

Have you ever studied friendship, -
sought its meaning and its worth?
Real sincere and lasting friendship,
all for all, can save this Earth!

Wars and strife bring grief and sorrow;
aggression only brings despair;
greed and avarice are wicked;
those who sanction them, - beware!

Brothers, sisters, I implore you
do not scorn the simple things
God has given us to cherish,
nor the joy that kindness brings!

Let us give and take together
as we go upon life's way;
let nought the bonds of friendship sever,
don't let tyranny hold sway!

Let us work to serve the purpose
for which God gave us the Earth!
Let us serve Him well and truly,
being friends for all we're worth!

N. Egbert Williamson

Friendships Blossom

Friendship is like a special flower
It touches the soul and fills with power
Many colours and kinds abound
But at times a rare one is found

Its precious beauty does not fade
Even when winter winds sweep across the glade
Its stem is built with truth and grace
And any problem will help you face

Hard times are greeted with a grin
Whether they are thick or thin
The generous hand the purse has swelled
Possessions are in common held

Under its petals you take shade
And in its tears swim or wade
Happy times remembered and shared
Or from downfall caught and spared

Search as you will and may
Real friends don't oft pass this way
If you have this treasure found
Hold it tight without a sound.

John Wynn

The Golden Years

Thank you for the Golden years,
years of love and of peace.
Thank you for your kindness, tolerance, your time
I would not have had these very happy years were it not for you,
you are so very thoughtful, in everything you do.
A warm human being, a friend, so caring, so innocent, so loyal, so true.
All these things are precious, they came with your soul.
Do not change, stay the same always for others will always envy
these treasures that God has entrusted to your care, knowing that
you will always tend them lovingly,
just as you tended me, in my time of need . . .

John Anderson

Colander Of Pain

Memories remain, unheeded, banished to the deepest crevice of the
mind, a constant reminiscence struggling to staunch the colander of
pain, where trust seeps through, forced by the bitterness of reality;
past chapters, irretrievable,
dripping ceaselessly; feelings stifled, choking, unwanted,
rage engulfs everything, leaving no survivor,
rage, the powerful protector, annihilates everything, achieves
nothing, drip, drip,
self-esteem, respect, once overflowing, now violated,
trickle unrestrained, broadening the ever-spreading pool of
desolation, darkness is welcoming,
sleep beckons sympathetically, sleep of a kind,
eyelids flicker restlessly, shutters against the storm of emotion
within; dream awakens nightmare,
burning sockets, still covered, drown in tears as consciousness
returns, drip, drip,
face damp against unfamiliar bed linen, crisp from its wrapper,
presses involuntarily downward,
yearning for warm familiarity, where only cold deceit still lingers.

Linda West

My Lily Among Thorns

Floating gently down the stream, Sweet Lily of the Valley
Floating so peacefully it would seem, you didn't have a worry,
Yet as I stare, the truth appears, such destruction is so rare,
They aim their pointed spurs at you and you don't seem to care.
Your petals torn, head held high, blood flows on and on,
Your soul screams, each eye gleams, tears fall like the rain,
Forming swirls of bloody salt, tears build up over all your years,
Rapidly running short.
I feel for you as I watch you die, so painfully, pointlessly wronged,
And wonder why they did to you all that they have done,
You died so sweet and innocent, they gloriously marched in triumph,
To them you never caused a dent of pain, or hurt, no wrong.
They surrounded you for far too long.
They'll choose your own revenge for you,
For causing seen and unseen pain,
As witness to your death my friend, wait for me above,
My Lily Among Thorns, My Love.

Rosalind Black

Lady Of The Night

Oh lady of the night, what opulence and heavenly sight, vision of
beauty, you are my delight.
Soft and serene, angel of my dream, will you be mine,
until the end of time.
And when I hold out my arms and call your name, will you fill my
heart with your incandescent flame.
Will you wrap your blanket around me, keep me warm and hold me
tight, and together we will make it through till the break of light.
Let me caress your celestial body, stroke your silken skin, see
your glowing face, oh how I admire your elegance and grace.
Oh how I adore to watch you wax and wane through the sensuous
hours of the night, then only to dream of your beauty, until you
return to sight
And lady of desire if I were to whisper softly in your ear, would
you kiss me gently, and wipe away my tear.
Oh how I love you so dear, to know you are always near, come say
you will love me too, and fill my soul with your colour blue

Russell T. Turner

Love Is

Little scraps of paper
With loving words enclosed
Make you feel so good inside
It's true, or so I'm told.

The magic words, "I Love You"
Work wonders for the soul.
It puts you on a pedestal
Without it you just fall.

A little child shall lead them
Are the good words of our Lord
It's little children who lead others
To utter those three little words.

Don't leave it too late to say you love someone
It has no meaning when they're gone
A touch, a smile, just a few kind words
Are all so much better than none.

Vera Ewers

Wise Old Woman

To Grandma, with love

Wise old woman, I hear you so
With your advice, I wish to grow
Through your eyes, I wish to see
To live forever, dance and be free

Wise old woman, you teach me life
How to cope with its struggles and strife
To fight I must, but to lose I must fear
And live each day as if death is near

Wise old woman, I love you so
Because of you, I can show
The world my heart, and your love it's caught
And teach generations the lessons you taught.

Kerry Ward

Joshua

The joy in my life is experienced through my child's eyes,
Watching him grow, laugh, play.
The four years have flown by so fast.
I thank God each day for blessing me with him,
He brings joy and laughter into all the lives he brushes by,
I watch on, taking all the credit, feeling very proud.
But it's not my success to hold,
He is himself, not just a part of me,
I can take nothing for granted,
He is a gift for my safekeeping, until he is old enough for his
   own care.
It is my role to guide and support him,
Encourage him to see all, form his own mind.
In only four short years he exudes all the qualities of a great man.
And so my life has been worthwhile in creating his life,
And so the cycle goes on - and on.

Anne-Marie Price

Only A Dream

As I slept a sleep that was so deep
I dreamt my love I chanced to meet
Embracing and sharing inner thoughts
We snuggled down in peace to watch
Sunset arriving gently before our eyes
Reddening a slowly darkening sky

As waves gently washed the pebbled beach
Nature her life's lesson began to teach
Then suddenly in natural shadow, there was light
As we remained embraced throughout the night

Then as I awoke I cried and cried
As all my senses to me had lied
For even dreams from me the facts of life can't hide
My own true love long since had died

E. G. Borwick

Nightmare

I wish I could take hold of lady luck's hand,
and try to persuade her to understand.
My head is heavy, my senses are dull,
death's having some fun with a spider and scull.
I'm walking a tightrope between fear and derision,
It's time to make up my mind and make a decision.
Below me a pit of snakes and strangers in dark places,
Out of a swirling mist come laughing leering faces.
Sinister figures threaten me with knives, guns, and swords,
Dusty old skeletons fall out of locked cupboards.
I'm haunted by ghosts from a dim distant past,
I now know this nightmare cannot possibly last.
I feel the warmth of a brand new day,
Take a fear from a heap and fold it away.
But now to a dungeon all dark and foreboding,
Climbing down the steps I feel I need goading.
From somewhere inside I hear someone moan,
Crouched in a corner weeps a child all alone.
In the dim light a small familiar face I can see,
I know who that child is; for that child is me.

Geraint Ingram

Holy Sacrifice

This is the Mass for which our forebears died
Holy Sacrifice and Sacrament
In which we take the bread He gave.
This is the mystery of Jesus crucified
Christ's command and testament
His gift to all he come to save.

In love and faith for near two thousand years
This command has been obeyed :
"Do this for my remembrance."
An offering of joy, an offering of tears,
In ecstasy and hope most humbly prayed,
For life's exits and its entrance.

In every place and time
This action has been made
For the crowning of a king,
For the healing of a crime,
At dawn's delight and evening shade
And for the marriage of a maid in Spring,
For a lifting of the darkness,
With a prayer in stillness.

Uvedale Tristram

Remember Odin

Far far, in the mists of time
Ancient warriors came to conquer this isle
With ships and sail and horns on their head
They rampaged this isle
Till all blood ran red.

Great Odin a King stood tall and erect
He lived his life over, now lost
Like a sunken ship wreck

Laying down his life, arms under his head
Closed now those eyes, for Odin is dead

A grave now to visit, another tourist attraction
But wait! Just a minute
Hold your breath for a fraction

Odin who lived, so strong and so brave
Deserved much more than those stormy waves
Spend an instant, a moment, even a sad smile

Remember this well
that this was once,
"Odin's Isle"

Hilary M. Crossley

Treasures

The Countryside covered in Velvet Snow,
The moon with all the stars in tow,
Autumn leaves of yellow and red
Covering the ground in natures bed.
Springs warm light showers,
The unfolding of the buds of flowers,
White shafts of light from the sun at dawn like
the cry of a baby being born.
The glory of a summers day,
Sand castles crumbling in the water's spray,
Glorious parks while on their stands come
Triumphant music from the bands.
The pleasure from the golden mile,
But nought can match a baby's smile.

Alan Davenport

Sea-Wife Sarah

Sea wife Sarah
Hair of wild sea weed, eyes of deep sea blue,
Many a strange shore I have seen
But always return to you.

Sea-wife Sarah
In my cockle kitchen, your songs of
Salt sea foam follow me
Like ghosts of drowned mariners
Wherever I should roam.

Sea-wife Sarah
Shimmering naked upon the sand
With shells and pearls plaited
In your hair and a starfish
In your hand.

A moon blackens a sea
Where once two lovers played
And beckons to its waters
My Sea-wife
My mermaid.

Andrea Selina Thomas

Payback

You want it all—give me a break
Another chance? More heartache
You hurt me once, never again
Cheryl then Jane, you'll never tame.
You think you know it all—you know nothing
You thought you had me—you have me not!
You hurt me, hurt me deep,
How could you leave me for her, you creep.
All I hear is you, you, you,
No more, you're dead, cold, blue.
Everything you said was lies—crap
Hey—sh** happens
"Payback" . . .

Amanda Brind

Three Sisters

A tale of two sisters who flew the nest
They went on their way to seek new zest
I thought for a time they would return
But the years slipped away oh how I did yearn
Then husbands and children came their way
And away they did stay
So far away across the water
Wishing the distance to be much shorter
To share in my joys to cry on my shoulder
But alas we are now much older
The years have gone the children have grown
And now the children have children of their own
I'm the third of three sisters
With a yearn in my heart
To have lived much closer right from the start
To share our sorrows and joys as one
And be three sisters at home again

Joy Fairchild

The Stray

He cursed the Stray that fouled his path
And trespassed on his new cut grass.

Each day it scavenged in his bin
That wretched scrap of speed and sin.

You haunt my days and nights he cried
For pity's sake it's time you died.

The warden came in his van
To end a life and he was glad.

He laughed to know his cunning trap
Would end the life of the little chap.

The little chap, yes that's the name
He used in death, head hung in shame.

R. Cocker

Water

Water so cool, so crystal and clear
Springs from the land, like Mother Earth's tear
Trickles down the mountainside
Filling streams and rivers wide,
Whirling and twisting flowing along,
Running swiftly, surging on,
Rushing and gushing over the fall,
Splashing and foaming lapping the wall,
Bubbling and swirling onward it goes
Gleaming and glowing in the sun's golden ray.
This is the water we use every day,
We take it for granted, few questions are asked
As it ripples and dances, caught in the breeze,
Racing and bobbing down to the seas.

Audrey Millership

Down Fantasia Way

Nature bequeaths
From the day one is born
We must follow the path of destiny
Inwardly hopeful - but outwardly worn!
Ever reaching for stars
Although landing halfway on the moon
Many end up flat on back
Frequenting - down - to earth bars!
For takers in life are many
Givers in minority
Vainly seek - the light
Whilst hypocrisy - greed - selfish desires
Lurk - in darkness - of the night!
Thus they can only seek salvation
As distant war drums play
Sadly - life for them is
But a forlorn dream - softly treading
Down a path - called fantasia way!

Harry F. Dickens

Cranborne Chase

I have strolled the woods and walked the paths
And crossed the fields in the aftermath
Of harvester and tractor and baler of hay.
I have done all these things, on a beautiful day.
I have breathed the scent of sun-warmed grass
And seen wild flowers nod their heads as I pass.
I have lain on the earth, the earth that I love
And watched the skylarks in the sky above.
I have seen roses and honeysuckle entwined in the hedgerows
And watched the gulls swoop on the newly turned furrows.
I have picked wild blackberries grown huge undisturbed
And seen tiny wrens dart about unperturbed.
I have seen butterflies shiver as they start to alight
And watched the red sunset as day yields to night.
I have felt the soft night wind on my face
And felt the urge to quicken my pace.
But stayed transfixed by the stars above
My beautiful earth, the earth that I love.

Barbara Anne Smith

Defeat Of Evil

The people's spirit raises up with might,
A new battle now they will fight.
With the return of Arthur The King.
The destruction of Drug Lords He will bring.
The evil doers will not succeed,
No more poison in veins that bleed.
There will be nowhere for them to hide,
For the spirit of Christ in people will abide.
Satan, your reign is over, it is through,
Judgement Day is coming I assure you.
The darkness will be lifted from the people's eyes
No more corruption, no more lies.
For these evils of what you lead,
Make God-fearing people and their children bleed.
The spirit of England will remain and dwell,
Once more, Satan, you'll be cast down to hell.

Pat Russell

The Last Tide

A small boat at her mooring in the grey dawn light,
Her bright blue awning protects her from the night.
The ripples round her bow are like music to the ear,
She is sweetly swaying as the day becomes clear.

Her heart within her engine wonders who will come,
To catch the tide, to feel the wind, the sea her soul has won.
Though the birds and fish are waking, so busy with their lives
No one comes to free her, and creaking, she sighs.

Someone must have heard her, the anchor chain is free,
Her blue bow is pointing to the deep and waiting sea.
She does not pause, she cannot think, only longing to be there
No helmsman is needed, the weather bright and fair.

Many tides may come and go, the sea her soul reclaims,
Though her mooring is empty her shadow remains,
And happy in that harbour, a better place than this,
No more winds to toss her, the tides she cannot miss.

Ann P. Vesey-FitzGerald

"Home is the Lady"

I've visited Crete and Kos and Rhodes
Egypt's Sphynx and Sunny Palestine,
Madeira where sweet the wines flow
I've watched the dawn come up along the line
From Colorado to San Diego.

Paris was pavement hot in late July,
And provincial light was artist bright
For perfect painting of sunflowers
Sitting in a lavender haze in Grasse
Dreaming away the daylong hours.

Yet of all the wonderful places I've been to see
Staffordshire is home for me

Jean Banks

What Do You Think Of Me

I have not a clue what you are thinking of me.
Sitting close to me so faithfully.
We sit together in our own thoughts and never say a word.
You are smiling a little and nothing can be heard.
It is comforting you are here.
You don't have to speak I know you love me dear.
We both know we are here together and words
Don't have to be spoken.
We find happiness in the peace unbroken.
The silence of love is all around and is understood by me.
This is how we live in perfect harmony.
What you think of me does not matter really
Because I will always love you so dearly.

Barbara Douglas

The World

I adore the moon that shines in night sky
I adore the sun at its hottest as noon flies by
I adore still lakes that inspire peace from within
And I adore birds that make nature so deep
I adore trees, the wind and the rain
I adore life, we have so much to gain
I adore the mind, the body, the soul
And I adore the world that makes me feel whole

Stephanie Brown

During Wind And Rain

For the day was broke
With a clap and a flash.
As one by one left their play
And sought to find a warm abode.

The whistling of wind, waking the branches
And scaring the leaves.
Of a cold, hard fall of poignant rain,
Beating down on the once dry land.

Dull faces gazing sadly out of the window.
As outside the land, is torn and destroyed.
Everywhere deserted, abandoned,
While above, the storm battles and tears and decays.

I long to go out, to smile and succeed
For here I'll be winning, determined, no fall.
I will laugh at the wind and scorn at the rain.
And stay 'til the end and relish the joy.

Deborah Helen Johnston

a tðo senyœr tðo honyœr
(Honour To Whom Honour Is Due)

Few things in the realm of honour are more
Significant than this French expression,
Since we seldom see honour being done
To those to whom honour is due but soar

They can never to Alpine heights truly.
To make matters worse, toadies, all over,
Genuflect before them under veneer
Of myriad pretexts shamelessly.

That superlatively long word, used by
Shakespeare, 'honorificabilitudinitatibus'
Meaning 'honourableness', is a rebus
Which they can't resolve, all loafers workshy.

Millions of mortals accomplish what is
Merely the appurtenance and semblance
As they need not sweat for it or penance
But show only external expertise.

'Nosce Teipsum' — know thyself — is the way
To explore the right penetralia
The inner, real prosopopoeia
Of the temple of soul the whole to fay.

Madhukar L. Wadikar

The Toy Box

In the corner of the room stood a big blue box
Stencilled with puppets and a clown,
With a lift-up lid and a lining inside
Where games and toys abound.
A battered tin soldier which has seen better days,
A fort and a clockwork mouse,
A farmyard with animals, a tractor too,
Three chairs and a table from an old dolls house.
A small rag doll and a soft green frog,
An elderly bear looking quite forlorn,
A ball, a skipping rope, a spinning top
And a handsome rabbit with his jumper torn.
Many little people have been delighted by this box,
Many hours wiled away in play,
But quite which toy has been played with most
is very difficult to say.

Susan Small

The Butterfly

I saw a butterfly today
As on the garden bench I lay.
It landed softly on my nose, and seemed to say,
"I don't suppose you'd come with me and play?"
Away it fluttered through the flowers,
I pursued, we played for hours.
Chasing, skipping, jumping high,
Trying to catch that butterfly.
I was having so much fun
I did not see the harm I'd done,
Until I heard an angry shout
"What is that kitten all about?"
I ran and hid behind the shed
And peeping out with fear and dread,
Saw flowers scattered all around,
Squashed and broken on the ground.
The butterfly, it waved goodbye,
And fluttered up into the sky.
With all around me in a flap
I stayed low, and had a nap.

Rosemary A. Ingles

Resurrection

If I had died 'ere this, I would have flown
Straight to my Lord, clad in my winding sheet.
But now, I'm just a little pile of ash,
Nestling within my modest funeral urn,
Soon to be scattered on the Surrey hills,
My ash to merge into that ancient soil.

And is this, then, God's purpose? This the end?
But look again in His good time: the hour
When ash and dust will raise a living flower,
Warmed by the sun and nurtured by each shower.

Frances Dobsen

Friend?

I have one eye, but I don't see
Yet most everyone stares at me
Though I can be offensive, I mean no harm
I can make you cry through my charm

Emotions range from bad to good
Exactly as I knew they could
New stories I can now unfold
But you will see they are ages old

I can both be silent, yet full of natter
We can both talk together, it won't matter
While you are speaking I won't hear
Whilst through my tones you'll prick up your ear

I'll tell you stories from around the world
And on your doorstep the news unfurled
This fount of knowledge, you ask, who can it be?
In reply, 'tis simple, I'm your T.V.

Rex Pilbeam

Our Queen 70 Years

Golden years have slipped away
Fond - memories Linger on.
There is so much we would like to say
Of the marvellous things you have done.

It is a wonderful thing to achieve this age
To give so much pleasure to so many
A shining example to young and old
A lovely mum and a granny

So today must be a special day
No birthday could mean so much
The Nation is with you all the way
To know you are well is all we ask

Happy birthday to you Our Queen
With many more to come.
A day we will all remember
Shining like the morning sun.

William Banks

Song Of The Swan

Rippling, rippling, waters of earth
May I ask you one question—when was your birth?
For since you have given me nothing but pleasure.
You are my home, my life, and my treasure.

Rippling, rippling, water so cool.
You are not stagnant like many a pool.
Leaves gently float by, reeds bend beneath you.
Dragonflies dart past from a summer sky of blue.

Rippling, rippling, water so clear.
Cool gentle waterfall, white foaming weir.
Willows bow down their heads washing their hair
As you clean and caress them with a dear mother's care.

Babbling, boiling, water so dank.
Flooding the countryside, breaking each bank.
Torrent of fury, speeding towards the sea.
No time for anyone, not even me.

Rippling, rippling, water of Spring.
Subsided and peaceful, greeting my offspring.
Giving of yourself, giving me pleasure.
You are my home, my life and my treasure.

Peter D. Purbrick

Storms Of The Soul

Hail stones blow hard against the soul
and beat furiously against the mind,
Gale force winds disturb the peaceful day
and unsettle everything they find.

Thunder rolls into a hollow heart
and the angry echoes sound,
A black cloud closes in thick and fast
and soon it is all around.

Bolts of lightning strike in haste
and lash out at anyone,
Suddenly all is silent and calm
but the storm has not gone.

A moment's grace to breathe a heavy sigh
and listen to the whispering air,
A moment for two weary eyes to rest
and another trying not to care.

In the darkness there is a piercing scream
and it is a scream of living pain,
Lightning strikes twice and thunder struck
as teardrops fall down like heavy rain.

Kathleen Speed

Time

Every second wakening or sleep, turns
to minutes ticking with sounds of despair.
Thoughts in the silence without your voice
stab the heart with pangs of pain unfair.

Cold are the nights without you, chill
winds, dull thoughts of what were happy days.
The weeks are veiled in shrouds of mist,
the months only remind me of your loving ways.

Anniversaries bringing memories come and go,
opening the scars of loss and love,
searing through the human defences, even
knowing you are safe in Heaven above.

Years can roll by but never erase the
suffering of being torn asunder, nor yet destroy
the pleasure and love we still together share.
Time alone cannot surpass that earthly joy.

The ages of man must always cease
in the eons of infinity to abide.
My fervent hope for eternity is to
hold you tight and forget I cried.

Geoff Powell

How Many Words

How many words can I find to say
Just how I feel in my heart
I'll try to discover and tell to you too
Though I just don't know where I can start

Care is the first word, just four letters long
With cosset and pamper behind
Emotion and tenderness, filled full of joy
Ecstatic and losing one's mind

Euphoric and dreamy, fragile and shy
Full of wonder at thoughts of your charms
Blissful, devoted, besotted and coy
Always happy to be in your arms

Contented and peaceful, happy to know
I have found a treasure so rare
Wanting to give you all that I am
Wanting my life to share

Filling my day with thoughts of pure joy
These gifts from heaven above
Are small things alone but when put together
They make up the biggest word - LOVE.

Rosemary Atherley

Shopping In The Supermarket

When I'm shopping in a supermarket
And pushing a trolley around,
Things are never where I expect them,
So I always cover a lot of ground!

Tins are here, boxes are there,
Not forgetting the packets and crates,
And I believe that some trolley pushers
Should be wearing their 'L' plates!

There's an assistant on the shop floor,
Trying to open a cardboard box,
It would seem with all the trolleys and baskets about
That assistant is in for some knocks!

Another assistant is pricing goods,
With tickets from a small machine,
And yet another is stamping prices on tins,
As I go past to check the prices I've seen.

I once more survey this busy, bustling world
As I make my way to the till,
And now there's only one problem left,
That is having enough money to pay the bill!

Rachel Johnson

What Are We Doing To Creation

What are we doing to creation
The leaves shake and wither
Their secret powers of tales of the world
Hide under their precious flowers

But the petals exposed to the damaged sun

Claim the rays
Of torture and soon to die with all of us
The creation bursts asunder

God gave us power to think
Dying trade spotted leaves, wrench
At my heart and soon fallen trees will crunch the forest floor

No heart beat more, no saviour's ear
All are gone to the car
A broken leaf tells more of sin under the sun
Of silicon repair and severe danger for all who dare

Run their car
For a justice higher than the wheels of fortune
Which creates man from the stars
Sings out amongst the crowns of trees
Of starvation, thirst and the death of God.

Glynis Klein

The Anxiety Complex

Whoever you are, sweet girl of desire,
Of great heart, soul, and spirit of fire,
Who tries so hard, to be gentle kind and good,
Puts others first, without question, as an angel would;
Who weeps and weeps, at emotional strain
And if there is no one there, try, try, again
To fight the waves of tears, anguish and stress,
With the help of a friend, buy a new dress,
To go out for a while with a person of trust,
Maybe call for a meal, and linger, if you must.
Every little action helps to quell the darkest of deeds.
To create a new understanding will help sow the seeds,
For a brighter future, and a great new life.
To put an end to all this trouble and strife.
There is no doubt, that with resolve and will
And with the help of those who love you still,
You will overcome the demons from hell
And will emerge pure and, well, only time will tell.

Richard Douglas Cartwright

Visions of Black

This colour black
where was it born?
Was it born in the night time sky
with glistening stars in among it?
Or was it born with the black bat
flip flapping its wings in the night sky?
Or was it born with the big black crow
with its feathers glistening in the sun?
Or a big black stallion
prancing around?
Or a little tiny black kitten?
No
it's the big wide pupils of an owl
while it's sitting and hooting all night.

Zelfie Newcombe (age 10)

A Moment Of Time

Time enough we have not, to do, and see the all,
A million years and more will pass, but our time we cannot stall,
A flicker and a moment, existence here and gone,
Time will come and time will go, but I'll not see it all,
Wind rain sun snow, seasons come and seasons go,
time stands still, or so it seems, time enough to fill my dreams,
But wait, I am beyond that I longed to come,
a flicker of time, no longer young,
Flickers of time forgotten, we will join them soon,
within this sphere of flickers, we have no more room,
Time is like the wind, here and gone, but not seen,
taking along our memories, and ruining our dreams,
No stopping and asking if we have done,
just carries on going like the stars and the sun,
Our time's at an end now, but what do we know,
it could be beginning, and this time, go slow.

F. R. Wood

Lovesick Suicide Note

While you're alive
I'd rather be dead and without you,
Than being alive and knowing about you,
As I am hijacked on the road to a heart,
My engine tampered and taken apart,
In a shipwreck my emotions scattered,
Lost in a glass place that constantly shatters,
While you're alive
I wish I never met you as you wish not to know me,
"They both lived happily ever after" if only!
I am the toy airplane that's crashing,
Not taken seriously and soon to find the dustbin,
I am the lame horse the owner forgot,
I am the lame horse with a broken leg and heart,
While you're alive
I am soon to be shot.

Lee Ingram

Why?

The pale moon from way on high
Looks down on the earth and wonders why
Could the folk below not change their life
Cease their ways of fighting, killing, and strife
Could not some-one, somewhere for a change
Instead of destroying, rebuild once again
    While I wonder, from afar,
The silent moon is joined by a star
Not a Christmas one who guided wise men
A truce for Christmas? All fighting to end?
Once more the sick, hungry, and cold,
Rest where they can, nothing to hold,
While we sing carols, in warmth, and light
And now and then give a thought to their plight
No tomorrow for some, so cold, and sad,
No tidings of joy, no wishes so glad
Let's stop the making of weapons to kill,
Some men get rich, the poor pay the bill
With their lives, homes, and all they hold dear,
For them not much hope of a happy New Year.

Phyl Adams

A Friend Is.....

A friend is someone who's always there,
Not someone who doesn't seem to care.
A friend shares everything, if you let her,
She doesn't discard you for something better.
A friend makes you laugh or just smile,
She doesn't ignore you for a long while.
A friend is someone that you're close to,
And she respects you, whatever you do.
A friend is someone with whom you're yourself,
Not hiding the real you, in a box, on a shelf.
A friend is someone whom you can trust,
Friendship shouldn't turn to dust.

Emma Sharp

The Sparrow

Pitiful urchin of the Sky, tatty and unrobed.
No Scion of Nobility of the feathered world.
Why no talent on thee has Nature bestowed?
No pompous display with thy feathers unfurled?
Surely art no classical warbler of the Skies,
With no melody to appease the mortal's ears.
Merely scoffing morsels with twittering cries
This way of survival few express any fears.
Dost thou envy the sweet song of the Skylark?
Or the Nightingale's melody in full trill?
In the Valley of Song they have left their mark,
Where thy vocal strains lie dormant, still.
No feathery plumes to enhance your hidden charms
Art thou a vagrant as we must surely surmise?
With thy feathered coat, so unruffled and calm,
Art thou just an exiled outcast from the Skies?
On roof-tops and hedge-rows, thou dost abide,
Embraced as Mother Nature's arms still extend,
Freedom of the air, enjoyed with impish pride,
Nature has much to offer, my feathered Friend.

Frederick William Westley

The Garden

If ever you walk and if ever you talk
'Neath the shade of a tree, at the sound of a bee
By chrysanthemums tall and a quaint waterfall
You'll hum that forever
Or if ever was never
You are in an English garden.
Weep by desolate shade
Where the birds give you aid
All in winter is bare
But still you can stare
On an English garden
For by hollyhocks grand you can quietly stand
For the birds of a feather they flock together
In an English garden.

Peter Buss

Evening Star

A cool green evening sky,
With bright star cast on high,
I think of you with love, and
Dream of times gone by,
When all was well and our world was kind,
And the dark deep shadows were far behind,
But waiting their time to bring sorrow and pain,
To turn bright days into sad ones again.
The star shines on in the realms above,
But I'm lost as I look to the sky for your love,
Your love has gone and my eyes are dim,
And I covet the star as it shines on high,
Does the diamond-bright light shine from darkening skies
With a message of love for a heart that still cries?

Ina Paterson

A Sailor Song

Each time I yearn to hear thy voice
And blessed by thought in knowing it well
Its gentle breath shall not cease
How much I find myself away thee
This ship that rides its endless sight
A thousand miles away thy side
Strong heart of thine I hear it beat
To send thy only love to sleep
How sweet them joys of yesterdays
Them happy smiles thy happy face
And feel them not that far away
And as we fear such savage waves
The echoes of each creeping wind
I hear thy voice and hear it sing
And in that dream sweet love was made
But not as sweet as that sweet day
What's gladly locked up in my thoughts
Themselves constant like thy charms
To dwell or grow that way upon
To thee from were I'm gone.

Brian Morris

Nothing In Particular

My heart goes crazy without you
I jump when the phone rings,
Hoping, praying it's you
Every time I'm disappointed
I check the mail first thing in the morning
Hoping, praying there'll be mail from you.
I retreat disappointed
I gaze at nothing in particular
Hoping, praying that you will appear
But there is only empty space before me.
I know deep inside me: You won't phone,
You won't write, you won't appear before me
And as I realize this, tears roll
Down my cheeks as I gaze at nothing in particular.

Saman Raniah Khan

The Power of Love

Well I tried, I really did,
I didn't want this, God forbid!
Unattachment my soul intent,
No, never, would I relent.

My concrete walls, not quite complete,
Were not prepared for this defeat.
They held up strong, they served me well,
They fought with dignity as they fell.

With heart in hand, and white flag flying.
I climbed through the rubble where my pride lay dying.
Vulnerable and weak, with no defences,
Our life, my captor, now commences.

So now the deadly deed is done,
The battle's over, you have won!
What now my love, what fate for me?
You have now to decide my destiny.

I. V. Rose

Loveless Lifetime

Hollow words with angry exchanges
We are poles apart and acting like strangers
It never used to be like this
Just one look, embrace, one kiss...
But now wherever you are near
I look for signs, perhaps a tear
But all I see is an empty shell
We know it's over but just won't tell
Living as shadows trapped within this world
Staying together just because we should
And now our lives have trundled past
Our hollow years set in a memory cast
As I stare down at your lifeless face
I know I'm free to live at my own pace
I may be old but I'm not done
At last my chance at life has come.

Nicola Carol Sell

Grave

'Tis a place of death
where many a sad moment have passed
Till dusk, till dawn
Does no pain ever escape
I have come here for forgiveness
I have come on a whim, not despair
Nor fear of what treachery has passed
I have come to bless sorrow upon futures
I have come to end it all

Craig J. Smith

Drought

There is an extreme water shortage,
They are calling it a drought,
When I turn my taps on nothing coming out.
They say it should be funny,
But I cannot raise a laugh.
I have to jump in with the goldfish,
When I want to have a bath.
For water, I'm drinking vintage french champagne,
Even when the water does come back,
On champagne I'll remain,
I'm washing in pure cider,
I'm shaving with milk stout
But what else can you do,
When the water has run out,
I'm now totally convinced
And of that there is no doubt,
That there is an extreme water shortage,
And it is definitely a drought.

F. C. Pelton

Oh! Good She's Home

In trying to do the things I ought,
I seem to make her more distraught.
The things I should have done it seems
never entered my wildest dreams.
Did you feed the dog? - "He wouldn't eat"
Have you watered my plants as a special treat?
You got in the washing, I can see.
I don't suppose it's been ironed, for me?
You forgot to give the dog his pill!
We're out tomorrow, now he'll be ill.
It's about this time I find my voice
(Not as if I can talk by choice)
"How did your day go"? I'm heard to say,
"You've been working up the shed all day"
She answered, not hearing what I'd been saying.
You met our grandson, is he out playing?
Did you give him food, when he got home?
I hope you didn't leave him alone.
By now my ears were tightly shut.
I love her and I'd tell her so, but——

Don Chaplin

Golden Prize

I stopped to watch the setting sun,
Wondering what miracles had just begun,
In awe, at why just I deserved
To have my human heart so served,
With such a filling feast as this,
And have my soul beset with bliss.
As I gaze on, my eyes absorb
The beauty of that lonely orb,
As it spins on through boundless space,
It finds the time to warm my face,
And take the chill from my cold hands,
While giving flowers to barren lands,
Growing grass on majestic mountains,
Leading me to magic fountains.
Showing me that life can be
Full of joy and running free,
Full of tears and full of hope,
Full of fears, yet I can cope. With this;
More fulfilling than the finest wine,
This golden prize that is just mine.

Ian James Elliott

Stolen Lives

Their parents were unpacking, the children were told to play
They were playing on the beach, such a bright and sunny day

Two hours they were searching, no evidence could be found
The parents didn't want to think the worst,
That their children had been drowned

Twelve days had gone by slowly, we felt so very grave
Until early one morning a child washed up near a cave

As the sun was rising, a jogger passing by
Caught a sight of something that almost made him cry

It was a child's body, swept up by the sea
The cruel sea had taken her, then brought her back to me

Just a few days later a little boy was found
Washed up by the water lying on the ground

Amanda Wakefield

Untitled

When I was very, very young I heard a vicious lie:
That one day you would go away
That one day you would die
Not a second I believed you
Not a second did I cry
If seeing is believing I'd only have to close my eyes
You told me to remember (though I wouldn't even try)
You won't be here forever to hold for me the sky
Then I was not so clever so I instantly replied
"What a bad, bad thing to say"
For I was just a child
But now I'm all alone
And I couldn't even smile
For when I'm on my own
The sky is just too high

Elina Fahmi

Friend

Who are you, my little one?
How much do you know?
I know you're mine
and you are, so very kind.
You have known all along
that in my heart your name is there.
Imprinted, stamped for good.
Before long you will be grown
and I feel that my heart will be broken for you,
you will have no barriers, everything will be open.
You are my friend, my little son.
You are my breath, my life and sun.
Because of you, my life is complete.
When I'm with you I can face defeat.
The best little friend I ever had.

Claudia Flaxton

The Hero

A man who is quiet, and never let's know
His feeling for life. A smile, an hello.
Of his finest intention, he has not a clue,
And without thought, he will see it through.

He could be there, next to you, in a crowd,
You would never guess, he won't shout aloud
He has no idea, that an hero he will be
But when the deeds done, his heart we will see

Whether saving children, cats, dogs or toads,
Or helping aged friends across the roads.
He's never likely to shout, hey look at me.
Only time knows, what he his going to be.

There's always something, to create distress,
This is when the hero, is at his best.
He never has a problem, stepping out of line.
But he'll always do it, just at the right time.

How does he find time, to listen to his friends.
An argument would see him, making amends.
Of any award, he would just give it a glance,
And be glad, he was there, to be given the chance.

Jack Preston

Happy Days

In days of long ago -
 When I was very young,
I used to climb the mountains
 and bask in the summer sun.

To hear the distant valley sounds
 and birds singing in the trees,
happiness was all about
 'twas more than bliss to me.

To see the trout in the mountain pools,
 and the lambs skipping o'er the lea.
This was my enchanted world
 and I miss it constantly.

Royston Lawrence

The Welsh Shawl

It still hangs in the hall—Mam's Shawl
Cuddled in it when small—Mam's Shawl
First faltering steps, painful fall, nursed better in
 —Mam's Shawl.

Christmas play, curtain call, little shepherd in
 —Mam's Shawl.
Grown tall, worldly wise, know it all,
Pause awhile in the quiet hall, gently touch
 —Mam's Shawl.

Pat Penrose

Parting

The time has come to say goodbye.
It's not an easy thing.
The love we shared just you and I
Did mean just everything.
But you did throw that love away
To be with others far away.
You broke my heart a million ways,
when you threw away those happy days.
All the laughter and the fun,
It had all only just begun.
The days were good and full of love.
But why, my love, did you have to cheat,
And lie to me?
The one who gave all
Their heart and soul to be with you.
A love, a home, a family.
I gave them up just for you.
There's no more I can give to you.
You have found your love is someone new.
So goodbye my love, I will not cry. I just keep on wondering why.

E. A. Haskey

The Glory Of Wiltshire

Oh! Wiltshire, County of hidden vales and plains,
Of old highways and winding leafy lanes,
Wooded vales where streams run deep,
And in Summer's sun, your valleys sleep.

Your rolling hills, crowned with trees,
Gentle breezes around them, that downward carries
Summer's perfumes of blossoms and grasses,
In the meadows below, buttercups and daisies in masses.

Tumbling brooks and the old mill-streams,
Shimmering in the sunlight, like old day-dreams.
You hold in your heart your beauty to yourself,
'Till an author writes of it, in a book on the shelf.

Little villages, their churches' lofty spires
Reaching up as landmarks that the swallow requires
As it visits you, Wiltshire, yet once again,
Singing its song, through sunshine or rain.

And so as you slumber, in Summer's warm sun,
As you have done since your time has begun,
We will enjoy beauty till our dying day,
And then we, still, in your green valley lay.

Dennis J. Cannings

I Hate Golf

I have caddied my way up the fairways
Finding balls in the plough and the scrub;
I have ne'er been so cold, quite insufferably cold
Trailing on from the Withy House Club.

The wind cuts my face like a dagger
I'm fighting a torrent of hail,
My cries go unheard, or ignored for
They're up on the green in a gale.

I can tolerate anything normal,
No elements hinder my path
If I know in the end I can always depend
On a fire and some tea and my bath.

But they tell me they're going to teach me,
At my driving and putting they scoff...
Though I've caddied all day and uphill all the way
I shall *never* know how to play golf..

When their balls whistle past me I shudder,
There's a tee in the mud at my feet.
My dog's dashed away - he's defying all rules
And retrieving it out of the wheat.

P. Moorhead

Alone

Dedicated to my husband who died 20-9-95

Peace came at last but you are gone
The warm hand-clasp and loving embrace
The empty chair - is there
But we are here who loved you
We recall the gifts you left
Imparted in your family.

The kind heart, the sympathy, the fun
The sad heart clings to these
Your memory lives.
The outer shell of you is left behind
A new whole shining frame is yours
No pain, no deafness, no failing health remains.

The tide has turned and you will find
In your new life the birds and flowers
you loved, in brighter, purer hues
Old friends and loved ones there
Welcoming
Joyful with songs once more.

Gloria

G. N. Havard

Prayer And Love Unites

Prayer unites all nations. It has no boundary
between race colour or creed. Prayer is a common
bond uniting all. Priests failing in their calling
through lust or greed are only humans doing
the devil's deeds,
instead of using God's call to reform us all. Let us
pray for everyone. Love and prayer is good for us and
unites all in love and peace.

E. C. Williams

Mother N

A winter morning's sun, casts its pale glow,
Across a sleeping land,
Blanketed with snow.

No rustle from the hedgerow, no birdsong from the trees.
Everything stripped bare,
By her chilling breeze.

Oh where is the wind, from the night before,
That scattered clouds across the sky
That threatened every door?

Has she also become exhausted, needing rest and sleep,
Having tired her raging mood,
That left the snows so deep?

And yet, the beauty of her power, can take your breath away,
The scene on this cold winters morning,
Her destructive moods betray.

Dave Kenyon

The Stranger

A blazing fire lit up the room,
As snow fell to the ground,
A homeless man with no-where to go,
Made not a single sound.

He had no money, no food or spare clothes,
But had a twinkle in his eye.
This man I said I've seen before,
But maybe it was just my mind.

I took him in and gave him food,
And then I made him warm,
He ate until he was content,
And asked if he could stay 'till morn.

He left in the morning without making a sound,
I wish that I could have done more,
If there's ever a day that he comes again
I'll make sure I will do more,

Because now I don't know if I knew him or not,
And maybe I never will,
But someone once said I will find out soon
I just have to wait until...

Kara Codd

Eyes

His eyes are the mirrors of his soul.
He looked within me and my heart he stole.
The passion and conquest in his eyes,
He many a time tried to disguise.

But he can't hide anything from me.
He doesn't realize what it is I see.
Beyond his eyes his heart doth lie,
And I see, and I hear it cry.

His eyes gently sparkle in the dark.
But his soul still cries out to me, hark!
The pain of love he lost.
In his eyes I see the cost.

His eyes mirror my reflection, and
The pain of his cold love rejection,
But love I will never hurt you
Look in my eyes and you'll see it's true.

Debbie Fitzgerald

A Star In The Dark

"One afternoon at Half Past Four,
My Son, you crossed that road
And forgot your green cross code,
Son, you could not have seen
That Jesus was there guarding thee,
Flashing lights, siren bells
Please Jesus make him well,
To heaven I glanced and prayed
"Please Jesus don't take my son away."
My prayer he answered
"To mother of a now blind son.
Even in his darkness,
Your eyes and your kindness.
This will be your son happiness"
Thank you Jesus, you saved my son.
"Please take care of him when I'll be gone."

G. Phillips

My New Home

I've been here a year, or so they say,
When I came I thought it was a holiday.
I sit in this chair day and night,
I'm here all alone there's no-one in sight.

They've all gone to bed and it's only eight,
But were all told, "it's ever so late".
I'm not going until after ten,
But at six o'clock they'll get me up again.

I'm so unhappy and feel so alone,
They say, "cheer up darling this is your home."
But I can't do this and I can't do that,
I'm not even allowed to have a cat.

How can this house be my home,
When I feel so sad and all alone.
Please dear God take me away,
And bring contentment into my day.

Shirley Ann Lambert

Untitled

Nowhere is home for a black plastic sack
Full of belongings from someone's back
Scattered across a strange room floor
Packed with the contents of a life once before
Sad and so helpless, with old dreams inside
Of a handsome groom, and a radiant bride
Now the sack lies with no cupboard or shelf
To empty the contents of its inner self
Even a clock is ticking within
The desolate darkness of the black sack's rim
Hurled in the bottom, snatched from my hand
Lies without love, my wedding band.
Now the black sack has left my address
I will have no fear, I must confess
For black sacks are lethal, their owners are too
Both could quite possibly suffocate you.

Lynda Lewis

Be Thankful

Do you ever wonder, what kind of life 'twould be,
If there was never any sunshine,
No flowers, no grass, no sea,
No friends or companions to cheer you on your way,
No loving arms to enfold you, at the end of the weary day,

No one to share your heartaches, laughter, joys and fears,
No gentle hand to caress you, to brush away your tears,
No sound of children's laughter as they go about their play,
No twinkling stars at night along the Milky Way,

No songbirds to wake you in the morning,
No moon to shine at night,
We take these things for granted, as though it is our right,
Let us dwell upon these things, as we go along life's way,
I will thank the Lord for all these gifts,
As I kneel down to pray.

Josephine S. Hill

The Priory

The priory stands erect and forlorn
Where once monks sang, new faith was born
These soaring pillars, toward heaven above
Resounded with sound, were filled with love

Where once stood a house of wisdom and light
The walls are in darkness, the windows no sight
Now all that remains are tumbled stones
That cover the graves of old bleached bones

A creeping mist comes to chill the air
With ghost-like fingertips to dampen my hair
How long I'd stood dreaming and gazing around
As the cold gripped my body, not making a sound

Reluctant at leaving, feet turned to lead
No caution taken of where they tread
The steps beneath, were jagged and wet
Blood formed in a pool, where flesh and stone met

House of my dreams, where the winds blow through
Moldering ruins, but the grass grows new
At night fall the monks and I do roam
The grounds of the priory; Forever our home

Lynn Harman

Soul Mate

As the pure and gentle dew drops,
Fall on green and welcoming plants,
Willing its security of moistness on dry leaves,
So as my heart, innocent and true,
Waiteth for thy dew of love,
Releasing purity together of the natural kind.

The flower in all its rays of beauty,
Humbly waiteth for the butterfly to fulfil its duty,
So waiteth I in sincerity of love and devotion,
claiming what is divine in friendship of mind,
It's a gift of time, love unrefined melts my heart,
Cleanses my thoughts of negativity in a world of mysticism.

My inner self, being naked
To the gift of life,
Love of an honest and pure form,
Two souls pure in the presence of higher beings,
Magical to the naked eye.
Climbing to higher existence of love and beauty
In one accord with the universe,
Expressing peace and joy in soul mate.

Jessie Moyo James

I Remember

When travel meant a journey on your bicycle
On foot, or perhaps a steam train for a treat,
Not motor ways, speeding and road-rage
Or gridlock on a system you can't beat.

When communication was a hand-written letter
Or a friend coming round to have a chat,
Not a fax or a message on an answer phone
An E-mail or anything like that.

When trust was given by a simple handshake
Good manners were what one naturally expected,
Everyone knew who their neighbours were
And age was something children still respected.

When gay still meant light-hearted and care-free
And ecstasy was just pure happiness,
When children could roam free and unmolested
For people's lives were not in such a mess.

Now as science and technology rush forward
Do we never stop to think about the cost?
For in the constant struggle for more progress
It seems to me there's something we have lost.

Ann Rickhuss

There Is Always Love

"Grey Hair?"
"No is yours?"
"Aching back?"
"Just a bit." "Do you need a walking stick?"
"I still want you."
"I want you too."
"Well we are not too old for love."

"Where does time go?"
"It's like a dream and if we scream,
Do you think that we wake up?"
"No my darling but don't despair,
For you I will always be there."
"And of course we are not too old for love."

"As you get older you get worse."
"Oh now, you like me that way."
"What are our plans for today?"
"Doctors first then we can play."
"Because we are not too old for love.
No, no we are not too old for love."

Dora Conway

Voices Of The Weather

I am the wind fiercely roaring.
Blowing down trees, and sending leaves soaring,
Hold onto your hats, and your brollies as well.
What I'm going to do next, you never can tell.

I am the rain, I never stop falling,
Wetting your feet, and soaking your clothing.
I make your shoes squelch, as you step in my puddles.
At the bus stop, wet people are standing in huddles.

I am the sun shining brightly all day,
If you don't cover up, you'll get burned with my rays.
I sparkle on the sea, and warm the sand.
Spend a while in my company, and you'll get nice and tanned.

I am the lightning, a wonderful sight.
You should see me flashing, especially at night,
Then comes the thunder, this noise some folk fear.
For miles and miles my echo you can hear.

I am the frost, I think folk call me Jack,
I sometimes forget the exact time to come back,
So please forgive me, if I have made you grieve,
You'll find my apology in the patterns I weave.

Jean Monteith

Vision Of Winter

Beautiful red sunset shining on a ground of white
Take me to your shining light
Trees bare dancing in the winter chill
Places untouched by human foot
Taking me higher
Drifting further and further into the unknown
An empty train station dimly lit
Evil out there on the street
Incoherent voices surrounding me
Is there an end?
Or is there a new beginning?
Softly I dream
As a red sky surrounds me
In fields of white I lie
A contented but bewildered soul
Wandering and wandering
In hopeless flight
Take me I am here
Lead me lead me
Into your guiding light.

P. A. Swidenbank

The Rubbish Tip

The gates open at eight,
In the summer they close really late,
The pleasant "Hellos",
The angry bellows,
Or maybe the odd "Thank You Mate!"

They come in cars
Some people think they're form Mars,
Black bags and metals
Some branches and flower petals
Maybe one day some gold bars.

After the day is done
And all the cars have been and gone
The office doors are shut,
On the big green hut
In a strange way today's been rather fun.

Now we are at home,
Sleeping and waiting for morning to come
The alarm clock rings
'Creak' go the bed springs
Another crazy day has begun.

E. F. Burrell

The River

Tinkle, trinkle, moon beams, sun rays.
A flowing River, calm!

Green grass, blue sky, fish swim.
A flowing River, why?

I sit and look, I sit and stare,
I ask myself, but no one's there.
A quiet place, it's all the same,
I need someone to take the blame.

Torrents of anguish, flowing like the River.
A tight feeling - a feeling of empty.

Something is missing, it's been taken away.
Inside I am hollow,
Inside I am grey.

I know that someday my chance will come.
My turn to stand up, to undo what was done.

It was my fault, it wasn't my fault.
Whose fault was it?
A flowing River.
Movement...
Now at peace!

Ruth Ann Ryan

Warwick Castle

It's a magnificent castle,
Full of beauty and magic.
A castle with a history,
From medieval times to the present day.

A castle visited by many,
Including Kings and Queens of past and present.
And Winston Churchill,
Before he was Prime Minister.

But now all that come are tourists,
From all over the world,
Who come to marvel at the castle,
And be transformed by its power.

When they walk through the gates,
They imagine what life was like,
Many years ago,
Behind those magical walls.

The parties that were given,
The clothes that were worn,
The food that was eaten,
At this mysterious castle of Warwick.

Sarah Wale

Flying Free

I wish I was a bird flying above the mountain and trees,
gliding higher and higher into the air,
Diving and gliding through the meadows, so green and fresh,
gliding free from all trouble and sorrow of the world,
through trees then gliding higher and higher.

Just glancing back only once, on the past and only landing once,
then flying high into the air gliding over mountains and trees,
weaving in and out of trees, overland so great and fresh and free,
just to be a bird, feeling the breeze on my face and through my wings,
just to love life as it is.

Flying high above the great oceans and streams and rivers.
Through all the different seasons, and all weathers, looking and
listening, to what is around above and below,
watching the trees through the seasons, some with flowers name,
smelling different aroma from the fields and flowers,
higher, higher, I go

Gliding through the air currents, gliding high with not a care
in the world. Being a free spirit, free of trouble, just to be free,
just to be happy with life as it should be, twirling and twisting
through all the land, free of worries, free from pain,
love and live life to the full.

Sharon Joy Wandless

Forest Deep

In the deepest darkest forests, where the trees are thick of leaf,
You stand within this shelter, feeling very small beneath.
No light to shine between the branches, so rich and lush the earth,
Just like another world within, no step or sound of mirth.

An eerie silence frightening, is there life within these giants?
An obvious hiding for the small, a place no more reliant,
Little creatures who are nocturnal, or who dig for their life's needs,
Would find no better comfort than within these massive reeds.

After your eyes have settled and begin to see what's there,
You realize this silence, 'tis you who is the scare.
Amongst the dank and darkness, a new World lies inside,
So many eyes are watching you, as they rush and try to hide.

The rabbits, badgers, moles and owls, the quietest of the World,
You see them peeping intensely, frightened faces you have stirred.
They were so happy left alone, they hid within this growth,
God planned this vegetation, it is He that ordered 'Soweth'.

You must leave these giant growths, they protect the very meek,
Why stop their special happiness, go to the light to seek.
You need the shining sunlight to give well-being to your mind,
Leave all this wondrous darkness, that was not meant for our mankind.

Lucy-May Bloxham

Fallen Burma Stars

It was only a tiny hole, such a pity it was between his sightless eyes
From a bullet, so there he lies. Blue eyes, still open wide
As if in disbelief or shocked surprise.
In his marbled hand a crumpled snap, one last desperate fumble
For the split-second, bitter-sweet joy
Of a farewell glance at his lovely wife and baby boy,
Before the final tumble into a swirling vortex of terminated breath,
To splash into a monsoon pool, beside the maggot-ridden carcass
Of a decomposing mule who also met an early death.
He was on the road to Mandalay,
No! Not the one where flying fishes play,
But where every pagoda was a fortress, each conduit
A seething nest of Samurai, screaming "Hirohito" and "Banzai".
So many of those Fourteenth Army boys sweated on,
Knowing that they would die in muted throes of agony,
With whispered sobs of "Mother" drowned by a peacock's mournful cry.
They soared to blazing heights of valour
And when they fell to earth like shooting stars,
Their sun-kissed cheeks a waxen pallor,
Surely Odin's angels swooped down to uplift them to Valhalla?

John Martin

Are You Innocent Until Proven Guilty

I'm innocent I shouted I've committed no crime,
What happened to innocent until proven guilty?
The jury decided guilty no doubt
The judge he agreed, he thought I was a lout

I got transferred to prison that day
Jail I thought but what the hell for?
I wasn't involved in the killing of them
Added all up there was a total of ten

75 years in prison the rest of my life
What about my children and my beautiful wife
The moment the police knocked on my door
My wife screamed my innocence and wept on the floor,

Now I am here trapped in this cell,
The truth I can no longer tell,
I take my final glance out the window so small
Then jump off the bed and let myself fall

Good riddance to life, all my love to my wife,
The ribbon 'round my neck causes no strife
I will be blue in the face and dead when I'm found
I smile as I go because I made no sound.

Michele Long

The Lonely Girl

The lonely girl felt cold and weak
She shivered in the rain
She needed water, food, and warmth
And tablets for her pains

The girl walked quickly in the streets
But quickly was not fast
If she could find nowhere to sleep
Her cold legs would not last

She was so thin, and starved from food
She knew she'd surely die
And with the thought of death so near
The girl began to cry

But as the girl took one more turn
She saw an unlocked shed
She staggered over to the door
And saw an old used bed

The girl was shocked, amazed, and scared
But still she crept inside
She touched the bed, it felt quite soft
But on she climbed and died

Helen Rossi

The Five Senses Of Racism

I can touch it, it is sticky everywhere
This pollutant, people
Breathing in breathing out
I can touch it, it is sticky everywhere.

I can see it, it is glaring everywhere
Sneering sneezing sitting places
Tells it all, in the media, in law, in education
I can see it, it is glaring everywhere.

I can taste it, it tastes biley
In my mouth, fairground, sportground
This gall exuding hatred, I can taste it
It is bile in my mouth.

I can smell it, it is stinking everywhere
At the stations, on the roads
In the busses, in the ferries
At the airports I can smell it
It is stinking everywhere.

I can feel it, it is heavy in the air
In the staff rooms, in the classrooms, in the dining-rooms
On the shop floors, I can feel it, it is heavy in the air.

Ibisiki Elizabeth Kalio

Dream Journey

As my head touches my pillow
The world as I know it starts to mellow.
I fly, I soar, I glide to heights
My dreams are mine what joyous delights
Flying ends, and I start to fall.
Rushing winds, am I scared, not at all
Tumbling, diving, free-wheeling what joy.
While awake a man, now I'm a boy
Fighting dragons, magic, dwarves and elves
Everyone laughing, enjoying themselves
Now I'm awake my dream has ended
My life journey has now been amended.

Rod Leung

Kim

"You must be out of your mind!" exclaimed my friend, Jean,
Having seen me with Kim, a drop-out who had been
Living rough, since he left home where he knew that he
Wasn't wanted. "You know," said Jean, "what sure beats me
Is what, on Earth, you see in that bedraggled Kim?
I'd not be seen out with him! Well, just look at him...
A sorry sight, ugly, charmless, dead awkward, too!
Give me his handsome brother, Rex, who dotes on you,
Is yours for the taking, the kind who has it all!
But no! For that scruffy Kim you've to go and fall!
Oh, I know love's proved to be blind. But, believe me,
In your case, love's deaf, dumb and blind... plus plumb crazy!
But then, a sucker for lame ducks you've always been;
To most of them you've been a soft touch." "Alright, Jean",
Said I, "Point taken. I know you mean well. But you're
Wasting both your time and your breath; for there's far more
To Kim than meets the eye! And so, I'd not change him,
Even if I could." At that moment in walked Kim...
There in his kind eyes I was mirrored without flaw;
Eyes which said: "I love you"... as Kim gave me his paw.

Jackie Holroyd

Brief Time Out

Oh that I might stay forever in this tranquil place,
Where all is peace and harmony - and space!
Where beauty abounds in the trees and the flowers
Enriching my life - gladdening my hours.
But there's a busy world out there
With noise and bustle and strife;
And I must cease my dreaming
And return to the maelstrom of life.

There is work to do, a cake to bake,
Bridges to cross, decisions to make.
Housework and gardening, reading and learning,
There's loving and caring and giving and sharing.
Letters to write, problems to face,
Involvement with the human race.
Alas, reluctantly I must leave this scene
But oh! - that I might just sit here and dream!

Margaret Cooling

The Artist

Let the artist begin with skill and grace
As he transforms the beauty of the face.
Start with the texture of the skin
Applying moisturizer wafer thin.
Then blend in colours dark and light
Making the skin glow in the night.
Highlight the cheeks, the chin, the nose
With just a subtle hint of rose.
Then to the eyes the most important part
With a pale glossy blue he makes a start.
Under the eyebrows shimmering and shining
And on the eyelids dark blue defining.
Mascara applied to make eyelashes thick
And under the eyes use a Kohl stick.
Then the final touch, the lips ruby red
And the undertaker's finished making up the dead.

Lynda M. Rice

Why Is It?

Why is it that I, was put upon this land?
Why is it that I, was born with two hands?
Why is it I look different? No-one looks the same.
Why is it that some people, treat life like a game?

And why do people argue, shout and disagree?
Why is it people kill? Please explain to me.
Why is it people can be cruel and heartless towards others?
Why is it we have families? Mums, Dads, Sisters, Brothers.

Why is it people act and do not show their real side?
Why is it that some people, we just cannot abide.
Why is it that some die, when other people live?
Why is it we prefer to take, and do not like to give?

So many questions and so little time,
To find out the answers before we die.
But one answer that I know is true,
My life wouldn't be the same without you!

Kirsty Noden

A Tale Of Woe

When the heavens pour forth their warmth
And petals sway shyly in the breeze
Will I come to thee
To tell of a time forlorn and adrift
Like a lone canoe in an ocean mist
A time when our arms no more embraced
And the winter's light showed not a trace
Of your radiant smile and your lovely face
Only the ash in an empty place
Where the clock chimes away the days

Kathleen Mannie

Re-Incarnation

Just like a flower being stripped in the breeze,
I'm losing my petals and soon I will freeze.
Without love, warmth or happiness its days are few;
It's no consolation but I feel your pain too.

I'm really not different - I can be like you too,
But why should I change? I believe to be true!
Look past my laughter, and mend my weakened heart;
It's shrivelling and dying - it's tearing me apart.

You've known me for years but still cannot see
My soul yearning and screaming to be set free;
A smile on the outside can often disguise
My heart breaking inside me, weeping soft cries.

The answers lie in your actions, no more I can do.
You've hurt me already and that hurt I feel too.
I've learnt to forgive you, but is it a mistake?
The real question to be answered is "Who is the fake?"

Patrice Kehoe

Sinjoe

Your hair would reflect the golden sun
as your loyal brown eyes rest under
Your silver fringe
One paw placed over the other
And your head laid down
As you dream about our heaven which
Doesn't exist.

Our heaven of fields with new green grass
Where fiery red poppies grow
With birds singing in the clear blue sky
And a crisp clean stream with nothing to tow

So hush my little baby
And let all of your worries be released
We will soon meet again
But until then
Sinjoe, my angel
Rest in peace.

Jessi Fox

Pebbles

Pebbles on the beach washed over by gallons of water each
day are like humans.
Humans are gradually being washed over by waves of
emotion and pressure,
Destroying all out reaching parts of our being,
Making us an altogether smoother, rounder shape.
No individual identity to go forth into a brand new day.
No-one able to express themselves to their full potential.
Minds wasting away, like cities in recession.
Just tatty remnants of what a full life can be.
We must stand together,
For as millions of pebbles make a wall, millions of people
make a world,
And by working together.
Not squabbling over stupid governmental arguments that no
one will ever comprehend.
We may just be able to create a big enough dam,
As to stop these waves destroying us forever!!
Save yourselves and your fellow humans.

Shaun Mellish

Skin-Changing

Old lives for new . . .
Old lives for new.
The chances to change are but few.
To discard one's old shell,
Can be a living hell.
But survive is what we must do.

New lives for old . . .
New lives for old.
Just the thought of it can be daunting.
To empty the soul
Of trouble, is the goal.
So the ghosts in the mind won't be haunting.

So we start once again,
Accepting the heartache and pain.
And maybe this time we may get it right
This is our last-gasp chance
To change skins and dance
And never give up on life's fight.

Penni Bancroft

Forever Young

I am old and wrinkled and sad inside
Because the beauty within cannot be seen outside

The mind's not so sharp, the faculties slide
Mother Nature invented aging in time
She had a liking for the fine wrinkled line.

The blue print of life says I must wind down
And look like I am wearing a permanent frown

But just beneath this wrinkly skin
Is a beautiful young woman looking out from within

Jean Madden

Heptonstall

The sun's glare, warped by heat,
bleaches cobbles down Smithwell Lane.
Approaching the shell of St. Thomas a Becket's,
a ginger swiss-roll of a cat
strolls nonchalantly by;
a buzzing ball of a bee,
humming to pollen, reminds me
of heat-hazed summers.

The church's mass of tombstones,
cracked as crossed-over-teeth,
jostle for position:

Wadsworth Joanna aged fifty-nine,
versus
Wadsworth Edmund one year and six months.

Ruth Goode

Insecurity

That afternoon I arrived home to an empty house.
I cried.
I locked my bedroom door and cried a little more.
It took time to get over that throbbing
pain which made my stomach sick,
and my body exhausted.
But like an instant curse had come over me,
I realized,
Everything she'd said was true.
I had insulted, criticized, hurt and
drove her to utter hatred.
Just so I could be accepted.
For a split second the knife on my
bed seemed to tell me something.
I knew I couldn't,
I thought I wouldn't,
But I did.
A moment later the throbbing pain
which had made my body ache all over, was gone.
And so was I.

Shona Lyons

The Castle

The great walls are in ruins
from the wars they did endure,
they fought off the invaders
to keep this country pure,
the battles of a century
in our medieval past,
but now the castle is empty
it rests in peace at last.

Through portholes, once, the arrows flew,
Pours only now the sun,
A sparrow makes his nest and home
in the barrel of a gun,
The gate that once did armies stop,
now lets the tourists through
to see how once the English fought,
to save this land for you.

N. Chilton

A Surgeon's Hands

In your hands you have the power over life and death,
With your skill you move the scalpel as an artist his brush,
With every stroke you caress the skin that is your canvas,
With each touch life comes ever nearer,
Until at last he is lifted from her body,
His tiny hands reaching out to yours.
In your hands the morning is red with glory,
And the world a kinder place.
In your hands you hold my son,
In your hands you hold my world.

Paul Hope

Invasion

Mammy and Daddy, please don't go out to-night,
Under my door I can see the light.
Please, I beg you, don't leave me here,
I'm filled with this dreadful ugly fear.
I hear the footsteps on the stairs,
I'm lying here, saying my prayers.
In he comes with that evil look,
My innocence and young life he has took.
I feel the tears stinging my eyes,
He says he won't hurt me, oh! What lies.
The weight of his body on top of mine,
It really hurts, but I try not to whine.
The whole of my body he explores,
The sweat on his forehead, down it pours.
This is a person I'm supposed to trust,
And all that's on his mind is filthy lust.
I feel so ashamed and dirty too,
But who can I tell, what can I do?

Tina Reddy

Society In Addiction

Eternal tides, pulsing, swelling,
carrying cares midst dross and flotsam.
Souls adrift on islands of floating misery,
wandering through oceans of multiplicity
reflecting brightness, now mirrored in future's hope.

Perpetual progression, churning, mixing,
shedding tensions, bringing understanding
to minds entrenched in compromised livery,
green and yellow, colours of simplicity and cowardice
that infiltrate society and limit life's scope.

Sun drenched valleys beneath clear blue skies
rippling waters, transfixing in their beauty.
Blossoms exuding intoxicating vapours,
hypnotizing olfactory sense with natural odours,
masking the malodorous cacophony of life.

Who decrees humanities inclinations now?
Not nature or personal requirement dictate
the ruminations of speculative advancement.
Society answers the call of mankind now,
caught in mutual addiction, unrelenting, cold.

John C. Riddle

Silent Witness

Five years have passed this quiet meadow green,
With grassland lush and covering the scene
Of offence and outrage enormity beyond belief,
Now blanketed verdant with blade and leaf.

When on the surface all is beauty and light,
Beneath is the testimony to an unjust fight.
This ground holds the secrets, the pain and the tears,
The bodies that lie here frozen with fear.

At dusk out of stillness a solitary blackbird's song,
Not a hymn but a melodious lament for all the wrong
That is beneath this pasture fallacious in impression,
Baring silent witness to the atrocity and oppression.

Will the world be told of this camouflaged place,
Where the earth became goddess of destiny for the human race.
And who will be there to make reparation,
No person living will amend the personal devastation.

In the distance the figures of children at play,
All hope for the future at their feet we will lay.
The events that were hidden must open a door,
To edify their actions from those who trod here before.

Rosalind Alexander

Down Amongst The Dead Men

An explosion so powerful ripped through the mine
my body crumpled amongst others
surely there's no hope,
for us they'll never find.
Men groaning in pain and openly they weep
women and children above ground
are dragged by the noise, rudely from their sleep.
Down here all is still,
we have no future,
our darkness is a tomb,
with coal dust and gas it will quickly fill.
Men cry out their loved ones' names
picturesque thoughts of wives and children
knowing they'll never see them again,
One by one the voices die off,
black silence all around,
disturbed only by a harsh cough.
No more voices come into my head
it doesn't much matter now
as I lie still amongst the dead

Michael Patrick Williams

Wilderness

The ordered suburb garden borders on absurd
Now that attitudes have hardened-off,
And our lives grown so unkempt with empty
Promises to each other and ourselves,
That a hopeless wilderness has sprung up
Between us - rampant with dry dead wood -
Diseased from years of neglect.
Too-long content with the too-small fruits
Of middle-age, we no longer rage
With passion at the changing of the seasons
Or have too many reasons to regret
That the flowers of our love have faded
To less coloured memories. For now
The poisoned sap of fear rises within us
That thorns might prick our fingers
Should we attempt judicious pruning -
For us, cosmetic thinning, rather than
Green buds of new beginning; for years
We've hedged our bets, uneasy that some
Future Autumn will find us leafless of ideas.

Derek J. Pluck

Best Of Breed

Jodey, our dog, gives us so much joy,
Fond memories to my husband, when he was a boy.
The dog he then owned and loved tenderly,
Romped over hills and dales so playfully.

Our "West Highland White" terrier, a wonderful breed,
So much character, no trouble to feed.
Chasing through our woods right up to the common,
Wet or fine, even if the ground is sodden.

The walk they take gives them both exercise,
But look out for anything he appears to despise.
Such a little white dog, coat close to the leaves,
Romps and bounds, seems so pleased

To be out and about all over the place,
Oh dear, he's lost, unable to be traced.
Much time is spent searching for him,
Seems endless, so very worrying.

Finding his own way home, such perfection.
Seems he had taken the wrong direction.
Our little white dog, how pleased we are to see
Him back home with us, tail wagging happily.

Laura Walmsley

If I Could

If I could, could only cry
will the tears help ease my pain?
Or will the shadow that forever haunts me
reach out and call my name?

If I could, could fly away
and leave the agony behind
will I have the courage to survive
with the power of peace of mind?

If I could, could only kill
by focusing on what I hate,
would committing that one deadly sin
be the open door to Murphy's fate?

If I could, could stop the suffering
and camouflage the hurt by a lie,
I'd sell my soul to the devil below
for a promise that no more will die.

If I could, could speak my mind
tell loved ones how I feel,
will my words have greater strength
than alcohol and pills?

Stephen Rosan

Untitled

Suspended by a delicate thread
From an intricate web
Life: The past, the future, and now.
Mock the past; pray for the future;
And live for now
Memories grasped in a tightly clenched hand
Aspiring dreams washed away
By tears of reality
Familiar tones resounding clearly
In echo chambers of the mind
And the heart
For both give life its meaning
And its irrelevance
Such is life
A cruel painting
Etched on the canvas of existence

Sheila Russell

Back End

Already seed heads rattle. Shake down their grains
among the russets and furls and fruits and feathers.
Here are hushed dawns with webs of fog, silent except
for berries of bird song in sharp windless air.
Aimless dandelion fluff and thistledown catch
in the crisps and wrinkles of curled leaves and shaggy nettles.

Time is of restful lights and slow fields,
amber reeds and rose hip glows, and glints
of sun through dew. And browns of ceasing growth.
The pallid bristle yields to the dark stuff of soft soil.
And the raging sunsets, the finale of summer's labours,
have an encore of premature dusks and increasing darks,
and ends of day.
End of summer.
Back end.

Ross Newton

Mrs. Mopp's Farewell

I've been a domestic cleaner
Since the end of my office career.
But today I'll dispense with the duster
'Cos my 60th birthday is here!

Each morning I've zealously laboured
With vigour and sometimes with zest
But today I'll hand over the Hoover,
Put my feet up and have a good rest.

I've tried very hard to keep floors clean
-My knees are perpetually bent-
But today I shall fold up the floor cloth
For retiring is now my intent!

Bathrooms have been quite a problem,
They've driven me "clean round the bend"
But today is my 60th birthday,
So on that note I'll cheerfully end.

N. M. Aldous

The Soldier

In the warmth of the desert, his gun in his hand,
Stands a brave British Soldier who awaits his command.
As he thinks of his family, his wife and his son.
He knows that today there's a job to be done.
To free the Kuwaits so he is told, to a soldier like him
This seems rather bold, he jumps in his tank
No time for delay, the order has come
We are off on our way
His heart it is pounding, his hands wet with sweat.
This is a day he will never forget.
The sand rose before him and into his view.
Came an Iraqi Soldier, a man just like you
He looked at him slowly, his gun in his hand
His eyes spoke the message, yes I understand,
Understand all the thoughts that go on in your head.
The sorrow about it is one of us will be dead.

Carol Bailey

Flowers Of Life

A lifetime of blossoms, of colours so rich,
A bouquet of memories to share.
Red roses of love, white daises to pick,
Making a chain of fond thoughts in your care.

Bright daffodils dancing to youth's graceful measure,
Bluebells to carpet the home of your dreams,
The pink of carnations becomes yours to treasure,
All wonderful blooms sewn into your seams.

The sun has shone down on your day to day tasks,
Freshened by fountains of warm summer rain.
When grey cloud made hazy your visionary mask,
The blue skies relieved your anguish and pain.

The flowers of a lifetime continue to grow,
The colours have brightened the dusk drawing nigh,
A rainbow of blossoms, Time's pleasures do show,
A breath of fresh air in the trials of life.

Ann Berry

Reverie

What so sweet as the stolen sleep
The guilty passion, first flush of rare experience
Fresh scent of the wind on the bare fell
When time stands still or is not counted.

But heavy the heart in the dappled light
On the grey lonely hill descending
Striving, in deepening shadows, to recreate
The unattainable ecstasy of past wonders.

John Arnold

The Hunt

"The Hunt is on" The Fox he cries,
Nowhere to run, Nowhere to hide,
If they catch him they'll tear him apart,
And his heart will stop.

"The Hunt is on" The Huntsmen cry,
Dogs, catch that Fox or you're going to die,
It's just Sport, We have such fun,
Catch the Fox, Kill the Fox, Then go home.

The Hunt is on and so I cry,
God help this Creature to survive,
Help him run fast, Help him stay free,
If not for him, then do it for me.

"The Hunt is on" The Fox he cries,
Nowhere to run, Nowhere to hide,
If they catch him they'll tear him apart,
And his heart Will....Stop.

Susan J. MacDonald

Single Parents

Sick and tired of being broke
single parenthood is no joke
government says we are the scum of the Earth.
Social security and no worth.
I know for a fact that this is not I
Socially acceptable if my husband had died
I chose to leave a life of mental cruelty
to bring my son up with love and normality
In rented accommodation I'd be living like a king
but to social security mortgages are not the right thing
They'd pay 200 quid a week rent to their heart's content
to pay or help with my mortgage 150 a month
I would have more help if I said it was for coke
Stuck in no man's land without friends or confidence
slave labour is all that is offered and I
have no choice 'cos need the coppers
All I hope is when I die my son will remember
the hardship and tears and most of all our happiness years
epitaph will read
the greatest single mother of all dead

Tracey Evans

The Landing

They came in their hordes to witness the scene
The place where the alien spaceship had been
Though no one confirmed this, they knew they were right
And they came in their cars all day long until night.

The ground was indented, the grass was charred black
With a well trodden path leading to the dirt track
Some trees had been broken, the fence was all down
And strangely shaped prints could be seen all around.

The police and the military blocked off the road
The scientist came taking samples that glowed
In their suits made of silver, with huge boots and hoods
They'd soon solve the mystery if anyone could.

Old Thomas the shepherd was keeping away
He'd been tending his sheep as he did night and day
And what he had seen as he tended his flock
Had turned his hair white overnight with the shock.

He'd witnessed the landing, he'd seen the strange beings
But he wouldn't be telling the law what he'd seen
No-one thought of Thomas as they went on their way
So he's kept it a secret right up to this day.

Barbara C. Parker

Mixed Up Emotions

Mixed up Emotions, deep in my Heart,
Mixed up Emotions, messed up my Thoughts,
Mixed up Emotions, when I try to get Sleep,
Mixed up Emotions, won't give me Peace,
Like weeds in the garden choking the Plants,
These mixed up Emotions, won't let me be.

Sometimes I feel like I'm drowning in the Sea,
When these mixed up Emotions wash over me,
When I touch your empty space, here by my Side,
And the memory of the Good times, you shared with me,
Makes me want you to come back, and Share more with me,
These mixed up Emotions won't let me be.

Sometimes I feel like Sailing across the Sea,
To get far away from these Feelings in me,
But even way out here across the Blue Sea,
These mixed up emotions are right here with me,
Mixed up Emotions, deep in my Heart,
Mixed up Emotions, messed up my Thoughts,
Mixed up Emotions, when I try to get sleep,
Mixed up Emotions, won't let me be.

Shirley May

The Choice Was Mine

I chose to go for a walk in the countryside
Gentle hills, peaceful valleys as far as the eye could see
Happy and contented, it felt magical to be surrounded
By tiny mountain streams, their waters running free

I strode along with purpose and vigour
As if in a perfect heaven where no tears were shed
An idyllic silence only momentarily being disturbed
As an aeroplane that moment chose to fly over - ahead

Plainly enjoying one another's company
A boy and girl on horseback smiled as they rode by
I guessed that they were two young lovers
Riding only at a canter, letting the rest of the world go by

From time to time I found myself at crossroads
At most of which stood a well worn sign
To walk straight ahead turn left or right
Which of three roads do I take, it seems the choice is mine

A single steeple pointed to the sky in the distance
I walked a little closer, a bell pealed quietly, so serene
I decided to go inside that church and say a prayer
For all the wonders of nature, today which had seen.

David Robert Screen

I Will . . . Will You

Would you climb a mountain, would you ford a stream,
Can you hear my music, will you be my dream,
Will you be my mother, will you be my child,
Will you give me sucker, will you drive me wild.

Will you make me happy, when I'm so sad,
Will you give me loving, when I'm good and bad.
Will you give me comfort, when I'm full of pain,
Will you clean my wounds, make me whole again.

All of these things, I'd do for you,
I'll fill your soul, with a love so true.
I'll try to be, I'll try to do,
I'll try anything, you want me to.

For you are the reason, the verse, the rhyme,
For the love of you, I swear I'd do time.
I'd better stop now, I'm getting depressed,
I miss you darling, all is emptiness.

I miss turning around, feeling you there,
I miss holding your body, so soft, so fair.
But most of all, I miss you as a whole,
Your body, your mind, your heart and your soul.

A. E. Clark

Punch And Judy Man

The crowd laughs out, the children sing
With all the wonder that he brings.
Amongst his audience he is King,
The Punch and Judy man.

No longer young or strong of heart,
But still he likes to be a part
Of every child who comes to see
His daily trips to fantasy.

But nighttime, when the crowds go home,
He often has to sit alone,
And gaze out at the distant sea
And think how different things might be.

He often wonders what became
Of one time dreams and future aims,
The carefree world of childhood games
And adult love with all its pain.

There is a love he keeps apart,
A private memory in his heart,
As once again tears fill his eyes
Shared only with those midnight skies.

Patrick O'Reilly

The Head Or The Heart

My Head or my heart, the actress or me,
If I showed him my heart, what then would he see?
A different person with different needs,
would he show me respect, or destroy me with greed?
If I let him inside to the true part of me....
would he use, and abuse, and the ultimate - Flee?
'Cos that's what I fear, when the hurt starts to win,
when I give him my trust, and it's nothing to him.
I don't think that he would on purpose be so,
but it's not always choice, just a deep heart-felt No!
I don't really think, though, that everyone tries
on purpose to bring so much pain in disguise,
But the way that we're made, the way that we act,
can destroy other people with our heart's lack of tact.
The feelings and pain felt by others in life
is often forgotten as we cope with our strife.
We get so wrapped up in our own private needs,
we forget all the pains that others' hearts heed.

If I followed my heart so much pain could be mine,
if I gave of myself all the shame would entwine.
But if I were careful and went with my head,
the shame and embarrassment would stay mine instead.

To follow my head seems much simpler I feel
But then, would it truly be one LESS pain to heal???

Colette Fox

Thinking

In a dreamless world our thoughts come into play,
Thoughts of the past, and of the present - and then
we say: We've thought.
Our mind is like a dictionary, where we try
To find the right words - and if we may
Let us on words play - we will erase the
thoughts, that like piercing splinters of lightening
fill our hearts with doubt and uncertainty,
cultivate memories of precious moments shared
of looks, and smiles, that cancel out a million miles.
Of hopes and wishes soon to be!
That will include just you and me!
Of how you look, and call my name,
and how I always feel the same.
Of wanting you and then you came.
But blissful summers will fly I'm sure.
The autumn mist so white and pure,
Like swirls of never ending smoke
Will take these thoughts, and then transfer them
Just to you, and so will disappear.

Iris J. Brown

Goodbye Mum

I try so hard to ease the pain
But the memory of losing you still remain
Each little thing I try to do
Brings memories flooding back of you,
They tell me time is sure to heal
From those who have lost and know how I feel
Remember good times, not suffering and pain
And try to live your life again,
This I am told so many times
From people trying to be kind,
One day maybe I will find the way
To look back once again and enjoy my day,
For I loved you dearly and told you so
Before it was time to let you go,
Perhaps we will both rest now, you and I
For one last time now I will say goodbye.

Chris Gardner

To Gillian

Our poets down the ages have extolled
Their lovers' beauties, praising to the skies
Those coral lips, that hair of burnished gold;
Those rosy cheeks, those blue and limpid eyes.
We lesser lights, who dabble at the brink
Of poesy, and marvel at the skill
Of greater minds, are pre-disposed to shrink
From putting pen to paper. But, dear Jill,
No net of woven words could ever snare
Your innate beauty, nor your charms convey.
Even the Bard of Avon, in despair,
Would look at you and throw his pen away.
If literary giants dare not try
To praise your charms in verse, what hope have I?

John Clark

The I.R.A.

Another Bomb has exploded, it made an almighty sound.
The building it was planted in, has tumbled to the ground.

People screaming, people crying, people lying all around.
People searching, people shouting, hoping to be found.

Death for many came swiftly, others lingered on.
Many with battered faces, some they had none.

The injuries were so horrific, it made people stare.
It made you inwardly sick, and wish you were not there.

So when the rescue was complete, and the dead lay on the floor.
The lonely task to tell begins, the police knock on your door.

You open up the shock to come, your loved one is no more . . .

A. L. Sutton

Santa's Letter

It's been almost a year since my last letter,
Not knowing what to do,
My world should now be better,
I'm passing it all down to you.

I've thought about what I'd ask,
Not knowing what to say,
I know you have a huge, big task,
But I'll ask you anyway.

All I want from you this year,
It's nothing much to say,
If you got it for my world.
I'd love you everyday

Peace upon this Earth,
Is what I ask from you,
I've asked you for this with my heart,
Please grant my wish comes true.

Danielle Friel

Sadness

I didn't want to come to school today,
All I wanted was to go far away.
The sneers and taunts are all too much for me,
Why can't those kids just let me be?

My fake illness fails, my mum knows my wails are untrue.
If only she knew what I was going through.
I enter the room, my head begins to pound.
I think maybe today happiness will be found.

But I was so wrong to think of better days,
A place where people don't laugh, jeer or gaze.
And again tonight I'll dream my perfect dream,
Watching a world of happiness flow by in a silver stream.

Shelley Williams

With Love From Grandma

The 21st of November
A day to remember
The day the twins were born
Two little lives were started
Their journey through life had begun

May they travel their roads in safety
May they only stumble not fall
May they follow their pathways bravely
With pride may they always walk tall

May they meet life with joy and with laughter
May the sun always shine through their tears
May there be stars in their heavens to guide them
May the moon shed its light through their years.

Noreen B. Miller

To Autumn

Stay with us Autumn, linger on a while.
Let's pause and assimilate your breathtaking beauty.
As setting sun dips in the west.
The hawthorn blazes with a crimson glow,
And racing clouds in cobalt sky
Set the back cloth to a scene of gold.
A myriad hues of brown, and yellow
green, and copper leaves
Cascade towards the ground.
And there on tree top a squirrel
Scurries, leaps and disappears.
With missel thrush engorged with holly berries
A woodcock noisily defends his territory.
Gurgling, splashing, brook meanders on
O'er pools and waterfalls.
A symphony of music invades the mind
I have to go and leave this wondrous interlude
As sadly soon the scene must fade.
The wind is colder, winter soon to come.
Autumn memories, forget me not.

G. Davies

For Better Or Worst?

Truth is a bitter pill to take
When just hanging on for old time's sake
You can see it in the eyes when the end is near
But fight back the negativity you fear
Your face cannot lie when emotions are dead
To walk in the door is the moment you dread
But compassion will hold you to something that's gone
And guilt-ridden feelings of acts that were wrong
So you stick it out so hearts you don't break
Though the world that you live in is nothing but fake
The path you are following, the ice is too thin
Pressure is great it's hard not to give in
With heart turned to ice the rot has begun
And everything stands in the way of the sun
You just live for tomorrow secret moments of lust
Compensate for the shame and betrayal of trust
You wonder where you will be in time span from now
How many stolen liaisons your luck will allow
Or should you resign to a life full of pain
With time to reflect. Would you do it again?

Susan Diane Shevlane

The Dolly Bird

Unlike the female bird, so drab against the male
Who gleams with courting colours that flash from head to tail,
In the human species, it's the female who'll be found
Wearing glowing colours, to select her hunting ground
With perfumes to intoxicate the gaily strutting males
Her air of such sweet innocence is a trick that seldom fails
She will lead him gently onwards, she will let him have his say
But if he's very bashful, then she'll gently show the way
Until he's feeling manly, then she'll make her play
By asking if he loves enough to name the day
Soon wedding bells are ringing and they are man and wife
But with the honeymoon all over she begins another life
She now becomes the ruler, she wears the wedding ring
For although he thinks he's master, he's just a puppet on a string
Too late he sees the pitfalls, the price he's had to pay
For the female's glowing colours have faded right away.

F. D. Fuller

Enchantment

When night fades into morning,
And the sun is riding high,
The song birds just awak'ning,
While butterflies dance by.
The air is filled with buzzing bees,
The soft breeze whistling through the trees,
And flowers nodding gracefully,
Beside a bubbling stream.
This is the time to pause and feel
Such peace and harmony,
'Tis nature's hand, and wonderland,
For all the world to see.
Is this not true enchantment,
And may it always be.
Renewal and refreshment,
For all eternity.

E. M. Willis

The Grass Is Greener

He roams his domain, as a free man.
No chains on his person, no curfew, no ban.
He follows his instincts, his life is his own.
A casual man, with a casual tone.

She's trapped by convention, her position is clear.
Confined to four walls, with little to fear.
She's needed by others, and plays her role well.
But is this really living, 'twixt heaven and hell.

One day she will find him, and capture his soul.
He'll fight like a lion, but at last he'll be whole.
His freedom no longer, he'll share all his life.
With a friend and lover, and somebody's wife.

Elaine Rixson

Memory

The tranquil sand
Broken by the fire blue
light of memory, madness.
Hypnotic and slender, cold
but comforting.

The ebb and tide of a fragile
life, tossed onto a shallow
and pitted shore.

Return to the sea my
fine blue stones, to your
ever evolving but beautiful
turmoil

For there you will grow
in the cold depths of
joy, surrounded but lonely
emphatic but open to receive.

An arched and smiling moon shall return to shine
upon me, and yes my
memory of
my blue, so blue Egyptian jewels.

L. G. Snell

Awaken

"A new day dawns bringing its power.
Endless blue skies penetrate a warmth
Created by the sun ascending in a
    perpetual motion of freedom.
The whispering spirit of night is lost
As the shadow lightens releasing its voice."

Peter R. Williams

When Will The Summer Come?

When will the summer come?
Days of flowers and birds and sun,
Lazy days of burnished sand, sea calm
As a pond - where children splash and play
Their shouting muted in the hot still air.
When will the summer come?
Soft coo of sleepy pigeons in
Still branches, where the scented limes
Shade the hard baked baldness
Of the well played field.
Oh summer- Come!
Too long this friendless, shut in winter -
We cannot live, each huddled round
His own small fitful fire.
May sun soon warm our dreary days
And draw us out into its light -
Then will we laugh, throw wide our windows
Doors and hearts, to greet the summer world of
Lovely melting buttercup daisy days.....

Polly Wates

Peace

I held a beautiful rose called peace
There in the palm of my hand.
Exquisitely I fingered it
And then I did command,
Oh! Fragrant rose why can't I find
Something in me like you?
So graceful, and majestic
Away from the cry, and hue.
I let the rose, slip from my hand
To its place, there on the bush
And I thought to myself again, and again
How peace; so conquers abuse.
I took the rose again in my hand
And, prayed to God right then
Why—can't the beauty of this flower
Be found more, in the hearts of men.

Ronald H. Holloway

Hellish Times Are Here

Look at the squalid ghettos of city dwellers
Spy the protruding bellies of "Kwashiokored" children
Scan the penurious peasants in tattered sweaters
See the beggarly breed of our stagnated societies
Espy the feeders in filthy "bukas" by garbage gutters
Scan their scraggy faces; victims of the hunger holocaust;
As want and thirst take toll on our hopeless homes
Oh! What a horrendous hacking of vanquished victims.

With this famine exterminating Somalian souls,
'Tis obvious hellish times are here.

Look at the rebellious rabble raiding daily
Count the genocidal garrotting in world theatres of war
See the craggy cabs on our laughing roads
Check the waterless taps and lightless wires
Millions relish dustbin crumbs of "yore years"
Others drink dreggy druss from gutter seas
In hospitals, dearth of drugs cripple doctors' duty
Oh! What a bounteous harvest of bestial blessings.

With this pogrom and arson by mercenary crowns,
For sure, hellish times are very much here.

Nick Adegwe-Oshomah

As You Travel Life's Road

As you travel life's road take a step at a time
Take each day as it comes
And accept what it brings
Its joys and its sorrows alike
And thank God as each day ends.

As you travel life's road you will probably find
The going is sometimes tough
With the will to survive and God by your side
Things will work out alright at the end.

Keep God on your side never cast Him aside
Help each other as you pass along
Always aim to please
And you'll find you'll succeed
As you travel life's road to the end.

So here's to your future may it be happy and bright
Hope it helps you to know that we care
Here's a wish just for you
That all your dreams will come true
And you'll triumph with effort along side.

Anastasia Grogan

Tomorrow

The wind is blowing, the rain is pelting down
on my window while I snuggle down
my mind starts to ponder of the years that
have flown by - and wonder who am I?

My life has been a struggle
For the kids I have done my best
What have I left?
Shall I let them do the rest?

But can I?
I am their mother and there is no other
The biggest pleasure in life is to be a wife and mother
So I carry on wondering, what is it all for?
Yet life itself opens another door.

My children will get married, and their children
I will see, a grandmother I will be.
God willing, life starts again
children's feet pelting like the rain

What a gift to be a mother
Life's not quite finished yet
I'll make to-morrow smiling there's a silver lining yet.

S. Lockwood

Lonesome Pine Column

Property and patents are mine,
published poems, wealth fine;
but half my teeth and thinning hair
and Grecian figure going to pear.

So what then,
at three score nine?
Without your love, just a lonesome pine.

Write and find me, you Vampress you
and if we're fit,
I'll bound be true.

Phil Manning

Voices On The Wind

Listen, can you hear them?
Voices on the wind: The sound of children playing,
Laughter, shouts of fun;
Calling to each other, singing in the sun.

Distant church bells ringing,
Drifting on the breeze:
A far-off aircraft winging
Far across the seas.

The hum of cars on motor ways,
The whistle of a train:
The gentle buzz of honey bees
The splash of falling rain.

The raucous noise of road works;
Marching soldiers feet:
Trumpets from a passing band
The rhythm and the beat.

The chorus of the gentle birds
Singing at day's end,
So very many different sounds
All voices on the wind.

Ellen Day

Untitled

I often get up and am feeling sad
One look at my kids and I am glad
Some days I'd like to give them a clout
Instead I holler, scream and shout
I'd give up my life, my whole existence
Nobody would get through that resistance
Without them my life wouldn't be worth living
So to them all my love I am giving
I want each of them to know their worth
For a mother knows her children are richer than the earth
They're like the flowers and the trees
Often you find them easy to please
The simplest things and they're full of smiles
For them I'd definitely walk a hundred miles
I'd probably get to mile number four
Then run out of breath and fall to the floor
So as you can see very clearly
I love my kids, I love them dearly

Marianne Doherty

The Mute Swan

With Golden hair
She sits on a chair
with a glare in her eye
Time is no problem for she welcomes it
money is nonexistent

Her clothes are wasted
But, her Golden hair falls on the back of her chair

She must be twenty
without an education to boast
So she sits and tastes the bitter sweet drink from the bar

Pink trousers and jacket are the only colourful part of her life
with a smile she lifts her thin bony body to the door.

Karen Sutherland

Winter's Secret

We sit in front of the fire and keep winter's chill outside.
And when it's night we go to bed and snuggle deep inside.
And warm and cosy, through the night, we sleep the hours away,
While Jack Frost and his children begin a nighttime's play.
With 'hide and seek' and 'catch me', Jack flies across the land,
Leaving a trail of silvery dust to give the children a hand.
Over hills and rivers and barns and rooftops high,
Merrily they skip and jump as after Jack they fly.
In the air are Ice Dragons with scales of purest white.
Instead of fire, their breath is cold and freezes all in sight.
The ponds and lakes and puddles are frozen in the night
And Snow Elves skate upon them, in furry suits of white.
While on the ground, the Ice Fairies, in sparkling silver gowns,
Are busy painting round the edge of all the leaves in towns.
And when their task is finished, they join the children's fun.
And on and on into the night, across the fields they run.
Then slowly creeping up the sky, to stop them in their flight,
The sun puts an end to play-time by bringing in day-light.
And in the morning, when we wake, we look outside and find
That all is glistening with the silver dust Jack left behind.

Janice Steele

From Abroad

Let me wander once more through the scenes of my childhood,
Let me savour the perfume of lilac and may,
Let me see the young lambs gaily frisk in the meadows,
Let me roll in the sweet-scented, newly-mown hay.
Let me climb Clent's green hills with their coating of bracken,
Treading red, narrow paths my young feet helped to wear,
Winding down to the pool hiding deep in the valley,
How often I bathed my tanned body in there!
Let me cup in my fingers the wriggling brown tad-poles,
Whose hap-less relations I captured for school,
Let me fancy I hear my old friends' gay young voices,
See their faces reflected with mine in the pool.
Let me gather the bluebells which carpet the woodlands,
And rest on the seat where I once carved my name,
Let me seek for the nests of the thrush and the blackbird
And peep at those bright, speckled eggs once again.
But, this Spring's speckled eggs will be grown, singing birds,
Ere my heart and my soul may be thus satisfied,
So in dreams I'll return to my loved haunts of youth,
Till the day my ship sails with the tide.

Vera Fertash

Long Sundays And Lonely Friends

Papier-maché people sit in rumbling rooms
Square-eyed into weekend scandal (inhaling washing fumes)
Smelly dogs drag pot-bellies on steamy jogs
As nearby petrol queues haunt early fog.

Torchlight sun spits light over yawning gardens
As suburbia vomits life over those it pardons
For supercilious passions with tasty mistress cars
And a burning lust for bawdy jokes and Sunday gurgling bars.

Bombs of lunch mushroom over drying streets
Urge the punch drunk home for sleepy treats
Where evergreen mums beckon sunny boys
To a feast of cabbage topped with apple-pie noise.

Later wine-sipped families cosy in candy coats
Attack hushed lanes to honour pompous boats
Sucking executive air crushed from pristine leaves
As they sail past with regular asthmatic heaves.

And here I sit in my window-box tower
Stealing pollen like a bee from a tawdry flower
Watching their private sun and honeyed frost
Their smug handshakes, hypocrisy and its cost!

Paul Hooper

For Bianca

Spring. A new bud bursts through the dew-stained morn
Its petals uncurl and stretch out strong
A delicate shade that only nature knows.
It is you.

Summer. I hear a laugh through the sunny haze
Bringing an extra glow to the glorious day
I feel the warmth, the love, the joy.
It is you.

Autumn. A rush of air above my head
I look up to the sky beyond
And see a dove soaring high.
It is you.

Winter. A snowflake flutters from the air
And lands gently on my hand
Its perfect crystal melts on the warmth of my skin
It is you.

Forever. Wherever I go, whatever I do
You are there to help me through
I see you, hear you, feel you, smell you;
A sweet taste that will linger forever more... You.

Susan Grande

Death

Death is like a whirlpool
It never ever ends
People are being killed
More people that God sends
Conscience, haunting
How could you live with it
That person should be living
Who really does deserve it
Children, adults, animals too
Is that the life your children should be born into!!

Carla Quarless

The Wolf

Swiftly, swiftly he moves along,
Gently, gently calling his song.
Running on air as he chases his prey,
Hunting at night, sleeping in day.

Grey as the rocks from head to toe,
Moving his ears to and fro.
Listening to sounds near and far,
Howling under the great North Star.

Hunting in packs in the dead of night,
For hours on end until morning light.
They've caught their food, they've made the kill,
And ate until they've had their fill.

Teeth like razors glinting white,
People run at the very sight.
These creatures do not want to fight,
All they want is a peaceful life.

Victoria Tincknell

To A Tree In Winter

Your branches are so many great arms lifted to praise;
Their ends like the palms turned outwards and upwards
in a gesture of offering.
As you stand there bare but erect you seem to say:
    'Here I am, naked now, but potentially vibrant and tingling
with life.
In time I shall show you something of myself.
Meanwhile, I wait in hope - bare, black and slimy green.
Only a few dead leaves quiver on my gnarled body -
    the rest is silence.
But beneath this bark life flows on endlessly, quietly,
    awaiting the Spring.'

Margaret Bradley

A Moment Alone

Harsh winds blows through my already cold body,
It carries my racing thoughts,
Like the whispering words of my serene mother on haunting,
sleepless nights.
Faint vision of land is unclear,
Mist covers it like a silver, silky sheet.

Fierce winds carry my problems away like a dandelion seed,
I come here to think, to cry or to be alone,
But in fact I am surrounded by white sea angels,
Dancing, swirling and diving.
The sun reflects a path of stars trapped beneath the surface,
It reaches out, touching my body,
Dethroning the uncomfortable chill from inside.

The beauty of the sea has hidden the ebbs and flows of the tide,
That has claimed the lives of many an unwary swimmer.
Behind me, dark, dank openings of mysterious caves,
And tunnels that plummet deep down,
Into the heart of the silent, secret cliffs.

I walk away, hearing the violent waves on the now empty rock,
I turn, my rock sinks into oblivion.
As the peaceful, endless sea rises and covers my secret cove.

Jodie Hobden

The Sea

Come dancing to the fingers of the sea—
Down sloping, shifting sands, thrilling
As icy spray caresses happy feet.
Be a child again, with your own sweet-willing.

Wander awhile, discovering sunlit pools—
Where treasures lie, just for the taking.
Listen, whilst under Heaven the sea gulls cry,
Their oft repeated warnings making.

Now, under clouds, as wind direction changes,
Retreat for shelter! Crabs are hiding, shells closing
While turbulent frothy waves rush in—
Over seaweed—feet—a greater haste imposing.

A sudden fear replaces mild content
As white mares e'en whiter cliffs are lashing
Urged by Poseidon, and on warfare bent—
Impatient 'stamping', manes and mantles flashing.

Beyond the storm-clouds hear the siren song
Of great sea whales that in the deeps are winging.
What would they tell of ocean's mysteries
If we but learned the meaning of their singing?

Mary C. Hastie

The Garden Plant

If I had to be a garden plant I'd want to be a tree
Something tall and stately - not a bit like me.
I could be a Cypress tree and stay forever green
Then little birds would nest in me and know they won't be seen

Couldn't be a Bonsai - No! That would never do me
They'd put me in a little dish that wasn't very roomy.
They'd wrap my branches up in wires and twist me out of shape
Into weird positions from which there's no escape.

I've seen some lovely fruit trees, especially the cherry...but
If I were in an orchard they would come and spray my berries.
I'd be showered from the air and such with strong insecticide.
Now that's the kind of treatment I simply can't abide.

Don't want to be in lovers lane down in the local park
Cos' lovers, they would come and cut great chunks out of my bark
I could be in someone's garden and they'd keep me trim and neat
And plant their little snowdrops down around my feet.

There are so many kinds of trees that I'd be spoiled for choice
But if I were a tree then I wouldn't have a voice.
I couldn't even say a word when doggies came to wee.
Here wait a minute! On second thought I think I'll just stay me.

Jean Swinton

Our Dog Ben

He was fourteen years old
Was our dog Ben
A labrador, quite grey and thin.
He kept escaping to go to the park
So we tied him up, but all he did was bark.
We took him for walks, my sons and I
Over the park night and day.
Then one day just by chance
From the house he escaped and ran to the park.
A woman in a van sealed his fate
She knocked down, then didn't wait.
We took him to the vet's
But because of his age
His bones wouldn't mend,
He couldn't be saved.

I gave my permission, there and then
To let him to go to Heaven,
Our Dog Ben.

Eileen Osborne

When I Die, When I Die

What I'll miss, when I die, when I die
The trees, the bees and all those cream teas,
when I die, when I die
The highs, the lows and all that grows,
when I die, when I die
The talks, the hawks and those romantic walks,
when I die, when I die,
The floors, the doors and the seashores,
when I die, when I die,
The blinks, the drinks and the saucy winks,
when I die, when I die,
The hells, the smells and the old church bells,
when I die, when I die,
The groans, the moans, especially my home,
when I die, when I die
But most of all my wife, her love, our son
when I d....

Frank Gregory

Dreaming

Hoping to win the lottery
What a hope this will be,
Have only had a tener which is no good to me
Just wonder how some people do it,
Or is there a fiddle somewhere?
Being straight and honest does not get me anywhere
Us poor OAP's have no money to spare,
I came into his world with nought
And in this very same way will go out
God does not answer my prayer
Nor can He hear my plea
The promoters take the biggest share
Which does not leave much for you or me,
I would like to be a big winner
But wonder now am I a sinner?

D. E. Kessell

Barbedwired Tears

The ruins of childhood, their life, never free
From barbedwired tears, unimaginable to me.
Loving memories of youth, that cannot be found,
They were stolen away, and buried in the ground,
Now their barbedwired tears keep their trespassers in
With their battered child dreams, destroyed by the sin.
And crying souls of torture and pain
Desperately fight to love life once again.
If only they had the power to control
The persons who were allowed to savage their soul,
And take away, with ferocious attack,
The right of their childhood, they'll never get back.
And bleeding wounds never heal, from the child's neglected years,
Because their souls still weep bloody barbedwired tears.

Michelle O'Flaherty

A Love Poem

I walked you past, and you never saw me
My blood rushed up to my head
And down, leaving a space in the middle.
I felt sick.

I love you, Joe,
But you never saw me,
I love you Joe,
But you couldn't care.

I could say I'd go to the end of the world
And all that sh** they went for in Shakespeare's time,
But the world has no end,
So there's no point.

I prefer to tell you
That I need you,
Without ever having had you,
Simply, that I love you.

For ever.

Kate Hartnoll

The Shortest Day

Hardly the sun has spread its glow
Across the sky, then the dim dusky cloak
Of night casts its grey shadow on the snow,
And o'er the winter landscape steals like smoke.

The shortest day that brings the longest night
Holds yet the promise of midsummer's noon;
Beyond the darkness shines the sun's full light;
Winter sleeps on, and spring will waken soon.

Sonia Cardwell

Bolatito

When I see the moon, I remember the calmness of your love.
When I see the sun, I remember the bright colours surrounding you.
When it rains, I remember the magnitude of my love for you.
Bola, word cannot describe the magnitude of my love for you.
You are everything and everything is you
You are the charm that can heal the wound in my heart
You are a source of inspiration
When I first met you, I thought it was a co-incidence.
But I was proven wrong, it was destiny by nature.
I see in you what I can't find in other women.
I mean a will that can move the immovable.
A will that can change the unchangeable.
A will that can make everything work.
You are the only woman after which my heart sought.
Bolatito, I can't stop loving you.
Happy Birthday!
Happy Birthday!!
Happy Birthday!!!

Oke Ebenezer Akinsanya

Always Your There

I feel you in the sun so warm,
I feel you in the cushioned lawn.
Everywhere I feel your touch,
loving, caring, in every depth.

I hear you in the morning song,
I hear you in the thunder strong.
Everywhere I hear your voice, so low,
in the rushing waters, the fountain flow.

I see you in the flowers, and bees.
I see you in the grass, and trees.
Everywhere I look you're there.
Sometimes distant, sometimes near.

I sense you in a salted tear,
I sense you and know you're near.
In my feeling, hearing, seeing, smelling,
You're there - within my very being.

Eileen C. Hines

Lost In History

I held my life in my hands
And curiously I watched
As moment by moment
The hours trickled through my fingers
To be lost forever
In the depths of time

The chances I did not see
They danced with the wind and laughed
As they hurried by
But I felt no regret
As my luck dripped in puddles around my feet
No thought to retreat

My days without order
Empty pages with no story to write
No memories, no conclusion
Another life to be lost in history

Juliet Hurn

One Too Many Mornings

The head on the pillow feels heavy and large,
Its daily duties it needs to discharge,
Another day of work and mistrust
Before the night returns us to dust.

The escape in the evenings is only short term,
No matter how long, the morning returns,
To fight the inevitable and hope for a change,
Just seems too hard for God to arrange.

Why should it be that work is so hard,
When every night it's so hard to discard,
The thought that the world seems so loaded,
And all the real messages mysteriously coded.

It seems so easy to shut down the brain,
Let all thoughts go, not try to restrain,
The real issues that don't go away,
Why is it so hard to face a fresh day?

Ted Garratt

Brown Eyes

The special love I have for you
Because you love me as you do
Fills my heart with so much pride
The innocent love your eyes can't hide

When you cuddle me real tight
Hopes and fears in dreams at night
Make me glad that you are mine
And you will be, for all time

Those big brown eyes, so full of life
Cheer me up in times of strife
Your soft, warm cheek against my face
Your loving words and sweet embrace

The mischief that you show at times
Make me more glad you are mine
You and your love are so alive
You're mine, I love you and you're only five!

Romana Harrison

Star Dreams

When the shadow of the rocking horse,
Has slowly faded away, and the terrors of reality
Have turned to silence, never-ending thoughts
Of joyful eternity, that will never be, shall begin.

Obsession, lost in the deepened hope
That somewhere was the birth of her dream.
Wishing, praying, staring at her star;
One day, one night, she will find the death of her fixation.

The fantasy she lives in kills the fallacy
That her angel already took away from her sorrowed soul.
She will not need the company of the dark rocking horse;
Reaching out her hand to the skies, she will a star was born.

Ewa Kolodziejska

Disappearing World

Tigers, once hunters, are hunted today
For expensive skins and head moulds, they don't care what they pay
With rifles and guns they are killed one by one
Until that terrible day when there will be none.

Whales and dolphins are mammals in the sea
That are killed for their oils, and that's all it could be
With dynamite and harpoons they are gone for good
Left in pain for hours pouring with blood.

Elephants are killed for their ivory tusks
They are beaten then killed and left in the dust
It doesn't really matter what age they may be
As long as they have tusks which can be sold over the sea.

Fishing is a sport for the man not the fish
All the man sees is some food on a dish
Although it's a business, it's a cruelty case too
And when the species have gone what do we do?

Pandas are endangered just like the rest
With black and white patches, it's what China like best
Although by the figures of the killing rate scale
You'd have though they'd have hated it just like the whale.

Sarah Woods

Moving Home

I wish I'd never had the thought
To move away from this house I bought
Not so many years ago
But oh my dear I love it so.

I'm tired of people coming to view
my home which I've loved from new
They turn their noses up and frown
In the hope to bring the house price down

The sign outside the door says 'sold'
You'll be happier, mum, I've oft been told
You'll learn to love the new house too
Just give it time, but still I'm blue

We're all packed up, we're moving today
I wish that they would let me stay
to linger through each empty room
of this dear house that I called home.

We're off to a larger, more roomy place
Because they said, "We need the space".
I've locked the door for the very last time
No more to enter this house which was mine

Edith Mackey

At Night

At night when the moon and stars are out,
From little children there's never a shout,
Because they are all tucked up in their beds,
With the blankets pulled over their heads.

At night when people are in bed,
And the animals are out instead,
Looking for food on which to feast,
A mouse or two to say the least.

At night when people are asleep,
And from children there's not a peep,
Goblins and fairies come out to play,
Over the hills and far away.

At night when everything is still,
A little bird hops on the windowsill,
He is there to let everyone know,
Morning's breeze is about to blow.

At the end of the night there comes dawn,
When people begin to stretch and yawn,
Into their rooms come beams of light,
Another twelve hours 'til another night.

Annmarie Teehan

Spring Time

Spring has sprung!
Lambing time begun
The leaves of green shine on the trees
A host of golden daffodils waves in the breeze
The birds they sing each morning new
Amid the early morning dew

Rebirth of life for granted we take
Amid the wars, the hue and cry
People every day will die

They force feed the cattle
Amid all their greed
Destroying all nature
Why don't they take heed

The sea it's polluted
Fish covered in oil
The things God he gave us
But alas man did spoil

Nature is a wondrous thing
As in the glory of early spring.

Pat Bredee

Twin Of Argentuil

In aeons gone we safely walked our streets.
No muggers, pushers, gangsters or dead beats.
Where leaves would fall and crime was small
And hearts were made of gold.
Where have all the good times gone?
The history books I'm told.

It seems like it was yesterday,
When the QE2 ran down that slide
And into the river Clyde.
The sound of the cranes working away.
Screeching and cracking, day after day.

Still the iron dragons slave
And vessels they create
Where brother Clyde the river runs
The sea of Ireland's came.

Sail on queen.
The sea will take you places
We have never seen.
You won't forget our people in your will.
We're just a small town. Twin of Argentuil.

Reece G. Toye

My Feathered Friend

One dark and cold freezing night
came a knock upon my door,
Undid the bolt, then the lock
to find there stood the law.

The constable had found a little bird
just lying in the gutter,
I thought him dead to my dismay
no sound from him did utter.

Later that night my thoughts were still
with my feathered friend,
A broken wing a twisted leg
all these I had to mend.

I fed him bacon, milk and bread
I've chewed up nuts and faggots,
Although I love this little bird
I could not chew up maggots.

This little bird now stands tall
his wing is on the mend,
Leaving me soon this I know
a healthy feathered friend.

Lillian M. Turner

We're All Here To Find The Way...

The song of life is short and sweet, and lived by all in many a street,
The ups and downs fill many a day for everyone to try and play.

There are so many here in life who run around and cause much strife,
But they know not that all is seen and are the ones who are so green.

If any here would like to know
For all that's done this light does show,
Responsible each one for every deed
That's done through time of grab and greed.

If we are wise, just stop and stare
Then seek to find the answers there.
All deep inside for all to find, for consolation, peace of mind.

If we would watch through every day
At everything that's made to play,
Then question much before the act,
Then see what's white and all that's black.

But we all find when looking back, perhaps we should have done this or that,
But what was done sufficed that time, was not a reason, nor the rhyme.

We are all here to find the way to do our best, make things to play,
But in the end if end that be, there's none to blame, but you and me...

Robert Philip Mead

Season's End

The fields are ready, for the Autumn plough,
And the wind has a bit more bite.
Oh! How the seasons change so fast, almost overnight.
The birds are growing thick their down,
The horses hair grows long. No more across the open fields,
Can you hear the cuckoo song. The lambing days have long gone by,
They have delivered their last birth.
The leaves are falling off the trees, and carpeting the earth.
Then as the winds get colder, they will bring with them the snow.
To transform the countryside, with holly and mistletoe.
The children will be out to play, with sleigh and a snowball fight.
Their laughter will ring through the air, to add to the wondrous
sight. With sleigh bells and Father Christmas,
Spreading peace and all his joy.
There'll be smiles of glee upon the face,
Of every girl and boy. It's the time that we call Christmas.
A time we cherish dear. For it's not only the last season,
But the end of another year.

Ernest G. Brooks

Just A Whisper Away

Ripples blew across the grass... to roll out a carpet of green,
breathing new life into my naked soul, then you walked into my dream.

The sun shone bright in the daylight sky... but dark clouds got in the way,
So I climbed right up to the mountain top, and chose a place to pray.

I felt sure you would ignore me... but you responded to my plight,
I asked you to send a friend to me, then you appeared in a beam of light.

I pleaded with you, sit by me... and you stretched out a blemished hand,
I quickly placed my trust in you, because I knew you would understand.

You shrouded me with a cloak of love... and offered to read my mind,
you helped to lift this cross from me, and assured me I'd been blind.

You showed me an enchanted world... and made me want to weep,
Then you offered me a sacred key, which made my life complete.

I had never felt that may before... or known such a worthy friend,
you brushed away my falling tears, and willed my heart to mend.

You said you were but a whisper away.. and you loved me very much,
so I offered to do some work for you, and threw away my old crutch.

I now feel peace and tranquillity... and have seen the rainbow's end,
so Jesus, I would like to thank you, for being my spiritual friend.

Barbara Johnson

The Christmas Fairy

Count the days to Christmas, cross them off one by one,
If only it was simple, the same for everyone.
Some will have a good time, for some it will be poor,
Is the sorrow never ending? Must it be forever more?

Can the Angel keep on smiling from the glitter on the tree,
Is she really happy? the way she looks to you and me.
Is her sad heart breaking as all below unfurls,
Or does she see a ray of hope for the children of the world?

She looks down on wondrous scenes of happiness and joy,
A family together, for every child a toy.
But secretly she hears the agonizing call
Of children who are hungry and her silent teardrops fall.

But still the Angel hopes for better days ahead,
When children everywhere lie safe and warm in bed.
The world may show compassion, give help to those in need,
Do away with selfishness, banish all the greed.

The children pack the Angel away until next year,
She knows that she is safe, needs nothing, has no fear.
Her faith in all humanity with help from up above
Sends her smiling once again, to wait, with hope and love.

Kay Carr

Lord Of Nature

What a destructive being man is to be
trusted, to be keeper of the earth.
To ignore the laws of nature when he sees
himself the greater and sees in himself
more than he is worth.

Oh Lord of nature, please take hold once
more and bring thy being once more to the fore.
Take charge and put asunder all those
who'd put thee under, to make them listen
with thy mighty roar.

Animal and beast so meek and mild, Mother
Nature clutch them to thy breast.
While man is driving wild an abandoned
restless child, putting all thy laws
completely to the test.

Destroyed exhausted man, by his own hand,
Will one day have to listen to the land.
To recognize thy worth and see an earthly
birth and work together with thee,
hand in hand.

Dennis Curley

Untitled

Some people haven't got a mom or dad
We are happy; they are sad.
When I hear about this subject it makes me really mad.
People living on the street even without a bite to eat.
No food, no money, no clothes to wear
can't you see now we need to share

Laura Johnson

Untitled

Lazy, hazy summer days,
filled with sun and idle ways,
singing birds and buzzing bees
and the gentle murmur of a distant breeze.

The season of strawberries and ice cream,
time to lounge around and dream,
thoughts of work you've left undone
your sole excuse? Of course the sun!

The summer evening fresh and cool,
the sun sets like an antique jewel.
Splendid colours splash the sky
and the remaining clouds are soaked in dye.

Louise Ann Chamberlain

If Only It Could Be

Born into this world,
We know of only love,
Cuddles, kisses we receive.
If only it could be.

No hatred in our minds so pure,
No nasty words we speak,
No evil wicked sights do we see,
If only it could be.

In a world as big as ours,
There is this great big rift,
of colour, religion, language and class.
Like the tides of the sea we drift,
We seem to be chained, but are waiting to be free.
If only it could be.

As we grow our minds understand.
What it would be like to live hand in hand.
At the end of the tunnel we see the light,
And all around me are my friends, both black and white.
Perhaps in our other world, hatred there will never be
If only it could be.

Catherine Cockburn

An Autumn Eve

Gently the darkness wraps us 'round,
  Slowly the night descends,
This day was filled with Nature's gifts
  But ling'ringly it ends.

Lovely it was at early dawn
  The radiant sun to see
As, blushing, she rose from out her bed,
  Lifting so gracefully.

Noon, too, brought joy—a fragrance sweet,
  Scent of the Wild Woodbine,
Of whose pure nectar I did taste,
  Richer than any wine.

Evening came then, with murmuring breeze,
  Stirring—but soft—the leaves,
Ruffling the lacy crests of corn
  Topping the golden sheaves.

Gently the darkness wraps us 'round,
  Slowly the night descends,
This day, so filled with Nature's gifts,
  Now lingeringly ends.

Harold A. Lane

We Were One

I, I count the teardrops
Hidden by your smile
I see your sadness
Sent into exile

I heard you whisper to a friend of ours
It was not true but who cares now
Not me

We were one, but now we're two again
We could have tried to make things better then
If you had time

You've packed your bags and soon will be gone
So don't be back to sing your song
'Cause I won't know you
I won't want to
We'll both know
There's someone new

I, I count the teardrops
Hidden by your smile
I see your sadness
Sent into exile

Daniel Lestat Barson

His Life

Forty long years ago, a young man sat with eyes sparkling, like a lake on a sunny day.
The sound of laughter surrounded him.
It was as bright, and as light, as the sound of church bells pealing.
It was his family.

Beside him there was a young woman.
Her golden hair, fell over her slender shoulders, like rays of sunlight.
He cherished this woman like a miser cherishes his gold.
She was his wife.

Six starry-eyed children played happily behind bushes and on top of trees.
They were like six little kittens discovering the secrets of nature.
He savoured the sound of their laughter and loved the sight of their fun and games.
These were his children.

Now, forty years later, a withered old man sits alone.
His eyes do not sparkle.
There is no children's laughter, or no young woman with golden hair to cherish.
He is all alone, and only the dull ding dong of the dirty grandfather clock breaks the
dreary silence.

His yesterday was.
His today is.
But his tomorrow, who knows.

Karen Ryan

Had Eve Said No

Green grass growing, streams a'flowing, sunshine all around,
Bees a'spooning, flowers blooming, bursting from the ground,
The cud is chewed with never a feud, no other beast they kill,
Nothing spoiling, no one toiling and all do eat their fill,
Trees weighted down with apples round, yet the Serpent he is lurking,
Remaining coiled lest he be foiled and forever he is smirking,
Adam wanders and meanders, who can know his mind,
He does not tire, he is afire for a maiden he would find,
His thoughts are pure, he is not dour, and should sweet Eve appear,
His eyes would rove from tip to toe and towards her he would veer,
Had she said no, there would be no blame and every day would be just the same,
It may be nice and the beasts may snore, but where's the spice, it's an awful bore!

C. Douglass

A Special Friend

When all seemed lost and luck forsaken, your spirit stirred to gently waken,
the part I thought had died in me, to love and care so tenderly.
My little angel from above, sent to give me hope and love.
When all seemed dark and black as night, your presence came to help my fight.

I miss you so, my one so dear, that even now I shed a tear.
As if on loan for two short years, to help to calm and soothe my fears.
I only hope that you have gone, to share your soul where love is strong.
To give to some the strength and caring, you gave when life was not worth bearing.

You touched the hearts of man and child, with perfect beauty and manner mild.
It seems as though you simply knew, my time of trouble at last was through.
Your gift to me on golden wings, put in perspective many things.
I hope that where you are right now, my love still fills your soul somehow

Lynn Santer

Prayer Of A Tree

O hear our plea, vile men that seek to uproot us.
Listen to the words of wisdom before you add yet another horror
    to your list of atrocities against Nature.

You were given the blue sparkling waters of the seas - but you defiled them.
Life in abundance lay beneath the waters - but you killed it.
Green, fertile earth was given to you freely - but you scorched it.
Fruit hung heavy on the branches - but you poisoned it.

And now, destructive man, you seek to destroy forest.
God made us. We were created by a Divine Intelligence and you,
    little man, would raise your axes against us.

From time immemorial we have sheltered you. We have helped to
    build your homes and have given you fruit and shade.

This is our work and we seek to live in harmony with all of God's creation.
But hear this, O man. You are deaf to all but the chink of money and
the blaring horn so you will not hear our cries of agony as our roots
    are torn from Mother Earth.

But our sorrow will not go unheeded. The Forces of Nature will weep
with us and, assuredly, as you will do unto us, so shall be done unto you.
Our cries will rent the heavens and in our anguish we shall curse you O man.
So that as our forest has been desolated, so shall the highway that
you build upon it bring destruction in its path.

P. Els

Divine Spirit

I kissed death this morning it came without warning.
It left just as sudden in such a blinding rush.
How my brow was cool, as my heart started pounding.
As I lay upon the waters tide, the meadow so deep and lush.
Angels gather about my head tasting my very essence.
As they place me softly to the ground. I am aware of their presence.

Whispers of traced out time, dust over my precious skin.
Perchance, you have saved me as my soul sings a sweet song.
Oh how I love you, angels of destiny protectors from sin.
Moments of sadness betrayed my soul, but now I am strong.
I drank the goodness it stained my lips, how my heart brims with happiness.
Of golden light guiding my path, to angels faces, beauty and finesse.

To opened gates of dreams untold, how angels laugh beneath the clouds.
I see star crossed lovers holding hands, of true love circling our world.
Sunbeams strobe across my eyes, music fills my ears deafening all earthly sounds.
Peace enveloped my body as reflective images flavoured my spirit as it twisted and twirled
Time summons my soul as I awake to water lilies gently framing my body.
Refreshed, I swim to shore aware of my brush with immortality and mortal decay.

Petra J. Watkin

"Of Mysteries, Monsters And Marriage!"

'Twas the summer of 1989, when we set of for North of the border we chartered
a boat in old Inverness, to search the dark Loch Ness water.

Well it rained every day that we were away, I drank juice of the barely and fished.
I got fairly tight, though my line felt no bite, just the sight of old Nessie I missed.

Yet out on that vast stretch of water, in a void, the land eerily misted,
the mind would play tricks, with the whiskey you'd slip,
back in time before humans existed.

Then the light starts to fade very gently. The loch, a huge inky black hole.
In that fathomless deep, like unconscious sleep, there's
Presence you feel with your soul.

The days slipped by so serenely, in that land of the drum and the fife.
Just two of us left in all of the world, and maybe a primeval life.

When at last we reached Fort Augustus, I asked an old man by the water.
If he'd seen the elusive great monster, he said "Seen,
I married its daughter!"

Peter Grassi

A New Baby

A new baby came to our house to-day. Warm and pink, in her cot she
lay. Tiny toes, on such tiny feet. Downy heir, surrounds a face so sweet.

I love her very tiny ears. And when she cries, there are no tears.
I'd love to kiss her tiny lips. And touch her tiny finger tips.

But when I go near this is said: 'Darling be careful, mind her head.'
So from afar I'll worship her. And hope she knows I really care.

I watch has grow-ups 'Bill and Coo'. Telling Mummy, 'she looks just
like you'. I don't know how that can be. For Grandma says she's like Daddy.

Tonight when they are fast asleep. Along the landing I will creep.
They will think I'm tucked up in bed. For they all call me 'sleepy-Head'.

So little sister, I say 'Good night!'. For I know, that they are
right. But soon, I know they day will come. When you and I, together shall run.

J. Danson

The Bird Watcher

Today I walked for miles around watching, listening to each lovely sound
Of goldfinches on the treetops high, the lark singing from its lovely sky
Red poles and siskens on the alder trees buzzing around like a swarm of bees
Occasionally dropping to the stream below the cool their throats which seemed aglow
Now to the bullfinch on the silver birch, the warbling of the cock so soft and rich

I love to linger here a while so I sit upon the old wood stile
With binoculars resting on my knee pondering now what else to see
The quietness now becomes acute, my instinct warns me what's afoot
A hawk circling high above, ready to pounce on the birds I love
As the hawk began to make its dive I prayed this time my birds survive
I jumped about my hands held high shouting cand waving at the sky
Then to my great delight the hawk flew off overcome with fright

Over the stile now to the heather beyond saw more birds feeding near a pond
Blue tits and chaffinches chirping away, this has really made my day
I carried on another mile, the antics of the rabbits made me smile
but then I thought that I must turn and head for home across the burn

Alexander Laird

From The Old To The Young

We've all got loads to tell you
If you'd only sit and stay
With a little bit of prompting
We'd have a lot to say.

We'd tell you of the good old days
Where all for just some pennies
We'd fill a bag of quite a size
With sherbet dabs and jellies.

We didn't have it quite like you
No high tech gear or such
We'd all make do, rehash or mend
And no one minded much.

At home we had to "watch our mouths"
Clips round the ear were the norm
We nevertheless turned out quite well
And I came top in our form.

Just tarry a while and be patient
With us seniors of varying years
There's a harvest to reap if you're wise enough
So give us the loan of your ears.

Jean King

Locked Out

A woman once did pass me by,
and as she went, I heard her cry.
I didn't know what it was all about.
But I heard her scream, I heard her shout.
Then suddenly, I realized,
and felt that I should sympathize.
For what this woman shouted out.
She'd shut her door and was locked out!
Well after that we tried and tried,
to find a way to get inside.
We pushed and pulled the door, but no,
this was not the way to go.
We tried the windows, to no avail,
in this task we'd surely fail.
And then, it happened, quite suddenly.
The woman did produce a key.
"Would this help?" She asked quite shyly.
"Probably", I said most slyly.
I let her in and locked the door,
she couldn't get out anymore.

Donna L. Sim

Birth Of A Poem

Silently you lie there so pristine and pure,
exposing before me your very virginity.
This I shall take, with care and dignity.

It will be neither lust, or rape,
but with gentleness and, consideration.

These feelings I have deep within me,
now turn to the unspoken words I shall use.
Upon your very soul I will write.

With care, and feeling I shall impart,
these words from deep within my heart.

Confusion and frustration you have caused,
but now the deed is done, my needs fulfilled.

You have served your purpose well,
no more time on this we shall dwell.
Between us the bond is made,
pain and anguish I feel no more.

As I let you slip slowly to the floor,
my gratitude I give virtuous page, for understanding.

This night I can rest once more,
and I will not curse anymore.

E. S. Mayne

Silent Thoughts

There's a hush of calm tranquillity in the quiet of the night
And a warm gentle wind bathes my cheeks on its destination flight
I sit by my open window - see innumerable stars in the sky
I think of uncountable blessings received from my Father on high
There's a feeling of closeness to the One up above
And my heart's overwhelmed with His wonderful love.

Amy Cooper

Me

This poem is about me, what do I like.
I like the sea
The fresh sea air blowing in over me
The unconquerable swell of the waves and tide,
The beautiful peace and calm of a silent sea.
I like the rolling green and verdant hills peacefully gliding
Over the landscape covered by patches of yellow and green and forests,
Where all the animals roam unseen.
I like the Queen, the pageantry,
The history of our fair land forget the family troubles and the like,
Just remember our past through this fair lady, battles, buildings,
Shows, literature, fashions, language, laws and many more to bring us
Where we stand today. I like to sleep to unwind, relax close my
Eyes and drift away on a starry blanket through the skies.
I like to eat, all those wonderful delicacies all
Around to make you fit, healthy and sound.
I like to drink, to down a flagon or two can make you feel swell
And well. I like to laugh, a little joke here and there with
Friends to share makes life worth living and giving. I like to read
All that knowledge at one's fingertips. A precious book, a tale
Unfolds, richness itself

Michael Kerr

Shadows

The first thing I remember, in the shadows, were angels around my head
They stood there quietly, guarding me when I was asleep in bed.
Throughout the years, in trials and tribulations, happiness and tears.
Others angels have appeared from out of the shadows.
Earthly forms, pouring the sunshine into my life.
Kindly souls who help when in need.
The memories of both past and present,
Touching me with thoughts of Love.
Filling me with their earthly deeds.
I pray to God for me to be an angel for someone else.
Standing at a child's bed, full of love and gentle care.
In a home, or hospital, garden anywhere.
Longing, waiting to be used,
As the angels watched and comforted me.
Many years ago, in the shadows

Betty Fuller

Grasmere To Rydal Water And Back

The walk to Rydal Water ought to sort a fit man from a fat man any day.
It's the first bit that's the worst bit up the ever climbing way.
Still the view of waters streaming, gleaming, teeming down the fell
From the high road shining brightly, make me sprightly, feeling well.

See the young lambs lightly springing, hear the chaffinches all singing.
And the rhododendrons blooming,
Springtime nature fast consuming,
In the distance rain clouds looming,
Memories are building, clinging as my boots on stones are ringing
What a perfect day remembered as we walk down on the way.

Passing Wordsworth's homes in Grasmere and in Rydal makes one choose
To think how many people pass here on the bridle way, with muse.
Cross the road, down by the lakeside, children playing by the shore.
Dogs excited and delighted swim for branches more and more.

Past the river, dogs a'quiver shaking spray and panting hard
Walking on the road to Grasmere if you pass here don't retard,
There's a cafe by the lakeside, buttered scones with jam for tea
Foreheads burning on returning, springtime days for you and me.

Alan Pace

Untitled

Oh child of mine, yet unborn.
Is there a father I can trust for you?
It seems I can't be sure.
I want to give you everything
Love from a mother
Love from a father
A safe family
With enough freedom not to smother.
But if I cannot trust a man to be your father
Then I will be both, for you I will kill
for you the world will be made to sit up
And pay attention.
For you will always know
A mother's love.
You will always know the truth
And I hope
You will always have the freedom
To share your love with others and be loved.

Jenny Wall

My Absent Dad

A lonely walk with falling leaves,
awakens me from my silent dreams,
I see a man with greying hair
I take a look but you're not there.
Then the pain that runs so deep
surfaces up and makes me weep
I wish I was your little girl once more,
to hold you tight as I did before.
But the only comfort that I now find
Are happy memories etched in my mind
For every time I find I'm happy,
Every time I find I'm sad.
I think of you, I dream of you
My ever loving absent dad.

Karen Dallas

The Frivolous Wind

Pulling at bin lids
    whistling through alleys
snarling and tugging
    chasing the leaves
Blasting sharp hailstones
    staccato on windows
pounding through chimneys
    with invisible ease,
Skimming the duck pond
    tormenting lithe Willows
grounding the Heron
    submerged to the knees
Clearing the Parks of discarded wrappers
    whisking and stirring making them fly
    to benches and tangle on trees.

D. M. Tills

Why Me

I often dream of yesterday
with sorrow in my heart.
Dancing lessons, Sunday walks,
oh how they were the start
of a life that I will never have,
snatched from me in my prime;
Dear Lord, Why me? I often ask
why didn't I have the time
to walk and dance and do the things
so many people do.
This illness took its hold on me
and now uncertainty looms.
To fight, be strong, look forward not back
I know this is the key,
but this still poses one big question;
Oh, Dear Lord, Why me?

Lorraine Jenkins

"Gratitude"

We walked through sunlit meadows when my Granddad held my hand
And he'd often call me "Princess" and he'd always understand
And I'd never be excluded from anything he planned
And I loved him

We would play at being fairies as we romped around the wood
He would bounce me on low branches, never told me to "be good"
And we'd pick the wild flowers, Granddad always said I could
And I loved him

He'd protect me from the others, he was always on my side
When I was bad he didn't care, his smile was just as wide
But when a score of years had gone my Granddad, sadly, died
And I missed him

So, Granddad, if you hear me, I just wanted to say
That your life made mine better, and I thought of you today
And to tell you in my heart we two are sometimes still at play
And I love you

Lorraine Phipps

Eclipse - The Dance With A Shadow

I cannot feel you. I cannot touch you.
Yet I can see your mysterious power with my eyes.
Inch by inch your shadowy veil creeps over the moon's countenance
Blotting out the lantern of the night sky.
Your black velvet mist shrouds her pale beauty until she fades from view.
Total Eclipse.

I cannot feel you. I cannot touch you.
I cannot see the golden orb, the ghostly galleon on the night sea.
You play with her - teasing her with your mystery
Until you tire of lingering and move quietly on to another time, another place
Where light will catch you out and you will dance again.
Elusive Shadow.

P. M. Darwood

My Season

Spring is coming, snowdrops peep, lambs are skipping by mother sheep.
Daffodils sway in the breeze, buds of green unfurl on trees.
Birds are building feathering nest, spring is the season I like best.
Summer comes, the weather's warm, wasps and bees begin to swarm,
Lazy days by sea, on sand, or people working on the land.
Mowing grass in meadow, field, ready for the winter yield.
Summer sun, lighter night, makes most folk happy, and bright.
Then comes Autumn, it's harvest time, nights creep in dark by nine.
Leaves on trees once were green, begin to mellow, a sight to be seen,
Then they fall upon the ground, underfoot a crunching sound!
Winter comes with regret, icy fingers, feet get wet.
Snowflakes fall, fun for child, not for the creatures in the wild.
They hunt for food, be it nut or berry,
Christmas comes along, and folk are merry.
Sending cards, buying toys, for Santa's coming, to girls and boys.
Roasting turkey, cooking pud, eating too much for our own good.
Warmest wishes, full of cheer, but I'll be glad when spring is here!

Sheila Rider

Reminiscence

The pace of life can be so fast, tight schedules can make one gasp
So given the chance I let the pores exude the feeling of utter solitude
To take time out let my thoughts just fly, allow the day to pass me by
To go at my pace just for once, ease my soul and let my thoughts bounce,

Around my head they bob and weave as all around me I perceive
The rustling leaves, the trickling stream, the scented air and the sunlit scene
To look around the woodland glade as the trials of life are allowed to be fade
To think of nought but what I see, a falling leaf, a quivering tree

Many years ago it was all like this, we had the time, we were at peace
But all that changed with this new age, time speeded up with each turning page
I yearn to be in yesterday, it now seems oh so far away
When we all had time for everyone and looked forward to the rising sun

To set a pace we'd all enjoy, each man and woman, girl and boy
To love thy neighbour as thyself, to lend a hand, not keep to oneself
But the wheel of life rolls on and on as we all head for the setting sun
So I take my chances so I don't miss, my times of solitude and bliss

George Ellison

This My Valley

Across the lonely moor I walked
the turf was soft beneath my feet.
Across the wide expanse of peat
I looked toward the valley down below
how could strangers understand
a land of which they did not know.

Peaceful miles of hills and dales
moorland mists, relentless gales,
winter snow and icy hail
bleating sheep, the silent grouse.
O'er the hills low hanging clouds
Exposed to wind and weather, a shepherd's house.

The first lamb, white and curly
on a blanket by a fire lay
early for a spring day.
Carpets of heather in purple and blue
dark green shoots pushing through
the yellow gorse its colour blazing forth
this was my land, the North.

Margret Battye

Thoughts

Thoughts, ideas, what are they?
They certainly can't be taken away!
And yet, they mean so much to us,
truly conceived without a fuss.

Am I as others? No, I am not.
The reason for this is not part of a plot.
For I am a being, unique of my sort;
Despite what was said in an Edinburgh Court!

Would I like to be, as others are?
No, I would not. Their minds are ajar
to thoughts and ideas which easily condemn.
I am a being, unique among men.

I make up my mind, as I want to do.
Not listen to others who say, "hey, you!
Do as you're told and things will be right."
Shouting and yelling, well into the night.

I am a being, unique with a soul.
Am I unique, or just part of the whole?
The answer to this, I just cannot find.
It's hidden deep, deep, in the back of my mind.

T. Matthews

The Anglers Day

At dawn, by a fast flowing river,
a lake, a canal, or a tranquil pool,
with a rod, line, hook and bait,
the angler settles down to wait,
using a tackle box as a stool.

With some sandwiches and a flask,
a huge brolly to keep off the rain,
the float it bobs and starts to sink,
just as ones about the take a drink,
lost it; bait up and start again.

A tug on the line, and angling skills are needed,
Because it's hooked this time, no doubt!
Then into the net the beauty unfurled,
of this creature from another world;
and that's what anglings all about.

A evening time in the local inn,
where angler's meet to hold sway,
landing that fish takes a longer duration,
and the size of it grows with imagination,
and always the monsters that got away.

Barbara Marsland

Living With Light

Hey, Mister Moon,
What makes you shine so bright?
So bright you're blinding my heart.
How are the stars,
That hang by your side?
They make me feel so apart.
Are all the fairground lights stuck in your skin?
Trapped in a hole so thin,
Not trying to escape at all.
Maybe it's Mother Nature's natural glow
Surviving the rain and snow,
She just loves a sunny day.
Oh little glow-bug,
Your light's a dream come true,
When you whisper words, like 'I love you'.
When I'm standing there, staring at the sky.
I ask the heavens, "Why, oh why?"

Hazel Miller

The Garden Leak

The garden has a water leak my dear
  So near the house, this is so drear.
A week I sit, a nervous wreck
  Water's rising above the deck.

I think of the African woman's plight.
  Sometimes miles shod through the night.
Each drop is precious, carried on head
  Here all this waste running under the shed.

What would she give for an instant tap?
  My meter doesn't give a rap.
What do we mean by civilizations?
  This is the tale of at least two nations
East and west in peace unite
  But black is black and white is white!

Annette Smith

Life

Isn't it funny, how life carries on.
It doesn't stop and wait for you
and its clock just keeps on ticking.
Something may seem boring, but
look for the good side of it because
when it is over you'll want to go back.
Memories are treasures of precious gold
which no one else can repeat. Treasure
them. If they fade, don't worry because
the most precious ones will never leave
your mind. Always remember the fun -
not the unhappiness that you had with
your memory. It doesn't do you any harm.
Listen to words of wisdom. When you
are wrong, accept your mistake; but
when you're right, stand your ground.
Lastly, love your loved ones when you are
with them, because nothing lasts forever
except love and memories.

Leonie Rickards

Yvette

When joy does bring a song to sing, its title is a name
Expressions of Cupid's love whose target is the same
You are to me that everything of which they always speak
Like Christmas hols and Birthday all within a week
You are the sun, you are the moon, when both are shining full
A Summer's day, the joy it brings when all seems wonderful
The beauty of the Autumn time with colours on the trees
A crisp night sky so full of stars, all in you I see
Winter comes and brings along a pureness with the snow
And though the days are short and cold, your inner warmth will glow
Within my heart there is a place that's set aside for you
Where lambs do play and birds do sing, as Spring starts all anew
Years have gone, as more will pass I never will forget
When joy does bring a song to sing, its title is Yvette

A. J. Wilson

The Squirrel

I have a stranger in my garden
I've not seen him here before.
He has bright eyes and a long fluffy tail
Grey fur and very tiny paws.

The birds' feeder is down, with holes in
and the nuts are strewn all around
He is running across the grass now
into the trees, with a leap and bound

The little rascal has not gone far
I can see his ears among the leaves
I will leave the nuts for him to find
but my poor birds won't be very pleased.

It was lovely of him to visit
but I must admit, you see,
I hope he doesn't come too often
It's too expensive, having him to tea.

Christine Jeffery

Lonely

The night you held me so tight
I couldn't help but feel special
Oh that wonderful night
When you won my heart and soul.

We were more than husband and wife
We were more than lovers
We were soul mates, I thought for life
But you've forgotten me for all the others

You no longer hold me tight
I'm just a body - no longer special
We don't make love all through the night
It's just kisses and sex = no bite

You sold me out
Left me in a hole
My heart is dead and cannot shout
About the pain of my dying soul.

Norreen White

Disease Of The Heart

Disease of the heart is not fat from a burger,
it's infatuation with a girl who is murder.
Blind to the chase, impure fascination,
she could be a tart, she could be salvation.

Whatever she is, she puts fizz in the bottle,
and you're shaken up and wresting the throttle.
She'll tease you, seduce you then put you aside,
others will see it, but the truth's still denied.

And so it begins, the painful decline,
when it's hurting so much, you're drowning in wine.
And she'll never notice the moods that you swing,
'cos your soul wears dark glasses, and she's just a pretty thing.

Danny Quinlan

Mother

She stands at the window with anticipation
     a smile on her face
A sweet smile that I who love her
     feel my eyes brim with tears.
A pang of fear and sadness
     the passing years.

You know your children well
     faults are forgiven
Happy faces a laugh a wave
     the kiss and hug of welcome
     is all you crave.

Now that you have gone
No more can I confide
Forever you will be
Woven in my memory.

Diana L. Towner

The Story Of Highwayman Joe

Highwayman Joe could be found in any weather
dressed in the most skintight black leather
his famous cry of "Stand and Deliver"
made many a lass go all of a quiver

With a pistol poised in his big hand
Joe was feared throughout the land
money, jewels he would take them all
even frail old Granny Smith's shawl

Joe's day of reckoning came one dark night
when his horse Alf suddenly took fright
they parted company in a leafy lane
and Joe was left in considerable pain

He'd fallen awkwardly on stony ground
and to make matters worse he then found
his lovely leather trousers had been split
leaving his undergarments exposed quite a bit

After years of keeping his identity concealed
Joe's manly assets were finally revealed
he decided it was time for a change of career
and now is a stripper at "Ye Olde Red Deer"

C. Childerley

Louise

I have always called you "Lou"
Although Louise is your name
To me it is something special
And will always mean the same
To you I have told my troubles
To you I have told my joys
Because I know I could depend
On "you" my faithful friend
You are my loving sister
Over the years you have treated me
With love and understanding
Listened patiently, sometimes you have been a mother
Sometimes a loving friend, I know whatever happens
or what the future sends we will always stick together
Never far apart, a special place is set aside
For "you" within my heart, for "Lou" - you have meant
So very much to me over the passing years
We have shared our sorrows, shared our tears
God willing we will go on sharing
For many - more - years.

Rose Colegate

Untitled

Grandma's in the garden, watering the flowers,
Grandpa's in the deck chair, wiling away the hours,
everywhere is peaceful, on this lovely sunny day,
when in comes Madalina, and drives our peace away.

Madalina frowns when she looks at me, for I am very plain,
she's my beautiful mother, who's also very vain.
"Sit up straight", she said, "Why don't you dress with care",
"Do you have to bite your nails?" "Why don't you style your hair?"

"I think it's time I took you back, and taught you how to dress"
Grandpa shouts, "Leave her alone, I like her looking a mess".
Then the doorbell sounded loudly, Madalina went to see,
and Grandpa said, "Don't worry, she'll not take you from me".

Then in came Madalina, her face was all alight
Philip has called to take me out, so I'm going home tonight.
Grandma looked at Grandpa, and Grandpa looked at me,
and relief on all our faces was there for all to see.

We waved them off at nighttime, we couldn't hardly wait,
I skipped along the garden path, and Grandpa locked the gate
"Come on in", says Grandma, "I think it's going to rain".
The log fire was burning brightly, and peace was with us again.

Beryl Dutton

Patricia

I saw your smile
as it climbed o'er the crest of a distant cloud,
And watched your eyes sparkle
as we drifted deep into the dawn,
I felt your gentle caress
as the breath of a new cradled babe,
And touched you.

Like a silent symphony
your thoughts breached that far trodden mile,
While in my dream
I awakened to wash away your tears,
So slumber now my little dove
with the ken of twenty-five years,
And reach for me.

E. Rendall

Innocent

Such a little fluff ball,
Cheeky yet polite,
A stroke is all it takes to protect you from his bite,
He was a little cherub,
Such a little friend,
but then toy guns came out as a trend,

Just a little bang, bang,
Just a little toy,
A cat can't be protected by just a little boy,
The fluffy tail is held,
The cats head meets the wall,
The blood a devil colour deserved for an evil fool,
"I've shot him dead, I've killed him?"

Just a little boy,
with just a little bang, bang,

Just a little toy?

Jenny O'Hara

Adulterous Love

You tell me you love me, you tell me you care
You tell me you need me, but I don't find you there
You tell me I hurt you with words so unkind
I don't mean to do so, but you've mixed up my mind

You tell me to wait, it can only take time
But I find this so hard, for I want you as mine
You tell me you miss me when I'm not around
So you know how I feel when you're not to be found

You tell me to cheer up, to be so much brighter
But how can I do this when my heart gets no lighter
So forgive me, sweetheart, for keep being down
But it's loving you so that gives me this frown

But maybe one day, I hope not too long
You'll say those sweet words "It's with you I belong"
And when that day comes I promise you this:
My love I will show you with more than a kiss

Vincent Smith

Gypsy Dancers

Ghostly music filled the valleys,
Strains of gypsy fiddlers, play.
Girls in whirling, swirling dresses,
Caught in the dance, and the,
— flickering array.

Down the lane came blackened miners,
From dirt and grime, and coal seams deep.
Pick and shovel were their partners.
Home a hovel, widows weep.

Marching forward, singers, voices.
Girls in arms to their delight.
Round and round the ribboned maypole.
Down the lane, and out of sight.

Sue Williams

Abbeylands - My Club

Why do I go every week to my club?
When I could frequent the pub!
Why do I trouble to go every Tuesday?
Could it be my best "news" day!
Why do I go, whatever the weather?
Because it is "Good" to get together.
Sometimes we have a speaker,
Sometimes we have a "quiz".
Some of our members, are "whiz" kids!
Sometimes we laugh, not at a serious matter,
Sometimes we have a jolly good natter!
"Get together's" during summer, when the club doesn't meet,
Quite a few parties, with "goodies" to eat!
The carol concert to look forward to,
Better than that, our Christmas dinner too!
My how the year soon goes by,
The 'A.G.M' is almost nigh.
Then we start all over again,
and pray that "Abbeylands" will always remain.

Dora May Smallridge

The Dabbler

In the days when old was good
Gone and forgotten those made of wood
We scrape, we polish with no elbow grease
Because there are sprays for practically every nook niche

So hard we try to review the old
From days gone by, so we are told
We watch the T.V. that tells us how
Have bought a big thing, can I start it now?
Get some sandpaper, scraper and wire wool
Work very hard, rubber gloves on and make it dull

Then rub dust, rub dust and more sanding
This darn job is never ending
Have break, cupa, biscuit a ciggi
Then back with gloves on to the nitty gritty
Oh my goodness is that the time
Tea is not ready and husband will whine
Oh what a dash, thank goodness for fridges and freezers
Have quick look for any tongue teasers
Well that is it for another day
Wash dishes, put feet up, but before put things away.

J. A. Rimmer

The Man Who Didn't Like His Face

In the mirror, he would not look
Or gaze upon a face
That made him sad and feel that he may be mad.

A face which didn't fit which he would change
Even if just a bit to look and be smiled at, smile and look back

I can change my face, it will be smiled at
I will change my face, not hide under that damn hat

No one knew what he had done changed the face, the one,
That face he'd never gaze upon

Wrapped in bandages week in, week out, slowly bruises disappear
Then one day, a face appears, not his face but a new man,
He cannot recognize, they cannot stigmatize
This face, what do you think, he can't ask you know
For no one knows him, a stranger now.
And meeting people he'd thought his foes
They talk among themselves aloud
Where is that man these days,
You know the one
The one, the lonely one
With the lovely face.

Roger Hayman

Anthology

Beyond the simple pleasure reading brings,
Beyond my little thoughts and daily round,
Beyond the realm of ordinary things,
Beyond the humble words my mind has found,
Beyond my dreams and fancy's flights,
Beyond my thoughts that no one hears,
Beyond the stillness of my nights,
Beyond my secret hopes and fears

To ponder now another's mind,
To sense the yearning in their heart,
To find wisdom of a different kind,
To learn the truths their words impart,
To share those special thoughts within,
To reach from this my lowly place,
To journey where another's been,
To touch their lives through time and space.

I hope, beyond this world where all have sinned,
Our souls may meet to share and be,
As many voices on the wind,
A truly great anthology!

Jules Willis

The Plan

So many years, each carefully laid and planned
For the time when life's tools are put away;
Reflected peace, from effort's waving wand
Was to be yours, with love, and time to play.

The joy of fruition, so quickly passed
With stumbling torment of a kindly man,
Frustrated, he with every turn outcast,
Living within the shambles of a plan.

This living movement of a heart, that beats
To feed a now bewildered, fuddled brain,
Is still a heart of love, which now entreats
Us all to understand, and treat the same.

Self is to him, the same as ever was;
To you, the partner now the gate is closed;
His smile and twinkle eye you see, because
The barrier of love is not opposed.

In the lonesome, silent hours of the night,
You dwell upon the plan that went astray;
Naught can you do to win the Alzheimer fight,
But try to live each moment, and each day.

Frank Hickson

Children Of Eight

Children of eight
Should be safe and sound
To laugh and play
To hop and skip
To be loved and cherished
Praised and encouraged
With bedtime stories
And nice warm beds

But some children of eight
Are never safe
Abused and battered
And kept out of sight
No love hugs or kisses
No praise or encouragement
Just silent rages
No bedtime stories
No warm beds.

Lost and bewildered with secrets to keep
How are these children ever to sleep.

Diane Gavin

Frustrations Of A Housewife

The day you decide to go to town,
you spill something on your gown.
Rush to change, then find the bus has gone,
stand and wait, what is your fate.
We will have to go on another date,
back to the house, drop the key,
bend down, slip and graze my knee.
At last I'm back indoors,
going about the family chores.
Oh no! The washing machine won't pump out,
I could just scream and shout.
Try to phone the engineer,
sorry, can't come today, I fear.
Oh dear let's make a cup of tea,
for nothing's going right for me.
You do not wish your time away,
but tomorrow must be a better day.

Doris Smart

Reverie

In my reverie I walked, through a grove of trees.
The leaves were a living flame.
I heard your voice upon the breeze;
I heard you call my name.
I stopp'd. I turn'd. I looked for you.
Through the shadows did appear
A flicker of light. It was then I knew
You had kept your word to be near.

You stood there in that silent place
Just beyond my fingertips.
I felt your breath upon my face
And your kiss upon my lips.
Was this just a trick of the light?
Or the longing in my memory?
Slowly you faded out of sight.
I walked on in my reverie.

Jacqueline Hanson

Feelings

There's a pain deep inside.
Feelings of hurt so hard to hide.
One moment I'm on such a high,
But now all I want to do is curl up and die.

Promises, promises so many he gave to me,
From his home across the sea.
My heart once whose, now is broken.
My life, my whole being was my love token.

Now I have to try to get on with my life.
Memories of what was said, cuts like a knife.
My love for him goes so deep.
I thought he was mine to keep!

Though days are so long and lonely,
From now the children are my one and only
The pain is sometimes so hard to handle,
I know no-one will ever re-light my candle.

Jayne Bardsley

Nightfall

An ebony velvet carpet, scattered with diamonds,
twilight from the moon shines though.
Open the curtains to view the skeleton fingers of
the tree branches tapping against the glass.
It is sun down,
It is moon rise.

Outside I hear dogs howling,
in unison with the wind.
Through the window, I see frosty rings,
clinging and grasping the moon.
It is the dead of night,
It is hours of darkness.

Jo White

Christmas

Once more the rush and bustle will begin,
The present buying, cards to write and send.
The problems come again as of last year,
What shall we give to brother, sister, friend.
The crackers we must get, the puddings too,
The cake, that must be made, and iced as well,
The fruit, the nuts, the sweets, we'll not forget,
As trees we decorate with balls and bells.
The holly must be fetched, the mistletoe,
The logs to give the fire warmth and light,
The turkey we must stuff, the mince pies bake,
Without these, nothing else would seem quite right.
But whilst all of these things we do prepare,
Let us not lose the meaning on the way,
Of what the Christmas message really means.
Of what the Christmas message has to say.
A heavenly babe came to this world
In manger lowly life did start.
And all of us today who seek,
Will find a place within his heart.

Constance J. Cooke

Louise

Soon you'll be leaving for sunnier places,
Where the sun always shines,
Like a thousand smiling faces.

A passion of love,
A passion to behold,
Let the story unfold.

It started with a kiss,
One I will surely miss,
So soft and warm,
A new love forlorn.

Your perfume was divine,
I wished that you'd be mine,
With your long blonde hair,
And your complexion so fair.

And now you're gone and left for good,
I only wish that I would,
Have told you how much you mean to me,
A little love but endlessly.

Gavin J. Docherty

Mopsey

A black tornado who has just blown in.
It's a poodle called 'Mopsey' - for her sin.
Though she's only a puppy she knows it all.
The world is her oyster and humans will fall
For her mischievous ways, and throw her a ball.
Those dark shiny eyes that peep through her curls
Are full of intelligence and pretty as pearls.
She'll sit when asked - if there's nothing better to do.
And tolerate grooming - when a reward is due.
'Mopsey' likes gardening - well bringing plants indoors.
Loving the feel of mud on nose and in paws.
She knows it's her duty to spread all the grime
Throughout the whole house - she's got plenty of time.
'Enjoy your puppy days Mopsey' whilst you can
Because for you there is a greater plan.
You're being taught to 'socialize' there is no doubt -
That one day 'Mopsey' you'll help a person out.
By being the 'ears' for one who cannot hear.
You'll always be loved and very much treasured
Faithfully giving total loyalty unmeasured.

Rhoda Cane

Christ's Love

10,000 and 10,000 times are you shown.
The supreme truth
You see it, or you choose not to see it;
Nothing complicated.
The grass grows, the rain falls. There are no secrets.
The ultimate mystery of truth and love,
Being one.
And the door opened;
The flowers in the vase,
The tea water boiling.
The special cups being special cups.
The spirit of the visit.
For emptiness links all and true emptiness is solid.
Between all, through all, in all is emptiness
That can be touched.
For Christ's love is the ether within which all exists.

Malcolm Thomas Taylor

Christmas Verses

When Robin sings on Christmas Day,
Each tuneful cadence seems to say,
"Rejoice to hear this wondrous thing,
Today is born The Savior King."

When peal the bells with merry chime -
As oft they do at Christmas time -
Good news! Good news we have to tell,
Jesus is born "Immanuel".

As silver stars, with mystic light,
Spread diamonds o'er the Christmas night,
Their whispering voices proudly say,
"It was a star that led the way."

As robin, bells, and stars repeat -
The Herald's joyful message sweet,
With angel choir, we too can sing -
A carol for the New Born King.

Idwal W. Evans

In Our Child's Eyes

She came to us with eyes that danced with pain
    and spoke to us with unsaid words,
Longing to hold us as she cried silent tears
    again and again,
We watched our wounded child
    and prepared to give our lives in her defence
Nothing could we do against an enemy unknown
    because we could not get beneath or around the barrier,
The wall she built around her took its toll
    and in our child's eyes we were no longer Gods,
We could not cure her tortured soul
    but suffered with her from some unknown ill,
Hence when the thorn of truth dug deep into our flesh
    and every year that passed we suffered still,
We cursed the devil who had caused her pain
    and wished him all that he had given her.

Linda Bedford

Change Of Plan

It's not the end of the world
    It's just a change of plan.
If God had wanted you to have this home
    He would have done all he can.
But he knew that there was a problem
    So his message he did send.
He couldn't shatter your dreams himself
    So he sent them through a friend
This does not mean the door has shut
    And your happiness is no more,
Because today is no different than yesterday
    You still have what you had before,
Bricks and mortar don't mean anything
    Deep down the value is nil,
You have what is most important
    Your family around you still.

Ruth Rowley

To Brood In Vexing And Vivid Mood

We are getting older my chum, getting older...
Our dressing gowns moulder
And we are slightly balder;
The artificial vortex compels to wobble
Sometimes we gulls or windy but never yodel.

A tiny grain in ocean waves
Like sage Einstein through our plays;
We pine at labour, we pant at sweat...
Limelight we catch from star the Great.

The brook of time strives always for perfection
And kernel's acme related to reflection;
Thus even this can't change persuasive sound
Which under hat of bogus mazy ground.

We've groped as fateful twilight so fetching day
And also early morning pretty maiden ray;
I'm sorry to hear that but sadly smile
And hitherto it isn't handy
To stick a dot fragile...

Yura Beliaev

Summer Holiday

It's summer now the sun is out
let's have a party, I hear you shout.
You feel so happy the days are long
you want to dance and sing a song.

We go away to have some fun
now our holiday really has begun,
children are playing, they dig in the sand.
We listen to music, a big brass band.

Hankies are knotted and laid on head.
Mother looks on and shudders with dread.
What do you look like embarrassing me?
Don't moan mother, we're by the sea.

We're going home, we've had our fun
we've swam in the sea, lain in the sun.
Our cases are packed and everyone's ready
it's a long way home; let's take it steady.

Linda Wood

Silent Victory

When the sky moves I move.
When the grass grows I grow.
When the people call I call back.
When God calls I can't turn back
The spirit helps me to make good choices.
When my mother calls I can't turn away.
I can't turn away from my future.

Valerie Farrington

Sunken Dreams

Searching for skeletons on dark winter nights,
images of rosebuds that never bloom,
Tears that fill all oceans, hushed by gales that chill.

Now my love has gone, all alone, my nights
are cold, my house is empty, here I stand
alone, stricken with fear, the pain that
grips only lonely men can know.

Dark nights where shadows reflected my
thoughts of you, illuminated by moon
silhouettes and candles that flicker whilst
The wind moans and groans, howling like mad
Dogs that lay by graves.

No more do I see your face,
No more do I touch your sweet tender lips
That taste like honey,
no more do I caress your warm flesh,
no more does the sun shine for me.

Paul J. Abbott

Reflections

How
How will I manage to survive
Old age is here yes I'm still alive
Mirrored reflections is that really me?
Saggy flesh, wrinkly dark-eyed mess
Topped with grey, see through hair lines
How
How will I manage, no work for me
Bills I cannot pay leaving untold misery
Unskilled, unloved, too old, too fat,
Wrong sex wrong hat
How
How will I manage when death raises
Its head
Staking his claim on what's well past
Its best
Even then, no dignity for me
My children or the state
Will have to bury me
How

Agnes Burgess-Hall

Darkness

Night has cast her mantle, concealing the world
and her minions from prying eyes.
Each one intent on their own pursuits,
Be it for good or evil.

The headlights of a car
Catch a couple in a freeze frame of desire.
They step into the protection of the hedgerow
For their clandestine meeting.

Hooded shadows commune with their furtive
Partners of the underworld, planning their deadly deeds.
A blood-curdling sound pierces the air,
Only cats in agony and ecstasy.
A haunting melancholy hoot of an owl,
A sign of death to the superstitious.

So love and death stalk the night,
Each pleased with the protection of darkness.
As a rat scampers away
And a stray rabbit is crushed by oncoming wheels,
The lovers kiss and make promises.

Jenny Gott

Flickering Shadows

Visions of flickering shadows from the past
Fleeting shadows that did not last

When Christmas was a boy child full of love
Kings, Shepherds and a star that shone above

I remember a child on their loving gran's lap
By the fire-side corner grandad's having a nap

They spoke of family and friends they did know
White Christmas!!! But was there always snow

On Christmas Eve a happy child goes to bed
To dream of a man with whiskers, dressed in red

At dawn a knobbly stocking brought great joy
Book, orange, apple, some nuts, a wooden toy

More presents downstairs by a sparkling tree
Just a little something for each of the family

Nostalgic aromas of good things to eat
Roast turkey, pies of sweet mince meat

The silver thrupenny bit in the Christmas pud
Fun and games with the family, it felt so good

These memories on my mind do cast
Fleeting, flickering shadows of the past

Dennis L. Seaman

Chilean Exile's Epilogue

Once upon a time there was
A river, an old dirt road
And a forest rhyme.
Once upon a time there was
A condor which saw the valleys
For the very last time.

Once, to the west of the Andes,
Down the lost El Prado mines,
We saw the world's Occident,
We saw the Southern Cross.

Once upon a time there was
So much poetry in our lives:
Epilogue of all my verses;
Because today I write down
Without much rhyming;
Only tracing the stars of Perseus;
In nights without rivers;
In nights without dirt roads;
In the saddest of all my nights.

Luis De Arias

Haven

Gentle fingers caress my face,
Wipe the tears from my eyes.
Your voice, soft and low,
Comforting music to my ears.
Tenderly, you enfold me
And shut out harsh reality.
Warmth, love and care,
I find in your embrace.
Gradually, my mind relaxes,
Tension, pain and sorrow disappear.
Safe in your arms,
I smile, a little smile.

G. M. Band

Before

You live in the moon
The white, mulled

alabaster of your eyes
stare down on me

among the capacities
of stars.

You are modest
about your voice

And now that I know who you are
You guide differently.

Lucy Elizabeth Gooderidge

We're Going Tonight

I can't believe the time has come
We're actually off tonight
The car is almost fully packed
"Mum don't forget my kite"!
We all long for this yearly event
And to Cornwall off we go
To a village so calm and peaceful
And a pace of life so slow
But the journey's the real excitement
For we set off at two in the morn—
All whispering as we climb in the car
Be careful not to touch that horn
And when we eventually get there
In the middle of the day
In our homey Cornish cottage
Feels like we've never been away
And it's always very sad
On the day that we come home
But we know deep down that one day
It will be our permanent home

Bernadette Crook

Missing

Missing the laughter and the pleasing
The touching and the teasing
The arguments and make-up
The sleeping and the wake-up
The planning and the doing
The dreams and their pursuing
Missing you.

Wynne McLaren

Untitled

Do not weep, do not cry
Those majestic trees no
Longer reach for the sky
What have we done?!

David N. Sivills

The Search

I've discovered everlasting night,
Where those other lost and lonely souls
The Sun and Moon no longer shine
But hide behind the tear-filled clouds,
Pretending they are strangers.

I've found the darkest underground
Where long-lost memories are stored
Disappearing 'neath the dust
Of chilling thoughts and cold despair
From unrequited lovers.

I've felt the coldness of the sea
And listened to the mournful cries
Of seabirds on their futile quest
For happiness in any place
To have a someone's caring.

I've known the pain of solitude,
A Cross that's difficult to bear
Yet search within my arid soul
For answers, where no questions are
To free me from this sadness.

D. R. Goodwin

Indian Summer

Silhouetted against the ecliptic sky
they writhe;
struggling, contorted sheaths
of flaying branches—
as unseasonable as the weather.

No crusty mornings, yet,
only mistiness
heralding Indian summer days.

Where are our chilling frosts,
our watery sunshine?
Where our fairy tale flurries
as Christmas approaches
and children's eyes grow wider,
their parents' nostalgic
for the colds of yesteryear?

Jenny Willis

General Burns

*In memory of General Burns; Late of the
Coldstream Guards*

O'er the hills and dales of England
Over deserts burning sands, crossing,
Mountains, spanning swelling rivers
For our Queen and Mother Land.
See the colours go before me
Battle honours scarred with glory.
Proud am I, proud the bold Coldstreamer
To the war with General Burns.

Eric T. Cowlin

Alive

While walking out, I chanced to see,
A beacon flash its light at me,
It winked, I blinked, oh can it be,
   Alive?

The foghorn sounds its plaintive call,
Across the sea to one and all,
Long, low, forlorn sound
Alive?

A starfish lies there, eagle-spread,
On moss strewn rocks, at water's edge,
Clinging lifeless, still as dead,
Alive?

I walk, I watch, I stop, I see.
Nature's wonders filling me,
With perfect peace, tranquillity
I'm so glad to be
Alive?

Edwina Burt

Parents

Parents are loving, precious, and true,
Their hearts are so special,
They'll always love you,
They help you, and guide you,
Through life's ups and downs,
They cherish, they care,
They will always be there,
You are the world to them,
And, they are to you,
When they are gone,
You have memories galore,
You treasure your parents,
   Forever more.

M. Roberts

The Voyage Through
The Passage Of Time

What once was young and free,
Turns to the mirror in disbelief,
The aged face of now,
Wrinkles full with tears.

Her husband dead,
Her children grown,
What has her life been for,
She no longer wants to live,
Locked up in this old persons' home.

Beauty and innocence,
Years since it's been here,
Time did take her happy face,
And fill it full of fear.

Lucy Ferre

Hands

Hands that stroke,
Hands that shiver,
Hands that do almost anything,
I am talking about hands.

Look at my hands,
Smooth and warm,
Feel my hands,
Soft and dry.

Hands that wave,
Hands that hold,
Hands that say hello and bye,
I am talking about hands.

Clare Louise Bowden

The Country Line

Line dancing's got us in its grip,
The light fantastic for to trip.
Bend your knee and swing your hip,
we're on a roll.
The music causes hearts to flip,
it hits the soul.

Stomping feet and tapping toes,
clapping hands—the rhythm flows.
Hooked on country fever grows,
the lines are weaving.
To and fro, we're all in rows,
the floor is heaving.

Feeling good, feeling fine.
This craze for action won't decline.
Young and old, we all entwine
to hit the beat.
We're buzzing on this country line
with dancing feet.

M. Cowie

Rescue Me!

I worship him both night and day.
He's trouble - so my friends all say.
The day we met is history
Forever etched in memory.
Not that handsome, short and slim,
He uses me and I use him.
To read my statement is so hard.
Please save me from my credit card!

M. Cowie

The Sleeping Garden

Snow fell silently
in the stillness of night,
The sleeping garden lies
under a blanket of white.
The rooftops and houses
are all covered too,
Yet chimney pots proudly
still stand out in view.

Snow's canopy of magic
has spread with delight,
The hedgerows and bushes
are peppered in white.
A solitary robin
is perched on the fence,
Yet the garden seems filled
with a muted silence.

Robert Kennedy Jones

India

Beside the track
The beggar sits
Near-clone to Egypt's ancient scribe
Parched and furrow-flesh
To landscape twin
As hollowed vessel in limbo-crook
To each unseeing,
Cratered eye

With sudden rush from rail-converge
Comes the panoply, the might
Roar and hiss and rattle and clank
Of fire and metal and coal and wood
That is India king-steam!
Each succeeding glassy-eye
Plays that beggar-image host
Upon the juddering monster-flank
Beyond humanity's survival-cling
High and proud without disdain
It marks the passing
Of king-steam!

R. J. Radley

When The Crow Comes

Take a toke
to feel the high,
A mental block
and time goes by.

The murdering hate
and the envy so green,
A pull of the trigger
the blissful scream.

To drill through the mind
to take the soul,
The physical pain
and the hate will go.

And when the crow comes
the darkness will fall,
Until the next toke
good night one-and-all.

Yvette Larkin

Untitled

Our children have more today
Much more than we ever had,
But when I think about it
Life wasn't all that bad,
Dinner was always at twelve
And then tea at half past three,
We had to be in on the dot,
But in between times we were free.
We played in the nearby woods
And down the country lanes,
We picked buttercups and bluebells
And made simple daisy chains.
We always had our freedom
Something our children lack,
Wouldn't it be wonderful
To give them their freedom back.

Norma Burns

The Willow

Droop and weep, my willow
Hanging low with stretching finger
Whilst I watch you from my pillow
In bed against the window

Nature gave you life
With colour gracious green
You have witnessed joy and strife
And generations seen

Now look into the stream below
The breeze distorts your image
Silently your leaves will drop
And float down to the village

In childhood play I pulled a branch
Whilst courting you hid our love
Now old age has me in its trance
I'm sure I'll see you from above

Ben Soulsby

When You're Feeling....

When you're feeling blue,
I'll still love you,
When you're feeling glum
I'll be your best chum,
When you're feeling good,
So you should,
When you feel old,
You won't be!
If you feel cold,
I'll wrap you in my arms,
If you feel alone just phone,
And remember!
Even if you're not smart,
You're always in my heart.

Sophia Haq

No Friend

In the seed of our beginning
Lies the story of our end,
Convoluted tracks to nowhere,
Time, the foe around each bend.

Time, the essence we can't cling to,
Time, when young we sometimes waste,
Time, the longer we dwell in it
Seems to pass with undue haste.

Time, a track we walk with limits,
Ever conscious of our end,
Never giving, always taking,
Never to be called a friend.

In memory we'll surely fade
When we are dead and gone,
But time which robs us of ourselves,
Goes on, and on, and on.

Graham Jones

White Horses

Lying on a sandy beach
Gazing at the ocean
Watching the waves—
White horses
Striding across the surface
One, after the other
Each unique in its own way
Without a jockey
Free to graze.

Nikki McDonald

Missing You

I miss the sun on my face
I miss you
I miss the wind in my hair
I miss you
I miss the leaves falling from
the trees
I miss you
I miss the snow falling making all
It touches sparkle
I miss you
I miss the touch of your hand
on my face
I miss you
I miss your lips touching mine
when we kiss
I miss you
I look to the day when we will
Be as one and then
I won't be missing you.

Lesley Andresen

Love Is A Dream

Life is reality,
love is a dream.
Longed for but hidden,
perhaps never seen.

My dream is a hope
stretching up to the sky.
Will love come
before I die?

Life is reality,
love is a star.
Glowing and sparkling
out of my reach way afar.

I have life, give me love.
The warmth of a smile.
A star in my hand,
please, just for awhile.

Margaret McSorley

Look Within

Discovering you; discovering me;
Suspended now in time,
The universe may ever turn
But we'll no further climb
If the meaning of this life,
As we pass from day to day,
Escapes us and we're unaware
Or turn the other way.
We maybe hold the vital key,
May never find the lock,
May never turn the eye within
That beats the earthly clock.
But, as the earth does turn,
Our thoughts rotate as well -
The mind is ever powerful
And holds a certain spell.
We must recognise this power,
It may obliterate all doors
So we must not abuse it,
This power that's mine and yours.

Anne Rogers

Stargazer

I looked up to the stars
and saw a constellation,
a symbol of love,
but I did not see a heart,

instead,

I looked into the stars
within those fiery hearts,
in the birthplace of beauty,
an explosion of light and love,

here

I searched the heavenly bodies,
for love and laughter,
for a guiding star,
for a fiery soul,
and I found you.

Adam Evan-Cook

The Spring

My love came to me in the spring
Like a stranger to my room,
Who woke me by singing
Of new delights.
Of glancing days and steady nights,
Journeys around the sun,
And life unfolding like a flower.

And dipping my hand into the stars,
I tried to pluck out the moon.
But all I had
When I withdrew my hand,
Were drops of silver
That scattered
As I wept.

Uzma Gardezi

Tears

The morning dew is tears today,
Mourning for the Dunblane babes.
The little children are no more,
Will not be knocking on your door.
The sun is dull in Dunblane today;
People just do not know what to say.
In their hearts they know not why
Their children have gone up to the sky.
Maybe someday, they will see the light.
Then they may know the reason why
And the sun will shine again.
But your tears will stay always,
Just like the morning dew.

R. Livesey

Man's Forest

In the deep, dense and dark,
eerie silent and still,
beats a faithful heart, but not,
by nature's will.

Trees of the forest
who strive to reach the light,
but must spend their days,
in perpetual night.

No blossom adorns their hair,
or sounds of birds on wing.
No rushing stream or babbling brook,
not a living thing.

No arms outstretched caress you
or lovers' initials bestow,
no warmth of human touch, as from
earth's breast you grow.

No sounds of children's laughter
or flowers around you strewed.
Destined to live your live
in quiet solitude.

Joan Hibbert

The Ozone Layer Depletes

The ozone layer depletes,
Yet nobody greets,
Why is it science doesn't understand,
The Ten Commandments stand,

If you're busy hitting me,
Instead of planting a fruit tree,
Then you're breaking a commandment,
That God to you had sent,

So you're at the first burning,
It's to add to your learning,
It was to you the Bible told,
So you could grow old,

Your churches in the Middle Ages,
Did not understand the Bible pages,
So they invented a word called hell,
That's the term of the burnings tell,

But it is simpler than that,
Obey the commandments, you silly bat,
Then you will see,
You really need to plant a tree.

Victor Parratt

My Gift To You

I would give you the
Flowers of early spring
Or a lark as it flies
High on the wing

I would give you the sun
As a warm summer day
Or a dancing breeze on
A field of hay

I would give you the
Colours that autumn brings
Golden leaves, misty mornings
All life's beautiful things

I would give you the moon
On a clear frosty night
Or a snow-clad forest
What a wondrous sight

But all I have to give
To you is myself and
A love that's ever true.

Margaret Bridge

But Love Has Gone

Spring, comes the buds
   the birds' song
   but love has gone

Summer, comes the flowers
   the trees with all their leaves
   the sun that shines
   to summer breeze
   but love has gone

Autumn, with its copper glow
   the golden leaves that
crumble low
   bareness of the trees that show
   but love has gone

Winter, with its frosty air
   bareness coldness every-where
Frozen ice like time so still.
   A voice that whispers so softly
   through the chill
   But love has gone
   But love has gone

Brenda Walton

A Day Of Dubious Delights In Devon

On a sunny day in summer
To the seaside I did go,
Of my manifold impressions
I'll inform you - blow by blow!

T-shirts with a vulgar logo,
Baseball caps and jeans of blue,
Buxom birds in garish "britches" -
They should see their own rear view!

When it rains those sultry snack bars
Ring with accents shrill and strange,
Querulous kids and moaning mothers
Placing peace beyond your range.

Coaches leave before the sun sets,
So sweet peace prevails once more,
There's an ozone scented stillness-
This I surely do adore.

With the moonlight on the harbour
Fragrant zephyrs fan the trees,
Vessels blithely bob at anchor
Gently pliant to the breeze.

Roy Perry

Spring Time

Come with me
Down a country lane,
See the wondrous miracle
Of a newborn Spring again.

Snowdrops nestle under trees
With little white nodding heads,
Nestled for warmth
In their earthly beds.

Then the shy little Violets
Show their pretty face,
With patches of blue
As delicate as the finest lace.

The Daffodil bud opens wide
To greet the shining sun,
With yellow dancing dresses
They tell us Spring has come.

The air is lightly perfumed
To match the shining day,
But all too soon
The days of Spring will fade away.

J. Brown

A Last Farewell

And so I say goodbye to summer
and to joy also to thee
I know that I shall miss you dearly
and wonder if you will miss me

Maybe the sun will shine tomorrow
Maybe I'll even laugh again
But I can see no end to sorrow
and so I say let fall the rain

No more to see the face I long for
No more to hear your sweet voice
But of time there is no more
We must part we have no choice

So let the rain fall it doesn't matter
the things I yearn for can never be
No more to hear your friendly chatter
and no more camaraderie.

Susan Richardson

War

We are at war, action severe,
A phrase to fill my heart with fear,
Missiles, scuds, rockets, mines,
Modern words, new designs,
Bombs with another name,
Kill, destroy, that is their aim.

A ships missile, a sniper's shot,
Somebody somewhere's copped that lot,
A buried or a floating mine,
Somewhere, somebody's last deadline,
We fight for armistice and peace,
We fight for armed combat to cease.

Fighting for the end of war,
Fighting to fight nevermore,
Somebody's dead, somebody's man,
Somebody's girl, somebody's son,
A mother, a father, a civilian,
Killed by somebody's someone.

Mary N. Bell

The Gulf War

Saddam Hussain must be insane
to think that he can run,
the quiet Kuwaitis off their land,
simply with the gun,
the free world will not accept this
as Hitler did find out:
Saddam will have to toe the line,
or simply just bow out
But being the tyrant that he is
he flew into a rage.
He destroyed the gulf economy
by setting wells ablaze,
but time will heal all wounds they say,
for one thing it is sure.
The free world will not accept,
a tyrant anymore

Leslie Sykes

Pearls

Pearls of wisdom
Pearls of light
Help us through the darkest night

Pearls of laughter
Pearls of love
Come to us from the Lord above

In our hearts these pearls exist
To help us on our way

And when we kneel and pray each night
These pearls are here to stay

James Manley

His Name Was Cuddles

Dedicated to My Little Ray of Sunshine

I had a one-in-a-million bird,
Who's sadly missed and gone.
But in my thoughts and in my heart,
A part of him goes on.
In my mind, I still see
My little bird run to me,
Hear him mimic my every word,
For he truly was an exceptional bird.
I have these photos by my bed,
Which make me feel so sad,
But they're also a reminder
Of the little gem I had.
As I write this poem,
A tribute to the end,
For I know I never will forget
my little feathered friend.

Angela Susan Glynn

The Melting Candle

The candle flickers in the night,
I shed tears thinking you just might,
Put everything right,
As the candle melts away,
I wonder if next time,
You just might stay.

Edna Al-Turki

Springtime

Wind and snow and rain have gone,
Blossoms on the bough.
Everywhere green shoots appear,
'Tis spring-time now.
Time for planting, time for sowing,
Seeds, and plants, and grain,
Sadly though, a frost appears
And down will come the rain,
Soon again the sun is shining,
People once again are smiling,
Looking up into the sky,
See a rainbow shining high
    upon a cloud!
Tiny, fluffy, clouds of blue,
Float across from me towards you,
God is still a revelation
And the wonder of creation
Still remains - forever new.

Mary Staniforth

The Minstrel

I sit here on this gallery
Playing on my lute,
Fifteen others along with me
On recorders, shawms and flute.

We sit above the Lords below,
Breathing in the fumes
From hearth and fire below us
Smoking up the room.

Playing here from noon till night,
Then on till break of day,
We strum and blow our instruments
To earn our yearly pay.

One day soon the time will come
I'll lose this skill I have,
Then someone else will play my songs
Upon the lute I love.

My music says it all for me,
Play soft, play fast, play loud.
Sitting here with all the rest
Alone, above the crowd.

Lynne Bates

The Visit

His pale green eyes shimmered,
Beneath his beetled brow.
Cold like icy nuggets
He seemed to know somehow.

"Why do you come?" he did ask,
Through cracked and broken teeth.
I stood silent watching
I could feel his hurt so deep.

He appeared to crumble slightly,
Then a stiffness came to his frame.
Did you know of his suffering?
Is that why you came?

No longer could I stay my tears.
My face was wet with brine,
Never did I know his agony,
But, he was a friend of mine.

I cannot bring him back to life,
Or rekindle his life's flame.
All I know, he was my friend,
That is why I came.

Eddie Smith

She's Got A Pair Of...

She's got a pair of eyes
just like two custard pies.

She's got a pair of lips
just like two greasy chips.

She's got a pair of hips
just like two battle ships.

She's got a pair of feet
just like two platers of meat.

Kayleigh Cope

First Day

It seemed like only yesterday
I gave birth to a tiny baby
But now you're four years old
And growing into a little lady

In her uniform of grey
I won't forget her face
As the teachers were leading her away
I must keep these tears at bay

So here I am in this silent house
Tears start to descend my face
You can even hear the mouse
Saying what a peaceful place

I know within my hearts of hearts
That she will be just fine
It's only first day at school
It will soon be home time!

Fiona Hanson

A Sense Of Space

A sense of place of where I am
A child into this world was born
To see the trees so live and worn
This country a leaf so torn
And of my place my heart dictates
Oh wisdom faith and trust
Be servants to a cause so just
New times are bright
The changing of the light
Compassion is the essence of its life
Respect for all a diamond cut
The flowers they bloom so much
Communication a sense of trust
Peace dictates dialogue just

Denys E. Claffey

Untitled

I'm here.
With you.
You don't look at me.
Can't you see me?
I'm dying, falling . . .
My heart is dead.
I'm silent.
Can you hear me?
If . . .
If I kiss you
Will you taste me?
No, I don't know the answers.
I'm scared.
Can you smell it?
Can you smell my fear?
So afraid,
Aren't you ever going to notice?
Can't you sense it?

Can't you feel that I'm here?

Lena Karlstrom

Flesh

Slicing, dicing, chopping, massacre
then cleanse it: lemon, vinegar, flour
fry, grill, boil, roast that meat
tender, rare, medium, well-done eat.

Michelle Welds

A Child

Why do they hurt me so
I'm only small
No place to go

They use me for their nasty games
I'm innocent
Don't know their names

They took me to a far off place
I cried and tried
To hide my face

I went to school to read and write
A gunman came
I was in fright

I ran straight home to mum and dad
Only to find
They're just as bad

One day when I become a man
I'll love my child
Do all I can...

M. E. Brook

The Flower Beneath The Stone

Come out sweet flower,
From beneath the stone,
And show the world your sweet petals
That you have grown.
Your beauty just surely be adorned,
Your tenderness and love reborn.

Come out sweet flower,
From beneath the stone,
And leave behind your heavy load.
For you are as precious,
As the gift of life,
Let your strength and your courage.
Guide you to the light.

Come out sweet flower,
From beneath the stone,
Can you not hear sweet nature's call;
Soft melodies beneath the sun,
We are all together,
Dancing as one.

Jennifer Chapman

War

The baby was born
 with no concept of hate.

The baby was an example
 of what love made.

The baby's experiences
 were totally new.

The baby had
 no political view.

The baby's first words
 are what he had heard.

The baby's first steps
 are what he had learnt.

The baby's future
 was untold.

But this baby
 never got old.

The gun was used
 to fire its shot.

It hit the baby
 in his cot.

Clare Spilka

Respect

Respect may only be gained
When the respect comes from
Within decent human feeling.
When the respect is sought and
Found in oneself - ability with
Determination - Then thrives and
drives the able mind to accept
And graciously expect more from
the Sunshine of the unfortunate
Few - for heaven can wait

Karen Anne Marie Matthias

Children

Depression is a sad and lonely pit,
deep and dark, no escape from it.
How then can I myself recover?
Where do I hope and love discover?

Mischief written over his face,
hers is full of sun and grace.
They bring happiness to my days
with their smiles and funny ways.

The funny things they do and say
make me happy every day.
My children are my life and love,
lent to me from Heaven above.

The ladder is placed for me to climb
from this hole to grow sublime.
Their arms reach out with love for me.
Without this love I would not be.

Thank you for their hearts that see,
their faith which never forsakes me.
Their life, love and warmth I cherish,
for them I live—depression will perish.

Sandra Burns

Lonely

Lonely,
That's all I seem to ever be.
To be lonely
Seems to be my destiny.
I can't find love
And believe me I've tried;
I can't find happiness
And I'm losing my pride.

Debbie Viner

Welcome To The World

Gentle as a summer breeze
Causing rustling in the trees
Yet another life beginning
Full of joy to parents bringing
Friends and family all around
Waiting for the slightest sound
Welcome baby Emily
Newest member of the family

Lots of laughter fun and tears
All will happen through the years
Children's ailments colds and flu
Still everyone is there for you
Helping hands and advice giving
Everything that's part of living
Growing up won't be so bad
Just you ask your Mum and Dad

Jean Salmon

Aggro-Vision

BSE from ITV,
All balls on the BBC,
Football here and tennis there,
Tortured balls fall everywhere.

Blood and gore drips channel four,
I cannot stomach anymore,
So my relief, from all this grief,
Is to enjoy more British beef.

A. Schulz

Love

Love is at your Mother's knee
A cuddle says she cares
A kiss to make it better
A hand to guide you up the stairs

Love is when your eyes shine bright
When two hearts beat together
And life seems rainbow coloured
No matter what the weather

Love is when you're old and grey
Remembering dreams lost past
When you were young and so in love
If only they could last

Love is all around us
It's deep within our hearts
We feel its healing power
When from loved ones we do part

Love is in our Maker's eyes
His love within us all
His love is there to welcome us
When we heed his call

Cindy Lansdell

Lust Not Love

There he stands proud and tall
My knight in shining armour
A battle of passion and love
You call it lust, not love.

He smiles
The waves crash against the rock
Waves of thought and desire
You call it lust, not love.

I long so much to feel his touch
But in my heart I know it is true
That I could never be with you.
You call it lust, not love.

Love or lust
What do these words mean?
Is it for real
Or just a dream?!!!

Fiona Quinn

Togetherness

I'm me,
Not you
or them,
not us
but me.

You're you
but I'm
not sure
if I
know you.

We're us
or them,
not me
or you
but us.

We're not
the same,
but now you
and I
are one.

Marianne E. Bull

October

As Autumn's early mists appear
At dawn on each fine day,
Cobwebs abound amid the flowers
Strung out from spray to spray.

And as the sun begins to rise
They shimmer clad in dew,
Like diamonds sparkling in the light
As each beam filters through.

Chrysanthemums of red and gold
And dahlias firmly staked,
Are now the borders' pride and joy
Midst beds all newly raked.

Bold squirrels steal the hazelnuts
Torn husks lie on the floor,
Their appetites replete they take
The surplus for their store.

When young I saw the Autumn scene
As climax of the year,
Now I grow old it just foretells
Of winter - cold and drear.

Freda G. Jolley

In Praise Of Venice

Venice! may your pleasures never wane,
Such the measure of your fame,
Even the sea seeks to claim
Your treasures in a deadly game.

What joy to see gondolas glide
On the waters grandly by,
Did ever mortal eye espy,
A scene more gracious or benign?

Venice! romantic nights and gala days.
While all around thy water ways,
Palladian splendour 'mid modern rage,
Symbolic of a golden age.

Here St. Marco chimes his pleasure,
At the passing of each hour,
This joyous sound from vantage high,
Pray let no evil act deny.

Alas, if perchance you hear a 'Sigh'
It's only from a 'Bridge' nearby,
Fearful lest the time be nigh,
When sea shall rise, and Venice die!

G. Nicklin

Grief

Don't hurry grief - just take your time
And know that love lives on
With every thought and every pain
And every hour gone.

Don't analyse the way you feel
Accept that you feel low
The wound of grief is very deep
And must have time to heal.

No-one can ever take from you
The memories within
So hug them close and let them grow
The memories will win.

Judy K. Rutherford

The Stormwalker

I am the Stormwalker,
I am your wildest dreams.
I am the Stormwalker,
nothing is what it seems.

Nothing stops me,
not thunder, lightning, rain.
No-one cares for me,
but I don't feel the pain.

Always running,
never in one place.
Others follow,
but they can't take the pace.

I am the Stormwalker,
I'm always around.
You won't hear me,
I don't make a sound.

Georgina June Susan Hayward

The Stream

Out of the darkness I saw a stream
Gleaming as it ran
and trickled to the deep
knelled pools - whilst the
moonbeams looked on.
Over the stream I espied a bridge
It deep in shadow lay
as if to shield the very
fish from their unsuspecting prey.

Stanley Harry Hill

Two Hearts

Two tender hearts
Can't live apart,
Two kindred souls
Will be as whole,
Such is the law - the nature's role.

Two hands together
be held forever,
Sweet loving words
Will fly like birds,
And bind two hearts by firmly threads.

Such love will grow,
it won't be slow,
It grows inside,
But not to hide
That feeling, which is thing of pride.

Two tender hearts
Are strong enough
To stand all storms,
Which life has brought
According to the will of Lord.

L. Dutchak

Equilibrium

Mind's own creations,
Stumble over feelings,
Causing countless confusion.

Misinterpretation,
Unwanted dreams,
Prepare for death of the mind.

Connect mind and soul,
Search for the inner battery,
Recharge fate.

Never-ending abyss of body,
Learning control of mind,
Sending stale messages.

Balanced feeling, balanced thought.
Afraid of different,
Afraid of normal,
Afraid of inside,
When inside is afraid to come out.

Sarah Hannaford-Hill

Untitled

What happened to our Village
Where once we used to play,
What happened to the fields of Corn
Those stacks of Golden hay.
Where did the leafy lanes go
That pretty babbling brook,
Why did they have to change it
The way it used to look.
No more those little Cottages
All standing side by side
The Oak Tree on the Village Green
Where we would love to hide.
That funny little corner shop
Was every child's delight,
Where we could spend our pennies
Every Friday Night.
They took away our memories,
They took away our pride,
But most of all they took away
Our lovely country-side....

Iris L. Preston

Depression?

I am unhappy,
I cannot say why,
I'm breaking down inside
I begin to cry,
I cannot live with myself
I'd rather just die,
I calm myself slowly
I heave one last sigh...

And I will pretend
That inside I am strong,
Mask the emotions
That have been weak for too long,
And never really give up hope
When the happiness is gone,
The depression is only in my mind
- I think nothing is wrong.

Jim Payne

Judging

Why do people judge everyone from the
first impressions,
    No one can do what they want
without someone judging them,
    Maybe in a good way,
    Maybe in a bad way,
But everyone gets judged,
    you and me,
we are all being judged
and we all are judging someone else.

Sarita Prem

335

Sweet Parting

Oh! Dear sweet Caroline
I fondly think of you,
And the times we spent together
And the things we used to do.

Gone are the happy days
That were yours and mine.
We were young and happy then
Then, days, they were divine.

Too swift the day did part,
You went your way
And I went mine
But with you darling went my heart.

So farewell sweet darling
May good fortune, always be thine.
For you have your love
And I have mine.

John Joseph Joyce

Just For You

I feel the earth beneath my feet
A gust of wind against my cheek
Flowers in bloom
And grass that's green
These are the things that I have seen
A walk in the park
The sound of a lark
Trees are swaying
Kids are playing
The air is clear
Summer is here
The skies are blue
I'd just like to say
I love you!!!

Laura McDermott

Release

Dedicated to my dear friend, Margaret

You walked away
To go to her
The excitement in your voice
Was almost to much to bear
Please don't go—

You have made love to her
Made plans
What a wonderful life
You will share
Please don't go—

There are things you both
Want to do
Get rid of the old
On with the new
Please don't go—

What you have done cannot be
changed
So now your life is rearranged
Off with the old on with the new
All for the better let's hope for me
Please don't stay—

Wendy MacLean

1995 Christmas Thought

This Christmas 1995,
I did not have the time of my life.
For all the time I was sad,
I would think about my little lad.

I will watch my tiny baby niece,
while she will crawl on her knees.
I'd cry and cry every night,
Until morning had broken daylight.

Elizabeth A. Fowler

The Mistress—Her Story!

I Hate your wife
Your perfect life
Your house for show—
No inner glow

I Hate the lies,
All the goodbyes
No need to go, you choose it so—
I feel so used, sad and confused

I Hate the nights
I'm left alone
Whilst you return—to her,
At home

I Hate this need
I have inside
This constant urge
To be at your side

V. K. Jones

Remorse

A rapid heart slackens,
Tears dry as movements occur,
A vision of a lonely world as
your present becomes your past.
But unlike before your certainty
Bewilders you
for your feelings are none, and
excitement is a rare as it is a
contemporary thing
you conspire as you look upon it
as though it is merely a waste
of precious time.

Veronica Shanley

Reaper, Reaper

I fear my time on earth is through
I know he comes for me
I say a prayer before I sleep
Reaper, reaper leave me be

But prayers, I know, will save me not
from the blade of his dreaded scythe
what can I do against this shade
Reaper, reaper I cannot fight

When morning comes and I still breathe
I know that I am free
but life is short, he will return
Reaper, reaper comes for me

Colin Aherne

Promises

Politicians make me irate,
with all the promises they do make.
Vote for us is what they say.
If you do, we will raise your pay.

Tax be sure will be reduced.
More work we will make for you.
Allowances will be increased,
that is if you vote for me.

Houses will be easier for you to buy,
because the mortgage will not be high.
All interest will be kept down,
so more you will get for your pound.

We will help the disabled and the old,
and keep you warm when it is cold.
The N.H.S. you will not lose.
If your vote is us you chose.

We believe and vote them in.
Then wait for the promises to begin.
But everything said, they do reverse,
and the loss we feel, is in our purse.

Joan Sayers

Heaven

Pretty yellow meadows,
Clear blue streams,
Beautiful colourful rainbows,
The most wonderful dreams,
Single pure white unicorn,
Sun shining all around,
Peace, love and happiness,
Angels song the only sound,
Fancy gates to let the good go in,
And keep out all the badness,
Everything in dreamy light,
There isn't any sadness,
Fluffy white clouds acts as cushions,
Spirits are all friends,
Heaven is a lovely place,
Where nothing ever ends.

Kelly Adams

Sweet Love

Sweet love
Sweet love
I have each day
Sweet love
Sweet love
I hold in my heart
Sweet love
Sweet love
her eyes so bright and light
Sweet love
Sweet love
She holds me tight
Sweet love
Sweet love
She holds my soul tight
Sweet love
Sweet love
We make love each night
Sweet love
Sweet love

Emma Louise O'Neil

Taurean Raging

My Taurean raging
my Scorpion sting
Feel alive with a aching
for the one hid within.

This Venus is rising
but Adonis, you're far
away from the feeling
in the depths of my heart

Come closer, come nearer
I bid you dear sir
so my vision is clearer
not as dark as it were.

This rashness, be it rare
this boldness, be it new
if I ride upon dare
could I gallop to you?

Patricia Cater

Psychic Aftermath

It was my first time that night,
I've never been read before.
Did it give me a fright
Or a feeling of great awe
To hear the psychic's might
And learn of what he saw.

No matter what my plight
I knew I'd return for more,
To understand what is right
And open a new door.

T. W. Parkin

Why Can't I Be Me?

Why can't I be me?
People say things that go deep,
that hurt and stick to me like skin,
that's why I can't be me.

Images fill my head all day,
you must do this and don't do that,
you're so cool and so funny
that's why I can't be me.

Sometimes I want to be you,
and you might want to be me,
all these thoughts flood my mind,
so how can I be me?

So why not follow all the rest,
who all talk, walk and look the same
should I change to be adored?
Deep down I know I need to be me.

Change, why should I?
I'm made the way I am,
accept or reject me,
but I'm going to be me.

Rachel Parkes

Silent Tears

Emptiness, loneliness
No-one to share my joy,
See the silent tears I cry
I've cried since I was a boy.

I'm trapped, trapped within
Deep in my soul,
No-one can set me free now
All that's left is the eternal hole.

Those tears still falling
Falling down my face,
As silent as they ever were
Glistening like lace.

My body is just a case now
Within it nothing lives,
My soul, thoughts and emotions
Are absent so nothing gives.

Alison Hool

The Tower

A raven's cry in moonlight
Sweeps shadow over stone,
His gaze of fire like ocean blue
Steals moments swiftly flown.
Each feather hides dark fantasy,
With heather beaded eyes;
Each strand of thunder softening,
As each swift moment flies.
The tides of night are poisoned
With shadow mingled pain—
The more the pleasure the greater need,
But tears will never stain.
Sleepy eyes in morning mist—
Fair day well hides its scorn.
The sun must bear the aftertaste,
As a raven flies at dawn.

Polly Clifford

Owls

The moon would rise,
The owls came out,
All be quiet and silent,
The trees would bluster,
When midnight struck,
Owls would fly over the moon,
Dawn would be coming,
Owls would fly back to their places,
Until midnight would strike again.

Andrew Spavins

Solace

No more to see your smiling face,
or hear your loving voice,
God called you home, you left a void,
in this, we had no choice,
one day dad, we'll meet again
around God's golden throne
Be happy, love, I hear you say,
some day we'll all go home.
They'll all be there, to welcome us
and make us once again
one great big happy family,
with no sickness, fear, or pain
so until then, we'll live our lives,
as best as any can,
until we're called, as those before,
by God, the son of man.

Eliz Soppitt

Makeup Of The Perfect Man

Take a pinch of laughter
And a lot of common sense
Take a well-thumbed wallet
And a pocketful of pence
Blend a sense of loyalty
With a bit of old world charm
And beat them all together
With a strong right arm.
Include a dash of style
With a bucketful of trust
Take away the cobwebs
And wipe away the dust
Then stir them once again
To get the perfect man
And as his loyal wife
I'm his greatest fan.

J. M. Gilchrist

Untitled

Silent sleeps the meadow,
amongst the weeping trees,
the wind blowing secrets
through the evergreens,
ripples form on water still,
feel the moonlit shadow,
whispering,
remember nights kill,
forces are drawn upon,
reminisce of things long gone,
night is now,
and will always be,
that is for me,
whispering,
remember nights kill,
and how the world weeps still....

Leah O'Brien

Untitled

She made her entrance gracefully,
a vision so serene.
Flowing hair of auburn,
her eyes, a flash of green.

Her style was one of elegance,
that made the whole crowd part.
Every man would envy
the one who stole her heart.

My heart skipped a dozen beats
at the vision I could see.
She had eyes for just one man.
That lucky man was me.

To my delight she kissed me.
My heart was filled with pride.
I was the envy of the world,
as I embraced my bride.

Michael Graham Tamblin

Untitled

Van Gogh who gave us sunflowers
And irises in spring,
Who lived and dwelled with miners
And people very poor.
He spent his time with
canvasses and paint,
in times he grew angry and irate.
Because no-one understood
the talent of this man.

Van Gogh in all his sorrow,
Knew time was here to borrow.
So he painted crows in a cornfield,
And then this man did part.

Jennifer Miller

Dove's Lament

The Silver Shimmer of glistening light
The Moonbeams dancing on the waters
My heart it fills with great delight
They must be the fairies' Daughters

The Silhouette of hills beyond
The waters still and calm
The Ghostly shadows on the pond
They can do no harm

See the mist slowly rising
it gives a golden glow
A beautiful day though not surprising
Dawn has broken now I must go

I will return you can be certain
To this place that I so love
Again I'll see the lake's mist curtain
I am the lonely Dove

Adrian Martin

Poetic Justice

Poetic justice
Death calls

A cruel hard
Legal law

Around the corner
a shadow falls

Another life ends
forever more

Can we stop this
death to crawl

Or shall we stay
here and die

Nicola Dunn

Dream Swimmer

I've suffered in dreams,
where limbs won't bend,
a reflection maybe
of a pain I cannot end,
suffering in dreams
each night and each day,
Looking for a hand
to lead me away.
Engulf me in thoughts
and I'll
oh, so softly tread,
I swim through the channels
of dreams in your head,
I am just a man,
drowning in pain,
no more than a dream,
unloved and unmade.

Stephen Rees

In The Greenhouse

The Carlisle train in March
plunges north through summer fields.
The smell of warm grass
pricks male skins alert.
'In the greenhouse' they tell us
'many things will change.'

'In Preston you can expect
vines, hibiscus, bougainvillea'
By the track the hardy hawthorn
is out, and in the second class
girls remove their clothes
dreaming of pregnancies
under northern oleanders.

No-one is actually saying
the hot countries will dry up,
the babies there will stop crying soon.
In the greenhouse, they tell us,
many things will change.
Everything, in fact, except Man.

Cyril Laming

In The Flow

When we're truly 'in the flow',
learning how to 'let it go'
Staying out of all the fuss
learning to be truly us.

Standing back and watching life
empathy for all the strife
Accepting life, letting it be
judging no-one, truly free.

Then life still goes up and down,
but your emotions stay on the ground,
Life wasn't meant to be a struggle
let's get out of all this trouble.

Teach our children at school today
to learn to live life everyday—
truly loving who they are
let them reach out and touch that star.

Sheri Green

Provence

Oh vineyard in the south of mine
Green grapes growing on the vine
Butterflies of many colours
Hover in the sky above us
Cicadas busy in the trees
Sun's rays shining through the leaves.
Farewell, oh vineyard of mine
Until we meet next summertime.

Patricia Rumble

Dunblane

For the mothers who bore
   their souls so bright,
For the mothers who saw
   nothing but light,
So sweet they are
   asleep at rest,
A child so innocent
   taken from the nest.

With all the love and comfort
   they'll receive,
As we feel their hearts,
   that they do grieve

But one day they'll see
   their angels so bright.
As their souls someday.
   They'll surely reunite.

Julie Adams

In The Cage

I reach towards the sky
banging my head on the thin metal bars.
I reach out towards the side,
Nothing,
Steel bars again,
The earth below me,
Steel bars again.
I'm totally trapped.
No door,
No window, to climb out.
I will never see a different
life, beyond these cold bars.
Instead I feel myself
Wasting away into the darkness.

Kasia Fiderkiewicz

Sober

Powerless over, shed a tear.
The situation, becomes clear.
It's now time to share and hear.
No more swimming in the beer.

Can I get myself in gear.
Seems the way has lost its cheer.
Which direction shall I steer.
Must hang on 'cause life is dear.

Why do I now feel this fear!
Do some people really leer?
Paranoia, I reached the rear.
Higher power I pray you're near.
Day by day becomes a year.
Gently problems disappear.
To others now I lend my ear,
On my face a smile I wear.

PJ Nesbitt

The Innocence Of A Child

A young, fair child,
Innocent as the dawn breaking.
Knows not what life holds for her,
For life is a rude awakening.
But let's not spoil it for her,
Let her have her fun.
She is just a little girl.
Let her play in the sun.
She knows not what death is,
Has no concept of time.
Takes an apple to school,
Sings her favourite rhyme.
Skipping through the meadows,
Picking wild flowers as she goes.
She is one little, sweet child,
like a young innocent rose.

Claire Stevenson

Untitled

Sad sad day today
I saw a friend die
Bleeding in the gutter
His cries for help unheeded
His pleading eyes not comprehending
His outstretched hands a futile action.

The death was painful, slow and brutal
The blood ran slowly to the drain
All around were cowed and weeping
No-one would ever be the same.

I saw him die that sunny day
As the murderers walked free
Oblivious to the pain of thousands
Oblivious to their needs.

His death was slow.
His name was law.

James Higgins

An Ode To Pont Nedd Fechan

Guardian "Angel"
Elysian kingdom!
Artist with easel
And brushes has come
To portray the waterfall walk.

Birdsong exquisite
Fills him with rapture
Mere paint on palette
Simply can't capture
The exuberance of the waterfall walk!

Verdant brocades
Overhang cataracts
And turbulent cascades.
Eternal insomniacs!
On the spectacular waterfall walk!

Impossible choices!
Totally astounded!
Heart rejoices!
Senses confounded!
By the splendour of the waterfall walk!

Frances D. Dring

Expression

If you were to write a letter,
You would realize the power
Of speech is closer to the brain
To manipulate.
For only is it the heart,
Which pumps the blood that writes
The unblemished truth,
I love you.

Helen E. M. West

It Runs On Smiles

The rocking chair we sit in,
Grandad, Teddy and Me,
Takes us all over the world,
And very often out to sea.

We pretend we're in a speed boat,
Or a bright red racing car,
A rocket or a spaceship,
We really travel far.

Sometimes we're flying to the moon,
Way up in outer space,
Or perhaps we are the Roman's,
Winning a chariot race.

We can imagine all sorts of things,
Sitting on Grandad's knee,
Snuggled in his rocking chair,
My old Teddy Bear and Me.

It's the safest place on earth I know,
We travel miles and miles,
It doesn't run on petrol, but,
It runs on Grandad's smiles.

Helen Murphy

Moonlight Rainbow

Moonlight rainbow
Drifting by,
Silvery moon
In velvet sky.

Stars like diamonds
In the dark,
Spanned by
Iridescent arc.

Just a glimpse,
Then lost to sight
In the magic
Of the night.

Maureen Roper

Angus the Ant

Angus the ant
Was tiny and black
always working
looking through sacks

Over the rubbish bag
to find a hole,
inside he crawled
then found a doll.

The doll was broken
her dress, tattered and torn
one arm was missing
her body, filled with corn.

Into the empty sugar bag
collecting all the grains
rushing back to tell the others
to collect all the remains

To the queen, he gave a bow
showing her all that he had found
one by one the soldiers marched
along the dirty ground.

Kay Devlin

The End?

The years are growing shorter
As time around me flies;
The world is getting smaller
And many babies cry.

The rape of mother nature
Should be considered crime;
But now, no need to worry,
It's only a matter of time.

I find it so ironic
In our struggle to survive,
All we manage is destruction
And hate's in overdrive.

Cherril Rae

Childhood

Adoration for this place I hold,
My life, my existence,
My forever land . . .
Refrain, I beg, from snatching me,
Soul and cerebral heart,
From this, my warmth, my joy.

Shadows refract endlessly,
Visions of my life,
Oh wide and lavish land,
Take me into thee,
Envelop my soul in your colours.

Capture me forever,
In thy hands.

D. Emma Davies

The Springtime Of Life

Oh to be young in the month of May.
Seventy years seem so far away,
the may blossom and spring flowers
bloom, all to be gone so soon.
But however many years
your life brings,
Never forget that lovely spring
When love and life
Walked hand in hand,
Now how quickly years have spanned.
Still in your heart there will remain,
Those sun-filled days so plain.

I. Dunn

Why?

Why are people racist?
Why do people fight?
Why should it be an issue
If you're black or if you're white?

Why do people murder?
Why do people steal?
Why do victims' families
Have to go through such ordeal?

Why do people deal in drugs?
Why does it sometimes kill?
Why does a person lose their life
Over the sake of a tiny pill?

Why do people joyride?
Why do they drink and drive?
Why must they be so reckless
And end so many lives?

Why do people do these things?
Why must they cause such pain?
Why can't they think of others?
So we can live in peace again.

Why?

N. Brown

Dreams Of Companionship

To be alone,
Always alone,
Living in a make-believe world,
A world of dreams,
A world of hopes,
Always alone,
In mind in thought
Wanting seeking companionship,
Living for this alone.

Rebecca A. L. House

Power Cut

Light fails suddenly
Assisted by candles.

We peer into outlines
Of blurred faces
Around the table.

Voices are now
Our strength

Though we know each other
We seem different.

Yellow elliptical light
With limiting glow
Warns us all to

Move carefully....

How grateful we are
To the candles!

Paul Lucas

Fair Hands

Fair hands, fair hands,
O what fair hands,
fair hands that have
guided me,
but those fair hands
have gone to sleep
and are no longer here
with me.
But one day I will close
my eyes and fair hands
I'll come to thee.

Anne Jackson

Dreams

The shadows that fall
Across sunlit walls.
In my room
I lie awake.
Staring into space
The inside of my eyes
Form clouds that turn into odd shapes.
The tiny electrical impulses
That make up dreams
Swim through my mind
At immeasurable speeds.
From these untouchable thoughts
We build our world
And all sorts
So when we create material things
It is only then
Can we touch our dreams

G. Wheeler

Life!

Life is a game,
and we all are playing.
Hoping to gain,
just like we were saying

Never make mistakes
for we must pay.
Hoping for a new something
to help us on our way.

Life is a game
Like daggers and knives.
Some can't take the pressures
and others thrive.

Life is good,
Life is bad,
make someone happy,
but never sad.

Nicola Gabrielle Wilkinson

A Little Prayer

I trust in God for He has said
"Ask and you shall receive"
I know that He will hear my prayer
And my doubts and fears relieve.

Katherine Sargent

The Lady

There was a lady that I loved
    Truly dear to me.
Nothing too much trouble
    And as happy as could be.

Her hair was like the harvest corn
    She had a heart of gold,
Any worries that we had
    She was the one we told.

Until one day—the Angels came
    Their wings of gossamer lace
You see they said they needed her
    In a higher place

Now sometimes when I'm walking
    And in the gentle breeze
I hear voices whispering
    "Don't forget me please".

And of course I never will
    There is to be no other
Because this lady that I loved
    Was naturally my mother.

Pam Griggs

The Nurse

To be a nurse is a wonderful gift
A gift sent from above
She's chosen from so many
For her strength, her skills, her love

Each day she works among the sick
Who really need her care
They turn to her for all support
And smile to see her there

A nurse can cry and feel the pain
And often wonders why!
The job she does is so in vain
And why her patients die

To be a nurse she must be strong
And hide the thoughts she feels
The days are hard the nights are long
And only God reveals

The reason for it all is this
The trials of life are rough
To be a nurse believe in this
Although the role is tough

Freddie Baker

A Rain Drop Is A New Life

Listen to the rain,
have you noticed
how each drop sounds;
singular
on its own.
Imagine if people
were like that
on their own
only coming together
to form puddles.

Listen harder
each drop making its own tune,
only making a song,
when they all fall together
no war
no conflict
each and every one.
Out on its own
reaching its own goal
the ground!

Emma Galvin

My Dog

I've got a little dog
And her name is Holly
She likes to run and play
Because she's very jolly

I love my little dog
She's really cool
but when she goes to the park
She's a real fool

She goes for a walk
And wants to go every day
But my dad puts his foot down
And says "No way."

She plays with her ball
And thinks she's very rough
But I would not mess with her
Because she's very tough

At bedtime
She's worn out
Because she's been
Here and about

Kieron McCormick

The Haunted

It's peaceful in my house,
No noise,
No sound,
Not even a mouse.

Could my mind be playing tricks?
Making noises,
Banging doors,
Or building bricks.

Things begin to move
From one shelf to another,
Clocks stop the ticking,
One after the other.

I could be paranoid,
For sitting all alone,
But who's whispering my name?
From midnight to dawn.

Is there someone watching me,
Every move I make?
Is this house haunted,
Or is my mind about to break?

Pauline Davies

Sensuality

Silky breath upon my neck
Lacy tongue; deep kisses
Velvet touches, satin strokes
Looming sexual wishes

Rouge flushes through my delicate skin
Ignites an ochre fire
Azure heights and aqua depths
A spectrum of desire

Rhythmic timpani heartbeats
Piano murmurs sweet
Plucking strings, muffled horn
An orchestra complete

Seeping scents of body musk
Fragrant camphor's lit
Embalming incense stimulates
A perfume composite

Drink my succulent juices
An hors d'oeuvre to appetize
Relish love's ambrosial fruits
And savour my sensual prize

N. Munchkin

Our Baby Derdrie

Our sweet little Derdrie
So peaceful up there
Looking down on us
From everywhere

When we heard she had left us
We all just fell apart
And because she was so well loved
She had broken many hearts.

The place is not the same
Because Derdrie is not here
And every time I think of her
Down my face rolls a tear

She had beautiful blonde hair
And skin as soft as fur
And we are all so proud
For what we did for her

And from the day you went
I have felt terrible pain
And I know my little Derdrie
I will see you soon again.

Ursula McCreesh

In Memory

The storms of war descending,
Whilst our youth were still at play,
They risked their lives defending
our right to be free each day.

They sacrificed their teenage fun,
For uniforms of blue,
The cricket bat for the sound of gun,
Their pleasures very few.

Their toys became the fighter plane,
The bomber in the sky,
The idea that never again,
Would young men need to die.

So many flew to paradise,
That we may live in peace,
Their sons now reach for the skies,
But our memories never cease.

Sheila V. Calderwood

Until We Meet Again

How sad is my heart that loves you
and silent are the tears that fall
but living life without you
is the hardest part of all
I hold you close within my heart
and there you will remain
to walk beside me every day
until we meet again.

Joanna Purdy

First Steps

I flip from my back
onto my tummy,
"oh look at me mummy"
I want to talk, I
want to walk
Ba Ba Baba I can
talk!, mummy bought
me a walker so I
can walk.
Backwards sidewards
oh what fun!, forwards
next then I can run.
Da Da Dada aren't I
clever, not 8 months yet
but 2 words together
not clever enough, not by
half. Hiya mama! Hiya dada!
Oh what a laugh
my first steps are so much fun.

Katrina Smith

Our Country

Alas, what a country we live in today
People working hard, for very poor pay
MP's arguing like a lot of kids
They should work together and not tell
fibs, promising us this and promising
us that, while pensioner's suffer
and they grow fat, grime and
muggins go on all around and when
it happens not a policeman is found
men degraded have to go to the dole,
while the government keeps saying we
are out of the hole. Our country was
once a beautiful place where everyone
had a smile on their face. All
it is now is worry and wan faces you
see all pale and gaunt. So let's pull
together we know we can win, and again
make our country a place we are
proud to live in.

A. Boddison

The Depths Of Unpredictability

Giant waves like monsters looming
crash as thunder, frightening, booming,
taking, giving life at will
and then serenely calm and still
with sunlight dancing on the palms
of ripples when they come to calm
alive and wondrous at its best
as infant upon mother's breast
but yet in deepest darkest depths
it seems the giant monsters kept
the secrets of the mighty sea
and unpredictability.

E. Proctor

Honour Bound

For James

Of finest steel they fashioned me
Burnished to their pride
A scabbard then was finely made
To place me there inside
Unsheathe me not without honour
Tarnish not nor blunt my edge
For I am that moment of truth
To this I shall in valour serve
Let not dishonour break me
Nor lay me to the ground
Till we both lie in silence
Forever honour bound
And when at last our story
To others will unfold
The truth that was our glory
made us brave and bold

Edward J. Costello

Christmas Gift

Little baby in a manger
  Lying soft and small,
To a father and a mother
  Worth much more than all.

Did they know those little palms
  Would receive a hole
With a nail to pierce them
  Tearing out its soul?

Was it this the way to show
  How to save a world,
With a little essence caught
  And to space out-hurled?

Father in the holy heavens
  Watching all with pain,
Could you find no better way
  To vouchsafe our gain?

C. G. Carpenter

A Stretch Of Mexican Gulf Shore

The great eloping waves
of the gulf waters
paint the shelly shore
a light, deep green
touched with sun yellow sparks.

The white horses run ahead
drawing the shell filled sand
beneath its surface
of rolling ripples
tossing its load.

Further and deeper
the expanse graduates
to a deep blue-grey
with outcrops of shape
on the horizon.

Sarah Louise

What If

What if all the world could be,
A better place for you and me,
What if we were free from war,
Where life is pleasant, not a chore,
What if children all could grow,
Safe from harm where 'ere they go,
What if, growing old, we find,
Food and warmth, have peace of mind,
What if we could stop all crime,
And live contented for all time,
What if this could only be,
With peace on earth eternally.

Roy Strange

Lady Alcoholic

The weeping woman cries,
a vile secret she hides
Of a devil's sick sin,
to what the story begin.

Two identities she keep,
one evil, one meek.
To meet like a mirror,
their lives are so bleak.

The weeping woman cries,
and her vile secret still hides.

D. Edwards

An Understanding Of A Girl

Nobody really understands me,
or the way I feel.
People joke about the way I am,
and what I look like.
The only way I can express,
my feelings, yes I do have them,
is in music, dance or poetry.
Sometimes I feel different,
like I'm trapped in my own world,
I am on my own, lonely,
everyone looks at me.
It's my fault, I get blamed,
it wasn't even my fault.
They say that I do bad things,
I steal, lie and cheat.
There are no things worse in life,
that they said I could do.

Celeste Knowles

Untitled

Hurt
Is in the snow white swan
so beautiful
but with its head bent down

Loneliness
is in the eyes of the clown
Now old and tired

Pain
is in the last leaf silently falling
only to be swallowed by the ground
and lost forever

In the November darkness
I stand by the endless sea
Hearing the waves whispering
words of new hope

I walk on
with my head bent down
as tears of hurt and pain
fall to the ground
and are lost forever

Katja Hansson

Granddad

One sunny August afternoon
Death came upon you far too soon
I heard the news concerning you
But did not think it could be true
Try to be strong and not to cry
Emotions are so hard to hide
All the family came to pay
Their last respects in their own way
You have to wonder how they felt
Remorse, regret, or racked with guilt
A visit while you were still here
A conscience that could then be clear.
I kissed you softly on your head
And thought of all the things you said
You looked so thin and seemed so frail
Your skin was cold and oh so pale
When my day comes I hope you'll wait
To meet me at heaven's gates
Death comes upon us all, I guess
rest in peace, good night, God bless

Philip Woodward

Untitled

His heart was filled with shame.
He was innocent.
She knew him.
She left him.
For him to spare him from
destroying her.
For her to spare her from
hating him.

Sigri M. Gaini

A Dolphin's Life

Amidst the clear water
A silhouette against the
Ever-darkening sky
Gliding through the waves
Beautiful and slender
Streamlined in every way
No cares no worries
Nothing but love and affection.

Twisting, turning, splashing
Through the waves
They mean no harm
Not to us
Not to anyone
So why, why do we do it.

Imagine you, you being caught
In a net
Your life suddenly disappearing
Before your eyes
There's someone to miss you
But there's no one to miss them.

Paul A. J. Ames

In The Night...

In the night when we were sleeping,
angels came to say good-bye.
It was moon around the city,
many drops of rain had come.
I was listening to water,
it was running through my thoughts.
All around I heard them calling,
but I left them and went off.
But the sun was hiding somewhere,
so I couldn't reach his smile.
I was walking lonely by,
trying to catch some truth in life.
Rain was singing song of flowers
Everybody heard the same.
Hope for sun, belief in sunset.
I got up and made a step.

Farida Mestek

Tiddles

I have a large ginger tom.
  He sits upon my lap,
No matter where I'm sitting,
  or even how I'm sat,
He makes himself quite at home,
  upon our antique chairs,
Wherever he gets up to go,
  He always leaves his hairs,
He sleeps upon my pillow,
  On my bed, if you please,
I'm glad he is a cleanly cat,
  He hasn't any fleas,
His coat is soft and silky,
  it feels like ermine fur,
His voice is always booming,
  He has the very deepest purr,
He makes our home his kingdom
  He thinks he lives in Zion,
but after all he is quite big,
  because our pet's a Lion.

  Bernard Jones-Baynam

By Chance

By chance I saw her laying there,
Alone.
In peace.
Her face serene.
Black eyes looking at the sky.
Her limbs resting.
Gently.
On belly shiny.
Then
Gently rolling
She slides
Silently.
Down beneath the waves.
She comes but once again.
But does not play.
She looks,
She listens,
And quietly,
She swims away.

  June Patterson

Without You

I felt a yearning deep inside,
My heart beat faster still.
There is no place to run or hide,
So let me dream my fill

Of sunny days and fun-filled nights,
Some romance that will linger on
As I debate the wrongs or rights,
My love for you grows strong

The winter evenings crisp and cold
And log fires burning brightly.
I cling to memories new and old,
Longing to hold you so tightly

  Brian Macro

The Ball

Sometimes I feel like a ball
like I'm round and so small
I can be bounced around the floor
kick ball, kick ball.
I can be squashed and popped
squish, squash, bang pop.
But I don't feel no harm.
I'm full of life and air
I can be bounced down some stairs.
I can be kicked into space
oh I wish I was a ball

  Laura Ainley

The Lonely Teddy Bear

In a bedroom behind closed doors,
A teddy bear sits and cries,
The tears well up and fall like rain,
From his big eyes.

But no one knows the reason,
Why he is so sad,
Or what words or actions,
Will then make him glad.

But hush, a noise, a movement,
From the floor below,
He stops his cries and grizzles,
His face begins to glow.

The bedroom door flies open,
The room it floods with light,
His master comes to bed at last,
He's happy for the night.

  Gary Duckmanton-Hibbs

ECLIPSE

When dawn breaks through
I awake and think of
summers past and winters too
you were at the helm
My soul was with you.

You were Jack and I was Jill
Until the storms came,
The tide changed
The moon was at its worst
It no longer shone.

  Dela MacFarlane

The Man From Kent

There was a man from Kent
Who walked around really bent
When he fell down
He picked up a pound
He walked along further
Met his mate who was nicknamed
Burglar
He lent his mate the pound
His mate was astounded
And said he was grounded
Which shocked the poor
  Man from Kent

  Clare Webster

Eric Cantona

Eric Cantona
yes he is good
but when he got red
he was in a bad mood,

This man shouted names
and never gave his mouth a rest
Eric came over the barrier
Putting the feet in the man's chest.

Eric was hit
with a nine month ban
people missed him
because he was the best in the land,

It was October the first
when Eric came back from the dead
and he was welcomed back
by Fred the red.

2-1 up
Liverpool was looking hot
but Eric saved the day
from the penalty spot.

  Brendan Mulgrew

Sue

She has long black flowing hair
and a pale complexion.
She seems to always be alone
with no real direction.
I witness a dream
from the depths of my mind.
She really is all alone
just one of a kind.
A great friend she is to me
if only lovers we could be.
Those brown eyes compliment
her flowing black hair.
She surely knows lovers or not
that I really do care.

  Craig Harris

Peace

Here today, we are but a whisper
in the breeze
The gifts of life and love are but
a fleeting reality
More potent when is past.
Till we should drift as with
the tide,
left glistening upon the shingle,
shimmering in the setting sun.
In life's rhythm with nature
we are as one at peace.

  E. A. Bryant

Conflicting Minds . . .

The swords of tongue did slash
And blood did scorn my land
My soldiers so quickly they dashed
And my memories, they turned to sand
I thought the war had ended
De-crippled and walked away
My heart I thought was mended
And my sorrows they kept at bay
But have those days from long ago
Now come here from the past
To come hit me with a tremendous blow
And wound me with its blast
For I was weak and cold back then
When my eyes would begin to weep
And now I am strong, so strong again
Yet, only in my sleep
'Twas a day of beginnings
Where the end would unfold
Where my new-found surroundings
Would now be untold.

  Kavita Sohanta

Untitled

Sitting in silence
Thinking about you
Shadows whirl around me
I don't know what to do
Why can't you be here?
I need you to dry my tears
To feel you close beside me
To kiss away my fears
Now all I have are memories
Locked inside my heart
I'll keep them safe and warm
for as long as we're apart
And then when we're together
I'll never let you go
For you to me are the only one
I just want to let you know
My love for you grows stronger
Every second of the day
And just how I feel about you
Words could never say.

  Ethna Quirke

Who

Who slept and did not pray
Who betrayed him with a kiss
Who said thirty pieces pay
Who decided then his worth.

Who wove the crown of thorns
Who made the seamless coat
Who covered his eyes that day
Who slapped and asked who smote.

Who spat and plucked his beard
Who gave him a reed to hold
Who poured him vinegar to drink
Who said the king of jews behold.

Who lied and followed afar
Who pierced his hands and feet
Who plunged the sword in to his side
Who thought the job's complete.

Who left these awful scars
Who stopped to look and stare
Who denies him still today
Who you? Oh, friend, prepare.

Maureen Love

A Journey Through My Mind

I sit here and watch
the world go by
I don't seem to matter
forgotten in the blink of an eye.
I used to wonder
why the others were free
had someone important
forgotten about me.
I'm lying in hospital
depressed and alone
that's when I decided
to write you this poem.
I pray and I hope
as I lie in this bed
that my thoughts and my dreams
will get outside my own head.
When you read this poem
if it's not too much to bare
please let me know that,
at least you care.

Nicola Raftery

Windows To The Soul

Staring straight at two green eyes,
Pain and heartache visible inside.
Unable to communicate,
Pretending life is really great.
Hoping, yearning, praying,
Displaying emotion without saying.
A heart that aches inside so deep,
A painful feeling one has to keep.
People think that life's just fine,
So why the hell are those eyes mine?

Maria Murphy

The Ghost Of Reason

Between the rusted gates of fate;
the seeds of time were sown
And watered by those then,
in their time known;
As they still are now by those
fully grown.

Some folk await Jesus;
Whilst others
Function like Cain.
But most live and die
as did Abel;
For a reason they can't
honestly explain!

Dave White

Positive

To Annette and Anna Lee

Atmosphere, relaxation, concentration
 then channel your creation:
Construction, reduction, addition,
 revision leading eventually,
or hopefully, to production
 and consumption. You are
what you earn, so earn
 lots and eat loads.

Get Your share of the limelight:
 Have Your slice of the cake
and be greeted by the
 round of applause You always knew
You deserved, because, like
 Everybody else, You know
you Are better than the rest!

Neil Cogavin

This World Is Ours

This world is ours to care for,
Each man should do his part,
We can't take it for granted,
It's time to make a start.

People out there are starving,
Dying every day,
I think we have to help them,
Or starvation's here to stay.

Victims of war and innocent men,
Just like you and me,
Out there in a no-man's land.
That's not how it should be.

Destruction all around them,
With nowhere left to hide,
And all for one crazy thing,
They're on a different side!

I know I want to help them,
I hope that you agree,
One day it might be too late,
And then where would we be?

Louise Foster

Blue Whale Wonders

Blue whale wonders,
Blue whale tales,
Such big wonders,
Such big tails,
If you hunt them,
They will die,
So don't bother trying,
Do you want to know why?
Blue whales are real.

Selasie Y. Ocloo

Don't Throw Your Life Away To Drugs

Life used to be full of dark tunnels,
with not even a glimpse of light
Shining through

Full of long roads and obstacles
running to.

Decision here decisions there . . .
But now I have reached the end
of the tunnels.

Completed the obstacle and made my
decisions.

There was light at the end of the
tunnel,
And my friends were waiting for
me at the end of the road.

Sonia Tingley

Hail October!

The Summer now has gone
And Autumn tints are showing.
Why is it so short,
The Summer that I love?

It seems no time at all
Since springtime shoots were growing.
It seems no time at all
With true blue skies above.

The nights are closing in.
No balmy evenings, glowing
With fragrant petals falling
Like feathers from a dove.

Instead the skies are grey now.
The sharper winds are blowing.
They bite against my cheek now
My hands will need a glove.

The early morning's cold,
Still dark, the cock is crowing
To welcome hours of daylight
With overtures of love.

Dorothea Kent

A Sense Of Isolation

I feel unwanted,
No-one wants to know me;
It's the way I look, I'm different,
In my own category.

I yearn for acceptance,
But rejection's all I gain;
Cast out for being different,
A pale smile cloaks my pain.

Frustration dwells within me,
My spirit tattered and torn;
Uncertain of my future,
A body wasted and worn.

In my dreams I am tormented,
Aspirations - I have none;
My life feels as though it has ended,
When it has only just begun.

Love me as I am,
See beyond this shell;
Don't victimize, or criticize,
Relieve this living hell.

F. E. Laine-Pearson

Remembering

She sits in the wheelchair
Alone, lost, forlorn
Remembering her children
The days they were born.

Their lives flash before her
Entwined with her own
The love flows around her
Although she's alone.

Arthritis impedes her
And walking is out
Long gone are the days
When she'd twist and shout.

But she can remember
Her twinkling feet
And the boys who adored her
The memories are sweet.

Her life's nearly over
With patience she waits
To walk again in heaven
Right through the pearly gates.

Myrtle Fishlock

You'll Never Walk Alone!

Why did it happen to you?
I don't understand,
all I wanted was to hold your hand.

How I cried when you had gone,
Everything just kept going wrong.
When I wondered what I would do,
I just kept thinking about you.

I wanted to cuddle you really tight,
But no one was there through the night.
I only wish you were at home,
Instead of us being all alone.

You only went to watch the game,
Now things will never be the same.
As I look up into the dark night sky,
I know you're up there somewhere high!

Joanne Bestall

Cobbles

I walk upon the cobbles,
My feet hard upon the stone.
How long have they been there,
One will never know.
How many people have been before me,
How many troubles they have seen.
The rain, wet and cold, falls hard
Upon the rough, uneven-coloured brick.
Now becoming dusk, I cannot see
But feel beneath my feet
The waywood home once more.

Marion Moylan

You Too Can Be A Fat Cat!

On my birthday, late last year
I became a real 'Old Dear'!
And reached the ripe old age of eighty,
Which in years is pretty weighty.
And one important thing to mention,
Then I had a rise in pension.
Lots of us who fought a war,
Were wondering what it all was for.
But now the Government sees sense,
And offers us some recompense.

But please don't get it spread around,
That my financial state is sound.
I hate the thought of any debtors
Or people sending begging letters.
At first I sought some sound advice,
Regarding safe investment price,
But now, each week I spend the lot
And let my future go to pot!
This spending makes my legs feel weak.
Twenty-five pence rise a week!

Reg Yearley

In The Wee Small Hours

I could sit beside you
Until the end of time
Watching your dear countenance
Glad that you are mine
Knowing, when you do awake
And open up your eyes
Your smile will be like a sunrise
That lights the morning skies
And as I watch you sleeping
The pictures come and go
Of all our years together
When our love could only grow
For to know you, is to love you
And I am truly blest
So I thank God for my fortune
And lay my head to rest.

June Davies

Untitled

A small tear finding its path
on my cheek... travelling ...
passing away into air
nothingness.... to be lost forever
why cannot sorrow?

A sigh escaping from my lips
as quickly as it can
never looking back...
never heard again
why cannot memories?

Thoughts racing with time
knowing no bounds
no distances...
no realities, just being...
why cannot I?

Priyadarshini R.

Summer

They should have named you Summer
With your eyes like fields of green
Shining like the summer sun
On some enchanted scene

They should have named you Summer
So I could bask in your sunlight
And knowing when the day is through
There waits a starlit night

They should have named you Summer
For while winter's still around
I'll listen for your whisper
And Summer's joyous sounds.

You'll never be a winter
An autumn or a spring
You'll always be a Summer
Cause that's the season that you bring.

Brian Cassidy

Fragments

Fragments of my heart
lying in pieces
where do I start?

Chasing shadows
of the past
heart still beating
- fast!

Pockets of joy
that holes have worn through
promises of love
that were never true.

Tiny pieces
I was left to pick up
fragile and clear
so far - and yet,
so near.

Pamela Speir

Time And Relevance

Time is only relevant
Whilst the clock is ticking

Tick Tock

Tick Tock

When the clock stops ticking
Time stops still

Tick

　Tock

But relevance continues

Rodney George Priest

I Want To Stay Here!

No! I don't want to go,
I've only just arrived,
And now you're taking me away,
What if it's cold out there,
I have nothing to keep me warm,
Please leave me here.

I can feel that you really love me,
Or else why would I be a start,
Yet you keep saying,
"I don't want it."
Am I now reduced to an it,
No meaning in my name,
No soul.

Something's pulling me deeper,
Deeper and deeper I go,
I struggle and hold on to the lining,
But my fingers are too small to grip,
I feel myself floating away,
And then I am still,
Lying on a dish and waiting to die.

J. L. Huckstepp

First Impressions

I chanced upon a magic place
With fragrance in the air
Then I stopped in awe at what I saw
A carpet lying there.

A rainbow's woven silky threads
All spun by nature's hand
And I stared in awe at what I saw
A painted wonderland.

A thousand slender little maids
In frocks of modest green
And I gasped in awe at what I saw
A sight I'd never seen.

A humble sea of gentle folk
Arranged in such a way
And I drowned in awe at what I saw
Before me on display.

I stood amidst the tulip fields
And drank the perfumed air
Then I cried in awe at what I saw
Such beauty everywhere.

Phillida Orr

Sharing And Caring

Less of I
And more of we,
More of us,
And less of me.

Would make this world
A better place,
For the young and old,
Of every race.

Enjoy all things,
Ignore all greed,
Share and care
For those in need.

I and me,
You'll be amused,
Are two selfish words
Most often used

More of giving,
And less taking,
This world would be,
Of excellent nothing.

Kathleen Blanchfield

Remember Me

If I should die,
  Remember Me.
For I would be up on high -
  The wind will be my silent sigh,
To let you know,
  That I will always see
You, as a part of me.

  Time will heal my space,
In your memories you'll see my face,
  I'll always watch over you -
In everything you do.
  If I should die,
Let me be, because I'll know
  You've remembered me.

Abida Haidar

Parting

Remnants of daylight linger
as our great romance fades.
The blossoms from trees drift
romantically past our faces.
We drift further apart.

The darkening hues of pink
reflect upon your face.
The clouds gather together
to become one.
We are now two.

The last light of day dies.
The colours disappear and
your face becomes dark,
to me, and us.
Our love died with the sun.

Jennifer Ramsay

It's A Wonderful Life

God has given me the chance . . .
To see another spring
To work the soil; and plant the seeds
And watch what nature brings

God has let me live to see
The sun rise in the sky
To smell a new mown lawn; and watch
Another day go by

Every day's a bonus
Now I've reached that certain age
I don't desire material things
I'm way beyond that stage

The hustle and the bustle
Of life's well into my past
I can potter . . . or just ponder now
Contentment's mine . . . at last

Sandra Brewerton

Praying Hands

Praying hands, what do they mean?
Peace and harmony to all who see
Comfort and love to those who need.

Draw loved ones close whilst in prayer
We think of them often over 'there'
Are they safe? Are they well?
Please can't somebody come and tell!

The waiting is awful
The time is long
Still in our thoughts—very strong!

Time goes on it passes by
Till the day we are by their sides
Then others pray and wonder the same
Till once more we meet again.

Pat Appleby

Miracles

Why must it take a miracle
For people to believe
That there is a God in heaven
Who looks after us in need
He's also there for all of us
Every single day
But why does it take a moment of need
For us to turn to him and pray
In a moment of danger
In a time of fear
Why then do we decide
That God is near
Why can't we pray
To God each day
And just thank him for our life
Be grateful that we are alive
If we do this every day
Then we won't need to be afraid
Don't wait until you need his help
Talk to him today

Marianne Whelan

No Rest Nor Turning

The sky is dark in every place
As the earth below
I think it wore the self-same face
Two thousand years ago

I think I have another home
No better place to find
For nothing save the thought of heaven
Is stirring in my mind

A good tree gives me shadow
And shelter from the rain
A precious voice is silent
And will not be heard again

I have climbed up by the hillside
And wandered by the sea
Move on move on is all I feel
For there is no rest for me

My sheep are feeding onwards
My dog sits watching by
I have wandered down the valley
And yet I know not why

Morag Anderson

A Green Prayer

Dwindling fields, and dwindling trees
Polluted rivers - polluted seas
Insecticide and acid rain
All man made, with what to gain?
Ponder primeval to present day
Scenes of awe, deer at play
To growing towns and winding roads
Super stores and new abodes
Sadness fills the heart, not mirth
What man has done to mother earth
Water forests, they disappear
Raging floods then appear
Destroying homes - destroying crop
Surely this damage has to stop
But question man on this mess
And blame is put on progress
But pray for strength to atone
For damage done to ozone
And also pray it's not too late
For damage done to abate

William Lea

Eventide

The golden sun shines on the corn,
We have worked to dusk, from dawn,
Harvest time arrives once more
Telling us the seasons o'er.

Now we see a building of rooks,
Perched upon the golden stooks,
The farmer wends his homeward way,
Thinking of another day.

Across the fields the rabbits play
Dashing past the stacks of hay,
Sinking slowly, the sun doth creep,
Silently she goes to sleep.

Ann Easton

Becoming Me

I sat in your oystered room
bare, barefaced, barefooted—
Passing you my dreams,
Opaque crystal balls,
Which you tenderly took
and broke open;

Releasing a bounty of Butterflies,
Doves of Divine desire
and a Hawk's-head of horror beside.

The crystal casing cauterized,
Jagged edges shredded
the skin beneath my feet.
When I was leaving,
blooded and laughing towards the water,
You lifted me
and washed my hands in saline sea.

Meriona Armstrong

Dreams

Dreams are my only escape
When I dream everything is great
everything is lovely
Not a bit of hate
In my dreams I am so free
Just like a dolphin in the sea
I go to a place way up high
It's worth more than diamonds.
And twinkles like a star in the sky
This is a place where others won't be
This is a place just for me.

Claire Longella Coady

Alone

The girl lost her father and mother
When she was very young
She didn't even have a brother
So she was alone, alone.

She didn't act the same
After this event
Forgot her own name
Because she was alone.

They put her in a room
All padded and white
So much like a tomb
While she was alone

They often said, "why?"
To the dead girl hanging
Not even a bye
From the girl who was alone

Her suicide note read
From by her side
"I would rather be dead,
Than to be totally alone."

Alison Waldram

Tomorrow

Tomorrow never comes
Nor will it ever really be,
Yet all those lost tomorrows
Become our history.
Time goes on and on forever
Like a dance that has no ending
With steps that take us nowhere
To a land of never never.
It is yesterday left behind
As we hope to reach a something
That is better than today
And which we all would love to find.
So is there still a future
When we reach the final bend
In life's road to the last gateway
To a new beginning, a new tomorrow,
Another time that has no end?

M. England

Death Of Humanity

Blood, Blood,
There was blood all around,
The sight was fiery red,
For Humanity was dead.....
That gave birth
To callousness and Inhumanity,
What more was left
Of the mighty Human race,
That was so bloodily
Soaked, in its own blood!
Was it all real?
The Blood?
The death of Humanity?
The hopelessness all around?
The life of humanity
Was killed!
What remained was
A mere ruin, of
A glorious past!!!

Anuradha Bachkaniwala

Laburnum Tree

You're picturesque when in bloom.
But who knows what you hide?
For your seeds are poisonous
And deadly and could kill anyone.
When eaten to their doom.
You look so beautiful as you hang,
And full of blossom in the sun.
Who can predict that the
Laburnum Tree is as poisonous
As you and me?

Carole Hirst

Children of the World of Nations

Children of the world
of nations all around
Should all be filled with happiness
Should all be safe and sound
There should not be a time you see
For suffering and pain
As they are all God's children
Who give his son in vain
Some children, they are happy
Some children, they are sad
For if the world were safer
I think they would be glad
for some there is no food you see
For some there is too much
Why can't there be a unity
Why can't there be some trust
For children are the future
Whatever come what may
So give them love and caring
To guide them on life's way

Linda Sheppard

The Stream Of Life

Where would we be without nature
That magic touching the earth
Like a stream of life that can travel
So every second of time there's a birth

Filling the earth with its wonders
Beauty the eyes now see
Blooming with life for a reason
Like the birds in the air flying free

But progress can bring many dangers
Disrupting what keeps us alive
Polluting the air and the water
And the vegetation we need to survive

So picture a world that's barren
No life on it at all
No milk from a cow, nothing to plough
Just a rock the shape of a ball

So let us not cut off a lifeline
By not all being aware
How much we depend on nature our friend
That stream of life that we share

Olive Walters

Grey

Opening the gigantic doors
disturbing the silent peace
A place that has been
left, deserted
The dust had settled
cobwebs all around
The lights don't work
nothing made a sound
A window is flapping
echoing through the house
The derelict building
looking so cold
rooms look dark
A haunted house
falling to the ground

Louise Kimmins

Another Love

I lose my mind in swirls of grey
as the day begins; time slipping by.
So we have met and shared and cared
but lives of others pierce between
and young ones unseeing
tread in hope.
When snatching moments
in selfish haste to laugh and love
as if alone;
question not the reasons why
to find in rainbows by and by.

Nicola Dudley

Blameless

Animals in cages locked away
with nothing to say, tested with
sprays and fatal displays, the lives
of creatures that God made.
They have no speech.
They have no choice.
They eat, breath and sleep.
Just how different are we?
This is not a game to them.
Will anyone ever take the
blame for what we won't
see again?

Kerry Griggs

Of Ships That Pass

Like the passing of summer
Goes a fading romance.
Once so bright and fair,
Now so cold and bare.
The warmth I used to know
Has faded like the afterglow
Of glorious sunset.

My heart sinks low,
I dread cold winter's blow.
The bleak grey days
And longer nights
That steal away
The sun's blessed light -
My spirit fails me.

I fill the hours with brush and pen
And 'broider flowers as I did when
My love was here to praise and bless
My every task with happiness.
'Twere not for music my days would be
An agonized plea for eternity.

R. Hopkins

It's Amazing

It's amazing how a caterpillar
So small and ugly
Can become a butterfly
Beautiful and heavenly.
Or how a little egg
Can become a bird,
Flying against the wind.
How a tiny wasp
Can become a sharp sting,
Or how a simple lump,
Can become a crying baby,
Whining through the night.
How you are gone,
But still here
And always will be.

Maria Wilson

Untitled

In a fragile human moment
where coverage is displayed
The angels come to smile.
And the hero then is made
A brave heart for a while
laying down the ultimate
With fortitude and style.

P. D. Jude

Jewels Of The Night

The sky full of wonder,
    for all to behold
"Sunrise and sunsets"
    a crescendo of gold
"Moonlight's radiance"
    love's eternal light
"Cascading stars"
    glittering jewels of the night
"billowing clouds"
    shed gentle tears of dew
To unveil nature's masterpiece
    to me and to you
"Lightning's flash"
    its lustrous streak
Opens "the sky to thunder"
    to loudly speak
These elements of wonder
    we truly applaud
All gifts to humanity
    by our "Saviour and Dear Lord"

Stanley Hayhurst

Extra Terrestrials

If this world were composed
Of merely mortal men,
Everything would stop
So be it, amen.

The world is filled
With extra people
What for?
I don't really know.

Perhaps,
If we ran out of people
The bell in the chapel
Would sit on the steeple.

And take on a mind of its own,
Like Bhudda or Jesus,
And rise beyond death
To a heaven unknown.

Brian Rosillard

Ripped Heart

The air I breath tastes salty
it reminds me of my stand.
Though not the air of childhood,
more the mood of foreign land.
Yet, it's mesmerism's gripping.

Where are you, my companions,
that for long I used to know?
While I sense a kind of friendship
so recent in its vow.
And it makes my heart do skipping.

I am timid that this language
might deny words of my mind.
There's no hope to ease the anguish-
will the future treat me kind?

But hush! I hear the calling
of the challenge to go on;
Bolt the need to cease complaining
to the things that might go wrong.
It's not me that does the ripping.

Matthias Perner

Yearning

Warm flesh I uncovered
your sweet touch I sensed
a joining imperfection
sweet smelling and tensed.

Filling the desirable
opening the locked
simultaneous motions
pure liberty is rocked.

Clear ecstasy and emotion
climatically aligned
last affectionate embraces
joined body and mind.

Kyle O'Connor

It's Not

It's not a poem,
    that does rhyme,
It's not a poem,
    just a time,
It's not a poem
    that we can sing,
It's not a poem,
    to make the bells ring,
It's not a poem,
    of war and hate,
It's not a poem,
    to make you wait,
It's just a poem from me,
to you to say how much I, love you.

Alison Neil

Time

Times change, people do
Minutes ticking, hours too
Drifting by, setting sail
Roses red, memories pale
Lost horizons, captured dreams
Silent please, tortured screams
Sun rising, moon aglow
Lots to do, much to know
Warm bodies, huddled together
Stormy skies, humid weather
Thunder rolling, clouds black
Humour found, personalities lack
Smiles broad, laughter rings
Love found, heart sings.

Dawn C.

Desperate

No one wants us old folks
When we are getting old
No one wants to house us
And we are left out in the cold

I only have till Sunday
Where I am living now
Soon I shall be out on the streets
But no one cares somehow

I've tried and tried the council
To give me a little flat
I do not ask for much in life
But they won't give me that

So I shall have to do my best
To find a place somewhere
Perhaps someone will offer me
A bed or cosy chair

Barbara Ball

Scrumpy Jack

There beneath my soul doth lie
a place where angels cannot fly,
where love is lost in seas of tears
and troubles wallow in shallow fears.

Deserts of time fill my mind,
sparkling seas of whisky and wine,
lost in dream of drunken rhymes,
riddles that rave of better times.

Falling down from standing up,
rolling around causing a muck.
Dancing, prancing singing a song,
a few more down and I'll be gone
to a better place where people smile
and there I shall stay for some while.

Russell Kingaby

Lord Mayor Treloar College

This college is wonderful
This college is great
I've made lots of friends
And now there's none left to make

The staff are really friendly
The carer's really kind
And if I had to mark this place
I'd give it nine out of nine

My lesson aren't too easy
But I know I won't get behind
Because the teachers do not mind
If I take extra time

If I had a choice
Of where I'd like to be
There's no college better
Than LMTC!

Helen O'Toole

What Is A Poem?

What is a poem I ask myself
as I gaily write today,
Is it just a part of me
I gladly give away?

Are these words that fill this page
My inner thoughts or dreams?
Are they lines I've read before
In books, by trickling streams.

I must confess when all is said
A poem seems to be,
Whatever comes into my heart
A thought I share with thee.

Linda Savage

The Artist

If I were but an artist
What beauty I'd create,
By putting brush to canvas
A whole new world I'd paint.

I would brush away the sorrow
From every breaking heart,
And paint the smiles on faces
Of those who have to part.

I would choose my colours carefully
That I may not offend,
The most sensitive of people
Whose shades most richly blend.

And in a blaze of colour
A canvas of gold cascade,
Would portray life's many blessings
Those colours which never fade.

Helen Evetts

Flight Of The Sea Gull

Oh, what is wrong with me,
I'm flying high above the sea,
Watching all the crested waves,
So powerful we are,
But slaves.
I'm soaring high above the sea,
It looks purple green to me
And underneath, in the world beneath
The starfish lie and shellfish die.
But in the winter, when rocks splinter,
The waves reach high and soak the sky
And me.
And now I fall into the depths
Where death awaits, I'm at the gates
Of eternity.
The sea is thirsty, it shows no mercy,
It swallows me,
I die in the sea.

Dean John Midgley

Absolute, Obsolete

No longer does the bird walk,
when it can fly.
No longer does the ape crawl,
when it can walk.
No longer does the man sigh,
when it can talk.
Now all of these are obsolete.

No longer do the mountains move,
when they can stand still.
No longer do the birds sing,
when they can talk.
No longer does man need make war,
when he can make love.
No longer does time stand still,
when it can move.
All of this is absolute.

Ian Colwyn

The World To Me

The sun shines in the sky
Your smile shines in my heart
And every time I'm near you
I wish we'd never part.

The rain falls down around us
As I shower you with my love
You're the meaning of me living
Sent from heaven above.

The moon caresses the night
As you caress me too
There is no meaning to living
When I am without you.

The wind blows so softly
As you whisper in my ear
The words you say so touching
I shed a single tear.

Nikki Hodgson

My Wish

I wish I'd been a lad,
A mate for my old dad.
We would have had such fun,
Playing football in the sun.

And as the years passed by,
We'd have gone fishing you and I.
Laughed and argued what was right,
From early morn till late at night.

But alas God gave you me,
One of four to bounce upon your knee.
Four daughters and a wife you see
To love you till eternity.

Linda Beatrice Yates

No Tears

Why am I so weary
Why has everything I once held so dear
Disappeared
Why when I cry out
Does nobody hear
Why do I fear
That my fate is near
That I stab myself
With sharp, pointed spears
Until no more tears
Only despair.

Each day I wind myself up
Like the wheels of a clock
Always turning, afraid to stop
My mind is spinning
I cannot think
This game I'm not winning
Into apathy I sink.

Heidi Warren

Have You Ever...?

Have you ever woken
to the sunlight
Streaming through your window
Drenching you in warmth
kissing your skin.

Have you ever dozed
to the rhythm of the rain
Gently tapping
Drawing you to drift
under its hypnosis.

Have you ever fallen
into deep slumber
staring at the sunset
a gentle breeze rocking you
willing you into another world?

Emma Mooney

Hair

The root is the beginning.

Nurtured and preened,
watered, tended,
caressed.

Its creeping tendrils stretch
and curl,
grasping an invisible trellis.

A dead tube growing.

Steven Todd

East Timor

There is a field
Brutality sows
With the corpses of a country.
And in that field
A river flows
With blood,
Mirroring tyranny
In shards of human tears,
Sharpening bones
Until daggers grow
And woken by stolen breath
The living will reap their harvest
And triumph over death.

Isla Boag

Celestial Beacons

Eternal life and wisdom
are the desires of man,
yet three score years and ten
foretell our allotted span.
Time traces storms and tranquilities
upon our mortal frame,
mirrored images reflecting that
age has won the game.
Internally the soul through
all the stress of life
with untold grace and beauty
will flourish and survive.
Death sweeps the decayed remnants
through the final gate.
The end seems all confusion,
Life is a debate.
But the souls of great men are stronger
though years and years pass by,
they shine through time eternal
like beacons in the sky.

Margaret I. Turner

Ancestors

God-like beings, serene, sublime;
Motivators in the dawn of Time.
Givers of Law and retribution dire.
Creators of crops and fire.
Those who said "Go seek and find".
"Increase and multiply your kind".
"Keep yet the rules of kindred clear".
"Nothing then have you to fear".
"Number the stars and weather lore"
"Honour those who have gone before".
"Raise up Ziggurat and Tell".
"Speak of your forefathers well".
"Salute those who blaze the trail".
"Be it they succeed; or fail".
"To the builders of wheel and keel;
"Sing a song of praise; and kneel".
Osiris, Buddha, and the Christus too;
Forget not what they did for you!
Protect thy child in the cradle well!
Of its descendants, nought can You tell!

J. Nolan

Alone

Everyone's gone,
I'm all alone,
Does anyone care?
That I'm on my own.

No one to talk to,
As the front door shuts,
Just me and the dog,
I think I'll go nuts.

My mum's in Egypt,
My dad's there too,
My brother's at a play,
What shall I do?

The doors are locked,
And shut very tight,
The lights are all on,
To make the house bright.

Is anyone out there?
I don't want to know,
Hiding in the bushes,
I wish he'd go!

Alison E. Webb

Sleep

These walls close around my world,
Darkness reigns here,
There is peace,
An inner calm,

Drifting . . .
My mind set loose,
No longer in control,
But for thoughts to roll,
To wander where they wish.
Freely.

Here is where I rest,
Content to lie,
No worries,
But for the sands of time to come,
And pass,
Over me . . .

Jonathan D. Chinn

Ignorance As Survival

It's better not to know
because what's the use of
knowing
when all there is to know
is not worth knowing.

Regardless of what I claim
Life will be more unbearable
because we'll all end up as
patients
in the Asylum we've created.

Marscha Penders

Walking The Tightrope

Walking the tightrope
Between good and bad
Walking the tightrope
Between happy and sad

Walking the tightrope
Afraid to fall
Walking the tightrope
It comes to us all

Walking the tightrope
We must balance our lives
And walk the tightrope
To the other side

Jim Cumpsty

Me And You

You say hello,
I hear goodbye.
I start to laugh,
You start to cry.

I say 'I'm sorry'
You hear me patronize.
You say you're happy
I see pain in your eyes.

You say you like it,
I say 'I don't'.
I say 'Let's go there',
You say 'I won't'

I am scared,
You are bold.
You offer your hand,
I shiver from the cold.

You were weak,
I was strong.
I was right,
You were wrong.

Rachel Start

Sky Watch

Have all the stars become old men?
Is all nature in decline
Is Pluto dead or without a head,
In his sad orb so fine.

A sheep has wandered from the fold
Now what next shall I do
Just wait and watch and wonder
Maybe she is wondering too.

What star is that, that star above.
That round about Neptune winds
It pushes, pushes firmly
And pulls him from behind

Live out the glories of this age
See the argonauts rise and roar
Of stern and keel and constant sail
Heard from the distant shore.

Tonight as I watch the mellow moon
Just mellowed out by time
Tonight in his five mooned citadel
Uranus gulps his wine

Katherine Teresa Weir

My Love For You

My fondness for you
Is like a fresh flower
It grows every day
Hour by hour

I look at you
With hope in my face
That one day we'll find
A love that won't waste

People won't let us
They say it's not right
To care for each other
Every day and all night

They say we're too different
To feel the same need
To show one another
Just what we mean

You make me feel happy
And very secure
I will always love you
Every day, more and more

Kerenza Spargo

I Dreamed A Dream

I dreamed a dream of you,
of silver meadows,
Blue cornflowers,
And a silver moon,
Shining in a midnight sky.

I dreamed of dancing
To a moonlit melody,
With you in my arms,
Just you and me.

I dreamed of stars,
Which sparkled in your eyes.
All this I dreamed.
And I dreamed I dreamed
A dream of you.

Kerry Smith

The Writer Of This Poem

The writer of this poem
Is brown as a bear
As tall as a mini bus
And she loves to share.

As fierce as a lion
As tidy as a gift shop
As giggly as a hyena
Art is her top.

Writing poems is a hobby
Shopping she enjoys
As organized as a bookshop
She has lots and lots of toys.

Now here is a message
I'd really like to send
I really have to go now
So bye, and here's the end.

Reshmee Rehal

Winter's Dawn

If I did not have lead feet
I would be quick to hold you
Caress and make you mine

But now you are gone
Like a bird set free
I just shout into the air
A quiet "I love you"

"I love you", three simple words
The tears roll down my face
Filled with the innermost turmoil
Purging my soul

But now you are gone
Like a bird set free
I am left with a heart ablaze
And a brief memory

Life is suspended
My soul is empty
Waiting to shine
Since that early winter's dawn

Victor McIntosh

Moon, Moon

Moon, Moon, what do I know?
Why does your light shine like so?

You're sometimes full, half or new,
You look like the last drop of dew.

I have a lot of questions to ask,
Of your beauty or is it a mask.

You look so good in a cloudy sky,
I know your beauty will never die.

Tausif Bhatty

Finished

I don't see you anymore,
No kiss as you close the door.
Have we really changed that much?
Have we lost the will to touch?
Every time I'm near you,
You seem to pull away.
Every time I talk to you,
You never know what to say.
We never share a secret,
Not even share a word.
The silences are hurting us,
Our words are never heard.
If we cannot share our feelings,
We number all our days.
We will say goodbye forever,
We will go our separate ways.

Joanne Sudell

Time Passes

Time passes by so quickly,
some might say
though I think of you
every day.

Pictures I can look at,
with a smile or a tear
but no longer, your voice
do I hear.

Longing to talk to you,
even more for you to listen
There is so much
I still need to say.

You were there for me
at the beginning
I hope you heard me
say, I love you,
at the end.

Clare Randle

Life

From North to South
And inside out
I wonder what
Life's all about

From Past to Present
And round and round
Life's just another big
Merry-go-round

From East to West
And top to bottom
Our lives' experiences
Will never be forgotten

From Life to Death
I can only but guess
We will know our true purpose
When we are laid to rest!

Audrey Imray

Silence

In response to silence,
No response necessary.
Silence the ultimate truth.
The seeker seeks.
When obtained,
No passing over.
The destroyer of truth,
Are they who foolishly,
Pass it over.
Unknowingly diminishes,
That which is real.
Then lives in secure,
Unknown falsity.

Mary White

Time

We all need time to sit and think
And watch the world go by
But time just passes with a blink
It doesn't wait for you or I

We all need time to ponder
To think of what to do
But in this world of wonder
Time is precious too

It ticks away the hours and days
The weeks and months roll on
And like our dreams of yesterday
The years have come and gone

Now we must make the most of time
For it's not here to stay
To move with it is not a crime
So we can't let it run away

Joan Power

Tee'd Off!

Some may say golf spoils a walk
Who are they to scoff and talk
They'll never master the perfect swings
Joys and sorrows of intricate things
The setting off in anticipation
Giving way to resignation
A shower of brollies in winter's grip
Birdie putts that sit on the lip
Summer days with mixed delights
Rabbit scrapes and insect bites
Screams of laughter and so much more
Between the nervous shouts of fore
Wayward shots, felling of trees
Addressing the ball with creaking knees
Missed the bunker by an inch or two
How you did it, you haven't a clue.
With nerves of steel, quick reaction
You find the green with satisfaction
But my favourite tee, don't tell a soul
Is always the welcoming nineteenth hole.

Sue J. Whittaker

Now

If I were a poet,
I'd pick up my pen.
I'd write of the fleet dancing swallows
and then,
when the grey clouds of winter
hung low in the sky,
I'd read through my verses
and let my heart fly
And all of Spring's freshness,
and Summer's bright hues,
I'd weave into words
so I never would lose,
no matter how lousy the weather
and drear,
the heart-soaring joy of
this time of the year.

Kathleen Herriott

A Wonderful Life

They say that life's a wonderland
of wondrous things to see, of
mountains high and valleys wide,
and feckless seas so free, to see
the clouds that scud along, like
chariots of fire, or the beauty
of a promised dawn, to end in
twilight hour, of winds that
blow like Pipes of Pan,
enough I think for any man.

C. Johnson

Cooper Bay - Antarctica

The moon - eyed sea wings across,
Its sapphire seas,
Once untouched,
Ah no, the years oh,
This place of silent, sapping shores,
Troubled by the claws,
Of a new world, unwilling
Man himself not believing
The frozen fields, slowly sinking.

The fast, fading snow melts,
The now familiar path,
Once untouched,
Ah no, the years, oh,
Lone echoes, lonely lost,
Amongst crying whales in a new world,
Their stories never told,
Blue seas reddened, bones sold.
Down their skulls the rain drops plough.

Douglas N. Crichton

Justice And Power

Say not of the untried,
Though tested in battle,
"Here's a man, a good man.
Encamped with the oppressed
He does injustice to none.
Had the world many like him."

Among all men search still,
For those few men of power,
Battered and scarred in common fights,
Yet whose biceps twitch and dilate,
And from whose pores and wounds
Ooze litres of brine and blood,
As they fight for the powerless.
Search for those
Whose roads are strewn
With the clean bones of injustice,
And whose corridors are littered
With the fresh bodies
Of nascent injustice.
To the world recommend these few.

Emeka Obiandu

Bordeaux

Smelly, dirty, rude.
Train station like a brothel.
Shouting men with naked tops.
Unsightly streets.
Rubbish everywhere.
Is this Bordeaux?

Foreign men eyeing bags
Ready to pickpocket.
Pretending to limp.
Drinking from unmarked bottles
Talking with slurs.
Sleeping like a coma.

Watch our bags.
Keep our guard up.
Trust no one.
Hate Bordeaux.
Glad to be leaving.
The dirtiness seeps in our pores.
If we leave, will this dirt leave us?

Belinda Chapman

Trust

Trust is a bridge
and a relationship is a car
If the trust goes the bridge goes
and the car won't travel too far

Brett Ingram

Away

You sailed away
in a boat built of steel
flying your blackest flag,
such a solemn day.

Tears are strong
in my eyes
I have felt pain
but it mustn't prolong.

Make the church bells ring
let the mourners come
let their voices sing.

For you have sailed away.

J. Sherwood

Gone Forever

Blackness appears
From nowhere,
All is empty inside
And as the coward runs,
The trees sway
In the light breeze.

He ran away
Into the black.
I knew then he'd never come back,
When he left
My burning hatred came forever.
I was hurt inside
Always, forever.

As the river flowed,
The secret was told.
My childhood gone
Battles already won.
But nobody wins the war.

Stacey Corbett

Was It All Meant To Be?

Young and free, young and free
Walking in the rain
I for you and you for me
Would we do it all again
If we were young and free
And didn't know the pain.

In my heart a sadness
Such longing, such regret,
Que sera sera
Was it all meant to be?
I never thought I'd ever say
I wish we'd never met.

Yet surely some of it was good
We had our moments, didn't we?
Que sera sera
Was it all meant to be?
One day when I come back home,
Will you be there for me?

Ruth Turner

Could It Be?

You did not know I watched you,
As we watched the late night show,
And thought I saw upon your face
The first shy blush of death.

In the flickers of the TV light
My guilty thought took secret flight:
Could it be that one day soon
I'd look across this friendly room
Gazing at an empty chair,
Remember how I watched you there,
And wonder that I did not know
I loved you so?

Marjorie Sandiford

Thoughtful

To sit
and think
what might have been.
To wonder
how it will end.
To find
that you have no control,
over destiny,
your mind
and your soul.
To realize
that it was just a lie,
when tears
will fill your streaming eyes.
To sit
and think
what might have been,
to wonder
how it will end...

Emma Waller

Castles On Quicksand

When I dream of tomorrow,
And now it could be.
I have a lover,
And a big castle by the sea.
But then I remember that,
You can't build castles on quicksand.
My dreams sink,
Whilst I sit and watch,
The world goes by but no one stops.
I'm sat alone,
My dreams lying on the ground,
People stamp all over my dreams.
No one cares no one makes a sound,
My eyes well up,
Does it show?
Are they tears?
I'll never know!

Donna Ashford

A Colour Flower

A field of colour,
a sea of red and yellow,
the flowers seem to float,
a burning flame in sight,
pollen carriers buzzing,
around and around,
when the night arrives,
the flowers change their tune,
no more do they whistle, in the wind,
but they hum in the silence,
of the cold black night,
until the dawn does break,
then the sky will buzz once more...

S. Robertson

Untitled

What is love, I don't know
Is it wanting you near
Is it knowing no fear
Or is it shedding a tear
I don't know.

What is love, I don't know
Is it holding you tight
On a cold lonely night
Or is it fleeing in fright
I don't know.

What is love, I should know
It is knowing you care
And wanting you there
It is being a pair
I do know.

Wendy Hooper

Love In Unity

Love is more than passing pleasure,
love is strong,
love is weak,
love is hard to keep.

Adelia Cloete

Fair, Fat And...

It crept up
Silently one day
Hanging in clusters
Like bunches of dumplings
Stuck together.

Trying to escape
From walls of restraint
Creeping over
Edging under
Suffocating.

Caught a glimpse in the mirror
And suddenly knew
The puppy fat
Grew up
Into a ferocious rotweiller
Straining at the collar
Biting the hand that feeds it
And nobody loves it.

Janice Taylor

For My Love Of Julie

For my love of Julie
I write my verse,
With heartfelt words
I can converse.
As she reads I hope she sees,
She's just the business,
The bee's knees!
But it's me who's buzzing,
And how I hum,
Adding up our good times,
Into one big sum.
And for my love of Julie,
I reflect in verse,
That still I long, oh how I long,
For me to be hers!

Graham Mitchell

Innocence Personified

Her eyes, they don't see colour,
Her world is black and white,
But she has the advantage
Of seeing all at night.

She doesn't understand much,
But then, she's still no fool,
For anything she has learnt
Has not been taught at school.

She's really full of innocence,
A joy to watch at play,
A quiet, shy companion,
Of sunshine, she's a ray.

Her conversations limited,
In fact, if truth be heard,
She only has a repertoire,
Of one quite simple word.

Her day is most spent sleeping,
Or doing this or that,
And if you haven't guessed by now,
This female is.... My cat

Colin Ross

A Little Plea

Just a little message
for those to help in need,
with all of your donations
our cause it will succeed,

Please help the little children
to live a life so full,
help rid of complications
to do, we tug and pull,

Our aim is for a better life
to living without pain,
enjoying games and sports
together this we'll aim,

So if we pull together
and with each other's trust,
we'll help the little children
of this, it is our must,

So please pull together
we will get enough,
to help to build the future
of our society, KRUF.

B. V. Dance

Reverie

I oft times wonder should I dare
When there is rain upon the air,
To go as Nature did intent,
And in complete abandonment.
Cavort and frolic in the showers,
Dancing amidst the Garden flowers.
Though this is but a dream for me,
Who knows! One day! Maybe.

Cecil Andrew

Our Natalie

As knowing glance,
Your perfect smile,
Tells us your beginning to learn.
These times are precious,
Your growing fast,
And they will not return.

What lies ahead,
For you who knows.
We can only wait and see,
So we will hold the memories
in our minds,
For you our Natalie.

And when your grown,
A women you will be,
The future is yours
And you hold the key.
So make good your life
And be proud steadfastly
And remember the good times
For us, our Natalie.

Paul Baker

Intimacy

In...timacy
Fallacy
I will blow a kiss softly
To you who are not answering
My soul is sore from aching
Aching in the emptiness of being
Listen!
Listen to it waiting
Waiting to give
The sap
The juices
Of my draining life
To whoever passes by

Sylvie Stainton

Resting

I'm wearing the sun,
it is such fun,
to while away the hours,

To watch the birds,
swoop and swerve,
and flit among the flowers,

Blue is the sky,
clouds roll by,
and disappear o'er yonder,

This is the life,
free from strife,
I've no wish to wander.

Marion Hewlett

Time

Slowly, slowly, from the chair,
Cannot hurry, wouldn't dare
Stiffly, straightening, oh the pain.
No! Seventy will not come again.

Age is precious, time to think,
Do not let your spirits sink,
Look back o'er the years gone by,
Remember, fondly, do not cry.

Memories, they all are good.
Remembering only as one should.
The happy things, the precious times.
Oh! I remember, all was fine.

Gently sit back, rest my eyes.
My time to go to paradise.
My life's been happy, fulfilled too,
Dear friends, I wish the same for you.

Mary Palmer

Farewell

The old man sits alone in the chair,
In his silent world he will wait
Waiting for someone who may care,
Knowing sorrow and eventual fate.

Endless time, full of thought
Each day, draining life away,
Thinking over the world he sought,
The only future is judgement day.

Things, that once were so futile,
Creating problems in his mind
Hoping not to be senile,
Each year slowly going blind.

Reaching for comfort out of the past
Re-living life is his mind's eye
Not knowing how long today will last,
He waits for the time to say good-bye.

Noreen Almond

Stationary Falling

See an echo
Feel a cry
Hear a brilliant vision
Black to white in contrast
Animated reason
Surround the whole
Enclose the one
Secure an open mind
Action asks of no reply
Except a trust in kind
Fortune follows
Persuasion leads
Logic theory is spoken law
Intense the sounding
Less now more
Square peg in circle rounding

Anthony S. Hyland

Thoughts Of Home

The pub was full, "the crack" was good
But my thoughts were far away
I was back home in Kilrush Town
It was Saint Patrick's Day

I can see the church, my mother too
She came down the steps to me
The wind blew cold from Francis Street
It came in from the sea

Two weeks ago my father died
And now he's laid to rest
Among the hills and valleys green
In the place he loved the best

This was the day when I must go
There was no work for me
My brother Jim had got the farm
Being the eldest of us three

Someone spoke, I turned around
My thoughts came back to earth
For Bonny Kathleen stood there
Her face creased up in mirth

Gerard Quirke

Daniel

Daniel was a man of courage,
All alone he prayed to God.
Never falt'ring nor complaining,
In the narrow way he trod.
Even in the den of lions,
Loyal to the one true God

Gwen Holmes

Golden Carpet

Golden carpet on the floor.
Leaves that blow from door to door
Gently lie, and then they go
Making way for winter snow.
As the seasons pass along
Where now is the birds' sweet song?
Snowdrops in the garden beds
Open up their tiny heads.
Daffodils will soon appear
Bringing with them springtime cheer.
Out will come our garden chairs,
Shops will show their summer wares
Back will go the garden chair,
Out will come our warmer ware.
Autumn comes around once more,
Golden carpet on the floor.

Hazel Hill

My Lady Fair

No party frock or coiffure hair
Has the lady, oh so fair
Green crushed velvet, bows and lace
For her frankly has no place
Yet she holds a love true
Smile of comfort when you're blue

Sharing the laughter, drying the tears
Love you give lasts treasured years
Time will fade, your beauty die
Often black clouds invade the sky
Store of riches you are indeed
You beside me, no other need

Never alone a warming glow
Forever from your presence flow
Love words sincere, live in mind
Forever last to end of time
No party frock or coiffure hair
Has the lady, oh so fair

Pearl Powell

No Cheers Just Tears

How did I get here
What did I do
Will I stay here forever
Without seeing you
Will these walls be my home
Will I sit here and die
Will they lock all the doors
Will they hear me cry

I want to get better
I honestly do
I can't go on living
Without seeing you
Please, help me fight
The longing, the pain
I love you too much
To drink ever again

Doreen Harrington

A Way Of Life

She rises bright and early.
Her day to start afresh
A woman of the world is she
My dearest darling Jess.

Though we have our ups and downs,
And have a tiff or two,
There's nothing like our making up
We start our lives anew.

Her greatest joy is this she'll say:
To play with children grand,
To keep and hold them to her breast,
And guide them safe by hand.

The moral of this poem is
Be true - be honest - kind.
To live and love become as child,
And ease your troubled mind.

D. Richardson

Friends

We met as strangers, years ago,
Soon become firm friends.
But too soon we had to part.
There is the great divide,
But not between us.

Where the blue of the sky,
Meets the blue of the sea
Where the shore kisses the sand.
There is a great divide,
But not between us.

I know not when we will meet again;
There is a great divide,
But not between us.
As too great friends we are.

L. Penney

The Fairground

My pappa owned a fairground
It was neat in every way
Oh how I love the sounds
My pappa used to say
Come, come step this way
Get your coconuts today
Ice cream and candy bars
Were two of the things I love
Riding on bright horses
Knocking down the cans
I loved it when my pappa
Placed a teddy bear in my hands
And when the fair was over
I would hear the town people say
Oh how I wish the fair was
Here, each and every day.

Jannette Chapman

The Child

When a child is born
It is a gift from God
The love between two people
Is sent from high above.

After the child is born
A mother's love is needed
The warmth and tenderness she gives
Will be for life, believe it.

Soon the child will be five years old
It's then time to go to school
To learn to read and write
Listen and obey the rules

When the child is all grown up
Ready to go it alone
Out into the big wild world
To wander and to roam.

Moira Emslie

Free Spirit

Somewhere - running through the trees
With hair flying in the breeze
Wild spirit, free of pain,
Can't see tears in the rain,
Energy pumping through
Muscles and sinew,
Mind clear and singing,
In the air birds are winging.
Breath hot as fire,
Life will not expire
Pure joy and freedom of will,
Whilst the rest of the world is still.

Julie A. Thompson

My Dad

I have your photo in my room
I talk to you each day,
I tell you all my troubles
and they seem to go away.
I tell you about poor Alec
And the burden seems to lift.
Oh! Dad how I miss you.
I wish you were here to-day.
You were kind and honest
Thoughtful and generous
A gentleman through and through
I was so proud to have
A Dad like you.
God bless until we meet again.

Olive M. Eaves

The Four Beautiful Seasons

I love the summer's heat,
And the winter's cold;
I love the spring when all is young,
And adore them when they're old.
So, each separate season
I would choose
To write a poem on.

I love the haze of summer
And the perfumes of the air.
Yet, I love the chill of winter
And the frosty everywhere...
I love the newness of springtime
When all the snow has gone;
And the colours of the autumn,
I adore them every one...

Each season I have chosen
Has a beauty all its own -
A poetically beautiful setting
For 'my English country home'.

Mary Pauline Winter

My Identical Twin - As We Part

You mirror my emotions
You understand my pain
You know about my frailties
You know my fears again.

I don't think I can do it
Survive without you here
You hold me up - not push me down
Believe in me - not jeer.

Happy we can always be
Together - not a rift
I love you with my heart and soul
This is my parting gift.

Lynne Rivers

You Said You

You said you knew
how I felt about you,
you said you wished
you felt that way too,
you said you hoped
we could stay friends,
but what you couldn't say
were the words, I love you.

You left, I cried
but I didn't know why
I wasn't the one for you,
you wanted much more than before
when I gave all my heart to you.

I don't know what went wrong,
whether we grew apart
or whether love was too strong.
One thing I do know
of one thing I'm sure,
there's a room in my heart
and you hold the key of the door.

Martin Stelges

Take My Hand

Your hand to me reach out.
Being unsure whether I should take it
Loving you, but left in doubt
Did you love me or did you fake it?

I'll never know now, so far away,
Images of a hand so strong
Taut urgently as if to say,
Come to me, dear, where you belong.

Your voice whispers softly in peace,
No suffering, no pain, no tears,
Come to now, troubles will cease,
For where I am there are no fears.

Lynda Long

To Mother

Oh, Mother just what have I done,
To feel the way I do.
Because there are so many things,
That I would like to say to you.
I'd like to turn the clock back,
And live my life again,
To be loved and really wanted,
Free from fear, or guilt or shame.
But looking back won't change things,
Or the way things are today,
Because the thing I wanted most in life
Is but a few short miles away.
So I'll just love you from a distance,
And see you when I can.
I love you more than words can say,
Don't forget, your loving daughter,
Ann.

Ann Timmins

The Inside That Counts!

My magic box is fashioned with
gems and pearls and real gold curls
with sparkling jewels, emerald balls
a cluster of diamonds, the finest silk.
A wall of rubies, sapphires and
opal stones the colour of milk.

In my magic box it would be
delightful for me,
if I could keep
Neil Armstrong's first leap.

When a baby first smiled.
The laughter of a child,
the sweet smell of a rose
the river when it flows.

Some really kind words,
the song of some birds.
A feather from a peacock tail,
a wish from a wishing well.

And just for good measure,
a helping hand I would treasure.

Tanya Caruana

The Game Of Life

You reach into darkness
Knowing nothing is there,
Just a deep empty cavern,
A hope and a prayer.

You still close your eyes,
In vain you are sure,
For something uncertain,
Behind a locked door.

Your patience is waning
And how your heart aches,
For someone to give you,
What everyone takes,

But this is the nature,
Of the games people play,
With rules to be broken,
And rules to obey.

And throughout this process,
We all have our turn,
To be taught our importance,
To be taught how to learn . . .

Lisa Courtier

Forgotten Friends

I look at the picture on the shelf
Remember the friends I had back then.
Remember their quirky habits—
Those that endeared me to them.

The best of friends,
Never a stronger group:
Loulla, Miguel, Wayne,
You only had to look

To see how close we were,
How strong the bond.
We thought it would last
I guess we were wrong.

We all went separate ways,
Some of us kept in touch.
I still see Matthew today,
Though only now and then—not much.

One by one, I stopped writing to them,
They stopped writing to me,
Back then we'd never have said
That forever could never be.

Mark Gunther

Watching - Dreaming

Sitting in the garden chair
Breathing in the breezy air,
I watch the insects large and small,
While dozing off as sleep befalls.

I see the bumblebee on clover hover.
The ants just racing for some cover.
Butterflies with colours bright,
Winging past on their last flight.

A snail curled tight within its shell,
Away from dangers, who can tell.
As I sit with eyes half closed,
I see ladybirds on flowers reposed.

Grasshoppers chirp in reeded grass.
The flowers close their petals at last.
The sun goes down and gnats appear,
In shady places a buzz I hear.

I must arise this end of day
From my dream where insects lay.

Beryl Smyter

Bittersweet Love

A woman is a taste of hell,
  A taste as sweet as wine.
A taste that men so often find,
  So bitter yet divine.

A woman can be sweet and kind,
  And then as cruel as fire.
To use a man to gain her ends,
  Then tread him in the mire.

Most women know not what they want,
  Nor seem to even care.
As long as they can break a heart,
  No pity do they spare.

A woman is like the sweetest rose,
  But look out for that thorn.
For it is sure to prick your hide,
  And tear your flesh with scorn.

All this I know yet do not care,
  For a woman is what I need.
But not just any one will do,
  It is for you I plead.

John M. Thomas

The Futility Of War

The stench of death was in the air
The ground covered with gore
Many a brave lad had died there
The futility of war

The faceless men pulling strings
Herding their men like cattle
With hatred and fear the only thing
Accompanying them to battle

Both sides fighting for common ends
To make this world a better place
Millions of lives they will expend
Even God averts his face

Many a wife will become a widow
No father for the child she bore
No dad to see his young son grow
The futility of war

And when the final battle's fought
And peace breaks out once more
Future generations must be taught
The futility of war

J. H. Allen

Time Is A Healer

People say that time will heal
But it's just not so
They also say that in time
All the hurting will go.

But my heart will always miss a beat
When someone mentions her name
Oh, I can't eat and I can't sleep
I guess I'll never be quite the same.

Life used to be so happy and gay
Then we drifted apart
I'll never forget those happy days
She will always be here in my heart.

So to those people who say
That time will heal
It's obvious that they don't know
The way I still feel.

P. R. Williams

The Modern World

See the people sitting there
All that they can do is stare
No one at all seems to care
That they face life in despair
They have no homes, no hope,
No life,
All they know is poverty,
Misery, and strife,

Their children cry
Their babies die
There is no sunshine
In their sky

To health and happiness
They have said good bye
I guess all they want to do is die

Elizabeth Mary Reid

Spring

Buds burst from branches,
Bird songs erupt,
Mosquito prances,
Ice hills corrupt.

Cloud crowd and clashing.
Rain fries tree top.
Fish return splashing,
New creatures hop.

Spring rushes onwards,
Earth's painting green,
Wet water down pours.
World's newborn sheen.

Kristina Holt

Seacliff

Rough sea pounds upon the rocks
Where cliffs tower high above
Home to Jackdaw and the Dove.
Clifftop thrusts into the air
Where Fulmar stiff wing glides
And Gannet on the current rides.
Fissures cleave the rugged rock
Kittiwakes noisily "kittiwaak" cry
As Auk and Puffin whirr by.
On grassy ledge and slope
Thrift, mallow and campion
Fine flowers looking champion.
Upon weather worn ledges
Guillemots all in a row
Whilst Shags nest far below.
I stride over these lofty cliffs
Open, airy, wild and free
And let their spirit speak to me.

Malcolm S. Arnott

Stolen Treasures

To lose a child, I can't explain
The feeling deep within of pain,
Our precious children on life's crest.
Prematurely laid to rest.
Life will never be the same,
For people living in Dunblane.

Sixteen angel faces,
And a teacher brave and kind,
Let's not forget the memories
Each one has left behind.

Grief is a dreadful burden,
A weight upon the heart,
Such emptiness we feel inside,
When those we love depart.

Are we expected to forgive,
Is this the reason why we live,
To test the strength of our endurance
And look to God for reassurance.

Jennifer Parker

Two Rooms

Across from a ten room
mansion for two
One room, our cloakroom
One room, our sitting room
One room, our dining room
One room, our kitchen
One room, our washroom
One room, our bedroom
One room . . .
On Saturdays
The score of us and the baby
Take the mattress outside
Under the heat of the sun
And kill bedbugs
Outside—the other room

Odalo Kio

Pills

Pills tae mak'ye fat
An' pills tae slim ye doon
There's even pills tae stop ye
When ye'r birlin roon' and roon'
There's pills tae cure yer tummy aches
An' pills tae mak'ye sleep
An' mair tae wauk ye up again
If yer sleep becomes o'er deep
There's pills tae tak awa'yer pain
Nae maitter where it's stingin'
An' mak ye feel a richt again
Ev'n when ye jist feel "hingin"
When somethin's stoonin' onywhere
Jist reach oot fur "the pills"
Whit a blessin' we have a cure
Fur a' oor little ills
Sic a nuisance it can be
When ye suffer frae cystitis
But noo there is a new disease
A' think it's ca'd Pillitis.

Margaret Johnston

The First Impression

The impression one gives
Is one that lasts forever.
One that starts a chain
To bring two hearts together.
To succumb to the other,
Sending the notion as if to bother.
With the motion that starts the chain
Of joy, of love, of pain
One that a mind cannot contain.

Rob Tapley

With Love . . . To Him

I have learnt to trust,
Only him.
A secret lust,
Over him.
I wake in the night,
Thinking of him.
My bright candlelight,
Burns for him.
A sweet gentle smile,
Blossoms for him.
And all this while,
Just for him.
A sense of security,
When I'm with him.
A gentle kiss,
Lives for him.
My heart's beating,
With love . . . to him.

Jennifer A. Hayes

School Prayer

In this house of learning
May God reside,
May teachers and children
Work happily side by side.

As the fleeting years pass
And the mould is cast,
May all the memories
and friendships
forever last.

Kathleen M. White

Passing Clouds

Clear skies of forget-me-not blue,
Clouds like balls of cotton,
Glimpsed for a moment, then swept away
And at once they are forgotten.

Constantly changing in shape and form
The clouds rush swiftly by,
Tearing themselves apart as they race
Across the brilliant sky.

Now a monster, now a bird,
Silhouettes constantly changing:
A never ending picture show
For ever re-arranging.

Here on earth we are much like clouds
Always in such a hurry.
Never stopping to wonder why,
Or learning not to worry.

Life has so much to offer us
If we only give it a chance,
So have good look at the clouds today,
Not just a passing glance.

Patricia Stockdale

Dooms Day

Is the world the same,
I ask myself each day,
For I have lived a long, long, time,
In this place I have to stay.

I wonder is there life outside,
Are there any people there,
Since they dropped that final bomb,
All I feel is deep despair.

And yet I can't remain,
I must find my destiny,
I might die of radiation,
But at least I will be free.

Ruth Doyle

The Weeping Willow

The weeping willow
weeps because summer is over,
drooping over the ground
like a sulking child,
that summer has gone.

Lemony leaves sweep past the willow,
like twirling ballerinas,
the willow mourns,
her leaves are
crumbling,
   withering,
      twirling
to the ground,
only to be crunched
by passing feet.

Suzanne Roberts

Do Blondes Have More Fun?

Miss Peroxide,
Standing there
Hand on thigh
posing.

Bimbo, dimbo, living in limbo.
Waiting,
For anything that's male.

Clichéd baby
A species that will never die out.

Hollowed out statue.
With a smile like cultured silk.
Black ink eyes.

Experienced, yet, quivering child
Is what blokes see.
Oh, honey, protect me.

Heidi Ortmann

The Mangroves

Kawau preens
snake neck
bent
and
dragon beak
shuffles
feathers
softly through yesterday
tomorrow
today slippery
sided channel winds
water sly
mangroves grope
from crab hold mud
old
stubble
breathes
with spawning ocean.

Julia Yearsley

Music Lover!

You, are like a musician,
   you touch chords,
play the right rifts,
   and hit the top notes
in a pianissimo . . .
   that the ultimate
crescendo is reached . . .
   our bodies entangled
in eclectic flow . . .
   my veins rhythmically pulsate
and my nerve-endings, tingle
   with the intermezzo.

Jan King

Kathleen

With Irish brogue on one's tongue,
That is how your name is sung,
At tenors lips your name it hung,
From Irish loins you were sprung.

Spanish mix shows in your grace,
Young Colleen with a fresh face,
No make-up or lipstick show,
To spoil complexions that do glow.

Now in the autumn of your days,
Deep in thought you sit and gaze,
At your life in different ways,
Hoping memories do not haze.

Then I look into your face,
A young Colleen with Spanish grace.

K. R. Hirons

Memories

Think back to 19...
Then onward through the years
All the happy times together.
Filled with laughter joy and tears
Take it slowly as you ponder
All the little thing's we've done
At the time were so exciting
And gave us so much fun
I am happy dear for both of us.
The past has been just fine
Now to day I hope especially
You will have a lovely time.

Norman Mew

Cancer Clinic

We sit
in lines,
look nonchalant,
Flick desultory pages,
chat,
watch, in ferny forests
diversionary fishes
dart.

Fish that in lit tanks
glow,
silver and blue,
red, gold
and black
and black

And Black.

Mary Markwell

The Tyrant

The tyrant rapes and plunders,
This land he does not own,
His armies all seem brainwashed,
An evil seed is sown.

A brilliant army is amassed,
To keep the foe at bay,
His army get well beaten,
So turn and run away.

We think that war is over,
That we have peace at last,
But the tyrant sends his army out,
Innocents they blast.

Other countries go to help,
To feed and clothe each day,
But as another baby dies,
The tyrant gets away.

Dave Maxfield

Untitled

Glacier of my soul
melting - sun bound- to the thrill

Dancing Daisies
upward growing
Pleasure throwing
freedom in the eye of a book
Beholder.

My vast mountainous range of dreams
escape with Dove wings flying south.

Emma Campen

Free Choice

Only the abnormal
Can legitimately claim
Not to have free choice

The rest of us
Have free choice
To be or not to be
That is always the question

How often do we hear
That "I did this"
Because "so and so"
Made me do it

How often do we claim
I was forced
I was influenced
I was made to

Even at gun point
We still have a choice
To live or to die

Anna C. Mupawaenda

Untitled

'Tis a funny world we live in
of tents 'n' tops, o' pens and pots
materialism, opinion
insult or compliment, who knows
not I
do 2, do twenty?
what is wrong what's right?
Things left things lost
the ways of peoples turn to ghosts
still here to tend the future.

D. Russell

The Empty Place

No one to share the table
Just an empty chair I see,
No one to share the music
Sitting on the old settee.

No more cosy lunches
In some quaint hotel bar,
Or meeting at the Half Way Inn
When I had travelled far.

No one to share the rambles
Along the lanes or by the sea;
No one to help with shopping
Or make the early morning tea.

I see you in the garden
Resting in the old deck chair,
I see you in the kitchen
Making meals for us to share.

I think about you daily,
Hold your picture in its case;
Now all I have are memories
To fill this empty place.

Barbara Doherty

Your Spirit Lives On

As my body lays in its surround,
My spirit lives on it holds no bound.
I am not alone others are here,
You cannot see me I cannot appear.
If I visit you any time or place,
You would not know I leave no trace.
Death may scare but do not fear,
Your spirit lives on and I will be near.

Trevor Codd

Dawn To Dusk

At six o'clock in the morning
The sun rises to bring a new day
The birds start cheeping
As people awaken to start their day
As the morning progresses, the sun
Reaches its maximum height in the sky
Birds are playing overhead
The temperature is at its highest
The sun begins to go down
People arrive home to settle down
for the evening
The birds return to their nest
Finally, the sun is gone
The sky is dark
That is the end of the day.

Keith Bandy

The Rascal

What would we do without him?
What would our lives be like?
Without our little rascal,
Who gives us so much fright,
He's always into mischief,
He keeps us on the run,
He really thinks he's 'Jack the Lad',
When banging on his drum.
He always throws a tantrum,
When he can't get his way.
If mum is very busy,
Dad's not there to play.
He has such wily, cute ways,
Knows he'll always win.
'Cos, we love him very dearly.
A weakness, we give in.
When it comes to bedtime,
We say "Oh thank you God,"
For our lovely little rascal,
Who's now in land of Nod.

M. E. Owen

The Hobo

What good are words in flowery prose
to an embittered, haunted life?
Words won't fill his belly up
or ease his pain and strife.
Words won't keep him warm at night
When rain beats on the ground
Words won't give him freedom
from this awful life he's found
Words so full of promises
for him,...none will come true
they cannot shield his body
as a biting wind cut's through.
No knights in gleaming armour
or maidens fine and fair
no tower with Rapunzel in
to let down golden hair.
Just cold and thirst and hunger
to mar his every day.
What good are words in flower prose
they just get in the way.

Lesley Stockley

Xmas

A babe in Bethlehem,
A bright star above.
Hope, joy, peace and love.

An angel on the Xmas tree,
Hope in our hearts
There'll always be.

Families together,
A smile, a tear,
Joy in having loved ones near.

Windows bright,
Lights on the snow.
Happy children, faces aglow.

Friends send greetings,
A smile, a prayer,
Peace forever, everywhere.

Church bells ring out,
Carols we sing,
God's love envelops everything.

Dorothy F. Steer

Lost

Lost inside,
My foolish pride,
Of when the war had ended.
Still memories
Of death and blood,
Bombs from the sky
Descended.

Army planes,
Green and brown,
Missionary,
Traps of netting,
Opposition coming near,
New bombs
In the making.

Livvy Kimpton

Wise Advice

There was a gipsy wise,
She told me straight and true,
Love is not for finding,
'Tis for the taking of.
A stolen kiss gives far more pleasure
Than one that's freely given.
Enjoy the chase and make no haste,
Lay your snares with care,
Until in your arms he's driven.
And best of all you let him think
That he has freely given.

E. A. Condron

Useless - Just Like Me!

At the time the world seems useless,
Useless, just like me.
I ask myself in fear,
"When will I be set free?"
Every step I take in misery,
Every breath, I breathe in woe.
Where my heart is to take me,
I don't want to know.
My tears are a symbol of my mourning,
My thoughts are a colour of grey.
If this is just a game,
My anxiety votes not to play.
Recovery doesn't seem possible,
Happiness is never to be.
I suppose I'll just have to carry on,
Being plain and simple me!

Jessica Wilson

A Friend

Do you know my grandmother used
to have a saying;
May be it came from a song.
It was this; make new friends, but
keep the old.
One is silver but the other's gold.
We are living very different lives
We used to be playmates,
since that fell through.
We'll always be soul mates.
No matter how far apart we are, or
what's going on in our lives.
Grinning with pure joy.
"Soul mates for ever."
They shook hands on it.

Genowefa Ziarko

Weep Not

Weep not little willow tree
pale dormant in the hollow.
Accept this phase as destiny.
Comfort stems from certainty
assurance of tomorrow.

Has no one ever whispered
the changing season's tale
when nature's breath of spring evolves
from winter's icy gale?

The sun will warmly kiss your limbs
like a lover's soft caress.
Warm breezes gently will arouse
small buds of life within your breast.

So weep not little willow tree
nor hang your head in sorrow.
Sleep patiently and you will see
a fragrant dawn unfold tomorrow.

Marie Somerset

60 Plus

To reach the age of sixty on its
own is quite a treat and though
we know were getting old, we're
really at our peak. The things that
used to worry us no more are they
a bother. Instead we're searching
for activities to wile away the
hours, and in due course we join
a club that caters for our needs.
We play bowls or dance or paint,
we really have it made, and if we
have a pain or ache,
We laugh it off and blame it on
old age

Eileen Vinters

Precious Memories

Memories crowd of other days
When I walked life's road with you
Beside the sea, the hills and dales
In moonlight and in morning's dew
And when the sun was in the sky
Shadows played among the trees
In the flowing of the breeze
No words needed for we knew
Your dear heart was knit to mine
And new deal heart memories cling
  you are gone
    and I am left just looking on
      alone in time
You are not gone, indoors memories crowd

G. Camp

Timelessness

Of all creations
Surrounding us
We think ourselves
To be the stars

Yet how mistaken
We all are
To limit the grandeur
Of all around

Nothing's created
And none is graded
As we're all potential
Manifestations

Egos at large
Cause us all to judge
And expect things
To turn and budge

The reality is
That reality is myth
As all is shifting
In time and mist.....

Mary Attard

A Mother's Prayer

God we pray
see us through
to another day

Guide us in all we do
through the day and night

Let us remember always
the good to be had in
life

Things that cost nothing
like a smile or a kiss
Happiness a baby's love,
and at the end of the day
the thankfulness to kneel and
pray

Florence Williams

Autumn

O look and view on yonder hill
The trees of autumn shed their leaves,
Across the fields the golden sheaves
Are stacked before they go to mill.
The farmer standing calm and still
Looks aloft unto the eaves
And dreams of fortune in his sheaves
When they are ground in yonder mill.
And all around is peace and calm
And now he goes into his farm,
Labour done, sits down to rest
And takes his paper in his hands
While his young wife behind him
stands;
It is the hour they love the best.

B. Wright

Lament

My heart is wrung with sorrow.
My brow is lined with care
The hands once firm now tremble
With each imagined scare
My footsteps slow and weary
Though half my span not gone
Oh which of many turnings
Led me to this wrong.

James Phelan Girvin

An Ode To Mental Illness

My life is black
There is no sky
I just lie back
Days pass me by.

I sometimes lie in bed and think
of empty thoughts and notions,
I never seem to eat or drink
I have no motivation.

I just wish I could take a pill
That would help me carry on.
I lie and lie so very still
perhaps my day has gone.

Ruth Doyle

Visions Of Life

When I look outside my window,
I see so many things,
the birds that sit upon a tree,
the children on their swings;
The people with their shopping,
the stars that shine above,
the traffic bustling to and fro,
the couples so in love.
And yet I never wondered,
the beauty there could be,
for my life has been in darkness,
since I was only three.
But now I look around me
and gaze up to the sky,
for now my blindness has been cured,
I'm so happy I could cry.

Ruth Doyle

Hearing

What is sound?
They say it's all around
But I have never seen it
Is it square or oblong
Or really no shape at all
Does it float down like a feather
Or bounce just like a ball
It's something we take for granted
When we have ears that hear
To those who live in a silent world
It's akin to dread and fear
Can you talk quite normal
To those that are close by
And feel a fool when you answer
With the wrong reply
Please bear with us, it's not our fault
We cannot right a wrong
For sound to us is what we hear
Not the sound for which we long

G. A. Van De Voorde

Meditation

Endless thoughts, like mayflies,
Skim the moving stream
Emerging from nowhere,
To captivate the mind.

Ego-centred shadows,
Drawing like magnets,
Hypnotic and alluring,
They dominate the dance.

Let them all go softly,
Shrinking and fading,
Drift with murmuring senses
Into velvet depths.

Here, time has no meaning
There is only now.

Joyce Drackett-Case

The Scream

The abyss so deep,
the silent scream so loud,
the hurting so intense,
the eyes so frightened,
the wall so high,
the fright too much,
the night too black,
the shame too deep
covered over,
buried,
never to emerge again
to see the light of day.

Patricia McAuliffe

Young Hazel

Young Hazel standing in her raincoat
Forlorn amidst the tumbling rain
She somehow looks so wistful
I long to soothe away her pain

My sad maiden of the raindrops
A depth of beauties hidden there
Keep the heart that loves you
My Hazel young and very fair

If you're ever sad or lonely
And the world shows little care
Remember then to turn to me
My Madonna of the dark brown hair

I'll not let you wander lonely
With rainspots on that lovely brow
For I only want to love you
And steal away your heart somehow

I'll fold my arms around you
To calm the beating of your heart
And the truth that's in our love
Will live should life itself depart

John Donald Jebb

Weather Vain

The same old drops are falling,
like the tear drops from my eyes,
and the leaves are disbelieving,
with a distant season cry,
I can only branch into my life,
with a reason to begin,
and my only crying way out,
is to start my life again,
it's winters way of saying,
that life's not always black,
and a way of make-believing,
something better's coming back,
and you always must believe in,
the seasons they are few,
but it's equally important,
to hold your point of view.

Sandy Lees

The Awakening

My world had slipped.
The abyss was deep.
Could I come home
Once more to peace.
Yes, God has given
A second chance.
To a mortal soul
Whose life was lost
In the unknown.
I see again the rolling tide
And love is still a wondrous thing
So don't despair
God is always around
To help us pray
For happier times

Emily Cooley

Sea gulls

If only I had wings
Like the sea gulls over the sea,
I would no transport need
To go to Italy.

If only I could be
One with sands and sea and sky,
Less conceited than those monkeys are,
And yet could fly so high -

They all have the same outfit,
No rivalry and no strife,
But all have the same heavenly wings;
This is their blessed life!

If only I were such a heavenly
Creature that could fly -
Be one with water, wind, and sky.

Ida Potter

Only You!

Dedicated to my sister, Denise Cattermole

There's someone who's special
In so many ways
And gives me attention
And even praise.

And her love is the sunshine
That brightens my day
She brings only love
And brings the hate away

You're someone who's there
When my spirits are low
With her warmth and love
That constantly show

I'm proud to have
A sister like you
Someone who's special
And always true

Weather it's right
Or even wrong
You're always there
Standing strong!

Christina Cattermole

Suffering

Our lives can be empty
Lives can be dead
Jesus collapsed on the cross
His blood had been shed

Why do we have to suffer
Cannot all be the same
This is the answer
Jesus used it to rise again

Suffering can save the soul
He said I make broken people whole
Some day we shall understand pain
Know it is eternal life to gain

D. Dean

Adagio

Don't say this time
This perfect time
This time from nowhere
Is wasted
Or that I may not enter
The secret door of blue
Beyond the cruel boundaries of love
Almost invisible
Tired of flight
Two butterflies suspended
Above a sea of glass

Margaret Froud

Apocalypse

Innocence prepares, sinners repent,
The world stands deficient in belief,
Apocalypse in sight,
So many lacking in armour,
Return to the womb,
The vagabonds of infinity,
To the afterlife we assume.
Solitary, our souls lie dormant,
To us impeccable, oblivion the fear,
Realization the end is near,
Shall it be the beginning of an era,
Or the end of existence,
A remainder left behind,
Some may reminisce,
But a definite rendezvous,
Of which we remain unable to change,
To talk of purgatory,
Our souls no longer range...

Viola Hughes

The Fairies' Dance

In the moonlight bright and clear
Oh so wonderful, oh so dear
Hopping and dancing on the grass
With their shoes of crystal glass
Danced the fairies
Golden are their dresses
Shining are their tresses
Oh so wonderful they do look
In their tiny little nook.

Claire Ellison

Untitled

A willow bends
But it doesn't break
A heart can mend
A new life you make

But you never forget
The roots of love
Deep down they hold
Like the heaven above

When water falls
The ripples they make
Like the rings of love
On the shores they break

A beauty surrounds you
Everyone can see
And in my loneliest of hearts
If only you could be

I would treasure you forever
Perhaps one day you'll see

Gavin Young

An Ex-Patient

She thought I looked so cute
as I settled on her knee,
But I was getting ready
for a much long-needed pee!

She then decided to check me,
for signs of fleas or mites.
I had had enough of that
so I clawed and ripped her tights.

With the shock of this, she let me go
to run about the room,
While I was being so naughty
she quickly grabbed a broom!

I knew from this my time was up,
and the game I played must stop.
She picked me up, and told me off
but then gave me a choccie drop!

Sara Gardner (Veterinary Nurse)

And To All My Felines

O creature of exquisite grace
with mystic beauty in thy face,
who came into my home and heart
of my life to be a part,
who gave to thee that honey'd purr,
that golden eye, that silken fur,
set slender legs on nimble feet,
soft sleeking, sunlight seeking, fleet?
How oft have I, in loneliness,
sore needing solace after stress,
embraced thy softness, held it near,
and whispered in attentive ear
of all the problems and the strife
that oft beset this human life,
and, telling thus to one so true,
have found, in peace, my hopes renew.
O little cat, thou may'st not know
just Who it was that made thee so,
but I do know, and all life's way
shall humbly thank Him every day.

W. Slater

Sam

Pearl drop tears fall down my face
As I cry my tears of pain
Sorrow washes down my cheeks
Each time I hear your name.
All I have left is memories
Now you're not by my side
I wish that you were still with me
I wish you'd never died.

If you hadn't borne the pain alone
If you'd only ever asked,
If I'd only heard your cries for help
Your sorrow might have passed.
Instead you kept the pain inside
Too proud to turn to friends
If you'd only told the way you felt
You might not have known the end.

Emily Bumby

Shadows (Three Japanese Haiku)

Shadows in Autumn,
deep and long, walking ahead,
my own steps in theirs.

Our imagining,
like the shadows before us,
dreams that mark our way.

Shadows in Autumn,
cast by the Son's wondrous light,
illuminating.

P. E. Coppen

Life

What is life?
It's given to us for free
But would we choose it
If we could pick it from a tree?

What is life?
They say it's what we do
But have we any choice
I'm asking you!

What is life?
It's sometimes hard to take
We smile through good and bad
For others sakes!

What is life?
A pathway through the years
Alone or with others
It ends and then there are tears!

That's life!

Doreen Fay

The Angel

Do you believe in Angels?
I most certainly do
I spoke to one, the other night
That angel dear, was you.

With your neat trim figure
Personality too,
All men would be happy
If all angels were like you.

Just one kiss from an angel's lips
To me would be a treat
If it ever came true for me
My heart would miss a beat.

When I get to heaven
I'd think, my life was not in vain
Especially if I were to meet,
An angel named Elaine.

It would remind me of my time on earth
Of things I've done, and seen.
Memories that mean so much to me
Like my angelic beauty Queen.

Frank King

Rapprochement

Standing alone in shimmering haze
An island in a playful sea
Fearful when high tide is reached
Lest its solitude be breached

Unresponsive to siren calls
From dancing flotsam all around
Drifting where the flow dictates
Away from where reality waits

Forbidding face impedes advances
Protective mask a masquerade
A ploy to keep the world at bay
To hide a centre of softest clay

Remoteness caused by seismic shock
Wary of the heaving swell
In depths conflicting forces surge
With mainstream it may once more merge

The stony facade will slowly fade
Returning at last from whence it came
Estrangement drawing to an end
Encroachment greeted as a friend

Robert Warren Reed

Memories

Fairest England, that I love,
Dear to me, where'er I rove;
Pray to thee I'll soon return
From foreign clime, where earth burn.

To know again thy pleasant fields,
Where troubled mind to beauty yields;
Or sit beside thy mossy streams,
Would satisfy my fondest dreams.

Let me hear the song of bird,
'Midst thy leafy hedgerows, heard,
Trilling forth his song of praise
To God, amidst thy woodland ways.

To walk the paths that ever wend
'Neath the rustling boughs, that bend
With every gust of wind that blows
A great desire within me grows.

Let me gaze upon thy hills,
Whose grandeur, awe in me instills;
Or on thy placid lakes, reflecting
The magic sky with sun a-setting.

Rennie Kirby

Sailing

The hiss of waves,
the heavy silence
of the night,
far above me
A meteor streaks
Across the sky,
A fiery lance
Just passing by,
Phosphorescence in the sea
Shimmering trails of light,
Plankton spawn
The shapes of fish
The silky coming
Of the dawn,
Gone, the heavy
Silence of the night.

Andrew W. Shiston

Equal Shares

How precious time is
But do we count its worth.
Each day the waking angel,
Presses coins in our hand.
The rich and poor all
Receive equal shares alike.
Everyone must spend them
Before the curfew bell
And ask themselves the question
Did I spend them well?

R. De B. Hovell

The Fourth Season

My eyes were full of landscape,
All contours covered in white,
The air was crisp and chilling,
The blue sky startling and bright,
The countryside was covered,
Like the icing on a cake,
It slowly woke from a dreamy sleep,
Ice and crystal shimmering on the lake,
Icicles hanging down,
Like jewels dripping from the trees,
Sparkling, glimmering droplets,
Shivering in the breeze,
Red Robins adding colour,
To the white and snowy ground,
The beauty of winter has now been found.

Pam Williams

47, 48, 49

It's that time of the night again
You sit with pen and paper ready
Yes you have, no you haven't
You start to feel unsteady.

You have one, then have two
You check and check again
If there's three you've even a tenner
Oh! It's such a pain.

Let's try next week, you never know
We could get four or five
So there we sit, fingers crossed
And suddenly come alive.

The balls are juggled, out they pop
One, two, three, and four
Two more numbers for the Jack
And life will change forevermore.

Five and six we've won the lottery
You check and scream that's what you do
We were lucky this time round
You never know, "It could be you".

Jane Foster

My Window

I sit by my window
And look at the view
The sea rolling by
Thinking of you

Looking at the sea
Has a calming effect
Giving the troubled mind
Time to reflect

Sometimes it's calm
With a mirrored silence
Sometimes it's wild
With a feeling of violence

If you could join me
And look at the sea
You'd feel much better
You'd love what you see

Nancy Wilkie

With My Nose

I can smell a fresh cut lawn,
and a day newly born.
Or maybe! it is Christmas time,
oranges, cigars, and wine.
Fresh ground coffee,
homemade toffee.
Fir cones, burning in the hearth.
Powdered baby, from its bath.
Wallflowers in the summer sun.
Evening primrose, when day is done.
In the dusk,
the scent of musk.
Violets, that never should,
ever be taken from a wood.
Wet earth, and fallen leaves,
dancing in the heady breeze.
Tangy pine,
smells divine.
But! always when I smell a rose,
I am glad that God gave me a nose.

J. Purbrick

My Prayer

To die is but to live again.
And I can't wait to see,
the smile on my "Dear Lords" face,
when he welcomes me,
He died to save us all you know,
He was just thirty three,
it's hard to think he gave his life,
for others such as me.

Joyce Barrett

Waiting

All your life you sit and wait
You never know what for
Then one day a little boy
Comes knocking at your door

Hello Grandma he says
I'm Stephen how do you do
It's taken God a long time
To send me to you

You see the face of an angel
In this boy so pure and bright
I know now when I pray to God
He hears my prayers at night

The wait is over now
This little boy is here
All my love I give him
Because he is so dear

Jean Davison

Uncaring

Is it nothing to you
All ye that pass by.
Do you not the flowers see?
Or the beauty of the sky?

Is it nothing to you
All ye that pass by.
Each day, week, year.
Left empty as they fly.

Is it nothing to you
All ye that pass by.
That hate has taken root
And stands faceless nigh

Is it nothing to you
All ye that pass by.
That a little love given.
May save a life "try"

Is it nothing to you
All ye that pass by.
That urgent call "cry"
Was yours not answered "why"

Norman W. Bracey,
Chelsea Pensioner

Seven Magpies

One for sorrow, so they relate
But not on this, your wedding date.
Two for joy was simply grand,
Now at your resting place I stand.
Three a letter, for you no more -
How still they lie, inside the door.
Four a boy, though you had two,
One storeman and a scholar true.
Five for silver, just like your hair
So proudly bourne in your armchair.
Six for Gold, your wedding ring
Blessed in church, one final thing -
Seven a secret never told,
To you, we never did get old.
Now as free spirits
Through the fields you fly,
Like seven magpies playing
That I did Espy!

T. G. Bloodworth

The Storm

Black clouds forming
while the wind is roaring
The thunder crashes by.
The Rain comes slamming down.
"I wonder", when the storm is o'er,
"Whether" we will see blue sky,
The lightning strikes -
I wonder where
Its power lands below
will it be on the hill tops
Forest, or stream below.

A. S. Moore

Words

Tunes in your head
Come alive with your hands,
Pluck a string,
Bang a drum,
Blow a trumpet,
All make a sound.
Bring all these together
a song is born.
Now find the words
and a singer to note,
bring alive rhythm and sound.

Lesley White

Why?

The sun always shines,
The rain always falls,
A flower withers and dies,
Why?

Green leaves turn brown,
Blue oceans turn black,
A river runs dry,
Why?

A car moves too fast,
A puppy is killed,
A happy child cries,
Why?

Dreams become fears,
A smile becomes tears,
A love begins to die,
Why?

A planet is hurting
A world without mercy,
Man does not try,
Why?

Marvyn B. Candler

Poet

What, can one expect
From your 'loom'...?
A tangled 'weft'...
To form a 'tapestry' - in tune...?

A tune, to soothe
All listening ears...
To words of love;
Or passions - lost - in tears

Shed not always, in grief, or pain:
As is their normal want;
But also tears of joy - to gain:
From life's baptismal font.

The gifts from heaven,
That in richness - earth abound:
Move they ever, the eager pen:
To capture, each murmuring sound.

So!... O Poet: compose in mind:
Your tuneful words, for aye;
Speech - transient - as the wind;
Words - forever - will stay.

Lawson Henry Brookes

Too Many Empty Plates

I've eaten too much apple pie,
I've eaten too many buns,
The ice-cream was delicious,
But now there's no more fun.

There's too many empty plates,
Too many empty plates,
It's too late to ask for a cake,
There's too many empty plates.

The orange squash has now all gone,
So has the lemon, too,
Mum and dads, gone down the pub.
And you ask me why I'm blue.

Mum said, "Do the washing up"
Dad said, "Dry them dry"
I do not like the washing up
And here's the reason why

There's too many empty plates
Too many empty plates,
I might make too many breaks
On too many empty plates.

P. R. A. Somerville

Do Hurry

O come on dad,
The film will start,
No second cup of tea.
Please hurry up mum,
The film will start,
Your face looks fine to me.
Let's speed up brother mine,
The film will start,
All comic books must wait.
Do be quick sister dear,
The film will start,
He won't forget your date.
Gathered safely at the door.
One final look to check.
On no I've seen the film before.

Jackie Billett

Mortality

So suddenly we reach
From flashing days of certain life,
With body strong and thick—
So straight
A future we will see is right,
Our heritage to leave.

To this, a canopy of fear
And shame—
That we did mould this screaming,
Death's-head horror of a world.
Fear we now sag, or nod, and droop
A scaly thin thatched head.
A swelling gut, a purpling vein—
From then—the future all to win
Is but a moment to our end
And shame.

Owen Dan Jones

Katherine, My Muse

You are the wonder of your sex
the epithet of womanhood,
a lit candle no one dare vex
because no one could.
All conquered hearts wished
they had kissed
this Venice of femininity.
Consenting to warm my cold heart
we make love, unbridled and unrivalled.
Like an eternal infant,
I am shielded from the nightmares
of living on my own
and dying alone.
You are no longer just in my prayers
or in my dreams,
but the centre of my entire life
the reason for my being.
Marry me, Katherine
and be my wife.

Julian Wall Hayes

To My Wife

Light and springy are her steps
A pearl that shines up from the depths
Her hair is fair and softly curled
She lightens up our dull old world
Shrugging off advancing years
She sets example to her peers
Life's problems she takes in her stride
Her doubts and troubles tends to hide
To me she shows great tenderness
And patience with my sometimes stress
To all she shows her love of life
This lovely lady is my wife.

John Thomas

Ode To A Rose

Rose O Rose so fine a flower
Blooming bright upon yon bower,
Your fragrant perfume fills the air
Rose dear Rose so fine and fair.

Those tender petals smooth as silk
Some perchance pure white as milk,
Brilliant reds like burning fire
O Rose of you I'll never tire.

Beads of crystal from the dew
On your leaves of soft green hue,
Sparkling clear as teardrops tender
Rose O Rose so full of splendour.

Such is the Rose with colours bright
Lasting beauty from morn till night,
Brightening each dismal day
O Rose sweet Rose so gay.

The emblem fair of this our land
Sown no doubt by God's own hand
Fairest bloom for thee I pray
Rose my Rose, don't fade away.

Doris Vellam

The Orphan Child

When I was made an orphan child,
And left to fend and grow up wild,
I found myself just roaming round,
At night my bed was on the ground,

So cherish all that life can send,
And hope this beauty will never end,
To wake and feel the morning dew,
See spiders' webs so pearly too,

I've wandered far across this land,
Yet not a friend to lend a hand,
And the only things that I possess,
Are my health and happiness.

So as the evening turns to night,
And the moon sheds its eerie light,
Now the mist rolls across the ground,
And listen to nocturnal sounds,

As the dawn creeps through the skies,
To the morning chorus I arise,
And all the birds they seem to say,
It's time to start another day,

D. G. Foster

Why?

Why can the deaf not hear?
Why can the blind not see?
Why can the lame not walk?
Why does this have to be?

They cannot hear the rain,
they cannot see the sea.
They cannot walk together,
why does this have to be?

Why is their life so silent?
Why is darkness all they see?
Why is their life so motionless?
Why does this have to be?

What have they done to deserve this?
What terrible crime could it be?
Why can't we all be the same?
and Walk and Hear and See?

Sue Rudin

Elaine

Emeralds perhaps if I were a King,
Lamb, if I'd be a shepherd bring,
As I am a wise man
I offer no emeralds, no lamb,
Nothing more than
Ever thoughtful. It is the best I can.

Ian E. Goddard

Time Passing By

The clock hands rotate
Second minute hour
The taste in my head
Turning distinctly sour
Another minute lived
Still no nearer
Yet another minute gone
Still no clearer
Time ever present
Stopping for nothing or no-one
Another night passed
Another rising sun
Time travelling forward
Where do I go from here?
Perimeters of time so fine
Yet life is so unclear
The ticking echoes in an empty heart
The working parts long since gone
The clock hands will always go round
But the time I show is wrong.

Glen Walker

The Wobbly Tooth

I had a wobbly tooth one day,
It really was quite funny,
And when it popped out of my mouth,
I hoped for pocket money.

I placed it under my pillow,
Thinking a fairy would appear.
I thought I was a clever girl,
"Oh" what a good idea!

I waited oh so patiently,
It soon must be the hour,
Please hurry Tooth Fairy and visit me,
To leave my money shower.

But Grandma told me no fairy comes,
Unless you are asleep,
So I think I'd better close my eyes,
Or maybe one last peep?

J. M. Yates

The World Around Us

Sometimes the world seems wrong,
So many bad things around.
Hurting people so helpless,
Who never make a sound.

The cry of tiny voices,
Ring around inside my head.
The cries for help,
Their needs which are unsaid.

So many people die,
As a mistake of others.
Just take a look around us,
See if anyone bothers.

I just sit and think,
What help can we give.
If we stopped the wars,
Then they all would live.

Tracey Coverdale

Just To Be There With You

On planes I will fly
Over sea I will sail
On land I will run
Just to be there with you

Through snow I will crawl
Over hills I will climb
Through fire I will walk
Just to be there with you

Through wars I will fight
On horseback I will ride
Will fight the wild cat
Just to be there with you

I would kill my best friend
I would fight to the end
I would give my last breath
Just to be there with you

But life can be mean
My life is a dream
I know we'll never meet
For a film star you're sweet

Susan Davies

Hindsight

You never see the changes day to day.
You have to step back to find
What's going on,
On your own front doorstep.
Look! (Unless you're blind).
Don't take a love for granted
Easy come, easy go.
Because all you will find
What's in the mind isn't really so.
Pay attention to the little things
Every day, every night.
Just try a little harder
To make everything all right.
Take hold of yourself.
There's nobody else
Can do it
For you.
Learn from what you've seen by day
And dreamt of during your night.

Steve J. Collier

Washing Up

I return to the sunlit kitchen.
From the bowl of glistening suds
Steam warms my face.
I mop automatically
Scraped stacked dishes,
A forest of cutlery;
And nurse in my mind
The frail aged body,
Once proud in her independence,
No longer able to help herself or me.
In the light of her weakness
My chore becomes my privilege.

Audrey Stapley

Temper

Brows furrowed, storm brewing
Tension mounting, as anger grows
The first signs appearing
Hear that heavy breathing
Moaning, groaning louder
Cutting, lashing, fiercely howling
Eyes flashing, steely cruel
A final whip, then energy spent
A softer breeze of breath apparent
Calmer now, we'll all sleep easy
With that violent storm at last abated.

Pat Royle

Loved With Love

Living together
As lovers do
Living entranced
With each other

Time is lost
To love and loving
Sublime excitement
Heading for utopia

Lovers' desires
Can be commands
But love is love
So give and be given

But mind love is fickle
If love is lost
Search now and find
Another lover tonight.

Jamie Williams

Untitled

Father Christmas won't be long
With his sack so full and strong
So full of gifts for you and me
Oh! What a Christmas this will be

Sweets and chocolates; crisps and meat
Golly me it's such a treat
Christmas lights and candles too
Decorations and mistletoe through

Underneath the Christmas tree
All the presents we will see
One for all the family
Oh how I wonder what they can be

The big night has now come
I cannot sleep I feel so numb
Then suddenly I wake and see
Lots of presents left for me

Susan Bowen

Acid Angels

Where is your angel now?
I break down when no one's around
To see this narcotic pain,
My halo crashing on the ground,
Worn out wings and vacant eyes
Where I used to shine,
Even my soul has abandoned me,
She ran away with a real angel
So real he made her whole,
She was my only possession,
Now he's all I can depend on,
They are the raft I cling to
Will their weight drag me down?
If I drown
I take them both with me,
Our lungs red raw
Filled with salty, stinging sea
To rust my silver skin,
My glitter washes away,
Reality is pain.

Carol Murray

The Sailor

The night was wild and stormy
the night that he was lost.
   Now all was still and quiet
except for the gentle lot of waves.
How bright the stars doth shine.
Who is this God that changes
mild to wild.
   It is the way to test
our faith, and make us worthy
of his heavenly home.

Nehaita Morgan

Therese

I love to lie among the wild flowers
In the field beyond the town
And to listen for the Church Bells
To tell me when it's noon.

To watch my father fishing
By the sparkling bright trout stream
Fills my heart with joy and gladness
He's my King and I'm his Queen.

I love to lie among the wild flowers
When sun is way up high
And reaches gold-tipped fingers
To warm me where I lie.

Summer perfumes drift and wander
Summer's haze is all around
I close my eyes and dream a little
In the field beyond the town.

Evening comes on shadowed feet.
It's time for us to roam
Back along the little path
That leads us to our home.

Kay Keating Cullen

Don't Ever

Don't ever lose that little smile
that says, I love you Dad

Don't ever lose that little frown
that says I've just been bad

Don't ever lose that puzzled look
that says I wish I knew

Don't ever tell that little lie
then wish that it were true

Don't ever fear the dark of night
as long as I am around

Don't ever lose your funny laugh
it's such a silly sound

Don't ever break a poor man's heart
to satisfy a whim

Don't ever jump into a pool
before you learn to swim

With all these rules I give you
you think life will be sad
but I don't want to lose you
because I am just your Dad.

Martin Morrell

The Countryside

Just outside the busy town
lies a land, unspoilt by man
as perfect as when time began—
a blanket of green and chequered brown.

Cattle grazing in the fields
wildlife's everywhere you go,
lambs skip playfully—to and fro
and rabbits eat the farmers' yields.

A stream dawdles down a hill
unhurried in this land of peace—
where God has granted us a lease
and time is almost standing still.

Trees standing side by side
not yet cut down for their wood
but growing old as they should—
so tall and wise and full of pride.

The air is fresh—so clean and pure,
invigorating heart and soul—
relieving stresses of life's toll
and worries trouble you no more.

Geoff Durham

Untitled

I am a wounded soldier
I am fighting for the course
I am fighting for the truth
And am fighting for the sword
And I swear by the devil
And I swear by the Lord
Am fighting for the truth
Am fighting for the course.

Am living on bread and water
And am waiting for the order
From behind these bricks and mortar
Am preparing for the slaughter
No I can't recall the reasons
For this war I am in
But love and hatred
Are such powerful things.

Mark Bridgeman

Untitled

Eyes of green,
Burning bright,
Eyes of magic,
Mystic light,
Now so sad,
Left so cold,
Lost to love,
Grown so old,
Never to find,
What was lost,
Left alone,
At such a cost.
Misted, frozen,
Lost the past,
Left alone,
In sadness vast.

Alison Smith

The Silent Sky

A thousand twinkling stars,
Shining in the silent sky.
Each one a dream.
One night so bright,
The next obscured by cloud.
Some already dead,
The rest waiting
To be touched
By hands so gentle
They will not break.
I know one star
Belongs to me;
What I do not know
Is how to reach it.

K. Heidi Johnston

Hunting

Stop the hunting,
is what I say.
For man kills animals,
every day.

Stop the killing,
now! I say,
Let them live,
another day.

Stop the slaughter,
is what people cry.
But still man shoots,
and still they die.

Stop it now,
for it's not fair.
Surely out there
Someone must care.

Bethan Roller

Captain For A Day

Down upon the swollen river,
On a make shift raft of timber,
Acting out the role of Captain,
Stands a small boy known as Tommy.

Brave the young boy with his cut lass,
Hoisting up the jolly roger,
floating now to deeper water.
Unaware and not much caring.

From the wood those fibres loosen,
Escaping free the match stick timber,
Tommy falls to depths unyielding,
Cries now muffled by lungs of water,

Pity his folks at home unknowing,
Also Tommy who's life has ended,
Laid there now in a watery graveyard,
Silt and weed's his body covering.

C. F. Vernon

Teenage Wonder

Once, I could laugh with you,
tickle you,
play hide and seek,
tease too,
Fly you thru' the sky
floating on the world
of happiness and innocence,
Cuddle and hug.
Now you look at me
and wonder -
wonder why,
why did I change
wonder where
has this magic gone,
senility is not breached yet -
yet, no more do I do the things
that made us equal
in your sight.

Jack Ryan

The Group

Sitting in the van, we talked.
Lying in the van, we laughed.
Speaking of things we'd done before
Somewhere back there in the past.
Drooling over bottles, we giggle.
Talking about love, we ponder.
Truths coming out, we speak our mind.
With alcohol dragging us under.
What about love or lust?
Just not agreeing, we argue
Do what we want, feel how we can.
Saying to who what we want to
Swigging back tonic and gin.
Feeling quite happy with friends
Now I'm content, I smile.
And I'm hoping that this never ends.

Alexandra Clare Lymer

Untitled

It's quiet now the heat has passed
And sanity prevails at last
When ugly rumour raised its head
The unions tiny voice was dead

The press for selfish reasons show
The truth they did not want to know
They smeared and spat in vicious tone
At nothing! If the truth were known

Oh! We know the men were wrong
Their right to discipline was gone
But Oh! What silly childish prose
About a noose that never was

Tom F. Elliott

A Cottage For Sale

A broken fence, a gate with no latch
An old fashioned cottage
With the roof well thatched
Tiny windows, two down and two up
And one that keeps banging
Because it won't shut
A door that needs painting
And old rusty nails
And on a board a cottage for sale
Now this sweet old lady
Will be leaving soon
For a long time ago here
She spent her honeymoon
For now she's alone
And all on her own
This little old cottage
She once called home.

Jill Hale

My Roundelay

As the ripples of a pool circle
    round in bigger curls
and the spring comes drifting lightly
    with its gentle swings and swirls,
how my heart it is so happy
    for again I see it all,
with my little one beside me
    just in case he might fall.

The pleasure of the past life
    comes now into view,
with the golden-headed rod
    and the silver-headed dew.
I thank God that he is with me
    as I do my daily task,
and my little one's beside me
    as we sit upon the grass.

Sally Crook-Ford

Kitchen Lament

Why must fitted kitchens be
designed by men of six foot three
while I am only five foot tall
and cannot reach the shelves at all?
Straining up to get the bread,
tins come tumbling on my head.
When I'm working at the sink
it's not as easy as you'd think
to peel the spuds and wash the veg
with armpits jammed down on the edge.
As for work tops, it's a devil
rolling dough at shoulder level.
Concealed lighting shining bright
shades the cupboard doors from sight.
If one I should forget to close
I get a bang upon the nose.
To reach the cupboards 'neath the sink
is hell when knees are on the blink.
Complain, you say! They'd only mutter
"another letter from a nutter!"

Freda Pryor

Cheating Death

I went to a place called death once,
not very long ago,
I went to a place called death once,
when I did not want to go,
to prayers I clung,
to life I hung,
not for me was that dark place,
not even pain made death a grace.

Lorette Poland

My Father

My father was a little man
His stature it was small
But as his heart was full of love
He seemed like 10 feet tall
He could be strict he could be mean
He could get really mad
But then he'd smile and be contrite
And then I'd think he's not so bad.
He was so kind and generous
He was so loving too
He loved his wife and family
Was honest through and through
He is no longer with us
The angels came to call
They took my dad to heaven
Where he stands true and tall
I really miss my dad so much
It really seems unfair
We don't appreciate what we've got
Until it's no longer there.

Elizabeth Gardner

His World

The penguin, puffin and mole
He made each perfect for their role...
The hippo, platypus and giraffe are
Often "good for a laugh"
Our Lord - though holy - has given us
Laughter to enable us to live...
"Happily ever after"...

Patricia Lawrence

The Autumn

The hibernation comes at last,
The Autumn leaves come swirling
fast,
The birds fly off to warmer places,
And here come these cold, red faces.
The squirrels store,
More and more.
The leaves don't exist,
And the hedgehogs must have a very
long list,
Of what they want to store.
The acorns fall,
For the squirrels to store
with berries.
Crispy leaves upon the ground,
Make a lovely crunching sound.

Emma Louise Ward

Reflections

Festooned with garlands of my past
So heavy that they scar my neck
And pull down on my face
Making me stare at the floor
Disgraced
Don't want to wear them anymore

Don't want to see the black of earth
But the umbrella blue of sky
Retracting into night
Scared into submission, fearful
At the sight
Of lamenting cloud eyes, tearful

But I can only see reflections
Broken shards of mirror dreams
Lie festering at my feet
And the images are scattered
Obsolete
Deranged and shattered
Yet I know a piece is missing
For my view is incomplete

Stephanie Metcalf

Skin Deep

I saw the forest from a distance,
Its beauty moved me deeply.
Its height, depth, vivid green
Spoke all of strength and power.
Then I moved in closer
I moved beneath the trees and
Found that all about me now
Was rot, corruption everywhere.
I smelt decay in every breath,
And trembled in the suffocating air,
I saw the ivy clinging to the trees,
Sucking away at life so slowly,
The worm, the tiny insects eating there
way through everything around.
All I touched showed signs of death.
And I was glad to leave the forest.
To try to make myself forget that there
I'd seen a picture drawn of life.

Esther Graham

All New . . . Amazing Stories

Ten tall tales.
Nine nauseating nasties,
Eight horrifying hauntings,
Seven sinister secrets,
Six sickly scenarios,
Five fiery fiends,
Four forceful phantoms,
Three threatening tigers,
Two troubling tasks,
One kiss from a vampire,
One carrion empire,

All new . . . amazing stories,
Their lusts and their glories.

Colin Edge

Stands Alone

So we move on
yet the kindled smile reminds
when, silence stands alone
and days linger
momentarily stilled
with memories aglow
the cloaks of us to reveal
a hidden truth
the past
the true companion
so you are remembered
and separate paths become
retraced via this
that stands alone
your memory

Leslie Downton

Sadie

A rescue dog
She came to us
Settled in
Without a fuss

A large black dog
With a cold wet nose
Drags me from my bed
And out she goes

Whatever the weather
Through fields she walks
By trees she sniffs - aha
She has the scent of a fox

She is beautiful
And we are her pack
She is a saint
No quality does she lack

Jean Dodd

Love

Love can be annoying
Love can be kind
Love can be great
Leave your troubles behind.

Love can be a nuisance
And get on your nerves
There's a straight path to follow
Or one with curves.

Love can be normal
At a perfect rate
Or love can be exciting
You've got a date!

Love can be romantic
The perfect thing
Think of a wedding day
The diamond ring!

Nishma Manek

Thoughts

A sudden thought came to my mind.
A tear ran down my face.
A burning inside told me,
It was you my thoughts had wandered to.

For years no love or affection,
For years no loving kiss,

Reserved from eternal bliss.
And this a thought to chance my life
To detour thoughts of loneliness
To bring thoughts of happiness again,
    So beautiful a thought.

A thought to delight the mind
    Often so hard to find.

To see you so full of charms
Makes me want you in my arms
    to love.
And if a thought to take a chance
A kiss, a caress, a loving romance.

Max Martin

The Lonely Dog

The lonely dog is looking for a friend,
He's barking and talking,
He wants you again.

The lonely dog wants you to play,
When you throw the ball,
He won't go away.

The lonely dog won't go home,
He's crying all the way,
In the cold freezing snow.

The lonely dog sits by the fire,
He looks so sad,
But he really looks tired.

The lonely dog is getting old,
You don't know what to do,
You will have to let him go.

Geraldine Bond

The Snowman

I'm a cold old snowman
Who is melting away in the
intense heat.
I'm a cold old snowman
who is waiting for somebody
to give me a home.
I'm just a snowman
who wants to go home.

Roberta Cooper

Tony

You came into my life that day.
No different from the rest.
But the moment I laid eyes on you,
Transformed into the best.
Everything I wanted
Is wrapped up in your being,
Every sense my body has
Awakes, when you I'm seeing.
Tony, you're the only one,
My one and only one,
Life itself began that day,
The day the lights came on
You walked into my life that day,
And all I see is you,
And me as well, of course that is
Because one and one makes two!

Lynda Kirkbride

Lithium Emotions

Nerve-ends numb and my
    pleasure points dead,
Paranoia plays with the
    chemicals in my head.
Floating on a cloud
    far from the sun,
Yellowing my life-line
    and my metabolic lithium.

Stutter starting doctors take a
    hammer to my skull,
I think that this would hurt if
    my senses weren't dull.
Sunset sight is great delight
    to medical profession.
Sunset sight is not to sleep, but
    deeper down depression.

A lawn mower cutting through my mind
    could cause less destruction.
I tear my heart out with my
    Lithium emotions.

Iain Maloney

Bombardment Poem

Snipers strike across the street,
People terrified of their fate.
Why do countries always fight?
Knowing of the consequences
It will bring.
Do they know of the effects?
Do they really care?
Do they see the mutilated bodies
Lying helpless on the ground?
Grief, tears and distress
Take a toll on their lives.
Disfiguration of their country
Gives them no hope for the future.
Imminent armaments surround them all.
Why do they bother to live their lives
If they are so close to death?
There are so many questions
Surrounding wars.
But who has the answers, the solutions,
The peace? No-one knows.

L. White

Life . . .

Life is like a flower
It blooms then dies away,
Life is like a light
It's bright then darkness appears,
Life is like a person
It's young and then grows old,
Life is like your love
It's strong then is no more.

Emma Crane

Battle

There is trouble in our midst,
We face our greatest challenge yet.
The path is long and difficult
And the time of the battle is set.

The enemy is wild and fierce,
They never shed a tear.
Keep your weapons close to you.
And hide away your fears.

Pull the ground from under their feet
And beat them to the floor.
The flesh and souls of our enemies
Must remain no more.

Your finest hour is about to begin,
None of this will be easy.
The battlefield is fresh and green,
Ready for our glory.
Many will die, few will live,
We fight for King and Country.
We won't stop until we drop,
This battle will be a beauty.

Andrew Lowe

Ode To My Love

Shall I paint a picture of you,
I'll never get past your eyes.
Gentian blue—they are sketched,
    By an angel in disguise.
Your face, a lovely face, its lines
    Etched in my heart.
And yet as I come to draw it,
    the picture will not start . . .

Shall I paint the glory, of what
    You are to me,
Laughter lines, and greying temples,
    The wonder that I see . . .
I will not need a paintbrush,
    Just one that will not cease,
And there—unfold in sweet description,
    as my masterpiece.

Chris Coulton

Thursdays

He sits alone, he smokes a fag,
He sips his tea, he takes a drag,
Time slips by, he sits and sighs,
He thinks about the day he'll die.
He wants to go, but outside it's cold,
He wants his story to be told.
The world is his through a window pane,
He wants to get on an endless train.
He pours more tea, he stirs it round,
He does it all without a sound
He wants to sleep, he wants to cry,
He wants to shout, he wants to die.
He breathes in deep, it's glorious day,
He stands, he pays, he walks away.

Robert Swift

Untitled

Little girl,
Waiting to grow,
But scared to know,
What the future holds,
It happens so fast,
You're no longer a child,
When you feel the pain,
It hurts in your heart,
It feels like an end,
But it's just the beginning,
A journey to take,
So long for a child,
No longer a child.

Rebecca Morris

Second Birth

Gently she counts her steps
Gracefully paced like a lion
In her belly an embryo speaks
Thy cry of pain in darkness
Sucking life fluid.

Patiently
In thy dark room wait
Lo! Demons stand my way
Preparing for dinner feast.

Oh! Open thy door of light
Guide and show me bright
My Lord give me sight
Reaching out my safety.

Thy word, oh... listen thee
Eternal name of my light
Only nectar of pure waters
Sipping will merge in Thee
Into Thy light supreme.

Walter Sato

I Sing My Songs

I sing my songs into the lonely night,
to the moon, to the stars so bright,
I sing and sing, I don't know why
I feel so good, I feel so high.

I hope my songs go far, so far,
so far as the loneliest star,
to lonely people to warm their heart,
to give them hope, a happy start.

I sing my songs into the lonely night,
to the moon, to the stars so bright,
and the angels, they sing with me,
how wonderful my songs can be.

C. J. Chamberlain

The Dream

One day, when I was talking to my nan,
when out came this weird looking man.
He was wearing bits of junk,
so I knew he was a punk.
He shouted at me, saying,
"Your money or your life!"
And he held out a large knife.
I wanted to pull his hair,
but he shouted, "You dare!"
I started to scream,
then mum woke me from my dream.

Taslima Rasul

Whisper

Softly, listen can you hear?
So quietly the future whispers.
But now how to get there?
Deep inside I know I'm here.
I can feel myself laughing.
Patience is a virtue, it's true.
I laugh with a hearty roar,
From deep inside I laugh once more.
You see it's me,
At last I see, I am my past,
Although it passed,
I live in the present,
Under the trees.
The breeze eases the pain.
Don't restrain, feel the pain,
Heal the soul, the whole.
Life's a drug.
Give me a hug,
The healing drug.

Ann Starkie

My Box

I will put in my box...
The sweet penny whistle tune
Hovering over the Irish sea.
The shivering reflection of
The sunset in the water at night.

I will put in my box...
The dust of a glistening fairy's
Wing and the war of the century,
So it cannot get out and
Kill millions.

I will put in my box...
The rainbow of life so every time,
I slide down it I can put things
Right for people and animals
With the magic of the gold.

I will put in my box...
The magic of a unicorn to start
A new day.
The North star to brighten my night.
It's all magic in my box.

Hannah Christine Buckland

As Life Unfolds

Though the river be wide,
and the ocean be deep,
and the birds fly free,
there'll always be a place
for thee and me.

Why not be as free as a bee,
and as absurd as a bird,
it's all part of this life on earth,
and leads to much mirth.

There is plenty of strife,
at all times of life,
and though the violence is rife,
I carry no knife.

Some do their best
to quell the unrest,
but when some are apart,
they take it to heart.

As life unfolds, we all behold
the best and the worst,
whichever comes first.

David Carress

My Mixed-Up Family

I've got a big fat mum,
who's as skinny as a rake,
my dad is really handsome,
but his looks are fake.

My two baby sisters
are hasty and they're smelly.
They never watch T.V.,
but are always watching telly.

My two little brothers
are lovely and they're kind,
at school they're always forward,
but at home they are behind.

My granny and my gramps
sadly passed away,
they're visiting tomorrow,
and staying the whole day.

And me of course I'm perfect,
as perfect as can be,
I've never met a living soul,
as wonderful as me.

Shelley Meredith

Spring

The best part of the year is spring
When crocus come up in a ring,
Daffodils hold their heads up high,
To catch the sun right in the eye.

Time to seed and plant and grow,
Ready for your summer show,
Work hard, keep the weeds at bay
Slug pellets don't forget to lay.

The pussy willow are now in bud,
Rivers and streams are a flood,
A season for new growth to bring,
You know the time, it is spring.

Sandra Pike

Untitled

I'm seeing the other side,
of darkness and despair.
The likes of so much evil
that nothing can compare.
Stranded in the wilderness
with nothing else there.
Trapped in my mind,
where solitude scares.
But to find myself
I must reside there,
and travel through its depths
like I just don't care.
I must face the demons
of my mind's lair,
and pass through the doorway,
where things are bright and fair,
And when I pass through,
I'll live my whole life there.
A long hard battle
which will end this nightmare.

C. K. Mancini

Happy Retirement

Cathy's been a cleaner now
For near on twenty years,
You always know when she's around
From the singing in your ears.
You have cleaned and dusted
This old folk's home for so long,
We will all be very sorry
On the day that you are gone,
We hope you have happy memories
Of working here with us,
You only live around the corner
So pop in and visit us,
Now we have knitted you a mouse
To send you on your way,
Well it beats the mop and bucket
You carried with you each day,
So now as you retire
Put your feet up for a rest
And put on Tina Turner
Because you're simply the best.

D. M. Baker

Somebody Died

Somebody died
But the clouds kept on moving

Somebody's ill
But the sun keeps on shining

Somebody laughs
But the wars keep on raging

A wedding takes place
Everyone's happy

Somebody died
And the clouds keep on moving

Susan Eggleton

Emerald Isle

Life is but a narrow road
Of shattered hopes and dreams,
Life is but a broken heart
An endless string of tears,
Life is but another bomb
That pierces someone's joy,
Life is what we've made it be;
In this so called Emerald Isle.

Michelle Madden

As The Darkness Loves The Light

The day before yesterday
she loved a man
with all she had and could.
She was a woman.

Yesterday
she loved a woman
with all they both had and could.
She was a woman to a woman.

Today
she loves a woman
with all she has not and cannot.
She is a man to a woman.

But tomorrow?
Will she love a man
as a man loves another man
if she will, she will love him
with all she can but has not.

D. Springer

A Daughter's Gift

She gave me something beautiful
To keep me here,
To bind me to the earth with love,
Ignoring age and illness,
As if the slender thread
On which our lives suspend
Would never break.

This season's roses on the tiny bush
Will soon be dead
But, nurtured well,
Buds will spring again
And bloom beyond the darkness.

Jean Sly

Christmas Tide

Soon it will be Christmas again
November the 5th it's bonfire night
All good things will come and go
What it is I give, give, give
I like the silvery stars at night
Here's a prayer for you and me
All in all they remind
Me of Christmas joy
And other good things too.

Frances McLean Atkinson

Andromeda

Stranded; trapped; chained
To the rock of my heart's fixation:
At the mercy of love's strictures.
If the dragon came, this Andromeda
Would welcome his power to devour;
Would pray for oblivion - yet
Would know that the pain would
Remain beyond
For I am Andromeda in chains,
And Perseus is dead.

Jill Curtis

366

Untitled

The Light, The Light
It calls me, So Bright
I can't resist it
I have to follow it
Where is it leading me to.

Where is my body
I've left it behind
I'm floating, and happy
My pain is all gone
I am only my soul.

I am not afraid
I feel the presence of others
Lost long ago, they greet me
I am warm and glowing
Peace surrounds me.

I try to look back
I only see tears
Do not grieve me
I belong here now
I will watch over you.

Heather Hopper

Set You Free

Set you free
From my mind
I gotta be cruel
To be kind

You're in my mind
All of the time
The only place
Where you can be mine

I've waited and waited
For so long
The only place
Where I belong

I want it all
I want it so much
I'm letting go
Just one more touch

To keep my dreams
Alive with you
To let me start
A life anew

Helen Paszyn

Quo Vadis, Morituri?
(Whither Goes Thou, Mortals?)

A person is a paradox,
When one is really two -
The ego presented to the world
And the quintessential 'you.'

If a soul has any form,
What then would be the size?
For nothing can be measured
By judgement, hand or eyes.

Your soul is but a blend
Of all that you have been -
Great with gracious goodness,
Or small and grossly obscene.

God's wisdom is apparent here,
For no-one can foretell -
Will there be surprise in Heaven?
Or the stunning stock of hell?

No matter how others saw you
Or if you performed well
When your time is finally up,
Then only you will tell.

J. Clarke

Why

Why does man have to create wars,
and tear our world asunder?
Why is man so full of hate,
Why does he pillage and plunder?
Why does man have to set his bombs
So that they injure and maim?
And why can't man admit he was wrong,
Why can't he accept the blame?
All over the world, there is suffering
Of one kind or another,
So why can't man live in peace
and harmony, like brother to brother?

E. V. Helman

Mum's Poem

Look for me in the soft gentle rain.
Look for me in a song's sweet refrain
In the sunset in the skies
Look for me in a baby's eyes
Everywhere you will see
Fond sweet memories of me
Don't cry for me, I am still here
All around so do not fear.
The sands of time
will not erase
The memories of our bygone days.

Rose Smith

Lily And Florence

Lil and Flo went out
Together you know
Down to the park
They had such a lark

On to the pond they go
Look at the ducks says Flo
It won't make me ill says Lil
No says Flo didn't you know

The girls like to stare
Their heads almost bare
With hardly any hair,
But they don't care

They laugh and giggle,
Do lots of wiggles
Then get lots of tickles
But never get niggled

Eleven months is Lil
Five months our Flo
They're good girls you know
Our Lily and Flo

Shirley Lilian Bryan

Be There

You ask me
Why are you here?

You ask me
What's it all about?

But I have no doubt as,

If you were not there
Who would stand up for me,

If you were not there
Who would cheer for me,

If you were not there
Who would shed a tear for me,

If you were not there
Why would I want to be.

Catherine D. Nugent

The Last Rose

Nature fights each spring anew
To fill the garden green,
All the colours of the rainbow grew
Where once the snow had been.

Summer comes and with the light
The flowers and the fruits of season,
Fill the air with scent at night.
To gather them seems treason.

Autumn with us once again
The dark nights closing down each day,
Growing cooler by the hour
The flowers try to stay.

They lose their battle with the frost
A lonely rosebud stays,
I picked it, gave it to my love
To remind her of those summer days.

K. Parkinson

Waiting

They all sat round,
Waiting
For the meal.
Some spoke
Some questioned
But few really understood -
All, were waiting.
At last He spoke
but no one really heard
those words so meaningful
that they would be said so
many times again.
They were still waiting -
for an explanation
But it had already been said:
They ate -
They drank -
All were sad; but
only some knew why
And Our Lord -
He, was waiting.

Iris Rigazzi-Tarling

I Said Goodbye

I said goodbye to you today
no-one heard, not even you
I said it as I passed your house,
so softly no-one knew.
I said goodbye to the memories
of a love I thought you'd shared
And then I turned and walked away
As if I'd never cared.
I said goodbye to all I had
And all I ever knew.
But even as I said goodbye
I knew I still loved you.

Julie Taylor

Grandad

Big, strong, tall and fine
so reliable; all the time.
Never ever was a bore,
Ever faithful, ever sure.

While you're busy; wash and clatter,
Grandad fills you up with laughter.
When the night is getting creepy
Grandad's sure to tell a story.

If you think you're just a flop
Grandad's sure to lift you up;
always there to raise your spirits
with his funny, funny lyrics.

Aniema Violet Medekong

Thinking

What a beautiful world
As I sit by the sea.
God made it all
For you and for me
His hands never tired
His heart full of love
To give all a chance
To do some good.
He must be sad sometimes
To see how we fail
But never forsakes us
He knows we are frail.
One day we will meet
This wonderful God
Let's pray for forgiveness
And the beauty we've got.

Lily Merrilla Sinclair

The Christening

We have gathered here
With our children today
To have them baptized
In the Lord God's way

Children are born
So meek and mild
Let's give love and care
To our new child

We stand in God's house
With the next generation
The family together
In celebration

Let's give our thanks
Think of children in need
We don't have to worry
We don't have to plead

Richard Jones

Untitled

My love for life is so sweet
Makes some nights so I can't sleep
I dream of all things good and bad
And all the things I love and have
When my life has been and done
At least I crammed in lots of fun

Chris Blake

Verses To A Baby Boy On His Christening

On this your dedication day
Sweet baby undefiled
Upon your birth and early life
The Lord has surely smiled

For you are blessed with parents kind
And joy attends each day
Family love is yours to share
God-Parents for your pray

But babyhood will pass too soon
As you become a lad
Then years will roll on steadily
With good times and with bad

For the good times thank your Maker
In the bad times seek his aid
And you will find that life somehow
Gets better when you've prayed

Remember his Commandments too
No better guide you'll find
To help you live your life at peace
With God and all Mankind

W. A. N. Ferguson

Before The Crack Of Dawn

Someone stole the Moon.
The longest night.
Heavy, dark and scary.
Only owls were hacking in the night,
Tearing the blackness apart,
Like a wolf, the sea was breathing
And the wind was deadly whistling.
Someone stole the Moon,
Spilled the celestial milk
Away souls withered with waiting...
Roosters were long ago wiped out,
Their song left unsung.

And the dawn needed just so little,
Before it was unlocked.

Vladislav Danailov Katzarski

An Invention Of Mine

It's like king Midas
With His touch of Gold
All the things I have
Are the things I hold

and the things I make are limitless
My imagination is completely free
But if I close my eyes
Those things I made will cease to be

So I am God and God is me
Or that's the way it seems
I can bring dead men back to life
And make lakes into streams

So maybe there isn't a God at all
Maybe he's only something I can see
And in which case, if I invented God,
Then who invented me.

Mark Jeffery

A Toddler's Frustration

Will I ever grow up tall,
to be just 'like my dad'?
At nearly two, I'm still quite small,
I really do get mad.
'Cos everything I want so much
is never on the floor,
I'm always told I mustn't touch,
it's really quite a bore.

Everything is always 'No!'
And that can be quite tough.
I've even tried on tippy-toe
but my arms aren't long enough.

I've tried to climb on chairs and bed,
but someone always sees;
or else I fall and bump my head,
and graze my arms and knees.

So life is hard for one so small
in these frustrating stages.
I don't think I will grow at all,
or else it will take ages.

M. E. Linney

Left Alone

Why does he have to go
My tears already begin to flow
His bag is packed and done
We were two, now we're one
The door is open, now it's shut
This really is the deepest cut
My mind is numb, I cannot think
Why has he broken this loving link
Will I ever come alive
His first school day and only five.

J. McKernon

VESPER

o f
searing
scorching
tresses
shorn
rests   RA
t o
spy
domed
minaret   spire   softly   soaring
silhouette 'gainst the gath'ring hues
the weary contract workers who
breasted the infinite blue through
myriad routes like flints to
magnets fly dazed and dreaming
                    m
            u   a
hied these h   n motley moths
charmed by a   candle   glow

Miguel Balboa D'Mendoza

Drugs

What pleasures do drugs give?
Sometimes I wonder.
It makes one's life miserable and dry,
So why should a person try?

But some youngsters say
They want to look cool.
But I think they are
The biggest fool.

People get addicted to it
And lose their precious lives,
But they don't care
Till they cannot bare
The misery, the addiction and diseases.

So why should people try?
Though they know they'll die.
I sometimes wonder why?

Rabia Shah

Matthew

It seems like only yesterday
The nursing sister came to say,
What I'd been waiting hours to hear,
That you'd arrived, and what a dear,
My grandson born that day.

I held you at an hour old,
Wrapped up warm against the cold.
You didn't even make a sound,
Just looked at me with eyes so round.
My blessings were tenfold.

A bond was made right then and there.
You knew that I would love and care.
Though no words were ever spoken,
It's a bond that can't be broken,
And our love we'll always share.

I only hope I live to see
You grow up tall, just like a tree.
To watch you grow into a man.
To see you strive, hard as you can,
To be the best that you can be.

S. P. Gillott

I Wish Upon

I wish upon a wishing star,
So very nice and bright.
I wish upon you because,
You're so nice and bright.

Sharon Cook

Seasons

Flowers budding, hatchlings chirping,
Green is everywhere,
Each day anew with morning dew,
Spring is in the air.

The sun is high in bright blue sky,
Butterflies abound,
Children play in ocean spray,
Making happy summer sounds.

Leaves tumble down to waiting ground,
Reds, russets, gold,
There to delight, a glorious sight,
Autumn now unfolds.

The trees are bare, snow everywhere,
Freezing where it lays,
Changing all the eye can see,
On frosty winter days.

K. S. Richardson

Rainbows And Rain

A rainbow so beautiful,
Each Unique colour,
A well defined arch, .
No more, no less.

Rain so free,
Soft to the touch,
Yet coldly felt,
No more, no less.

Colours so bright,
Freeness so cold,
Rain is needed,
But a rainbow is wanted.

R. Lewis

The Children

I wonder if your children knew,
The stresses, the strains, the worry,
They put you through.

You're up at midnight,
Still up at dawn,
O, please go to sleep
At least 'til morn.

The sun comes up,
The children wake,
And life goes on,
And still they take.

You love your children,
You always will,
And always remember,
They were your will.

Jennifer Studholme

Morning

Watching clouds rolling down
The mountains white with snow
High above the sleepy town
Rain like teardrops flow
Sitting by the water's edge
Waiting for the sun to rise
Primroses grow beside the hedge
Little birds and dragonflies
Daffodils sway in the breeze
Tall trees without their leaves
Another morning of a new day
Close my eyes and try to pray
I hope today will never end
Thoughts of love to you I send.

Brenda Shaw

Oh! That I May See

Have we ever thought
how the world would appear
if we found ourselves blind
no sight - far or near.
To live all alone
inside one's own head -
with no visuals around
to recall living or dead.

Though seasons will change
and gardens will glow;
the skies will change colour -
for rain or for snow.
The daffodils all yellow
bring hope to mankind;
but there's nothing but darkness
for the sightless or blind.

As God is the One who
promised us light -
then we plead and we pray
He assist in our plight.

Mary Mullally

Santa's Cruise

Laughter song tears and smiles.
Every year you travel those miles
A twinkling eye a helpful hand
Elves and fairies make their stand.

Robins fly, angels cry
With love not sadness for you and I
Snowmen smile, reindeer prance
Warmth and love, take a closer glance

The ground now covered, sky now clear
Silvery crystals of angel's hair
Footsteps harsh the crystal breaks
Nature or man's mistake?

Still you care, still you come
Children adults everyone
Gifts for pleasure, gifts for joy
Candies, poems, fruit and toys

A jeer of laughter Ho! Ho! Ho!
Dancer Prancer away we go
A soulful song, rousing cheer
Away you fly to return next year

K. Gray

Separate Togetherness

Let me lie here
Next to you but not
to sip the sea's breath
with effortlessness.

Allow me the stillness
of that of a rock
which time could erode
if left here long enough.

Let's just lie.
Not thinking, not speaking.
Untouching.
Not wearing each other's souls
but bearing our own selves.
No weaving, no delving
or swimming there sinking
through the rhythmic tide
of each other's minds.

Let's just try
tasting not wasting
this moment we're living.

Debra Jayne Hunston

Friend To Friend

I send this poem
to let you know,
how rare it is for me,
to take a soul
and call it friend
that's what I see in thee,
your love of life
and joyous laugh
make me smile inside,
it's just so good
to have you, friend,
I'll cherish you with pride.
no wealth of gifts
can I bestow,
just little things
that please,
so treat me as your
comfy chair,
and rest in me with ease.

Shirley Lynn Kent

The One

Raise my hopes
And let me fall.
Been here and there
And done it all.
Round again
And back to one.
Dreams are near
Then they're gone.
Melt my heart
Make me freeze.
Let me down
With so much ease.
Drag me down
With just a word
Shout so loud
I can't be heard
Hide my tears
For fear you'll see.
Here I am
The broken me.

Debbie Faizey

What Is It?

I love them,
I eat them,
I have one for lunch,
They are not like apples,
They do not crunch.
You pull back the skin to
make it peel,
If you have a large one it is
almost a meal!
   What is it?
An orange.

Samantha Fairhead

Thoughts Of An African Youth

I am all alone
A stranger in my own home
For I am torn between two worlds
The modern and my own.

I want the things from the films
But they seem to only bring sin,
To a culture that forbids
Me to even dream.

The despair is not mine alone
For we are many that are so,
That have all our hopes
Forever to stay cold.

Oduntan Ibironke Oyefuga

Howsham

Stones
In the grass
Standing

Head high leaning weeds
Meet the winds of Paradise
Soughing through
The green leaf'd spring
On a high, quiet English hill

There is no returning
From this place

Soft chatterings
On the air subside
Like swarms
Of falling fire flies

The closed community
Waits
Till the trespasser
Drops the latch
On the heavy church-yard gate.

Audrey E. Greaves

What Is Love

What is Love,
It's full of Pain.
My Heart beats fast,
When I call his name.
I can see his face,
How it hurts me so.
Full of warmth,
When he held me tight.

You think of the past,
To keep you going.
And do many things,
to try and forget.
No regrets,
No remorse,
What is love,
it's full of Pain,
but, I'd do it again.

Jill Coombes

20 Seconds Ago

20 seconds ago
I was mean
Now I have changed
And everyone knows

20 seconds ago
I was different
Now I have changed
That's the way the world goes

20 seconds ago
No time to lose
Because I am getting old
And now I must choose
The path to hell or to heaven
For angels or for the devil
Am I bad or am I good
To be or not to be
I should be good!

Danielle Marie Levy

Let's Part

Love smiles, let's part,
in deceit,
when we meet
it blankets the guilt.

Damian Gerard Coyle

Museum

Kingdoms rise and kingdoms fall
The rivers flow and then they stall
Greek, Roman, Nok, Inca and Gaul
Egyptian, Israel, Ming enthral
So now in hallowed case and echoed hall
We trek and muse through each portal
And passing by respect we pay
To ancestors who bloomed one day
Now set in shows of artefact
And artistry once great now cracked
Once lost beneath a desert sand
Unveiled by our collecting hand
Revered as memories of might
And glory dim in distant light
But as we wonder at the years
They whisper to our inner fears
Their lives were once invincible
Brought down by pride's hot crucible
We will one day be in case
Admired by some yet unborn race.

G. B. Langley

Passion

Inside my body of desire,
Is a passion of love,
That burns like fire.
The warmth of our bodies,
The flame's will ignite,
The fire will burn,
From sheer delight.
Your arms will caress me,
Our bodies entwine,
Our lips touch with passion,
From feeling divine.
Today we have given our bodies as one.
Intimate feelings of love has begun,
It could last forever, or end in a day.
But the memory stay's with you.
When life slips away.

Patricia Mulvihill

Solitude

The only sound, the falling rain,
It rattles at my window.
I turn to you within my sleep,
But find only my pillow.
For solitude, my only friend,
Accompanies me now,
Since you have left me all alone
To struggle on somehow.
And, yet, within my loneliness
A light shines through the grey
For all I wanted was for you to find
True happiness someday.
The cost to me, it matters not
If joy is yours to be.
So, we walk onwards, hand in hand,
Solitude and me.

Robert E. Sharman

Squirrels

It was a cold wet evening
The leaves a rustic brown
The autumn has arrived now
The squirrels forage around

They gather all the nuts near
And build them in a hill
The winter it is coming
Now the squirrels have their fill

They bury deep and hibernate
And miss the winter snow
Then springtime they will wake again
And back to play they go.

Florence Shanahan

Untitled

The day is lost to night
and night is stolen by day
if I hold you forever tight
could you promise to stay?
Night is made for loving
but day returns too soon
no more loving
under shadow of the moon.
With day comes reality
cold hard fact
our love a fatality
my heart pain racked.

Melanie J. Cochrane

The Squirrel Red

Each night I lay in my bed
Thinking of the Squirrel Red
With his bushy tail and twinkling eyes
He climbs the trees way up high
He builds a home to keep him warm
And to protect him from the human storm
He is so shy and we know why
So please help to save the Squirrel Red
So that they don't end up dead.

Grace Louise Brayshaw

The Frost

Silently it comes,
In the stillness of the night,
Covering and disguising
Everything that's in its sight.
Trees turn to silver,
Still no one hears,
And tiny captured dew drops
Sparkle, like a thousand million tears.
The patterns it makes on the windows
Like stars, twinkle and shine
Oh! How I love this silent beauty
That catches everything in time.

Maureen Beech

Enough Of Love

I thought it was meant to be,
I thought we should be together,
The first time I saw you smiled at me
And I thought it would last forever.

I remember walking along the sand
In the still moonlit night,
I remember walking hand in hand
And everything seemed just right.

But as the wind changed direction,
And as the sea turned its tide,
So did your affection,
And that knock blew my pride.

As I look up to the stars above,
I know now I was stupid,
So now I've had enough of love
And quite enough of Cupid.

D. J. Denis

Cranefly

Little dusk dancers
Bobbing in the breeze
Humming among gravestones
And tiger grass.
Tiny fairies
Just visible
As the grey shroud falls
And then like
A passing thought
Touch your face and are gone

Joanna Davey

Memories Of A Carefree Childhood In The Country

Christmas log hissing days
Mistletoe kissing days
Fond reminiscing days
When we were young.

Easter Egg rolling days
Clear cuckoo-calling days
Frisky gambolling days
When we were young.

Merry mad May days
Hawthorn and hay days
Wish you could stay days
When we were young.

Oh! for those lazy days
Buttercup and daisy days
High summer hazy days
When we were young.

Now all those days are gone
And fond memory lingers on
Golden days in the sun
When we were young

Lila Jackson

The Teacher's Talking

The teacher's talking,
But I hear no word,
I look out the window
And see a New World.
No more troubles, worries or problems
They've all gone for good.
I find myself flying
In a land that feels good.
Friends playing, no more shouting
With an atmosphere that's the best,
  But the wind starts to blow,
  And the land starts to go
I find myself back at school,
No games to play,
No words to say,
Sat all alone again,
But, if I dream hard enough
Maybe one day I'll find,
The Land that's Hidden
Behind all Time...

Michelle Evans

Just Don't Do It

This is a generation
Planed off by ecstasy,
Reduced to a uniform pulp,
There are no tests,
Hierarchies of quality are gone,
Characters ponder silently
Where their potentials went
And the unexceptional
Fill the vacuum
With their desperate noise;

Night shifts in a factory
Day shifts on a Sega,
You keep buying Polo shirts
Because you'll never afford
A polo horse,
Every virtual facet
Of your ambitions you buy
Saps the zest to really do it,
Treadmill economics
To keep you running, not moving.

James McHenry

Out Of The Land

Out of the land
Her ancestral voices sent her
Head, spinning,
Her womb ripped.
Out of the tenements
Babies were spilling

Into the concrete.
Lips smacked of blood
And suckling noises,

The milk dust flying
In hell's dry wind.

The roaring of storm
In her ears.
And in you
The roaring
As she stares
Into the darkness.

Now she holds the silence
like a prayer.

Maureen Cropley

Silent Journey

I look over the wilderness
  And the way begone
Loneliness sneaks into my heart
  Time stands still
My mind cries out,
  For the ones I love
My despair keeps me from hearing
  Maybe I hear an answer
But time doesn't permit certainty

I look over the wilderness
  And the way ungone
    To my destined journey

Sigridur Sigmundsdottir

The Gentle Breeze

I sang a lovely melody,
To a very gentle breeze,
She played a kind of sensual game,
And teased the words from me.

I hummed a tiny little tune,
To the gentle breeze that blew,
She took my sweetest note away,
To show the milky moon.

I softly sung a lullaby,
To the evenings gentle breeze,
She cried a gentle tear away,
Then touched a star for me.

I sang a gentle love song,
To my sweet and gentle breeze,
She gently stole my love away,
And blew a kiss to me.

Julie Grantham

The Butterfly

I'm just a little butterfly
And sometimes like to settle
On the many leaves so green,
Or pretty coloured petal.
For when the Summer sun shines bright
I like to spend the hours
Watching birds and humming bees
Flit among the flowers.
But when the Summer sun has gone
I know that I will die,
And rest among the flowers I knew,
As a little butterfly.

F. A. Barnes

Gypsy In My Soul

I must away—'tis time to go
Whither—whither—I do not know
The sap has risen in my soul
What then—is my chosen role

The countryside calls
The open road beckons
Time to go—waste not a second
What is it within my soul
A romany spirit—I behold

Still reaching far—within my heart
Old time stirrings—time to part
On and on I've got to go
Whatever—hail or rain or snow

Oh Romany just let me be
Content in spirit to be me
But oh—the calls of yesterday
I feel are in my heart to stay.

Elizabeth Beckinsale

Autumn Memories

Autumn is a mellow month,
That brings back memories,
Of lovers' trysts, and swirling mists,
Secret meetings, that first kiss.

The tired sun slips behind the hill,
The wind declines, the woods are still,
A squirrel rushes to his home,
But I don't move, I sit alone.

Feelings of nostalgia stir,
A silent voice is calling,
As if somehow, somewhere, someone,
Is giving Earth a warning.

The burning ember of dark November,
Now lingers in the air,
And the hooting of a distant owl,
Warns us to prepare.

Mighty trees, whispers on the breeze,
But weather is on its way,
The icy fingers of Winter,
Their visit soon shall pay.

Sandra Clayton

A Bed Wetting

Sparrow hawks sang in her pillows,
Her bed rocked like the solent,
Changing a little girl
Who wet the bed
Into a frightened nymph a pool.

Sharon Gatfield

Friends

Friends are people who share all
  the riches in life,
Friends will help you through all
  your troubles and strife.
Don't ever mistake the love you feel,
  when all your friends are near,
Cherish all the moments filled
  with love and cheer.

Not only welcome new friends,
  but be a friend yourself.
You never know when someone may
  need your loving help.
There'll never be a time when you
  will not need a friend.
So make the most of everyone
  to have a happy end.

Julie Looker

Elvis We'll Remember You

In 1935 a king was born to be,
A king of rock 'n roll
his name is Elvis Presley.

But in 1977 the king of
rock 'n roll did die,
he's now gone to make
his music, in the heavens
in the sky.

He left us with his music
and with his memory,
he will always be remembered
and go down in history.

The greatest rock 'n roller
that ever lived to be,
we'll always be so loyal
and always true to thee
yes you're still the greatest
  Elvis Presley.
  Michael J. Dyer

The Stone Of Destiny

This stone has caused an argument
To which place will it be sent
To a castle or a village fair?
Where is its resting place,

I tell you now, does it matter where
This stone will finally end
What power has it, it's only stone.
No life has it my friend

In this our final days on earth
We need a "rock" that's true
But I believe in Christ my Lord
He'll be a rock to you.

Trust not in stones which have no life
Nor bodies made of clay.
But trust-in-God who knows your way
He is the Bread of Life.

This life we need with a capital "L"
on this our storm-tossed world.
So trust in God he'll see you through
Until your journey's end.
  A. Hillan

Untitled

You're the Prince of my heart
The other half of my soul
I'll never let you go
Just as a knight in shining armour
From the pages of a fairy tale
You came a-chargin'
Into my life to bestow upon me
The touch of love
You swept me away
With whispered promises
Displays of passion, and
Within your arms
I've found a haven
A sense of belonging
In a word . . . home.
  Nasima Ali

Rivers

Gliding ducks in a dither
Going up and down the river
Croaking frogs
As mad as hogs!
Swishing pike - looking for prey
A nice fat fish will make his day.
Kingfishers zooming by
Too fast for the naked eye.
  Jeffery Gore

Fickle Emotions

Like a warm summer breeze
A tender kiss sweeps over me
Emotions slowly swell within
Craving liberty.

Hues of smoky purple haze
Swirl around subconscious thoughts,
As kisses melt increasing doubts
And worries wrought.

Colours of a vivid hue,
Bursting, blundering uncontrolled.
Fiery feelings seemingly
Forever taking hold.

Passion finally unfolded
Into peaceful, tranquil mood,
Remnants of ebbing emotions
Quietly subdued.
  Christine Barrow

My Friend

I have a friend who follows me
And he rarely leaves my side,
That he really loves me
Can in no way be denied.

He doesn't ask for much in life
And makes few demands of me,
He's quite happy with some cuddles
And something nice for his tea.

He is very clean and tidy
And he makes no mess at all,
He sits and listens to me
And comes running when I call.

Jack has lovely amber eyes
And with him I am smitten,
He has four legs and a tail,
My gorgeous black and white kitten.
  Carolyn Warner

Hands

What bliss to have a hand to hold
Throughout life's busy days
It gives us strength to carry on
In oh so many ways
Brings comfort in our sorrows
And joy when things go well
And hope for our tomorrow
Where love and peace may dwell
The sweet hands of the ones we love
The soft hand of a child
The healing hands of those who care
Are needed all the while
  Monica Wilson

Drifting

I feel that I am drifting, drifting
  yet know not where I go
Encushioned in safe and gentle arms
  above the Earth below.

Drifting in effortless movement
  I feel I don't belong
To Earth's pulsating human crowd
  This noisy, unheeding throng,

So I drift in idle wonders
  In safe and warm embrace
Viewing from somewhere far away
  This tide in time and space.

Then as I go idly drifting
  O'er this world far above
Compassionate prayers envelop me
  For huge downpours of love.
  B. F. Smyth

Reflections

Yesterday, the years of yesterday
Where have you gone.
You passed by me like a
Rolling stone, not stopping
For me.

You left me behind whilst
I was in my prime.
But then I was too busy
To mind.

On looking back now at
Aged sixty-three, the
Times were not easy, upwards
Of twenty-three.

On reflections I realize we
Had the best years.
No, not young again would
I like to be.
I am quite content to plod along
At sixty-three.
  M. Waters

It Was Love At First Sight (Gina)

Gina, they say love is blind
but I can say what I saw was divine
you and me turned against reality
is this love in our dreams?

You're the fire inside me
still I can't find the words to say
someday I'll make my move
to make my love known to you

It's love in my first thoughts
when I'm at your abode
stuck in life's strangle holds
I'm caught in boundaries untold

When I first met your eyes
è stato un amore a prima vista
it was love at first sight

Oggi ti amo più di ieri
ma, meno di domani
Today I love you more than yesterday
but, less than tomorrow.
  Clive Ayton Bell

Chinese Whispers

Pleasures of the past,
Corrupt the happenings of today,
Hidden secrets revealed,
But told in a different way.

A chain reaction of events,
Unveils such a surprise.
A listener's interpretation,
Results in exaggerated lies.

The revelation of the truth,
Becomes the first step to delusion.
The friendly spy goes unobserved,
Breaking the ethics of intrusion.

Their ears act as processors,
The new information is arranged,
They twist and adjust the expressions,
And suddenly the story has changed.

A condition of which we're all guilty,
Which has most impact on the listener.
The aftermath is bitter and hostile,
As a result of the Chinese whispers.
  Wayne Gilby

Grace

I would give the stars to you,
  for one sweet tender glance,
I would give a flower with dew,
  for just that other chance,
I could dream from dawn to noon,
  without a thought or care.
If you would tell me softly, soon,
  a world that we might share.
I could wait a lifetime dear,
  just to see you smile.
Instead I shed a lonely tear,
  and walk a long, long mile.
I have waited many years,
  for love that never came.
Maybe you're no longer there,
  the law of years to blame.
But some day maybe we can meet,
  as the sun meets the distant sea.
And wish and hope your heart will beat
  just as passionately for me

Norman Burles

Set Me Free...

Soaring high
Into the sky
That's where I'd like to be
No trouble or care
- Part of the air -
Please let me go - set me free

Like a bird on the wing
I'd chirrup and sing
Then rest on a soft downy cloud
Swoop high and low
Through wind, rain and snow
Then 'light on a field newly ploughed

Flying so far
To furthest star
My wings completely unfurled
Please, let me be
Let me go - set me free
To discover the rest of my world

Sheila Clapham

The Unwelcome Visitor

It comes around in dead of night,
Wakes you up, gives you a fright,
Sneaks in bed when cold and damp,
That awful dreaded thing called cramp.

He pinches leg and foot and stump,
Really hurts, and makes you jump.
When I awake at morning light,
I'm twice as tired as I was last night.

Place your foot upon the floor,
But my legs standing by the door.
Oh fellow amps have you a cure
To stop him coming back round here.

Margaret Vinall-Burnett

Mortal Man

Could we paint the rainbow?
Put the blush upon the rose
Place a smile upon a baby
As he lies in sweet repose
Can we make each tiny dewdrop
Put the leaf upon the tree
Weave the tiny spider's web
Put the sting into the bee
Could we make the crashing thunder
Hold back fury of the sea
Such puny hands would thwart us
Oh what fools we mortals be!

Edna Knight-Jones

Future Imperfect

Yes I have loved you
naked in the rain
and dressed in summer

Though we have loved
we will not woo again

Yet I have loved you
naked in the rain
and dressed in summer

David Hodges

The Window

In the darkness of the hour
In the tiredness of my day
I look through the window
And quietly wonder away
On the brim of my new thoughts
I gather up some things
But then I drop them down again
From the uncertain sting
In this place of mind
Where I go to every day
I notice that nothing
Has ever really changed
I hear a voice
High-pitched calling
That brings me back to life
And I shut the window softly
But it's always in my mind

Tresha Costa

Love's Impossibilities

Maybe it is true
That the ravages of life
Make a stone of the heart.
If it is so
Then this is surely one of life's
Most enduring tragedies.

Everyone has a whole to fill.
A little kindness,
A little tenderness,
And the black can change to blue;
The dark stone even soften
To an emerald hue,

And a sunny snow-filled
Late Autumn morning
Radiates
New possibilities
Of a coming Spring.

Kieran D. O'Malley

Metamorphosis

In the depth of Winter,
Not long ago,
I surveyed the world
Whose sombre bleakness
Matched my dark despair.
There was no life,
No light,
No hope;
And I wept.
But now I look again
And see a changing world.
The first green shoots
Have forced their way
Through once-frozen earth
And promise life
And light
And hope.
Now I rejoice,
For soon it will be Spring.

Marguerite Elliott

The Price Of Life?

For each life born, another dies,
One family laughs, one family cries,
One family celebrates that day.
One family now can only pray.

One family smiles ignoring cost
One family counts what it has lost.
One family laughed and then it cried,
For life was born and then it died.

Louise Cotton

Astral Flight

Running wildly, searching someone
Break the silence, make it end.
Any race, in any language
Just a voice with mine to blend.
Panic, fear, no sense or reason
My tortured soul remains in flight
Constant sun, no change of season
Burnt, white ash, reflecting light.
Now, only sky meets bare horizon
Lashing waves meet empty shores
Black clouds gather, blend together
Lightning flashes, thunder roars
Buildings blasted, desolation,
Wandering lonely isolation,
Aimless lost no destination,
Screaming loud recrimination.
Obscenities and accusations
Loudly pounding palpitations
Violently I'm tossed and shaken
Sweating, frightened, I awaken.

Alexandra B. B. Mills

Memories

Memories are something
We can never never lose,
But sadly they are something
We cannot always choose.

So very many memories
Often make us glad,
But sometimes there are memories
Which only make us sad.

Our lives continue onwards
With interest and with change.
Life can be most exciting
But also very strange.

How frequently we wish
That the pleasures of today
Will stay with us forever,
And never pass away.

Our aim should be that every day
For happiness to strive.
Then our supply of memories
Make us glad to be alive.

Barbara Rhona Thompson

Print Room Pressures

From the print room window oft I gaze,
It's furnished with a lovely view,
When Pedro strolls into the room
And says there's work to do.

He asks what date we're working on,
How soon will it be cleared?
He says the air is very moist,
For the time of year.

The next two dates are now complete,
The pressure's really on,
I say I'll try and work 'till six,
But by five I will be gone.

Scott T. McLennan

My Best Friend

My husband is my best friend
I share with him each day
as through his life we wend
each one in their own way

When in the valley deep
or on the mountain top
at nighttime when I can't sleep
he helps my fears to stop

That little conversation
that helps to clear the mind
is to me that special thing
our marriages do find

A good husband is worth having
but today they're hard to find
if you like me have got one
to him be loving and kind

Maureen Dawson

My Life

As I lay alone under the stars,
I remember when I was young,
I thought I could reach the stars,
when I grew up,

But now I know,
I shall never reach the stars above,
hold the moon like a torch,
grasp the sun like a lamp,

Now I know I'll never grow so big,
to reach the stars,
all I know is that all I can do
is still dream,
and wait till the day I'm called above.

Tanya Mulryan-McNally

My Dear Cleo

Oh dearest friend with heart so bold
With swishing tail, your wet cold nose
What can I do to make you well
For ten long years my loving pal.

To open dear my eyes once more
And find you standing by the door
Your rough old tongue my face does find
That doggy breath, but I don't mind.

What shall I do with you not there
To pat your head and brush your hair
I'm sure dear God will spare you pain
And send you home to me again.

But if dear friend it's not to be
This breaking heart that beats in me
Will grieve forever deep inside
Still not ashamed to say I cried.

F. G. Hayward

Shattered Dreams

He left them all alone without a
care or thought
He hurt them both so badly
when only love they sought
He didn't understand them
nor listen to their plea
He didn't want to hold them
or sit them on his knee
He turned his back and left
without a backward glance
He walked away forever
there is no second chance
Their love he turned away
without so much a care
Two sad and lonely children
whose father is not there.

Joan Alcock

The Gardener's Friend

I have a friend comes to my aid,
The moment that I get my spade,
Two bright eyes are watching me,
From a twig of a nearby tree.

As I carefully turn the soil,
He watches as I slowly toil,
Then dives down oh so suddenly,
For something I cannot even see.

He keeps my garden clear of pests,
And, when I take my little rests,
He hops upon my spade and sings,
Of valentines, and fairy things.

Robin, with your breast so red,
Sitting quietly o'er my head,
Thank you for your cheerful aid,
The moment that I get my spade.

O. M. Brailee

The Carob Tree In The Rock

Long slender branches
Stretching up and out
In all directions.
Like the splash in the water
From a falling stone.

You are a splash of life
From the seed
Some hurrying bird
Let fall into the split
Grey rock.

And now
From breath the stern silver cliffs
I see your spreading
magnificence,
And know that life
Is stronger than
Stone.

Naomi Kerer

Venus Rising

Let me sing to you
O daughter of the sea
rising from the waves
veiled in a pale white haze
let me memorize
the timeless glow
of grey-blue eyes
that gently fix my gaze
let me praise your gracious ways
for they touch the heart
more than words can ever say
let me chase down sunlit rays
that caress your golden hair
as you glide silently
to the highest stair
let me forever hold
these dancing images of you
like a reverie in blue
clasped firmly to my yearning soul

Robert Solomon

Catalyst

Imagination oceans of thought
Like a butterfly in a net
The dream is caught

A new creation the old has gone
Changed from within a soothing balm
The inner flame burns like the sun

Thoughts have power the catalyst
In the etheric the creation is formed
The dream is blessed

Ian Barton

You Were . . . You Are

You were the breeze,
That blew those petals away,
Clean into the air,
Sent them on their way,
You were the one,
That turned out the light,
A shadow,
Creeping away into the night,
You were the one,
That meant so very much,
A voice that still echoes,
Traces of your touch,
You were the rain,
That touched my skin,
You were the intensity,
That left an ember,
That smoulders within.

Susan Lau

The Cool Wind

The cool wind moves
When a woman smiles
Free wind moves within
When the night that falls
You hear the calls
Falling to each whim
A dance, a tune, a light
From the silver spoons
For they rest upon the floor
I feel the night air in my bones.
Well warm me up
For I cannot touch the cool wind alone.
For when one laughs there is a path
And when the leaves fall from the trees
The shine horse has all the push
But the cool wind is free.

Peter K. Ward

Is There Really Life Up There?

I watch the moon that shines so bright,
That silvery beacon in the night,
And wonder, as I stand and stare,
Is there really life up there?
To avoid our hunt they must be small,
Have hardly any size at all!
We've wandered round but no-one seen,
No eight-eyed monsters coloured green.
If they exist they must be tiny
And very dark, they can't be shiny
Or we'd have seen them all aglow,
But no-one has, not that I know.
Microscopic they must be
And so this thought occurs to me,
Perhaps, like us, they're in a fix,
The place is run by lunar-tics!

Robbie J. Pettitt

Autumn's Kiss

I was kissed by autumn,
And it reminded me of the berries
That blush on the trees.

I was cooled by the breeze
That gave flight to tawny leaves.
And warmed by golden sunlight
That bathed and healed my sorrow.

I rested on the grass, and wrapped
My happiness around me;
And slept among the carefully
Woven thread of autumn's web,
That sparkled with dew.

I was kissed by autumn
And it reminded me of you.

Linda Surman

Spent

It's first a letter
Sealed yet unposted
Sitting on a mantelpiece
Awaiting delivery

It's now unwanted
Been stored away
Like a raincoat
In a heat wave

It's now a bottle
Long uncorked
A wine for the breathing
A vinegary vapour

It's now worn out
Been neglected
A wedding dress
For the likes of Miss Haversham

It's finally a cake
An occasion forgotten
The memory disgorged
A feast for the birds.

Martin James Patrick D'Evelin

My Autumn

It's that time of year again,
The cooler nights, those misty dawns,
The dewdrops on the spiders' webs -
The fallen leaves upon the lawns.

The smell of Autumn in the air,
The yellowing tones for all to see,
Scarlet berries on the bush -
Ripe plums and apples on the tree.

Whilst tidying up a flower bed
My friend the robin in the tree,
Watched me from his shadowy perch,
Quietly whistling just for me.

He watched and whistled for some time,
And then flew down to search the soil,
In and out of plants he hopped -
Finding grubs disturbed by toil.

And underneath the drooping leaves
In the damp and cooling ground,
To my delight - for next year's show,
Some tiny seedlings I had found.

Margaret A. Porritt

"Ode to Age"

We all are getting older
It really is a bore
When you find you can no longer do
The things you did before

There was tennis, there was dancing
And swimming from the shore
The leaping on your bike
To go shopping in the store

Then milking cows and making hay
And working on the land
Going overseas for holidays
And playing in a band

Now you cannot see and cannot hear
And walking is quite hard
Our strides are only inches,
Where they used to be a yard

But looking back on all your life
Brings memories galore
Which make you wish that you could say
"Please Sir" I want some more

Dorothy Longley

Growing

Maybe, you'll always be young
And never have to earn your keep
To dress accordingly
Choose your words.
You'll never have to play the game
Or love but one woman
Father children
Force a smile.
Never develop aches and pains
Or lose your hair and teeth
Entertain to be sociable
Wash dishes to be noble.
Pretend to like modern music.
Forced to listen to small talk
To understand what went wrong
And put it right, till next time.
You'll never just want to read a book
And close the bedroom door
Curl up warm and snugly
You'll always be young, maybe.

Ilan Bar-Nathan

Friendship

Friendship is a wonderful thing
It makes you feel aglow
My heart it seems to sing
Just hope my happiness shows.
I know I like the warmth of the sun
And friends like you as well
When all is said and done
To know you is simply swell.
A friend is worth a fortune
Far more than money can buy
Someone when you need them
Is always standing close by.
I thank the Lord for finding you
Or was it the other way
For me it is something new
Just hope it's here to stay.
Material things are worthless
They only fade away
But friendship even under stress
Will remain alive always.

J. D. Groundsell

Live For Today

Live for today
    It comes not again,
Let not your mind dwell
    On yesterday's pain.

We cannot re-live
    The joys and the sorrows,
We only can hope
    For the better tomorrows.

So enjoy the bright moments
    That might pass your way,
Forget the dark patches -
    Just live for today.

D. Vera Johnson

The Dump

There were rusty creasy taps
Stood beside some cricket bats.
Broken lamps and broken sinks,
Toilet chains and rusty links,
Smelly broken rubbish tins,
Washing machines and black bins,
Old and broken window frames
Lorries, cars and huge cranes,
In the corner lay broken clocks
And in the mud were rusty locks

Katie White

When Love Hath An End

To live a life
Tho' feel half-dead.
The curse of rejection,
A hell! All fear and dread.
Flagitious fortune:
On whose shoulders, metered out,
Can easeful overthrow
Spirits even strong, once stout.
'Twill sickle hearts
Wrench out all hope,
And drove the vanquished
Wretched o'er the slope.
To have all control
Torn from one's grasp.
Love's joys, ordained to soothe,
Then formed to rasp.
O! Fie on fate, when trust
And kinship in a spouse has fled!
The sacred vows: then desolate
And empty, as the marriage bed.

John Archer

Radiance

The happiness which radiates from you,
Seeps into the essence of my soul,
Giving me warmth and courage,
Keeping the cold chill of loneliness,
From my door.

Wayne Bilbrough

Making Love

When with my body I thee worship
Then worlds collide above,
And angel hands descend to play
The violins of love.
And as the music soars away
Beyond the hills of time,
The Gods upon Olympus smile
And bless this love divine.
Your breath like galleons on fire
Burns on my waiting lips,
And waves of milk and honey flow
Beneath your pounding hips.
There is no land, there is no sea,
The earth is merged in sky.
There is no time, there is no space,
Like moths, our spirits fly—
Then suddenly, there's stillness,
Hands caress and gently creep
With a sigh, wrapped in a smile
Round lovers as they sleep.

P. M. Parlour

Who Knows?

If you could see inside my mind
So many troubled things you'd find
So many things that I don't know
So many feelings I can't show

So many things that I can't see
So many things I want to be
But I just cannot work it out
I don't know what it's all about

Is it okay to be afraid?
To have a doubt or fear
And sometimes let emotions show
Or even shed a tear?

I don't know what the answer is
I don't know what to say
I'm travelling down the road of life
But I do not know the way.

Elon W. Charles

He Is My Father

Hatred boiled in my bosom
But love burnt in His
Both my Creator and Counsellor
For He is my Father

When in Adam I rebelled
He cast me not away
Instead, A Saviour He promised
Because He is my Father

Through all the prophets
My Salvation He foretold
At my behest, His only Son He sent
Just because He is my Father

And so my death He died
My debts He paid
Oh what a love, so great
That's why He is my Father.

Nobert Amaraegbu

Lea

Lying lazily in a field
gazing into a pure blue sky
Cotton clouds are revealed
Beautiful butterflies dancing by

Shining golden is the sun
water trickling down the stream
children playing having fun
am I floating in a dream?

Birds soar through the trees
Lips of mine release a sigh
gentle whispers form a breeze
as hours of time wind on by

Startled only by their sound
Now it's time to be on my way
Tiny creatures buzzing around
I'll keep this picture from today

A. Craig

Ben

You came and went so quickly
Like a flicker in the night.
You were so brave, so beautiful,
You tried so hard to fight.
God only takes the very best,
To be with him at his side
But the day he chose to take you
We just broke down and cried.
But now you will be free from pain
Free to laugh and play
But rest assured dear Benjamin
We will be together again one day

E. Meek

A Child

You look at me,
You turn instantly
I know I'm not pretty,
I'm only a child

But still you sneak a look
I see that pity in your eye
I may be a child
But I don't need your pity
What I need is your smile.

A smile that means so much to me,
Just to show you care,
That you could show me love,
Love that means more than pity,
So much more to me,
Yes, I'm only a child,
Only another retarded child.

P. Devlin

Gale

Brown leaves running,
Town dust whirling,
Roof smoke leaning,
In an autumn gale.

Back gates swinging,
Loose lids crashing,
High tiles sliding,
In an autumn gale.

Rain clouds speeding,
Pale sun gleaming,
Sharp showers biting,
In a winter's gale.

Sea walls creaking,
Rivers rising,
Drains o'erflowing,
In a winter's gale.

Thick blinds pulling,
Bright fires lighting,
Humans hiding -
From a winter's gale.

Eileen Sier

Our Mum

She did her very best for us
And gave her love without a fuss
She cared and helped whenever she could
Kind and loving, who thought only good
We loved our Mum.

She left us for a better place
The empty void is hard to face
We shall ever remember her gentle ways
They will sustain us all our days.
We loved our Mum.

She went to meet past loved ones
As will we when our time comes
All will be joyous love once more
We shall know what life was for.
We loved our Mum.

Daphne Morey Choppen

Nature's Wonder

Tiny seeds are scattered,
Upon our mother earth.
Warm rain gently falling,
Bringing forth new birth.
Green leaves quickly sprouting,
Spring is on its way.
Flowers sturdily growing,
Nurtured by sun's ray.
Nature's many wonders,
Jewels of the ground.
Nature's gift of beauty,
Does ever us surround.

Mary Jones

Self Pity Or Reality

I'm the unluckiest man they know of,
or that's what they say about me,
whatever I do seems to turn out wrong,
It can only happen to me.

My life seems just one big disaster,
I can't seem to get it right,
this long and lonely road I walk,
there's no light I see in sight.

My hope is to be successful,
and lead a happy life,
is that too much to ask,
for my children and my wife?

M. White

To The Love Of My Life

There's a rose outside my
window
It reminds me so much
of you
that rose will fade and
die my love
but that will never
happen to you
the memories you give me
now, my love
will last forevermore

Eric Evans

Alter Ego

Dreams are suspect, the senses lie,
reacting from the stimuli
of my conniving brain.
And yet my principles permit
a crazy Hamlet to admit
the doubt that I restrain.

Freud has pronounced and I obey,
Darwin and Pavlov have their say,
Descartes will let me be.
The Masters call the tune and set
my motions, like a marionette,
to dance my destiny.

But like an incubus I keep
a Hamlet to disturb my sleep
and nag of other things
undreamt of by these latter day
Horatios - who know by they
have robbed the tombs of kings.

Jennifer Couroucli

A Mediocre Poem

I pondered ...
                    ... silent as a cloud ...
How tall we've built our symbols
... the things that make us proud
Ingenious, engineering ...
Industrious, pioneering ...

Creative, like the river
cuts a wound into the rock
We build the bigger, brighter
for it's only scale we cannot mock
Swarming like the busy bees
we copy, flatter, everkeen
Cloning more, but even better still
to appease our fickle queen

For inspiration and the soul
there's no market in these days
We all but learn too early
"Mediocre" always pays

Ahmed Khan

"Falling Snow"

I see snowflakes falling
From the sky,
I'm getting old,
It's cold, I cry.
The sound of children
In the park,
Playing snowballs,
For a lark.
They make a snowman
With my scarf.
First I smile.
Then I laugh,
Thinking back, when I was a boy
Toboggan, sliding, spills of joy.
Life speedily passes by,
Gentle snowflakes fall from the sky.

Max Doyle

Christmas Bells

We welcome Christmas here once more,
The joy to families bring,
As we sit round the Christmas tree,
Unwrapping all our things,
The holly bush heavy with snow,
And sleigh rides through the town,
A celebrated birthday,
For our king that once got crowned,
Christmas bells, oh Christmas bells,
You hear my singing voice,
We will put our hands together,
Everybody will rejoice,
For all the festive food we eat,
To all our friends we toast,
Pulling all those crackers,
Before the turkey roast,
We will say our prayers for everyone,
Whether near or far,
As little robin chirps away,
Under that special star.

Norma Clarke

Thoughts of Love

The sea is calm,
The air is cool,
Tonight we will be together until
Cupid plays the fool.
Your smile is cute,
Your voice is sweet,
our minds together beat as one
giant heartbeat.
Your eyes bring a smile for every
blink you make,
So please make your move
before you set my heart beating.

J. L. Evans

Picture On The Wall

The Portraits in the hallway,
Hanging, on the wall.
It tells a tale of history,
Of answering the call.
It tells a tale of freedom,
Of how we won the war.
For if they had not fought to win,
Old England would be o'er.
The poor old soldiers died,
Fighting for us all.
But they will live in memory,
By the picture on the wall.

Eleanor Upperdine

Going Away

Leaving behind the one I love
The one for whom I care,
The friendship that formed unknowingly
The one we'll always share.
The sadness as we part
Going far, far away.
The losing of the chance
of things we had to say.
The hiding of the tears
We didn't hug or kiss,
The fun I had with you
The things I'll always miss.
Goodbye until next time
but we will meet again,
until then, my special friend
how do I forget the pain?

Nina Islam

Hearing The News Of Dad's Death

I lived in a flat in London
Working nine to five hours
In the Civil Service,
When it happened.
The fag-in-mouth Landlord
Called me to his creepy room
One dark, pitiful night.
"It's about your father. He's..."
(There was a long pause)
I said, "Dead?"
He nodded.
I lay awake all night.
The next morning the traffic was busy.
(Funny how the world didn't stop)
I went to see a Welsh girl
Who I was in love with.
(But she didn't love me)
She asked if I wanted a boiled egg.
I said, "No, thanks."

Roy Iliffe

Untitled

It's so cold
You can feel the icy
Fingers of winter
Pierce your blood
Like a sliver of cold steel
It eats into your very soul
Leaving you shivering
Teeth chattering
You hug yourself in
An effort to get warm
But you fail
You go home
And curl up in front
Of a warm fire
Slippers on
A hot drink warming
Your ice cold finger tips
The warmth spreads down
To your toes
At last you're warm again.

Miriam Staker

Eternity

Across the baking sand we run
Beneath a shimmering sun
To an oasis of blue horizon
Soaring towards the sky.

Splashing the swirling blue deep,
We turn and hold each other
Your wet lips - so full and sweet
Beneath your breast, a soft heartbeat

Swept away by your spell
Crashing surf encircles above.
An island of love, amongst the swell
As you drown me in your love

Hugh O'Donnell

First Love

To be in love, in love like this
I'm telling you, it's utter bliss
The two of us alone together
We'll go on for ever and ever
I love you more than words can say
I love you more and more each day
We'll go on for ever and ever
Will we part, no way, not ever
I tell you this I do not lie
A love like ours will never die

Julie Steele

Transformation

In a pretty country village
A small thatched cottage stands,
Derelict and empty,
On a tiny plot of land.

It must have looked so lovely
When it had some-one to care.
It was so sad to see it
In need of much repair.

One day an artist painted it
As he thought it once had been.
Now set in a beautiful garden,
It became a lovely scene.

Yet nothing had been taken
From the character it held,
Just a little restored beauty,
To where, once, someone had dwelled.

Now, within a lovely frame,
This remarkable picture stands.
A derelict country cottage,
Transformed by an artists hands.

Brenda Thorne

When We Become One

Watching you closely
I see in your eyes
burning desire,
they hold no disguise.

Your smooth curving smile
that captures my voice,
enchanting my thoughts,
I've no other choice

You... like the wind
Me... like a flower
Each breath that you take
withdraws all my power

I couldn't start to tell you
the ache my heart feels,
My passion for you
it feels so unreal.

Now look to the future
for it has begun.
I await that moment
when we become one.

Tammy Chester

Questions

When I come home
Tired hungry and torn
I pull up a chair
With you all snug and warm

As I unwind
I softly caress your skin
As I open the covers
Let the romance begin

Will you make me laugh
Will you make me cry
Will you mess up my emotions
Will you leave me high and dry
Will you tell the truth
Will you be full of sin
Will my heart be on fire
Well let the adventure begin

Does the heroin find love
Do the good guys win
There are so many questions
Well the answers lie within

M. Smith

377

Life

If you get hurt it ebbs away,
If you die it does not stay.

A passable ticket to this world,
A breath untouched but all disturbed.

A subject for a poetry class,
An object in a looking glass.

A soul contained beneath the skin,
The life inside, the one within.

A continuous experience, one to share
A man, a woman who both will care.

Life not death and not much more,
A story, a spirit, a closed, open door.

Clare Green

Mountains

Here exists
a vast and terrifying peace
in the constantly changing
light of the sun's tide;
a sprawling network
of miniature continents
distantly related to the horizon,
blasted like moon mosses
from centipede worlds
high in the stratosphere
of altered time and space.

Nik Morgan

Untitled

I wish I could take the pain from you
Oh how I wish with all my heart
Knowing that special friend of yours
Is soon from you to part.

Try to remember the good times
You shared with one another
And you must always remember
He wouldn't want you to suffer.

This world is full of evil things
But he will feel no pain
He'll go to doggie heaven
And have everything to gain.

We don't know what kinda life he had
But this you know is true
You gave him everything you could
In the short time he had with you.

Don't fret my love, don't fret no more
He will soon be fast asleep
And all those treasured memories
Are forever yours to keep.

Amanda Dean

Loves Insecurity

To love again —— once love is sworn,
Risks bleeding heart and soul once torn
Sleeplessness that kindles thought
Of bitter lessons earlier taught.
Trust given as a priceless gift
Another's weighted soul to lift
To chance perhaps awesome pain
To feel the touch of love again.
But if you lose, will you survive
Though only live not be alive.
Burning like some raging fire,
Flames powered by pure desire.
Has temptation proved to much?
And this feeling simply lust.
But trust and love did prevail
Tearing down doubts dark veil.
A kiss, that taste of ecstasy
To end loves insecurity.

Phil Prosser

War Games

I watched a boy with interest
As he played out with his friend
A game of war and Indians
A game of let's pretend

But one day I think he'll realize
When he grows to be a man
What war and death has done to us
To avoid it if he can

The boys and men who went to war
Most likely did the same
Not knowing that in some years' time
It would be real and not a game

If words could solve our problems
Then would the fighting cease?
This I hope for years to come
That we can live in peace!

J. Freeborough

Untitled

Oh lady solitude I embrace you
You are the pathway of God's few.
Tranquillity and peace lie therein
Who dedicate their lives to Him.

Oh lady solitude 'tis you I love
Listening quietly to the Lord above.
God uses you to speak to me
My soul rejoice thanking thee.

Oh lady solitude have no fear
Surround me in your mantle here
Enclosed in God's loving care
No troubles do I have to bear.

J. F. Napier

'Life'

Beauty can be found
   in oh so many things
Amongst the most amazing
   a pair of insect wings
A filigree of colour of
   every shade and hue
And movements quite
   Incredible to folks
like me and you

Pat Groot

Untitled

My heart can never say goodbye
Because I love you so
And whenever I've been with you
I never want to go

So many will make it sordid
This love that means so much
Even now just thinking of you
Makes me hunger for your touch

We shall prove them wrong my love
As the weeks go speeding by
I've told you that my love will last
Even beyond the day I die

This tremendous force which binds us
Against my strongest will
In spite of all my common sense
Is growing deeper still

I cannot help keep thinking back
To that fateful winter's night
But in spite of all my worrying
To love you - I know is right

Margaret E. Budgett

Ode To Ire

Oh, Ire you emerald evergreen land,
   of deep dark earth rain soaked sod.
Oh tortured, tortured soul of man,
   Why, oh why have you forsaken God.
Why; sup and drink from Satan's hand,
   Who; bends you to his twisted rod.
Cast of his painful shackled band,
   live in peace, love, and en-joy.
      God's evergreen land.

John Turner

Maelstrom

Frustration grows within my head,
Phrases fighting - no repose.
All those things I might have said,
If equipped to so compose.

Unused words required invention
To ease the uproar in my mind,
To comfort and allay confusion,
But no such solace can I find.

I struggle with this gnawing ache,
Inadequate as one struck mute.
I plead for aid, for my God's sake,
Whoever He be, can He refute?

Then at last, I gain perception,
Turmoil gone - oil on the sea.
There is no need for this commotion,
For I am you, and you are me.

As one, we need no author's pen
To relate those inner notions.
Our poetry belongs in Heaven
And transcends life's blackish oceans.

Andrew Guy Homfray

The Lady Of The Wood

The lady of the wood
Sat still, not a word
She wasn't to be seen
She wasn't to be heard.

She sat in the corner
Of the wood, on her own
But deep in her heart
She was never alone.

Coralie Hartigan

Civil Times

Come with me my little one,
Away from this beating drum,
Let the soldiers fight their way
You'll only die if you stay.

War, oh this bloody war,
Bodies lying across the floor,
Fine men they once were,
With tears, they became a blur.

Houses, fields, burn to ashes,
Looters, suffer leather lashes,
Shells shake this rocky ground,
With cries of pain, from all around.

The smell of cordite powder,
As the gunfire echoes louder,
Charge after charge dulls the pain,
With inch by inch of land they gain.

Let's go, let's flee this bloody war,
You won't suffer this no more,
Come with me my little one,
Before we and this bloody war are done.

D. Honeysett

La Mer

Few saw her arrive
Although precise in her daily habit
She was so part of life as not to
expect an audience,
The hem of her salt green dress
brushed the golden sharpness of the
carpet below.
She stayed to see the ebbs and flows
of the next few hours knowing that
whatever the fate of mortals
the issue of her neaps and bores
would reverberate throughout.

Steph Needham

Love

I sat on my bed thinking of you
I pulled back my curtains
It wasn't you
I'm still here waiting
From this day on
I want to see you
but you're in the wrong.
You're the one, the one for me
I love you but do you love me?
Please come round here
We need to talk
about our problems on a walk.
I can't stop thinking of you
I want to see you before you die
So come here quick
we'll say our goodbyes.

Lisa Waterman

World Of Despair

The world is here
it holds us all
we still destroy it
soon we will fall

We destroy our world
we kill each other
they strive for peace
why do they bother

The world is at war
at war with one,
destruction inevitable
no one will have won

The bombs still blast
they're wrecking lives
but in our hearts we see
for peace the world strives.

The world is at peace
our balance is there
we and the world are one
no longer is there despair

Lee Nicholls

Untitled

From the dark
There was light
From the light
There was hope
From the hope
There was opportunity
From the opportunity
There was reward

From the dark
There was no reward
From no reward
There was no hope
From no hope
There was only the dark

N. Hartigan

War

Echoes from a distant war
still ringing down the years.
Driftwood on a blood red shore
still bringing back our fears.

A candle in the wind of death
still burning bright and fierce.
Blown out in the final breath
of a man who's heart we pierce.

A field of poppies in full bloom
nurtured by grief and tears.
Loved ones deep in mortal gloom
lost voices no one hears.

Men kill men in wars of hate
lessons are not learned.
Peace laid in the fire grate
hopes are scorched and burned.

The child of war is born again
torn screaming from the womb
to die in rage of tortured pain
and laid coldly in it's tomb.

Trevor Downing

The One I Love...

As birds sing
I think of you.
For you are the one I love.

When not singing
I think of no-one
For there is no-one to love.

As he lays me to sleep
He waits with eyes open
For nothing shall be wrong
Whilst my light is there.

He is my light and my life
For he is the one I love
When awake my light is still there
For I am the one he loves.

Our love is special
A spark that shall burn forever
Our flame will die
When he leaves me sleeping

I will wait...
For that time to come.

Susannah Craig

Ghost

The old door creaked,
With an echoing groan,
The cold wind blew,
And a horrible moan...

Was sent through the house,
Making everything clatter,
The place shook with terror,
The windows all shattered.

Then straight through the wall,
Flew a horrible spook,
Dust filled the room,
And make everyone choke.

The spook was quite quick,
And nobody saw,
Him infiltrate,
Through the rock solid floor.

It had glowering eyes,
And quick light feet,
But nowt did it say,
For that ghost was a sheet.

Liam Thatcher

Tomorrow Never Comes

She sat in the corner weeping,
Not with pain but with sorrow,
She knew this scene so well,
That drunken, hard voice of that man
She once loved,
How could this be true?
She thought with hurt and guilt,
Maybe this was her fault,
Maybe somewhere along the line
She'd done something wrong,
She thought of the past
That trust that never lasts,
"I'll leave him tomorrow," she wept,
But tomorrow never comes.

Tammy Louise Davies

The Greatest Deed I Can Do

Today is tomorrow
What I am - I will be,
What I desire - I will have
If I want to, I can.

Life presents what it will
And that is as far as it can go,
The master of my destiny is - I
I will be as I choose.

Tomorrow will be as I dream
I will reach the stars,
I will see the land beyond
Adventure will be mine.

The greatest deed I can do
Is action today,
Then I will live and love
And in that - I will be.

Tafadzwa Muparadzi

Bereft

I took a vow of poverty
Gave away my property
Silver and gold I sold
Nothing remained Tear-stained
Bereft of all I possessed
Depressed I wanted you

I took a vow of chastity
Denounced all my curiosity
Never to conspire with desire
Goodbye vanity Hello banality
Bereft of all that obsessed
Transgressed I desired you

I took a vow of obedience
Denying self and confidence
No choice No inner voice
Now compliant and undefiant
Bereft of all things expressed
Distressed I needed you

Austen A. Penlington

With Me

You did not die,
Because you are with me,
Inside me and around me,
The pain of losing you,
is more than I can take.

I see you before me,
around me, in everything I do,
you're in my mind,
you will never leave me,
because I love you,
and you love me.

Anna Dickson

A Stray Bitch

She's a border collie
With a doleful eye
Sweet natured she is
And a friend of mine

An orphan, no owner
Just two years old
Picked up by the police
In Yarmouth I'm told

To Potter Heigham they took her
To the R.S.P.C.A
Two thousand are gassed
Every week they say

We paid ten pounds
Just to save her life
But what a friend we have
Me and my wife.

Philip Knight

Believe

Underneath the moon I dream,
Far away from here I see,
There lies a peaceful place to be,
It's somewhere you can share with me,
It's somewhere, out there,
If you believe.

Kai Wootton

Lovers

I love my life with you,
Each and every day,
All the things you seem to do,
In your own special way.

I love you in the morning,
When the sleep is in your eyes,
I love the look upon your face,
When I give you a surprise.

I love the way you smile at me,
When you're relaxing in your chair,
And when I reach out to touch you,
I know you're always there.

I love the little things you do,
To please me in your way,
And how you always seem to know,
The very words to say.

I know I'll always love you,
And with you I'll be content,
Because I know the love we share,
Has been heaven sent.

Doreen Southall

"To My Mother"

You are to me, so very special,
Like no-one else could be,
You're part of my world
And part of my heart
But mostly part of me.
You brought me into this very world
And then you showed the way,
You've always cared and listened
Whenever - night or day.
You're the one who gave birth to me,
Which no-one else could do
And that is why I want to say
So many thanks to you.
I want to say so many things
Which I don't know how to do
But I think there's a line which sums
Them up,
And that is
"I Love You."

Ciara Kelly

Nostalgia

A Country walk, a timeless joy
Long remembered since a boy
Sunday afternoons were good,
Sunday School, then through the wood
To pick some bluebells (in the Spring)
What a beautiful, fragrant thing!
Celandines and cowslips grew,
Many then, but now, so few.
Birds would sing high in the sky,
Couldn't place them, wonder why.
Through the wood and over fields
Much more beauty now revealed;
Calves and cows and ponies too,
Ewes with lambs, almost new.
Grass and trees, tender, green,
What does all this beauty mean?
It means that Mother Nature will,
Every day give us a thrill
Of life and colour on a walk
That we'll remember and forever talk

Howard John

Little White Lies

Lying—what a lie,
Everyone must lie,
Little white lies!
See, lying is survival.

Lies, lies, lies.
They grow you see,
deeper and deeper,
Until the truth dies!

Little white lies.
Are no longer,
They grow until,
You are no longer.

Tammara Michelle Wilband

Beaching At Silver

To me
The sand was the sea,
Shifting and moving,
Rearing and biting the bit,
Making rippling waves over my toes,
Stretching forever,
A vast domain
With great waves
Towering over its hidden treasures,
Swallowing up the watery shore,
For in the sun
Water glowed golden,
And grains tinted with blue.

Elaine Kenny

"Beauty In A Cage"

Wings flexed once, then twice
Searching eyes cast to grey skies
Dreams of spirals in the air
Not below his friends free cries.

Arched head peering through
The grey criss cross of his cage
Condemned to live this way
Life that truly is a stage.

Thoughts of better days
Run across dry sunlit plains
South African plateaus
Green canopies, sporadic rains.

Tell me why it's so
This thing of beauty should be
Forced to exist, not live
For the likes of you and me?

Debbie Warrier

Eyes of My Shoes

Lying beneath my feet,
the slow swish of the water-wheel
runs in a dream;
clear blue water, a dusky mill,
the damp scented room
still lies below.

A man grows older,
weaves the magic spell of the mill,
harvests memories:
A ginger cat lying in the corner,
a donkey runs the grind-store.
Here I am standing on stillness,
listening to silence.

Jenni Clark

I Will Lift Up Mine Eyes . . .

All will gaze on flaming glories
At sunset or at dawn.
I find beauty e'en more wondrous
In skies all lined and drawn.
Though my soul be filled with rapture
By fleecy baby cloud,
Trailing like celestial garment —
Such joys are for the crowd
Give to me the fleeting splendours
Of streaks of tender green.
These, though shown to me so rarely,
Treasured are when seen.
Or the shapes of hills and castles,
Or dragons drenched with gore,
Oft repeated cloud formations,
Yet varied evermore.
And this once the wordy wise ones
An insight true have shown —
Names like cumulus and nimbus
Breathe magic all their own.

Ronald Lee

Parting Gesture

Grateful thanks
for the tanks.
A barrel up each nostril
will foster
a soldier of fortunate unease,
unfortunate orphans
readily unwilling to please.
Fences of pretence
built on
the sly smiles of indifference.
Signatures of ruptured
unity,
Mine's a Kalashnikov
tanks for the memory?

Christopher Kewell

My Mother

A mother, have I,
Who is a fairy,
A mild nature, has she,
Which helps her to be merry.

I am lucky indeed,
To get a sweet Mother,
When I am in need -
Of her, she senses it earlier

She gives me kiss,
Kiss of lovely roses,
When I feel her miss,
Think, I am in a loss.

I love her rather,
Than anything else,
She is a mother,
Of all my senses.

K. Anuja

I Saw You

I saw you last night
You were a star shining in the sky
I saw you last night
You were smiling, a sparkle in your eye

I felt you last night
Felt your breath upon my face
I felt you last night
Felt your energy and your grace

I needed you last night
Needed to feel your touch
I needed you last night
Needed to love you so much

I heard you last night
Heard you call my name
I heard you last night
Your words eased my pain

I missed you last night
But your memory lingers still
I missed you last night
I love you and I always will

Tony Hucks

Untitled

Times when this human heart
  needs for warm embrace.
Yet barren hours do not leave me barren
  nor pull of pain
    nor suffering's pierce
  bleed dry my life.

In moments - still gather
  my juices that feed the
  fruit to ripen
  and to share.

Catriona MacPherson

Destiny

The air is stuffy: it stifles,
My walk is slow and stiff,
This limp it hinders my thinking,
My thinking is slow like my pace.
The leaves are swept by the wind,
They decay as the warm rain falls,
It soaks through my trousers and skin,
My throat becomes dry like before.
They say my hair is too long,
It's true it gets in the way,
Like spiders it crosses my face,
Like spaghetti collects at my mouth.
I'm here if you wish to find me,
My leaves are a path in the dark.

Anita Clarke

Broken Promises

Still and quiet remains the air
The town all tired and cold
Whilst time ticks by without a care
The daylight is getting old.

Light returns so the streets now fill
A package is seen nearby
Ticking away, its aim to kill
Innocence, not knowing why.

Destruction! Despair takes over
Smoke and debris fill the air
Women and children take cover
Time goes on without a care.

A number of people have died
To change this what can be done?
Politics is choosing to hide
But innocent people must run.

Jaime Austin

Erin

How green are the cloves,
In this land of Eire?
How wild are the rovers
In this country of desire?

  Are its fairy tales true?
  Ghosts, Goblins, an' all
  Enchanting skies of blue
  Leprechauns blowing their horns.

The wailing of the banshee
In the dark of the night
Eyes peering at you
Bodies out of sight.

  'Tis grand to belong
  To this beautiful land.
  With legends such as this
  Sure you're the envy of any man.

Sinead Davison

"If Only"

No matter what happens,
as you go through life,
with all the happiness you find,
go the stress, and the strife.

We'll make mistakes which
we wish we could atone,
but at one stage in life,
you will be alone.

Oh, if only I had done this,
oh, if only I had done that,
would it have changed our lives?
Only the Lord knows that.

Don't mope and shut yourself in,
and wonder what life's all about,
get out there and make new friends,
enjoy life, and get yourself out.

With your new friends and God,
who is there every day,
You'll find a new peace in church,
when you sing hymns and pray.

T. M. Harrison

My Summer Love

I'll never forget last summer,
that summer of 95,
When your warmth, your smile,
and your tenderness
Brought my whole body alive.

Now that summer is over,
I'm no longer wanted,
feeling sad and alone,
All I'm left with are memories,
and your voice at the end of a phone.

Rachel Richards

Freedom

Freedom is the greatest gift
and if I died tomorrow,
I'd know I really did exist
life's not an empty hollow.

Compound fractures I've received
so many, I've stopped counting,
now so strong, so positive
I'd climb the big Rock Candy mountain

My spirit has been freed at last,
make way for it's direction,
elusive it might be, my heart,
I'm drunk on resurrection.

Marian J. Rutherford

Untitled

The wind stilled for a moment,
Each flower bowed its head.
And everywhere was silent,
The man on the cross was dead.

He'd claimed to be a saviour,
They said it was a lie,
And so they hung him on a cross,
He was condemned to die.

They took away his body,
And wrapped him in a shroud,
So bravely had he passed away,
His courage never failed.

That Friday was a black day,
On Sunday shone a light,
The Son of God rose up again,
To guide us to do right.

To steer us from temptation,
A cross, a crown, a thorn,
And all that happened years ago,
When Easter day was born.

Christina Thorpe

New Relationships

I sit alone and think of you
it's all so wonderful and new
I wonder if you feel the same
it feels so good with you

The early days of being together
finding out about who we are
a tender touch, a gentle kiss
a melting look across a bar

I'm scared to want you too much
in case it all goes wrong
I'd like this to be good for us
my feelings for us are strong

At last we're here holding each other
as close as two people can be
I'll take each day as it comes now
we'll just have to wait and see

New relationships always bring
old fears, new hopes and dreams
the risk of getting hurt again
is never as bad as it seems

Dianne Rodgers

"A Wild Orchestra"

At 5:30 a.m. he returned with his
orchestra of notes

After a long harsh winter, his song
filled the still dawn,

He awakened our depressed souls
and promised us love, peace, and
hope for springtime,

Each note thrilled and stunned the
echoes of time, and like time itself
he sang onwards with gay abandon,
proud and true,

To whom or to what was his song
intended? It seems like he had
a harem of lovers and with such

command stilled them into submission,
what arrogance, he was pompous
and forthright

at 5:55 a.m. a still earth returned,
silence abounded and I thought
about my life.

Nikola Merrigan

Bathroom Blues!

I'm sitting in the smallest room
In quiet concentration.
I thought that I could be alone
At least for the duration,
But children don't play by the rules
And come bounding up the stairs
And barge right in and crowd around
And modesty despairs.
Now as I sit here I must act
As referee and consoler.
There is no peace in the smallest room
For any young child's mother!

Eilis Breathnach

Always Memories

Always to me, you will be
The loving, caring husband I remember.
So many memories recalled,
Cherished within my mind,
Of how perfect our marriage was.
Things went wrong and I walked away.
Turned my back on the only man
Who'd ever done everything for me.
Time passed, I thought of you still,
Were you happy with your life?
All I ever wanted, your happiness.
Reflecting on knowledge gained
Since our parting,
I know now, all too late,
What a mistake I made.
I cannot turn back the clock.
I cannot say sorry to you.
Since you have taken your soul
To the Angels.

Zoë Fail

Untitled

Sitting on the pier
Staring out to sea
Wondering what's ahead
What's in this life for me

Trying to understand
What I feel inside
My emotions come and go
Like the movement of the tide.

I look up at the birds
High up in the sky
Fighting wind and rain
Trying hard and fly.

They soar they glide
Move from left to right
Trying to survive this world
I know they'll be all night.

I feel just like those birds
I want more from life not less
Wondering what's ahead; well
I'll be ok; I guess.

Rauley

Shattered Dreams

Shattered Glass
Broken into a million pieces
Checking for cuts
On passing pilgrims
A terror bomb
Fire engine on the scene
Condemnation from all angles
Press reporting in
Mindless murder without borders
Lost lives, shattered dreams
Politicians playing political games

Bryan Heavey

Four Different Horses

Red Rose is a quiet horse
For a lady to ride,
Jog-trotting on the bypass
Or even through the countryside.

Wolf is a hunter
All strong and tough;
Day long he will cantor
Not tumble or fall.

Black Magic's a race horse;
Disappeared like a will-of-the-wisp.
With the wind in her mane
To speed past the winning line.

But munching and chewing all
In a field of green clover
Stands Brownie the cart horse,
Whose labour is over.

Laura Campbell

The Snowman

He's out there in my garden,
With a scarf on and a hat,
He's very white and shiny,
He's also very fat.

He's got lovely big potato eyes,
And a turned-up parsnip nose,
He's got a carroty sort of grin,
But no shoes are on his toes.

He's out there every morning.
Although, he's getting thinner
Perhaps he'd like to come inside,
And share our Christmas dinner.

Oh, my snowman's gone today,
I don't know how he'll see,
He's left his eyes and nose behind,
Underneath our apple tree.

Francis Bryant

Karen

My name is Karen,
I'm such a bad'an,
Always after boys,
An I like a little love,
But not all lovely dove,
All in all,
I like them all,
Who like to have some fun.

Karen Ward

The Mountaineer

It stands there,
Reverberating, majestic
Silhouetted,
Piercing the midnight sky
Relentless, without mercy,
Challenging to justify.
The spirit of this mountain
Breathes life into his soul,
With passion and endurance
He begins his final goal, —
To climb this vicious beauty
In its entirety, —
To satisfy his fervent need; —
This is my loved one's destiny,
For guidance and protection
I ask the Lord above: —
Don't let this mountain claim him,
He is mine, —
My one true love.

Pauline Barnes

Infinity

Thinking about infinity,
never coming back here,
for once I've gone
where will I be where.

If only I had
the elixir of youth
I'm frightened with
thoughts of death
that's the truth.

For granted I take
my life here on earth,
wishing the years
over again from birth.

Joan Middleton

FALLEN

Lost
and seeking asylum
of life I abstain.
Alone
my own assassin
I confess all,
Anxious
to apportion the blame.

Bizarre
a banished angel
cutting to the core.
Acquitting
without caution
every aspiration,
Defying
my demise and life's desecration.

Samantha Howard

The Depth Of Beauty

Ships at night in harbour
At rest from tossing waves,
Recline in glowing ardour
From sunset on the caves.

With funnels gently oozing,
The drifting smoke doth float
Into colours soothing,
Each cloud, a painted moat.

How tranquil as the gulls fly,
The trippers stand and stare,
Then twilight warns that night's nigh,
So record these sights so rare.

Only artistic contrasts
On canvas tells the scene,
No change from days gone past,
Perchance, an enlarged screen.

John Webb

As I Recall Those First Few Words

As I recall those first few words
And the smile as you spoke to me,
I often wondered how it would be
If we had never met,
Perhaps there would be no sunny days
No starry nights lasting long,
No one to care what the future brought
Or be there if things went wrong,
All the things I remember,
But the one thing I'll never forget,
That love in your eyes
That captured my heart
The glorious day that we met.

Donita Lois Guile

Alone

She walks through grassy glade
single flower in her hand
her eyes hold a sorrow
what pain weighs this vision.

She stops and wets the flower
with a tear
she falls to her knees
her mouth opens in silent pain
hand tightens against petals
and the flower drops
not moving she sits
her face aged three fold
what grief she carries.

Her life dies behind
beyond be a tunnel without light
the flower she tries to revive
but its life is lost
shed another tear
to a broken stem.

Kevin Campbell

Blue Bells Chantny Land

The cottage on the side of the wood
looks in to the blue bell wood
Blue Bells stretching all the way
This is what I see to day,
There was an old water pump
at the top of the hill, I really
don't think it's there still
The cottage is very old they say
it goes back a long long way.
Francis Chantny lived, not far away
a milk lad he was in his day
He went to Norton church to pray
and took milk round every day.
He went to London to make his way
and so he did, so they say, Francis
Chantny was a clever lad Old Norton
over had a Old Norton is a lovely
place full of dignity and grace.

Bea Mackereth

"Contrasts"

I drew back the curtains
And to my delight
The city I lived in
Was all clothed in white
An Ethereal Scene
A city of Light

Our hearts are a-glow
'Cause we're cosy and warm
But what of the Blizzards
Others face in the storm
There are the frail and the sick
Unable to Cope
The trendless and the "Druggies"
Devoid of all hope

Life is made up of
Pendulum swings
One day you are up
The next in the wings

L. T. Macdonald

Memories

Let's take a walk down memory lane
To shops with tainted window pane
To hold your hand, to sit on grass
Such nice memories of the past
We walk with frames
Our sight remains, along with the glow
inside our hearts
We needn't speak, a look says it all.

Miriam Elias

My Prayer

Dear Lord I hope you hear this prayer,
I need your help so bad,
You see there's something that I'd like
something I've never had
this favour that I ask of you
Will surely break no miles
Just let me guess the numbers
of the score draws on the pools.
I wouldn't want to win a lot
About five hundred thou.
I know just what I'd do with it
In fact it's half spent now.
I'd buy a pub, my local bar,
Where everyone could mingle
let no one in who wasn't male
and tall, dark, young and single
but if you cannot help me Lord,
I won't be sad at all,
if you tell me where the cross goes,
when I fill in spot the ball.

Jacqueline Foster

I Am So In Love

I am so deep in love, I'm so deep in
thought,
My mind's a playground of foolish
thoughts,
He's my boat, the waves I ride
on,
He's my night, my morning, my
daytime,
That boy is the light who clears
the darkness,
Who gives me joy and relieves
my blindness,
The one who has my most powerful
source,
My joy, my gift, my love, my
heart.

Joanne Billson

"Young Days"

Young years pass oh so fast
Always thinking they will last.
Camping down memory lane
In your arms till dawn came
Orders came for sailing again
"Oh heartbroken and sad."
Could not wait for that
Handsome lad.

Jean Partridge

'Love Courage'

"Sky is her name
Stars are exploding in her eyes
And blue moons are floating
As she stares into paradise

Our passions come as a soul dance
Sweet sweat and flesh
Tasted upon the tongues of our fire

To quench and to feed
Those hungry stars
So much desire

Sky looked from paradise away
And tears I saw came wet upon her face
The blue moons emptying out her cry
As she began to say..."

    "Love courage
    Excite me with your gift
    Spice me with your gift
    Caress me with your gift

    Suffocate me".

Marc Paul Graham

Untitled

I dream a dream of a hot summer's
day, for the love I once had that
drifted away.

Like a rose late in bloom faded
and weeping or the last ray of
sunset, her heart nearly sleeping

The shadow of night this time I
must fear brings the heartbreak
of love ever 'creasingly near

So take heed my own lust,
My love it must pray
I dream a dream of a hot summer's day

Geraint Wyn Owen

Seasons Of Love

Spring and distant music heard
Soft voice beckons, almost purred
Music swelling, a startled fawn
Voice compelling as love is born

Roses bloom in summer sun
Violins leap, skip and run
Beating hearts in exquisite tempo
Pristine melody for loves crescendo

Music fading, as leaves are falling
Roses dying, and heart keeps calling
Voice discordant, and violent sigh
As this love prepares to die

Soft lips hard, part no more
Soft wind stir, start to roar
Snow flakes fall, soft white bed
Music fading, love is dead

Victor Reynolds

Our Earth

Oh earth you are so beautiful.
And man is so unkind,
They cause havoc in your waters,
Environmentally most are blind,
You have so many wonders
And you share them with us all.
But still pollution rises
And destruction does not fall.
Green people try to help you,
And fight your worthwhile cause,
But you must feel the turmoil from
From mindlessness and wars
Oh earth you are so lovely,
And man should care for you,
If you ever lose your fight for life,
What would all people do.
Dear earth with hidden strength,
That comes from deep within,
You are the master of us all,
Your time will come again.

Laureen Sykes

The Last Centurion

With head bowed low the soldier stood
So low he looked in shame
Around him lay the dead and dying
But he himself was not to blame.

His comrades had fought hard that day
The enemy had been stronger
The blood that spurt from his wound
He could not live much longer.

Beside him lay a golden bird
An emblem he knew well
One last salute he gave
Then on earth no more to dwell.

Joyce Boast

A Message for You

I said a prayer for
you today,
even though you are
far away.
My thoughts are
with you all the time.
You and your brother
will always be mine.
May Jesus watch over
you in every way
and keep you safe,
both night and day.
I love you, and miss
you, may Jesus keep
you in His arms, until
we meet amongst His
charms.

Lorraine Pritchard

The Profound Dream

From the steps of my redoubt
    With questing gaze cast about
Seeking source of light and song
    Then I behold the celestial throng.
And with bounding joy then I see
    My dearly beloved approaching me
From their midst with ethereal grace
    Hastening to our trysting place
Encircled in her warm embrace
    A loving smile upon her face
One tender kiss, she then moves on
    Beyond the shores of rubicon

Willie Aistrop

Winter's Edge

An imitation spring arrives
after a downpour of rain.
A teasing sun boasts its
black reflection
in shallow pavement pools,
torturing the eye
with pleasure.
Birds ruffle feathers
in anticipation of an easy feed,
yet winter's barely
reached its limitation.
Wait for the yawn
then take arms
against the white invasion.

E. R. Skinner

Space

Black as night
All year round
Quiet and still
Without a sound.

A shooting star
Falls from above
With power and grace
Like the great white dove.

The planets orbit
A big bright star
Slowly rotating
From afar

The man in the moon
With his solemn face
Endlessly looks out
Into that world called
Space.

Deirdre Cronin

Untitled

One November morning as I gazed
out my window. The frost was
like a blanket covering the
grass. Then suddenly the sun
came out, and as each part of
the frost had melted on the grass,
I saw what looked like jewels
glaring at me I run out to touch
each our and as I did each glaring
drop melted in my hand I felt
once more like a child hoping
one might be a magic one I could
keep for me.

Josephine Foley

Sea Birds Isle

Gannets; many, old and young live atop
These island cliffs with flat outcrop.
Steep angle dive, at speed, for prey,
Older birds now blind-at-hitting-spray.
Gannets native to this isle,
Others come and reconcile.
Blind birds remain... atop the rock.
Die and into sea do drop.
Meanwhile young feed old,
Gather round, if night is cold.
Young seen trying out their wings.
To leave, each must fly or foreboding.
Unless they do, cannot return
To top of rock; precipitous burn,
Some leave and land on sea,
Cannot fly off - become Sharks Tea.

Mary Josephine Carroll

My Rebecca

When you hurt, I feel it too,
When you laugh, I laugh with you,
When you rest, I watch you sleep,
When you play, I watch you peep!

I feel a love I never knew,
My life, my love was made for you
Your beauty shines above all skies
And diamonds sparkle in your eyes.

Your smile can make the hardest day
Seem a thousand miles away,
A cuddle gives me so much pleasure
And thoughts I will forever treasure.

I thank you for the sleepless nights,
The felt tip pen that's on your tights,
The endless nappies, shouts and screams
And wallpaper lifted at the seams!

So little one of mine, I say,
I love you more and more each day,
An angel living on this earth —
You'll never know how much you're worth.

Lynn Clarke

Journey

The future slips into the present
Like sea on to the sand,
While the past sails by
With a cargo of experience.

We cannot halt the passing,
We can only watch.
We can only learn.
Storing treasured memories,
Letting go of the pain.

We travel on.
A little older
A little wiser.

Miren Patricia Roberts

Untitled

The loss of a life can be painful
but what if that life is your own,
a witness of a destruction,
a death of all you've ever known.
The blade clutched in the hand,
Will stab deeply into the soul,
The anger, the hurt, the confusion
-
trying to let go.
The eyes will hold the sorrow
the tears will be cried alone,
That sorrow will be covered by curtains
Those curtains will be forever closed.
The questions will remain unanswered,
For where is the sense
to dwell upon the unknown
- to ask those questions,
to which the answers will never
can never, be told.

Lyndsey Kalaher

The Wolf

This great beast
With flashing eyes
When the full moon comes
Hear his howling cries

With his furry tail
And his swift paws
See his sharp white teeth
And his tearing claws

See his smooth fur coat
And his pointed ears
When the sun comes up
How he disappears

Down in his den
There he sleeps
Until another night
When out he will creep

Kieran Leckey

Autumn

Autumn comes and autumn goes,
And silent trees in woodland rows,
Await the coming of the snows,
And mighty gales of winter

The fallen leaves so crisp and brown,
Upon the path are strewn around,
Have richly carpeted the ground
Before the frosts of winter

Philip Dilworth Harrison

Yesterday

I remember you walking into my life
as though it were yesterday
and in a sense it was
the yesterday of my world
the world before
where I dreamt of the future
before the world that is
where I dream of the past.
Yesterday
when light and dark merged
when boundaries blurred
and time ceased to beat
the rhythm of my existence
when lust and love
truth and deceit
reality and myth
became one-sided coins
the currency of my confusion.
I remember when you walked into my life.
Yesterday.

Peter Mullin

In Memory

In memory
of my broken heart
reaching out to your soul
to grant thee a meaningful life
to cherish and love till the doomsday
until the sun rises upon my gloomy day
and a rainbow appears in a fine sky

In memory
of my broken heart
betrayal from thee devastated me
sending a knife to my bleeding life
torn apart in an agonizing breath
apathy from thee towards tenderness from me

And what is left, is only
unforgettable memory
of my broken heart...

Ruwaida Safa

Creatures Of The Meadow

Down in the meadow, where the butterflies play,
And the bees are gathering nectar from the flowers,
The clover and the buttercups are all out in bloom.
And the sun seems to shine there for hours.

The "Pee wit" calls to her chicks on the ground
As she swoops about, up above.
She gets so excited if anyone goes near
As she protects them with motherly love.

The cows walk about, as they graze in the field,
Their only concern is their food.
In the distance you may hear a cuckoo call
As she flies across the sky to the woods.

The meadow is home to animals big and small,
The hedgehog and weasel, the stoat and the mole,
They are all very busy looking after their young.
And the rabbits leave their burrows, to bask in the sun.

When the heat of the day is cooling, and the evening shadows play,
The flowers of the meadow seem to close and fade away.
When the colours in the sky glow from the setting sun,
The creatures of the meadow come out for food and fun.

Annie Dorothy Alcock

The Big Bang

It was all started with a big bang, so the scientists say
    But I believe God stepped in, in a very special way.
He made it round this Earth of ours,
    With his artistic set of powers.
He created beasts, fish, birds and man,
    Trees, flowers, sea and land for the use of man.
So let us give him the praise,
    And take care of this world where cattle graze.
If we don't respect this Earth of ours,
    The Big Bang will return with all of its powers.
It needs us all to play our part,
    If we are to preserve God's wonderful work of art.

M. E. Ashley

Understanding Me

Why don't you realize that I want to be
left alone today.

Stop bothering me, your voice just crowds
my mind when I am trying to think of other
things.

You will never understand me because I
don't want to be understood, I find that
the art of being mysterious makes me who I am.

Even I don't understand myself sometimes,
it's becoming another life of mine.

Living in another dimension, another world,
another time.

Lesley-Ann Ross

Late Spring

Spring came late this year -
But it was worth the wait.
For when the blossoms came -
The best I've ever seen
Hung bold and bright against the new spring green
The horse chestnut tree holds its candle blossom high
Its branches reaching to the sky -
Large bird nest in these tall trees
Catkins on the silver birch shimmer in the breeze.
The magnolia and the cherry tree
Have had a bumper year
The morning chorus of the birds is music to my ear
Small birds nest contentedly in green and leafy bowers
And down below - a carpet -
Of nature's new spring flowers.

June Mimms

Granddad

An ode to my granddad, a dear old man
Who'd be glad to help you in any way he can.
He's the kindest man you'd ever meet,
and when you see him, it's a king you'll greet.
He's had his shares of ups and downs
but never once stooped to the ground
to a grandad warm, and a grandad
true, we are you're family and
    we love you true.

Nadine Carnie

Embrace

I shook of the impulse, the impulse to embrace
As with downcast eyes he averted his face
Is he just shy, or thinks he's too old
Perhaps he thought I was being too bold
I felt the forced grimace, which was saving my pride
When all the while I wanted to hide
The deep freezing hurt at the cold goodbye

Never again was the kiss proffered
To the lips or the cheek that had not been offered
Until many years later when he'd travelled through life
On the way acquiring a child and a wife
He put his arms around me and drew me aside
Pulling me close as he bent to confide

I have something to tell you, he finally stated
I stood there waiting with breath that was bated
I love you, he told me, there it's done
With tears in my voice I answered
I love you too, my beloved son

Patricia Pegg

Looking Out

Here I am sitting behind the blinds, I
watch the rich and the poor, boys and girls
    passing by, yet I sit watching out but
they cannot see in at my face of lost love.
    I watched her walk by with her dark hair
    bound up, her face was rosy and soft as
velvet. She walked closer to the window
    as I looked out at her. Looking in and
smiling, it was the most beautiful sight I've
            ever seen.
    Day after day I watched for her presence
once again. As time went on I saw her no
more. I sit and dream of the same girl I saw
    that day, the girl I feel in love with but never
saw again. As the blinds close so do my eyes
    and everything is dark, as I reopen my eyes
    I see nothing but the darkness of the sky
    around me. I am alone and have gone for
ever, to a place where I will surely meet her for
            the last time.

Paul McFadyen

Gifts From God

Love is liken to a rose.
Day by day it grows.
Each petal opens to reveal its wonder.
It is a joyous spell to be under.
In the garden a rose is a delight.
This another of God's beautiful sights.

So with love that grows day by day.
If watered and fed will stay.
Caring, sharing and giving,
Love's awakening and living.

The rose is the early morning sun
catches the rays, we see spiders have spun
their webs by the mornings light.
So with love it is a delight.

If love is hidden away
eventually it dies, it cannot stay.
A rose if picked and left to dry
it too will shrivel up and die.
They are both a gift from heaven
when truly given.

Jan P. Carmichael

My Prayer

And if when I've travelled the road
I find I have done a good deed
Helped someone carry their load
Or maybe a fellow in need
I'll say life's been worth living
What joy I have reaped on the way
Finding pleasure in giving a lift to a soul
Gone astray

These are the things which will cheer me
By these I'll have gained my reward
Knowing that heaven's been near me
And I have been blessed by the Lord

To give unto others such pleasure
As I have been able to give
With no heed to more earthly treasure
Than the need of wanting to give.

Dorothy Harkcom

As Dusk Falls

As dusk falls over the mountains so green,
Such breathless beauty is still to be seen.
Cows, horses, and sheep, are still grazing there,
As all the beauty of God's earth we share.
While the birds fly homeward to their nest
There is such peace and calm and rest.
The wind still rustles right through the trees,
Making a calm and almost silent breeze.
The sun sets so slowly over the hill
In a blaze of colour, and clouds so still.
Quiet trees stand there, so erect and tall,
As we sit listening to the last bird's call.
Tomorrow will dawn another new day,
But things will go on in the same old way.
God will surround our life with His beauty still,
May we thank Him always and do His Will.

Eunice C. Squire

Answers

Believe, make me believe, in what I hear you say
Say, say anything as I only hear what I want
Want, everyone has but don't dare express
Express our feelings to each other, what we need to do,
  as we are lost without
Without touch that is, the feeling of closeness and security
Security, what we need to find
Find the answers to my questions, impossible as the
  meanings are deep in the heart
Heart, where does the research start?

Sarah Pratley

Spring

As melting snow seeps slowly underground,
To join the stream and flow down to the sea,
New tender shoots of plants are all around -
Snowdrop, primrose and wood anemone.
The sun's pale rays caress the floral show.
Then blossoms turn their heads toward the light
And wait in expectation. For they know
The child who's born that day will bring delight.
Within the cradle Adam coos and sighs.
But when the newborn sees the sheltered glade
His gurgling laughter fills the air and skies.
The blooms rejoice. His future has been laid.
The tumbling stream acclaims that happy boy
While oak and ash unfurl their leaves in joy.

Evelyn Golding

My Heart Sings!

I love all beauteous things!
Thus wrote the poet, but did not tell us more.
My beauteous things are many. I will tell of just a few.
Buttercups and daisies, they are the children's flowers;
Not welcomed by the farmer, so they spring up everywhere.
I taught a little child to make a daisy chain to wear
In her soft golden hair.
Suddenly one summer morn,
A miracle amid the corn!
A cloud of poppies, beauteous things!
I laugh aloud and shout with glee
And applaud their defiance merrily.

In a temple of beauty I softly tread,
Bluebells around me scent the breeze,
Pillars and roof are the beautiful trees.
The rainbow hangs 'twixt earth and sky, ethereal beauty from on high.
The glories of the sunset bold are my jewels of ruby and gold,
Stars are my diamonds, my silver the moon.
"I love all beauteous things".
  And my heart sings!

Irene Dickens

Untitled

I sit and I ponder "What's life all about?"
Sometimes I'm happy, at times in great doubt
The master has fashioned a heaven on earth
Why can't we see it for what it is worth
The flower, the green grass, the hills and the trees
The creatures who dwell on the land, in the seas
What makes us so sure that we're always right
When all we can do is to kill and to fight
The Garden of Eden was spoiled by man's greed
So much of which has been passed to his seed
So I wonder when viewing the great master's plan
What does he think of this thing he called man?

Kathleen Rastall

A Body Of Fear

As a tear caresses her naked eye,
the salt tastes bitter against her tender lips.
Bitter like the feelings within her,
A feeling that's forever burning away inside.

As she watches the night fold up,
the deep black clouds redeem the moonlit sky.
She alone within a confused mind,
wanting to escape the frozen body that's no longer hers.

An infant's cry escapes from her soft, icy lips;
but it's a woman's body that's seized in time.
A woman who is trapped screaming,
tormented inside her own lifeless shell.

The shell is just a timeless void,
but without her mind to comfort her,
She will gently slip away,
Into her own silent world.

Emily Roberts

O There You Are

O there you are!
I see you now
Beyond the boughs of wearied trees.
In tears of crystalline snow -
A vision of you.
And then you slowly melt away,
"Earth to Earth" - a distant voice prays.

O there you are!
I hear you now
Haunting me, lovingly,
Your translucent smile embracing my mind.
The hopes we have - the hopes we had
In dreams now I only find.

O there you are.
But you're not the same.
As silent as our memories.
As invisible as the cruel air
That holds me inside an empty corpse.
O welcome the day, when I will silently say -
O there you are! I'm here to stay.

Louise A. Crabtree

Waves

The wave retreats to its home of discontentment,
It stirs restlessly until its energies are gathered,
Forward it lunges,
All efforts amounted then spent in one determined journey,
It throws its body of true raw
spirit out onto the vast sands in a passionate embrace,
Surrendering itself desperately in an attempt to escape,
Its bony foamy fingers stretch and
reach helplessly for the shore,
Victorious for a second,
Detached it seems from its invincible master,
Time pauses,
However the teasing taste of freedom
is soon to be withdrawn,
Reluctantly the wave is dragged
backwards into its deep blue ruler,
It rolls and sighs,
The calm waters settle,
Yet the resentment and passion of the seas are momentarily calmed,
It schemes and rages deep within its own depths of fury.

Mariam Khan

The First Day As A G.A.

The milkman's rattling the bottles,
the cat's trying to get in, it's 5 o'clock in the morning
and my first day in the kitchen
I hope I don't lie in.

Only 3 hours to go, what shall I do?
It's only twenty miles to Grandma's
She'll say I've got the flu.
It's too late, I'll have to go. I got out of
bed at eight and walked to the hotel gate.

"In you come", said the chef at the gate, "I could
hardly wait to see you mate. There's the sink,
there's the pan and after you have polished that
there's my very dirty van. You will give my van a treat
looking at the speed you travel on them feet

Then there's the windows they're a little grim.
Watch out for the ladder and the old man Jim.

That's enough wake up that prat! Watch out.
Kick that cat." It was ten when I got in; my hands were
sore, my feet red raw. My dad went off his
head, and for some reason I was sent straight to bed!

J. Burton

Trapped

"Life is too short for cheap wine" he said,
and our children, well be are champagne
but if we could have our lives over once more
Would we go down the same paths again?

Decisions are 'oh so important,
rights and wrongs are not known till the end
It's the wrong ones that tear our hearts open
and these are the hardest to mend.

Sometimes through life you meet someone
the conversation, understanding feels good,
It's true my heart skips a beat on these days
Sharing kisses, and walks through the wood

Do not think of a moment that I haven't thought
of how close I have wanted to be,
wrapped around each other in a sea of silk
together just you and me!

But those dreams can go on forever
and I'm sure you will never be mine,
so live for each moment and don't shut me out
for life is too short for cheap wine.

Sheila Hanna

It's Never Too Late To Say Goodbye

We met each other when I was three
You were wee just like me
For seven long years we were together
Yet you grew up and I never.

You were my pal, my buddy, my friend
You were my dog, you know man's best friend
Then one day you made a mistake
You were punished, your life was the stake.

Six years on I still think of you
And the times we had
And even though I know you are dead
In my heart you'll live to the end.

This is why I write this today
To you, my one, my true, my very first dog
To let my heart lay you to rest
And finally say goodbye to an old dear friend.

Even though I now have another
And I love her as I loved you
I promise to you as I write this today
That saying goodbye doesn't mean I'll ever forget you.

Colleen Keenan

The Boy

I often see him in the street,
three years old, a tiny mite.
The first time I saw him
I looked around for his mother
but now I know he's there on his own.

I've been told his father has gone
His mother's been left to bring up the child
Don't think his dad will be back now.
A parent at sixteen, he couldn't cope

The boy's so 'street wise' a real 'live wire'
cheeky and confident, but cute just the same
Hanging around with kids a lot older
they'll educate him on the ways to survive.

I've heard his mother drinks with a vengeance
can't say I'm surprised after what's happened to her.
Dirty and smelling, the boy doesn't know better
sooner or later he'll be taken into 'care'.

But what will become of his broken young mother
there's no-one to take care of her then she'll be the one in the
gutter people ignoring her depth of despair.

Christina Lindsay

Untitled

It is with a great big pride
That in this Forest I do abide,
With the beech, the oak and the Seven Bore
Handed down from days of yore;
The mighty oak with its wood so bold
Saved us all in days of old,
Pounded by the waves in the stormy seas
Blasted with cannon balls by the enemies.
But the ships that were built with the Forest oak
Saved us from the tyrants yoke.
So that we could roam unfettered and free
In this glorious forestry.

A. Shurmer

A Bit O Scottish Poetry From Avril McGregor (Fae Dundee)

I'd like tae pen ye a poem
But I dunno what tae say
My heid's a full a nonsense
Swinging' awa northward wad gae
Eh've jist pit doon a few lines
Ye dinna need tae fret.
This poetry comp
Is affy hard
A'll still be here at eight.
The house door swings in the yaird outside
In front o' the fire on a Setterday night that's right.
Ae day I thocht I'd dump it in the bin
Nae wey! I couldna stuff it in.

Avril MacGregor

Untitled

Why is it when things are bad, they just get worse
Or is it me, do I hold a curse?
Why is it you don't love me anymore?
Maybe you never really did before.
Why is it things are never as they seem
Like in a nightmare or in a dream?
Why do the moon and stars look so inviting?
Nothing in my life is ever exciting.
Why do the sea tides never stop turning,
Like my pain, heartache and yearning?
I think I hate you, no that's not true.
I used to,
But now you're just a memory stored in my mind
From another place, another time.

Jill Elliott

The Modern Gran

When working mothers are bemoaning their plight about the
uphill struggle to get the balance right.
I wish they'd spare a thought for a significant other, namely
the working still young grandmother.
Their task is harder it's an ongoing fight to fit everything in
a schedule that's tight.
Maybe still a wife with a hubby whose glad, he can now be
a husband not a worn out dad.
This woman has guilt trips bigger than a house,
trying to be gran, mother, career woman and spouse.

A trendy grandmother can surf the internet, play basketball
and even hit the net.
She buys you cool clothes, knows which label is best, can
dance to Boyzone and the rest.
But if she's like me there's a struggle inside, a struggle
between memories old values and pride.
Can time be found to bake and to knit, and to sew dollies
clothes that actually fit.
Can she muster the energy to have the little ones to sleep,
to bandage sore knee's, dry tears when they weep.
If you're like me you'll do your best, there's always time for
love and cuddles never mind the rest.

Wendy Marie Walton

If Only..........

You and I my love shared so much
A wink, a smile, a secret touch
You were part of my life for so long
Now you're gone and it seems so wrong

I wasn't there when you felt so bad
When your mind was confused and you were sad
You took your life and gave way to despair
I should have reminded you I'm here and I care

I wish I had known you were troubled and lonely
But it's too late now for saying if only
I fervently wish I had known of your pain
Just maybe your life wouldn't have ended in vain

Like the words of our song, the rainbow has ended
Wherever you are, my love I am sending
I hope you've found the peace that you sought
Thanks for the memories, they are locked deep in my heart.

Angela Monk

Feeling Low (Lowgy)

People, people, people.
doctors, professors, lecturers and top managers.
From all places, major and minor
Forming part and parcel of the grand diners
Raising profile in praises and songs,
In tune with the high plane
   where they belong

But oh-Lord, how my heart sank,
like a heavy silver pan
Down to the level where ocean
meets the land.
Out of tunes with the music they sang.
Hiding little despair prayers between
my hands.
Asking "God, why me? Why them?"
Or may be, I should go.
To where I belong
there should I stay
down the market bingo place.

K. C.

The Virgoan

A child of Virgo is for all so easy to perceive;
Such child will always, through her life, so utterly believe
That every task required of her, and every problem met,
Must with perfection be performed, so there is no regret
Or imperfection marring any duty to be done;
Oh no! With Mercury in charge each challenge must be won.

Each day she must accomplish so much more than any other.
She drives herself so hard, much more than father, sister, brother,
Who, born beneath the other signs, less structured and demanding,
Have tried but failed to instil in her a sense of understanding
That they would love her just as much if she did fall from grace,
And drive herself not quite so hard - live at a slower pace.

But what if, to achieve that goal
She save herself, but lose her soul?

Elizabeth S. Smith

Gramps

Why do I adore, the stars up above,
When they twinkle and sparkle the way I love,
When you're alone and think no-one cares,
Look at the stars they'll always be there,
Stars are so perfect in every way,
If only stars would come out at day,
Then if you're ever alone and sad,
They'll remind you of memories and good times you've had,
Maybe the reason I love these little lamps,
Is because they remind me of you Gramps,
Because now when I see a twinkle in the sky,
I remember the twinkle you had in your eye!

Claire Ellis

Sonnet To Loneliness At Christmas

Young and alone was I; alas! One Christmas night -
"Praying that God would preserve my sanity;"
"Behold! Faith freed me from that melancholy plight."
With praise I thanked heaven for hearing my plea.
My thoughts then in childhood did merrily flow -
To those family parties of yesteryear;
Mid ghost music, Laughter, Echoing low.
"Thro' this bright star of hope: Reborn to rear"
"It was Jesus!" "Who cares for you and me,"
Bringing a message for us all to share
In deeds of kindness, love, humility;
As along life's unknown pathway we bear;
"So if, like you, we do remember that lonely one,"
"Then in true "Festive Spirit," "we will double our fun".

E. S. Clark

Valhalla

Odin, O Odin great God of the north,
In the halls of Valhalla, the place of my birth.
The trumpet has sounded, the death knell is done,
I've fulfilled what I started, the battle I've won.
My family before me, like a great spreading vine.
They know how I've loved them, they will always be mine.
The wind changed direction, it is North that it blows.
The Valkyrie are riding over soft clouds of snow.
I'm ready to enter the vast halls of light,
I, who fought and who loved, now surrender my life.
With my sword in my hand and my dog at my feet,
The race now is over, my lifetime complete.
Odin, O Odin great God of the north,
I've returned to Valhalla, to the place of my birth.

Christine Pascall

Respect...

Life has its own means of time!
Once a child, not a care in the world
Play, sleep and eat the menu of the day.
Now just a memory.
Through the hustle and bustle of a
faceless crowd walk I.
Destination still not known.
Wiser with age I take up life's gauntlet
known as 'employment'
Life goes on...
Today, other persona carry the gauntlet
Behold, you still see a wise old man.
His wisdom is given for young to hear and
'act' upon,
This service is free to all - all who
wish to listen.
But remember, one day you will change places...

James J. Connolly

A Dog's Grief

My Master's gone, I do not understand
Why I no longer hear his voice or feel his gentle hand,
He did not say "Stay there till I return"
So is he never coming home?
All I can do is sit and wait
Patiently by the garden gate,
Watching the people hurrying by,
Hoping one of them will cry,
"I'm home old mate."

The time has passed; I do not know how long,
Why did he leave me on my own, did I do something wrong?
Now memories are fading fast,
The pictures in my mind don't last,
But I still have to sit and wait
Patiently by the garden gate,
Watching the people hurrying by,
Just in case someone will cry,
"I'm home old mate."

Freda Maw

Traffic Cones

Traffic cones are here to stay
There always on the motor way
Miles and miles of red painted cones
They never seem to take them away.
The sign appears to keep to the left
The lanes are closed—but no work is in progress
I think they are put there just to confuse
To make just one lane for the motorist to use
Why make them red? Why not yellow or green?
And go one step further and stand gnomes in between.

Even our 'local' has a cone or two.
They stand getting cold out by the loo'
One day I will paint them illuminous green
So when it is dark they will clearly be seen.
A 'Patron' got one, it was quite a surprise
When the landlord presented it as a prize
He thought he would get a drink or two
Not just a cone that stood by the loo.

P. Schlaepfer

Our Sky

Oh wondrous clear blue sky with
white billowing clouds floating by,
the summer sun shining by day
night-time, the moon and milky way.

Along with hundreds of tiny stars
higher up Jupiter, Venus, and Mars,
with thunder rolls and lighting flashes,
from the sky, the rain lashes, and dashes.

That's how it has been since time began
then due to the intelligence of man,
across our skies the planes, and rocket booms
as they succeeded putting man on the moon.

Where will it end, no-one knows since
man's intelligence grows, and grows,
I pray for skies full of peace, for
the killing of mankind makes me weep.

Philomena Malik

Starting Over

I stand alone all by myself
Collecting my thoughts and thinking hard
I hold out my hand, no-one's there
I sit, I wonder, I begin to stare
My mind is racing, my thoughts nowhere
My life's a mess, nothing's clear
I cannot listen, I do not hear
I want to cry and scream and shout
Life's not fair, let me break out
My heart is breaking, can't stop the pain
Am I really starting over again
I get up and begin to walk about
Waiting for the sun to come out
Another day dawning, but what's in store
Me on my own once more.

Beverley Douglas

The Earth Fights Back

As we rip open the vale of night,
The earth unleashes its power and might,
As the blood oozes from the wound in the sky,
I cower in fear from where the wolves lie,

The oceans erupt from the nocturnal rest,
The rain pelts down upon my heaving chest,
The wind screams out its shrieking cry,
I run for my life from where the wolves lie

Torrid skies boom out their thunderous roar
I drop to my knees on the crumbling floor,
Succumbed to the darkness I wait to die,
Caught in the lair, where the wolves lie.

Carl Robinson

Through The Eyes Of A Child

I once was a dreamer that dreamt all day
About a future of happiness in every way
About when I grew up I could laugh
But that ended abruptly because I gave up.

I once was an astronaut that flew through the stars
Passed the heavens, Venus and Mars
Gliding into beauty, I loved cruising
When I woke up I had severe bruising.

I once was a soldier
That fought out at wars
I came back to reality
When I was kicked through a door.

I once was an actor that paraded on stages
In costumes, on film of many ages
Till a fateful day I was beat
And couldn't sit down for a week

I once was a dreamer that dreamt all day
The ultimate penalty I had to pay
To escape this reality I couldn't condone
When I was found I was stone cold.

Mark MacDonald

Rosary Of Thorns

In silence, empty minds do sit
And stare its own shadow
Cast, half on the wall, half
On the fire place, with flames
Lapping warmly in its own light

Shadow, bent and humped
With age, each movement slow.
As the aged mind sits empty
In the dim light of the now
Struggling flame in the pit
Of the open fire.

Shadowed fingers, warped with pain
Move slowly through a rosary;
Each bead a prayer, each prayer
A silent scream of pain and time long past

Time now, displays its handy craft
As empty mind sits waiting
His only companion, pain.
And a black mirrored image
Half on the wall, half on the fire place.

Michael John McGlynn

The Victim

I've learnt to live with going to school,
With that bully making me look like a fool!
I try so hard to keep out of his way,
But there he is every day.

Biff's his name,
All their names sound the same,
'Give me your money!' he said,
God, I wish I was dead!

I never get support,
That bully will never get caught.
I'm too scared to tell the teacher,
He just says he'll soon leave you alone.

Mum says she'll sort him out,
But all she'll do is shout.
He will just walk away,
And demand more money the next day.

I wish I could leave this school,
I wish I could die!
But all I can do is sit at home,
And cry!

Rachel M. Ferguson

The Sunset

Have you ever seen the beauty of a sunset, that golden crown that
glorifies the sky?
The dappled clouds spread out around it like the wings of angels,
the beauty of it brings a teardrop to the eyes.
The splendour of a sunset over the ocean making it sparkle like a
million little diamonds bright, or the sunset casting a gentle
glow over a waving cornfield making it an extra special night.
No matter where you look there's beauty all around you such
loveliness for one and all to see,
What better sight is there than the sunset behind a tall majestic tree?
The sunset to me brings such contentment, for no matter where you
are or what you do, to stop for just a moment to gaze in awe and
wonder at a sunset brings such peace and calmness too.
All around the world you can see a sunset, you never get two
sunsets that are the same, they are an expression of love from
God above, so by enjoying their beauty—what better way is there to
glorify His name?

Melinda Evans

Wipe Away Your Tears

Never stayed long I know, never had time to say Goodbye!
Each child born is only on loan, just some are here longer than others,
It was not my time to stay on earth to grow and play as the years go by.
I am happy in Heaven it's where I want to be.
Look at the sky at night the stars are not there to make the night bright.
Each star is a child, some to be born, some to stay and shine
so bright over each one of you as you sleep at night.
Wipe your eyes please don't cry. One day we will be together
just you wait and see.

Sharon Andrea Cattell

Lieutenant Deathword

I am a wanted poet; I always wring words by the rough of their necks,
I misplace colons and abuse silent W's.

I stab thoughts at people without
first preparing them by word of mouth.
I have language in a vice all my own. But today,
I am confronted by the nation's chief lieutenant and word regulator:

Lieutenant Deathword. Yes I. Confess your atrocious crimes
to this word defence unit. I am Lieutenant Deathword - how dare you
corrupt our language?

Why don't you cross your t's? Don't talk,
I do all the talking here.
You are under arrest on suspicion of lynching the word 'culture' by
its second syllable; violating a full-stop, and
stabbing four consonants

without provocation. Understand? We must rid
society of your kind - insensitive word merchants like you
must be punished. You have no roots, no heritage, no big

tradition. Don't write in my presence. This is enough.
Leave me. Take him away.
Hang him publicly from a fully-taut P.

Barry Mansfield

Autumn Trees

Autumn creeps in, gently at first, with shorter days and darker dawns.
And trees cast their cloaks of reds, golds and browns.
It happens everywhere, each village, town and city.
They can't be picked up and replaced, more's the pity,
As they fall gracefully to the ground, a carpet to make.
Signals extra work for the gardener, out come the gloves and rake.
It's the end of life for these vibrantly coloured leaves.
But not death, just hibernation for the deciduous trees.
For evergreens it's very different; their leaves are always there.
They're not left looking forlorn, stark or bare.
Some trees in Autumn have berries to display.
Not only pretty, but food for the birds on a cold Winter's day.
Autumn, oh Autumn, how beautiful you are.
And busy Mother Nature begins to prepare
To make a plentiful harvest for creatures great and small.
Before winter is upon us, our coldest season of all.

Elizabeth Parker

Time

The days drag on, there's not much to do.
The nights are lonely, I just think about you.
But here I am, with many others.
All together like sisters and brothers.
Tears have fallen, smiles have shone.
My emotions grow dry, they have almost gone.
But I build up my strength and full of hope.
That this is not life for a few K's of dope.
It seems unfair and such a shame.
We are not guilty or even to blame.
I pray that true justice will save our grace.
And the man that did this will be in our place.
I feel in my heart that things will be fine.
I just wait for the healer and the healer is time.

Claire Martin

The Matriarch

Standing in the darkness, silently they mourn their loss,
confusion and sorrow gratefully shrouded by the night.
Giant grey shadows gathered around the fallen one,
a still and lifeless sight . . .
A baby touches tenderly with its trunk and wonders why,
his mother does not answer to his plaintive cries?
Majestic and composed in grief she watches from a distance,
her beloved sister's life extinct, another orphan in existence.
Between the deeply-etched lines of age,
her knowing eyes weighed heavy
Her trunk wrapped itself around the calf, his little legs unsteady.
She rubbed his face in comfort and pulled him to her side,
For now her love must nurture him, if he was to survive . . .
Suddenly she gained new strength and held her head up high,
This madness had to stop soon or her race would surely die!
Man, for all his actions, surely one day must atone!
For now, the right to live, the fight to live,
  Was theirs and theirs alone . . .

Gillian Fail

Modern Day

Have you noticed the traffic that's using our roads
The cars and buses and lorries with overloads.
It's hard to find a place to cross, the old folk wait and wait,
and when the traffic passes by you can feel the place vibrate.
They used to send a lot by rail, it seems so long ago
but now we seem to have it all pass by our front door.

They talk about the environment and not to drop your litter
but with all the muck that lorries chuck out it's no wonder
people are bitter
We have to put up with daily the fumes and with the noise
It cannot be doing any good to our young girls and boys.
So why don't they give the old folk a break and clear our roads
and use again the railway track to carry their heavy loads.

Mal Roberts

Waiting

From sleepless bed to garden gate
The world the breaking dawn awaits
'Cross my shoulders, aching—fears
As pale fingers of the dawn appears
Squeezed from breast, heart, broken sigh
Just o'er the field a lone dog's cry
Does he also know despair?
No one, really, sorrow's share!
Happiness rubs off on others
Other's trials! No one bothers.
Alone I stand at quiet dawn
All hope and faith are almost gone.
When, as if in answer to my prayer
The voice I love, "Why standing there?"
Anger, sorrow, all forgotten
No recriminations twist us are spoken!
Fears, untold, all are gone!
But, how to make my peace with God?

E. Gardiner

Greedy Dog

This dog will eat anything!
Apple cores and bacon fat
milk you poured out for the cat,
she likes the string that ties the roast
And relishes hot buttered toast,
hide your chocolates, she's a thief
She'll even eat your handkerchief,
and if you don't like sudden shocks
Carefully conceal your socks,
leave some soup without a lid
And you'll wish you never did,
when you think she must be full
You find her gobbling bits of wool,
orange peel or paper bags
Dusters and old cleaning rags,

This dog will eat anything.

Except for mushrooms and cucumber
Now what is wrong with those, I wonder?

Melanie Rich

Thoughts

Crisp mornings and bright days,
A welcome sight in many ways,
Winter approaches but time for reflection,
Of carefree days, summer perfection.

Sylvia Ellis

Mother Dear

Mother dear on a September's morn,
To you and my dad, a baby was born
Through all of it all, there could have been danger
But you risked it I know, for this little stranger.
You gave me life, you named me
You looked after me well
There's so many good memories and stories to tell.
Out of love you made me whole
You made me safe and kept me warm
Mother dear you gave me life
With you beside, there is no strife.
The talks we've had, the secrets we've shared
You only listened because you cared.
You showed me every colour and creed.
And gave me everything that I will need.
You showed me love and devotion and the secrets of your potion
Without you here, there is no laughter
And you always leave yourself for after.
You should know this as we start
Mother, you're in my heart, and for you, I am here
Because you're so special, My Mother Dear.

Lesley Symons

The Mirror Of Your Soul

As a person looks into a mirror
the reflection of your face
from a small child, reflects
the beauty of innocence, which
reflects your soul.
As you look into a mirror when you
are a teenager, the good, bad and
indifference, reflects in your moods.
Then the soul looks distant in
distorted reflection in a mirror
when a person falls in love
they look in the mirror they radiate
happiness so the soul radiates good.
When a person loses someone
they love they look into the mirror
the sadness of the soul is felt
when a person is growing old
they look into a mirror and are
at peace with their soul because
they know that they will soon meet their maker.

Gloria Chamberlain

Untitled

Within my tomb of silence
I speak to you by signs
Are you listening by your senses
As my thoughts reach out to you
I use my eyes to let you know my inward soul revealed
Please use your eyes to see me as then I can be whole.

Elizabeth Pringle

War

Mars, God of war, why do you give us your flames,
the ability to raise such suffering and pain

Do you line us all up on your table of death,
and shoot us cruelly,
one by one,
so we all may burn like the flames of the sun.

We don't need you, War,
your heartache and pain,
your nuclear missiles,
your bombs dropped from planes

Brother War, you have no conscience, no peace, no love,
your heart is hard as stone,
so take your bombs and missiles
Go. And leave us alone.

Lisa Johnstone

Time

What a wonderful thing time is
It fills every day and every night,
With endless effort like a kite
Soaring higher and higher in the breeze,
Being carried with such ease.

Every tick of a clock every beat of a heart,
Not one second is lost!
Time has a place in all things for everyone
Time for work, and time for fun,
And takes account of what we've done.

Time to think, time to act,
Time to reflect on this and that.
Time to be happy, time to be sad.
Time to be sorry, time to be glad
Time to repent for days ill spent.

Time marches on, or so we are told,
And makes itself known, when we grow old.
Whatever we do, wherever we may be,
Time marches on for you and for me.

Lilian Collins

Betrayal

Anguish.
A closed door.
Breathless whispered voices,
The click of the receiver.
Another assignation?
Doubt, pain like a leaden stomach chumming ball.

Betrayal
An inner scream,
A continuous waking nightmare.
The house, the love of many years,
our precious children, the treasured
objects shared are dust and ashes in my mouth.
His heart has gone leaving
empty words - mechanical actions - an artificial life.
Some old familiar patterns
still remain; like actors we carry out our roles.
Hedged about by courtesy we smile
Only the lies, deceit, distrust are real.
The broken promises, the empty life.
His desires are for his lover and the pain endures.

Sheila A. Read

The Better Way

Lord—what can I tell those who say you aren't real
How can I show them they're wrong?
When science is given the credit for being,
The acclaim, that to You should belong.
Should I shout aggressively at them
Should I rant—and roar—and rave?
Or should I turn quietly from them
Let them find out themselves, that You save?
Should I tell them they're not worth the bother
Should I turn away when they grieve?
Accuse them of bringing it all on themselves
If they ask for my help—should I leave?
I know Lord—You wouldn't desert them,
Your example shows that's not the way;
So I'll opt to stay close 'til I'm needed,
Like You did—whilst I learned to pray.
I'll reach out, if I think it will help them,
I'll keep to the path—then they'll know,
That the light of the Lord will shine for them,
When they realize the better way to go.

Ivy Squires

Was I Ever

Was I ever born to be
Master of my destiny?
Or was the script already written
That I should live my life this smitten?
The yellow days were all too short
Whilst the long dark nights I fought
Seemed like a never-ending pit
Filled with panic, fear and hurt.
Could I have played it differently
That fellow players did not pity me?
On life's stage—there's no rehearsal—
Every act is universal.
To the final curtain call—I'll play my role
With the Director in full control.

Linda Roberts

A Look In The Mirror

Drifting over yesterday thoughts, remembering
forgotten dreams. Far off lands once knew, of
places past and present walked, and thoughts
of childhood fancies, Christmas days and
Turkey roasts, of Easter bunnies and chocolate
goodies, of summer days and flowery meadows, of
fishing trips, life's telltale lines.
A face smiles and hides, life's hidden
memories of parents loved and lost, of children
flown the nest.
Oh God is this a test?
I look in your eyes and what do I see?
I see me...

Carl B. Pemberton

Drugs 'N' Guns

He lived as a gangsta, he hung out with thugs
He loved alcohol, money and dealing drugs
He thought what he was doing, was a lot of fun
Because of this he died by the gun
I feel something about this, should be done.

There should be more lectures
that taking drugs isn't a game
A lot of lives are being wasted
and it's a great shame.

I feel strongly that guns should be banned
Every community should lend a hand
We need to get through to the people who do this
Drugs can kill, if only people knew this

Drugs can't solve problems, they make things worse
They make you hallucinate, it's like a curse.
I'm desperate to show my point of view
And I give my respect to others who speak out too.

Selina Ditta

The Storm Inside

The sun is setting over the sea
The sea is as calm as it could be
But underneath its twisting, turning
The storm is coming, my stomach churning.

Standing on the sandy shore
My fear grows more and more and more
The waves start crashing in
The storm is about to begin

The thunder begins to roar
My heart starts to soar
Does he love me, does he not?
Do I like the answers I have got?

The lightning starts flashing
My heart he is smashing
There is so much turmoil inside of me
I adore him so why can't he see.

The sun has settled over the sea
The sea as calm as it could be
The quiet shore I stand beside
The only storm there was is the one inside.

Linda M. Murray

My Child

I wish that I could make you see,
Just how much you mean to me,
Through all your trouble and your strife.
I'm here to live with you for life

Your smell, your touch, your pain and joy,
I'll be your keeper and your toy,
I'm here through smiles and also tears,
I'll be here, when needed, throughout the years,

When you smile my heart skips a beat,
When school's out, my arms you'll greet,
And when you've grown and flown the nest,
Only then will I have the final test.

I'll have to let you go at last,
To discover life, wether slow or fast,
For you to make your choices of life,
To become a mother, or perhaps a wife.

But on whatever choices you decide,
There is one rule I will abide,
To love you forever, whatever may be,
My darling child, I live for thee.

Jackie Evans

Carrots And Clover

Bobby bunny small and brown
sleeping soundly underground.

In the morning up with the sun
time to hop and skip and run.

It's 12 o'clock and time to eat!
carrots, clover, what a treat.

As it gets late and time goes by
there is a darkening of the sky.

Now Bobby's played and had his fill
as the sun sinks slowly behind the hill.

Time once again to go to bed
for bunnies must lay down their heads.

And dream sweet dreams all through the night
until the early morning light.

Then once again when it is day
Bobby will come out to play.

Shaun Gilbertson

A Sentence Of Death, No Apologies Please

The ocean waves, to the sands of Time, this world of ours, not yours,
not mine. New Horizons, beyond mountains high or fading dreams, in
the beckoning sky? Valleys of moonshine, where deep rivers run, to
buttercup meadows, of rich golden sun. Sweet, fragrant roses, tease
summers cool breeze, mysteries of the earth, entwined in the trees.
Mother natures beauty, a delicate flower. The seasons of life,
awesome power. Freedom to live, where wild eagles fly,
yet, crimes we commit, destined to Die.
All the magic and wonder, in children's eyes,
pure, innocent believers, of false promises and lies.
Their visions, their dreams, painfully stolen away,
in their dying world, cursed with decay,
what is your answer, to the child that asks WHY?
Do you expect any pity, when you breakdown and cry.
The truth is, as always, too difficult to bear.
The ultimate question, did we really CARE,
for our suffering world, through mankind's abuse, When accused of our
crimes, we have no excuse. All too apparent, A Sentence of Death,
worthless apologies, No beginning please.

Our world that needs justice, what kind of criminals are we.

Michelle O'Flaherty

England

Over rivers, valleys and snow clad mountains, through highways, byways
and down by the fountains, although I have travelled far and near,
none have I found so sweet and so fair as this beautiful rose that is
England, none can compare.

Patrick Milling

Our House

Our house is unassuming, it isn't large or grand,
Just a modern semi, with a garden and some land.
It's made of bricks and mortar and all the usual things.
But that's not most important, it's the joy the inside brings.
It takes a lot of love and care to make a house a home,
A place where you are welcome when there's nowhere else to roam.
The doors are always open to welcome all within,
With friendly voice and cheerful face and sometimes a cheeky grin!
Through windows comes the light of God, to brighten up our lives,
A light that never falters, however dark the skies,
The heat and warmth within the walls give comfort, love and care,
Not just to ourselves alone, with others we like to share.
Outside in Spring and Summer, the flowers appear and bloom,
A sign of God's creation surrounds our every room.
Not just inside, but outside too, there's hope and joy and love,
The gift of God's creation, sent down from heaven above.
So, if your house is not like ours, with "welcome" on the mat,
Just pause a while... Stop, think and act... And you can make it
just like that.

Doreen Cragg

The Wonders Of A Garden

I love to be in my garden whatever the season may be,
There are always plenty of things to do and wonderful sights to see,
As spring, with her promise of awakening bulbs and plants,
Starts the growing season again, and the birds on wing
Stop to sing, all is fresh, bright and clean.

A kaleidoscope of colour, it's summertime once more.
The tall sunflowers, as if to say 'hello', look in through the door.
The veggie patch looks neat and clean, the baby cabbages vibrant green,
The waving silks on the sweet corn grow,
They sway like cobwebs when the breezes blow.

As we slide into autumn new wonders appear,
The leaves on the trees turn from green
To colours of brown orange and red,
As an artist's palette when well clad.
To see the structure of the trees standing bare,
When not long ago green leaves fluttered there.

Winter's arrived, nature's hand has painted the garden with snow
Little snowdrops and crocuses peep through the soil.
The yellow and red of the dogwoods stand proudly in their right
To make the winter garden a most wonderful sight.

Margaret Kinshott

One Day

Every time you say you don't love me a tiny piece
of me breaks off and disappears,
And soon you'll say you don't love me once more,
and I will just fade away.
And you won't even notice that I've gone,
My heart is screaming for you to love me,
Just for a little time off my worthless life,
When we look into each other's eyes I can see
that we are meant to be,
But you just don't realize it,
Will you ever?
Yes!
One day you're going to look at me and see that
all this time you have been a fool,
And how could you ever have not noticed the
love you have for me....
Well one day

Emma Logan

Winter

As the leaves change and start to die
You know that winter is on the way.
Gloomy days and long dark nights,
It seems forever before it gets light.
Snow covered ground and ice on the pond,
Even the birds seem to lose their song.
People hurrying to get out from the cold,
To the warmth of the fire and comfort of home.
A snowdrop appears showing the first sign of Spring,
And the dawn of a new year begins over again.

Louise Jane Neal

Loch Lochy

The view across loch lochy
falls into many moods,
The clouds hang down and
cover the hills,
hiding them from view.
When it's dark and grey with heavy rain,
Cascading down the mountains,
Forming many waterfalls,
God's natural water fountain.
The sound of water echoes down,
Streams and babbling brooks,
which carry on to find their way,
into the swelling loch.
The rain will stop, the clouds will clear,
And the scene will change in time.
The mountains sheer will re-appear.
Bathed in bright sunshine.
This beauty spot, a breathtaking view,
is a creation of God, for me and you.

Elizabeth Horgan

Time To Change

There must be meaning in this pointlessness we call living,
We must have faith in humanity
However pointless it seems,
We stand in judgment
Of those we know nothing about,
We hate, fear or ridicule
That which we do not, or cannot understand,
We fight battles for our ancestors
Wars over feuds long since forgotten,
We hate without knowing why
But cannot love the same way,
What is life if we cannot give without taking
Cannot love without being loved,
We hate, steal, rape and kill
And still call ourselves civilised,
We live in a beautiful world
With only one flaw . . . us,
It's time to change.

Marc Adams

Golden Memories

I take a look down memory lane,
And think of my childhood days again.
The golden days when I was a lad,
To think of the happy times I had.

Remember the days of the horse and plough?
The blacksmith's hammer and anvil silent now.
I used to pump the bellows till the fire was red.
Now the coals are black and dead.

Remember the shepherd looking tattered and old?
Herding his flock from downs to fold.
The sheep dog working from left to right,
His only companion from morn till night.

Remember Monday's wash day again?
Please let it be sunny, please no rain,
The copper, the mangle and the great big tub,
And the old wash board for the collars to scrub.

Remember the candle to light you to bed?
Up those wooden stairs to rest your head.
The days I remember most were olden,
But those days to me were golden.

Victor Gilbert

Seasons

Alas! Another year has passed,
As winter slips away beneath its cloak of frost,
Though, still, the evil deeds of men hold sway,
Defiant in the mould of Nature's way.
When with her once again, have came and gone
Events imbibed in life's cocoon,
A trail of births and lives and deaths forlorn,
Is hitherto enacted... to be forgotten soon.

To weave a cycle into history's schemes,
That so reflects the nuance of perpetual dreams,
Of latent life that beckons resurrection from the deep,
Disturbed again by echoes from compelling sleep
That so incites the active equinox of Spring,
With all its force and wetness, crops to bring
To bear on hungry mouths the substances of toil,
Infused with human sweat on Summer's soil.

When, by its rape, the fruits of husbandry is wrest,
To bare the seeds of Nature's future boon, lest
They chant survival's issue and recite its worth,
And so excite to riot Autumn's will
For struggle, in the guise of constant birth,
Persists, while evils that beset Man linger still.

Errol C. McKenzie

Rhiannon

Rhiannon, my white lady, rides upon dreams and ocean,
celebrates the ordinary transit, or, shaking foam,
beckons to mystery. Under a brazen sky
her three birds circle, bold wings beating:
green as a destination, silver as hope;
gold as a sunbeam splashing down
on furlong billows.

The bright noon climbs. Rhiannon descends to plunder
the shell-scattered fastness,
trading vision for a fair wind. The ship ploughs furrows,
plants the long mile.

At midnight, surge and thunder of uncharted waters
will call her up. Her white horse races dolphins.
Like flakes of pearl we skim
the plunging salt-sea meadows.

I am the mariner chasing a fantasy
with a fateful concubine,
Rhiannon, my white lady. The ship moves on,
prints out a friendly shadow
to dapple Atlantis and the questioning shore.

Jennifer Brice

Come The Dawn

Come the dawn, as well it must
When all the earth lies beneath the dust
If man pursues self destructive course
And does so, without remorse

Come the Dawn, of man's demise
With total destruction from the skies
No more trees, no more Fields, the stench is rife
No Babbling Brook, No sign of life

Come the Dawn, of man's awakening
To the horror of his creating
Turn back now, too late tomorrow
There is no more time to borrow

Then come the Dawn, the sun will shine
Once more upon this world divine
When Man's creative mind turns once more
To health and Happiness, and things we Adore
Come That DAWN

Gilbert H. Waudby

Food Riot

Shedding tears and voiceless gestures
a deeply, deeply saddened call.
While desperate poverty starts to fall
Unpleasantly people walking by
not even turning one blind eye.
Of bodies so painfully thin
as if it were a major sin.
Children and families of all ages
dressed in rags from live magazine pages.
Their sad eyes and driving emotion
in tense frustration, delivering commotion
low-toned voices, gentle and quiet
going any length for a food riot.
These people lead a life of hunger
fragile, feeble, fears among them.
If we cared for are friends from the start
It wouldn't now hurt from my aching heart.

Jenny Jones

Magical Thoughts

Hang the holly, shut the shop, close the office door.
It's Christmas Day tomorrow there'll be no work in store.

Sitting with the family, new baby on your knee,
All shiny eyes with Christmas lights reflected from the tree.

At fifty now a grandma three times over, life is full,
Exactly how it should be tiring, but never dull.

The family reminisce while sharing a glass or two,
How good or bad the year has been, but we've all seen it through

It's quiet when at last they leave with presents under arms
and christmas pies and chocolates tucked into little palms.

You close the door and then you know you suddenly believe,
there's never a place so magical as home on Christmas Eve.

Pamela June Houghton

The Combination Of Light And Shadow

Light differs from shadow
Shadow differs from light
But one without the other,
Just would not be right.

A world without shadow,
Would be as bright as the sun,
But a world without even a little light,
Would just be dark and dumb.

So have I sit in the classroom,
Thinking what to do,
Because this earth just wouldn't be the same,
If we didn't have the two.

Rebecca Hogarth

Untitled

Why did Daddy leave us, Mummy
Oh, why did he go away?
Mummy, is it funny
Is it just a game you play?
Who's going to play at soldiers,
Who am I going to fight,
Now Daddy's gone
Who's going to tuck me in at night?
I thought daddies only had to leave
When God wanted to see them,
So why, Mummy, do you grieve
When Daddy's not gone to Him?
Peter said my Daddy's having an affair,
And he said, Mummy, you don't care,
Is an affair very bad
And when this thing he's had,
Will he come home to love me,
And tuck me in my bed,
Will things be like they used to be?
You haven't listened, Mummy, to a single word I've said.

M. Monks

Thoughts Of An Aged Man

The aged man, a shrunken skeletal figure,
A shadow of a once strong man,
His prominent veins pumped full of tobaccoey blood,
His skin wrinkled and crumpled,
Hanging from dry and brittle bones
Warped and gnarled with time and work.

The hair upon his head, grey and receding,
Under which are the last remnants of memories
In a slowly fading mind, mixed with
Jumbled tales of times gone by.

He moves, shuffling around the cluttered furniture
In old and tattered slippers, worn yet comfortable.
After propping up the battered cushions he
Slowly lowers himself into his chair,
An aged armchair situated in a corner of a poorly lit room
Placed amidst all his worldly goods.
Then he slowly drifts off into the oblivion called sleep.

Sarah Collett

I'll Miss You

When you die -
can I please whisper in your coffin,
so morbid and cold.
When you die -
can I please touch the warm mahogany,
so gallant and bold.
When you die -
can I please lie down beside you,
and feel your frozen features so blissfully blue.
I'll miss you.

Sharon Pargeter

Family Ties And Family Trees

Hear the whispers of the rustling leaves
of family ties, and family trees
of sisters, brothers, mums and dads
the greatest of friends, a family has
Uncles, aunts, cousins, and all
each to be there, should you fall
words of wisdom, and jokes galore
that's what I feel a family's for;
to be with each and everyone
in early morn, or as day is done
to show each other, how much we care
it's the wonderful loving of a family fare
I'm glad to have a family true
that's you and I and me and you
it's never too late to seek or find
a family so warm, so loving and kind
say goodbye to loneliness, and you will see
you too have a family, just waiting to be.

Lavina

In Peace

The baby lay, like a china doll
Peaceful in sleep, forever gone,
No-one knows the pain endured
By this child, born so pure,
What made this man turn so bad
To beat to death this little lad,
Who was born to love and cherish
In someone's hands he was to perish,
His bright blue eyes showing so much love
A soft white skin of a beautiful dove,
He is now safe, away from danger
With our Lord! Jesus! Our gracious saviour,
With guardian angels watching over
This bundle of love, all in clover,
His sad life has now ended
His broken body has now been mended,
With love and happiness, with friends around
As he lay in the ground,
The rest for everyone, in peace.

Leslie Stones

The Rose

The rose sits upon the windowsill in a class of its own.
Its elegant structure is refreshing to see.
Protecting its colourful, fragile petals with its sharp thorns,
The rose will be wise for an eternity.
Its wonderful aroma cleanses the soul.
Its vibrant life is precious to me.
The rose's presence brings tranquillity.

Jessica Morton

Christ-Mass

Christmas is . . . Children, turkey, plum-pudding,
scarlet berried holly, soft green mistle-toe,
Church bells a-ringing, heavenly singing,
rosy-red cheeks, white flakes of snow.
Christmas is . . . Thankfulness for things bright and beautiful,
God's creatures around us, His birds on the wing,
Christmas is . . . Remembering the smile that has left us,
the touch of the hand, soft lips on the cheek.
Christmas is . . . Caring for those who are with us,
the lonely, the grieving, the sick and the weak.
Christmas is . . . A baby conceived out of loving
into a world of beauty and sin.
Christmas is . . . Jesus, our Lord and Saviour,
sent to forgive us, born to be King.

Herbert G. Taylor

My Artist

My Artist, she sits and dreams,
Looking at the world and all the things
That fill our lives, but some never notice,
Too quick, too shallow, some think it hopeless.

Hills and trees, hedgerow and thorn,
Grass in the meadow, fields of corn,
Bridge over brook, just take a look,
Another page in the artist's book.

Pastel, pencil, brush and paint,
Building images, dark and faint,
Using her skills for as long as it takes her,
From the eye to the hand, brush to the paper.

Taking her cue from feelings inside,
Lets imagination reach out wide,
Mixing colours and textures for people to see,
The wonder and skill of her artistry.

A brief insight indeed, this may well be,
In the life of my artist, for it is she,
Who brings much joy to many others,
And fills my life with so many colours.

Vince Povey

Set In My Ways

The sun setting beyond the hills,
Sky the colour of daffodils.
And time it ticked itself away,
The end of another golden day.
Walking and pondering back across the moor,
Opening the heavy oak door.
It's been so long now, I'm set in my ways,
I'll carry on like this till my dying days.
The sun still setting in the window,
Like a picture in a frame.
I've seen that sunset so many times,
To me it always looks the same.
Completing tasks like a clockwork soldier,
Signs that say I'm getting older.
I'll keep on working till the end of my days,
All because I'm set in my ways.

Laura Kennedy

Dream Catcher

Catch me this dream and help me to sanity.
Light me a flare, leave me not to calamity.
Calm the wild waves and harness its power,
Abandon me not in my imaginary tower.

Unquiet mind holding tremulous' thoughts;
Rejection, dejection, expand to hold court.
Are dreams just a mirage to nurture our yearnings.
Does madness hold sway, searing and burning;
Like passion that needs a reciprocal mate
Screams like a vixen her feelings to sate.

Now visions come softly gently ironing hurt mind,
Emotion becalmed, resting, sleeping, perhaps blind.
Love on a seesaw or a giant pair of scales
Dipping, adjusting, now on a windmill with sails.
Thought pictures by night, come, what do they mean.
Help me to sanity, catch me this dream.

Janet Bradley

The Window Of Life

As I look through the window, many people I do see,
All too busy in their own lives, that they don't notice me,
I look at all the faces, so different yet the same,
Some take life so seriously, others treat it as a game,
Children play so happy, not knowing what lies ahead,
An old man in an alley, a cardboard box for a bed,
Some kids on a street corner, all get really high,
Their poor heartbroken mothers can only sit and cry,
As I draw the curtains, I thank God for what I've got,
I'm luckier than others, even if I haven't got a lot.

Caroline Waddell

Inner Self

I've said too much, yet I hardly spoke.
And my mind swims with the unspoken words,
That could change everything.
My thoughts stay with me.
I will not know the path they may have led me down.
I carry on as I am, reviling only little,
For my feelings are strong.
From experience I have learned that I can have great impact,
With words formed deep in my heart.
But the impact I have I do not take pleasure in.
Unknown to others is my inner self.
Caged off is the person in me who is a crying soul.
My only fear is that this soul, which I hide,
Screams louder each day.
To be understood is its wish, noticed and accepted.
Yet others in my surroundings,
Discard the type of opinion it holds.
This is my reason to withdraw it.
It's time will come to be realized.

Elizabeth Sage

Circle Of Life

As I stroll along this life of mine,
where will I be at the end of time.
Is there a God in the Heavens above,
what is he made of, forgiveness and love.
Or are we alone with no soul to seek,
hiding in hell where no-one will peak.
I close my eyes and rest my head,
Is there no peace until we're eventually dead.
Then where do we go after that final day,
to take our judgement come what may.
What have we learnt from this life of ours,
to hate, to love, the balance of powers.
To return to where we previously came,
to be sent right back again and again.
Is there a conclusion to this worldly cause,
the refining of love, the removal of flaws.
These are the questions that fill my time,
as I stroll along this life of mine.

Robert E. Ovington

The Mind

Your mind holds the future, the present, the past
It stores all of your memories, from day one to the last,
It's your own private film, which give instant replay
You can watch yourself grow, to whom you are today.
You can relive your triumphs, the laughter, the pain.
And see the mistakes you made on the way
How many times have you heard people say
I wish I knew then what I know today.
Unfortunately wisdom comes with the passing years
You've done things you can't change, when it's finally here.
But now it's the present, you're more wiser, mature
The future can wait, there's no rush anymore.
You've learned through the years, life can be a bitch.
So the time is now, catch up on what you've missed.
Look back into your mind, and as the years unfold,
Go for some of your dreams that were put on hold.
No one can turn back time before that long rest,
So among all your memories, make the present the best.

J. Monk

They're Here

They're here, they're there, they might just be,
But will it come together which is unfortunately,
They're big, they're small
The horrible and tall,
They're triangle, they're square
Oh my God what a mare,
The world, the space
The apocalypse on race,
This came together with a bump and a bang,
And so he said it the Lord himself might hang.

Nick Taylor

Memories

How I remember those times in the past,
How sad is the feeling that it never lasts.
Tears are forgotten, only memories remain.
Gone is the feeling in that safe domain.
Childhood experiences from which we all learn,
Often memories from which we must mourn.
Youthful adventures advantageous sometimes,
Unfortunately often we pay for our crimes.
So to adulthood we enter brave but afraid,
We try to remember the debts that we've paid.
We battle, we struggle to carve out a life,
But all we end up with is a whole lot of strife.
After trying and trying in vain, now we are old and
only in pain.
What is the next step, I hear you ask?
It's simply we merely just remove our mask!

Amanda Jane Date

Birdie Bird

Birdie Bird came from a land far away,
She must have travelled by night and day,
She landed in the fore court where the main sold cars,
Swooping to earth with fluttering eyes
And displaying her beautiful silvery wings,
Oh! How the mind thinks of many things.

You are coming home with me, the maid said,
Puss puss and Boogie will love you too,
They will need you, just as I need you,
Puss puss and Boogie were less than certain,
They chased her around the house and up the curtain.
She thought the maid's hair was a nest,
For that is where she came to rest.

Chrissie Murphy

Joseph's Lullaby

Joseph go to sleep my love
Look at the stars and the moon above
Joseph close your eyes of blue
I hope that all your dreams come true

Joseph go to sleep my son
night time is here but morning will come

you are your Mummy's pride and joy
you are your Daddy's golden boy

Now go to sleep, I hate to nag
But Mummy really needs a fag.

Wendy Churchill & Emily Carter

Release From The Inner Scream

Midnight chimes loudly for the last time
For the pain is deafening to the young ears.
In a flight of hope the blood is still.
The street lights glisten off it like a
Pool of glass on the roadside.
A woman screams as she runs to the
Lifeless corpse.
The heart is silent.
The devil claims another victim as the
Bodily heat escapes into the spirit
Of the cold dark night air.
The soul too escapes from this the house of pain.
The arms can be seen like an
Ancient scripture of pain and suffering.
The cuts are deep in body and mind.

The parents answer the knock at the door.
Policemen stand there with a hardened tear.
No words are spoken but the silence tells all.

Adam Levick

In Bed

Inside my head I feel the gathering storm
Though nothing on the outside can be heard
I see the wise trees feel a strange alarm
Like me they feel a warning of great harm
And gather in their leaves the startling birds
Who feels as I do something in their minds
That warns of coming piercing killing winds
A whisper gathering sound as it draws near
Stars behind their cloud veils now disappear
Soon with full force the tempest breaks
Before its God-sent power all nature quakes
Accept that something rules our days
In inexplicable and humbling ways
No man has yet been born
So stupid as to treat with scorn
The miracle of each breaking dawn.
Scientist can smugly give the reasons
For the ever-changing seasons
Yet all admit it's not a plan
That ever was devised by man

Rosaleen O'Shea

Untitled

Flowers are beautiful
Flowers are love
A symbol of life
A sign from above.
There is no above
There is no below
So why do these beautiful flowers still grow?
In the winter time
They wither away
But all of us know
They'll grow back someday,
To show all their blossoms
To show all their glare,
To show that our flowers
Will always be there.

Tim Channelle

Christmas

Santa is coming with lots of toys
for little girls and little boys
dolls and prams, a doll's house too
and games that can be played by two

There's bikes to ride, and boats to sail
and kites that have a very long tail
some nurses' clothes and doctors' things
and books to read about all kinds of things

So remember children Christmas Eve
hang up your stocking (and what must you leave)
a something for Santa to help him along
so his work through the night won't take him so long

B. Bourgaize

The Lottery

Forty nine balls, tossing in a drum
Celebrity presses the button with his thumb
Who's going to be the lucky winner this week??
My mouth goes dry and my knees go weak.
I grab my ticket, the balls drop one by one
Just six balls is the lucky sum.
One and seven to me, and eight and nine,
Numbers looked to me, just fine,
Seventeen and eighteen popped out fast,
It's going to be my lucky week at last
Just the Bonus ball, now just keep cool
I started giggling I did feel a fool.
Out it popped, it was number four
Sweating and trembling I sank to the floor.
I've done it at last I cried with glee,
But it was last week's ticket Oh silly silly me.

Patricia Youngs

Is This The World?

Maybe the beautiful world
We'd all craved to live in happily
Born into the great unknown
Full of promises and treachery
Gazing into the beauties of the blue skies
Lost in wandering thoughts of the deep seas,
ocean floors, landscapes of beauties, deserts, forests
and mountains harbouring wonderful creatures,
Creatures we've vowed to exterminate
Lands we've decided to make desolate where is the peace today?
Take this and eat it, take this and drink it
This is my peace I have given unto you
The peace that slips through our fingers
Closer to the peace we yearn for further adrift the
Peace of humanity, away into the
great beyond! We the great women and men, dangers allure us
Greater are the men and women who can
Be granted the serenity to accept things,
That courage to change things that could be transformed,
and the almighty wisdom to accept all. Where is the world of
tomorrow!!

Eddie B. Onwubolu

Fear Not I Am With You

I am the warmth from a ray of sun, the rush of the cool breeze.
The opening of a brand new flower, the movement in the trees.
I am the rain before the storm, the calm and still of night.
I am the field of lush green grass, the mountains of great height
I am the frost of winter time, the dew the morning brings.
The movement of the wildlife, the song the blackbird sings.
I am the fog so damp and dull, yet the gleaming white of snow.
The crops that yield at harvest time, for you to reap and sow.
I am your rivers gently flowing, your current of the sea.
The songs upon the radio, the pictures on T.V.
I am the brilliant bright sunset, the dusk as evening falls.
I am with you constantly, I am your four walls.
I am the darkness of the night, the diamonds in the sky.
I am your first 'good morning', your last minute, your 'good bye'.
I fill your day from start to end, your season, month and year
I am with you, I am life, you do not have to fear.

Samantha Parkinson

Untitled

All the words I've ever said are true
I'm grateful for the day that I met you
Our friendship that we have is very strong
And friendship of this kind cannot be wrong
The warmest pillow is your welcome breast
It's the only place I find my treasured rest
You give me quiet when others offer none
You give me peace when a wretched day is done.

Heather Lilian Neale

A Child's Thoughts

To stand on a bridge looking down on the road
    Watching the traffic go by
Holding mum's hand as there we would stand
    And a gleam would come into my eye

When I grow up that's what I will be
    A Lorry driver hauling his load
Going to places that I've never been
    Travelling the country by road

Now that I'm grown up, a driver am I
    But that gleam in my eye has now gone
Not wanting to travel the country by road
    For its not where my heart now belongs

As darkness draws near and day turns to night
    A man in one place he should be
Not in a Lorry travelling the road
    But at home with his family

Alan Kettridge

First Love

Two people met many years ago
Adolescent emotions, too young to know,
For what they had they'd never equal,
First love they say, it has no sequel.

So burning cinders remain alight,
How did those ashes first ignite?
Our love was brief, then came the tears,
If only we'd met in later years.

I've played this part as best I know.
But the rules are harsh, the game so slow,
But love's no game, I knew the cost,
For I can never win, if it's you I've lost.

So what did lead to our demise?
Those long summer nights with stars in our eyes,
Why did the laughter begin to fray,
And the crystal skies begin to grey.

How could I devise this "set?"
The stage being when we first met,
The "scenes" our time we spent together,
And the "epilogue" losing you forever.

Mick J. Wickham

Armenia

A city stood complete
With very busy streets
Houses here houses there
Houses there, were everywhere
Now they've gone and all is quiet.
Sound would gladden the heart of all
In the midst of all the smokey fall
Where is Armenia why did it fall?
The world far and wide heard the people's call.
Hearts were moved to give them aid
Because of the terrible price they paid
All were mourning a loved one's call
They crying there, was for one and all.
Armenia, Armenia, we saw you fall
The God above heard the people's call
Said the way was open for all
Armenia though fallen will rise again
Armenians though Solemn will smile again.

Elma Calder

Come Back

Now that you've gone no words can describe
The hurt I hide and emptiness inside.
My dreams they were shattered,
I've cried a thousand tears,
But you had your reasons,
And you had your fears.

You came so far I can't believe you've gone,
It won't be the same but I have to go on.
If my heart is broken will I get through,
Or will I give up and then follow you.

I sit and listen, your voice fills my heart,
I hope one day you will reclaim your part.
For no one can fill the place where you stood,
Unless you return and come back for good.

Samantha Rudge

Life Trial

Please save my sanity,
In this thick forest of humanity.
All I see is chaos and confusion,
Broken dreams and disillusions.

Help me through this murky mire.
As I'm dragged down by my own selfish desires.
Stand by me while I conquer my fear,
So when I look in life's mirror it's more clear.

A. Henderson

Masquerade

Many times I've watched the world go by
Different feelings come and go
When I gaze into the mirror
Who's staring back - I just don't know.

I listened to every word you spoke
You taught me to be strong
The advice you gave will stay with me
You showed me right from wrong.

My life is like an open book
You know my every page
You said there's nothing to be scared of
So why am I afraid?

Many times I've thought about you
And of the things you've said
I've found the strength inside myself
Those fears are laid to rest.

"Don't hide behind your feelings
Stop acting this charade
Just trust what you believe in
Don't live a masquerade."

Stuart Robb

Skippy

What in the world would I do without you.
My dear little four-legged friend.
You always meet me and greet me with love
When the end of a long day is through,
We roam the hills together,
You trot by my side down the lane,
We play hide and seek in the meadow,
Then you race me back home again,
We sit by the fire in the evening,
Your head resting on my knee,
You gaze into my eyes and I realize,
What a treasure you are to me,
We have been together for many years.
And will be till the end.
But what in this world
Will I do without you,
My dear little four-legged friend.

Ida Bradbury

Is Anyone There?

Never ending are the sun rays,
Tears from the skies fall no more.
Skeletons roam from site to site in order to find food,
Their only purpose in life is life, but for how long?

Infants in distress once again, their mouths are dry,
Years have passed, how long are they expected to carry on?
Their pleas for help are answered for now,
What is to be done when we hear no longer?

Are they punished for some unjustified sins?
Forgiveness is easier than to see them suffer.
Babes exist for two years or less,
Families weep for the ones they have loved and lost.

Their struggle for life is everlasting, always praying for tomorrow,
One fortunate day the skies will shed plenty of tears.
Life is precious now, it is valued more
When there is something to live for,
Will they be skeletons forever, or normal living beings?

Olabisi Akinola

The Fading Of Love

He retreated into the scarlet dusk,
Taking with him my life, my soul.
The numbness of my very being
Displayed, for all, to see, in whole.

There seemed no future,
No safe way forward,
Without the shadow,
No certain to-morrow.

Powerless to deny the unreal emotions,
Festering to-wards a lonely existence.
Perhaps eternity may change its direction
And grant some hope of a heavenly distance.

Mabel Robertson

Home

The summer crazed garden sprawled, unconfined.
Green smothered gravel, all quiet as a mouse
in the clashing of colour, pale columbine twined
with ivy reaching the rotting tree house
where once two would hide, until called for tea
then scrambled to race, leafy branches astir
so still, in their sorrow when four became three.
Life rang the changes that left only mother.

Trebles of children piercing her reverie
striking a chord of distant delight, yet
in tune with malaise and dusty redundancy
old faded chintz, and misty grey net.
After final appraisal events followed fast
decidedly 'all for the best' hers alone,
the empty house echoed lament for the past
heart sure, there is nowhere better than home.

Sheila Manley

Life Support Machine

Five days went missing from my life
Like death the spirit survived but where?
The angels did not visit me while I slept
Nor God to comfort me—was He there?

Five days in darkness, time stood still.
Was I in my mother's womb ready to travel and prepare for birth?
It is hard for a new-born child to live.
They have to fight and await God's will.

My life hangs in the balance,
Will I live or will I die?
It's the life support machine which races
And doctors fighting as I lie.

Now the dark is gone and I can see a light
As my eyes become accustomed to visions though dim.
A nurse is holding my hand and saying
"My Goodness, you did give us all a fright!"

Joyce Corner

The Triangle

When we are like this, apart
There is a space within my heart
A secret precious space
That is filled with an image of your face,
Our love grows stronger and more true,
For every day is an adventure new.
And now our triangle is complete
The bond of love so pure, so neat
No man could have what I have dear
Two people who love me more each year.

D. Martin

Everlasting Love

My love for you is like a river,
Everlasting and ever-flowing,
Your every touch makes me shiver,
But why I'll never know.
As long as the stars line the night sky,
And the birds can still fly,
Whether you're right or wrong,
I'll be there to help you be strong.
I can't tear my heart away from you,
Because you're deep within my soul,
You say it's something I must do,
But you fill my once empty hole,
I can't tell you this love I feel for you,
Although it's something I must do,
Nothing will keep me from your charms,
I'll always be right there in your arms.
You're every beat of my heart,
And I hope we never part,
It's something I hope we never have to do,
For both me and you.

C. A. Smith

Our Mothers

Our Mothers bear the pain of childbirth
The pain that brings us light of day
We cause such pain and they still love us
The love that guides us on our way.

Those gentle hands that do our bidding
Those arms that hold us when we cry
We fall, get hurt and Mum comes running
She prays for us when night comes high.

She teaches us what is right from wrong
She gives us what no other can
Then comes the day we say goodbye
It's Mum day she laid the plain.

So look into your Mother's eyes
And hear her heave a sigh
As the album she looks through
Of those wondrous years gone by.

James H. Oliver

Dunblane 1996

Eyes, bright as pools of sparkling water,
Someone's son, someone's daughter,
Laughing and playing,
Unaware of approaching slaughter.
Laughter turns to cries of pain,
As the gun fires, and fires again,
This, this is the awful slaughter,
Of someone's son, someone's daughter.

Where's my friend, my Mum, my Dad,
What is happening, this feels so bad,
I try to hide, but his eyes they follow,
The room spins round, the sound is hollow.

All is still now, nobody moves,
There's just silence, and then sobs,
No laughter now, but tears like sparkling water,
Of someone's son, someone's daughter.

Barbara Quimby

Should I Kill Myself Today

I awoke this morning looked up to the sky,
and began to wonder should I live or die.
I looked at the ceiling, I looked at the floor.
I looked all around me then did it once more.
Then remembering the good times out numbered the bad,
it started me thinking life isn't that bad.
So I picked myself up and I'm happy to say.
No! I don't think I'll kill myself today.

Kathleen Doyle

I Just Can't Bear To Give You Up

As I rock my baby fast to sleep
Into a dream world oh so deep,
As I look at your face and your warm embrace
I just can't bear to give you up.

If any more bills come this week
A foster home for you I'll seek,
For someone to look after you and someone to care
'Cause the way Mammy's doing it just isn't fair.

I love you very dearly and I know you love me too
But Mammy has to give you up and get help for us two
People keep saying "No don't give her up"
But with no one to help me I just cannot cope.

You're a bundle of joy and a very happy child
But you're so sweet and nice you deserve to be spoiled
And so darling child I will miss you with all of my heart
You are my first newly born and now we have to part.

I promise you baby in about a year or two
Mammy will return to take care of you, and
I'll love you and spoil you like all mothers should do
And we'll stay together forever, yes just me and you.

Elaine Neary

Eagle Flight

As I float through the misty sky.
I can feel the clouds on my cheek.
I fly higher. I can feel the warm sun.
Drying out my feathers.
I can hear two birds singing below me.

I wonder what they are singing.
They have a nice song.
The sun is going down.
I can see the migrating swallows.
It's unusual for them to be out at night.

It's dark early. I will go to my eyrie.
I can smell the wet leaves.
I can smell mice too.
I'm hungry. I'll get one.
I dash down and get it.
Back to the eyrie.

Ross McKeever

The Tear

There's a big tear rolling down my cheek,
A tear just like a stain.
But this tear browns what sorrow is,
This tear has felt some pain.
This tear has had some good times,
It's had some bad as well.
For this tear has seen heaven,
And this tear has seen hell.
This tear is really special.
And it's important too.
But why it's really special
Is because it falls for you.

James Ashe

Untitled

The teddy, a toy a present to give,
To be loved, hugged and cuddled for as long as you love,
He may become thread bare or even lose an eye,
But you lose your teddy with grief you will sigh.

Some teddies are discarded and put to one side,
If they were alive I'm sure they would hide,
In some dark corner away from your view,
But not ever once would they stop loving you.

So go out and find him and hold him quite tight,
And please never let him go out of your sight,
My darling, my love let me make you aware,
That all I want to be is your teddy bear.

Christopher Carter

Sweet Tranquillity

I strolled through a shady glen and felt the damp moss
Springing beneath my feet, as I walked across
To the edge of a pool, in the cool of the day,
And a deer justly startled wondered away.

O, sweet tranquillity calm and serene
I stood there in silence and gazed at the scene.
Then the silence was shattered as a bird fluttered by
Singing its roundelay into the sky.

My eyes lifted skywards following its flight
Into the firmament blue and bright.
Then the deer I had startled peeped through the trees
As the leaves gently rippled in the cool breeze.

I walked from the forest feeling at rest,
Breathing the clean air sweet and fresh.
This earth so glorious, seeing eyes to behold,
God reigns above us and His creatures are loved.

Mary Roberts Cunliffe

Waking Ocean

As the night fades away and it grows lighter
a new day unfolds and gets steadily brighter
the dawn of colour, deep coral and red
slowly evolves to bright pink hues instead

The sun sparkles jewel like on the waking ocean
climbing higher and higher in silent motion
beneath the surface the ocean world wakes
whilst over rocks a crested wave breaks

Under the water is a kingdom unknown
with a life and a power all of its own
multi-coloured fish, corals and plants
are there to be seen but most don't get the chance

Dolphins leap and dash through the blue
near a far off paradise too good to be true
an island alone with bright golden sand
lush green trees where underneath it's pleasant to stand

And look out over the ocean of blue and green
the most beautiful place that I've ever seen

Sarah Cooper

Thoughts Upon A Sonnet (Sonnet)

What is worse than rambling poetic verse
On a subject which demands an essay?
The readers and critics who heed us, curse,
Or worse - they just throw the damned thing away!
Poet, confine your finest mental thought
Into the boundaries of a sonnet -
One hundred and twenty syllables ought
To refashion your meanings upon it.
Philosophical thoughts in fourteen lines -
Metaphysical decasyllables!
Depths of thought equal poetic defines;
And sincerity greatly ennobles...
One completed, beautiful thought is joy:
In a poet's hand; a delicate toy.

S. Wilfred Croxtall

Untitled

The paving stones of years gone by
Just lie there dormant, as children's cries
of hopscotch, kick can echo through
but the children of today say there
is nothing to do.
Where I live there should be
fields and trees, but nothing flutters
in the breeze, there is concrete blocks
and factories too, there is nothing
here for me or for you.
And as I walk through these
concrete fields I see the outcome
of their yield, there is mayhem, carnage,
drug taking too, but the children keep
saying they have nothing to do.

M. A. Young

Teamwork

The heart and the mind may work together as one,
with unity and trust numerous jobs can be done.
Working as allies instead of old foes,
"What can't be done?" is the question to pose.

An example of this is when the heart said "It's love!"
fluttering softly like a little white dove.
The mind then said "Wait, let's just be sure,
before we let anyone in through the door".

The heart then thinks back to when it's been hurt before,
and now knows the reason it's bolted the door.
The mind and the heart in unison then,
decide whether or not to let this person in.

Both are agreed that the vibes feel so good,
and let this person enter? They think they should.
With a heart that's so warm and beauty so fine,
to not let her enter would be seen as a crime.

A. S. Hearn

Where Is My Life

Nature, an infinite orb of purity and innocence
Enraptured by the gods both Christian and Classical;
Fate, fortune, all the same, unsurpassed by providence.
We'll be surrounded by the auras of the Divine and Natural.
The feelings, they flood in,
The depression, a mode of such a negative realisation.
Nerves jumping as if due to a sin.
What has caused this depressed, hated situation,
Feelings of a need to commit suicide,
To end this life and start anew elsewhere;
To let the pure soul leave and the corrupt body to decide.
My mind covered, my mind dead, my soul lacking,
Where is my heavenly conclusion?
I feel no presence, no tapped-up believing.
Desertion, not wanting a belief; therefore a restricted protection.
Nature, a belief, a way of life, a pleasure not to disturb.

Tom H. N. Bishop

The Way Of Power 1996

Elevate yourself from the wickedness of oppression,
see through the eyes of the oppressor,
meet the hypocrite sat in his
seat of power,
fascism towards the people on
every hour.

To hear the people plea
is just another form of ridicule
to his own stance,
grant us our need in these oh troubled times,
and ask yourself the question is not
the tool of your power the instrument
of all end to mankind.

We see our views as being
views with no windows,
to us the people of your undoubted ego,
bring us now the truth to our own future,
and let us once again hear your lies
to our own answer.

Nigel Howard Dalby

A Wish

If I were granted just one wish
I think I'd choose to be a fish
My pond would have a snug, dry feeling
While the rain made rings on my pale green ceiling.

Barry Devetta

Addiction

I am addicted,
but not to the heady taste of alcohol,
nor to the pulsating rush of ecstasy
as it courses through my veins.
Silence is my drug!
The tranquillity of solitude,
the serenity of noiselessness,
As in the silence I face myself!
Here I, and only my mind exists,
Alive, without pressure from others.
Silence is my sanctuary!
Where I can be myself,
untouched by others' thoughts or criticisms.
I choose solitude without regret,
Revelling in silent living harmony,
Opening my mind to a million, trillion
soaring rainbow dreams and thoughts.
I renounce the insanity of constant, inane chatter.
I pledge my soul to silence,
To the peaceful paths of spiritual addiction.

Jennifer Flynn

The Sacrifice

1942 young men where going out to war
They were not yet really quite mature
It wasn't their choice, they had to go
Brave young men they had to show
Terrible times they went through
Their youthful years were taboo
Sad parents saying goodbye
To all of their sons they knew might die
They should be treated better and paid their dues
Not looked down on because a small pension gives them the blues
They just accept with grace what they get
And have to be careful not to get into debt
This country could have been under a different rule
If it wasn't for men, some only a few years out of school
So many didn't come back, and those that did with their haver sacks
Were embraced by their family and lovers
And maybe they had also lost brothers
We must appreciate the elderly everywhere
Show respect, show we care
It is they who helped save this nation and gave us our salvation.

Jessica Looke

The Gift Of Our Land

Our promised land, so brown, so red;
parched, cracked, with heat so strong.
'What are you doing, my children?'
Cries mother earth.
'Where are you, child, where are you?'

I am here for everyone to love.
Come back, dear one, come back.
I showed you the way.
Together we have seen flood and fire
leaving their torrid scars behind,
burning into my soul.

The sweet glory of early morning hues,
tall gums stretching to clear blue skies,
your beauty springing forth,
a softness which has been hidden away;
an everlasting wonder of Nature's realm,
bringing peace and joy to our hearts again.

Elizabeth Game

Sonnet

How long can I survive with memories?
For though our love affair is long since past
The mind-felt sentiment will ever last.
Pleasure an ever fainter tremor is
And hands-lips senses are but knowledge massed
For future satisfaction. Yet the brain
Evaluates. Cursed poignancy, in vain
You reappear. He is forever lost.
Yet now when I desire no other's kiss
And lonely am depressed, my mind I'll cast
On days when ecstasy was all my pain
In man and woman's sweet experiences.
A once indulgence in love's full repast
Will feed me still when I am old and sane.

Carolyn A. Drury

The Rock, The Soul

The rock is harassed from every direction
The wind, rain and sea at their discretion
Its foundations are strong but the pounding is bright
Just like in life as you fight for your right
To love one and all and to live your life through
But the devil's around just waiting for you
To make a mistake at your weakest point
Just pray to God for your soul to anoint
He'll pound at your heart and tear at your soul
Just pray to God for to keep your life whole
His evil is strong but God's love is stronger
And in all of us now it will go on for longer
A time will soon come when the devil will perish
And love and happiness in this world we will cherish...

John Wright

The Sea-Bird

The 'Ha-Ha' bird balanced in the wind.
From his rooftop height he glowered down.
People did come and people did go,
Breathless, battling against storm,
But the 'Ha-Ha' bird mocked, "Ha-Ha"
From up high.

The 'Ha-Ha' bird balanced in the wind.
From his rooftop height he glowered down.
Boats came in, and boats went out,
Salt-sprayed, charging against tide.
But the 'Ha-Ha' bird mocked, "Ha-Ha",
From up high.

The 'Ha-Ha' bird balanced in the wind.
From his rooftop height he glowered down.
The house by the pier is now empty, forlorn,
Alone, brooding against the gales.
But the 'Ha-Ha' bird mocked "Ha-Ha",
From up high.

Judith E. Symon

Nature's Remedy

Off the beaten track
and down the winding lane,
there I find my solace
in the countryside again.

Weary of the world
its hustle and its bustle,
I turn to nature
as my shining example.

Slow down, stand and stare
listen to the peace and quiet lurking there.

Then with renewed vigour
I retrace my steps again,
back to my busy day
along life's winding lane.

S. Newton

Where Did The Peace Go?

It took so long to get it,
But seconds to destroy it,
The peace was here for all to see,
Everyone said they wanted it.
But a few people looked,
And it seems I'm mistook,
The ceasefire has suddenly ended.

What's going to happen now?
Nobody seems to know how,
To get the peace started again.
How can we get things the same?
So they're proud to say their country's name,
Let Ireland stand re-united again!

Claire Dornan

Philosophical

The timeless ages of our God,
Do they exist forever?
Can we believe the end of God is never?

It seems my human mind,
(So limited its range)
Cannot stretch forth and grasp this fact.
A universe without Mankind,
A measureless line of ceaseless years
Of everlasting, rolling spheres,
Devoid of laughter and of tears;
For Man will be no more,
No rich, no poor.

Shall we be spirits in eternal space?
Shall we behold God's loving face?
Can we know what Fate awaits us
Far away on an unknown shore?
Can we know, or do we care no more?

We can humbly trust in Him
Who sent His Son to earth
To die in agony to prove love's worth.

Daphne Stephenson

Spring

When I opened my spring box out streamed
A swirl of fresh air,
A pack of baby lambs,
The fun fairs,
The circus,
Lots of lovely, colourful, fabulous flowers,
New life and new beginnings,
The birds singing,
People going for walks
Me feeling happy, jolly, cheerful and glad,
The sun coming out happy and jolly,
The first holy communion,
The green leaves of the trees.
Spring is here.

Catherine Himer

July 13th

July.... it came so quick! My first time it was you know
I had it all planned, nothing too big
but just to say what a marvellous couple they make.

I almost lost them... the rings that is. But I knew where they were.
She thought I had lost them, the bride I mean,
I finally pulled them out of my pocket!

The worried moment "I now pronounce you man and wife" he said
It was all over.

The Restaurant. Next was the lunch
It was soon my turn. I stood up. I could feel my face going red
my ears burning. Finally it was all over

A big sigh I made... You did not let us down they said
But it was the red jelly part!!??!!
Next I had to take the guest book round

The Evening. They all came, my part was over
I had a couple of dances with the bride, but I had all the fun
The disco, the drinks, the dancing and most of all, my job

In the end, it is just a memory never to be forgotten
Just... July 13th 1996, the day my dad, Keith, and Margaret were married.

I WAS THE BEST MAN.

Stephen Eves

Tender Heart

Oh! Tender heart, that feels another's pain
And sees another's welfare as its gain,
There is no greater gift God gives to man.
Than that his heart should understand Gods plan.
To feel for others with an open hand
And lift their burden, show, you understand.

Oh! Loving heart, a gift from God to you
Happy are you, when helping someone through;
When times are hard and they have lost their way
You give out cheer, you understand their day
And God our father works his will through you
Lifting a soul from deep despair, that's true.

Oh! Heart, so burdened with another's care, you cannot carry all
life's ills, not dare, to lift life's burdens from these souls alone,
but only by the strength and guidance known to those whose hearts are
bound to God in Christ whose own dear heart was broken, sacrificed.

So live your days, give up your pain to God, to that great lover of
our souls, who wants that we should work in love and gratitude by
helping others, as we always should; we must stay always by our
saviours side and in his love and wondrous grace abide.

W. Herbert G. Palfrey

Bella

You came to me so small and frail, and measured six inches from head
to tail. Your favourite spot was the palm of my hand, a beautiful
lump of white and tan.

Oh! How I loved my sweet little dear, the thought of rearing you
filled me with fear. Your presence gave me great joy and love,
faithful and loving, sent from above.

For I was so lonely before I had you, my life was so dreary, my
friends were so few. Yet! You were so artful, and funny, and wise,
who could deny you with those brown eyes?

Everyone loved you, and children galore would run up and my drive
and knock on the door. They'd take you for walkies most every day,
then off to the meadows, there you would play.

I gave you the best in life that I could, for dear, you deserved it,
you were so good. When I was poorly, you sensed it, my dear - and
would snuggle up close to me ever so near.

If the doorbell rang, you went before - in case there was danger for
me at the door. There were many times hurt and pain, but we both
endured it, again and again.

But one day my sweet "Bella" was so very ill, she was put to sleep,
her heart now still. She was beautiful and loving, loyal and true,
the most lovely part of my life was you, dear Bella.

M. F. Williams

The Lost Kingdom Of Angkor

In Kambuja, where bridgeless Mekong flows,
Ka-Kup uprears its rugged peak, and, sighing,
Mourns for the lost glory of a former age
Swiftly from misty past the Khmers came;
Built Angkor Thom, a city of the plains.
To it leads a causeway, beneath the arms
And feet of giants who pull Vasuki,
The earth-encircling serpent they have grasped.
But mightiest of the galleries and towers,
Rival to the Solomon-built temple,
Near perfect as the Parthenon of Greece,
Stands Angkor Wat, reflected in its moat.
   Suryarvanam, great king of Kambuja
Built Angkor Wat, his tomb and testament,
That overflying gods may see and know
That they were worshipped here by Khmers great,
Proud people of an empire long since gone:
For as sudden as this people came from misty past
They vanished without trace, mysteriously,
Except for these slave-hewn memories in stone.

Arthur Howard Cross

Dunblane, Nowhere To Run, Nowhere To Hide

The memories, the horror, and the trauma.
   When will it stop,
is there an end? The happy times
The hugs, and the chats
   Who could ever have imagined,
It would all be over so quickly.
   What could possibly drive someone,
So insane, that they resort to this,
   Not only did they take their own life,
But seventeen others as well.
   We have no pity for him,
And the only thing we feel,
   Is anger and hate!
No one understands what led him to this,
   Only that they had no right,
To take it out, on such innocent young children,
   Who had their whole lives ahead of them!

   With nowhere to run, and nowhere to hide,
   What was there left for them?

(A parent's memories, thoughts and feelings)
Donna Peachey

Drugs Have No Hold

What is all the fuss about? It's plain for all to see.
I don't have a problem, it has no hold on me.

Shaking, Sweating, Gaunt, Gray faced. Oh, what can it be
It's not the drugs, I'm sure of that, they have no hold on me.

I can fly like Batman, can even hold back the sea.
The voices in my head and the rush, it's all just meant to be.
Yet I don't have to worry, it has no hold on me.

I'm acting out of character, is all you seem to say.
That I don't know what I'm doing, it happens every day.
I tell you I'm just tired, oh why can't you see
I've said it once, I'll say it again, it has no hold on me.

I stole, you said. No borrowed, you were not there to ask.
It is such a problem? It's done, it's in the past.
Ok give me some money, I can get it back you see.
I know you don't believe that it has no hold on me.

The lights went out, what happened? Is this an angel I can see?
What do you mean my time is up and you've come to set me free?
Free from what I ask you? Were You Too Blind To See?
The drugs they were no problem, as they had no hold on me.

Diana Slater

Spring

Spring is a maid, attired in green,
She glides about the earth unseen.
And as she passes by each flower, she
touches them, and has the power to
make them grow.
As we pass across the sweet and dewy grass,
We pause to say "What lovely flowers,"
but do not think who has the powers
to make those blossoms grow so fair,
and spread their perfume through the air.

Eileen Gibson

Dave

Suddenly you are acting single;
Footloose and fancy-free,
And all these plans you're making
They don't include me.
Whether it's thinking about a holiday
Or planning your career,
Or talking about somewhere to live,
I don't seem to be there.
And you don't appear to be bothered
Where I've been or with who;
As long as you still have a girlfriend
It's of no importance to you.
But I don't want to be your best friend,
A lover who is only part-time.
If that's all you want in the future
I have to stop,
And think about mine.

Loretta Fennell

Xanadu

In Porlock Town did Doctor Brown,
A lovely mansion see,
Where ran the River Lyn thro' Lynton Town,
Down to an oil-polluted sea.

The slick of oil was ten miles long,
In Milford Haven the stricken tanker lay,
Upon the rocks, the winds so strong,
The salvage tugs were held at bay.

Across the sea in Milford, Skomer and Skiddo,
The sea birds, Gillemots, Gulls and Skewers too,
Are covered in oil, and must be rescued soon,
The Super-tanker was dragged off the rocks, by Noon.

She lost half her cargo (70,000 barrels) into the sea,
The ancient hills and forests too, and the lea,
And lovely gardens of delight,
Where grow the Rhododendron and Azalea bright.

With varied shades of brown and green,
And perfumed roses there are seen,
The oil slick has reached Lundy Island,
And sea birds are dying by the Thousand.

R. P. H. Fleming

Untitled

Oh summer dawn which brings the sound
of birds where songs announce the morn
Humble sparrow, lark or dove whose cries
reach to the heavens above, the king of
earth of leaves and wood, the gentle silence
'ere the flood of summer sunshine reaches out
to lighten all with golden glove.

That I may sit alone this morn and view
the wonders being born, God's creatures
great and small, a stir on leaf, in bower,
on stately fir, the gentle murmur of the bee,
of butterflies upon the tree, oh God
provider of the flowers, thank you
for making so much ours.

Frederick C. Puffitt

Daisies On The Frontier

There are daisies on the frontier now
No marks to show this was a slaughter zone
A bleak stretch of land
That has smothered its past
Burying it deep beneath
A cover of inoffensive weeds

History sighs over this silent field
Whispering elegies for young men in uniforms
Weaned on patriotism and glory
Mowed down like blades of grass
A generation of boys
Harvested for Nationalism

Warped strains of humanity
Have defended their pride
With the blood of their youth
And to what end?
To ensure freedom and peace
For the daisies on the frontier

Jane M. Hall

Pain And Joy!!

The day has come at last it's here.
This huge big lump will disappear.
I'll soon be able to see my feet,
Lie on my tummy! Oh what a treat.

I hope it's quick with little pain
I'm never going through all this again,
The morning sickness, the heartburn at night,
It's just been one big endless fight.

Maybe if 'he' or 'she' was planned
And "Daddy" was here to hold my hand.
I wouldn't be feeling so much dread
With mixed emotions running through my head.

I've already been blessed with two wee boys
I'm used to mess and lots of noise,
I just didn't think I'd see the day
I'd be lying here again in this way.

Well, all the worry, fear and dread
Has already gone right out my head
Cause here she is oh what a thrill!!
I've got myself a beautiful baby girl.

Linda Thomson

The Blue Earth

Two lands of white far apart,
Proud, silent; unending day,
Or night beneath the quiet stars.
So near? Light, light years away.

Or forest lands flooded, deep
Beneath their canopies of green,
Where creatures in the night, sleep,
Or of the day, hide unseen.

And high above the desert bleak,
Or Northern rugged highland hills,
The eagle soars from lofty peak.
Its lonely cry the thin air fills.

Proud mountain ranges linking arms
Like sentinels, guarding the way,
Towering o'er valleys deep or lonely farms,
Grazing herds or lambs at play.

Turbulent seas or oceans serene,
Mountain streams or rivers in flood.
Green fields, red earth, all Nature's scenes,
O, lovely blue earth....you're looking good.

Anthony Smith

My Grandson

I saw you for one week, young man, sixteen years ago
I held you in my arms each day and you will never know
The heartache when I said goodbye, and sealed it with a kiss
I thought my heart would break to think of all the years I'd miss.
You were a tiny bundle then, today you're near a man,
But, we have never met again, since your life began.
I pray life has been kind to you and brought you every joy
You're my grandson, but to me you're still that tiny baby boy.
It's sad we never knew each other over all these years
But I know the home that took you in shared love and joy and tears
But I hope, boy, when you wonder who your mother was and why
Did she give you up, you're told she loved you, so young man please try
To forgive her, for it was the hardest thing she had to do
'Cos she wanted what was best for her first born son, love, you.

Pat McBrine

Angel

Nothing is more beautiful than when an angel sings
with stardust on her golden hair and moonlight on her wings
My mind and day were dull and grey when into my life she flew
My life it changed, when you appeared, to lift me from the gloom
You blew away the cobwebs that pinned me to the wall
I broke free to fly with you the day I heard your call
(I haven't any choice with the sweetness of your voice)
As nothing is more beautiful than when an angel sings
With stardust on her golden hair and moonlight on her wings
You take me to the heavens when I'm close to you
You spread your wings, and show me things, that change my point of view
You're my dream, you're my angel, your wings are pure white snow
Which take me to the heavens, and from whom I can't let go
(Or I'll fall, yes I'll fall, but I'm falling for you)

Hear the beating of my heart, from the beating of your wings
Nothing is more beautiful than when an angel sings.

Mark Mawston

Ascent

Through such dreary days of despair a deathly dream awakens in me,
frozen and forever, these drained ragged veins run dry then disappear.
Impaled upon this splintered cross, reflected holiness through a
shattered mirror, the questioned answer greeted with silence, a mirage,
no truth instills such fear as the end, goodbye, the solemn shedding
of the final tear; as the end, goodbye, the tranquil fading of the final breath.

Yet beyond the curtain I still go on alone, as just one;
and though the storm may pass, no cracks invite the saviour
to devour the boundless nightmare of the mind,
my mind, caught in the perennial prison of this perished corpse.

So pale and haggard now, red rivers drown my desire;
enlightenment explodes through my head, splits this agonized soul
in two: the walking dead and the living truth—suffering cleanses—
and, elevated to a pure plateau of perfected penance,
I see the Way Out.

Neil Bristow

Time Descends

Move silently through the distant growth, winding and screaming,
times faster than light itself. The constant battle that
all shall renew, the ignorant suffering, we cannot keep up. Is this
fate, do all the people go crazy through the ticking of one's
heart not knowing whether tomorrow can be fulfilled? A losing battle,
a task to belief impatience. Do all believers dwell and become lost
through the roots of time? We are all level in our race,
some may fall behind—either deceased or drifting dimension hypocrites.
To die is also to win. The knowledge of one takes hold in space.
Time dies with age, remaining somewhere hidden in the distant time
travelling mind to where time began with age, and will end. Turning
and turning, rumbling her presence remaining adrift, world famous,
an old legend not just an enemy but a saviour. Long past the end of
the world she will live a conqueror of all, untouchable. I pace
amongst the battle grounds that time has left, and I myself will
conquer within time. Yet now I have to live with it. This is the
moment of war, I have come to understand my strength. She has no
sympathy, a cold blooded bandit, I have no time. I will die and
she will live, but I will live within.

Matthew Gill

405

In A Biblical Sense

If there's a heaven, I cannot repel
Trust in thy saviour or endeth in hell
Is there a God? Do you know what he's saying?
Questions unanswered, shall I start praying?

Profits are chanting "We know what's best"
Give us your souls and we'll lay them to rest
Murder relinquished and sinners go free
Sounds ideal for a criminal to be.

Community's wrecked, but Christ gives a damn
This is the act of the creator of man.
Bow to your knees, give two minutes silence
Read the good book, forget all the violence.

You've tasted temptations, now just show regret
Satan he's laughing, but Jesus respects
Stop enjoying life, for Lucifer is strong
Stick with the Lord for he's never wrong.

The end is near, it's time to choose
If I die impure, will I really lose?
If I keep the faith, my curiosity will end
For the Messiah claims he's my best friend.

Mark Leonard

The Body

This wonderful thing we call "Body",
Is made up of lots of little things,
hard things called bone which support it
and tendons that look just like strings.

Body moves around with its muscles
they move it from this place to that,
muscles move our bodies faster than elephants
but not quite as fast as a cat.

There's red stuff called blood, inside body
it moves through the vessels inside,
blood is what keeps body going
with other things that dive in for the ride.

Everything in body is connected
tendons join muscle to bone,
different tissues cover this bit and that bit
and blood doesn't flow on its own.

We all must be grateful to body
there's nothing we could quite use instead,
because without all these bits and their functions
we'd just be this thing that's called Dead

Nichola Carless

We Knew This Man

We knew this man
So gentle and kind
What a lovely family he's leaving behind

We knew this man
With a heart of gold
Who had love and affection, and many dreams
untold

We knew this man
So tender and true
Never a bad word of all those he knew

We knew this man
So strong, yet so small
By just being himself was respected by all.

We knew this man
With heartfelt love
Now watches us all from the heavens above

We knew this man
With all good things life can convey
So we have come here to say
Sweet farewell "to Edwin" today

Audrey Joy Humm

A Stroll Through Bluebell Woods

I wandered slowly o'er the dell,
Between the trees so tall,
When my eyes beheld a deep blue sea
Of elegant bluebell.

They gathered together round the trees,
And in between the grass,
Their slender stems swaying in the breeze,
Bells fluttering as I passed.

A picture of beauty rare indeed.
Painted by nature's hand.
With colours all blending brown, blue, and green,
Cascading o'er the land.

As I strolled on that summer's day,
The sun glinting through the trees,
I felt as though I'd walked o'er heaven's highway,
My spirit soared, my heart was pleased.

Cyril G. Button

America

Fifty states born to be great
America this is you;
From Atlantic to Pacific shore, through a tapestry of time,
Threads the Everglades floor to Niagara's shore
In nature's work so fine.
Like a vast great hand, this fertile land beckoned one and all;
And people of many countries, were quick to take the call;
They found the Red Man waiting, brave warrior, fearless foe!
But fate decreed, another breed, should flood the land and grow.
And so they join together, to people this vast place,
The mountains and the valleys, the forests and the lakes.
A heritage of wildlife, of culture rich and rare,
The proud and mighty Redwood tree,
The chipmunk and the Bear.
And now America today strives for a greater prize,
Man's most exciting journey, to reach the outer skies;
May Wisdom, Faith and Courage, guide them as they go;
And if it is God's purpose;
New Worlds to us they will show.

Brenda Pascall

Life

People begin life
    from the moment they are born.
We cannot choose to be on this earth.
Growing up we must do.
The obstacles we face
will all be brand new.
Life can be good, bad, happy or sad.
It can also be precious or cruel.
Decisions and choices will
    be made at some stage.
Older people may be wiser
    because of their age.
Heartache and dilemmas
are part of life too. The world
will be nothing unless we all try. But
it's a well known fact that eventually we must die.

Lisa Timney

Nobby Who??

I remember as I sat with rattle, scarf and hat
The winger had the ball, the nifty Nobby Hall
He rounded two, then three - his sight at goal was free
His boot came down with might - to the home fans great delight
To them he was a God but he hadn't seen the sod -
His shot was sliced and high - it flew into the sky
It hit some poor old chap - right squarely in the lap
The stars that night came early as I was stretched off to Purley
When I came round, I said, "Why am I in this bed"?
Then I remembered Nobby's cracker had hit me in the knacker!
An honour was the pain; to the nurse I did explain
But as they swell and grew - she said, "Nobby Who"??

R. M. Reed

406

Come, Rejoice, It's Eastertide

Nature stirs from winter slumber,
Green leaves clothe the bare-branched trees!
Daffodils, their buds just bursting,
Nod their heads in gentle breeze!

Orchards, bright with apple blossom,
Pink and white, like love's young bride!
Grace the countryside with colour,
Come, rejoice, it's Eastertide!

Through the dawn, alive with chirping,
Come those creatures on the wing!
Hunt their prey, to feed their fledglings,
Helpless, hungry, hatched in spring!

Springtime brings romantic notions,
Easter bonnets, Easter brides!
Bells are ringing, rings on fingers!
Come, rejoice, it's Eastertide!

All is rising, life renewing!
Bright with spring's adorning pride!
From the body, free the spirit!
Come, rejoice, it's Eastertide!

John Austen Stokes

Adolescence

The childhood fear at the back of your mind
Is hard to get rid of, but easy to find.
Defending the feelings is easily said,
As is ignoring the pain in your head.
A distraction will put the confusion on hold,
Like a small burst of heat in the freezing cold.
It feels as though comfort is lifetimes away
And that pain will persist, day after day.
You try to dismiss it, and persevere,
But no help releases that childhood fear.

Jade Threlfall

"Sad, Sad World"

Oh foolish people why must you be
Full of hate and brutality.
Fighting and killing by the score
Bringing sorrow and grief
What for! What for!
This world was given to live in peace
Bring this bloodshed to a cease.
Life is a gift, you have no right
To take it away in a senseless fight.
Death, destruction, violence, pain.
A world full of hate is all that you'll gain.
What good is a world that is full of hate?
Curb your greed before it's too late,
Live peaceably as God intended you for.
In a United World—forevermore.

Eileen Mosley

Gently Towards Winter

Autumn leaves adorn the trees,
The swallows now are gone,
We savour in our memory
Caressing summer sun,
Soon the leaves will softly fall
Covering lanes and meadows green
And feathered friends will change their song
From melody to hungry plea.
Cobweb mists hang over shores
And valleys like a cloak.
Morning air is chill and damp.
Lazily curls the chimney smoke.
The heathers faded on the moor.
The bracken crisp and brown.
So soon the mountains will display
Their glistening snowy crown.

Marjorie Curtis

The Bag-Woman

Look over there a poor and wretched sight indeed.
My word, why yes. I know her, it is I'm sure.
I haven't seen her around for years and years.
She's changed of course from times gone by
When she was young her eyes were bright and full of life.
I tell you now she used to be a "looker" then.
She dressed in vivid greens and blues, in reds and yellows in lilac
too. Always clean she smelt so good, of lavender fields and mountain
pines. Her long seductive shiny hair rustled softly in gentle winds.
Full of energy and life she rushed around from dawn 'til dusk.

But see her now a wretched soul,
Clad in sombre rags of grey and brown, with crawling things upon her flesh.

A fetid air surrounds her too, the stench of someone dying.
Her hair a tangled, matted, mess, and arid flaking desert skin.
What calamity befell her; what sorry stories can she tell?
Who broke her heart and caused her so much pain and sorrow?
What gave her face that empty, hopeless haunted look?
Why does she sit there all alone in this our Multi-Universe?
When she was young she had a name, now let me see;
Yes, I remember now, they called her Earth or was it Mother Nature then?

Adrian Blake

The Church Mouse

I wonder why folk think church mice are poor?
'Cos I have always had enough - and more.
Kept by my Christian friends, I'm treated well, and truth to tell
I'm getting fat with idling time away,
And not being forced to search for food all day.

Tomorrow, listed in the magazine
Communion for St. James is what I've seen.
The celebrant, in vestments rich and red will break the bread
He sometimes drops a portion just for me,
I'm one of God's small creatures don't you see?

Last week I heard them talking during tea
A man to church was coming to see me.
They all discussed me - all that blessèd crowd, I felt so proud.
I thought - "perhaps the Bishop or the Dean!"
Such dignitaries I have rarely seen.

The man they talked about is here - mid. week,
With tins containing food, I had a peek.
He placed them 'neath the pipes with loving care, oh! such fine fare.

I ate a lot, but now I'm sick! I'm crying!

It didn't agree with me, I think I'm dying, d-y-i-n-g, d-y....

Jessie Edwards

My Angel

Angels come in many guises, many shapes and many sizes,
Mine is shaped like any man, two busy legs, two willing hands,
Since 'Parkinsons' gave me a call, I can use neither hand at all,
If I need food, I'm not alone, his hand manipulates the spoon,
When nature calls, he too will come, to wipe my nose, or wipe my bum,
When bedsores come to plague my day, his gentle care takes them away,
He helps me walk the garden path, and wash my face, gives me a bath,
He combs the hair upon my head, he lifts me in and out of bed,
Does the shopping at full speed, anticipates my every need,
He does the housework, cooks the meals, and always knows just how it
feels for me to aye depend on him, to tend my each and every whim,
Yet, never once does he complain, to serve me is his only aim,
He wears a smile upon his face, and makes our home a happy place,
He showers me each day with love, he must have come from heaven above
To love and care and wait on me, and yet, he's nothing much to see,
But, somewhere in God's mighty plan, he made an angel of my man,

Yes, I wrote this all by myself, on his W. P. up on the shelf,
With pencil held in jaws so tight, I, with great effort this poem did write,
To tell the whole world if I can, my angel is a normal man,
Who since retiring's had to be an angel and a nurse to me.

Jean Smith

A Journey

The train, when moving clickerty clack
Always forwards, with its carriages down the track;
Passing sleepy village and town
Darkness has quickly fallen down!
How fast the train goes up hills and dales
Silently passing through the vales,
We are on our way! We are on our way!
Look past the cattle asleep in the hay,
The train slips by the braes and locks
Passing, unloading ships in the docks.
Stopping at stations along the route
Porters collecting and dropping their loot
How wonderful to see the dawn breaking
Passengers from their sleep are waking!
Is the train stopping at last?
Only to let another train past!
Here's the train turning, the final bend
Alas! Sadly bringing our journey to its end.

Jean C. Watson

The Soldier

Tall and sturdy stands the soldier
Tough and smart stands the soldier
A gun and a knife, a kid and a wife
Maybe he will see them maybe he will not
If his number is called and he must die
His wife will weep his wife will cry
But who cares?
He is only a soldier not even a sergeant
Who cares?

Dead and lifeless lies the soldier
Six foot under lies the soldier
No good being brave
When you're lying in your grave
Surrounded by wood and soil
But who cares?
He was only a soldier.

Michael A. J. Fawcett

For An Ailing Friend

A positive thought is what you need,
When meeting trouble or strife;
A friendly thought, to aid the lead,
Of a caring and wonderful wife.

My God goes with you, strong and stern,
As you meet this, your next dire test;
You'll conquer this one, in its turn,
It's part of life, your quest.

Think only hard, think only strong,
This battle is yours to meet;
However grim, however long,
Remember that victory's sweet.

Martin J. H. Fisher

Insomnia

When dawn awakes to lift the sky,
And sleep once more deserts my eye;
I look towards a brighter light,
That helps me through the darkest night
When tossing, turning, sleep evades,
And horror through my mind parades.
All worries, small in daylight hours,
Grow larger with the nighttime powers
Which stretch the sleepless mind, to see
Dark contrasts to what life should be.
Exaggerated woes and strife,
Which are not there in daily life,
Attend the night, when nought around
Distracts, and all concerns compound.
I know that I should thank the Lord,
For all the good in life He's poured,
But only dawn and sunlight's beams
Can shrink these wild thoughts to "sweet dreams".

E. Tomlinson

Fire Down Below

Does it happen, inconceivably, and do you ever think
That your cruise might be abandoned and you'd end up in the drink
That like sailors through the ages you'd be teet'ring on the brink,
Well it happens, yes it happened, I was there.

Not a moment of confusion, just a ripple, first of mirth,
For the thought of a disaster was the farthest thing on earth,
But they called the captain, then the crew, the passengers changed berth,
When the smoke rolled, filled the ship's hold, and the air.

With the yellow of life jackets and with faces sickly green,
With soot blackened men in hard hats dashing all around the scene.
The majority smile bravely but there's panic in between:
Fire fighting is disquieting, so beware.

Hours later, tired and shaken, but the roll call says 'all here'
Food and laughter long forgotten, what has happened isn't clear,
There is water in the cabins: Was Omega really near?
Though unduly, yes quite truly, never fear.

Doreen Sowden

A Valedictory, My Broken Heart

Sweetest love you have parted like a flame quenched by water,
why are you abandoning me?
What have I done to receive my tragic death?
Why are you relinquish so quick it is not near day?
I must hear from you everyday in the hour for a minute there are many days,
I felt like a beautiful red rose with you in a lonely field, it felt astonishing
I now feel like an old and tired rose looking for my love,
Our love is too strong to be broken
When the sun shines I will think of you,
you are part of my enchanting dream.

Nada Hussain

Hateful Love

See this man who lies before me, his body softened beneath the folds
of the sheets. Here are his smooth lips - how many times have they
smiled fondly, and uttered tender words to me at the setting of the
sun? These are the hands that have loved and caressed me, easing me
through this surreal existence. They are the hands which struck my
virginity from me, paying me off with a new, deeper love.
Now I am sore and weary.
What is this feeling that commands me, a sensation so strong that it
squeezes my heart and moistens my eyes? My love consumes me, pains
me. Here are the eyes that have beheld my naked body.
Finally to close in dissatisfaction and renunciation.
This night, which was born of a blow, has died of a blow.
Maybe I'll find a place to nestle, within this hurtful plain,
where so many others must have been before.
Perhaps I should run, and escape the emotions which imprison me.
But where would I go? Back to the hands that clothed and fed me,
in my youth? Those hands are now withered and withdrawn, and their
love has evaporated, like juice from a fruit grown old. I am lost in
a turmoiled maze of loving hatred.
I will remain here, and make my home from thorny affections.

Rosie Major

I Dreamed That The Moon Had Fallen To Earth

Rain fell and darkness covered the sky like a black sheet.
I heard a great cry, like the voice of rolling thunders saying:
the end of the world has come.
I froze. Where were my family?
I searched around in vain, but I could see no one.
I called but no one answered. I was alone in a silent world.
Then there was a loud bang and the Earth shook with rage.
I ran petrified for my safety.
I clung breathless to a chestnut tree, clinging for my dear life.
I looked fearfully at the black sky, and saw a gigantic silver dish
come falling down to Earth. I heard a huge crash and the Earth fell,
crumbling. Lightning shot through the sky and tore the Earth in half.
It tore me too. I screamed aloud in pain and called for help.
But then... someone heard my cry.
Someone lifted me and planted my feet on a new Earth.
Where I could feel no pain, and cry no more.
Where I could be glad and breathe freely, and live for Eternity.
I dreamed that the moon had fallen to Earth.

Martha Obozua

Untitled

Part of me is him, yet none of him is me.
People say 'obsession' but I say 'love'.
Without him I'm empty.
Reality is nothing, imagination is everything
If he knew, he'd laugh - I'd cry
People believe in miracles, where's my miracle?
He makes me glow, a word from him to me -
Eternal happiness, amazing feelings,
Then I crash, with huge pain to reality
And realise I love him, I feel him in my heart
But he is perfect and I am me.

Teresa Maguire

You!

You, gave in yourself - and outwardly
Such things that could never be replaced.
And when looking into someone else's eyes
A picture reflects - it's your face.
I place myself - and fall into
Someone else's arms,
Tho it's in your arms - where I long to be
Safe and away from harm
I kiss another - only to bluff my kiss
And whisper in their ear,
Tho it will always be you - forever I'll miss
You whom I long to draw near.
I touch another - and then linger
Then slowly embrace their skin,
I close my eyes - then drift away
For it's you - whom I want to let in.
I greet another - and put
A smile upon my face,
Then reflecting back - straight back at me
Again I see your face.

Nina-Marie Walker

Escape

To walk carelessly, over the fields
  Of the leafy countryside.
To linger on the river bank,
  Or to sail out on the morning tide.
To remove the shackles of despair
  And fly off to some distant land.
To free one's mind, of doubt and fear,
  Then turn again, when homeward bound.
For if you dream eternally,
  Your dreams become reality.

R. A. Bennett

Trouble And Strife

You're working hard all through your life
Just to keep a happy wife
You buy a house and run a car
Sometimes you think you've gone too far

It's pay for this and pay for that
If you don't pay you're just a rat
The wife keeps nagging all the while
Now and then you'd think she'd smile

Off to the seaside for a break
There's not a lot of give and take
When you have a blazing row
It's back to mum - O, Lord and how

You and her, you hardly speak
It's murder getting through the week
But after all is said and done
You're still together, no-one's won

No looking back on goes your life
And you've still got the trouble and strife
Think happy thoughts and you'll be glad
She's still the best you ever had.

K. A. Batham

The Song Of Living Pain

When passion dies from someone's eyes the love they had is lost,
And the bleeding tears flow through the years turn cold and wet
like frost... Like rewinding film flows through the mind it must
also flow through the heart, remembering times but time never
remembers only you and your broken heart.

With each day that brings refreshing winds blowing closer to the
frame, with understanding sighs it fills the eyes, remembering all
the pain.. When remembering joys of long loved days and thoughts
that fill the heart - perhaps a look a glance perchance these
thoughts will never part.

For you are conscious living soul which absorbs every feeling felt
like the star like shape, a flake of snow that snow will start to melt

  But never stopping to adjust the song remains the same,
  Our instrumental heart recites the song of living pain..

Pain played through the heart itself obstructs the thinking mind,
And the mind can't work out on its own without the heart inside.

Phil Carroll

Winter

Unbidden from the frozen plains the North wind blows,
The land is dead, the earth sterile, nothing grows,
No tender bud, no infant shoot to lift the soul,
Nor eaglet small or life renewed with roe deer's foal.
The harsh snows fall and hoarfrost lies on dormant bough
Lone sparrows forage far and near, eager now,
To dine on hard-won berries from dried-out sprig,
Or some neglected relic from frenzied dig.
Then joy, with nature's birth, the heart and spirits soar,
The virgin land exults to feel the sun once more,
Harsh winds no longer blow, tender snowdrops bravely grow,
And on the new green naked sward, free from frozen tundra's blast,
Grow with gentle warmth's reward, the flowers of spring at last.

Evelyn Wickens

Animals Have Feelings

Staring through my sad eyes, wondering how many days I have left
How many hours left to suffer, before my painful death
How many cruel and heartless experiments, until the day I die
How many cold and lonely nights in pain, how many tears must I cry
To you I'm just a dumb animal, a prisoner in a cell.
To test all your products before the market stalls can sell
Needles do hurt as you should know, and bleach does burn your eyes
Can't you hear the pain I'm screaming, how many more must I try
I cry each lonely tear, I'm a person I am, I'm me
I dream at night that I am home, running wild and free
I see the spring meadows, and lie in the shade under the trees
I see my friends and family, I'm home where I long to be
But here in a cage I now must stay, until they've finished torturing me
And here I lie, I'm dying, I'm lifeless but now I'm free

Amanda Woodcock

Dawn

Hello Dawn, yes it's me again - waiting for you all alone,
Hey now don't be sad, you know I'm getting used to being on my own.
Well Dawn, what shall we do with this bright new day?
There's got to be something or God wouldn't have sent it my way.
Don't start to panic - silly old me.
It's the weekend again and once more I am free,
But free to do what and free to go where?
When there's no one to talk to and no one to care.
I'm sorry Dawn, that's enough of this sorrow.
You've brought a shining new day and there'll be another tomorrow.
I'll tell you what Dawn - you and I will take a walk
together down the lane,
We'll look at the flowers, snowdrops, primroses,
celandines - you see I know them all by name.
We'll say 'Good Morning' to the cows and the birds up in the tree
Then we'll wander slowly home again, you and me.
Someday perhaps, I'll find a friend, companion, lover
And we'll share all the wonders of nature together.
Until then Dawn, it's just you and me,
But one day with luck I hope there'll be three.

V. J. Wingate

Grey Days

It's a cruel world when born into poverty
The daily tasks for a mere child just reality
Then you grow up only to find
That your way of life is so unkind
you then marry and think the
    world a far better place
But, no even then with an ugly face

Rearing its head it strikes again
And you lose your loved ones to the pain

Patrica Wood

Honours Pre-Soccer

In days of old, when knights where bold
and football wasn't invented
The favourite sport was jousting
They earned their honours ousting.

To get their rivals on the spot
They had to use their lance a lot
once this achieved, with skill and grace
a greater Hazard had to face.

For back at home and full of ire
awaits a dragon breathing fire
For like their counterparts today
The wives of yore would have their say

Instead of tasty snacks in sight
For tired steed and weary knight
Across the moat a voice would float
Your ousting about just gets my goat.

Florence Pilkington

Lonely Old Man

Times were hard but people cared
Friends were good and food was shared.
Money scarce and jobs were few.
But how I wish I'd lived like you.

But you're old now and in a world
Where people are wicked and cruel to the old.
And no one cares about each other.
You're someone's father and someone's brother.

You live your life in poverty and fear.
No one cares, no one comes near.
I look at you and feel so sad.
You look so frail and yet your glad.

You'll not be long this cruel life
You'll soon be back beside your wife
So you'll struggle on another year.
You know somehow your time is near.

You've lived your life at ninety four
And soon won't be lonely anymore.

Lynn Byers

Addiction

A huddled figure in the corner,
dilated pupils stare in space,
needle marks command thin arms,
bewildered expression on a misused face.
People stare, but never stop,
they've got their own ideas,
about the addicts of today,
not many shed real tears.
Shaking hands outstretched in plea,
most will try not to see,
a pusher appears but there's no cash,
as if a vision, gone in a flash.
Sweat runs down the rigid frame,
breath by breath a call in vain,
a small voice begs with one last try,
stop press, and one more dies.

Wendy Blundell

Daddy

Smiles and laughter echo through my head.
Memories of Mum, eight years dead.
I remember Daddy crying at the side of the grave,
As I held his hand and tried to be brave.
Not one teardrop fell from my eye. I had to be strong, wasn't to cry.
The sobs would come later, when I was alone.
Safe in my room and warm in my home.
At night I'd hear Daddy crying in pain, wishing Mum was with us again.
The pulse of my heart would then skip a beat,
As across the hall I'd hear his feet.
The door would open and I'd squeeze my eyes tight.
He is my daddy, but this can't be right.
I loved my Mum, and when she took bad,
All she would say was, "Look after Dad."
"You're a big girl now, so just be strong.
I've got Cancer and I won't be here long."
Daddy is a good man, people have said.
But when the night comes, he creeps to my bed.
It hurts when he touches, but I fight the pain.
So why does he do this? Please someone explain!!!

Kenneth Boyle

City People

Tall man walks briskly down a street.
Black hat and black suit help engulf him in the shadows,
as he turns into the darkness between the looming mass of
concrete and steel and despair.
Sunlight at the end of the tunnel—escape for the rich man,
to places more pleasant and green, and safe and clean and habitable.
    Scurry, the rich man, scurry past your conscience, and forget,
    Forget the pain in their expressions, the wrinkles in their hides.
    Forget the tortured souls we stare in at, through their eyes.

Longing for acceptance by society,
they turn to anything for a momentary pause in reality.
Old man sings to his invisible friend,
and waves to tall, rich man as he passes by
Offers him a swig, but rich man's indifference is taken as a refusal.
Old man is offended, and the hurt pours out in his tears.
Nobody loves him. Almost.

Still sobbing, conversing inanely between hiccups
with invisible friend, old man
feebly tucks himself in for the night, in his cardboard.

Nina Walsh

Bobby

Bobby Joe: Roberta, to call her by her name,
    Was five years old and happy before the bad man came.
Her bright blue eyes are dim now, her smile is seen no more,
    Her rosy cheeks are pale and thin, unlike they were before.

She never skips, or jumps or runs, nor leaves her mother's side,
    He said he had some sweets for her, and now she knows he lied,
She can't remember details like the colour of his hair,
    I wonder if she can, but then, perhaps she doesn't dare.

She was found alone and blood stained, half-naked and confused,
    Her tiny body violated; broken; ripped; abused;
Her little mind in turmoil, she called her mum in vain,
    Now all she can remember is the day the bad man came.

Gone are her childish memories of fun with girls and boys
    At her birthday-party, with all her brand-new toys,
Gone are the games and laughter, gone are the bed-time dreams,
    All that remains for Bobby, are the nightmares and the screams.

They caught him, then they jailed him, and courtesy of the state
    They handed re-habilitation to him on a plate,
They spent thousands to provide him with every little thing,
. . . They should look into Roberta's eyes, and let the bad man swing!

Marion E. Halliday

410

Autumn Poem

Many of the leaves fall on the hard ground,
When they fall from the sky they don't make a sound.
Cobwebs shining like silver stars,
People not able to start up their cars.

Conkers falling off the trees,
Children going to play in the leaves.
Everybody wraps up warm,
Just in case there is a storm.

The leaves turn a darkish red,
They're often floating around my head.
Warm steam comes from your mouth,
I bet the weather's warmer down in the south.

Charlotte Gardner (written age 10)

My Diamond Jubilee

For full sixty years I have travelled,
Hoping none of them have been in vain.
Today I look back through the storm-clouds,
See again the sun follow the rain.
The going wasn't always so easy
Many times I have floundered and failed,
But faith, hope and charity led me
O'er paths which with courage I hailed.

From the cross I drew strength for the labour
I'd been trained to expect my life through.
Many others had managed before me
So I knew I should make the grade, too.
I've had crosses to bear and much sorrow,
But what human being has not?
The joys and the blessings were many
And made somewhat easy my lot.

Today we are gathered together
To celebrate sixty years and to say -
"Thank You, Lord, for all You have done
To bring me to this jubilant day."

Dominic Mary Lynch

Dead Again

Hard, harsh, cold.
Still and sombre.
Dead.
Reincarnated by a solitary match.
Burning in the dark.
Life - reproducing, changing, moving, breathing.
Taking long sip-full of cold night air.
Generating warm poison.
Generating warm light.
Radiating heat.
The two shadow stretchers reach high into the vast nothing.
Creating rivers of pain,
Flowing away into the dark.
Washing their tall bodies with their own blood,
Extinguished through lack of fuel.
Dead again.
Waxed cotton - candle - burnt cotton - wax.

Gemma White

Sunday Morning

Cats on the bed and bells in the distance,
forget about yesterday;
tea on the doorstep, the garden ablaze
with today's sunshine -
masses of gold and rubies on trees,
aquamarine sky,
cat - warmed ankles,
forget about slippers.
Don't feel the threat of common sense worries,
dull banal colours of everyday life.
Sunday sunshine and furry cats' cheeks
brush my teacup,
copper, sapphires, rubies and gold
are all for me now.

Manuela Sava

Ocean Blue

I can look at the ocean and it only reminds me of you
The way the water ripples is like your spine
Water brushes over the rocks
Like when you rub your body up against mine
The movement of water in one direction with many curves
It's like your body embraced in mine
I am the bed below with my many corals
I look up at you as you protect me from the outside world
You are the water that covers me
Drift through me with your thousand ripples
When tide goes out you leave me once again
Rocks stand so still and cold waiting for the ocean
If you were the ocean you would come back
Rap your arms around me and swallow me up
We are just like the ocean.

Lorraine MacArthur

Changing Seasons

The grass is growing very high
The trees are in full bloom,
Young birds are learning how to fly
The sun fills every room.

Football and rugby have now passed
Tennis and cricket are here at last,
The evenings are now getting light
The children will not sleep at night.

Holidays makers fill our beaches
Roads are filled, car brakes screeches,
Young lambs are having their last fling,
Yes summer has taken over from spring.

M. Prince

Convenience Food

Tonight I heard a red fox bark,
A harsh, staccato cry,
And smelled his scent on the April breeze
As he went slinking by.

The ducks and hens, within their pen
Won't be disturbed tonight,
And little lambs, beside their dams
Can sleep 'til morning light.

For when I heard the red fox bark
Across the playing field
He was eating scraps, where earlier
A picnic had been held.

Why should he waste his energy
Hunting for his prey,
When human beings will provide
Such a tasty "take away."

Betty Bowles

Patience

Patience is a job, life sometimes pays to do.
I've waited and I've waited, but still my wages due.
Patience is our enemy, a respectable friend as well.
Patience boxes you in, inside we anxiously dwell.

Patience is of discipline, we wait under our own command.
Some people wait forever, never reaching their promise land.
So patience is our teacher, learning what our wait has brought,
And patience is an asset . . . for dreams that can't be bought.

Patience is a good thing, too much becomes a crime.
Like patiently waiting forever, so not getting to work on time.
Damn that train,
And damn that bus,
All these people,
Oh! What a fuss.
Why couldn't someone be patient for me?
Well I guess there could be someone,
I'll just have to wait and see!

John Finch

411

Memories

I remember a time you said you cared,
Intimate moments we both shared.
Thoughts of you released in my head,
All the things you once said.

Memories tell of the past,
I thought love was supposed to last!
I wish I could hold you once again.
Only you could take away this pain.

I could only hope and pray
That you'll return one day
I know it's a dream that won't come true,
But I can't stop loving you!

Emma-Jayne Carty

My Most Treasured Gift

When God, He planned to make this world,
He gave us, for our pleasure,
Many, many pleasant things,
For us on earth to treasure,
Yet all of them, we seem to take
There, in our daily stride,
But there's one treasure I hold so dear
Which fills my heart with pride.
It was one of His creations,
I'm sure meant for above,
For I never knew such beauty
Could be filled with so much love.
He sprinkled His creation,
The greatest one by far,
With very special qualities
That shine, just like a star.
Then He went and named you
Unlike any other,
Dear God, I truly thank you
For my dearest, darling Mother.

Linda J. Archer

Abortion

Can you hear me Mum?
I'm in here you know.
I love you Mum.
I can't wait to see you.
We can do things
Go swimming and all the things you like.
Where are we going today?
Are we going on a bus or in a taxi?
Will it be hot or cold?
Are we there yet?
What's going on?
Who are all these people?
What's happening?
Mum it hurts.
What's that bright light?
And those hands?
I'm dying Mum.
Don't you love me?
What are you doing?
I love you Mum.

Tamara Crosland

Sicilian Summer

So hot! So hot! It's too hot even to think.
Long black shadows across the terrace link
the contrasting terra cotta red floor
with the green leaves, shining even more,
in the bright early morning light,
after the short, sharp showers during the night,
everything is clean and sparkling.
In the distance some dogs are barking;
however they are too far away to disturb the ear,
but near enough to make it clear,
that someone is climbing the dusty lane,
winding up the hillside to our domain.

Grace Holgate

Rapture Of Emotional State

Torrid whirls of colour encase me, burning oranges singe my emotions,
Placid rivers of green drown me, blinded yellows force fear into my eyes,

And yet the fear is of nothing animate or inanimate,

People surround me, weaving, twisted and
Rearranged faces stretch close to mine,
My frustration reflected in them,

I am incorporate in them, an un-oiled mechanical component,

They are the environment that I am engulfed in. Yet I feel as if
I am in a void, an abyss, incapable of emotions, devoid of passion,
Sentiment, and impulses of agonizing anguish.

Numb to all, yet aware of all.
Incapable of feeling, yet not able to do anything other than suffer in
The cave of my mind that is swallowed by the black nightmare of my own
Perplexed emotional memories.

They leave me.

All that is animate, all that is capable of any form of love, all
That could ever survive the torment and torture, fades.

Now they are gone—the colours, the faces, the company. I am alone,
In solitude, left to be digested by the black intestine of life.

Tara Barton

Woburn Abbey

Driving through the country lanes intoxicated by the view,
Inhaling deeply rich aromas carried on the summer breeze.
Trembling in anticipation savouring every scene anew,
In nature's own cathedral garden with God's choir in the trees.

Inside the abbey grounds again, the tranquil splendour of the place,
Dissolved away my fears and pain, leaving me speechless with emotion.
The memories flood each step I take on ground which royalty did grace,
And ancient monks in sacred order tended with such deep devotion.

Adjusting to the timeless beauty, gazing at a tree-lined lake,
Where golden carp in great profusion swim majestically along.
Protected from the angling masses, baited hooks they never take,
The pampered monsters rise to feed from fingers of admiring throng.

Hordes of people now arriving flock towards the stately home,
Oblivious to the glorious gardens, dazzled by the treasures there.

All unaware that history dwells beneath the velvet lawns they roam,
Where long dead friars rest serenely with their spirits in God's care

The late sun's heat-haze shimmering softly lends the park a ghostly glow,
Whilst grazing deer appear to float as knee-high mist drifts gently through.
Lost in silent admiration at this most amazing show,
With heavy heart I now depart, whispering low my sad adieu.

Frank Smiley

A Walk In The Woods

Wandering for no particular reason
Hand in hand along a beckoning path
Following as if guided by a hidden emotion
Caring for naught whatever the season.

Did you capture the sound of the glistening tree
Standing there agape, wondrous of its glory,
Seeming familiar with waving arms in directions many
Giving the feeling of strength and courage and accepting whatever may be.

Distant rustlings that are really quite near
Remains hidden under the freely given camouflage
Their secrets known only to those in the towering canopy
Generations sustained season after season able to live without fear

A circle is cleared, with a green matted carpet dotted around are tiny
Blooms, their faces pointed, to the warming sun protected by their
Leafy friends, from the breeze that bends them low.
Waiting for the early morning, their lives renewed by the tiny dew droplet.

Time to leave along a different track.
In body and spirit the direction is new.
The dark clouds of your minds to mingle with those far above.
The tall visions all around, whispering softly *they will be back.*

C. Whan

Reflections

Occasional visits and holding of hands
Lunches, talking, walking on sands
Being together yet so far apart
Two people caring but where do they start
Putting things right that maybe are wrong
Things that are put up with for far too long
Fate - I believe - takes a hand if they wait
Silently waiting at far distant gate
Hush - if you listen you may hear her call
Telling them - now - jump over that wall
But trouble is things have gone on for too long
And now they are scared to put right the wrong
So gently and slowly they're feeling their way
And together they'll be - maybe - one day.

Sue Wyatt

Then And Now

There was a time when the world was at war,
families were in danger, they were very poor.
Down in the trenches there was a bang!
But the soldier's marched on a hymn they sang.
Their faces were grey from lack of light,
and still they marched on, they had to fight.
To the front they ran and fought,
some were killed, and some were caught.
When the soldier's returned and those who did not,
heroes they are, and wont be forgot.
And to this day it still remains,
a sacrifice for all, a silly game.

Gary Allen

Principle

There are still folk here about, who well remember
When principle ruled as king,
But in this present climate, here today,
Not many heed that valued thing,

But choose to live a bitter-sweet life,
Yet not ever count the cost,
Averted eyes no longer seek,
Those many souls, so recent lost,

So 'all hail', then to that Merry Band,
Who live by rules, then still,
A good, and wholly, fulfilling life,
With stout heart, and fighting will,

To the die hard folk, nor yet so young,
This spirit fosters strong,
And principle, still the vanguard,
To a fading breed ere long,

Faithful too in heart, and still strong of mind,
Head proudly held on high,
Sweet thoughts of happy yesteryears,
Not yet ready to bid principle, goodbye!

Dennis J. Taylor

The Boy-Next-Door

I got so mad at the boy next-door,
When I was playing shops.
With empty tins, on a plank of wood
Which he kept knocking off.

I punched him, and I stamped my foot,
I gave him such a fright,
When I said my first swear word,
I saw him no more that night.

But he called again next morning,
To carry my books to school,
Well, I've always liked the boy next-door.
But he shouldn't have been a fool.

So he said that he was sorry,
And gave me a quick kiss,
But I was only five years old,
And he was only six.

Yvonne Watson

Lucifer

The devil came up from the bowels of the earth,
And said there's not enough sin,
You can't go to hell 'less you're really bad,
'cause I won't let you in,
And you can't go to heaven, if you've sinned a little,
'cause God's a fussy man.
And if you can't go to heaven and you can't go to hell,
Well, I guess you're in a jam.
You'll be stuck in the middle and it's not very nice,
You'll end up a ghost or a poltergeist,
Throwing things around, you'll be awfully mad,
That you weren't all good, or you weren't all bad,
So get out there and do your worst,
Join us in hell, you won't be the first,
There's M.P.'s and Vicars and royalty's not rare,
There's lots who thought they'd be going elsewhere,
But remember when you're here, you're down here to stay,
There's no getting up and walking away,
You'll be treated cruel, but don't think that's not fair,
I'm only doing to you what you did to people up there.

Keith McGill

The Love In Our Hearts

Where there is Love, Life is so bright,
Where there is Love, the day will Shine,
Where there is Love, there is a song,
To help things that go wrong,
Where there is Love, there is a smile,
To keep peace of Love in our Hearts.
A tranquil place where turmoils cease.
Love changes darkness to light in our hearts,
So blest are those who walk with God,
With God's own Love, in all mankind,
Men will help us to walk in peace again.

Jean Forster

The Room

There's a room with a view
Filled with sinking sadness
She's a mess now
Tired of selling pictures to the rich
Who have the frames to surround them
She held tight to her dreams
The truth had told too many lies
Chalky taste of pills and stiffness in her throat
Floating in that room with a view
Longing for colours and bright lights
Tears and torment
Wishing she had the strength not to leave
What about the flowers
Be free butterfly a voice in her head
The flowers will lie down
Mothers in the ground
A silence haunts the room
With much love but no view.

L. Chapman

When Dawn Breaks

I go to bed and lie awake
Lie and wait for dawn to break
Until it does I'll think on
Then all my fears will be gone
I feel so empty
and so alone
Wishing I had someone
To call my own
Someone to say I love you
Someone to say I care
Someone to say I'll always be there
I hope the day will come for me
When these three things will happen for me
Until they do I'll lie and wait
for dawn to break

Gillian Williams

I'm The One For You

My heart has many functions
loving you is one
my hands have many fingers
Caressing you is fun.
My body is an instrument within
your hands I play
and I begin to love you more
with every passing day.

My feet are large and awkward
but if reason to be known
the larger the better as the quicker I get home.

My lips are round and luscious and are always pursued for you.
When you're lying in my arms, kissing is all my lips will do.

My eyes portray my feelings, emotions and my fears
The thought of ever losing you brings me close to tears.

My head has many hairs, of different colours range
the greys as I grow older just signify a change.

But as the years pass by and the older I become
I'll always remain there with you.
Because you're the chosen one.

Carmel Dermody-Lawrence

The Birth Of Christ

Christ's birth in a manger
on a cold December day,
The glory of this miracle
was never lost in any way.

Getting together to celebrate
the birth of this child divine,
Church bells ringing, children singing,
one day in the year that stays the same.

The sharing of presents from the Christmas
tree, laden with bells and toys, brings
Fun and laughter from everyone
as we all give thanks and sing.

All the preparations and excitement
shared with family and friends,
Brings forth such great happiness
that never really ends.

Christ's birth will never be forgotten
as long as we shall live,
Our children will long remember
the pleasure His birth still gives.

Mollie C. Elborough

I Still Love You, My First Love

With reasons restored in the depths of our minds,
    for the rainbow of wishes we made.
With a regular heartbeat of various kinds,
    in a whirlwind we're forced to create.

As dreamers stay dreaming for many a day,
    their fancies coloured and bright.
Our love may be treasured in many a way,
    as the darkness embraces the light.

Take wisdom in body, and body in mind,
    age is a symbol of grace.
But to flee from the truth makes it harder to find,
    and a sin that all hearts have to face.

Our reason for failing must never be known,
    but the pride of our winning is said.
Young ones must listen to words of the old,
    as the living make room for the dead.

Our hearts will unite in the love they denied,
    as it's true we were meant to be one.
Deny them the patience and tears that we cried,
    we won't ever regret what we've done.

Amanda Ayoola

Memories

There is a mistiness on the ocean
Ships go sailing by, birds skim over the water
Sea reflecting sun and sky, peace all around us
Beauty we do not always see
If we would take a little in our souls
And let the worries be
There will be a new tomorrow
So we can carry on
Life we know becomes too much
There are things that have to be done
So as each day comes, store a little beauty away
And in those bad moments, bring it out and let it stay
If life must be worthwhile
We will have softness as we go along
It may be in the things around us
Or a very plaintiff song
Like an incident remembered
'Twas pleasant we recall
Loving...living...laughing...giving
Sweet memories most of all

K. Mead

Jewels In The Sky

Opal like the milky way,
Diamonds like the stars,
The sky the blue of sapphire,
A wonder from afar,
Topaz like the golden sun,
Shades of ruby blending bright,
The darking sky of amethyst,
with lightning flashing white,
The moon like some gigantic pearl,
so far.
Yet man as touched, the dawn with streaks
of silver,
This earth we love so much.

G. Haydon

For Sir Winston Churchill

written on the day he was committed to the earth

Where I lie; people will come here and muse on greatness
Tell them I gathered mine - from the hearts of the Brave
My people! These little people - I have loved
Rallied and goaded into the fray of battle in war
Still I despair for them, for the Bread of peace -
So hard won - falls from the tables of vigilance
to break as it falls on the floors of misuse
Could I but speak in vigour of life again.
Not! from this inaction called death
I would implore these my people I have loved!
Gather even the crumbs
They are the whole of the bread
That men and nations must live by.

Elizabeth A. Kerr

God's Love

Jesus sends the flowers
Jesus sends the rain
Jesus sends his power
To the earth again
All the power of Jesus
The power of His love
His children on earth that know Him
Touched by His love
The sky and sea acknowledge Him
Walking the earth right now
The Holy Spirit guides us
Showing us who is the king of kings
The King of Glory now
The Prince of Peace, ever loving Father, very God of
    all God's children and every knee shall bow
Under the shadow of His wings forever bless His Holy name.

Jude Goodwin

The Way The World Revolves

Have you ever felt that feeling
That sad and regretful feeling
When you wish you could turn back time
So that you could make things just fine
Or when you are weak
And wish you had the strength you seek
Or when you've said something you want to take back
But then you're glad
That you did say what you said
And you did do what you did
Because if we could take things back
Then life wouldn't be the way it is.

Kirsty Kennedy

Still Waiting

Why do you behave in the way that you do?
What makes you an angel of the morning hours
   and then a monster, an animal, a vicious beast
   of the night?
Why do you no longer love and respect me?
Where have you gone to?
Why are you lost?
Can't you see the pain and anguish in my face?..
Why do you make me suffer and weep?
I love you but you care no longer!
What now means the world to you will soon disintegrate
Where will you be, who will you turn to when your
   'mates' disown you?

How long can I wait in anticipation for your return?
How long?... Before I too am past caring.

R. K. Samra

My Teacher's Magnet

My teacher locked me in a cell.
With a magnet that looked like a giant bell.
She said if you don't find anything metal
You'll live in there with just a kettle.
So I pointed the magnet towards a chair.
It was broken and battered but I didn't care.
It came straight for the magnet and stuck right there.
In came a cable along with a table.
That was rusty and dusty and stuck to the chair,
A box of staples jagged and labled these are all Mables glued
   to the table.
So there I was, my arms felt dead.
My feet were aching and so was my head.
All of a sudden I fell with a clatter and a shatter right down
   to the floor.
The magnet gave way like a balloon without air.
My teacher came in oh life isn't fair.
Well done, she said, you need a treat.
So she put a box of magnets right down by my feet.

Katie McCambridge

Joseph

It's now two years since the day you were born,
our lives did move on, but oh how we still mourn
for your such short life spent in my womb,
never to see daylight just the stars and the moon,
up in the sky you seem so far away,
we hope that you're happy, in God's garden you play.

Your baby brother helps us to be strong,
We know you are watching, guiding us along,
we love and we miss you
The pain is still great,
But we did our very best for you little mate.

One reason or another you weren't meant to be,
you stepped aside for a new pregnancy,
Our first little boy you will always be,
big brother for Christian
and another new life,
(one day, we will see!!!)

Alaina Deans

Outside Of Your Dream

Why are you standing outside of your dream?
Did you think the hard day would be kinder this time?
Bring the sun with life's motive together again
By the altar where hope stands with light's strongest beams?

You're standing, you're waiting, you're hoping; it seems
That fear lurks behind your brave, outward grin.
I won't let you out, and it won't keep you in.

Or did loneliness rush at your heart just to win
And by conquering dreams make this nightmare begin?

Dead leaves lie behind you, dead leaves lie ahead.
But this moment's unsoldered—just a fragile gold thread
Spilling out in vast sequins
Where the crowned trees divide.

Splendour past timely notice in the present denied.

Life that hit and run dealer in and out of your dream
Has swapped you his shadow out on which you still lean
Fearing truths without end, true to no end of fears

While your dreams keep on standing
In a race against tears.

Julie Blake

Posthumous Portraits Yesterday's Children

Who were these flowers? Conceived of love
Blossoming in life's garden of loveliness
Soft, gentle, of captivating pose
Likened to an English rose. Who were you.

As blossoms dance April air
These blooms softness unaware
Burst forth radiance to behold
Melting in a blush of gold.

Silken blooms, where did thy beauty grace
Some gracious ball on gown trimmed with lace
Twirling elegantly romantic hours
Turning heads of other flowers.

Petals of velvet, buds of flame
Naught is known whence you came
Naught is known the in-between
Or just what might have been

Flowers of beauty, captured evermore
Passing years have marked no final score
Time has not condemned thy handsome face
Not until your likeness falls from grace who where you?

E. A. Audsley

A Sailor's Dream

I dream, I see an anchor.
It calls to mind my toil,
Which causes me once again to leave
My home, my native soil.

I dream, I see a heart
So full of love for me
Reaching across tides of memories
Over the beautiful raging sea.

I dream, I see a cross
The symbol of my faith,
Reminding me of my family
On that safe home shore, they wait.

I dream, and yes, these things are real.
I can almost feel and touch
These things within my restless dream,
These things that mean so much

Yet there's a restless spirit in me
It never lets me be,
It calls to me forever
Like the beautiful raging sea.

James A. Kells

Lament Of Mother Earth

Mother Earth weeps, save me, she cries
from Man's insanity.
War, starvation, pollution, I did not create
this inhumanity.
I gave it life for man to flourish,
bore grain and fruit from which to nourish
themselves, and then without even thinking
of what they do,
They strip and degrade me and leave me bare.
My acid tears falling everywhere,
Adding to already polluted seas
and turning black the leaves of crops and trees.
My only hope lies with those few
Who care, and will, I'm sure
Come to my rescue.
Till then, patiently I wait,
To see the outcome of my fate.

Shirley Parker

Words

Words can make you happy or sad too
Take you high or even low
You can jumble them manipulate them
Sentence them together and watch
As they start to flow
Write a love letter tender
And sweet two hearts entwined
As they meet.
Shattered words can break your
Spirit destroy you with a chosen few.
Use them, abuse them, shuffle to and through
Play scrabble or even crosswords
To stimulate the mind
Use for beauty or to be unkind
Love them or hate them
They can not be ignored
Words, words, words

Margaret Hamilton

In Absentia

A sentiment of loneliness, all the while
I talk to her and I talk to him, conversations in my head.
There's a world in my mind, I travel to each night
And I'm pulled into this world when I'm losing sight.

Surrounded by Jacaranda, in my ivory tower
This valley where I used to run to, I sensed it then
A human lynx in circumspect
Reticence and secrecy, expressed in monotone.

Time changes circumstance
And I fall, sometimes, in a fathomless reverie
Knowing not what passes by me
Then I long like the weeping willow
To lapse to the depth of shallow.

Helon Begum

Freedom

It's said that blood is thicker than water
And Pride in one's country should not falter,
This I can observe, this I can understand
I wholly support this cause in any land.

But to take a life in the face of Religion
And say that it is right, for the cause of the mission,
A mission belonging only to the I.R.A.
A pack of animals who kill and run away.

They should be caught and made to pay
For the misery they cause in the most ghastly way,
I have no support for this cause, but I do care
The I.R.A. are scum who hide in their lair.

One day Ireland will have peace once more
No more fighting or killing on the Irish shore,
The British flag will fly with pride
Ahead of the people who will no longer have to hide.

Kevin Wildish

No Emotion

I don't know why I feel this way
Just emptiness and nothing to say
Each day I dig into my mind, searching my soul
To see what I have to find
Why can't I laugh, why can't I cry
Give me wings and let me fly
Just flesh and bone I feel so alone
There's something missing
Like a garden without a flower
Like a politician without power
I'm locked inside my body
Hundred different keys struggling to set me free
There's something I need to discover
Help me pull away the cover, I feel I don't exist
Like rain without water, like fire without a flame
Am I playing a hide and seek game?
Am I going to explode? Someone give me the code
Why can't I laugh, why can't I cry
Give me wings and let me fly
Help me discover, someone pull away the cover.

Jemila Khan

Untitled

The children of the world
Look up trouble man and learn to pray for the
lovely world to stay what right has man to kill
a little child that want to sleep and play to
live another day put your guns away God
tired and gone to rest he said o man you are a
pest you have made this world an awful mess
so look up trouble man and let the children
of the world eat sleep and play that wants to
live another day

D. W. Young

The Travelling Willberry

It's getting dark and getting cold, the wind and
the rain begins to blow.
There I walk with nowhere to go, the South of the City
is nobody's home, to me it is my only abode.
I passed one day down "Bakers Lane", to
see an old friend who'd gone insane.
He lived life in the lane, but life in the lane drive him insane.
I said, "My friend, how's things with you?" Too cold
to speak with a nod, and a wink, he came over and muttered,
"Will you help me sleep, forever and ever so I'll never blink?"
Too cold to talk I walked on by, Mother of God the life
he had was not as sore, well what
the Hell, that's the score you win and
lose in the game of life, my friend
he lost the life he lived, another night
another day of scrounging and begging is
the only way, I scrounge and beg
until my day, because there is no other way.
I'll see a light that might shine bright,
I guess I'll have to wait and see

Dale Kookcoo O'Donnell

Untitled

Life is hard from the moment you are conceived
You are in danger from life's infections and diseases
Then finally your time has come for you to be born
(They dig your grave with a spade, but you can't see this)
Most of your life is forlorn
Through your childhood you'll be scorned
And when you get to your teens you try to achieve
Then when it finally dawned (on you)
It's too late, old age has crept up on you
(You know it's true)
So when you finally die, only the person who truly cared
As he takes you in his arms, at the gates of Heaven with the brethren
For he gave us his life, so try and make your life
what he gave to you, helping others as he has helped you
You know this to be true

Mark Bernard Thorpe

Mighty Oak

Oh tall, majestic, pillared trunk with arms
    outstretched so high
With crisp and golden withering leaves against
    Autumnal sky
Did you once stand on open land with grazing
    cows nearby?

For now your mighty structure stands midst
    busy tarmacked roads,
Near huge metallic monster trucks
    transporting covered loads.
Near red-bricked homes and garden gnomes
    and ponds with ornamental toads.

Oh solid, tower, whose branches rise
In loy'lty still 'neath Autumn skies.
Your beauty stands in spoilt lands
With grace that never dies!

    Chris Bircher

The Old Clock Tower

Old clock tower majestic and grand
Your four faces survey the surrounding land

In recent years there has been
An addition to the nearby scene
For locals and others to spend their leisure
I know they will have much pleasure
On the village bowling green

Long ago beneath your turreted tower
I used to spend many a happy hour

Just listening to your hourly chimes
In days gone by and happier times.

    A. C. Neill

Dawn

When the sun begins to break
And its rays begin to flow
And the earth begins to colour
The sky bathes in a golden glow

When the sun comes up
The cockerels start to crow
All the farmers start to wake
And the cows start to low

When the sun's fingers appear on the horizon
The earth begins to light
The fields have just a touch of yellow
Oh! What a breathtaking sight

When the sun infiltrates the night
And rapidly turn to day
The countless hours of the night
Just seem to fade away

When the sun comes up
Birds wake up just like the wren
But soon the night time arrives
For dawn to come again

    Claire O'Shaughnessy

Untitled

Why are we here? What's it all for?
We're born into what? Yet we still make more.
All the little children filling little holes
Of the little lives of us lonely little souls.
But all sorts of things keep us going
We just carry on without knowing.
But we still carry on thinking we know
The reasons why we go with the flow.
We've got to be here but we don't know why
Always striving for something, and God how we try.
Just when you think you've got it and you're job is nearly done
You turn around and it's all gone. Your struggles just begun.

    Lorraine Daniels

Leave Me Alone

Just get out of my head,
I don't want you in there anymore.
Just get out of my head,
You're hurting me.
Leave me alone, I hate you;
You're not there when I need you.
Stop haunting me—making me dream,
Get out of my head—please.
And you don't even phone—so don't even bother,
Have to cry on my own.
Have to force myself to despise you,
So I'm asking you to leave;
Pick you from my brain, savour you, tear you apart.
Like you did me,
    and throw you away!

    Karen Ashton

Salar

A thousand miles to travel to the pool where she was spawned,
A hundred rocky falls she'll leap and a hundred more beyond,
Tired as a weary pilgrim; rheotropism guides her course
Though high the frothing cataracts fearsome the water's force.

Her journey almost mastered; the last leap; only one,
She's tossed and thrown back in the foam her courage almost gone,
The turbulent pool is deep and cool
Those bruises it does soothe
Then one brave effort gains her goal the nursery of her youth,

Her eggs she sheds
Her strength is spent,
Her species safe she dies content,
So high a price she's had to pay but nature can be cruel that way,
Inert she floats where life began,

And Life Begins All O'er Again.

    Ellen Black

To Those Who Will Never Understand

I'm going to find my daughter, wherever she may be,
No one has the right nor power to ever try and stop me.
For my daughter is my life, no one can understand,
There's nothing that can substitute, nothing on this land.
She was my reason for everything, and I wanted nothing more,
She gave me hope and happiness, like no one could before.
Without her I'm so empty, I have no purpose left at all,
She is all that matters, I have to be there when she calls.
In life she was so perfect, in death I hope at peace,
She left me in a prison, with just one chance of release.
So leave me be to die this way, it isn't suicide,
Just the only option my daughter left me when she died.
I love her so unselfishly, I could never love that way again,
I lived a life so happy, now that life reduced to pain.
I see her still so clearly and I hear her laugh and cry,
I need so much to hold her, I can only do that if I die.
I created such perfection, my only dream came true,
I lived my life, it's over now, just one thing left to do
So let me die with dignity, I have one last request,
To let Louise and I, in God's arms both be blest.

    Jayne Rawlings

Friend

When times are bad and things go wrong,
And it feels the whole world is closing in,
And there is no point in carrying on,
It's a time like this you need a friend.
Someone you can talk to
And can help you see it through the end.
Someone you can trust and confide in
And tell your innermost secrets to.
Without a friend you're nothing.
Friendship is the most precious thing in life.
To have nobody and be all alone
Is the saddest story ever told.
Don't hide away from the world,
Go out and find a friend you can call your own.

    Deirdre Campbell

Tears For Love

Why was it that you left me, how could you let me go,
After all you were my mother, you should have loved me more.
They came and talked and took me, you cried and hugged and felt despair,
Please sign we have to go now, you could run and hide, please find somewhere.
So small and young and helpless, you never saw me smile,
You said you couldn't keep me, at least not for a while.
You never came to see me, to take me home again,
I hated life without you, struggling with my pain.
Living here and living there, always on the move,
Meetings and decisions, what exactly did they prove.
I often sat and dreamt of you, and wondered do you care,
If only I could find you, there's so much I need to share.
Disruptive and beyond control, they didn't comprehend,
With you was what I needed, if I was ever going to mend.
Lonely, sad and homeless, with plenty time to think,
Please return to find me, before I finally sink.

Vivienne McDonagh

To Lisa

A fairylike creature, so pale, and so slim
Her hair frames her face, like a mantilla of gold;
Like a butterfly, she alights so softly, now here, then gone,
She should have been a ballet dancer; Swan Lake, Sleeping Beauty, tales of old,
Lily of the valley, little snowdrop, blooming in the summer sun
Too soon, to soon, our youth takes flight, one should grasp, and hold it with both hands,
I could cry, to think, how carelessly, we treat our precious treasure.
Our innocence and childlike trust, gone, gone forever,
Gone the magic days of youth, belief in Santa - disillusion
Rainbow bridge - the land of dreams
Then the awakening - stark reality, fitting into the scheme of things
Facing up to all Life's hand-outs, but holding on to youth and dreams
Never letting problems floor you, fight back bravely and you'll win thro'
Never admit the passing of the years, no matter how fast they roll,
Keep Peter Pan in your body, and also in your soul.

Marjorie Pearce

The Child Has Learnt To Speak

Imagination running wild, as if the mind of witless child,
Who lives by love alone, but free, as in its own adversity,
Dispatched to lands of fantasy, to land on feelings, fancy free,
Travelling to what parts they reach, planting ideas to beseech,
So they will grow in nature's quest, maturing only where they rest,
Nurtured, cultured, filled with zest, built-in time which can infest,
But when invested, knows no bounds, frightening ideas which astound,
Leaving marks, as if a seed, planted only to be freed,
However, likely to succeed, when sought with selfishness and greed,
As when a child has grown in stature, mature in knowledge, slow but sure,
Whose mind which once would dwindle carelessly and now runs wild, down time, to see
what lies at ends of rainbows spectrum, better still, where rainbows come from,
Out of blue, where raindrops shine, immortal spines hung in a mind,
To grow, as if with sunshine warmed, nurtured ideas gently swarm,
To make imagination peak, formed, the child has learnt to speak.

Mark Abrahams

Quiet Thoughts

One day as I sat thinking under the shade of the old apple tree, something stirred deep within me, and my thoughts returned to thee.
I remembered the day we strolled hand in hand, and shared such a spiritual need. We were caught in a love that was never planned, we knew that it just could not be. Deeper and deeper our souls intertwined, the power of our love was so divine.
The time passed by so quickly, we knew we had to part. There will always be a place for you deep down in the corner of my heart.
I close my eyes and feel you near, and know I will always love you my dear. My love is returned, of that I am sure, never demanding, forever pure.
My favourite place must surely be under the shade of the old apple tree, where quietly my thoughts return to thee.

Janet K. Cox

Food For Thought!

I'm having guests to lunch today... what to give them I can't say.
No way am I 'Cordon Bleu'... well I only wish I were!
Something simple would be good... paté starter, then I would
Roast a joint of beef... or should I take notice of what's said
"Don't eat beef, you could be dead! Better make a different choice".
When at the door I hear a voice... "Hello dear we're off to Spain,
Could you mind our house again? Oh and could you use this meat?
Cook it for your luncheon meat I believe you're doing today".
"Oh I don't know what to say..." "Not a word! Just cook this lamb,
Oh and here's a bit of ham. Goodbye dear and thanks again
For looking after number ten!" Problem solved... well that's good
news, Offers like that I can't refuse. Starter, main course sorted
out. Oh my goodness what about afters, desserts, what you will?
Trifle? No that makes me ill. Well just look here, am I in clover?
In the fridge I've got Pavlova! Great! But I really must get on,
I told them to be here for one... and it's ten-thirty now... wow!

Anne Pearson

Another Black Wednesday

Newspapers these days are full of stories that happen time and time again
Today though is so different, for I can't help but feel the pain
For March 13th is just too much, the tears rise inside my eyes
I need to get my thoughts out now, before I break down and cry

For in a little Scottish school, in the quiet village of Dunblane
Sixteen helpless children are by a gunman shot and slain
He killed with no sign of mercy, struck without a warning
Gunshots burst right through the calm of another blood-soaked morning

I now search myself within, but can't find the reasons why
These children were taken before it was their rightful time to die
Now as their parents face their loss, we lay yet another wreath
I ask who will take responsibility for their suffering and their grief

For society now is so screwed up, in two month's time who'll really care
About the poor souls lost today, for it happened elsewhere
And no-one wants to count the cost, even God for this won't take the blame
Though I feel their pain, I share the shame, for I know I'll soon forget their names.

Steven Kirwan

If Life Were A Garden...

If life were a garden
Weed out the badness, evil and hatred
While let the goodness flourish and thrive yet trim and tailor as you wish
And put us in our place
For an unkempt rose bush is as ugly as a creeping vine
Let me live in harmony with nature
And blossom from a mere seed to growing roots to sprouting buds
And become what I may
For I cannot choose where I am sown
Nor who I am
But how I live?
This is left for myself to decide
And when I die may I return from where I came without bitterness in my soul
For I will be the foundation for others to build upon
And return all that was given to me
This is the definition of a good life.

Daniel Baxter

The Hurt; The Anger Which Turns To Love

I'm hurting, I'm angry he told me he loved me, but boy!! did you hurt me

I walked with anger for as long as I could remember, the anger
which ate my inside away

The hurt was continuous, the hurt was pain, there was no reason for what
I had experienced, but I knew one day God would remove all this pain.

The tears I cried, the sleepless nights I had, the loneliness I felt
again, I knew all this would melt; one day I received this letter which
made me feel better, better to understand the behaviour of who wrote
this letter.

At first I read it and it meant nothing to me, I read it again and
saw the understanding of how I should be. The anger, the hurt
started to lift, lifted in such a big way; the anger, the hurt has
now turned to love and loving you is all I can say.

Loraine Sherwood-Ellis

Pollution

God made the earth in six days, on the seventh day he rested,
Everything was perfect, nothing could be bested.
The earth was lush and green, the oceans the deepest blue.
He even made the animals and birds of every hue,
But then he made man who scorned the earth both sea and land,
Forever greedy for more, more, more he stole the bounties from nature's store.
Where once rivers and lakes were clear and sparkling,
Man's pollution made them dank and darkening.
Making them so unhealthy, just so someone can be wealthy,
Even when we know it's unwise, we still continue to pollute our skies.
We cut down trees we know are needed - conservationists' cries go unheeded
The media, TV and Radio, daily bombard us with what we lose.
The acid rain our crops our cities,
No one listens, no one pities,
Now the time has come to awaken, so no more liberties can be taken-
And maybe the next generation can put a stop to the exploitation.

Donna O'Loughlin

Eve Of Culloden (15th April 1746)

Ride off the battlefield fair drummer boy.
Ere long in twain shalt we be!
Long dusk and twilight besets this ground
Sodden in foul deeds,
Where nonchalant emotions arise
To curse at the accursed!
Tarry not like the jaded bracken
Lying trodden in the bloodied earth.
For the magnitude of this manslaughter
Is nought to the battle that will ensue.
So offer thyself to thy maker,
For thou art pristine and true.
Then recover the miles that we have trod,
Over which my heart doth fly,
To the warm stone bosom of a kitchen fire
Where the hounds in sorrow lie.
Go now! Lest your drum should cease to roll
But remember at Culloden, how great shall be the toll!

David Green

My Treasures

My treasures are not diamonds and pearls
But memories of bliss near a sea, sun-kissed
And forests deep with caskets of jewels
In stars above
Glistening cobwebs at early dawn
The golden glow of snow on sunset mountain top
And the pink proud Pyranees from flight deck
Homeward bound

The magical sound of tumbling waterfall
From cliffs gleaming silvery diamonds
The coolness and peace of caves
With icy chandeliers of tears
The welcoming radiant smile from a friend
The pearl of greatest price, wisdom
And knowledge of Life!

Audrey Adsett

The Surviving Stag

The grey mist settles high above the heath clad moor
The hill is now a safe haven
For welcome rest has come at last.
His gasping breath could easily enfold to darker depths,
When panic would return.
The eyes are glazed while for a moment, one senses tears could fall
The animal is all but lost, no running left.
It does not know how many fell behind.
The guns were plenty that day.
They did their job. Alas the hunted had escaped.
It was but a miracle as from his majestic stance
He could no longer keep.
Now lowering and toning into the brushwood
It would survive for yet another day.

Donald W. Sutherland

Christmas

Why can't everyday be like Christmas?
That's what the people say,
But to make everyday like Christmas.
First, we must all learn to pray.
We need everyday to love and care,
To give and take,
And learn how to share.

The life that God gave us is meant to be,
Happy and caring,
Loving and free,
Don't waste time thinking of things you have not,
Please, just be grateful for what you have got.
Life is only lent to us.
Don't take it as your right.
Be contented with life's beauty
That is within your sight.

Jan Bourne

Succession

The Darkness descends, comes the Canopy of night,
Following the Day that gave us Light,
But the Gloom is lifted by Luminosity,
What can the truth behind your dazzling secrets be?

Silver Moon aloft, impressive as a Bride in the Sky,
As smaller twinkling stars like Bridesmaids stand by,
So pleasing a pattern shown on Heavens Canvas tonight,
But what is latent, I wonder, beyond our Human sight.

Shining Trinkets of Night, your time is but Brief,
You'll steal from the daylight, as would a thief,
The Dawn will hide where you have been,
As Heaven prepares for her next scene.

What a measure of mystery is Time and Space,
Akin to the riddle of the Human race,
Seeming Insignificant...in a World so Vast,
Yet relevant all into this Universe Cast.

There is so much of Mystic within the Night,
More magic still, as the sky turns bright,
Such secrets beyond our faculties Range,
Except that all things... Are subject to change.

Eileen Cristchlow

The Man With The White Walking Stick

One lovely summer's day standing at the entrance of the park,
The sun shone, the birds sang.
I looked up at the lovely blue sky and thought,
"What a lovely day". Then walking towards me came a man
Holding a white walking stick.

His features were lean and drawn but the lady holding his arm
Guiding him past me was full of charm.
I heard her speak in a kindly voice
But did not hear his reply to her, the tears in my eyes
For he was holding a white walking stick.
I looked up at the lovely blue sky,
Saw the birds flying high, people passing by.
I was so thankful I could plant my feet firmly on the ground,
Go where I pleased and had no need of a "white walking stick".

Now when I see the beautiful colours of the flowers, the green grass,
Magnificent tall trees, the waves of the sea,
Moon and stars at night, I am so thankful
I have been bestowed with two precious things,
More precious than gold: two eyes that can see,
And have no need of a "white walking stick".

E. Jares

Pollarded

He spreads out in the water, pouring her from the taps
to cleanse himself of her chameleon indecision.
She tugs his ropes carelessly through cold, thick cloud
His taut skin whipped by stings of frozen wind.

He threads his hypodermic needles with sutures of crimson cord.
Then chews a hand of six inch steel nails,
spitting out the rubble remnants of his teeth and tongue.
Now his life is sieved and almost boiled away.

The pain in him is the hurt of her.
Her frustrations pumice her tender skin.
His nonchalance blisters her flesh.
Unconsciously deadly, euphemistic smiles...

Artificial happiness is developed
like memories on photographic paper.
Through the chemical water she slowly rises.
He washes off the acid from her smile.

She mangles him between her teeth,
treading undaintily on his softly-carpeted heart.
He will wear his red mittens with her love.
She will keep him in a golden cage and feed him cockroaches.

Jeff Gardiner

A Down and Out

He stood, he looked, he wondered,
Should he stop or go on by?
The fiver in the gutter,
Had suddenly caught his eye.
It would buy him food for supper
Or a drink when he felt low
A million thoughts raced through his head.
Surely no-one would ever know.
He bent and clutched it in his hand
And slowly turned around
Then he saw a frail, old woman
Eyes searching on the ground.
He hadn't always been down and out
Living rough out in the cold.
Beneath that scruffy clothing
There beat a heart of gold
Gently he touched her on the arm
He saw the fear in her eye
He handed back the fiver
And was glad he hadn't passed by

Marcia Wigham

In Loving Memory

I stood among the crowd that day.
Not knowing where to look.
I thought of you my darling
An ever open book.
I said 'My God it isn't fair'
What life is left we cannot share.
So now I look towards our son
And think, what would his dad have done.
He would have clasped him by the hand
And gone to seek some promised land
'Promised Land', what does it mean?
Showing my son that the pasture is green?
How do I tell him that life isn't bad
When all he longs for is his dad.
Maybe one day he will think aloud
I must do that, my dad would be proud.
And then there's our daughter, your pride and joy
You loved her as much as you loved our boy
I'll set things in order with a smile on my face
And then one day your steps I will trace.

Hazel Diane Black

Peter John

My one true friend my one real pal
The one who knew me oh! So well.
My little faults he overlooked
As long as his dinner was properly cooked.

He loved his children One, Two, Three
He loved his wife! Oh yes that's me.
He loved his friends. He was a good mate
Always tried to keep a date,
Ever early, never late.

His Grandchildren were his special joy
Two girls so pretty and a precious boy.
His love for them was tender and true,
If only he could be here for you
To watch you grow on Earth below.

If there's a Heaven I'm sure he'll know
And keep an eye on all of you.
But most of all I hope he can see
How very much he really meant to me.

I have an ache inside my heart
Which only love can be a part.

Gillian Husbands

Innocence In Torment

Look into his face, the face of a survivor.
An innocent face, yet thwart with torment.
Look into his empty staring eyes, deep, dark and wanting.
See him standing barefoot on sandy, dry, sharp gravel.
Grappling with his thoughts, examining his dilemma.
What choice, a poor offering.
This lonely existence or a slow death.

Youthfulness has fled, his lot aged him beyond his years.
He stands and pleads, bereft of words.
Silently longing for love, the love only a mother can give.
Yet he is deprived of this need, through no fault of his own.
The pain of suffering, pangs of hunger continue to devour his
    young body.
Abandoned by man he endures this agony bravely, silently.
He knows no other life, only endurance.
Life has left him with nought but an instinct to survive.

For him is there a future, a destiny, a life?
Or, is death just waiting to rescue him, cruelly waiting
To release him from his torment, his indignity?
Is there hope for this poor broken child?
If only Lord.

Carolyn Foggin

The Doors

I see a door ahead of me, a door of wood laced with spiders' silks,
A door splintering, decaying, dying.
Behind the door is the past, what has been.
I see blood running as water, men crying, bodies burning,
    wives mourning;
There is a stench of rotting flesh, which the rats feast upon,
And the silence of death is broken only by echoes of gunshot.

I see a door ahead of me, a door of glass that is no shield to me,
A dull, clouded door that would shatter easily.
Behind the door is the present, what is now.
I see the sands of time running out for the starving forests,
choking, the endangered dying;
I smell nothing, yet I know that radioactive toxins are hiding
    around every corner, waiting to destroy me.
I hear an orphan weeping for the world around him.

I see a door ahead of me, a metal door, strong and protecting,
A shining, trustworthy door that glints in the sunlight.
Behind the door is the future, what is yet to be,
You may ask what is behind the third door;
My friend, the door is a tempestuous illusion, there is no door

Vicky Sampson

Untitled

Along came a man into my life
Who made me a promise that I'd be his wife
Three children we had and a lifetime to share
Gentle and kind it seemed like he'd care

It stayed like that for quite a long while
Then all of a sudden he adopted a new style
He hit me and hurt me and called me bad names
He had an affair and played silly mind games

He lied through his teeth as he hit with his fist
Then he'd say sorry and gave me a kiss
He made me feel dirty, degraded and abused
And while in his bed I was there to be used

I'm leaving I told him and I'm leaving today
He nodded and laughed in his usual way
You're jealous and stupid it's all in your head
Why should I hurt you was all that he said

I was battered and bruised in more ways than one
And you'd never regret anything that you'd done
You hurt me so badly, the scars went so deep
But now when I see you not a tear would I weep.

Lydia Hellear

Feelings

I don't know why I'm still with you
It's just a habit I guess,
I don't know if I feel the same
As when we first met.

But then, nothing else mattered
It was just you and me,
the feelings we had for each other
seemed as if they were to last forever.

It's too hard to tell you
that I'm feeling this way.
But the feelings I had for you at the beginning
Can't have gone away.

I have to look inside my soul
Forgive me, it might take some time,
But you have to make sure that what you find
Makes sense to you in heart and mind.

Rebecca Jane Morris

For May

Today I did cry, and I shed a tear,
as my eyes they caught sight of a little old dear.

She was lying in bed, so pale and so thin,
covering her body just a layer of skin.

My heart it did doubt this God up above,
'cos this wasn't mercy and this wasn't love.

In her eyes I could see she wanted to die.
I sat by her bed and asked myself Why?

All I could do was give her a drink,
hold her hand tight and try not to think.

As I go to my bed and turn off the light,
to her I do wish, a peaceful Goodnight!

Elaine Fowler

"Pip"

I am me, sitting here alone
At this table on my own.
My dog is close beside me
Her chin is on my knee
Her eyes are so full of love
She truly does love me.
I wonder what her life is
She can't go out alone
She cannot ever want to go 'shopping'
Only she loves to roam
Providing that I'm beside or near
So she does not get lost
And the pleasure in her tail is shown
That "this human is the one that rescued me when I was all alone".
And when I think of her foxy tail wagging proud and high
I know I'm never on my own
It's always Pip and I.

Linda Watson

Venus' Stranger Angel Cries

Come swim with the lost swans of heavenly grace.
May they fly along the sunset
into your open arms
past golden suggestions now left behind.
A burning wing no longer has the power
to douse the glow of the present
for it only strives to catch a past moment
as a lingering lament from a lonely soul.
Come fly with the lone angels of earthly glory.
How they yearn to hold the power
and grow beyond their siren.
The foreseen have a past welcomed by all generations,
but only the timeless can see a future
torn from an everlasting eye.

Doug Tolley

Winter's Beauty

Aconites and Snowdrops blooming
together in moss and grass,
Carpeting the woods
Between tall trees stretching heavenwards,
Could heaven be more beautiful?

The bright yellow of the aconites turned gold
In the winter's sun,
Sharpened by the pure white of snowdrops
Their little heads waving in the breeze

The carpet spills over into the Churchyard
Elsie gathers twigs,
She treads carefully between the tombstones
So as not to hurt the flowers.

She loves sticking for her fire, especially
When freeing flowers
So they bloom to the greater glory of God,
And help others to see the miracle of creation.

People come from far and near to this quiet spot.
Hidden on the wolds,
It has other charms as the seasons change
Not only Elsie thanks God for its beauty.

Elsie Pescod

Summer Symphony

As I wandered by the water's edge,
I heard the phalarope in the sedge,
Above my head the whimbrel's trill,
The gulls cawing from the hill,
And from the shore the sound of sea
Came wafting on the breeze to me.

I saw the oyster catchers fly,
Their screams and calls piercing the sky.
A tiny wren sang out his heart,
Doing his bit, playing his part,
While starlings sat there in a row
Discussing the next place to go.

A tractor ploughing far away
Sounded rather hoarse that day,
And from the farm the dogs and cattle
Must surely have been doing battle,
But no! They just wanted to be
Part of the summer symphony.

Sheila Arnskov

My Pen

When I take up my pen in the morning
It's such a wonderful start to the day
I know it will help me understand
Myself in a strange kind of way

For it helps put my life in order
Sweeping my doubts away
So that I can look up and go on
Making sense of my life for today

Reading words written by great authors
Laughing and having some fun
Listening to songs recorded by man
Thinking a new day's just begun

Birds singing songs in the morning
Knowing another day has begun
Watching the sunrise come over the hill
See the flowers, walk for miles in the sun

For happiness is held in a moment
Like the bird it was born to fly
Leaving us a memory to cling too
Some times happiness makes us cry

Elizabeth Hunter

Only The Wind

As they were sleeping the riot was stirring.
A voice, less distant, daring and bellowing:
"Charge, all my kind, all you that have fire
To plunder and beat, to scatter and raze.
What fools made secure
Tonight we make waste."

Closer it came, that unstoppable army
Gathering force, nearer and nearer.
Torturing trees; breaking birds.
Demented horses trapped by fences
Called back to dogs
That whimpered in doorways.

The shaken sleepers sat up, silent.
Every nerve within them jagged.
Heard the rebels shake the windows.
Covers closer, switches clicking;
Yesterday's books
And the light flickering.

Nancy E. Hughes

One Day

One day we will walk hand in hand.
One day we will stroll across the beach.
one day we will look into each other's eyes.
one day we will sigh at the same time and smile.
one day we will hold each other tight,
neither of us dare to let go.
One day, yes, maybe one day.

C. Russell

Anger
(A Dialogue Between Anger, Mask And Flower)

'Who minds if I see your face or not?'
Said anger in peevish tones most hot.
'Hidden there behind your mask.
I shall really take to task.'

'Who minds if I smile or frown?'
Said two blank eyes looking down.
'Broken bottles, paper litter,
All too often I am bitter.'

'Who minds if I flower or not?'
Said one small poppy in a pot.
'So much pesticide and dirt.
My soul strives for far less hurt.'

'Who minds if we come or go?'
Said two together in furious woe.
'Confound you both!' Anger calls.
'I care! I care! I care about you all.'

Elizabeth Mullarkey

The Mariner's Mate

In the dockyard, late at night,
When cranes are immobile and signals bright,
I wander alone in a crumbling shed,
With starlight twinkling, above my head.
The roofs have been gone now, for many a year,
But no one seems to shed a tear.
Unless of course it's the ancient tar,
Whose only joy now is his local bar,

He's passed his time for going to sea,
And the only real pal he's got is me,
He's always reminiscing, the time that's passed.
When he stood before that great oaken mast.
And went to places far and near,
Composing his stories to tell over beer.

There's no one left now to tell his yarns to,
Unless he turns to his pet cockatoo,
Or maybe me, but there's no fun in that,
I only listen, 'cause I'm his cat!!

Ted Garnham

The Lonely Hours

The ghost in my soul, with you in my prison,
I pray as I close my eyes, I need him, in life,
Not in my mind's vision.

Please give me strength, and give me hope,
yesterday's time is my only antidote.
Let time go quickly, like the speed of light,
I say this to you, each and every night.

Not for today but for tomorrow, every picture my mind contains,
No time apart, will make a difference,
My feelings remain the same.

You gave us words, God, to do as we pleased,
I write to make me feel better,
It pleases me at the end of the day,
To sit down and write him a letter.

So if you can hear my prayer tonight,
For a moment, let me drown in his soul,
I'd give my last hours, on this earth,
Just to have him, at this moment to hold.

Deana Wright

A Time To Say Thank You

Now is the time to say thank you for those days long ago
When you felt for me, helped and looked for the way to go
To say thank you for warding off the fear of failure and
    speeding me on my way.
To say thank you when nobody cared
Save you to show me the way.

Passing clouds of time have brought illness.
But all in the goodness of time acceptance of what is, and the
    will to live is all.
Love of a different kind you show.
That you and I will ever know
Not seen but always there
Brother and Sister to always care.

Ronald Paradine

Stencil

The colours of silver grey and pearl attach to the edges of my vision
as I awaken to another day where once there was life
and now the pain sears my spine and creeps into my brain
as I remember you are not here
where can you be now that you have left this world
are you dissipated, are you feeling were you once real
did we really love and touch and believe
what happened to the morrow
the one in which we entrusted our lives
till it took you away after promising me that you would be here
where is the reasoning for which I search in the early hours
of darkness when you are again so real
that I could almost feel and attune my sensors
to the karmic stencillings echoing in the shadows
show me that life is not so fragile so that once again
I can believe that the years had a meaning
and a strength beyond the power of this earth.

Karen Thomson

Drifting Emotions

Sitting here wondering, am I letting life pass me by?
There's scenery, greenery, a great big open sky
A quick glance is all I give not realizing its worth
For if not for them, my life would be—
A glum place here on earth.

The week begins but still I hope, the weekend will come fast
But in years to come, I guess I'd wish to go back to the past
It's time to stop and look around and cherish where we live
The world around us and each day, the pleasures that it gives.

Let worries pass, and happiness rise—take each minute slow
Lots of memories we then keep when it's time for us to go
O' heavenly father hear my plea I'm sorry for my haste
I've only just learned to love and laugh, and never live to waste!

Katherine Cheer

I Wish

I wish I was a bird who could fly so free
I wish I was a bird 'cause I wouldn't be me.
I wish I was a wave upon the open sea
I wish I was a wave 'cause I couldn't see me.
I wish I was a star in the dark night sky
I wish I was a star, so far I would fly.
I wish I was a candle burning on through the night
I wish I was a candle with an endless light.
I wish that I was far away, as far as I could go
I wish that I was far away, with nobody I know
I wish that I could see into some people's minds
I wish that I could see through what you hide behind
I wish that I could hear the voice inside your head
I wish that I could hear, I can't because I'm dead.
I wish I was a bird who could fly so free
I wish I was a bird 'cause I wouldn't be me.

Beverley Hughes

Happiness

H is for happiness, a gift for us all.
A is allowing the thought to free fall - as
P is the person you truly could be - and
P stands for peace, but please also see - that
I is the infinite wisdom you hold - as
N are the negatives, now please be bold - because
E the experiences you choose to release - so
S is the success you deservedly reap - another
S takes you towards the solution - that
Happiness is all part of your evolution.

Valery L. Coburn

A Place With Nature

Come with me to the place with nature,
I'll take you there.
Shelter from the blustering wind,
Just to breathe in fresh air.
The heavy gusts blur my vision,
But I still walk on alone without you.
Share with me the place of nature,
And watch all the season's change.
New buds on naked branches,
Awaiting the call of spring, in their dormant months,
The season's swirling and turning,
The darkness of winter months into the light of spring.
Come with me to the place with nature.
I'll take you there.
See the serenity so calm,
Where the Blackbird and Robin are my only friends,
They come up to me so close singing their song.
Solitude of separateness,
Away from all the crowds of people's clutter, and chaos of traffic.
Escape into tranquillity with nature's freedom.

Lou Crouch

What A World

The planet earth is a beautiful place,
I am a human I'm ashamed to say,
My people are called the human race,
And we will destroy it all one day.

We pollute land, sea and air,
As the ice caps melt we have our warning,
Most of us just don't care,
We can call it global warming.

The destruction goes on year after year,
Forests disappear and animals die,
Until it becomes irreversible we fear,
And just a few of us even ask why.

I'll leave it to the others, it'll be o.k,
I can't go out now to get a suntan,
But I look forward to another sunny day,
Why worry, after all I'm only "Human"?.

Brian W. Fitzpatrick

Baby Blues

She never stops crying, long monotonous screams.
The essence of nightmares, not the nectar of dreams.
With no choice I listen, not knowing what to do.
Put two fingers in my ears, but the noise still gets through.
Fed, winded and changed her, gently rocked her to sleep.
Lay her down in her cradle, from the room tried to creep.
Before I'd walked through the door, she'd started to cry.
I carried on walking, beyond questioning why.
She has to stop crying, I can't cope anymore.
Guilty thoughts fill my mind, my emotions are raw.

I've been to the doctor, she's perfectly normal.
But whatever that means my life's in a turmoil.
It resembles a ride on a Merry Go Round.
Where I cannot get off, put my feet on the ground.
How I longed for a child our happiness complete.
A perfect family, with a baby so sweet.
Now I hide in my bed as her cries drill through my brain.
Where's the bonding of love, my heart only feels pain.
Somebody please help me, my depression is real.
I should want my baby, but that's not how I feel.

Stella Beasley

Meddling With Time Travel

Like a rose lost in time,
Borne into the wrong one in fact; thus
creating a mad flurry of confusion beyond wildest belief.
Her tormented soul cannot interpret the scenes, events and
happenings that take place,
For she hath been educated in the old ways of life.
Her remaining hope and faith so lies still in God himself.

Sara Sherif

Schizophrenia

Feelings of torture in my mind.
Won't somebody help me?
Like looking in a mirror I am seeing an evil part of me, but
It was the nurse who I had really seen.
Why did they leave me in darkness?
This is terrifying.
I need help.
What is wrong with me?
I don't know what I am doing - where are my shoes?
This is hell on earth - help!
People are going to harm me. I must attack them
Before they get the chance to attack me.
A kick for the doc and a black eye for the nurse,
I later found out.
What is the day? What is the time?
Is this torture never going to end?
I shouted, "Rape", when the doctor gave me an injection.
I thought it was rape.
Now I understand those terrible feelings were
Caused by Schizophrenia.

Christine Doherty

Flowers

Daffodils peeping at me
Tulips are blowing free
Every tiny little flower
Is awakening this hour

Yellow and red, purple and white
Are turning their heads towards the light
Some will be gathered ready to sell
And spread around their lovely smell.

Then as daylight passes
Gathered in their floral art classes
Ladies with all their loving care
Use every flower there is to spare

With all the skill within their power
They bring out the best in every flower
But no matter how hard anyone tries
The special magic in the garden lies.

Lorna Wong

My Friend

My friend is a faithful friend
She is kind, caring and loving
I am glad that she is my friend

My friend is a faithful friend
She is always happy, nice and good to me

  I wonder why

My friend is a faithful friend
She likes being cheerful, helpful, and thoughtful
I like a friend who is like that to me

Telika Brown

Menopausal Me

I'm on the change, it's clear to me
Always so tired and ill you see
Aches and pains I have so many,
And always wanting to spend a penny,
Scared to go out, bored staying in
It's a wonder to me I stay off the gin.
Tablets I take for this and that,
And when I get angry I kick the cat.
I pray each night this phase to end
So to the shop me they can send,
To get the bargains and have a chat
'Bout nothing, particular, just this and that.
I look in the mirror, but hate the reflection
It's not my face, but the face of dejection.
I had such a full and jolly face,
Now such a grimace has taken its place
Oh, it would be heaven if I could just
On my own take a walk or ride on the bus.
They say I'll do all these things in time
But I can't believe them in my frame of mind.

Thelma Bywater

Remembrance Of My Mother

A mother's love is something to treasure
From the moment of birth,
This contact brings a warming glow
Felt by infant and mother.
As you grow older protected by her
Knowing the heartache she must endure.
Keeping her feelings all locked inside
Perhaps never to be told,
She would not hurt you for a pot of gold.
As you spread your wings ready to fly,
How many times has she been told,
"It's time to let go."
Hoping the partner you choose in life
Can match her love and understanding.
Then she will realize that you are no longer hers.
But always hopes you will have
"A special place in your heart for her."

Ena Pullen

Senses

Cool, still, quiet, on that walk along the drive.
For one second or two, silence, no automation.
Yet as I heard my footsteps fall
a pheasant let out his mating call,
and was that star, his eye?...Imagination?

A smell of grass just cut, bulbs now blooming.
A rustle of leaves from last year, dead not fallen.
Bleating lambs for mother's milk hungry,
from somewhere far a fox was calling.

A distant train heard, then it was gone.
Quiet again, then a blackbird in song.
Five minutes or six to walk the drive,
so glad that I walked and did not ride.
For my senses reel as I look at the sky.
Pink into grey, darkening...oh I'm glad I'm alive.

Faith M. Perry

That Man Might Love Himself—Herself

Then came the shrieks of horror
Thunderous showers and cries of agony
Naked and ashamed man stood may crawled
  the divided self.
Fomentations of self-hatred and shame
His Mortal Reign—to bring death to paradise.
Then came a messenger from God with a simple prayer.
That mankind might love—Himself—Herself
Since Iago could distinguish 'twixt a benefit
  and an injury
Nothing more—Nothing less—just that man right love himself

Raymond Martin Hanagan

Father's Footsteps

To stay, you'll be involved in crime
Never what I had in mind
Trouble follows the life we lead
No ethics, or morals, only greed.

Another cigarette, as I concentrate
Stale taste ignored, while I debate
The easy life's clouding my vision
But I know I've got to make a decision.

You're only nine, but time's of the essence
With the latest robbery planned in your presence
Your Dad's confused, his eyes fill with tears
It's hard to explain my future fears.

But the signs are there, for all to see
School truancy and the shoplifting spree
Bulging pockets, as you breeze in the door
Vivid warnings I'd be a fool to ignore
Pointless to start my usual inquisition
I know it's time to make my decision!

Eleanor O'Brien

Walking On The Wind

Sometimes, when the wind is in my hair
And I can taste the cold touch of an icy breeze,
I hear him calling me.
His voice whispering my name,
Drawing me into my dreams.
I rise from the hard damp ground
Caressed by this majestic spirit.
It cradles me in its bosom
And my soul dances on the air.
The whole earth opens up to my heart, and
My heart opens to her,
And I know the day will come
When I will be free,
Walking on the wind.

Anouska Charles

Untitled

Burning coals
in the place you entered
without asking.
Huge young eyes full of
bewildered trust
staring up at you
while your fingers graze
on pasture which is not yet ready.
Fiery lava running down
child's flesh:
The result of the bullet
hitting its target.
Whispered promises; seductions,
as you try to ease the pain.
A look in your eyes
I do not understand, which tells me only
that you will return.
Burning coals
in the place which has smouldered
beyond all feeling.

Shonagh R. Dubsky

A New Beginning

My favourite season is the Spring
It simply makes me want to sing,
Just like birds up in the trees
Whose feathers ruffle in the breeze.

Goodbye to Winter and the dark
Time to greet the tuneful lark,
Mornings and evenings both get lighter
And the sun seems so much brighter.

Flowers burst forth in regal splendour
Led by the snowdrop so small and tender,
Soon there are daffodils and tulips too
Filling the garden with their vibrant hue.

Spring is the time of Easter and joy
Happiness for every girl and boy,
Chocolate eggs they can be found
And hot cross buns are abound.

This time of year plants begin to grow
Hibernation is over and animals show,
Everywhere seems like heaven on earth
A time of renewal, a time of birth.

Maureen Daniel

A Countryman's Song Of The Seasons

Sing me a song of springtime
When the blossom hangs heavy on tree
And the celandine, aconite and wood violet,
Bloom sweetly for all to see.

Sing me a song of summer
When the sun rides high in the sky
And the fields are wet with dew and mist
And the lark sings gaily on high

Sing me a song of harvest
When the wains are piled high with corn
Drawn home by gentle shire horses
Who've worked to twilight, from dawn.

Sing me a song of autumn
When leaves fall russet and gold
And cobwebs sparkle with diamonds
On hedgerows frosted with cold.

Sing me a song of winter
When snow lies deep all around
And icicles hang from roof-top tree
And nothing stirs in the ground.

Iris M. Willis

Friendship

To have a friend who is true and sincere
Is worth more than riches or gold,
Someone to turn to, someone to trust,
A friend can be young or old.

Someone on whom you can always depend,
A friend always cares about you,
And if you are feeling worried or sad
Turns the grey skies into blue.

A friend brings love and warmth to your heart,
Brings sunshine into your day,
Makes the world feel a happier place
With warm friendly words to say.

True friendship is a wonderful thing,
You can feel it right from the start,
It lasts forever, year after year
'Coz true friendship comes straight from the heart.

There's always someone who's needing a friend,
Maybe someone who's living alone,
The world would be a much happier place
If everyone helped 'a someone'.

Edna Gallacher

My Precious Child

Precious child of the universe, walk with me across the Earth,
through hottest sands and deepest snow,
through eternity shall our true love go.
Through mighty winds and stormy seas,
through rolling hills and dancing trees.
Walk with me our souls at ease.

Walk with me through tribal lands, the warming glow, the tender hands,
the rising breeze, the summer time, the gift of natures herbs and wine.
The peaceful nights, the moonlit hours, humid rain and scented flowers
walk with me through gentle showers.

Run with me through grassy planes, through April gales and country
lanes, through Autumn leaves and ocean waves, through mountain
streams and crystal caves.
Run with me by ancient walls, by mighty oaks and waterfalls,
by rocky cliffs and creatures wild, run with me my precious child.

Fly with me through magic skies, sweet voices singing lullabies,
the diving birds and butterflies, the song around, our spirits rise.
We set off into distant space, and leave the troubled human race,
we tour the cosmos, race the stars, and leave our origins afar.
The journey starts, to know we thirst, my precious child of the universe.

Alan Haynes

Just A Voice

I will not look upon those eyes again.
For evil fills them.—Seeps through them, breathes and lives in them.
And I will not call thy name again.
For that is the name Satan hides behind,
that is the name that when called gathers all sins.
That is the name I loathe.
And no more tears shall I shed in front or because of you.
For I will not let thy know thy have hurt me.
Even in the depths of my pain and hurt.
For even in that depth I know that I shall rise.
My soul may be silent but not dead. It lives on—and grows.
And as thy cruel, heartless thoughts beat against me, I learn how to
survive—how to make them rebound from me as if never felt.
I become a body of steel—slowly but surely.
You have made me what I am—cautious, afraid to let one in
come close . . . but I grow strong.
From me my light shines on—and you are only a voice now.
That grows dimmer . . . dimmer . . . like my youthful years
. . . as those who love me drive me on . . .
As I grow older . . . wiser . . . I grow strong.

Sheila-Marie Egan

Race

Race the constitutional unceasing time
envelop the wind and subdue the brain
close in on the mundane atmosphere
and let me be seen again, remove the formal veneer
and let the tension subside and my life decide.

By a river that is my place or riding a horse with extreme grace
or perhaps running along an open meadow
feeling the penetrating sun, and cool breeze on my face, or maybe
I would like to be in a pensive mood
sitting by a lake, or on the back of a
motorbike at twilight with darkness
impending and freedom looming and
feeling the peace of the dove while I cling to my beloved one

I realize my life will soon change radically,
am I capable to endeavour change
or to grasp what life has to offer or suppresses!
What could I possibly do, perhaps I
will have to join the ever swelling "government queue" or worse still
spend the rest of my days wondering if I could have enjoyed a complete
state of bliss while I spend some mundane time at the office

Nicola Quinn

The One You Should Love

A mother should be loving, a mother should be kind.
Just like I am, and just like mine.
To be there whenever, come what may.
Until you're grown up, and want to go away
she'll say do this, she'll say do that,
but all we do is give her back chat
she smacks us, but does she care.
To answer her back, but would we dare
She's there when we laugh, she's there when we hurt.
She's there to clean us up, when we're covered in dirt.
But, she loves us, let no man take that apart.
This loving mum, who has a loving heart.
Mothers are there in the morn, to keep us at our pace.
She even keeps us clean, when we have a dirty face.
We play her up, but does she mind
that's when mums are very kind.
So look after your mum, she's a great pleasure.
I haven't got a mum, so I haven't had that treasure
So be good to her when she's frail and old.
Because she's your best friend, a great piece of gold.

Carol Williams

Regrets

I stare in the mirror is that really me I see
Or just some stranger looking back at me

With aching heart, no crocodile tears
What have I done with the passing years

Did I achieve what I set out to do
Or stumbled through life without any clue

Did I try and take the world by storm
Or stayed out of the cold and tried to stay warm

Did I really let all those years slip by
Didn't actually get any where, didn't really try

Has my past and future been written and told
Or is it just because I'm getting old

Is it really me standing there
That old man with greying hair.

Ronald Woods

As Darkness Fades Away

At night the skies are black and blue,
Sparkling stars twinkling too.
The bright white moon shines upon the trees
And the night's cold dripping rain falls upon leaves.
Chilling breezes of the night seep through doors
And twilights reflect on bedroom floors
Shadows form on pavements, ceilings, walls and waterfalls.

The wind whispers, whistles and moves in mysterious ways,
It blows and flows and glides through waves.
The ocean simmers down and silhouettes disappear
Whilst owls glare at strangers who dare to go near.
Palm trees begin to sway as darkness fades away
And the moon hides in darkness until the next day.

Sheeva Moshiri

Blackbird Solo

The sky was dark and wintry
And yet I had a song.
It was a lonely blackbird, so sweet and clear and strong.
No prompting did he need, no audience to cheer.
And yet how sweet his simple tune, so delicate and clear
It lifted up my lonely heart, it brought such peace and calm
This one solitary black bird that sang a heavenly psalm
And as I stood and listened, quietly watching there,
I was filled with peace, for love had come to share
This one precious moment of stark reality
That spoke untold wonder profoundly just to me
So sweet little bird of song go on singing still
your magic notes invade the air, they bring such hope that will
pour into a lonely soul that was a lonely place
so sing and sing your solo, my heart you now embrace.

Enid Butler

Memories

I look through old photographs,
Some with tears, some with smiles,
I know that although you've left our lives,
You'll never leave my heart.

The love I felt, and indeed still feel,
Is unconditional and eternal,
You were an important part of our lives for so long,
You brought us joy and happiness.

I can't help asking myself little questions,
Like where did you go and why,
Just when I realized I needed you.

The face that's in my dreams is yours,
Yesterday's my memories,
The last time I heard your voice
Is the last time I knew true happiness.

You taught me to see the right from the wrong,
Just look at what I have become,
Can't you see yourself in me?
I miss you so.

Laura Gebbie

Visions

When I think of a puppy's nose,
Or a dewdrop on a rose petal,
And the dimple in the cheek of a baby,
The sigh of the wind in the trees,
And the laughter in the mouths of children,
Or the music in the background,
Floating over the rooftops,
And the beauty of old churches,
I look at the mountains
That fill my window,
And see,
Her!

Hyrum Oliver Heywood

Fortune

There stands an empty little apple tree
Motionless and solemn in its orchard cell.
It bears no fruit or blossoms, that you can see.
But watches incompetent and jealous

Of surrounding Oak and Elm, fat and proud,
Although smothered and with ivy overcome.
Trickling sun brings cold comfort amongst this crowd.
The apple tree is lonely in its shame.

And in the brittle days, cruelly gnarled,
Will it, withered, reflect upon things denied?
Or bitterly accept, by nature's stake mauled
Time brings no change. Is never forgiven.

Nicola O'Connor

Love Is

Love is being thoughtful and kind
To all those people around you,
Love is for giving
To those less fortunate than yourself.
Love is caring and sharing.
One's children and grandchildren too.
Love is for friendship, and helping those in need.
Love is for patience,
For those who wear you down.
Love is not to look away,
When someone you love goes astray.
Love is lending a helping hand,
When jobs have got to be done.
Love is a shoulder to cry on,
When something's gone terribly wrong.
Love is a nice big smile, to cheer people who are sad or alone.
Love is a wave of the hand,
For those who can't get out of their homes

E. A. Malpass

Dial 141 For Pervert

Sad man staring at the telephone,
if he calls her now, will she be alone?
Receiver in one hand, transmitter in the other;
fat, bald and forty-five -
still lives with his mother.
He doesn't mean to scare her, he just needs to hear her voice,
but she's not allowed the luxury of choice.
His breathing gets faster,
his palm sweaty and hot
as he desperately imagines he's something he's not.
She hangs up and shudders, feeling nervous on her own.
He sighs in relief and wipes down his touch-tone phone.

Michaela Wadsworth

Sunshine

Bright rays dance their polka,
on the webs diamond dusting of dew.
Fledglings raise feathery heads
to join the eager choir.

The woman turns to her sleeping lover
and gazes in awe,
at the face that fills her life.

A sigh escapes—
as a butterfly slips the catchers net
and he extends a gentle hand
to enfold the breasts that still shimmer,
with the night's kisses.

Alicia Hughes

Collection Of Favourite Words

Oriental antiquities, silhouettes and labyrinths
Opaque manoeuvres, sophisticated madness
Psychopathic fantasy, confusion and illusion
Desire and obsession, precious emotions
Miscellaneous vibrations, simultaneous orgasms
Unique hemispheres, Dali-esque surrealism
Seductive caresses, virgin anxiety
Chameleon absurd, eternally cynical
Profane or insane, occult masturbation
Simulated stimulation, beautiful whores
Echoing diagnosis, passion fruit pseudonym
Hallucinating sorbet, palindromic theorems
Rampant plagiarism, infinite repercussions
Lesbian sexuality, explicit sensuality
Writhing in ecstasy, exotic erotic obelisk
Existential rhythm, sarcastic love
Cryptic exhibitionist, radical critique
Esoteric posturing, linguistic perversion

Russell Harrod

Black Sheep

Smash her head,
against a wall.
Abusive names,
they shout and call.
Knock her then,
from left to right.
She closes her eyes,
and squeezes tight.
Seem to always,
pinch her stuff.
When will they realize,
she's had enough.
She's sick and tired,
of their bitchy ways.
Hates going to school,
for every five days.
She tries to tell people, who don't want to know.
They don't or won't listen, of things she has to show.
So nobody would, play with her.
The dark girl with, the afro hair.

Katy Hunter

Expressions of Love

Closer closer your lips next to mine,
make love to me Darling, one more time.

The days pass too quickly, the night hours too,
when is there time for just me and just you?

Closer closer your breath mixed with mine,
Kiss me, touch me, as our bodies entwine.

Angels go riding on rainbows of gold,
like children and lovers their secrets unfold.

Foaming jade horses and diamonds so bright,
ride the waves of passion long into the night.

The bells and the cymbals are crashing so loud,
The Stallions are pounding - so tall and so proud.

Eros and Cupid are now by our side,
with arrows of Love so deep and so wide.

Longer and harder, like the shot from a gun,
Onwards and upwards, until we are done.

Susan M. E. Pretty

Untitled

Big brother Dave was about to leave school
Although he wasn't a genius, he was no fool
To be a miner was the family tradition
But our Dave decided he had more ambition.
A family meeting was called to see what could be done
Many thoughts about our Dave and decided it could be fun!
Mum said, "His brains are in his trousers and not his hat!"
His girlfriend sniggered and agreed with that.
Uncle Harold, who's always jolly and hearty
Suggested he join a political party
Dad said, "He once went out with the local tart,
So if he goes into politics, he's off to a good start!
He fornicates, cheats and lies like hell,
That'll go down with the journalist well!"
"Well I've no idea at all" said aunty Pat
"He could be a lawyer, but he's too honest for that!"
Uncle Steve said, "Well, it's a pity he's not gay,
He could get into the priesthood, any day"
Dave said, "I'll not be a miner and work down a hole,
I'd rather be a government artist and draw the dole!"

Valerie Lionis

Eternal Night

Whispers of love in the deep of the night,
 passionate kisses with care.
 The warming inside or erotic delight,
 so pure is this love that we share.
Entwined our position, encased in my thighs,
 the heat of the strengthening fires.
 Ever exploring the silence of eyes,
 adhere to their wanting desire.
Caressed be the body so close to my own,
 the taste of your flesh on my tongue.
In time was our bliss to the tune we have known,
 so sweet be the song we have sung.
I lay in your power, for ever it seems,
 contentment fulfilling me through.
 We sleep till the morning with promise of dreams,
 enriched with the pleasure of you.
Embraced as we were, we awake to the dawn,
 the gentleness pleases and calms.
 Now as we encourage this love that is born,
 feel safe and at rest in my arms.

Caroline Gardener

Belied With False Compare

Not a bull she is
More Jeanne d'Arc than John
With her laky districts
And several sisters in the south

Two hills of brown moor she has
And below her navel
An exciting triangle of thick hair -
Like forest openly awaiting my coming

I struggle and glide to please her
And recognize my failing, again
When finally I fall over her mental cliffs
Of Dover

Malte Tschirschky

Self Pity

Once I'm dead, I'm not responsible -
or so it seems. That's the attraction.
Dead fathers cannot pay, nor suffer bouts
Of guilt or insecurity.
However old your family may be,
The sense that you're responsible,
That their well-being is a function
of your own, is inescapable.
I'm sick of it! I'm not equipped, I find,
To bear the loads of others -
I cannot bear my own, or scarcely.
The pen will clatter from my lifeless hand,
And now I wish it over, soon,
With people weeping o'er my grave,
Or pissing in it.
I seem to be the focus, or the fount,
Of so much misery and pain.

Anthony L. Brace

The Groper

He's small and fat, his face is round,
His arse is one foot from the ground,
His eyes light up, each time he sees
A nice round arse or pair of knees,
He likes to pinch, and probe and poke,
And thinks that it is a big joke,
He goes around from bar to bar,
And watches the girls, as they have a jar.
He sneaks right up, and has a feel
And can't understand "what's the big deal"?
But someday soon, the time will come,
When time is called, on this little bum
And when that faithful day does call,
They will nail his arse against the wall,
And say goodbye once and for all.
To this little prick, with no cares at all.

John Meade

True Love

Caress my body, feel my soul
Feel my burning skin
Feel my breasts, feel my love
Feel and don't give in,
Kiss my body hard with your tender lips
Slide your soothing tongue down unto my hips
Let's play games, let's make love,
With passion and with lust,
Let's discover one another,
And give each other trust,
Let's play together, laugh together
Do things as a team
Let's do the things we want to do
That other people dream
For we are one, you and me
And will never be apart
As husband and wife, we love each other
With all our hearts

Janice Buchan

Somebody

Set amidst an evening pub the conversation stirs
And all eyes, they look upon the girl as she recounts her tale
To the boy in the faded shirt she is merely the girl
with the faint moustache
But to her lover at her side, she is a sweet and cheeky enchantress
Inhibited by groups her manner is coy, but he knows she is
by no means shy,
And to her best friend she is admirably intelligent and strong,
She listens to problems and makes them no more,
She likes the way she is very laid-back with the same taste for
onion crisps and having a laugh,
But the girl to her left really can't stand her, to her she is a
bimbo with a childish humour,
Her make-up is thick, she can be a right b****, the way she clings
to her boyfriend makes her sick,
Him in the corner, he secretly adores her, she is so cultured and chic
With rubies for lips, her porcelain face so distant, she can give
such an air of mystique
So these people gathered round her, but who really knows her?
To each she is unique
She's the same face under different guises
The same person with many disguises
But all her friends know her in a different light.

Lisa Clare Merone

The Truth About Man

Late at night is when I shed my tears,
I picture my whole life, hopes and fears.
You see I feel my heart torn in two,
when I see our animals suffer and don't know what to do.
Mankind is no more than cruel, too obsessed with power and rule.
When I see dolphins panic and cry, drowning in drift nets waiting to die,
A feeling enters me, one I can't explain, I feel much regret, hate and pain.
Gorrillas' hands taken away, never again to feel the light of day.
Tigers penises cut off with knives
when they should have been used to create new lives.
Orphaned babies wander the land because
their mothers were killed by the human hand.
Live baby calves on the roads for hours,
when they should be in fields enjoying the flowers.
Elephants only crime is their tusks so white,
poachers come and hack at night.
Baby seals heads bashed in, why?
Because they have such beautiful skin.
'Mankind' what an ironic word to give!,
When 'kind man' cruelly kills all creatures that live.

Carla Marie Linnette

Tree People

Don't look at me like a piece of s***
I'm fighting for you and your children you ignorant git.

Maybe not now but in years to come
You'll all look back on this and see what we've done to bring
to the world's attention.
The Acid Rain, the Ozone Layer and the slow demise of our Green Belt
replaced by pollution and industry
The cars all so many just keep coming and coming
Can't you people see were friends not the enemy.

For crying out load we want to help
Stop polluting our streams, our earth and our heavens.

Money magnets obviously don't want to know
Clean Air and clean streams in the bank account don't show.

All they see just like everybody else are Hippies up a tree
Anti sociables with long hair and dirty cloths.

They miss our object but really they know
Just like us they have Scientists, Accountants and Annalists
on the pay-roll.

Clive John Reid

429

The Secret

The sun is slowly burning,
eating itself away.
The world can't remain forever turning,
bringing us night and day.

The clouds are no longer white and fluffy,
but grey and weighed down with tears.
They rain on us, but what we fail to see
They cry out their hopes and fears.

The tall grass sways with the song of the wind
humming and swaying.
Every day always praying
that one day we'll read the words.

The trees strive to reach the sun,
they know the secret that's hidden.
They try to find a reason; just one,
but in this world freedom's forbidden.

So we'll carry on each day with our small lives,
not knowing the answer to why?
Mother Nature can only pray
we'll wake up to the truth one day.

Debbie Shilling

The Visit

I love to visit "Scotland",
The scenery is stunning
Each mountain quite spectacular
Cool streams forever running.

Driving around those winding roads
By beautiful "Loch Lomond"
What a beautiful sight by day and night,
The highlands and the lowland.

This beautiful and splendid land
Is a privilege to see,
It makes me very humble,
Insignificant, and wee.

But would I feel so passionate
If I lived there all year round,
Would I take it all for granted,
Never notice sights or sounds?

It doesn't stop me feeling sad,
And when leaving, filled with pain
My only consolation is
I can return again.

Jean Silverthorne

Night Life

We watched out for a big bright moon,
A light to guide our way,
For we must travel far tonight,
To a place so far away.

Our costume that of winter black,
Our boots of autumnal brown,
Our make-up that of a ghostly stare,
Just like the face of the moon.

The time is right, the wind has come,
Our guiding light is shining strong,
A thrust... a lurch and up we go,
Flying free and full of song.

For we must travel good and long
To celebrate this night. To dance, to scare,
To freak and kill under this dark
Cloth of night sky.

What was that... A light... A bird,
Oh no... So little time to scatter,
We whispered, we huddled,
... then gone forever.

Mary L. O'Grady

Happiness

Happiness they tell me is a great thing, yet when I try to achieve it,
they tell me it can wait.

Go for that career, go for the car, go for the house and the CD player.
Aim for goals so high that even God herself would find it hard.
Enjoy life, meet with friends or one of the many lovers that you have,
but don't get too involved, because there's plenty of time for that.

Of course I listened, it was an exciting choice.

It's ten years on and I have my career, that I'm not so thrilled about.
I have a car that can do nought to sixty in five seconds flat, but
there's no road around here that allows me to do that speed. I have
a large house with only myself living in and a CD player that should
be playing the kind of songs that you need a partner to share with.

Don't be a fool to believe that happiness will wait for you just
around the corner, while you deal with the more important things in life.

Michelle McKenna

The Remembered Places

We will come back to the remembered places
To the woodland paths, the glow of primroses
The sea of bluebells breathing their perfume around the trees.
A deer lies browsing on the warm earth
We stroke his firm brown coat
His nostrils twitch but he has no fear.
Little brown rabbits scamper across the paths
Intent on their own affairs
Our footsteps do not disturb them.
We suddenly feel very alive - we chase each other along the paths
We run and run and Run!
We lie down in the bracken, looking in wonder at the blueness of the sky.
There is no Time, no Hurry, no Noise.
One day we will come back to the remembered places
We will come back.

Joan Clement Jones

The Waterhole

All was activity at the Waterhole, zebras drinking with their foals,
Shy impala, tall giraffe, water buffalo and their calves,
Old baboon, sly raccoon, drinking together 'neath a silvery moon,
Noisy ostrich and her brood, fish below digesting food,
Tall, tall elephant with a swaying trunk, looking like some city drunk
Grumpy warthog and wild dog, crocodile lying like a rag,
The rhinos, the hippos, the Thompson gazelles, hyenas, the jackals,
  the monkeys as well.

Each showing in their delight, the pleasure at drinking at the pool
  that night,
But soon delight would turn to fear, death for one was very near,
A lion is crouching in the tall, tall grass, waiting for his meal to pass,
Comes a gnu ambling slow, fate had struck her final blow,
A mighty roar, a mighty leap, cry of the terror stricken beast,
The King was enjoying his midnight feast with one mighty blow of a
  savage paw,
He was upholding his right, his law.

Brian Rysdale

It's A Hard Life

If you're feeling lonely and about to cry,
If you don't want to live, but you want to die.
If the nights are getting longer as the days are drawing in,
If you want that happy feeling, but all you get is grim.

If your troubles seem to weigh a ton no matter how big or small,
If whenever you get to the top of a mountain you always seem to fall.
If every friend you've had in life has turned behind your back,
If people tell you there is light in the tunnel, but all you see is black.

If people say they love you, but the word they mean is hate,
If you and every dream you've had seem to be separated by a bolted gate.
If every time you see yourself you feel the need to change,
If every time someone looks at you, you think they think you're strange.

If every if of this poem was true you'd have no life at all,
so next time you climb the mountain of life you know there's no need to fall.

Sarah Chambers

430

THOUGHT

Oh! Wondrous, wondrous my secretive mind,
How can I get hold of you when you're soaring,
through the boundary of space and time.
    As you pass through the myriads of events,
    Past, present and the distant future time,
    You behold them all in your creative mind.
Oh! Wondrous, wondrous my secretive mind,
nobody can see you embrace you or touch,
Even in my best I only know you so much.
    wisdom and knowledge I know you embrace,
    On paper with pencil I can draw your face,
    But that isn't all that you have in your store;
The excellence mercy beauty and fame,
The honour revulsion in your inner frame.

Victor Dehtiar

Forward

Standing alone in 'Centenary Square'
A monument larger than life.
A puzzle to many,
A history to some
And a sign to those who stare.

Look at the crowd making up this work,
The people are using their skills
From early crude works
To industries small
The "Brummies" have moved on ahead.

And now as they stand taller in height,
Their skills have been changing again.
They are forging their futures
Far brighter ones now
To greater things ahead.

E. A. Thrupp

Children

Children are such loving things
They bring so much joy
To those around them every day
That little girl and boy
I have two children of my own
And I can tell you I should know
They can bring so much love and joy
But also tears along the way
But being a mother you understand
Especially when they hold out their hands
Their needs are great, their hearts are big
Especially when they give you lots of hugs
And kisses.
But most of all that little smile
It just makes life so worthwhile
I love my children very much, so this is
For them with that tender touch called love.

Margaret Oakley

Humming and Whispering

Humming and whispering
The river calls my name
Telling me to listen to my wisdom
Telling me to forget the pain

Walking, just walking
In tune with my heart
In the darkness the river shouts my name
Promising that paradise will start

Thinking, just thinking
The water cools my fears
Reflecting a light to guide my path
To look forward to the future years

Humming and whispering
The river sings my name
Asking me to stop and feel the flow
We are but the same.

Richard Gabbrielli

The Reason For Dreams

Now I awoke just then,
And wish I could dream that dream again,

Who was there, I just don't know
Where did all my dream just go.

I knew all pieces, every one,
And just like that my dream was gone.

I search for the pieces I can find,
But they just can't get back to mind.

I know I was there and how I felt good,
But I just can't remember, I wish I could.
I don't know why or when or how,
Or where my dream could be right now.
It's there somewhere, all a shatter
And now I believe it just doesn't matter,
For now my eyes are open wide
All day my dream feels warm inside.

Bronagh Herbert

Mountain

The path to happiness may be a steep mountain
You may have to walk in the pouring rain
You may lose your shoes,
and cut your feet on the rocks
You may come across boulders blocking your path
You may stumble and have to restart your climb
You may have to carry the weight of confusion
But the beauty of the view at the top
Will echo so deeply in your soul
That every trace of suffering will be forgotten.

Catherine O'Connor

Myself

Gemini lady hard to catch, gemini lady, weary to watch
Gemini lady won't you stop! Always trying to beat the clock.
Full of talent, ideas over flow.
No patience whatever with folk who are slow.

She needs all the eyes of a spider to use
All the limbs of an octopus she can use too.
For all the things she plans to do.
Six jobs are not too many for her, two is not enough I fear.

Just like a butterfly flitting around
Out in the sunshine - covering ground.
"Oh why can't we live without sleep" she cries
While vainly she struggles to keep open her eyes!

Gemini ladies are people apart when old in years still young in heart.
Lovers of nature and sweet solitude
Of wide open spaces and deep old woods
With many old trees, where birds fly around
And carpets of violets cover the ground.

"A good night's sleep"? - "people die in bed!"
"Time is awasting" is what she said
"Relax" - they say "Well not today! Can't change the gemini lady."

Naomi Ruth Burden

Absent Shadow

Faithful shadow, which forest do you roam?
Whose body do you call home?
Patient eyes and soulful gaze.
In tune with every step.
Forever watchful, always near.
Brave little heart, full of courage.
Trusting eyes reflecting love.
Kindred spirit, forgive me.
Death's dark veil has swallowed you up.
Gentle extension of my soul
I lost you in the lonely night.
But I will find you in the warmth of day.

Elizabeth Anne Pearson

Thursday

Two o'clock in the afternoon
Hope you'll be arriving soon
Up all night worrying about this
Realizing that I was out of practice
So you 'phoned me up to make the date
Didn't realize you'd be this late
Arrangements were made perfectly clear
Yet still you are not here

Ten minutes more and then I'll leave
How you can be this long I can't believe
Unable to think what could be keeping you
Right now your arrival time is overdue
Suddenly, just as I'm about to split
Deliverance comes as you finally make it
All previous worries are instantly forgotten
Your arrival always stops me feeling rotten

Simon Hodge

Art

A way of showing one's emotions
Putting things in their right proportions
Long lines, short lines
Some thick, some faint
A brush, some paper
And the wonderful ability to paint.

Joe Maratty

A Fisherman's Tale

The concrete jungle is left behind
As I take a few moments to empty my mind
Sometimes work can be fine
But this is quality time
And at last the chance to unwind

The lure of the river is powerful and strong
It's surrounding beauty, the birds and their song
Yes life can be bliss
On a day just like this
But it never seems to last long

And so I begin my meandering walk
No matter how great the creatures I stalk
If I'm asked I'll just say
The monster got away
Well you know how fishermen talk

Please answer me, God, all the questions I ask
That appear in my thoughts in between casts
Save me from hostility
Give me peace and tranquillity
To enjoy my short life while it lasts

Alan Beasley

Who And What Am I?

An oak am I, tall and strong
Firmly I stand
Though the wind breaks my boughs when the storm lasts long

A tiny field mouse sometimes am I
Mustn't be noticed, I'm timid and shy
I'll hide in a corner living in fear
And scuttle away when someone draws near

I'm a fast running stream continually flowing
No time to rest, must keep on going

A blanket I'll be to keep you warm
I'll wrap tight around you, keep you free from harm

I can act the fool, I can play the clown
Though tears may flow when the mask is down

Am I friend or foe, nursemaid or mother
Perhaps in sweet moments a helpless lover

All these things sometimes I'll be
For all these things are part of me.

M. S. Batty

Blessings

When you're burdened with life, and can't find The Way,
With a friend share your troubles, very soon they will say
Count your blessings, dear friend, I'm sure you have many,
There's no person alive that hasn't got any.

There's Good Health and Strength to name but just two,
The beauty of Nature, it's all around you,
Get out, say "Hello!, to the people you meet,
Interests you'll find down every street.

Then, very quickly, the day will be done,
And you will forget how it all began,
You'll be pleasantly tired and ready for bed,
Or may be exhausted and feel half dead,

But whichever it is at the end of the day,
Take a look at your life, you'll find The Way.
Put away all your cares, and in a while
Tomorrow will come, greet it with a smile,

Count the blessings, that you have been told,
Are all around you to have and to hold,
Sit yourself down and quietly reflect,
What is from life that you really expect?

Mary Elizabeth Biggs

Memories

O, Spirit of Forgetfulness, free my Memories.
Cast them to the Winds, scatter them to the Clouds,
The Clouds that adorn the sky with beauties,
Ever changing shape and kind, Cirrus and Cumulous,
Storm-laden or faery-feathered, drifting or menacing.

Or cast them to the Seas, to ride the waves
That drift, on hidden shores, or rage against stern rocks
Thunderous and terrible, scouring the coast,
To be devoured by sharks or whales, or nibbled at by shrimps,
Or hidden in coral reefs or sunken galleons long lost.

Or fling them far on to mountainous peaks
To perish in crevasses, gorges, waterfalls or lakes,
Or freeze on gleaming glaciers that, at evening's end,
Turn from grey to rose, as though the water at its base
Had been a river of sparkling rosé wine.
Or let them hide in snow snared caves
Impaled on glittering stalactites.

Or cast them to the sands, arid Deserts of the World,
Wind-torn, forever changing shape,
BUT, O, Spirit of Forgetfulness, disperse my Memories.

Ruth Sudbury-Palmer

Who Knows

In a vast black airless vacuum
With a million twinkling lights
Who knows how many planets
Who knows how many lives.

Look to the stars my children
Turn your face to the skies
There's a memory out there beckoning
If only we knew why.

In a place where our whole lifetime
Is the blinking of an eye
Not one thing goes un-noticed
From birth to death, through life.

Look to the stars my children
Turn your face to the skies
There's what our memories long for, that's the reason why.

When the learning is all over
When time is right for moving on
This life may well be over, but a better ones begun.

So look to the stars my children. Turn your face to the skies.
For that where your ancestors came from
That's where your future lies.

L. Wharton

Favourite Things

I love to watch a rainbow in the heavens after rain
I love to see the sunshine struggle through the clouds again
I love to watch the swallows dipping 'cross the dewy lawn,
On curving wings they circle when the day is newly born.
I love to see a puppy or a kitten at its play
And to watch the crimson sunset close in death the eyes of day.
A velvet rosebud opening with its fragrance sweet and rare
Gently blending with the colours of the other flowers there.
I love to see the puddles caused by heavy storms and rain
And the holes the raindrops make which quickly close again.
But best of all I love to be beside a winter fire
where crackling logs send showers of sparks forever rising higher
And to be surrounded by my family and my friends
Is a pleasure and a sweetness and a joy that never ends.

Jean Murrey

Restitution

Buried face down in a field of lost souls,
I felt death bearing down on me.
Its indiscriminate harvest knew no bounds,
In this place of torment and misery.

So I caressed the moment as if it was my last,
And prayed for forgiveness as I held to my gun.
For I had felt hatred this day for fellow man,
In this bloody battlefield called 'The Somme'.

The cold now incapable of subduing the pain,
Let the full intensity of my wounds come to light.
For it was with bayonets mounted we'd each met our foe,
And with vigour we'd each won our fight.

In agony I then strained my head up from the mud,
Desperate in the hope of seeing my enemy dead.
But to the shrill scream of a falling bomb,
He looked me back without a single word said.

At which point then our anger dissipated,
And between us all hostilities did cease.
And in that brief moment till the shell finally struck,
Two war weary soldier's knew peace!

Paul Richard Taylor

Mametx

A whistle screams, shattering the still calm air.
Smell the terror in our communion with hell
Officer shouts, we all pour out.
My stomach knots awaiting the shots.
We move forward in shocking line abreast.
We start to fall in gouts of crimson and pink.
Hysterical thoughts of glory sear my terrified mind.
No honour in this nightmare come to life.
Will there be someone to wake me.
I lie in gut and gore on blood-soaked ground.
My inside obscenely plain for all to see.
No words can explain the screaming pain.
Take me home sweet oblivion.

Mark Simms

The Black Heart

Black and deathly, it is my curse
Hell 'hath surely known no worse
For this evil beats within
Taints my soul, burns my skin
'Tis evil as none ever seen
It feeds on me, picks me clean
Robs me of my poisoned mind
It numbs me, strikes me blind
The death bell tolls, sombre and slow
Funereal shadows dance in the snow
Grotesque caricatures that mock my soul
Leading me to the only way I know
A dark procession remains for me
Yet even hell will not set me free
I suffer this pain that will tear me apart
Stemming from my cold, black heart.

Lee Wood

Rekindled Torches

I am lost like a snowflake falling
To receive news of you
I am swept up into a vault of frenzy
The thought, dancing on the winds billowing breath
Prana
Future, past, prana,
Life, live, live,
Guts, tugs, what is left
No explaining
Up again I climb
Your white-tipped mountains
Snowy powdered snow spirits
Spirit of the hearts
Desires
Magic onto another dimension
Our words, a poet's heart
Rekindled torches
A tunnel's end
Light!
Reality again to live.

Pat Van Ravenstein Cleveland

Keepers Cottage

At the end of a secluded lane, in the area of Pease Pottage,
Is situated a very old quaint cottage;
Built in the early 18th century,
Was used as a meeting place for the rich gentry.

In those days the structure was soundly built,
Due to ground erosion, has now a slight tilt;
It has cork-screwed chimneys, a total of three,
Climbing up the facial wall is a Jacaranda Tree.

The entrance to the cottage has a stable type door,
As you go inside, the hall has a parquet floor;
Most of the furniture is made of mahogany or teak,
In the sitting room is a rocking chair that has an occasional squeak.

All the rooms have oak beams going across the ceiling,
Log fires glowing, giving off a warm feeling;
Within the cottage are antiques galore,
Mainly of the 18th century, and some even before.

The old meeting room that was used in the olden days
Was entered by a door at the top of two small stairways;
The door has not been opened since the last meeting ended;
On the 17 August 1897, when the final rich man was suspended.

Andrew S. Rymer

Must Be Love

Beneath the stars and beneath the trees
All I can see is
you.

Looking at each other across a crowd
this must be love,
they say

In my mind night and day,
In and out of school through each and every lesson
All I can think about is, you.

That day I held your hand made me feel so sad
knowing that any minute now it will be over.

The littlest things we argue about enemies must be lovers
they say.

The glimpse of your eyes makes my heart jump.
The bitterness and shyness we both have
shows me I care for you.
But the hurtful things you say to me

That make me cry

Our friends say it must be love but now I think

It Must Be Love.

Neesha Patel

433

The Unwanted Invader

As life goes by, we work and strive,
for material things to enrich our lives.
Searching for goods that shine and please,
forgetting the pleasure from a summer's breeze.

A better home, a new car, more money,
never quite satisfied, isn't that funny.
You work even harder, life's a chore,
stress builds up, but you still want more.

You wake up one morning, feeling quite ill,
"I'll pop to the doctor, he'll give me a pill.
There's concern on his face, he wants you to rest
and return on Thursday for another test."

The news is bad, it's cancer you see,
"Oh no, this can't be happening to me!"
It's the one thing in life that you must face,
the unwanted invader that you have to embrace.

Some days you'll think it's so unfair
but family and friends will always be there.
Your mirror of life has a new reflection,
things you thought were important, gave no protection!!!

J. E. Webb

The Solitude Of The Sea

I could sit for an eternity,
entranced by the white water.
Crashing onto these sands

My mind in a maze having not the means to escape.
I glance at a sand lizard scurrying across pebbles
to its sanctuary under a shell,
I am not alone in finding security at the sea.

A battered plastic bottle drifts out to sea.
I wish I could drift away so effortlessly
If only life were so simple

I feel an aura surrounding.
A tidal wave of calmness
washing over me, breaking me loose

I skim flat stones
over the barrelling waves and I feel lifted

I return to a tranquil state of mind
feeling rejuvenated and refreshed
like the salt spray of the sea.

As I turn to look back becoming aware of my footsteps
swallowed by the thirsty sea.

Lesley Anne Paul

My Son

My son has grown, from child to man,
I still help him, when I can,
But seventeen years is an age unknown,
'Tis when a youth is fully grown,
No need to listen anymore
To what I say, he knows the score.

One hair must not be out of place,
His walk is not without a trace
Of mirrored actions as he moves,
To show us how his manhood proves.

He used to climb upon my knee,
And listen, very carefully,
To tales untold and tales well read,
Before I tucked him into bed.

I taught him how to write his name,
I placed his picture in a frame,
I combed his hair and tied his shoes,
I kissed his knees when they were bruised.

Such days I knew, would have to end,
I've lost my child, but found a friend.

Philippa C. Benacs

The Spirit Of Nature

The reddening sky as it heralds the dawn
Proclaims here am I to the ears of the corn
My spirit is there, in the mist o'er the trees,
Your skin feels my touch, when it's kissed by the breeze

My voice is the fox as he barks in his lair,
The colours of spring are the clothes that I wear
The myriad sparkles of sunlight you see
On the stream, are the jewels that God gave to me

I dance in the moonlight on the shores of the tarn
I rest with the owl as he sleeps in the barn
I live with the eagle, the badger, the deer
You say you can't see me, but I'm always here

Within and without, above and below
I stand there beside you, wherever you go.
Your quest is to find me, but 'ere you do start
Just close your eyes and open your heart.

David F. Simms

A Baby Boy

Your baby boy is here,
now it's the day we can all cheer,
the lads are probably having a beer,
you are watching your baby's little bed,
wondering if he'll be alright,
and how old he'll be when he flies his first kite,
wondering how tall he will grow,
and will you be able to keep him in tow,
will he be a six footer,
and will he be a looker,
well the future's about to be,
full of fun as a family.

Tracy Davison

Nature

Nature is part of the universe
As we see it revealed in the Spring
When the trees and the shrubs show their buddings
And the free birds of note start to sing.

In Summer, we relish its splendour
With the arrival of butterflies and bees
While they're busy distributing pollen
That later brings fruit to the trees.

In Autumn, the fruits of their labours
Are safely collected and stored
Away from the cold spell of Winter
Awaiting the Springtime once more.

As we study the mysteries of nature
Supervised by our Great Lord and King
Then we wait with reserved expectations
Not knowing what the New Year might bring.

Maurice O'Connell

Innocence

Tell me little one,
What do you see?
Do you see magic in life's mystery?
Is it a giant's breath, rustling the trees?
Are fairies riding on the backs of bees?

Would you like to bounce the golden ball
That's so high in the sky?
Catch the sunbeams as they go scurrying by?

Smell the scent from the flowers,
The pollen tickling your nose.
Chase the thistledown wherever it blows.

Do you hear the birds singing your name?
You can make life such a wonderful game,
So, little one, in innocence play
And in treasured memories,
The magic will stay.

Jean A. Henderson

Erratic Pessimism

As the day draws to an end and I retire
My mind is still racing as I sit through the mire
The ups and downs of the previous epoch
Create a bombardment of thoughts focusing on the hiccups
Predicaments both trifling and momentous
Their resolve never clear of my conscience
The trials and tribulations of a day at the office
Every effort, in the eyes of the boss, never seems to suffice
The mountainous workload I am continually climbing
Contrasts the slippery slope on which I am sliding
Business and personal quandary coming to a head
All my time and effort can't put them to bed
Continual uncertainly is chipping away at me
Leaving a shadow of the man I used to be
The concept of ending it all up seems more appealing
To rid me of the daily dread I am persistently feeling
But I awaken to a brilliant new morning
And dismiss the feelings that I am hoarding
A strength of purpose fills my being
As Mother nature forges in me a believing
For each new day brings with it a new encounter
And I am a visionary not a doubter

Tom Hearne

Winter Paradise

My feet sink loud into the frosted crust
and guilt and joy run tingling through my breast,
to spoil such beauty, yet to be there,
to see such wonder, I feel blessed.

To watch the sun rise over snow-kissed fields
and see its fire spread through sky and sea,
to stand transfixed as wandering sheep turn gold,
is something close to heaven for me.

Nestling farms are swathed in white before me,
tractors lie discarded, all is peace.
From hilly slope and furrowed earth birds rise
on silent wing, as suddenly released.

I have fled from busy town to peace
of country roads and pallid silver lochs,
with little water-birds and fishing boats,
heathered hills, sea, sand and rocks.

Pollution now exchanged for pure fresh air,
the 'Top Ten' tunes, for gulls and curlews cry.
For me this lonely shore and the rising sun
is truly paradise before I die.

Sylvia Stewart

Lighten Our Darkness

Florrie had a little lamp,
Its flame was strong and bright.
Through the barracks of Scutari Camp
She carried it at night.

It gladdened many a soldier's heart
Wounded in the Crimea,
And was to play a symbolic part
As the new century drew near.

We maintained a twentieth century flame,
'Til its dimming and its dying
Indicated when the tories came
A selling and a buying.

We dote on paper sent in reams.
The faceless trim the wick.
Such moves intended, so it seems,
To blind us to the sick.

At the flickering flames decease
Another century draws nearer.
The turkish lamp's a museum piece
And the ending of an era.

Harriet B. Spilman

Uplifting For The Soul!

Have you wandered far away from the Lord?
Sweeter comforts will soon be restored;
For the Joy Of Christ outweighs everything-
When on His 'Loving Arms' you cling!

The Comfort Of God will soon draw near;
Contrite, humble Prayers To Him are dear.
Whose is the weakest, sorest complaint?
Repentance-soon melts the soul's 'Dark Decent'

Pretensions have No Place with Thee;
Just Come to Him on bended knee.
Let Him be your Strength and Stay;
Soon 'Lifted Up' and Nothing to pay!

Has your Faith then Still lost its Cheer?
Hold on fast-those 'dark clouds' will soon disappear;
Let the 'Storm' and the loud thunder roll-
Peace Be Still-He Comforts your 'Drooping Soul'!

He Will Sweeten every 'Bitter Cup'
Each Time you 'Fall' He Lifts you up:
Upon His Promises you shall stand-
Upheld by His Faithful, Omnipotent Hand!

Josephine Raison

Helpful Neighbour

God put an angel here on earth
In our hour of need.
She came into our humble lives,
She is a friend indeed.

She never tires of helping us,
Our welfare's her concern
This lady from the house next door
Her place in heaven has earned.

She calls in every morning
With a 'cuppa' and a smile
Always ready and willing
To go that 'extra' mile.

She comes too in the evenings
To see we're locked in tight
Makes our Ovaltine or Horlick's, to ensure a restful night
Years of sacrificial service, with community in mind
Keeps our neighbour on the road
Where true happiness she'll find.

She didn't just 'come' into our lives
She was well and truly sent.
When God promised His just reward, we know for whom He meant.

Maureen E. Todd

The Perfect Kiss

Sometime in the night when the land is still
Your dreams take command and escape beyond your will
This is when she strikes and never does she miss
That haunting little angel with the perfect kiss

She picks you from slumber and flies to the sky
Scorching through the atmosphere that angel and I
We rest upon the clouds and now I have my wish
I hold the little angel with the perfect kiss

I look into her eyes and tell her that I care
She sings out that she loves me and will always be there
Her arms enfold around me and now I'm in my bliss
Entwined with the little angel with the perfect kiss

Suddenly she stops and flees towards the stars
She circles round of Saturn and dances round of Mars
I spring to try and catch her but all I know is this
I've lost my little angel with the perfect kiss

Dawn comes oh so quickly, the owl bows down to sleep
I open up my eyes but soon begin to weep
Lament for love that's passed and what I sure will miss
Goodbye my little angel with the perfect kiss

John Paul Wilding

Dad

These feelings I've never been able to keep inside,
You know I loved you from the start until the day you died,
I will love you forever and remember you for eternity,
I know I loved you as much as you loved me.

You made me feel happy when I was feeling sad,
You made me feel good when I was feeling bad,
You made me feel like the best person on earth,
I know you loved me right from my birth.

You were always better than expected,
You were always there for me, I was never rejected,
You gave me so much comfort and love,
I know you'll be happy in the heavens above.

I've never ever wanted you to go away,
I've never wanted you to go through any pain,
You always gave me everything with love and with care,
When you weren't feeling good I'd always be there.

Dad you were the best Dad I could've ever had,
Dad you always made me feel so glad,
Now it's time for me to say goodbye,
I try to wear a smile but just seem to cry.

Francesca Fleming

Full Cycle

The seasons are unchanging as year follows on year
But it can be wintertime in summer when you lose someone dear

The spring arrives unfailingly but it means not much to you
You seem to be oblivious to green shades of every hue

The summer comes long afterward to thaw and melt your heart
You suddenly notice beauty around
A different life begins to start

Autumn's flaming colours persuade you life is worth living
You give thanks for family and friends
With their loving and their giving

Life begins to become more precious
When you realize how short it can be
So when winter arrives - you face it head on
And get used to saying "I" and not "we"

Finally the last icicles have melted with the news of a newborn child
And all the love and the name lives on wintertime now
becomes more mild

As season follows season - you begin to realize
Autumn years can be golden although you have to part
And summertime will come in winter
When you keep springtime in your heart

Audrey Mitchell

Reality In A Dream

As I lay down too sleep at night
I dream about life around me.

A flower which was once living,
breathing and growing
deprived of its life
for the beauty of its likelihood.

A fish that once swum free in the ocean,
caught and served up on a plate,
slaughter for food.

All over the world people are dying
being killed for the greed of another.

I feel so lost and alone
as if I'm laying in a deserted desert.

I look up to the sky for help
only to see an angel with a bow and arrow
looking for its next victim.
"Take me, please take me!"

I close my eyes and cry, I know now
we are living in hell!
When we die we go to heaven.

Kim Sibley

Magic Moments

A vision of warmth creeps into the mind
An illusion of comfort lightens the load
A softening of eyes to which others are blind
The warmth of a smile, a message in code
A questioning look, a touch of the hand
A certain aroma, a sense of delight
A feeling of time trickling like sand
To live days and weeks for just the sight
Of a certain physique, the sound of a voice
The painful thud of the heart when the telephone rings
To be needed, wanted, to have always that choice
To lie entwined, arms encircled, so that the body sings
Cries out in ecstasy, acknowledging its need,
Desire sated, contented, aching heart fulfilled,
To take again and again, to delight in the greed
Of a joining of souls and all painful thoughts stilled
A meeting of minds, and a burning desire,
To be cherished, caressed, and to bask in the glory,
Of travelling through time, the whole being on fire
Is not right or wrong, but simply love's story.

Rosa Montague

Four Legged Friends

A dog is a man's best friend, they say,
To some that may be true,
But the happiest part of all my days,
Is always spent with you.

You are my horse, my trustworthy pal,
For now, I give you my heart,
I'll always be near you, come what may,
And I swear that we never shall part.

Who do I turn to, my secrets to tell,
When I feel lonely and blue?
Who keeps me fit as a well-tuned bell?
No one, "Dear Madam", but you.

Well-fed and watered, and groomed to a sheen,
is all you really require,
But a daily cantor, like a well-oiled machine,
Two hearts with one desire.

To ride the wind in fresh green fields,
You and I together,
In dreams we ford the icy streams,
To reach the purple heather.

Doreen Blades

To My Love

I have not lived in vain
Having your children was such a gain
And having loved you through and through
Bears repeating as it's true

The ups and downs and times apart
Were evened out by a constant heart
Beating for you, with you, but not without you
'Cause it's joined to yours from the start.

Will you please walk again on the shore
Where we sealed that sacred tryst before?

T. Hughes-Ellis

Something For Me

Bricks and mortar, nothing more,
Inside I'm fighting another war;
Disappointment silenced by a happy smile,
Hand me some courage, just for a while;
Bake me a cake and make me new,
Build me a land while I wait in the queue;
Give me those roses, I'll throw them away,
I never saw roses and the truth doesn't pay;
Burn those books, the words are too loud,
It's hurting my ears, come away from the crowd;
Give me a vote and I'll give you new life,
Those were never my lies; but whose was the knife?

Claire M. Taylor

Autumn

White frothy clouds in a candy-pink sky
Give way to an azure plane.
Brown leafy paths, damp underfoot,
Nature's tapestry on view again.

Meandering rills play their melody
And frosted webs quiver in time.
Riparian antics disturb the undergrowth
Flora and fauna emerge through the rime.

Morning mists emit incandescent hues
Enshrouding the woodland ways,
Earth holds on to its precious gift of beauty
Just for a few more days.

Tall majestic trees, autumnal coloured
Dappled shadows on the floor below,
Cascading leaves dance on breezes
Telling summer it's time to go.

Sue Curd

Untitled

Do or do not do,
Calls Thee Eternal Priest,
So long, so old thou heavenly list.
I whisper: To the taverns mist.
Let the wine flow and carry on the feast.

Mehdi Shafii

Summer In My Heart

Love is like a summer's day,
The sunshine and the flowers,
The light that takes all the gloom away,
And brings blue skies instead of showers.

The birds in song, a butterfly in flight,
The feeling of warmth on your back,
You are my sun, the warmth in my heart,
With you, happiness I cannot lack.

So sweet is the air with children singing,
Don't you know the joy you're bringing?

If I could describe a summer's day,
Your love is what I would say.

And so my love, it's you I cherish,
Without your love, my summer would perish.

They say the sun can never die,
When people love, like you and I.

Michael G. Clare

Preparation

The town's still noisy with last minute shoppers
buying wine, toys, and party poppers
Turkey stuffing, that one forgot
a bunch of holly, that must be the lot.

Lights shine from windows bright
Listen, children's laughter rings though the night
On the radio carols play
getting ready for Christmas day.

Inside the family all gathered round
Last minute decorations to be found
Missing bulb from the fairy light
and the star on the tree is not quite right.

At last the children are asleep upstairs
Now to relax from all the day's cares
Take a look outside at the silent night
One star in the sky shining so bright.

Time to remember the stable forlorn
And Jesus Christ, who for us was born.
The kings and shepherds were in no doubt
That He is what Christmas is all about.

Bronwyn Dunnett

The Mersey Sound

As you sit here by the riverside, you'll hear the Mersey sound
and see a panorama as "Queens" and "Empress" glide -
straight into "princes" dock - rising on the tide
we've built a new cathedral where heavenly voices sing
and we've even got a tunnel - that was opened by a king
A "Liver" bird, pigeons at Pierhead
but the "Liver" Bird is never heard!
Flower girls and barrow boys - you could be down at Kew
and, if we look and sound inscrutable we've lots of pathos too
we've got the lot, we made the scene, we've comics by the score
'Tis said you have to be one - that's Liverpool folklore!
There's a brashness and a humour, that's seldom found elsewhere
it's years of working on the docks, insisting we still care
of keeping it alive - for this is Merseyside!
We've so much to be proud of, singers who've played it cool
who made a name here and abroad - and they all came from the Pool
and many strange tales told, of Lime street in its glory
and ladies who were bold!
We've many colours, races and creeds, and "scouse" is one of our
favourite feeds
so drop by and look around you and you'll hear the "Mazy" sound.

M. Griffiths

Death

He sat in his chair with ease. At his foot was Sounder, his
faithful companion, his only companion. The wood crackled in the fire
as its sparks flew into the air. Alone they sat in the quiet of the
night. The house was dead, it had been that way for over five years.

He began to rock as he scratched the ear of his friendly partner.
He sat up late that night, rocking and thinking, silently as though
the world had never heard sound before. Later on, he managed to drag
his weary bones one last time to the bed where he lay, peacefully.
Beside him lay his devoted pal. Who too lay down to rest. The two
slept silently through the night. So silent was their sleep it seemed
as though the whole world had stopped moving at their very feet.

When the first glimmer of light tiptoed through the open window,
a ray was cast upon the two sleeping silhouettes. They slept on
peacefully. For a different light is what they saw. It filled their
thoughts and souls with a happiness they had never felt before.
Quietly, they drifted off together, past all evil and sorrow they
had ever known.

Later that day, when the sun was high and the world was alive, a
smile could be seen upon their faces. A smile so calming it looked
heavenly. For there, lay the bodies of a frayed old man and a weary
dog together, in happiness.

Shireen Khattak

Shadows Of Death

The morning dew glistened brightly on the green grass,
And in the silence of the morning, the river gently flowing,
A cloud of mist circling over the waters still surface,
The valley was alive with all the aspects of spring.

The water rippled gently, as a breeze blew a path through the mist,
Birds sang happily in the leafy branches of the trees,
Embankments cascading handfuls of flowers, reflecting in the glassy water,
As the mist parted, a new vision could be seen.

The swans, so graceful, gliding on the waters surface,
Like married couples holding hands, their necks entwined,
In the peace and tranquillity of the valley they danced for each other,
Showing their love, in love's own way.

Then as if by a cruel fate the female was dead,
Darkness cast shadows over the once beautiful valley,
The trees filled with sadness, like statues of stone,
The meadows and embankments held only wilted flowers.

The females mate, mourned for love's own loss,
Now he was suffering and the valley suffered too,
The bony, twisted branches of the trees, grasping at the life that was left,
The swan was to suffer no longer and joined his true love in death.

Jeanette Marshall

Save Nature

A little boy once had a strange dream
He saw gloomy desolate and dreadful scenes
First he saw a barren land
That must have been a greedy man
Who took away all the trees
The wood from the forest he has seized
Then he heard cries of animals
They were killed and nature was dull
Next he saw smoke and people suffering
In pollution we all will sink
Man builds big industries
Some workers suffer from diseases
He crushes a beautiful flower
Only to erect the same old tower
He ignores wild life
And later cuts them with a knife
The boy wonders if we can save nature
Yes, we must for our future
All is lost if nature is destroyed
Let's hope tomorrow we do not cry

Shital Morjaria

Enchanted Voyage

I saw a wondrous sailing ship
Dipping through a moonlit sea
And dreamt the treasure in her hold
Could thrill me to eternity

Not tall but dainty was her trim
And fair for all the world to see
Her silvered passage through the waves
Enthralled, entranced, enraptured me

Marooned, I had not dared to think
She'd turn towards my shadowed place
But moonbeams wrought a magic spell
And joined our stars in time and space -

Enchanted voyages we went
Yet scarcely seemed to leave the shore
Our journey through love's firmament
Will live with me forevermore.

Forevermore I saw us sail
Far beyond all mortal bounds
Cast in a moon-dripped fairy spell
In realms where shimmering moon-thoughts dwell

Michael Hildred

Good Guidance

Hatred is a sinful emotion,
Not to be fostered or taught,
To turn our cheek is the proper devotion,
And revenge must never be sought,

Go with peace, understanding and teach love,
Never hide nor harbour a grudge,
Always seek the good guidance from above,
And upon others never act as judge,

Pray for help, to guide those that need most,
Listen carefully, but no side stand upon,
Try the Christian approach to the problem,
Follow good teachings and the commandments act on,

God's good words must be your only weapon,
Upon violence you never must stray,
With good faith you must surely rely on,
And on the right road you will stay,

Remember hatred is a sinful emotion,
Never to be adopted or taught,
To turn your cheek is the proper devotion,
And revenge must never be sought.

Michael John Hurley

Our Garden

We love our little garden 'though it isn't very big,
There's just enough to potter in 'though not enough to dig,
We fill in all the spaces with this and that and those,
And anyone who calls on us is welcome to a rose,
There's a willow in the middle where it's nice and cool to sit,
And a fish pond with a lily and a plastic duck in it,
The fish looked lovely swimming round and grew so nice and fat,
But they're no more I'm sad to say; why? You'll have to ask the cat,
The birds come for their titbits from many miles around,
We like to sit and watch them, trying not to make a sound,
We also have a lot of frogs who come out in the rain,
There's always lots to look at even through the window pane.

Joan Rogers

Courage

Courage is a must for us, who travel the road of life
With its ups and downs, its tears and joys, and peace and tranquillity
So thank our God who gives us life and blessings all from above
For the gifts are God are priceless, let us all use them here...
See the beauty of an early morn, with the sun rising high in the sky,
Hear a blackbird sing in the old apple tree, you know that God is nigh

On through the day the hours pass away, till we come to the evening anew.
Catch a glimpse of the first evening star, high in the heavens above,
Stand and stare, say a prayer to your Father above, who gives
us these treasures with love, so it will be day out and day in
Just think how lucky you are, to live and to laugh, to love most
of all, and give what is best from your heart.

Thank you Father above, sing His praises with love,
And promise to do better things,
With a prayer in your heart just carry on,
Along life's road, straight back to Him.

K. M. Biddle

Nineteen Ninety-Four

Ten years too early George,
that's all that's wrong.
Big Brother watches everyone and all that goes on.
Poverty on the outside and riches for the rich
Non-conformists beaten up lay bleeding in the ditch.
Little beeps identify where your car can be found
imprisonment for anyone who hangs out in a crowd.
Soon there'll be no talking and our minds will disappear.
Not tomorrow but give it, perhaps,
Another ten odd years.

White-washed walls scream "Read me?" But there's nothing to be read...
Those with minds scream "Kill me?" But the others are all dead...
The book's near completion if you look at the central core:
George Orwell's minute mistake;
It's Nineteen Ninety-Four.

Joanne Lee

Lost In Winter

With a turning of the season, the afternoon slips into night
and the losing of the light transforms the homeward journey.
What was sustaining joy of changing scene
and colour combination, the eye's delight, is instead
a road race, chasing anonymous red glows on the road ahead.
The world is lost to the lonely traveller, trapped in a moving pool of light,
as bus or train pushes onward into night.
No longer the passing green and gold of nature's treasure:
lawns, leaves, light lost.
We look in upon ourselves unseeing, unconnected,
forced into an inner world coloured by the losses of the past.
Looking in or looking out in darkness;
we stare unseeing at our own reflection in the glass.
Beyond, the darkness holds the same forms as before
but losing touch, we're out of touch
until, uneasy, we discover, like the blind,
that touch reveals what darkness hides.
No longer lost in Winter's monochrome and melancholic mind,
but joining, holding, dancing in a new dimension,
unafraid to leave the light behind.

Lottie Hewitson

The Cherry Spray

The breath of spring blows softly down
the glittering acres of the sea,
for winter's tides have turned, and larks
sing to the blue infinity.

Beside the gentle foaming edge
of shallow falling waves, I stand
in silent dream and watch the dark
shadows drifting on the sand.

How swiftly see them change from gloom
to gaiety, like dancing moods
which chase across my heart, leaving
little but their solitudes.

Around my feet, the gentle ripples
play in pools of golden light,
while laughing children in the foam
tumble white to softer white.

Now visions fade, and darkness falls
to close the blue fringed eyes of day,
how brief this dream, when through the night
crimson stains the cherry spray.

Jean Mary Orr

Oh Dear - He's Married Now!

I want to say goodnight right now
Pity you are not here
Midnight, moonlight, mist and love
Oh, why can't you hear
What I have to say to you, when I need to speak
Of dreams, of love, of wanting you
Tomorrow will not do!

Morning is not conducive to warmth and comfort
Softness, care and love
And bed and curling close,
Wrapping limbs, dimness, soft confusion.

Morning is lightness, clarity
Office desks and competence
Hard chairs, efficiency,
Cool, rational talk of love
As if it were an ordinary thing
Stripped of the surreality of night
I can't wait until tomorrow
I want to tell you now!

Jacqueline Wright

Teenager

Sometimes I feel like shouting out in anger,
Sometimes I want to let out tears,
Sometimes I feel so wild and free,
Sometimes I feel quite happy.

My parents think a genius of me,
Expecting A's on my report,
They don't accept B's or C's,
They just want me to be the best.

Sometimes I feel like a slave in the house,
Washing the dishes, mopping the floor.
My parents say it's best for me,
But I am just too blind to see.

Because I love to chat to my friends,
I'm always on the phone.
To me the phone is like a friend,
But to my parents a huge phone bill.

My room is always a mess,
I can't even find my bed.
My parents wonder how I can live there,
I tell them it's the best place on earth.

Ethel Okorji

Spider

And now the spider's work is done,
Each glittering, dangerous strand is spun.
    She breathes and relaxes a little shutting each of her eight eyes in turn,

As it is her hundredth time she has no more to learn.
    Just waiting for the chosen one to come to her,
She picks up one of her complex legs and smooths down her
    hair-like fur.

The white silver birch tree looks beautiful in the morning light,
And the small insect is flying straight into eternal night.
    It is caught in the diamond dew prison.
And the spider from her hiding place has already risen.
    She wraps it in her silky cloth—taking great care,
And before she goes further—utters a small prayer.
    God pardons her as nature's course must always carry on,
But then the sunlight filters . . . And then it is gone.
    The hand comes from a boy and crushes her almost perfect
    body like tissue paper,
Then he laughs and runs—happy because of the pain he made her,
She lays crushed and still after wondering why? What was it was for?
And God looks down from above with scorn, coughs and says no more.

Natasha Bruce

Drifting And Dreaming

I drift around from town to town
And upon my brow there lies a frown.
I sit alone. Not a friend to call my own.
In doorways and alleys and on pavements too.
Just me and my shadow sharing the same old view.
My hands in my pockets and my eyes fixed to the ground.
Thinking to myself what I could buy if I had a couple of pound
A sandwich or two and a cup of tea.
Please dear Lord let someone take pity on me
Come nighttime I don't know what to do. It's then I really feel
The cold and my skin goes so blue
I climb into my cardboard box and put newspaper all around
Dreaming about tomorrow and wondering
Will I ever again lift my head up off the ground
My family and I have long since parted that's when
I fell to pieces and was left broken-hearted.
Through no fault of my own I was left without a home
So dear Lord be with me whilst I am living in this hell
And maybe tomorrow someone somewhere will show me
That little bit of heaven I once knew so well.

Valerie Thorpe

Longing

Come to me when dreams enfold me
and stay with me, the long night thro,
For I am weary of the lonely days,
and with the longing that I have for you,

Come lay you, oh so close beside me.
Let me feel you near me, oh and then
The memory of the night will help me
Face my lonely world again.

Until you come there is no joy in living,
The world for has lost its glow
And I have nothing worth the giving until I cease to suffer so.

And when you come bring with you
The happiness and joy that once we knew
Dreams will seem like reality
When I am once again with you and when our dreaming tryst is over
And you return to your strange world apart,
Take with you all my love and longing and hold it to your silent heart.
So come to me when I am dreaming, happy together we will be
The long night thro, for I am so weary of the lonely days,
And with the loving that I have for you.

Ivy Louise Audley

439

What Good Is A Heart

What good is a heart when it's always broken
What good is a heart when it's torn apart,
What good is a heart when all it does is crumble,
Will the mending ever start?

To give it to anyone is foolish,
To mistreat it could leave you in pain,
To abandon it could leave you lonely,
Making it harder to start again.

Why does it hurt so much when you receive that first blow,
Why does the pain linger on for days even weeks on end,
Why doesn't the pain stop, will it ever end?

The only protection is to build up a wall,
preparing it for when you receive the fall.
It's better not to have one, I think do,
To avoid getting hurt don't let go.
Keep it safe never give it away,
But lonely ever you will stay.

Wenona Elie

Jack Frost

When Jack Frost throws his coat of steel
Across the cold grey stream,
And a sprinkling of icing on the grass
And pathways can be seen.
We know it's time to don our hats
Our scarves and mittens too,
Warm boots and socks upon our feet
As we go out our friends to meet.

The air is cold our noses red
Curtains are drawn on those still abed,
The mist so silent creeps away
And the Earth awakens to a glorious day.
Birds start to sing and take flight
As the sun bathes the land in a glistening light,
Jack Frost bows and turns to leave
For again tonight his spell he'll weave.

Diane P. Magrath

Grandma

I pray to you most nights, I hope you can hear,
Between everything I say there's always a tear,
All the bad times I'll regret,
But the good times I'll never forget,
For me you have always been there,
And when God took you it was so unfair,
I'll always have a broken heart which will never mend,
You were not just my grandma, you were my best friend,
Today's your birthday, no cards we can give to you,
No cuddles warm and true,
All that is left to say
Is how we wish you were here on the special day,
Lie down and rest,
You've gone to the place which is the best.

Sarah Smith

Inspired

It's early morning, I lie in bed
Jumbled words whirl inside my head.
What are they saying, what do they mean?
Was I asleep or was it a dream
My body cries out, I am so tired
But my unconscious mind has become inspired -
To write a Poem for you

Pick up paper, pen by bed
What were those words inside my head
I cannot think now I'm awake
Jotted words on paper no sense do make
Back to sleep, I am so tired
As I slip away my unconscious mind inspired -
To Dream a Poem for you.

A. M. Moseley

What Will Tomorrow Bring

I lie here on my bed,
Thinking of what might happen tomorrow,
What will tomorrow bring,
happiness, sadness, love or joy

We can't ever predict what tomorrow will bring,
we have to take what is given to us with a smile,
we can't ever look back.

What happens today,
won't happen tomorrow,
we have to take everyday one step at a time.

We may wake up tomorrow a different person.
Some people never wake up or see another day,
We are lucky for what we are and where we live,
we can't ever change people for what they are
     or what they look like.

We have to respect and love people wherever,
     or whoever they are,
from the bottom of our heart.

Sarah Spinks

Night Life

One and two, baby done a pooh,
three and four, baby done some more.

Baby start to whimper, baby start to cry,
wakes her mummy and daddy up,
Mummy gives a sigh.

"I did it last, your turn now."
Daddy not too sure of this,
feeling sick now.

Daddy take the nappy, drop it in the bin.
Put another clean one on and tuck the baby in.

Nighty - night baby,
Nighty - night daughter,
baby go to sleep again,
Three, two, one.

Daddy back in bed now, Mummy gets a cuddle,
baby is awake again, lying in a puddle.

Up you get, Mummy, baby done a wee.
No sleep for you tonight, no siree!

Kelly Marie Bentham

The Heron's Cry

When night enwraps the river in its blue embrace
and gently dusts away the trees and reeds
and only just allows the shiver of the stars
to be reflected in the deep...
When sounds become hush hush
the rustle of birds wings
the lapping lisp of waves
is all we hear,
I lie in wait: the heron must be near.

I just lie still and concentrate
and stay awake. Until
a sudden splash! Its feet lash out.
I hear its wings unfold
and my mind's eye
can see its slender beak.
It opens and yes, there it is:
the heron's cry!
Its rawness tears the night apart.
Just once. Then silence closes over it.
Now I can sleep. —

Ena Okma

Slender Thread

Emotion covers her like the clothes she wears
and attracts my fond and sensitive eyes
which peer deeper than superficial stare
to the tangled tapestry of her soul-
a delicate pattern, woven and complex
of bright colour mix and dark background mood
to reveal outward signs that somehow reflect
a gentle rage which is simmering within.

Glib-spoken voice shoots a measured wit
that stretches across labyrinth paths to foil
the unfeeling who would callously inflict
lasting hurt with their trespass words;
but tame laughter and wild tears
occur or follow with each twist and turn
in pursuit of self-worth, and stalked by fear
of this tenuous life, in an uncertain world...

Kevan Beach

Crystalline Pain

Pondering, on how strange it is,
That in one tiny drop of crystal
Can be condensed
Years of mindless frustration.

The build-up to that swell of water,
The ease with which it slips away,
Sliding slowly down a path of turmoil,
Then dropping away, forever lost.

The pain, the loss, the grief,
All there, in pure liquid form.
The comforting coldness as it slips away,
Leaving just a silent memory.

Yearning for just one more,
Longing to set another free,
But pain has built its barrier;
Frustration reigns once more.

Jhone Cunnane

The Lamp-Lit Lives Of The Young

The tears of God frozen into stars,
By the cold indifference of cosmic delight,
Steer to salvation the saints of the city
Who rage along roads of crumbling pity,
Their towers recede into the derelict night.

The lamp-lit lives of the young,
Scattered across streets like sacred stones,
Temples dressed in tattered sleep
And the ragged dreams of a raging tongue.

Every storm-beaten stone is a story untold,
Fossilized by the stare of an arrogant eye,
Or the hapless sigh of the passer-by
Who proffers a prayer of pocket gold,
Then looks to the light of the star-meshed sky.

Dean Poland

The Killers Of The Sea

Red puffs of cloud appear in the dark blue sea
as the harpoon struck with such force
To break through any object in its path
The killers just sit there, watch and laugh.

The whale without a hope of survival
Struggles with every last ounce to swim free.
But the killers have him now
The killers of the sea.

The mighty warrior is dragged upon the boat
And there he is slit from tail to throat.
Deep under the sea you can hear the school cry and yelp
Knowing that nothing will ever help.

That mighty whale is now someone's tea
All because of those killers, those killers of the sea.

Eleanor Ann Jones

In The Arms Of Sleep

The ending of the days, the beginning of new fears
The constant lies that are told, the forever falling tears
And the secrets that I hold cannot remain the same,
Because you don't ever seem to feel the agonizing pain.

Well I'm tired of this day, 'cause this day seems to repeat itself,
As my whole painful life and there's this knife which cuts deeper,
By every second of the hour.

So glad you left me here alone
If you stare long enough at this hourglass
You'll see the sand has turned to stone
I think time has frozen still
Now I feel immortal.

Now the night sky has fallen,
But I can't hear you calling me,
I close my eyes and there you are,
You see I'm not that burnt out falling star
Well this time the knife had cut too deep
And finally I'm in the arms of sleep.

Daphne Sofroniou

Time And Tide

For Steven

We walked, my little boy and I,
    along the sand...
    he held my hand
"Dad, nobody's ever been here before"
So we made our footprints along the shore.

    We wrote our names
    in the sand,
in giant letters... on our new land.

"Can we build a castle - will you show me how,"
"Let me finish it myself, 'cos I know now"

And as we played and laughed and walked,
the tide came in, and it was time to go.

He walked, my boy, this time with his,
    along the sand,
    hand in hand.
"Dad, nobody's ever been here before"
And life went on... along the shore.

Joe Devine

In The Name Of Love

Oh, beloved Aphrodite, Emerald jewel of hope
And Celestine herald of the Saffron dawn,
I do wholeheartedly and humbly implore you
In this dark night of shipwrecked human souls,
To remember how you, too, have loved and lost
And wept oceans of grief over your own twin flame, Adonis.

Even the greatest of us, like Solomon,
Whilst choosing wisdom over power or wealth
Have so oft' estranged ourselves from you, my love.

Oh yes! How we curse the sun for going in
When it's only our own clouds getting in the way
Of this ever-shining orb of transcendent golden light!

Do not forsake us, I beg of you; arouse the heavenly host.
Let love again rule the court, the camp, the grove
And fill our cups with that rare spirit
Of empathic human fellowship and chivalry.
And stir the embers of the sacred and eternal flame
Through the jests and antics and the chansons d'amour
Of your merry bands of troubadours.

Oh, Aphrodite, I raise my glass: "To you, and to the golden dawn."

Eric Twose

The Holiday

I decide to plan a holiday to give myself a boost
Just a week away—somewhere comfortable to stay
Peace and quiet relaxing in the sun
A few pleasant walks I thought that would be fun.

The time came around I didn't feel well
It was pouring with rain—oh! what the hell.
A trip to Hythe by taxi I had chosen the wrong day
The shops closed at one—what more can I say.

I spent a pleasant hour returned the way I came
To my surprise the sun came out turned out a lovely day.
Despite the awful weather some pleasant memories stay
Of kind and friendly people—I may go back that way.

Rita Snaith

Untitled

Are you missing your memories, are you missing your ways?
Are you missing the long and hot sunny days?
Are you missing the moments when you felt good inside
Are you missing contentment in spirit and mind?

Are you searching for love, are you searching for pride?
Are you searching for somewhere, somewhere to hide?
Are you searching for worries, are you searching for lies?
Are you searching for reasons, and reasons and whys?

Are you wishing you'd stayed, stayed in our lives?
Are you looking for sorrow and listening for cries?
Are you watching us closely and tasting your tears?
Are you wishing for peace, forgetting your fears?

Are you wishing your heart would continue to beat?
And your battles would cease to end in defeat
And your wishes and dreams may all fade away
But my memories of you forever will stay.

N. J. Darley

My Feelings

I often sit and wonder,
Why I'm still here with you.
As there's no real love around us
And I'm left feeling blue.

You show no real affection.
If I touch you, you push me away,
I try to tell you how I feel.
But you smirk and my nerves start to fray.

How I wish I could change you,
But that's an impossible task.
As you're set in your old fashioned ways
But please try is all that I ask.

Do take heed of my warning
As this will be my last,
As I'll just find me another
And you'll be the man of my past.

B. Green

Memories

We lift the lids of memory, each box a special treasure
And pick out things that bring a smile and please
A gleam of eye, a touch, those years do measure
Into reverie we sink, eyes dim, at ease.

And in that peaceful mood those friends of yore
Join in the mists of time and are with you
Search through those memories, you'll find many more
But make sure that those rich memories are true.

Were those summers all filled with joy and fun
With tennis to play and cricket to enjoy
Was weather hot and did hair bleach in the sun
When you were just a girl and I a boy.

There was also pain and grief if truth be told
But we always paint our memories in gold.

Gordon Jack Crisp

Starlight

Bright shone the starlight on that still Judean morn,
Casting its radiance on the lowly born.
Through the open doorway shepherds gaze with wondering awe,
On the Christ child sleeping on His bed of straw.

Bright shone the starlight on the wise men from afar,
Journeying onward by this God given star.
Then before the infant knelt in worship to adore,
Laid their gifts so costly on the stone flagged floor

Bright is the starlight shining down on us today.
Guarding and guiding those who see its rays
Straight from Bethlehem's manger to the hill of Calvary.
Now the infant Jesus, Christ the Lord is He.

Eunice Hulley

Lonely

I sit here alone in the gloaming,
My family are all far away,
With only the night sounds around me.
And I sigh for another lost day.

Dim scenes from the past come before me,
Long forgotten voices I hear
As I sit here alone in the darkness
And sigh for another lost year.

How quickly time rushes by us,
How quickly the years have fled
As I sit here alone at midnight
And remember friends long since dead.

There is always the hope of tomorrow,
Perhaps someone will call or just phone.
And as I sit here by the fireside
I'll find that I'm not really alone.

Such are the thoughts of an old man
Whose life span ebbs slowly away.
As I sit here alone and deserted
And dread facing another lonely day.

Michael C. McCann

Sweet Music At Dawn

Shimmering white clouds across the sky,
caught by the early morning sun,
as it shines through the tiny wisps of dawn,
to the sparkling gems in the grass below.

Then as if by a sign the sweet call of a bird,
followed by one, then two and then all,
and suddenly the air is filled with a crescendo of music,
that sweeps you, carries you, up to the skies.

Till it seems as if all the birds in the world
have joined in to sing the sweet song of the dawn.
Then as if by a mutual signal they stop,
and you are left breathless and filled with great awe,
wondering how these tiny birds of the air,
can sing the most beautiful songs you have heard.

Maureen Lake

Till Dawn

Till dawn does let us speak freely,
let us stay quiet in our solitude
before time calls,
for silence is tremendous in
darkness so still
but dawn will come rushing to
fetch away peace and darkness.

Till dawn does let us speak freely,
talk only in telepathic language
that we know.
For we must enjoy these last
moments of night,
for the dawn will come quickly
to fetch away darkness, peace and solitude.

James L. G. Verrier

The Tree

Kissed by the sky, caressed in the ground,
Majestic tall, erect, profound,
Boughs heavy laden, sway in the breeze,
Bright red berries, dark green leaves,
Giving shelter to birds in song,
Stopping to look, as I walk along,
Sun shines through making you glow,
Rain pours down helping you grow,
Strong and sturdy, loved by the earth,
Absorbing its nourishment giving you birth,
Wonderful, notorious beautiful tree,
Endearing, elegant, gloriously free.

Christine Russell

A Painted Reflection Of Life

Hanging high above our expectation
We glare into a world of another mind.
Every picture has its own story to tell
With each colour is a different thought.
Each painter explains his life by brush.
To stand peacefully and admire with joy
To capture a beautiful memory
With such grace and detail.
A world without art would be sorrowful.

Lynette Dunn

Bobi

My lovely little cat of Silvery Grey
Warmed my heart with his winning way
As I rested my head in his silken fur
And heard his happy sonorous purr
I loved him so!

His little padded paws on my shoulders would go
Because he wanted to let me know
That in his own little pussy way
There's no other way that he could say
He loved me so!

We played a game with his ping-pong ball
He ran and scampered along the hall
He dribbled the ball against the wall
That I scarcely saw the ball at all!
I loved him so!

The memory of Bobi always with me stays
Of those sweet and playful happy days
'Tis ten long years since we had to part
But his little pussy paws are etched on my heart
I loved him so!

Eva Smith

The Old Canadian Cabin

The old log cabin, nestled on the hill,
Knows that winter cold and bitter winds
Will follow the gentle month of Indian Summer.
The strong log walls still stand.

The roof was first to go,
Weakened by the weight of many snows,
Crashing at last to the floor it sheltered for so many years.
Hands that built the cabin have long since turned so dust.

Dreams filled the cabin long ago,
Dreams of golden acres ripening under the summer sun,
And of children who would play on the great flat rock
That still forms the forever doorstep.

Relentless seasons have changed the once green logs
To bleached white bones upon the virgin sod,
The dreams are gone, leaving the rotting logs,
The only monument to what once had been.

When frost brings red and yellow to the trees
Bright spirits dance across the cold winter sky,
Dust and smoke hang upon the breeze,
And Nature knows that everything must die.

Mary Lancaster

Golden Man

Where are you now, we are apart! Specks of dust scattered
on the silver sand.
The boy, the man that held my hand, that grasped my heart
within a band of happiness and love and helped me stand
Against all adversity and sorrow.

Where are you now, my love, my man?
Father, grandfather that held my hand
That loved your offspring and was so proud
Of all achievement of worth?
Scattered by us amongst the surf.

Where are you now, my love, my man?
Not for you the sodden turf,
But scattered by wind and sea and surf.
And so I hope by this last deed
A measure of my love you'll heed.

Where are you now, my love, my man?
My heart is broken as I can
No longer feel, or hold your hand.
Just wait for me on the silver sand
That I may join you, when I can,
My life, my love, my golden man.

L. E. Perren

Dawn Breaks

The little church proudly
sits high on the hill, shadows
on tombstones are all very still
an eerie sight on this moonlit night
awaiting patiently for morning light,
laughter from children wake up at dawn,
dew drops on grass on the tombstone lawn.
A radiant bride a smile on her face,
a beautiful wedding about to take place,
grandparents, watch from their graves
below, remembering their wedding years ago,
the church bells are ringing loud and clear
the ring on her finger is very sincere,
My babe has grown into a beautiful
bride, a handsome groom is now by
her side, my little girl's grown,
that's plain to see, no one
in that church is prouder than me.

Averil Millman

Reece

Reece was too young to know right from wrong,
He did not understand what was going on,
Taken from you in such a cruel way,
His spirit will be with you night and day,
The love that was given by you to him,
Was something special, it came from within,
No more pain will he have to fear,
Knowing you loved him, he will hold that so dear.

Catherine Papworth

York Minster

It stands so magnificent.
So high, so wide,
It seems it surely touches the sky.
They come in their millions
To visit this place,
And stand to wonder
At its size and grace.
They gaze entranced
At the window of the rose,
Which stood defiant when beheld.
Lightening struck like a dagger from the sky.
And tongues of flame leapt on high
York Minster on fire "Oh no" they cry.
Restored majestic, still she stands
She reigns supreme throughout the land.
Glory to God and all mankind.

P. Barrett

Michael

When you were young and daily growing,
I prayed the angels down to guard you, never knowing
that you could not recognise them.   You always turned away.
Yet in my heart I knew that you would come to God one day.
Your given name was Michael and in my dreaming
I saw you brandishing the judgment sword with others screaming
You fought my mothering and love.   You always turned away.
Yet in my heart I knew that you would come to God one day.
When you started school you were always cast the fool.
Mocked and taunted, driven to flaunt the rules.
And forced to live in a solitary vacuum.   You always turned away.
Yet in my heart I knew that you would come to God one day.
Then came the day when the sword became a gun.
A deadly weapon, bought you said, for fun.
Again I bade the angels guide you in your play.
Because I knew that you would come to God one day.

And when you stood, lonely and blood red,
among the bodies massacred and dead,
saying "God made me do it".   And you did not turn away.
I knew that you had come to Him that day.

Brenda M. Orrell

Word Waves

When life answers,
    The selfish cravings of a heart,
Does it smile,
    Putting love close, but so far apart?
When a soul laughs,
    What does the world do, but kick it back down?
When a life forms,
    Will it so live, or murderously drown?
When a god lives,
    Does it secretly, hate or abhor?
In my soul-cage,
    I'll secretly, cry evermore.

Marc Easton

The Hero

Bless the hero, let him in,
Far away from the challenge of sin,
For he is our saviour, our martyr, our Christ,
We have tried it without him but it cannot work,

Split forever by the forces of time,
Compelled to drift through a vast eternity,
Crying endlessly to stop with a longing to continue,
And still in the night the child cries.

And yet I felt as I walked that long dusty track,
Understanding that feeling never, yet wanting it more,
Still I kept going, wondering how I could have stopped,
And yet continued.

The lights are glowing, yet showing no way,
Passing taverns full of wayfaring travellers,
Who ask nothing but a gentle blanket of kindly oblivion,
To escape the perils of the journey,
And the unknown destination.

Terence Love

A Prayer For Peace

Come, God, and cleanse the sins of man from earth
With soft sweet water falling from the skies,
Your raindrops have baptized us since our birth,
Mixed with the tears that flow from tired eyes.
Come, purge this earth of man's horrific deeds,
Expel the hate and falsehood deep within
Which threatens peace, denies the poor their needs,
False peace which nuclear weapons underpin.
This planet earth, polluted, poisoned, raped,
Bears witness to the boor and beast in men,
The murder that men do in God's good name
A younger generations does again.
So come, good God, our sanity restore,
Root out the sin that makes a god of war.

John Stephenson

Ode To A Misogynist

You're a thief!
You stole my years, and, in tears,
I think of everything I might have done,
Every place I might have gone,
Every friend I might have made,
Every love I might have found.

You're a liar!
You vowed your love would never changed,
every year grow strong,
yet now you say you never loved
and cannot stand to share even one moment more,
here with me.

You're a sadist!
You revelled in my agony, gloried in your power to hurt,
gloated when, finally, I questioned the very reason for me to be.

You're a murderer!
You are killing my love for you,
for this I thank you, gratefully.
By destroying my love for you,
You are setting me free!

Maureen Delenian

The Writer's Circle

I've joined a writer's circle, it's a smashing thing to do,
You write out all your bits and bobs,
And on Monday read them through.

Ian is so helpful, he puts you right on track,
And your colleagues give you good ideas
To use when you get back.

You dash home in a hurry,
Change all your ifs to buts,
You alter this, and alter that, and end up going nuts.

No use, no use, you cry, I'll have to change the lot,
But wait, inspiration hits you, you've come up with a plot.

You dash to the computer,
Type it out like mad,
This is a real corker, the best I've ever had.

Can't wait till Monday comes,
To read it out in class,
And hear the gasps of amazement, I'm not such a silly ass.

You gaze at the screen in wonder,
Too overcome to speak,
And then you hit the wrong key, and your work goes up the creek.

Susan Belcher

For You

For you, I dedicate these words.

You were the crutch I could lean on,
When all I wanted to do was crawl.

You were my inspirational friend,
In the moment of my torment.

You were the bridge I could cross,
When the chasm of despair became too wide.

You were the light to guide my path,
When darkness shrouded my eyes.

You filled me with self esteem,
When I became racked with self doubt.

For you are my spirit, my strength, my comfort
And my inspiration.

They say that beauty is in the eye of the beholder
And I feel that I just have to tell you,
That you have set my heart on fire,
And when I look into your eyes
I see the love, I feel the love.
I want you in my life,
In my life always.

C. A. Smith

Wonders Of The Sea

Waves riding high, life in the sea
sheltering wonders unseen,
Rocks standing fast, coral reefs
spreading to unknown life such
beauty could only be seen.

Sharks seeking their prey
shell fish like castles, yet moving
gracefully
Darkness as with light gave sanctuary
to unsolved mysteries of the sea

Earth trembles, waves brought destruction
as Ice flows gave warnings
Thunder and lightning ruled the sky
Larks gave comfort, sea gulls just
Gliding the waves gracefully

Looking upwards to the sky
clouds rolled by casting shadows
on the ground.
Cliffs stood firm, sea shoves brought
memories to all around.

J. S. Mitchell

Thoughts Of Spring

The birds sat on the trees so bare,
Not a bud was showing there.
The clouds in the sky were hanging low.
I thought, perhaps there may be snow.

Sea gulls flapped their wings in flight
And screeched their sea gulls cry.
As if they were showing off their might.
To the smaller birds on high.

And as they swooped down to the ground
The birds both big and small.
Looked for food scattered around.
In answer to their call.

You see these birds must be fed.
All the year long
And the way they thank you
is by joyful song.

And as they sit on the trees so high.
The chorus that they sing
is for us to keep our spirits high,
For soon it will be spring.

V. Butcher

The World

I love the world
Its beautiful creatures,
Big or small, the lion, the tiger,
even the ant,
I love them all
But most of all I love the world.

I hate the world,
I hate the way man lives on it,
And makes cars which pollute,
And destroy the landscape
I hate man,
But I really do love the world.

I love the world,
The bright green grass
The sound of birds singing in the trees,
The bright blue sea, the fluffy white clouds,
But I also love the world a lot
So could we keep it please?

Paul Ives

Winter Dreams

I sat there, in the corner, and drifted off to sleep.
To dream of Winter scenes, and the crispness that it brings.
The Autumn leaves drift gently down,
Green, Gold and Orange upon the ground.
As Winter's hand stretches out, the wind and rain is all about.
It lashes hard upon the ground, branches twist, and turn-around.
The coldness soon comes, settling in.
Bringing snowflakes scurrying down.
Spreading crispness on the ground.
Robins dash too and fro, pecking at the ice and snow.
The long, wintry nights drag on, birds seem to have lost their song.
But soon the sun comes shining through.
Spring has come, and all is new.
Buds and shoots come forth, bringing colour to our thoughts.
I look around, and thank the Lord for giving me my sight and sound.
Smell and thought, all anew.

Joyce Bassett

Heaven

The purple skies I lie beneath, rain with purple showers,
and sleeping knights with dozing minds, rest in high-rise towers.
Pinkish shades with lemon tints, run through rippled waters,
and castle walls are bedded round, by flowers and their daughters.

Beating down across the land, while perching on the mountains,
the sunshine laughs with jolly gnomes, that stand on leaping fountains.
Carousels of pony rides, that trot along in tune,
dance around the stars at night, and round about the moon.

Glazing windows break the walls, rimmed with golden edging,
and round the castle boundaries grow, a sparkled silver hedging.
The birds around the garden fly, and sing with all their glory,
this fairy palace stands alone, each room still holds a story.

When I leave I dream to live in my eternal land,
with friends I've lost who've gone before, in a home made just of sand.
A place of rest my heaven lies, this castle in the sky,
with pretty flowers, dozing knights, and water running by.

Victoria Jayne Mercer

What Happens, Asks My Little Gnome

I sat and watched the world today, the little birds at play
The flowers seemed to dance for me as I dreamed the day away
Just then my little gnome came by on a magical unicorn
Your wildlife is in danger, and may not see tomorrow dawn.

What happens when the elephant's tusks are beads for you and me
What happens when the dolphin's dance no longer on the sea
What happens when the tiger's eye looks coldly from the wall
What happens when the wondrous sounds of the whale are no more.

The ivory beads around your neck will bow our heads in shame
And when the dolphin's dance is gone, we have only ourselves to blame
A tear will fall from the tiger's eye, and we'll drown in their pain.
And when the whales no longer call, life will never be the same.

Our wildlife, said my little gnome, needs help from you and me
Go, walk with the elephants, and see the tigers running free
Go, dance with the dolphins, hear the whales and be reborn
Before they are as rare as this magical unicorn.

Maureen Gentry-Evans

Just My Caz

The time we ourselves have spent working hard together,
Bonding our love for each other to a peak.
Out in the cold but within the open warmth of your arms.
Your understanding can be and never will be like yours.
We together we will be one, one love, one force together,
We will fight the force against us.
These words I put to paper will stay in our minds always and forever.
I think of you and love you so very much.
"As one will always have time"
As one force of love
"The force", "The Fight"
"Together To Stay"
"Marry Me Babe".

Paul B. Falloon

A Vision

She's lovely and her beauty charms
So when she smiles in her own way,
As though she opened wide her arms
And sunshine filled your heart that day.

You feel a gentle tenderness,
A sharing of a deep content
A kindly word like a caress,
A comfort and a blessing sent.

And as you gaze into her eyes
Attraction melts all awkwardness.
Their candid humour does surprise.
A feeling of great happiness.
More beauty shining in her hair
And lips that promise sheer delight.
What joy that just by being there
Makes me believe that all is right.

Oh, smile again Madonna fair!
Enrich my eyes, caress my heart.
For longingly I gaze and stare
Yet know that we must stay apart.

Graham Ryan

Life

All my life
I'd hoped for a big jolly man
To whom I could be a dutiful wife
And have children a half-score
And life would sure not be a bore
I'd live in the country
With roses round the door
And a cat or two - no more
With a shaggy dog and ponies galore
I would want for nothing more

But life's not like that
I had to score with a different bat
I've had to work in the big city
For years and years which is rather a pity

So the mistress of a married man
Was never part of the plan
So in sophisticated clothes
A smile on my face
I hide my woes
And dance on my toes

Ann Hill

Stanley McPann

There is a man named Stanley McPann
His eyes are as black as coal
He lives in the slums of London town
And is always on the dole

His cap is torn, his shoes are worn
And his coat is falling to bits
He walks over to a lush green park
And on a bench he sits

He's a lonely sort of man is Stan
With his feet tucked into the grass
He sits around looking up the birds
And watching people pass

Some folk think he's an evil man
With a knife hidden beneath his coat
He's the most evil man that has ever lived
Yet he creeps about like a stout

One day it seems his luck will change
And no longer will he be poor
He'll be living his life on an island of dreams
And Stanley McPann he will be no more

Simon Fisher

Hope

The glimmer of hope has been extinguished.
All black, except for the swirling smokiness that was hope.
Now it fills the air, choking me.
It permeates the darkness, tainting the sanctuary.

And the smoke threatens, filling and overfilling the void left by hope
The gap has been overcompensated and, as surely as the hope vanished,
the despair set in, and now smoke overwhelms me.

I have a choice.
To suffocate, or to open the window.
But the choice is not simple.
My body disobeys my mind.
My mind also disobeys my mind.
It tells my body to open the window, but simultaneously, it will not
will it to do so.

So I am doomed, by myself, to suffer, maybe to die.
I have sealed my own fate.
The perpetrator and the victim.
Survival of the fittest, and I am killing myself.

Yvonne Abrahams

A Melancholy Refrain

Whilst falling deep in reverie, through the casement one could see
the younger birds though in full growth, frolicking and sallying forth
endeavour sometimes come to nought. Then in hope, beaks open wide,
mother thrusting deep inside, the food for which perhaps she fought.

A furtive movement down below reveals a peril unforeseen
a feline monster, even though replenished from her bowl, has been
prompted by nature to devour some living creature this very hour.
Crouched along the grass with claw distended, but even though
the ancient instinct there to slay, and sate the blood just come what may.

The pretty paws with which she may have pushed a ball in innocent play.
Sheathed in fur, no menace here. Romping around so merrily
whilst tickling her stomach in a spree.
No longer harmless. Pads unreal. She slashes skywards, claws
unsheathed, razor sharp like barbs of steel. Perilous. Fatal. No repeal.

Open beaked, awaiting still, for sustenance from Mother's bill
the chick receives the coup de grace. Mother knows she must out pace
the approaching danger ever present. Remorseful but in swift ascent.

Accepting nature's ruthless fate. No other recourse but to wait, the
coming year when time will heal, her loss perchance to feel, again
the love of motherhood. God is rarely understood.

William Glasson

Settings Of Perfection

"C'mon let's go"!
"Where"?
"I dunno, let's just get out of here".

A dimly lit corridor with ceilings that never ended lead our
Path and portal, a quick gaze and swiftly to the next dependable shadow.
Thriftier than I my consort left seven of himself behind that
followed at a slower pace; all of a different colour returning
to the one. A reassuring smile broader than the face it resided met
me and slowed my pant, the welcome breeze dried my brow to
salt and made my hair feel as wet as my appetite.
A successful affair with other seekers of divine consciousness
payed passage to put our hollow guts to silence and walk this alien
land unvexed.
A time of understanding, and peace, and love, and
loneliness had unveiled itself upon us, and a sense of perplexity
drove us forward and apart and together again until the hatching
of the day made freaks of us and seclusion and sanctuary
together was the only escape from a wretched reality.

Gareth James Williams

Come To The Fair

Come and hear the wonders of the happy fairground sound,
Gaily coloured carousels are spinning round and round.
Misery and sadness have to run away and hide
While children scream and laugh as they try out every ride.
Big Dippers and Chair-o-Planes are lit up in the sky,
Roller Coasters go so fast they almost seem to fly.
Lovers share their candy floss, while walking hand in hand,
Older folk sit chatting while they listen to the band.
Bumper cars are bumping to the children's sheer delight,
Strong men with the hammer hit the peg with all their might;
If the bell rings then you'll see a smile light up their face
As another muscle man steps up to take their place.
When you look around you'll notice laughing everywhere,
So why don't you come and lose your worries at the fair?

James Hardaker

The Squire

A squire is walking down the street,
Only 20 years old but still very neat,
Polished new shoes upon his feet,
Polite to everyone that he meets.
A brand new suit of deep jet black,
And a coloured waistcoat with a golden back,
A sparkling white shirt
With not one spot of dirt.
A bow tie to match the suit,
And a warm camel jacket in the car boot,
His car is a Porsche in red,
But the cost does not stop him being fed.
As I see him climb into the driver's seat,
My heart begins to beat,
How can he not see,
Middle class people like you or me.

Caroline Woolfrey

The Beginning

With brief respite late winter sun
Unburdens faint unyielding light,
To make a show for April's glow
And birds upon their maiden flight,
With ever joyful beating wing
And hearts that herald songs of spring.

Dear love, the sweetest fields of green
And hedgerows keen to burst anew
Bring forth a need to share,
When other springs have brought their own despair.

But now, the sun again shines bright and clear
And Daffodils abound in stately and haphazard way
So brief and yet so beautiful a stay,
But never a more dear or welcome sight
For you at last are here,
To fill my word with summer's golden light.

Sheila Lear

My Visit To Earth

Being a stranger on this planet,
People here, they call it 'Earth'
I have to face a certain limit -
Once life starts with so-called 'Birth'.

Divided then in different sections:
Childhood, grown-ups, rich men, poor men
I follow rules in all directions -
Using the talents I've been given.

Within a short time, things are changing:
I am old soon, cannot run anymore
Weakness keeps me from arranging
Leisure-travels to another shore.

Achievements of mine, mostly accepted
By my friends and fellows here
At last, a coffin is selected,
I die, and simply disappear.

Ellen Poldrugo

Just A Dream

I had a dream the other day
I had walked along the milky way
Up to the heaven's beyond and far
Able to touch each twinkling star.

Was this the way heaven or only Mars
Drifting upwards along a path of stars,
Passing the moon and its bright light
Upwards and onwards through the night.

What a wonder this journey was for me
Full of surprise and tranquillity,
At last I felt at peace
No more worries, what a blessed release.

Just me and the stars, the night and the moon
Don't let this dream end, not yet, it's too soon
Please don't send me back to earth for a while
The stars and the moon, they make me smile.

Too soon I'll awake, and the dream will be gone
My trip to the heavens all over and done
Back to reality with a sudden bump
The wonders I saw, left my throat choked with a lump.

Jean McCoy

Doreen

The taste of life has been bitter,
The love of my life has been lost,
I walk the streets alone again,
No ones shoulder to cry tears on.

She saw me coming up the street,
Took pity on me, knocked me off my feet,
Love is life, incomplete.
No more coming,
No more to meet.

I was out cold on the floor,
cry out for help, Huh!
Say no more,
Doreen was there.

Night after night, bed to be battled,
Infatuated by my presence, down like a dog,
Watch out for that fire, burning log.

I get older, these days and into the night
Merry widow, O! Say what a night,
Long gone are that days of sorrow, no!! I won't be back,
Tomorrow, sad days end, Doreen!!

John Francis Davidson

Coming Home

Cruise liners adorn the picturesque harbours
Of palm tree laden Caribbean Islands
Colourful species of birds and vegetation
Amidst, dancing to vibrant steel bands

Oriental gardens, neon lights markets beckon
Breathtaking views of Hong Kong Harbour from peak
Thailand's floating market, temples, golden buddha
India's Taj Mahal, Singapore's Sentosa in humid heat

Anemones upon Australia's great barrier reef
Spectacular views of fish darting to and fro
Sydney Opera House, the Harbour Bridge
Rain forests, kangaroos, pineapples down below

African Zulu dancers, Egypt's pyramids
Rome's Colosseum, Paris' Montmartre
America's Liberty, Broadway and Manhattan
But England is in my heart

Thatched cottages, Yorkshire Dales and castles
Steeped in history, a land of stately homes
Buckingham Palace, houses of parliament, pageantry unrivalled
Home is sacred, wherever one doth roam

Diana Cramp

We Are Rich Indeed

Oh! What a wonderful world we live in,
If only people would see.
With its flowers and birds and beautiful trees,
What's more, these things are free.
The rich blue of the sky,
With cotton wool clouds passing by,
and the gentle caress of the breeze,
The song of the bird and hum of the bee.
So happy in flight to be free,
As we look and we listen
To these wonderful gifts,
In these terrible times of greed,
Be happy and thankful for the
  greatest gift of all:
The one who planted the seed.

Dorothy Simpson

Know Thyself

If you fall from position, as your relation, I get elated.
Odd? May be, but the cause and the effect are related.
My eyes are eternally engaged to find fault with others,
What about the fault with your own self? Who bothers?

It is said: the car, while driving, to view
Is the one behind the one in front of you;
So is the self. It is you that needs scrutiny,
Look at yourself, leave no bit, not even tiny.

Know thyself: Socrates would advise you,
The subject person, indeed, is you to view.

Jahangir Shahnawaz

Pride

Your hair is your crowning glory something I will not deny
The beautiful red highlights seem to lighten up the sky
At twenty you were worried as it receded from your brow
I told you I still loved you, you seemed to doubt my word
But there it stayed throughout our lives a half inch off your brow
You would stand in front of the mirror and examine every hair
In fact I think you counted them to see how many there were
It became a family joke as every one passed your chair
They would reach out and stroke it telling you it was still there
You came in from work one day I could only stand and stare
I had it shaved for charity was what you said to me
The family thought it funny I could only agree
As it grew back in all curly it was a sight to see
People passed you on the street and didn't recognise
The man who had lived amongst them for most of their lives
You decided it was better to wear it under a hat
That was until the wind blew it from your head
You raced it down the street the hat could only win
As it headed for the canal and went down with a spin
the bargee whose head it landed on looked up with a grin

Elizabeth Bell Hewitt

80 Years Ago

I sat down in the park,
Beneath the marble plynth,
and I noticed it was covered in such names!
Gerald, Mark and Philip, John, Joseph, Paul and More!
All local men, who died in vain
in the 14-18 war.

They had not come from grand homes
With heat and running water;
home entertainment had not shown its face;
Undernourished, they did not grow tall,
But they were prepared to die for all
To keep the future for the human race

And as they fell in the deep black mud
They turned their face to the stars above,
Sir! Please tell mother I sent my love...
Then silently they found their rest,
Young English men of the very best!!!

Norma Grey

The Beauty Of The Sea

The mountain breeze blows gentle thoughts across my mind
Of days long gone, just shadows now of ghosts left behind
Sweet childhood memories swirl mistily before me
Happy faces, happy voices in the place I long to be
Daffodils dance merrily around me
They bow their heads with an air of serenity
Green fields lie scattered all about me
But nothing can compare with the beauty of the sea.

The morning sun spreads golden light before me
Sweet scented air enfolds a carpet of tranquillity
White clouds embrace the still blue sky
So pleasing to the heart, enchanting to the eye
Majestic mountains rise up to kiss the morning air
Nature's garden in full bloom and beauty everywhere
Pleasures in abundance stretch before me
But nothing can compare with the beauty of the sea.

Maureen Harrison

Au Revoir

Now the last chance has flown.
No more the downcast head into coastal winds,
As we seek the side walkers on the shore.
No more salt-licked lips, bitter ranking
To start the flow of saliva onto punished tongue.
Oyster catchers screaming our leaving
As they hover over the shoreline.
Beak sand deep searching, thrust for prey.
To leave this scene, yet to return.
Unchanging tide, well placed memories.
Till the sun comes out again on lazy summer days,
Heat mist skyward now, draws the chill into the Bay.
Au revoir.

Anne Melling

The South China Seas

As I looked out on the South China Seas
With their gentle swell and very light breeze
Junks and sampans were dotted everywhere
Some in triangles some in squares.

What are they doing? someone is heard to say
They're fishing of course with nets they do lay
The boats zig and zag but soon that will stop
To reel in their nets and gather the stock.

But now all the boats are coming together
The sea is changing and so is the weather
So it's full speed ahead back to their haven
With boats that are low and heavily laden.

The junks in the bay are pulling down sail
To ride out the storm a force ten gale
But at last it has passed and the sun is shining
With the sea again gleaming like a silver lining.

T. W. Hutchison

Comfort Of A Friend

Did the songbirds ever sing you a song?
Did they ever help you to get along?
Did the sun ever shine when you were blue,
And you knew it was shining especially for you?

Did you ever laugh when you wanted to cry?
Did you ever live when you wanted to die?
Did you ever stay sober when you should have been drunk?
Did the boat stay afloat when it should have sunk?

Have you ever won a fight you should have lost?
Have you ever seen an angel when it should have been a ghost?
Have you ever whispered when you wanted to shout?
Have you ever wondered what it's all about?

Did you ever find comfort in your best friend?
Did they talk till your broken heart was on the mend?
Did you ever wonder who to turn to?
I hope it's me, because I'll always need you.

Cheryl Hamilton

Loneliest Hour

A shooting star over head,
a dying man begins drawing his final breath,
in no-man's land, with the surrounding smell of death.
Feeling life slipping out of his reach,
his heart is slowing down to only a few beats.

The veil of death begins to cover his face,
the reaper is coming, taking him and his comrades
to another place.
The sound of gunfire carries beyond his ear,
thinking of his children, shedding a tear.

The loneliest hour of his life,
laid there waiting for death to arrive,
His eyes close, never to open again,
their deaths were not to have been in vain.

In eighty years to come, poppies shall grow,
where he and his comrades fell in the snow.
The poppies will bloom and flower,
for the men who died in their loneliest hour.

C. Leith

Rest In Peace To Survive The Chaos

The life I live is not a lie,
Just a masking of the truth.
But what's the cost of such deception,
When I look in the mirror do I see my reflection?

Is the truth I hide now buried forever,
The real me dead and gone?
Was my soul too weak to survive the test,
A mercy killing for the best?

And so what you see before you today
Is all there remains to be seen.
An image created, an empty shell,
My soul at peace, nothing left to sell.

Beth Whiskerd

Watchful Architect

Oh misty morn of Autumn day,
with air so pure and golden ray,
revealing gossamer silken thread,
amid the brambles and privet hedge.

Woven veils in terraced rows,
intricately built, with pride, they grow;
and rounded hall with a hundred rooms,
stands out, to dominate the building boom.

Their beauty, made I know not how,
in the foliage and on the bough.
Held in suspension, by single threads,
set to claim one who least suspects!

Mary Day

Is This Goodbye?

The feelings that run wild through my mind and out of sight,
Feelings of such hopelessness and feelings of such fright,
I don't want to imagine living without you by my side
I want to stop these thoughts that your feelings have all died.
I can't stand the way we argue, I can't do it anymore
My mind is so mixed up and my heart is getting sore
I'll do anything and more for you, you know I always will,
So let down your defences and tell me how you feel.
Please don't take out hassles and your stresses all on me,
If you really paid attention, how sad I was you'd see,
I never want to lose you but you're driving me away,
I don't know where we're going but I really want to stay,
Can't you see you're hurting me, you're tearing me apart
I'd lie for you, I'd die for you—You're breaking up my heart.
Treat me as an equal, not something off the floor
Come lay with me, come stay with me, come love me now once more.
I know that I'm not perfect and sometimes I am to blame
You loved me once the way I am. Can't you once again?

Stephanie Pinder

Castles Within

Your home is your castle, a fact I am told,
Inheritance for offsprings when labelled as old!
Where then is my inheritance? I question, I sigh,
No job so no income, Alas! I can't buy . . .

My Castle is the streets, a roof woven with stars,
My bedroom's a doorway lit up by your cars.
My food is by chance, if there's some to be found,
Little and unoften my heart sinks to the ground.

I remember a Castle, in my dreams as I sleep,
A fairy tale or reality, I'm not sure as I weep,
Yet I gladden in spirit as with a kindness I'm blessed,
As a parcel I'm handed, now I'm a person well dressed!

A thick wool jumper, shoes, socks, hat and coat,
Gloves for my blue hands a warm scarf for my throat.
Jewels indeed for a king with no crown,
My doorway Is my castle, I'm no longer down . . .

Yes the kindness of others are with me this night,
As the winds howl around me I know I must fight,
(Armed with food for the body, now clothed warm to the feet)

For . . . all those who are homeless and their castle's The Street . . .

B. Carr

Appetite For Destruction

Swirling endlessly; suspended infinity
A sleepless reserve with isolated dreamers
Glassy depths own a fearful temper
Unexplored heights surrounded by nebulous mist
The Flawless Architect satisfies his desire.

Thoughtless neglect; Inanimate minds
Convoluted masses drenched in corruption
Hopeless ambitions fade like a timeless moment
Onlookers and passers-by captivated by the collapse
They once awed with wonder, now they wonder why.

Unsuccessful experiments, thorough investigations
Poetic injustices haunt the starving innocent
Chemistry: The study of pollution
Now award yourselves with the severest penalties
Once perfect, now withering, decaying, perishing.

Immediate action; prevention required
National disaster on an international scale
Panic buttons depressed: Danger - Red Alert
Can our evergreen heritage be restored?
Six days to create, a lifetime to destroy.

Andrew D. Hurley

Those Were The Days

I sit here alone, looking out to sea,
I am thinking of the life, that used to be,
There were no jet aircraft flying in the sky,
No loud roar of motorcars, passing me by.

There was no fear of muggings out on the street,
Only a lonely old policeman, slowly pounding his beat,
The youngsters thought of the many things they could do,
Unlike today's youth, hiding in corners and sniffing glue.

Doors and windows could be left open wide,
Family and friends would be welcome to come inside,
Today we are scared of what we might find,
Of theft and damage, in a home left behind.

There was no way of knowing if some men were gay,
or did we hear of some women acting that way,
Or of drugs smuggled in, which were destined to kill,
Only of drugs prescribed, when we were ill.

I look back and think of those good old days,
Which we thought they were, in our sort of way,
Who knows, perhaps my parents have sat here like me,
Thinking of their past, that used to be.

Leonard J. Negus

449

The Sands Of Time

Walking on the sands of time,
The world's oceans to be mine.
Wind flows through my hair,
Whispers, secrets everywhere.
Waves crash, an endless flow,
Never stopping, newly grown.
The depths of the ocean, locked by a key,
Creatures of the deep, never free.
Footsteps left in the sands,
Wandering through the pastured lands.
Sands of time clasping tight,
The seasons flow through day and night.
Holding in the future, present and past,
Lingering on, their shadows cast.
The world ends where the sun rose,
The door to freedom is always closed.
Trees forsaken, by the death,
Of the last person's lonely breath.
A new world, the old to fade,
For the sands of time to be made.

Sarah-Louise Elizabeth Hamlyn

Finland Farewell

Farewell to your forests, all virgin and green,
Farewell to your cities, the finest I've seen,
And to your islands like jewels most rare
In archipelagos rugged and bare;
I'll long for the Arctic horizons so vast,
Where big rivers flow and whose currents are fast,
Also Helsinki and Tampere too,
Kuusamo, Koli and Punkaharju;
Farewell to your lakes whether east, south or west,
Farewell to my Finland, your land I love best.

J. J. R. Cockburn

The Fisherman

Flowing, flowing, the river's flowing
On its journey to the sea
And on its banks the men stand waiting
To catch the fish, that swim so free

They stand for hours casting their lines
In the sunshine, cold or rain
And if they fail to catch their prize
They'll return tomorrow, and start again

To us it's just a relaxing hobby
To them it's a war, of patience and tactics
To lure the fish to a waiting hook
And take it from freedom, to a waiting basket

To then go home with pride and achievement
That years of experience won the day.
But to spoil it all with that same old story
By telling their friends of the ones that got away

Robert Sibbald

Looking Ahead To: A Wonderful Cleansed Earth

What sheer beauty to behold,
The towering mountains, oh so bold,
Nooks and crags and snow-white peaks,
And many wandering, grazing sheep.

Far in the valley down below,
Sparkling, rushing, all a glow,
Water weaving, cool and clear
Over large stepping stones and weir.

On either side, tall waving trees,
Across the meadow, humming bees.
The sun sheds rays of warmth and light,
A group of birds hover, then take flight.

The scene is one of serenity and peace,
For God has caused all wars to cease.
No more will 'man' pollute the land,
The earth is cleansed by God's own hand.

F. Cooke

There Is A Better Way

He was a keep-fit fanatic,
Black belt Judo, a jog in the gym,
A swim in the pool, then a walk in the woods with me.

We climbed Knocknarea one magical summer evening
And Benbulben was next on the agenda.

Mountains inspired in him a sense of culture,
And he assured me of his deep affection
For the plays of Samuel Beckett,
And casually discussed the merits
Of "Endgame" and "Waiting for Godot".

I felt a sense of déjà-vu
And wondered what was his endgame,
And why Godot inspired him to wait.

After a long night of interminable boredom,
When I fluctuated between "The Cry" by Edvard Munch
And the blessed relief of hara-kiri,
He presented me with a video, "There is a Better Way"
And as the P.V.P'S and the B.V.P'S came tumbling down
Around my ears, like my illusions, I realized that it was pyramids,
Not mountains, that inspired him and that *his* way was "Amway"!

Kitsy Brady

Pages Of Treasure

Where do you start, when you wish to read,
There are Libraries and Book Shops, full for your need.
Words all on paper, stories to tell,
Books on a shelf, many to sell.

Find a special moment to sit and relax,
Especially for exams, should you wish to pass.
Books full of treasure, and knowledge to share,
Stored in books, some very rare.

Books full of mystery, some full of love,
Words whispered softly from God above.
Thrillers and mysteries, history so deep,
Many good stories for you just to keep.

So many interests and hobbies too,
All stored in pages just for you.
Words making chapters, to give so much pleasure,
Authors, sharing all their thoughts to measure.

If you can make time, pages to turn,
You'll find stories of wisdom, so much to learn,
To bring to mind a story told,
For you to store in your mind and hold.

Sandra Bramall

Trapped

A sunken face
A dark cloud
A lonely place
No one allowed

If I open up and let you in
I'll destroy my only friend
The one who tells me food is a sin

Is it for attention?
But I know that's so untrue
I'm caught in a trap
Yet no one understands just what I'm going through

I live in guilt yet I can't explain
Death draws nearer
As each day is spent in constant pain
In fact I want to eat but it seems so hard to do
As I'm frightened of becoming someone new

Food I long to enjoy
Yet my friend won't allow me to
All it does is destroy
And I wouldn't wish it upon you.

Alyson Bointon

With None To Share

Long I sit my thoughts despair
alone in silence . . . with none to share
My hopes, desires all seem forsaken
Comes the dawn as night has spaken
Words of love . . . with none to share
My dream it seems will ne'er come true
for ever leaving, ever parting
  ever losing, ever marking
Times we had when still we cared
I find it hard with none to share
My trust, my fears, my true devotion
with a friend whose heart's emotion
Gave her love to one who sits
and waits alone . . . with none to share

Garry Courtnell

Charming Elusive Confident Confidant Who?

Oh perfect husband, dearest person to my heart
I never can be with you, we have to stay apart.
Feelings always near the surface, never to betray.
You wouldn't have me with you, wouldn't let me stay.

Oh perfect husband, ideal family man, the time we
spent together, was any ever mine? If we could
spend tomorrow just like yesterday, but thankfully
my memories will never go away.

So perfect husband, I truly understand why you
chose the other woman whose ring is on your
hand. You chose the other woman, only yours to
choose, cherish the other woman, her love you'll
never lose, and stay the perfect husband, it was
never meant to be. Most perfect, perfect husband,
if you had chosen me.

Sheila Toms

If God Went On Strike

The world would stop turning
If God went on strike
There would be no day, only night
And everything would be dark not bright
There would be no sun or no moon
And the rain would no longer fall
In fact there would be nothing at all
The rivers and seas would all dry up
And the stars would no longer shine
And there would be no winter or summer time
Time would stop, it would come to a halt
And the world would curl up and die
And so would you and I.

Cherie L. Langslaff

Beauty And Us

Dad had a motorcycle combination.
A Beauty, he'd proudly say, B.S.A.
Engine very impressive.
Roared, when kicked into action.
Can't remember how many horses we had.
Thundering, Big, and strong.
Pulled us to our destination.

We liked going to Brighton.
50 miles there, 50 miles back.
An easy run for our journey.
Crawling through Tooting and Croydon.
Warming up to Dorking, and Crawley beyond.
To the new duel carriage way.
Thottle open, picking up speed.
Pounding along so excitingly.
AA, Patrol, salutes, coming fast.
Whines and Zoomsssss going past.
The deep steady throb of the engine.
Humming and tuned, strangely calming, satisfying.
As we lick the miles to Brighton town.

Joyce Barry

All My Love

I love you so, I love you so
And every day my love does grow,
My love is bigger than a tree
And it will burn eternally,

The symbol of love is a beautiful red heart
And if you were to leave mine would fall apart,
There are many different ways of showing your love
And one day if you do it, it may raise you above,

I held it all back in the dark
When all it needed was a single spark,
When you're near me the clouds do part
And let the sun shine on my heart,

Your eyes are like a river
"Oh" they make me shiver,
All the time I was in the dark
And when I saw you I felt the spark.

Phillip J. Howarth

Virgin Of Life

The days of your years will collide with strife,
You'll forever remain a virgin of life, they'll accumulate
with hustle bustle all you'll see is life's little tussle.
It will utter no words not a hush—and capture you
till you capsize in a blush—and all your senses
shall hurry, rush, until your heart is trampled—with a crush.
The days of your youth will collide with strife,
You'll forever remain a virgin of life. You'll seek
A night—that remains disguised in a day, you'll never
speak wise words to say, forever you'll be unwise
Tempted—and shall stay that way, until knowledge
You do regain, and so shall cease innocence and
You shall begin to feel human pain—if forbid
Knowledge you do not—cannot regain, then you'll
Forever dwell in the clutches of the tempted and
Unwise and your innocence—immaturity no matter
How hard you try to mask it—shall always
Be your true disguise.
The days of your years will collide with strife,
You'll forever remain a virgin of life.

Amanda Salmon

Kick Off

Football! Not for poets you might think
but after the game there is always the drink
then to discuss the next game
to plot your strategy and achieve fame
all who play want the cup
that's what keeps them on the up and up
no one is defeated they enjoy the game
from start to finish the mud and the pain
the support of the fans who never let them down
following faithfully from town to town
no game is as great than when you hold up the cup
you know you've made it, you are on the up cheers!

Daphne Mahoney

Childhood

Childhood—with its everlasting summers.
Snow in winter, sledging with our cheeks aglow.
Rules to be obeyed without enquiry.
Safe and sure our lives were—children long ago
Parents, we were certain, always loved us—
Planned and worried, shielding us from harm unknown.
Food we did not care for—and our manners.
Sunday school, and being in the dark alone.
Time crept by—anticipation endless—
For Christmas, Easter, birthdays, two weeks by the sea,
For visitors and visits—and the pleasures
Of cosy fireside, a book or toast for tea.
How we longed for time to push us forward
To the adult world we thought so free and fine
All that haste—and we would lose forever
The simple joys and sorrows of that childhood time.

H. Brenda Allan

Josh's Green Wellies

There was a boy called Josh, who had wellies bright green.
They were the most peculiar wellies that anyone had ever seen.

Then one night when he went to bed strange things began inside his head
The wellies went dancing around the room, the wellies blew smoke and then zoom.

They shot to the ceiling up and down, as Josh stepped inside in his dressing gown.
Instead of walking through the door, the wellies zoomed right off the floor.

They flew to the moon and back again, Josh said these wellies must be insane
As soon as Josh looked at his wrecked old roof, Josh heard the sound of a horse's hoof.

To his amazement he was in Cowboyland, there were cowboys' guns and lots of sand.
He was riding on a horse dark brown, as it rode along right out of town.

As the dust flew at his heels, he felt the need of a decent meal.
So he stopped off at Burger king, then voices around him began to sing.

He was at a party in a smart waistcoat. The party was on a big speed boat.
Everyone was having fun, so Josh started to dance with everyone.

After many more adventures it finally began to end, as little Josh in his wellies started to descend.
As soon as his feet touched the floor, he heard his mum open the door.

Josh quickly jumped inside his bed. What a day! As he lay down his head.
Stacey Mahoney

Hellas The Forgotten Land

Once three thousand years ago there was a beautiful place. The air was fresh, the water crystal clear and the land rugged and green. The life force then was of great intelligence, strength and understanding, with deep religious and spiritual roots. The Ancient Greeks were a far superior race then any other who walked the Earth. The first to discover and teach mathematics, physics and philosophy. They invented the Olympic Games and believed a healthy body equalled a healthy and intelligent mind! But now as I look out over Athens in the 20th Century, it is hard to believe that such a race ever existed. For the smog looms over the city, slowly suffocating and threatening the existence of Athens. Even the very trees that line the tiny, dusty streets lower their heads in despair, as if the very life was being sucked out of them. Whatever could have happened to this forgotten land? Where are the twelve Greek gods now? Why has no one been sent to rescue the people and the city of Athens? But the Greek people still dance and sing, they still laugh and drink and toast their beloved Greece of yesteryears. The world no longer acknowledges them as a great power, only as a poor relation to Europe. They have only the past to salute and give them comfort, as the future is a dark and frightening place. "We live for today" they say. "Not like you English" and down another Svinaki. But who can blame them certainly not I. I stand and salute their spirit and zest for living! They still are that strong, intelligent and spiritual race. And when Churchill spoke to the people in 1944, to commend the Greeks over their victory against the Germans he said, "The Greeks died like heroes and the heroes died like Greeks". Turkey may have robbed them of their future in the 15th Century, but Greece is fighting to change her destiny! I hope and pray she succeeds, as the world owes much to Greece and the Greek people!
Angela Kells

King

Born is a child of confusion, talent, was life in a world of illusion. The essence and quality betrayed him as one, they danced just one dance yet he solely outshone. He was fragile and innocent his youth was dried, susceptible to pain and often he cried.

Like rags to riches a little boy, so secluded, they focused on stardom yet the sadness protruded. He was hounded by the leeches that fed on his fame, he lost all trust but was never to blame. As he is crowned eccentric with burdens to bare, to nourish a battered childhood, does anyone care?

A lifestyle was taunted envied and misconceived, bubbles of oxygen and dead bones bereaved. "I was there to change the world", tears and madness and sorrow unfurled. As the reign terror unleashed in Neverland, who was there to hold his hand?

I have spoken of innocence, the description so true, the tabloids are written for only a few. He cares for the children, he invests in their future, there are rivers of blood that are making us richer. As his feet move, intellect pauses, repetition strays, martyrs fight for such causes.

A current of majesty infects friend and foe, as the tide does it flow. Execution of dance you have stolen my sin, hereditary complexion for our next of kin. The rhythm, the lyrics, the creator, the creation, the grace of a king has swept the nation. Reflect again as a slave bids you pose, a subtle kiss and the death of rose. To collide with insanity all morals retained, a little last, all eternity gained. You have taught me the courage that once was my fear, you have shown me success, a saviour of tears.

When inspiration creates me, will you be there? When life is my punishment, when life isn't fair? Continue to dance, heal as you sing, you deserve heavenly riches for you are the king.
Laura Nolan

The Still Of The Morn

As I walk along this narrow country lane, rays from the early morning sun break through patches of mist and fading rain.
The tall grass sways slightly, caressed by a light breeze, and capped by a layer of shimmering morning dew.
I paused for a few moments to admire the peaceable panoramic view.

I catch my breath; as I see a rabbit scurry across the path.
Silently, and oblivious to my presence it stops..... listens, then scampers off into the tall grass.

The sound of a croaking frog suddenly broke the stilled silence of this peaceful early morn',
In the distance I hear a faint, new sound.. I shudder slightly as the
sound becomes clearer and nearer.. It is the sound of a hunting horn.

I look and listen, but remained quite still,
Then I saw the fox running down the hill.
Not far behind I saw the baying hounds, then the sound of many hooves pounding the ground.

Soon they were gone and out of my sight,
But... I couldn't help keep thinking of the foxes plight.
Hunted, then chased, until tired legs give way,
It knows that it's life, could end this very day.

Panting, and shaking with fear at every breath,
It still seeks a way from inevitable death.
The dogs know no better, they're trained to kill!
I turn away, in my stomach I feel quite ill.

Not a bullet to the brain, or even the heart, but savagely ripped, until torn apart.
The last cry of the fox, as the hunters stand by,
unfeeling... Unrelenting... They watch the fox die....

John Banks

Remembering

When I lay in my bed, what goes on in my head? - I remember the days and the years
The childhood I had, which I lived to the full, when the laughter would bring me to tears
Little faces of friends that I no longer see, but remember them well, life was good
If you just shut your eyes you can see them all there and you'd wish them all back if you could
Bygone days, sunny moments, holidays by the sea, with my bucket and spade I would play
I remember those times - oh so well, all the memories are there to this day
Looking back on my youth, it seems far away now, but I'll never forget childhood dreams
They will always be there, I will look back and smile, I'll recall them - especially the screams...
Of delight in the playground when I was at school, all those faces familiar to see
I will treasure the memories, the names I still know, but those children have grown - just like me
Whenever you're blue, now you know what to do, you can think yourself back and just smile
You may be grown up and more wiser inside, but you'll always be that small child.

Valerie Jean Pocock

The Death Of God

To smash to shards the memory of that day and turn all truth to lie,
For on that day when prayer denied, those who dared to pray,
To tear all heaven down to earth and tear down all God's sky,
For on that day when the damned did pray, my Gods bowed their heads and cried,
I saw men of iron and men of steel and men that would not bow.
All illusion shattered, all my heroes cowed
Who would bend a knee to no man, reduced to tears of deep despair, the pain of death so real,
To find life in one crushed child each man would sell his life and with the devil deal
Tearing at the smothering earth with bare and bloody hands, case hardened miners cried,
On that day and in that place my Gods forever died,
And then I knew that iron hard men aren't iron hard men and there was no God to care,
My Gods had died with torn out hearts and I returned the Reaper's stare,
I knew of death and understood, of innocence forever robbed,
For it took from me that youthful place and stole from me my God,
In that place nature's justice by fate and chance denied,
The lives of her own innocents, my Gods they knelt and cried,
In that place called Aberfan my God most surely died

Alan Ryder

Untitled

You died and I didn't believe it, it wasn't real you were still alive
but it felt like you had gone on holiday!
I'd lie in bed and cry myself to sleep, I'd dream and dream about all
the nice days out together we had, then I'd wake and think, it was a
dream, I'm not going to see you again, no more days out, and then cry again.
I'd write to you, and write poems to let the pain go away.
It lasted for ages and all I did was cry because you weren't with me anymore.
I got over it after a while but I didn't forget about you, I thought about you every day!
Christmas came and I was so upset that you weren't here, when New Year's
arrived I went upstairs and cried while everyone else went and had a
drink for you, but I couldn't because I'd start crying and everyone else would.
Then your birthday came, you would have been 73 so we all went out for a drink, I cried again.
I think about you all the time and want to just scream because I want you back so much!

Amanda O'Hare

My Corgis

"One dog's enough for anybody",
Father said,—so we had Bob.
He lived and died, I cried, tears flowed.
Within a week there had to be
Another puppy sold to me.

Aged eight weeks along came Boyo
Born for life of love and sorrow.
He soldiered on—not ailment free,
Nor knowing he'd be one of three.
But always my dear boy was he.

Taffy joined us—gift of joy,
Of wondrous face, my angel boy.
Personality unique
Sweet by nature though not meek.
Carefree little puppy he, with stolid dog for company.

Two red white corgis smart as paint,
Then in came Tessa, older, quaint,
A rescue dog but ne'er a saint.
She eyed my boys, said "you stay there",
And promptly sat in my best chair.

G. M. Bond

Autumn Confusion

Leaves dancing from the trees,
Lie golden crisp on the ground.
Grass so green, 'tis freshly grown,
Birds sing on, the air so warm.

The wonder of a coloured sky
Shades of pink, smooth and rough,
The moon hangs high amid the stars,
Like a giant powder puff.

Little primrose peeping up
Uncertain when to bloom.
Seeing the lush berried holly
Realize they've come too soon.

Water scarce in the reservoir,
Children lightly clad,
Holes in the ozone layer
Have set the seasons mad.

As we bask in clement heat,
And welcome summer's intrusion,
Someone should tell the birds and plants
Thus avoid confusion.

Joan Blake

At 40

A milestone reached,
And fate has etched away the mark
That tells how far to go.
And so,
You sit a while and ponder, on your weary feet
That have trudged the purgatory of time
Scarred with anger, pain and hate
With love, and joy.
Don't wait too late
Before they swell, too sore to move
And if, by chance, a fellow traveller comes by
A friendly smile, a merry laugh
A twinkle in her eye.
Don't hesitate
To pass with her a weary mile,
Or two
And share the evening's sun
Before it fades from view

And when your journey's end's in sight
Ponder then, life's weary plight

Mary Rose Everan

Lonely?

Sometimes it gets so lonely, in the chasms of your mind,
And you think you're going crazy, when no comfort you can find,
It seems there is no place on earth, no where for you to turn,
And you simply want to cry—or die, as your heart begins to churn,
You scream out for a reason, as to why you feel this way,
And when silence gives you nothing, it increases your dismay.
Self pity overwhelms you, and consumes you head to toe,
Because you put your faith in someone, who you knew would have to go.
How many times within your life, has someone let you down,
And in return for your concern, have you been rewarded with a frown?
Well it's no surprise to me, that you suffer like you do,
For in my younger days, I used to suffer like that too.
But that was before I learned, to recognize my plight,
For I discovered The Solution, and began to see The Light,
I know now why I suffered, why I tortured myself so,
It was because I was ignorant, to what I needed to know.
I now never feel alone, for I've recognized The Lord,
And He is ever near me, when I listen to His word.
He said, "My sheep hear my voice," and if you listen—you can too,
So don't be sad and lonely—read the Bible when you're blue!

Philip John Barber

The Lady Of The Lake

When the summer sun sinks low, and the twilight shadows fall,
When the peace and still of evening, yields to the curlew's lonesome call,
When these calm and tranquil waters, adopt a shimmering hue,
It is then she is most enticing, almost hypnotizing.
As she glides and swirls around me, in her mystic gown of blue.

Far and wide I have travelled, much beauty I have seen,
But there is none quite like the sunset, beyond these Isles of green.
Right here amongst the tall reeds, she has reigned supreme,
Bathed in mystery, and legend,
Lough Erne's enchanted queen.

It is here I will always find her, in a hooded cloak and veil,
Keeping watch over nature's providence, and the solitary boats that sail.
Betrothed, to the Erne forever, only momentarily mine.
A fleeting passage of beauty like the evening wind that sighs.

The full bloom scent of a summer night, rides on the whispering breeze
While the small birds from their daytime chores, wing homeward to the trees,
When I like they, move on from here, and on some other shore do wake,
My thoughts will stray, to a moonlit way,
And the lady at the lake.

Anne Eves

My Budgie

Turquoise budgie in your cage, such difference to my life you've made,
Six weeks old when first you came, no possessions, minus name,
Fluffy feathers just like down, now you wear them like a crown,
Suspicion filled your little eye every time I passed you by.
Spoke to you for one whole week, still you uttered not a tweet,
Then next day your head I spied, tilted slightly to one side,
All at once a little squeak came from out your tiny beak.
To me it was the sweetest sound, beady eyes followed me round.
Confidence at last I'd gained from your little fragile frame,
Frightened feelings, lonely too, I had shared them all with you.
You got bolder soon I found as I let you fly around,
Perching on my hand, and head, warmth and joy to me you spread.
Minute, tiny, lovely thing, oh, what happiness you bring,
Climbing ladders, ringing bells, sharpening beak on seashore shell.
Bathing, preening, feeding too, what a busy day for you.
In between you chatter on, chirping, talking, it's such fun.
I was lonely till you came, now my life is not the same,
Little creature out of shell, you have cast a magic spell,
Little creature, turquoise blue, you're for me and I'm for you.

Maud Hurford

My Country Walk

Over the bridge and over the hill,
The river below looks very still,
Down the hill on the other side
I need a rambler to be my guide.

Gathering wild flowers by the stream,
On the water the sun did gleam
Revealing fish and dragon-fly,
Above my head the bright blue sky.

Walking slowly through the copse,
I gazed up into the tree tops,
One or two birds I hoped to see
Startled, they flew away from me.

Once more into the sunlight I came
Over the meadow which had a frame,
Of hawthorn hedge and also bramble.
In such a meadow I love to ramble.

Over the style to the lane beyond
In the distance I saw a pond
On which ducks were swimming round and round
My walk has finished, I'm homeward bound.

Ruth Neighbour

My Lady Of The Night

What could I see, what better sight
Than my lady of the night.
A vision pure in every way
Oh, where is she by light of day.
My Lady.

Her touch is gentle, her voice serene
It's as though she were a dream
How I do ache when we're apart
Speed on the night and ease my heart
My Lady.

My sadness comes from my despair
When she's not there for me to care
But as night doth come, my pulse does race
In promise of our warm embrace.
My Lady.

Her eyes do shine upon my sight
Like golden rays of orient light
She gives herself in every way
It's with such memory, I pass my day.
She's my lady of the night.

Colin P. W. Meggison

What Dreams May Come

Take me to the grave
with the poetry of the brave, to save me
where the thick creeping weeds tie down
my soul to enslave me.
Let the words of wisdom manifest the Knife's
to cut the roots from my heart, and my lives
and my dreams.
To go on a journey through Eternal realms
once unlocked, no barriers, no bounds.
Where sounds need no hearing or heeding
or pleading.
Where touch needs no embracing of arms,
or holding tight in our palms.
Where a voice once spoken, and whispered
in your ear, becomes a soft velvet futurity
in which to disappear.

What dreams may come
never to be told
only for the spirit
and Poets of old.

Carole Anne Boone

Winter Days

Faces spring unbidden, like flowers, from the dust of my memory;
Trusty perennials, watered by the soft - hard haphazard rains of my tears.
Scented with Summers past.
Petals of the joys that haunt me in the grip of a Winter
Which contracts my heart.
A cold iron vice of icy thoughts and leaden sorrows.

The faces open out into rosy smiles.
And the magic music of eternal words of warmth
Works its charm as ever,
Gradually dissolving the crystals in a gentle thaw.

And when the garden is full of colour and fragrance,
My mind immersed,
I feel happy and secure.

I know that my secret garden will always be there.
It cannot wither and die,
However cold the winds of my emotions blow.

Caroline O'Hare

Ode To Shakespeare

Long, long ago in days of old
There was a poet with talent untold.
He became a playwright whom everyone knew,
He wrote Hamlet, and Romeo and Juliet too.
The Globe Theatre was host to them all.
The Balcony was full and packed were the stalls.
From the 16th century through to today,
Famous, Shakespeare will always stay.

Claire Ward

A Yokin's Wark

O' fit a bonnie mornin' Meg, ye'll mebbe gi' us a haun
Tae clean the road-side burnie, it's dammin up wi san'
Ye'll better tak' a shuffel lass an I'll tak' scythe an spad,
We'll mebbe get it feenished afore the midgies start gaun mad.

It wi'd be Friday I'nt it lass? Losh the days gyang by richt fest
We'll hae tae gyang tae the mert sometime an see fit's takin' place.
I hear that nowt are affa chape bit sheep are affa dear,
Gweed sakes it's nae gweed kennin fit's happenin' ony mair.

We'll Meg it maun be lowsin' time, this ditchin's richt sair wark
I dinna ken aboot you lass bit I'll sweer I could wring oot my sark.
The sweat's bin halin' aff mi, mu buits are foo o' dubs,
Hash harkin tae the peasies Meg, it's music tae yer lugs.

Yer mither 'ill hae the denner ready, she'll be feenished mukkin the hens,
An' as Lady Priscilla fae up the road wad say,
"We shall just have our hands to cleanse."
Yer tattie soup's jist gran Jean, I'll hae a suppie mair,
Fill up Megs bowel an a lass, for she's bin warkin' sair.

Audrey Fowler

Life Is Just A Door To Death . . .

Life is just a door to death some people might well say,
Because when your starving in the cold there seems no other way.
When there's a war just round the corner poverty in distant lands,
There seems no way there is a God to take you in His hands.

When the world around is troubled and a black man hates a white,
When just a silly argument makes a country want to fight.
When people turn to drugs or drink to get away from life,
It seems there's no one good enough to take away their strife.

Only when they find Jesus will they find an inner peace,
When all their problems, thoughts and worries can be released.
When they open up their hearts and let Jesus in,
They'll know that day to start a-fresh and He'll wash away their sin.

And then the world won't look so bad they'll see a better way,
The smile upon a small child's face will brighten up their day.
They'll discover how to serve their God their daily life to live,
And know that death's the door to life, to God the glory give!

Anna Firth

455

The Bombing

This is the man, who starts it all off,
Who gives the order, in a discreet little cough.
This is the man who tells the men,
Who tells them to set the bomb for ten.

This is the man, who creates the bomb;
The police get a tip, but this man has gone.
This is the man who places destruction;
Without thinking, placing devastation.

This is the man who detonates death,
Who runs away while no one is left.
This is the man who committed a crime;
A mass slaughterer - he'll do it again another time.

This is the man -
Does he dare?
Should he do it again?
He doesn't care.

Andy Foster

Pathos (Or Tender Love And Understanding)

Pathos came from the skies but he didn't stay long,
He didn't like what he saw,
The sight of man hanging by a rope,
His poor toes pointing accusingly to the spoilt earth,
Brackish water you can not drink in with your eyes
Flesh you can not eat, so greedily devoured, containing no pity,
Acrid air you can not breathe, burning away the soul of a world
This world never to know from beginning to terrible end,
    a moment's peace
How beautiful it looked from way above,
A dead animal may look fine till you turn it over,
Then you see the maggots underneath.

Joanne Robins

Bus Stop

Hey! There's a queue!
Now I must race to find a place
Along the street that's free of feet,
Where I can stop and let some off,
But not one on.

Complicity creates a queue;
The civic instinct of the few
Who like to think they know their place,
Just where they are, how near, how far,
Who's first, who's last, what's next or past,
Who's left behind, who's taken for a ride.

What fools! Their destinations I decide.
I have my etiquette, my pride.
I am a bus! And I refuse
To carry those who stand in queues.

Rosemary A. Thomas

Roller Coaster

Swooping through the sky,
Clattering over rusty tracks,
Swirling in a corkscrew,
Racing so fast it beats a whistling wind.

Up and down whizzing like a tornado,
Bang! And a sudden stop!
Lunging from side to side
Nearly reaching heaven,
Spiralling with terror like a sky demon.

Hurtling through tunnels with creepy sounds,
Going fast and slow and swirling round,
Sickly feelings and spooky pictures
And the carriage flies on into ghostly darkness.

And then twirling through the water,
Tumbling under cascades.
Splashing icy water and making lots of foam,
And with a final deathly plummet
We realise we are home!

Alexander Cherry

The Cruel Sea

How calm and clear the water looks today
If only you could stay, and watch the white
    bubbly foam when the tide comes in.
Sometimes the breakers are so big, the
    surfers ride on them.

But oh, I know how cruel can be that
    beautiful sea.
If only it could talk, and tell its tale of
    sunken ships, and drowned men.
Of tragedies, and storms with darkened skies.
You wouldn't then think only of its beauty.
But would say, "Yes, that name is true,
    it really is 'The Cruel Sea'."

Marjorie Davies

Untitled

Once upon-a-time my heart was in two,
But now it's a whole and,
made especially for you,
if you love me and treat me right
I'm sure to love you every day and night

Now that you've gone
my life is in pieces
no tender loving
which your heart it teaches
to love someone is such,
a great feeling
when it's someone like you
it hurts to see you leaving.

Emma Capell

Lost Child Within

Naive no, lost innocence no,
People see a little child,
hair, two eyes, a mouth.
But they do not see the calling
spirit crying out for healing.
Her eyes look so sad, so helpless.
Though through the mist I reach out to her,
she cannot hear me.
Her spirit trapped behind a false attire,
a front, to protect, but a lost child.
She does not know that I can help,
she will not come out - hurt too many times, afraid.
But one day, when she's grown,
freedom she will find and a hope to hold.
She will be her own, have her own.
She will find healing for her wounds
and a love for her heart.
When her lost child is found...

Bebe Holden

Danny Boy

Oh Danny, my Danny it's trouble you are,
Is it because you are missing your da?
I shouldn't have clouted you, come near to me
And you'll have a wee taste of my dish of hot tea.
I'll darn up your breeks if it takes me all night,
So stop your poor sobbing, you'll soon feel all right.
How about going to visit your gran?
I've saved up enough for the fare, so we can.
I'll just check the money I've got in my bag,
So dry all your tears, here's a clean bit of rag.
Well, we've got just enough, it's for you and for me,
The driver will take you for half 'cos you're wee.
I'll boil up some praties, they'll make you feel warm.
We must start fairly early, as soon as it's dawn.
Now give me your breeks, I'll get darning quite soon,
At Granny's you'll not have to share my bedroom.
Now, whisht, don't you cry, you can share if you wish.
Don't worry my wean, what's an old broken dish?
I never did like it. Soon we'll be away:
Don't forget all your prayers, you'll see Da one fine day.

V. Peers

The Genes Of Attila

Stand too you Iceni, you Briton, you Celt,
Look you cross the water, old danger is felt!
The Saxon is rumbling, seeking power o'er us all,
The Genes of Attila, our serfdom its goal!

Look you to your past, its lessons are clear,
Uncloud the memories, relive the fear!
Attila wants Europe; by war, not won still,
But with guile and great cunning, achieve it he will!

Remember, remember the millions who paid,
Just a short generation since grandfather gave.
His bayonet and berry lie 'neath Dunkirk's sand,
Don't tell me 'tis forgot or politically unsound!

Throughout the millennium the hun's eyeballed our land;
Now gullible leaders assuage his demands!
A thorn in his side, we fought his enslaving,
Remember when Chamberlain brought proof of his devilling?

Attila the Hun once roared down from the plains,
He raped and he pillaged, he lied and he slayed!
Wake up fellow Briton and see what I say,
The Genes of Attila course stronger this day!

Robert Giles

War

An angry sky, a setting sun
A wounded soldier, a loaded gun
A blood-soaked body. A helpless cry.
Another's dying, for someone's lie,
Who's at fault? Who's to blame?

The politicians, they're all the same.
Where are they? Now bullets are flying.
Where are they? Now we're all dying.
Head keeping low Promise to keep.
Lying in a puddle waiting for sleep.
Wet and cold. Mud to the knees.
Hear our plight and help us please!

"Your Country Needs You" the talking finished.
War is declared, but an end is wished.
The war is over, it's come to an end.
Dead to be buried, funerals to attend.
Awaiting destination, lump in throat.
My family waiting, it said in note.
Welcome home, with open arms.
It's all over, so thank our charms.

Stephen Charles

My Dream

My dream is for peace and happiness
In a world without famine or war
Where children have enough to eat
In countries near and far.

My dream is for joy and contentment
In everyone young and old,
With people safe from earthquake and fire
And other horrors untold.

My dream is to save all the rain forests
and flowers and butterflies rare,
Save the animals from extinction
And put a 'patch' in the ozone layer.

My dream is for all of the people,
Black, yellow, brown and white
To live together in harmony
When the outlook would always be bright.

I hope someday my dream will come true,
What a wonderful world this will be,
Enough food, clean air and homes for all,
This is the dream for me.

Marian K. Smith

Butterfly

Don't hold me down, just let me play,
For I might up and fly away.

Love's so strong that it can crush,
And that world be the last of us.

They say it makes the world go round,
But not if it's flattened on the ground.

So lighten up, don't make me cry.
And I will be your butterfly.

Happy and carefree all day long,
Just wanting to fill your heart with song.

J. Rosholm-Olesen

No Longer

He is no longer mine.
Mine is no longer the body
That awakens the passion buried deep inside of him,
That burns the desire in his heart and soul.
The part of him that cries out in the night
For my touch, my comfort, my love,
Had died.
The raging flame that fiercely burned for me and me alone,
Had ebbed and slowly diminished.
His eyes, deep dark pools of mysterious power and wisdom,
Full of forgotten secrets, hidden pain and broken dreams,
No longer gaze into my own with such heat, it numbs the senses.
The way he held me in his arms; safe, strong and powerful
With an overwhelming intensity and determination
To keep me captive for all eternity and beyond.
The breathtaking moment of unchained ecstasy, helplessness,
Total loss of control when love, passion and urgency
Captivate imagination and reality,
Emotions beyond restraint,
But, no longer.

Tanya-Marie Steutel

Colour Me Pink

We hide in a rage behind layers of beige,
Permed, powdered, and pressed.
So different from us,
Said Miss Beal and Miss Buss,
yet there are hundreds and thousands of 'us',
Permed, powdered, pressed and pleated.
I must powder my nose, said Miss Briggs,
With a smile, for I think I have won,
a considerable sum.
Although I do know it is a sin to have more,
I think I will break, this inexorable law,
For the rest of my days I will change
all my ways.
So colour me pink.

June Oliver

The Panda

Something which stays in your mind,
is something gentle and kind.

For the panda that lives on this earth,
a creature which lives from birth.

A panda is now a rare sight,
With its warm black and white fur.
Making no errors, or doing no harm,
this is surely to occur.

The world is full of rights and wrongs.
But do we all know that the panda belongs?
As the bamboo shoots go down, and exported into town.
The pandas now die of starvation.
But money comes into conversation.

So do we really care about the real world, the outer
World we rarely see?
Or do we care about money and business.
Or a world for wildlife. For you and me?

Clare Turner

Upon Your Leaving

Fly my little one fly,
Soar to where man's hand cannot reach.
Find yourself in a valley of calm,
Or winging low on a sun kissed beach.
Take your beauty away from man,
Let him realise his loss for now.
Glide to the edge of your own domain,
Rest your wings on a frond kissed bough.
Turn your head and see what the
World has become without you.
What man has made of his kingdom,
When his own rule is untrue.
Don't pity us for we bring on ourselves,
The tyranny we impose on others.
Please don't damn us all to your leaving,
For the sake of us all being brothers.
Don't take your flight forever away,
And leave your freedom to burn.
But when you deem we have suffered enough,
Fly swiftly upon your return.

Hogarth

The Christening

Dear baby Emily Grace,
With bright eyes and smiling face,
Your mother's joy, and father's pride,
Grandma and Granddad just can't hide
The delight and thrill of you three,
Another treasure for the family tree.

This your very first special day,
Family and friends gathered to pray
That angels will guard and Jesus will guide.
God take your hand and stay by your side.
Grandma and Granddad will always be there
To share your happiness or burdens you bear.

Written on the occasion of the Christening
of Emily Grace, our first grandchild - daughter
to our eldest son.

Janet Boxell

Empty Heart

Swimming in the river of dreams,
  All I can see is your reflection.
I start to think what our life means,
  we are so close yet all I feel is rejection.

These days are getting harder,
  more difficult everyday.
All that keeps me going is your laughter
  and that I love you in every way.

Then suddenly it has gone,
  I have been brought back to reality,
The distance now between us is so long
  My world is empty why have you left me?

Louise O'Brien

In The Hands Of Time

Mirror mirror, as I look I see.
Surely? Not I who reflect on thee.
For upon this face of which you bear,
is a woman of old with silvering hair,
her features appear quite frail and gaunt.
Why is it I - she chose to haunt.
Her lips snowy-white, her eyes stone-grey.
Why is she here? What has she to say?
I turned my head and hoped in vain, that this
woman's face would not remain.
But taking a glance, I could clearly see,
this frightful old woman's a reflection of me.
If only I'd known how time would fly.
I'd have made the most of each day gone by.
Don't put off tomorrow what can be done today,
for soon like me, you'll be old and grey.

Jean Hill

When someone that you love so much...

When someone that you love so much
just turns and walks away
you feel as though your life is through
and you can't face another day
and when you know he loves you
and your parting should not be
you feel as though the light has gone
and it's much too dark to see
but keep that light burnt brightly
and maybe one fine day
that love that was so special
will come again to stay

J. Nolan

Spare Change

The sad eyed beggar
sits in the street
pennies of pity scattered round his feet
people walk past and don't react
trying hard not to make eye contact

Hungry and homeless is his plea
he asks passers by
if they've got 10p
hands in pockets
the public don't give
but they don't understand
he too has to live

So let me take you by the hand
and lead you through the streets of sorrow
I'll show you something today
that'll still be there tomorrow

Gregor Park

School Life

School life's driving me out of my mind.
School life's making me sick.
I want to go home,
home, home to mum,
'cause school life's breaking me in bits.
Monday morning,
the bell went clanging.
I felt so sleepy,
that I went on yawning.
But by the count of three,
I was up on my feet,
and had my bath,
with half a bucketful.
After my hasty bath,
I dressed my naked back.
Breakfast tastes so funny,
gives me an upset tummy.
I want to go home,
home, home to mum,
'cause school life's making me sick.

Obal Otu

The Real You?

The nights they bring such pleasure,
for in my dreams I see your solid perfect self.
You stand and hold your hand out to my face,
those fingers stroking, stroking, loving.
To see your eyes with thoughts and sun-a-brimming,
and creases as your mouth turns to a smile.
I'm yours you say and hold me to your love.
The mornings they bring such pain,
for awake I see your bitter angry self.
You stand with hand held hotly to my face,
those fingers warning, telling, hating.
To see your eyes with danger, storms-a-brewing,
and creases as your mouth turns to a sneer.
You're mine you say and drag me to your side.
My dreams they bring such hope of things to come,
my days they leave me numb.

Caroline Jones

This Motherland

She's beautiful, she's lovely,
This country that is ours,
Entrusted to our care
With her Mountains, Plains and Bowers.

But oh! How we've betrayed that trust
Through selfishness and greed,
Corrupted and polluted her,
Ignored her dire need.

We must stand firm and stop the rot
Of Vandal-ridden strife,
Effectuate, with wisdom,
Peace and virtue into life;

A life where fear does not hold sway
And trust is prevalent,
Where each for other has a mind
And all are well content.

When we can laud, with truth, this land
For which so many died,
Then we can all walk tall again
And lift our heads with pride.

Annabel F. Barnes

Memory And Memories

Did you tell me? Tell me more
What these things are really for.
Did you tell me? Should I know
Where it is I've got to go?
Did you tell me? I ask you
What is next? What must I do?

Thinking back to times of yore
Childhood joys in pinafore.
Thinking back to later scenes
Courting days, and all that means.
Thinking back to married joys
Our own children and their toys.

Now I'm old and sit a lot
In my chair, my favourite spot.
Happy when it's peaceful here
Or when grandson's noise I hear.
For contentment is great gain.
Helps through joy and also pain. But remember:
Though I'm old and memory's gone
Memories stay, I'm not alone.

Sylvia J. Hill

My England

A country cottage, with lime-washed walls,
Wisteria round the door,
With pussy sitting on the mat,
  To welcome one and all.

An autumn ride upon my bike,
Upward toward the moor.
To clamber on the rocks, and gaze,
For miles, o'er field and moor.

To trample through the purple heather,
The bright yellow gorse avoiding,
And see the ponies motionless.
Thy have no cares like us.

And riding on through village street,
Past post office and store,
But wait, I must just stop a while,
Cream teas, I see on this door.

I must press on, for home awaits,
With wife and family,
What joy to be a part of this.
Old England, we enjoy.

R. S. Warren

His Peaceful Tones

Within his soul he yearns to play a tone of tranquil peace, to see
that you and I can live and hope for war to cease.
Its sound uplifts me once again to write to what I know, to have
and hold a better life is where we want to go.

It's up to us to make this stand and even end the fight, to take this
land that lies in dark and turn it into light.
Let's quell the rage that lies within and put our minds at ease, to
pray that we all take this chance and rise up off our knees.

But who are they who hide themselves and seek to keep it on to
kill and maim the ones we know until our peace is gone.
They do not ever say the words that we would like to hear, but just
the same this cherished land has cost us very dear.

If this is the sound of a peaceful time may the moment never end,
from a frightened and endangered life it's time for us to mend.
Meaningful and from the heart, thoughtful and inspired, just take
away this damning pain and all that's not desired.

Brian Campbell

Willow Weep

Oh weeping willow, willow weep, for all those souls within thy keep,
They battled on the soil beneath your head, they fought in vain
and now are dead.
Their armour clangs on stormy nights, the flash of lightning
on swords it strikes, the battle cry of boys and men
rings out upon the night again.
The thunder rolls out distant drums, the enemy of death
he slowly comes, ignoring them in anguish cry,
he marches through their ranks, they die.
The frightened sound of horses' neighs rise up upon a windy day,
the banners fly above their heads, they rise and trample
on the dead.
Flashing swords on lances break, heavy are the hearts that ache,
as they battle hard in vain, their bodies fall on crimson plains.
Oh weeping willow, willow weep, now shield these souls
within thy keep. Let no wind or stormy rain disturb these
gallant souls again.

Rita Maher

To A Dying Man

Oh weary one! Oh weary one! Do hold your head up high,
You go to meet your maker deep within the sky.
You've weathered troubles here on earth each day,
Always seeking but for what we pray.
It seems to me, we strive and strain
and bungle dearly, what we gain.
Mighty one, you must look down and wonder how it all began
This land of greed and evil so ruinous of man.

Oh troubled one! Oh troubled one! Do you yearn to leave this place
And live with heavenly angels of goodness and of grace.
Resolute you served your brothers well
So pray and plead to go to heaven not to hell,
That loved ones will reunite and follow thee
To that eternal place we all would wish to see.

Oh joyous one! Oh joyous one! Your time to leave is near,
There within to dwell amongst the spirits dear.
A shining light to guide you to eternity and care
To a glory far beyond, that one day all might share.

T. Chaplin

Life

In life we all have lessons to learn, and treadmills to tread,
We all need a worthy hand, an inspiring pat on the head,
Life is full of great expectations, joys and the unknown,
We have to search, learn and listen until we inside are fully grown
For we are the future, we choose what and who we want to be,
For some this will come naturally others will need guidance to see,
Life is a lesson that will last all of your life and more,
But remember always take advantage of luck knocking on your door.
We live our lives and try to do what's best for everyone all told
But suddenly we're not young, we're starting to grow old,
The moral to this verse on life is easy for all to see,
Let your dreams come true, let your hearts live to be free

T. A. Harrowing

Broken Bonds

I feel a loss, a deep, dark hole,
Reaching to the depths of my soul,
The warmth of love is frozen still,
When you were taken against your will.

And at that moment you were snatched from me,
The ties were snapped and you were free,
To wander happily, who knows where,
As I reflect on whether you still care.

You were my confidante and my friend,
I never wanted the intimacy to end,
So I thank you for every precious memory,
And hope I returned the gifts you gave to me.

So cruelly taken when my heart was light,
I still wait for you, day and night,
I look and listen for you longingly,
But you're not there to reassure me.

Only the silence comes screaming back,
To torture me with what I most lack,
And painfully stab me into reality,
And that this was always meant to be.

Phil Johnson

The Ideal Pet?

Percy is potty on poodles,
Diana just dotes on these dogs:
  "Oh, isn't he sweet
  On his dainty wee feet?"
(I think he'd look better in clogs).

Bernard is barmy on budgies,
Brenda's just bats on these birds:
  "You should just hear him talk!"
  (To me it's a squawk,
I am sure they imagine the words).

Kenneth is crazy on kittens,
Cora just coos over cats:
  "What lovely soft fur,
  And doesn't she purr!"
(I just keep them for dealing with rats).

My own favourite pet is no songster,
Nor buries he bones in a hole,
  He utters no sound
  As he swims round and round,
My goldfish all bright in his bowl!

Barbara Hoy

Birth And Renewal On Easter Day!

Dear longed-for one that through me writhes and strains
In waves of water, hard incessant pains;
Soon from this expectant agony
Will come my innocent baby,
And heartfelt joy to parents and relations -
Our stake in the eternity of nations.

Thus can we cast away greed and dross
Be born again, greater from the loss
Of covetousness, ignoring our neighbour,
Because in claustrophobic workplaces we labour.
Love comes to dwell in us that can be born again,
Renews life like virgin snow, pure dropping rain!

Now heaven-sent tiny miracle, kicking limbs in air,
Blue eyes, pink cheeks, soft lips, bright wispy hair,
Innocence, gladness, radiance all entwined
From fond memory of faith and hope behind!
Here lives our own gift from God, our pride,
Our first child to nurse, protect and guide.

Darling, littlest baby as we clasp you close to our heart,
We vow to love, guard and treasure until our ways must part!

Annie Beaven

Reflections Of Time And Love

When, in the solitude of loneliness,
  Whispers the voice of another time,
How can we hear the voice of love
  Over the outrage of fears?

The calling of our yesterdays
  of another time and place,
The brief kiss of happiness brushes the cheek of joy.

The hands of time and patience,
  The nakedness of memory,
Dance in the mind of long ago,
  The heat of passion tempts the ego of when and where.

Call to me over the longings of my yesterdays,
Remember the hand that held and caressed your soul,
Remember the love of him who clings
  like dew upon the dawn of time.

Reach over the canyon of my younger years,
  Wipe from my eyes the fog of my tears,
Bring once again a smile to my face,
  Whisper softly to my soul
of another time and place.

Patricia Holland

Untitled

How is it possible to live a life
Free from distress, from sorrow?
To sit in our warm comfortable homes,
While people not far away must beg and borrow.

How can we justify a life free from starvation?
A life of ease and little pain.
When a child of this earth is crawling around
Pleading, crying, dying, dust in his mouth, insane.

Not insanity but life, ebbing away
Before our very eyes. How can I sit
In my comfortable home, knowing, knowing
They are dying.

People stand in the house of power
Dictating what must be.
Their bellies full and fat, thinking
Only of their power and authority

What good is a crown to a dying child?
What good a comfortable home?
When all he wants is a bowl of rice,
A slice of bread, a hand, so he doesn't die alone.

Judith Baines

Retirement From Commerce

The spirit of free enterprise pervaded through the land
In the year of 48 you joined the Hauser band.
Many changes you have witnessed, the transition of rail from steam
Now the diesel and electric, they both reign supreme.

As a captain of the industry you joined in common cause
To ensure the company prospered, to obey the basic laws.
Respected by competitors a legend to the end
In the world of freight forwarding you have made many a friend.

Two score years and ten have passed and you did not fail
Forming a network of branches, developing Hauser Rail.
Your achievements they are legion, we have only named but two
Mere words cannot express the debt the company owes to you.

Inspiring younger people to go and try for gold
You helped to forge endeavour, you did not break the mould.
Over zealous branch directors you sometimes had to face
Your expertise and knowledge are impossible to replace.

Your marathon is over, you have won your race
It's time for a well-earned rest as retirement you embrace.
When you tee off up the fairway golfing iron in your hand
Spare a thought for all your colleagues here in Hauser's band.

Bryan Corless

Through Our Eyes

We look around us, and what do we see?
We see the world full of misery.
The starving, the hungry and the poor,
Waiting for an open door.
Each day a new hurdle we have to face.
Wondering if we can all keep pace.
But there's no need to feel so sad.
Things aren't really all that bad,
Share your troubles with a friend,
When you feel you're at your end
You don't have to be filled with sorrow,
Just look forward to tomorrow.
A new day dawns, when things look brighter,
And your mood seems somewhat lighter,
A cheerful grin, a smiling face.
Makes you realize you can win this race.

L. Birdman

Leaving Life

The night stars fell like fireflies at my feet
and the full moon tenderly kissed my cheek
Infinite peace brushed my cooling skin
and awe at this place softened my pain

I have left love behind, poor bedraggled love
wrapped in tears and memories of mistakes
Here there is no past nor future either
only a present of great and glittering stars

I have come from weeping life to silent death
my soul wrapped firmly in light and love
The torture of black deep pain forgotten
my body whole again and bright in perfection

The stars tumbled and crunched underfoot
and the moon sat like a hat on my bowed head
My soul is like music along the Milky Way
and I am where I should be, complete in death

Jacki Larcombe

Those Missing Years

So many years were spent apart
The years we missed tug at my heart
those missing years never can be found
lost childhood tears and laughter abound
to share our troubles in teenage years
and talk of our dreams and of our fears
those missing years are lost for good
but look to the future we must we should
we found one another after years apart
one brother two sisters with love in our hearts
to know each other after all these years
has brought about some joyful tears
those missing years are lost I know
we won't look back and time will show
we will share laughter our dreams and our fears,
but we can never replace those missing years

Jill Cox

Bad Reds

Red, red, from the flames of hell,
A coloured warning, a death spell.
A war, a devil, a Nazi flag,
Blood, wine, a snake-skin handbag.
The blazing sun, red-raw meat,
A pencil, a pen, a death sheet.
A coffin, a desert, an un-washed deck,
A bite from a vampire that gives you a pain
in the neck.
An extremely unlucky day,
A bill, a cheque you have to pay.
A thief, a murder, a disgraceful sin,
A fairy's dying because you're so mean.
A ghost, a witch, a large ogre,
A bad-luck charm, a pain, a roar.
Someone's left dying on the floor.

Louise Hickling

Life

This life of ebb tides,
Drawing back from existence,
Come the morning, ending the persistence
A nagging doubt in one's ability,
To cope with any further subsistence

But to gain any momentum on a Gravely track,
Finding the smooth spots doesn't negate the fact,
That advancement is not always by the smooth way,
But often from bump to dip instead,
Through the valleys of abandonment to hills of attack,
Until one reaches the summit of accomplishment

From that dizzy height regaled,
There gorged on one's own self esteem,
In the triumphal splendour of critics' hails,
Make all the mistakes of pride and gain,
Remaining still a man to the end, frail.

Frank Sanderson

Living Together In Harmony

How wonderful our life on this earth would be
If we could all live together in harmony.
Never to fear famine flood or war
Nobody rich and nobody poor
But all caring and sharing equally
For the common good of the family.
By family I mean the human race
Which we are destroying at a terrible pace
For the poverty, the famine, and fighting goes on
And for many their hopes and dreams have gone
But to show us the way there is only one
Why else did he sacrifice his only son
So why don't we listen and understand
That we need him to lead us by the hand
Back into that world how he meant it to be
All living together in harmony.

M. E. Turner

Bridie

I see a difference in her at last,
The years are quickly rolling past.
Her once proud head is sinking low,
She tires quick and is now slow,
Sleeping where once she could not stop,
Hunting and chasing until she would drop.

A tinge of grey surrounds her face,
That coal black lustre fading without trace.
A better friend you could not find,
Asking nothing, unselfishly kind,
Greeting me always rapturously,
Unconditional love and servility.

Sometimes I glance at her and see,
She has not much time left with me,
The tears will come - but not just yet,
Some precious time still left with my pet.

Jennifer Precious

Destruction

They came in the evening of a new decade,
Snow lay on the ground and on the branches of the trees,
Nature had made patterns of ferns on the window panes,
Inside the house one could hear the murmur of male voices,
The rasping sound of saws and chopping of wood,
Then rushing to the door I stood AGHAST!
Seeing man wrench arm from arm of tree
Which shivered in the frosty air, then CRASHED!
Then branches that for many days had held light and shade
Had sheltered creatures on the earth and heavens
In death now laid.
Children regardless heaved wood away for fuel
Thinking not of the past nor feeling the passing moment cruel.

So must an old world, tottering and insane,
Be tortured by being pruned then nobly LIVE AGAIN.

Evelyn Metcalfe

Stimulations

A sense of stimulation enhanced by the charming impact of
all surrounding. The scenery faded to subconscious
and remained, like a simmering sun, slowing, washed in a
finery of blurred scarlets, pinks, orange and grey.

A sense of expectation, tinged with
anticipation of thoughts held, yet hurriedly converging.
All that is, that's going to be and more.
The vine pregnant, the laden apple orchard, the
horsechestnut, half
encased in its prickly cocoon glimpsing
a contrasting rich mahogany fruit.

A sweet caress of movement, consuming
emitting, ebbing, above and around
Many memories, many sights and
sounds, minute in time and beyond their appreciation.
A small twig swiftly snatched out the river's side, sent with it
spirit resurrected, in a neverending dance of freedom.

Our world of fleeting entwinements, a depth to each and every caress.
An artist, a painter, the sculptor or perhaps, engrossed, altering
dimension and form, individual on the escaped horizon of our
ongoing landscapes.

Kate Newman

Ageing

I looked in the mirror and what did I see,
an old wrinkled woman,
Not me Not me.

Teeth so white and hair that shone,
All gone All gone

Eyes so bright and skin so fair,
Not there Not there

Muscles supple - nice straight back,
Now slack Now slack

Body slim and tummy flat,
Now fat Now fat

Full of hope with nothing bad,
Now sad Now sad

Where did they go, those years between,
Unseen Unseen

Life's gone by and now I see,
It's me it's me

Patricia Bassett

May I?

Young. Fresh. Alive.
There was a game we played out in the yard
When we were five.

It went: you are a train, a plane, a pair of scissors
A bunny hop, till I say stop.
If you forgot to cry the words - "May I?"
Then as you know - no go.

So many decades on I now perceive
We still play that game.
Our lives are but a re-run of before.
We are such fools to think the rules
Do not apply to us.

Success or fail, smile or rail
We are postman, lawyer, doctor - on the factory floor
To think that we dictate our fate is so absurd.
We can no more explain why such a thing was done
Or what was for - no word.

But he knows. That gentle voice who at our final sigh says
Stop! Come back!

You never said "May I."

Barbara M. Byrne

Tune In Your Mind

Treat your mind like a video
Record only what will enhance your life
Like wavebands tuned to radio
They can bring either happiness or strife

Tune in your mind like a video
To what is pleasant to both see and hear
You'll find that in life's heights and lows
It will bring joy throughout the years

The mind, like an activated video
Dictates only what is recorded within
Violence and wars may erupt like volcanoes
But only with peace and love can your life begin

Be wise and tune thoughts as you would a video
To what is good and nice to see
As years roll by you won't feel so low
If your mind is untrammelled and carefree

L. G. Lynch

South Downs

When light and shade had just been made
And clouds began to move,
A whisper floating on the earth
Rose to the throne above -
A message from the shadows
To their Lord of night and day,
They said "We'll serve you truly,
"But we sometimes long to play."

Their prayer was heard. The downs appeared
Out of the ocean bed,
Over the smooth and springy turf
Gladly the shadows sped.
Low curves against the sky line,
The downs are there today,
A playground for the shadows,
That will never fade away.

Helen Bell

Reflections

Our lives from Birth to Death
    are mere reflections of ourselves,
Our thoughts, our dreams, our hopes
    are mere reflections of ourselves,
The way we act, the things we do, the words we say
    are mere reflections of ourselves,
Other people's actions, deeds and words to us
    are mere reflections of ourselves,
So it does well to put in front of life's mirror
    which is a mere reflection of ourselves,
All those actions, words and thoughts we wish
    to be a true reflection of ourselves.

Michael Mortlock

The Yearly Clock

Mother Earth is awakening now it is Spring,
The bulbs are endeavouring their jewels for to show,
The bird on the bough, its nest it is building,
While now is the time many seeds to sow.

We welcome the Summer in her outfit of green,
Such shading the artists' palates never have seen.
The sun at its highest shines down from above,
On the children who frolic - it's the time that they love.

Suddenly it's Autumn, the days are now waning,
The orchard is laden with fruit that is ripening,
The rivers are swollen, the salmon are leaping,
The hum of the harvester from the gort we are hearing.

Alas and alack, the axle has turned,
The cold, the damp and the snow have returned,
But right in the middle we have a great feast
That's celebrated for centuries and never has ceased.

Kathleen Moloney

The Fountain Of Youth

The fountain of youth is something,
That some search for in desperation.
But the fountain is there for everyone,
In every generation.

We know that age comes to all of us,
As the carpet of time is unrolled.
But although we all grow older,
We do not have to grow old.

There are those of course amongst us,
Who, sadly for them, may scorn.
They're the ones who have never known youth
For they were old when they were born.

And there are the Peter Pans and Wendys,
On whom age never seems to bear.
They've drank deep of the fountain's magic,
Some not knowing it was there.

They're the ones that really know youth,
And don't have to search to find.
They know that youth is not a time, or place,
But is simply a state of mind.

H. Gratton

3 Hours Of Guard Duty

A half hour after midnight,
   everyone safely out of sight;
The ghost of the shadows haunts the light,
   and I alone dare the night.

The ashes of winter's breeze haunts and glides through the trees,
He calls me! - a ghostly chant.
Would I dare? Would I care?
He whispers! a faceless pant.
Would I dare? Should I care?

He waits for me around every corner,
I dare him to act, seeking an encounter,
He seeks his mate; he lies in wait,
   circling around - me as bait!

Without fear - I fall back and hide for cover.
He who walks, glides and stalks - there
   - is gracefully crossing the bridge!

The bridge between our two worlds, my dear sirs.
He stands there - pauses, rightfully mocking,
Since this is his dimension and woe he who treads there, beware!!!

Yaeer Yehezkel

From A He To A She

As the dawn breaks, a figure fights free.
Plain apparel;
loose and ill fitting;
he emerges from his place of birth and stretches lazily.

As he looks around, he perceives female beauty.
Blinding colours;
compact shapes;
yet he feels the need to join the throng and do his duty.

Hiding his discomfort and uncertainty,
he assumes the male classic stature.
Then moving slowly and with caution,
he proceeds to join the cast of nature.

For most of his life the caterpillar remains unaltered,
but his discomfort with his shape remains the same.
Until he feels the need is overpowering,
to return itself to that from whence it came.

As the dawn breaks, a figure fights free.
Rainbow colours;
gossamer wings;
and the butterfly discards his shell and resumes his life as she.

T-J Evans

Parable Of The Seasons

Winter - dark and damp and dreary:
All the world is lifeless, weary; trees are leafless, stark.
But to this cold world, frost-frozen,
God still gives His Child, His Chosen -
Light to chase the dark.

Spring-time - now new life is waking:
Fresh young blades and buds are making
Green mist, Nature's breath.
Though He dies, a lone seed planted,
Endless life to Christ is granted, vanquisher of death.

Summer-eyes are tricked by heat-haze:
Brief warm nights and long hot dog-days, blue and gold and brown.
As the grain is fast maturing,
So God's Kingdom, strong, enduring, puts its roots deep down.

Autumn is the year's fulfilling:
All our ploughing, weeding, drilling,
Proves worthwhile at last.
So the pain of Christ's travailing
In the end will be availing -
Heaven won, suffering past.

David Gurney

No Doubt!

How can I doubt my faith in God? with beauty all around,
The birds that sing in chorus, what a lovely sound!
They chirrup and they twitter, whilst flying overhead.
And sing a song of thanks to me, just for some crumbs of bread.

How can I doubt my faith in God,? Who gives both day and night,
The evening sky at sunset, what a radiant sight!
A blaze of glorious colour, too wondrous to be told,
So many varied colours, from grey to shining gold.

How can I doubt my faith in God? Who gives us cooling rain,
Majestic trees and grass so lush, in every country lane.
Greens and browns of every shade, none could make it so,
Except our great Creator, who made it long ago.

How can I doubt my faith in God? Who gives so much to me,
The laughing eyes of children, good friends and family,
The creatures that surround me, gifts of speech and sight,
Wisdom too, that I might know, what is wrong and right.

I cannot doubt my faith in God, when I look around,
Considering such marvels, such beauty to be found.
In so many places, How can I not believe?
And give thanks, from my heart, for all that I receive!

S. Wright

Inner Turmoil

The day starts off as ordinary as any other -
Shower, breakfast and dressing powerfully.
A look in the mirror, "Oh! Can that be me?"
Looking so confident, you wink to yourself, then
   go on your way.

Walking briskly along the path, thinking of what's ahead,
Remembering what you have learned. Going through it
   in your mind
To get through this day, just smile and be yourself.
As the sight that greets you looms ahead,
Your stomach starts churning, though it's not been fed.

The smile wavers as you stumble, but you move on determinedly.
Thoughts come more rapidly and fast, chasing confidence to pass.
Palms start sweating, head is pounding,
A few more steps and the ground starts spinning.
Finally making it through the door, to the seat that's vacant,
You almost hit the floor.

When the prim voice says, "Class, you may commence",
Pick up the paper and think where to begin.
What is it about exams that makes us need to pass?

Christine H. Wilson

Revealed In Passing

Death is just passing away,
On the roadway to heaven's bright lights,
where the angels are happy and gay
as they languish in realms of delight.

Hell they say is here on earth
as we struggle from day to day,
each one of us searching for solace
but none of us finding the way

Losing a loved one is sad,
it fills our hearts with distress
but you need not worry if the above be true
then we are the one's in a mess
for Nanny (Mary) is safely in God's company,
surrounded by His awesome might,
while we are left here on our own,
to continue the devilish fight.

Janet Wile

The Princess Maud

The memory and smell that still reminds me of hell,
is travelling on "The Princess Maud"
From Dublin's North Wall to the Liverpool Docks,
and vice versa on the way back.
Travelling with the cows there was never any rows
As passengers were always sick, from the rocking of the ship
And the smell of cow s-ite, which wafted through the night.
Sea sickness and babies crying
Every body around looked dying.
Minutes turned to hours people of the floor rolling all about.
Tea was like bog water
Oh! How you envied those cows for slaughter.
You surely wished that you were dead
When they unloaded at Birkenhead.
Landing in the cold grey dawn of Liverpool
You knew then you were an awful fool
That did not stay at school.

Bernadette McGrath

Turn Off The Sun

Turn off the Sun and pull down the Moon
The life that we had has ended too soon
The love that we felt the passion we knew
Has all been snuffed out because I've lost you
The promise of joy, the hopes of my heart
Will all come to nought for we have to part
One moment you're living, the next you are dead
You've left me in darkness with a future I dread
You were my life's anchor, my reason to be,
My heartbeat, my lifeblood, you're still part of me
The love you have left me will help me get through
A light for my pathway that leads me to you
With our souls reunited, our new life begun
We'll put back the Moon and turn on the Sun

Terry Meredith

A New Tomorrow

Soon the world will see a new millennium,
And maybe man can learn to love,
And live in hope again.

No babes to starve and die while politicians lie,
No needy and neglected by people we respected,
If man just cared for man,
And did away with sham.

If one power cried enough,
No war no weapons no riches can replace
The trust we lost.

Then ask the child what we could do for them,
In this their new millennium

Their hopes their dreams, the future that they share,
With one voice they all answer,
Show you care.

Margaret Smith

Yesterday

It only seemed like yesterday
    When the angels came and took
my son away.
    Even when shopping I'd stand and cry.
    People would look and wonder why.
    Relations kept saying that time
would heal.
    But no one can know how I feel
Oh why did angels have to come
    And take away my precious son.

Sometimes in bed I'd lie awake
    Then I'd cry and my body would shake
    My husband would wake and hold me near
    In his arms to chase away my fears
People say they understand
    But they never held his little hand they never touched his tiny
toes or even kissed his button nose
    Time does seem to have gone on by
But there are times when I still cry
    For in my body there is life again
    And I can't help wondering if it'll be the same.

Lindy M. Clark

Derwentwater

It rained and rained,
There was mist,
The mountains were hidden
Guarded by greystones of lakeland.

Rain stopped, sun shone,
Mist disappeared, lake appeared.
Its blue water
Carried me to the mountains.

I had climbed them
Years ago, the memory
Took me now to the summit.
Thank God for memories.

Quickly the sun disappeared,
More rain poured heavily
Reminding one of life's changing scenes.
Across the sky came the rainbow.

Thank God for this beauty,
Give us strength to protect it
And time to enjoy it.

E. Pescod

Promise

To dream the dream of a thousand Isles,

Of water lapping upon craggy shore.
That sea of endless motion, calm and strong,
Warmed by the sun, sea becomes clouds, changing
shape and form, working down upon a changing world.
Breath of earth guides each raindrop to its destination.

Flower, lift your head to welcome within your body

That which is essence to all.
Wondrous is the beautiful bloom that excites the
Senses and revitalizes the spirit to all it touches,
As winter casts a darkened shadow,
Sleep keeps safe its tender charge.

Spring brings the marriage of sun on earth

To bring forth the return of life.
Summer heralds the strength, vitality and promise in all its glory.
Autumn, bringer of future gifts, so precious is this time,
In darkened days that precious flower will be
In the hearts and dreams of all it has given pleasure to.

P. Chapple

Treasured Memories

Hands to hold and noses to wipe.
The laughter, the fun and the tears.
The terrible twos four times around.
And the paddies in those first years.

Your first days at school and the sadness I felt.
Letting go in those early school years.
All the concerts I've seen and the parts you all played.
Just remembering them brings me to tears.

The cuts and the bruises, the coughs and the colds.
The scratches, the tears and the bumps.
And I've sat by your beds for many a day.
With the chicken pox, measles and mumps.

Now you're all growing up and it makes me feel old.
But I smile when I hear myself say.
"That music's too loud. Will you please turn it down?"
It's the same thing my mum used to say.

Now you've given me so many memories.
Your achievements, your let downs, your fears.
And now I just want to say "thank you".
For letting me share all those years.

Carol Young

The Secret Garden

We talk over coffee and shape our belief,
Both of us, perhaps hide pain underneath,
From work each day I hurry home,
Knowing I'll hear your voice on the phone,
"Just good friends?" Yes that's right!
The heart on my sleeve tucked well out of sight,
When alone, my true feelings I will impart,
Knowing there's a seed planted in my heart.
Afraid to water it, or let it bloom,
Afraid for you I would be too soon,
The other day when we walked God's land,
I felt the temptation to hold your hand.
I must not rush, or get in your way
So I'll just stand back and let you have the last say.
Me, I'll just smile and say.
"He's my best friend" and turn away.
Will I get hurt?, will I feel pain?
Well that's when I'll start sifting
The soil again.

Joyce Davidson

Nowhere Road

I left in the sunshine and I'm still leaving now and it's dusk.
Moonlight. Engine idling. Tick, tick, tick, tick.
I fidget. I feel sick to the Radio Man's drivelling drone.
Nowhere Road. Traffic cone.
I feel agitated, aggravated.

I left with the sun still shining. Now guided my moonbeams.
On Nowhere Road with gasoline dreams.
Engine idling. Tick, tick, tick, tick. Metronome
Nowhere Road. Road of cones. Radio phone-in.
I really feel agitated, aggravated.

My mirror sees a snake of white light.
My eyes see a lighted wall of red.
Engine idling. Tick, tick, tick, tick.
Tick, tick, tick in my head
White light snake. Lighted wall of red.

My head on my shoulder. Hard shoulder. Diesel picnic.
I was going somewhere and now I'm going nowhere.
Roads go everywhere but Nowhere Road.
Where am I going? Am I still getting there? Road? Nowhere Road?
Where? Why?

Andy Pollard

Sight

As I walked down this windy road,
A million things I see,
Flowers, trees and bumble bees, are all crowding me.

Sight is such an amazing thing,
Please bring it back to me.

The sea wind blows my long brown hair,
The sand blows in my eyes,
No longer I can see the morning sun rise.

Sight is such an amazing thing,
Please bring it back to me.

All I can remember is the last thing that I saw,
Which was the sea hurdling against the Black Rock shore.
I wish that I could see back into the past, the past that
I never saw.

Sight is such an amazing thing,
Please bring it back to me.

Sandra Hartford

You Asked Where God Was On That Day

You asked where God was on that horrible day,
when that evil gun man blew the children away.
Did he hide his head in shame,
or like us, did he share our pain.

Please don't blame God for the evil done,
remember, he sacrificed his only son
To make things better, for us on earth,
so we'll never die, but get a re-birth.

He gave us the will, to make our own choice,
to ask for love, and salvation, he gave us a voice.
It's man who makes wars, maims, and kills,
it's man that's responsible for all our ills.

He gave us a beautiful world, and a will to toil,
but what do we do, we contaminate and spoil.
So don't blame God for the evil we do,
remember Jesus's message, that God loves You.

Rita M. Hough

Grass—The Field Of Battle

Constant contest: stretching, straining:
   Permanent racing—morning to night;
     For the victor, the great prize—the chance to grow free,
     The loser condemned to a death in the shade.

     Insects troop by, unaware of the race
     Yet blades battle on whilst the day twice repeats;
   As the breeze blows cold westwards, pushing wars towards dusk,
Time for a rest as the target moves round.

Dawn poses new threats: the hard-hearted frost
   Devouring all life within its iced range.
     The grass relents warring, turns all strength to life;
     The final stand ends with all blades thrown down.

Simon Boice

Hull's Poet

And now there can be no more High Windows,
no more Whitsun Weddings,
no more lines that cut like knives,
or warm like glowing fire,
with words that not so much inspire,
(although they do), but seem to hold me captive,
as if in awe of someone with so fine a sense of time.

To think he lived but half an hour's walk from here,
to be so near, and yet so far away,
a fellow citizen, living and working in my home town,
a poet of such wide renown, he could have been the laureate.
And now he's gone, passed on, down the long slide to happiness,
and there inside the local press, halfway down the page it read,
'Hull's poet, Philip Larkin, - dead'.

John Fairclough

Oh! England, My England!

Land of my birth and boyhood days,
I remember still, your charming ways,
'Twas here, that I first knew a true mother's love,
And heard the soft croon of a cooing dove,
Whilst the wind a-whispering amongst the trees,
A message to the birds, trilling songs on the breeze,
It's time for mating, it's time for love.
   "Oh! England! My England!"

Thy sons have sailed the seas of 'yore'.
And fought for England's name,
Bringing wealth and fame to England's shore,
"Long may she reign!"
In war, God to her glory came,
He gave her strength for victory,
In blood he wrote her name in fame.
And made her "MOTHER OF THE FREE!"
   "Oh! England! My England!"

   G. L. Cripps

Just War

What is the meaning of War,
I only know of death that is on par.
Men went to war because of the slave age,
To free all human beings from bondage.
Men went to war because of women,
For Cleopatra was desirable to all men.
Men went to war because of land,
And yet there is so much on hand.
Men went to war for the sake of religion
Yet the same God is worshipped by a nation.
Men went to war because of man's colour,
Yet we are men with so much valour.
Men went to war for the sake of freedom
For man wants to move freely in his kingdom.

   John Naideo

The January Gale

It happened at night as most fearsome things do
I awoke with a fright, I hadn't a clue
To the sound that I heard.
It came roaring along, like a monstrous train,
Gathering speed, and force, was all its aim,
I shivered, and trembled, with fear.
I thought the end of the world was near.

The roofs of the buildings it tore off on the way.
What a devastating scene there was the next day.

It ravaged the county, as well as the town,
Some tenement building, razed to the ground.
Trees in their thousands, all blown down.

The damage it caused, was hard to assess
Not everyone tells, of their plight and distress
The January gale, that came with such might,
The January gale, that came in the night.

   Ann Muir Hush

Untitled

Cows are simply wonderfully warm creatures.
Hay is simply greatness.
The moon has simply caught fire.
A woman has simply come down the horse
and tied it to a tree.
The tree has simply fallen down
and the horse has run away.
The woman has simply died of the wounds.

The moon has simply burnt out.
The hay has simply grown.
The cows have simply caught fire.
It has turned out like a wonderful day.
"It is a wonderful day, isn't it", they say
and go humble every time.

   Maria Gardner

God's Error

Over a hundred million years ago
God said "Let's make earth," so
He made the trees and made the flowers
Made time out of minutes and hours
He made pigs, sheep and cows
Males and females, boars and sows
He made rivers flow into seas
Made ants, spiders and bumblebees
He made the land and the sky
He gave birds wings so they could fly
He made the clouds and the sun
God was having a lot of fun
He made night dark and day light
He gave some creatures the power to fight
He made some stars and a moon
By this time he was running out of room
He made the countries to split earth up
With hot in the middle and cold on top
But then God made a silly mistake
He made people, what a thing to make

   Donna Stevens

Homeless

I am lost, I have no direction, I have nowhere to live
I have no possessions and nothing but my love to give
I see you go about your business every single day
You are always very busy as you go along your way
I ask of you nothing except perhaps a smile
You grant me this I am grateful everyone else keeps me in denial
I live to see you daily with your shiny smiley face
It keeps me out of trouble and from causing myself disgrace
I am going now to pick the best flower that I can find
And I am going to give it to you my dear for being so kind
Because I cannot make this homeless journey on my own
And I thank you kind lady for the happiness seeds you have sown

   Gary Liles

The Five Senses

Beauty is in the beholder's eye, we are told.
This ancient adage may be true, but hold,
And think about those who cannot see,
The blind to whom a scene or tree
Or colour has no meaning but who,
See with their ears, surely sound has beauty too.
Bird song, laughter, favourite tunes, to name a few.
But what of those who are bereft
Of sight and hearing, what is left?
The sense of touch has beauty of its own
A kittens fur, polished wood, a piece of stone.
And then add the sense of smell,
There must be beauty here as well
Flowers' scent, wood smoke, make us sigh
With delight, as does the smell of Mother's apple pie
And lastly, the wonderful sense of taste,
Ensures that the best of food never goes to waste.

   Bernard R. Bass

The Dirge

We are The Forgotten People:
Once we were Young - Cried, laughed, sang
And counted Not the days.
We fell in love, mated, some not.
All lived a life of service to Our Country, Our Heritage.

Life is for living and we lived it to the Full.
Those busy battling beautiful balmy days;
Tasting the heights, savouring the depths,
Caring for the Old.
Till - one day - Wham, Bang!! We were the Old.

We were assured, and foolishly believed
Old age would be Stable, Secure, Serene.
Alas! Alack! The Wheel has turned full Circle.
Insensitivity, Instability, Insecurity for us
The Forgotten People, the Over Seventy-Fives.

   Genial Octogenarian

Feelings Of The Heart

The road is long when the heart feels pain,
  And we think we'll never love again.
A wall of scars from times unspoken,
  Fortifies a heart so easily broken,
Never again will it come to be,
  That love's emotions will trouble me.

For many years these words were true,
  Till the day fate introduced me to you.
Just a kiss, that's all it took,
  For hidden feelings to pop out and look.

The demolition of thoughts now lays bare,
  The fortified heart to warmly care.
Now love's blood pumps through each vein,
  What was once hidden by a smile, lives again.
It's pain, it's joy, it's wondrous glow,
  I now hold out for the world to know,
That everything I say and do
  Is done because I'm so in love with you.

  Joyce Davidson

Rwanda

I never thought I knew you
Until I saw your eyes.
While flicking channels
Through unsequenced babble,
The split second image held
And locked your eyes with mine
Briefly.
Oh God! How sickening, how horrible.
Turn it off! Turn it off!
I don't want to see your images of war Rwanda.
Let me hide in safe indifference
From your eyes,
Your death eyes,
Your black, black death eyes
That follow, probe, haunt, disturb
Compel me to watch, to see
To feel
The horror,
The slash of steel, the stench of death,
The burning pyre of infant flesh.
Is Coronation Street on yet?

  Joanna B. Cowley

No Need To Be Afraid

I asked the Master, with some deep fear
How shall I feel when death is near?
Shall I flounder in depths unknown
In pain, or torment, all alone.

Shall I cling on to memories sweet
And beg my heart - don't cease to beat!
Shall I in panic plead for life
Forgetting all its pain and strife.

And when at last I know I'm dead
What will I find to rest my head.
In cold damp caverns shall I roam,
Shall nought but darkness be my home?

The Master smiled and said with mirth
You found no terror at your birth.
But light and warmth and comfort too,
With arms to shield and cradle you.

And love to help you live and grow
The answers you already know.
"Fear not my child," the Master said,
"There is always life - you are never dead."

  P. E. Stacey

World War II 1943 The London Blitz
Hutch Played The Piano On The Radio

Warm in my bath I listened to "Hutch"
About this old war I didn't care much.
Scrubbed good and hard and felt ever so clean.
And thought, there's no hurry, then hell: the siren.
With one hectic splash I jumped out of the tub,
Hardly dare waiting my body to rub.
Pajamas kept slipping, the elastic was broke,
If I'd waited to pin them I might go up in smoke.
Rushed down the stairs, my heart sick with fear,
Cursing the Huns as I heard them fly near.
On gaining the cellar, regaining my breath
I proceeded to guard against catching my death.
Over my pajamas my girdle I slipped,
To hold me together in case I got "pipped."
I then stuck my feet into warm woolly boots
Still hearing the siren's sharp blood-curdling hoots,
And at last a warm coat and some wool in each ear,
I sat praying and shaking awaiting "All Clear."

  Maureen Kinsman

Current Affairs

He's got money, looks and charm,
She's blonde, blue-eyed and fun.
They drink, they chat and, well, that's that . . .

She sits at home
Working on the bank balance
Making impossibilities possible to afford.
She puts another shirt on the ironing board.
She's ironed, she's washed, she's cleaned,
She's exhausted . . . but she doesn't sit down.

She switches the oven on,
Makes a casserole and opens a tin
Which she knows will end up in the bin
With the rest of her self-respect.

"Good day at the office, dear?"

Six months ago that was me.
I got through it, while his dinners burned.
Then he returned on bended knee,
Only not so wealthy—he'd lost his charm.

But revenge is sweet
In another man's arms . . .

  Gwyneth M. Glascodine

Motherhood (To Be A Mother
Is A Vital Role In Life)

To be a Mother can be the hardest role on earth.
The easy part I'd say is giving birth.
We can bring our children up really very well.
But how they will turn out no one can ever tell.

A child needs a very stable life.
We try to protect them from trouble and strife.
But one day they will have to stand on their own two feet.
So we must prepare them for things in life they will meet.

The rewards of motherhood are thousand fold.
But no one can prepare you, well, I wasn't told!
The love of a child and the trust that they give
Really makes life worthwhile—that's how I want to live.

I want to be a mother who loves her child so strong.
So that at any age we will still get along.
I know it won't be easy—I don't expect it to be.
It is the most extraordinary feeling, having your own flesh
and blood on your knee.

I pray to the Lord for guidance for this very special role.
To be a perfect mother has to be my goal.
Yes, to be a mother is the hardest role on earth.
But I'm very glad for this special gift and that's the gift of birth.

  Edith Meldrum Cooke

467

Not On That Day - I Wasn't There

It wasn't me, I was not there
Such abuse, such despair
It wasn't me, I am not she
I've got to get out there and look for me
The time has come, I must get back
I can't turn round, it's not strength I lack
Self belief I need to see
I need to find, look after me
It's time to reach out and try to catch
All that pretending can't be a match
Surely not? I must be worth more
Don't judge the people, look at the core

I'm losing, they're losing, that's for sure
But how can they trust me to swallow the cure?
Damage was done, a sad state of mind
I know there's no antidote any could find
But I'm not such a bad girl, or so they all say
But it wasn't me there, not on that day

Yvonne A. Forbes

Odessa

Odessa is a pearl of South!
It on the Black Sea coast stands,
I like your beaches full of sounds,
And playing children on the sands.

The chilly sea is tender under sun,
With coming of the night,
The moon makes silver line on waves that run,
Then rising sun presents again its lovely light.

The chilly light of moon
It throws on the sea
Is changing to the hottest noon.
And all the people at the sea love it, including me.

Aleksey Orishich

Leukaemia Research

Medical Researchers perform stringent tests,
Standards ultimately exceeding their best;
Their accuracy for detail will astound,
For into the future a cure must be found.

The suffering and pain one has to endure,
If only someone could find a cure;
Please make a donation but don't count the cost,
The battle against Leukaemia must not be lost.

Do unto others as you would have others do,
As we are all one family including you;
Help Leukaemia Research win again,
The battle for victory is never in vain.

Love and affection comes from the heart,
Remedial treatment is always a start;
Thank you for helping this worthy cause,
Your generous gifts deserve applause.

Malcolm Goat

A Footpath

A narrow field, with rim of trodden soil
  Where once, we strolled in peace at end of day,
To taste the freedom from day's work and toil
  With nature and ourselves in mood so gay;
The footpath led to forest so serene,
  Where bluebells formed a carpet near our feet,
The rippling stream below enhanced the scene
  And summer breezes through the leaves did meet;
The hardened path, to us, was world's highway
  For it was trodden by our kith and kin
To home and love, where brightness led the way
  And open door was refuge from all sin.
Alas, the footpath now is overgrown—
The cottage, dark and lifeless on its own.

Margaret A. Evans

A Golden Sunset

As night is fast approaching
I look across the bay,
At a beautiful golden sunset.
Colours in bright array.

  I listen to the silence
  At this peaceful time of day,
  And on the far horizon
  The sun is sinking far away.

    The evening seems quiet and tranquil,
    A lone bird on the wing.
    As he glides home to the warmth of the nest
    To the world a chorus he sings.

    The coming together of sea and sky
    On this clear and balmy night
    Awakes my soul to the wonders of nature,
    And this golden band of pure delight.

Sylvia Hall

Wonderful Day

It's a wonderful day,
I'm watching the birds that sing and
The lambs that play.
The sun's shining so very bright,
Everywhere's full of colour and light.
The farmer surveys his fruitful fields,
The reaper sharpens the scythe he wields.
Colourful insects slowly flutter by,
The beauty of the day brings a tear to my eye.

Matthew Pearce

The Blackout

The blackout is darkness,
In a cave with bats,
Black oil spilt on a pool of light,
Fear tips itself all over the moon,
The sun and my eyes,
Danger spills into my mind,
Earth worms climb up the back of my neck,
Blackout is pure black ink in my path,
It is blackness, blindness,
It is silence in the middle of a speech,
Danger and fear are the blackout,
Pin pricks of light show fear in people's eyes,
It is friends who don't care,
It is under water trying to get to the top,
Swimming and swimming without hope,
It is under the bed,
I can't get out of the darkness help!,
It is a nest covered in black bees,
It is a black cover over my eyes,
My black guinea pigs feet walking over my face.

Rebecca Hilliker

A Saddened World

Innocence in a child's eye.
Why did sixteen angels die?
What drove a man to do this sin,
Questions you want to ask, were do you begin?
Angels born young and true.
Their only sin to go to school.
The love of a teacher could not save
These innocent children who he slayed.
She also died by the maniac's gun:
We ask God what could have been done.
Why didn't he stop him in his wake,
Why seventeen lives he had to take,
In Dunblane a city mourns:
Mothers and fathers, their lives are torn.
A nation weeps, we're all in grief
For seventeen lives no one could keep.
We'll send our love like all the rest.
And only say God takes the "best".

Julie Palmer

Old Lostock

What once stood tall and proud and strong
A hive of activity, of labours long
Is now a hollow, empty shell
The axe has fallen—a jobless hell

Where once worked thousands now are few
Machines all gone, no wares to view
Was it us, are we to blame
No longer matters, what a crying shame

The hopes, the fears, the laughter and tears
The times we had throughout the years
Those days are gone seems a long time past
But unlike the memories, the jobs didn't last

And still we reflect on our working life
Hoping never again to endure such strife
A time for sitting and taking stock
Those were the days back in Old Lostock

Neil Hopper

The Poplars

Tall poplars stand stark against
    the Winter's evening sky
The distant lights encircling their
    meagre tresses like a crown
There they tower like unrobed princes
Away and high above the industrial town.

But when summer comes
Their green plumes sway beneath an azure sky
And although the noisy traffic flows beyond
All one can hear on passing is a sigh

Sheila Clarke

When

When days die babes at winter's hands
And shadows hunt the freezing land.
When nature wipes its pallet clean
And sadness stalks the ground again.
When clouds won't let the sunlight through
When I'm a world away from you.

I picture beauty in my mind
And see your face before my eyes.
I smell your hair and touch your skin
A candle light where you have been,
A memory etched inside my head
A soul for to search when I am dead.

When I'm alone and silence reigns
Your blood pumps purpose through my veins.
Each thought I have of you is laid
A home of which our life is made
And unto love I will be true
When I'm a world away from you.

Giles Upton

Him...

I wish we'd talk more, I wish he'd talk to me,
When I close my eyes, it's always him I see.
His mysterious face and his lovely brown hair
With his baggy blue jumper I can't help but stare!
I love him so much, in every possible way
I see him so often, almost every day.
We have been friends since I was around ten
I've always liked him, even back then.
I love the Scottish accent I hear when he talks
I melt inside even at the way he walks.
When I see him come by my heart misses a beat
My legs turn to jelly and so do my feet.
I want to hold him and hug him and squeeze him tight,
And never let go like in my dreams at night.
When I see him at school and he looks at me
He stares in a nice way, my mouth drops to my knees
I love him so much and I wish he loved me
But we are just friends that is plain to see.

Abby Donald

Didn't I Always

Didn't I always say, that one of the nice
things about being married, was
having someone to cuddle up to in bed.
Now the bed is too big and so cold.
Didn't I always like to see you,
sitting in your own armchair by the fire,
smiling into my face, making the whole
room feel warm, cheerful and secure.
Now your empty chair makes me afraid in
a cold bleak world.
And didn't I always like to feel your hand
holding mine, as we walked down the street,
We didn't mind the rain in our faces, or the
cold nip of frost in the air, we were happy.
Now there is no soft touch, nothing to hold
but the shopping bag, nothing to feel but
the harsh reality that I am alone.
Didn't I always wish, that when the time
came, we could still be together,
Oh my dear, didn't I, always.

Elizabeth Bell

After Life Fantasy

The harmonic sound of an angel's wings,
Is one of the highlights that real life brings.
Death, not an ugly word, but one that is sad,
Not one that is lonely or one that is bad.
A subject mysterious, the future unknown.
A time we must face, and usually alone.
Do we enter a world alive and new, or remain in a sky that is calm
and blue? No problems arise, no worries or stress, No T.V. dramas
where lives are a mess. Reunited families, happy again, like
wilting flowers in light summer rain
A land called heaven if there is such a place.
A world to accept us, regardless of race
My dream of love is alive like the sea
An invisible door with a time lock, not a key.
A wave washing a pebble from the shade of a palm,
Taking it far into the ocean to protect it from harm
so when this world closes and our lives cease
I feel we'll be accepted to a new one of peace
The people we've lost, don't class as dead
Their spirits have moved on to a new future ahead.

Kelly Pailes

My Dear Old Granddad

In his prime my granddad was as energetic as I could say,
But as the nights got colder,
And the days grew longer,
My dear old granddad weakened day by day.

My granddad is now no longer,
For he passed away not long ago,
I wish I could tell him the things I wished,
But how was I to know.

If only I hear myself say,
If only he still lived and never went away,
Death comes to us all his time had come,
But I was the one feeling hurt and numb.

I admire his courage he tried to show,
But I could see straight through the lie,
Deep down I did know,
This man I loved was just as scared as I.

Life goes on as it was before,
But where does that leave me,
It leaves me bitter and sore,
But what has happened has happened, it's better left be!

Jodie Abrahams

The End Of A Life Time

For the last time maybe I stand,
eyes set on that mountain grand.
A whispered word and I turn to see,
those loving eyes observing me.

With heavy heart I hold her tight,
a trickling tear affects my sight.
Soothed by kind and loving phrases
sadly fearful of distant places.

The mountain covered in darkened cloud,
the air is cold and I am old.
How much longer can I last.
My thoughts all muddled in the past.

The doom of life is heavy now,
rocked by the swaying tide.
Of everlasting love for her,
my fair eternal bride.

Farewell this life that I have lived
with all its tribulations.
Farewell that girl that I have loved,
through all the generations.

Alwyn James

The End Of An Era, The Birth Of A New Era

Folks have come, and folks have gone,
Poorly people we have made healthy and strong,
But now the city hospital will be no more,
It's merely just an empty core,
Empty wards and sighing walls,
No more bells and no more calls.
But don't let us sigh,
And don't let us cry,
For it's off to Tadcaster Road,
To our brand new abode,
All is new, and all is bright,
It really is a wonderful sight,
"St. Helens" is our new name,
Our "Crue" will bring us lots of fame,
Nestled there among the trees,
People enjoying afternoon teas,
No more will we think, it's a pity,
That we have left behind the city,
So "goodbye" to the old, and "hello" to the new,
And all the very best to "Kath Ward and her Crew."

Peggy Meehan

Ye Olde Oak Tree

What's the matter
my dear old tree?
Are you tired and
knackered just like me?

Is your trunk emaciated
just like mine?
Are you dying
before your time?

Well I'm hanging on
as long as can be
So don't give up
Keep going with me,

You losing your leaves
Me losing my hair
We'll soon be bald
But we won't care.

'Cos we've got each other as down the years we trot
Then we'll be buried and left to rot.

Your coat will cover me lovely tree of mine
And we'll stay together till the end of time.

Elizabeth Goodwin

Night Journey

Night, hovering like a huge black bird
Keeps the distant hills and trees from view.

And we, heads resting on walls or window-panes,
Look out to see a twilight star
Or see the moths beat on the glass,
Pick out the headlight of a distant car
And still wait.

Fingers lie audaciously on sofa cushions
Tracing out pathways with a nail.
Eyelids drop and gaping jaws hang slack
Before the cosy fire.

Until the roll of tyres and hiss of brakes disturbs us
And we clamber out, to sit and sleep again.
Hiding in the darkness of a van.

I watched your head bobbing on a seat back
Like a dingy on the swell of the sea.
Your hair riding like waves across your arm.
I heard your silent breaths
Rustling over the seat covers.

David Salisbury

Travels Without A Donkey

In the footsteps of Stevenson, we set out
To retrace his route of long about.
Le Monastier was the starting place
From where we hastened upon our chase.
Daily we heard the cuckoo's call
As we made our way through woodland tall.
The valleys lush with grasses green,
The heights from which, rooftops gleam.
We walked each day at a regular pace,
For "Modestine" our thoughts did grace.
Across the mountain plains of gold,
We followed the standing stones of old.
And rested at the "Lady of our Snows",
For spiritual refreshment, heaven knows?
Onward we trekked as true we could
And completed the journey as we knew we would.
For Stevenson, it was his life's direction,
And for us it quelled our fascination,
From this rural land of dreams be said,
Our memories like his travels, will never be dead!

Adrian Coombes

Second Sight

In the breathless, silent portent, that comes before each dawn,
In the tranquil hours of early morning light
As the fading stars bow gracefully in farewell to the night,
In the ghostly misty valleys that lie waiting for the sun, I see you
A kaleidoscope of colour, sparkling 'neath the golden rays
Silver webs with dewy strands, reflected hues.
Mother Earth awakens smiling to another day.
Through the rising vapour disappearing with the dew, I see you
In the constant chatter of a stream that rushes through the glade,
In the solitude that isolates my heart.
At the thought of never holding you I'm lonely and afraid
Through the timeless limbo of the years we've been apart, I see you.
In the autumn evening painted russet by the early sunset,
In the twilight of the day and of my years,
As the afterglow of the receding light surrounds me,
And the moon arises banishing my fears, I see you.
From the perfect, flawless, loveliness, you radiate within
You created an emotion strong and true.
There are many facets to my love that only time may heal
But through all my days, in ev'rything I do and feel, I see you.

John C. Walsh

Red Rose Of Destiny

She skated in circles, around and around
  But for skate upon ice
  There was no other sound
Ever faster and faster, as though in a race
  A red rose in her hand
  Frozen tears on her face

They'd been skating partners, but now he lay dead
  His brilliant white shirt
  Like the rose, was now red
He'd brought her the roses, to tell her 'goodbye'
  That he'd found a new partner
  But instead,—he would die!

The ice on the pond had worn dangerously thin
  And the thorns of the rose
  Pierced her pale, frozen skin
A crack rent the air—she was gone in a trice
  Now the lovely red rose
  Lies forlorn on the ice
  J. Jacks

The Western Disease

Buy a little something.
Feel better for the treat.

Turn the telly on.

Make another cup of coffee.

Forget your dreams as you wake.

We live in a state of denial;
Bland, passionless societies
Filling the gift of time
With empty distractions and surrogate deities.

We've ripped our myths from our psyches.
We've edited ceremony from our lives.
We've replaced religion with feel good causes
And truth with lies.

On a bed of incestuous osmosis
Sister faith and brother science have conceived
A shining new order
Of materialism and greed.

We've nothing to live for.
We've nothing to die for.

It's the Western disease.
  Paul Quarry

"A Personal Thought"

The Past

We Cannot change the past but we can learn from the mistakes we consider we may have made. To dwell on them only inhibits our ability to deal with the present.

The Present

Live for now, having learnt a little from the past. We must give all of ourselves to the present, to those we love, to ourselves, enjoy this time, for the present is here and now, it is certain it will not return, for in the future this time will be in the past too. Leave happy memories of now.

The Future

We cannot predict the future, only hope, perhaps if we have a God, pray. The way we are and the love we give now and in the future can help those we love and ourselves cope with whatever the future may be.
We cannot live for what could be, for our greatest fears may never happen.
  Colin L. Bowen

Loneliness

There is nothing quite so sad as being lonely and living
  on your own
No one ever visits or even telephones

The days are oh so long, the nights even longer too
Is there nothing anyone can do?

If you have a neighbour living on their own
Just think how lonely they are and call or even phone.

Never think for a moment, it will never happen to me
Just wait until you are older, then we shall see.

It will not take a moment to give a little smile or even stop
  for a chat
For just a little while.

Just to stop and say, "My you do look well", and to see
  the look of happiness
Their face will foretell.

There it did not take a moment of your precious time
Perhaps you could do it all again another time.
  G. M. D. Stacey

My Leadweight Heart

My trusting nature often leads me into danger.
And, my blind folded wit prevents my heart from
warning. Now, the time has come for my old weary
heart to stop tearing apart and start loving once more.
So, my tender, weary heart, from you I'll never part.

My lead-weight heart lies in a house where night never
ends. It lies there awaiting for the love it once knew,
in a time long ago, when the smallest star in the sky
seemed bright in the darkest of nights.
It lies here trapped, for the need of know-how to rekindle its
fire starting its drum-like beat.
That's when night becomes day, once more.
  Nora Galvin

Trevor

His heart is made of the purest gold,
A beautiful face that will never grow old,
Strong arms around me that hold me tight,
With the softest voice, he will say "My darling good night",
Velvet blue eyes that glisten like stars in the evening sky,
A radiant smile for whoever passes by,
His hair golden, yet tinged with grey,
And hands so scarred by the toil of the day,
Imagine the feeling of happiness and pride,
Our arms locked together as we stand side by side,
This love sent from heaven,
Sturdier than the mighty oak tree,
I thank the Lord each night on bended knees,
For Trevor choosing me.
  Elizabeth Spencer Smith

Friendship In The War

Lying miserable cold and lonely,
Dreaming of opened doors to faraway places,
Watching as the hands of the clock
Move to past, present and future. Time is slow.
Suddenly a rush of hooves,
A flying mane, and there she was,
Neighing, as she paused beside my window.
And thrusting her head through the frame,
Rubbing her nose against me,
Like an adoring puppy.
And I am not ashamed to say
That as I put my arms around her,
Knowing that I here, tired, wounded, and away from home
Among strangers, I had made a friend.
The only of thousands, one who loves and cares,
And so, as she gives, I return
Her everlasting love and friendship.
An idol in the war.
  Michelle Kirrane

The Derelict House

Once it stood proud on the corner of a busy main road.
Gleaming, shining, new bricks and mortar,
Bright new curtains, furniture, garden looking like it ought to
The shop that was part of it flourished - family too.
People came, chattered, purchased that which was new.

Then came retirement, shop closed down,
Owners did as all pensioners do.
A journey to shop, and wander round town,
One day they went a journey too far,
Alas, they died in a horribly crashed car.

House stood empty, was put up for sale, but didn't go,
Too large for young folk, old ones didn't want to know,
Each day it becomes more trashed,
Yobs, its very heart have smashed.
Curtains hang all tattered and torn.
No more will the windows shine in the dawn,
It makes one cry, as day after day,
It stands there, a monument to distress and decay.

Kathleen Collins

Purple

The sun in the sky on an unclouded twilight
All fades away then turns to night
Purple is suffering, sorrow and grief
Purple is royal; high rank like a chief
The juice of a beetroot, swirled on a plate
The feeling of strength and the feeling of hate
The colour of the wrapper on my favourite sweet
The colour I become, when not close to the heat.
My favourite colour's not red and not blue
My favourite is purple. Is yours too?

Rebekah McAteer

Ember Days

A thousand sparkling crystals hang on dainty jewelled strand
Along the golden hedgerows in autumn's magic land.
Red and amber leaves aglow, slowly drifting down
Adding their adornment to Mother Nature's gown.
The swallows long have left the skies in search of warmer climes
But still their memory lingers on, in lazy summer times.
Seasons come and seasons turn, time passing, never slow.
Age advancing swiftly, as down life's path we go.
Days are crisper, edged with rime, night is getting strong,
The sun so weak and feeble, can't hold back winter long.
This mellow season, rich and full, has not yet given way
To time's old age, stark and white, as a mid-winter's day.
Echoed by the season's change once more our hearts will sing,
As our future hopes and dreams awaits the coming of the spring.
Hoarding precious memories, we count each passing day
Until that joyous burst of life when once again we'll say
"Welcome!" to each bud and shoot, "Welcome!" re-born earth
As Mother Nature blesses us with her glorious re-birth.

Patricia M. Manfield

Strange Life

On the return I gazed over the high mountains,
Snow-tipped and glowing in all their rugged splendour.
And I remember the smile on the glowing face,
The recognition in the dazzled eye,
And the bridge as it swayed over the white water.
And I remember peace in the honeycombed meadow,
The sweet scent of summer, the bright distant sun.
Yet I was confused as the kingfisher dived clearly
Into the shallow waters, and the larch sang high
In the sycamore tree, as the waves crashed ashore,
The seaweed tossed, dolphins played, I felt a restlessness,
Of one who has nothing, yet wants everything.
For always there is something missing, a piece of the puzzle
That won't quite fit. And I remember the discontent,
As the wind whipped to a frenzy, changing the scenery
As easily as if a landscape painter had whipped all the colours
together, blurring the face, obscuring the memory
Strange how suddenly things change.

Gail MacDonald

Meg

Far off, the isles where I have never been,
Sea-nourished by warm currents, isolated,
But home for you, whom I had never seen
Since you were golden-haired, whose smile melted
My heart with that soft look - always
A sweet challenge to my younger days.

Often you called to me to come
To your far island in the West, but I
Had found excuses nearer home.
We exchanged cards as Christmases went by,
Then finally these festive missives ceased:
I did not know - how could I? - you had died.

But now, upon the wash of distant tides
And on the shore just rising from the sea,
A blue-eyed mermaid shiningly resides
In that far isle - looking just as, to me,
You looked in those long years ago:
The Meg whom I once loved to know.

Humphrey Wynn

Love (From The Eyes Of Another)

You let me slip through your hands.
The babe in arms gone from your life.
Your pain I could not understand.
The wrenching parting, the widowed wife.

How could a life so young, so tender,
Comprehend such surrender?

Then death took you into his arms.
Cutting the chord from which I came.
All alone, fate mapped out in a child's palms.
The future could never be the same.

Now as a man life from me is born.
Her hair surrounds the sweetest face.
Will she journey through life in the cloak I've worn,
Or will she find the happy loving place?
The place I fear too much to find,
Others might uncover my true mind.

Love left me when your heart grew silent,
Your body quite cold, life gone from your face.
Love left me then, replaced by silence,
When you flew away to a better place.

S. P. Lacey

The Hills Of Home

The hills of home are calling
    And I am far away
I hear them call above the thrall
    And know I cannot stay
The memories from childhood days
    Are strong in heart and mind
And pull me ever homeward
    To days of Auld Lang Syne
It seems like only yesterday
    When we all played together
Through springtime days and summer haze
    O'er bracken fields and heather
Now some are gone and I reflect
    on how far I have wandered
From here to there and back again
    How much time I have squandered
When I recall the things I've seen and people I've encountered
Some were bad and some were sad but most were happy chapters
    Now time has flown and age creeps on and I no longer roam
My final journey takes me back to see the hills of home.

Helen Macdonald

Ageless Love

The sun so warm, a gentle breeze in my hair
Takes me back when I was 14 and had not a care.
It was then I met Maurice, the love of my life
I lived on daydreams of becoming his wife
For two years we shared our life and our love
We were young, hadn't lived, love wasn't enough.
We quarrelled and parted and went separate ways,
How could I live without him - I lived life in a daze.
But then I recovered to live life again
Though I knew I would never get over the pain.
We made separate lives, had kids, life went on
Till many years later life as I knew it had gone.
I was alone, I was widowed and Maurice divorced
Memories and feelings of my first love were restored.
After twenty seven years our love was beyond compare.
We dated, got engaged and became an inseparable pair.
We just got married and I at last became his wife
So lucky our love survived, we'll walk together for the rest
    of our life.

Susan Joyce Bardsley

Untitled

If you have faith it will enable you to have
such strength, when in times of sorrow and sadness.

To see beyond life without fear,
To love life with such passion that overwhelms us.
To see beauty and to cherish life's treasures preciously.

I thank God for the contentment I feel in my
heart.

All those priceless gifts one has love, peace,
Strength and vision.

Sandra Stote

The First Christmas

A little brown mouse crept out of the hay.
She felt something special was coming her way;
So she watched and she waited
And as she sat there,
The sound of sweet singing came down the night air,
And a little grey donkey came in from the street.
He felt something special was guiding his feet;
So he watched and he waited
And as he stood there,
The sound of bells ringing came on the night air.
Then a little white dove flew in from the night.
She knew something special has guiding her flight;
So she watched and she waited,
And called from her height.

Then the stable was warmed with a new kind of light
That feeling so special was with them to stay;
And they knew they had witnessed
    The First Christmas Day.

E. P. Boothby

I Miss You

Strange that they all meant so much less to you
those beautiful moments that we shared,
and sad to think that every time you held me close,
deep down inside you never cared.
I believed every single word you said to me,
I believed every promise in your kiss
I know now they were lies you were telling me,
but they're lies I'm really going to miss.

I can't listen to the records we used to listen to,
I can't visit the places we used to go.
I can't read the letters you sent to me.
Every word of them hits me with a blow.
Sometimes I hate you for the things you've done,
but the hatred I feel never lasts
My present and my future are so empty now,
because my heart is still living in the past.

Nicola Robert

Dad

I remember when you used to hold
my hand sitting side by side building castles in the sand.
    I remember when bath time used to
be fun, and playing in the garden seeing you run.
    Did the sun really shine brighter
then did the grass really look greener when,
    You would take me by the hand
and we would build castles in the sand?
    My childhood did not belong to
me alone it belonged to both you and I.
    And when I think back to
those days I remember a bluer sky.
    You gave your love and time
so freely; you were so generous
    Now the memories of that
time are so very precious.
    Father, dad and pop are such very special words; they are
filled with love and tenderness and hold together the world.
    There are so many ways to say father I love you dearly.
Dad, you must realise your daughter's words are said sincerely.

Sharon Wiggins

A Light Shed On Autumn

Blue crystal dew drops,
Glimmering as the early red sun
catches their sparkling tips.
The smell of fruit and warm flowers,
Carries on the tip of the fervent
breeze with ardent passion.
Dead leaves and burned bark lay
scattered carelessly on the damp twinkling grass.
Serene silence is broken by the songs of passing birds.
The trees appear black against the
Grey/blue sky, withholding no disguising leaves,
Mournful and desolate.
The throbbing hum of distant tractors
sounds like the Earth is breathing,
Inhaling the scents of Autumn.
Puddles of moving mists reflect
nothing but the grey heavens above,
The juices of unappreciated apples seep from the fruit,
Bubbling and frothing, letting off a sweet fragrance.
A light shed on Autumn.

Louise C. Occomore

The Weather

What's happened to the weather; it's the worst for fifty years
Here in Dumfries and Galloway it has brought us all to tears
We're all hemmed in with all this snow which is lovely looking out
How are we going to get to work, we ask ourselves with doubt.

We start to dig and make a path to clear the snow away
So vans and cars can make a move in time to start the day
Busy trying very hard and doing all they can
The local folk are happy to see the delivery van.

The weather is a subject which affects each one of us
It's something boffins ponder over and make an awful fuss
There is no power here on earth that can alter mother nature
As each season shows us who's in charge over every other creature.

Dumfries has made the national news because of all the snow
And when it starts to thaw and melt wherever will it go
Down from the hills and into the Nith the river will be wide
And the folks along the white sands will take everything in their stride.

Once again we're back to normal as the sun begins to shine
And so this ends this little tale and also ends this rhyme
Regarding our favourite subject which we all in turn discuss
I'll really have to hurry now; I'm off to catch the bus.

Betty Stewart

The Little Old Lady

There's a little old lady sits, in her old rocking chair,
With her shawl round her shoulders, and silvery hair.
She looks so sad, as she rocks to and fro'
She feels no one cares, or wants to know.

She sits by the window, she feels happier there,
Watching the people go by, some just look and stare.
The postman stops by, she thinks, 'someone's remembered today'
But he slowly turns, and walks away.
She sheds a tear, just a few pages would do,
To know someone cares, and thinks of you.

A small girl passes by, and looks in at the gate,
On her way to school, she mustn't be late.
She smiles and waves, and then hurries on,
And then all too soon, she is gone.

The day seems so long, as the old lady sits there,
Rocking herself, in her old rocking chair.
She longs for someone to knock at the door,
Just for a chat, nothing more.
But no one comes by, and nobody calls,
And she's alone once more, in her own four walls.

Margaret Platt

The Most Beautiful Day Of Them All

The soft frilly lace,
As I hold to my face,
The most beautiful lovely white gown.
My heart full of you, In my mind, 'Yes I Do',
As the cool Chapel Aisle I walk down.

The white veil gently flows,
Silk ribbons and bows,
Right down to the small wedding shoes.
My heart full of you, In my mind, 'Yes I Do'.
The boquette and garter ribbon of blues.

As I walk to the Alter,
Not one step to faulter,
And there be with you, my fine Groom.
My heart full of you, In my mind, 'Yes I Do',
From this wedding day on, until doom.

This beautiful day,
In my heart it will stay,
For surely this is the best day of my life.
My heart full of you, In God's house, vowed, 'I Do',
For dear husband, I'm so glad, I'm your wife.

Linda Hayes

The Footpath Across The Meadows

The footpath across the meadows, through the fields,
Where the wild flowers grow,
There village sweethearts walk to dream

The dreams all sweethearts know.
We walked that path one June night
At the closing of the day.
There were flower fragrances on the breeze

From the blossoms on the May.
There was magic that night in the starlight,
That June night you walked with me.
And from the meadows a little brown bird

Sang a beautiful rhapsody.
A nightingale serenaded the twilight
From the meadow were the wild flowers grow
When you and I were sweethearts

That June night long ago.
You and I are now reaching life's twilight
But our love is just as sweet and true
As it was on that wonderful June night
When I walked the footpath with you.

A. M. Bell

Summer Dreams

Drifting and dreaming the whole day through,
Dreaming that Summer's come back anew;
Dreaming of sunshine and happy days,
And trips o'er the sands with a friend to play.

The rain now beats on the window panes,
When will the sunshine come back again?
The wind blows aloft in the chimneys tall.
Flowers are sleeping, awaiting the call:

Of warm summer days when the skies are blue,
And soft summer breezes that call to you:
To come out to play near a tranquil sea.
When summer returns how happy we'll be.

Mary Pickles

The Toy Box

Magic container of childhood things,
Of sunshine and happy days.
The growing and changing through the years
In so many different ways.

Special reminder of times now past,
A children's treasure chest.
Still with favourite memories there
Of toys they loved the best.

Contents varying, time goes by,
And now we're up to date.
New generation quickly growing
At an alarming rate.

Magic container of childhood dreams,
Of happiness and fun.
Remembered now with joy and love
Each and every one.

Doreen Wilson

The Empty Goal

Look at me, mirror, as I stand erect
The surgeon's sculpt'd me in so many parts
My eyes, my lips, my breasts, my legs
Have all been changed to fashion's way
The wrinkles have been lasered flat
And years of worry have just fled my face
Genes have been transplanted too
To make me clever, many viewed.
An athlete I've become, musician too.
Now I'm the most intelligent and pretty person ever
I have achieved my goal and I can live forever

Alas, the treatment has been done for all
The image that I strived to gain
Serves me no better than before
A clone, I stand before you in a deep despair
And see myself reflected back once more

Hilary Ingle

Eve Of War

At the Eve of War I sit all depressed,
At the thought of bodies "laid to rest",
With thoughts of loved ones waiting at home
Feeling in a world of anxiety, all alone.

The soldiers' nails bitten - with time to spare,
Are wondering how they each will fare.
The doctors and nurses 'all clean and right'
Are wondering will this be a 'bloody night'?

The Sergeants kept busy with 'tactics' and such,
Are hoping their fears don't show too much.
The Generals are making their last minute plans
Of fields of war in these strange lands.

The clock is ticking ever loud 'Tick Tock',
It seems to say 'Time is the enemy, do not mock'.
And now the day of battle has finally come,
"Where is God? - Where is my Mum"

Carol Nichols

A Plea For Peace

All we want in Northern Ireland is peace
And we are pleading to the Lord above
To ask all of those involved
To show some brotherly love
Peace for Northern Ireland
Is something we all demand
We've had twenty five years of troubles
And it's all that we can stand
We want no more funerals
No more widows and orphans left to cry
And we are appealing to all concerned
Please give peace another try
Peace to us all is so important
Without it we can hardly exist
Take a look at our beautiful scenery
There's something the tourists cannot resist
So let's all stand together
Regardless of colour creed or class
And say aloud "give peace another chance"
And we will make it last.

John D. Johnston

I Had A Dream

I had a dream the other day.
That I could change the world
I'd give all men dignity equality for all.

To the far east I'd give priority
I'd sow the land with wheat
Abandon all forms of torture
And give the people peace.

The lonely need some comfort
I'd visit them each day.
Console them in their troubles
And give them a brighter day.

To the blind I'd sing a melody
And to the deaf I'd bring some cheer.
I'd abandon all abortions
And let God's children live.

I'd drive hatred from all men's hearts
Put love, and kindness there
Then there would be a better world
Where people all would care

Patricia McAteer

P's And Q's

If you remember please
You'll maybe get your way.
If you remember thank you,
that's all you'll need to say.

If you remember P's and Q's
you'll always have a friend,
you'll always know you're welcome here
until your visit's end.

If you behave the proper way
you'll find that life is fun
you'll always have a happy time,
and not upset someone.

Manners are a key in life
they open many doors
they'll help you through some awkward times,
treat them just like laws.

Remember this small poem
when you get in a state
don't say that manners don't belong,
use yours at any rate.

Mary-Jane Allen

On The Toll Bridge At Old Shoreham

Eddies form the wooden pilings swirling to the north.
The tide is on the make as dusk draws in.
Raucous sea-birds squabbling from the mud flats sally forth,
Their feeding done for this tide. Now the turn of fish and crabs begin.

Trenches form the lug-worm diggers fill and tumble down.
The river broadens. Bridges need their span.
A tidal stranded boat begins to swing toward the town.
An old Grey Heron fishes. As evening comes less fearful of man.

Mullet rings are dancing 'round a floating scrap of food.
A Sea Bass splashes gently close to shore.
I stand alone, and silent, while the river is renewed.
Absorbing the emotions; reversals of the ebbing of before.

Would that my existence flowed eternally as yours,
And not this solitary tide I live:
One hard earned high, one tired low, then nature's ancient laws
Decree my time is over. Rebirth for man is not for her to give.

Jim Scott

Memories

It's only a strip of blue water that separates you from me,
If you wanted to, you could take a boat, and sail across that sea.
Or better still, just close your eyes, and think of days gone by,
When you and I would walk by streams, where all the dragons fly.
Remember the hill where we used to go, where all the daisies are,
And how it took our breath away, to look and see so far?
Those hills and dales are still there now, for one and all to see,
The sturdy oak and copper beech, the nottled elder tree.
Don't think of these as days gone by, never to come again.
For like the memory of someone loved, or the lilt of an old refrain,
Even the seas of time can't erase these treasures in our heart,
And like the hand I reach with now, you will always be a part.

J. Toms

Acts Of The Apostles Chapter 2 Verse 17

'Twas no enchanted evening, just a busy thoroughfare
I spied her, lithe and lissome, in the throng
I marvelled that her beauty made no others stand and stare
Oh! How they rudely jostled her along.

I hoped she would confront me, I would gladly step aside
She did and how my thoughts began to dance
For in her smile a thousand prospects would not be denied
Encapsulated in that fleeting glance.

Did sweet liaisons beckon in some far exotic clime?
Romantic aspirations joined as one?
Alas! Just flights of fancy, no excursions on cloud nine
She turned her eyes - too quickly she was gone.

Yet long will I remember her, quite hopelessly it seems
Her world and mine, too many years between
"Our young men shall see visions and our old men shall dream dreams"
Could this be what the Scriptures also mean?

Alf Parry

To My Grandmother

Winter branches, stark and bare, looking forward to the Spring
having so many years, I look back and to my memory cling
Rolling hills of Devon, rich red earth, my short legs hidden
in grass so green, Daisy, Buttercup pink Clover ridden.
My beloved Grandmother, low on forehead, back to front, old cloth cap
rough hessian sack, tied apron wise to protect her lap.
Patiently waiting, her most prized and loved possession
Seventeen, large gentle South Devon cows - all sweet perfection
on low wooden stool, her head resting on heaving rust red side.
Mouse quiet, on mound of yellow straw, I sit mesmerized.
Cream milk, foaming, dancing like thunder rain, into silvered pail.
Hay tinged breath rising, mist like, clink of chain, swish of tail.
Knurled fingers working, soft voice coaxing her cud-chewing herd
Far away, long ago an Inn, full, no room to offer, no bread
Came the Baby, to another warm earthly cattle stall
Bringing that message to the world, Peace be with you one and all.

Betty H. Bucknell

Perhaps

The rays of sunlight stroke my face . . .
    Sweet kisses from the sky,
And motionless peep through my lids . . .
    So pensive do I lie,
In wonderment my thoughts at play . . .
    To what the day unfolds,
Perhaps today good fortune reigns . . .
    Perhaps today brings gold.

Then all my senses waken . . .
    In a union to embrace,
Another day is gifted me . . .
    Experiences to face,
    And in anticipation . . .
        Perhaps positively knew,
    Perhaps today's tomorrow . . .
        Where my promises come true.

But if perhaps I err . . .
    In fantasizing all my dreams
Perhaps that time is yet to come . . .
    Perhaps . . . or so it seems.
        Marisol S. Franklin

Rain

Pitter, patter falls the rain
Tapping on the window pane
Running into cracks and gutters
Down the drain it gurgles and splutters

Gently at first, then gathering strength
Tiny droplets grow in length
Bouncing on paths, soaking the ground
Sending people scurrying round

Ruthlessly lashing at chimneys and trees
Flattening grasses and splashing leaves
Causing creatures to shake and shiver
While birds on the wing are all of dither

Swelling streams as on they go
Down to the rivers where they overflow
On to the mouth of the estuary
Swirling onward to join the sea.

Swelling waves that pound the sand
Quenching the thirst of a dry parched land
Fading now, their fury dying
Teardrops of rain, the angels were crying
        Pamela Frances Williams

Ella

My name is not lovie, sweetheart or love
My name is Ella as stated above

I am not senile I am not insane
so the least you can do is call me by name

My name is Ella I live in a home,
I had to give up the one that I own.

You see I got old and that is a crime,
I had to give up all that was mine.

Please be gentle, don't be unkind
I may be old but I still have my mind

I sit in the chair and do what I'm told
It doesn't do to admit you are old

You're got out of bed and given your food
but you do not protest in case it seems rude.

I don't ask for much, just a little time,
which is all on your side and little on mine.

I no longer choose what I want to do,
it is all decided by nurses like you.
        Rosemarie Bassingthwaighte

The Hunchback

If only I had been born straight
I would not have this grotesque gait,
A figure of scorn and ridicule,
taunted, despised like a fool.

This twisted tongue and drooping lips'
no fair maid will ever kiss.
My soul is sad, full of shame,
the hump on my back fills me with pain.

Small in stature, ugly in shape,
surely descendant from the Ape.
I will take this burden onto the grave,
I am not free, I am a slave.

The curtain of dusk falls each night, covers my shame, hides me from sight.
The sun comes up to herald the dawn, my cry to heaven! Why was I born?

Ugly misshapen creature from hell, time of day to ring the bell,
Sanctuary, Sanctuary, hear my cry! For "Esmeralda" I would die.

A daily whipping is my lot, to ring those bells I had forgot,
locked in a "pillory" for all to see, there is no pity, not for me.

I cast a dark shadow upon the wall, my prayer is answered,
It is nightfall.
        Yvonne Delaney

The Seasons

In the bleak winter days the land is cold and bare
Cold north winds brings the snow, warm days are so rare
Snow ploughs clear the roads of snow but here comes another shower
Oh dreary days of winter when shall we see the flowers.

In the freshness of spring's morning air the birds do sing again
Happy is their dawn chorus now and many join in sweet refrain
Fields of daffodils we see a carpet of yellow flowers
In the fens the tulips bloom thanks to the April showers

Glorious days of summer are here with us at last
Now for the holidays we planned we spend our hard-earned cash
Many will fly to foreign parts, strange and rugged lands to see
Others will stay nearer home or visit Mablethorpe by the sea

Many combines we see in fields down on the farm
Tractors and trailers to transport the corn back to the barns
Gone are the days of reapers and binders and work done by hand
And wagons and horses carrying the harvest home of the land

Autumn is the most wonderful and glorious of seasons to see
The splendour of the colours makes it a favourite with me
And if I should pass the heavenly gate the wonders of heaven to see
May the memories of the wonderful seasons on earth remain with me
        H. Skinn

Ode To The Boss

Why do we keep Jesus for Sundays, and do what we want in the week?
We abuse, ill-use and ignore him, don't you think it's a bit of a cheek?
When we're happy, his name's never mentioned,
But as soon as the sad tears appear,
It's out with the Bible and Prayer Book,
And expect him to lend us his ear.
At the start of our lives we are carried, to a Church in our Parents' arms,
At the end we are laid out before him, does this ring a bell with alarm?
In the middle he's a passing fancy,
And at times a bit of a bind.
Sometimes we would rather be doing,
Sinful things with the rest of mankind.
When we're sick of the world that's around us, and friends are letting us down.
So we yell, and we swear and get angry, and spend hours wearing a frown,
What a blessing the good Lord in Heaven,
Doesn't sulk, and cause a fuss,
Imagine the World's state of panic,
If our Father reacted like us!
So next time that life seems a doddle, give the Boss up in Heaven a treat,
Smile and offer him laughter, for the blessings he's laid at your feet.
        Margaret Derbyshire

Psalm Of Adoration

Like a cat I curl in the comfort of Your kindly arm,
Safe from harm,
Sensing the warmth of Your touch,
You, seeing my need.

I came to You in the silence of my loneliness,
Seeking succour:
And You received me, rejected me not.

As a murmuring wind is Your voice to my ears,
Soothing my soul, calming and quieting my heart.

How often have I strayed,
Only returning when hungry and cold
To find You, as always
Waiting to welcome me to Your hearth,
Your hands outstretched, offering me nourishment.

In Your homely presence, I eat my fill,
Quenching my thirst in the fountain of Your love
And then, restored, at peace,
I lie in adoration at your feet,
My good and gracious Lord.

J. C. Wellings

The Terminus

A solitary pigeon, struts across the buffered floor.
But, busy minded people, his personage ignore.
Everyone is rushing, going somewhere, coming back.
An air of expectation, as the train creeps up the track.

Lovers, friends, and family, wait shivering, in the night,
Standing by the 'Coke' machine, that's luminous and bright.
Lurking in the darkness, is a man with 'Shoddy' clothes,
Puffing at the 'Dog Ends', and begging, as he goes.

From somewhere in the rafters, where the ornate pillars stand,
A mumbled sound of 'Jargon', circulates the platform grand,
It's the 'Ancient' Tannoy System, British Rail
   still keeps in tow,
Reeling off, the destinations, what it says, we do not know.

At last from laden carriages, the tired travellers step.
With suitcases, and bulging bags, by eager folk they're met.
And when the spell of leisure time is over,
   don't you cry.
Well, just a tear, see you next year, God willing,
   and Goodbye.

Heather Overfield

Our Max

I thought we'd bought a healthy pet
He's nearly two and still suffering yet
At thirteen weeks old we found his hips bad
But we still loved our beautiful lad
At five months old he had his first op.
So on three legs he had to hop
Eight weeks later he has to go back
They said his elbow had gone alas! Alack
So he had this done he was hopping again
But once more it will ease all his pain
We thought at nine months he would have to go
But we've done our best 'cos we love him so
Eighteen month old his tendon has gone
our poor Max everything has gone wrong
They took him back replaced tendon with wire
He's also been castrated, Max will never sire
This was our greatest dream it was a sin
Now we'll never see any puppies of him
October 1996 he'll be two years old
He's big and beautiful and very bold.

L. J. Moreland

Memories

My memories are lovely melodies engraved upon my heart.
But like the distance sound of sweet violins.
Sometimes cause tears to start.

Memories of those yesterdays
When my world was clear and bright skies always blue.
No clouds in view and I still had my sight

Primroses in a woodland glade
Sweet violets in the lane
Butterflies with wings displayed
Rainbows after rain, honeysuckle in the hedgerow
Red roses by the door
Wall flowers perfumed by the sun's glow
These are memories precious stored
My memories are lovely melodies
And indeed a treasure store

For the things I knew and loved so well
They let me see once more
But shed no tears for my yesteryears
I know the Lord meant them to be
Golden threads for interweaving into life's rich tapestry.

A. M. Bell

Old And Useless

They looked after their children all their life
He was a good Father, she was a good wife
They tended and nursed them while they were small
And watched them growing, become strong and tall
Both were worn and tired, when the Children left Home
Then he passed away, she was alone
She needed someone, she became old and weary
Her everyday Life was cold and dreary
So she turned to her Children for Comfort and Love
But they were not bothered, it was not enough
When she said needs them, 'cause' she can't cope,
They shouted at her: That's the end of the Rope,
You are old and useless and your Mind starts to roam,
We've got no Choice, you'll go to a Home.
They drove her away and took her there
And they did all that without any care
Her arms, they ached for her Children's Embrace
But all that was left were the Tears on her Face.
She died alone, without Love and no Rest,
And her Children said proudly: We Did Our Best.

Ingrid Bockman

Look

"Splosive" sun and "sceptred" star,
Jewelled gems that gleam afar.
Mystic worlds and far-off life.
Free from care and woe and strife?
O art thou heaven or hell?
Delirious joy or empty shell?
Dew clasped crystals clear and bright.
I shall see thee every night.
I shall wonder how and why
Thou art up there in the sky
Moon of beauty cool and calm.
I can touch thee with an arm, trace with fingers long and firm.
Soft rays bathe me in return.
Craters etched by giant hand.
Perhaps from some far-off land?
Timeless face peers on and on.
Even perhaps when we have gone?
Mighty universe go slow. Eternity is yours and so.
When we hear that joyous call, and so we will one and all.
And obey "His" wondrous will.
I shall love thee still 'o' still.

Diana Fay Ford-Wetton

Untitled

It's been a long time
since I met somebody so fine
but now he is here
and thank God not queer
amazing to see
for him to fall in love with someone like me.
To my heart he has found the key
and he can be sure
    that I will never flee.

So hold me tight
and wish we might
be together forever in sight.

Rea Hoffmann

Seasons Of Love

Walk with me thro' the springtime of love
Hold my hand as we go
See the flowers as they come thro' the earth
As 'the soft winds gently' blow.

Stroll with me, in the summer of love
Hear the lark sing his song.
Smell the perfume of beautiful flowers
There is nothing in our love can go wrong

As we are now in the autumn of love
Sorrows and joy we did share.
The leaves from the trees, are falling, my love
A hint of frost in the air.

Now we have reached the winter of love
And still smell the perfume rare.
And happy we've been together, my love
Though snow-white be our hair.

Helen Stainsby

Stolen Memories

We've laughed together,
We've cried together,
As close friends do.
Long summer days,
Cosy winter evenings,
Holidays shared, children's birthdays, anniversaries,
Make memories to cherish,
A complete recall.

No aroma of flowers,
Or a smile from the bride,
No hugs of congratulations,
Or the sounds of their vows,
No capturing of the atmosphere,
Locked safe in the mind forever,
Photographs show only fragments of moments past,
The years will roll away and somewhere, someone
Will weep for a stolen memory.

Christine Rusby

African Hope

The sizzling sun sets, its day's work done,
Tormented chills take over, cold torture for some,
Night sidewalks are full of the living corpse,
In black townships, the future backwards walks,
Coloured bodies twitch with nightmarish dreams,
No hope for Africa, replica of life it seems,
They grow no crops, the lands too dry,
Few crimes are committed, so tell me why?
If the sun could cry and turn to rain,
Life becomes saner, green and sweeter the grain,
Worry never leaves them, sickness, abuse and toil,
Such a wonderful land, but immature the soil,
Their livestock larder is poached by foreign men,
Who try to hide their guilt, but return again,
Oh please, dear God, show them you're real,
And remove those hopeless pains they feel,
Future plans urgently needed and ability to cope,
I pray all rich world leaders give Africa hope.

Mick E. Baker

Letting Go

Is this joy, when stretch-marked skin feels empty,
And parting-pains give rise to inadequacy and loss?
When golden headed angel, with chubby legs and unsure feet,
Finds playschool play and 'doh and sand
More fun than quiet nursery rhymes by the fire?
When sand-haired youngster runs to join the gang
On asphalt ground, without a backward glance,
Then journeys further on with endless mates
And embarrassment to give the embrace
That 'till now has been umbilical.
Or is joy when familiar clutter moves to
Redbrick city, and B.T. Line becomes the only
Conduit of nutrient news and long-haired, long-legged girl
Knows what is best to eat and wear?

If this is joy, then give me the pain
Of sleepless nights and constant vigil,
Of wash-tubs full of dirty socks and kit,
Of pans of potatoes to feed a growing frame,
Of itemized phone bills and endless rows
Accompanied by loud, loud music.

Jennifer Potter

The Last One In The Picture

The frame is brown, and edged with gold
A long forgotten story told
Sepia images stare at me
Others' moments of history
A camera captured and took its fill
The only moment when time stood still
Four people in a wedding group
Post war clothes, macs and suits
Dreams and hopes locked away
Within the wooden frame they lay
The scene will live forever, held in time and space
Unlike the four within, that time has now erased
She was the first to go, the one that gave me life
The second gave me strength, the one beside his wife
The third witnessed the day, the time, the place
From the fragmented group, remained just one lone face
For years he bore witness to the story of the past
He brought colour to the sepia picture, underneath the glass
Now the memories are sealed away, and hung upon the wall
As the last one in the picture has made his final call

Barbara Hinchen

Fifty Years After A Visit To An Emptied Dachau

Just thinking of each of the aspects of that era of Evil
Still blights and warps me.

The magnitude, the brutality,
The fact that horror was an accepted norm!
The filth and the stench.
The hunger, the cold and the pain.
The abysmal helplessness.
The dread,
The humiliation,
The degrading indignities,
The curdling, futile anger.

Malevolent inhumanity and barbaric savagery
Were calculated, debated, weighed and selected
By humans
As behaviour codes
Towards other humans.
Still others implemented those codes.

And that is why, to this day,
As a human,
I shrivel.

Nomi Zuckerman

The Time Of The End

The time has come to walk that path,
    that path that signifies the end.
The soft chant of angels surround me as I step
    through the gateway to heaven.
Is this real or am I dreaming?
Visions pass my eyes
    of youth and prime through to age,
The friends I have had to help me accomplish my
    dreams and ambitions,
The family I have had to guide me on my way.
Memories both good and bad,
    now echo through my head.
I leave this world with no regrets,
    and step into another with a clear conscience.

Gemma Priestley

Father

Old man lying wasted with agitated emotion,
Apparently lucid, wait see the confusion dimming his eyes,
Icicle encrusted fog dismantling his life,
Circling faster, faster, his life, children, wife;

Once indestructible now unable to fight,
His life glue melting away before us,
Deserving greater dignity not this hell,
What does he feel behind that fragile shell;

Drug-induced coma stills his limbs,
Realization finally breaks through his senses,
In front of strangers all his fears bared,
Painfully he mutters "I'm scared, I'm scared";

At last the peace has returned,
All suffering evaporated, his soul released,
Outside the December day feels cold and long,
Now it is for me to learn to be strong.

M. Baddley

Hope

In America a man used to sit by a phone
In Russia it happened too.
Just one ring and the switch would be thrown
the end of me and you.

In Germany a wall kept families apart
and in South Africa intolerance was rife.
Imagine the feelings people had in their heart
when oppression gave way to new life.

All over the World we're beginning to see
leaders known for their hard-line stance;
coming together with an old enemy
to give peaceful methods a chance.

Many have paid the ultimate price
for someone to hear their voice.
We must not forget the sacrifice
to achieve freedom, equality and choice.

Sally Millett

Untitled

I'm lost without doghairs coming from you
I've 'hoovered' them up but not 'you'
I still want you Peg, your doghairs as well
Bless you love, it's giving me hell
The desire for you keeps coming to me
All the things you'd do, like going out to see
The butcher, the coalman, the milkman as well
I'll miss you my love, as they ring the bell
Oh Peggy, my Peggy, I did love you so
It's hard to believe you have had to go

I hope to a God love who'll take care of you for me
Please God, be there God, then my Peggy I will see
And she will not be gone forever
    Peggy God bless you

Eileen Girling

Ocean

A deep green mystery moved by the moon
A dark blue rage with silver white horses
Inviting forbidding, unfathomable, enigmatic
A limbo of unknowingness, unfamiliarity
A fascination undefined
Leaving a gap between expectation and execution
Between yearning and reality
Through which the imagination has room to squeeze
A place with no politics, no churches, no vanity, no sadness
No human likes being in the ocean too long
We are mostly water but we are not waterproof
We don't always swim, we plunge, we drift, we sink and drown
We descend in the current restless flow of change
With its own laws darkness and light
Reality is an ocean we take away in teacups
We wave at those aboard big white ships
And send our earthly messages encased in glass
And the tide takes them away and brings them back
The tide takes them away and brings them back
Tide takes them away and brings them back
Takes them away and brings them back.

Julia Wallis-Bradford

'Call-Up'

(Written on Remembrance Day 11-11-96)

He was only a boy
But not for him youth's joy.
The second world war had begun
His duty to king and country must be done.
As brother and sister we were close.
So please don't ask me how I felt.
When with his 'call-up' papers in my hand I knelt.
"Please God look after my brother", I have no other.
With heavy hearts we awaited the dreaded train.
We tried to jest but all in vain.
'Tis true we know not what the morrow has in store.
Do we ever really think I may be no more?
But on that cold, sad day as at the
station we stood, it must be said
The gruesome thought kept turning in my head.
Tomorrow he could be dead.
Such is war.
Please no more.

May Park

Choose Life

It's a little bit battered, and a little bit worn,
but I don't think you'll find any pages torn.

The first few pages are a little hard to get,
as it seems to be written in Scottish dialect.

Give it some time. Give it some thought.
The next thing you know, that's how you'll talk.

Sometimes it's scary. Some times it's crude.
It's always shocking and quite often rude.

It's based on reality and it makes you realize—
there are thousands of people that the masses despise.

But the one thing it does for you once it's read and done—
You realize there's no big difference between you and them.

And it's not what they do, it's not about shooting up.
It about letting things go and to Hell with the lot.

We are running our lives as we're told how to do.
Age old conformity that we don't question—Do you?

Life is a journey—Do you go for a ride?
At the end of the day, only You can decide.

Johan V'haley

Time For Me

Time to laugh, time to cry,
Time to fly high in the sky,
To free my spirit, to have peace of mind
And the healing power,
That comes from him, my lover.

The healing rays to heal the world
The world down there that suffers so,
Hold my hand, give me the strength
And memories that I may need,
To take with me, when I go back
Where I belong.
Ambar

Gipsy Girl

Gipsy girl with jet black hair,
With merry eyes without a care,
With pearly teeth and laughing lips,
A rebel to the finger tips.

Gipsy girl with skin tanned brown,
With torn cloak and tattered gown,
Bright red berries you do eat,
And shoes have never shod your feet.

Beside the brook with sparkling foam,
You make your simple, happy home,
You work while lovely sunlight gleams,
And 'neath the trees you dream your dreams.

They call you poor, Oh Gipsy girl,
Because you've neither gold nor pearl,
But 'neath your rags they do not see,
Your heart beats deep, and rich and free.

So Gipsy girl with jet black hair,
With merry eyes without a care,
You're richer far than they who say
"Poor Gipsy girl" - so sad - so gay.
Margaret Parker

Temper

Heels are clicking, fingers tapping,
Hold your tongue, control its snapping.
Harsh words in haste you can't take back.
And yet you feel you must attack.
You're hard and cold and often cruel.
Your tongue a sharp and wicked tool.
Your foe is hurt and quite defeated.
Your devil task is now completed.
The storm is gone, the damage done
And you are the defeated one.
Ann West

The Star's Story

Pale moonlight through an open door,
Making patterns on the marble floor,
No sound, or movement from outside,
Yet on that night a mother cried,
For her first born baby child, that died.

A million stars from far above,
All shone down eternal love,
But one stood out most clear and bright,
It was a truly wondrous sight,
The secret of the night.

A beam of light caressed the ground,
The mother's baby boy was found,
For as she looked into the glare,
She knew that it was he, up there,
Of him, someone is taking care.

So if you've lost someone you love,
Look toward the heavens above,
For every man, woman or child that dies,
A new star appears up in the skies,
So mother dear, please dry your eyes.
Richard Norburn

Winter's Morn

Stark trees in silhouetted form, against a clear blue sky,
Biting wind that stings the cheek, and brings a tear to eye.

Rose hips and berries shining red, cling to twigs stripped bare,
A nose that glows, breath that steams upon the frosty air.

Ivy grasping to the bark of mighty oaks that stand,
Like sentinels or guardians of England's pleasant land.

Creatures hastily foraging, in winter's shortened day,
Right now the heady days of summer, seem a long, long way away.

The sun shines bright yet weakened rays afford the earth no heat,
Birds gleaning food, where are they can, to shelter soon retreat.

Puddles frozen to their base. Frost glistening in the sun,
The stream that flows a slower pace, as if it race is won.

Such a tranquil world is this, as earth seeks solitude,
Where noise and haste, the very stuff of life all seem to be subdued.

Whisper softly, tread light your step, as you greet the frosty dawn,
Lest you should stir her very soul, upon the winter's morn.
Delia Cowell

The Promise

Frozen snow is slowly melting, as the sun starts to shine,
Pools of water gradually appearing, for the ground water is like wine,
Spring lambs running, leaping then skipping, so glad to be here,
Each species bringing forth their young, it happens this time of year,
In spring fields and meadows, green shoots come out of virgin snow,
Stretching infant heads towards a cloudy sky, quickly starting to grow.

And as precious water soaks into wet sodden earth,
Then evaporating into crispy fresh air, our earthly mother gives birth,
Terra firma nourishes little snowdrops, crocus are blooming too,
Soon will come golden daffodils, other flowers will join the queue,
Birds are busy nesting, expecting, young will soon be here,
Sudden movements in the forest, it is the hastening of a dear.

Now trees so sleepily resting, are about to awake,
Backwards and forwards swaying, in cold winds they shake,
Young leaves are sprouting, for magnificent deciduous to wear,
For throughout frozen winter months, their branches stark and bare,
New life is beginning everywhere we look,
Forming part of priceless promises written in our Holy Book,

As every bud that opens, each small chick, like darts in the skies,
Standing in awe and amazement, witnessing miracles unfold before my eyes.
Josephine Smith

Heaven Can Wait

Heaven can wait - I told myself, as I stood outside the gates.
I'm not ready yet - it's not my time - now this is tempting fate.
It started with a 'nap' you see, then it turned into a doze.
A deep, deep sleep - then unconsciousness! - Blimey! I'm comatose.

I tried to wake up, but to no avail - then I saw this shining bright light.
I was like a moth drawn to a light bulb, feeling safe from the darkest night.
I felt that I had gone back in time, seeing friends and family.
I knew I didn't belong there, I knew it was not for me.

That's when I went to see Peter, he is the angel who 'guards the gate'
I told him straight that I didn't belong, I told him 'heaven can wait'
I'm too young Peter - there has been a mistake - I'm a woman in her prime.
Someone has made a big 'faux-pas', wrong place definitely wrong time.

Wake up! Wake up - I heard someone yell, and get the smelling salts out.
Alright, alright I am awake! Blimey - you don't have to shout.
But we could not wake you up - we thought you were dead!
You looked so peaceful curled up in your bed.

Oh! - What a dream - it seemed so real.
I really thought it was true.
But I was dead drunk - and I had passed right out.
'Cos I really had drunk quite a few.
Marilyn Ruse

Nobody Cared

The old man huddled against the churchyard wall
The cold icy wind chilled his careworn face
The people hurrying by noticed not at all
Too eager to get to their own fireplace

The old man in slumber, dreamed of yesteryear
Of glowing fire, of child, and loving wife
They had long gone, those people he'd held most dear
Leaving no will to live, no lust for life

Came the dawn, with eyes closed in death the old man lay
His threadbare coat sodden with the driving rain
What a shame, what a shame, I heard people say
But he had no need of their pity
He was free at last from his grief, his pain

If only a helping hand had been held out with warmth and love
Instead of hurrying by or just stopping to stare
There may have been one less lost soul in heaven above
But nobody cared, nobody cared

    K. Whitley

Out There

Is there other life out there?
I believe there is, but know not where.
There are the people who have seen
Flying saucers, men coloured green
Some say they've been aboard their craft,
Many laugh, say they're daft,
I myself believe it's true,
Believe they could visit me or you.
I read the books, I watch the films
I hear of sightings in their millions.
And as there is life on this earth
Could not another race have had its birth?
I believe they'll come when we show willing
To end the wars and stop the killings.
And when they do I know we'll find
They will bring real wisdom to mankind.

    Tracey Plane

School's Out

It's good to be back, so good to be here,
I've been away so long, cried all my tears.
Taken for a fool, taken for a ride,
But now I'm back, with some fire inside.

Yes, you put me down, cheated on a friend,
Told all those lies, right up to the end.
It took a long, long time, to heal the pain,
The good news is I've started living again.

As each pain in my body, does slowly subside,
The pain in my heart, walks but one step behind.
Now, looking to the future, the past forgotten not spurned,
My life, going forward, with all lessons well learned.

    Bob Perrie

A Poem For My Love

  For you my love,
I have become a poem that cannot be recited,
I have become a song that cannot be sang.
  Why?
Because I cannot express my love for you
as well as I could have when I was with you.

I miss your wild careless laughter,
  the evenings you spent comforting me
when my life seemed a disaster.
  I love you for being there for me.

Indeed I have become a poem that can't be recited.

How well can I express my gratitude
  to God for it all would never have existed.
How best can I express my gratitude
  to you my love, for being there for me even when you
  were restricted.

    Olgar Walusimbi

When I Am Gone

Dedicated to my son Billy

Don't weep for me when I am gone
Hold each other close and carry on.
I loved you all each and every one
At last I now join my beloved son.
The day he left me my heart was broken
I wasn't there to hear his last words spoken.
All through this life my heart was sore
My dearest son's face I would see no more.
A heart that is broken will never mend
The pain is with you right to the end.
How much I missed him could never be told,
This only son of mine who never grew old.
When at last I see him once again,
Only then will my heart be free from pain.
We'll hold each other close never more to part
There will be no more tears, only joy in our hearts.
Don't weep for me when my life is done,
Be happy for me I'm now with my son.

    Elizabeth Tees

Truth

Morning hath a new dawn brought
And the truth that is
That stands on up quickening the man
And the tone of face aglow deplete of fear
And seethe thru the marrow relaxing the mind
A false I knew afore
That truth must taste as gall
But evidence doth contradict
A father's tearful joy and mother's distraught look
As son to truth confess but daughter the truth deny
Guilty straighten heavy laden thus lift
And conscience in bond at freedom set
Fallacy is the monster myth the cancer
Foundation of being being their fodder
Men of courage have sought to fight
Those of knowledge pledged to find
To kill and to cure the damage
Truth enthroned shall liberate by force
Those held in bond by fear of false
New morning hath dawn brought anew

    Okorie Chinyere Nwamazi Sylvanus

The Great No-Money Land

I used to walk in happy dream
  Enjoying sun and sea
No thoughts of money in my head
  The world seemed friends with me.

But I have moved to harsher scenes
  Where money seems the God
Where Youth just waits with begging hands
  Till Age is 'neath the sod.

Where the author or the poet finds
  No value on his skill
There's just one gauge of each man's worth
  What money's in his till.

They say they'll fight for their beliefs
  But their loyalty is strained
They only know one principle
  A few pounds lost or gained.

Do they ever think of how they'll go
  No keys or purse in hand
But penniless and in a shroud
  To the great No-Money-Land?

    Edith Phair

Destined To Die

Taken down in your prime,
Gone before time,
You'll never really know,
How I'm missing you now.

As time passes by,
All I can do is sigh,
My life is what you made,
Yet I had to sit and watch yours fade.

Nothing I could do would help you,
And still more suffer like you,
Sometimes they don't even know,
Yet when they do they'll hit all-time low.

To die before you're young,
Before your time is done,
Still things to finish, things to say,
But nothing you can do can let you stay,

You're destined to die,
Only you really know why,
Nobody can help you now,
Because nobody knows how.

S. J. Hopton

Nature's Way

A tree stands tall, its branches
laced against the sky. A pair of
magpies nesting there way up
high. The grey squirrel innocent
of their fate, have many young,
prey to the magpies, who devour
them one by one.

Walking in the park, one day
I was compelled to look up,
I saw what seemed to me,
a drama unexpectedly, nature's way.
A squirrel escaped death,
when his predators were too near.
A cat climbed the tree,
and sensed the squirrel's fear.

The cat stalked the magpies,
until they moved back,
quickly - the squirrel jumped from tree to tree,
agile to the sway - this time still free

Rosalyn C. Ellis

Time, Light And Far Off Places

Time, light and far off places
Give me a feeling I can't explain,
A wistful joy of unknown pleasure,
My spirit hits the sky again.

Time is past and time is future
The distance of the clock reveals
Memories and hope and longing
Each passing year, more thoughts it steals.

Light's the food that feeds your brain,
And swims the surface of your eye,
Light's the drug that heals your hurt,
Prescribed by God from heaven on high

Far off places draw my soul
Toward a land I don't know where,
Every place, an El Dorado
Where I can dwell without a care.

Time, light and far off places,
Are the elements of my salvation
I'll question not their strange effect,
Just thank the Lord for their creation.

Stephen Owens

Star

Oh Silver Loved One out in space
You could have had all my light years,
Eternal, bright and shining like the Milky Way,
Never bruised or crazed by the heavy meteorites of grief.

But there were newer stars in your firmament,
Hard and white and newer; and privileged because of that.
My long-travelled matter shattered with the blast of your rejection,
Disturbed the Universe with hurtling fragments of my disintegrated soul.

But we orbited Heaven for such a long time, once,
'Tis fitting my dust should glimmer and gleam,
And gleam and glimmer,
As it falls softly and eternally, amongst the stars.

Maureen Rosemary Ross-Ferguson

Feelings

Fans revolving dancing scheme, shaking earth, till ecstasy passionate warmth
Brazilian feeling, lay back sit relax getting your grip of the sunshine feeling.
Ecstasy pauses a scratch for records of a D.J. playing. Brazilian grounds will
Rule, measuring passing physique till hands of time dissolve forever loving
Dancing feet, till hands of ecstasy pull the clock back to Pele's mastering.
So blowing the whistle now sadness comes a match more painful yet revealing,
To hit any ceiling sadness swings hands for more believing is your eyes'
curtain to a pass of disbelieving. Itching for support to hear all samba
Beat, don't know any drum which can't part sadness from the sun.
Slow scoring without glory, digs feeling of sadness and makes the
Sun come down. Earth of ecstasy will topple fantasy for any days not having
Soccer tropically, which highs from physique get your grip of saddening feelings
Singings through a street, more Brazilian feeling isn't more unique. Don't
Blame the moonlight when the card of red walks a shallow head for
Tonight. And nothing stops Brazil if anger tonight makes them a
Moonlight thrill. Other days Brazil are the best team seen for years.
Careca a specialist when it comes to a power volley. Flowers that
Have taste for the mean machines is fever Brazil.

Shaun Turner

The Stamp Collector

Old Joe was a philatelist, a cheerful sort of bloke,
He didn't earn much money and was permanently broke.
When friends flew off to sunny Spain, he'd sit in his back yard,
With sun umbrella, crate of beer, life wasn't really hard.

He'd look through all his albums, he loved the stamps from Spain.
In his imagination, he'd be over there again.
One stamp showed the Alhambra, another an old mill,
He'd look at Barcelona from the fortress on the hill.

In Spain they'd stagger out of bed, with bleary eyes and aching head.
Their skin all burnt from too much sun, their stomachs bad—'Twas not much fun.

Returning home, they waited hours at the crowded Spanish airport,
While Joe slept happily in bed, at peace, without a care-thought.
When they got back and told their friends how lovely it was there,
Joe merely smiled, he'd seen more Spain from his old garden chair.

Frederick Atkins

The Reducing Mind

Two eyes through a window gazing, two lenses which front a shadowed mind.
Sigh from the heart, you, man from window staring;
Flash back to youth and days of your non-caring.
Your zenith reached, long gone is schoolboy lazing, now to all important happenings
you are blind.

You, woman sitting by my side, should I know you? Why are you crying?
Your hair so white, yet eyes which hold a sparkle,
I discern you from somewhere, though your manner is cool;
You resemble another, my sweetheart, my bride, but she was much younger with eyes
not so prying.

Mirrored through the window clearly, brow so lined with wrinkles deep.
With memories persisting from channels of darkness.
Recalling life's reason and creating a spark, less
The spirit abandon that God did create; and oblivion
through shadow deem be my fate.

Ron Fereday

We Are Here

I am an alien, flirting with space,
Keeping an eye on the whole human race,
You will never know how your race was conceived,
Heed what I tell you, it must be believed.
You caused us great pain, many eons ago,
As bacteria you grew, the best that we know.
No cure could we find to stem your death flow.
Our minds were made up, you just had to go.
We found you this planet, the one you call earth,
And then let you multiply, for what it was worth.
You've blocked out the sun, with your fumes
and your smoke, a lot don't believe,
They think it's a joke.
The end is quite near, you're killing the one thing
You should hold most dear.
The sun is your life force, this you all know,
For reasons most baffling, you're letting it go.
No need for attack, or for you to defend,
We'll come and take over, when you all reach your end.

J. A. Bowers

In And Through God's Creation

There are so many simple yet good things to do,
But where does one start to see them all through?
And so many really nice thoughts to express,
But how to begin without getting in a mess?

Then there's so much of beautiful Nature everywhere
And so much of its vitality it's eager to share.
Its resilience and strength always daily urging on
Its aspirations to achieve, whether short term or long!

Oh Nature, I wish I could produce like you -
Reach out, reveal, expound as you do;
But yes, of course I can, quite easily
By asking the God of all things to create also through me.

P. M. Warren

Stolen Lives

Sodden kilts, threadbare and torn
Bloodied feet, through punishment borne
Haggardly tired at prides lowest ebb.
Delirious dreams of a dry straw bed

Three days tramping with kith and kin
Surviving a conflict no scotsman can win
Countless families perishing by the sword
All on the whim of your southern landlord

Razing your home, livestock and means too
Ranting and raving over right of Feu
Parchment demands slapped in your face
Advising disappearance without a trace

Soon the west coast shall come within sight
We can steal to the harbour with cover of night
There's freedom beyond this gaelic strife
Possessions none, but a new chance at life

Andrew Connelly

A Summer Morning

The hills in the distance, their peaks in the clouds,
Such a peaceful existence away from the crowds.
A warm summer morning, the countryside's calm,
A lark sings a warning, she sounds the alarm.
The sheep are all grazing the lambs friskily play,
The cows are just gazing at the hills far away.
The school bell is tolling, the children they laugh,
A horse is just foaling a cow licks her calf.

The bees are all busily buzzing around,
A snail oh so slowly slides over the ground.
As I gaze at such beauty, all cares far away,
I feel it my duty to give thanks, and say
To my Lord and creator, I'm glad I was born
To be part of nature on this bright summer morn.

Shirley Honywill

Thoughts

The sun sinks slowly as the day grows old,
The sky is blue, and yet the air is cold.
The clouds are puffs of white, like cotton soft,
Drifting slowly, lazily, there aloft,
And here a bird glides on a current past,
Its wings outstretched, to make the moment last.
It soars and dives, in ecstasy of joy,
Alone, at peace, where no-one can annoy.
Could I, as well forget the daily grind,
Wipe all the trivia from my laden mind,
And fly, carefree, against the heavenly blue,
In bliss, that here below, I never knew
But still, perhaps the freedom may not stay,
For even birds to bigger birds are prey.
So, with a sigh, I just enjoy the sight,
And wander home, as day reverts to night.
Thank God for eyes, that for a little while,
Can warm my heart with sights that so beguile!

Barbara Hussey

Homeless Children

Homeless Children on the streets
All they want is something to Eat
The rich walk past as these children beg
All they want is a nice warm bed.
With no warm cosy home to stay in
Just a small blanket to lay in
All they want is a Mum and Dad
But that's a life they have never had
With no clean clothes to wear
No one to cut or wash their hair
Doesn't anyone care?

Suzanne Twilley

Sailing From Wood To Ruby

Hello sailor, my sailor joy.
I was a young girl, you a young sailor boy.
We've been through calm and stormy weather,
you and me together.
You and me, then there were three, then four.
Happy days full and busy!
Now three and four have flown the nest
Out of the door! Their lives ahead, full and busy! Busy!
Now there's just us two, we've always been true
To one another.
Change of life oh! What a strife, another
Hurdle in one's life!
I'm still a mother and a wife.
Oh! To be free, shall I flee?
Would that really be me?
Oh! What do I hear? The grandchildren are here!
Happy days again, full and busy! Busy!
Now! Don't get into a tizzy tizzy!
Where did I put that... busy Lizzie?

Jean A. Roberts

My Room Welcomes Me Back

The doll-house lies abandoned,
Golden-locked beauties loll bedraggled;
The faceless teddy-bear rests on the bed,
My golly-wog is standing without a head.
The air is still, it smells musty,
Everything is as I left it, but is dusty.

Opening the door and peering in my room,
Fragrant memories, in my mind, loom.
I reminisce the blissful hours,
Spend here playing and dreaming of stars.
I vividly recall the shadows at night,
My fears, my nightmares, my mother's plight.

Looking back, I realize I have grown
Faster than I had ever known...
And now I have a visitor standing beside me
My pretty little daughter grinning mischievously.

Sanam Singh

Fight For Death

Come be brave, the posters say,
Fight and kill and still get pay.
But what these posters do not store
Is all about the blood and gore.

Fight for your country, it needs you!
But your family needs you too.
Come have something to tell the wife
About how you stole some soldier's life.

This is how to shoot a gun.
Pull the trigger, let's have fun.
Wished you'd listened to what the wife said.
Too late now mate - bang - you're dead.

This is what war's all about,
Poverty, hunger, constant drought.
A bang on the door get you up from bed;
"Sorry lady, your husband's dead".

So fight for your country, as they say;
Help increase the undertakes' pay.
Don't just sit there with the wife,
Come to the front line - end your life.

Lawrence Phillips

I See You

I see you God, in the buds, in the trees.
In the sun, in the sky.
In the green of the fields.
In all that is good, and all that yields.

You're there in the peaceful break of day.
And there in a newborn baby's cry.
When someone in despair needs a helping hand.
And there, when sunsets at even stand.

There, everywhere, if we could only see.
In the sweetened tone of the singing bird.
Even in the buzzing of a droning bee.
We accept, Your sound and presence with glee.

Even to the blind, Your sound is heard
And to the deaf, without a word.
But those who do not want to see.
Have each and every faculty.

But close their eyes, to what they won't.
And shut there ears, to do's and don't's.
The glory felt, by us who see.
Sadly for them can never be.

Mary Gore

Motherhood (To Be A Mother Is A Vital Role In A Tripper)

I have been a tripper all my life.
In my youth, and until I became a wife.
I would trip on a pavement, or over a stone.
When these things happen, you are never alone.

Once in the town centre, I fell on my knees.
I think I may have slipped on some leaves.
My hand-bag flew open all the contents fell out
There was money, and powder, all scattered about.

A very kind post-man came to my aid.
He picked it all up. It looked like a raid.
I stuffed it pack as fast as I could and went on my way.
Thank you, thank you, was all I could say.

I went to the shops, one fine sunny day.
I was striding along, without a care, as they say.
Suddenly I hit the pavement, and was flat out
She has fainted, a woman said. No tripped I heard a man shout.

Up I got, to buy bottles of tonic and gin
If I had dropped them, it would have been a sin.
So, I must take care how I walk.
Or be more sedate. Just sit and talk!

Joan Francis

Dogs Don't Cry, Do They?

Frenzied seeking, as daylight fades,
afraid and alone, in darkening shades.

Like a storm-tossed dove, blown from her loft.
Like a bolting rabbit, fears the burrow is lost.

Like the wind in the hay, this way and that.
Like the swift stealth, of the sleek stalking cat.

Like thundering hooves, galloping fast,
the thump of his heart, pounds with each gasp.

Like a swan taking flight, sprinting on water,
his senses searching, lest he fail or falter.

Homeward he speeds, yet to cross over,
that dangerous divide, that smooth slippery boulder.

Those hurtling wheels, towards him raced,
like lightning struck, no more could he chase.

His body torn and broken, thrust up and flung aside.
He felt his lifeblood ebbing, weary sorrow deep inside.

Upon a grassy bank he fell, in the freshness of the dew.
So weak and all a'shiver, that scent of death he knew.

Eyes now still and wide, the image of his master kept.
A glistening teardrop welled, a hushed whimper as he wept.

Frank Payne

"Turn About"

Fancy car and made-up face
How do you feel now she's in your place
Gone are the days of household chores
Now you're in her job and she has yours
It used to be you, with briefcase in hand
But she wanted that too, so she took a stand
You were the work force, but now she's there too
There is no job on earth that she won't try to do
Engineer, Pilot, Prime Minister too
You sit and think, it should have been you
But you took it for granted, that you were the best
She slipped in beside you, as you took a rest
She loves the fight, the challenge, the power
From lying a plane to installing a shower
You should have listened when she was unhappy
You should have washed up, or changed that nappy
If you'd made her feel special, gave credit where due
She may not have wanted to work, just like you
A fancy car with a made-up face
How do you feel, now she's taken your place

Lesley-Anne Lloyd

Your Smile Means So Much

Your smile is very precious,
And it's absolutely free,
It is the most marvellous gift,
That God has given you and me.

A smile can bring deep happiness,
In times of great distress,
A smile can bring such joy,
To everyone as you pass them by.

A smile can change your world around,
So give your smile it's worth a mile,
So give it all awhile, so laugh, and smile,
It can make life so much more worthwhile.

A little smile however small, will help someone
As they struggle on. The world would be a better place,
If everyone just smiled. So can I say make sure
You smile each and every day.

No matter where you are, be it north, east, south or
West, remember always bring your smile with you
As you travel along life's way. And you and your
Smile will come triumphantly through.

Umelda Havard

"God's Good"

It's morning, I wake to "another day"
"God's Good" - He has had his way.
The sunlight shines - it's oh so bright
The birds are singing - it's sheer delight
Whatever I do with myself today
I have been given "another day"
More beautiful than the yesterday.
Then comes the night all peaceful and dark
I wonder if tomorrow I'll hear the lark?
"God's Good" - If He has his say.
I will awake to "Another Day"

Ethel Spence

Flying Free

Have you ever wondered
How the dragonfly appears,
Sun shining through its wings
Like multi-coloured tears?
It's one of Nature's miracles
Just watch and see it fly,
Those wings of fragile gossamer
Soaring to the sky.
You wouldn't think it started life
In a dark cocoon-like shell
Which fell back in the water
As Nature wove its spell.
So it is with people
When their days on Earth are through,
Whether their time was long
Or whether their years were few.
They can't come back to tell us
Where they are and what they see,
For they too have finished with their shells
And now are flying free.

Joan Corney

Aids

Innocence Of The Child
Born to this world with blessed cheer,
Am I a newborn cherished so dear.
To be loved and cared I have no fear,
That those who attend me will always be near.

Dreams so pleasant and joyful are mine,
Happy, beautiful, gentle and kind,
The love I receive forms images divine,
That reflections of these shall be locked in my mind.

Experience Of The Mother
Your life so new fills me with sadness,
A babe's plight that drives me to madness,
Times of joy and times of sorrow,
Of these both should follow

However your young life is plagued with infection,
As yet there is no cure for your affliction,
Agony, despair, torment and woe.
These are the feelings that I know will not go.

Nicola N. Walker

The Midnight Garden

In the midnight garden the moon
shines, the stars twinkle and glitter.
All over the world the grass is gleaming brightly,
from the moon above.

You see big green eyes of foxes.
The badgers come out of their hiding places.

The shadows of night make
faces and the trees
shake like waving hands.
They wave to me but no one
else can see.

In the midnight garden is
the place to be.

Hayley Frampton

Untitled

It's a word of God creations
Fills your heart with temptations
It's the truth and honest power
We live on it every hour.

Two people has the same feeling
Just like a deep out healing.
It leads to a warm passion
An irresistible emotional attraction

When you near to the one you love
Your world is a happy just like a dove,
No-one will ever share,
Your feelings will be eternal and very rare.

Hatred and jealousy can ruin lives
It burns inside just like two pair of knives
Today's world is full of temptations
Confusion leads to complications.

Why is it God love is so strong,
Nothing in that world can break that bond,
Needing your feelings as long as I live.
My soul is yours until death does its trick

Nafeesa Ali

Freedom To Darkness

Wildlife is free for the deer,
The moment of life is waiting,
He runs with a stride that's beautiful and mild,
Feet proud as he runs with the fear of a life being ended.
The hunter spies with a glance from his heartless eyes,
As he pulls the trigger the bullet fires out like a flame from a fire.
The young and life-full deer
Slides and glides roughly on the pouring flesh blood,
The deer tragically falls, with the look of the eyes
He lifts his head but it heavily falls
As he flickers his green glassy eyes

His life is now gone, gone, gone forever.

As the wind howls through the forgotten ears
Of the death spotted red glowing deer.

Rachael Murray

A Tangible Fear!

It comes alive with fear and hate,
The being within is a reprobate,
Its guilt and shame are eating away
At her heart and soul, day by day.

Her consciousness reels with the burning ache
Of passions that swell for her own life's sake,
Anger and fear are always close by,
At night her eyes lift up to the sky.

The hope that she seeks keeps drifting away,
Her heart it does sink as dark comes her way,
The terror she feels is so real, as it grows
That her body lies rigid, with fear of the unknown!

Susan Henning

My Darling

My love for you goes deeper than any ocean sea
My heart belongs to you alone
And you're the one that holds the key
We will be together always, of that you can be sure
And I will be here waiting when you walk though the door
I could never live without you
I don't even want to try, 'cause if you ever left me
I would surely die
So when this is over we will never part
'Cause if it happened over again
You would really break my heart
I need you here right by my side, so keep on being strong
There's only 10 weeks left to go; that isn't very long
So just remember that I love you and I'm waiting here
For you to come back home to me and wipe away my tears.

Colleen Weston

Mental Block

The textbook on my oaken desk
Lies open to Pythagoras,
I choke my pen to quell my fears,
This cursed Euclid's drawing tears.
The numbers blind me, strain me, daze me,
Logarithms, sine, and roots amaze me.

Never will I grasp this skill,
It's Satan's art, it's overkill.
My only wish is to be free
To view the Sphinx aesthetically.
Arithmetic is fine for some,
For me it's merely cumbersome.

Clouds descend before my eyes,
In math there is no compromise.
My plaint comes not from stress alone,
It's rigour that I can't condone.
Life's not the sum of absolutes
So damn your fractions and square roots!

Michal Tal

Untitled

A young boy lies bearing pain and cold
At home they say he is brave and bold
As he lies on his stomach in mud knee deep
His eyes are heavy through lack of sleep

His sight remains in just one eye
He looks around at boys who lie
In mud face down for their glory and fame
At home no ones hold of the pain

Of blood and shooting all around
Of dead men next to them on the ground
Shoot to kill is their law
For there's no room for sentiment in this bloody war

Tracy Joynes

Away, At The Seaside 1956 Ad

Away, at the seaside, far from home
is where my soul-mate perhaps may roam.
I soon perceived the sea of blue,
those happy waves knew what to do.

Away, at the seaside, my memory lingers.
With birds appointed as their singers
I heard the orchestras of the mighty seas
playing such beautiful melodies.

We touched the breeze, and tasted brine,
the seaweed had that aroma fine.
As darkness came as from hand switch,
we knew we'd had the full sandwich.

Thomas Anthony Liddell

The Sea Of Life

The Powerful sea speaks to me
It tells me things I ought to know
And what I must do and where I must go.
The strength of the sea is frightening to me
Threatening, fascinating, powerful, calming and beautiful.
Like the trees, only God can make the seas.
His power is everywhere
Not only in the seas
But in every living thing.
If we listen, we will hear
And his voice is always clear.
Telling us what we must do,
If we want to live a new
In a state of bliss and pleasure
When this world is gone forever
Only with God will we get full measure.
This world is fast passing
Our lives are short lasting
Just like a spark of lightening in the sky
Spans the story of life for you and I.

Proinseas Nic Iomhair Muinerchain

Think On

When the stresses of life burden you down,
And all in the world seem to act like clowns.
When you ask of yourself, is this all there is? Think on.
You could be lame, or deaf, or blind,
You could be "ashes blowing in the wind".
Think on my friend, what have you got?
You've got your loved ones, young and old,
You're not having to live out in the cold.
You've got the wind, the rain, the sun.
You've got life, like everyone.
Be grateful for it, be thankful too,
Thank God for all the things you can do.
Think of those less fortunate than you,
Who have no-one to ever talk to.
Who have no roof above their heads,
And nowhere they can put a bed, except a dank, dark open
Doorway, or some cold windy, draughty, porchway.
Think on: Be smart, and make a vow, you'll accept life as it
is, right now. Without a murmur or a moan,
Or else, too soon, that life is "gone".

Kathleen L. Norris

Do Not Forget The Ones You Love

Echoes of the past, like wispy Autumn days,
Looking back to times past as though in a smoke-filled haze,
People you have loved but no longer see,
It seemed as though it was only yesterday that you frolicked
in the trees,

Distant sunsets slowly closing in,
Waiting for nightfall to begin,
In the half light you remember yesterdays,
A long time ago yet somehow not far away.

Life moves on, new people to meet,
New conversations to greet,
Ideas, opinions, laughter and tears,
Emotions passing with the years,

But love grows deeper for the people you care,
Oh how you wish they could always be near,
But life takes them away to distant places,
You picture in your mind their lovely faces,

So say goodbye but keep them in your heart,
And in that way you never really part.

Derek Rose

Aye Bonnie Scotland

Was it the magic of the mountains
That stole my heart away
Or the falling of the snowflakes on a cold and winters day.
Was it just the height of summer
Sun kissed purple plain
That drew my very soul back to Scotland once again

Was it the mystery of Loch Lomond
Or the poetry of Robbie Burns
I only know I lost my heart to a place my body yearns
Was it the magic of the people
The echo in the air
Of Scottish accents, gretna green tranquillity everywhere.

Or was it the magic of the moment
I lost my heart and soul
The salmon in abundance, the greatness of the shoal
Whatever the reason
Magic or not
I'll come back again, Aye Bonnie Scotland
I lost my heart and there it shall remain.

Jeanne E. Quinn

The Chestnut Tree

It stands erect through every season
Queries neither rhyme nor reason
Sleeps through winter's darkest days
Stirs to warmth of Spring's sunrays
Seems to know it's time to wake
As shoots of green begin to break
Pearly flowers with drooping heads
Adorn the swaying branches
Strong winds scatter all around
A floral carpet on the ground
Its canopy of verdant leaves
Bring welcome shade in summer
The rustle of autumnal breezes
Make a crunchy carpet underfoot
Delightful hues our eyes behold
Wondrous shades of russet, brown and gold
This bounteous tree gives other joys
Raining conkers down on playful girls and boys
As colder days onward creep
Enjoy again, dear tree, your well earned winter sleep

Iris Owen

"War '96"

Sent to a place, there to revoke;
Surely where the tears provoke thoughts
of longing, not belonging, alien: race
across the tarmac face of understanding.
How many limbs can we expend? Foot —
slogging through the waste of crass mis-handling.
Metallic force takes no account of flesh
And bone, reaching the outer space of
   lucrative cash-landing.

Margaret Ward

Moribund William

Staring at me from beyond the Styx,
His eyes like birds in a cave,
Cheek bones like coffins from which hung
The funereal skin, the mask of death,
The cachectic remnant of who he was;
His cheerfulness now eerie and obscene,
Were it not innocent,
His childish pleasure at being wheeled around
Refreshing, were it not putrid
His naïve belief in promises and summer
All that remains.
He told me of great briny voyages,
Of naked White Russians in Canada,
Of drunken Americans in Guam,
Of elephant legs in India.
I told him he would be alright,
And he agreed.

David John Armstrong

Plea

I am filled with doubts and griefs and fears
About present, past, and future years
This depression pushes me to tears,
And I need you.

Sometimes I yearn for I-know-not-what
These daily struggles seem all for naught
I think about the battles yet to be fought,
And I need you.

I have so many hopes and dreams
Without you they are yet unweaned
I have neither the strength nor courage it seems.
And I need you.

I'll shout from the roof-tops that I love you and want you
I'll do anything to prove that it's true
For without you, my whole life is blue.
And I need you.

Mojisola Ogunsulire

Abbey Ruins

Speak to me of times past.
I lay my hands on your body
Trying desperately to sense
Some echoes of days
When you were alive
With the peace of God.
I can feel some intangible
Threads of calmness
That I cannot grasp
But am weary for.
A single-minded purpose built you
For the glory of God.
Little now remains but in your very skeleton
I nevertheless strive to feel the kernel of your being.
Surely you must still contain empowered by centuries
Those soaring notes of praise and service
To bring peace for a brief moment when man has turned his face
Towards self indulgence. Reach down through the years
With the very essence of your soul touch me with your serenity.
Speak to me of peace!

Michael Clewes

Our Granddad

When I see him, he's always smiling.
When he smiles, he always smiles with a happy grin.
He's loving and gentle and when he smiles, we all smile.
He's clever and active and he always has been.
Even Levi, his dog, loves him.
He's churpy all the time, even when he is poorly.
When Granddad is with us, fun days are definitely filled.
As we surround him, we definitely smile.
These enjoyable moments, we'll always treasure.
You can see in his eyes a look of warmth.
A lot of great big hugs, and a lot of kisses.
And a million of great wishes, as we blow him kisses.
A twinkle gleams in his eyes, of course it's happiness.
Tall, "Like Me", says I Claire.
Active, "Like Me", says I Michael.
Funny, "Like Me", says I Kelly.
Your Personality, "Like Me", says I Lauren.
And soon they'll be one more Grandchild who'll take after you.
We're all like our Granddad.
We want to say, Granddad, "We Love You."

Claire Wiggins

Your Inhibitions

The only thing that interests me is a thing that I can't do,
I want to be allowed to live
As myself -
Not someone else
Not You.

Me is a thing I cannot be
I'm bound by your resistance,
I've been assimilated, differences disliked
Don't think about me
I'm not you.

Hi! I'm doing my best now,
To be like all the rest
Differences apart,
Not quite the same at heart
But trying.

Now you'll like me better;
Sharper, fitter, bright new sweater
Still perspiring sadly, (that's not sweat but sweeter),
Myself weeping away
Acceptable, still cheaper.

Heather Crossan

The Bogeyman Is Coming!!!

When I was very young,
My dad told me about the bogeyman.
He said if you sneezed three times in a row, he'd come to get you!
Once I did just that,
When I found out my allergy to cats.
Then I thought I'd met my doom,
So I went and cowered in my room.
I couldn't sleep for days on end,
Until I thought:—"Hang about, what if the bogeyman's my friend?
Although he's supposed to be big and hairy,
What if he's as gentle as a fairy?"
Now I think he's really alright,
That he wouldn't snarl or bite,
I don't have nightmares or bad thoughts about him now,
I just fall asleep at night, he doesn't give me a fright.
He's gone right out of my head, I just imagine he's dead.
Just admit that he isn't real, right?
So now I'd better say good night,
And on your way out,
Would you please turn out the light? Good Night!

Dawson Thomas

Holly Unites With Ivy

And so the union continues through modern times and old
Retaining still past traditions in name for us
to care for and hold

The Holly and the Ivy a linking of nature's own
Symbolic of life's momentum
extending our devotion to the lost felines
found

A protection that's often misconstrued
But you must allow us this volition
A freedom of one's beliefs should be exercised
within England's laws

As the years advance give our children
the opportunity to make their own
informed decisions
Then a future in harmony can be assured
Reintroducing the title 'Great Britain'
And only then will it be richly deserved

A contentment to be shared among we living here
And those lands connected by the 'cord'
Beneath earth's international waters

John C. Maddison

Friend

Into your life I arrived as a friend,
And when you came to meet me,
A passion followed.
You changed me from a friend to your lover.
But when you finished with me as your toy.
You became tired and grew bored with me.

And like the change of tides,
We grew apart,
And like the earth and moon,
We orbited each other, but failed to cross in path.

We needed each other,
Or so thought,
But the love I so much persisted
Another love you found, you bought.

And so the past friendship came,
"Back to normal" as it were,
But I still blame myself,
Because what I wanted to care and to be,
You felt for him
And where was the friend for me?

Ian Mitchell

Exams

Are they worth the trouble?
Do I really care?
Do I need to know a sperm has less chromosomes than a root hair?
Revision last forever,
Exams last a few days,
But when you're in the exam, the revision's just a haze,
Bitumen's used for tarring roads,
Or was that kerosine, oh well, it's just,
17 marks, oh no!
I must rock my little brain out,
I know it's in there somewhere,
Then think again, maybe it's not, maybe my brain is, yes bare!
Exams are now over, and yet now I know I passed,
I really only skimmed through
Next year I'll never last,
So when I get older,
And become an MP,
I'll ban exams forever,
So kids won't suffer like me!

Jemma Saville

Little People

Leprechauns, goblins and little fairies too
Are all around us, don't you know
They take good care of you
So if you see a baby with freckles on its face,
You'll know the fairies all have kissed it
Of these there are no trace.

They are such little people, so be careful where you tread,
They do their work and magic when we're tucked
up in our bed,
I never believed in little people, but now I have no doubt
Because the world is full of magical things
And the sun is always out.

It must be all the magic dust
They scatter all around
It's a shame we cannot see them
But they're nowhere to be found.

S. A. Williams

My Baby

My baby was lying waiting to live
And I sat waiting, wanting to give
Love and affection like all fathers would
Only the best that I ever could
Whilst loving his mother my future wife
Through all the bad times troubles and strife
But he can't be with us where he's gone to live
And I can't hold him and kiss his small cheeks
But I'll always love him as long as I'm here
Because the thoughts of my baby to me are so dear.

Darren Kiff

Get Off, Bad Show - Boo!!

You're not funny anymore!
(the wallpaper falls off...)

Rather
like an antiquated comedienne
whose jokes have dried up;
what was once beautiful
has become monotonous and tasteless,
what was once funny
has become tedious and sour
(the comedian walks off...)

Rather
like burning embers
finally ceasing to exist;
a relationship that once embraced affection and knowing
has become arid and misunderstood,
a skill that once tickled psyche and persona
has become tame and unwanted
(the person goes off...)

Blaze

D. N. A.

We hear a lot these days
About the stuff of life
Called D. N. A.
Such a simple thing,
Made up of four chemicals.
And tells them what to do,
And when to do it,
So we are all alike,
and I am just the same
As a leopard, or a plumb tree,
And a whale is just the same
As a fly, but put together
In a different order.

What I really want to know is,
Who decided the order in the first place?

H. V. K. Knaggs

Untitled

A seat of episcopal power
lets me perceive by the eye,
Your translucent but glowing complexion.
I humbly watch you from afar,
So as not to stultify myself
Temptation burns like a fire,
And you're a fire I cannot resist.
Your phantasmal power shines
Perpetually upon me.
And I cannot help but be drawn
toward your stupendous Aura.
I am lorn without your words of endearment
Do not let us dissever,
but if we do, I'll love you forever.

Alexandra Wildy

White Crystals

From still sky they fall
White crystals from heaven born
Shrouding our earth
With glistening bright sheet
Scenery altered - cold
Though beautifully neat.

With treading feet
We scar their glows
As man and beast
Their movement slows
Trekking their way through heaps of flows
Crystals now marred, earths flesh exposed.

Then white turns grey
As crystals decay
With ice now forming
Clear waters then running
So all white crystals disappear
Yet will they return - next year.

R. A. Court-Hampton

Untitled

I slowly look in front and see
A charred body that is facing me
None will ever know his name
But for that who is to blame?
Maybe it was the Government
On weapons our money was spent,
Or was it just people like me and you
'Cos of the evil things we do?

Now I am tired, I can run no more
My head is aching, my feet are sore
So I sit down amongst the waste
And with every breath I get a taste
Of the sad future of this world
And finally under a stone I have curled
to die in peace, no longer in war
I close my eyes, become a stranger once more.

M. Brady

God's Gifts

Open wide with wonder, are the eyes that look and see
While strolling in the country lanes, God made, for you and me
The beauty of the flowers, gently swaying in the breeze
The sky in many shades of blue, he made for us, to please
He worked for us for six whole days, the seventh he did rest
The singing birds, the buzzing bees, he really gave his best
So open up those dreamy eyes, look, and really see
Don't take it all for granted, blue skies, and leafy trees
Birds so sweetly singing, as they flit from bough to bough
Sweet scented flowers, running streams, look and see them now.

W. Taberham

Untitled

What is it child? What do you see? Why do you sit in melancholy?
What can have happened in your life? What harmed you so? Why so much
strife? What can I do? Is there no balm? I want to help, keep you
from harm, I'll pick you up, blow under your chin, hold you close,
breathe you in. Your sad, sad eyes bring tears to mine,
I plead with God, 'Please let me find the key I need to this child's
heart her sadness grips, tears me apart!
Child of my heart can you not see just how much you mean to me?
Do you not know you're like a star,
You shine for me and I've come so far to love you and to hold you
tight, to give you hugs so that you might one day see the world was
made for you and me. The world shines clean and bright and good, as
God intended that it should, but you must look your world to find,
I would, but cannot give you mine. There is a life out there you know
just wait a while until you grow. Don't shut yourself in, don't keep
the world out, don't cringe in your cot, don't wait for the clout,
but wait for your time, and it will come soon,
My little Sunita, muy bulgia nay toom.

Diana McGrady

Judge Me Not

"Order: Order: All Rise"
The voice echoes, like the aftermath; bringing a chill to the atmosphere.
As I the Highest in Authority infiltrates the inhabited chambers.
To the commoner, I am known as simple, magistrate or judge.
To then elite; adjudicator, expert connoisseur.
All walks of life situate themselves before me; with one thing in customary;
Illegality!....
With the aid of my two abettor solicitors;
Who have rehearsed their part in this cavort.
One to vindicate the appellant,
The other to arraign arbitration without plausible dilemmas.

Listening to the monotonous rigmarole; and on and on; mutter, mutter, mutter.
The thrill of just banging the hammer; interrupting the nattering and shouting,
"Life In Bondage: To The Gallows! Hang Him High Till Dead!";
Appeals to my better nature.
For I see it; who ever stands before me should suffer the maximum punishment.
Be he innocent or guilty; for he should not have got caught.
But; alas, the cat has got to give the mouse a sporting chance.
Then I'll make judgement quick and swift....

Sidney Hall

So Many Things Are Unexplained

Where did those voices come from, playing with my mind?
Telling me their secrets, helping me to find
the solution of this planet, the conclusion of this Earth.
With music the centre point, starting with its birth.
They made me a founder member, these people in my brain,
They told me they were watching when I was going through such pain.
They told me I had passed the most important test of all.
I passed with flying colours and was invited to the Ball.
The test of life itself is a challenge, can't you see.
I am not the only one, there's others just like me.
But some are much less fortunate. They entered the test and lost.
They couldn't jump the hurdle, so now they're paying the cost.
They tried to reach the sky, but came crashing down to the ground.
They tried to get too high. Now there's doctors all around.
But they don't seem to understand about their anguish and pain,
About their beautiful thoughts, they just class them all INSANE.

Minette McFarlane

Drift Away

My eyes open to another day
Tomorrow circling within my head
With yesterday trailing not too far behind.

I search for my dreams
I begin to stumble over yesterday
Turning to seek tomorrow
But you're too far away
Yet worst of all, I have lost today

Laying myself down to bed
Tomorrow becomes today
Then I rest my head
Thoughts of yesterday
I have found out where today was!
But I let it drift away.

Aden Faulkner

Illness

I lie dreaming
A colossus felled by ancient neglect
Half buried in sands
Which swirl and drift around my pitted body,
Eroding me,
Blanking out my features.
My sightless eyes dust bowls to trap their eddies
My ears, nose and all my extremities
Blunted by these unforgiving grains.
Time and the ageing winds of fortune
Have brought me thus low.
No clarion call within me now remains.
My voice a gravel grinder, toneless as a drain.

Christopher Dunn

A Friend So True

To love you like the way I do,
A friend you've been, so kind, so true,
This time you'll be so far away,
I'll miss you so much every day.

Wipe away the tears, you'd say,
I'm only a short phone call away,
But it's easier said than done, you know,
Leaving a friend who has to go.

Enjoy your time in the sun,
And I hope you have heaps of fun,
You deserve life's best with what you've been through,
But you'll always end up smiling because you are you.

Thanks to you there's a different me,
It's long ago what I used to be,
I'm stronger, more mature and not so scared,
Only because you took the time to care.

Denise Barbour

Sunday Dinner

Mum can I leave the table now? No you can just sit there
Till everyone has finished, just sit there on your chair
We have this every weekend, they all come round for tea,
Everyone laughs and talks, that's all except for me

There's uncle George; he's sitting there picking at his peas
If that were me, Dad would look and say, son eat all your greens
There's auntie Dot; her hair is red, and all she does is talk
Look at her waving all that food round on her fork
There's uncle Jim; his nose is long, he always has a rash
Look at him now, he's got potato hanging from his tash
Uncle Reg is worst of all, his mouth it seems so big
His false teeth clatter up and down, he eats just like a pig

Why doesn't Dad say to them, Eat your greens, don't wave your fork
Wipe your chin, sit up straight and when your mouth's full
Please don't talk?
Every Sunday we have this, they all come round for tea
But why is there one rule for them and another rule for me?

Mags Tate

Untitled

He was one in a million; someone unique.
Told lots of tall stories but with 'tongue in cheek.'
He was gentle, yet strong.
Loved by all he knew.
If I have half his qualities,
I will see this life through.

As his little recruits, we went through our paces,
In all of us, he left endearing traces.
How watched over his garden, like a hen, over her chicks.
When he wasn't doing this, he was chopping up sticks.

He was the greatest; a rare old lad,
He was just wonderful.
He was my dear old Dad.

Eva Dunn

Autumn

Autumn is frost,
Autumn is trees,
Autumn is all those wet leaves.
It's Halloween
And colder nights,
Sometimes conker fights
I play 'til at least seven o'clock
Then I put on my fancy witch's frock.
On bonfire night the firework display
Is my favourite part of the day.
Then I go to bed,
Thinking of the wonderful Autumn I've had.

Lynn Ferguson

My Super "M-A-A"

My dear "M-A-A,"
You're the golden wealth in our life.
You're so precious "M-A-A!"
We felt secure in your affection,
Although we were so little.
So far as I can remember,
We played outside and if anything happened to us,
We would run - run and go to you for comfort.
Before I came of age
God, you took away my "M-A-A!"
I can't find the "M-A-A," I love.
She left us so suddenly
And her smile has gone forever.
I pray for you "M-A-A."
God bless, we love you always.
You're everything to me
My super "M-A-A."

M. Shafiullah

Susannah

I've never seen a child so fair,
Golden sand is in your hair.
Beautiful, and full of laughter,
Were you an answer to a prayer?

A dainty child, without a care,
So fairy like, and sweet and rare,
With golden curls that flow so free,
I know that God's been good to me.

When you twirl round that garden tree,
The little birds sing happily,
They know they're safe, because you're sweet,
And little cats sit at your feet.

A little star that shines at night,
With eyes so bright, and full of light,
Your pinkish roses, covered in dew,
I never tire to look at you.

A little dancer, in the snow,
A precious stone that's all aglow,
My love for you, you'll never know.
What would I do? if you should go?

Julia Ann Holliday

The Consciousness Of God

Like the chrysalis that breaks forth
After its dark winter's night
Is my sleeping spirit
Buried in the earth of toil and much doing

Outwardly, seasons visit, leaves fall and fall
A compost settles over the weary soul
The once ploughed ground lies fallow
Encrusted by time

Yet, He who holds seasons in His hand visits
There is a rustling overhead
A moving in the bushes
A warm spring breeze thaws the winter's freeze

Helpless in the fallow ground
The plough of God wreaks havoc
Exposed to light and air
The hidden spores of life evolve
At last! The chrysalis becomes a butterfly

Jude Martin Dunne

Autumn

Outside the wind is blowing, it's whipping
Through the boughs, the trees are really trying to hold their
Heads up proud, to sit so warm and cosy, and watch what's
Going on, I feel the autumn's coming, it really
Won't be long, we'll see the greens turn into red,
A lovely sight for sure when summer goes and nods its head
And shuts another door, then soon another Christmas,
A Peter Pan type time, when thoughts
Will turn to snowmen
Fast gone the autumn time, but just before it disappears I
Beg you take the time to really look at autumn
When the land must go to sleep
And you too may see the beauty
Should you want to take a peek
How very very lovely as winter comes along,
As fast as autumn's coming quite soon it will be gone

B. K. Watson

Summer Rain

The rain brings out an emotion,
Like a strange hypnotic potion.
Cars in the road make sounds like the sea
Lapping gently onto a bed of sand.
Your body starts to float, head spun in a dream,
Up to the clouds, then back to the land.
Forever being drawn out into the street,
Like standing on a cliff, staring out at the ocean.
Feeling tired, just wanting to sleep.
Need no tablets, no counting sheep.
Just stand at the window, look out on the day.
Everything wet, river swollen.
Another summer's day has been stolen.

J. M. Bright

"A Stroll Along The Shore"

As we walk along life's shore so many
things we see
Tiny coves where we can hide and very
quietly be
Little rocks where we can rest before we
go our way
And little bays of courage to help us face
the day.

In the harbour of our lives, our anchor
must be firm.
So we can face the storms of life without
undue concern
The tides of time so quickly change, the waves
of life roll by
"Come" let us walk the shore with Him
who is always nigh.

Elizabeth Want

First Home

Oh little house so cosy and so dear,
How many happy times we had here,
Times full of laughter and sweet song,
Wondering where the next penny would come along,
Little place where I never felt afraid.
When once inside all my worries and problems fade,
This place I never will forget,
So I leave with sorrow and regret.

Carol Gibson

Life's Too Short

Life's too short to quarrel — this is what we say.
Yet we forget this saying — nearly every day.
We are so quick — with hurtful remarks to make,
Never willing to give an inch — demanding to take.

If only we could stop and think — before we speak,
If only we could find peace — and not trouble seek,
There would be an end to wars — no trouble round about,
Life would be so good — no one would shout.

The world would be a better place — for all of us to live,
We could stay together — each other help we'd give,
But this is just a dream — but we can play a part,
It always takes two people — for a quarrel to start.

K. J. Havard

Untitled

Don't push me so close
You know that it hurts.
Yes, I'm angry, with me too.
My crumpled up shell has done its time
Its contents beyond man's repair
Just talk to me Nurse, the way you once did.
About life, you men and my bladder
Yes, you joked about that
made me feel 'good' where I was 'bad'
and cleaned me so I was myself again.

I'm still in this shell
I know I don't talk and do the things I don't want to
It's no wish of mine to test you this way
I know you do all you can.

Don't push me so hard, have I changed all that much?
Do your actions say what you now feel for me?
I still have a mind, even though I don't talk
full of thoughts, in actions and dreams.

Stephanie Whyte

Childhood Memories Of A Country Girl

Horses working the fields flat
Gentle giants to look up at
Dandelion heads blown in the sky
Games of hopscotch and I-spy

Walks to the village shop
Hand tightly clutching a penny
For thin sticks of black liquorice
With a bag of yellow sherbet

Jack Frost's patterns across the window
Hedges white, cocoon by spiders' webs
Sledging in the cold snow
Wet trousers, cold fingers-owch!

Seaside donkey rides, bucket, spade
Scent of bluebells in the glade
Making daisy chains in the green meadow
Joy when tying shoe laces into a bow

Time goes by so fast
Fifty years have passed
When learnt knit and purl
Just memories of a country girl

Mary Mycock

What Makes Good Poetry

For what is to and for?
For what is ebb and tide?
For what is T. S. Eliot
For the reader cannot find.

For what is form and content?
For what is strength or depth?
For what untanglement necessary
For the eyes the mind does accept.

For what is poetry needed?
If a fool can cheat the eye
For strength and form, content and depth
With my pen I can disguise.

S. A. Forrester

Divine Music

What mortal music has been heard more fair
Than David's psalms unto the Lord his King?
Tumultuous Saul was stilled to hear him sing
And play upon his harp a gentle air.
Is there a song more free of worldly care
Than that, upon a starlit night in spring,
The nightingale's clear silvery voice does bring
Uplifting men his rapturous ease to share?
The most sublime terrestrial melody
Has beauty less than heaven's minutest sound;
No earthy soul in holy ecstasy
Can hear celestial notes of harmony.
  Where songs of faith with love and hope abound
  Then, here on earth, the God of joy is found.

Robert H. Williams

Spring

The dismal days of winter pass
Now spring is on its way
A pale, weak sun peeps through the clouds
- Its rays of light, as if to say -

"Wake up! you sleepy dull grey earth
Let me warm you, give you life,
Hear you sing, rejoice the birth
Of summer" - on its way at last.

Birds and bees and long warm days
Tall green trees and flowers ablaze
- With every colour to behold
A sight so pleasing it unfolds -

A feeling of great warmth and love
A peace surrounds us, whilst above
The blue sky stretches, clouds depart
Happiness lifts up the heart

Spirits high, we sing in tune
Summer days will follow soon
Goodbye to sadness, hurt and pain
When winter leaves us, spring is here again

Patricia Ann Graham

What Of It

The lorries backing,
The Guinea Pigs squealing,
The syringes squirting,
The Scientist working,
The needles stabbing,
The money, greedy money,
The sad little lost souls,
The steel work surfaces,
The sterile walls,
The clean tiles on the floor,
The stagnant smell of the drinking wells,
Cages, row upon row of cages,
The extreme harshness of too much authority,
Not fair of life,
The excruciating pain and cringes
Of the lonely little souls.

Wesley Pascoe

Hands

Work-worn, rough and chapped,
Yet tender, as they surround
His precious new son.
Years later, hands still rough and worn
Turn the pages of a story book.
Dirty, strong, determined hands
Show eager, young hands how to fix.
Hands working together, old and young
Young, strong hands now writing,
Working hard, achieving.
A strong handshake, proud father
Grasps the hand of his son.
Well done!
Amidst the cries of newborn babes
A loving hand reaches out
To touch the soft hand
Of his precious new son;
As a rough, feeble, shaking hand
Lovingly strokes his precious grandchild.

Alison Humphreys

The Recipe Of Life

The melting pot is brimming,
with harmony and joy.
The recipe is so unique,
for every girl and boy.
Add the warmth of a loving heart,
and watch the mixture swell.
Fold in happiness and laughter,
they blend so very well.
Add love for every race and creed,
and our land will flourish too.
Knead with tenderness and humour,
and the world will smile with you.
Sprinkle seeds of compassion,
so the rich give to the poor.
Especially add a sprig of time,
that's what we all hope for.
When ready to serve add the zest of life,
for everyone large and small.
Garnish with peace and contentment,
serve liberally to all!

Val MacFadyen

The Arena

You have shared this mine field
Felt the recoil of my explosive indiscretions
Felt pain burning like shrapnel in your ever faithful heart.
You have been lost behind my smoke-screens
Felt the stinging of tears in undeserving eyes.
Sometimes even hoped that one final battle's volley
Might blank your mind of me forever.
Yet never once have you stepped into the safety zone
You stand firm by your own choice, within the arena.

Brian Curtis

Why Do We

As I look so far across a diamond clear ocean
I can't explain this peaceful emotion.
I cast my eyes to soft clouds in the sky,
I close my eyes, breathe deeply and sigh.
I wish every day I could feel this free,
I've never experienced such great harmony.

Then all peace is lifted, and I realize
that our world is dying, I can hear its cries.
Why cut down the forests that provide us clean air?
We know we are wrong, but don't seem to care.
Our land is so precious, it's all we have got,
If we keep on this way we shall wipe out the lot.

So listen to your emotions and they will make sense,
We're killing ourselves at our own expense.

Emily Rice

Oh! Black Rock

Unmoved, untouched, alone you've stood,
since time began, at the edge of the seam
a grey lump of solid granite rock,
defying the powers of the mighty Atlantic,
though your shape might often change,
like the long centuries you've been through,
your heart is still dependable and strong,
home to millions of little sea creatures,
green moss and barnacles cling to your roof,
you're a seat for humans on hot days,
immune, impregnable, you stand aloof,
from the furious waves that lash you,
for though tides and winds keep changing,
you're forever still, a landmark, my black rock.

Eileen Sexton

Chair

Dedicated to my Mam and Dad who have always been there for me.

Sitting alone in my room, the solitude envelopes me.
Then out of my gloom, Arms suddenly enfold me.
I knew not where they came from, but my loneliness subsided.
The warmth I seemed to feel, seemed to lift my spirits high.
Looking out of my window, the sky reached out and touched me.
Clearing my cloudy mind, the sun came out and warmed me.
I didn't have a care, I floated round the room,
Not knowing how or where, then I felt my chair,
Whose arms they were around me
Whose legs had sprouted wings
And love it did surround me.
Then it suddenly hit me
That although it could not be,
This was not my imagination;
It somehow had to be.

Marjorie Fletcher

Look Remember Me

I am the unnoticeable one
I am the one nobody cared,
I can see you, you can't see me.....
Simple.
I hear you chatting about football.
But me, I am alone with nobody to care -
no sympathy.
You see me walking in the same coat
every day and shoes.
And you sometimes wave to me.
But I can't say anything, I am too nervous.
I am the unnoticeable one....
about whom nobody cared.

Richard Rose

Lines On Limitation

I climbed with a friend the hill of Filopapou
on a blowy Sunday afternoon,
but not before we'd had some ouzo first.
Up we went, wondering a little, just why we did it.
Then on top, at the Roman ruin, commanding
Athena's shrine, we were alone for
just a time before some Germans came.
I turned and looked at grey-blue Imitos,
lying to my right, a giant seal,
wallowing in the cloudy sea.
Head and tail obscured by billowing waves,
it waited, watchful across the scattered
city, cupped within the chambered hills.
I looked and knew. My hand picked up the brush
I use at home, and at once, my mind
put down in paint - which coal grey, and how to touch it,
when to dare some ochre to bring the blue alive?
That's called technique," I told myself,
which I lack in words, and which
my heart so longs to speak.

John F. Flynn

The Ways Of Sin

Leading me down a path ever winding,
Chemical cadavers and celestial infusions
Swirl and frolic among the lilies;
Chasing their shadow makers
Where angels fear to tread.

Floating through the milling crowds
Drowning in bloodstone finery and words unspoken,
I grease my lips with the sweat and toil
Of any souls I cross,
Where angels fear to tread.

Ministers of darkened delight do haunt me,
Whispering words drenched in the wailing echoes
Of suppressed divinity,
Guiding the willing
Down that path ever winding....

Stacy Richardson

Breathing Freedom

In last light's loneliness I walked the beach,
This boundless beach, this beach of timeless charm,
And realized I was beyond the reach
Of civilized sound, beyond technology's harm.
I waded through the wearied ends of waves,
Around me thrashing, crashing, rippling, receding,
And kicked water as a child behaves,
Wilfully, wrathfully, and needing leading, pleading.
I stopped, and turned, and scanned the white-tipped
Breakers fleeing frantically from Fiji.
Amid surging surf and water whisked and whipped,
I breathed freedom fresh from the foaming sea!
Ah! That this moment would forever survive,
This momentary thrill of being alive!

James Humphreys

The Flower

The Flower of the flock they called you
while I was Standing there,
I pretended I was not hurt nor did I care.

But the thought is still inside me,
the way I felt that day,
You made me want to hide my face away.

But now I look in the mirror
I'm thankful for what I see,
The face God gave me
Is there in front of me.
I smile to myself and say
How Silly I was that day,
It's the only face I'll get and
I know it's here to stay.

Jan Stanley McBride

School Days

Children start school at five years old.
They try to be brave and very bold.

The first day at school is very trying.
All the strange faces, some end up crying.

As they settle into a new routine,
Their mums miss them a lot it would seem.

Then comes the time for junior school,
When the children have grown and try to keep cool.

More independent the parents would say,
Getting themselves ready for the school day.

They learn more and more as they grow.
Don't need mum's help now, you know.

Senior school is the final stage,
Before they start work, and earn a wage.

How fast our children grow and mature.
The pain and gain the parents endure.

L. Bradbury

Life and Dreams

In life there is truth, in life there are lies,
eventually nuclear, when everyone dies!
In dreams there is fantasy, violence and hope,
in life there is liquor, anguish and dope.
The dreams become life, the life becomes dreams,
but it's never quite what one hopes, so it seems.
A house or a job? A family or new dreams?
Then eventually death! Whatever that means.
If dreaming is life, then life is a dream?
Whatever it is, it's not very clean,
and if that is true, then life isn't just,
so who do we love? And who do we trust?

Kevin P. Morley

Distance!

I am surrounded by millions,
yet I am completely alone.
I bear the objective voice of thousands,
yet I stand in silence,
People are walking round my head
shouting and yelling their views their ideas,
and my thoughts are drowned out by this
dreadful sound
I am trapped with these monsters,
These so called humans.
and I am falling deeper and deeper into
despair,
with no guide wire or helping hand to
pull me out.
They think they know me,
but not even I know me anymore.

Linzie Winton

To Margaret

When I stop and think of the time I spend with you
I think of all the lovely things in life that's warm and true
The flowers, the trees a warm summer's
  breeze, the sea rolling in to the shore

With these things in my heart I think of you
and the love you give me so warm and true

A woman with a love to help me through my lonely hours
A woman whose love blossoms like the flower
A woman with a love as strong as the sea
A woman who's given her heart to me
Her life is my life and I love her so it's a
pity in a way the world will never know
for it's her love that makes the flowers grow
Her love is the force that drives
  the sea to the shore
This woman whose life and love I adore

Jack Neal

An Irish Cry Of Old

The Emerald Isle was not so green,
but darkened by disaster.
Social patterns changed it seemed,
no singing songs and laughter.
Irishmen were burdened, stricken by despair.
Battered by the shadow of the blight.
Dignity was far from captured, nothing to declare.
Survival, death defying fight.
The crippled soil of Ireland,
A cultural decline.
Ancestor's savaged by starvation,
frightened by the killing time.
A promise of the new land called.
For many emigrated.
An ultimatum forced upon them,
as their land disintegrated.
Overpowered by the sight, of natural confusion.
Patriotism torn apart, a country lost for pace.
Affected and injured by disillusion.
A horror they had to face.

Nigel Kiely

Our White World

Just like a fleecy blanket
The snow lays thick and white,
With footprints in the pathways
left by travellers of the night.
Small birds hop through the branches
Of the trees now cold and bare -
but beautiful lace patterns
of ice and snow lay there.
Early morning cobwebs sparkle in the sun -
hanging like bright jewels -
whilst spiders wait to run.
Our world's now white and beautiful -
and the children have great fun -
But I like many others -
Prefer the Summer sun!

N. A. Hill

Thoughts

There's something I've been wondering almost all my life.
Is this world a real one with all its pain and strife?
War and want is all the rage, there is no freedom
just this cage.
The news is full of doom and gloom,
Not much light in this dark room.
Blood, frustration, tears and fears,
so little hope through these sad years.
Smiles these days seem far and few if only we could start anew!
Give ourselves another chance to join together in life's dance.
Imagine peace and joy for all,
each could rise, no man would fall.
Food for every little one, No more arms,
No bomb! No Gun!
Is there a choice in this great scheme?
Is this illusion?
all just part of someone's dream.
A nightmare maybe whilst we sleep.
When we awake, a world to keep?

Barbara Baldwin

A Little Treasure

She sat by the river bank
Watching the clear water flow,
Her thoughts were with the one she loved
Who had now gone far away.

Her heart was filled with sadness
There were tears, unhappiness and anguish,
No more love and laughter filled the air
Her lover had gone and found another.

He told her that he loved her
Promised never to depart,
She would always be his treasure
His life, his love, always and forever.

She would always have her memories
Also time would heal the pain,
Then there was her little secret
An unborn child to remind her of his name.

Susan Baxter

Awakening Nature

"Woo-Woo!" said the wind as it blew a cloud away;
"Ha-Ha!" laughed the sun, "It's the first spring day,"
"Ssss-Ssss!" said the snow as it melted away,
And there peeped the wee little flower!

"Rustle!" said the leaves, all shining in new green;
"Buz-z-z!" said the bumble bee, "Is there honey for my Queen?"
"Twitter-twee!" sang the bird, "What a winter it has been!"
And there peeped two little flowers!

The wind sighed softly, and the clouds sailed above,
The sun shone warmly, and the birds sang of love,
Bees buzzed busily; the leaves hid a dove,
And there was a whole field of flowers

Pauline D'Roza

494

Stop The Torture!

Young life, young life, ripped sadistically from the womb
torn to pieces in agony, butchered by the knife
before in pieces being exposed
to chemicals, poisons, gas, fire and acid.
I tell you: at this very moment
the soul of the tiny child still lives
and no preposterous statement
by the living can alter this.

And the animals, the furry and the feathered,
the scaled and unscaled living creatures
that I have scattered
throughout the corners of the earth,
ye now massacre and torture,
rip and slice while still alive
and inflict those indescribable pains
no being should ever suffer.

Damn ye, men and women of this earth.
I made the earth a jewel in the night;
and ye have turned it
into the sewers and torture chambers of hell.

Paul C. Sandison

I Was A Stranger In A Strange Land

'Twas a golden peal of trumpets that awakened me
From a sleep of a thousand years.
'Twas the muffled beat of a drum that awakened me
From a dream of a thousand years.

'Twas a strange land I woke to,
A world of a thousand fears.
'Twas a land of Sorcery I awoke to,
A world of a thousand Seers.

'Twas a world of magic and potions,
A land I should not have seen.
'Twas a world of colour and emotions,
A land that should never have been.

'Twas as a stranger I walked here,
Awakened by a spell from the deep.
'Twas magical chants that kept me here,
Awakened from a dream-filled sleep.

'Twas the trill of a lark on a wing
That slipped me back to my dream-filled sleep.
'Twas the beat of a butterfly wing
That slipped me back to my ancient Keep.

Sandra Lesley Dow

The Lion Roar

The rolling waves tossed and curled all covered in foam
This I saw as I did roam,
Along the beach upon mile and mile,
Without a field hedge pond or style.

Slowly and surely it covered the sand,
With a thundering alike the promenade band
And crowds shouting and clapping with glee,
But no it was the wild cruel sea.

The sand and pebbles just lay there to die,
Comforted by the darkening sky,
And a moon so bright which seemed to say,
I'm helping the sea to find its way,

Perhaps a hope if winds were anew,
Knowing the way in which they blew,
Perhaps they could try and hold the sea back,
But no the sea was there to attack.

Like a lion ready to prance on its prey,
Before a chance of something to say,
Along the beach the sea was abating,
And slowly slowly suffocating.

S. G. White

The Trenches

Walking with fear, knee deep in mud and slush.
Places where water is waist high.
Mud is not mud for it is dead bodies mashed into one.
The stench of the trench the horrible smell.
It's enough to make any one shrill.
"Keep your head down boys", that's all you hear.
See the enemy upon the line.
Aim, Fire, Bang.
The enemy is dead.
Shells exploding, bodies everywhere.
Bobbie your best mate Robbie your pal.
Killed dead mashed with the mud.
The sides of the trench have given away
This God forsaken hell hole will have its day.
I will keep fighting day after day.
For victory for gold.
My hopes are high my feet in mud
Cold defenceless I shiver with fear
As I put my life upon the line for Robbie and Bobbie my pals.

Louise Simpson

The Subliminal Allegory Of Marksbury

I'd be a highwayman's woman,
I'd ride a black horse,
A stallion,
That rears against a moonlit horizon and summons
  a rider of quality,

Of strength,
to bear the weight of pride,
To ride against the name of justice,
To hear the call of a woman's love,
Yes,
I'd be a highwayman's woman.

Sharon Dowding

Rwanda

We should cry for every human being
in Rwanda, and those who've joined the dead.
Marching like ghosts from evil men: fleeing,

Hungry and frightened. Searching for a bed
to lay their weary bodies. Heads bowed low.
Searching for "The Red Cross" where they'll be fed.

Cholera has dealt them a mighty blow.
Each little corpse within its grave; until
Kind people bring water and seeds to sow.

There are lots of tiny stomachs there to fill.
There's a living hell going on over there.
If everyone gave some money they will

See their lives improve, and that people care
about them. There'll be laughter everywhere.

Denise Russell

I Broke My Toes on Sunday, and Thought They'd....

I broke my toes on Sunday, and thought they'd broke right off.
I hopped just like a mad dog, and all Andy did was scoff.
He said it wasn't possible, and that it couldn't be true.
But when I took my boot off, my poor foot turned quite blue.
The pain it was unbearable, I prayed it wouldn't last,
My son he called an ambulance and they turned up pretty fast
They took me off to hospital to have an X ray,
Thank God for national health, and I didn't have to pay.
They loaned me two of their crutches, so I could get around,
They said it wasn't difficult, but that's not what I found.
The crutches they went one way, my body went another,
They said it would be easy, but I found it such a bother.
I went back to the hospital, to get a plaster cast.
My foot cocooned in cotton wool, I could get around at last.
The pain is still unbearable and that I have got to rest.
I have a lot of work to do, and I will do my best.
I hope it will be over soon, and I will be back to normal
With two good feet and ten good toes, and everything back on formal.

Gwen Vernon

495

V. E. Day

Today is the day we remember the war
To remember the pain, the sorrow and gore.
Men in their uniforms, children in rags
Thousands of soldiers waving their flags.

Soldiers on land, soldiers at sea
They were all there to fight for you and for me.
The courage and strength shown by all
As the bullets and shrapnel began to fall.

Families waiting in the camps of death
All of them wondering if they had gasped their last breath.
Queuing in a live waiting to die
Wondering how and wondering why.

Bodies all around, the smell and the stench
Whether in the streets or in a trench.
The pain of being wounded with no one around
The thought of dying and to never be found.

Precious lives that were wasted and thrown away
Who was to blame and who will pay.
We must all say a prayer and spare a brought
For the ones that died, the one's that fought.

Martin Farnsworth

Last Summer

I left you last summer, it's etched in your mind.
You've hated me since, and thought me unkind.
Now you've found another to even the score,
We're back where we started - only worse than before.

We've been friends and lovers, it's truthful to say.
Yet fraught with disasters - it was always that way.
Love conquers all, or so I am told.
So why all the effort, to make it unfold?

It eluded us always, and caused us great sorrow.
For we never could fathom, nor plan our tomorrow.
I know that I love you - I have for so long.
But you loved me weak, and now I am strong.

I love you for you, I wanted no other.
But differences matter - to you, more than ever.
Will you always remember, deep in your heart,
It was I loved you best, even now we're apart?

I left you last summer, it's etched in your mind.
You've hated me since, and thought me unkind.
But today you came to me, and loved me again.
And whatever may happen, my love will remain.

Karen Phillis

Happy Easter

It's springtime once again,
It's time for renewal and rebirth;
New beginnings and fresh visions,
Altered states of consciousness.

Fresh thinking, inner probing,
Self - awareness and discovery;
Self enlightenment, new awakenings,
Self knowledge and fresh stirrings

Within the depths and centres
Of our beings, selves, psyches;
the mind, our thoughts and spirit,
Our emotions, feelings, sentiments.

A sense of well-being, the 'feel good factor',
Thoughts of otherness, feelings of compassion;
Words of warmth, looks that heal,
Acts of caring, sharing, service.

Self - denial and self - sacrifice,
Gentleness, patience, tolerance;
So that our better and higher selves
May reach out to the other parts of our whole.

K. K. Kempt

God's Tailored Pie

With the ashes, and breath, the liquid, and heat in the sky
God baketh us all, into this great almighty pie
As the tools of his great mind, are but ruled by the weather
He says unto us all, "Please Come Hither"

He rotates this pie, with His great big hands
And tells us "We Must Share, This Crust Called Our Land"
He lets the heat bake us, until we are brown
Then His breath blows, to cool us all down

The Master of time, then smiles and frowns
Shall I eat this pie up? Or shall I put it back down?
Because He is so very kind in mind
We are placed back onto His wheel in time

The speed is so fast, we are sent into flight
Our flight is but a circle, or any shape of his might
And our never ending, is always in God's sight

Once more, the Great Tailor of our land
Puts us back on His potter's stand
He says "I will rebake you, with my great big hands
As you are all worthy of tasting our crusty land"

Catherine Evans James-Thompson

Roll of Thunder

In the distance cries, a roll of thunder
  Can hardly hear myself, above the waves
In the distant skies, a cloud of anger
  How many of mankind can we save?

The birds are flying south, the birds are leaving
  Is more danger coming? Are we doomed?
Did we make this happen? Us, the humans
  Is this the life for us, which we ourselves have groomed?

Maybe, if we cleanse our souls in the water
  Maybe then we can all start anew
We can all join hands, sons and daughters,
  Like new flowers soaking in morning dew

Come little children, see what we've done to you
  we couldn't even get the art of killing right
Instead there's suffering, it becomes your friend
  As the day fades into night

In the distance cries, a roll of thunder
  can hardly hear me screaming, above the waves
In the distant skies, a cloud of anger
  How many of mankind should be saved?

Amber S. Kelly

Worry and Hope

When life has you reeling with pain and despair
Your heart it is broken with worry and care
When friends and relations are nowhere in sight,
Just pray to the Lord, He will care for your plight.

When life is a struggle, each day brings you pain.
When life gets you down, you are feeling the strain.
Just turn to the Lord, He will lighten your load.
He'll guide you, and help you, to find the right road.

When people and places are getting you down,
You're with the wrong people, you're in the wrong town.
Just look on the bright side, your life will soon change.
The Lord, He still loves you, He'll loosen your chains.

Just look for the rainbow that lights up the sky.
It's there as a comfort to help you and I.
When the rain clouds have passed and the rainbow shines there,
Your spirit will lighten, you'll be free from all care.

So praise be to God who cares for us all
He is the Good Shepherd, He is there when we fall,
And remember the rainbow shining brightly above.
It's there to remind us we'll always have Love.

Mary Wilson

My Love

For you, my love is a cool, cool stream
For when I sleep, of you I dream
As the raindrops fall from up above
You have wholeheartedly all my love

For you, my love is a raging river
With you, the snow won't make me shiver
As the rays of the sun beat down upon us
I would stay with you always, without a fuss

For you, my love is a tall wide mountain
Overflowing, like a giant fountain
Free as a bird, flying high in the air
To you, beloved, no one can compare

For you, my love is as rich as the earth and oh so dark
Strong and straight, like an oak tree bark
Acorns fall and waste away
My love for you will never stray.

For you, my love is the sky so blue
The love I have is completely true
Like the moon that shines up in the sky
My love for you will never die.

Valerie Deering

Sweet England

Sweet England, you shall always be
A comfort deep inside of me.
Although I know you not so well,
You have a word or two to tell.

Sweet England, with your throne and Queen,
The Royal Crown Jewels there to be seen
Is but a sweet reminder, so
We can recall the past you know.

Sweet England, with your castles of old,
Each one a memory to unfold;
A fresh, enchanting countryside,
Which takes our souls on some sweet ride.

Sweet England, please remain the way,
You've always been to this day,
With your traditions through each town,
From North, right to the South Down.

Beyond the Channel we may see
France, just how it used to be.
Each battle fought, each battle won,
Is in Sweet England's ancient song.

Susan Wieland

Fading Light

Take a road all sticky wet
Take a look in the trawlers net
Watch the sun sink in the sea
Watch the water cover me.

Green hills that rise from the land
The beauty not touched by man
Walk alone through the mist at night
Walk out of the back door of life.

Dream about gunfire in the sky
Pray for those who have died
Open your heart for those who left this life
Hope you never reach the fading light.

Feel the grass below your feet
You have the life but won't retreat
Get deafness drunk by life's horn
Start to live when your soul is born.

Out the old give birth to new
Life is sweeter on life's brew
Madness grows from deep down
No chance left when the axe is ground.

M. W. Bramley

Mystical Mermares

The vision of the mermare is beheld by very few
As they're shy and timid creatures I'll share my story with you
While alone in a boat I saw some, a rare and wondrous sight
With coats like sealskin and sharp eyes so large and bright

Though glimpsed only for a few seconds, my memory is full of awe
Muscular bodies are similar to racehorses, with the finest Arabian Jaw
Their ears were erect and short, so compact and neat
Swimming oh so gracefully with four gigantic feet
Yet not hooves beneath their fetlocks, but webbed. More like a swan

Suddenly nostrils flared and ears twitched, all too soon they were
gone, effortlessly they galooshed away, with the swish of dolphin-like
tails submerging submare like, more akin to a school of whales

Most were virginal lippizana white, though some had appaloosas spots
Rapidly they faded from view, as does television's diminishing dot
Figments of the imagination? Though pondered I've dismissed the
thought as on moonlight nights with the sea becalmed, you can
occasionally hear a snort and there were cobwebs on the water, or fine
translucent mane I suppose the best I can hope for is one day to
see them again

G. H. Ellott

Sometimes...

Sometimes it's there so clearly
I can see it rolling by,
The first rays of the brightest sun
In an ethereal, azure sky.
The grass still wet with morning's dew
Its fresh, refreshing smells,
Enveloping all and everything
As it from its green carpet swells.

The dark dense clouds of flocks of birds as they settle, once more to fly,
The sound and the beating of their wings electrically charge the sky.

The silence that is not silent as all nature reawakes,
Shedding her dusky gown to bathe in low hung mists on a thousand lakes.

A feast for all the senses to set the soul ablaze,
The miracle of the world's rebirth seen rising through the haze.

But though I am a witness to this majestic sight,
I cannot be free to share its joy in my youth of eternal night
A night so without colours
Waiting for day to free and
Light to splash onto the canvas of life.
"Oh bright dawn come to me".

Joanne Lindley

Garden Party

"Daaaahling!! — Fancy seeing you here —
I thought this would be an exclusive do, dear!"
(Unfortunately I thought that too, dear — how wrong can one be?)
"Of course I would not have dreamt of coming
but dearest Jonno insisted on slumming!"
(So now I've been lumbered with your bumming — why must it be me?)
"My gown cost a bomb — what do you think?
— Of course I'm always divine in pink!"
(In my opinion you need a shrink — in more ways than one.)
"See — it fits me superbly! — don't you think it's fantastic,
though my latest smart diet is nothing too drastic!"
(It's a mercy indeed they've invented elastic, but do have your fun.)
"Your little frock is wearing quite well,
it could almost pass for a Norman Hartnell!"
(And I'm sorely tempted now to tell you, with whom you are present!)
"O.K. now! — I'd best get on my feet —
there may just be someone important to meet!"
(Ain't that the truth! — but I'm going to retreat, — you ignorant peasant!)
So come on doggies, let's go inside and find a cosy place to hide.
When one's gates are open wide — life can be most unpleasant!

Mary E. Campbell

497

Second Time Around

When little more than a child myself,
I experienced giving birth,
Overwhelmed with love, for this tiny soul,
Now heaven was here on earth.

My first born was a cute little girl,
With hair like ripened corn,
Her eyes so full of expression,
To her, anyone would warm.

As time went on I was to be blessed,
With more daughters, just as sweet,
Loving them all exactly the same,
And dressing them all so neat.

My son he was the last to arrive,
With his typical boyish ways,
Dismantling everything in sight,
Yes! Those were happy days.

Grandchildren now sit on my knee,
Bringing joy that is profound,
Making me just as proud,
The second time around.

Shirley Ann Lewis

Mystical Haven

I think of some places I'd like to be.
Sometimes it's difficult, even for me.
I float all around, and look from above.
I fly with the sea gulls, searching for Love.
What's that I see? Look, straight ahead:
A Mystical Haven ... Well ... Maybe!
"Take me there!", I cry with delight,
Blinking through the tears blurring my sight.
Then I see them at last, galloping around,
Their white, shining coats
Their proud, pointed headgear.
"Come down; join us", they seem to say.
So I swoop down amongst them
And they nuzzle up close,
Showing me they care.
"Come with us!", they whinny.
"This love is for free.
It's yours without asking."
Pure love - at last - that's only for me.

Lyn Oliver

The Seed Of Hope

The plant it sheds another leaf
It one time so grand
It stood upright and full of life
Fed by a loving hand

With extra love and tender care
Less solemn it would be
But the leaves have lost their glossy shine
The plant, I feel, is me

When new life starts in fresh new soil
With tender care it thrives
Without that special caring touch
In time this new life dies

If tendered in the best surround
And kept that way for life
The plant will flourish, make its roots
Then show itself with pride

If all the leaves fall to the ground
And show but just the stem
Then we must plant new seeds of hope
And form that love again.

Diane Richards

Barney

Many stories can be told of how man's best friend is his dog
For five long years now my friend has been - a faithful black and tan
We meet at dawn to trudge the fields
And at that hour we find our peace
The birds sing to us - they tell a tale
The robin follows - we know him well
And across the way - the woodpecker drills
Down the hill a pheasant calls - a warning call?
The squirrel scatters up the trees and
Catkins tremble in the breeze
Here and there are rabbit runs - Barney chases
All in fun.
The clouds will give the game away
Of what we can expect to-day!
But all too soon it's time to return
To the warmest welcome in the land!
Two special people wait for me
With a slice of toast and a cup of tea
So say goodbye - and off to work
For Barney does not belong to me you see!!

Mary Tout

The Morning After

Blue sky's shadow on a fresh green earth awakens the dream of a night.
Sunbeam flicker and cobwebs glitter and wood smoke climbs to a height
while a thrash sings to its audience the world.
Bacon crackles and coffee brews, a new day's problems present.
And after the storms and thunder roll the sun fingers its way to
this earth and gathers the tears she cried.

Maria Mulholland

Depression!

Got no job, got no money, this damn life, it ain't so funny.
Hang around all day feeling blue, don't know what the hell to do.

Not much left now, as I can see, no one to understand me.
Feel all alone, most of the time, what's gone wrong with this world of mine.

Want to vanish, want to hide, sometimes feel like suicide.
What have I done that's been so bad, to take away everything I had.

Don't want people trying to be kind, I want to be alone, am I loosing my mind.
This nightmare in my head I see, it won't be long it's killing me.

Saw psychiatrist, hospital I was sent, took some pills and had shock treatment.
It did not work, still feel so low, but I have nowhere else for me to go.

What's the point in going on, now my mind has nearly gone,
I can't sleep when I go to bed, for God sake demon get out of my head.

Have I cracked, gone down the drain, yes I think I have become insane.
It could be weeks or even less, I must be released from this tangled mess.

Must talk to someone, for it's too late, before this hell can seal my fate.
They say the darkest hour is before the dawn, well, it's all dark
and I wish I'd never been born.

Trevor M. Tompkin

It's Not Over John

One day while John lay deep in stone
A voice came thru his blaring headphones
It screamed "John I am God, turn this damn thing low
I have a mission on which you soon must go
You must blow apart banks with words not tanks,
Hang monarchs and popes, with jokes not robe,
Start a brave new world with only a pen,
Tell a tale so noble and worthy of men,
That the rot on my children will stop."
So John tuned in his mind (he was the tuned in kind)
And led his now pious ass to the hills,
Where holy in loneliness he lived alone to decipher what loneliness filled.
A hermit, a fool, a strange wild-eyed jewel, his mission began with a bang
while strangling an impeccable priest with his faith
He stopped when a mocking bird sang.
The song had a chorus, a verse and a break, a verse and a chorus and theme.
It reminded John of an old rock song "To frame a schizo"
Now he dies each night with a curse and a scream.

Clayton Richardson

Recipe For Old Age

Ingredients:
Some warmth and comfort - a nice cup of tea
This basic ingredient I think will suit me
Just enough money to pay my way
With a little bit over to fritter away,
A bunch of mixed flowers - a Rose or two.
A bit of gardening to see me through
A measure of Romance - a book or two,
One very good friend I can matter to
A sprinkling of love and a few kisses too
A flavour which no one can overdo
Mix altogether with morning dew
And a little fun to dispel any blues,
The taste of this mixture should be quite delicious
Although of course it is purely fictitious.

C. Petchey

Morning

The sounds of day come fading in
A hum that's like a gentle whispering
To hear the world slowly awakening
The sound of every single living thing
The scent that settles when the wind is resting
To taste the air of morning breathing
The only time you'll ever know this feeling
As dusk holds on the remaining evening.

Andy Collenette

Soliloquy On Pain And Suffering

I can see God's care in the rain, wind and sun,
That heralds each season and its fruits follow on,
Man can praise the Lord for the fullness of the earth,
For life in all its glory and wonder of each new birth.

But why does God allow suffering and pain?
Is a question often asked time and time again.
I don't think there is an answer for sure,
Just many caring people trying to find a cure.

When medicine has done all it can possibly do
It's still hard and lonely - who will help us see it through?
Does God care? I wonder. My mind goes on and on
Until at last I'm faced with God's own beloved Son.

Suffering anguish and insult, His body wracked with pain,
His love, costly and selfless, given freely in order to gain
Our way back to God - to set believers free,
To be with Him one glorious day, free from pain and misery.

I'll turn to the Saviour and His resurrection power,
Accept the pain and learn to trust Him through each hour,
See Him in family love and friends along the way,
Claim His love, strength and peace to rely on each day.

Lilian M. Lamb

The Soldier's Testament

I found him in Masada, in a cave below the wall, above
the Dead were lying beneath the sky.
An old man from the Galilee, a stooped and broken greying Jew.

Well he squinted, and he stumbled - saying "Have you come
to take my life?"

He had the truth on his wrists. He had the truth in his eyes,
all the truth the Caesar wished to hear.

He spoke. "I made my testimony for Israel - and Israel alone -
all my words were true, till evil Saul for glory's sake
fostered his lies, proffering them for pagan eyes. Vinegar, in
place of wine."

He cried out and he clutched the air, and fell upon the
stony ground.

I left him where I found him in the cave below the wall.
An old man from the Galilee, a stooped and broken greying Jew.

S. Sinclair

The Romany And The Burglar

One miserable Monday morning a Romany crossed my path,
told me many wonderful things
pierced my loneliness, released my smile, sold me a charm
and was arrested.

One bright Sunday evening a burglar entered my garden shed,
brazenly smirked, gave me his name
'No crime's been committed,' the policeman said.

The latter shattered my peace of mind.
The Romany's gentle, accurate, kind
words lifted me
for a while.

Her 'crime'? Selling the charm?
The burglar, with many convictions, doing such harm
walked free - smiling at me.
His eyes were steel; her gift was real.
I know which one I'd rather be!

Annette Borrill

Granddad

You're falling asleep as I rustle your hair,
You grin and you smile as you take me by there,
The place I know well,
The place I feel safe,
The place where I come when I'm filled with grace.
I really love you,
Not that I show,
Granddad you're the best,
And I want you to know.

Andrew Read

No Rights For Us

We're herded in and out,
But we cannot shout.

We're sprayed with horrible stuff,
Till we've really had enough.

We're bought and sold, stamped so bold,
Then we're left to graze.

We may be shipped abroad,
Cramped together on board.

Lorry after Lorry, kind people only see our eyes.
If only we could cry, when knowing it's goodbye.

Then they may have pity on us,
The men who do all this,
We're too stupid to rebel against the human race.
When will it ever stop?
Solutions must be found,
If only we could keep ourselves
Firmly on the ground.

Christine Miller

The Day Of The Hangman

Amidst the tumults of unrest and uncertainty
In the wake of kidnappings and ritual murders
Rooted in the savour of the nouveau rich
Incensed by the siege of the new pentecostals
Who preach wealth and prosperity
And set the stage for confusion and conflagration

The hatchet of the hangman rivets round every neck
As the devilish cauldron of greed and wealth
Boils deep in the conscience of the masses
The cabalistic gang of mindless miscreants
Seeking fame, fortune and favour at all costs
Must ride out the tide of wealth without sweat

These cannibals hold firm on rituals and cults
Mortgaging loved ones as pawns for power and positions
Desperate for control and command of politics and polemics
With masked faces of deceit basking in magnificent fortresses
But as the day of Karma dawns with the wreath of justice
Atonement with blood is drawn with the sword of Damocles

Anelechi B. Chukuezi

499

Dusk till Dawn

To the moon at night I feel strangely drawn
No child of light - a lunar pawn
When dusk has come and day is over
Out sneaks the moon like a secret lover.

Night holds a magic all of its own
A mystical wonder in me is born
The shadows dance and tease the light
That magical, wonderful beautiful night

Everything changing, nothing stays still
Soon the cold light of day the shadows fill
Another hour and day shines bright
Another day until the night.

Jane Anne McKloud

Untitled

Like all new mothers sat at home
I watch my baby grow alone
The days, the weeks, all starts the same
First beds, then dishes, then feed the wean.
My life's an endless carousel
Of household duties that are hell
I've never had that sense of pride
In no dirty washing left to hide
But if I stop and think a while
The time spent sharing a perfect smile
With my darling little son
Work's soon forgotten - my heart is won.

Jane McCairn

Oh! Friend

As the ashes hit the tray.
And as the filter creeps away,
thoughts begin to entwine
while we seek that rare shrine,
from where our lazy brain cells,
lose the reaper as he fells
empty spaces not our soul
for we shall regain control.

Light brings light and fear brings fear.
We'll cherish light and draw near to the place we seek to find
that brings us to know our mind.
You so pure like skylark song
offer strength and love so strong,
We are like one; why is this?
When all I give is my kiss.

Nothing sexual or lustful, a friendship so powerful.
I cannot start to comprehend
Why you have me as a friend.
Since that time we shared such truth I feel as one loving youth,
Ready to live all anew, My dear friend, 'tis thanks to you!

Rory O'Connor

I Dreamt

I dreamt of a corpse,
Being exposed on the road;
Exposed on the road, to the wind and the rain.
I dreamt that the corpse
Was of someone I knew;
Someone I knew, I would not know again.

I dreamt of a place,
Where I'll go after death;
Where I'll go after death, is a place in my dreams.
I dreamt that my life,
Will be gone when I die;
Gone when I die, or that's how it seems.

I dreamt of a world,
With good women and men;
Good women and men, who murder and kill.
I dreamt that the world,
Would come to its senses;
Come to its senses, and one day it will.

Brendan Martin

Hope!

I wrack my brain to make it think:
That I might find the precious link,
The thought to set the World to right.
Could I but learn - know how
To make my brain cells turn.

Thinking is done by everyone,
But what an awful mess we make!
Torture and bombs, fraud and fake,
Pollution of mind, pillage and rape.
From our karma there's no escape.

In silent pause, in mystic space
I preen my soul and seek for grace:
But will my virtue a difference make?
Heathen or holy, what is to be taught
To set the World to right?

We need to learn to think and be aware:
To change our ignorance, to give up fear,
To show all beings that we care.
For we are now such a blight - that
God leaves us to our well-earned plight!

Robert P. Mills

If Only

I dreamed one night of a perfect world
with no sorrow, tears or strife,
where all nations helped one another,
to live a better life,
where everyone lived in harmony
regardless of colour or creed
and children were loved, parents respected,
the natural resources never neglected.
But then I awoke in the cold light of day
and realised that life on earth will always stay this way
until all people know their worth
then maybe we shall make a start to build Utopia here on Earth

E. M. Windsor

A Lasting Thought

To think, when thoughts are hard to find,
About some aspects of the mind;
To glide along the water-flow
When gravity pulls from below.
All this and more one can contain
Within the complex human brain.
Yet searching far, and farther out
To find what it is all about
Must often seem, at least to me,
A goal that none will ever see
    In all its fullness.

Maxwell Royle

Mother

Mother, keep me from the witches,
Mother, save me from the bomb,
Mother, keep the darkness far away,
don't let them get me Mum,
Mother, keep me warm on winter's nights,
Mother nurse me when I am sick,
Mother protect me from the evil ones
Every low down dirty trick,
The storm does not frighten me protected by dear mother's charms
Nothing now can hurt me, I am safe within my mother's arms
Come fire thunder, hail and rain, come tigers strong and free
Not these nor any other foe shall separate you from me
Mother, you've always been there rocking me gently to sleep,
When the good Lord take you from me Mum
    I shall not cease to weep,
Mother, you are wonderful, loving gentle fair and kind
More cherished than life itself a greater love is hard to find
A summer's day a freshly mown lawn,
The sun is blazing hot and true just lying in the
    idle bliss, mother, I love you.

David Isaac

The Tempest

A distant clap of thunder rolls incessantly,
And lightning flash illuminates a threatening sky.
The sombre clouds await to unleash their fury on undulating waters.
Dark storm clouds gather at enormous velocity
And break upon the waters shattering its serenity
Coercing to bend it to the will with ruthless savagery.
Protracting, roaring, screaming waves with daunted melody
Whiplashes the forbidding rocks which gouge the leadened sky,
Where screeching gulls re-echo with abandoned torturous cry.
A misty mantle weaves its cloak around the murky creek
Where unseen dangers lurk among the foils of the deep.
When ocean fathoms merciless their inmost secrets keep
From warring souls upon their wakes
And challenge all who seek to be its master,
Alas, no one can tame its arrogant sway
Until suddenly, the storm abates and dies away and all is peace.

Wendy Holford

Look Remember Me

I am the unnoticeable one
I am the one nobody cared,
I can see you, you can't see me.....
Simple.
I hear you chatting about football.
But me, I am alone with nobody to care —
no sympathy.
You see me walking in the same coat
every day and shoes.
And you sometimes wave to me.
But I can't say anything, I am too nervous.
I am the unnoticeable one....
about whom nobody cared.

Richard Rose

ANNIE

i thought
with an acquired scepticism
that someone
described as you were described
would prove
so much wishful thinking
on my part
delight to find
my love in mental desert saw
a kindred light
taut with fixèd soul who felt
on similar lines
a telepathic joy of shared belief
in oneness

organic life
in turn makes nomads of us all
and disallows
too long a tarrying in each mental oasis
the desert beckons
before we part let us
drink deep

Robin Davies

Bullying

I see the bullies advancing towards me. I see their
horrible expression as they prepare to pound me. Why?
What is the point of it?

I feel them punch me, kick me, bang my head
against the wall and then they hit me with my own ball.

I taste the blood after they punched me. This
really hurts me but they can't seem to see.

I hear them taunt and torment and make fun of my
clothes. Bullies are people that I really loathe.

I try to pretend that I am not scared, but if I do
that they just beat me up even more.
Why is it happening to me?

Oliver Shooter

This World Of Ours

This world of ours in terrible pain
With air pollution and acid rain
We hack and mine and chop down trees
We're bringing this land down on her knees
With nuclear power and chemical waste
To destroy this world we seem in such haste
When we annihilate what we've been given
How can we expect to be forgiven
Listen all to what I say
To save this planet there must be a way
It will be hard; this we all know
But we have to care; there's nowhere else to go.

Ursula Bass

Walk In The Park

Walking slowly in the dark through the streets into the park.
Sitting lonely on a bench one old man and his friend
Talking quietly of old times, singing songs and telling rhymes.
Now I'm walking home from here, it's not too far, it's not too near.
Back to my room and loud T.V., back to noise and reality.
It's nice to walk on lonely streets when all is dark and
all asleep, hear the silence
Feel the dark, oh how I long for my walk in the park.

Catherine Doran

Memories

I searched the hallows of my mind
To retrace back into time
Dormant thoughts were lying there
I brought them out, to give them air.

Childhood days when cars were rare
When Horse and Carts, brought our wares
And lights would flicker, with an eerie glow
As the old Lamplighter, went to and fro.

Saturday was a special treat
We got one whole penny for the week
A farthing for a candy bar
A farthing for sweets, from a big glass jar.

With Orange rope, We learned to skip
And we played with top and Whip
There were Tramcars with open tops
And a lovely smell, from the Baker's shop

I wondered back to childhood days
They were more content in every way
Oh, what memories I did find
When I searched the hollows of my mind.

P. Epps

White Man's Whiskey

Dream time was woken and killed where it slept.
Promises were broken but the threats were all kept.
Your things that excited me, now reject and disgust me,
To be a friend, I am not ready yet.

Oh, and what you'll do, to rule me
You, your God, and white man's whiskey.

The bush that brings us roses, brings us thorns as well,
I was really trying to get to you, but time will never tell.
Foul mouth children void of dreams shoot down sparrows,
and dam up streams.
I dreamed of that yacht again, moored somewhere hot again,
my birth and the place that I fell.

Oh and what you'll do to rule me
You, your God, and white man's whiskey

She had a kiss that could bring life to the dead,
Memories I will keep, long after life has fled.
When it is all said and done, and I have drunk
all their whiskey,
Will someone ever remember me?

Ronald Sinclair

My Day At The Fair

I sit alone in my old rocking chair
remembering the day I went to the fair
it was there I met my true love, he was so shy
now I am left with a sad tear in my eye.

My folks are all gone, they were so old
no one is left belonging the fold
the children have gone, each on their way
to start a new life, for them I do pray.

I turn back a page in my memory's eye
recall the days so long gone by
my way to school in a clatter of clogs
we trudge each day over cobbles and bogs.

At Sunday School we knelt to pray
and sang he hymns just as today
as we sang the hymns of praise
it was a light on our darkest days.

And so I sit in my old rocking chair
dreaming of my day at the fair
but time moves on we all grow old
till no one is left belonging the fold.

Daisy Cooper

Security

A mother awaits to greet her new chicks.
She listens to the sound of tapping and kicks.
A tiny form of life slowly cracks its shell.
The anxious mother waits while all goes well.
Slowly the crack develops into small holes.
Revealing a fragile naked body coloured like a rose.
A cry for help frustrated and weak.
Mother answers her cries by tapping her beak
The chick now free spreads its tiny wings.
Its little eyes stare curiously while its mother sings.

Karen Melody Roberts

Gladioli

I sat there, deep among my scarlet flowers
which bled from the vase and over the table.
I sat there in all that fire engine red
and let the colour bleach me, drain me.

I thought of you during those moments
my eyes closed, blood pumping through my eyelids.
Petals thundered over me, sank into my skin;
they possessed me like a furious death.

The violence of their colour was all around me
like an enormous, floating wound.
My power, my fury, my passion
exploded wildly with your memory.

I sat there with my hair caked in blood,
with a million crushed petals forlornly lying.
The green stalks, like bold spears in the vase
grinned mockingly.

Mrs. N. Fenwick

Prayer Before Birth

I am not yet born; O hear me;
let not the gremlins, goblins and witches
or the bloodsucking snakes or ogres
come near me. Save me from
sinking sea, or in a car crash and also
save me from crashing in a plane.

I am not yet born; provide me
with family and friends, sunlight and darkness.
Provide me with food and water, creatures
and living things. Provide me with warm
shelter and a clean world,
teach me to read and write.
God keep me safe.

Sally Doleman

Crush

His smile, his eyes
I'll not forget
His hug, his kiss
Brings out the sighs

I loved this man with all my heart
But they just said it was a crush
How could they know what I felt inside
For my lonely heart had been hit by a dart.

I walked around in such a daze
Hoping he would be the one I'd see
For he was the key to open up
A head so filled like such a maze

To see his smile upon his face
Was sure to warm this heart of mine
I'll not forget him I am so sure
For my heart was always so sure to race.

Helen Bennett

A Barren Land

Yesterday morning I awoke.
Drawing back the curtains I saw a mass of white but there in the
Corner a little touch of green caught my eye.
Looking closer I saw sixteen tiny shoots poking through the
White mass.
Spring was on the way...
New beginnings.

Later that morning the elements released a violent snowstorm.

On returning home I found my sixteen tiny shoots had perished....
No match for such conditions.

This morning I awoke.
Drawing back the curtains I saw a mass of white but there was
No green.

Now I sit here wondering what might have been.
Would those tiny shoots have grown into beautiful roses...shrinking
Violets...strong sturdy thistles...
Who knows
After all it takes an assortment of flowers to make a garden
To be proud of.

A garden to remember.

Ann Kidd

Time Gone

The sand of time slips slowly down the hourglass of life,
I think of joy and happiness, of trouble and of strife,
I look back and reminisce of times long past and gone,
Of things done right, but oh, what pain if things go terribly wrong.
What changes could I have made to have improved my lot,
And if I had made changes would I have what I've now got,
Or would I still be wandering down life's long weary road
With not a soul to care about, and none to share my load,
Instead I've got a family, a house, a wife, a home,
And in the life that's left to me I need never walk alone,
There's my children and my grandchildren and my ever-loving wife,
So sand, please slip more slowly down that hourglass of life.

Colin R. Hollman

Wrong Judgement

Don't judge people by the colour of their skin,
Where they're going or where they've 'bin',
What they do or what they don't,
If they will or if they won't,
We all have feelings - you and me,
Let's think about others and then we'll see,
Peace in the world, a change in life,
To some this world is like a giant knife,
One unkind comment can be like a stab in the back,
For certain this shows there is one thing we lack,
A judgement on people,
A judgement on all,
Let's stop the judging and love one and all

Gemma Delfino

Sweet Release

I sat out in the sun
The warmth to ease my pain
He passed me by
He smiled at me.
I did not know his name.

As holding out his hand
He bid me follow.
I should have been afraid
But no fear came.

He held my hand
Above my head flew swallows
I walked with him
He softly spoke my name.

I sat out in the sun in body only,
My soul he took
Relieving me from pain,
And flying free above
The summer swallow
My soul soars high above and lives again.

Shirley Whittaker

Redundancy

Sixteen years overcome the fears
The anxiety the nerves and the politics
Starting again leaving the friends
The colleagues and the comfort zone
Feeling alone unsure and doubting
The knowledge the skills and the judgement
Achievements awards successes forgotten
Past glories distant memories fading

Hit by the axe had to make tracks
Facing the fear, facing the facts
It happened its true could happen to you
Sacred! Not any longer

Now made a start given me heart
Finding my feet feeling the part
Working again making new friends
Swelling with pride no need to hide
The memories inside

Dignity respect growing stronger
The past is the past the futures ahead
Life now worth living fears put to bed.

Paul Sainsbury

The Cotswold Way Saga

'Twas summer, ninety-six, quite late,
Sixth of September was the date,
Two stalwart travellers took the path
From Chipping Campden down to Bath
Unknown the road from day to day
They bravely faced the Cotswold Way.
Unarmed against all beasts and foes,
And disregarding blistered toes
Our fearless pair, with heads held high,
Trod forth each day, 'till night was nigh;
Through wind and storm and torrid heat
With heavy packs and pain-racked feet.
Their only thoughts—the goal ahead,
Their only wish—a simple bed
To rest their weary limbs a while
Blot out that endless final mile.
In years to come, all folk will read
With awe and wonder, of the deed,
Of two—who, heedless of the weather
Finished up in "Bath"—together.

Monica Boothroyd

Friendship - No Ties

I tried so hard to help you, I know I let you down
Seems I wasn't strong enough to keep you homeward bound
Tried so to keep you safe, to ease your troubled mind
I let you down so badly, I must have been so blind

We sat and talked for ages, it seemed like years and years
Felt so very rotten watching you shed your tears
Why wasn't I much stronger? Why couldn't I hold you up?
Why couldn't I keep you going? In me you put all your trust

You stroked my face with caring hands "Please help me babe" you cried
I felt so useless as I watched your watering eyes
Felt so much pain on your behalf, wanted to be so near
You squeezed my hand so tightly, for your troubled mind I feared

Now you're gone, left me feeling guilty and alone
Feeling pretty useless, my mind a heavy drone
One last thought I have for you, calm, peace, quiet
But sad, sad, memories of friendship, no more burning fire.

Patricia J. Smith

Gertrude

She lay in the hospital bed, a bag of bones,
and a face so distorted by life.
None of us knew if she was a spinster, or a mother or wife.
No visitors ever came to see her, there was no sign of a family.
She lay there for weeks in Death's shadow,
hardly caring to notice or see.
Then Janet appeared before her, like a magical and friendly light.
Perhaps for a few precious moments, her life became decidedly bright.
She now had one good friend in this cruel world,
a girl who brought her gifts and warmth and love.
Goodbye then, dear old Trudy, we hope you are with the Lord up above.

Alan Heath

Did We Make It Home?

When the walk to your chair, and the length of your hair,
give you a glint in your stair, and take you back over there.

Dressed in black, and ready to fight,
he was farmer by day, and our enemy at night,
We smoked to get high, and to believe the lie,
that the good old U.S. of A were gonna save the day,
and blast communism away.

And now as I sit here alone,
I think back of the guys, of the blood, and the lies,
my God I can still hear their cries.

Hueys fade away, but will be back again today,
and as I break out in a sweat, I realize I'm a vet,
who can never free myself of the Vietnam debt.

John Adam Gray

Yellow Rose

Sometime, way back then - my yellow rose had died
silently it slipped away - un-noticed, nobody cried.

Unable to thrive in the darkness - it bowed its head in shade
then quietly began to ebb away - as its spirit began to fade.

Living in the dusk of life's shadow - a cold and lonely place
no hope could thrive within its heart - or reflect upon its face.

For how can we live without promise - or survive without a dream
tap the strength that lies within - understand who we have been.

Nothing tangible now remains - to mark where my Rose once grew
but I who cared, remember still - keep the imagine safe and true.

For the heart remembers all things - preserved truths will never die
memories through our life remain - 'til as one, with our spirit, they'll fly.

An afternoon of moments shared - scent of roses in the air
a photograph from far away - a poem to show you care.

Dried roses in a dusty church - past and present merge as one
timeless ties that bind us now - to those people we'll become.

Each feature and expression - memorized for me to find
pressed between the pages - of the book within my mind.

Jenny Pierce

Our Mind

Lie in bed awake, mind still on the go,
Does it ever stop? Will we ever know
What about our dreams? Our mind must assist,
Typing out old memories and ambitions in a list,
Our mind is a computer, upgraded every day,
By knowledge and awareness with things people do say,
What about reincarnation? Do our minds change as well?
But what about regression? We remember what happened so well,
How can we be sure the world is not a fake?
And not our mind creating a picture that won't ever break,
Perhaps whatever we imagine, or think of, or can do,
Is something in the mind transmitting ability to you?
You'd think with all the technology placed inside the mind,
That it would not be able to be squashed and packed inside,
Have you ever thought, you are not you?
Your mind's in control of whatever it chooses you to do,
One thing I know is, as long as you live,
The mind is just yours, something you cannot give,
Transplants with organs, limbs, whatever they like,
But the mind won't be transferred
The mind is yours for life.

Nicola Hewson

Domestic Chaos

Rubber boots in the hallway,
Clutter on the stairs
Why is it, I look at this?
It reduces me to tears

Washing, ironing, I do hate,
Washing up as well,
To have a bit more time for leisure
Would make me feel real swell!

Hoovering up the bedrooms
Is what I now must do,
But when it comes to dusting
I blow and say "that will do"!

I had my grandson for the day
He likes me to have a cuddle,
He runs to me with open arms,
So I live in one big muddle!

If I win the lottery on a Saturday night
It's off to the travel agents to book myself a flight
To sun-drenched shores and palm trees
I'm sure this would help my arthritic knees!

Ann Knight

The Flying Machine

The man with his marvellous Flying machine,
were both, the most wonderful things to be seen.
He wore brown leather suit with white flying scarf,
no-one could ever look smarter, not by half.

The large goggles he wore to protect his eyes,
looked as if they were as big as two pork pies.
From the Hanger his plane they pulled out with pride.
We saw how courageously he climbed inside.

It was gleaming bright, painted in silver grey.
What a beautiful plane, when put on display!
To win the races and show us its paces,
it had eight wings and struts with crossed braces.

Four pairs of wings on top, and four pairs each side.
The man inside waved as he started to ride,
Six yards down the runway it went, when it crashed,
nearly everything on it was broken or smashed,

From under the pile came the man with a smile.
Although impressive the wings were excessive.
An important point, without doubt, he had proved,
out of eight pairs of wings, six could be removed.

Norman J. Holmes

Little Rosebuds In Early Springtime.....

Little Rosebuds - why so soon
when the dew is still around
little Rosebuds - spring just starting
when showers and little lambs abound

Wind and clouds and frosty mornings
need careful treading on new sown grass.
Into summer - sunshine and blossom
and the first hard days will pass

Warm and cosy, birds in treetops
Skies of blue and soft white cloud
Little Rosebuds you are blooming and
your parents are so proud

Hours to days and days to weeks
the flickering flame grows stronger,
week by week and into months,
that haunting fear no longer of each passing hour

Little smiles appearing on the sweetest of small faces
prayers and tears are answered, now we're really going places
Patience, love and understanding, last 2 yrs have flown,
since you made your early debut, our Rosebuds are full blown.

Glenda Le Masurier

Laughing Moon Water Wakes A Deep Sleep

The runes are cast, the cards are spread;
Candles flicker, gemstones shimmer.
Incense burning, charcoal glows;
Shaman, dragon raise the soul.

Sly is black, no stars tonight,
All is calm, black cat awaits.
Drifting back on sea of smolle
I wallen to myself.

See the white horse come to me,
Gently taking me aloft
On wings of purest love.
To realm of high priestess.

The moon, the sun are temperance joined.
Mann, lagu and Ing are one.
Rainbow cubes arch the sky
Leading to the we' moon way.

Laughing moon water greets the day,
Extinguishes the flames of night,
And dances up a healing ray
Of orange and yellow light.

Lisa Naylor

My Mother

When I was young life was good
happiness all through my childhood
Then mum got sick and died
that night Dad and I cried, and cried

My brothers were too young to understand
that God had called Mum.
He took her by the hand
to take her to a land above
that knows no sorrow or pain
only laughter and love

A beautiful land all sunshine and sand
were loved ones walk hand in hand
She will wait for us there with open arms
and a smile she will wear, my mother's love
once again I can share

I miss her every day, still don't understand
why she was taken from me
Perhaps it was her beauty, everyone could see
now that she is in heaven
she will never suffer again

M. Miller

God Below

I hear the call
Saying 'The tides of my love will drown all your
Sorrow'
But I was told the story about the boy who cried
'wolf'
You locked away your secrets in cages of steel
But along with my burdens I set them free.
Your love was a mere concept of immorality
And the concept grew in shame,
Whilst your cups overflowed with the promises
You made.
You nurtured fields of humanity,
But I walked through barren desert lands
And the choice was mine.
You became a pretence for what lay within,
And because of this,
Your throne,
At least in my palace,
Lies in dust.
Lust is a concept of stark reality.

Jag Khurana

Conscience

How often do we yearn for better things
and more riches always crave?
Blinkered in quests to change our fate
We tread all underfoot in the rat race,

Never seeing the tears until too late!

Destroying Trees, Wildlife, and Countryside,
The air we breathe with Traffic fumes,
Rushing here and rushing there,
In concrete towns like Graveyard stones,

Never having time to spare!

Child abuse, Murder and Mugging abound,
mis-use of Drugs to get that buzz,
corruption, Pornography, get-rich-quick schemes,
selfish, thoughtless hurtful deeds
have nothing to do with us it seems!

Where gone has caring for our Fellow man
Before we act, just stop and think,
About the consequence of impatience,
Kind words and Smiles, is that all it takes?

To soothe attacks of conscience.

M. E. Watkiss

To Victoria

Eighteen years have come and gone
Since we first set eyes on you,
A tiny babe with jet black hair,
With a Mum whose love shone through.

You may not have grown so very tall
Though eighteen years have passed,
But our hopes and aspirations
You certainly have surpassed!

You stand poised on the brink of adulthood
Looking forward with the freshness of youth.
The future promise of all things good
Is held in this moment of truth.

Glance back now and then at your childhood
And cherish the good times gone by
No one can deny you your memories,
They are yours and will never die.

We wish you good luck and happiness
In all you decide to do
And as you travel along life's wonderful road
May our love and support follow you.

B. G. Busolini

Who

It's will you mind my child for me
    while I go out to work.
Will you run an errand for me,
Can you mend Sonnie's shirt.
Will you do this, will you do that,
They ask me all the time,
And if it rains, please take my
    washing off the line.
Some people say you are a fool to let them
    treat you so.
But they don't understand you see,
They just don't seem to know,
That now my family's all grown up,
Well, I have lots of time,
Besides I am their mother,
And mothers just don't mind.
Many years it's been since I first wrote these words,
Now I am growing old and cannot do so much,
So my family do jobs for me instead,
And always keep in touch.

D. Osborne

Ode To Dalmatia

Softly shimmering sunshine filters through leafy trees.
The soft air stirs around us, stirred by a gentle breeze.
The beauty of the songbird, high in the bough above,
His lilting voice so sweet, such joy,
Wonderful sounds of love.

White clouds high in a blue, blue sky,
Look down on a turquoise sea.
Soft waves roll to a beautiful shore.
For such beauty, Lord, we thank thee.

Joyce Port

Rain Outside My Window

I sit alone in silent tears.
Raindrops teasing through my years,
and as before I stop, I stare
at nothing, and oh what I see there.
A fly with fretful beating wing
it stops and stays, then sings.
My heart is drenched with something here,
I stop, I stare, I stop, look here.
I see a world with none so dear,
of what I see as I stare
at nothing, all around me hear,
a silence teasing through my years,
A lonely beam, alone it strays
Shining silver, through my window, pains,
I see a sight with monstrous grace,
With lonely heart that has no trace
of hope and of wishful intent,
just pain and love and honour bent

Declan Sheehan

Yvonne My Best Friend

Even though you are not here
I often feel that you are near
It's been years since you've been gone
Although it doesn't seem that long

At Christmas time I think of you
When skies are grey, when skies are blue
When fields are full of pretty flowers
I sit and wile away the hours

Then on that fateful day
When God took you far away
I locked myself away and cried
I thought that everyone had lied

But then they put you in the ground
Our crying was the only sound
Then I knew you'd really gone
I sat and sang our favourite song

Caroline Penfold

"Troubles"

A chill cold, looking over the blue line of the sea
And there is a boat far out on the horizon
To India or some other distant place.

The wind blows

I am perfectly still, have cast my worries
For a moment, to the surface of the ocean
And forgotten - temporarily.
The sail on the edge is where I am,
Is me - for now, but nothing lasts.

The sun is on his way, westward I think
To light the tops of trees in America.
My! What a wonder: One of God's, you know.

The little island in the bay is gold
And everything is gold, except the specs
Of the white birds dancing in the suns end.

I will rise soon. I will loose tranquillity.
    R. F. Elder

Can You Imagine

Can you imagine a world with no sun
    Can you imagine a world with no moon.

Can you imagine a world being dark
    Can you imagine a tree with no bark.

Can you imagine living in a river
    Can you imagine a snake with no sliver.

Can you imagine the world in the sea
    Can you imagine a world with out me.
    Laura Thompson Harper

Cloak Of Silver

Enchantment awaits in a summer sky
An eloquent silver bird soars high
Gracefully winging blithely in the air
Happily singing with elegant flair

O silver bird with magnetic powers
Gliding thru' a vale of flowers
The stately serene queen of trees
The silver birch - softly rustles in the breeze

Silver birch, silver bird, silver sky
A soft zephyr whispers with a sigh
Beside the silver waters a fairy land
Amid the peaceful meadows of lakeland

The noon-day sun glorifies the earth
And the wind of change is full of mirth
The silver rivers and mountain streams
All of which fulfils my dreams

A silver sea laps the shores of England
So richly adorned in fairest green England
    Anne Cooper

The Fallen Snow

Another day is dawning, it's the end of the night,
You draw back the curtains, and see a wondrous sight,
It fell from the sky without a sound,
It covers like icing every inch of the ground,
It colours the grass, a brilliant shade of white,
It glistens on the trees like tiny lights,
So perfect and smooth, a new creation.
It's as if every creature on earth has gone on vacation,
But there on the fence, sitting alone and proud,
Is a little robin, singing his song out loud,
It's as if he's trying to let you know
The beauty of the fallen snow.
It's so clean and pure, like the virgin birth,
Sprinkled from heaven here on earth,
Everywhere you look it's a brilliant white,
Sparkling like glitter, such a beautiful sight.
    M. I. Goodwin

Untitled

It's a word of God creations
Fills your heart with temptations
It's the truth and honest power
We live on it every hour.

Two people has the same feeling
Just like a deep out healing.
It leads to a warm passion
An irresistible emotional attraction

When you near to the one you love
Your world is a happy just like a dove,
No-one will ever share,
Your feelings will be eternal and very rare.

Hatred and jealousy can ruin lives
It burns inside just like two pair of knives
Today's world is full of temptations
Confusion leads to complications.

Why is it God love is so strong,
Nothing in that world can break that bond,
Needing your feelings as long as I live.
My soul is yours until death does its trick
    Nafeesa Ali

The Schizophrenia Of Love

You are there, arms outstretched
Beckoning me to come into you
To fight and struggle is futile
My guard is down and I have no other defences
I come to you like a moth to a flame
You engulf me and we become one living breathing organism
One heartbeat
You are love
In a lot of ways you resemble fire
You cannot be touched, yet whoever you touch you affect
You are uncontrollable and will not leave without a fight
When you are finally extinguished, the surface you touched is never the same
Sometimes toughened
Sometimes dead
But always, always scarred
You are both the personification of beauty and evil incarnate
When you are good you create a euphoria undreamt of
Yet when you are bad you could reduce a forest to a pile of ash
You must be worshipped, respected, but never taken for granted.
    Darren Dean

Looking Back On Miss Proctor

Now - you cannot write poetry properly dear
If you can't make it scan right, you see.
You cannot write poetry this way at all
You must write it in four lines - not three.

It must flow, it must rhyme, you must take more time,
Be careful, just think - does it gel, does it scan, does it flow
Does it tell you a story, so we understand
The power of that pen that you hold in your hand.

What's that girls? You don't know what to write - how very trite
With brains like yours, girls, we'll be here all the night!
Oh! why am I saddled, why am I so laden
With people so dense and no i-mag-i-na-tion?

You've plenty of stories and know all their uses
You come to me daily and call them "excuses"
Of why you are late, why the homework's not done
Why you cannot go swimming, and from the gym you do run.

You've got plenty of stories up there in your head
So put it on paper and think about what I said.
Just make sure that it scans, that it flows, make it gel
Oh drat it! It's home time and there goes the bell.
    S. M. Lucas

Colours

When I think of colours there's four
that spring to mind: red, yellow,
Black and green, of these I will define.

When I think of red I see the
blood of Christ and how they
nailed him to the cross and
took away his life.

When I think of yellow I see the
cowards that put him there and
left him to die without a
thought or care.

When I think of black I see life
after death and the place that
he was taken to where he did resurrect.

When I think of green I know
his life goes on for he's our
heavenly father and his power is so strong.

Ernest Hiddleston

Apocalypse

Shapeless shadows 'cross the moonlit night
Creating fears of old,
Who can stand before such fright?
Or be he of the bold.
Stark bare forms of winter trees
Stare out on formless land,
Not even the slightest breath of breeze,
No sign of human hand,
Were they horses riding 'cross the sky?
Or fantasy I see?
Were four horseman riding by
And did they stop for me?
Should I reach to touch the sky
Or look the other way?
Would the horsemen pass me by
And leave me here to stay?
Four riders on their deadly course
Looking down on me.
But did I see one on a pure white horse
Smile down and set me free?

Margaret Cox

Ring In The New

The new year's come
Let's start this year
With resolutions new,
To greet each day with a great big smile and
Try so hard to do - all the tasks
That need to be done with all the good will
We can, be kind and helpful to all we meet
We must love our fellow man!

With our God's help we all can face,
And be glad for another new day;
To do the things that we forgot to do
In the time of yesterday!
And with God's love he'll give us all
The strength and help we ask
To help ourselves and strangers
As we go along life's path!

So look forward to a great new year
Be thankful for this brand new start
Be pleased that you can start each day
Knowing God is within your heart!

Teresa Wyatt

Verses to the Destine

I who am dead a long time ago and unknowable
and wrote this verse in darkness and in light
at a time where air earth and skies were warble;
the pitiless time filled of crafty sins delight.

I care not who dreams to sway in an air of glory
or whose sword will conquer the boiling earth
or which child's thwack has razed the fool's destiny.
The nifty child is father of the man of life and death.

Oh poor pride with blithe and blithesomeness
pour rewards of those who shall dare to claim award
in one society, in storm and tempest and in ruthlessness
for some good thoughts of the some bad thought's reward.

But hope little think little of these ratty men
who fail to view the time as it passes ploughing
here and there; but today toil their minds till when
may clasp them because their lack lustre eye sidling.

Oh Earth Mother of snakes with double tongue
and out in the dark together near gloat at the writer's tomb
whose spirit was on some rocks a mourned ancient virtue
but with full of truth the rock slide under the dumb.

A. Roushias

Home

At home I feel so cosy and warm,
    When winter's here, I'm safe from a storm,
    With mum and dad and David too,
        A feeling of love, too good to be true.

The hard things in life are easier here.
    It's mum who worries, who's always so dear.
        She washes, she irons, she cooks and she cleans,
            Until our sweet home's so spotless, it beams.

No problems for me, no bills to be paid,
    My time is my own, I'm totally made.
        A pair who have worked to give me it all,
            Who will pick me up whenever I fall.

I want to say thanks for all that you've done,
    In darkness you always show me the sun.
        Parents who strive to give me the best,
            I want to say thanks, you're better than the rest.

You've been there for me from the very beginning.
    You've done a good-job to stop me from sinning.
        My love for you will never depart,
            For you hold the key, the key to my heart.

Angela Ashworth

Pillbox

Pills for this and pills for that;
Pills to make you slim,
Pills to make you fat,
Pills to take between meals,
Pills to take the lot!
Pills to take at bedtime,
Pills you have forgot,
Pills that make you younger,
In no time at all,
Pills to make you bigger
When you're feeling small,
Pink pills, blue pills, some coloured red,
For every part of your body,
Not just for your head.
Pills to make you happy,
Pills that make you sad,
Pills for all the family,
Pills that are just for dad.
Large pills, small pills, any size will do,
But don't forget too many pills are not so good for you.

Eva Pilbrow

My Case Against E.C.T.

Captured by aliens? A prisoner of war?
What are these mindless experiments for?
In a room full of zombies, awaiting my turn
for electrical currents my memories to burn.
Treatment not torture psychiatrists claim,
please ask your patients if they feel the same.

I imagine these currents have damaged my soul
killing off pieces that were part of a whole.
They are probably far-fetched and unfounded fears
but of my son's teenage life I have lost several years.
From this experience alone I can't be the same
to wake up and not to know my own name.

Janet Craig

A Loving Mother

You're a young man out on the street
Come into the kitchen and feel the heat.
All too easy to blush and shy away
None too easy to make it through the day.
To be a young man and uncertain whilst equals seem to know
It is times like this when your mother will know.

Manhood! Did I do right or did I do wrong
Did I make a decision or was I dragged in headlong.
When swirling in the rapids of my life
Finding I no longer have a wife.
Where are my friends, married, moved or dead,
My Mother never forgot the friends she had fed.

From the boy who blushed to the youth who never saw danger,
To the man who inherited her strength and controlled his anger.
Her love has got me through all these days
And she showed it in so many ways.
Now school is out, my Mother is no more
But I will never forget the Mother I will worship for evermore.

Kevin Wilks

Deceived

A foe, he is, more than the friend he ought to be
A bond, I thought, yet he the enemy
Attacked, destroyed my life, he tore my heart from me
Like war, the fight, that love was meant to be

For many moons I struggled to hold on
Too blind to see the truth that love was gone
A fool, I was, to trust emotions deep and strong
I should have known inside that it was wrong

Now bare within me lies the coldest night
No hope is left, no spirit to commence the fight
I drown, for straws I grasp with all my might
Would there be darkness if there was no light?

Surrender? Never shall he see my ache
I'd rather die unveiling him as fake
What's pain, for the amount I take
Is worth it for another lover's sake

Deceived I was, by his appearance, by his word
He was of beauty and of class unheard
Never again shall I believe my eyes
For mis'ry and betrayal in their verdict lies.

Gina Geiger

Elegy

I am not dead. I did not die.
I have merely passed on,
into another room of another world.
Push open the door and enter the room.
Feel my presence and be comforted.
Be not sad,
For I am in the Garden of Paradise walking with the angels.
Now close the door and leave the room.
Be joyful.
For life is for the living and the best is yet to come.

Linda Runeckles

Mother Miracles

Thy gift of life received from God
For nine months I was blest,
My child was one with me
Joined by a cord of flesh
Two hearts did beat, two souls did shine
One was my child's, the other was mine
Within my womb a spirit of fire
Clothed in flesh and filled with desire
Entered this world naked and divine
The cord was severed, the miracle was mine
You came into this world with a cry of distress
To face the material and do your best
Challenge this life with a humble heart
Never lose faith God takes your part
These words, with love, I give to you
Forgive, share, be kind
And all that's good returns anew
And will give you peace of mind

Mary Ann Paterson

The Last Good-Bye

Good-bye dear sister Mary
   your life is past
We loved you to the very last.

We'll not weep for you
   but courage take
And love each other for your sake.

Sweet memories of you will always remain,
But one day, in paradise
   we'll meet again

Susan Alberta Varnham

All That Was Left

As he sits in a daze from his waterlogged eyes
Under the matted grey web of hair his mind it cries
For youth, and woodlands where once he'd played
And under a roof where he once had stayed
Under a roof of thatch, bone dry,
With a peephole in the attic that looked out to the sky.
He remembered the family's first motor car
And thought back to the moths he had kept in a jar
On a piano by a photograph
Of his Ma and Pa, that made him laugh.

But now as he comes back to the present day
He looks at his hands which have withered away
And imagines an ant climbing with difficulty
Over the lumps of veins he could see
He chuckles and ripples pass down his face
He was at the close of his human race
At last as he picked up his glass for a drink
He realized all that was left was to sit and think.

Jo Logue

Wishing For Snow

We watch the weatherman every day
To see if there's any snow on the way.
Sure enough the weatherman says,
A cold front's due in the next few days.

Christmas is just a few days away,
Please let there be snow on Christmas day.
Excitement grows as the days pass by,
But no sign of snow for you or I.

The canal is frozen, first time in years,
Icicles hang like frozen tears,
Christmas day comes, and Santa does too,
But the snow doesn't come for me or you.

On waking one morning and rubbing my eyes,
I open the curtains, and what a surprise!
Everything's covered in a blanket of white,
Untouched and unspoilt, not a footprint in sight.

Helen Bellamy

The Tide

I stood where my feet were lapped by the sea,
Watching my Life-tide deposit debris.
Alone on the shores of my fragile existence,
Watching the waters retreat to the distance.

Footprints I made, erased from the sand.
No proof that I walked here, except where I stand.
I delve in the pickings at the high-water line,
Searching for meaning in the season that's mine.

Briefly, I find it,
But brief is our day.
'Fore the tide rushes back,
And cleans it away.

Laura A M Stewart

Death

Captured by a mystery
Seized by unknown visitors
Interrogated by devilish delights
Almost like a raindrop as it pounds the once vibrant hearts
A newness, a light, a confusion quite impossible to describe
The pain and hurt being the only remains of such a
vibrant loss of beauty
Irreparable
A journey from one universe to another.
A change in matter
Striking screaming, showing its overwhelming power
Disappearing
Disappeared
Gone, lost forever

Rachel Gaster

Untitled

You couldn't ever become mine because you belong elsewhere
But every time you needed me I was always there
I didn't mean to hurt you but I'd have thought you'd understand
To me you promised nothing but a lot you did demand
I did all that I could to show you that I care
I told you that our lives together we would share
You became very insecure for a reason that I don't know
You tried your best to hide it but at times I'd really show
Please try to believe the love I feel for you
And show me that you care and that you love me too
Sometimes I sit and wonder what would happen if we part
The only thing I'd be left with is a broken heart
How many times can a person get hurt and feel like dying
And then pick up the pieces and again carry on trying
I didn't think what you felt was as much as this
And if I ever left you what we have you'd really miss
There's no turning back now we've come this far together
And for your sake as well as mine I hope it lasts forever

Mary Priddice

Beauty In Australia

The sky is of the deepest blue
Reflections in the sea are too,
Also the big jacaranda tree
Deep purple, blue as it can be,
These pretty flowers all come first
Before the green leaves form and burst.

Around the electric pole geraniums grow
Pale or deep pink make a lovely show,
In botanic gardens, herbs and such,
The notice says "Please do not touch,"
Parrots feed on the fig tree seed
There is plenty for every need.

Oranges and lemons grow next door
The biggest fruit I ever saw.
I still wake early every morn
And hear birds start to sing at dawn,
A blackbird from the top of a tree
Sounds like he's singing just for me.

Lucy M. Johnson

Judy And Rabbi Jones

Judy feeds the pigeons every day - she's eighty-three
and just as tall as Rabbi Jones - from Clapham
Toby saw her goldfish once - they were in her pond
when he went to fetch the ball
'She was talking to the shed' he said
we all laughed

Judy was a little girl once - and pretty
When she was young everybody loved her
except Rabbi Jones - from Clapham
who didn't know of her existence

Judy didn't even shed a tear
when Rabbi Jones died one October morning
in the park - in Clapham
she wasn't there as they buried him
she just smiled serenely in the cemetery
Mid November she still wasn't there
why should she be - 'Judy lives in Dorking
just down the road from me', so Grandpa said
we all laughed - except Judy
she wasn't there

Simon J. Durrant

Happy Talk

Happiness is a state of mind, in contented
surroundings it is easy to find.

This earth we are on for such a short time
why make life a long hard climb?

Problems are not just there - problems are
created, so why not share?

Conversation is such an easy step, what
has happened - did we all forget?

People are lazy, they don't want to talk
the TV is on they just sit and gawk.

If we all took an interest in life and each other
life would be fun, and go on with no fuss or bother.

So next time you feel like hiding away
don't make a move or go for a walk

Remember this motto!
Stop, think and talk

Lesley Ann McCarthy

Walking the Streets

People say......
That prostitutes should be stopped
Walking the streets with hardly any top
Wiggling their bums with a slight shake
Walking the streets till it's almost late
But that's all red-tape
Think how many people
Are arrested for rape
And the children
Who are used and abused
And the police haven't always got someone to accuse
Prostitutes help keep down sexual attacks
By simply making a living
On their backs
This is not fiction, it's facts
Good girls go to heaven
Is what they say
She replied
Bad girls go all the way.

Ronnie Mitchell

Life Is Precious

I lost my best friend, it was a sad day
Something happened and he passed away,
From that moment I withered inside,
My emotions coming and going just like the tide,
Days were long and nights were cold
Without a hug or hand to hold,
Many times I've asked why couldn't it be me
I have no strength, a weaker person you'll never see,
Why were you selfish to leave me alone
One minute here, the next you're gone,
But time doesn't stand still, the days pass by
The tears get less, no more I cry,
And just like winter turns to spring
The pain dies, of happy memories I sing,
I'm here alone but I've found the strength
To carry on, life is precious at any length,
And although, my friend, we've had to part
You'll always be near, here in my heart.

Linda Webster

Bosnia

Little houses in rows; all similar
gerry-built, gimcrack affairs.
Card houses, we called you and scoffed
at your petty suburban airs.

Oh! Desolate gaunt-eyed houses
huddled in broken-backed heaps,
still terror struck, sightlessly staring
while death clothed in flames round you leaps.

Charred bones of rafter-arms pointing
in silent reproach to the sky,
the children you once protected
now shelterless, terrorised die.

Nesta Moore

Black Friday

Hustle and bustle of expectancy, it's Friday
Going home, going out, enjoyment,
Happy people, dreaming, it's Friday,
An atmosphere, silence, a shout,
Explosion, screams, panic it's Friday,
Blood, devastation, chaos,
140 hurt, children wounded, maimed it's Friday,
Victims fleeing, choking, crying,
A bomb an I.R.A. bomb it's Friday,
Fleets of ambulance screeching,
Terror in faces, Doctors running, it's Friday,
The news, the horror, we feel what they feel, it's Friday,
Why? Why? Evil people,
We can see the blood, terror, trauma, it's Friday,
They kill children, they don't care,
Why do they want to kill? It's Friday,
Maybe we should kill them all,
It could have been us, it's Friday,
The I.R.A. are cowards, killers,
Such anger, hatred, shattered peace, it's Black Friday.

Jean Ellershaw

November's Gone

The sun beats down upon the arid ground,
Dead leaves cling stubbornly to sodden twigs,
Parched and timid dogs seek frantically for shade
Without a sound.
Winter's come
Wind etched and sun bleached bones can here
And there be found.
A robin shrills impatiently whilst someone digs.
Goats feed on cardboard cartons lying around.
I'll soon be home
Evening shadows slowly climb a sand and
Ancient mound,
Above the door, all green and red a holly sprig,
A camel train passes by somewhere bound.

Peter Hanlon

A Child's Nightmare

Nightmares, horrible dreams, hearses to take me away,
Mongol children already dead coming to ask me to play.
Mother on the telephone, is she asking someone to call to take
Me to some dark creepy grave where I cannot escape
Men in black cloaks, black beards, grey faces to suffocate?

Wake up screaming all of a shake
Mummy, come quickly, I've got tummy-ache.

I don't trust no one, I feel insecure,
That man is coming to mend the chair
That I'm blamed for breaking, I'll hide in the corn
It's like a forest, I'll stay here till morn
That man, he will skin me although I'm alive
And probably also he'll pull out my eyes.

I'll run with my cushion and sit by the mill
Which now is a ruin, but I see children still
Playing around me and swinging on posts
They're not normal children, just more of the ghosts.

May Booth

"Shattered"

Shattered, like a broken windscreen
the crazed fragments of me
Somehow hanging together
by an invisible film
On the framework of my flesh and bones
waiting for the inevitable jerk
to disintegrate my life before me,
like ashes in the path of the prevailing wind.

Kathryn Hodgkinson-Szommer

Anonymous Destination

Life is a mystery, disclosed to none,
A wilted rose under the blazing sun.
With bare feet and empty hands,
We tread on the blazing sands.
With weak pride and endless desperation,
We try to find our Anonymous Destination.

In a subdued storm of life, we're all drifting away,
Hanging onto the rope of desires, hoping it will never fray,
Even though we're worn to a frazzle by our tainted lust,
But still we chase the ashes of bliss in the dust.
And when the barren heart blazes with guilt, it cries out for rain.
Sometimes tears cannot extinguish a burning heart, but
enhance the pain.

When we choke back the tears of dismay, thus
A dim roar of silence moans inside us.
But the shadows of woe keep crawling behind.
We follow the traces of destiny, when thoughts go blind.
As we walk through this weary trail of frustration,
We discover, life is a trial, not an Anonymous Destination.

Shazia Khan

A Shadow Of Doubt

Who is it?
Who's there?
Who's following me?
Please go,
Leave me alone,
Leave me be.
I've done nothing wrong
And I've nothing to say,
Please, whoever you are, please go away.
I must find a place now, to hide
Nowhere to run,
Nowhere you can't find.
I panic now
And tired, I'm slow.
Wait,
Stand,
Look!
For it's you... my shadow.

Denise A. Scott-Flounders

Waiting

The bed seems to become part of you.
Every experience becomes imprinted on
your mind, this last for all eternity
The memories so clear and so difficult to forget
The days so long they never end
People come and go, yet you stay
Somehow suspended there.

You hear people laugh and wish that you
Could laugh too. Then you start to think and
Wish that you could go to the places
that you did before

But no-one would be there
the same place, different people,
Those you once knew have gone to
greener pastures and you are still
the same, lying there in that bed, wishing...

Wishing for the end to come
Just lying there, waiting.

Suzanne C. Whiteley

Homage To Nature

I meditate along the winding path
Grassy, glassy, mulchy
Of recent rains the aftermath.

Silence breaks way down a little
With hidden view it's vague yet brittle.

I pause to peer through forest thicket:
I listen to the eerie sound
Of water somewhere near my ground.

The mist is rising faster now:
A shaft of light creeps through the bough ahead of me;
the sky I see
Glimmering, shimmering sunlight pale:
I pause on pebble, rock and shale.
A crazy waterfall of hail like snow
Dashes, crashes to slower flow
And quietude of pool below.

A rainbow then appears across that fall:
An iridescent offering; a barrier
To nature's impenetrable wall.

I gaze and gaze enchanted and awe-shrouded
The mystery beyond remaining clouded.

Helen Anna Zurlinden

Crowborough Hill

I walked up the hill
To Crowborough Town.
Not a pence in my purse
But on the pavement.
Shining bright a 5 pence piece.
I picked it up and gazed at it
And went on walking
The steep climb up Crowborough Hill
To Crowborough Town.
Alas when in Crowborough Town,
What could I buy for my five pence?
Not a coffee or a bread roll.
I stood on the pavement,
And there outside a shop
A charity box
Give to the sunshine home. Children who are blind
So I slipped the five pence in the box
It's like the widow and her mite
I have been blessed with my sight.
And I will pray for the children who are blind.

Grace Baldwin

Vigil

I wasn't there
When the gossamer thread
That bound your world to mine
Was severed by your final, laboured breath.
They were not my lips that kissed your eyelids
Sealed by earthly mortality,
My mother did, but I wasn't there.
Alone, I sat in my dark world, clock watching,
Waiting for the news I feared would surely come.
And when it did, I cried the cry
That brought my loved one running to my side.
Oh, how I held him tight,
Desperately craving his body-rhythm that beats...
I am alive, I am alive.
And when they carried you shoulder high,
Beneath a garland of roses, trussed and wired
In a parody of life,
I walked behind, yet I knew you were not there
My beloved breath of Yorkshire air.

Rachel Bull

Life

All my dreams are shattered.
I've been bruised and battered.
My future blew away
On one windy day.
With it, it took my heart and soul
And left me in a deep dark hole.
Suddenly the smile left my face,
Now not even a whisper or a trace.
My world is somewhere in the distance,
It ran away from me in an instance.
Somewhere between life and death is a line.
Maybe soon, I will cross mine.

Nadia Sahir

Age Is Timeless, Time Is Ageless

Age is nothing special
It just happens when you're old
Like a wine that's in its prime
Or a nugget of ancient gold

And time is only something
That happens in your mind
As you remember all the things you've lost
And all you wish to find

But the trees know age is timeless
As they ring another year
Protectors of the seasoned land
That holds a planet dear

And the birds know time is ageless
As they dance upon the dawn
And that for every moment passed away
Another one is born

John Wadsworth

Seeds of Happiness?

She lays the foundation to her new life in the sun
A one way ticket to scenic beauty that befits her own
As her seeds of self-righteousness grown.
Observers wonder if flowers like her could
survive in such heat.
So she arrives and is surrounded by an array
Of flowers, raising their heads to greet her
Such an introduction in her new life only
adds to the complacency.
Doesn't she realize the higher she is on her own,
the harder she will fall . . .
alone.
Who will replace the fallen petals on this mimosa?
Too late she realizes that petals which have
been pulled from the heart, never regrow.

Rihana Basheer

Strength

I need a strength
When pride and vain conceit
Boils up in spite
And angry heat.
I need a strength
When problems causes
My tongue to lie
And spill deceit.
I need a strength
When self importance
Fills my head
And I forget the roots from which I'm bred.
I need a strength
When lust and greediness
Fills heart and mind
Without thought for those in dire distress.
I need a strength
That I may see the light
Which opens wide my eyes
That once saw only night.

Olive Samuel

They Ask Me

They ask me brusquely
If I wrote, am writing, or write anything.
My answer is three brusque no's.
"Wasted talent", they sneer, and leave.

"Wasted talent!"
What talent have I,
Lost between two languages?
I winked at Telugu,
And English winks at me
A bilingual tragedy -
I have no key . . . . .

"What are you writing?"
"Words."
But words are words are words,
Not great writing,
Though they pass for it at present.

In the beginning was the word in the West,
The OUM of the East is not even a word,
But a strange creative sound
The little of Hindu wisdom.
Shell

N. A. Yajulu

The Silent Stalker

Is it he, who passes by,
With measured step, and twisted lip?
Dark glasses shade his murky eyes.
My thudding heartbeats dip, and flip,
As from my sight he slides away,
To hide, until some other day.

What does he carry in that bag,
That dangles from his bony hand?
Is it my death-knell hidden there?
Pistol, knife, or just a strand
Of rope, to tighten round my throat,
As into black oblivion I float?

Or could it be that woman.
Who loiters on the corner there?
From her black raincoat hood,
Protrudes a pointed nose, and wispy hair.
That shabby handbag on her arm,
What does it hold, to do me harm?

Freda E. Allen

The Death Of A Mouse

Have you ever seen a cat then compared it to a mouse?
The cat has might
so he thinks he's right,
but a mouse walks timid about the house.

The mouse is a hungry wee fellow, he don't even know he's a pest,
he'll scurry around
until he has found
some food to take back to his nest.

The cat drinks milk, eats fish and meat, but the mouse he must succumb,
to abide,
with a rumbling inside,
and hope for the left-over crumb.

Brave mouse thought "I must fight that cat, much against my wish,
tonight I'll be sure of something to eat . . .
I'll beat him to his dish."

So with a heart much bigger than he, he crept out of his hole,
but that very night
he lost the fight
and never reached his goal . . .
brave hungry mouse "God rest your soul."

E. Pratt

Untitled

I walk in sleep through waters deeper by far
Than ocean's darkest reaches,
And in this profoundness where I am
abiding in endless spaces out of Time,
Wherein my shadow may encounter its premise.
Veiled in attire no earthly eye may see to this blessed place
Of retire I flee.

Constant in motion,
Ever changing in circumstance and renewal pervading in this immensity,
Which in Time may not be conceived of in flesh,
Nor bear witness to the wonders of this creation
Melting all in the fulfilment of His design.

We sing in union with the stars His praise
Where no night nor day may end this peace.

O Great Spirit that cast away my bones,
And rendered my flesh to dust,
Thou who brought me hither from the mouths of dragons,
And thence from the cold womb of earth I wore in sleep
To these cosmic reaches blessed before I am,
And from whence I am come reborn likened unto Thine own substance
To reside forever in Thy keep.

Anthony John Doyle

Brother of Mine

Come here my brother, come and take my side,
All is on the game and the fates are ours to ride,
On this day we will surely taste success or defeat,
Dogs and cowards may run, but we shall stand and not retreat.
The skies are black and the power of the thunder can be felt
   throughout the ground,
And on the earth, blood and death lie nearly all around,
But come closer my brother, come brother take my hand,
A pact of strength let it be, for us to defend our land.
For I know you not, and have never seen your face,
But such strong silent actions define your nobility and grace.
Countrymen are we and I love you with all my heart,
Together then, together, and let us into this bloody battle depart.
And now, as the noise of battle, its tortured song has begun,
My thoughts turn to death, has the race of my life finished its run.
For if death calls my name, and from this day on I will no longer live,
Then I will taste the bitter poison, and for my people, my life I will give.
For if, with my countrymen side by side together we will stand,
Then no death will I find finer, no resting place so grand.
So come here my brother, come and take my side,
All is on the game and the fates are ours to ride.

Malcolm McAndrew

Pillbox

Pills for this and pills for that;
Pills to make you slim,
Pills to make you fat,
Pills to take between meals,
Pills to take the lot!
Pills to take at bedtime,
Pills you have forgot,
Pills that make you younger,
In no time at all,
Pills to make you bigger
When you're feeling small,
Pink pills, blue pills, some coloured red,
For every part of your body,
Not just for your head.
Pills to make you happy,
Pills that make you sad,
Pills for all the family,
Pills that are just for dad.
Large pills, small pills, any size will do,
But don't forget too many pills are not so good for you.

Eva Pilbrow

The Exam

Waiting for the exam to begin, nerves start to tingle.
Tick Tock goes the clock.
Time to begin your exam.
Open paper; take a deep breath; Tick Tock Tick Tock.
Finding questions to do; Tick Tock Tick Tock.
Twenty minutes have passed, and questions done are none!
Panic takes over; face starts sweating.
Tick Tock Tick Tock.
Wait a minute, you know the answer to this one.
Rush! Rush! Rush!
Relaxation and confidence take over.
Here's another question you know, and another.
Tick Tock Tick Tock.
You've finished with ten minutes spare.
At the ceiling and paper you stare.
Oh no!
You've only answered seven of a needed eleven.
Rush! Rush! Rush!
Tick Tock Tick Tock; time up!
Out of your eye comes a tear; oh well, there's always next year!

S. V. Sewoke

Forest Lament

Once there was a world of green harmonies
Gently set in a time honoured peace,
Where little things moved with a quiet purpose
And bustle and fear were strangers.
Only sometimes came the great dark shadow
Heralding the heavy approach of monstrous beasts,
But dull of understanding in those early days,
Causing distress to none but the unwary.

Palms waved their flagged leaves, tattered in the sunlight.
Great trees and plants intertwined,
Vied with each other in reaching to the stars,
While everywhere a thousand different muted
Humming sounds of green, deepened and darkened,
Flashed into yellow, splashed onto shadow-flecks.

Now it is no more.
Only the trees in the deep wood could tell the legend
Of men who hacked and tore at the heart of things,
Of the mighty monarchs who now lie deep, deep down.
There is a sadness in the forest
'or all now hear the sighing in the tress.

E. Farrell

Sustenance

See all those foodstuffs on the shelves -
Which do we want and which do we need?
We can help ourselves.

We can help ourselves, our families to feed.
Fill a trolley or two, expense no object;
But is this greed?

But is this greed when the starving collect
Food grains which fall from another's bowl,
And keep them, unchecked?

Keep them, unchecked, and hope that the weakened soul
Will allow its human frame to survive
Until the saner people of the world regain control.

Christine E. Coleman

Whispers of the Past

Flowers grow on earth where lovers have trodden
through centuries unheard,
And left no path of trodden violets and rows of their daisy
chains,
The same blue skies blanket like a canopy,
Hiding the lovers from the stars that have peeped on
secret and on stolen hearts,
With time and dust those footprints have long since
vanished,
Where you and I first walked hand in hand,
Down those cherished lanes that wove our hearts with
love,
Lasting through time until we join the lovers of the past,
As lovers lane hides beneath the dust of time,
And the stars will never tell our secrets to those who
follow us,
With the same words on lips that caress and spell the
words of love,
I once said to you.

Ronald Walker

The Mist Of Sorrow

What has Dunblane done to warrant such grief?
The whole World stood silent in disbelief.
Those wee Angels with faces so bright
Have gone to their God in raiment white.

What does one say to a Parent grieving
Words are superfluous to a heart that's heaving.
The will of Allah, God or Jove
His prerogative betimes is hard to probe.

One day in the future, all will unfold
But for now, it is torment untold
Those wee Seraphs; with no wiles only love
Watch down on those sorrowing from Heaven above.

My heart is heavy as I pen this
But the Weans live now in a state of bliss,
To those bereft, this is comfort cold
No warm bodies to hug and hold.

'Infamy' has to be Hamilton's name,
The curse of him is akin to Cain,
A Father am I, so grieved that I cry,
The question I put is "why, why, why?"

Padraig O'Daoirin

Constance, My Constance

Such poise and beauty rarely seen
climbing high and wide over trellis and screen.
Laughing at the world with gay abandon
throwing out buds, it seems, completely at random.
In the early morning dew you are so coy
but in the mid-day sun, in full bloom, what a joy.
Your perfume, like myrrh, so heady, so sweet
and with your soft pink petals you are complete.
Towering high above me into the sky
there's none to compare with Constance, my Constance Spry.

Lesley Wright

Best Cure For Fleas?

I woke up one morning covered in lumps.
Went to the doctor, who felt these bumps.
He said, "They're fleas; they had you last night
They had a feast, 'My God', did they bite!
You must have animals, pets of some sort;
This is were you got them, this is what you've caught.
The best cure is simple so have o fear
Just don't bother washing for at least a year.
No need to brush your teeth, or do your hair
And take, no notice of hygienic care.
People won't mind you smelling for a while,
You may stink at first and whiff a bit vile,
But my remedy will cure those fleas
And garlic is a food you should eat as you please.
Curry and chilly also raw onions too
Anything spicy and hot will also do
You see, the fleas will not like this taste
And will leave your body with terrific haste,
So take my advice for 12 months and have no fear
'Coz if it doesn't work, you can try a cream ——
    I've got some here!
            Stephen Fountain

The Abused Child

Alone in the darkness the frightened child cried.
No one came to hold her, no arms opened wide.
The room was all blackness. She whimpered in fear,
And down one soft cheek - past the bruise - stole a tear
The cold house was empty. They'd left her alone.
She trembled with fear when she heard them come home.
Drunken and fighting, they crashed through the hall.
They fought in their room - she could hear through the wall.
Cold, hungry, whimpering, afraid they might hear -
She crammed her small fist in her mouth, filled with fear.
But some sound that she made penetrated the wall,
And her door was flung wide. He stormed in from the hall.
"Here's something to cry for!" His fist struck her cheek.
"No daddy! Don't hurt me," - but he liked the weak.
It made him feel brave when he menaced his child,
He punched her and kicked her, his eyes laughing - wild.
And when she lay still, crumpled up on the floor,
"I'm sorry," he said. "It won't happen no more."

This time, it was over! This time was the last!
His child lay beyond pain. Her small life had passed.
            Joanna Deacon

Leanne

Is your hair long, fair, curly or short?
How tall are you now? Do you give me a thought?
For I think of you, at school and at play.
Are you laughing and loved, did you have a good day?

Do you walk in the park, feed ducks on the lake?
Get covered in flour, as you help Mummy bake.
Do your eyelashes sweep your pale lovely cheeks?
As dreamless and pure your innocence sleeps.

Whilst far away alone in the dark,
I dream you're walking with me in the park.
Your Mummy looks back, they forget don't you know?
That children and granddads walk awfully slow.

When I awake it's not the old life.
Of Grandma, Granddad, Husband and Wife.
For today, that only happens in dreams,
All you need now is a Mummy it seems.

So, for us little one, there'll be no today,
But tomorrow is yours, have a great day,
While I hope and pray, before your life is done,
Your grandchild and you get to walk in the sun.
            Derek Forward Davies

Apron Strings

I realize my children have a life now of their own.
It's natural they've flown the nest, they both are fully grown.
I try my best not to interfere - I know I don't succeed.
It's hard to come to terms - it's not a mother they now need.

I only want them to be happy, have lives of relative ease
But after years of putting them first, myself I cannot please.
I fill my days with trivia. Keeping busy is the thing.
I just can't relax until they give me a little ring.

I can tell by their voices if things are not alright.
They don't want to worry me. But then I get uptight.
I imagine the worst and worry, I never do things by half.
Then next day they sound better as they give a little laugh.

I don't want to know their business - it's nowt to do with me
But when they sound so happy - I feel I've won the lottery.
Will it ever get better - does the worry ever ease?
I hope it does - I know it does - please! - Please! - Please!

But if a choice were given, would I really do without
The offspring I have mothered - of course not, there's no doubt
For to obtain for them "Health and Happiness" is all that I ask.
I'd climb the highest mountain and do the hardest task!
            Sheila Davies

My Son's Ted

Poor old Ted - he's had his day, he's getting very old,
he used to be the pride and joy, of my last born baby boy.

He played with it most every day, from it he never parted,
until one day he lost it, and he was broken hearted.

Poor little lad - he was so sad, but not for very long,
because it was returned to him, and made him very glad.

Time has passed - my son's grown up, now he has a bride,
poor old Ted - he's left behind, been pushed on to one side.

I picked him up - took a look, and got out my old knitting book,
I made some clothes in green and red, also a hat to sit on his head.

He really does look very swell,
What comes next? - well time will tell.

I'm going to save it for the day, for when my son comes in to say,
"Mum, do you still have my old bear?
'Cause we're going to have a son and heir."
            M. Impey

Winter's Magic

Like silhouettes the trees project black against the winter sky
While frost that shines like diamonds upon the earth doth lie
The glow of winter's setting sun in the season that is cold
Transforms the world of colour into orange, black and gold
The damp cold mist of winter that swirls across the distant hills
Transfiguring the bush and tree, to portray artistic skills
Of statues carved in marble stone all rising from the earth
While cold winds blow to echo sound of merriment and mirth
Snowflakes fall and settle, shedding a white blanket on the ground
To enhance mysterious silence, muffling every sound
The virgin snow lies deep, hiding all the treasures caught below
'Til spring returns promise of life, with radiance and glow
            Valerie Evans

Car

If we are all sane, and, mostly we are,
Then why must we have the abominable car?
The car is a thing. Our planet, it destroys,
all because people must have their new toys.
The engine is a pollutant. By its fumes, it kills,
its functions are all taxable, hence spiralling bills.
The countryside is raped, destroyed for more roads.
Tarmac is delivered in ever-increasing loads.
Where will it all end? This folly of ours,
This folly called love, a love for our cars.
            K. Chamberlain

Good Morning

Good morning John, Good Morning Archie,
Walking again today?
Summer, Autumn, Winter, Spring,
Where do you go, by the way?

Are you with us, the so-called sane,
Or safe in mind in a far off place,
Where only a very faint refrain,
Of "normality" pierces the haze?

Unbalanced, inadequate are the judgements given,
"There but for the Grace of God" say we,
Perhaps God's Grace is really your heaven,
Of private make believe.

We, the "coping" plodders on,
Must do the right and proper thing,
To soldier on with our rigid lives,
Perhaps forgetting the why to sing.

We must supply the place of care,
To house "poor" John and Archie,
Yet the real truth, too heavy to bear,
Is that we are the captured army.

E. L. M. Gibson

Music

The music was poignant and beautiful.
It rose above the horizon
and encircled Humanity.

A profound stillness overcame me,
intricate, powerful patterns
seared my body.

From the depths and farness of Time
all people past and future paths
flowed wherein I stood entranced
and inextricably bound.

I looked down at my hands
and found a Universe of Light.
I closed my eyes,
looked into my heart
and found Joyous Rhythms in the Stillness,
beating,
greeting,
weeping,
sleeping,
deep within Humanity.

Maggi L. Thomason-Macleod

In Love Again

Are there voices in your head
Chanting Latin in your mind
Are there Arabs, Sikhs and Nepalese
With accents unrefined

Are there silverfish in sunlight
Glinting fast before your eyes
Shimmer, going, coming, leaving
Never grasped, elusivised

Are your thoughts like sunk-stone ripples
Always fleeting, never caught
Disappearing as they're growing
Hiding deeper as they're sought

Are kaleidoscopes of wonder
Crackerjacking in your head
Is your tongue forever speaking
But your thoughts remain unsaid

Are you floating on a bubble
Pink champagning to the sky
Are you breathing effervescence
As you are, then, so am I.

Tess Good-O'Brien

Cone Song

Twenty-two traffic cones, stretched across the road,
Made a milk-float skid and shed its messy dairy load.
"Now we need a couple more!" Paddy hollered to Clive,
Who quickly ran his barrow up and made it twenty-five.

Twenty-five traffic cones in a curving row
Kept the morning rush-hour moving nice and slow.
"Would y'ever bring a couple more!" Paddy hollered to Shorty,
Who quickly backed the van up - and then there were forty.

Forty muddy traffic cones in the dark, wet night
Cuddled close together and deciding that they might
Make some baby conelets, cuddled close some more.
Next morning Paddy hollered, "Jaze! Now there's a thousand and four."

A thousand happy traffic cones paralysed the route.
Drivers shook their fists and cursed and furiously did hoot.
Paddy hollered, strolling past as if on Brighton prom,
"And there's a thousand more, boys, where that little lot come from."

Adrian Vale

Lost Life

All alone she wonders why, still these tears she does cry.
Now an empty soul, a lonely woman without a goal.
That magic sparkle's gone, the one which had once twinkled on in the
    proud daddy's eye.
He'd felt it too, a pain that was thought only she knew.
Not understanding why he can't stop her helpless cry.
For their baby she'd let die.
Motherhood had once felt so good, just like she'd always dreamt it would.
This empty mother does so regret that lost love for their unborn
    baby she'll never be able to forget.
Her regretful tears still don't stop, they keep on falling drop by drop.
Each and every time she looks at him, she remembers the life that
    had once felt warm deep within.
Growing day by day, a life that would have been perfect in every way.
Will these tears ever stop or will they keep on falling drop by drop.

Carla Geraldine Newton

HOPE

HOPE is ever eternal, for every one of us,
An entity to call on, when we feel we must.
We always HOPE for a healthy life, to all newly born,
Then HOPE their childhood is enjoyed, as it follows on.
There's always HOPE for their success during their school studies,
Giving further HOPE towards a good career, with seldom any worries.
We HOPE they'll meet someone to love, and HOPE they'll also marry,
To bring fresh HOPE every day, from children crying "mummy".
There's always HOPE from everyone, for others in distress,
For without HOPE, what would we do, when we're in a mess?
There's HOPE for peace and HOPE for joy, also tranquillity.
There's always HOPE for everyone, until eternity.

John White

Runaway

There was a girl on the street today, she said she was a runaway,
"How old are you?" I asked her then, the girl replied "I am but ten"
"D'you want to go for a bite to eat? Oh don't worry, it'll be my treat".
"That's very kind of you" she yelped, I was just glad that I could help.
It began to rain, so we ran inside, and then she began to confide.
The little girl was called Jenny, she told me she was one of many
who lived and wandered about the streets, who begged and searched
for things to eat.
She said her mum was never home, she had to cope all on her own
The council found out she was alone, and threatened to put her in a home.
And then Jenny began to cry, she said she didn't want to lie.
Jenny had been taking drugs, and was wanted by a gang of thugs.
I asked if she would let me help, she said she could manage by herself.
She then produced a stanley knife, and in the cafe, she took her life.
The ten-year-old, living rough, decided she had had enough.
So the next time you meet a runaway, stop and think back to this day.
Think of what it would be like, on the streets, day and night.
Don't complain about your home, it's better than being on your own.

Lyndsay-Marie McDonaugh

A Winter's Tale

Winds howl and shudder throughout the house
floors a tremble squeaks from mouse
windows rattle, doors they creak
winter's here, winter's bleak

The skies grow dark with snow and hail
the cattle cry, the cattle wail
for soon the land be powdered white
winter's here, winter's fight

Jack Frost has cast his wintry hand
across the fields, across the land
the trees are bare, no leaves in sight
winter's here, winter's night

Lakes and rivers held cold and fast
winter's now and winter's past
their icy cavern's deep in chill
winter's here, winter still.

F. G. Hinshelwood

When I Was A Child

When I was a child,
I wanted to be wild,
I wanted to be free...to be just me.

I hated that red dress
it made me feel distressed
I got cold chills, when I had to wear frills,
and oh...no! When out come the bow,
But Ah! When I reached Granma
"By all means...wear your jeans,
I put on my gym shoes, then watched the news
Went for a hike...then rode my brother's bike.
Oh! To be free...and be just me.
Then I'd return...inside I'd burn
mother had come, put my hair in a bun
gave me that dress...that brought back stress.
Another day I'd have to play
the game of taking the blame.

Angie Kenway

Understanding A Loss

Death is never an easy thing,
Grief and sorrow it does bring.
Tears and sadness for someone dear,
Now they are gone and no longer here
But, if there was pain, it's gone far away,
Free from the torture, day after day.
And if there was age, one must accept
That life has been lived and promises kept.
Tragedy, we know, is a terrible thing,
Anguish and shock it has to bring.
But death must be seen in a different light,
Heaven must be a beautiful sight.
For the Lord takes all, good and bad,
So try to understand and not be too sad.

Sue-Anne Gatt Coleiro

The Consoling Friend

You were meant to console me,
To erase the sorrows that shroud over me.
Your sympathy was the balm to my torments.
You said, be strong, good friend,
Be courageous, my sister.
Be this, be that......
Persevere till the sadness disintegrates.

But your doubtful face
Distorted those words of prudence.

You seemed to care very deeply -
My woes were as thorns in your life.
Your devotion to me was divine,
Or so it seemed to my tearful eyes.
You claimed that you would be always near -
But looking up, I saw no shadow of yours.

Tahmeena Gani

"My Eyes"

My eyes are weary, tired and sad,
They have seen the misery of his world,
Children, land and animals suffering.
My eyes cry out to see the world, full
Of laughter, green pastures, the birds flying
Free of toxin, oh, a sight to see, my eyes so sad.

Where has the love for children gone,
Their hunger is the world gone wrong.
The trees are going, the animals fleeing,
Will there ever be a forest, full of animals
Free and frolicking, flower blooming, bees
Buzzing, will a child be well enough to
See these acts of nature growing.
Oh, my eyes, will you ever smile again.

Oh, world please listen, and start to act,
We have to start and make this world,
A place for our children, clean of air,
Their tummies full, and most of all, to see their eyes, happy,
healthy and full of promise. Then my eyes will not be weary,
tired and sad.

Patricia Fisk

Refusal in Slumber

Refusal in slumber, great self denied.
Eyes, ignorant of wakings
Open and view the world
For armed with bags of power
We carry each an invisible hunchback
Which after wakings, guides destiny to concord.

I, in my solitary cry
The metamorphosis observed

These crowds of mouths
Wrapped in wonders are dumb men to witness the years.

O Nshi of the stream valley
Hold me; take me to the land strange where lads
Rehearse the songs of the beginnings

I am listening behind the dark waters
Leaning on a lioness
Studying the days and mysteries
At the birthday of Earth
And we learnt of wonders and orderliness
Like the pregnancy of the virgin

Tomorrow shall Christ come, world without ends.

David Ugba

Soul Spectrum

Speak to me with your soul, not your mind
For once you were whole, now you are blind
We had no corruption, we had loving eyes
The purity of wonder without disguise

Recall when you were a child beauty so thrilling
The world was all yours, you knew nothing of killing
Now there is evil as a child you didn't know
The purpose of your birth is that you're here to grow

Man has laws so corrupt I tell you no lie
For when you were born, you were born to die
Think of our happiness like blossoms never last
In all of your decaying you will remember the past

The oracle is in the water where my mind is flowing
There is spirit of light, a seed that is growing
When the mind in our brain has not been affected
You may go to the light to be resurrected

So who will compare themselves to the good word
For it is so bright if the word can be heard
Is God he or she or the word as the light
Visualize the spectrum, follow insight

Terence E. Mallinder

Tragedy

I sat by your side, saw your life ebb away
I should have cried, wishing you'd stay.
You looked so at peace, so innocent and free.
I never felt more at ease, how can this be?

You were my lover but now you've gone
There can be no other, it's been you for so long
Could I betray you as you lie in your grave?
I'll never replace you, I'll remain forever brave.

I'll replace the flowers, never throw them away.
Remember the hours we spent your last day
I'll never let the memory of you slip away
But now you're in eternity and that's where you'll stay.

I never wanted you to see me cry
But I don't want to be haunted so I'll say goodbye!

Juliette Seel

'Springtime'

Springtime is here again, after the winter chills
to show us again, that everything has arrived as planned,
and flowers in perfect colour renewed and looking great.
to be admired by everyone whatever they feel or do,
and to bring so much happiness and food for animals too,
Just as the seasons come and go.
And winter is getting high, with snow and chills anew,
Ah! But the season's now gone
and we want another to come.

D. J. Ford

Heavenly Sphere

With no parsimony the man plays with music and
So magical and harmonious is the blend.
With blissful feelings our souls ascend,
Pure and perfect the sound may be in the end.

Source of desires tending to go deeper,
Deep emotions like joy and grief all together
Enter the spirit and body like a symphony,
And mixed feelings mingle with our memory.

Clouds of sweetness and tender happiness
Weave around our imagination like lace
And give a pleasant escape to the mind.

Nectar of life, so noble and beautiful
Renders our dreams quite meaningful
So as to the man, no more he is blind.

Marie Castagna

My Special Friend

He never appears in human form,
In animal or in bird.
There's no shape to cast a shadow,
Nor voice to speak a word.

He'll sometimes show me sadness,
So I'll not go there again.
He also shows me endless love,
When life seems all in vain.

And if I'm walking down a lonely road
With no blue skies, flowers or trees,
He'll come to me and bring with him
Bird songs, petals and a warm summer breeze.

My heart is filled with love for him,
For in everything we share.
He is a piece of all I've seen,
I've known or been aware.

He is the guardian of my whole future
And the ghost of all my past.
He's my special friend and mine alone,
So long as life shall last.

E. J. Walton

Untitled

Now that I am young I don't want to grow old
thinking about it makes me go cold.
I'll get lots of wrinkles and lose all my hair
Mother nature is just not being fair
I might lose my mind and be put in a home
Which really quite truthfully won't be my own
Some people say it isn't that bad
But if that is true how come grandma is sad
My children and grandchildren won't visit that much
I'm sure they will think I am quite out of touch
But inside my head I'll know the truth
That I was once young and fun in my youth.

Nicola Davis

Untitled

If there's something so strong you can feel it inside
Hold on to it tight else away it will slide
If your heart is full of love and light
Don't chuck it away else you will feel plight
Love is life and life should be fun
But when it goes away so does your sun
When love disappears you're left like a shell
All dead inside which makes life all hell
Like last week's rubbish you get chucked away
When instead you just want to stay
It's hard to let go of what is your life line
But when you do it hurts and you don't seem to shine
When something's so good you just can't let go
But it suddenly slips and you go down with a blow
You can't always give up what feels so right
Or at least not until you've put up a fight
When you've lost the battle you feel really bad
Inside you feel anger but mostly you're sad
When it's done, it's done; when it's gone, it's past
But that love inside will always last.

Susie Porter

Blackpool Seasons

Yes, and the winter came;
And the sad listless leaves were swept away
trodden in low, lanc puddles
underneath my feet; and I sat down and cried.
My mind as heavy as the grey clouds above;
My mind was lead. And the old closed places
with the boards across; yes, and the winter came.

Another year older and we think of the winter,
Then things will be different;
the people that we scorn, flock in their numbers
in ridiculous hats - as we look down our noses.
Streaming towards and away from those golden postered sands,
crowding those places that we longed to be opened
and, once opened, avoid.

So we all work harder to get more money
to throw away; and the nights are too light;
and we think of the winter with a feeling
verging almost on nostalgia; yes, and the winter came.

Thank goodness Spain is not the same; no, the winter never came...

Elizabeth Hobson

Love

Does the world evolve around love?
Was it implanted in our souls by God above?

This emotion, until aroused, is securely bound
And releases steadily when a suitable partner is found.
Like a flower that blossoms in response to a season
That withers and dies in times of trouble, without reason.

And sprouting again it gradually blooms, lacking all fears
When the essential element it searched for, finally appears.

The rest of its time it will happily spend
Entwined with the other, on which it will always depend.

Claire Hall

Lucy Pucie

Lucy Pucie has come to stay
for a three week holiday.
Her coat is white.
Her eyes all green.
She's the prettiest cat you've ever seen.
She eats my plants
And sleeps all day.
When evening comes she starts to play.
Leaping from window sill to
chair her toy mice thrown
up in the air, she makes
me laugh I love her so,
The holiday's over and she
goes home, and I am sad
and all alone.

Dee Parkinson

Time Passing By

An empty sensation fills me
struck by little arrows I dream
to stand on a hill on my own
to look into the empty space
to feel the wind blow towards away
time races restlessly past me.

I must have stood there forever
when suddenly I saw your face
so fresh that roses turned grey
so soft that feathers turned stony
so gentle, so happy, so gay
yet so strong that my feelings I gave away.

Boris N. Liedtke

Tears Of Happiness

Winter brings out a dull coldness to the earth
But still every second there's a baby's birth.
A happy and joyful day for the mother and father,
Life will be good a long time after.

The baby doth say its very first words,
The first ones spoken since its birth.
Its first steps bring joy to the family near,
And to the mother and the father, brings a tear.

Its life after that should be long and happy,
With its very own mam'e and pap'e.
With an odd tear shed for all the sad times,
But happiness will overrule all of these fears.

When it grows up and has a family of its own,
It will remember the days when it was bold.
Its life will flash by with the young once near,
And again the shed of happy tears.

Nicolette Taylor

Tears

A night at the ballet
started it all
as though the swirling passion
of the music ran through their veins
and would not be quenched
even by the crescendo at the end.

"I'd rather go to hell with you
than heaven without" he said
and so they remained lovers
at the periphery of life, meeting
when their paths perchanced to cross.

A routine call when distance - as usual -
divided them, gave the news.
"I have a problem. Can't remember things.
It's so frustrating. How damn silly"
And month by month the memory got worse.
Soon she will not remember him at all
but he will remember her
and cry - yes - all of his tears.

John Dicks

Untitled

The old lady huddled in tattered coat
Sits alone
Dull skies, chilling winds, her sole companions.
What mysteries invade her mind now,
What was she before
Before she came to this quiet place
Where visitors stare but no words pass their lips.
Sometimes she wonders
Why do they look - then quickly avert their eyes,
Smiling to each other, but not to her.
What secrets do they share, but not with her.
They told her to come for a rest,
But that was years ago.
She's still here - they still smile
And she wonders why.

Sheila Carboni

Passion Tide

Wet sand between toes, squelchy and soft
Stepping on seaweed, slimy and green.
In the light of the moon, two lovers lost.

Waves gently lapping, edging in the shale
Tide and wind laughing, as they scrape it back again.
Salt water washed pebbles, making grated noises
Shadows in the moonlight dart upon the water.

Lovers lingering longer, arms and legs entwined
Never heard the thunder or the sudden changing tide
Lightening flashes streaking across the darkened sky
Two lovers lost, as angry waves leap high.

In the stillness of the dawn, before the sea-gulls call
Gentle lapping waters wash traces of the storm.
Salted pebbles murmur about the night before
They know where the lovers are, lost beyond the shore.

Olive Bridle

Behind Bars

Here I sit watching through the window pane,
The birds in the trees and children playing in the lane,

They do not know how free they are, I hope they'll never be
Imprisoned on the other side just like me.

I know it won't be permanent, but no matter how hard I try
I count the days and weeks, and hours that I will have to lie.

I know there's many people who never get about,
For years and years, they sit resigned, I have not any doubt,

That when my time for walking comes, I'll really appreciate,
The many people in the world on the other side of the gate.

I'll know when I walk free again, for I know that I will see
With different eyes those moments when I am free.

J. A. Knott

Rooftops

A view across rooftops, a certain kind of magic holds,
Beneath each one, what diverse tales of intrigue unfold?
Rooftops, slates, tiles, reds, greens, dingy greys,
Steeped in history, yet yielding to our modern days.

Rooftops above attics, concealing dusty family treasures,
A rooftop view is surely one of life's simple pleasures;
Rooftops, steep, stark, outlined against threatening sky,
Covering, protecting, keeping our precious dwellings dry.

Rooftops sparkling in the rain, water sliding down,
Shelter for those tired souls, hurrying home from town;
Rooftops, clad with snow, and glistening purest white,
So strangely changed after just one cold frosty night.

Rooftops in summer, creaking, expanding 'neath midday heat,
Rooftops in the fall, shrouded in mist, shapes incomplete;
Rooftops in spring, reaching up for air, fresh and clean,
A land of rooftops, a world set apart for that special dream.

Jan Falla

Good-Bye

She was in agony as a bullet of pain
Shot up her arm.
The pain thrilled her: As if she craved it.
She sat, and stared in awe
At the red liquid flowing from her body.

She had felt the anger beginning to grow
Inside her many months ago.
It was the creation of a new life, an evil life.
This anger had taken over her body and soul,
And now it was killing her.
She thought about the happy times,
When she loved and was loved.
But her wonderful life had crumbled around her,
Leaving her alone.

She slashed at her arms a second time
And began to cry, but it was no use.
She had reached the point of no return.
Her body became an island,
Surrounded by a sea of blood and tears.

Kerry Davies

The Roup

The auctioneer shouts a gither roon
The roups begun at Erchiestoon.

Hens and bantams and a braw crawin cock
A guse an a ganner an a fat broon deuk
A puckle fine stirks an a auld milkin coo
Twa three black faced yowes and a saddleback soo.

Tilley lamps, lantrens, kettills and a black porritch pot
Tables, chairs, beds an a auld grandfaither clock
Kists and girnels, harness an traps
Hyowes an spads, besoms and rakes
Wire and nails and troughs and hakes.

A battered auld Fergie that's served weel and true
Harras an barras cairts an tyres
Broadcast spreaders an binnels fer byres
Sacks an scales and tattie sculls
And pride o place a Thrashin mull.

Hey and strae, neeps and hashers.
Posts and strainers, fiddles and tapners
Happers and plucks, haimmers an pails.
And loads o fine firewid a fer sale.

Silence reigns faur ense there wis steer
Aye gane are the days of yester year.

L. M. McIntosh

Dawn Of A Silent Spring

This planet will surely become a lifeless place,
Due to greed and demands of the human race,
No wild animals prowling, no birds to sing,
We are heading towards a silent spring.

Governments demand economies to expand,
Putting more pressure on our precious land,
This human folly will surely bring,
A barren wilderness, a silent spring.

People of all colour, religion, and creed,
Must slow down demand, cut out their greed,
To all branches of nature, humans must cling,
To halt the progress of a silent spring.

Why must man, just for capital gain,
Destroy the forests, produce acid rain,
In his quest for power, man will be king,
Of a lifeless landscape, a silent spring.

The seeds we are sowing of self-destruction,
Will be more disastrous than any volcanic eruption,
Leaf-less trees, no bird on the wing,
Can we survive a silent spring.

Graham Longden

The Lottery (Of Life)

Every week we all wait in line
Silently praying, please let it be mine
Housewives, lawyers one and all
Glued to the telly watching the ball

Sitting there with eyes aglow
All six balls appear in a row
The tension, the terror, sheer despair
Am I really a millionaire

A call to Camelot then ensues
And they confirm the goodly news
In those few moments life stands still
Will it change things, I'm sure it will

No more living from hand to hand
Life from now will be so grand
Holidays, cars, a yacht, a plane
No, life will never be the same again

Life is a lottery, a game of chance
It can lead us a merry dance
Let's do as we will with our newfound wealth
But will it bring us happiness or good health?

Robert Grant Brown

Romantically Insane

An unquenchable thirst for women
(The excuse of the eternal bachelor)
"I always get bored and restless"
(The admission of a complex man)

"You need to give the more space"
(The words of a man looking hassled)
"You deserve someone better than me"
(Said the man looking for an excuse)

"You never know what's going to happen"
(The voice of insecurity and indecision)
"I really can't plan that far ahead"
(Somebody looking for somebody else)

"I struggle with relationships"
(This is really a one night stand)
"This really wasn't supposed to happen"
(Everything went exactly to plan)

"It's never felt like this before"
(Because it's never been done before)
"I've been waiting to do this for ages"
(I've been waiting to do this for ages!)

Roland Guy

Adam And Eve

I met with a guy called Adam in the park last week,
Wandering through the daffodils the wind
Swayed heavily about the heat of golden sunlight.
He struck me as very handsome, being the first
And all. They say you never forget your first.

I sat there on the rickety bench watching
Him move through the flowers, bobbing
Like a butterfly, I imagined pulling his wings,
Having him wriggle in my hand
Helpless and hungry for wind and flight.
The new spring sun clothed my neck
With a pleasurable breath. For a second,
Just a moment, I closed my eyes, caught between
The cold earth bench and the biting light.
I closed my eyes to pleasure,

In the beginning fruity and juicy
But after the first bite there was no other.
I opened my eyes and Adam was gone.
My neck ached and the breaking day
Signalled another way out of paradise.

Ruth Bourke

A Poem Is Good to Be Read

It's good for the living
And is good for our dead.
It goes on forever
Weather's cold right now,
But soon it will be spring
Where flowers bloom and birds will sing.
So love one another all year through,
Where ups and downs will worry you.
But with our love
Things will go right
All the day and night
Our Lord with us
And by our side
So we can go through the
Year with pride.

G. H. Care

Too Late For The Sun

You were never as old as I am now,
Yet it was I had youth enough to spare.
My life touched yours for such a little while,
But time enough for love to spark and flare.
Now, my magician gone, enchantment fled
I have no silver wand that I can raise;
No miracle will bring your voice again,
No loved hand will soothe the weary days.
Sometimes an echo of the time passed by
Whispers to me and you are near once more.
Then I can smile and face the world anew -
Remember happy days long gone before.
Too late for the sun we enjoyed the moon.
I came too late, my love. You came too soon.

Natalie Thomas

Dreaming

Dream not of today, but of the past or future yet to come.
Fond memories of people past, and present there are some.

Mother, Father gone but still they linger on in reminiscences
of Joy and Sorrow, as life still goes on.

Where do all the Nightmares go as with the night comes dawn.
Swept away by sweet dreams when another day is born.

Ambitions it is said are Dreams but Ambitions I have none
except maybe to say that all my Dreams I've done.

But time is only borrowed and ambitions and dreams change
So maybe one day when the time is right my future I can arrange.

And so I keep on dreaming the past is far behind.
I look forward to the future and the joy of life I find.

Sheila Storr

Growing Up in a Sceptic's Eyes

Look at the young ones, how their eyes shine,
Why are they so different from yours and mine.
What do they know that we have forgot?
Do they see the light that we cannot?
And why does it fade the older they get,
Like a deadening disease we haven't found yet.
Before too long innocence is only fondly remembered,
Our childhood ideals lie dismembered.
Corrupted by race, religion and greed,
The embers of intolerance are the fire we feed.
When I was a child I saw pictures of men burning books,
I remember the hysteria and cold angry looks.
I still can't understand this manner of hate.
In these pictures do we see mankind's fate.
To hate someone enough to wipe out his thought
Is like being the first to point the gun and fire the shot.
Can I stand by my ideals come what may,
Can I look in the mirror and ask myself to say
What of you? Would you stand by and look?
Are you the kind to burn a book?

Alan Milby

The Tide Of Life

As the sunlight hides her lies,
Her tortured tears begin to dry,
No one hears her cry,
Then her feelings start to untie.

Does her mind collide with the tide,
Yes, but it will subside,
Or—maybe memories that were just supplied.

Dank air envelopes her nubile body,
Lies flood her veins like poison,
Searching to devour her very soul,

She's standing just like a flower,
And all are fixed by her power,
And yet so obscene, not meaning to demean
She—is only thirteen.

Emma Rutherford

I Want

I want to be by myself sometimes
I want to be alone.
I want to be on my own
to be free from you all.

I want to love you
without loving you too much,
I want to be here for you
but I want to be away somewhere,
I don't know where.

But I will always be near you
wherever you go, I will be there.

I just want you all to know
I loved every minute of your lives
and I wish to know you are happy, in love,
which is the best love of all
as we have loved each other all our lives.

J. Moore

My Family

When as a boy of tender years, my Aunts and Uncles lived very near
Every year they came bearing presents and cheer
The magic of Christmas they created, became so beautifully clear.

Party games were played by my Aunts who laughed and giggled,
And sometimes got a little pickled.
My Uncles in a circle sitting on the floor
Sang sad songs of comrades they lost in the war.
As a finale before going home they sang just one more.
'I don't want to be a Soldier. I don't want to go to war.'

On leave in the second war, I visited each Aunt in turn,
Was given a hug plus five bob and wished a speedy return.

I still visit them at Christmas, though not so very near
I hope they found the magic they gave me down here.
When I left the Cemetery it became much colder,
And voices whispering on the breeze were singing
'I don't want to be a soldier.'

K. Merchant

Heaven And Hell

You created us all in your image - but we're not equal,
Slipping from your grip - we just fall,
The fires of hell are burning - as we get nearer,
Satan's hand out held - we feel his claws.

I've called to you alone - with a broken heart,
A world veiled by tears - torn apart.
Famine war and trickery - you put us to the test,
Where are we left to turn to who knows best.

Where are the times in the night - when I need you,
Where are the answers - I pray
Bleeding and torn we all live in this madness.
Stumbling and starting to fall
Living our lives in a time filled with darkness,
Is heaven like hell, for us all

Dallas Wilson

A Poet Born?

I was a child awakened by a storm
my cat was heard crying outside forlorn,
and when my mother would not heed my plea
by letting my pet back inside with me
My frustrations I vented out in rhyme
the poet inside me was born, aged nine.
That moment I've remembered through the years
still using verse to show my joys or fears.
This option gives freedom for thoughts to fly
above all else like a bird in the sky.
Sometimes the words just flow straight from the heart
but others they stumble right from the start.
Myself I lose while sorting what I feel
and writing it down makes it very real.
The gift of expression is there to use
be it in prose or verse I'm free to choose.
That's part of the challenge of poetry,
finding out individuality.
When I write poems they make me feel whole
because they are me and come from my soul.

Linda Bagnall

The Ship That Slipped Its Moorings

Friendship - what does it mean,
Where does the ship come onto the scene.
The friend part was right, but where were the morals
All I seemed to gain was heartache and sorrows.

I had a friend, a friend so rare
but she stepped on my 'waters', how did she dare.
My mind's still confused and in a terrible muddle,
My heart is torn and life's a dreadful struggle.

The 'ship' from my friend has sailed away,
It left its safe harbour, it ended that day.
That was the day that she broke my heart,
And from my life 'so sad' she must now depart.

I miss her now, I probably always will
my friendship and love she did kill,
She Trod on my 'waters' and my heart did drown
Will I smile again, or will I always frown?

Rekindle this friendship - I'm not so sure
The ship is still missing, maybe forevermore.

Tracy Bessey

Hope

Sat here, wondering what to do next,
Knowing that life doesn't run to a text.
Ups and downs, there's plenty around,
Looking for problems, there's plenty to be found.
You have to wonder what it's all about,
At the same time, wanting to scream and shout.
'Why are we here?' 'What is the meaning?'
'Is life real?' or 'Are we just dreaming?'
The same routine day after day,
Must get out, must be a way.
It's hard to imagine how life could be,
You shut your eyes, not wanting to see.
But yet, there's hope, a positive thought,
The negative vibes should always be fought,
There's always someone worse off than you,
Not easy to remember, when you're feeling blue.
Look, the sun is out, the birds are singing,
Answer that phone, a friend could be ringing.
A light is on, there's hope at last,
I'll go and grab it, before it flies past.

H. E. Piggott

The Death Of Life

The stillness of the blood in my veins,
pains my unbeating heart.
And as my final breath hangs on free flowing chains,
my fear is that for now we must part.
What waits in the shadows of death's lifeless kiss,
shows no sign of afterlife, of the life I know I shall miss.
For I cannot take you with me,
though your hand is in my own.
Please my darling, forgive me,
for against my will I must leave alone.
The oblivion of our separation,
is the death of the life that we share.
But look to the life within your memory,
and as sure as the sun,
you will see me standing there.
May I serve as a companion,
when darkened nights grow cold.
I will always be your partner,
remember the face of my soul.

Brendan Pollitt

One Life

We only have one life; there is no dress rehearsal
We none of us have time to study our lines
We often never say what we really feel in our hearts
And yet an angry word can often slip from our lips easily
Our feelings get bruised
And our dreams crushed
We all sometimes hurt one another without meaning to
And yet most of us are capable of such love and compassion
Enabling us to give friendship and comfort
To our fellow human beings
We are all jewels
In life's rich pattern
And although some may appear to shine more brightly
In truth we all have the same worth
We all have a starring role in this play called life
We must not judge one another by our costumes or the
    scenery that surrounds us
The best we can hope for is a long run; with many curtain calls
And that when the final curtain falls
We leave the audience thoughtful and smiling

Kim Harrison

Alone

Each morning as my eyes open,
It's the same.
I feel empty, life is meaningless.
What used to be a happy, fun-loving person,
Is now hollow, barely alive.
The days stretch out before me.
Long, tiresome
Nothing to look forward to.
Hunger comes rarely.
Surrounding me, other people's perfect lives.
Not mine, not me
When I was with him,
I was alive, carefree, content.
Nothing could hurt me
But now our love is gone
I ache for him,
For his smile, his touch.
I know I will never feel the same.
He was my life,
And now I'm alone.

Chantelle Ashby

The Moon And I

Just a short verse
I feel inclined
The subject, the moon
Combined with my mind.
For the moon you see
Has a power on me
An energy twisting with heat
And when it is full
I am crazed with a passion
And the whole town can hear my heart beat.
But you must understand
That we go hand in hand
Though I tell you this tale with despair
And to let you all in
To this secret I sing
Is something I never would dare.

Lara Yeolanda Semeraro

Only My Friend

So you think you have all the answers.
Well you feel it's fun to try.
Until the end of forever, you will always ask why
the only one who ever cared, you would rush away.
Always and forever a game to play today
you think tomorrow will never come
but I tell you, my friend, it will
and when he lands fool, in control, will be you, still,
control of what, an empty space, where none would ever dare to be
so, no one came to be controlled, by one so sensitive as you
would you ever understand why all were so scared of you
you are the dream maker, oh yes, all things for all
how could anyone deny it feelings wall to wall.
But how long will the dream last this time, my weary friend
you want control, you take control, I humbly hand you all
for in your pleasure, you lose the treasure of feelings without end.
Until the time you crush in pursuit of pleasure, my dearest friend.

Sue E. Henderson

"The Eyes of Hunger"

The eyes of a child, full of hunger
Who will feed her, or heal her pain,
She knows no anger, she is a child
Will she ever trust again?
Before the bombs, she laughed and played
She knows not why she feels such pain.
No food, no water for her tiny frame
She falls down weeping, surrendering to pain.
The eyes of hunger slowly close
She is at peace at last, the hunger finally gone.
This earth we walk, this air we breathe
Who will save her now?
Oh, mankind, what have you done?
The eyes of a child we see no more!

Patricia Fisk

Him The Boy

The child inside begins to weep,
For better days and peaceful sleep,
And riches gained beyond compare,
To live his life without a care.

He does not understand the rules,
The world outside is full of fools,
His feeling are all ones of rage,
He reads a book, tears a page.

Within her womb he was safe and sound,
Inside the walls they could not hound,
Decisions then he did not make,
But mother did just for his sake.

The easy option one might say,
To admit his feet are made of clay.
His frustration, weakness, hope and joy,
He the man, him the boy.

Sian E. Davies

"An engine house where time....."

An engine house where time stands still,
No raucous diesels ere lorded it here.
The gentle giant that powered yon mill
Toiled in silence, for fifty year.

Now for the engine they are but a dream,
The days when it lived, its life blood steam.
The days and nights when its silent power
Was used by man in his industrial tower.

But all is not lost to this noble machine,
As it slumbers in shadows and sunlight beams.
It's still well cared for, its brass-work gleams,
It's oiled, and greased, and its paint-work cleaned.

Preserved as a tribute to the pioneers,
To Watt, Trevithick, and their peers.
To the men and machines of Steams' heroic past,
For this old engine, works finished at last.

Brian A. Prowse

Daddy

Daddy, are you there?
I thought I heard you calling.
Maybe that is just wishful thinking on my part.
Sometimes I feel, I sense and smell you.
People ridicule experiences that I feel with all my heart.
They don't realize that memories are really not enough.
Get on with your life, you are young so be tough.
If only I could but I miss you so much.
Love and security was what could be sensed by your touch.
On the day you died, we mourned and we cried.
Life has never been easy since that dreadful day.

Mummy's still here, she misses you lots.
Now I'm all grown up and ready to marry.
I hope you'll be beside me on my wedding day.
As a child I remember you called us tiny tots.
There's so much I long to tell you.
Well, I guess you already know, I'll love you for the rest of my days,
Daddy, and I'm sorry you had to go. This world is such a very big
place and sometimes we get lost on our way. Watch over,
protect and guide me in all that I do and say.

Sharon McCabe

I Give You

I give you the oceans in calm and storm,
    With waves that dance in the air;
I give you the showers and the winds
    And summer days, warm and fair.
I give you the rainbow that springs from the sun,
    The clouds that drift slowly by;
I give you the vision of anger and peace,
    With beauty to feed the mind's eye.

I give you the buzz of the insects,
    The drone of a plane overhead;
I give you a night beneath the stars,
    Another snuggled warm in a bed.
I give you the flowers, the bushes and trees,
    The birds and the beasts of the field;
I give you a crop of wishes and dreams
    With the pleasures each harvest will yield.

I give you a heart to fill up with love,
    The chance of a life free from cares;
All these things I gladly will give,
    If you will give Me your prayers.

May Park

The Battle Lost

Struggling to complete,
Playing to compete,
Working, never resting,
Never stopping, never jesting.

You are told to work
Making you shirk
Responsibilities, have them!
You have none, you avoid them.

They want you to be good!
All you want is food.
Nagging, everlasting, they don't stop,
You lie constantly, eyeing the clock!

You watch T.V. at home,
You let your parents come.
Ignoring them, hating them,
You failed. You have no shame.

All they wanted was you to be good. The Best!

Marryat Stevens

"Man's Progression"

The land we tread, the land we feel,
with the Lord, we fail to deal.
The seas, the lakes, the rivers and ponds,
we fish, we swim, we skate upon.
The mountains for views, we look upon.
From whence they came, we dwell not on.
The skies, the clouds of white, grey and blue,
to look at in wonder, not I or you!
The sky at night, a sight to behold,
The moon and stars in a big black hole.
The Lord created this wondrous earth.
Which we take for granted with fun and mirth!
We care not of chemicals into rivers are dumped.
We care not of rockets, into clouds they bump.
We care not of trees, being hacked to the ground!
It might behold us all, to take a look around,
because of this, when no more we see, you and I;
for sadly then, it will be a time to die.
Sadly we give no thought to the MAN,
who created this world and left it in our hands.

Elizabeth Prothero

Be Still . . . Listen

And poet weeps
as chars of human rags
are carted, dropped in foetid hole.

Yet still he weeps
on countries green that rainbows lose,
where scars run deep and vogue boutiques
show cosmic pools from modern spools:

Those shapeless ghouls, ragless and still,
numb running sheep that carted still
are topped in putrid hole

Now poet dares to bare his soul
'kin trumpets blare of Jericho'

Ne'er still he cries
"Reign peace on earth
for ye men of goodwill . . . "

But drowning skies
weep on a million flare . . . Still!

Maria Dolores Kirkop

Ode For The World To Be Struck Dumb

What use are words?
When all they do is
Break the unsuspecting heart
And dampen starry eyes.

I'd gladly lose my lonely peasant tongue;
An example to men,
Light of mind,
And, oh, too free of speech.

The beauty of a silent ear,
An ancient slave freed from infinite grief,
Saved the pain of sweet God's voices,
Gently whispering their savage goodbyes.

Ode for the world to be struck dumb.
And all language, to perish on our illiterate smiles.

Take my voice and I'll be forever,
Blissful in my ignorance.

Oonagh Brady

Hampshire Rivers

Poplar and willow lined
they smoothly,
meandering,
ripple their way seawards.
Gentle and crystal clear,
weeds waving,
speckled trout filled
sleekly, fishily swimming.
Calm, placid and quiet,
smooth flowing
they gently move
south to their salty homelands.
Paddling place for children
their weirs;
picnic places
for families being happy.
Escape for men fishing, relaxing
at peace. Their world with nature communing.
Such beauty slow flowing, just curving,
quietly through meadows of gently sloping downlands.

Pat Rees

Timeless Time

A child wanders amongst the rock pools,
As such has been for a million years and more,
For here is home, it's where we live,
Or, it could be, on some far and distant shore.
And the timeless joy, come look and see,
Some beautiful creature of God's creation,
Accepted as is, as is as was,
And simple, innocent, childish fascination.
Look out there, where sea and sky are joined
What lies beyond is but child's imagination.
Time on time, yet mysteries still remain.
'Tis time on timeless time of Revelations.
Some revealed, though not yet understood,
By the wisest intellectuals in the land.
For how can we mere mortals,
Ever! expect to know what God has planned.
He has promised, all will be revealed
Before the passing of the age.
Whilst angels watch over everything we do,
This is nought but yet another page.

J. H. Evans

A Hidden Poet

She walks down the street every day,
She's totally normal in every way,
She's not really mad, not really weird,
She fears the same things that we've always feared,
But she holds a secret and no one would know it,
That inside her heart is a hidden poet,
Life goes on and people die,
You take a deep breath, release a sign,
You climb up so high, you fall to the ground,
Your ears start to thump with every sound,
But she holds a secret and never will show it,
That inside her heart is a hidden poet,
She looked so happy but also so glum,
While walking so slow, inside she would run,
She doesn't look different, just totally strange,
Any odd thing she'd always arrange,
But she holds a talent and never will grow it,
When inside her heart is a hidden poet.

Marie Ready

Time...

Time will never stop and watch
Though years go sailing by
Time will never keep those lives, who surely are to die,
And yet we find a tiny space,
To keep those years inside,
To surely prove to everyone
We've lived a happy life.
And because our life is precious
We only have one chance,
One Sunrise in the morning,
One endlessness to dusk.
And when we reach our final dreams
Time still carries on,
Never stopping just to glance
In case the time is wrong
And yet in life we pass our pleasure,
From father on to son,
And when we're gone, we only hope
Those dreams will carry on.

Debbie Pattison

My Motherland

So much corruption greed and starvation
The suffering is so much the pain the same
So we seek salvation

Oh such leaders without foresight
So blind they have turned our day to night
A barefoot kid walking to school
Unknown to him what tomorrow brings

They invent strategies to suffer the common man
But one man's invention is another man's intervention
Three decades ago the 'biafran' war had destroyed the people
How could my people face this again
All the struggle over the past would be in vain

Home sweet home she is blessed with all mother nature
has to offer, yet she weeps in pain
as she fears everything is down the drain
And so where do we go from here
They say if it ain't broke don't try to fix it
But if it's shattered, how do you fix it?

Enoh Agege

Wishing

I often wish that I could do,
Things impossible, for you,
My sight is good, it should not be,
That you could fail in sight, not me,
My age is sixty years this Fall,
But you my son, no age at all,
Of all our gifts I am sure I'm right,
There's none more precious than the gift of sight.
We with sight so clear and bright,
Forget to think of others' plight,
There are operations, this is so,
But when things go wrong, it leaves us low,
For months we wait, improvement to come,
Before you can have the other done,
You battle on, take it in your stride,
While I myself feel sick inside,
But I know you and how you try,
And deep within there's a clear mind's eye,
Your mind's eye, will see you through,
in everything you have to do.

Doreen Drummond

Life

Life is full of mysteries
Full of happiness and pain.
But even though we learn by mistakes
We'd repeat them all over again.
The many nights of anguish
Which continue over the weeks,
The many sleepless nights and tears,
Fallen down one's cheeks.
It can happen to anyone of us,
Today, or maybe tomorrow.
First, you feel the pain inside,
Followed by tears of sorrow.
It's as though you've been stabbed in the back.
the knife twisted round and round.
No-one can feel the pain but yourself;
And you need not make a sound.
But the pain you really do feel it.
And there's nothing you can do.
Except, maybe look to tomorrow,
Which maybe brighter and happier for you.

Anne Thomas

Untitled

Looking closely into their eyes,
I know so little about their lives;
Once ageless figures I looked upon,
Their eternal being suddenly gone.
Much frailer now than ever before,
What can I see as I gaze once more;
How must they feel when we talk months ahead,
What would we learn if their minds could be read.
To no longer plan for the years to come,
But to sit and remember all they have done;
Of dreams youth made and goals that were set,
Ambitions achieved and those not met.
I paid no attention to the tales that they told,
I never thought that they would really grow old.
Will it be for me like it is for them,
Will my children's children repeat it again,
Telling tales that they don't want to hear
Stories of old, year by year
To look in the mirror and see their eyes,
Still knowing so little about their lives.

Julie Heeley

"Memories"

In a foreign land where he chose to roam
An angel came one day to take him home
So full of life, and dreams, our lovely son
Laughing, loving, but too soon gone,
I wonder, can he see the tears that fall
Each evening when we go to call
Does he hear the birds sing in the trees
That sway gently o'er him in the breeze
So quiet now, no slamming door
No shouts of laughter, no music roar,
No noisy friends the house to fill
Memories, shadows everywhere still!
And yet! This winter will not forever last
Soon the future will become the past
Again to look upon the face we love so dear
Forever at peace, no more tears.

Mary Boland

The Sea

The sea the sea the roaring sea,
It cares not that we stand there,
With howling wind blowing through our hair,
With large waves comes stones and wrack,
Then draws nearly half of these back,
Screeching gulls fly overhead,
With sharp eyes on those throwing bread,
As the tide receded and the wind dropped,
The throwing of the flotsam and jetsam stopped.
Now exposed is shingle and sand,
Where not long ago mighty rollers would land
Be careful be careful don't venture too far,
Waves still race up and sweep over the bar,
Swirling waters now wash the sand clean,
And now not a sign where footprints had been
Ever so slowly the tide draws back,
And small gullies it leaves in its track,
What a wonderful day this has been to behold,
Watching nature's forces unfold.

N. DeBreanski

He Was Mine . . .

I thought it could last forever
The one great love of my life.
Did he promise me anything - never!
I'll never become his wife.

How do we get involved
With those we have to share?
It's a fact, never to be solved
We shouldn't but why do we care?

Children play a major part,
We mustn't hurt or leave them.
So sorry, my love, you can have my heart,
But anything else is forbidden.

Why did I love him so much?
We hardly had any time.
I'll never forget his love, or touch
He was mine . . . for a while.

Lorraine Roddy

Untitled

Someone to tend me when I was small,
Someone to watch me when I grew tall,
Someone who taught me right from wrong,
Someone who put me to bed with a song,
And leave me in comfort with a night light.
someone to get me up for the day
Someone I know I can never repay
Someone I loved more than any other
That someone was simply mother

K. Foster

Promise Fulfilled

No rain to assuage earth's thirst
Not even a mist to lay the dust
The gardens just as parched as we
Yielded but little husbandry.
A cup of tea could no more suffice
Unless it was very cold - with ice!

Day after day of relentless heat
Sweating bodies and swollen feet.
Not a cloud in the blue, blue sky
Not a breath of wind to cause a sigh
through the leaves of the trees, so still
No rain the reservoirs to fill.

Were we being punished for complaints of rain?
As we're wont to do, time and time again
But no, our God did not forget
For at last came welcome, glorious wet.
His promise fulfilled, our needs supplied
Our thankfulness we should not hide.

Jean Haffenden

Why? (on visiting Normandy war graves)

Oh God, why did there have to be a war?
Such destruction of human flesh
Was any good purpose served at all?

Beneath lush green turf decayed bones lie
Of those who were given no option
How many of them would have chosen to die?

"Theirs was the Glory" we have many times read
But does such a glory compensate
For the rich full life they would have led?

It's hard to believe that so many men died
On the threshold of manhood.
Oh God, was such a wastage justified?

Today we talk blandly of the "Chosen Few"
But it doesn't appear a few to me
Cold white crosses row upon row
Oh surely God these should not be?

Joan D. Armitage

Maddie

You were such a cute ball of yellow fur
The day we chose you at the cat and dog home
Having travelled ever so far
We named you Madelaine, Maddie for short
A pretty name for you, or so we thought
Little did we know that lovely summer's day
That you had rather wild ways
Naming you Maddie was an appropriate name
You were not an easy puppy to train
Three years of obedience classes did not do the trick
All you want to do is play and lick
We still love you even with your eccentric ways
You are a one off what more can we say
The people who gave you away
Don't know what they are missing
Their loss is our gain, more with each passing day
Your endless love and devotion
Is worth putting up with the garden devastation
Holes dug in the lawn, plants uprooted
Maddie you drive us to utter distraction.

C. Findlay

The Experience Of Love

T oday I sit here all alone waiting for him.
H e who was once my true love. That
E vening when I saw the last of him.

E very day I sit and wait for that man who lifted up my heart and then broke it.
X mas was the best of all, the presents he gave me, he gives me no more.
P eople used to smile and greet us. Now they greet me on my own.
E very night when I go and put the kettle on for one, when I am used to two.
R emembering the good times we had, memories is all I have to comfort me.
I n bed at night it feels so cold when I am used to his warmth.
E ven though I have the memories of him it is not the same as seeing him in reality.
N ow my heart is beginning to heal, I know for sure it won't heal completely. The
C ause of him leaving me is a story never to be solved.
E very day I wait and wish that he would get in touch.

O ver the months I have had relationships but they will never be the same.
F riends buy me flowers and candy just to make me smile again.

L ove is the most powerful emotion.
O ther men have asked my hand in marriage, but I turn them down.
V arious people tell me you only live life once. I just take
E ach day as it comes.

Stephanie Peters

I Owe It All To Animals

I owe it all to animals, I don't know why
It's just the feelings there and really high
Sweet little pets, hamsters, insects and other little pets
Big loving animals who care and stay to guard
Ones who like playing in my backyard
Creative, imaginary or realistic
Once my friend Johnny had this said to him
"Johnny, I thought you were better than to go and buy a big Red Setter"
It was then put on a trial period and he was looked after and brought
people lots of joy

This happened to lots of my friends, tiny hamsters to five foot rattle snakes
Personally I bought out the pet shops of all these animals and cared ever since
For caring it can be very rewarding and brings lots of joy
But remember a pet is not a toy
It is a living soul
Treat it with goodwill and give it a caring home
I guess what I am trying to say, is
Care and think before taking on
One day you might owe it all to your pets just like me!

Emily Chiappini

A Reality

Walking along the neat gravestones I feel really down,
So depressed I've come to visit the loneliest part of town,
Look at this one, a 3-year-old boy gone from this life before he could start,
And the verse below it of his parents, died of a broken heart,
Further along I come to another,
A nice black headstone there for a 25-year-old mother,
This one here is for an 18-year-old lad,
And right next door is for a 38-year-old dad,
I sit on a bench and try to take it all in,
As an old shuffling lady walks past me to put still fresh flowers in the overflowing bin,
She slowly arrives at a faded old headstone and lovingly puts new flowers in the pot,
The sweat pours down my face the day is so hot,
Then it hits me, what the hell am I doing here?
What right have I to feel sorry for myself, it's insulting for the
left loved ones who never fail to appear,
All these dead people I bet wished they were where I am now,
It's as if they are saying: get on with your life, take it day by day, you'll get through it somehow,
So I start to feel better and head for the gate,
And reader, if you are ever depressed, visit a graveyard and read of
life's casualties. You'll feel better, I know you will, mate.

Roy Walters

The Moon

It had been raining, it's stopped now.
I got out of my bed and looked at the silvery full moon
The moon was shining on the silvery raindrops hanging from the tree.
In the pond I saw the fish swimming about in the moon's shadow.
The clouds were white with the moon splitting them apart.
The water was shimmering silver with the moon's bright sparkle
The street lights were nothing compared to the moon's light.
I went to bed dreaming of the moon.

Andrew Kay

Blossom

There is a soft sheet of golden grain,
By the river-side, where daffodils remain,
Underneath the sea-blue sky,
Where white clouds go sailing by.

A ripple of waves on the pebbled shore,
And trees full of fruit from the week before,
Below the cliffs that stand so high,
Gently sleep as evening draws nigh.

A silent rustle from the Whisper Wood,
As the day decides to shed its bud,
And say hello to the sapphire sky,
To sing the clouds their lullaby.

Jenny Harold

The Sun, Moon And Stars

The marriage of the sun and moon is an enviable one,
The day is blessed with the sun's warmth and light.
And, he shies away at night to let the moon
display her splendor along with her children, the stars
her light guides them across the galaxy but a few
stray into the black holes, where they are consumed by
the harrowing darkness.
And on these nights when she mourns the death
of her young one, the clouds comfort her as a veil
from the night; she becomes a crescent.
As she cries, the mist hangs over the ground, covering
everything in its path.
On the eclipse they come together as one and you can
see her shining bright and clear on the night of
the birth of her stars.

Fauzia Rizvi

The Sketcher At Lukov

She evades them a while, tucked away
beneath the trees, off the fitful path.
Head angling back now her gaze absorbs
the infirmity of the plank bridge carrying
its flimsy surmise to bold stone stacks.
She gleans the ruins, others clamber.

Only a bright delicacy permitted by her eyes
claims her solidity for womanhood as she sketches.
She casts lines into the past of the strategic hollow,
the brick supported stones, the weathered walls
that aspire to and crave horizontal assurance.
She craves assurance too, but is left stranded
like the walls, her lines failing to catch a glimmer
of the sieges, feasts, peasants and pecking poultry.
Her eye is replete with suggestions and tales
failed by her hand, harried by her judgements.
The mocking light silting through the lettuce green
Spring leaves glitter its perfection on even drab
stones before registering as leaden smudges.

Gregory Jones

Us Three

My friends and I are having a romp
Round the park today.
Our owners said, "Now just behave!"
But we're in a mood for Play!

Ben's got the ball, so it's free for all.
Tackle him, round and round.
Rosie's squashed and lying quite flat
But Bunty's holding her ground.

Whilst the ladies chat, no holding back,
The ball is just alive,
Three happy dogs play on and on
From four to half past five.

Now it's time to trot off home,
A moment here for sorrow.
But never mind, O musketeers,
There'll always be tomorrow!

Valerie Barton

Undaunted

Some folks mock us;
Their cacophonic guffaw, a painful pause.

Obviously, our thatched roofs are frail,
The nondescript mud wall now rats' trail,
No incandescent lamp for the night.
We stumble and fumble in fright;
Groping and moping.

Though our progress is imperceptible,
We remain resolute and incorruptible.

We shall neither equivocate nor falter
Before their disparaging negative verbiage.
Like the eagles, we'll soar above the altar,
Into the vast, boundless sky of this age;
No encumbrances of spatio-temporal cage.

From our ruins shall emerge edifice
Of grandeur. From our crumpy mounds
Shall mighty oaks grow in wonder,
For we refused to go under and yonder...

Dan G. Awe

Of Fountains And Fantasy

Excitedly, busily jockeying for position,
rising higher, ever higher - until spouting
    yet spent with effort
momentum ceases, exuberance wanes
    leaves energy panting.

Residual damp, heightened plumes, fragile,
gently wind borne - weave a ghostly
    travelling curtain
stealthily drawing across space, only to
    dissolve into nothingness, uncertain.

Below, a shimmering carpet forms, pinpoints
of silver sparkle, laid firmly
    yet disappearing in vulnerability.
All is perpetuity, unceasing, subtly changing
    cycles, linkage of continuity.

M. Atkinson

Real Friend

He is at the finishing of his play,
It is the evening of the day.
Like the setting sun, he is going to the horizon.
At the time of ending of a heated day.

He says I walk alone, and
Not found anyone at unevenness.
Got many friends of fair-weather,
All of them were blind of covetousness.

Who are you? At last of happiness -
Stand beside me, when I am penniless.
I say to him, to heave a sigh -
Oh! My poor friend you can trust me.

Nasrin Zahan

For Jimmy

I turned my gaze towards the limitless
Expanse of grey
The sea stretched before me
Heaving in unrelenting turmoil
Giant foaming barriers, fiercely guarding
The depths
Waves crash upon the rocks

Sunlight reflected on a calm green ocean
Fragmenting into a myriad of sparkling
Diamonds
Dancing in uncontrolled gaiety
Radiating warmth and pleasure
Waves sigh on golden sands

Jane Bauld

The Bold Young Knight

The sky was dark, dim and cold
that one young knight stood proud and bold.
One hundred foe he had to fight
steadfast steed with reigns held tight.

His battle cry so strong and brave
on this day he'd see his grave,
he charged with pride and valour he
let noble Lord and martyr be.

All battle scarred and weary now
he bid his foe defiant bow,
with head raised high he saw his chance
blooded arm held tight his lance.

He fought and thrust with all his might
his foe could not believe their sight,
but fatal wound he had sustained
his heart that beat so strong now wained.

Sixty nine he killed that day
those who stood in righteous way,
true, a knight, a king at best
honoured now he's laid to rest.

Ivan Faith

The Gallant Soldiers

The Mars hauled out the siege artillery
Amidst cheers and encomiums.
They waved the freedom flag proudly,
The bravest men of this time.

They sang songs of justice,
Of fairness and of equality,
Each thirsty for the traitors blood.
They read messages of hope,
Of love and of a better tomorrow,
Unmindful of the thorny roads.

They fought, they bled, they wailed, some died,
The gallant soldiers for liberty.
Some cried, some fled, some slumped, some swooped.
They remain as always most undaunted.

Though the path they tread be rough,
Though the sacrifice to make be much,
One day, one bright summer day,
They shall sing the victory song.

Bassey Isoh

The Spider's Web

Delicate fusions of gossamer thread
woven across the sky
back and forth like jewelled stars
giving shape to the spider's web.

Patterns of eternal thoughts and strife
invisible links which join
hand in hand as if to form
the necklace or life.

Delicate, yet deadly paves the way
for dreams must first be spun
and ladders climbed
to reach the light of day.

Each step demands a great respect
and inner thoughts are known
across the Universe
to where all promises are kept.

And something which was once begun
can never be devoured
for where the spider's web is joined
a whole new life transpired.

N. Smith

For Your Christening

A baby born one summer's day
Seemed like you'd never come
With innocence and peace you lay
And love for everyone.

The bluest eyes I've ever seen
A smile that's cute and coy
Could only be dear baby dean
A darling little boy.

I want to watch you slowly grow
Into a happy child
To know you, help you, watch you
Breathe contentment, calm and mild.

So be happy little baby
For your life has just begun
May your days be filled with sunshine
My precious Godson

Beverly E. Pearce

Winter

Like a horse in a frenzy
Wild with rage
The winter weather
Turned like a page

A page in a book
of a season so old
with days full of darkness
and always so cold

The sky bleak and grey
The clouds scatter rain
The weak sun's glow gone
To shine is such pain.

Jane M. Smith

Metamorphosis

After long dull hours of waiting
Through the mist the sun will gleam,
Snow will melt disclosing flowers
Ice turn into bubbling stream
Sleeping nature, once foreboding
Wakes and tells us of her dream.

After whirlwind, storm and tempest
Comes a gentle cooling breeze
Bowing down the lazy grass heads
Whispering, tickling to tease,
Buds the barest branch will soften,
Out of thistles fly the bees.

Noel Sargant

Jack, You Were That One Star

*Dedicated to dear 'Jack' who was known
everywhere, especially Brean,*

Jack, you were that one star
That put a smile upon everyone's face,
Jack, you were that one star
Everyone you met, in any place,
You listened to their troubles,
You turned a frown into a smile
Jack you were that one star,
Shining in life so bright,
You were my soul mate, and dear friend,
Although inside you were a lonely man,
Jack, you gave your 'all' to the end.
I shall miss you Jack, your advice, your guiding hand.
You will not be forgotten Jack
The wind will whisper your name
As I walk at Brean, Somerset, along the sand.

Ruth Dunstan

Advent

Blue clouds in the dark night
A dappling of colours;
Blinking flashes of lightning
A Christmas light monotone;
Whistling easterlies blowin' wet
A dry spell redeemed;
Tingling smells of rusty freshness
A water-dust melee uncovered;
Thundering rhythms in the night silence
A skydance, mead for the Gods;
Swaying trees like dry laundry
A joyous exodus to greenery;
Tap tap on my zinc roofing
Like a cobbler's hammer routine;
Barechested, a cold poet on the balcony
A cardinal moment to capture;

Heralds the coming of the new rain.
Ogbogu Ubaka

Because He Claimed

Because he claimed to be the son of God, Jesus was flogged.
Pilate, what did you do handing over to soldiers this innocent jew?
On his head they put a crown of thorns, this man you crucify is the
savior of the world. You put on him a purple robe, he's struck upon
the face for all the human race. Why!! For you and I, he came to die.
As he hung on the cross he said, "Father forgive them for they know not
what they do." This sacrifice was special; it was for me and you that
whosoever believes in him shall not perish but have eternal life,
(John Ch.3: v.16) he became the human sacrificial lamb; this
was in God's plan! Then all was completed so that the scripture would
be fulfilled. Jesus said "I am thirsty"; water they gave him not, with
vinegar they soaked a sponge, put it on a stalk of the hyssop. When
Jesus received the drink, He was near the end. Can you hear my friend,
he bowed his head. Jesus was dead. How cruel people can be. Jesus
loved us so much. He died to set us free, that our sins might
pardoned be. One of the soldiers after Jesus hung his head. Pierced
Jesus's side bringing a flow of blood and water. He had already died.
They divided his garments and cast lots for his clothing. Is this
horror story true?? I believe it. It's up to you.

And we complain.
Hilda France

Nothing's Left And Nothing's Right

Like a bank account in January my life is empty because you're not here,
Like a will held in probate my life's on hold because you're not here,
Like a story without a moral my life is meaningless because you're not here,
Like a joke without a punch line my life is pointless because you're not here,
Like a criminal evading justice my life is full of desperation because you're not here,
Like a tiger lacking stripes I'm not complete because you're not here,
I've given my heart to a man that didn't want it,
I've given my soul to a man who has no use for it,
I've given my love, my life to a man with no comprehension of the power he holds,
He who is no longer in my life holds it in his hands,
Please give me back my life, the others are all lost my heart, my soul, my happiness, my ability to love,
I know how much you love me through you couldn't see it too.
The things that I am missing are yours without a doubt,
But you don't know you have them so you cannot cast them out,
If you took time to look inside yourself you'd be surprised at what you'll find
But if you did I know for sure you'd be back by my side
Ann Pearson

A Daughter Of Suffolk

I am the daughter of Suffolk soil,
Of humble birth and humble toil,
My heritage the sun-drenched corn,
The luscious grass, the heavenly morn.
I roam again the leafy lanes
Where as a child we played such games,
And paddled in the sparkling streams,
More often now in happy dreams.
Could I pull the curtain back
And frolic in that lovely stack.
The joys that were, remain with me,
The blackberry bush, the hawthorn tree,
The mushrooms on the dewy meadow,
And marshmallows a heavenly yellow.
The Suffolk punch, so strong and proud,
It makes me want to sing out loud.
Oh thank thee Lord, for all the joys
You gave us then as girls and boys.
Ruby Robertson

Day After Day

From a distance his shadow is proud, defined and understood.
Why therefore does the owner live outside of life's brotherhood?
Has he not still the same blood or was it all put to waste?
Did he really throw it all away or did other hands help haste?

Paper promises, paper love hang on the ignorant surroundings.
Paper people, paper minds follow what they're told is their horizon.
The scene is desperate and is perfectly set for its photocopy image to go,
But our truth is only repeated lies, so it's easy to pretend not to know.

I've learned what I was told I would learn, and now what follows
For the broken man and soul is only long forgiven sins and sorrows.
But who'd tell the nearing man his tears make no sense?
Fear is the virtue of the man who's only fear is violence.

So leaning my eyes away from his cold stare, and in the darkness of midday,
I pull the rags of clothing and start on my pointless journey my way.
For the point I set out to make is forgotten. Is that not unholy absurd?
Especially when the point I set out to make was not and will never be heard.

Lifting his voice from the enveloping fog of such deep profound thoughts,
Whispering to be acknowledged but not exercising the vocal chords.
I replied slowly before we wandered off dangerously close to the end.
Unlike the diaries of the loved man, I didn't know a name, but a friend.
Karl Hulme

Biographies
of
Poets

ABBOTT, CHRISTINE
[b.] 3 May 1951, London; [ed.] Degree 2.1 Social Sciences at the age of 41; [occ.] Tutor in F.E. I teach Literacy.; [oth. writ.] Article for newspapers, I have written my life in poetry as yet its not been published.; [pers.] I write poetry about my life to help me cope with my own feelings in order to be whole so if within my words you feel sadness, laughter and joy, I know it has all been worth it.; [a.] London

ABBOTT, TINA ROSEMARY
[b.] 1 October 1979, Canterbury; [p.] Rosemary Abbott, Charles Abbott; [ed.] Simon Langton Girls School, Canterbury, Kent; [pers.] This poem is dedicated to my close Uncle Roy, who died suddenly at the age of forty-five. He is missed greatly.; [a.] Whitstable, Kent

ABRAHAM, KELVIN
[pen.] Kelvin; [b.] 16/09/66, Dominica (Wi); [p.] Josephine, Patrick; [ch.] Kyhan; [ed.] St John's Roman Catholic School, Waltham Forest College, East Ham College of Further Education; [occ.] student; [pers.] The world is full of richness. Let's enjoy it without destroying it. My inspiration comes from the love and respect that I have for humanity and the earth.; [a.] Stratford, London

ABRAHAMS, JODIE
[b.] 14 October 1981, London; [p.] Helene and Tony Abrahams; [ed.] Still at Chancellors Schools Brookmanspark; [occ.] School girl; [oth. writ.] Nothing published; [a.] Brookmans Pl, Hertfordshire

ABRAHAMS, MARK
[b.] 25 May 1952, Botesdale; [m.] Barbara; [ch.] Kate, Victoria; [occ.] Chartered Surveyor and 'Architect'-working for N.H.S.; [memb.] Associate of the Royal Institution of Chartered Surveyors and Member of the Association of Planning Supervisors; [hon.] Architectural Design Awards; [oth. writ.] My work is extensive including poetry, music, songs, books and plays which are gradually being edited for publication.; [pers.] Spanning all subjects for all ages, my writing delves into the deepest meaning of existence but maintains a light heartedness enabling difficult subjects to be more easily interpreted. Influenced by those I love and my experienced by those I love and my experiences, my work is the essence of life.; [a.] Norwich, Norfolk, UK

ACMAN, LORIETO
[b.] 10/12/51, Iligan City; [p.] Vicente Acman and Geronima Virtudazo; [m.] Grace Mary Mercado Acman, 22 Dec. 1990; [ch.] Patrick Joseph Acman, Frances Josephine Acman, Lorigrace Acman; [pers.] Simply stop planting the seeds of steel.; [a.] Initao, Misamis Oriental

ADEGBESAN, GBOLADE
[pen.] Gbolie; [b.] 24 November 1975, Ibadan, Nigeria; [ed.] Abadina College Ibadan, University of Ibadan (U.I.); [occ.] student; [oth. writ.] (List of poems, short stories, plays, and novels all unpublished); [pers.] I strive to reflect the oddities of nature and human standards with other aspects of human's strivings in connection with his environment thereby evolving a conclusion that transcends its face value but deep in reasoning and full of meanings.; [a.] Ibadan

ADERIBIGBE, J. AYO
[pen.] Olorun Ara; [b.] 17 April 1937, Gbongan; [p.] Mr. & Mrs. S. A. Aderibigbe; [m.] Phebean Olufunmilayo Aderibigbe, 17 December 1966; [ch.] Adesola, Olusayo, Oyeduntan, Adesubomi; [ed.] St. Andrew's College, Oyo Nigeria, St. Paul's Anglican School, Gbongan Nigeria; [occ.] gardening; [memb.] Christian Benevolent Group, St. Paul's Ang. Cathedral, Gbongan and Nigeria Union of Pensioners, Ayedaade Branch, Gbongan; [hon.] Teachers' Certificate Grade two.; [oth. writ.] 1.Novels: Robbery in God's Name and Angelina. 2.Poetry: 12-14 short poems and The Dais (A Satirical Epic) 3.Auto-biography: Here So Far. None of which was published due to unfavourable conditions / unconducive environment. [pers.] "The Still Small Voice"; [a.] Gbongan, Osun

AISTROP, WILLIE
[b.] 20 April 1922, Sheffield; [p.] Willie, Doris May; [m.] Florence Sheila (deceased May 8th 1993), were married 2 April 1966; [ch.] Alan Stephen, step-son; Kathryn, step-daughter; [ed.] Council School; [occ.] retired; [memb.] Wales Jubilee Social Club & Institute, Shallownest Miners Welfare Club, Stoodbroke Community Centre (Dance Sect.), Darnall Community Centre (Dance Sect.); [oth. writ.] Short verses for relatives and friends for social occasions and for my late wife's demise anniversary; the long and latest poem inspired by the beauty of my first glimpse of the Scottish Highlands, January 8th 1996.; [pers.] My father and mother acquired a home on a new council est. When I became school age there was not a school in the vicinity. When my sister was nearing school age, my parents transferred to an area with school in the vicinity, therefore I was late starting school. Mother taught me to read via newspapers. I left school one week prior to fourteenth birthday. Commenced work in a rolling mill on fourteenth birthday. Dancing is the love of my life. Courtesy is an admirable companion.; [a.] Sheffield, South Yorkshire

AKINSANYA, OKE
[pen.] Akin Oke; [b.] 11/05/65, Ile-Ife; [p.] Akinlayo and Comfort Oke; [ed.] Adventist Grammar School, Ede, Nigeria; Obafemi Awolowo University, Ile-Ife, Nigeria; [occ.] Management Consultancy and Business; [memb.] Member Oyo State House of Assembly (1992-1993); Associate member Nigerian Institute of Management; member, Nigerian Marketing Association; [hon.] B.A. Hons (philosophy) - 1989; Post Graduate Diploma in Management Studies (DMS) - 1992; Masters in Business Administration (MBA) - 1996; [pers.] "Always allow events to take their natural course". I have been greatly influenced by the situation and events in which I find myself in life.; [a.] Ibadam, Nigeria

ALCOCK, JOAN C.
[pen.] Cecilia Allan; [occ.] Registered Nurse - Young Physically Disabled; [pers.] I am inspired by experience of life and all that it may bring.

ALDER, GWENDOLINE
[b.] 15 August 1920, London; [p.] Lionel and Elizabeth Osborne; [m.] Albert, 12 December 1942; [ch.] Michael, David and John; [ed.] Various Army Schools and St. Frideswides Girls School, didcot, Oxon; [occ.] Housewife; [memb.] Milverton Horticultural Society and R.S.P.B.; [hon.] R.S.A. Certificates for English; [pers.] My poetry is all spontaneous and from the heart.; [a.] Taunton, Somerset

ALDRIDGE, DAPHNE JEAN
[b.] 17 May 1934, Balham; [p.] Florence May, Alfred Frank Aldridge; [m.] Peter Aldridge, 1 May 1954; [ch.] Andrew Peter; [ed.] Ravenstone Secondary School; [occ.] Retired; [oth. writ.] Few poems published in Local Social Club Magazine "Logogram"; [pers.] The base of every thought is poetry; [a.] Welling, Bexsley, Kent

ALDRIDGE, KATHLEEN I.
[pen.] Kate, Katie; [b.] 16 May 1923, Stalham, Norfolk; [p.] William Woodbine and Rachel Althea Sandell; [m.] George Aldridge, 25 March 1978; [ch.] Grahamy Stuart Leslie, Vanda Kathleen and Trevor Stanley; [ed.] Northwalsham High School, Norfolk gained Cambridge School Leaving Certificate 1939; [occ.] Retired; [oth. writ.] "Eastern England" published in "Poetry in Motion Eastern 1994", The Pig on the Wall published in "Island Moods and Reflections 1995.", "Our Eva" to be published in "Jewels of the Imagination 1996/97"; [pers.] Time is the most valuable asset anyone can have may it be used wisely and economically, with love and care; [a.] Cambridge, Cambridgeshire

ALEXANDER, ROSALIND
[pen.] Rosalind Alexander; [b.] 5 March 1950, Birmingham; [p.] Ella and Alec; [ch.] 1 Daughter, Victoria Helen; [ed.] 1. Marsh Hill Girls Grammar/Tech., Erdington, Birmingham, England, 2. Birmingham College of Food; [occ.] Voluntary Worker; [oth. writ.] War Crime - Between a Laugh and a Tear, unpublished poetry for personal pleasure; [pers.] Dedicated to Clint

Williamson, your work has meant so much to so many, may you continue making this world a better place for a long time to come.; [a.] Den Haag, Netherlands

ALEXANDER, STUART
[b.] 13 June 1964, Leeds; [p.] Kenneth and Winnifred Alexander; [m.] Susan Catherine Alexander, 31 August 1985; [ch.] Marc Scott and Rachel Dawn Alexander; [ed.] Agnes Stewart C of E; [occ.] Retail Store Manager Leeds Industrial Cooperative Society; [oth. writ.] First attempt: In poetry competition I have more poems written.; [pers.] I consider my poems to be true to life in that you just don't know what will happen next. I strive to amuse.; [a.] Leeds, West Yorkshire

ALFNES, INNI
[b.] 1 April 1976, Jerusalem; [occ.] Student; [pers.] Through my writings I try to understand and reflect on human ideology, the relationships between good and evil, past and future, and so discover new ways of thought and a deeper insight of microcosmos within macrocosmos.; [a.] London

ALI, NASIMA
[b.] 16 July 1975, Birmingham; [p.] Jerina Ali; [ed.] Wilson Stuart School Then Onto College (Hereward); [occ.] Student; [memb.] Book Clubs; [hon.] Have won Various Medals for Sports over the years but nothing for me my writing until this. I'm very proud, to achieve this type of merit.; [oth. writ.] Do write all kinds of poems and short stories, yet nothing published until now.; [pers.] This poem I sent was inspired by someone very special to me. Now, always and forever. My poems are a reflection of who I am, without them I would be a 'closed book'.; [a.] Birmingham

ALI, SHUMAILA
[pen.] Mala; [b.] 25 Jan 1972, Karachi; [p.] father: Kalimullah, mother: Mumtaz Kalim; [m.] husband: Nadeem Ali, 22 Dec 1992; [ch.] one daughter: Amaniah Ali; [ed.] St. Joseph's College, BA in Economics & Maths; [occ.] housewife; [memb.] Table Tennis Club, Bradford; [hon.] Bachelor of Arts in Economics and Maths; [oth. writ.] A booklet titled 'Ode She Wrote', comprising about 20 poems (each one titled individually), yet to be published. Several proses, too.; [pers.] My writing portrays my moods and the way I have felt the life around me. They all carry a moral point of view. 'Good Art is a miracle blessed by God on the mankind through His blessed people'.; [a.] Birmingham, West Midland

ALLEN, DONNA LEE
[b.] Nurnberg, Germany; [p.] Clarence Dale and Florence E. Myers; [m.] Woolsey Allen, 25 June 1977; [ed.] King's Park Primary School, Lurgan Girls' Junior High School, Lurgan Technical College, Lurgan, County Armagh, Northern Ireland; [occ.] Secretary School Board of Manatee County; [oth. writ.] Two poems published, winter 1997, sparrowgrass poetry forum, additional two poems to be published, summer 1997, sparrowgrass poetry forum anthology books, "Treasured poems of America"; [pers.] Writing poetry is truly an inspirational experience, and I hope to pass them along to others because there is nothing more brilliant than reading poetry to brighten one's day. When stressed, to write a poem, gives me a great release on life that I feel the whole world has been lifted off my shoulders.; [a.] Lurgan, Armagh

AMARAEGBU, NOBERT
[pen.] Odinaka; [b.] 04/06/72, Abgejah, Nkoerre L.G.A.; [p.] Andrew and Justina Amaraegbu; [ed.] Pri: Central Sch. Abejah, Sec: St. Mary's Seminary Umuowa, Orlu, Tert: St. Joseph Major Seminary, Ikot Ekpene; [occ.] Reporter, "Project '97'" Grapevine Communications; [oth. writ.] Meditations on the Lord's Prayer (Unpublished book), several unpublished articles; [pers.] I am a staunch opposer of modernity for in its lack of transcendence, in its atheism and anti-theism, in its moral relativism, in its autonomy, it furiously rejects the reality of God as a heteronomy. I have always tried to reflect this in my writings.; [a.] Lagos, Nigeria

AMARAL, TANYA
[b.] 13 November 1978, London; [p.] Antonio Amaral, Maria Amaral; [ed.] Convent of Jesus and Mary Language College; [occ.] A'level English, History, Government and Politics, Portugese Student; [hon.] 10 passes at GCSE Level, A/S Level Pass for English; [oth. writ.] Collection of Personal poems.; [pers.] In my poems I feel it's important to demonstrate emotions that readers can recognize and relate to. I have been emotionally influenced by personal experience.; [a.] Harlesden, London

AMBLAVANEY, HELENE
[b.] 05/08/75, Seychelles; [occ.] Receptionist Telephone Operator

ANDERSON, MORAG
[b.] 8 March 1946, Isle of Lewis; [p.] Ian and Mary McKay; [m.] Ian Anderson, 8 February 1974; [ch.] Two; [ed.] Secondary School; [occ.] Due to ill health none was a Stewardess; [memb.] Life Boat Church of Scotland Green peace; [hon.] I do some charity. Red cross life boat etc.; [oth. writ.] Poems published by local papers one poem published by Anchor Book; [pers.] I was both in a small village on the Isle of Lewis. I do love writing poetry especially when I'm depressed.; [a.] Liverpool, Ross-shire

ANGILLEY, BRICE
[b.] 7 October 1941; [m.] Mary Angilley, 30 March 1996; [pers.] This poem "My Love" is dedicated to my wife Mary on the occasion of our marriage.; [a.] Saint Austell, Cornwall

ANTONIOU, CHRIS
[b.] 6 March 1964, London; [p.] Anthony and Emily; [m.] Chrisonlla, 25 September 1994; [ed.] Comprehensive and further education with correspondence school; [occ.] Civil Servant; [memb.] Royal Naval Association; [hon.] Home office Craft Show Award (poetry section) Contribution to my Unit award at work, 2 other awards from my work; [oth. writ.] Short Story "A Dawn in Egypt" not yet sent to competitions. Our City Streets Won Best Editors Award International Library of Poetry.; [pers.] I express my life and beliefs through my work. And if people can say that that poem was a message of love, war etc, and can relate to it there I am content with my work.; [a.] London

ANUJA, KARAN
[pen.] Dinju; [b.] 29 March 1983, Trivandrum; [p.] R. Krishanan (Exe. Engineer, Electri-City Board) and Dr. V. Sobha (Head of the Dept. Environmental Sciences, Kerala University); [ed.] School student (IX Std.), Holy Angel's Convent School, Trivandrum; [occ.] Studying in IX Standard; Holy Angel's Convent School; [hon.] Won first prize for Science exhibitions in District level and was honoured by Sri. Chithra Thirunal Institute and Seaweed research Association, Madras for dance competitions. [oth. writ.] Some poems published in local magazines (English and Malayalam); [pers.] I have been influenced by my mother's character. I want to reflect her character through this poem. Writing poems makes me happy.; [a.] Trivandrum, South India

APPLETON, CLAIRE
[b.] 4 July 1982, Caerphilly; [p.] Michelle Appleton; [ed.] Still at School, St. Cenydd Camp; [memb.] Y.M.C.A.; [hon.] Had an award for my poem Carousel Young Writers; [oth. writ.] Recently had a poem published by my school for Young Writers Carousel, S. Wales.; [pers.] The poem that I have entered is a very special to me has it was dedicated to my dad who has recently passed away.; [a.] Caerphilly, Mid-Glam

ARCHER, MRS. LINDA JOYCE
[pen.] Mrs. L. J. Archer; [b.] 27 October 1952, London, England; [p.] Mr. Reginald and Mrs. Doreen Maynard; [m.] Mr. John David Archer, 23 December 1988; [ch.] Christopher, Georgina, Catherine and Michael; [ed.] Comprehensive School Member; [occ.] Housewife Mother, care Assistant to son poet author Lyricist; [memb.] The Child Growth Foundation, The international Songwriter Association Ireland; [hon.] The International Library of Poetry, Editors Choice

Award, "Every Child Is Special"; [oth. writ.] 4 other poems published plus another 3 to followed by Rivacre Ltd. Cheshire England since April 1996 I has penned Lyrics to 43 country songs. The 1st of which has just been completed and is in Nashville for consideration. Children book in test run at this point in time.; [pers.] I write for both children and adults. My dream is to become a lyricist. Though will never give up writing for children or adult poetry. I believe my writing to be a gift. My greatest influence is life itself. I love feel so therefore I am.; [a.] Hornchurch, Essex

ARMSTRONG, DAVID JOHN
[b.] 22 June 1972, Carrick Fergus; [ed.] Royal Belfast Academical Institution, Queen's University, Belfast; [occ.] Hospital Doctor; [memb.] Various Sports Clubs and Local interest Groups; [hon.] Medical prizes; [oth. writ.] Poems in anthologies and local reviews, short stories, local history.; [pers.] Influences - classical literature, the romantic poets, Hector Hugh Munro ("Saki") George Orwell.; [a.] Carrick Fergus, Antrim

ARNOLD, LISA CHARLOTTE
[pen.] L. C. Arnold; [b.] 21 October 1965, Cheltenham; [p.] Colin and Sheila Davies; [m.] Michael Alen Arnold, 13 December 1986; [ch.] Two children boy 8, girl 3; [ed.] 0-Level Eng Lit, 0-Level Eng. Lag. Geography, 0-Level History, 0-Level Art, 0-Level; [occ.] Housewife; [oth. writ.] 5 poems in 5 anthologies. Destiny - my own anthology booklet; [pers.] With my poetry and writing I try to communicate with the heart and soul of other human beings.; [a.] Cheltenham, Glos

ARULANANDOM, FREDERICA
[b.] 11 September 1975, Malaysia; [p.] Fred Arulanandom, Lucy Arulanandom; [ed.] St. Christopher's School (Malaysia), International School of Penang, Uplands (Malaysia); [occ.] Student; [memb.] The Alliance Francaise (Malaysia); [hon.] Distinction in grade 5, theory of music (piano); [oth. writ.] Several poems and stories published in school magazines.; [pers.] My poems often reflect my moods and the way in which I look at life and world.; [a.] Salford, Manchester

ÅSELL, VANESSA
[b.] 13 April 1978, Malmo, Sweden; [p.] Anders Åsell, Maria Åsell; [ed.] 7 years in Stocksund, Sweden 5 years at Benjamin Franklin International School, Barcelona; [occ.] Student in 12th grade at Benjamin Franklin Int. School, Barcelona; [memb.] Amnesty International; [hon.] Honor Rolls for High Standard of Academic Excellence, Ecis Award for International Understanding; [oth. writ.] For 7 years I have been writing in my journals, every day has been documented in 37 journals. Poetry for the literary magazine at school; [pers.] I admire Martin Luther King Jr. and I was very inspired to write after studying the civil rights movement, especially the Black Movement and the Montgomery Bus Boycott, 1955.; [a.] Barcelona, Cataluna

ASHLEY, MARJORIE EDWINA
[b.] 19 March 1933, Bolton, Lancs; [p.] Father - Dental Surgeon, Winifred Castelle Ashley; [ed.] Artist former member of Bolton and Blackpool Society; [occ.] Retired Children's Nurse; [memb.] R. E. G. Blind; [hon.] Diploma, for teaching handicap children Nursery Diploma; [oth. writ.] Poems; [pers.] Walk a low with guide Dog. Church poet. Arts and crafts started first guide Company in England for mentally handicapped girls goes primary; [a.] Saint Anne's, Lancs Nr Blackpool, Fyled Coast

ATKINSON, MARIANNE
[pen.] Marianne Atkinson; [b.] Hornsea, E. Yks; [ch.] Son and Daughter; [ed.] Higher (Dip H. Educ.) Hemberside University; [memb.] Haltem Price Art Group Cottingham E. Yks; [oth. writ.] Other poetry short stories; [pers.] Artist/crafts person. Some merits/sales in both. No published writings as yet. Imaginative, creative, with a strong interest in Observing all life around me. Enjoying the many colours in nature.; [a.] Hull, East Yorkshire

ATWAL, HARMINDER K.
[b.] 25 November 1979, Leicester, United Kingdom; [p.] B. S. Atwal and S. K. Atwal; [ed.] Currently a student at College; [pers.] Much of my inspiration comes from recent songwriters. Poetry can also help to express inner feelings.; [a.] Leicester, Leicestershire

AUSTIN, JAIME
[b.] 7 July 1978, Harrow; [p.] Barbara Austin; [m.] (Engaged) Russell Cox; [ed.] Barnhill Secondary School, Walford High School, Ealing Tertiary College; [occ.] Student; [oth. writ.] Various short stories, a story called "A Joint Betrayal" earning me a WH Smiths certificate of commendation; [pers.] I use both my poetry and stories to express myself, and my views on issues over which I have no control. My own life has influenced most of my work.; [a.] Ashford, Middlesex

AWE, DAN
[b.] 20th November 1956, Benin, Nigeria; [p.] James and Grace Awe; [ed.] Araromi Baptist Primary School, Lagos; Ibadan City Academy, Ibadan; University of Ibadan, Ibadan; University of Lagos, Ibadan; [occ.] Business Consultancy; [memb.] Nigerian Union Journalism, Corps for Education Advancement; [oth. writ.] screenplay writing, e.g. Entangled (1997); [pers.] Love will forever conquer hate and knowledge will forever govern ignorance.; [a.] Lagos, Nigeria

BACHKANIWALA, ANURADHA
[pen.] Anu; [b.] 28 September 1969, Surat; [p.] Kanti, Usha Master; [m.] Harish, 2 February 1990; [ch.] Prem, Dimple; [ed.] Commerce graduate; [occ.] Housewife and designer; [memb.] Royal Park Resort, Sterling, RCI Resorts.; [hon.] Several articles and poems published in different magazines got prize for them and received a lot of appreciation.; [oth. writ.] A collection of 100 poems to be published in the book form. Name of the book: "In Between Life And Death". (My poems covers all the feeling that comes in between life and death.); [pers.] Dreams and life, though confined to the 4 walls of your house, are free. Thoughts can never be imprisoned, for, they take the form of words, and with the help of your pen, they give life to your dreams and meaning to your life.; [a.] Surat, India

BAGNALL, MRS. LINDA
[b.] 23 December 1958, Fulford, York; [p.] John and Irene Kemp; [m.] John Bagnall, 24 May 1980; [ch.] Rebecca and Lisa; [ed.] Poppleton Road Primary School, Tadcaster Grammar School, York College of Arts and Technology; [occ.] "Little School" Pre-School Group Owner and Organizer (NNEB); [pers.] I am thrilled to have my first published poem which I would like to dedicate to my family who I love dearly.; [a.] Haxby York, N. Yorks

BAILEY, M. W.
[pen.] Popeye; [b.] 4 November 1952, Thurnscoe; [p.] Eric Bailey and Hilda Bailey; [m.] Divorced; [ch.] Richard, Alan and Simon; [ed.] Comprehensive; [occ.] Labourer/Factory worker; [oth. writ.] Untitled poems published in "Red Hot Lovers" by Anchor Books; [pers.] All the words are felt in my heart but put there by the woman I love, Christine Wall who greatly inspires me to put pen to paper.; [a.] Retford, Notts

BAKER, DAWN
[pen.] Twiggy; [b.] 13 September 1963, Plymouth; [p.] David Rogers and Betty Rogers; [m.] James Baker, 20 September 1986; [ed.] Efford Secondary, Modern School, Efford Plymouth; [occ.] Domestic Asst. 15, years; [oth. writ.] None, this is my first competition; [pers.] There's an old saying, no one can take our memories away. When I wrote this poem it was for someone with whom I worked for many years, we had laughs, also tears, but stayed friends for many years.; [a.] Plymouth, Devon

BAKER, LESLEY
[b.] 24 June 1945, Hillingdon, Middx; [p.] Jean and Victor Cooper; [m.] Raymond, 31 July 1965; [ch.] Simon, Andrew and Lisa; [ed.] Harlington S. M.

School; [occ.] Administrative Assistant; [memb.] Psoriatic Arthropathy Alliance; [oth. writ.] Several poems published in anthologies.; [pers.] In my writing I try to reflect on the joys and sorrows of life.; [a.] Street, Somerset

BAKER, ROBERT
[b.] 25 January 1946, Bristol; [p.] George and Hilda Baker; [m.] Sylvia Anne, 9 November 1968; [ch.] Paul James, Michelle Louise; [ed.] St. David's College Bristol (1962), Bristol Polytechnic; [occ.] Computer Software Manager; [memb.] British Computer Society (M.B.C.S.); [oth. writ.] Many poems written but none, until now, submitted for publication.; [pers.] Influenced by many poets but primarily the romantics, specifically wordsworth. My main poetic theme is pantheism, encompassing spirituality, immortality, nature and childhood.; [a.] North Walsham, Norfolk

BALL, CHARLES JOSEPH MANTON
[pen.] Wordsworth; [b.] 13 January 1970, Congleton; [p.] George Joseph Ball, Rosemary Anneball; [m.] Angela Michelle Ball (nee Maines), 25 March 1995; [ed.] Astbury C. of E. Primary school, Heathfield High School, Congleton. Heathfield High Six Form Centre. Hartford Art College, Northwich.; [occ.] Postman.; [memb.] Congleton Snooker Club. Congleton Park Bowling Club. Congleton Coronation Bowling Club. Walkers Bingo Club, Hanley; [hon.] Runner-up Cyril Tonge Memorial Trophy 1995, Congleton Top Boy Swimmer 1978. Congleton Horticultural Society Best Marrow Grower 1986, 1992.; [oth. writ.] Three poems published in anthologies by anchor books. For poems published in anthologies by Triumph House.; [pers.] Poetry to me is, a picturesque statement of ones influences and desires, written in a humorous and challenging way to attract others to read and share your inner sanctuary of literary thoughts, hopefully gaining enjoyment and satisfaction from it.; [a.] Congleton, Cheshire

BAXTER, DANIEL
[pen.] Michael Noble; [b.] August 26, 1978, London, England; [p.] Mary and Michael Baxter; [ed.] Lower Canada College (Grades 3-7), Ashbury College (Grades 8-12); [occ.] Student; [pers.] I wrote "If Life Were A Garden" when I was 14 yrs. old. I am currently collecting my more recent poetry and insights to form a novel I have been greatly influenced by Molliere, Voltaire, Dickens, and Bronte.; [a.] Ottawa, Ontario, Canada

BEALE, ELIZABETH ANNE
[b.] 22 January 1942, Bedfordshire; [ed.] Grammar School Bedford, Mander College Bedford, Diploma in Psychology; [occ.] Writing poems; [oth. writ.] Several poems published over 30 yrs. Parnasus publications and competitions. (N.B. I have never won a prize.); [pers.] My poems strive to form simplicity out of complexity of human emotions. I have been influenced by Brian Patten.; [a.] Flitwick, Beds

BELL, MR. GRAHAM RONALD
[pen.] Alexander Topcliffe; [b.] 13 October 1972, Leeds; [p.] Mr. Ronald Bell and Mrs. Margaret Bell; [m.] Miss Anju Kumar (Fiancee), to be married in spring 1997; [ed.] Snaith school, Selby Tertiary College, Magdalene Collage, Oxford; [occ.] Unable to work as a result of chronic I'll health; [memb.] Member of the Magdalene Association graduate of the Royal Society of Chemistry Member of both Oxford and Cambridge Universities; [hon.] BA (Hons) in Natural Sciences, Christie prize for Natural Sciences (Cambridge), scholar of Magdalene College, Cambridge (ie. Elected into a Scholarship for Excellence in University Exams); [oth. writ.] Poem Published in "Pure Poetry", a forward press anthology, Scientific Research Papers Published in International Journals (e.g. "Faraday Transactions" and "Molecular Physics"); [pers.] I am inspired by the likes of zola and flaubert I relish the study of the human spirit.; [a.] Leatherhead, Surrey

BELL, MARY NIGHTINGALE
[b.] 11 October 1930, Easington, Colliery; [p.] Frances May and Albert Duff; [m.] Jim, 18 March 1950; [ch.] 3 - 2 daughters and 1 son; [ed.] Easington Colliery Infants and Junior Seaham Harbour Girl's Grammar; [occ.] Retired State Enrolled Nurse; [hon.] I proposed Durham Litfest and was awarded a medieval garland from Denise Robertson for it. I was visited by Princess Helen of Romania after she read my sit poetry; [oth. writ.] Several poems published in local papers. Many short stories and a novel which I should see about getting published. Most are about the pit life of the area in which I have always lived.; [pers.] I have been greatly influenced by my father (dead for 31 years). He had learnt poems at school (which was paid 6 days a week) and I could receive all the nursery rhymes and children's poems before going to school. He was a pitman.; [a.] Easington Colliery, Peterlee, Durham

BENACS, PHILIPPA C.
[b.] 7 May 1944, Birkenhead; [p.] William George and Ethel Townson; [m.] George Benacs, 14 June 1986; [ch.] Mark Edward, Kathryn Jane; [ed.] Secondary School and Carlet Park College of Further Education; [occ.] Rest Home Proprietress, Bunkers Bounty Rest Home; [oth. writ.] Names of poems: Old Father Time and Hush My Baby, Name of anthology: Between A Laugh and a Tear. Name of poem: Snowflakes, name of Anthology: Jewels of the Imagination. Published by the International Society of Poets.; [pers.] From an early age I have taken pleasure in putting pen to paper. Expressing myself in rhyme. Now at 52 yrs. of age, I am truly delighted to be recognized as a poet. I believe a poem is not a poem unless it rhymes. The subjects vary, but my main theme has always been of my family. They are my inspiration and loved dearly.; [a.] Blackpool, Lancashire

BENNETT, HELEN
[b.] 6 November 1976, Slough; [p.] John Bennett, Pauline Hounsome; [ed.] Westgate School, Slough Middlesex Training Center Hayes; [occ.] Child Carer; [hon.] Guides- Baden Powell- Highest award in guiding; [oth. writ.] None- this is my first publication; [pers.] My writing has been greatly influenced by my friends and family, who I'm entirely grateful to. My greatest thanks goes to my Godmother Pam Hounsome and my grandfather George Hounsome for all their encouragement and support, without them this poem would never be.; [a.] Slough, Berkshire

BENNETT, RICHARD HEDLEY
[pen.] "Bakewell Burt"; [b.] 21 May 1949, Bakewell; [oth. writ.] "Tomorrow", "The Quiet One", "The Little Royal (Bakewell Show)", "Blackberry", "The One", "Thought for Easter", "Alcohol", "The Fishermen" published in various anthologies dating from 1994; [pers.] I'm a local, born and Bred- my great grandfather being the landlord of the Devonshire arms on Church Alley. My poems are nature or creation based - in the belief that that which was given for free - and to be shared by all - can never be overshadowed.; [a.] Bakewell, Derbyshire

BENZAQUEN, DINA D.
[pen.] Dee De La Roca; [b.] 3 February 1975, Gibraltar; [p.] Esther and Samuel Benzaquen; [ed.] Westside Comprehensive School, Gibrattor. Bury College, Manchester. Currently of King's College. University of London; [occ.] I am an undergraduate student reading French and Hispanic Studies; [memb.] University of London Debating Society, King's College French Society; [oth. writ.] My ultimate ambition would be to publish a book of Anglo-Hispanic poetry.; [pers.] In my writing I like blending fantasy with reality. Sometimes, it is too realistic other times it is too fantastic. But after all, fantasy in what makes life worth living and reality reminds us what life is all about.; [a.] Gibraltar

BERRY, ANTOINE L.
[b.] 30 May 1943, Saint Christopher; [p.] Anthony and Mary Berry; [m.] Carol Berry, December 1967 and December 1977; [ch.] Two daughter and three sons; [ed.] Bachelor of Arts Degree (Sociology and The Arts) and master of Philosophy (Sociology of Public Administration) Brighton University and the O.U.; [occ.] Manager - Policy and Strategy (Local Government); [oth. writ.] Many poems in various styles (But Publication not Previously Sought); [pers.] I believe strongly in social justice and personal choices. I try to reflect this philosophy as work in stoping social policy and as a magistrate in tempering justice with humanity. These themes are also evident in the poetry I write and enjoy reading.; [a.] Reading, Berkshire

BERRY, MICHAEL PATRICK
[pen.] Paddy Berry; [b.] 4 August 1961, Blackburn; [p.] John and Maureen Berry; [m.] Joanne Berry, 11 February 1995; [ch.] Daniel James John Berry; [ed.] St Edmund Arrowsmith's RC. Blackburn Lancashire; [occ.] Chef; [memb.] Just a humble member of the Human Race; [hon.] "Nothing of Note"; [oth. writ.] I have had some work, published by Anchor book's. (I have only ever sent four bit's of work out. So I am as pleased as punch to of been selected by you folk); [pers.] The words that tumble from my brain of love of life, of thing's never quiet gained, having people reading my simple script, I thank you all, be blessed with peace.; [a.] Accrington, Lancashire

BINSTED, CHRISTOPHER MATTHEW
[b.] 16 August 1975, Epsom; [p.] Colette Binsted and Adrian Binsted; [ed.] Glyn School, De Montfort University Milton Keynes; [occ.] Student (Architecture); [hon.] BA (Hons.) Architecture Riba Part One; [oth. writ.] 'Simon's Honour' - short story and editorial in Ebba's scrip (magazine of Glyn School Epsom). And 'looking, seeing, interpreting - subjective immersion in the built environment'.; [pers.] Enjoy your emotions, they are the only things that are truly your own.; [a.] Ewell, Surrey

BIRCH, EUNICE
[b.] 19 July 1940, Blackburn, Lancashire; [ch.] Justin and Ashley (2 sons); [ed.] B/Burn High, Leeds Teacher Training College; [occ.] Retired; [hon.] Junior Teacher N.N.E.B. Tutor, Church Pianist Foster Mother.; [oth. writ.] 'Deafness', 'War In The East' - published by Triumph House 1996; [pers.] I try to convey personal feeling re animals, and attitudes toward fellow men. Personal feelings re life's UPS and downs; [a.] York, North Yorks

BISHOP, JOHN R.
[b.] 31 December 1935, Fulham; [m.] Dorothy O'Brien, 5 September 1959; [ch.] Teresa Clare, Catherine Helen; [ed.] Lord Wandsworth College, Oriel College, Oxford; [occ.] Chief Examiner, A level General Studies; [memb.] Former director of Studies, Liverpool College; [pers.] 'Expatriate' was one of of a series of poems written when I taught in Uganda. I prefer writing verse to doing crosswords.; [a.] Liverpool, Merseyside

BISHOP, TOM HUGH NIALL
[b.] 13/08/73, Beckenham; [p.] Rev. A. P. Bishop, Mrs. R. I. Bishop; [ed.] Newlands Manor School, Seaford, East Sussex, University of North London, Huntingdon Regional College; [occ.] Mature Student; [oth. writ.] Several poems published in "A Postcard From Murmansk"; [pers.] My poetry has been influenced by the metaphysical poets Marvell and Carew. I try to illustrate the lateral actions of the mind, mankind's influence on nature and the world in which we live.; [a.] Huntingdon, Cambs

BLACK, ELLEN
[b.] Balinluig Perthshire, Scotland; [occ.] Housewife; [oth. writ.] Six poems published in poetry International 1974; [pers.] My writing, is influenced by my great love of animals and nature.; [a.] Southwaite Nr Carlisle, Cumbria

BLACKBURN, EDWINA
[b.] London; [oth. writ.] Poetry and verse, short stories, two half finished novels, nothing published.; [pers.] Our planet is weeping as we declimate her creatures and environment, we should treasure her and treat her gently before we muddle ourselves into a wasteland.; [a.] Salisbury, Wilthshire

BLACKMAN, STEVE
[b.] 9 October 1959, Crowborough; [occ.] Railwayman; [a.] Crowborough, East Sussex

BLACKWELL, BRIAN
[b.] 20 July 1935, Oxford; [ch.] 4 Children; [ed.] Southfield Grammar School, Oxford, Universities of Bristol, Leicester and Bradford; [occ.] Retired Lecturer: Taught Biology and Psychology in schools, F.E. and H.E. Colleges. Now teach (P/T) Management Psychology in Minsk Univ., Visiting Lecturer still at Minsk University of Linguistics (Belarus); [memb.] British Humanist Association, Labour Party, Standing Advisory Council for Religious Education (Leeds City Council); [hon.] B.Sc. Bristol Univ., P.G.S.C. Leicester Univ., and Adv. Dip. Psych., and Soc. of Education and M.Sc. Bradford University; [oth. writ.] 1.) For feeding poor Grandma, Aramby Press, ISBN 900462 206 (1996), 2.) The smile of lies, New Hope International, ISBN 0903610 191 (1996); [pers.] I strive to challenge the appalling elitism and selfishness in society with my poetry. I abhor exploitation. I maintain that the hierarchies of major religions are a major cause of many of the world's problems. (Marathon Runner throughout my 50s!); [a.] Leeds, W. Yorkshire

BLAKE, JOAN
[b.] 12 March 1946, Gorey; [p.] Roger and Alice Doherty; [m.] John Blake, 30 March 1974; [ch.] Alison, Jonathan, Dwayne, Beverley, Melissa; [occ.] Farmer, Housewife and full time mother; [memb.] Gorey Writer's Group, Mother's Union, "Community Alert" Group; [oth. writ.] "Family Value", "Spiritual Attraction", other poems published in Local magazines; [pers.] By painting pictures with words, I hope to stimulate a greater awareness of our beautiful countryside and the wonder of creation.; [a.] Gorey, Wexford, Ireland

BLAKE, JULIE
[pen.] Julie Krivinia, Julie Blakrywinia; [b.] 27 May 1950, Sheffield ; [ed.] Abbeydale Grammar School, Sheffield Hallam University; [occ.] Student of Creative Writing, Sheffield University; [hon.] B.A.(Hons) English Studies, 1983, Sheffield University Certificate in Theatre Arts, 1984; [oth. writ.] Poems published in University and other magazines. Two short self-published collections - "The Locked-Out Psalm" 1975, "Sharing Tables" 1977. Currently working on a longer collection entitled "The Secret of Feminine Spirit".; [pers.] My theme is the obstinacy of human yearnings thwarted by material entanglement. "Outside of Your Dream" is posthumously dedicated to Phil Ford, a soul-searching friend who died tragically at 29. I perform my poetry in aid of Chernobyl. My favorite poet is Baudelaire, whom I read in the original French.; [a.] Sheffield, South Yorkshire

BLANCHFIELD, MRS. KATHLEEN
[p.] Catherine and John Glendon (Deceased); [m.] Michael Blanchfield, 14 August 1969; [ch.] Denise, Marie, Caroline and Michelle; [ed.] Primary, Bonnettstown National School, Secondary Education Kilkenny, City, Vocational, School; [occ.] Housewife and mother writing short stories and poetry in my spare time; [hon.] Two achievements for, National Letter, short story writing from "An Post", 1995-1996 and received book with letters published each year, at a special awards ceremony in Dublins writers Museum; [oth. writ.] Writing some short stories and poetry in my spare time. One poem published in the anthology "Between a laugh and a tear in 1996.; [pers.] I appreciate the blessings of each day, and thank God for a healthy husband and family. I love writing, and my inspiration comes from my own feelings within as I study wonder of life itself.; [a.] Acragar, Ballyragget, Co Kilkenny, Eire

BLANQUEZ, ALEXANDRA
[pen.] Alex Hunyadi; [b.] 3 March 1976, Andalucia, Spain; [p.] Jose Holmes Blanquez, Maria Dolores Rodriguez; [m.] Engaged to James Logan; [ch.] Not yet, but loads of pets; [ed.] Ecoles Francaises de Seville, I.N.B. Murillo, Borough of Manhattan, Community College (New York); [occ.] A bit of this, a bit of that...; [memb.] Club Nautico (Sevilla) - Penfriends Writing Group (Limerick, Ireland), Member in the Cathedral of Sevilles Choir - Mensa; [hon.] 5 prizes in school competition (Poetry and short stories), 2 prizes in theatre production, 3 regional prizes in Poetry Competitions (Spain); [oth. writ.] Collaboration in Penfriends Book "Scratches in the Wall" (My story "Ohnaka and the Kayal"); [pers.] I am born every day, I die every day. I am twenty-six earth - years old. Raised in Spain, I have lived in too many countries. Where tomorrow?; [a.] Seville, Spain

BLUNDELL, WENDY E.
[b.] 23 July 1961, London; [m.] Brian Blundell, 29 November 1986; [ch.] David, Brian Blundell; [occ.] Elephant Keeper, Blair Drummond Safari Park; [memb.] (A.B.W.A.K.), Association British Wild Animal Keepers; [hon.] Certificate in Animal Management; [oth. writ.] 'Clwyd' published in Welsh poets; [a.] Thornhill, Stirling, Perthshire

BODENSTEIN, JUHA
[b.] 30 January 1953, Heilbronn; [p.] Lydia and Albert Walter; [m.] Helmut C. Bodenstein, 28 July 1974; [ch.] 2, Felicity and David; [ed.] Leaving Certificate in Munich, unfinished studies in music; [occ.] Poet and Housewife; [oth. writ.] Published, 'Liehend' by R.G.V. Fischer - Veilag, Frank - furt, 1995, poetry and prose in magazines, newspapers, literary magazines, several poems in anthologies; [pers.] I am amongst the last Romantics - or a Romantic of a new kind...; [a.] Cloorgee, Co Mayo, Foxford

BODRUL, ONJALI
[pen.] Shiba; [b.] 21 February 1981, Newcastle-upon-Tyne; [p.] Salma Bodrul and Syed Bodrul; [ed.] Currently studying for eleven GCSE's also attends Newham Academy of Music to play the double bass; [oth. writ.] I also write stories, as well as other poems — this is my first poem ever to be published.; [pers.] My poems reflect the world as I see it, and how I wish it was. I strongly believe that we, as humans, need to stop fighting with each other, and take into account, the things we overlook as unimportant.; [a.] East Ham, London

BOLAM, C. L.
[pen.] Catherine Middlemas; [b.] 3 August 1912, Alnwick; [p.] Robert and Katherine Middlemas; [m.] Robert George Bolam, July 1935; [ch.] Peter Bolam, Anne Bolam; [ed.] Sherborne School for Girls; [occ.] Retired; [pers.] This was written at school many years ago. There are no hills in Sherborne.; [a.] Rothbury, Northumberland

BOLTON, WILLIAM ERNEST
[b.] 20 March 1908, Wrexham; [p.] William and E. Bolton (Deceased); [m.] Violet (Deceased), 26 October 1929; [ch.] Vernon Owen Bolton; [ed.] Council School Buckley; [occ.] Retired October 28, 1972; [hon.] Stella Atois Local award 50 yrs service Deacon and Elder Long Service Award, meals on wheels 24 yrs MBE, 24th July 1996, by the Queen Chester Chron and Manweb Man of the Year; [a.] Buckley, Flints

BOND, G. MARY
[b.] 11 April 1937, Brixham; [p.] George Bond, Hilda Bond; [ed.] Paignton Secondary Modern, South Devon College, Torquay; [occ.] Domiciliary Care Agency Proprietor; [memb.] Lapsed Member of Church and other choirs due to pressure or work; [hon.] Various connected with career; [oth. writ.] A few unpublished poems.; [pers.] In caring for the elderly, I find poetry a useful means of jogging aged and failing memories. A pleasure restored to me by a dear friend.; [a.] Brixham, Devon

BOND, WALTER
[b.] 22 April 1953, Manchester; [p.] Walter and Margaret Bond; [m.] Elizabeth Jeanne, 25 August 1973; [ch.] Steven and Natasha; [ed.] Didsbury Technical High School; [occ.] Agricultural Contractor; [memb.] Served with the British Army for 15 years; [hon.] 65M UN Medal (Cyprus); [pers.] I believe that the poet is the modern story teller. A good poem will make sure events are remembered.; [a.] Lincoln, Lincs

BONHAM-NOYLE, KYRSTI
[b.] 3 March 1980, Swansea; [p.] A. and M. Calonyddaear-Noyle; [ed.] Home Educated; [pers.] In 1990, when I was 10, I moved from Wales with my family to a remote wind-swept island called Inishfree off the coast of Donegal. I'm nearly 17 now, and I'll be moving back to Wales shortly to go to college to build on my home education; [a.] Llanelli, Carmarthenshire

BONNER, AINE
[b.] 3 October 1982, Letterkenny; [p.] Francis and Teresa Bonner; [ed.] Arranmore National School #1, currently studying at "Gairmscoil Mhic Diarmada" on the island half way through; [occ.] 3rd year student; [memb.] Hola! (Royal Mail Penpal Club) Arranmore Island Rowing Club, Ceoltort Eireann. (Traditional Musicians); [oth. writ.] Several poems, songs and currently writing a short story.; [pers.] In my writing I like to bring out the feelings of people around me. I like to relate to the readers and produce a piece of work which they feel they can understand as apart of life. I am influenced by those around me.; [a.] Co Donegal

BORRILL, ANNETTE
[b.] 23 September 1946, Old Leake, Boston, Lincs; [m.] Michael Borrill, 24 October 1970; [ch.] Kate - 25 yrs; [ed.] I studied as a mature student at Boston College and with Nottingham University. In 1993 I obtained my Cert. Ed. (Adults) I taught Communication Skills at Boston College from 1984-1995. My work involved working with overseas students studying English, Special Needs students, Hospitality and Catering students, Health and Social Care courses and 'A' level students. I also worked with women returners and was Adult Basic Education Tutor and Co-ordinator for several years; [oth. writ.] Articles published: 'Lincolnshire Life' magazine, 'Loneliness' article in local newspaper, several poems in various anthologies, won $100 (editor's prize) in 'Dear Sir' magazine, poem on bullying was used by the 'Anti-Bullying' campaign based in London - and acknowledged by 'Childline' - it was also published; [pers.] "Words are a powerful, often abused, tool. I would like to think my words give a voice to some of those seldom listened to in our society. I write 'soul to soul' - rather than on an intellectual level. My late Grandfather, Bill Herd, was my inspiration to start writing."; [a.] Boston, Lincolnshire

BORWICK, MR. E. G.
[b.] 12 July 1941, Kirkwall, Orkney; [p.] George and Betsy Borwick; [m.] Mrs. J. L. Borwick, 20 March 1964; [ch.] James, William, Susan, Edward; [ed.] Educated at the Kirkwall Grammer School, Kirkwall Orkney; [occ.] Police Constable, A.E.A.C.; [memb.] Society of Amateur Artists; [oth. writ.] Christmas Questions "The International Society of Poets" The Survivor, Christmas Questions, Maid of the Seas "Flight 103" poetry now; [a.] Thurso, Caithness, Scotland

BOWEN, COLIN L.
[b.] 7 March 1944, Winchester; [p.] Leonard George, Ellen Elizabeth; [m.] Penny Anne, 10 December 1965; [ch.] Nicola Lian, Clayton Lee, Fiona; [occ.] Retired Professional Fire Fighter, now Psychiatric Nursing Assistant; [hon.] FSLS and GC Medel; [oth. writ.] 'Love Can Be Many Things' as of this date unpublished; [pers.] Writings based on life's experiences.; [a.] Hayling Island, Hampshire

BOWENS-JONES, BOBBIE
[b.] 17 January 1962, Islington; [ch.] Genna (18), Penni (15), Chloe (9), Kallie (6); [occ.] Writer; [pers.] It has always been my ambition to write, with much inspiration from my children. It is my wish to make them proud.; [a.] Tumbridgewells, Kent

BOWERS, JOHN
[pen.] Leighton James; [b.] 18 April 1946, Britain; [p.] Deceased; [m.] Pamela, 28 April 1990; [ch.] Boy, girl; [ed.] Secondary Modern City and Guilds 5 yrs. Pass.; [occ.] Disabled dug to serious lung problems; [hon.] After numerous attempts to children published whose remains were to say how good my work is, they have there own poets.; [oth. writ.] 50 poems typed on safety for children. Birth poetry, Bereavement poetry, almost anything.; [pers.] I feel that my work could be very beneficial, especially, in the times we live in.; [a.] N-u-L, Britain

BOXELL, JANET ANN
[pen.] Janet Ann Boxell; [b.] 22 July 1935, Street, Somerset; [p.] Charlie and Hilda Reed; [m.] Derek Sydney Boxell, 26 May 1958; [ch.] Timothy Sean and Neil Simon; [ed.] St. Louis Convent, Glastonbury, Somerset; [occ.] Company Sec and Director; [memb.] The Inner Wheel Club, Haslemere; [oth. writ.] Only to personal friends and family; [pers.] Expression in words of one's emotions.; [a.] Haslemere, Surrey

BRADBURY, IDA
[pen.] Ida; [b.] 25 November 1908, Burnley, Lanc; [p.] William M. Bradbury and Geraldine Bradbury; [occ.] Retired Shop Assistant; [memb.] Park Lane Operatic Society, Padiham Municipal Choir; [pers.] The love of poetry and singing has kept me happy and young at in heart.; [a.] Hitchin, Herts

BRADLEY, T. J.
[b.] 31 March 1936, B'ham; [m.] Lilian Mary, 3 July 1954; [ch.] Three boys; [ed.] St. Mary's RC; [occ.] L/ Rover - Engineering Co-ordinator; [oth. writ.] Short story, several poems published also travel articles in magazine.; [pers.] 'I never get serious'; [a.] B'ham, Warwickshire

BRADY, MISS LISA
[pen.] Lisa Brady; [b.] 2 January 1971, Liverpool; [p.] Daphney Turner and Tony Turner; [m.] Michael Thomas Knox; [ch.] Phillip, Andrew and Alicia; [ed.] New Heys Comprehensive School, Allerton, Liverpool; [occ.] Sales Person, for Dixon's stores, Liverpool; [hon.] Certificate of Achievement in successfully completing a full time retail induction course, in October 1996, Authorized by Dr Jon Stephenson and General Manager of Dixon's Stores, Mr. Graeme Hughes; [pers.] Poetry brings me closer, to describing the "real world" through my inner-self, sharing my thoughts and expressing personal view points with others. "Time For Thought" was wrote for my dear mother, Daphney to delegate Inspiration to overcome her problems.; [a.] Allerton, Liverpool, Merseyside

BRAHIMI, ALIA
[b.] 15 May 1980, Kansas, USA; [p.] Farouk and Kathleen Brahimi; [ed.] Government School in Algeria, Foley's Grammar School, Cyprus, St. Christopher's School, Bahrain, Stowe School, Buckingham; [occ.] A-level student at Stowe, History, English, Theatre Studies; [hon.] Assisted place at Stowe School Scholarship (Partial); [a.] London

BREATHNACH, EILIS
[b.] 6 August 1961, Burton-on-Trent; [p.] Thomas and Marie Brennan; [m.] Shane Walsh, August 6, 1988; [ch.] Thomas and Oran; [ed.] Knock N.S. Conent-of-Mercy, Borris-in-Ossory (Qualified Nursery Nurse and Montessori Teacher); [occ.] Mother and Housewife; [memb.] Aras Chronain (Irish Cultural Center) Clondalkin and Aras Chronain Patchwork Group; [pers.] Inspiration for my poetry comes from my family and everyday events.; [a.] Clondalkin,, Dublin, Ireland

BREIGE, CRILLY
[b.] 25th July 1975, Swatragh; [p.] Mary and Bernard; [ed.] Secondary, Higher Education; [memb.] athletic clubs; [oth. writ.] purely for personal pleasure; [pers.] I live for today.; [a.] Swatragh, Londonderry

BRIGHT, JOHN
[b.] 10 October 1970, Barnet, Herts; [p.] Mary Bright; [ed.] East Barnet Secondary School; [occ.] P/T Self employed Decorator/Gardener; [hon.] English Literature 'O' level Grade A; [pers.] My poems tend to express how I felt at the time of writing, and how personally I am affected by the subject.; [a.] Palmers Green

BRIND, AMANDA
[pen.] Christ Knight; [b.] 31 March 1976, Rush Green; [p.] Margaret and Grammar Hall; [m.] Kevin Brind, 14 October 1995; [ed.] Bromfords Secondary Sch., Southend Enterprise Training College; [occ.] Trainee

Financial Controller; [memb.] English Heritage, WWF; [hon.] Diploma in Business Administration; [oth. writ.] A total of eight poems published in various different publications.; [pers.] I would like to dedicate this, my eight personal achievement to my family and friends, especially my husband Kevin...with love.; [a.] Wickford, Essex

BROCKLEHURST, KRISTA MICAELA
[b.] 11 April 1981, Tameside; [p.] Mike Brocklehurst; [m.] Angie Brocklehurst; [ed.] Thornsett Primary New Mills Comprehensive Latimer School; [oth. writ.] Poems published in other anthologies; [pers.] Poems help me express my feelings and experiences.; [a.] Village Isham, Northants

BROMLEY-DAVIES, MICHELLE
[b.] 5 June 1955, Bishop, Auckland; [p.] Harold Davies, Eleanor Davies; [m.] Clive Vinnicombe, 1974 to 1994; [ch.] Carl Vinnicombe, Steven Vinnicombe; [ed.] Leeholme Secondary School, Bishop Auckland, Darlington Technical College, BP Auckland Technical College; [occ.] Probation Service Officer Durham county Probation Service; [memb.] Dyslexic Institute, Institute of Advanced Motorists, National Association of Probation Officers; [hon.] Studied A level Psychology, A level Sociology, NCFE Counselling Certificate; [oth. writ.] Several poems awaiting publication in a personal anthology, several poems published in a local women's monthly magazine.; [pers.] My work is written from the heart and reflects an inner spiritual awareness of beauty, relationship and love. It also enables a gentle feminine perspective of women moving towards equality, respect and freedom in all aspects of life.; [a.] Newton Aycliffe, Co Durham

BROOK, MARGARET ELIZABETH
[pen.] Maggie Brook; [b.] 2 January 1950, Birmingham, England; [p.] Sid and Gene Ryman; [m.] David Brook, 26 March 1983; [ch.] Angela Dee Lenny and Barbara Ann Brook; [ed.] Great Barr Comprehensive School; [occ.] Foster parent; [memb.] The Blues Band/ Manfreds Fan Club (Ready); [oth. writ.] Poem "In These Days" published in recent Anthology - `Word Of Mouth' by poetry today; [pers.] As one of Jehovah's witnesses, I care about people and get much inspiration for my poems and songs from the bible together with the plight of people today.; [a.] Shanklin, Isle of Wight

BROOKER, ANNE
[pen.] Megan Rolfe-Brookes; [p.] Linday Brooker, Bill Brooker (Journalist); [m.] Frederick Brookes, 17 March 1992; [ed.] Our Lady's Convent Hildenborough - Bexleyheath Technical High for girls; [occ.] Writer/Cat Breeder; [memb.] Various Chow Clubs F.A.B.; [hon.] 1st - Cadbury's National Essay Comp; [oth. writ.] Poetry and short stories, published in Australia (Sydney Morning Herald etc); [pers.] I was virtually reared on cabell and Shakespeare, and tend to write about the mystical aspects of life, and man's inhumanity to man.; [a.] Mkt Rasen, Lincs

BROOKES, KATE
[b.] 7 March 1964, Cambridge; [p.] Mary and Tony Fowler; [m.] Paul Brookes, 6 April 1996; [ed.] Willingham Primary School, Cottenham Village College, Cambridge College of Further Education.; [occ.] Unemployed, but I am a Nanny—between contracts; [memb.] Redditch Folk Club, Trinity Church Choir, With my husband, I am in Redditch Otters swimming Club for the Disabled (my husband is blind, but I am fully sighted).; [hon.] Caring skills in the community, 6 Different Training certificates, in the Scout Movement, I am a Cub Leader and Beaver Leader; [oth. writ.] Had a poem in "New Poetry 1981" had letters in "Cambridge Evening News" constantly for years. Had true story published in "Take a Break" magazine August 1996. Short true story in an anthology of pet stories - called "Tips and Tails", 1988; [pers.] I have wanted to be a writer since I was a child. The idea of other people reading and enjoying something I have written fills me with pride. I want to be a poet and author.; [a.] Redditch, Worcestershire

BROOKES, LAWSON HENRY
[pen.] Lawson Henry; [b.] 7 November 1911, B'ham, England; [p.] Ada and Harry Brookes; [m.] Olive (Deceased), August 1935; [ch.] Alan John and Anthony Lawson; [ed.] Self taught music, literature, drawing and painting; [occ.] Retired, Music and Writing; [memb.] Antique Collectors club, Cello in several orchestra; [hon.] Royal Marine War Service Medals; [oth. writ.] Poems of the Austrians outback, several short stories by Zola and Balzac put to UFRSE Numerous poems on all subjects; [pers.] I am driven alone by a perpetual urge to put in towards, a better understanding of my self, and my fellow humans and originality in all my work; [a.] Broadway, Worcs

BROWN, BERNARD
[b.] 1933; [ed.] Two years in the Royal Navy were followed by a RADA scholarship; [occ.] 40 years as an actor, touring the world with the RSC and Old Vic, and performing on TV and Radio; [pers.] Now retired, he enjoys sailing and looking after his disabled wife, Joycie, at their Emsworth home. His first poem to be published, "Through a Glass Darkly", appeared in *Quiet Moments*.; [a.] Emsworth, Hants

BROWN, JEAN
[pen.] Eujeanie; [b.] 14 February 1937, Yorkshire; [ch.] Two sons, one daughter; [occ.] Design and make Christening Gowns; [oth. writ.] Non published, but lots in my memory box in my poems I try to write what I feel, also many of my verse are little piece of my life.; [pers.] When the window of life looks dull, make an effort to clean the window.; [a.] Leeds, Yorkshire

BROWN, PAULINE
[pen.] Donna Grey; [b.] 11/07/54, Liverpool; [p.] Edna and Lyndon Browne; [m.] Separated; [ch.] Lydon, Maria, Stephen Browne; [ed.] St. James Comprehensive , Charles Woolton College, Sight and Sound College; [occ.] Housewife; [hon.] Diploma for Secretary work; [oth. writ.] I have four other poems: "All Alone", "Little Mo", "Autumn Leaves", "Reflections"; [pers.] I am a single parent who has a big family and a lot of friends. I have been writing poetry for a long time.; [a.] Liverpool, Lancs

BROWN, STEPHANIE
[b.] 5 February 1980, Birmingham; [p.] Sharon Smith and Karl Brown; [ed.] GCSE's at Hodge Hill Girls's Secondary School, Joseph Chamberlain VIth Form College (Currently) for A-Levels.; [occ.] Student; [memb.] Bromsgrove and Redditch Athletics Club; [oth. writ.] Other poems have been written, but none have been published; [pers.] I feel that the best poems are those that have a different meaning each time they are read, this is why my favorite poems are by Wilfred Owen and Shakespeare.; [a.] Birmingham, West Midlands

BROWN, TELIKA ROCHELLA FORBES
[b.] 7 April 1987, Birmingham; [p.] Melanie Forbes, Michael Brown; [ed.] Welford Primary School; [occ.] Pupil; [pers.] Very sensitive child who is very interested in nature. An independent person who is aware of people's emotions. Enjoys dancing, singing, cooking, sports and reading. Enjoys playing with words on paper.; [a.] Handsworth, Birmingham

BROWNLEE, D. M. H.
[b.] 15 April 1907, Lurgan, Co Armagh; [ed.] Victoria College Belfast, Queen's University, Belfast; [occ.] Retired Teacher; [hon.] B.A. Honours, French and German, subsidiary subjects, English and Spanish, Higher Certificate of Education; [pers.] Motto: "Rejoice in the Lord greatly and again I say rejoice."; [a.] Stow-on-the-Wold, Glos

BROWNLESS, MISS TANYA
[b.] 23 August 1974, Dagenham, Essex; [p.] Mr. Robert Brownless, Ms. Sylvia Thompson; [ed.] Parsloes Manor Comprehensive, Barking and Dagenham College; [occ.] Care Assistant; [pers.] Many of my personal poems are reflected on my childhood memories, of which I can only express in writing; [a.] Dagenham, Essex

BRYAN, SHIRLEY L.
[b.] 25 July 1933, London; [p.] Harry Davison, Kate Davison; [m.] David Bryan, 25 November 1953; [ch.] David Paul, Stephen John and Jane Coral; [ed.] Saint Savour's School, London; [occ.] Receptionist; [memb.] Laindon Conservative Club; [oth. writ.] Onions and Bunions our florence 11/4/96 Jane our only daughter Tracy; [pers.] After the death of my father and the birth of my granddaughter Florence I wanted peace of mind. Writing poetry has given me this; [a.] Basildon, Essex

BRYANT, FRANCIS HAZEL
[b.] 14 September 1957, Surrey; [p.] Peter and Jean Murphy; [m.] Clive Bryant, 19 October 1996; [ed.] Yeoman's Bridge County School, Ash, Aldershot Hants; [occ.] Partner in a Printing Firm "Butterfly Press"; [pers.] I like to write poems that relate to circumstances and express feelings.

BUCKLEY, PHILIP HENRY
[b.] 2 February 1956, Bridlington; [p.] (Both Deceased) Wilfred and Cora; [m.] Divorced; [ch.] Laura Janine and Kerrie Leanne; [ed.] Lady Lumleys, Pickering, N. Yorks; [occ.] Technical Support Manager, Cussons (UK) Ltd, Nottm; [oth. writ.] Personal Collection of writings (poems nd lyrics) compiled over last 25 years - nothing published; [pers.] Writings based on personal experience, influenced most by rock/pop lyricists.; [a.] Burton-on-Trent, Staffs

BUCKNELL, BETTY H.
[b.] 17 April 1914, Newton, Abbot; [p.] Alice Amor Coleman, Joseph Coleman; [m.] Frank T. Bucknell L.R.I.B.A., 16 July 1938; [ch.] Wendy Julyan 13th, Timothy Bucknell, NCA; [ed.] Cumberland House School, Paighton Barnstaple Girls Grammar; [hon.] Exhibited Paintings with Southwest Art Soc.; [oth. writ.] Poem published in the Other Side Of The Mirror; [pers.] Very proud of six grandsons and great granddaughter I love the world.; [a.] Truro, Cornwall

BUCKTON, PAMELA
[b.] 10 October 1950, Shipley; [p.] Charles and Margaret Bagg; [m.] George Buckton, 1 July 1969; [ch.] Mark, Karl, Charles, Antony; [ed.] Woodend Sec., Modern Windhill, Shipley; [occ.] Just class from Yorkshire who has worked in the mills and then married and had my children; [oth. writ.] I have written childrens stories but never had any thing published; [pers.] I have tried to keep the magic alive, that life can offer I have been influenced by Enid Bligten and Beafrex Potter.; [a.] Shipley, West Yorks

BUFTON, JANE
[pen.] J. B.; [b.] 4 February 1964, Wirral; [p.] Sheila Bufton; [ed.] Woodchurch High School and within's Lane College, Wallasey, Merseyside; [occ.] Carer for the elderly; [oth. writ.] 24 other poems and nearly at the end of my first novel. Have wrote a short story two years ago for the Guild of Romance writers and was asked to join their organization but my heart is for poetry or songwriting.; [pers.] I only starting writing my poetry six months ago. Life is my influence. I hope that if my poetry is published it will bring a sense of calm to people who read it.; [a.] Birkenhead

BULL, RACHEL
[pen.] Rachel Bull; [b.] 16 March 1965, Eltham, SE London; [p.] James Tate, Maureen Tate; [m.] Laurence Bull, 8 April 1989; [ch.] James Bull, Grace Bull; [ed.] Haberdashers Askes Hatcham Girls School SE12, Camberwell School of Art and Crafts; [occ.] Visiting Music and Art Teacher; [oth. writ.] Nothing published, write and sing songs; [pers.] How can words convey the deep ache of losing a father? He has gone now, but his gift of creativity lives on in all who loved him.; [a.] Lee, London

BUNN, JEANETTE
[pen.] Kathrine Summers; [b.] 2-10-1942, Norwich; [p.] George and Doris Thompson; [m.] Alan Bunn, July 15th 1961; [ch.] Paul, David, and Ian; [ed.] Costessey Scondary Modern School, left at fifteen with no qualifications; [occ.] Housewife/writer; [oth. writ.] Eighteen published poems. Three short stories not published. Adult science fiction not yet finished.;

[pers.] I have read other people's work, and feel that most Poets have a great deal in common. They say beauty is in the eye of the beholder, with most poets this especially so. A concern for the environment. We may be peaceful dreamers, but it's a great pity more people are not like us. What a wonderful world it would be.; [a.] Norwich, Norfolk

BURDITT, KENNETH
[b.] 30/05/31, Market Harborough; [ed.] Market Harborough Grammar School; [occ.] retired; [memb.] International Society of Poets; [hon.] Award of Excellence and Editor's Awards (poetry); [oth. writ.] several poems published in local newspapers and anthologies including: "Voices on the Wind", "Awaken to a Dream", "Jewels of the Imagination"; [pers.] Enjoy reflecting the present day happenings and events in my writings; [a.] Rugby, Warwickshire

BURGAN, ANNE
[b.] 18 February 1962; [p.] Joseph McShane, Ethna McShane; [m.] Christopher Burgan, 28 July 1989; [ch.] Enya Burgan; [ed.] Hollies FCJ Grammar, Xaverian 6th Form College, Manchester University, Crewe and Alsager College; [occ.] Primary College Teacher; [hon.] Combined studies B.A. Honours (English Literature, Education and Classical Civilization); [pers.] Make the most of the living years. Don't be afraid to follow your dream!; [a.] Sale, Cheshire

BURKE, JANE
[pen.] Jane Peters; [b.] 19/04/62, St. Helens; [m.] Peter John Burke, 30/03/85; [ch.] Charlotte Jane, Rachel Victoria, and Benjamin Peter Thomas; [pers.] The written word can be inspiring to those who read it. If something that is written by one is strong enough to evoke change in the thought of others or re-direction of their very lives. This shows the true power of our language and the way we can use it to better effect. This is my dream to strive for in all my work.; [a.] Rural Fylde, Lancashire

BURRELL, MRS. ESTHER FAYE
[pen.] Mrs. Esther Faye Burrell; [b.] 24 June 1974, King's Lynn; [p.] Mr. and Mrs. F. A. Sturman; [m.] Mr. Steven Burrell, 3 December 1994; [ch.] Shawna; [ed.] Flitcham V.A. Primary School, Flitcham Springwood High School, King's Lynn; [occ.] Unemployed; [oth. writ.] Between You And Me, Travelling Soul, Christmas Child, none in other papers or magazines; [pers.] Ideas enter my head so suddenly that I have to have a pen and some paper near me.; [a.] Fakenham, Norfolk

BUTCHER, VIOLET
[b.] 21 October 1921, Exeter, Devon; [p.] Ted Owens, Edith Owens; [m.] William Butcher (Deceased), 27 August 1988; [ed.] Council Cofe; [occ.] Retired; [oth. writ.] Several poems in church magazines.; [pers.] I love and read poetry all the time.; [a.] Exeter, Devon

BUTTON, CYRIL GEORGE
[b.] 5 June 1931, Merthyr Vale; [p.] Ernest William Button, Phyllis May Button; [m.] Margaret Rose Button, 11 August 1954; [ch.] Wendy Michelle Carl; [ed.] Quakers Yard Grammer School, BA (Open) 1988, F. E. Cert. 1988; [occ.] Personal Home Tutor English, Maths; [memb.] Open University Graduate Association, Army Cadet Force Association; [oth. writ.] "Aberfan" after the disaster and a poem in connection with the `Hongkong Sevens Rugby Competition' - which was read on radio - Wales; [pers.] I greatly admired my father for his ability to recite very long poems, particularly those of Rudyard Kipling. I find poetry reading and writing very relaxing.; [a.] Merthyr, Mid-Glamorgan

CAINES, HAZEL
[b.] 21 January 1956, Mickley, Northum, Berland; [p.] Andrew and the late Martha Dawson Thirtle; [m.] Michael Robert Caines, 18 June 1977; [ed.] Prudhoe County Secondary School; [occ.] Housewife; [oth. writ.] I write poems for Relaxation; [pers.] Dedicated with love to my mum the late Martha Dawson Thirtle born 04-05-30, died 26-12-96 of 37, Errington Place Prudhoe; [a.] North Cumberland

CALDWELL, ERIC
[b.] 24-03-53; Limavady, N.I.; [m.] Ann Marie Caldwell; 22 July 1994; [ch.] Eric and Fiona (previous marriage); [ed.] Limavady Technical College; [occ.] Custody Officer, Royal Courts of Justice; [memb.] Freemason, Goldfish Society of Great Britain, British Motorcycle Federation Member, Herts Masonic Sports Association; [oth. writ.] various poetry on all subjects; poem published in The Other Side of the Mirror, 1996; Editor's Choice Award; [pers.] Reflections, heartaches, desires, all are states of mind and who are we to awaken the sleeping tiger in all of us. I have been greatly influenced by Seamus Heaney and Ted Hughes; [a.] Enfield, Middlesex.

CAMERON, MARY
[b.] 15 May 1927, Glasgow; [p.] Christina and Alfred Radcliffe; [m.] Jim Cameron-Deceased, 31 July 1976; [ed.] Senior Secondary School left at fourteen years of age to become a wage earner; [occ.] Retired; [memb.] Just anything to do with retirement clubs. And gardening magazines and Church activities; [oth. writ.] Couple of other poems never, sent them to anyone; [pers.] I like to write about Scotland, as I don't know about other places, although I would love to stretch myself further; [a.] Cumbernauld, North Lanarkshire

CAMPBELL, EDWIN
[b.] 24 January 1943, Frizington; [p.] Mary and John Campbell; [ed.] I was educated at Frizington St. Paul's School; [occ.] Not working due to ill health; [memb.] The only membership I have is, Frizington Working Men's Club; [hon.] I have received plenty of Domino trophies and a couple of Pool trophies.; [oth. writ.] I love writing poetry inspired by the Lake District and the walks I go on with my brothers dog. I like playing snooker and dominoes at the club.; [pers.] Frizington; [a.] Frizington, Cumbria

CAMPBELL, KEVIN
[b.] 30 April 1965, Co Kildare; [m.] Annabelle, 27 September 1996; [occ.] Aux Nurse; [hon.] This will be my first publication; [oth. writ.] Poems, short stories; [a.] Clane, Co. Kildare, Eire

CAMPBELL, MARY ELIZABETH
[b.] Glasgow; [p.] Thomas Wilson Mackay, Violet Mackay; [m.] Robert L. Campbell, 11 December 1970; [ed.] North Kelvinside Senior Secondary School, Langside College, Glasgow; [occ.] Housewife, Previously N.H.S. Administration: (Ill Health Forced Early "Retirement"); [memb.] Harbour Arts Society, Irvine, Ayrshire; [hon.] Business Administration Certificate of Proficiency. (Nothing of note Education Terminated at Early Age because of Shortage of Family Income.; [oth. writ.] One limerick published in "loony toons limericks," an Arrival Press book. Several short poems and letters published in newspapers. Countless personalized greeting cards as `Favours' for people. I do the illustration then as well as the verse but mainly just for their pleasure - and mine!; [pers.] I value beauty, happiness and laughter and therefore endeavour to contribute to this as best I can.; [a.] Stevenston, Ayrshire

CANDLER, MARVYN
[pen.] Marvyn B. Candler; [b.] 25 March 1971, Thetford; [p.] Gwendeline Candler, Barry Candler; [ed.] Rosemary Musker High School; [occ.] Production Operative; [memb.] Poetry Now, Poetry Today; [hon.] Editors Choice award, from last years Competition; [oth. writ.] Several other poems published in various anthologies and magazines.; [pers.] It is my intention to create a better understanding of both life and each other. I also believe that through my poems I can release the inner see it that Owells within us all.; [a.] Thetford, Norfolk

CAPELL, EMMA
[b.] 2 August 1980, Worksop; [p.] Carol Capell, Philip Capell; [ed.] Attended Portland Comprehensive School for Five Years; [occ.] Waitress, Regancy Hotel; [memb.] Langoid Libairay; [hon.] First Aid Certificate Most of the Life-Saving Awards; [pers.] My first attempt to publish any poetry. I hope to publish many more.; [a.] Worksop, Nottinghamshire

CARLESS, ROBYN
[pen.] Robyn Danielle; [b.] 9 June 1972, Birmingham; [p.] Monica Nield; [m.] John Carless, 23 October 1993; [ed.] Ladywood Comprehensive School, Staffordshire College; [occ.] Care Assistant; [hon.] Diploma, NVQ One; [oth. writ.] Written several poems, songs, short story and a children's book; [pers.] I believe that people should be open to questions about life and it's meaning. Also to be more aware of one's emotions. I hope to encourage this in my writing.; [a.] Birmingham, Warwickshire

CARR, MRS. GLORIA L.
[pen.] Glor; [b.] 29 January 1958, Anglo Portuguese, India; [p.] Mr. and Mrs. D'Cruze; [ch.] Daniel Glenn and Joshua Alex; [ed.] St. Mary's Convent and Thomas Bennett Comprehensive, R.S.A in Word 6 microsoft.; [occ.] Registered Nurse Learning Difficulties.; [memb.] U.K.C.C. and R.C.N.; [oth. writ.] Poetry and prose but never forwarded anyway for publication.; [pers.] I enjoy a lot of arts and my writing is based on my thoughts and feelings. Love various music and enjoy doing home furnishings and decorating myself.; [a.] Trowbridge, Kiltshire

CARSWELL, JENNIFER
[pen.] Jennifer Dove; [b.] 6 December 1937, Brentwood; [p.] Dora and John Dove; [ch.] 4 Daughters; [ed.] Queens Park School Eswestry Shropshire; [occ.] Disabled; [oth. writ.] Other poems but never entered anything for publication before; [pers.] I love words and the way they are presented; [a.] Bodmin, Cornwall

CARTER, TIM
[pen.] T. C. Lewis; [b.] 14 June 1957, London ; [p.] Eric and Irene Carter; [ed.] Masters Degree in Business Administration; [occ.] Contract Manager; [oth. writ.] Other Poetry; [pers.] Writing is a wonderful way to bring light into the world.; [a.] Clevedon, N. Somerset

CERI, SHIRLEY
[b.] 28 May 1977, Oxford; [ed.] North Oxfordshire College and School of Art; [hon.] BTEC 1st diploma in art and design, BTEC National diploma in Photography, City and guilds in Communication Skills; [oth. writ.] "Glimpse Of The Fairy" appeared in local newspaper. I've written other fantasy poems; [pers.] I enjoy writing fantasy poems as it's a form of escapism for me and I think everyone should escape out of their lives once in a while to magical places that need to be discovered.; [a.] Bicester, Oxfordshire

CHADWICK, JOYCE
[b.] 5 November 1937, Tunstall; [p.] Robert and Elizabeth; [occ.] Enamel Kiln Cranker; [oth. writ.] Bob-The-Collie (First Poem), Bob-The-Collie (Its a Dog's Life); [a.] Tunstall, Staffordshire

CHAPLIN, MRS. THEA URSULA
[b.] 17 April 1928, Chelsea, London; [p.] O. Albert and D. Albert; [m.] Ex Husband now deceased, 27 June 1953; [ch.] Nicholas and Claire; [ed.] Convent of the Sacred Heart Pitmans Secretarial College; [occ.] Retired Personnel Manager; [memb.] Current Minehead Painters Group; [oth. writ.] None at present - though have thoughts of writing a book.; [pers.] My outlook on life has been influenced by my traumatic marriage and consequent divorce - giving me, a deeper appreciation of life and all the joy and love it still holds.; [a.] Minehead, Somerset

CHAPMAN, JANNETTE GEORGINA
[pen.] Rose-Lee; [b.] 21/09/70; [p.] Joseph Grand, Violet Grand; [m.] Gordon Dennis Chapman, 16/10/93; [ch.] Joshua (5), Kieran (2); [ed.] Shotton Hall Comprehensive School; [occ.] Unemployed, typist - Housewife; [oth. writ.] This is the first poem that I have ever submitted to anyone and after reading the outcome over and over, it is now that I realize the importance of my ability.; [pers.] My writing comes from my heart and must hold some meaning to life. I enjoy what I do and hope that in the future others will too; [a.] Peterlee, Durham

CHAPPLE, LYNNE CREES
[b.] 14 October 1956, Bristol; [p.] Robert Crees, Edna Crees; [m.] Ian Chapple, 3 June 1981; [ch.] Bobbie Jay, Jeremy Ross and Scott Eddie; [ed.] Withywood Comprehensive, East Bristol Institute of Adult Education; [occ.] Clerical Officer; [memb.] 'The Penny Pinchers' - charity fund raisers for Children's Hospice South West. Active Campaigner for the Preservation of the remainder of Bristol Lido.; [hon.] Distinction - Communication Skills; [oth. writ.] Several stories and letters printed in local newspaper.; [pers.] Poetry - what a truly wonderful way, to communicate and convey; [a.] Bristol, Bristol

CHARD, SALLY-ANNE
[b.] 27 January 1968, Lyme Regis; [p.] Larry and Rita Chard; [ed.] Woodroffe Grammar, then when I left school, went to Weymouth College and did Y.T.S. in (Care) W.; [occ.] Fetterler Ceramics, Axminster; [oth. writ.] I have my own book of poems published, called feelings about love, prayers and life of today. I also write songs, plays, and children's stories, but they have not been published yet.; [pers.] My influenced in poetry, came from the love of my family and friends, and the love from my granddad Street who was a well known and loved man in Lyme Regis. He was best known as (Buffey Street). I still miss him very much.; [a.] Lyme Regis, Dorset

CHARLES, ANOUSKA ALEXANDRA
[b.] 6 October 1979, Lichfield; [p.] Sandra E. Howell and Ian C. Charles; [ed.] Hagley Park High School, Rugeley, Aelfgar Post - 16 Centre, Rugeley; [occ.] A-level student (Full time); [a.] Hill Ridware, Staffordshire

CHARLES, ELON
[b.] 22 June 1965, London; [ed.] Wandsworth Boys Comprehensive 1976-1982, South Thames College 1982-83, 1993-95; [occ.] Sales Advisor, Royal Mail; [oth. writ.] No published work; [pers.] My poetry is a reflection of the various emotions I experience during my life. I try to incorporate aspects within my poems which will enable the reader, whoever they may be, to identify with and relate to.; [a.] London

CHARLESWORTH, JODIE LETITIA
[pen.] Jodie Letitia Charlesworth; [b.] 15 April 1982, Ponterfract; [p.] Ms. Deryn Deleyes Charlesworth, Frank; [ed.] Student; [pers.] I've wrote a couple of poems but only noticed I had this talent on the arrival of your letter. I'd like to write a book of poems or a novel before the age of 22. And Jack will always be my inspiration!; [a.] Upton, W. Yorkshire

CHARLTON, DAWN
[b.] 14 January 1962, Belgium; [p.] Walter and Florence Charlton; [m.] Fiancee: Alvin Strang; [ch.] Leanne and Davis; [ed.] Peterhead Academy; [occ.] Accountant in Fishing Industry; [pers.] My poems reflect how sad love can often be. We strive to obtain perfection within our relationships but everyone's perception of perfection is different.; [a.] Mintlaw, Aberdeenshire

CHARLTON, MRS. LYNNE
[b.] 2 June 1950, Ilkeston; [m.] 9 May 1970; [ed.] Michael House School; [occ.] Housewife; [memb.] Hilltop (A.O.G.) Chapel Fan Club Memberships 5 altogether; [hon.] Eistedfod, and 2 Poetry Awards; [oth. writ.] Several poems in small books; [pers.] I write poetry to help others now and after I have gone and I am God inspired mainly.; [a.] Ilkeston, Derbyshire

CHEASLEY, CARRIE
[b.] 19 December 1977, Colchester; [p.] Kenny Cheasley, Sandra Gant; [m.] Steve Baines; [ch.] Marty Cheasley - 3; [ed.] I never finished school, or done any exams. I left school to have son at 15 I had my high school at, Colbaynes High School; [occ.] Mother; [oth. writ.] I have one poem published by Andrew Head, called, 'Sea Of Romance'. The book titled 'One Small Step'. I have also written other unpublished poems, which I hope, one day will be published.; [pers.] I believe, anyone can be a poet, they just have to took for the main ingredient, deep within themselves, and let inspiration lead the way.; [a.] Saint Osyth, Essex

CHEER, KATHERINE
[b.] 26 February 1971, Basildon; [p.] Lauretta and Bernard Cheer; [ed.] St. Anselms Roman Catholic School, Basildon College of Further Education; [occ.] Administration Assistant; [pers.] Poetry is made easier with writings from the heart.; [a.] Basildon, Essex

CHILTON, NEIL WILLIAM
[b.] 28 April 1957, Lichfield; [p.] Maurice Chilton, Pamela Chilton; [m.] Divorced; [ch.] Stephen and Samuel Chilton; [ed.] Pelsall Comp Cannock Tech; [occ.] Welder; [hon.] City and Guilds; [oth. writ.] A few, none published; [pers.] Hold onto your dreams, one day they will be the only thing you've got left.; [a.] Stafford, Staffordshire

CHOHAN, MRS. SIONA MARCELLA
[b.] 1 May 1971, Seychelles; [p.] Jinette Henriette and Mr. Oddvar Vindedal; [m.] Mr. Saleem Chohan, 19 March 1991; [ch.] Adam Chohan; [occ.] Hairdresser; [pers.] My writings illustrate the fascination I have of the creation of human life. Reading and writing poems is also a strong way of expressing my inner feelings.; [a.] Birmingham, West Midlands

CHOPPEN, DAPHNE MOREY
[pen.] Daphne Morey-Choppen; [b.] April 21, 1933, Vicarage Lane, Stubbington; [p.] George and Viola Morey; [m.] Divorced; [ch.] Nicholas William.; [ed.] Fareham Secondary Girls School Portsmouth College of Art; [occ.] Part time ceramics painter; [memb.] Former member of the stubbington art group.; [oth. writ.] This is my first attempt.; [pers.] I am the eldest of eight children six brothers and a sister. The death of my mother inspired me to write my poem.; [a.] Fareham, Hants

CHUDASAMA, KIMEL
[b.] 5 February 1982, London; [p.] Mr. and Mrs. Chudasama

CHUKUEZI, DR. ANELECHI
[b.] 31/01/45, Umudim; [p.] Felix Chukuezi, Malinda Chukuezi; [m.] Comfort Chukuezi, 31/01/70; [ch.] Chinaemeze, Chukuemeka, Nmeoma, Anelechi; [ed.] Government College, Umuasha, Nigeria, University of Lagos, Nigeria, Institute of Laryngology and Otology, London, Royal College of Surgeons of Edinburgh, Scotland; [occ.] Medical Director and Chief Consultant Otorhinolaryngologist, Federal Medical Centre, Owerr, Nigeria; [memb.] Nigeria Medical Association, Nigerian Cancer Society, Nigerian Society for Speech and Hearing, Society for Promotion of IGBO Language and Culture, Nigerian Society for the Handicapped, British Society of Audiology, Member New York Academy of Science; [hon.] Oxford University Press Drama Prize for Best IGBO Play, Best IGBO Drama Award by Society for Promotion of IGBO language and culture, Knighthood (KSC) Knight of St Christopher conferred by the Angelican Diocese of Owerr, Nigeria; [oth. writ.] Books: "Udo Kamma" - first ever published IGBO play - Oxford University Press - 1974, "Aku Feohaa" - IGBO play - Oxford University Press 1980, "Akwa Nwa" - IGBO play - African University Press 1979, "Ako Bundu" - IGBO poetry - Longmans Publishers 1987, "Okihas Grandfathers Tale" - MBAA Publishers, "Waiting For Destiny" - MBAA Publishers; [pers.] I try to be honest in all my life undertakings. In my writings I try to reach out to the people, to touch their lives and attempt to influence rectification towards good life, justice and equity.; [a.] Umudim, Nigeria

CHURCH, SHARON
[b.] 10 October 1964, Swindon; [p.] Colin Clinch, Josie Head; [ch.] Kim Church, Nikki Church; [occ.] Hotel Management (Student in Interior Design); [oth. writ.] A diary of poems as yet read only by my children; [pers.] The poem was inspired by spiritual meditation, helping me from one chapter in life to another and dedicated to Vincent who's shown me the magic and frustration love is...; [a.] Swindon, Wilts

CLACHRIE, JANE OSBORNE
[b.] 20 May 1908, Ayr, Scotland; [p.] Joseph and Maria Clachrie (Deceased); [ed.] Newton Academy Ary Scotland; [occ.] Retired; [oth. writ.] Several poems in church magazines and one in Australian "Nursing Home" magazine. (Still writing poems) always willing to learn more.; [pers.] Before retiring traveled on holidays to Australia, various European countries and United Kingdom. Was clerkess for 32 years. And 13 years in Erays Carpet Factory and other jobs the same firm 45 years altogether.; [a.] Ayr, Ayrshire

CLAFFEY, DENYSE
[b.] 23 March 1962, Borough of Lambert, London; [p.] Eileen Stannes, Michael Paul Claffey; [ch.] Marcus Claffey; [ed.] Taylors Hill Galway, Tathmines Senior College.; [occ.] Poet, Artist, Jungian Psychotherapist; [memb.] Irish United Nations, Association, Green Peace, Irish Association Jungian, Psychotherapists.; [hon.] Diploma in Jungian Psychology/Psychotherapy.; [oth. writ.] Other poems unpublished; [pers.] I believe that would peace is attainable I feel concern for the future of humanity and our beautiful planet mother Earth and all the life she contains.; [a.] Dublin, Ireland

CLANISTER, LILIAN
[b.] 20/01/32, Liverpool; [p.] Beatrice and Charles Ellis; [m.] Philip, 29/05/53; [ch.] 2 sons; [ed.] Elementary; [occ.] Retired; [oth. writ.] Poems (sad and humorous, odes, ditties, verses for all types of floral tributes), Poems about world incidents and happenings; [pers.] I am motivated to write verse by things both seen and said, finding all thoughts pass through my mind in verse and prose form. I find great joy in the beauty of words.; [a.] Warrington County, Cheshire

CLAPHAM, SHEILA
[pen.] Sheila; [b.] 10 November 1942, London; [p.] Charles and Ethel Nicholls (Both deceased); [m.] Richard Victor, 3 June 1967; [ch.] Peter Charles and Julia Carol Clapham; [ed.] Secondary Modern, Ruckholt Manor; [occ.] Partner - Driving School; [memb.] Kingston Bagpuize Amateur Dramatic Group; [hon.] Silver Cup - Best Actress - Four Shires Festival 1985 - Amateur Dramatics; [oth. writ.] Many poems, including "Love" published in Between A Laugh And A Tear and "My Dad" published in The Other Side Of The Mirror, both issued by The International Society of Poets.; [pers.] This poem was inspired by my friend Kathy in the beautiful surroundings of Hayling Island. However I still need coffee to wake me in the mornings and thereafter my fluffy dog slippers still keep my feet warm!; [a.] Oxford, Oxfordshire

CLARE, MICHAEL G.
[b.] 2 August 1961, Lanark; [p.] George Clare, Helen Clare; [m.] Living with Partner - Claudine; [ch.] Jessica (Born May '96), Gerard (Born January '84 Previous Marriage); [ed.] St. Margaret's High, Airdrie. O'Grade, Accounts, Arithmetic, Economics, English, Modern Studies; [occ.] Production Operative, Boots contract manufacturing, Airdrie; [memb.] Ex Member: Pitlochry Golf Club, Pitlochry, Perthshire, Scotland; [oth. writ.] I always wrote poems for pleasure. Only now have I decided to take it seriously.; [pers.] I called upon the innocence of childhood for this poem, where all eyes are filled with beauty, and where hearts are full of God intentions.; [a.] Airdrie, North Lanarkshire

CLARK, ANNE
[b.] 2 May 1939, Bristol; [m.] Gerald, 26 December 1964; [ed.] Grammar School 6-0 levels dip of Social Studies, S. E. N. and member of Mensa; [occ.] Disabled ex-Nurse; [memb.] Mensa, I am a church going christian; [oth. writ.] This is the 3rd poem published Drugs, Truth and I Remember Christmases Of lifty Years Ago.; [pers.] Drugs was written because I feel its such an awful trap that people fall into perhaps without thinking about it. I hope this verse will make someone think.; [a.] Cwmbran, Gwent

CLARK, CAROLE
[b.] 26 September 1947, London; [p.] Leonard Haines, Winifred Haines; [m.] Harry Clark, 3 February 1968; [ch.] Nicola Jane, Stuart Jason; [ed.] Bishops Park (Central) School Fulham, London; [occ.] Freelance Secretary; [oth. writ.] None published; [pers.] My poetry usually reflects my own personal experiences or the feelings of those close to me. I was greatly encouraged in my writing by my English teacher at senior school.; [a.] Fulham, London

CLARK, JENNI
[b.] 28 August 1982, Reading; [p.] Lynne and Graham Clark; [occ.] Pupil of South Bromsgrove School; [oth. writ.] None published; [pers.] My school is built on the site of an old flax mill whose pond still exists. A poetry workshop led by Eleanor Cooke looked at this feature and 'The Eyes of my Shoes' was the result of my efforts; [a.] Alvechurch, Worcestershire

CLARK, LINDA MARGARET
[pen.] Lindy Lu; [b.] 14 September 1953, Dorset; [p.] Elenor and Earnest Joy; [m.] John Paul Clark, 24 June 1978; [ch.] Four Daughters; [occ.] Housewife; [oth. writ.] Why - Every Where Farewell - Words, Happy Birthday Dad, All Alone - To My Dad, Granddad - Love, Another day -loneliness; [a.] Bournemouth, Dorset

CLARK, MRS. MARGARET ANN
[pen.] Sandee Ainge; [b.] 24 September 1942, Northampton; [p.] Charles Merrey, Edna Merrey; [m.] Edmond Charles Clark, 20 July 1976 (Deceased); [ed.] Kingsthorpe Secondary School, Northampton College; [occ.] Professional; [memb.] WRVS Northampton, Victory Services Club London; [oth. writ.] Written several poems had one published 1996 in (Between A Laugh And A Tear), I have been writing since the age of fourteen; [pers.] I admire the great poets and read their great works often; [a.] Northampton, Northants

CLARKE, ANITA
[b.] 29 January 1968, Dudley, West Mids; [p.] Geoffrey and Janet Clarke; [ed.] Kingswinford Comprehensive School, University of Essex, University of Leeds, University of Durham, Stourbridge College of Technology and Art; [occ.] Full time post-graduate student (MA in Applied Social Studies and Social Work); [memb.] World Society for the Protection of Animals, Liberty Campaign for Bears, World Wide Fund for Nature, National Assoc of Probation Officers; [hon.] B.A. Hons in English and European Literature, Post Graduate Certificate of Education, Teaching English as a Foreign Language Qualification; [oth. writ.] Have been writing for pleasure for fourteen years. This is my first published work.; [pers.] I attempt to capture a gothic, macabre, mysterious, fantasy atmosphere in my poetry. I am inspired by J.R.R Tolkien, Edgar Allan Poe and film noir. "There is more to life than reality".; [a.] Kingswinford, West Mids

CLARKE, NORMA EILEEN
[pen.] "Val"; [b.] 5 May 1938, Sutton Colefield; [p.] Lillian and Charles Hughes; [m.] Richard Christopher Clarke, 10 January 1959; [ch.] Angela, Mark, Natalie, Amanda; [ed.] Secondary Modern School, Lea Village Sheldon Birmingham 33; [occ.] Housewife; [memb.] "The Guild of International songwriters and Composers"; [hon.] "Mother of the Year" for having the most interests in one's life. Still hold title by the people paper and Oxo Company; [oth. writ.] Written 200 songs, consisting of, rock 'n roll, rap, reggae, ballads, country carols, heavy metal, dance disco, M.O.R. jazz, blues, soul, my poems and songs are of true life; [pers.] Eldest child of 11 children, mother died, when I was 15. Leaving 7 school children and 3 babies. The youngest was 1 year old, she died giving birth to him at Marston Green Maturnity Hospital.; [a.] Coleshill, Solihull

CLEGG, PATRICK MICHAEL
[b.] 25/06/68, Coventry; [p.] Patrick Joseph, Marie Kathrine; [ch.] Jenna Kimberley Morgan, Aaron Patrick Morgan; [ed.] R.C. State Schools; [occ.] Unemployed; [memb.] MENSA; [pers.] Be happy.; [a.] Coventry, Warwickshire

CLEVELAND, PAT
[pen.] Path; [b.] 23 June 1950, New York, USA; [p.] Lady Bird Cleveland, John Johnston; [m.] Paul Van Ravenstein, 30 June 1984; [ch.] Noel and Anna; [ed.] Art School, Painting Sculpture Fashion Illustration and Design, Dance, Acting, Mime, Hatha Yoga, Meditation, Screen Writing; [occ.] Run away and photo model mother wife writer, lover of life; [hon.] Mother of the red cross Italy best Actress in a TV Commercial Italy, Best International Run Away Model, Best Choriographer for a TV show Italy; [oth. writ.] At the moment, working on several screen plays, short stories and my love is in poetry, I have just started on the path of writing as expression of the self.; [pers.] Love is the greatest force in all the world, let it speak through our poetry.; [a.] Stresa, Italy

CLOUGH, CATHERINE
[b.] 2 June 1922, Alvechurch, Worcs; [m.] Peter Clough, 19 July 1947; [ch.] Three; [ed.] Private School, Secretarial College; [occ.] Caring Grandmother to eight; [oth. writ.] Childrens Poem accepted and used by BBC in 1950s - nothing else submitted for publication!; [pers.] I have written poetry and stories for as long as I can remember, mostly factual and inspired by characters. Experiences and places which have influenced my long life.; [a.] Bromsgrove, Worcs

COADY, CLAIRE LONGELLA
[b.] 14 December 1978, London; [p.] Annette Coady, Peter Coady; [ed.] Study Business and Finance Advance at Northwest London College; [memb.] Falham Swimming and Gym, David Loyd Tennis Club; [hon.] Swimming Awards, 50 Metres, 100 Metres, Bronze, Silver and Gold, Poetry Award from Burlington Danes School; [oth. writ.] I write poems as a hobby but I've had a few poems in local papers and magazines.; [pers.] I've always been a very deep person and I find the best way to express myself is through poetry.; [a.] London

COATH, JOHN P. H.
[b.] 30 July 1928, Paignton; [p.] George and Dorothy Coath; [ed.] Torquay, Grammar School for Boys, St Luke's College, Exeter. Qualification, Exeter University Teaching Certificate BA. (Hons) Open University L.T.C.L.; [occ.] Retired; [memb.] Devonshire Association, Torquay Natural History Society; [pers.] Though a keen enthusiast for literature. I am primarily a musician with a considerable number of compositions to my credit. Although retired from full-time teaching, still take private pupils and am organist of the local Anglican Church; [a.] Torquay, Devon

COCKERILL, B.
[pen.] Cockenill, Je, Suis; [b.] 9 October 1947, Cromer; [p.] Zena and Arthur Cockerill; [ch.] Carina, Gregory, Ryan Cockrill; [ed.] Fakenham Grammar, Norfolk only 7 levels; [occ.] Tax Consultant and Beach Bum; [memb.] None other than Life membership of humans; [hon.] Best slave of the year Sheringham 1969; [oth. writ.] Children's Books - yet to be published tears of a dawn novel - yet to be published. Neutron Bomb Nobel - Sci-Fi yet to be published.; [pers.] I am green having seen to problems we are getting in world into I equate with the indian ides of earth - man.; [a.] Great Yarmouth, Norfolk

COLLINS, EMMA
[b.] 2 January 1983, Portsmouth; [p.] Patrica Tolliday and Jeff Collins; [ed.] May Field School and Stage Coach School of the performing arts; [occ.] In training to become actress/singer; [pers.] I enjoy writing song's and poems and my dream is to have a book of my own one day!; [a.] Portsmouth

COLLINS, JANE
[b.] 31 October 1980, Rep. of Ireland; [p.] Anthony Collins, Margaret Franklin; [ed.] Primary Education at Cornamaddy N.S. Athlone, Secondary Education at Our Lady's Bower, Athlone; [occ.] Student at Our Lady's Bower Secondary School Athlone; [hon.] Selection as a semi-finalist in the 1996 International Open Amateur Poetry Competition is Jane's first literary achievement; [oth. writ.] The poem "Live" is Jane's first published work. She was aged 15 years when she wrote it; [a.] Athlone, Westmeath, Rep. of Ireland

COMLEY, MARY
[b.] Cuckfield, Sussex, England; [p.] Lionel and Eleanor Peake; [m.] Robert Comley, September 8, 1990; [ch.] Stephen Anne and Clare; [ed.] Convent Educated Lourdes Mount, Ealing St. Josephs, Read-

ing Berkshire. I am not a Catholic but a Pentecostal Christian; [occ.] Homemaker and Enthusiastic pet owner and people encourager?; [memb.] Immigrated to Australia - flying through the Darwin cyclone and didn't surprise my U.K. friends!; [hon.] Distinction and credits H.Sc Standard. Elocution medal, honour in sports, running cup several times - I've awarded myself and overcoming medal of life's traumas to hopefully result in a character to bless"; [oth. writ.] Reading Evening Post published hundreds of my letters and a few human interest articles. I have this year sent my poems to friends here and overseas, ministries overseas a good respond; [pers.] I survived a very traumatic childhood, hence life for many years was a series of awesome knocks, the results from learning to respond rightly created growth and later in a building relationship with my Creator blessings flowed!; [a.] Glenthompson, Victoria, Australia

CONNERTY, CLARE
[b.] 8 May 1982, Cheltenham; [p.] Christopher and Pat Connerty; [ed.] St. Edward's School, Cheltenham; [occ.] Student; [pers.] Thanks to everyone, especially Mum, Dad, Sallyanne, and my friends for all your support - I couldn't have done it without you!; [a.] Cheltenham, Glos

CONNING, JOHN GILBERT
[pen.] Phantom Poet; [b.] 2 May 1949, Stewarton; [p.] John Conning and Jean Shedden; [m.] Susan Miller, 2 March 1972; [ch.] Michelle, Paul, Jay Gilbert; [ed.] Stewarton High Kilmarnock College of Engineering; [occ.] Musician Composer; [hon.] From the poetry club L.T.D. 3043086 commendations. Poets of the year 1995 illustrated Poet of the year 1995 song writer of the year 1996. For "Love At First Sight."; [oth. writ.] Published in fourteen anthologies, local magazines, charity print and radio reading. Recorded poetry to music cassette "Tale of a Tail".; [pers.] Words and music flow like a river of ink from my pens. Portraying life's blood stream as a picture show from my veins.; [a.] Luton, Bedfordshire

CONNOLLY, JAMES
[b.] 11 November 1939, Dublin; [p.] Edward Connolly, Mary Connolly; [m.] Veronica White, 8 July 1961; [ch.] Valerie Mary, Amanda Ann; [ed.] St James C.B.S., Dublin; [occ.] Plumbing Heating Engineer; [oth. writ.] Numerous poems (unpublished); [pers.] Poetry is the voice of the soul; [a.] Reigate, Surrey

CONNOLLY, JAMES
[b.] 8 July 1944, Rochdale; [p.] Peter John and Mary Connolly; [ed.] St. Gabriels RC School, 49-59, Extension courses, Roman History Latin (at present); [occ.] Sales Consultant with the Canada Life Assurance Co; [memb.] Local Crown, Green Bowling Club, Previous Rochdale Cine Club, Local Interest, Civic History, Reading many Historical also Autobiography; [hon.] Rochdale Cine Club comps, also Rochdale Metro Crown Bowling Competition 1986, various awards at workers exam's and others. Recent winner of a poetry competition, Council of Poetry; [oth. writ.] Sixty poems hoped to be published in the future. Complete history of both parents family (just finished and in print) many letters sent to the local paper (whom I got your details from). Short story; [pers.] I have been writing for a number of years. Having traveled the globe, I now enjoy gardening (pot-patios). In meeting people I love to discuss many topics. Listening to the manner which people often speak the poem 'Eloquence' was founded.; [a.] Rochdale, Lancs

COOKE, EDITH
[pen.] Edith Meldrum Cooke; [b.] 30 November 1944, Sunderland; [p.] Hannah and Thomas John Meldrum; [m.] Gordon, 22 December 1962; [ch.] Four sons, 1 daughter; [ed.] Secondary Modern School; [occ.] Housewife; [oth. writ.] Had three poems published for Arrival Press in three very different anthologies.; [pers.] Only just started writing poetry since March 1996, had all published so far. Favorite is Christian Poetry as I am a born again Christian. Have postered a couple of children adopted one and had a one late in life hence Motherhood is near to my heart.; [a.] Sunderland, Tyne and Wear

COOKE, FLORENCE ELLEN NORA
[pen.] N. Cooke; [b.] 20 September 1916, Clapton, London; [p.] Mr. Percival Northcote, Mrs. Eva Northcote; [m.] Summer 1948; [ch.] Two boy and girl; [ed.] Fleet Road Central School Hampstead NWZ, London; [occ.] Retired; [hon.] A bible for good conduct; [oth. writ.] I write letters to people in all walks of life - have done so for years. Many clergy - some royalty - the popofilm stars.; [pers.] The bible is a wonderful book and since the age of 44 years I have been studying it - have learnt a great deal, and at 80 years I'm still studying and learning! It is never too late to learn.; [a.] Guildford, Surrey

COOPER, ANNE
[pen.] Anne Marie; [b.] 27 December 1916, Maryport, Cumbria; [p.] John and Jane Minkella; [m.] Herbert Cooper, 28 September 1940; [ch.] Carl; [ed.] Church of England School; [occ.] Retired; [oth. writ.] Various poems published; [pers.] Inspiration for my poems stems from years spent in the English lake district, the philosophy of spiritualism helps me to write spiritual verse and to serve others to the best of my ability.; [a.] Carlisle, Cumbria

COOPER, NORA KATHLEEN
[b.] 14 August 1934, Glossop; [p.] Edgar Hallam, Ellen Hallam; [m.] George Ernest Cooper, 11 July 1953; [ch.] Norman, Leslie, Derek, Joy, Diane and Roger; [ed.] Whitfield School, Glossop, West End School, Glossop, Derbyshire; [occ.] Farmers Wife; [oth. writ.] Several poems published.; [pers.] I am just very happy to have my poems published, and hope someone enjoy's reading them.; [a.] New Mills, High Peak, Derbyshire

CORNER, JOYCE
[b.] 14 May 1921, Etchingham, Sx; [p.] Charles and Kathleen Back; [m.] Charles Gordon Corner (2nd Marriage), 31 August 1959; [ch.] Roger, Anita T. Jenny (1st Marriage), Jill (2nd Marriage); [ed.] Convent of the Holy Child, Hasting, East Sussex; [occ.] Housewife; [memb.] The Laburnum Centre Lyon Street, Bognor Regis West Sussex, Tutor for five years until 1995 to the Centre's Creative Writing Class; [oth. writ.] Poem in book "A Taste Of The South", Title of poem "The Pastoral Scene", story "The Third Party" in book "Paper Clips", Children's book "Bertie The Little Red Car", I have contributed to National Magazines Newspapers and children comics; [pers.] My first husband, Peter Cavanagh Impressionist, a leading Entertainer of his day. He was a firm favourite of the Royal Family. My second husband Charles Gordon Corner was a Fleet Street Journalist. My favourite author is Jane Austen. I like descriptive pieces on the countryside.; [a.] Bognor Regis, West Sussex

COSTANZA, LISA
[b.] 1 April 1985, Taunton; [p.] Bronwen and Raffaele; [memb.] Griffin Association (Sport); [a.] Street, Somerset

COSTELLO, EDWARD
[b.] 19-9-1926; Waterford-Eire; [p.] Edward and Sara; [m.] Catherine; 1949; [ch.] Jacqueline and Catherine; [ed.] Taught by nuns for six years in Convent, four and a half years in Monastery School by Christian Brothers; [occ.] retired; racing carriage builder; [hon.] Editor's Choice Award as author of "Dunblane" in Quiet Moments; [oth. writ.] "Dunblane" published and many others unpublished-not yet submitted; [pers.] My greatest pleasure apart from writing my poems is the pleasure I'm told others get in reading them. I have to thank the nuns for teaching me to write poetry and God the gift of inspiration. I wrote many poems for servicemen to send home during World War II; [a.] Bushey-Waterford, Hertfordshire.

COTTON, LOUISE
[b.] 4 May 1971, Nocton, Lincs; [p.] Pamela Wilson, David Wilson; [m.] Richard Cotton, 25 May 1991; [ch.] Lewis Richard, Jamey Louise; [ed.] South Leas Comprehensive, Scunthorpe; [occ.] Mother; [memb.] Local Pre-School Committee; [oth. writ.] Many other poems but this is first attempt at publication; [pers.] This is for my husband and family for all their inspiration.; [a.] Bagshot, Surrey

COVERDALE, TRACEY
[b.] 17 February 1978, Whitby; [p.] David and Hilda Coverdale; [ed.] Setton C.P. School (Primary) Caedmon School, Whitby Community College, From 1st September 1997 Derby College of Nursing; [occ.] Care Assistant; [pers.] All the poems that I have wrote come from my heart, telling my feelings of others.; [a.] Staithes, Cleveland

COWELL, PAUL LAURENCE
[b.] 7 January 1959, County Durham; [p.] Norman and Doris Cowell; [m.] Ava Cowell (Nee Pattison), 6 October 1979; [ch.] Tanya Ava and Phillip Paul; [ed.] England and France, International Business and European History; [occ.] International Marketing; [oth. writ.] A private Portfolio of poems and short stories exist, largely inspired by, or written for my wife and children. Work on a first serious novel has commenced.; [pers.] As technology and profit rule our world, mankind fails to recognize its true potential for greatness through nobleness of spirit. I hope my writing reminds that long - remembered pleasures of ten are simple, and that man's Genesis was originally divine. May we learn always from our mistakes.; [a.] Fraddon, Cornwall

COX, MARGARET
[b.] 30 June 1940, Northfleet, Kent; [p.] Daisy Snelling and Ron Snelling; [m.] Geoffrey Cox, 25 January 1958; [ch.] Stephen Cox and Mark Cox, Debbie Cox; [ed.] Hall Rd School For Girls - 1 Northfleet. State enrolled nurse; [occ.] Retired/Sen.; [oth. writ.] First submission other writing for personal pleasure and friendly reading.; [pers.] "Tragedy, deepens ones respect of life when sprinkled with hope" This I truly believe.; [a.] Gravesend, Kent

COYLE, DAMIAN GERARD
[b.] 8 April 1965, Belfast; [p.] Patrick J. Coyle, Jean C. Curran; [ed.] North West College of Further and Higher Education, University of Ulster - Theatre Studies; [occ.] Actor, Theatre Direction - (Resting) - Writer; [oth. writ.] Several poems published in poetry now, Arrival Press, Anchor Books.; [pers.] Casus Belli, all men have fears, the brave put aside their fears and go forward, sometimes to death, but always to victory.; [a.] Derry, Derry

CRABTREE, LOUISE
[b.] 12 July 1974, Leeds; [p.] Roger Crabtree, Cheryll Cole; [ed.] St. Ursula's High School Bristol Plymouth University; [occ.] English Teacher in Japan; [hon.] BSC (Comb) Hons Psychology First Prize - Short story Eisteddford, Third Place - Poem Eisteddford; [oth. writ.] Poem "Loss" to be published this year; [pers.] For a poet, a poem does not always bring a life of riches, but always a richness of life; [a.] Bristol, Avon

CRACKNELL, MARIA
[pen.] Marla Frank; [b.] 9 October 1975, Welwyn Garden City; [p.] Richard and Susan Cracknell; [ed.] Presdales Secondary School for girls, Didn't go on to further education; [occ.] Shop Assistant in home Town, Ware, Herts; [hon.] Other publications; [oth. writ.] I have written a book that I, one day, hope to get published. I have another poem published, and hope to get other work published too.; [pers.] Thanks to the continuous love and support of my loving family, I have persevered in putting my work forward, I thank them. I have been influenced by poets such as: W.B. Yeats, John Keats etc...The poetry that I write comes from deep within my heart, and I hope it will influence peoples lives.; [a.] Ware, Herts

CRANE, EMMA
[b.] 14 November 1979, Wolverhampton; [p.] David and Susan Crane; [ed.] Redhill Primary School and Blake High School; [occ.] Student at Blake High School, I also have a Saturday job in a fruit and vegetable shop; [memb.] Blake High School Chamber Choir and the Staffordshire County Choir; [oth. writ.] My poem "One Little Calf" was published in 1996, in the book titled "Beyond the Horizon".; [pers.] I am the eldest of seven girls in my family, I have a love for animals and enjoy singing and performing in stage shows.; [a.] Cannock, Staffordshire

CRAWFORD, ALEXANDER
[b.] 30 May 1943, Carlisle; [p.] Scottish; [m.] Brenda Ann Crawford, 5 July 1980; [ed.] Carlisle Grammar School, Cumbria College of Art and Design. RAF Medical Colleges of Nursing; [occ.] Writer; [memb.] Royal Air Force Mountain Rescue Association. British Gordon Setter Club; [hon.] Meritorious Service Award for rescuing injured climbers in Snowdonia whilst in service with RAF Search and Rescue Helicopters (22 Sqn. RAF Valley); [oth. writ.] Autobiography 'Audible Glue' Novels: 'Mush Mumkin' - 'Hill Troop' - and currently 'Sand in my Shreddies' regular writings for the British Gordon Setter Club... 'For the good of the breed... and all it stands for....'; [pers.] Proud of my 'Border Heritage' I strive to save as much as I can for my God-children so they may enjoy it as I have.; [a.] Carlisle, Cumbria

CRAWLEY, MICHAEL
[b.] 1 September 1936, Belfast, NI; [p.] Thomas and Helen; [m.] Betty, 31 March 1962; [ch.] Two boys and one girl; [ed.] The Christian Brothers School, Newry Co Down, Northern Ireland; [occ.] Engineer Self Employed; [memb.] Midland Counties ABA Staffordshire ABA; [hon.] For Sports, Boxing Cross Country Coaching, Shooting, Internation Team Manager and Coach, England University Boxing Team, guest on Turkish TV about Sport Boxing China TV about Sports Boxing, Radio; [oth. writ.] Reports of boxing tournament for newspapers; [pers.] I enjoy writing short stories and poems, for fun I also enjoy reading poetry. It make me feel relaxed and happy.; [a.] Kidsgrove, Staffordshire

CRICHTON, DOUGLAS N.
[b.] 25 October 1976, Guernsey; [p.] Robert and Sue Crichton; [ed.] All Hallows School, Dorset, Kent University (history); [occ.] Student; [memb.] Debating Society (Kent University) History Society; [hon.] Poem "La Coupe" published in 1995 Hilton Head Anthology "Poetic Inspirations" it received a "Special Commendation"; [oth. writ.] Predominantly poetry written about "Lost Love" and the progression of human society nature and the natural world. Are also important.; [pers.] Greatly influenced by poetry of Thomas Hardy and Byron. I try to write personal, emotional and honest poetry from which others can relate their own personal experiences.; [a.] Jersey

CROSSLEY, MRS. PEGGY
[pen.] Peggy C.; [b.] 9 August 1913, London, SW; [p.] Minnie and Frederick King; [m.] Dr. Edgar Crossley, 20 October 1984; [ed.] Surrey College, Pitman's Business College; [occ.] Retired; [memb.] Crown Road Baptist Church, Sutton Royal National Lifeboat Institution; [oth. writ.] Articles/Short stories published in employer's Magazines Articles and reports in Church magazines; [pers.] I am a committed Christian and my poetic skill is a gift from God. My life has been richly blessed and I hope that I pass/blessing on/to those I meet in the course of the day.; [a.] Wallington, Surrey

CROWE, ZAIDIE
[b.] 12 June 1958, Sheffield; [p.] Merdel and Alburn Crowe; [ch.] Idehen Christy; [ed.] B.A. (hons) and LL.M London University; [occ.] Policy and Research Officer - Kente; [oth. writ.] Short stories, poems; [pers.] To write what I see, hear/taste/feel. Others in society see/hear/taste/feel....and to write the echoes and reflections.; [a.] Wembley, Middlesex

CROXTALL, STANLEY WILFRED
[pen.] S. Wilfred Croxtall/St. Angelo; [b.] 28 July 1936, Plymouth, Devon; [p.] Grace Croxtall and Lawrence Stanley Croxtall; [m.] Bren Croxtall, 30 March 1974; [ed.] Westcotes Secondary Modern Leicester (Et Al), Open University (Social Sciences); [occ.] Retired Civil Servant; [memb.] Loyal Company of Town Criers, National Geographic Society R.S.P.B.; [oth. writ.] Poetry reviewer in national magazine, local poetry critic and writing workshop tutor. Co-authoring reference book on Psychology.; [pers.] "Subjectivity Perpetuates the imperfections of mankind: We ought, therefore, to be more diligent in our quest for truth."; [a.] South Wigston, Leicestershire

CULLER, KAY
[pen.] Audrey James; [b.] 4 October 1930, Co. Dublin; [p.] John and Ellen Keating; [m.] John Culler, 8 January 1957; [ch.] Audrey and James; [ed.] Primary - Co. Wicklow, Secondary - Co. Wicklow; [occ.] Disabled in a wheelchair; [memb.] Management Committee in Ardeen Cheshire Home; [hon.] First for a poem on Programme Live at three on Irish Television pictures made of my poems. Which were bought by Australians and Canadians. Poems in a frame was presented to the President of Ireland.; [oth. writ.] Lots of poems, "Wheelchair Lament", "Coblattin Wood", "Gloria Dei", to name put a few.; [pers.] I won a diploma in London out of 52 countries for wheelchair lament.; [a.] Shillelagh, Wicklow

CUMMINS, TOM
[b.] 30 April 1961, London; [p.] Thomas, Kathleen Cummins; [ch.] 1 girl - Sian-Marie; [ed.] Ambrose Fleming Secondary School; [occ.] Fabricator; [oth. writ.] Persona Stills, which want the world to know.; [pers.] 'Being' life is a chemical reaction wanting to happen.; [a.] Enfield, Middlesex

CURD, SUE
[b.] North London; [occ.] Ambulance Escort for Local Authority's Social Services Department; [memb.] Royal British Legion Women's Section, Lancastrian Drama Club, Local Lay Visitors Association; [hon.] Several Medals for Tap Dancing, Mensa Challenge Certificate; [oth. writ.] Two others poems published.; [pers.] I get my inspiration from the world of nature, and anything else that is wondrous.; [a.] Enfield, Middlesex

CURLEY, DENNIS
[b.] 25 July 1946, Chorley; [p.] Desmond Curley, Vera Curley; [m.] Christine Ann Bland, 25 October 1969; [ed.] Southlands High Chorley Technical College Wigan; [occ.] Artist Glass Engraver, Glass Retail; [memb.] Craft Member Guild of Glass Engraves; [hon.] Craft Status of Guild Glass Engraves One Man Exhibitions of Paintings and Glass, Honarth Art Gallery, Accrington and Samlesbury Hall, Preston; [oth. writ.] Beauty - voices on the wind. - Scottish mountain loch and glen - PLGA for life, and others local magazine.; [pers.] I try to reflect the beauty of the world and the seasons my love for the birds and the animals - and thoughts to find peace within.; [a.] Euxton, Chorley, Lancashire

CUTTING, JOSEPHINE
[b.] 21 June 1957, Kingston-upon-Thames; [p.] Kenneth Cutting, Barbara Cutting; [ed.] La Retraite Convent, Salisbury, Hereford College of Education; [occ.] Life Education Manager Wiltshire (Drug Prevention Work); [memb.] Mensa; [hon.] Certificate in Education Master of Arts Degree; [pers.] I derive my inspiration from nature. I am to reflect through my writing a sense of wonder and to the capture the silent power that nature words.; [a.] Bath, South and East Somerset

CUTTS, NOELINE IRIS
[pen.] Iris, or Noeline Cutts; [b.] 16 July 38, Otahuhu, NZ; [p.] Mrs. B. Thorley, Mr. G. Thorley (Deceased); [ch.] Lance, Sandi, Jasmine, Juliette, Tim; [ed.] Three years secondary, school certificate, 4 papers NZCB - Accounting; [occ.] Accounts Payable UGNC; [memb.] Distinguished member or International Library of Poetry, Victim Support; [hon.] Semi finals for 'Quite Moments', Semi finals for 'Lasting Calm'. Distinguished member of International Library of Poetry, one of 10 poets on "The Sound of Poetry"; [oth. writ.] "My Garden in verse and adverse". The language of love - book 1, The language of love - book 2; [pers.] I want to have the world a better place than I found it.; [a.] Auckland, New Zealand

DA COSTA, MARIA
[b.] 12 August 1936, Cabo Frio; [p.] Aracy, Nazareth Machado; [m.] Carlos Eduardo, 26 November 1960; [ch.] Carlos Eduardo, Teresa, Claudia, Paula; three granddaughters: Stephanie, Rebecca and Caroline; [memb.] Friend of the Royal Academy and National Art Collections Fund; [oth. writ.] "A Bouquet of Memories" (book), "Breath of Life" (35 poems in English and Portuguese), editorial team of "Leonora Age Concern Special", supporting poetry and short stories. (Magazine); [pers.] Do not let precious moments of your life be grabbed by life like strong winds in a stormy day...live them to the fullest, time never returns.; [a.] London

DALBY, NIGEL HOWARD
[b.] 17 November 1963, Huddersfield; [p.] Eva and Vincent Dalby; [m.] (Fiance) Dominique; [ch.] Shawn Dalby; [ed.] Newsome High School, left without knowing my qualifications; [occ.] Was unemployed. Now my trade is a catering butcher; [memb.] Cricket player for Nott's Amateur Cricket Club; [hon.] Just general sporting Trophies in Cricket and Boxing; [oth. writ.] I have never bothered to send my poem's to any publishers. The poem's of mine are kept private at home.; [pers.] My personal thoughts are given in my work. "Inspiration is from oneself not from anyone else." "Thoughts can differ with every second."; [a.] Nottingham, Nottinghamshire

DALLAS, KAREN
[b.] 10 July 1962, Beckenham; [p.] Ivan and Sandra Stock; [m.] Jim Clifford; [ch.] Ben, Tom, Jim and Jessica; [ed.] Woodlands Secondary; [occ.] Housewife; [oth. writ.] First poem published last year in an anthology "The Other Side of the mirror"; [Pers.] This poem is dedicated to my late father - the greatest inspiration of my life.; [a.] Gillingham, Kent

DANCE, MISS EUNICE
[pen.] Eunice; [b.] 13 June 1911, Reading; [p.] Mr. Sydney Christopher Dance, Mrs. Eunice Eva Agnes Dance; [ed.] Grovelands Comprehensive School, W. Reading; [occ.] Retired Nurse, Housekeeper; [memb.] Life-long Methodist, Officer of Girl's Life Brigade, Later Girl's Brigade (40 years), also Ass. Artist Guild; [hon.] Many for painting; [oth. writ.] A number of short poems and one longer work.; [pers.] Usually my works have a family background, looking back with gratitude, or in time of difficulty or sorrow.; [a.] Reading, Berkshire

DANIEL, MAUREEN
[b.] 9 January 1953, Ilford; [p.] Herbert and Elsie Daniel; [ed.] Beal Grammar; [memb.] Clacton Hospital League of Friends; [hon.] O.N.C. Public Administration; [oth. writ.] I have had my work printed in various publications.; [pers.] Humour is a major part of my life and I enjoy adding a sense of fun to my poems.; [a.] Clacton-on-Sea, Essex

DANKS, J. GEOFFREY
[b.] 2 December 1953, Netherton; [p.] Albert Danks, Mary Danks; [occ.] Civil Servant; [memb.] Crescent Theatre Birmingham; [a.] Dudley, West Midlands

D'ARK, MR. RONALD
[b.] 19 April 1936, Lexden, Essex; [p.] Sidney D'Ark and May D'Ark; [m.] Daphne D'Ark, 16 November 1968; [ch.] Helen now in Germany and Liam in Leeds; [ed.] Wandsworth Grammar, after compulsory call-up to obtained GCE 'A' Levels in English, Eng. Lit. and History plus RAF Teaching of touchtyping and shorthand for journalism later; [occ.] Hors-De-Combat with Epilepsy from Public Relations 'A' High Level; [memb.] (Note: All are now defunct); [oth. writ.] News and feature articles in local, national and international press, TV, radio, top-rate journals plus poetry in Scarborough's evening news and the book, 'Poetry Now', in 1993, have written sufficient poems for solo book publication; [pers.] Although governed by fate, most are lucky to have the faculties admired in my poem - gifts seldom valued until lost. We're more lucky if, like me at my age, they all keep going! Whatever we look like physically we cannot gain respect without having self-respect for our bodies - its the start of happiness.; [a.] Scarborough, North Yorkshire

DARLING, VALERIE
[b.] 14 September 1939, Swindon; [p.] Walter James and Lilian May Cozens; [m.] Leslie Victor Darling, 15 August 1959; [ch.] Paul, Robert and Neil Darling; [ed.] Pound Lane Secondary Modern School,

Willesden, London N.W. 10; [occ.] Housewife; [pers.] My poems are greatly influenced by my love for my husband and my three beloved sons and grandchildren. Benjamin (7), Emily (5); [a.] Dawlish, Devon

DASMAL, LAYLA
[pen.] Layla Kaycif; [b.] 2 September 1971, Dubai; [ed.] Oxford University, Pembroke College, Degree in Arabic, Literature; [occ.] PhD Oxford, Pembroke, Arabic Lit. (also aspiring singer/songwriter and creative writer); [memb.] Also enjoy painting - have done series of nudes in mixed media which I hope to use as a basis for possible development in that field.; [oth. writ.] 2 screenplays, several poems, several songs, started novel entitled "The Palmer"; [pers.] I feel that creative pursuits and intellectual fulfillment are my only real drives and I find is frustrating and 5th of a golden cage existence to have such diverse something, conflicting aspirations.; [a.] London

DATTA, JIA LAL
[b.] 12 October 1924, Tarntaran, India; [p.] Manohar Lal Datta; [m.] Bimla Rani Datta; [ch.] Two sons, one daughter, eight grandchildren; [ed.] M.A.B.T.; [occ.] Retired Teacher; [hon.] U.P. Govt. (India) 1988 award on my book 'short stories' (Urdu), Punjab Govt. (India) 1995 award on my Urdu Poetry Book called 'Raks-E-Saba'; [oth. writ.] Call To Prayer (poetry), Adoring Breeze, (poetry), Gulfashan (Urdu Poems) 4. Haroof-E-Jabeen (Urdu Poems); [pers.] My english and urdu poems are regularly being published in National Newspapers and Magazines in India.; [a.] Hounslow, Middlesex

DAVEY, JOANNA
[pen.] Jo Hanna; [b.] 15 March 1966, Huddersfield; [p.] Reverend Eric Davey and Joan Davey; [ed.] Kings Comprehensive School Wakefield District College Bradford and Ilkley Community College; [occ.] Mobile Beauty Therapist; [oth. writ.] Several poems on a number of subjects; [pers.] My poems are personal perceptions on the experiences in my life. It is self expression. I have no choice but to reach for pen and paper to share my thoughts with others; [a.] Wakefield, West Yorkshire

DAVIDSON, JOHN FRANCIS
[pen.] Little Scotty; [b.] 26 April 1942, Aberdeen; [p.] Mr. and Mrs. Geddes; [m.] Doreen Chalmers, 26 October 1974; [ch.] Gary Phimister (step son); [ed.] No higher but learning computing; [occ.] DIS; [memb.] Mecca Bingo Glasgow Ranges Fan; [hon.] Saved 2 boys life's from a Carbon Monoxide Cave in England 1973; [oth. writ.] Dustin My Pocket, Second Time Around, The Pages of Time, Just Another Day, The Endless Night, A Thousand Wishes; [pers.] I find poetry is good for the mind, it also helps when someone is ill to recite it to them.; [a.] Clydebank, Dumbartonshire

DAVIDSON, JOYCE
[b.] 21 May 1942, Aberdeen, Scotland; [p.] James and Mabel Stuart; [ch.] 1 boy and 2 girls, 2 grandchildren; [ed.] Secondary education attended classes and gained 5 "O" levels; [occ.] Cook at a local night club; [oth. writ.] A short story published in a magazine many years ago. One poem published earlier in 1996; [pers.] I see myself as an incurable romantic and tend to show this in my writing. I write the way I feel so therefore most of my work reflects my mood.; [a.] Turriff, Aberdeenshire

DAVIES, DAWN EMMA
[pen.] D. Emma Davies; [b.] 3 August 1974, St. Asaph; [p.] John Davies, Anne Davies; [ed.] Ysgol Emrys-Ap-Iwan, Abergele, N.E.W.I., Wrexham (University of Wales College); [occ.] Primary School Teacher, Abergele, N-Wales; [hon.] B. Ed Honours (English and History); [oth. writ.] Several poems all unpublished; [pers.] I write all of my poems from personal experiences.; [a.] Rhuddlan, Denbighshire

DAVIES, MR. DENNIS N.
[b.] 20 February 1937, West Bromwich; [p.] Edith and William Davies; [m.] Marie Davies, 16 June 1962; [ch.] Jason; [ed.] Church of England; [occ.] Production Operator; [oth. writ.] Other side of the

mirror by the International Library of Poetry contained poem Inner Peace other writings published by anchor books plus Poetry Guild; [pers.] Born in West Bromwich served in the British Army in the Middle West moved to Telford in 1965. Worked at G.K.N Sankey for 31 yrs took up poetry writing putting feelings to paper, when William my dog died.; [a.] Telford, Shropshire

DAVIES, MRS. EUNICE
[m.] Harry Davies; [memb.] Member Allied Dancing Association (Both my husband and I are qualified Teachers of Ballroom Dancing); [oth. writ.] Short stories, also, entered National Magazines, and newspaper competitions winning several prizes from time to time.; [pers.] Enjoy a most busy and interesting life. Attend and take interest in local borough council meetings, also, National and world events. Share many happy occasions with husband, relatives and close friends.; [a.] Runcorn, Cheshire

DAVIES, ROBIN
[b.] Ceylon; [ed.] L.S.E. (London School of Economics); [occ.] Prof. of Economics Sarajevo; [oth. writ.] Academic Journals Newspaper Articles; [a.] Bellevue, Geneva, Switzerland

DAVIES, TAMMY LOUISE
[b.] 19 August 1980, Rhondda; [p.] Graham and Gina Davies; [ed.] Porth County Comprehensive School; [occ.] Staying at School to do my A. Levels, O levels; [hon.] Gained compact certificate. Distinction award. In keyboard skills, also Religious Education Project has been submitted to W.J.E.C. due to work being of such a high standard.; [pers.] Writing poetry gives me a great sense of enjoyment and I hope the people who read them will also gain enjoyment from them.; [a.] Trealaw, Mid-Glam

DAVIES, VALERIE ANN
[pen.] Val Davies; [b.] 25 September 1931, N. London; [p.] Leonard Kiff and Florence Kiff; [m.] Charles Frederick Davies, 14 June 1952; [ch.] Clare, Howard and Diane; [ed.] Bromley Grammar School; [occ.] Retired; [memb.] Christ Church, Cheltenham, Mother's Union, Cheltenham Choral Society; [oth. writ.] "To Charles" - a collection of poems; [pers.] I started writing poetry in 1995 following the sudden death of my husband, expressing my emotions and subsequent belief that with God all in the end will be well.; [a.] Cheltenham, Gloucestershire

DAVIES, WILLIAM THOMAS
[pen.] Glyn Davies; [p.] Elsie Jane, Ben; [m.] Olive Irene; [ch.] Diana, Lynne, Anne; [ed.] Hendrefadog (Comp.); [occ.] Retired; [oth. writ.] The Walking Stick Man (Novel), Fatal Perfume (Novel), Handsome Is (Short Story), Little Billy and the Runaways (Children's Story); [pers.] Frailty, holds no fear for the frail. Only the strong.; [a.] Caerphilly, Mid-Glam

DAVISON, ANNE M.
[pen.] A.M.E.; [b.] 8 August 1961, Dublin; [p.] Catherine and Thomas Fetherston; [m.] Phillip J. Davison, 21 August 1987; [ch.] Stephen and Lauren; [ed.] St. Paul's Secondary School and Free University of Ireland; [occ.] Music Kindergarten Assistant (Lesson Park Sch of Music); [memb.] HXT Musical Society now and then Production Co. Shadow of the cross folk group; [hon.] Gold medalist in drama and speaking of verse and prose from the London Academy of music and dramatic art; [oth. writ.] Emphasis on poetry with a small amount of prose. Poem "Loves First Flavours" to be published this spring through the International Library of Poetry (Anthology).; [pers.] Truth may be found in beauty, which is why poetry often bears its fruits.; [a.] Co Dublin, Dublin

DAVISON, TRACY ANNE
[b.] 28 May 1980, Epsom; [p.] Linda Sibley and Brian Davison; [ed.] The Beacon Secondary School Banstead; [occ.] Student; [hon.] Gymnastic Award Tang Su Do in Martial Arts up to Yellow Belt, Two awards given, Certificate for 24th famine from World Vision for two years.; [oth. writ.] Many others written for pleasure.; [pers.] I enjoy putting my feelings into words. It helps me deal with my depression which I have suffered from for

some time. I feel a sense of achievement in doing them.; [a.] Tadworth, Surrey

DAWSON, BRENDA JANE ELLEN
[pen.] B. Clark; [b.] 24 July 1953, Dartford, Kent; [p.] Doreen Clark and Frank Clark; [ed.] Secondary Modern School for Girls A-Level Art; [occ.] Visual Merchandiser Assistant Manager (Display); [hon.] Highly commended for MM Illustration Art and Painting - exhibited at White Chapel Gallery. Still painting on a private basis, exhibited at Ilangili, Wildfowl Trust; [oth. writ.] Many poems written for personal use and to close friends and as an experience of many facets in my life.; [pers.] The power of the pen is great - reading is not only a pleasure but healer of the soul, helping many people in many ways.; [a.] Llanelli, Carmarthenshire

DAWSON, JACK
[b.] 4 February 1925, Leeds; [m.] May 1977; [occ.] Retired Tailor; [memb.] H.M.S. Howe (Ass), Burma Star (Ass.); [hon.] Burma Star Pacific Star and War Medals; [pers.] Often seeing the lighter side of life and reflecting it in poems and stories, more than 50 at the moment.; [a.] Leeds, Yorkshire

DAWTRY, RHODA
[b.] 17 June 1911, Wolverhampton; [p.] Mr. and Mrs. Dawtry; [ed.] St. Annes Convent High School, Birmingham, Sisters of Mercy; [occ.] Retired (music); [memb.] National Trust, R.Digest, Book Club, History Club; [oth. writ.] A private book for family and friends of poems, privately published.; [pers.] Loving all my life - Music, Art and the simple pleasures of the Countryside.; [a.] Wellington, West Midlands

DAY, CHARLI
[b.] 7 July 1979; [occ.] A level student; [pers.] When words are straight from your heart, time will never erode their beauty.; [a.] Windlesham, Surrey

DEAN, AMANDA
[b.] 9 December 1964, Luton, Bedfordshire; [p.] Rowland Dean and Brenda Dean; [m.] Robert Jancsics; [ch.] Kristina and Nichola; [ed.] Stockwood High (Luton) Barnfield College; [memb.] Taido Karate Club; [oth. writ.] Several poems published with another book company; [pers.] I would like to thank my boy friend Rob for having confidence in me where others failed. May my children Kristina and Nichola enjoy reading my poetry when they get older. A message to all poets, it doesn't have to be shakespeare to be good. And I love you dad.; [a.] Barton-le-Clay, Bedford

DE ARIAS, LUIS
[pen.] Luis De Arias; [b.] 31 January 1952, Chile; [p.] Federico and Maria Melly; [m.] Maria Teresa Loyola, 17 February 1972; [ch.] Marcelo, Carol, Mary, Daniel; [ed.] History, Literature, Philosophy Graduated in the University of Chile in 1974; [occ.] Postman - Royal Mail 55 Barrack Rd Northampton NN1 1AA; [oth. writ.] "Azalea" Surrealist Fantasy-Unpublished - currently writing autobiography "The Quiet Room"; [pers.] "I call upon the spirit of mankind to evolve and reach our true destiny - the discovery of our own souls and that nothing else does matter but the beauty of just being."; [a.] Northampton, Northamptonshire

DE BREANSKI, MR N.
[b.] 20 March 1920, Guernsey, CI; [p.] English; [m.] English; [ed.] Secondary School Education; [occ.] Retired; [pers.] I have lived near the sea most of my life and I am very much influenced by all of its moods.; [a.] Maidstone, Kent

DE SOUSA, JORGE AUGUSTO AMORIM
[b.] 27 May, Belem, Brazil; [p.] Stelio Elleres De Sousa and Cleide Amorim De Sousa; [ed.] Degrees in English by the Univ. of California of Los Angeles (UCLA) and in Linguistics by the University of Toronto, Canada; [occ.] Teacher of English, Portuguese and Spanish, as second languages; [hon.] Certificate of Proficiency in English by the University of Michigan USA; [oth. writ.] Several poems in Portuguese, English and one in French, also some short stories and essays-never published.; [pers.] Most of my writing is about feelings - this fascinating rainbow. To me, they are the soul of a poem and make every poet humanly more human.; [a.] London

DEANS, ALAINA
[b.] 3 June 1969, Halton, Nr Ayl; [p.] Ivan Parsons, Frances Parsons; [m.] Joseph Deans, 13 February 1993; [ch.] Joseph, Edward, Christian Mario; [ed.] The Grange County Secondary School Aylesbury Bucks; [occ.] Housewife; [oth. writ.] Poems I've composed for family and close friends, none have been submitted for publication. I didn't think I had a talent although people have told me otherwise.; [pers.] My poems come straight from the heart and are not pre-planned. The words just happen, so I quickly grab a pen and some paper and write. They are written to give help and comfort and to express my inner most thoughts for myself and others.; [a.] Aylesbury, Buckinghamshire

DEHTIAR, VICTOR
[b.] 18 April 1921 raine; [p.] Ukrainian; [m.] Eva Mary British, 31 July 1948; [ch.] Two; [ed.] Three years of four year College of Mining Engineering Technical College in Ukraine; [occ.] Retired; [oth. writ.] Autobiography, Five Hymns and other poems not published; [pers.] Planet Earth is just a garden of Primordial Divine being, the God. Who from the beginning of time sow the seeds of Human race to grow. To grow not only in stature but in wisdom and understanding, that we may learn to live in harmony, peace, charity, love and hope. Then through His eternal redeeming love we may became his adopted children or at least the citizens of His Eternal Kingdom.; [a.] Swansea, Swansea

DENHAM, PAM
[b.] 13 October 1950, Middridge, Co Durham; [p.] Ena Foster and Arthur Young; [m.] Kevin; [ch.] Mark, Richard and Craig; [ed.] Shildon County Infants Shildon County Juniors. Spenny Moor Grammar Technical School, Co. Durham; [occ.] House Wife - Part time student; [memb.] G.C.S.E., R.E. and English; [hon.] Several poems and short stories.; [a.] Shildon, Durham

DENNIS, MS. JILLIAN LISA
[b.] 3 September 1970, Hillingdon; [p.] Mr. Michael West and Mrs. Patricia West; [m.] Divorced; [ed.] 8 Olevels 1 Alevel (English lit) Diploma - children's fiction and freelance journalism; [occ.] Police officer; [hon.] 8 Olewels, 1 Alevel English, 2 Diplomas - children's fiction and journalism; [pers.] I write real life, not only pleasant things - but the things that hurt...; [a.] Worthing, Sussex

DERRY, CLAIRE
[b.] 19 February 1987, Munster, Germany; [p.] Andy Derry and Lynne Derry; [ed.] Amesbury Junior School; [occ.] School Girl; [pers.] My Grandma Pam wrote lots of poems and she has influenced me in my writing. I wrote this one no memory of her the say after she died.; [a.] Amesbury, Wiltshire

DICKENS, MR. HARRY F.
[pen.] Charlesmore; [b.] 20 July 1923, Stourbridge, West Midlands; [p.] Squire and Anne Dickens; [m.] June 1966, Divorced 1973; [ed.] Orchard Lane (Comp. Stourbridge West Midlands - but mainly self educated through Royal Naval Service and deep insight study into all fine works of art; [occ.] Self Employed (Boarding House And Flat Owner); [memb.] Royal English Poetry Society 22 Betterton Street London WC2H and distinguished member of the International Library of Poetry Sittingbourne Kent; [hon.] Prize Awards for writing several letters of controversial nature such as the return of the stocks for punishable offences against the elderly and children legalization of brothels for street Clearance and Great passion for the Big Band Sound; [oth. writ.] Poems already published, Cuckoo Love Anthology (Voices on the Wind and Future poems of note awaiting publication - may I quote? - Is this what if really is all about a life?; [pers.] I see it all within my mind - and gather fruits of a different kind - for what is he that lives in sin does he never realize just as with the roll of a ball or toss of a coin life - could be on call just give it a spin!; [a.] Blackpool, Lancs

DICKINSON, CHRISTINA LOUISE
[pen.] Christina Dickinson; [b.] 9 August 1985,
Grimsby; [p.] John Dickinson, Yvonne Dickinson; [ed.] Bursar Street Primary, Cleethorpes, Matthew Humberstone School, Cleethorpes; [occ.] Student; [hon.] Two literature awards for poetry and English from school. Aged 10 years.; [pers.] I enjoy reading fictional stories and writing poetry, one day hoping to have more published.; [a.] Cleethorpes, NE Lincolnshire

DICKINSON, FRANK
[b.] 1929, Bradford; [p.] Hilda, Ernest (Deceased); [m.] Jean Dargue, 20 March 1953; [ch.] Mick, John, Philip; [ed.] Bradford Hanson Grammar School, Blackmans School; [occ.] Retired (Police-officer); [memb.] 'Bronte Society', 'Eccsleshill Local History Group' Bradford 'Platform' Poetry Reading Group; [oth. writ.] A few poems published. Many local history research articles published in local and published in local and national magazines. Articles on soccer history in supported magazine (Bradford City); [pers.] I have been influenced by the 1st war poets - I Wilfred Owens - Isaac Rosenberg in particular. Nature poetry appeals to me - also the Georgian Poets. I try to emulate their ideals.; [a.] Bradford, W. Yorks

DICKINSON, MRS. MAVIS
[b.] 18 March 1932, Northumberland; [p.] Henry Cookson, and Hilda Cookson; [m.] Divorced, 17 December 1952; [ch.] Lynne, Steven, Ann, Stuart; [ed.] Secondary Modern School, Morpeth Commercial College, and Nurses Preliminary Training School; [occ.] Housewife, now retired; [oth. writ.] Several poems published in other anthologies.; [pers.] I simply write about life, therefore my poems are diverse. I see beauty, sadness, laughter, hope. All of these things, I write about in my poems!; [a.] Lichfield, Staffordshire

DICKSON, ANNA
[b.] 11 August 1973, Leicester; [p.] Keith Dickson and Jo Dickson; [ed.] Leicester Grammar, Loughborough, College of Art and Design, Sheffield College; [pers.] I would like to dedicate my poem to my father, for whom it is written. And to thank my mother for being there for me throughout.; [a.] Stoneygate, Leicestershire

DITTA, SELINA
[b.] 28 February 1983, Bradford; [p.] Mansoor (Father), Shahnaz (Mother); [ed.] Rossefield Primary Shaw House Secondary; [oth. writ.] I have recited my poems in public, but have not submitted any for publication.; [pers.] I used to write imaginative poems when I was younger. Now I write about something that inspires, or concerns me. Drug's guns was written about the dangers of life on the street and is dedicated to the late American rap artist Tupac Shakur; [a.] Bradford, West Yorkshire

DIXON, GEMMA
[b.] 16 April 1983, Middlesbrough; [p.] Cliff and Tina; [ed.] Currently in year 9 in Acklam Grange Comprehensive School, Middlesbrough; [occ.] School Girl; [memb.] Dovecot Youth Theatre, Stockton; [hon.] Grade III Speech and Drama (Merit), Grade V Group Acting (Honours) - London College of Music; [oth. writ.] Have just completed Compilation of poems and stories on the theme of "Christmas" written over the last 3 years, which I hope to get published.; [pers.] Poetry is my way of expressing my feelings to the world.; [a.] Middlesbrough, Cleveland

DO, THANDAR-KHIN
[b.] 10 February 1978, Burma; [p.] Khin Maung Do, Nilar Do; [ed.] Leisure and Tourism, Bromley College; [occ.] Student; [hon.] Intermediate GHVQ, Leisure and Tourism; [pers.] Dedicated to my granddad. I strongly believe that my words and my creation came from the root of my emotions.; [a.] Bromley, Kent

DOBSEN, FRANCES ELIZABETH
[pen.] Biddy Froth as Sub-Editor of "Sphinx"; [b.] 23 February 1912, Wallasey, Cheshire; [p.] John and Alice Gaskill; [m.] Edward Dobsen, 3 July 1948; [ch.] Celia Haxlon and Paul Dobsen; [ed.] Wallasey High School, University of Liverpool - English and
Education Departments foll. by 36 years of teaching, ages 5-18; [occ.] Retired teacher (I am now 84 years old); [memb.] At University -Cox of Women's Boat Club, later varied literary, sport and political groups. Now - Women's Institute, Choir, Over 60's keep fit.; [hon.] B.A. Honours in Language and Literature at Liverpool University 1930-1934; [oth. writ.] Numerous stories and poems, including several sonnets, loughish, religious poems etc. (Poor sight now Glaucoma); [pers.] A prized possession of mine is an original letter from John Lockwood Kipling to my grandfather, announcing the birth of Rudyard Kipling. My grandmother was Elizabeth Kipling, J.L.K's sister.; [a.] Bramley, Nr. Guildford, Surrey

DOCKERY, SARAH JAYNE
[pen.] Sarah Dockery; [b.] 3 October 1982, Sutton Coldfield; [p.] Terry and Barbara; [ed.] Highclare School (Erdington) Commencing ACSE Coursework September '97; [occ.] Student; [memb.] Mensa, School Hockey Team; [hon.] Form Prize (School) 2 years 5 Royal Academy of Dancing Certificates, A.S.A Swimming Challenge Gold Award; [oth. writ.] Writings for school and private pleasure; [pers.] My hope is that through my poems, people will find peace and love in their lives.; [a.] Sutton Coldfield, West Midlands

DOHERTY, ANNIE
[b.] 29 October 1946, Letter Clonmany; [p.] Bernard and Kathleen McLaughlin; [m.] Patrick Joseph, 3 September 1970; [ch.] Brian, Martin, Anthony, Annette, Patrick and Michael; [ed.] Primary School; [occ.] Housewife; [oth. writ.] This is the third anthology in which I've had my poems printed, was a runner up in 1994 Drogheda 800 Comp., (In Ireland), a Book of my poems called "Penned into submission" which I've had printed out myself currently on sale.; [pers.] I've loved writing since I was at school and the feeling of anticipation on opening my exercise back and revealing an unwritten page and the ever thrilling scent of new paper has never left me like a starving person offered a meal I can't wait to set stuck in.; [a.] Letter Clonmany, Lifford, Co. Donegal, Ireland

DOHERTY, BARBARA
[pen.] "Bara Dane"; [b.] 25 August 1918, Wilmslow, Cheshire; [p.] Charles Edward Holt, Bertha Holt; [m.] Douglas John Doherty, 28, July 1945; [ch.] John Bryan, Rose Anne, Susan Gay; [ed.] Wilmslow Preparatory School Stockport High School, Cheshire Manchester School of Art, 3 years course, Auxiliary Territorial service (3 1/2 yrs), No. 1 MTTC (Camberley) March 1942 - September 1945; [occ.] Ex-housewife, Widow; [memb.] WRVS - Civil Defence, Women's Institute-Harlech, (24 years); [oth. writ.] The British Broadcasting Co. accepted three of my poems for "Listen with Mother" one was broadcast. Two poems printed in "Brethyn Cartret" our WI Magazine.; [pers.] I love the countryside, the Flora and Fauna, also the beauty of each season poetry and music give me so much pleasure.; [a.] Harlech, Gwynedd

DOHERTY, MARIANNE
[pen.] Marianne Lea; [b.] 29 December 1969, W. Midlands; [p.] Alice and Steve Lea; [m.] Michael Doherty; [ch.] Michael, Tammy, Shannon, Hayleigh, Kirsty; [oth. writ.] "My First Bike" published in voices on the wind. Many unpublished poems hopefully going into my own book.; [pers.] My poem is sent with all my love to: Michael Tammy - Shannon - Hayleigh and Kirsty Doherty. Love from Mom; [a.] Birmingham, West Midlands

DORKINGS, SARAH E.
[b.] 24 January 1969, Lewes, E Sussex; [p.] William Dorkings and Ann Dorkings; [ed.] Lewes Priory School, Lewes Technical College; [oth. writ.] With "Friendship" being my first published poem, I am encouraged to share some of my many other poems written; [pers.] My poems are written from my heart to reflect my experiences of life. "Friendship" was written after a visit from an old school friend whom I hadn't seen for years. It was when she left that I realized the importance of true friendship and was inspired to write.; [a.] Lewes, East Sussex

DOUGALL, SHEILA FRANCES
[b.] 22 August 1960, Aberdeen; [p.] Margaret Alexander, James Alexander (Deceased); [m.] Graeme Buchan Dougall, 31 May 1984; [ch.] Heather-Anne and Craig Buchan Dougall; [ed.] 4 O'levels, City and Guilds, 70611, First Aid; [occ.] Part time cook and housewife; [memb.] Cat Clubs,, Line Dancing, Darts; [hon.] Dart trophies, Ear Rosettes; [oth. writ.] None viewed by public eye.; [pers.] I write about life as it happens or experienced.; [a.] Dyce, Aberdeen, Scotland

DOUGLAS, GWEN
[b.] 5 October 1948, Hull; [p.] Kenneth and Jean Hayzen; [m.] Edward Douglas, 15 July 1995; [ed.] Estcourt High School for Girls. Hull College of Technology, Hull College of Humberside; [occ.] Chemical Anaylst at Smith and Nephew Medical, Hull; [oth. writ.] Several poems published by Anchor Books Poetry now., The International Library of Poetry, The Hilton House Publishers, Anthology Series; [pers.] Poetry should not be obscure and difficult to understand. A poet should be able to reach out to people and touch a certain nerve or emotion. Poetry of the people should be for the people.; [a.] Hull, East Yorkshire

DOWDING, SHARON
[pen.] Phagos; [b.] March 1970, Paulton; [p.] Ruth Edditts, Francis Dowding; [occ.] Horticulturalist; [hon.] 29 awards for Floral Displays from the Bath in Bloom Committee; [pers.] Influenced by the writings of Philip Carr-Gomm and of dragons my work reflects my knowledge of lore at its many stages.; [a.] Bath, Avon

DOWNS, SAMANTHA
[pen.] Sam; [b.] 17 November 1978, Billinge; [p.] Susan Oakes and Fred Downs, my Grandma, Mrs. S.E. Downs; [ed.] Wigan College; [occ.] Student; studying G.N.V.Q. leisure and tourism intermediate; Virgin Cinemas, Wigan; [pers.] The poem here written by myself has been created from deep memorable feelings I've experienced in my life. I've connected these feelings through the symbol of each yearly season mentioned; [a.] Wigan, Lancashire.

DRACKETT-CASE, JOYCE
[pen.] Joy Drackett-Case, Joy De Case; [b.] Newmarket; [p.] Herbert and Mary Drackett-Case; [m.] Edgar Clements; [ch.] Maxwell and Susan Clements; [ed.] Kingston-on-Thames; [occ.] Artist and Housewife; [memb.] Associate Royal Ulster Academy, Past Pres. Ulster Society of Women Artists, Vice Pres and Chairman Ulster, Water Color Society, Student of School Philosophy; [hon.] Twice Recipient Perpetual Trophy-Ulster, Society Women Artists (Paint Under Joy Clements); [oth. writ.] Article published in local magazine "Mandalas" and poem attend creative writing class and am doing correspondence course.; [pers.] "No Man Is An Island", we are all part of the great universal consciousness, but most of us are asleep and unaware. Poetry and art can awaken.; [a.] Newtownabbey, Antrim

DRAKE, JO-ANN
[b.] 9 April 1982, Cork; [p.] Billy, Josie Drake; [ed.] 2nd year in Colaiste Eoin Youghal; [hon.] This is my first; [oth. writ.] None that are known of at the moment but have written over 200.; [pers.] The greatest influence in my life, to this point, are my feelings and that shows in all my poems.; [a.] Youghal, Cork

DRAYSEY, JACKIE
[b.] West Midlands; [p.] Mary and Gordon Williams; [m.] John; [ch.] Sally; [memb.] Member of the National Society of Poets; [oth. writ.] Several poems published and illustrated.; [pers.] When words rise I have to write them down. This a choiceless path for me.; [a.] Arden, West Midlands

DRUMMOND, DOREEN
[pen.] Doreen Drummond; [b.] 1 October 1935, Brighouse; [p.] The Late Thomas and Kathleen Paviour; [m.] Divorced; [ch.] Steven, Paul, Croft; [ed.] St. James, brighouse, Longroyde, Junior, Rastrick, Rastrick Common, Secondary Modern

School, Brighouse; [occ.] Retired; [oth. writ.] Several poems published in Brighouse "Echo" paper.; [pers.] I write what I feel, when I feel strongly about something, I always put it into verse. I am influenced by where I live, and what I see, I am only a few miles from Bronte Country.; [a.] Brighouse, Yorkshire

DUGUID, SALLY
[b.] 20 May 1978; [pers.] This is a poem about memories, love if it doesn't break you it will make you stronger.; [a.] Uckfield, East Sussex

DULSON, CATHERINE E.
[pen.] Catherine Dulson; [b.] 23 April 1957, Scunthorpe; [p.] William I. Reynolds and Bernice B. Reynolds; [m.] Stuart P. Dulson, 23 May 1987; [ch.] Samantha and Adam; [ed.] High Ridge Comprehensive School Scunthorpe; [occ.] House wife; [oth. writ.] Several poems written during my latter school years and since, but only for my pleasure, nothing published.; [pers.] To achieve what has always seemed a distant goal, to complete and hopefully publish my own book of poetry.; [a.] Scunthorpe, North Lincolnshire

DUNN, BRIAN
[b.] 22 March 1937, Plymstock; [m.] Julia Christabel, 25 October 1965; [ch.] Tracey John, Joantha Caroline, Alexander James; [ed.] Birkenhead School; [occ.] Recently Retired; [memb.] Port Sunlight Players, Church Lads' and Church Girls' Brigade; [hon.] NODA 35 yrs. Medal and Bars; [oth. writ.] Letters and articles in House Journals and Parish magazines; [pers.] Poetry for pleasure, not pretention.; [a.] Birkenhead, Merseyside

DUNN, DERRICK DELORNO
[b.] 17/08/70, B'ham; [p.] Jeff & Oreta Dunn; [ed.] Audley Junior School, Sir Wilfred Martineau (C.S.), Aston Arts (College), Wolverhampton University (Current); [occ.] Part time library assistant - Bloomsbury Nechells; [memb] of a fiction writing class at Stonehall, Acocks Green for five years; [hon.] School and class monitor, awarded for rugby, played Sunday football for a brief spell until back problem, also indoor football at Aston Villa Leisure Centre; [oth. writ.] Never published other than a joke in 1978 in a comic called Whizzer & Chips. Hopefully this is a start. However, I have performed on several occasions, notably council open days.; [pers.] I want to leave the globe the flowers of my creativity, connoting that its bedded seeds are owed to the workings of the universe.; [a.] B'ham, West Midlands

DUNN, ELEANOR
[pen.] Eleanor Brandes (when single); [b.] Birkenhead; [p.] Charles and May Brandes; [m.] James Dunn; [ch.] David-Jaymie & Paul; [ed.] Prenton Secondary School, Laird Art School; [occ.] housewife, poet, writer; [memb.] Poetic License, One Eyed City Poets, Poetry Society (London); [hon.] Editor's Choice Award, International Society Poets, Jeff Roberts (Lyric Award), Talent and Ass. (Lyric Award), prize from Robbie Burns Society, Award for Art; [oth. writ.] Children's stories, Ghost stories, Horror stories, 32 poems published since March 95, Magazine SA poems published 3 newspaper pieces of writing and two songs published.; [pers.] I love to get my thoughts down on paper. I love to write. Influenced by Robert Servile Alfred Noyes. I write many long funny monologues, unfortunately too long to publish. I have a very active mind which speaks poetry to me all the time. I like to feel my poems bring a little happiness to people. [a.] Birkenhead, Merseyside

DUNN, MRS. IRIS
[pen.] I. Dunn; [b.] 8 October 1925, Rugeley, Staffs; [p.] Mable and Joseph Flowers; [m.] Mr. Joseph Dunn, 27 December 1948; [ch.] Two girls, one son; [ed.] Rugeley, Church of England, Primary and Relgar Comprehensive Schools; [occ.] Housewife; [hon.] Editor's Choice Award 1996; [oth. writ.] Poem for mother's day "Bonds of Love".; [pers.] I like to write poetry when the mood takes me mostly about people and the beauties of nature, to take my mind away from the stress of this world today.; [a.] Seaford, East Sussex

DUNNE, REV. JUDE MARTIN
[b.] 5 June 1948, Cork, Irl.; [p.] James (Deceased) and Margaret Dunne; [m.] Mary Dunne, 22 September 1990; [ch.] Jude Leslie and Jacinta Elizabeth; [ed.] B.TH. Jacksonville Theological Seminary, Florida, U.S. (Irish Satellite), M.A. candidate, candidate for Counsellor with Assoc. Christian Counsellors, Irl.; [occ.] Programme Mngr. J.T.S. Irish Satellite; [memb.] Association of Christian Counsellors (Irl); [oth. writ.] Currently preparing a booklet of Penned Poetry. A desire to publish penned short stories; [pers.] An expression of the heart is my intention through 'words' in poetry, so others may be lifted up and catch 'hope' to go on living fruitfully.; [a.] Cork, Ireland

DUNNE, MARY
[b.] 11 January 1926, Liverpool; [p.] Robert and Bridget Davies; [m.] John Dunne, 26 December 1953; [ch.] Paul, Angela and Brian; [ed.] Our Ladys Eldon St Liverpool; [occ.] Senior Citizen; [pers.] I started writing poetry after I retired. Most of my poems reflect the past events in my life; [a.] Welshpool, Powys

DUNSTAN, RUTH
[pen.] Ruth Dunstan; [b.] 27 February 1938, Saltash, Cornwall; [p.] Edward John Dunstan - Rita Dunstan; [m.] Wilfred Tomlin (Divorced), 28 February 1959; [ch.] Kent Tomlin, Paul Tomlin, Dawn Tomlin; [ed.] Secondary Modern; [occ.] Early Retirement from being a Court Usher; [hon.] Served in WRNS 1957-1961 - 18 months Abroad in Malta-Met Queen mother in WRNS 1957 HMTS dauntless reading, berks - also met the late Gracie Fields in Capri whilst serving in the WRNS - in Malta; [oth. writ.] Served 12 years as a Court Usher in Birmingham have always been composing lyrics, ballads, verse for over 30 years; [pers.] I've always been poetical-have compiled several small booklets of verse-also a large book of lyrical verse, religious verse titled "Walk in Faith" I also dabble in oil painting-mainly seascapes - I am a very deep spiritual person love the sea-but live inland.; [a.] Solihull, West Midlands

DURHAM, GEOFF
[b.] 18 September 1967, Staffordshire; [p.] Mrs. Barbara Hollins, Mr. Terry Durham; [ed.] Trinity C.E. High School, Cauldon College of F.E., Staffordshire Polytechnic; [occ.] Admin/Technical Assistant Newcastle Borough Council; [hon.] HNC in Public Administration; [oth. writ.] "What In A Smile" International Library of Poetry, "Night" Poetry Today, "Scarecrow" Poetry Now.; [pers.] Poetry brings out my true feelings it is something I really enjoy and hope that others enjoy reading them.; [a.] Newcastle, Staffordshire

DUTTON, BERYL
[b.] 10 September 1946, Newscastle, Staffs; [p.] Frances and Wilfred Alcock; [m.] Christopher Dutton (Deceased), 24 October 1964; [ch.] Julie, Debbie, Lorraine; [ed.] Secondary Modern; [occ.] Care Assistant; [hon.] Award of Merit for Piano Playing; [oth. writ.] Many but none published; [pers.] A situation can arouse a sense of feeling which can be wrote in verse.; [a.] Grange-over-Sands, Cumbria

DYER, ROBERT
[pen.] J. Antboz; [b.] 23 February 1960, Govan; [p.] Richard Dyer, Ellen Dyer; [m.] Agnes (Nan) Wilson, 24 January 1997; [ch.] Louisa, Maria; [ed.] St. Cuthberts, Johnston Anniesland College James Watt College; [occ.] Welder; [memb.] Dunoon Tipplers Appreciation Society; [oth. writ.] I divide my time between landscape painting and writing short poems; [pers.] Without the support and affection of my family I would not have made it through the storms; [a.] Sandbank, Argyll

ECCLES, THOMAS
[b.] 28 June, Corby; [p.] Margaret and Joseph; [ed.] Our Lady and Pope John School Corby; [occ.] Knitter in the Hosiery Trade; [memb.] Thai Boxing, Now Training for Instructor in Silat Martial Arts Instructor; [hon.] Several Awards in Boxing during my time in the Arm with the 2nd Royal Anglina Reat; [oth.

writ.] This poem is my first attempt to have a poem published but I have written many poems for my own pleasure reflecting my thoughts.; [pers.] You only live once, live it to your fuel potential, look at life!; [a.] Corby, Northants

EDDERSHAW, MARGARET
[b.] 26 November 1943, Westham, Sussex; [ed.] Bexhill Grammar, University of Manchester; [occ.] Retired Previously Sen. Lecturer in Theatre Studies, Lancaster University.; [hon.] B.A. Hons. Drama (Man.), M. Litt. (Lancs.); [oth. writ.] "Grand Fashionable Nights" (history of theatre in Kendal), "Performing Brecht" (Routledge 1996), five plays, incl. "Penelope's Web", performed by author in London, 1991, two poems pub. in ...the buzz... (Manchester).; [pers.] This poem is dedicated to my sister, Liza Pragnell, Fashion designers and Journalist , Murdered in Paris, December 1995.; [a.] Lancaster, Lancs

EDGE, COLIN
[b.] 4 May 1966, Darlington; [p.] Peter David Edge, Patricia Anne Edge; [m.] Michelle Grant; [ch.] Mathew, Misty; [ed.] Comprehensive School; [occ.] Police Officer; [hon.] Studying for BSC(Hons) degree in Policing and Police studies - embracing Psychologically, Criminology and Social Science Areas.; [oth. writ.] Continuing to write a book of short horror studies and a fictional book based on police work entitled: "The Blue Bubble"; [pers.] Currently researching "Bystander Intervention" for my BSC (hons) degree in Policing studies.; [a.] Erith, Kent

EDWARDS, BRIAN ROWLAND
[b.] 16 May 1934, Brighton; [p.] English; [m.] Separated, 1963; [ch.] Four; [ed.] Professional/Technical Building Surveyor; [occ.] Technical Manager; [memb.] Fellow the Chartered Institute of Building FCIOB.; [oth. writ.] Romanian Promises Securitate Songstress (both yet to be published); [pers.] Widely travelled. Lived for a short time in Soviet Union, working there for 2 years, particularly interested in Romania. Enjoy writing about personal relationships.; [a.] Luton, Beds

EGGLETON, SUSAN
[b.] 9 February 1959, London; [p.] Dorothy and Peter Tomlin; [m.] Kimberly Eggleton, 31 January 1976; [ch.] Nichola Joanne and Wayne Liam; [ed.] Richard Jefferies Comprehensive School, Park High School; [occ.] Senior Customer Service, Representative; [pers.] As this is my first published piece I am hopeful that it will be the catalyst to my writing, both poetic and novelistic, career.; [a.] Swindon, Wiltshire

EL-HADIDI, LINA
[pen.] Linapeare; [b.] 13 May 1969, Kuwait/Egyptian National; [p.] Mohammed El-Hadidi and Rouaida Zokoy; [ed.] English Literature Graduate/University of Damascus - Syria; [occ.] Secretary/Bank of Kuwait and the Middle East; [memb.] Marine Club - Kuwait; [hon.] English Literature Certificate from University of Damascus; [oth. writ.] Several articles published in Local Newspapers and Syrian Newspapers. Poems published in Local magazines.; [pers.] "This poem is dedicated to my everlasting inspiration: Alex James (member/blur band). It's good to bring back to life the pure and honest feelings of romance which are mostly unexisted in this artificial world."; [a.] Kuwait, Kuwait

ELIE, WENONA
[b.] 7 June 1975, Forest Gate, London; [ed.] St Angela's Ursuline Convent, New Vic Sixthform College, Luton University; [occ.] Student, and Writer; [hon.] Certificates, medals and trophies for Contemporary Dancing, produced a twenty minute Magazine Programme, which was broadcasted on Cable Television; [oth. writ.] Published short stories in college magazine. Called Excell.; [pers.] I have a passion for writing, not just poetry but for fiction. Hope to be a successful author and scriptwriter. And hope to share my work with the world.; [a.] Luton, Bedfordshire

ELLIOTT, THOMAS FLEMING
[b.] 28 November 1918, Glasgow; [p.] Jeanie Campbell, James Elliott; [ed.] Albert Higher Glade Springburn Glasgow; [occ.] Retired; [memb.] British Limblees Exservice man's Ass., Cumnor Cricket Club;

[hon.] 1939 Star France, Defence with free French General service Deep-Sea-Diver; [oth. writ.] A few little poetry efforts.; [pers.] History is the key to life. My favorite places: The Cotswolae, The River Thames, The Cote D'Azur; [a.] Oxford, Oxon

ELLOTT, GUY HEWITT
[pen.] Hewitt Ellott; [b.] 2 September 1959, Redhill; [p.] James Ellott, Jeannie Hewitt Ellott; [m.] Caroline June; [ch.] Joanne, Sarah, Megan and Jake; [ed.] The College Of Life; [occ.] Motor Vehicle Examinations and Medication; [memb.] Royal British Legion, Green Peace; [oth. writ.] Eglathius ring super tankers, Cave men ruled O.K; [pers.] "Genethon" The writing's on the walls.; [a.] Horley, Surrey

ENDLAR, TOBY S.
[p.] Louis Endlar and Sophia (Nee Lawrence); [occ.] Accountant (Retired); [memb.] Chartered Secretaries and Administrators, Chartered Institute of Arbitrators, Institute of Management, Instit. of Financial Accountants, Instit. of Company Accountants, Society of Amateur Artists; [hon.] F.C.I.S. - A.I.Arb. - M.B.I.M. - A.F.A. - A.S.C.A.; [pers.] "The Pen is Mightier than the Sword." In considering the works of Robert Burns one cannot fail to be emotionally moved by the intensity of his love for all humanity and his hatred of suffering. He used his poetry as penned ammunition against hypocrisy and cruelty, but many were poems that inspired awareness of beauty. His works are an inspiration to would - be poets who feel that they have something to say, and try to find the best way to say it. He has certainly inspired me.; [a.] Glasgow, Lanarkshire

EPPS, PEARL MOLVINA
[pen.] Molvina; [b.] 30 March 1921, Plymouth; [p.] John - Violet Simpson; [m.] John Epps, 13 December 1941; [ch.] Five; [ed.] St Johns School Plymouth; [occ.] Housewife widowed; [oth. writ.] A poem for the Queen of her Silver Jubilee, it was published in the local press; [pers.] A romantic at heart, in my day Wordsworth and Longfellow were my influence. My philosophy is "if you can't do a good turn, never do a bad one".; [a.] Swansea, Glam

EVANS, IDWAL WILLIAM
[b.] 3 August 1902, Llanelli; [p.] William Evans, Edith Handley; [m.] Eva C. Evans, 28 April 1956; [ch.] Idwal William; [ed.] Council School Newton Abbot Oldham, Bury (Lancs) Ashton Under Lyne, Totham (Essex) Boston (Lincs) Seacombe (Cheshire); [occ.] Retired Salvation Army Officer; [pers.] In 1922 I was commissioned as a Salvation Army officer and served on active service for over forty five years in England and Wales.; [a.] Brightlingsea, Essex

EVANS, JACKIE
[b.] 12 December 1968, London; [p.] Michael and Rosemary Evans; [m.] Partner: Mark Nelson together since 2 July 1984; [ch.] Rianna Jodeci; [ed.] Eliot Bank Primary School, Sydenham Girls Comprehensive both in Syndenham, London; [occ.] Lithographic Printer; [pers.] This is my first poem to be published. I am an ordinary working mum, who enjoys writing for pleasure. I am honoured that my poem has been chosen.; [a.] London, Catford

EVANS, MANDY ELIZABETH
[pen.] Amanda Pyke, M. E. Evans; [b.] 29 October 1967, Barnet; [p.] Dennis Evans, Irene Evans; [ch.] Stephanie Taylor, Samantha Taylor; [ed.] Mount Grace School, Potters Bar Oaklands College, Borehamwood; [occ.] Mature Student going to University to study writing and publishing with philosophy; [memb.] Member of Potters Bar, Spiritualist Church, Oaklands Student Union; [oth. writ.] Writing first novel at present. Putting a collection of inspired poems together also written short stories for magazine publication without success so far.; [pers.] My poems are inspired by my spirit guides and my friends who attend the church. It is with hope, that my words reach out and touch the many, who read them.; [a.] Borehamwood, Hertfordshire

EVANS, TRACEY
[pen.] Poet Evans; [b.] 14 September 1963, Neath, W Glam; [p.] Eifion Evans, Maureen Evans; [ch.] Ricky

Phillip Evans; [ed.] Aberaman Primary School, Aberdane Girls Grammar School, Ystrad Mynacy College Fe; [occ.] Student; [memb.] Institute of Supervision, Management; [oth. writ.] Several poems this is the first one to be published; [pers.] My achievement has been due so the love any inspiration of my grandparents especially Emrys Evans and William Henry Rowe sadly deceased and to Uncle Brynmore who himself is a writer and poet and is always there to offer encouragement.; [a.] Aberaman, Mid-Glam

EVENDEN, CLINTON
[pen.] Clint Edwards; [b.] 11 June 1979, W. G. City; [p.] Sandra Williams; [ed.] Barnwell Secondary; [occ.] A level student; [memb.] Vice - Chairman of Sixth Form Committee; [hon.] The duke of Edinburgh Award and the Institute of Management award for public speaking; [oth. writ.] Many poems and prose including "A Critic Of An Expressionless State", "My Designer Bliss," and "Liquid Desires".; [pers.] As civilized beings, we are chained to the hopeless tradition of rebuilding our self-esteem, while being totally aware of the worthlessness of everything.; [a.] Stevenage, Hertfordshire

EVERAN, MARY-ROSE
[b.] 6 October 1962; [m.] Brian MacAllister; [ch.] Sam MacAllister; [occ.] Technical Writer; [oth. writ.] Technical manuals and articles, short stories; [pers.] Influenced by my beloved mother who sadly didn't live to see my work published.; [a.] Dublin, Ireland

EVES, ANNE
[b.] 5 April 1964, Enniskillen; [p.] Patrick Meehan, Mary Meehan; [m.] Michael, 20 October 1984; [ch.] Ryan Patrick, Emma Lorraine; [ed.] St. Fanchea's Intermediate, Secondary School for Girls; [occ.] Community Care Worker (Elderly Care); [memb.] U.K. Parkinson's Disease Society; [pers.] I am lucky enough to live in the heart of the beautiful Fermanagh Lakeland, a source of lavish natural beauty that changes with each season. My inspiration comes from there.; [a.] Kesh, Fermanagh

FAGAN, SARAH
[b.] 26 June 1979, Harrow; [p.] Susan Fagan and Michael Canney; [ed.] St Margret Clitherows Primary School, St Gregory's High School and Hendon College; [oth. writ.] I have had a few of my other poems read out on Kiss 100 fm radio station.; [pers.] I would like to thank all my family and friends for supporting me and giving me confidence in my writing of poetry.; [a.] Sudbury, Middlesex

FAIRCHILD, JOYCE MARGARET
[pen.] Joy Fairchild; [b.] 13 April 1941, Surrey; [p.] Florence and Thomas Willis; [m.] Brian John Fairchild, 30 July 1960; [ch.] Four - two sons and two daughters; [ed.] Chigwell Village Primary, Kingswood Secondary Modern Chigwell; [occ.] Healt Care Support, Care of the Elderly (Nurse); [memb.] Poetry now magazine; [hon.] B-Tech N.V.Q. care of the elderly, Anglia Polytechnic; [oth. writ.] "Forgotten" Medical Verse Memory Lane "Times of Joy", change "Growing with God", pride "Lifes Cycle", put the radio on "Faith in Society" tears of pain "Mightier than sword", "Lost Love The Other Side of the Mirror"; [pers.] A love to write what comes from the heart.; [a.] Chelmsford, Essex

FALLA, JAN
[b.] 7 October 1945, Guernsey, CI; [ch.] 2 in their twenties; [ed.] Ladies' College, Guernsey; [occ.] Secretary; [memb.] Member of Belles & Broomstick Female Morris Side; [oth. writ.] Collection of serious/humorous poems - hoping to get them published as a book fairly soon; [pers.] Other hobbies - playing the melodeon, tin whistle and bodhran, Irish dancing. Poetry started with making up humorous verses to well-known tunes, then went on to serious poetry. Ambition - to write a novel; [a.] St. Peter Port, Guernsey, CI

FANTHOM, GEORGINA
[b.] 20 August 1978, Wordsley; [p.] Robert Fanthom, Jackie Fanthom; [ed.] Weaverham High School, Sir John Deanes sixth form college, University Hospital Wales; [occ.] Physiotherapy student, Cardiff; [memb.]

University Hockey Team; [hon.] A levels in Biology, Chemistry and Psychology; [pers.] Poetry is my attempt at getting feelings and thoughts into words. My inspiration comes from many moments, places and people - I dedicate my poem to you, most of you know who you are.; [a.] Northwich, Cheshire

FARNSWORTH, MARTIN STUART
[b.] 30 July 1971, Nottingham; [p.] Eunice and David Farnsworth; [ed.] 'O' level English, Woodwork, Music, Math, Business Studies 1st certificate; [occ.] Unemployed; [memb.] Breadsall Country Club Hotel, Fitness and Leisure, Karate Association; [hon.] Classical Guitar - Grades 5, 6, 7, and 8; [oth. writ.] Going to bed, nature poems printed in the Nottingham Evening Post; [pers.] I enjoy composing poems and I am currently writing a thriller. I find my experiences in life have inspired my poetry.; [a.] Wollation, Nottingham

FAULL, CLAUDE
[pen.] Claude Faull; [b.] 29 June 1921, Beacon Camborne, Cornwall; [p.] William John Henry and Louie Faull (Deceased); [m.] Elizabeth Stella Faull, 15 January 1947; [ch.] Julian Scott and Elizabeth; [ed.] Elementary Joined Royal Navy 7-9-39 left R.J. 7-3-1953; [occ.] Senior Citizen; [memb.] Manchester Unity Independent order of Oddfellows, Freemason; [hon.] Service Medals only Russian Convoy Medal, Malta Star 1939-45 Medla, Atlantic Star, North Africa Star, Pacific Star end of war medal; [oth. writ.] Peace, or Perfect Peace (between a luagh and a tear); [pers.] I endeavour to do who others, that which I might wish, they should do unto me.; [a.] Redruth, Cornwall

FELLOWES, MISS JOY
[b.] 26 November 1945, Croydon; [p.] Sybil Fellowes, Claude Fellowes; [ed.] Secondary Modern; [occ.] Legal Secretary; [oth. writ.] Small book of poems published by Avon Books.; [pers.] I have enjoyed creating these poems and hope they bring pleasure and amusement to others.; [a.] Croydon, Surrey

FELTON HAZELL, TRUDI
[pen.] Trudi Felton; [b.] 12 October 1956, Stanley, Falkland Is.; [p.] Winifred and Anthony Felton; [m.] David Hazell, 28 June 1975; [ch.] Lee and Angela; [ed.] Taught until age 10 by a travelling teacher, then in Stanley I attended Stanley Senior School, Pretty Average Education really!; [occ.] Barmaiding Temporarily whilst awaiting full-time job. (I am an ex-policewoman - and will maybe return to that occupation...); [memb.] Falklands Conservation, Whale and Dolphin Conservation Soc.; [oth. writ.] A poem published by Triumph House Publishers. Some of my work has been published in our local Church Magazine.; [pers.] My writing grows from a love of the English language and the world around me. Music plays an important part in inspiring me - also as a Christian I gain a lot from my faith.; [a.] Stanley, Falkland Islands

FENTON, GERALDINE
[b.] 24 January 1960, Bammeen; [p.] Mary Carr; [m.] Graham Fenton; [ch.] Charlotte and Shannon; [ed.] St. Colman's Primary, Bammeen St. Mary's High School, Newry, Newry Technical College; [occ.] Housewife; [memb.] The friends and parents of St. Colman's Primary School Drumgreenagh, Rathfriland; [pers.] To revive memories and to enchant hearts of young and old I was influenced by man poets of the early and late era.; [a.] Rathfriland, Down

FEREDAY, RONALD BERTRAM
[pen.] Ron Fereday; [b.] 12 August 1930, Stourbridge, Worcs; [p.] Thomas Bertram, Hettie Esther (Nee Woodward); [m.] Gwendoline Olive (Nee Randall), 6 October 1952; [ch.] Martin; [ed.] Quarry Bank Sen. Boys and Stourbridge School of Art; [occ.] Retired (U.K.A.E.A. Winerith, Atomic Energy Est); [memb.] National Federation of Spiritual Healers, Dorset, Hants and Wilts Spiritual Healer Ass., British Legion, Southill Horticultural Society; [hon.] English/English Literature; [oth. writ.] Articles in N.F.S.H. "Healing Review" International: Australia Spiritual Healer Magazine, Books: Children's, 5 to 10 years "My Friend The Prince", Minerva Press: Healing, Meditation and Spiritual Philosophy "Three Faces of Spirit" Regency Press; [pers.] I find that contemplating the spiritual arouses compassion and deeper insight. We learn so much through the wisdom of others.; [a.] Weymouth, Dorset

FERGUSON, ALISTAIR JOHN
[b.] 7 April 1955; [p.] Jack and Peggy Ferguson; [m.] Jennifer Ferguson, 17 August 1992; [occ.] Retired Medically Royal Navy; [oth. writ.] Words, Life Is A Gift, My Lady, We Saw The Truth!, Who Knows, Face Reality, Life's Challenge, Who Is Kidding Who?; [pers.] No matter where you are on the ladder of life, there will always be someone above and below you. Enjoy what you have while you have it, it won't last forever.; [a.] Plymouth, Devon

FERNANDES, THOMAS HERBERT
[b.] 21 October 1933, Karachi, Pakistan; [p.] Ignatius Fernandes, Prudence Fernandes; [m.] Alma Regina Fernandes, 8 June 1958; [ch.] Daryl, Judyanna, Lynette, Llewelyn, Brendan; [ed.] St. Patrick's High School and St. Xavier's College, Karachi; [occ.] Accountant; [oth. writ.] Several poems; [pers.] I wrote the poem "The Only Straight Road to Happiness" because I felt dejected with the way people, the world over, were separated by social barriers. I must get emotionally involved with a subject before I start to write a poem.; [a.] New Cross, London

FINDLAY, SYLVIA EDNA
[pen.] Henrietta Valmore; [p.] Anne and Henry Morrell; [m.] Douglas Findlay; [ed.] Whickham County School, Whickham, Newcastle Tyne; [occ.] Local Government Clerk/Typist; [oth. writ.] Quite a number of poems, written. None published to date!; [pers.] A poem can personify and reveal the true feelings of the inner self. It can almost touch the soul!; [a.] Newcastle/ Tyne

FINKLEMAN, PAULINE
[pen.] Pauline Finkleman; [b.] 16 January 1934, London; [m.] Widow, 1970; [ch.] Gary F., Michael F., Tracey Kramer; [ed.] Secondary Modern School, Hairdresser; [occ.] Retired; [memb.] Hounslows Borough Association for Disabled People (Executive Committee Member), Brenford and Chiswick Action and Support Group; [hon.] Received Royalty from first publication; [oth. writ.] Two other poems previously printed by Poetry Now; [pers.] I am a widow aged 63 and wheelchair-bound as I suffer from multiple sclerosis which gives me the inspiration to write my poetry as I am no longer able-bodied.; [a.] London

FISHER, JANETTE
[pen.] Janette Fisher; [b.] 31 March 1959, Carlisle; [p.] Joseph Gardner, Beth Gardner; [m.] Joseph William Fisher, 26 March 1993; [ch.] Elizabeth Bunting, Amanda Bunting; [ed.] Harraby Comprehensive Carlisle, Carlisle College; [occ.] Accountants Assistant Studying to Gain Accounting Technician Status; [memb.] Carlisle United Supporters Club; [oth. writ.] Several poems published in anthologies by anchor books, one of my poems used as radio advertisement for local children's nursery.; [pers.] I write poetry for the love of it, in the hope that my poems have as much enjoyment to the reader as I do when writing them.; [a.] Carlisle, Cumbria

FISHER, SEAN
[b.] 20 October 1972, Swansea; [p.] Frank Fisher and Juanita Fisher; [ed.] Pentrehafod Comprehensive school, Swansea College, Tycoch; [occ.] Student Bahons Media/Drama/English; [oth. writ.] Community church centre poetry display conducted by the creative writing course I had attended. The poem's title was "Caine And Abel"; [pers.] I would just like to thank all my friends and family for their constant support and in particular Debra Rebecca and Andrew for having in the faith in what I always felt was an inadequate talent. Special thanks also to Peter Thabbit Jones my Mentor.; [a.] Swansea, West Glamorgan

FLAMSON, BARBARA FRANCES
[pen.] Barbara Frances; [b.] 17 September 1935, Whitwick, Leics; [p.] Mary and Thomas Wainwright; [m.] Denis Flamson, 26 October 1957; [ch.] Four: Stephen, Jacqueline, Michael, Simon; [ed.] Public School; [occ.] Housewife; [memb.] ISA International Songwriters Association, Limerick City Ireland; [hon.] An award for the words of a song, "My Pillow of Heartaches"; [oth. writ.] I have a book (childrens) published last year 1995.; [pers.] I started writing in 1982. I wrote my first poem, then started writing songs, then stories, I find a lot of pleasure in my writing. I always have the melody of a song in my head as I write the words.; [a.] Ashby-de-la-Louch

FLEMING, FRANCESCA
[b.] 9 February 1996, St. Bartholomews; [p.] Kathleen Nixon; [ed.] Woodbridge High School; [pers.] I dedicate this poem to Elaine Chapman, my best friend. I wrote this poem when her Dad Bill Chapman died. He treated me like I was his daughter, and felt like his daughter too, he was the dad I never had.; [a.] Woodford Green, Essex

FLEMING, RACHAEL E.
[b.] 28 December 1980, Hull; [p.] Tina and Vincent Fleming; [ed.] I went to Kingston High School and had my exams done there. I am doing very well in word processing though I have a distinction in that.; [occ.] I am not working at the moment.; [hon.] I have some certificates from St. John ambulance and some more certificates for school things.; [oth. writ.] I have no other writings except the teenage stories I have done at home no professional has seen them though its just long stories I make up which I hope one day could be a book.; [a.] Hull, E. Yorkshire

FLETCHER, HAYLEY DANIELLE
[pen.] Hayley Fletcher; [b.] 18 January 1984, Frimley; [p.] Larraine Fletcher; [ed.] Collingwood College; [occ.] Student; [pers.] I hope to ensure my writing has an inspiration for others and to encourage our generation to express your self will in making poems.; [a.] Lightwater, Surrey

FLETCHER, MARJORIE
[b.] 14-06-54 in England, one of ten children. [pers.] Dad (Joseph) and Mam (Violet) encouraged my ability to write what I feel. Married with three grown-up daughters, four grandchildren. My family inspire me. My poems are like a biography in rhyme. I would like to dedicate this poem to my Mam and Dad who have always been there for me.

FLOCKHART, CLAIRE
[pen.] Claireballe Flockhart; [b.] 5 January 1983, London; [p.] Mr. Harry Flockhart; [ed.] Edmonton County Secondary Lower School; [memb.] Drama group held on saturday's (Millfield House), T.K.U. held on wed for church; [hon.] Books from school for progress and achievement, hopefully I will someday be famous like Beehoven or Mozart who I greatly admire; [oth. writ.] I try to reflect and to write from the deepest of my heart which I write with my deepest passions and understanding; [pers.] I think that anybody can do anything they want to if they put their mind to it and try hard at what they are working towards they will succeed.; [a.] Northaw, Herts

FOLEY, JOSEPHINE
[b.] June 5, 1936, Ireland; [p.] Irish; [m.] Frank, February 24, 1984; [ed.] Convent School Orphanage, no Particular Education; [occ.] Housewife; [oth. writ.] The arrival of the plover in late winter early spring I heard the sound of rustle bells the sound so familiar the jingle of the plover they have just arrived as if to celebrate of spring.; [pers.] A spur of the moment decision to put pen to paper.; [a.] Ireland

FOLLETT, JOHN
[b.] 3 October 1944, Sherborne; [p.] 'Jack' Follett and Lorna Jollett; [ch.] Simon Christopher, Lorraine Victoria; [ed.] Bridport Colfox Comprehensive, Waymouth Technical College; [occ.] Singer Guitarist, Plumber; [memb.] Equity; [oth. writ.] "The Special Things" song recorded on LP 'Come On Over To My Place'; [pers.] In their many guises play a major part to the human. Detriment and his freedom of heart. To endeavor to recapture the essence of happiness once common to all of mankind, but then sadly lost in the passage of time.; [a.] Bridport, Dorset

FORD-WETTON, DIANA
[b.] 03/11/42, Birmingham; [p.] William Ford, Nell Ford; [m.] John Wetton, 20 May 1972; [ed.] Harrison Barrow Grammar Featherstone College, Former Air Stewardess, Birmingham Hospital Clerical Receptionist, travelled world wide; [occ.] Volunteer Counsellor (Breast); [memb.] Associate Stress Consultants; [hon.] Stress Counsellor, B.A. English Literature; [oth. writ.] Several poems, short stories; [pers.] I like to reflect man's inate godliness and joy in all things.; [a.] Grendon, Warwickshire

FORREST, HAZEL
[b.] 7 August 1950, Wallsend-on-Tyne; [p.] Audrey, Margaret, Helena & Richard, William Brooks; [m.] David Forrest, 12 December 1970; [ch.] Paul David Forrest; [occ.] Sales Distributor; [oth. writ.] poems published in local newspaper. Also in anthology 'Quiet Moments' poem 'Existence' recorded on tape 'The Sound of Poetry', 1996; [pers.] The spiritual preparation for writing a poem is influences by life itself. As long as there is life, I shall endeavor to write poetry.; [a.] Whitley Bay, Tyne & Wear

FORSTER, MRS. JEAN
[b.] 27 August 1953, Redhills, Exeter; [p.] Mr. Frank-Sidney Sercombe and Mrs. Emily Sercombe; [m.] Mr. John J. K. Forster, 8 September 1979; [ch.] Charles W. F. Forster; [ed.] Honiton Secondary School Honiton Devon; [occ.] Housewife; [memb.] N.A.C.C., B.D.A., County Library, Matalan, D.D.C., IFAW., Pet Rescue; [hon.] Webb Ivory, N.C.H. Children's Homes; [oth. writ.] "A Mother's Love", "Feelings", "The Festive Cheer", "Words From The Heart", "The Unforgotten Children", "Peace of Mind", "A Christmas Alphabet" Feelings in My Heart Down to Shore; [pers.] I first started writing poems when I join the "Seaton ladies choir" which gave we a inspiration to wanting to write. This will be my first peace which has been published.; [a.] Maryport, Cumbria

FOTHERINGHAM, KRISS
[pen.] Mr. Risk; [b.] 25 March 1980, Dundee; [p.] Diana Fotheringham, James Fotheringham; [ed.] Hipperholme Grammar; [occ.] Student; [oth. writ.] Over 400 unedited poems; [pers.] What's outside becomes my inside and what's inside is my poetry I was touched by the poems of Jim Morrison and since picked up the pen.; [a.] Halifax, West Yorkshire

FOUNTAIN, NIGEL STEPHEN
[b.] 4 January 1956, Luton; [p.] Dorothy Ellen, Alec; [m.] Christine Anne Fountain, 20 January 1996; [ch.] 1 Boy, 1 Girl grown-up; [ed.] Challney High for boys Luton Bedfordshire; [occ.] Security Dog Handler; [memb.] IWA, RAC; [hon.] Won many school prizes in poetry and writing competitions; [oth. writ.] 1,000's but never inclined to get any published; [pers.] 2 quotes! Always do your best and never do a man a bad turn. You don't have to do him a good turn just don't do him a bad one. Poetry is to be written, not necessarily to be read.; [a.] Burwell, Cambs

FRASER, LORRAINE DIANA
[pen.] Lorraine Diana Fraser; [b.] 19 May 1963, Montevideo - Uruguay, British Nationality; [p.] Charles Duncan Fraser, Ana Maria Fraser; [p.] Jonathan Fernando, Malasa Fraser; [ed.] Universidad da Republica Del Uruguay/Theather Teacher, Escuela Technica - Ipsiproda -Peru Informatic Technique; [occ.] Material Manager; [oth. writ.] Several poems, beginning at 9 years old, never published then. This is the first time.; [pers.] I think that writing is the best way to express our deep feelings, and help us to reflect of what we really felt. Also we can help other people, showing that even this world is getting cold, we can still have our heart warmth and sentimental.; [a.] Estoril, Portugal

FRECKLETON, SAMUEL
[b.] 31 March 1944, Manchester, Jamaica; [p.] Cyril and Eurelda Freckelton; [m.] Gleneta Freckelton, 28 May 1980; [ch.] Mark Phillips Freckelton; [ed.] Elementary; [oth. writ.] Unpublished short stories, unpublished TV Sitcom, unpublished TV Drama; [pers.] It is indeed a very great honour, and privilege to come to know of the International Library of Poetry, and yet

again to have learned that another one of my poems had been selected, thanking the selection committee. My thanks also to Managing Editor.; [a.] London, Wembley, Middlesex

FREEMAN, TANYA MICHELLE
[b.] 14 August 1978, Islington; [p.] Ellen and David Freeman; [a.] London

GALWAY, MIRIAM
[b.] 28/08/1939, Manchester; [p.] Arthur & Ivy Jones (both deceased); [m.] James Galway (now divorced), were married 18 June 1960; [ch.] Stephen (35), Timothy (33), Rebecca Joy (28); [ed.] Eccles Grammar School; [occ.] Retired Civil Servant - Court Service; [memb.] Ex-member Stewartby Amateur Operatic and Dramatic Society - Gilbert and Sullivan Productions and "The Pirates" singing group (variety of music performed for charity and community entertainment), left on move to Bristol; [oth. writ.] "Vintage Love" in 'The Other Side of the Mirror'; [pers.] My poetry expresses human situations, experiences, dilemmas and emotions. Also the important issues encountered on life's journey.; [a.] Bristol, Avon

GARDEZI, UZMA
[b.] 12 March 1973, Lahore, Pakistan; [p.] S. Ikram Gardezi, Zenie Gardezi; [ed.] Bancroft's School, Essex, England; Convent of Jesus & Mary, Karachi (O-levels); Karachi Grammar School, Karachi (A-levels); London School of Economics & Political Science B.Sc. (Econ.) Hons.; [occ.] banker, Deutsche Bank AG, Lahore.; [memb.] Chartered Institute of Bankers .; [hon.] English literature prize (A level), representing my school in international debates; [oth. writ.] Poems & articles published in local magazines, including an interview with Abdus Sattar Edhi—winner of the Ramon Magsaysay Award.; [pers.] In my writing I want to explore the infinite shadings of human emotions and to play with the beauty of words and images.; [a.] Lahore, Pakistan

GARDNER, MARIA
[b.] 4 January 1968, Vaala, Finland; [ch.] My first is Due in February 97; [ed.] English Philology and Linguistics, University of Tampere; [hon.] Prize in Local Writing Competition, 1993; [oth. writ.] Poems in finnish literary magazines and anthologies, a school book and university conference.; [pers.] If meaning was vague, there would be no variation. It is better to ask how than what.; [a.] Tampere, Finland

GEORGE, LINDA
[b.] 17.02.51, Gower, S. Wales; [p.] Anna and Robert William Phillips; [m.] Divorced; [ch.] Gaynor George, Anna George and Helen George; [ed.] Mynyddbach Comprehensive School for girls in Swansea, S. Wales; [occ.] Secretarial Administrator; [memb.] Member of "Runrig" Fan Club, "Distinguished Member" of The International Library of Poetry, member of "International Poetry Hall of Fame"; [hon.] Several passes in G.C.S.E. and typewriting and secretarial studies. I now hold two certificates for poetry issued to me for outstanding achievement in poetry (Editor's Choice Award); [oth. writ.] "That Special Moment" published in "The Other Side of the Mirror", "Forbidden Love", published in "Quiet Moments", "Holy Waters", published in "Jewels of the Imagination", "Forever", to be published in "Light of the World". I have written 50 poems to date. I am now promoting two of them to sell in aid of "Save the Children"; [pers.] The peaceful village of Llangennech in Dyfed, S. Wales gave me my first inspiration to write, when I met a wonderful person from there called Stuart Williams, who now owns, and will always own, my heart. I believe love is for the giving and not for the taking. I would love to have my inspirations published in one book. I also have musical talents and would love to sing to a live audience. I am now planning on writing a romantic novel. I believe in Jesus Christ and I know he will continue to shine his light on me.; [a.] Swansea, W. Glam

GIBSON, ELIZABETH LILIAN M.
[b.] 22 September 1940, Glasgow; [p.] Agnes McBride, John McBride; [m.] Divorced 1971; [ch.] Angus Gibson; [ed.] North Kelvinside Secondary,

Glasgow, Scottish College of Commerce, Jordanhill College of Education; [occ.] Retired Teacher; [memb.] Citizens' Theatre Society, Glasgow, Charles Rennie Mackintosh Society, Glasgow; [oth. writ.] Short stories, street/tenement poems; [pers.] Kindness, especially to other Partick Thistle supporters.; [a.] East Kilbride, Scotland

GILCHRIST, JOAN LLOYD
[b.] 17 September 1919, Liverpool; [p.] Norman and Florence Lloyd; [m.] Frank Gilchrist (Deceased), 13 September 1958; [ch.] Nicholas Lloyd Gilchrist; [ed.] Secondary Modern School leaving at age 14. Trained 1 year at Commercial College as secretary; [occ.] Retired secretary; [hon.] No honours. Have acted as secretary to the late sir Thomas Beecham and sir Malcolm Sargeant, worked in West Africa and Saudi Arabia; [oth. writ.] Poem published in "North West Chorus" and also "A Poetry Now Anthology" written life story going back 100 years, (not published); [pers.] Writing is my way of complete relaxation; [a.] Liverpool, Merseyside

GILHOOLY, SARAH
[b.] 14 February 1978, Enfield, Middlesex; [p.] Joan Gilhooly, Peter Gilhooly; [ed.] Cheshunt Grammar Senior School; [memb.] Dancing Club; [hon.] Levels Bronze up to Gold Bar Medals for Latin American Dancing; [oth. writ.] A selection of more of my own poems. Also verses written for personal greetings cards.; [pers.] For me pleasure is poetry. I find it a very good way of expressing the thoughts and feelings closest to my heart. You see words can be hard to express in real life, though when pen is put to paper the words come naturally without hesitation.; [a.] Hoddesdon, Hertfordshire

GIRLING, EILEEN
[b.] 13 April 1941, Beverley, East Yorks; [p.] Mable and Leslie Kemp; [m.] Nigel William Girling, 13 February 1988; [ch.] Philip 1963, Fiona 1965, John 1697; [ed.] Estcourt High School Hull; [hon.] Only an 'o' level grade B in human Biology Gained at Bluerley night college in 1979 when I was 38 yrs. old I am very interested in Genetics and other interests inc Astronomy; [oth. writ.] Two poems published in whispers in the wind and poetry now Yorkshire 1997, both triumph house.; [pers.] I have a very deep love and concern for all animal suffering especially by the cruelty of man believe animals are as important to God, as we are, I am vegetarian have two dogs and 5 cats and feed strays.; [a.] Beverley, East Yorkshire

GOAT, MALCOLM
[b.] 3 July 1944, Middlesbrough; [p.] Frank and Edna Goat (Both Deceased); [m.] Jean Goat (Barthram), 12 April 1971; [ch.] Veronica, Stephen; [ed.] Whinney Banks Secondary Modern Cleveland College of Further Education Longlands College of further education; [occ.] Retired (after 37 years with I.C.I. and Zeneca as a Chemical Technician); [hon.] City and Guilds Ordinary, advanced and post advanced diploma in chemical plant operations. 20 years, 25 years, 30 years and 35 years long service awards with I.C.I./Zeneca; [oth. writ.] Christmas Celebrations 1993 Mast Publications, Christmas Time 1994 British Poetry Review. Mast publications. Gifts of life. 1996 International Society of Poets. Several poems printed in our local village magazine and works news letters.; [pers.] Poetry helps one to relax. I also receive a great deal of satisfaction from completing a poem and am constantly on the look out for new themes and ideas.; [a.] Great Ayton, North Yorkshire

GOLT, SONIA
[pen.] Sonia Golt; [b.] 6 July 1945, Northern Ireland; [ch.] Samantha and Brendon; [occ.] Public Relation Director; [hon.] Flam Poetry North - a poetic recognition, Huddersfield ; [oth. writ.] C. Chronicle Newspaper - weekly article; [pers.] Started writing poetry six years ago. It was an internal impulse to put down my thoughts in paper, her feelings, past experiences, daily contacts with nature, her emotions. Being a "Carcerian" is a true romantic and this is very eminent in my poems. I write in a very human and natural form which is extremely expressive and shows great emotions.; [a.] Gibraltar

GOOD-O'BRIEN, TESS
[b.] 25 June 1961, Ireland; [m.] Des O'Brien, 13 May 1988; [ed.] Convent of Mercy Dungarvan, Ireland; [occ.] Local Government Officer. Prev: Financial Co's Bournemouth and Southampton; [hon.] Diploma Social Studies U.C.C.; [pers.] "Without purpose, we float, like foam, disintegrating further with each new impact"; [a.] Dungarvan, Waterford, Ireland

GOODERIDGE, LUCY
[b.] 17 April 1976, Mid-Glam; [p.] Roy Gooderidge, Mary Gooderidge; [ed.] St. Albans R.C. School Pontypool, Gwent Tertiary College - Pontypool; [occ.] Student hoping to attend Liverpool John Moores University; [pers.] My greatest influence is Sylvia Plath. I have written for pleasure since my early teens and intend to make it a part of my career 'before' was one of my first poems I seek not so much to sit down and 'compose' a poem but rather to write what is already within me.; [a.] Pontypool, Gwent

GOODMAN, CYRIL KENNETH
[pen.] Ken Goodman; [b.] 12 March 1923, Mobley, Leeds; [m.] Joyce, 21 September 1946; [ch.] One daughter Pamela; [ed.] Grammar School; [occ.] Retired; [memb.] Ex R.A.F. M.I.D., R.A.F. Associated, "Burma Star", Africa Star; [oth. writ.] Various poems when residing in Spain and appeared in this first British Pantomime performed in Spain and donated various amounts of money to Red Cross over 2000 pounds for heart machine and others from these shows (7 in all).; [pers.] Have appeared on T.V. as extra's and walk on part in various programs namely "Emmerdale, Coronation St, "Adleigh", "Main Chance, our kid and many more.; [a.] Morley, Yorkshire

GOODMAN, TERRY
[b.] 28 December 1950, Bristol; [p.] Ray and Marie; [m.] Mariea, 10 August 1984; [ed.] Brislington Comprehensive; [occ.] Betting Shop Manager; [oth. writ.] I've written poems for as long as I care to remember, this is the only one in print.; [pers.] I love the poems and short-stories of Dylan Thomas and the words and music of Robin Williamson.; [a.] Bristol, Avon

GOODWIN, MRS. JUDITH ROBERTA
[pen.] Jude; [b.] 28 July 1943, Penarth-Cogan; [p.] Mr. and Mrs. R. J. Hatton; [m.] Mr. Len Goodwin, 22 September 1962; [ch.] Scott Paul and Helen Faye Goodwin; [ed.] Secondary Modern Blogg's College, Newport Rd, Cardiff, Clark's College, Newport Road, Cardiff; [occ.] Managed House-Service Attendant; [oth. writ.] Previous writing in local and Borough church magazines; [pers.] I have a deep understanding of the way of God's word and teachings should be expressed in my poetry. I hope people by reading my work can see how beautiful God's love is.; [a.] Cardiff, Glamorgan

GOODWIN, MARION IRENE
[b.] 9 September 1950, Bracknell; [p.] Elsie and Percy Rollett; [m.] Dennis Goodwin, 8 March 1969; [ch.] Nikki Jane and Terry Neil; [ed.] Sandy Lane Infant's and Junior School Bracknell Borbugh Green Secondary School, Bracknell; [occ.] Housewife; [oth. writ.] Sixteen poems, published by small publishers; [pers.] I enjoy writing my poems and would like to share them with others.; [a.] Bracknell, Berkshire

GRANDE, SUSAN PATHANA
[b.] 26 April 1957, London; [p.] Mary H. Johnson, Donald Tennet; [m.] Raffaele L. Grande, 12 April 1990; [ch.] Bianca Louise (1978-1995), Angelo, Giorgio Vincenzo; [ed.] 1961-1966 Rochdale Convent School, 1966-1975 - Hulme, Grammar School for Girls, Oldham; [occ.] Restaurant Owner; [pers.] I wrote this poem for my daughter. Bianca shortly before she died in Sept. '95. To show her that she would always be with me. She has been an inspiration to me and all who knew her, throughout her short, but full life. She suffered from cancer since the age of 3, and undergone numerous illnesses with bravery and great dignity.; [a.] Rochdale, Lancs

GRANT, DIANA C. M.
[b.] 1937, Cheshire; [m.] Charles G. Grant, 27 January 1975; [ch.] Four daughter; [ed.] Secondary Modern/Grammar Hampshire/Dorset and life itself; [occ.] Housewife; [hon.] Small award for an essay when at school; [pers.] I am presently working on a book for children, planning a novel. My greatest love is poetry, which seems to come from an inner spirit, prompted by beauty, suffering, and all that touches the soul.; [a.] Bicester, Oxon

GRANTHAM, JULIE DAWN
[b.] 18 July 1964, Hertfordshire; [p.] Leonard Henry Willis, Margaret Willis; [m.] Terence Grantham, 17 March 1990; [ch.] Lee Terence, Joe Leonard William; [ed.] Carshalton High; [occ.] Housewife and invalid carer to my husband; [oth. writ.] Short stories for monthly womans magazines, anecdotes etc. have written many many poems. (None as yet sent anywhere, until now) I love poetry. Working on fiction novel at present.; [pers.] I have been a writer in an emotional capacity since I could write my fathers death and other "sadnesses" put my hand to paper forever. The world is not always nice - only sometimes! `Do today, the dream of yesterday, that waits for tomorrow' (Quotes: My own); [a.] Clacton-on-Sea, Essex

GRASSI, PETER
[b.] 26 October 1946, Bath, Avon; [m.] Fiance - Frances; [ch.] Oliver and Katie (Teenagers); [ed.] Oldfield Boys Schools, Bath; [occ.] Carpenter; [oth. writ.] Have written a book of humorous verse. (Unpublished as yet!) From my experiences while managing a restaurant in London from eight years.; [pers.] Only humans laugh and we're only human!; [a.] Mortlake, London

GRECH, JACQUELINE
[b.] 24 February 1966, Gozo; [p.] George and Kathleen; [m.] Louis, 9 October 1988; [ch.] Michelle; [ed.] Diploma in Medical Laboratory Technology; [occ.] Housewife; [pers.] Inspired by family links of love and the storms of life.; [a.] Victoria, Gozo

GREEN, JOHN WILLIAM
[pen.] John Green; [b.] 27 November 1951, Hermingham; [p.] Sidney Green, Margaret Green; [ed.] Debemham Comprehensive School, Suffolk College; [occ.] Garden Specialist; [memb.] (Melton Candidate) The Green Party. Friends of the Earth, green Peace, Ipswich animal rights, (Peaceful); [hon.] Joint Third Suffolk Music Festival 1966, maybe one year out and sang the hunting song this event was help I'm Ipswich; [oth. writ.] Written Articles in magazines, Lots of unpublished poems. I write about Environment and cruelty to animal other poems include - this mighty fortress sacred cow dance of death; [pers.] My poems reflect the cruel and wasteful side of life the extremes we go to, to make it possible, and this mad science that back it all up.; [a.] Melton, Woodbridge, Suffolk

GREENWAY, FREDERICK
[b.] 9 August 1923; [occ.] Retired Bank Manager; [memb.] Institute of Bankers RNLI. (Insmore Rescue)

GREER, ALAN JAMES
[b.] 8 August 1979, Magherafelt, N.I.; [p.] Colin Greer and Beth Greer; [ed.] Ballyclare High (Grammar); [occ.] Student; [memb.] Constitution Monarchy Association, Conservative Party, School Debating Society, School Public Speaking Society; [hon.] Winner of Somme Association Essay Competition - 1996; [pers.] In my writing I wish to ensure current and future generations understand and value the sacrifices made by so many this century in war, for the freedoms we enjoy today.; [a.] Ballyclare, Antrim

GREGORY, MR. ALAN G.
[b.] 29 August 1936, Leicester; [p.] George and Mabel Gregory; [m.] Jeanette Gregory, April 1966; [ch.] Helen and Douglas; [ed.] Secondary Modern; [occ.] Machine Operator; [oth. writ.] "Deception" which I believe was published by you in "Voices On The Wind". Other poems and songs unpublished; [pers.] I wish that in my younger day's I had learned how to read and write music. Perhaps then I could present my songs for publication; [a.] Narborough, Leicester

GREGORY, ERIC
[b.] 1 September 1921, Oldbury, West Midlands; [m.] Doreen (Deceased), 25 September 1943; [ch.] Janet, Keith; [ed.] Grammar School, Technical Colleges; [occ.] Retired Mechanical Engineer; [memb.] Tamworth Photographic Club; [pers.] Write for pleasure only.; [a.] Tamworth, Staffs

GREGORY, PAULINE ANN
[b.] 1 May 1943, Birmingham; [p.] Gladys and Harry Broadbent; [m.] John, 1 July 1961; [ch.] Gary and Lisa; [ed.] Comprehensive; [occ.] Housewife; [hon.] Certificates and Medals for Music and Dancing; [pers.] We should all slow down, take the time to look for a rainbow or we will miss the very best of our lives.; [a.] Birmingham, West Midlands

GREVELDING, KLAUS
[b.] 19 February 1953, Dueren; [p.] Hans and Elfriede Grevelding; [m.] Elke Grevelding, 13 May 1980; [ch.] Anna - 13, Sonja - 6; [ed.] Stift. Gymnasium (grammar), RWTH Archen; [occ.] Teacher St. Angela - Public School Dueren; [oth. writ.] Several poems and essays published in local papers and magazines, one in Voices On The Wind.; [pers.] Still love expressing my thoughts in verse.; [a.] Aachen, NRW, Germany

GRIFFITHS, AMY ELAINE
[b.] 15 January 1984; [p.] Tracy Jayne Griffiths, Steven Parker Griffiths; [ed.] Oakdale Comprehensive School; [memb.] Ballet and Modern dance club; [oth. writ.] "The Wind" a poem published in a book called "Hah Hey"; [pers.] I try to reflect my appreciation of nature in my poetry.; [a.] Blackhood, Caerphilly

GRIFFITHS, MR. H. G.
[b.] 24 August 1965; [p.] Michael and Cynthia; [ed.] Farneyclose School, 1976-1981, Wigston C.F.E., 1982; [occ.] I have worked in a low paying-scheme since '83; [memb.] Neo-Tech; [oth. writ.] Millennium prophecy and other poems about how the future will be!; [pers.] We are being used up by government and other Neocheating poppa boys. My poems must help to sink the B.O.A.T. (Burden on Advancing Technology!); [a.] Harborough, Leics

GRIFFITHS, IVY
[b.] 23 December 1919, Walsall; [p.] Ethel and Francis Craddock; [m.] William Griffiths, 29 January 1942 (Now Widowed); [ch.] Son and daughter; [ed.] Comprehensive Walsall Wood; [occ.] Telephone Operator now retired; [oth. writ.] I am trying to write my life story, of my early years, I have had several poems published in local magazines.; [a.] Burntwood, Stafford

GRIGGS, PAMELA MAUREEN
[pen.] Pam Griggs; [b.] 29 November 1942, Colchester; [p.] Edna Wilkins, Bernard Wilkins; [m.] Gordon Griggs, 6 February 1965; [ch.] Karl, Nicola and Jacqueline; [ed.] St. Helena Secondary Modern School for Girls; [occ.] Book keeper for Heather College Cabinet Makers; [oth. writ.] Several poems printed in local magazine and rhymes for plays school.; [pers.] I hope that my innermost feelings and inspirations can be of some comfort to others.; [a.] Halstead, Essex

GRUND, RICHARD L.
[b.] 25 February 1937, Minnesota; [p.] Clarence Grund, Virginia Grund; [m.] Ann Grund, 24 February 1989; [ch.] Tamsin, previous marriages - Gary, Kathy, Lisa, Patrick and Jo-Ann; [ed.] Reville High School, MN, USA, various US Colleges; [occ.] Computer Analyst; [oth. writ.] Poems published in Local magazines Placed well in short story, contest: Write for my family.; [pers.] Lived in Gil 21 yrs. I served 20 years in the USAF, I enjoy the strength and power of words and their ability to reflect the human emotion.; [a.] Newton St. Cyres, Devon

GUARDIOLA-RIVERA, OSCAR
[pen.] Edgar A. Croe; [b.] July 1969, Bogota; [p.] Oscar Guardiola, Haidy Rivera; [ed.] San Bartolome School, Universidad Javeriana, Aberdeen University; [occ.] Writer; [memb.] Maroa Poetry Group, Paranoic-Critical Society, Latin American Philosophy Movement; [hon.] Philosophy and Economic - Juridical Sci-

ences., 1993 'Amigos De Las Americas' Poetry Award; [oth. writ.] Poems, short stories, article and essays published in latin American newspapers and magazines. 'Poem for empty spaces' included in the forthcoming anthology 'Nothing Left Unsaid'.; [pers.] Drawing on the work of the surrealist movement and critical - realist theory, I strive to build up a critical poetry which deals with our world as it is, and intervenes in its transformation. Poetry is conceived as a true alternative to ideological ordinary language.; [a.] Inverurie, Aberdeenshire

GUNN, JOSEPHINE JEAN
[b.] 21 January 1927, Liverpool; [p.] Edward Brindley, Florence Brindley; [m.] Prof. Seamus Peadar Gunn, 6 October 1948; [ch.] Josephine Elizabeth, Florence Jennifer; [ed.] Laycock Society Girls, Trinity University; [occ.] Retired; [oth. writ.] Several poems published in local magazine.; [pers.] Poetry, the relinquishment of feeling.; [a.] Fraserburgh, Aberdeenshire

HADDEN, BRUCE
[pen.] Bruce Hadden; [b.] 9 April 1942, Surrey; [p.] John and Marsorie; [m.] Sylvia, 24 September 1992; [ch.] 1; [ed.] Cofe General University of Chambridge and Huddersfield; [occ.] Spiritual Consultant; [memb.] The Poetry Society; [hon.] BSc in computer information, CPC in Road Transport; [oth. writ.] Too many to list. But some published in Australia, and New Zealand and Britain.; [pers.] I would like one day to become a household name though I try to make people happy through my writings.; [a.] Batley, West Yorkshire

HAGUE, TANIA
[b.] 1 July 1958, Littleport, Cambs; [p.] Joan Nina Clarke; [m.] Richard Hague, 14 May 1996, (Divorced); [ch.] Adam Benjamin, Oliver Thomas; [ed.] Littleport Village College Wisbeach Technical College; [occ.] Housewife; [hon.] Isle of Ely Music Festival (Held 1st place for 3 years); [oth. writ.] I have written a great many poems and songs, though mainly for myself as a hobby.; [pers.] I believe words express so many feelings from the soul that we could not otherwise speak of and therefore enable us to reach into the heart of others.; [a.] York, Yorkshire

HALE, JILL
[b.] 4 March 1928, Crookman; [p.] Edith and Alfred Rolee; [m.] Widowed, 23 July 1949; [ch.] Elaine Ann; [ed.] Fleet Church of England School; [occ.] Retired; [memb.] Formerly Yateley Gardening Club; [oth. writ.] Several poems in church magazine 1 in national magazine.; [pers.] I write mainly country poems also Romantic poems and poems connected with memories.; [a.] Yateley, Hampshire

HALE, JULIA A.
[b.] 7 September 1960, West Bromwich; [ed.] BA Hons. (Graphic Design) and Diploma SW and Cert. Man; [occ.] Manager/Housing Association; [oth. writ.] Unpublished Poem and songs; [pers.] My inner self is expressed through my poems and songs, for others to understand who I am, so that we can share experiences of Life.; [a.] Kidderminster, Worcestershire

HALL, IAN
[b.] 8 April 1972, Newcastle upon Tyne; [p.] John Hall, Joyce Hall; [ed.] Parkview Comprehensive, Chester-le-Street; [oth. writ.] I have a book out in Summer 97 called *Alice Said* published by Minerva Press. Also a poem called "Love you love me" in *Between a Laugh and a Tear*, "Can you feel it" in *Poetry Now* Northeast 1997

HALL, SIDNEY CHARLES
[b.] 26 June 1968, Zimbabwe; [p.] Bertrem and Sophie Hall; [occ.] Student of Psychology; [memb.] Christian Life Centre; [oth. writ.] Desert Storm, Just A Thought, Forever Lost, Hopelessness, Remember?, Beauty Cast Out; [pers.] I am what I want to be and being what I am it has been a long journey from where I started, and arrived where I want to end. Yet always remaining in a state of becoming.

HALL, SYLVIA
[b.] 2 June 1945, Lowestoft; [p.] Marjorie, Sidney Bultitude; [m.] Divorced 1980, 25 March 1967; [ch.] Alison June and Christopher David; [ed.] Southolme

High School Lowestoft Suffolk; [occ.] Civil Servant; [memb.] Civil Servant Sports and Social Club (Committee member); [hon.] One of my many hobbies is swimming and I received an award for completing my 1/4 mile; [oth. writ.] 2 poems published "View From My Window" was published in a book called capital lines. "Jack" was published in a book called animal, vegetable and mineral. And a Xmas poem in my staff magazines.; [pers.] I try to introduce a spiritualness. In my poetry pointing out the real gifts. In life, especially the wonders of nature, and the joy of good health.; [a.] Romford, Essex

HAMBLY, MARILYN K.
[pen.] Kay Stammers; [b.] 15 October 1946, Glossop; [p.] Eileen Stammers (Deceased), Leslie Stammers; [m.] Peter Hambly, 24 August 1968; [ed.] King Edward VI Camp Hill School, Derbyshire College of Higher Education; [occ.] Principal Community Officer - Community Regeneration; [memb.] White Tower Writers Association, Royal Society of Health, Social Care Association.; [oth. writ.] "Flutterby", "An Ordinary Bucket", "Time Traveller", "Look Back with Love", "Childhood Dreams of Derbyshire", "Azalea Gardens at Muncaster Castle", "A Derbyshire Tale" all published in 1996 in various anthologies, including Voices on the Wind.; [pers.] Writing is a wonderful distraction from everyday worries and concerns. Ideas emerge, not to order, but from experiences, observation and feelings. Sharing the outcome with others is an added pleasure.; [a.] Ashleyhay, Matlock, Derbys

HAMEEDUDDIN, AYSHEA
[b.] 02.12.78; Basildon Hospital; [ed.] The Billericay School; [occ.] Student; [pers.] I try to capture sudden moments of inspiration and savour them through the written word; [a.] Billericay, Essex.

HAMER, LESLEY ERNA
[pen.] Lesley Erna Hamer; [b.] 14 October 1952, Halifax, West Yorkshire; [p.] Harold Stead and Annie Stead; [m.] Roy Hamer, 1 March 1971; [ch.] Louise and Noel; [ed.] Secondary Modern College Department of Pharmacy; [occ.] Pharmacy Technician; [memb.] Association of Pharmacy Technicians; [oth. writ.] Several poems, some prose also one or two comedy pieces. However 'twixt earth and heaven' is my first Nationality Published Work. My sonnet for Christine has been incorporated in a fund-raising card. For the local local hospice. Has raised to date; [pers.] El, 300. Both of my parents died when I was young. Being the youngest child of a large family. I spent some time with foster-parents, who have had a great influence on my writing. It is my ambition to write an autobiography.; [a.] Halifax, West Yorkshire

HAMLYN, SARAH
[pen.] Dannii Fox; [b.] 1 August 1984, St. Charles, MO; [p.] Keith Hamlyn, Yvonne Shirley Hamlyn; [ed.] Kesteven Girls Grammar School; [occ.] Student; [memb.] Harrowby Singers, St. Wulfram's Guides, Singing Group; [pers.] I enjoy writing poetry and I would still like to carry on. All my poetry is from my own feelings I have, whatever they may be: Love, anger, and sometimes, my dreams.; [a.] Grantham, Lincs

HANCOCK, SAMANTHA
[b.] 28 October 1969, Ipswich, Australia; [p.] Christopher and Dianne Hancock; [ed.] St. Scholastica's College; [occ.] Yacht Crew; [memb.] Royal Hong Kong Yacht Club; [pers.] Poetry is pure music for the soul.; [a.] Phuket, Thailand

HAROLD, JOHN-PAUL
[b.] 2 December 1976, North Shields; [p.] Kim and Paul Harold; [ed.] Beckfoot Grammar Bingley; [occ.] Student (eventually going to Aberystwyth); [oth. writ.] Some failed scripts and school mag. contributions aside, I wrote another 'poem' called "The Original Design". I mainly composed songs.; [pers.] Aleister Crowley said it all "Every man and woman is a star". I aim to be honest about myself and so what I write is often sombre, but I don't think it's depressing, I simply expect failure as much as I do joy.; [a.] Shipley, West Yorkshire

HARRIES, JONATHAN LLOYD
[b.] 11 June 1959, Wales; [p.] Derrick Harries, Jean Harries; [m.] Linda Maree Harries, 20 October 1984; [ch.] Elin Lloyd Harries, Gwenno Lloyd Harries; [ed.] Amman Valley Comprehensive, Swansea University, Trinity College, Carmarthen; [occ.] Head Teacher; [memb.] N.A.H.T.; [hon.] Hons. - Education Dip. H. E.; [oth. writ.] Poems - Novel in writing; [pers.] To understand the worth and value in people from the past to the present. In memory of Florence Harries.; [a.] Ammanford, Carmarthenshire

HARRIS, MISS SHARON
[b.] 21 November 1980, Weston super Mare; [p.] Phillip Harris, Elizabeth Harris; [ed.] Haygrove Comprehensive School - still attends at present; [occ.] Student but works part time in an Old People's Home; [hon.] Certificate and Distinction for introductory course of the Russian Language at School; [oth. writ.] One poem to promote Regional Charity and books I've put together but nothing that has been published.; [pers.] I want to say how pleased I am to be having my poem published. It's a great honour because I didn't think it would get published.; [a.] Bridgwater, Somerset

HARRISON, DAPHNE MARY EMILY
[b.] 5 May 1936, Wallington, Surrey; [p.] Mary and Albert Tegg; [m.] William Harrison, 29 March 1958; [ch.] Jane Mary Harrison, Richard John Harrison; [ed.] Secondary Modern School, High View, Wallington, Surrey; [occ.] Housewife; [oth. writ.] Several more poems.; [pers.] My inspiration for writing poems comes from my love of nature, and the wonderful world we live in. That God created "The Best of time is now."; [a.] Whitehaven, Cumbria

HARRISON, MAUREEN
[b.] 28 June 1950, Wallsend; [p.] Gladys Smith, Joseph Smith (Late); [m.] James Harrison, 20 March 1976; [ch.] Steven James; [ed.] Stephenson Memorial Girls School, Wallsend College; [occ.] Housewife (Ex Secretary); [memb.] World Book Club Transatlantic Pen Friends; [hon.] Poems published in magazines, semi-finalist in Duke of Edinburgh Award for songwriting at 15 years old (30,000 entries); [oth. writ.] Mostly songs, 4 recorded professionally on tape.; [pers.] I strive to capture nature's beauty in all its glory.; [a.] Whitehaven, Cumbria

HARRISON, PATRICK J.
[b.] 6 April 1933, Brighton, England; [p.] Charles W. Harrison and Bridget Harrison; [m.] Elizabeth Harrison, 30 March 1959; [ch.] Philomena, Patrice, Helen and Andrew; [ed.] St Josephs Secondary Borough High Street London S.E.I; [occ.] Solicitors Managing Clerk; [memb.] John Clare Society; [pers.] Love of poetry, particularly by John Clare. Intrest and Research into life and works of president truman research card no C4679 Harry S. Truman Library.; [a.] Shaftesbury, Dorset

HARRISON, PHILIP
[b.] 20 February 1956, Shipley, West Yorkshire; [m.] Teresa Harrison, 17 May 1980; [ed.] Bingley Grammar School; [occ.] Building Society Branch Manager; [memb.] Tavistock Rotary Club; [hon.] Fellow of the Chartered Institute of Bankers; [a.] Tavistock, Devon

HARROD, RUSSELL JOHN
[b.] 28 December 1963, Lowestoft, Suffolk; [m.] Madhu Prasad-Harrod, 2 October 1989; [ed.] University of Sheffield, (B.A.); [occ.] Accountant; [memb.] Chartered Institute of Public Finance and Accountancy, Amnesty International, Campaign for real Ale; [hon.] Editor's Choice Award from the International Society of Poets (1996) for "Entrelestrous de la Memoire" Runner-up in William Grant and Sons creative writing competition for Glenfiddich Whisky (1992); [oth. writ.] Poems published in "Voices On The Wind" (International Society of Poets, 1996), Arrival Press poets "Spring Collection" (1993), "Arc" (Sheffield University Students Union Poetry and Creative Writing Society (1985-1986); [pers.] My work is centred on two main themes: The agonies of love and surrealism. My best poems emerge by combining the two.; [a.] Burgess Hill, West Sussex

HARROP, HAZEL
[b.] Penrith; [m.] Martin Harrop, 18 December 1971; [ch.] Joanne and Deborah; [ed.] Penrith Grammar School and Mature O.J. Student in Final year of B.A. (hons) history.; [memb.] Mensa; [oth. writ.] Presently researching material for a book.; [a.] Ayton, Berwickshire

HARTFORD, SANDRA HELEN NORA
[pen.] Sandy; [b.] 1 April 1985, Royal Bucks, Aylesbury; [p.] Christian and Margaret Hartford; [ed.] Dundale JMI School Tring Tring Secondary School Tring; [occ.] School Girl year 7 Tring School; [memb.] Tring Swimming Club, Carter School Irish Dancing, Girl Guide, Church Choir; [hon.] S.P.I.A Primary Irish Dancing (all England 1995) champion Trophies (2) Plaques (6) Medals (60) in the last 2 yrs. member of Tring Swimming Club; [pers.] Poetry is a way of showing your feelings.; [a.] Tring, Herts

HARTSHORN, BARBARA
[b.] 18 January 1938, Holsworthy; [p.] Walter and Susan Symons; [m.] Geoffrey Hartshorn, 24 June 1956; [ch.] Three; [ed.] Holsworthy Secondary Modern, Holsworthy, Devon; [occ.] Housewife; [oth. writ.] Memories and 1945; [pers.] Born Holsworthy 1938. Maiden name Symons. Now live with my husband Geoff Hartshorn in Nuneaton, Warwickshire.; [a.] Nuneaton, Warwickshire

HARVEY, JOHN
[b.] 16 April 1933, Liverpool; [p.] Charles and Mary Harvey; [m.] Widower; [ch.] Julie, Barry, Steven, Mark, Jackie, Colin; [ed.] Our Lady of Mount Carmel, Secondary Modern School; [occ.] Un-employed; [oth. writ.] Many poems, plus a musical play entitled "The Boy Of The Forest" containing 17 songs. Unpublished.; [pers.] I am a big admirer of country music and also poems about the countryside. Rudyard Kipling is my favorite poet.; [a.] Liverpool, Merseyside

HASKEY, EILEEN ANN
[b.] 24 July 1936, Bulwell, Notts; [p.] Grace-Lilian and Charles Read; [m.] Eric William Haskey, 11 September 1954 (Deceased); [ch.] Philip, Diane and Susan; [ed.] Secondary School Bulwell Nottingham; [occ.] Domestic Cleaner; [memb.] Wine Club Balderton, Grove Dart Team Balderton, Serramics School, Clay Pole; [hon.] First second - third Wine Club awards, Ladies Summer Darts League winning trophy 1994; [oth. writ.] My first poem I submitted last year 1996 was printed in your book voices on the wind. And this is my second one to be printed in the book of, A Lasting Calm.; [pers.] I always loved reading poetry. From my school days. At Sunday School I always recited poetry for the church anniversary. My family and friends are very proud of me for having my poems printed; [a.] Newark, Nottingham

HASTINGS, MICHAELA
[pen.] Kayla; [b.] 4 July 1977, Yorkshire; [p.] Carol and John Hastings; [ed.] Pipers Corner School, Staffordshire University; [occ.] Student; [memb.] Stafford Athletic Union, Stafford Student Council; [pers.] The first pome I heard was Wordsworth, read by my Dad, since then my writing has been a release for my feelings and opinions, my writing is from my soul.; [a.] High Wycombe, Bucks

HAUNCH, V.
[pen.] Victoria Louise; [b.] 12 January 1980, England; [p.] Linda Haunch, George Haunch; [ed.] Broadgreen, Comprehensive School, Liverpool; [memb.] School Orchestra (Flute); [hon.] Liverpool Compact Award, The Associated Board of The Royal Schools of Music; [oth. writ.] GCSE Work; [pers.] I have been influenced by everything around me and past experiences. I am greatly inspired by various types of music and musicians.; [a.] Liverpool, Merseyside

HAWKINS, BRIAN
[b.] 27 May 1938, Huddersfield; [p.] Bill and Nellie Hawkins; [m.] Elizabeth Hawkins, 20 August 1960; [ch.] Allison and Marie; [ed.] Primary School; [occ.] Unemployed Builder; [oth. writ.] Many poems of various natures; [pers.] I enjoy writing poems and have done so for a number of years.

HAYES, STACEY
[pen.] Stacey Hayes; [b.] 19 September 1979, Cheshire; [p.] Craig Hayes; [ed.] Stamford High School and Warminster School; [occ.] Student; [memb.] Rotary Club and Amnesty International; [oth. writ.] School magazines; [pers.] It was written in remembrance of a friends untimely death.; [a.] Pershore, Worcestershire

HAYES, ZARA LOUISE
[b.] 12 January 1983, Wigan; [p.] Eileen and Bernard Hayes; [ed.] Lamberhead Primary School, Abraham Guest High School, Wigan; [occ.] School Girl; [memb.] Chris Noolfenden School of Dance, Orrell Operatic Society, and Abraham Guest School Council; [hon.] Various dancing awards in: Ballet, tap, modern jazz, character, lyrical and contemporary. School awards in all subjects, but special credit in English, Art, Drama and German; [pers.] I thoroughly enjoy writing poetry. I hope to write poetry that all people can relate to. From an early age I have been influenced by various literary sources.; [a.] Wigan

HAYMAN, ROGER JOHN
[pen.] Roger John Hayman; [b.] 26 February 1950, Morriston; [p.] William and Phyllis Hayman; [m.] Julia Marea Davies, 1 August 1990; [ch.] Eve, Carl, Rebecca; [ed.] Treachaf Sec. Mod. Swansea College of Art; [occ.] Mural Artist in Paint and Glass Sign and Graphics Manufacturer; [memb.] British Society of Master Glass Painters, Society of Artists and Designers of Wales, Member of the Worshipful Company of Glaziers and Painters of Glass; [hon.] First prize National Worshipful Company of Glaziers 1967 and 1968, Sir Arthur Evans travelling scholarship '69, City and Guilds Masters in Stained Glass '69, Swansea College of Art Degree, The Dylan Thomas Poetry award '70; [oth. writ.] Poems published in Poetry in Time Magazine '73, The Four Seasons Window Commission based on my own poem of life passing in 4 seasons, Bridgend Crematorium, National Eisleddford Poem Competition; [pers.] One's life can be changed by positive thought, using one's own karma to over ride the stress forced on one by insensitive people.; [a.] Swansea, West-Glamorgan

HAZELDINE, KAREN
[b.] 5 May 1979, Crewe; [p.] Robert and Hazel Hazeldine; [ed.] Victoria Community High School South Cheshire College; [occ.] Student; [memb.] Crewe Flyers Swimming Club; [a.] Crewe, Cheshire

HEALION, CARMEL
[b.] 21 July 1971, Tullamore, Offaly; [p.] Billy Healion and Maura Healion; [ed.] Killina Primary and Killina Presentation College; [occ.] Unemployed; [memb.] Rahan Womens Group, International Penfriends, Irish Pen Writers Group; [oth. writ.] Poems published in local newspapers. Book published in April 1996, entitled "Tears of Love and Laughter".; [pers.] "I adore nature and all the beauty around me. In my poetry I hope to reawaken the ability in every soul to appreciate love and life."; [a.] Tullamore, Offaly, Ireland

HEEKS, KATY
[b.] 19 March 1946, Hetton-le-Hole; [p.] Rosanna and Harold Seymour; [m.] Leonard Heeks, 15 June 1991; [ed.] Hetton Lyons Secondary Modern, Highbury Tech. Col. Portsmouth, Kirby College Middlesborough, Birmingham Polytechnic, William Booth College, London; [occ.] Day Care Manager; [oth. writ.] Several poems not yet submitted; [pers.] My work is among people and my poems are about people, reflecting their nature.; [a.] Birmingham, West Midlands

HEER, JASVEENA
[b.] 10 June 1982; [p.] Surinder Kaur Heer; [ed.] Mathematics ACSE Gained early at Harlington Community School; [pers.] This poem 'Darkness', was dedicated to Meena and Javed Shad. Though without Ravish Shabajee, (A friend) I would never had started poetry as he made me search within.; [a.] Hayes, Middlesex

HELMA, MR. E. V.
[b.] 29 June 1940, Eastbourne, Sx; [occ.] Housewife now I do tapestry and poems; [memb.] Save Our Wildlife Fund, Oxfam and Cancer Fund; [pers.] Most of the Poetry I have written is about true life today so that our children of the future can get an in sight of how it was in our time and strive to make the world a better place. Give me love peace and beauti of nature and I am content.; [a.] St. Annes, Lancashire

HEMMINGS, E.
[b.] 30 August 1932, Cumbria; [p.] Dorothy Wesley Rummey; [m.] T. Hemmings, 12 February 1955; [ch.] Peter, Carole, Crais, Patrick; [oth. writ.] Several poems published; [pers.] Most of my writings come from listening to people talking I'm a terrible eaves dropper; [a.] St. Brelade, Jersey, CI

HENDERSON, ANGELA
[b.] 13 May 1961, Edinburgh; [p.] Stella and Edward Henderson; [ed.] Firrhill High School, Edinburgh; [occ.] Shop Assistant, shoe fitter; [oth. writ.] "Question" - Awaken To A Dream, "The Towns News" - winner of the Town Crier Poetry Competition (Edinburgh), quite a few unpublished.; [pers.] I hope my poems will encourage thoughts and feelings of our time and will go on to do so in the future.; [a.] Edinburgh, Midlothian

HENSON, SUSANNA CLAIRE
[b.] 18 July 1977, Nottingham; [p.] Mr. and Mrs. J. Henson; [ed.] GCSE's at Holly Girt School, A levels, Notts Girl's High School, Art Foundation, South Notts; [occ.] Student - BA Hons. Fashion Design; [hon.] Duke of Edinburgh Awards; [oth. writ.] I have written a number of poems and I am currently in the process of writing a novel.; [pers.] I have been greatly influenced by contemporary American writers such as Jim carroll, Allen Ginsberg and Jack Kerovac; [a.] Nottingham, Nottinghamshire

HEPPINSTALL, PAULINE ANNE
[b.] 17 March 1964, Doncaster; [p.] Vera Heppinstall, Bernard Heppinstall; [ed.] Campsmouth High School, Doncaster, Granville College, Sheffield, Nottingham Trent University, Sheffield Hallam University; [occ.] Teacher - Design and Technology; [hon.] BA (Hons) in Visual Arts, P.G.C.E.; [pers.] I dedicate this written verse to the memory of my parents. My everlasting love. My work is purely representational, semi-autobiographical in nature - as perceived by my minds' eyes. 'Til then sweet fate.; [a.] Sheffield, South Yorkshire

HERBERT, JIM T. P.
[b.] 21 November 1962, Earls Court; [p.] Christine and Michael Herbert; [ed.] St. Thomas's Infant School (London), Wood Lane Junior School (London), Walter De Merton Junior (Watford), Leggatts Way Senior (Watf.), Art College (1 year) (Watford); [occ.] Unemployed (at the moment); [hon.] Nothing. I write for enjoyment and have never submitted any work before. I am a complete amateur, I'm afraid!; [oth. writ.] I write lots of poetry and songs, but, as already indicated, have never had anything published.; [pers.] Nothing special. I just love writing about life, my own or other peoples. My memories, experiences and lasting emotions influence my work. If my poetry makes people happy, I will be happier.; [a.] Watford, Hertfordshire

HEWETT, MISS JULIA RUTH
[pen.] Ruth Hewett; [b.] 10 November 1965, Hayle Cornwall; [p.] Barry and Pearl Hewett; [ed.] Bodmin Comprehensive School; [occ.] Self Employed Marketing Consultant (Since Feb. 1996); [oth. writ.] Occasional poems and rhymes written since early childhood; [pers.] I have always written for fun, but in later life find and aids relaxation and gives expression of the person.; [a.] Plymouth, Devon

HEWITT, ROGER MICHAEL
[b.] 22 March 1965, Eccleshall, Staffs; [p.] Michael and Elizabeth Hewitt; [m.] Tracey Hewitt, 5 June 1993; [ch.] Jamie Colledge Hewitt; [ed.] Graham Balfour High, Stafford College; [occ.] Area Sales Manager, Pioneer Concrete; [memb.] Licentiate of

City and Guilds, Chartered Institute of Building; [pers.] I write mainly to express my feelings for my wife.; [a.] Halesowen, West Midlands

HEYWOOD, HYRUM OLIVER
[b.] 6 October 1943, Salford; [p.] Nephi Dewsnup and Olive Heywood; [m.] Divorced; [ch.] Mark, Judith, Angela, Helen, Richard; [ed.] Stand Grammar, Manchester Grammar; [occ.] Ill Heath Retirement; [memb.] Clevedon Cricket Club N Guage Society National Geographical Society; [hon.] Mensa Certificate; [a.] Clevedon, North Somerset

HIBBERT, MRS. JOAN
[b.] 8 April, Romiley; [p.] Annie, John Booth; [m.] Derek Hibbert, 2 September 1961; [ch.] Steven Debra, Allison David; [ed.] Bredbury Secondary Girls School, now attending the Ridge Danyers College; [occ.] Home help; [memb.] National Trust; [hon.] Since 1991, 4 GCSEs, Bookkeeping, English Literature, English Language, Psychology; [occ.] I have wrote other poems but this is the first one I have sent in. Also I have wrote about Derek and myself when we walked the Parrine Way in 1990.; [pers.] I have loved and read poetry since I was a very little girl. I try to understand what the poet is saying in any form of written verse. Greatly influenced by the poems of Ella Wheeler Wilcox.; [a.] Stockport, Cheshire

HILDRED, MICHAEL
[b.] 27 January 1939, Grimsby, Lincs; [ch.] Patrick and Philippa; [ed.] 1949-56 Tadcaster Grammar School, 1956-60 Leeds College Of Art, 1960-61 Leeds College Of Art Teacher-Training, 1970-71 University of Leeds Institute of Education; [occ.] Full-Time Panther, mainly of landscape and flowers in oil or a crylic. Previous occ. 1963-71 head of Art Department Rowlinson Community school, Sheffield. 1971-91 Lecturer in Dept. of Aesthetic Studies, Moray House College of Education, Edinburgh; [memb.] Adel Squash Club, Leeds, Leeds Fine Art Society; [oth. writ.] 1965 "Is Sheffield Art - Conscious?" Sheffield Spectator. 1986 " Expressing Opinions Takes Practice Too" in Newsletter no. 2, Scottish Central Committee on Art 1986, "New Ways of Seeing" Report on Author's Courses in Critical Activity and Practical Art Appreciation for Schools. Moray House College of Ed. 1987, "New Ways Of Seeing" in Journal of Art and Design Ed. Vol 6 No 2,1989 "New Ways of Seeing" in Thristlewood, David (ed.) "Critical studies in Art and Design Education." Harlow, Longman; [pers.] Pride and pleasure in creativity, the power of love, wonder at the forms and patterns of life, celebration of humanity and the senses: These drive my poetry and my painting.; [a.] York, Yorkshire

HILL, BARBARA HELEN
[pen.] Barbara Helen Hill; [b.] 31 March 1942, London; [p.] Florence and Louigi Savino; [m.] Thomas Albert Hill, 24 October 1963; [ch.] Robert and Joanne; [ed.] Sir Hugh Tyddleton (Central) School, Clerkenwell; [occ.] Medical Secretary; [oth. writ.] Poem in "Voices On The Wind"; [pers.] Poetry is my way of expressing my inner feelings: Sometimes of love sometimes to expel pain of life for my grandchildren Jordan and Louie: For pleasure; [a.] Stevenage, Herts

HILL, STANLEY HARRY
[b.] 26 February 1930, Chesterfield, Derbyshire; [ed.] William Rhodes Boythorpe, Highfield Hall Newbold, Chesterfield Derbyshire, Also St. Helens Infants; [occ.] Retired Paintings, Salesman; [memb.] Byron Society (Honorary), Royal Horticultural Society, Orchid Society of Great Britain; [hon.] N.L.; [oth. writ.] Unpublished as yet.; [pers.] Overwhelmed.; [a.] London

HILLYARD, HAROLD S.
[b.] 8 January 1922, Great Yarmouth; [p.] Frank Hillyard, Lily Hillyard; [m.] Jo Sims, 4 August 1990; [ch.] Three stepchildren - David, Lisa and Andrew; [ed.] Elementary 1927 to 1936 then life, especially six war-years as a life guard, household calvary latterly A* pass in else English; [occ.] Retired; [memb.] Fellow and Past National Chairman British Association of Communicators in Business (formerly British Association of Industrial Editors) founder member the Country Players,

Wootton, Bedford; [hon.] The Federation of European Industrial Editors Associations (FEIEA) Award of Honour in 1979; [oth. writ.] Poetry performed (read) but unpublished, 30 years writing for house journals.; [pers.] The purpose of language is communication, Fail to do this and you are buying at the moon.; [a.] Wootton, Bedfordshire

HILTON-FOORD, KATHLEEN
[b.] February 17, 1903, Dover; [p.] Frederick and Kate Chatwin; [m.] Ernest A. Foord, October 29, 1924; [ch.] Sylvia, Peter, Daphne; [ed.] St. Mary's National School Terminated and working at 12 yrs. old; [occ.] Retired; [memb.] Life member Broadstairs Writers circle; [oth. writ.] 'Grannies Girl' copies to Oxford, Cambridge Dublin, Edinburgh Universities', The Survivor' copies Dover Library Brunel, Keele Universities. 'A little National School' copies Dover Library and Museum, 'A Little Bird Shop' life of Frederick Chatwin', taxidermist and musician, published in Bygone Kent.; [pers.] Never give up hope. Only started writing in mid-seventies.; [a.] Broadstairs, Kent

HIRONS, KEITH RICHARD
[pen.] Layne Woodway; [b.] 2 October 1946, Coventry; [p.] William and Kathleen Hirons; [m.] Divorced; [ch.] Two; [occ.] Voluntary Work; [memb.] Coventry Deaf Club, Local Sports Club; [oth. writ.] One published in the other side of the mirror, others published in local papers and magazines.; [pers.] I write what I feel at the time, trying to be accurate yet instill humor or a twist in the poems tail.; [a.] Coventry, W. Midlands

HODGSON, NIKKI
[b.] 2 July 1978, Taplow; [p.] John and Ann Hodgson; [ed.] Burnham Grammar School and then two years at East Berkshire College; [occ.] Resident Entertainer at Devon Valley Holiday Village; [memb.] Maidenhead Musical and Comeday Society, Bateman School of Dancing; [hon.] B. Tec National diploma in Performing Arts.; [pers.] My writings have always been influenced through my personal experiences and thoughts.; [a.] Slough, Berkshire

HOFFMAN, PAUL
[b.] 14 September 1960, Leigh, Lancs; [p.] Herbert Hoffman and Bessie Hoffman; [m.] Carole Lesley Hoffman, 27 September 1986; [ch.] Lauren Hoffman; [ed.] Fred Longworth County Secondary Tyldesley MC/R; [occ.] Long Distance Lorry Driver; [oth. writ.] Several poems published relating to trucking and life in the North.; [pers.] I try to write poetry with a trucking theme and its effect on my family life, often with a humorous or poignant message.; [a.] Wigan, Lancashire

HOLDWAY, KATY
[b.] 24 January 1983, Bath Hospital; [p.] Lesley and Ron Holdway; [ed.] George Ward School, Melksham; [hon.] Received a highly commended certificate for poetry; [oth. writ.] Write private poems and stories; [pers.] My feelings can be expressed more in poetry than in normal writing.; [a.] Melksham, Wiltshire

HOLLAND, PATRICIA B.
[pen.] Charlotte Alexandra Butler; [b.] 19 August 1943, Glace Bay, NS; [p.] Patrick and Olive Le Blanc; [m.] Robert C. Holland, 31 July 1983; [ch.] One girl and two boys; [ed.] High School; [occ.] Housewife, wife, mother, grandmother; [memb.] I belong to the Ladies Axillary of The Legion Branch 62; [hon.] I have not completed high school. The greatest award I have ever received was from my daughter when she was about 30 yrs old. She said that she was glad that I was her Mom!; [oth. writ.] I had a lot of poetry in a show box, which spanned over 30 yrs. Due to a house fire in 1987 in Ontario. I lost all my writings.; [pers.] I was a single mother back in the sixties. So when things got real hard. I wrote to get rid of the longings and fears. So with God's blessings, I have received many blessings. Thank you.; [a.] Louisboure, Cape Breton, Canada

HOLLERBACH, JAMES
[b.] 23 June 1975, Kettering, Northants; [p.] John and Mavis Hollerbach; [ed.] Bedford College of Higher Education, Amersham and Wycombe College; [occ.]

Freelance Textiles, Surface Pattern Designer; [hon.] (BTEC) Higher National Diploma in Textile Design; [oth. writ.] A number of unpublished poems.; [pers.] Personally, poetry is the vehicle that carries my emotions, a driving force for my expression.; [a.] Amersham, Buckinghamshire

HOLLINSHEAD, ROY
[b.] 13 May 1962, Islington, London; [p.] Hilda Hollinshead, Roy Harry Hollinshead; [ed.] Gilbert Miles Sec. Mod. School Redbridge Technical College; [occ.] Customer Services Operative; [pers.] My grateful acknowledgement and thanks to R.F. Kannemeyer, once acting head of Gilbert Miles, for fostering my interest in English; [a.] Dagenham, Essex

HOLMES, MRS. V.
[b.] 7 February 1942, Silchester; [p.] Mrs. Marshall; [m.] Mr. Holmes, 29 August 1981; [ed.] Three; [pers.] After the very sudden loss of my dear husband last December, unable to our goodbyes. I find writing verse helps me to express my feelings and allows me to say all those things I would so like to have told him.; [a.] Lincoln, Lincolnshire

HOMFRAY, ANDREW GUY
[b.] 25 July 1943, Birmingham; [p.] Samuel Lawrence and Alfreda Homfray; [m.] Andrea Homfray, 18 August 1962; [ch.] Faith Dawn, Lorne Angela, Adam Jolyon; [ed.] King Edwards Grammar School, Aston, Birmingham; [occ.] Painter and Decorator; [oth. writ.] Several other poems written but to date not offered for publication; [pers.] Majority of poems written during period of time whilst serving aboard ship during and following the Falklands War, with the Royal Navy.; [a.] Tinajo, Lanzarote, Canary Islands

HORGAN, ELIZABETH
[pen.] Elizabeth Dibb; [occ.] Housewife; [hon.] 3 Nursing Certificates 13 years nursing; [pers.] I hope my verses on nature will enable people to see life in a different light.; [a.] Dagenham, Essex

HORSFIELD
[b.] 30 March 1937, Aldershot; [p.] Both Death; [m.] Divorced; [ch.] 2 Boys - 40 and 25; [ed.] Due to parents not getting on, with my 3 sisters I spent 5 years in a special school in Yorkshire left at 16.; [occ.] I am a prison Auxiliary H.M.P. Winchester

HORSTED, LEE
[b.] 22 November 1976, Cheltenham; [p.] Michael Horsted and Gillian Horsted; [ed.] Alton College; [pers.] While writing my work it becomes hard not to sink in my own thoughts, I hope readers will find a similar difficulty.; [a.] Bordon, Hampshire

HOUSE, PAULINE
[b.] 11 November 1957, Offham; [p.] James Rose, Kathleen Rose; [m.] Brian House, 17 August 1974; [ch.] Gavin Aaron and Zoe Fiona; [occ.] Housewife; [a.] Snodland, Kent

HOVELL, R. DE B.
[b.] 19/11/39, Worthing; [p.] Arthur and Stephenie Hovell; [m.] Jacqueline Hovell, 19/02/63; [ch.] 2; [ed.] Dover College, RMA Sandhurst; [occ.] Gentleman; [memb.] Thin Raft Poetics; [oth. writ.] Various poems and articles; [pers.] To attempt to understand and reconcile the rhythm of the seasons with life.; [a.] Upper Basildon, Berkshire

HOWARD, JILL
[pen.] Jill Howard; [b.] 31 March 1933, Harrow on Hill, Middx; [p.] Arthur and Edith Howard; [m.] John Marshall (Second Marriage), 28 March 1980; [ch.] 3 - Mark, Sarah, Joanna Pashley; [ed.] Sacred Heart High School; [occ.] Housewife; [memb.] In the nos. I was a member of "Geoids," a Gilbert and Sullivan Amateur Operatic Society; [hon.] Scholarship to Trinity College of Music; [oth. writ.] I have several unpublished poems.; [pers.] Writing poetry is my greatest pleasure. It is the only time I feel I am really myself. Neither wife, daughter or mother!; [a.] Grawtham, Lincs

HOWELL, DEBBIE ALICE
[b.] 19 December 1964, Rochford; [p.] Pauline and James Shaw; [m.] Keith Anthony Howell, 4 Novem-

ber 1995; [ch.] James, Laura, Dawn Rhiane; [ed.] Housewife; [pers.] I have enjoyed writing for years. Now is my time to share a little of this, with you.; [a.] Redditch, Worcestershire

HUGHES, HAYLEY
[pen.] Risen Hay; [b.] 14 June 1979; Birkenhead; [p.] Eric and Sheila Hughes; [ed.] Eastway Primary School, Weatherhead High School; [occ.] Training for child and environmental care [hon.] Twenty certificates including: first aid, German, mathematics, computers, business studies; [oth.writ.] "In Memory of Terry," published in Sunlight and Shadows; [pers.] Education sometimes, to some people like myself, is governed by other people's behavior which affects our lives; Expression and poetry is my way of release; [a.] Wallasey, Wirral, Merseyside

HULL, SARA
[b.] 16 June 1987, Portsmouth; [p.] David Hull, Maureen Hull; [ed.] Glastry College; [occ.] Student; [memb.] Environmental Club, Poetry Club, Scripture Club; [hon.] History and English Awards; [oth. writ.] I once wrote a poem for a blue peter competition about a tiger cub, but it didn't get entered.; [pers.] I try to write poems with emotional feelings. Sometimes I describe objects or use my imagination when I write.; [a.] Newtownards, Down, Northern Ireland

HULME, KARL
[b.] 24 August 1980, Poole; [p.] Ashley Hulme, Jennifer Hulme; [ed.] Ferndown Upper School; [occ.] Student; [hon.] Dorset Young Composer 1995; [pers.] My major interest is in writing, arranging and performing my own songs.; [a.] Ferndown, Dorset

HUMM, AUDREY JOY
[b.] 22 May 1944, Colchester; [p.] Mr. and Mrs. C. G. Plowright; [m.] Edwin (Deceased 1995), 7 December 1963; [ch.] 5 and 7 grandchildren; [ed.] Secondary Modern; [oth. writ.] I have written many poems, purely for my own pleasure if something touches my heart then I just sit and write a poem, I just like to put my feelings down on paper, and what nicer way could it be than poetically.; [pers.] I had a lot of sadness in my young childhood, married a wonderful man, I had a wonderful family, we shared an abundance of good times, I'll always miss and love Edwin to whom my poem was dedicated.; [a.] Colchester, Essex

HUMPHREYS, BRIAN LEWIS
[b.] 15 August 1933, Swindon, Wilts; [p.] Lewis and Kathleen Humphreys; [m.] Widow, 18 October 1989; [ch.] Two, Boy - Ian, 1963, Girl - Susan, 1966; [ed.] Upper Stratton Senior School; [occ.] Retired - Ex Work Study Engineer; [memb.] Lapsed Corporate Member of Institute Manngimens Services; [oth. writ.] I have an ambition to write book reflecting my own life (brought up in orphanage etc.); [pers.] My marriage in 1989 to Ruby was my second marriage. I have a boy - Ian-1963, a girl - Susan-1966 from an earlier marriage.; [a.] Harlow, Essex

HUNT, MARY WARD
[b.] 14 January 1913, Wadenhoe; [p.] Capt. George Ward Hunt, Daisy Ward Hunt; [ed.] Queen Anne's School Caversham St. Elphin's Darley Dale Derby Art School; [occ.] Retired, Am an OAP. Former owner Wadenhoe Equitation School Stud.; [memb.] East of England Show Society, Bedford Cat Club, Anchor press, Gardening Clubs, Welsh pony and Cob Society; [hon.] Numerous Show Ring awards for Jersey Cattle, ponies, and cats bred the famous, Wadenhoe Team of International Driving ponies who represented Gr Britain, and who won numerous Wembley Awards have just published my Life story in verse. Am also an artist; [oth. writ.] In numerous anthologies for both stories and verse; [pers.] Was influenced in my youth by the collected sporting verse of Will. H. Ogilvie. Also learn journalism under my English Teacher at St. Elphin's Wrote stories and poems from childhood. Could read fluently by the age of 5.; [a.] Wadenhoe, Northamptonshire

HUNTER, P. G.
[pen.] Pauline, Gladys; [b.] 22 April 1934, Erpingham, Nr Gromer; [p.] Billy, Edith Folkard; [m.] Ronald Frank Hunter, 9 January 1954; [ch.] Steve, Karen,

Maria; [ed.] School Saywood Park Modern High School, Kings Lynn Norfolk; [occ.] Domestic Supervisor at GEH have retired 2 years ago

HURLEY, ANDREW D.
[b.] 29 April 1969, Liscard, Wallasey; [p.] William and Norma Hurley; [ed.] The Mosslands School, Wirral Metropolitan College, Marconi Information Technology Centre; [occ.] Clerical Officer and Freelance Photographer; [memb.] Wallasey Amateur Photographic Society; [oth. writ.] Several C.C.M. Reviews published in Direction Magazine, and author of "Wirral and Chester: What To See, What To Do, What To Photograph"; [pers.] My attitude should be the same as that of Christ Jesus: He made himself nothing and humbled himself. He became obedient to death - even death on a cross! Therefore God exalted him to the highest place.; [a.] Wallasey, Merseyside

HURST, SUE
[b.] 9 August 1938, Wokingham; [p.] Alfred and Mary Elson; [m.] David William Hurst, 1 August 1992 (Widowed); [ch.] John Michael, Sharon Joanne, Kevin James and Mark Timothy; [ed.] Kendrick Girls Grammar School; [occ.] Debtors Technical Officer at the Royal Berkshire Hospital; [pers.] I have scribbled poetry for many years but have never done any thing with it until my husband persuaded me to enter this competition. I enjoy writing poetry.; [a.] Reading, Berkshire

HUSSAIN, FATIMA
[b.] 2 August 1979, Manchester; [p.] Dr. Iftikhar Hussain, Ume Kalsoom; [ed.] I did my A levels in 1996, Islamic International Medical College, Islamabad, Pakistan; [occ.] Student of Medicine; [hon.] Several prizes for general English language, few for debates and declamation contests and one for an English Essay competition in school.; [oth. writ.] Many others poems and a few short stories, none of them yet evaluated or published. (Except for a couple in a school magazine).; [pers.] Playing cricket with words is the most enjoyable past time, provided one has enough vocabulary for the batting, enough expression for the fielding and enough imagination for the roaring crowd. I try my best to concentrate the most intense emotions in my poetry....; [a.] Dukinfield, Cheshire

HUSSAIN, NADA
[pen.] Nud; [b.] 20 June 1982, Abergavveny; [p.] Manzoor and Azra Hussain; [ed.] I have just started my First Year in G.C.S.E.'s and hoping to sit my exams in 1998.; [occ.] Student; [hon.] I have won many competitions in writing.; [a.] Abertillery, Gwent

HUTCHISON, JOHN THOMAS WETHERLY
[pen.] John Hutchison; [b.] 15 September 1930, Ellon, Scotland; [m.] 12 September 1959; [ch.] Jeffrey, Andrew, Heather Sophie; [ed.] Secondary; [occ.] Retired (O.A.P.); [memb.] The 8th Destroyer Association; [oth. writ.] Quiet a number of other poems, also, very recently completed the writing of my biography, which contains all my poems.; [pers.] I endeavour to express, the visual beauty and tender loving thoughts, I feel within me, both mentally and physically.; [a.] Worthing, W. Sussex

HYLAND, ANTHONY
[b.] 27 March 1965, London; [ed.] Alleyns School, (1978-79 Eastern Junior High, Conn., USA); [occ.] Theatre Producer/Director, Agent; [memb.] Directors Guild and Great Britain, Equity, Mensa, Players' Theatre, Sportsmen's Association; [hon.] Hons. Certificate for Languages (USA), Dist. for Classics (UK), Shinto Karate (25 yrs.) 3rd Dan Renshi; [oth. writ.] Play/Film scripts, ongoing over the past 15 yrs.; [pers.] Greek and Egyptian Classicist. Philosophy - Homer, Aeschylus, Euclidi Mako Taraki, Jung. "1997 Thought - 'In Defeat Malice, In Victory Revenge'"; [a.] Streatham, London

ILIFFE, ROY
[b.] 16 January 1949, Leicester; [p.] Mr. Walter Iliffe (Deceased), Mrs. Dorothy Vera Iliffe; [ed.] Gothlaxton Grammar School, Wigston, Leics, I CSE, 'O' levels, 3 'A' Levels, Honours Degree in Politics, University College Swansea, University of Wales, at present in year two of Certificate in the Art and Craft of writing

course at Leicester University; [occ.] Library Assistant; [memb.] Member of Theatre Writers Union, Leicestershire Playwrights, Wide Angle (A Local Film Group); [hon.] My Play "The Tramp" won first prize in the 1987 Lantern theatre trust play writing competition. My Play "The Hump" won first prize in the Salford One Act Play (Authors) competition 1992 and first Prize in the understanding Literary Magazine (Edinburgh) Play Competition 1993; [oth. writ.] Comedy Sketches for Central TV (3 Broadcast), two short plays for Radio Leicester, five one act plays (All Performed by Amateur Drama Groups) and two full length stage plays. Co-writer of a soap for cable TV and a film script.; [pers.] After years of writing plays and acting my interest in poetry was rekindled when I joined a writing course at Leicester University - If the emotions are controlled and disciplined, it helps the poem to be profound and true.; [a.] Leicester, Leicestershire

INGRAM, BRETT
[pen.] Brettley; [b.] 19/08/1971, Aldershot; [p.] Len & Sandra Ingram; [ed.] Beauchamps Comprehensive; [occ.] Builder, budding poet/child's author; [pers.] In sometime in everyone's life they have experienced some kind of sadness through love loss of some sort, and my poems are my emotions through my love loss put into words to help you come to terms with yours, I hope.; [a.] Wickford, Essex

INGRAM, LEE
[pen.] Lee Ingram; [b.] 5 November 1970, Leicester; [p.] Glenis Ingram, Dennis Ingram; [ed.] Wycliffe Community Collage; [occ.] Unemployed; [hon.] (I was 12) 1 Boxing medal and (I was 10) Football medal; [pers.] If anyone can relate to my poems, or I can communicate through my poetry then I am extremely gratified. If you are as me, one who never had enough self belief, then don't let anyone or yourself choke your beliefs. Let them breath...cut to the chase. Influences - any deep and meaningful poetry, lyrics, and life experiences. I am most peaceful when writing.; [a.] Leicester, Leicestershire

IRWIN, OLIVE
[pen.] Olive Irwin; [b.] 22 December 1972, Ireland, Leitrim; [p.] William and Emma Irwin; [ed.] Secretarial course (1992), Art and Design course (1994-95), Computer (Word Processing) City and Guilds (1996), Sligo Grammer Leaving cert (1992) School; [occ.] Doing art work painting; [memb.] The Book Club of Ireland; [hon.] Business Awareness Awards 1989 "Irish Life" received a certificate and plaque. Art: Dromahair show every year winning 1st and 2nd and 3rd places in some sections.; [pers.] I think all poetry comes from within our self. Listen to your heart and you will know.; [a.] Springvilla, Dromahair, Leitrim, Ireland

ISAAC, DAVID
[b.] 12 July 1969, Manchester; [ed.] Cheadle Hulme School, University of Sheffield; [occ.] Solicitor; [memb.] Manchester United F.C., Lancashire C.C.C.; [hon.] Cheshire County Cricket (under 18), Cheshire County Lacrosse (under 18); [a.] Manchester, Greater Manchester

JACKSON, LILA
[pen.] Lila Jackson; [b.] 16 April 1942, Co. Armagh, N. Ireland; [p.] James Wilkinson, Edna Wilkinson; [ed.] Dungannon High School for Girls 1) Now Royal School, Dungannon), 2) Nurse Training at Royal Victoria Hospital (Post-Grad), 3) University of Ulster, Jordans Town Campus; [occ.] (Retired) Health Visitor Bangor, Co. Down; [memb.] 1) Health Visitors Association (N.I.), 2) Women's Forum Executive Committee (N.I.), 3) Assistant Public Relations Officer for O'Neill Country Historical Society, 4) belfast Ladies' Choir; [hon.] English Literature, Music also R.G.N., R.G.M., Q.I.D.N.S., P.W.T., H.V. Cert., N.E.B.S.S.; [oth. writ.] 1) Poems published in local and mainland anthologies. 2) Pictorial History with captions of local area. 3) Items for local newspaper 4) Aricles for local historical magazine.; [pers.] My writings mostly recall a happy and beigh childhood in a shall rural village - "The Moy" - in Co. Tyrone. In them, Nostalgia turns into reflection of the purpose of existence and what people are striving toward. I have always liked poetry to rhyme.; [a.] Bangor, Down

JAMES, JESSIE
[pen.] Jessie Moyo; [b.] 19/07/58, Jamaica; [p.] Delroy James, Doreen Johnson; [ch.] Adrian, Obe, Rudoh, Issa, Tumpe; [ed.] Jamaica Primary & Secondary Schools 1965-73, Handsworth College 1982-96, Bookkeeping, English, Child Care/Pre-Nursing, Radio Journalism; [occ.] Recently qualified as a Nursery Nurse; [memb.] Newtown & Aston youth mentoring project, Centenary International Fund Raising Committee; [hon.] BTEC National - Diploma in Nursery Nursing & Caring; [oth. writ.] I am currently involved in a project which is publishing an anthology of poems from the black community writers. I have also written a collection of Caribbean short stories for children - to be published in the near future. I am currently a finalist in a BBC Radio Play Competition. I am a singer, songwriter with a group, Culture & Family. We perform at various community events in and around Britain. A lot of my writings are still unpublished. I am currently recording an album of songs.; [pers.] I believe in a higher Supreme Force and try to live a life of high moral standard. I grew up with my grandmother, a strong God fearing woman who taught me a shining example of good moral living and a godly life so I try to reflect true experiences and knowledge within my writing; [a.] Birmingham, West Midlands

JEBB, JOHN DONALD
[pen.] Paddy; [b.] 19 November 1915, Babyhackamore; [p.] John Thomas Jebb, Helena Jane Jebb; [m.] Hazel Nora Elizabeth, 28 September 1940; [ch.] Three daughter, one son; [ed.] Qualified as an Aircraft Engineer, took a level in English Literature; [occ.] Retired 81 years of age; [memb.] Cross country and track medals and Cups (running); [hon.] Africa Star and Clasp, 3 other other medals; [oth. writ.] 90 poems some good some not so; [pers.] A lifetime in the Royal Air Force.; [a.] Shrewsbury, Shropshire

JEFFREY, MRS. LYNN
[pen.] Lynn Jeffrey, LJ; [b.] 30 March 1950, Dorking; [p.] Mr. and Mrs. G. Hutson; [m.] Mr. Peter Jeffrey, 7 November 1987; [ch.] Karen, David and Mark Hutching; [ed.] Secondary School and Secretarial College; [occ.] Assembly and housewife; [oth. writ.] Am writing a book of poems, for personal gratification.; [pers.] My inspiration is music and art, people such a Bowie, godley and creme, and the destruction of the world my greatest love is Thesea; [a.] Tadworth, Surrey

JENKINS, LISA
[b.] 19 May 1980; [p.] Mary Jenkins, Royston Jenkins; [ed.] Kingsmead High School Hednesford, Cannock, Cannock Chase Technical College; [occ.] Student - Cannock Chase Technical College; [memb.] Aquarius - Disco Setters - Disco; [pers.] My poems are a way of expressing my feelings.; [a.] Cannock, Staffordshire

JENKINS, LORRAINE
[b.] 11 September 1969, Altrincham; [p.] Laurence and Shiela Walton; [m.] David Jenkins, 17 September 1994; [ed.] New Mills School, Stockport College; [occ.] Music Teacher; [memb.] Multiple Sclerosis Society, graduate member of the Institute of Export; [hon.] Music and dance; [pers.] Now I can no longer do, I teach. Time spells use not waste.; [a.] Chapel-en-le-Frith, High Peak

JENKINSON, ANDREW NEAL
[pen.] Andy Kinson; [b.] 16 September 1937, Newcastle upon Tyne; [p.] John and Violet Jenkinson; [m.] Olive Jenkinson, 28 September 1968; [ch.] Valerie (Step Daughter) 3 Grand Children 4 grand children; [ed.] Whitley Bay Grammar School; [occ.] Circulation Administrator; [memb.] Seaford (Sussex) Constitutional Club Wallington Bowling Club; [hon.] One poem entered in St. Mary's Church, Beddington's Monthly Magazine; [oth. writ.] Many of which have been seen solely by family and close friends.; [pers.] I find great comfort in the ability to express my deepest thoughts - although somewhat profound - at times. To create a work which gives pleasure and food for thought to the reader is a blessing and privilege.; [a.] Wallington, Surrey

JOHN, SARAH LOUISE
[b.] 2 November 1975, Maesleg; [p.] Gregory John, Anne John; [ed.] Maesleg Comprehensive School, Maesleg College, Bridgend College; [occ.] Overworked, Underpaid Slave for Revlon; [pers.] We each have a destiny and mine is to write poems and stories for my pleasure.; [a.] Maesleg, South Wales

JOHNSON, LAURA
[b.] 24 December 1986, Birmingham; [ed.] Water Orton Primary; [pers.] My inspiration for this poem was seeing homeless people in town. I don't think that it is fair that some people have got so much and others have nothing my favorite poet is Alan Ahlberg.; [a.] Birmingham, West Midlands

JOHNSON, RACHEL
[b.] June 1951, Hull; [ed.] Hull College of Further Education; [occ.] Clerk (Hull City Council); [hon.] Have advanced qualifications in shorthand typing and the BTEC in Public Administration; [oth. writ.] Have written a number of poems and was first published in 'Voices On The Wind' (1996); [pers.] I prefer to write in a light-hearted vein about the simple or mundane things in life.; [a.] Hull, East Yorks

JOHNSTON, JOHN
[b.] 28 June 1937, Portaferry; [p.] Alexander Johnston, Teresa Johnston; [m.] Sarah Johnston, 23 April 1962; [ch.] Johna, Teresa, James, Hugh; [ed.] St. Patricks High School Down Patrick Co. Down; [occ.] Farmer; [oth. writ.] This is only my second attempt at poetry, my first poem about local Portaferry was published by Tim Sharp Peterborough last year.; [a.] Portaferry, Down

JONES, ALUN
[b.] 20 July 1947, Liverpool; [p.] Charles Greenslade Jones and Edith; [m.] Ann, 13 June 1970; [ch.] Maxine and Shelley and Rachael; [ed.] Sec Mod in Liverpool did not take any exams (too busy playing football); [occ.] Investment Consultant Ex Stage and Television Prop Man; [memb.] Institute of Financial Advisers, F.A. Soccers Coach; [hon.] FA Football, Coaching Badge, Essay and Hand writing, Award 1964. Liverpool under IS's boxing champion 1962; [oth. writ.] The Rabbit Hutch (School Play) unpublished poems, like in a box (modern nativity) for Patrick (Tribute in Memorium); [pers.] May your knees never knock at the doors of fear - do not give way to intimidation. My greatest influences were C.J. Oneill S.M. (Royal Court Theatre) Bill Shankly and Denis Potter; [a.] Pudsey, W. Yorks

JONES, CARLY SAMANTHA
[b.] 23 November 1981, Lancaster; [p.] Ian and Alison Jones; [ed.] At Secondary School; [memb.] Manchester United F.C.!!!!; [hon.] Many. Yet to be achieved!!; [oth. writ.] None published; [pers.] There is no strength like inner strength!; [a.] Kirkby Lonsdale, Lancashire

JONES, ELIZABETH
[b.] 1 September 1972, Church Village; [p.] David and Patricia Jones; [m.] Fiance: Mark Stephens; [ed.] Pencoed Comprehensive, University of Wales Newport; [occ.] Student Teacher (Primary); [memb.] St. David's Players, Royal Life Saving Society; [hon.] Currently studying for Bed (Hons) Primary; [oth. writ.] Several articles in school magazine, letters to magazines; [pers.] My poetry is influenced by things that have affected my life or subjects and events that I find moving.; [a.] Pencoed, Mid-Glamorgan

JONES, ELIZABETH MARY
[pen.] Elizabeth Jones; [b.] 30 March 1944, Ballymoney; [p.] The late Robert, and Rose McConachie; [m.] Des Jones, 25 July 1973; [ch.] Alan, Lynn, Bryan, Alastair and Trejor; [ed.] Ballycastle Grammar School, Royal Victoria Hospital, Belfast, The John Radcliffe Hospital - Midwifery Nuffield Maternity Home and Churchill Hospital Oxford; [occ.] Staff Nurse; [hon.] State Registered Nurse, State Certified Midwife; [oth. writ.] Other poems previously published Christmas Bells, The River Bush, The Fly Adventure, So Simple and So Great, Past Rays of Country Life, The Century of the Car, The Small Orphan Boy, Friends and Friendship, A Little Snowflake, Irish Men - Honest and True; [pers.] I like to show the warmth and beauty of Ireland and its people in the words of these poems. So often in our country - evil people and their actions get all the publicity. The good and kind deeds go unnoticed.; [a.] Magherafelt, London Derry

JONES, GARETH
[b.] 24 May 1979, Wordsley; [p.] Val Jones, Keith Jones; [ed.] Buck Pool Secondary School; [occ.] Assembley Feeder (upholstery); [pers.] I look at poetry as a release. My poems show all my feelings and emotions. I have been influenced by John Lennon, Don McLean, Noel Gallagher.; [a.] Stourbridge, West Midlands

JONES, HEATHER-JAY G.
[b.] 27 January 1979, London; [p.] Viv and Eric Jones; [ed.] Sylvia Young Theatre School; [occ.] Actress; [memb.] Equity the green room; [hon.] Various dance and drama awards including East Grinstead Silver Medal; [pers.] In my poetry I try to show my feelings about life which I hope will to some extent reflect those of the reader.; [a.] Purley, Surrey

JONES, RICHARD
[b.] 23 April 1963, Rhondda Valleys; [p.] Ivor Jones, Myra Jones; [m.] Mandy Teresa Jones, 29 March 1986; [ch.] Luke, Ryan, Nathan, Regan; [ed.] Porth Countly Comprehensive; [occ.] Bus driver; [oth. writ.] Poems for family and friends my aim, to write a poem for every event and occasion.; [pers.] My poems show how I feel about, family or political, military, Religion, Love for nature and my fellow man and have been influenced by my marriage and more so by the birth of our four children.

JONES, ROBERT DAVID
[pen.] Robert Kennedy Jones; [b.] 19 May 1943, Ebbw Vale; [p.] Oswald Jones, Kathleen Jones; [ed.] EBBW Vale, County Grammar School, Caerleon Training College; [occ.] Retired Primary School Teacher; [memb.] Wymeswold Players Drama Group, The Wolds Choir; [pers.] My inspiration comes from observing nature. I have been greatly influenced by the works of William Wordsworth and Thomas Gray Wymeswold; [a.] Nr Loughborough, Leics

JONES, SAM
[pen.] Sammy J.; [b.] 1 April 1965, Bentley; [ed.] The Petersfield School open university; [occ.] Writer Student; [memb.] Mensa Hackney Scuba Club; [oth. writ.] Surviving Life published in The Memory Bird (by Virago) previously produced/edited areas singles newsletter for mensa; [pers.] Once met, never forgot and if you see someone without a smile give them one.; [a.] Petersfield, Hampshire

JORDAN, NATALIE
[b.] 11/05/82; [p.] Barrie and Margaret Jordan; [ed.] Beginning GCSE courses at secondary school; [occ.] student; [memb.] World Wide Fund for Nature (WWF), Cats Protection League, Animals' Vigilantes, Tiger Trust; [oth. writ.] A poem published in a small booklet by Animals' Vigilantes. Currently finishing my first novel; [pers.] I aim to bring the suffering of animals to our attention.; [a.] Dagenham, Essex

JOYCE, JOHN JOSEPH
[pen.] J. J.; [b.] 13 October 1938, Dartford; [p.] Michael Joyce, Mary Ann Joyce; [m.] Sandra Ann Joyce, 3 November 1962; [ch.] Linda, John, Anthony; [ed.] Secondary Modern; [occ.] Unemployed, disabled; [oth. writ.] Poems, letters (None published).; [pers.] Though one is physically handicapped, I feel that I still can contribute to society generally by your help. By publishing my work.; [a.] Farnborough, Hampshire

JOYCE, PATRICIA
[pen.] Trish Joyce; [b.] 23 June 1935, Western Australia; [p.] Walter Silvester, Mavis Herbert; [m.] Kevin Joyce, 27 September 1952; [ch.] Rhondale "Lee" Brendan Michael, Gary Stephen, Degra Ann, Alan Phillip, Warren Gregory, Jeremy Lawrence and Daniel Raymond; [ed.] Perth Girls High School and Hartill's

Commercial college; [occ.] "Traveller"; [memb.] W.A. Genealogy Society Austin Seven Club Dove Camper Club (W.A.) Campervan and Motor Home Club of Australia, Perth Writers Group; [oth. writ.] As editor of Dove Camper Club Newsletter - produced in Verse. Published own book "smile awhile" subtitled "A Family Affair" dealing with antics of a growing family - (To Get My Revenge) have also written many children's poems (As yet unpublished).; [pers.] I basically write all my poetry with a humorous twist at the end because I believe laughter is the best medicine and there is far too much trouble and sorrow in the world.; [a.] Wilson, Western Australia, Australia

JOYCE, TERENCE JOSEPH
[b.] 25 May 1939, Dublin; [p.] Anna Josephine Joyce; [ed.] Fear and Ignorance, Irish Style; [occ.] Semi-retired in France where I came to live 1973; [pers.] If music is the language of the soul, poetry is the song of the intellect from which it springs. When the two become married in one, divorce could never be contemplated because peace would be lost. From the peace within the peace exterior is constructed.; [a.] Le Colombier, Plessala, Cotes D'Armor, France

JOYNER, JOANNE
[b.] 22 June 1981, Galway; [p.] David and Ann Joyner; [occ.] Second - Level Student; [a.] Tuam, Galway, ROI

JUDD, CAROL M.
[b.] 20 October 1943, South Wigston; [m.] Keith Anthony Judd, 4 June 1966; [ch.] Clare and Simon Judd; [ed.] Royal College of Nursing, Open University; [occ.] Psychotherapist/Hypnotherapist; [memb.] The National Assoc. of Counselors, Hypnotherapists and Psychotherapist, graduate member - British Psychological Society, British Complementary Medicine Association; [hon.] Honors Degrees in Psychology, State Registered Nurse, State Registered Clinical Nurse Teacher; [oth. writ.] Editorials for local Newspapers.; [pers.] We each make an inner, as well as, outer journey through life, which may become fraught with difficulties. I wrote this poem to assist one person's inner journey - to move them beyond despair. I hope it will speak to others'.; [a.] Bishops Stortford, Herts

JUNOR, MRS. EULALEE
[b.] 11 January 1928, Jamaica; [p.] Luther Brooks - Ivy Brooks; [m.] Victor V. Junor, 24 December; [ch.] Three; [ed.] Secondary (College); [occ.] Asst. Speech Therapist; [oth. writ.] Songs; [pers.] I am a Christian, and I, I have been writing poems. Since 1995. Never wrote poems before until one night I had this vision to do so. Residing in this country for 42 years.; [a.] Ilford, Essex

KALIO, ELIZABETH IBISIKI
[b.] 4 December 1960, Nigeria; [p.] Christiana Kalio, Edmund Kalio; [ch.] David Soibi, Christine Belema; [ed.] University of Sheffield, MED University of Ife, Regina Caeli T.T. College, College of Education; [occ.] Primary School Teacher KS2; [memb.] British Educational Management and Administration Society (BEMAS), Black Heart Publishing; [oth. writ.] "The Mushroom Child" published in a volume (UK), articles in the `Nigeria Standard'; [pers.] Out of the abundance of my daily experiences, I open the gates of my feelings to share with the human race. My greatest inspiration to write sprang from my rich African cultural background.; [a.] Ealing, Middlesex

KANE, CATHERINE
[b.] 11 May 1936, Glasgow; [occ.] Art/Drama Student; [hon.] A level English Certificate and Art 'O' level gained; [oth. writ.] I still write poetry and at the present, I am writing a book about my experience of life in Glasgow in the 1940's up until present day.; [pers.] I believe if you have a talent for expressing your ideas through writing then you have a special gift. To be used and cherished Catherine Kane 24 Swinton Place.; [a.] Glasgow, Cardonald, Scotland

KANE, MRS. MARY G.
[pen.] Mary G. Kane; [b.] 5 October 1925, Clyne/Neath, W. Glam; [p.] Luke John, Gwendoline John;

[m.] William Edward Kane, 28 August 1948; [ch.] Paul, Andrew, Deborah, Sharon; [ed.] Elementary; [occ.] Housewife, (Retired); [memb.] Elim City Temple Pentecostal Church Swansea, Fellowship of Christian Writers, Evangelical Alliance, Ex. A.T.S. Organization S.P.U.C. Pro-Life; [oth. writ.] Twenty one poems published in anthologies, four of which have reached the semi finals in competitions.; [pers.] In my writing I strive to touch on current trends in society, I have been greatly influenced by my strong Christian Faith.; [a.] Swansea, West Glamorgan

KARLSTROM, LENA
[b.] 15 May 1980, Tromso; [a.] Tromso, Australia

KATZARSKI, VLADISLAB
[b.] 15/01/1966, Sofia; [p.] Danail Katzarski, Trayanka Katzarski (M); [m.] Anellia Peterova Velinova-Katzarski, 19/11/1993, [ch.] Omana Vladislav Katzarski; [ed.] State University of Sofia "Kliment Ohridski"; [occ.] Journalist; [hon.] 1st prize in the Balkan Literature Competition for Poetry 1996; [a.] Sofia, Bulgaria

KEATS, SARA
[b.] 17 January 1972, London; [p.] Helen and Louis Keats; [ch.] Kaya, Karma, Karizma and Cosmos; [ed.] Collingham Tutors, London College of Printing; [occ.] Writer; [oth. writ.] To be published shortly.; [pers.] My words come from the raw feelings one experiences from sadness to hatred and spirituality and love.

KEHOE, PATRICE
[pen.] Halley Hetfield; [b.] 22 January 1979, Dublin; [p.] John and Katherine Kehoe; [ed.] St. Leo's College, Carlow; [occ.] Student sitting leaving certificate in June; [memb.] (HO) School Hockey Team; [hon.] Junior certificate, Sports awards and Medals in Athletic, Hockey, Gymnastics; [pers.] Poetry is a door to the soul only you can open influenced by Irish poets Yeats and Kavanagh.; [a.] Baltinglass, Wicklow, Ireland

KELLS, ANGELA
[b.] 15 July 1962, Crawley; [p.] Colin and Williamina Kells; [m.] Niko Georgantopoulos, 19 July 1997; [occ.] Assistant Accountant; [memb.] (AAT) Association of Accounting Technicians; [pers.] I met my fiance in Zakyntuos and subsequently spent one year in Greece, which inspired me to write "Hellas The Forgotten Land".; [a.] Crawley, Sussex

KELLS, JAMES A.
[b.] 27 July 1947, Dublin; [p.] James and Bridget Kells, (Deceased); [m.] Cindy (My Lady), March 1991; [ch.] Five year old son Troy; [ed.] Self educated through books etc., Formal Education Secondary Level; [occ.] Merchant Seaman, (Retired early through injury); [oth. writ.] Previously I have had some short stories, poems and childrens stories published.; [pers.] I have been told that I had a lot of myself into my poems as "A Sailors Dream" reflects. However I say I write from life.; [a.] London

KELLY, CIARA
[pen.] Ciara Kelly; [b.] 17 August 1979, Dublin; [p.] Brendan and Teresa Kelly; [ed.] Loreto Secondary School, Balbriggan, Co Dublin; [occ.] 6th year student in Loreto Secondary School; [memb.] Digges Lane - The College of Dance, Dublin; [hon.] Various awards for performing arts and dance. Various school achievements also; [oth. writ.] Various poems unpublished; [pers.] To my family, relatives and friends, thank you for being there for me. You all mean so much to me. My poems are influenced by family, friends, surroundings, experiences and feelings.; [a.] Naul, Dublin, Eire

KEMPT, KEVIN KEITH
[b.] 10 March 1938, K.G.F. Mysore State, South India; [p.] Percival and Rosamund Kempt; [m.] Yvonne Philomena Kempt, 6 January 1968; [ch.] Two grown up daughters; [ed.] 6 "O" level G.C.E. passes Ex-Ecclesiastical Student with a Theological, Philosophical, Psychological Sociological and widely read background; [occ.] Retired Civil Servant after 24 years plus with the D.S.S.; [oth. writ.] Book-

Living: Poetry and thoughts published by Minerva Press 1995, Poem: A Living Legend, Anthology: The New Voices Anthology published by Minerva Press 1994, Poem: Do This In Memory of Me, Book: Anthology, Christian Verse, Published by Triumph House from East Anglia; [pers.] This author is a Eurasian by Ethnic Origin and has been a British Citizen for the last 24 years. He has a deep interest in and an expanding knowledge of not only the Christian tradition, but also of all religions. East and West mystical truth and harmony are his life's way and work.; [a.] Tottenham, London

KENNEDY, ANN
[pen.] Ann Mahon; [p.] John Mahon and Annie Mahon (Dead); [m.] Alan; [ch.] Sinead Lorraine, Ailish Darragh and Marc; [ed.] Scoil Josephian Parnell V.E.C. also Whitehall House Senior College; [occ.] Hosuewife I worked as book keeper for Hart Brennan, Co. Accountants along with other office duties; [hon.] Two certificates for English R.S.A. and department of education. Also one for commerce; [oth. writ.] Short stories

KENNEDY, TERENCE KEVIN
[pen.] T. K. Kennedy; [b.] 10 February 1959, Liverpool; [p.] Michael Kennedy, Helen Kennedy; [m.] Irene Kennedy, 8 March 1980; [ch.] Linsey, Terence, Shaun, Kevin; [ed.] St. Augustines School Riversdale Technical College; [occ.] Civil Engineer; [memb.] Incorporated Engineer (Institution of Water and Environmental Management); [hon.] ONC Civil Engineering, HNC Civil Engineering; [oth. writ.] Publication of poem in (Poetry now anthology); [pers.] I write to inspire people, to relay a message worthy of understanding whether it be fact or fiction.; [a.] Liverpool, Lancashire

KENNY, SIMON
[b.] 4 June 1973, St. Heuer, Jersey; [p.] John Kenny, Linda Kenny; [ed.] Highlands College (Jersey), Lampeter University; [occ.] Stuyding Philosophical/Religious Studies at Lampeter (BA); [memb.] Adyar Library Madras, Lampeter Squash Club; [oth. writ.] Travel diary written as a teenager published in Jersey Evening Post; [pers.] Preparing for death, by learning to actually live. Humans can stop pretending to be lemmings and realize they do have wings to fly. This for me would be a true lasting calm.; [a.] St. Helier, Jersey

KENT, SHIRLEY LYNN
[pen.] Suga; [b.] 25 July 1957, Skipton; [p.] Derek and Zona Johnson; [m.] Barry Kent; [ch.] One son; [occ.] Freelance B.H.S. (Reg) Rising Instructor; [oth. Writ.] Inner Cry, Mother To Son, Dunblane, Faith, Easter Parting, Fear; [pers.] Favorite writing is Desiderata, May Ehrmann.; [a.] Skipton, North Yorks

KERR, ELIZABETH ANN
[pen.] Am De Vizard; [b.] 1 July 1914, Stockport; [p.] Winifred Peter Hanratty; [m.] Bernard Kerr, 8 October 1938; [ch.] Anthony, Mary; [ed.] Our Lady's Catholic School Stockport; [oth. writ.] My own, Auto biography and direrifs unpublished; [pers.] I was a member of united nation's Association: Manchester 1946 Branch - was delegated to African Affairs Committee where I met many African's delicated to their cause. "He who lights one candle to show in the darkness of the mind is a prince amongst men.; [a.] Stockport, Cheshire

KHATTAK, MISS SHIREEN
[b.] 23 April 1983, Riyadh, Saudi Arabia; [p.] Abdul Samad Khattak & Vivienne Khattak; [ed.] Saudi Arabian International School—Riyadh (American section), Overseas Pakistani Foundation (O.P.F.), Girls College Islamabad; [occ.] school girl; [memb.] Alliance Francaise d'Islamabad; [oth. writ.] Panjab Middle schooling project (short story competition), Pakistan National Council of the Arts (PNCA), National Gallery Mural Painting; [pers.] Being the great, great, great, great granddaughter of Pathan warrior and poet Khushal Khan Khattack, it is an honour and a pleasure to be accepted as a contributor to this international anthology.; [a.] Islamabad, Pakistan

KHURANA, JAG
[b.] 18 September 1974, Birmingham; [p.] Mr. H. Khurana and Mrs. R. Khurana; [ed.] Leasowes High School, King Edwards VI Sixth Form College, Stourbridge, University of Central Lancashire - Preston; [occ.] Student; [hon.] B.A. (Hons) English Literary Studies; [pers.] Take the rules, the givens, the unquestioned, and interrogate them until you transcend their limits. There is always more to be said, to be done, to be thought; [a.] Halesowen, Dudley

KIELY, NIGEL
[b.] 26 January 1969, Ernville, Cork City; [p.] Jane and Sean Kiely; [ed.] St. Patricks Boys National Sch., Mayfield Community School; [occ.] Manufacturing Operator for Philips C.S.S.; [memb.] Currently studying for a Diploma in Journalism; [oth. writ.] This is my first publication.; [pers.] A poem comes from the heart, it is mixed with some creative emotions and finally touched up with a spiritual rhythm. It's purpose - to live on forever.; [a.] Mayfield, Cork

KILGOUR, MILTON
[b.] 11 August 1967, New Zealand, New Plymouth; [p.] Jim Kilgour, Nola Bright; [m.] Karen June Summers, (to be Kilgour) coming up: 22 February 1997; [ch.] Jesse Aaron Burton; [ed.] New Plymouth Boys High School New Plymouth, New Zealand; [occ.] Estate Manager; [pers.] Simple things can mean so much and when it brings happiness to others, I am glad my poem contributes.; [a.] Virginia Water, Surrey

KING, JAN
[pen.] Jan King; [b.] 14 December 1952, Matfa, Malta; [p.] Mr. B. A. Seiboth and Mrs. M. E. Blake; [m.] Russell Brown, partner; [ch.] Paul - 9; [ed.] Boarding School - 'Upton Hall' - College (Newark Tech), 1996 Nottingham Trent University; [occ.] Mature Student, BA (hons) Social Sciences; [memb.] Book Club, Music Club, Arts and Crafts Club; [hon.] Diploma in Beauty Theraphy (A.A.B.Th.) 'O' Levels and 'A' Levels; [oth. writ.] I have written poetry since I was teenager, but I have never tried to have any published before.; [pers.] I have always been very interested in poetry, art and crafts. My other interest in criminology and I hope to qualify as a criminologist in 1999.; [a.] Muston, Nottingham

KING, SHEILA BEATRICE
[b.] 5 October 1929, Bromley; [p.] Archibald Rumph, Hilda Rumph; [m.] Stanley Frederick King, 4 April 1953; [ch.] 2 Sons - William King and Matthew King; [ed.] Bromley Grammar School, Clarks College; [occ.] Retired - Bromley Magistrates' Court; [oth. writ.] Several poems published.; [pers.] Master of the spoken word and English Language. Brilliant humerous communicator. Ray Moore, broadcaster. They say you are dead but I think you are circling "Gatport Airwick".; [a.] Bromley, Kent

KIO, ODALO
[pen.] Ali; [b.] 7 July 1974, Benin City, Nigeria; [p.] Benjamin Kio (deceased), Agatha Kio; [ed.] University of Benin Staff Primary School, University of Benin Demonstration Secondary School, Presently - Part 5 Law Student, University of Benin, Nigeria; [occ.] Student; [memb.] St. Alberts Cath. Church Mass Choir, University of Benin, Ugbowo Campus; Zone 6 Youth Movement, St. Alberts Cath. Church, Uniben, Ugbowo; Editor Kampus Mirror mag. Uniben; President OD'AL & Assoc. Public Relations & Image Consultants, Benin City; [oth. writ.] "Our Culture", published in "Rake" mag. - a literary Forum 1989; "Bang!", published in "Virtue", a youth mag.; as well as over 60 unpublished poems and commentaries; [pers.] God gives talent, and talent should be used positively and in bringing out the beauty in the simple things of life.; [a.] Benin City, Nigeria

KIRK, HEATH
[b.] 17 August 1976, Doncaster; [p.] John D. Kirk, Christine E. Kirk; [ed.] Read School, Drax, Thorne Grammar School, Manchester Met. University (English); [occ.] Student; [memb.] Contemporary Rock Band - "Persuasion"; [a.] Thorne Doncaster, South Yorkshire

KISLINGBURY
[pen.] Tressie; [b.] 19 May 1919, Colnbrook; [m.] Arthur, 25 January 1942; [ch.] Christopher, Adrian; [occ.] Housewife

KIZRAK, FILIZ
[b.] 29 December 1978, London; [p.] Mr. B Kizrak and Mrs. N Kizrak; [ed.] Elizabeth Garrett Anderson Secondary School and currently at Enfield College, studying Business and finance; [occ.] Student; [oth. writ.] I have written a lot of personnel poems for my own use, in order to keep special events in my life memorable.; [pers.] Writing poems releases my inner feelings about life and it's obstacles, including the very deep feeling of love.; [a.] Woodgreen, London

KNIBBS-HUGHES, VERONICA
[b.] 3 December 1952, Jamaica; [p.] Zechariah Haynes and Myrtle Haynes; [m.] David Hughes, 20 August 1983; [ch.] Alexander, Joel and Dionne; [ed.] Dick Sheppard School (Comprehensive) University College Hospital; [occ.] Assistant Residential Manager (Croydon Social Services); [oth. writ.] I have used my poetry in my job work, as a medium to communicate to others. (See example) please return S.A.E. enclosed.; [pers.] My desire to write poems comes from, strong feeling, such as, love, anger, pain frustration, self pity, happiness, observations etc. But when I start writing my ideas/vision often changes.; [a.] Croydon, Surrey

KNOWLES, VICTORIA
[b.] 1 October 1975, Norwich; [p.] Marianne and David Knowles; [ed.] Hellesdon High School Norwich City College - A levels University of East Anglia; [occ.] Student of Law; [memb.] Amnesty International University Law Society; [hon.] Norfolk County Scholar Award for a levels; [oth. writ.] This is the first piece sent off.; [pers.] I believe through the power of the pen, no man can truly ignore his own feelings, his owns dreams, and his own fears.; [a.] Norwich, Norfolk

KOLODZIEJSKA, IWA
[b.] 22 April 1981, London; [p.] Magda Kolodziejska, Marian Kolodziejska; [ed.] Francis Holland School, (Graham Terrace); [occ.] Student; [hon.] Poet Lureate, ('95-'96) (of school); [oth. writ.] Other poems - unpublished; [pers.] I use my poetry to express what I am feeling, about the people around me and life in general poetry acts as a person who listens to the good and bad which is released into the open.; [a.] London

KRAJINA, SARA
[b.] 4 January 1973, Sarajevo; [p.] Smiljka and Mijo Krajina; [ed.] BA/BSC English and Media Studies (combined Degree), University of North London, 1 year acting Course Diploma - Mountview Theatre School, High School Diploma - Sarajevo (Equ. to a-level); [occ.] Student I'm doing the final year of my degree course; [memb.] Women's basketball team at my University, Various fitness Clubs in London, Flamenco Dancing at "Dance works Studios" in London; [hon.] See "Education" above; [oth. writ.] I've only recently started to write and this was my very first attempt to be noticed. However, I'm beginning to think more seriously about writing poetry as well as short stories and perhaps even a novel one day. English is my second language, so using english words to express myself is quite a challenge, but its the one that I'm only too happy to accept.; [pers.] Although coming from a country that's been turn apart by the war, I still believe in love and its powers to heal the wounds and make this world a better place for all of us. My inspiration comes from life itself and its my search is for beauty in all things of life. I'm forever intrigued by what the future holds, I'm trying to learn from the past, but I'm lost comfortable at the present times.; [a.] London

KYRIACOU, MRS. KATHLEEN
[b.] Swansea; [ch.] Twin daughters - Anna and Mary; [ed.] School Teacher after being Educated at Glanmor Grammar School for Girls and Swansea Teacher's College; [oth. writ.] An article for a local magazine; [pers.] I do my best to try to make sad people happy by listening to their troubles and by giving them words of comfort.; [a.] Finsbury Park, London

LACEY, SUSAN PATRICIA
[pen.] Georgia Austin; [b.] 1 February 1968, Bridport; [p.] Maurice Lacey, Patricia Lacey; [ed.] Woodroffe School, Lyme Regis, Weymouth College; [occ.] Bakery Assistant; [memb.] BHRA, British House Rabbits Association; [pers.] My writing reflects my own experiences and the inspiration of those around me.; [a.] Bridport, Dorset

LACK, ERNEST N. H.
[pen.] Ayli; [b.] 17 August 1923, Prome; [p.] Col. and Mrs. L. A. H. Lack, I.M.S.; [m.] Elizabeth Lack, 13 January 1953; [ch.] Three; [ed.] Daniel Stewart's College, Edinburgh, Edinburgh University; [occ.] Retired; [oth. writ.] The Lack Saga (a private publication); [pers.] Let yourself not be swayed into criticising other countries, other cultures until and unless you have lived abroad long enough to be able to take a long critical look at your own country, culture.; [a.] Hannover, Lindemannallee 15, Germany

LACOUCHIE, ALAIN
[b.] 28 May 1946, Liroges, France; [ch.] Aurelie Lacouchie; [ed.] LMCEE gay Lussac (Lioroges), Liroes University of Arts; [occ.] Teacher; [memb.] Contribution to several and magazines (manly poetry) such as friches, Traces, Nowelle Tour De Feu, Le Cri D'os, Retro-Viseur etc. Several drawings published in these review exhibition of photograph and paintings in France. Actor and producer of - theatre group for more than 10 years.; [oth. writ.] Several books the two last ones are: "Les Rapaces" Birds of Prey) with a special drawing by Noel Myles (Bradford Challenge winner London 1987 and "Les Autoura" Huis Clos" (My every days in camera) To be published "Rimageset Magie" and "Entrowert - Enttrevu (with black and white photos and poems; [pers.] Life and death this grief of living like desire and this everlasting question of death. Is every glitter if desire what we call happiness! And then?; [a.] Liroges, France

LAMB, LILIAN MAY
[b.] 12 February 1909, Liverpool; [p.] Alice Argyle and William Argyle; [m.] George Edward Lamb, 8 April 1933; [ch.] Veronica Jane; [ed.] Several Junior and Secondary School Leaving at Age 14; [oth. writ.] Poems published in local church magazines; [pers.] I started writing poetry in my seventies as I became increasingly housebound. I firmly believe it was a gift from God to help fill the hours. For my philosophy in life, I quote from a poem: "I am aware of God's son who gave his life to save me and claimed my love, life and service for all eternity."; [a.] Wolverhampton, West Midlands

LAMING, CYRIL
[ed.] Purley Grammar School, Cambridge Univ.; [occ.] University Teacher; [memb.] Royal Society of Arts (Fellow), Institution of Mechanical Engineers (Fellow); [hon.] Hobbes Prize, 1991 (Royal Aeronautical Soc.); [oth. writ.] Mainly technical - but unpublished poetry of course; [pers.] I distrust professional poets, and believe that poetry's true head of steam arises from the prosaic lives we all lead. Through poetry, we each seek our own hidden agenda.; [a.] Highgate, London

LANE, MISS GEMMA LOUISE
[b.] 23 March 1984, Ascot; [p.] Graham Lane, Susan Lane; [ed.] Frogmore Community School; [occ.] School Student; [a.] Camberley, Surrey

LANE, RACHEL
[b.] 15 September 1976, Lydney; [p.] Derek Lane, Kathleen Lane; [ed.] Severn Banks County Primary School, Lydney, Whitecross School, Lydney.; [occ.] Book Keeper, St. Michael's Square, Gloucester.; [oth. writ.] The heart of the hunter, published in world of words, by anchor books.; [pers.] Go beyond what you see, write the very atmosphere itself. Then blend it together.; [a.] Lydney, Gloucester

LANGHORN-HOOLIHAN, CAROLE
[pen.] Carole Langhorn-Hoolihan; [b.] 7 August 1953, Stockton ; [p.] Norma and Ken Langhorn; [m.] John P. Hoolihan Jr., 2 September 1990; [occ.] Television Production Assistant/Radio News Presenter; [oth. writ.] Freelance writer for national newspaper in V.A.E. writing weekly article on computers, other poems - some written when I was 14 yrs. old in a school exercise book and lost in London in the 70's!;

[pers.] As spiritual awareness increases I hope that individuals apply their personal beliefs and principles to their areas of business so that we can see a significant move to what author, James Redfield describes as an enlightened capitalism, following a new business ethic of lowering prices as a conscious statement of where we want the economy to go.; [a.] Nr Faringdon, Oxfordshire

LANGRIDGE, CAROLYN
[b.] 23 September 1972, Rinteln, Germany; [p.] Caroline and Michael Langridge; [ch.] Amie Langridge; [occ.] House Mom; [hon.] This is a personal goal, I wanted to achieve, getting one of my poems published, and hopefully the first of many.; [oth. writ.] This poem is dedicated to my Nan who passed away - Ellen Langridge, and I wrote it for her husband, my Granddad, John Langridge.; [pers.] I write I feel in my heart, I find emotions are a great influence to write about.; [a.] Southend, Essex

LANGSTAFF, CHERIE LISA
[b.] 10 November 1960, Nuneaton; [p.] Reg and Doreen Rowley; [m.] Christopher Paul Langstaff, 10 November 1982; [ed.] Hartshill High School; [occ.] Housewife; [oth. writ.] Have written many poems and stories since I was 11 yrs old; [pers.] I strive to bring happiness to the world with my poems and have been greatly influenced by the works of Helen Stenier Rice.; [a.] Coventry, West Midlands

LANSFIELD, DONNA
[b.] 3 April 1959, England; [m.] Stephen Lansfield, 18 October 1980; [ch.] Stacey Dean Terrieanne; [ed.] State School Tottenham County; [occ.] Housewife; [hon.] I have been published before and I won a certificate of merit for my work.; [oth. writ.] Finding Me - was my first ever entry and was published last year; [pers.] I have always loved and written poetry, but I had never entered anything until last year. I was given a certificate of merit and my first publication. It was such a proud day for me.; [a.] Hatfield, Herts

LAURIE, STEVEN
[pen.] S.W.L.; [b.] 7 January 1977, Glasgow; [p.] John, Micheline Laurie; [ed.] St. Ninians High School; [oth. writ.] Nothing published; [pers.] Politeness helps but patience is necessary.; [a.] Glasgow

LAWSON, AGNES
[pen.] Agnes Burns Lawson; [b.] 29/12/1919, Fife, Scotland; [p.] James and Margaret Lawson; [m.] Desmond E. Weeks, 22/02/1946; [ch.] 1 son, 2 daughters; [ed.] Secondary; [occ.] Housewife; [oth. writ.] 5 manuscripts: "Theoretic Theology", "Lyrics", "Romance - Children's Stories", "100 Progressive Spiritual Readings", "Epic Poetical Mythology"; had greeting card poems published by Wilson Firm; [pers.] My flesh is but a shaded bower, my spirit free my shining hour.; [a.] Hillingdon Heath, Middlesex

LAWSON, MR. PETER L.
[pen.] Peter Lawson; [b.] 23 January 1935, Bradford; [p.] James Leonard, Vera Patrica; [m.] Violet Mary Tudge, 24 February 1962; [ch.] Peter Andrew, Fiona Ann; [ed.] Woodend And Bingley The Collage; [occ.] Retired; [memb.] National Trust; [pers.] If my writing gives pleasure to others then I am amply rewarded.; [a.] Bonton-le-Lands, Lancashire

LEATHER, MARGARET MARY
[b.] 30 July 1939, St. Helens, Lancs; [p.] Joseph and Monica Twist; [m.] Joseph Thomas Edward (Ted) Leather, 21 July 1962; [ch.] Mark, Jacqui, Chris, Nicola, Kady; [ed.] Notre Dame High School, St. Helens, Lancs., Mount Pleasant Teacher Training College, Liverpool; [occ.] Retired Teacher; [memb.] Cottage Garden Society, Leather Family History Society, R.S.P.B.; [oth. writ.] Six other published poems in general anthologies. First poem published 1994.; [a.] Warrington, Cheshire

LEDGER, WILLIAM A.
[b.] 9 September 1917, Brinsley; [p.] The Late Adelaide and William Ledger; [m.] The Late Elizabeth Ann Ledger (Nee Vallance), 13 September 1941; [ch.] Ann and Denis; [ed.] Brinsley Infants, Brinsley Church of England Elementary; [occ.] Retired miner;

[oth. writ.] "The Brinsley that I love" my only poem, has been hung in the council chamber at Brinsley.

LEE, LISANNE
[b.] 27 October 1982, Glasgow, Scotland; [p.] Yuk Lan Lee, Shui Lun Lee; [ed.] King's Meadow, Bicester Community College; [pers.] Thank-you, Miss. Philips for encouraging me and giving me the wonderful chance to write a poem like this.; [a.] Bicester, Oxfordshire

LEE, REBECCA
[pen.] Rebecca Lee; [b.] 23 June 1982, Portsmouth Hants, England; [p.] Rosemary and Mark Lee; [ed.] Up to the age of 8 I went to a private village school, from the age of 8 up until now I go to Wykeham House School in Fareham, at the age of 16 I hope to go to a dancing college or stage college; [occ.] At School; [memb.] I am a member of 'Southampton Arts' dance school, the netball and rounders team at Wykeham House and I am also a member of many animal charities such as 'Respect for Animals'; [hon.] Over the past years I have achieved many awards, i.e., for dancing Ballet, Tap, Modern, Greek, National, Character and song and dance. Singing folk songs and songs from films and musicals. Drama for producing my own duologue with the help of my best friend Sarah; [oth. writ.] I have also written the poems, 'Love is...,' 'Looking out of my Window' and 'They don't Understand.' I also wrote a duologue called 'The Runaway Orphans' for the Fareham Drama Festival, with my friend Sarah Lambert-Humble from School.; [pers.] 'The Bull Fight' expresses my views and opinions an animal cruelty such as Bull fighting. I am very against all forms of animal cruelty and try hard to fight for animals' rights. I wish people would be less selfish about allowing animals to suffer for their own enjoyment and vanity.; [a.] Fareham, Hampshire

LEE, ROSALIND
[pen.] Rosalind Lee; [b.] 24 January 1953, Cardiff; [m.] Gerald Lee, 19 February 1977; [occ.] Secretary; [pers.] To write poetry, is a wonderful way to express your innermost thoughts and imagination.; [a.] Malpas, Newport

LEEDER, WILLIAM J.
[pen.] Old Bill "AG"; [b.] 3 January 1926, Tottington; [p.] George and Alice; [m.] Cynthia (Deceased), 26 February 1944; [ch.] Norman (52), Christopher; [ed.] Sec. and Modern, Watton, Norfolk; [occ.] O.A.P. disabled; [memb.] Swaffham Ex-servicemens club; [oth. writ.] The New Man, My Mirror Quiet Moments, The Old Man, published by the International Library of Poetry; [pers.] The poems are memories of some of the missions is flew on as an 18 year old rear gunner on a Lancaster Bomber in World War II. Lest we forget we who flew can't.; [a.] Swaffan, Norfolk

LEHTORANTA, TIINA
[b.] 4 June 1965, Kuopio, Finland; [ed.] M.A. (English), The University of Helsinki 1996; [occ.] English Teacher (TEFL); [hon.] 1995 Honeywell Futurist Competition Finalist; [oth. writ.] Poems for anthologies by arrival press and poetry now magazine.; [a.] Helsinki, Finland

LEIGH, TARAH
[pen.] Tarah Melmoth; [b.] 30 August 1974, Tiverton; [p.] Janice Meltmoth; [m.] David Leigh, 21 September 1996; [ch.] Lewis; [ed.] Tiverton Comprehensive; [occ.] Fulltime mother; [oth. writ.] Published in the other side of the mirror; [pers.] I always write about feelings with emotion and peace as a main element.; [a.] Tiverton, Devon

LEIGHTON, AMANDA
[b.] 14 March 1961, Leominster, Herefordshire; [ed.] BA (Hons) Philosophy and Psychology, Warwick University; [occ.] Ex Local Government Officer; [oth. writ.] 'In House' guides, booklets and promotional material on local government, a writer of poetry since childhood.; [pers.] The search for truth and wisdom compels me. My fascination with the mysteries of life and universe has led me along many paths through philosophy and various religions. I aim to set people thinking.; [a.] Leominster, Herefordshire

LEONARD, MARK
[b.] 12 February 1974, Bristol; [p.] Terry and Marlene Leonard; [ed.] Merrywood Comprehensive School; [occ.] Warehouse Operative; [oth. writ.] Unfortunately I have had no other work published as of yet. I have wrote several songs, and hope to make a career of this.; [pers.] Poetry reflects the greatfulness of life. As long as there's life there will always be great poetry.; [a.] Bristol, Avon

LETCH, PETER
[b.] 17 October 1979, Rochford, Essex; [p.] Jill Letch and Fred Letch; [ed.] Brampton Manor School; [pers.] I have been influenced by various poetry written by Marc Bolan from his book "Warlock of Love". Also lyrics from Jim Morrison and John Lennon.; [a.] East Ham, London

LEUNG, ROD
[b.] 22 October 1976, Enfield; [p.] Steve Leung, Mazy Leung; [ed.] St. Francis De Sales - Tottenham, St. Ignatius College - Enfield, Portsmouth University; [occ.] Biology student; [pers.] My poems come straight from the heart, what I see, what I feel, what I believe, what I am.; [a.] Tottenham, London

LEVICK, ADAM
[b.] 2 November 1977, Tamworth; [p.] Elaine Levick; [ed.] Queen Elizabeths Mercian School Tamworth; [occ.] Photography student hoping to go to University September '97; [pers.] Dedicated to my good friend Caesar Lengua, thank you.; [a.] Tamworth, Staffs

LEWIS, DAVID JOHN
[pen.] Dave; [b.] 15 September 1951, Hornsey, North London; [p.] Sylvia and Brinley Lewis; [ed.] Priory Vale Sec. Mod Crouch End London N. 8; [occ.] Unemployed; [oth. writ.] I have written a few poems based on my personal life and people in it.; [pers.] Life is not a rehearsal take every opportunity as I do now to thank family and friends for their inspiration and encouragement. Remember words from the heart are words of truth.; [a.] Iver Heath, South Bucks

LIDDELL, THOMAS A.
[b.] 23 November 1933, York; [p.] Thomas and Eileen Liddell; [m.] Divorced; [ed.] Nunthorpe Grammar School York; [occ.] Retired instrument maker; [memb.] Ex member of York Chess Club, Ex member of York Railway Institute Boxing Section, Ex member Prescot and Knotty Ash Chess Club Liverpool; [hon.] Two Awards won at Chess 1973 Kirkby open York Schools Boxing Champion at my weight member of York Youth Boxing Team 1950; [oth. writ.] Won editor's choice award for poem published in "The Other Side Of The Mirror" and entitled "The Steam Express 1946; [pers.] Played jail (traditional) solo piano for 14 years every saturday night in the same public house never missed one night. A record that will take some beating, poem about this later.; [a.] York, Yorkshire

LIGHTFOOT, MARGARET
[b.] 19 December 1948, Westminster; [p.] George Lightfoot and Florence Lightfoot; [ed.] Mary Boon Secondary Modern for Girls; [oth. writ.] Three poems in three anthologies; [pers.] I strive to give pleasure to others in my writing.; [a.] London

LINDROTH, KATARINA
[b.] 25 August 1978, Sweden; [p.] Rosalino Lindroth, Mats Lindroth; [m.] Sophie Lindroth; [ed.] Christ's Hospital Boarding School, Horsham, West Sussex; [occ.] Student of English (Lang. and Lit.), French and Russian A-levels; [memb.] 2 Choirs and 2 Orchestras at school, RAF section of combined cadets force, Dramatic Society (Shakespeare) and Dance; [pers.] My philosophy - there are no limits to your dreams but there is every reason to try and fulfill them.; [a.] Reading, Berkshire

LINDSAY, ROBERT JAMES
[b.] 10 May 1944, Belfast; [p.] James William and Lillian Lindsay; [m.] Thelma (Edwards), 01/04/67; [ch.] James Israel, Joel, Selina; [a.] "Lacken" Carryduff, Co. Down, N.I.

LINNETTE, CARLA MARIE
[b.] 25 September 1974, Liverpool; [p.] Maureen McHarron; [ed.] Notre Dame High School; [occ.] Civil Servant; [pers.] Cats open their eyes when darkness falls and through that darkness nothing is hidden from their sight, in fact its when darkness covers the land that their sight becomes so acute.; [a.] Liverpool, Lancs

LINNEY, MISS BARBARA ANN
[pen.] Barbara Ann Linney; [b.] 29 August 1939, Rfd Hill, Surrey; [p.] Deceased; [ch.] Susa, Angela, David; [ed.] GSCE; [occ.] Unemployed; [memb.] Library; [oth. writ.] Biography sent to International Library of Poetry; [pers.] What you can't do today their's always another day.; [a.] Kidderminster, Worcs

LLEWELLYN, ADELA
[pen.] Adela Llewellyn; [b.] 2 March 1924; [p.] William George and Edith Gladys Waterman; [m.] Leslie Vivian Llewellyn, 16 August 1952; [ch.] Ann, Gwyn, Mark, Gareth, Glenys; [oth. writ.] Since Feb. of past year I have had fourteen other poems published in books and have written others I intend to send.; [pers.] I love the story's of Thomas Hardy also William Barns writings as for poetry it has to be patience strong for her gentleness and Pam Ayres for her sense of fun.; [a.] Poole, Dorset

LLOYD, JACQUELINE CHERYL
[pen.] Jacqueline Cheryl Lloyd; [b.] 9 February 1977; [p.] Heather, Michael Leech; [m.] Christopher Lloyd, 20 April 1996; [ch.] Jonathan, Neal, Lloyd; [ed.] Ammanford Comprehensive School Amman Valley Comprehensive; [occ.] Housewife, mother to loving son Jonathan born 26-9-96; [hon.] 6 GCSES, NVQ in caring certificates on Health Care; [oth. writ.] As yet none of my others have been published.; [pers.] I share an insight, that through my blindness I did not see, true happiness, in todays world, does come free, it is as rare and precious as the morning breeze the love that surrounds me through my family.; [a.] Llanelli, Carmarthenshire

LLOYD, JUSTIN
[pen.] J. D. Ratt; [b.] 23 February 1971, Ilford; [p.] Gloria and Trevor Lloyd; [m.] To be! Angie Donnely, soon; [ch.] Jade Zara Zinia Lloyd; [ed.] Park School, Rayliegh Palmers Sixth Form, Grays; [occ.] I prayer, studies at moment with cartoon and Illustration; [oth. writ.] None as yet, this is my first.; [pers.] This poem was written about the meeting of two kindred spirits, Angie and myself. I was a singer in a band: Maelstrom, the pub was "The Worlds End" Tilbury, my life was changed by her beauty.; [a.] Dagenham, Essex

LOCK, MAXINE
[b.] 12 March 1963, Somerset; [p.] Terence Knowles, Shirley Knowles; [m.] Martin Lock, 5 February 1996; [ch.] Jay Nicholas, Romy Annalise; [ed.] Huish Episcopi Comprehensive, Langport, Somerset; [occ.] Housewife/Mother; [oth. writ.] Poem published - Southwest poets - 1994; [pers.] For me poetry represents the flight of the spoken word. Within it I share the empathy I feel for all human emotions.; [a.] Taunton, Somerset

LOCKWOOD, POET
[b.] 22/12/38, Portsmouth; [p.] Elderly but ill, working class; [m.] divorced at 52 years; [ch.] Grown son and daughter, now with children; [ed.] Ordinary, developing a natural talent at 30 yrs for house, interior, and garden design; [occ.] disabled with arthritis at 50 yrs, ex-psychiatric nurse; [hon.] 'Nil, but huge spread in the Portsmouth Evening News, (Sheila's Eye For Design) with photos of property and garden; [oth. writ.] My first, but the odd ones stuck in a drawer over the years.; [pers.] Previous hobbies, house renovations and interior design, six in total. Present property completed in August 1996. I am now contemplating writing a book.; [a.] Waterlooville, Hants

LOCKWOOD, ROY
[b.] 6 July 1951; [pers.] I wrote this poem after my wife passed away, to try and bring comfort to my children, friends, and relatives. It was my daughters wish that I submit it for publishing in the hope that it might help others in similar situations.

LOGUE, JOSEPHINE ANN
[b.] 13 May 1962, Jersey; [p.] Francis and Margaret Gautier; [m.] Robert Logue, 25 February 1994; [ch.] James Logue; [ed.] Jersey College for girls; [occ.] Senior Trust and Company Administrator; [a.] Saint Saviour, Jersey

LOMAS, AMANDA
[pen.] Amanda Lomas; [b.] 22 September 1968, Barking; [p.] Pauline Lomas and Andrew Lomas; [m.] Partner - Stuart Kay; [ed.] Chelmsford County High for Girls, Leeds Polytechnic; [occ.] Contract Accountant, Bradford Hospitals NHS Trust; [memb.] 1) Health care Financial Management Association, 2) Chartered Institute of Public Finance and Accountancy; [hon.] Several Sporting Achievements in Swimmer, Net ball, Hockey and Skiing; [pers.] "Remember that great love and great achievements involve great risk", "When opportunity knocks - invite it to stay to dinner".; [a.] Calverley, W. Yorks, Leeds

LONG, LYNDA
[b.] 15 February 1949, Lincolnshire; [p.] William and Edith Prew; [m.] Peter, 3 September 1966; [ch.] Amanda Kevin Janette; [occ.] Housewife; [oth. writ.] Several poems published in magazines and newsletters.; [pers.] I find writing poetry to be a very satisfying and enjoyable way of expressing inner thoughts and emotions. I am greatly encouraged by my family.; [a.] Evesham, Worcestershire

LONGDEN, GRAHAM
[b.] 8 May 1937, Bournheath; [p.] James Longden, Minnie Longden; [m.] Doreen Longden, 14 September 1957; [ch.] Mark, Paul, James; [memb.] Woodland Trust; [a.] Bromsgrove, Worcs

LONGUEIRA, YVONNE M.
[pen.] Brat, Y.M.L., Squirt, Babushca; [b.] 20 September 1976, Mary Mount; [p.] Mr. and Mrs. A. C. Longueira; [ed.] Matriculation from the National School of the Arts, currently at S.A. Home College in Johannesberg; [occ.] Artist/Photographer/Waitress; [oth. writ.] Poems and short stories published in Matric Year Book; [pers.] Life is what you make it. People think they are sane but only you yourself are sane and everyone else is insane.; [a.] Alberton, South Africa

LOVE, TERENCE
[b.] 24 February 1954, Norwich; [p.] May and Walter Love; [m.] Diane Elizabeth; [ch.] Emily and Annastasia Love; [occ.] Tele Communications Consultant; [memb.] Committee Member of the St. Matthew Society; [oth. writ.] Many poems and a novel; [pers.] I write to examine and understand those thoughts, feelings, emotions and actions that make us human within the setting of the cosmos.; [a.] Norwich, Norfolk, NR35 2QW

LOWDER, MARGUERITE LONGSTAFF
[b.] 11 January 1941, Sunderland; [p.] Ivy and Henry Longstaff; [m.] Walter, 15 August 1959; [ch.] Paul, Nigel, Mark; [ed.] Chester Road Secondary Modern School, Sunderland, Co. Durham; [occ.] Housewife and Mother; [memb.] Member of The Church of England; [hon.] Swimming achieved Smile badge age 31 yrs.; [pers.] My poetry verse is about life and nature.

LOWE, ANDREW
[b.] 21 June 1978, Geneva; [ed.] International School of Geneva - La Chataigneraie; [occ.] Media Student at Kingston College; [memb.] Kingston Hospital Radio; [pers.] The power of writing is unlimited, whether it is used for the benefit of good or evil though it is Nowadays sometimes hard to make the difference.; [a.] Surbiton, Surrey

LOWES, VICTORIA
[b.] 15 March 1982, Durham; [p.] Terrene and Dorothy Lowes; [ed.] Mill Hill County Primary School, Allertonshire Secondary School and Northallerton College work in partnership with each other.; [occ.] Still at school - Northallerton College; [memb.] Phoenix Club - Work along with deaf children and Beverley School, Middlebrough; [oth. writ.] Several articles published in church magazines, several poems printed in other anthologies (poetry now); [pers.] Due to my young age, I aim high so that people will take me seriously.; [a.] Northall Erton, North Yorkshire

LUCAS, JUNE
[b.] 22 June 1932, Colnbrook; [m.] Frank, 28 August 1954; [ch.] Kevin and Jocelyn and 6 grandchildren; [ed.] Church of England School; [occ.] Supermarket Cashier; [memb.] Bowls, 30 years a brown owl; [hon.] 30 year award for brownies top of the Windsor and Maidenhead League for Bowls; [oth. writ.] Writes children's short stories; [pers.] Like to write plays for my Brownie Pack; [a.] Horton, Berkshire

LUCAS, PAUL
[occ.] Retired; [memb.] Member of the Livery; [hon.] Design Management Award, Royal Society of Arts; [oth. writ.] 'The Other Side Of The Mirror', 'Between A Laugh And A Tear.'

LUCAS-FOSTER, ROSEMARIA
[b.] 11 September 1954, Budapest; [p.] Louis-Lajos Lukacs, Rozalia Katai; [m.] Divorced; [ch.] Laura Victoria Stephens Gately; [ed.] Abroad, Lambert College; [occ.] Mother and student; [pers.] Forever is Eternity but Eternity is only the passing of Time, Time however is the Father of everything we hold Divine...; [a.] Tulse Hill, London

LUFFLUM, PAULA D. O.
[b.] 25 June 1982, Cannock, England; [p.] Mrs. C. D. Lufflum; [ed.] Kingsmead Comprehensive Hednesford; [occ.] School Girl; [memb.] School Amateur Dramatics WWF, Rainbow House (Children Mosace); [hon.] Not yet; [oth. writ.] Poems published in poetry now, Anchor Books; [pers.] After losing my dad, I started writing my thoughts down. This has been a great comfort to me.; [a.] Hednesford, Staffs

LUKIC, MILENA
[b.] 9 April 1982, Zadar, Yugoslavia; [p.] Radmila Lukic, (Step dad) George Arkinic; [ed.] Weston Favell Upper School; [memb.] I play basketball for county (N'ptonshire), under 15 girls; [hon.] I've been in the paper because, 1) Our school won a trip to France by the 'Shuttle', 2) Went to Sainsbury's with headmaster to collect paintings, 3) Helping at an old age pentioners party, 4) same as 3 again the next year; [oth. writ.] When I was 11 yrs. old, I wrote a poem and it got put in the school library.; [a.] Northampton, Northamptonshire

LUNOE, SANDY
[pen.] Sandy; [b.] 12 July 1938, England; [m.] Bjorn Lunoe, 28 July 1959; [ch.] Three; [ed.] Heriot Watt University, Edinburgh; [occ.] Pharmacist and Dreamer University Lecturer; [memb.] Pharm. Soc: (Gt. Britain and Norway) Limerick Club, Norway (Committee Member) (Honorary), Amnesty International; [hon.] Pharmacy (Univ) (UK and Norway) London Academy of Music and Dramatic Arts (Lamda) Silver Medal Honorary member of Limerick Club, Norway, and have won many poetry competitions in Norway; [oth. writ.] Many poems published in Norwegian Books, magazines, and newspapers; [pers.] Cleverness means nothing, kindness means all!; [a.] Sandvik, Norway

LYNCH SR., MERCEDES
[pen.] Arma; [b.] 4 May 1926, Ballyjamesduff; [p.] James Lynch, Julia Lynch; [occ.] Retired Religious; [memb.] Loreto order; [a.] Ballyjamesduff, Co. Cavan, Letterkenny

LYONS, SHONA
[b.] 30 October 1981, Wexford, Ireland; [p.] Phil and Ann Lyons; [ed.] currently attending second level education; [occ.] student; [hon.] Guildhall School of Music and Drama (Grade Prelim—grade 6 incl.), Part in BBC's production of "Life in Early Times"; [oth. writ.] currently writing an autobiography; [pers.] Writing is a passion which comes from within.; [a.] Wexford, Ireland

MACDONALD, GAIL E.
[b.] 30 March 1977, Wick; [p.] Mr. and Mrs. R. G. MacDonald; [ed.] Wick High School 1989-1995, currently at Central College of Commerce, Glasgow; [occ.] Student; [oth. writ.] Various works published by International Society of Poets, the Poetry Guild and Poetry Now. Also local publications Inc. - tribute to Tomscott, Scotia Review and Wickwards.; [pers.] Most of my writing comes from personal experience

or what I happen to be feeling at the time.; [a.] Wick, Caithness

MACDONALD, MARK
[b.] 29 October 1971, Bramley, Leeds; [p.] Nadine Raper, Iain MacDonald; [ed.] John Smeaton Community High School; [occ.] Sales Assistant Tesco Crossgates; [oth. writ.] This is the first time I have sent in a poem but have been writing for about fifteen or 50 years. I've been writing more for fun that anything else.; [pers.] To quote aerosmith "Life is a journey, not a destination." I feel, experience what you can as to inspire you as a person to develop into the best you can be; [a.] Leeds, Yorkshire

MACDONALD, NORMAN
[pen.] Norman MacDonald; [b.] 6 August 1934, Isle of Skye; [p.] Andrew and Kate MacDonald (Both Deceased); [ed.] Received elementary education at two schools in the Isle of Skye, leaving at 16 years; [occ.] Retired Police Constable Cheshire Constabulary and Greater Manchester Police; [memb.] From 1963 to 1973 was exhibiting Member with the Grosvenor Art Society of Chester; [oth. writ.] Art reviews published in County newspapers. Have submitted project items on strategic Planning and 'Vision For Year 2010', relative to regeneration of Stockport; [pers.] Having completed over 34 years police service, I feel my observations on people and their diverse lifestyles has been greatly enhanced towards expressing myself as a visual artist and exponent of the written word.; [a.] Stockport, Cheshire

MACFARLANE, AUDREY DELA
[pen.] Dela MacFarlane; [b.] 27 September 1923, Liphook, Hampshire; [p.] Edwin Warrington, Emily Warrington (Nee Prior); [m.] Robert MacFarlane - divorced after 38 years, 1941, 2nd John Brierly - divorced, 1985; [ch.] 2; [ed.] Started at school overlooked by Cathedral Endly accomprehensive as it would be called now.; [occ.] No work as such retired but have plenty to do - belong to; [memb.] Chichester Film and Video Makers; [hon.] Silver Awards for Films and 2 Cups Associated with the club; [oth. writ.] Poem in another book, writing in local paper.; [pers.] From the age of seven brought up in Chichester cemetery lodge - playground among the headstones. The lodge built 1858 had no frills, I like writing poetry from the soul. Born Librarian creative and artistic creature, and a thinker. Love all things beautiful.; [a.] Chichester, West Sussex

MACLEOD, CHRISTINE
[b.] 5 March 1939, Stornoway; [p.] Malcolm MacArthur, Mary MacArthur; [m.] John MacLeod, 16 April 1963; [ch.] Mary, Rachel, Patricia, Malcolm, Norman and Esther; [ed.] The Nicolson Institute, Stornoway, The Glasgow School, of Speech Therapy; [occ.] Speech and Language Therapist; [memb.] Church Member; [oth. writ.] Poems published in local and Scottish Magazines; [pers.] I endeavour to highlight the spiritual aspect of life in my writing. I have taken interest in 18th and 19th century writers, and have musical interest.; [a.] Stornoway, Isle of Lewis

MAGALLONA, JENNIFER
[b.] 14 March 1981, Newham; [ed.] Currently undergoing the second year of my G.C.S.E.'s at Cannon Palmer Catholic School, Seven Kings (15 years old); [occ.] Student; [memb.] Rollerbrowl Romford Y.B.C. (Youth Bowling Club); [pers.] I'd like to thank my father (R.B. Magallona) and my brother Vincent for always encouraging my creative talents. I love you both. "Knowledge is power!"; [a.] Ilford, Essex

MAGER, LESLEY
[pen.] Lesley Mager; [b.] 2 June 1955, Raf Vegburg, Germany; [p.] Ron and Audrey Dunn; [m.] Harry Mager, 11 September 1976; [ch.] Deborah, Stuart, Anthony Mager; [ed.] R.A.F. Schools Hong Kong Derwent Lower School RAF Henlow, Etonbury Secondary, Arlesey Beds; [occ.] Axillary Nurse, Herts Cheshire Home; [memb.] WolfWatch R.S.P.B., owns Clifton Wildlife Rescue; [oth. writ.] Currently I am writing a poetry book. But I have never had anything published.; [pers.] Never loose hope, because eventually things do improve, and life does get better.; [a.] Shefford, Bedfordshire

MAHER, THOMAS
[pen.] Michael Thomas; [b.] 15/11/36, Knotty Ash, M-side; [p.] Catherine, Joseph Maher; [m.] Brenda Maher, 1 July 1958; [ch.] Three sons, five daughters; [ed.] St. Edwards School O.S.T., Broadgreen, Liverpool, 14 Merseyside; [occ.] Writer (part time), I am a disabled person; [memb.] (G.M.F.B.U.A.) P.P.F.; [oth. writ.] short stories, articles, some poems published; [pers.] My poetic efforts are in the main for my own reading, in them I have tried to express my own observations of life, as they appear to me to be.; [a.] Knowsley Village, Merseyside

MAINE, MS. PENNY
[b.] 25/05/52, London; [ed.] Local Primary & Comprehensive 1 'A' level, 5 'O' levels, 3 CSEs, D.H.P. Hypnotherapy; [occ.] Song writer and Author of Children's Spiritual Adventure books; [memb.] G.I.S.C. Member of the Guild of International Songwriters and Composers; [oth. writ.] 3 children's spiritual adventure books called Magic Room, Magic Lands and Magic Life with story tape and nine songs: 1. Do You Know You're Special, 2. It Is Time, 3. Land of Dreams, 4. True Love of Friendship, 5. Healing Hands, 6. Magic Lands, 7. Rainbow Bears, 8. Tick Tock, 9. Simon & Perry. As yet to be published, hopefully this year.; [pers.] I believe that every child is a gift from God and it is every adult's responsibility to: teach, nurture, love, and guide that child to adulthood, with the highest motivation for each child to reach their fullest potential for the cycle to continue.; [a.] Stevenage, Hertfordshire

MALL, SURJIT
[b.] 10 August 1969, Glasgow, Scotland; [m.] Uijay Komar Mall, 20 March 1993; [ch.] Shaun; [occ.] Practice Manager; [oth. writ.] Several poems that I have recently written which I have not yet forwarded for publication.; [pers.] I believe that good poetry starts from gut instinct before it is thought over in the mind.; [a.] Birmingham, West Midlands

MALLICK, DAVE
[b.] 22 May 1978, Wolverhampton; [p.] Susan, Prasun; [ed.] Codsall High School; [occ.] Student; [hon.] 'A' level music, 'A' level economics, 'A' level general studies; [oth. writ.] Musicals, songs, pieces for orchestras.; [pers.] My musical and lyrical inspiration is John Lennon, my songs and poetry attempt to reflect the feelings of my generation.; [a.] Wolverhampton, West Midlands

MARSH, DAVID
[b.] 27 March 1967, Bushey; [ch.] Kelly and Chloe; [ed.] Watford Boys Grammar School; [occ.] Pensions Administrator, Rank Xerox; [memb.] Watford Amateur Boxing Club; [oth. writ.] Watford Palace Theatre Young Play write Award; [pers.] True inspiration can come for but a moment - always seize the moment.; [a.] Bushey, Herts

MARSH, JANET ROSE
[b.] 5 February 1959, Poplar, London; [p.] Jessie and Herbert Marsh; [ed.] St. Pauls Way School E.3; [occ.] Receptionist, 'The Gentry' Canary Wharf; [oth. writ.] Poems published in Christian Anthologies; [pers.] This poem is written about 'Robert' the one I adore, and sadly he will never know 'He holds the key!'; [a.] Bow, London

MARSHALL, ANDREW
[pen.] Popeye; [b.] 2 May 1975, Giruan; [p.] Ian Marshall; [m.] Margaret Ross; [ed.] Secondary; [occ.] Unemployed; [oth. writ.] Junkies Paradise published; [pers.] I try to write about life today as I see it; [a.] Dalmellington, Ayrshire

MARSHALL, JEANETTE
[b.] 3 December 1979, West Yorkshire; [p.] Michael and Carol Marshall; [ed.] South Craven Secondary School and Training in Hotel and Catering Training Company; [occ.] Apprentice Chief; [hon.] Five G.C.S.E.'s and Two certificates in Catering at present; [oth. writ.] Various poems published in magazines. Also in local village newsletter.; [pers.] I am influenced by everyday life and write about my own experiences and visions.; [a.] Keighley, West Yorkshire

MARSHALL, MICHELLE
[pen.] Andrea Lane; [b.] 11 September 1977, Oxford; [a.] Kidlington, Oxfordshire

MARTIN, ADRIAN
[b.] 29 July 1959, Chesterfield; [p.] Barbara Rose Marie Martin, Roy Arthur Martin; [m.] Gabriella Martin, 27 December 1993; [ch.] Wayne, Rachel, Simon, Clair, Joseph, John, Robert; [ed.] Chapel-en-le-Frith School, High Peak College Buxton; [occ.] Security Officer; [memb.] British Red Cross; [oth. writ.] Unpublished, The Sorrow of Dunblane (Poem), The Lakes (Poem), Winter (Poem), Summertime (Poem), The Open Cast (Poem); [pers.] I started writing poems as the only way I could express my emotions, at nineteen years old, it started as a pastime to take my mind off things that were happening through my life. A means of escape.; [a.] Chesterfield, Derbyshire

MARTIN, BRENDAN
[pen.] Voisier, Spiv, Breno.; [b.] 21 July 1959, Mullingar, Ireland; [p.] Kevin and Maisie Martin; [m.] Monica Nee Foley, 14 November 1986; [ch.] Paul Aidan and Kim-Lisa; [ed.] Primary and C.B.S. Secondary Mullingar County Westmeath, Ireland; [occ.] Telecommunications Technician.; [memb.] Catholic Boy Scouts of Ireland, Extel Golf Society; [hon.] 10 year Service Award for Scouting.; [oth. writ.] Two volumes of my poems and songs called 'Smaointe' and 'Withered Words', neither of which have been published; [pers.] Dreams are not real, life is, and much stricter. Death is the conqueror, but Love is the Victor. Breno.; [a.] Clondalkin, Dublin, Ireland

MARTIN, CLAIRE LOUISE
[b.] 18 August 1976, Chelmsford; [p.] Susan and Christopher Martin; [ed.] St Benedict's (R.C.) College, Colchester Institute; [pers.] I wrote my poem "Time" in August of '96. When I was arrested. I have continued to write from the heart about my experiences here. My mother and father have inspired me to use my time here in a Moroccan prison to capture moments of particular emotion to share with others.; [a.] Colchester, Essex

MARTIN, ERNEST
[pen.] Ernie Martin; [b.] 1 January 1927, Middlesbrough; [m.] Violet Lily Douthwat, 11 August 1952; [ch.] Roy, Linda, Glen, David, Tracy; [ed.] Basic - from age 6 to 14 years, Programed to work in local steel Industries, (Main Education from Life); [occ.] Retired; [memb.] International Society of Poets; [hon.] 2 Special Commendation from Hilton House Poet of the Year, 1996, Editor's Choice award, International Society of Poets, 1996, (Medals - from War Time Service - Royal Navy); [oth. writ.] Poems and short stories in a local disabled mag. over a number of years. Two, 50,000 and word novels, unpublished, numerous poems published in anthologies; [pers.] Having spent, most of my working life. On overseas construction projects, in managements a lot of my poems, reflect and identify with their world people's quality of life, my humble childhood - of the means test era of the 1920-30's (Now back with a vengeance); [a.] Malton, N. Yorkshire

MARTIN, JOHN
[b.] 29 March 1923, Calcutta; [ed.] St. Xavier's College, Calcutta, Kettering Grammar School; [occ.] Retired Accountant; [memb.] Royak Air Force Association Stirling Aircraft Association. Probus, Parkinsons Disease Society. Age Concern, Pensioner's Parliament; [hon.] Medals for 1939/45 War Service on U.K. bomber airfields and air-strips in Burma and the Pacific Islands. Medals, certificates and cash prizes in poetry competitions including the International Society of Poets.; [oth. writ.] Short stories, contributions to and illustrations for books on Service life. Many poems published in various Anthologies and the press, magazine articles etc.; [pers.] Having served in the R.A.F. form 1942, to 1947, on a theme of "Lest we Forget", many of my writings are reminders of the suffering, sacrifice and heroism of the British during the war, all in vain, because the freedom that we fought for has gone down the Brussels drain. Consequently I am very anti EC. Greatly influenced by the poet John Clare.; [a.] Kettering, Northants

MARTIN, PEARL
[b.] 11 September 1967, Cork, Ireland; [p.] Eugene and Peggy Martin; [ed.] Scoil Mhuire, Templemore, Co. Tipperary, Ireland; [occ.] Bar Managers; [oth. writ.] Small collection of poetry and short stories, yet to be published.; [pers.] My inspiration comes from everyday happenings in my immediate surroundings. I have been greatly influenced by well known Irish poets W. B. Yeats and Patrick Kavanagh.; [a.] Templemore, Tipperary, Ireland

MASKILL, RITA
[b.] 27 August 1955, Chesterfield; [p.] Gertrude Jones, Clifford Jones; [m.] Peter Maskill, 28 May 1982; [ch.] Barry, Steven, Anthony, Allan, Wayne, Tammy; [ed.] Moorfield Comprehensive School, Bolsover, Chesterfield; [occ.] Housewife; [memb.] International Society of Poets; [hon.] Editors Choice Award; [oth. writ.] Several poems published in books.; [pers.] I dedicate this poem ("A Fishy Tale") to my daughter Tammy, who is the light of my life, and not just a dream.; [a.] Tredegar, Gwent, S. Wales

MASSIAH, LOUIS
[b.] 18/04/1940; [ch.] 4 children; [oth. writ.] I have written several poems and hope to publish a book one day.; [pers.] I get my inspiration to write from the ever changing happenings in the world today.; [a.] London

MATEER, MICHELLE
[b.] 20 October 1979, Kent; [p.] Marion Mateer; [ed.] Stanley Deason School Brighton College of Technology; [occ.] Student; [oth. writ.] Many as yet unpublished poems; [pers.] I find I get my inspiration from every day life and those around me. I only wish that I could write about happier things; [a.] Brighton, East Essex

MAUBEC, PATRICIA ANNE
[b.] 29 June 1942, Bombay, India; [p.] Lewis Twinn, Barbara Twinn; [m.] Serge Jean Maubec M.B.E., 2 April 1980 (2nd Marriage); [ch.] Sara Jane, David James (1st Marr.); [ed.] St. Joseph's Marist Convent, Barnstaple, Devon, Pitman's Secretarial College, Southampton Row, London; [hon.] English, Art, Music, Speech and Drama, Ballet; [a.] Forest, Guernsey, CI

MAVIN, MRS. MARGARET SHIELA
[pen.] Shiela Mavin; [b.] 20 June 1953, Edinburgh; [p.] Deceased; [m.] James, 3rd marriage, 1 October 1988; [ch.] Faith 25 years, Stewart 24 years; [ed.] General 'O' L 'M' Level Education, MND Business Student with French; [occ.] Correspondence Student; [memb.] Association of Accounting Technicians; [hon.] Have several awards in accountancy and secretarial and business and language studies; [oth. writ.] Used in local works but refused to enter any in National Awards until now.; [pers.] Keep on trying, do not base on anybody, everything I write is on experience, feelings and emotions. Went through deep depression and alcoholism.; [a.] Melrose, Roxburghshire

MCALPINE, ANDREW
[b.] 19 December 1956, Glasgow; [p.] William and Ileen McAlpine; [m.] Renee McAlpine, 9 April 1977; [ch.] Andrew, Karen, Kristy and Paul; [ed.] General Education N.C. Electronics; [occ.] Unemployed (currently Treasure of Autistic Holiday Home Trust); [memb.] National Autistic Society; [hon.] N.C. Scotvec Award in Electronics related studies.; [oth. writ.] This is my first poem; [pers.] I my trying to change the world's ignorance to handicaps in particular Autism, in my poems to show a positive side to it, this was what inspired me.; [a.] Glasgow, Strathclyde

MCBRIDE, JAN STANLEY
[pen.] Jan Stanley McBride; [b.] 17/04/42, Kilrush, Co. Clare, Eire; [p.] David and Mary Lowe; [m.] the late Philip Stanley, 13/07/63, and John McBride, 17/10/92; [ch.] Caroline, Philip - deceased, Sharon, Lee; [ed.] Convent School Kilrush, Co Clare Eire Intermediate, Cert and (Tec) School, Cert for Catering; [occ.] Housewife; [memb.] Letterkenny Writers Group, Co Donegal; [hon.] several poems printed in local papers

and magazines; [pers.] Born in Kilrush Co Clare a tailor's and dressmaker's daughter, one of 13 children, one deceased. Talk and write what is in my heart, not influenced by any poet; [a.] Carrigart, Co. Donegal, Eire

MCCABE, LEE
[b.] 1 October 1971, Cardiff; [p.] Christine Mitchell, Roger McCabe; [m.] Lisa McCabe, 20 July 1996; [ed.] Llanrumney High School, Llanrumney, Cardiff; [occ.] Electronic Engineer; [memb.] Greenpeace; [pers.] Nearly all my poems are about actual events that have happened in my life, and I take my inspiration from people close to me or the environment. My greatest influence has been James Douglas Morrison.; [a.] Cardiff, South Glamorgan

MCCALL, ALISON
[b.] 29 July 1975, Irvine, Ayrshire; [p.] Anne McCall, Gordon I. McCall; [ed.] Castle Douglas High School University of Glasgow; [occ.] Student; [a.] Castle Douglas, Dumfries, Galloway

MCCARROLL, NORMAN
[b.] 29 February 1928, Belfast; [p.] Capt. R McCarroll - Hettie McCarroll; [m.] Stephanie McGrattan, 28 August 1952; [ch.] Catherine, Wendy and David; [ed.] Bangor Central PE School, Co. Down Bangor Technical College Co. Down College of Marine Engineering Liverpool. College of Art, Dublin School of Philosophy and Natural Science Dublin; [occ.] Served 12 years in merchant navy Engineer Surveyor with Insurance Co. past; [memb.] Institute of Marine Engineers Engineering and Scientific Association of Ireland Royal Society of Antiquities of Ireland Shrewsbury Croquet Club; [hon.] Pursuer Cup for Lecture first class ministry of transport certificate (Steam); [oth. writ.] Several poems and articles published in company magazine and church magazine several lectures; [pers.] He was inspired by events happening in the world and was always searching for the inner meaning of life.; [a.] Shrewsbury, Shropshire

MCCLINTON, JANET LYNN
[pen.] Jaye; [b.] 9 November 1956, St. Helens; [p.] Joseph Wharton, Jean Wharton; [m.] Frederick William McClinton, 28 March 1987; [ch.] Heather Ruth McClinton, Martha Leanne McClinton, Esther Jay McClinton; [ed.] All Girls High School, Robins Lane, St. Helens; [occ.] Housewife/Cleaner for British Telecom; [memb.] Christian Fellowship Revival Centres International; [oth. writ.] Mainly poems for the fellowship in which I have been a part of for nearly fifteen years.; [pers.] I started to write poetry whilst expecting my first child Heather Ruth. I conveyed my joy in having Heather in that very first poem. I wrote many more of life, hard-ships and the beauty of the experience of life inspired by my own growth of it and by the poet patience strong.; [a.] Morecambe, Lancashire

MCCOY, JEAN
[pen.] Jean McCoy; [b.] 23 April 1942, Royton, England; [p.] Wilfred and Ivy Bartram; [m.] Bernard McCoy, 17 October 1987; [ch.] Step daughter - Allison Wilson; [ed.] St. Annes C. of E., Secondary Modern; [occ.] Medically Retired Social Worker; [memb.] Four Seasons, Exclusive Club, Portugal. Local Social and Sports Club; [hon.] Editors Choice Award for Outstanding Achievement in Poetry presented by the International Society of Poets; [oth. writ.] I have written short stories for children - with illustrations. I have had some of my poetry published by "Triumph House," I have had my poems published in our local paper. I have had letters published as well as poetry in our local paper.; [pers.] I really enjoy reading and writing poetry. I write about anything, and everything. I do hope that in my poetry, when people read it, they get a message from it, and enjoy it, as well, growing up, growing older and finding out what life is all about, expressing it in poetry.; [a.] Oldham, Lancashire

MCDADE, ENID JENNY
[pen.] Genial Octogenarian; [b.] 23 July 1908, Manchester; [p.] Allan A. Durward, Catherine Maslen;

[m.] Robert McDade (Deceased), 26 March 1935; [ch.] 4 Daughters - 10 grandchildren - 8 great grandchildren; [ed.] Primary Schools - Newkilpatrick, Bearsden Nr Glasgow 2 years - Bothwell Primary (1), Lanarkshire, Hamilton Academy Lanarkshire 2 years, Cuthbertson 2 years Glasgow S Side, Queens Park Secondary, Glasgow (4 years); [occ.] Retired (Sc and T), Retired (Company Secretary Director - Civil Engineering Ltd. Co.); [memb.] On executive Committee of Chinese Elderly Association Edinburgh; [oth. writ.] Tales of a Great Grandmother - not submitted My Life Story (not completed) one poem published in local community monthly magazine; [pers.] Think carefully before making a decision, then go all out to make it come true. If you fail, shrug it off. At least you tried! Be versatile Exercise mind and body to keep fit.; [a.] Edinburgh, Midlothian

MCDERMOTT, IRENE E.
[pen.] Rene McDermott; [oth. writ.] Several poems published in local and works magazine's a was very honored some years ago, when Sir John Betjeman Congratulated me on the Sensitivity of my work.; [pers.] I write about things that concern me, be it cruelty to animals of conflicts of war. Not being competitive, I write mostly for friends, who say "It Made Me Laugh", or "It Made Me Cry", depending on the subject. Is this a play on emotions, I ask myself.; [a.] Harron Weany, Middlesex

MCDONAGH, VIVIENNE
[b.] 7 September 1950, Wigan; [p.] Josephine Powell, Henry Myatt; [m.] Patrick McDonagh, 12 August 1984; [ch.] Victoria; [ed.] St. Thomas more girls school Salford Polytechnic College; [occ.] Social Worker; [memb.] BASW (British Assoc. of Social Workers); [hon.] NNEB (Nursery Nursing) CRCCYP (Residential Child Care Cert.:) Cert: in Sdvanced Management. (Diploma in Social Work - hopefully June 97; [oth. writ.] Short stories for magazines currently writing a novel.; [pers.] I believe that every human being has talent some are more fortunate in having it recognized.; [a.] Braintree, Essex

MCDONALD, BRIAN
[pen.] David Ash; [b.] 27 January 1977, Donegal; [p.] Daniel and Kathleen McDonald; [ed.] Carndonagh Community School; [occ.] Fisherman; [memb.] Book Club of Ireland; [oth. writ.] Two poems published in school magazine, other work as of yet has been unseen.; [pers.] Most thoughts are conflicts with other thoughts but a few make perfect sense and become poetry.; [a.] L'Derry, Derry

MCDONALD, JACQUELINE
[pen.] Mary George; [b.] 12 February 1952; [p.] Mary and George James; [m.] Edwin McDonald, 4 December 1969; [ch.] Michelle and Stephen; [occ.] Cleaning Supervisor; [oth. writ.] As poetry is a hobby for me I have several other unpublished poems for the enjoyment of friends and family; [pers.] I was inspired to write satarical poetry by friends and family and then encourage to branch out in other areas and hope my poetry gives pleasure to all who read it.; [a.] Belfast, Antrim

MCFADYEN, PAUL
[b.] 30 March 1972, Tyne and Wear; [p.] Thomas and June McFadyen; [ed.] Hebburn Comprehensive, South Tyneside College Hebburn, Newcastle College of Arts and Technology; [occ.] Mechanical Engineer; [pers.] I gain great pleasure in writing. I hope when others read my work it brings joy and pleasure to them also. To read my work you should not read with your eyes, but with all my heart. To understand my work you begin to understand me.; [a.] Hebburn, Tyne and Wear

MCFARLANE, MINETTE
[b.] 31 October 1961, Brighton, Sussex; [p.] Anna and Ian McFarlane; [ed.] Varndean Grammar School for Girls; [occ.] All round artist; [memb.] Tip Top Club; [hon.] Certificate for "Enthusiasm" in the Junior School; [oth. writ.] Plenty of poems, yet unpublished. This one's the only poem ever been shown.; [pers.] Never, ever, give up on your dreams.; [a.] Hove, Sussex

MCGINLAY, JOHN O'BRIEN
[b.] 24 November 1954, Ayr; [p.] McGregor and Cathrine, McGinlay; [m.] Isabel McGinlay, 3 March 1973; [ch.] John and Christine McGinlay; [ed.] Dalmellington High School, Ayrshire; [occ.] Unemployed, (Ex Miner) Labourer; [oth. writ.] Previously written various poems, until now never submitted any for evaluation.; [pers.] Alas if on life's paths to journey's end. Emotions were a matter of choice, we would travel the prettier route.; [a.] Glasgow, Strathclyde

MCGINLEY, MARIE
[b.] 18 September 1979, Dublin; [p.] John McGinley, Mary McGinley; [ed.] St. John's Girl's National School, Dublin until 1989, since 1989, European School, Karlsruhe, German; [occ.] Student; [hon.] Won a week's visit to Lisbon as prize winner in Essay competition organized by portuguese ministry of education; [oth. writ.] Three articles for "Early Times" an Education newspaper; [a.] Dettenheim, Germany

MCGINN, TOMMY
[pen.] In The Clouds; [b.] 10 April 1934, Augher; [m.] 1961; [ch.] Four grown up; [occ.] Semie retired; [a.] Aughnacley, Tyrone

MCGOWAN, STEVEN
[b.] 30 November 1968, Liverpool; [p.] Mary Thorne, John Thorne; [ed.] Campion High School, Liverpool, 1 English O'Level C.S.E. in art; [occ.] Van Driver for Sayer The Bakery; [memb.] T.G.W.U. The Sefton Arms Free Mason Society; [hon.] 100 meters swimming certificate and won a Rafael once; [oth. writ.] Wrote poems for "The Scottie Press" when I was 10. A parish newsletter published weekly on Scotland Road.; [pers.] Without trying to sound too deep, I enjoy poetry, writing and drama because it doesn't discriminate, class, age colour, creed, anyone can write it or read it or enjoy it. Poetry is the nearest thing we've got to world harmony.; [a.] Liverpool, Merseyside

MCGURGAN, CORNELIUS
[b.] 24 March 1966, Draperstown; [p.] Pat McGurgan, Katie McGurgan; [ed.] St. Marys Primary, St. Colms High, both Draperstown; [occ.] Farm labourer; [oth. writ.] I have written a few scripts that may suit T.V. or film, but so far I haven't done anything about them.; [a.] Draperstown, Derry

MCINTOSH, VICTOR
[b.] 14 May 1959; [p.] Eric McIntosh, Mavis McIntosh; [hon.] Old and New Testament Bible Studies; [pers.] Acknowledge God every morning and give him thanks with praise every night.; [a.] London

MCKENZIE, ERROL
[b.] 16/05/48, West Indies; [p.] James Augustus McKenzie, Miriam McKenzie; [m.] Lurline McKenzie, December 16, 1967; [ch.] Sean, Tanya, Alistair & Leon; [ed.] Hillcroft School, London; Open University, Milton Keynes; [occ.] Petro-Chemical Engineer, Freelance Consultant; [memb.] The Writers Bureau, Manchester, The Writers Guild of America-East, The Institute of Chemical Engineers; [hon.] Bachelor of Arts Degree (Chemistry Bias); [oth. writ.] First novel being finalised for publication in 1997. Numerous unpublished poems and short stories.; [pers.] To be a beacon of inspiration to my fellow men and women of this earth, and to utilize the gift of writing to make a difference in the lives of those less fortunate than myself.; [a.] Sanderstead, Surrey

MC KEOWN, ANTHONY THOMAS
[b.] 16/02/72, Belfast; [p.] Marie Mc Keown, Tony Mc Keown; [ed.] St. Malachy's college, Queen's University of Belfast, University of Ulster at Colgraine; [hon.] B.A. Honours Degree in English and Modern History; [oth. writ.] Several unpublished poems, M.A. Dissertation on Michael Longley's poetry; [a.] Belfast, Antrim

MCKLOUD, JANE
[pen.] Jane McCairn; [b.] 24 June 1969, Greenock; [p.] James McCairn and Jane McCairn; [m.] Heath Richard McKloud, 4 August 1990; [ch.] Andrew James and Emily Jane; [ed.] Notre Dame High School, Dumbarton Glasgow Western College of Nursing and Midwifery; [occ.] Casualty Staff Nurse; [memb.] British Organ Donation Society; [pers.] At the end of the day comes the night.; [a.] Greenock, Renfrewshire

MCKOY, XHOLA
[b.] 26 October 1981, London; [p.] Valerie Webster & Ian Steele; [ed.] Winchmore Secondary School, Winchmore Hill, London; [occ.] student; [memb.] recruitment in modeling and grooming school. Featured School. Featured in Lexton.; [hon.] Excellent effort and attainment in English. Achievement in catwalk modelling.; [oth. writ.] Several poems written as hobbies and enjoyment.

MCLAREN, MISS VALMAI
[b.] 24 September 1944, New Zealand; [occ.] Secretary; [memb.] Guild of International Songwriters and Composers; [pers.] I seek to open both heart and mind to the beauty of creation and bring enjoyment to those unable to see for themselves the pleasures so freely available all around us in this unique world in which we live.; [a.] Finchley, London

MCLAUGHLIN, JOANNE
[b.] 16 September 1974, L'derry; [p.] Simone O'Donnell; [ed.] Thornhill College, Saint Mary's College, Magee University; [occ.] Student; [memb.] Renewal Action in Youth First Aid; [hon.] Attendance, first aid; [oth. writ.] I have a collection of my own poetry. This is my first time showing them, and getting one published; [pers.] My talent I gained from my grandfather O'Donnell, my motivation from my mother to whom I owe a great deal, as to all those I'll always love; [a.] Derry, L'derry

MCMULLEN, RUTH
[b.] 2 May 1954, York ; [ed.] Mill Mount Grammar, York to A-Level; [occ.] Local Co-Ordinator and visitor for family fund trust for disabled children; [hon.] Certificate in Therapeutic application of the arts in therapy and education; [oth. writ.] Poetry and article contributions to the guild for psychological studies, USA.; [pers.] My poetry comes mostly from my own feelings, observations, experiences and reflections. I try to search my soul and to reach out to others souls too.; [a.] Holland-on-Sea, Essex

MCNAMARA, JACQUELINE
[b.] 24 December 1978, Cork, Ireland; [ed.] Convent of Mercy, Kinsale, Co. Cork Kinsale Community School Leaving Certificate Level; [occ.] Student; [memb.] Amnesty International; [oth. writ.] 56 unpublished poems; [pers.] I dare to discuss the issues that others won't even think about.; [a.] Kinsale, Cork

MCNULTY, PATRICIA
[pen.] Trish; [b.] 17 March 1944, Bolton; [p.] Deceased; [m.] Divorced; [ed.] Secondary Modern School; [occ.] Packer Machine Opp.; [pers.] Just had a poem entitled (Mum) in your hardback between a laugh and a tear and I'm really pleased to have had it published.; [a.] Bolton, Lancs

MEAD, KAY
[pen.] Kay Mead; [b.] 7 July 1914, Lancashire ; [p.] Mr. and Mrs. J. H. Nightingale; [m.] Douglas Mead, 1952; [ch.] One son; [ed.] High School Commercial Studies, Bookkeeping Art, Draughtswoman; [occ.] Retired; [memb.] Floral art, Cubs and Scouts, Art Teacher; [oth. writ.] "Still Moments" Vantage Press Inc. 516 West 34 St, New York N.Y. 1001; [pers.] Kay Mead was born in Lancashire, England. She won her first prize for poetry when she was seven years old. She attended local schools and was attached to the Royal Air Force during World War II. There she assisted in the rehabilitation of returned prisoners of war. After the war she decided to travel and went to South Africa, where she met and married Douglas Mead, a South African Air Force Officer. They had one son, with whom Mrs. Mead now operates a landscape gardening business. Despite a busy career, she finds time to be involved in gardening, reading, cooking, painting, floral art, and walking. She feels that each of her poems is inspired by incidents in her own life and her love of God and his creation. Kay Mead lives in Natal, Republic of South Africa.; [a.] Scottburgh, South Africa

MEADE, JOHN
[b.] 13 April 1958, Martinstown; [p.] Margaret and James D. Meade; [m.] Mary Meade (Deceased), 22 March 1986; [ch.] John and Aoife; [ed.] Martinstown National School, Kilmallock Sec. School; [occ.] Soldier; [a.] UK

MEADE, MICHAEL
[pen.] M. Meade; [b.] 7 July 1933, Liverpool; [p.] William J. Meade, Annie Meade; [m.] Brenda Meade, 10 November 1992; [ch.] (Previous Marriage) Michael, John, Lorraine; [ed.] Secondary Modern, St. Aloysuis, R.C. Huyton, Lancs; [occ.] Retired; [memb.] Ex Civil Defence Club, British Legion; [oth. writ.] Several poems, for songs, one songs on R.N.L.I. tape for charity. Called, Oil Rig Man, published in Scotland.; [pers.] I tend to write from personal experiences, influenced by the University of Life.; [a.] Heswall, Merseyside

MEDEKONG, ANIEMA
[pen.] Violet; [b.] 20 July 1975, Nigeria; [p.]Ann Medekong (British) and Okon Medekong (Nigerian); [ed.] Federal Girls' College, Calabar, Nigeria; University of Calabar, Nigeria; [occ.] Student, Industrial Chemistry Undergraduate; [memb.] Music and Literary Club, Federal Girl's College, Calabar, Nigeria; [hon.] Drama award, Abak, Nigeria.; [oth. writ.] several unpublished poems, short novel—"Sunita"—1987 unpublished, "Grandad" is a reflection of my English granddad.; [pers.] Life; from birth to death, is a great inspiration to every poetic soul. I believe that in every soul is bestowed a poetic gift.; [a.] Oron, Nigeria

MENDOZA, MIGUEL
[b.] 8 May 1945, Guiuan, East Samar, Philippines; [p.] Quirico D. Mendoza-Candida C. Balboa; [m.] Sylvia Son Mendoza, 25 July 1970; [ch.] Kim, Ivy, Haji, Mae & Vida; [ed.]Master of Arts in Teaching (University of the Philippines); [occ.] English Instructor (Training Centre Language Wing, Bahrain Defence Force, State of Bahrain); [memb.] Pi Gamma Mu (International Social Science Honor Society—Alpha Chapter) Philippine Association for Vocational Education, Knights of Columbus; [hon.] UP-BVE Scholar, College Scholar (University of the Philippines), Bronze Thanks Badge (Boys Scouts of the Philippines), Twentieth Century Achievement Award from the American Biographical Institute for Career Achievements and Social Contributions; [oth. writ.] "Of These Sunblest Isles" (A Collections of poems on Bahrain), "Other Poems" Instructional Modules in Developing Reading Skills; [pers.] That in sharing my poems—the very essence of my being and sparked by Divine gifts received, I touch hearts, enlighten minds, enrich lives, enhance creativity and leave a lasting legacy to humanity.; [a.] Guiuan, East Samar, The Philippines

MERCER, JOHN S.
[pen.] John Mercer; [b.] April 1938, Belfast; [m.] Audrey Byers, 30 July 1964; [ch.] Rosalind and Joanne; [ed.] Belfast High School and Stranmillis College Belfast; [occ.] Freelance Musician, Examiner, Tutor; [hon.] B.A. Open University LGSM on Piano Accompaniment, LTCL in Organ; [oth. writ.] Several poems published by Salopian Poetry Society - poem accepted for poetry no Ulsted Pub 1997 (Anthology).; [pers.] Organist and Choirmaster for over 40 years/founder of Belfast Operatic Company and Belmont Drama Group. Retired after teaching for 35 years.; [a.] Newtownabbey, Antrim

MERRIGAN, NIKOLA
[b.] 19 February 1946, Dublin; [p.] Dr. Michael O'Donnell and Joey; [m.] Patrick Merrigan, 14 November 1968; [ch.] Michael Patrick, Nicholas and Richard; [ed.] Our Lady's School, Templelogue St. Louis, Ruthmines, St. Marys, Arklow; [occ.] Freelance Water Colour Artist; [oth. writ.] Never published any of my poetry before; [pers.] The nuns in school said I was always day dreaming, I still do, and escape from real life with my painting and poetry. I like to reflect on life from the outside.; [a.] Cork, Eire

MEZAKS, MRS. DOROTHY
[pen.] Dorothy Mezaks (Mrs.); [b.] 5 June 1922, Shirebrook; [p.] Harry Kells, Alice Kells; [m.] Evalds Mezaks, 29 March 1952; [ch.] Linda; [ed.] Manor Grammar School Exeter University; [occ.] Retired; [memb.] Clipstone Social Club Notts; [hon.] Served in the W.A.A.F. attained rank of Corporal 1942-1946-7; [oth. writ.] 3 poems published by arrival press of 2nd World War. 2 in Local Paper, Chronicle Ad: Mansfield.; [pers.] A soft answer turneth away wrath. But grievous words stir up anger, from - The Wisdom of Solomon.; [a.] Mansfield-Woodhouse, Nottinghamshire

MIDDLETON, JOAN
[pen.] Joan Flint; [b.] 29 July, Market Harborough; [p.] Phylis Flint and Harry Flint; [ch.] Tina Whitbread, Steven Whitbread; [ed.] Market Harborough High School; [occ.] Fashions; [memb.] Swimming Club, Gardening Club; [oth. writ.] Children's stories creative writing unpublished; [pers.] To give peace of mind in reading my poems how to feel life and realize the importance of living.; [a.] West Bridgeford, Notts

MILLING, PATRICK
[b.] 28 April 1922, Clonmel; [p.] (father) Michael, (mother) Mary; [m.] separated, married 1944; [ch.] five; [ed.] Clonmel High School, Tipperary Ireland until age 17; [occ.] retired.; [a.] London

MILLS, DONNA
[b.] 19 July 1971, Dorking; [p.] Valerie and Terry Halls; [m.] Paul Richard Mills, June 8, 1993; [ch.] Four; [ed.] Howard of Effingham School; [occ.] Housewife; [pers.] My mother died in 1989. I was very close to her. I wrote this and other poem's to help me come to terms with the pain of losing a parent.; [a.] Bookham, Surrey

MILNE, NATHAN ANTHONY
[pen.] Nathan Anthony Milne; [b.] 22 March 1967, Cleethorpes; [p.] Len Milne, Pauline Milne; [m.] Deborah MacDonald Kerr Milne, 16 November 1996; [ed.] Mathew Humberstone Comprehensive School; [occ.] Stevedore; [hon.] N.E.B.O.S.H, Occupational Health and Safety; [pers.] I'm a poet and I did not know it! Sometimes in life you don't miss things until they've gone.; [a.] Grimsby, North East Lincs

MITCHELL, MISS EDNA MAY
[b.] 5 May 1922, London, England; [p.] Charlotte and Fredrick Mitchell; [ed.] Ordinary School; [occ.] Retired; [oth. writ.] Write stories.; [pers.] To talk or speculate in philosophical manner.; [a.] London

MITCHELL, RONNIE E.
[pen.] Frenchie; [b.] 3 November 1967, Lambeth; [p.] Granville Gayle and Carol Gayle; [m.] Rosemary Griffith; [ch.] Liam Sharp and Dean Griffith; [ed.] Sir Walter St Johns; [occ.] Laser Operator St Mary Cray Orpington, Kent; [memb.] Bingo, Snooker and The Librarie; [oth. writ.] I have had several poems and published in local magazines and a few newspapers; [pers.] If a man has money. Don't look up to him and if a man hasn't got any money don't look down on him the man with no shoes. Should cry for the man with no feet.; [a.] St. Mary Cray, Kent

MOBEEN, ABDA
[b.] 14 October 1980, Burnley, Lancs; [p.] Saleem Akhtar, Mohd Sadiq; [ed.] Walshaw High School studying 9 G.C.S.E. subjects; [occ.] Student; [oth. writ.] Poem published in "One Way Ticket" anthology; [pers.] Allah is the one I would like to thank and praise for the gift he has given me. I have greatly been influenced by friends and by the one and only (God); [a.] Burnley, Lancashire

MOHAMMED, AYAN
[pen.] Gill, Dolores Gill, Patrick Redford; [b.] 21 August 1977, Somalia; [p.] Halima Jama, Farah Mohammed; [ed.] Completed Secondary High School in St. Mary's High School in Liverpool now I attend college at Mabel Flatener College doing Health and Social care course; [occ.] Student; [memb.] I am member of Somali Community Association in Liverpool. I help children to learn Somali, English; [hon.] During the High School I have been awarded a

lot of certificates such as Youth Award, Scheme Bronze Award which was for personal and Social Competence on date October 1993.; [oth. writ.] I wrote a story about my experience in the civil war in Somalia in Miss Magazine 1993 on it happen to me page. I have been awarded I always like write about my own experience.; [pers.] I arrived England on 21 November 1991. Started school and make many friends. I am socialized person. My hobbies are reading, writing poems I also enjoy going out with my friends in my spare time.; [a.] Liverpool, Toxteth

MONK, BEATE
[pen.] Beate Monk; [b.] 13 January 1965, Willich, Germany; [p.] Anita and Josef Himmel; [m.] Stuart James Monk, 4 January 1986; [ch.] Sean Karl (25 May 1987) Halley Marie Louise (17 February 1990); [ed.] Kindergarten teacher went to school in Germany, never really had a chance to practice my profession. I brought up my children first.; [occ.] I now started as an assistant in a day care center and nursery for children.; [oth. writ.] None published "My Favorite Time Of Year", was the first ever poem I had the bottle to enter in my entire life, and I can't believe it's a semi finalist.; [pers.] I write about my life as a mother, housewife, private person, the pain and the joy. There's always something to be learned "If" we're humble enough. I found myself constantly worrying and rushing. I made myself stop writings down and found beauty where I never expected to find any before; [a.] Lower Quinton, Warwickshire

MONTAGUE, ROSA
[b.] 20 January 1956, Newcastle on Tyne; [ch.] Four; [ed.] Student at University of Northumbria, (Sociology); [occ.] Project Worker in a Womens Hostel

MONTEITH, JEAN
[pen.] Luci; [b.] 1 September 1937, Carrickadartans; [p.] Ruby and Alex Sproule; [m.] Kenneth Monteith, 19 December 1956; [ch.] 6 sons and 2 daughters and 5 grandchildren; [ed.] Small Country School called Garvetagh; [occ.] Housewife; [memb.] St. John Ambulance Sunday School Teacher, C.E.F. helper; [hon.] St. John Ambulance public First Aid Exam award and caring for the; sick. [Level 1]; [oth. writ.] 8 poems published, I am working on a children's story.; [pers.] I enjoy putting my thoughts in rhyme, and I am very happy when folk enjoy my poems.; [a.] Castlederg, Tyrone

MOORE, MR. A. S.
[pen.] Arthur; [b.] 18 May 1917, Poplar, London; [ed.] Elementary School; [occ.] Retired disabled O.A.P.; [memb.] Ex. special constable long service med and met, Police, Master Builder Hosp. Service App 15 years 1st Class Tech 1st Aid Cert. Life, Saving Cert at 12 years old; [hon.] Army H.S. Medal D.B. Med

MOORE, DONNA
[b.] 28 November 1979; [p.] Peter David John, Karen Elizabeth; [ed.] Haksham Community College; [occ.] Student, a levels; [pers.] My premature brother Alex was my inspiration during his first 14 months of life in the John Radcliffe Hospital fighting for his life. The family and nurses have pulled him through.; [a.] Haksham, E. Sussex

MOORE, S. F.
[pen.] Sandy Felicity; [b.] 11 October 1962, Britain; [p.] David and Shirley Huyton; [m.] Mr. Roy Moore, 21 December 1995; [ch.] Rachel and Luke; [ed.] Three O'Levels, Five C.S.E.'s, City and Guilds in Hairdressing and Make-up (Ramsey Grammar School I.O.M. College of further Education); [occ.] Beautician and Crossing Patrol Lady; [oth. writ.] Several poems written throughout my life, inspired either through my emotions or my surroundings. Poem printed in road safety magazine (I.O.M.); [pers.] To enable mankind to become aware of their physical and spiritual selves bringing peace and tranquility.; [a.] Douglas, Isle of Man

MORAN, ORIANA
[b.] 3 March 1977, Tralee; [p.] Daniel V. Moran, Bridget Moran; [ed.] St. John's Secondary School Tralee, Co. Kerry, Tralee RTC, Co. Kerry; [occ.] Student of languages and marketing; [a.] Tralee, Kerry, Ireland

MORGAN, DARREN GEOFFREY
[b.] 16 November 1969, Newport; [p.] Geoffrey and Kay Morgan; [ed.] Risca Comprehensive School, New Port College of Further Education; [occ.] Carpenter and Joiner; [memb.] Risca W.M.C.; [hon.] City and Guilds Carpentry and Joinery Advanced C+G CxJ.; [pers.] I consider myself more a lyricist than poet. I wrote this pisces in 1984 when I was 14 years old I have only started writing again in the last 12 months in this time I have gathered 100 pieces.; [a.] Risca, Gwent

MORGAN, NIK
[b.] 31 March 1962, Norwich; [p.] David Morgan/Jean Morgan; [ed.] University of Wales; [occ.] Poet and Artist; [hon.] English Lit. B.A. 1983, English M.A. 1986, Exhibitions - St. David's Hall, Cardiff. Freuds, London/Oxford. Edinburgh Festival 1994. International Biennial of Humour and Satire, Bulgaria, 1995.; [oth. writ.] Poems published in various small press magazines. Poetry and illustrations appear in "Grandchildren of Albion", an anthology of contemporary poetry - 1992.; [pers.] In my work I am attempting to rediscover a sense of the magical. I have been influenced mainly by surrealism, Dylan Thomas, and Mervyn Peake.; [a.] Penarth, South Glamorgan

MORJARIA, SHITAL
[b.] 30 April 1973, Kenya; [p.] R. G. Morjaria, Sumitra Morjaria; [ed.] Post graduate (Masters) in M.A. English Literature; [occ.] Associate Editor in A Syndication Comp - Children's Columns; [hon.] Gold Medalist for B.A. English Literature from Osmania University; [oth. writ.] Few Poems, Comic Stories, and Articles for children published; [pers.] I live by the motto that behind every dark cloud there is a silver lining... thanks Mom!; [a.] Hyderabad, India

MORLEY, KEVIN P.
[b.] 21 May 1958, Old Windsor, Berks; [p.] Hugh Morley, Shirley Morley; [occ.] In Enforced retirement due to back injury; [oth. writ.] Amateur Theatre reviews for a local paper. A number of unpublished poems. I am currently working on my first novel.; [pers.] My poetry usually reflects my current emotional state and my personal view of the world in general, and my views on world conservation - particularly animals specifically. I also paint.; [a.] Gloucester

MORRIS, CHARLOTTE ANNE
[b.] 11 February 1982, Wolverhampton; [p.] Barbara and David Morris; [ed.] St. Dominics School, Brewood; [oth. writ.] I've written several poems but have not before entered any in competitions or had them published.; [pers.] My writing describes my emotions and the way I feel at the time. I often feel the only time I can communicate my heart's true thoughts is through poetry.; [a.] Stafford, Staffordshire

MORRISON, MIKE
[b.] 4 May 1949, Huntly; [p.] Gordon, and Mary Morrison; [m.] Kate Morrison, 19 July 1973; [ch.] Ross Morrison; [ed.] M.A. (Hons) History DIP. Guidance and Counselling Aberdeen, Scotland; [occ.] School Teacher; [oth. writ.] Editor Gordon School Magazine "The Tower and the Linden Tree" 1968; [pers.] I enjoy the work of Dylan Thomas and Bob Dylan.; [a.] Inverness, Highland

MORRISON, SHELLEY
[pen.] Shelley Morrison; [b.] 5 June 1983, Birmingham; [p.] Gail Morrison; [ed.] Abbey Primary, Movilla High School, Newtownards; [occ.] School pupil; [hon.] 11 Gins Brigade Awards (2 1st Marching, 2 Top Gin, 2 Efficiency, 2 1st D.T.D.T., 1st or 2nd Drilldown, P.E., Bookmark). Two Mensa Certificates, Movilla High School Year 8 Endeavor cup and 89 Achievement. 4 C.T.C. Awards, 1 Pupils Council Award. I'm currently a monitor.; [oth. writ.] I published horror story.; [pers.] I'm delighted I sent in my poem just for the fun of it. My mum is proud of me.; [a.] Newtownards, Down

MOSHIRI, SHEEVA
[b.] 13 June 1980, London; [p.] Afsaneh Moshiri and Jubin Moshiri; [ed.] St Margaret's school (in Hampstead); [occ.] Studying French, Spanish and Art A levels at Francis Holland (Clarence Gate); [memb.]

Cumberland Lawn Tennis Club; [pers.] Sometimes when I feel stressed I like to write poems as they give me the sensation of freedom from my most inner emotions.; [a.] London, Middlesex

MOSLEY, EILEEN
[pen.] Emily Anne; [b.] 5 September 1941, Leeds; [p.] Mary and Clifford Rosendale (Adopted); [m.] Roy Mosley, 25 September 1960; [ch.] David Roy, Gareth John; [ed.] Lower Wortley County Village School Education; [occ.] Housewife; [memb.] Filey Art Society Palette Painting Group; [oth. writ.] None published; [pers.] The influences of my life have been - the bronte sisters whom I greatly admire and the painting of daniel sherring, also the American artist Bob Ross.; [a.] Filey, North Yorkshire

MOULTON, R. J.
[b.] 17 December 1932, Winterbourne; [p.] Annie Louise Moulton, Lionel John Moulton; [m.] Sylvia May Moulton, 5 April 1958; [ch.] Pauline and Paula; [ed.] Chirping Sodbury Grammar School; [occ.] Farmer; [oth. writ.] Trudy, Dun Milkin, Huggin The Moos, Calne Road Chaos, Grandfather, Diversification; [pers.] I like to write about animals and the countryside for others to laugh or shed a tear at.; [a.] Corsham, Wilts

MULLARKEY, ELIZABETH
[b.] 13 December 1935, Durham City; [p.] Ray Thomas Norman and Bessie Norman; [m.] Terence Denzil Mullarkey, 14 July 1969; [ed.] Durham High School 1945-1948, Craigmount School, Scone Palace, Scone, Perth, Scotland 1948-1951, The Middlesex Hospital, London, 1954-1958; [occ.] Retired; [memb.] Life Member Bronte Literacy Society, Member the Middlesex Hospital Nurses Benevolent Fund. Member of Ruddington Woman's Institute; [oth. writ.] Some short stories, odes and poems first publication of nursing article in the Nursing Mirror 1906's.; [pers.] The influence of my father Raymond Thomas Norman and The Brontes urge me to write my thoughts for others to feel.; [a.] Ruddington, Nottinghamshire

MULRYAN-MCNALLY, TANYA
[b.] 28 July 1982, Dublin, Ireland; [p.] Thomas McNally; [ed.] Melview Primary School Longford, Acoil Mhuire Convent Secondary School Longford; [occ.] Student; [memb.] Photo Club-Karate Club - Environmental Groups; [hon.] Short story published in school magazine, various sports awards; [oth. writ.] Short stories; [pers.] The wish is the father of the thought and the thought is the father of the deed.; [a.] Longford, Longford

MUPAWAENDA, ANNA CLETTER
[pen.] Princess; [b.] 45 yrs. old, Zimbabwe; [p.] Ellen and Cuthbert Mubviri; [m.] Divorced; [ch.] Tsungai and Kudzai; [ed.] Bsc. (Sociology) Honours MED (Adult Education), NCT, CBT; [occ.] Administrator, IDS, University of Zimbabwe; [memb.] Member of the Commonwealth Association for the Education and Training of Adults - I and the Chairperson of the Executive Committee; [hon.] On the 1996 Award for Business Training - Competence Based Training - Sponsored by USAID; [oth. writ.] Written several poems since 1995. They are not published. Will be looking for a publisher. Have started writing a novel.; [pers.] I draw the attention of humankind to the truth and their responsibility to themselves and others. Excuses have no room in my world. People have to face facts.; [a.] Harare, Zimbabwe

MURPHY, CHRISSIE LILLIAN
[b.] 22 March 1922, Liverpool; [p.] Hannah Batt and William Colpitts; [m.] George Thomas, 23 April 1943; [ch.] Christopher David and Elizabeth; [ed.] College Commercial College; [occ.] Living?; [oth. writ.] 10 years trying to write about a young girl's life from the start of the century, all the changes, material and other wise.; [pers.] My life is darkness, from day 'til night. Until your letter came to my door and flooded my spirit with light once more thank you.; [a.] Southampton, Hants

MURPHY, JEANETTE
[b.] 2 October 1940, Rhondda Valley; [p.] Albert Edward Johnson; [m.] Patrick David Murphy, 27 January 1962; [ch.] Sharon Valerie and Kathryn Marie; [ed.] Grammar School; [occ.] Retired; [memb.]

Flackwell Heath Good Companions; [a.] High Wycombe, Bucks

MURPHY, MARGARET ROSE
[b.] 02/07/1952, South Africa; [p.] Basil and Sheila Combrinck; [m.] James Joseph Murphy, 20/12/1986; [ch.] Alioa, Natasha and Sinead; [ed.] Trafalgar High School, Cape Town, South Africa; [occ.] Accident and Emergency Receptionist, Barnet General Hospital; [pers.] Greatest influence in my life is my grandparents Bernard and Florence Combrinck.

MURPHY, MARIA
[b.] 25 January 1980, Cork, Ireland; [p.] Pat and Wadreen Murphy; [ed.] Colaiste an Chradibhin, Fermoy Co. Cork, Watergrasshill National School; [occ.] Student; [pers.] When I wrote this poem I was at my lowest ebb due to illness. I hope it reaches those who are depressed and let's them know that they are not alone.; [a.] Watergrasshill, Cork, Ireland

MURPHY, MRS. P. A.
[b.] 12 March 34, Bucks; [p.] Lily and Frank Matthews; [m.] Edward Murphy, 15 October 1955; [ch.] 3 Sons, 2 daughters; [ed.] Slough High School; [occ.] Retired District Nurse; [oth. writ.] "Why" already being published; [pers.] I admire patience strong and would like to produce similar work with a more up to date version - am able to produce verse on a regular basis.; [a.] Bicester, Oxon

MURRAY-BORBJERG, KIRSTEN
[pen.] KM-B; [b.] 8 October 1985, Whitley Bay; [p.] Alison Murray, Hennig Borbjerg; [ed.] South Wellfield First school, Valley Gardens Middle School, Whitley Bay North Tyneside; [occ.] Student; [pers.] I am II and I wrote the poem when I was 10. I am working hard to overcome my Dyslexia, and this competition has been very encouraging. Allan Ahlberg is my poetic hero and inspiration.; [a.] Whitley Bay, North Tyneside

NAIDOO, JOHN
[pen.] John Naidoo; [b.] 1 November 1933, Durban, South Africa; [p.] Narappa Naidoo; [m.] Jagathambal (Deceased), 27 September 1957; [ch.] One son and one daughter; [ed.] Sastri College - South Africa and Natal University South Africa, British Rail Examination Distinction - 1st and 2nd year; [occ.] Retired; [memb.] At present engaged in voluntary work at British Red Cross, Benson Primary School, Croydon, John Ruskin College, Croydon; [oth. writ.] Wrote about 25 poems as an hobby.; [pers.] I try to bring to the notice of world starvation among children in the third world and "unnecessary" wars.; [a.] Croydon, Surrey

NAYLOR, LISA
[b.] 15 February 1970, Blackpool; [ed.] Durham University, Open University; [occ.] Health and Education; [hon.] Lamda Speech and Acting B.A. (hons) Social Studies; [oth. writ.] Short stories for motorblue magazines; [pers.] Influenced by paganism and the power of positive thought.; [a.] Knott-end-on-Sea, Lancashire

NEARY, ELAINE
[b.] 17 June 1982, Kilkenny, Ireland; [p.] James Neary, Elizabeth Neary; [occ.] Student - Loreto Convent, Secondary School, Kilkenny; [hon.] Awards for Dancing; [oth. writ.] Personal poetry; [a.] Kilkenny, Kilkenny

NEGUS, LEONARD J.
[b.] 27 December 1921, London; [p.] William and Sarah; [m.] Eileen, 20 April 1946; [ch.] 1 Boy and 2 Girls; [ed.] Elementary School Numerous Scholarships passed; [occ.] O.A.P; [memb.] Chairman of the Bedfordshire and Buckinghamshire Branch of the Aircrew Association; [hon.] War Campaign Medals Awarded Commission in R.A.F.; [oth. writ.] Other poems I have written refer to the war years. I flew as a wop/ag in the pathfinder force of bomber command. Therefore most of my poems reflect on the experiences encountered by aircrews.; [pers.] I try to create poems which reflect or relate to certain incidents which occur on holidays etc.; [a.] Luton, Bedfordshire

NEIGHBOUR, RUTH NORA
[b.] 16 March 1921, Halstead, Kent; [p.] William James Luck, Mabel Luck; [m.] Sidney John

Neighbour, 17 May 1958; [ch.] One adopted son Martin; [ed.] I only went to School, in what was commonly known then as Council Schools; [occ.] Retired and partly an invalid; [a.] Slough, Berks

NEWMAN, JENNY
[pen.] Jennyen; [b.] 4 July 1948, Gloucester; [p.] Jim and Lilian Eatough; [m.] Divorced; [ch.] 1 Son and 1 daughter; [ed.] Ribston Hall High School for Girls; [occ.] Accounts Clerk, Wellman Graham Ltd.; [oth. writ.] One so far published in poets premiere.; [pers.] I have only been writing rhymes for the past 16 months, I find it a very therapeutic day of coping with the stresses of life. Writing your thoughts on paper puts things in perspective and gives pleasure.; [a.] Gloucester, Gloshire

NEWMAN, ROBERT
[pen.] Arjay; [b.] 21 March 1938, E Twickenham; [ed.] Gainsborough Rd-Sec/Modern School Richmond; [occ.] General Builder Self employed; [memb.] P.M. Baron Carleton Masonic Lodge; [oth. writ.] Untold children's stories and poems - submitted but never published; [pers.] I like kids and I like people and life.; [a.] Isleworth, Middx

NEWTON, JULIA MERCER
[b.] 8 December 1982, St. Helens; [p.] Ernie Mercer, Mary Newton-Mercer; [ed.] Rivington County Primary School St. Helens, Cowley High School, St. Helens; [occ.] Student; [memb.] Royal Academy of Dancing, The Citadel Youth Theatre Company St. Helens elizabeth Hill School of Dance and Drama; [hon.] Grade One Violin Exam. RAD Ballet exams Pre Primary - Elementary, I.S.T.D. Top Exams Pre Primary - Elementary, I.S.T.D. Modern exams Pre Primary - Pre-Elementary, ISTD Jazz exams Bronze and Silver; [oth. writ.] My books include: Eat Your Sprouts, Murder at Mersham Mission and Outcast. My other writings include many poems and regular articles for the school magazine.; [a.] St. Helens, Merseyside

NEWTON, STEPHANIE
[b.] 31 May 1938, Yorkshire; [p.] Claude and Adelaide Lightfoot; [m.] David Newton, 8 July 1961; [ch.] Christina May; [occ.] Retired; [memb.] Friends of the earth, W-W.F. Dr. Hadwen Trust For Humane Medical Research; [oth. writ.] Some poems published in magazines and local newspapers; [pers.] I have been a keen environmentalist for many years and do everything I possibly can to help make our beautiful planet a safer place for future generations.; [a.] Sandhurst, Berkshire

NICHOLLS, ELIZABETH
[pen.] Liz Nicholls; [b.] 10 June 1961, Stockport; [ed.] The Manchester Metropolitan University; [occ.] Person-Centred Counsellor; [memb.] Local Art Class; [oth. writ.] Paper submitted for publication in Professional Journal; [pers.] My writing is a part of my search for psychological and spiritual growth.; [a.] Stockport, Cheshire

NICHOLLS, MRS. MEDINA
[b.] 7 October 1938, England; [p.] Cecelia and Charles Houlder; [m.] Brian Richard Nicholls, 4 April 1959; [ch.] Debbie, Mark, Craig; [ed.] Old Know Rd, Sec./Mod. School; [occ.] Kitchen Assistant Wrekin Nursing Home; [hon.] City Guilds, Pet Shop Management and Livestock, Pet Shop Manager 11 yrs.; [oth. writ.] Book called Inspirational Verse, 500 copies printed to raise funds for churches.; [pers.] I feel very privileged to have been given this wonderful gift to express my feelings in my writing.; [a.] Dawley, Shropshire

NICHOLS, CAROL PATRICIA
[pen.] Carol Langford; [b.] 21/08/41, Prescot, Lancs, England; [p.] Joan & Leslie John Langford; [m.] T. John Nichols, 06/06/73; [ed.] In Billinge in Lancs St Mary's, also in Ireland in Dublin and in Sligo, Interested in Operatics and acting and have Compere'd shows as well as taking part in them. Have had an exhibition of Watercolours. Won Most Original Print Competition twice and Best slide four times in our Foto Club.; [memb.] Kennel Club in Gibraltar, Gibraltar Photographic Society; [hon.] Best Colour Portfolio, Best Colour Print; [oth. writ.] "A Mothers

Prayer", "After the Storm", "Visitors", Fotos for advertising for Mackley Tri com. Pictures for the Safety at Sea Magazine.

NICKOLLS, MISS N. L.
[pen.] Norma Lyn Nickolls; [b.] 21 July 1944, Oxford; [p.] Mr. N. and Mrs. D. Nickolls; [ed.] Ordinary Comprehensive West Oxford Secondary Modern; [occ.] Self employed Agent of Leaflet Distribution; [pers.] Can write poetry anytime my poetry is influenced by seeing and hearing of life around me.; [a.] Oxford

NICOLSON, PENNILUCK
[pen.] Penni-Luck; [b.] 16 February 1946, Dundee, Scotland; [p.] James/Margaret McGinnis; [m.] John Nicolson, 30 August 1985; [ch.] 3 daughters - 6 sons; [ed.] Studying Social Science at open university, other education Lawside Academy Dundee; [occ.] Disabled; [oth. writ.] This is my first published writing - but many are waiting already written in the wings, have been too busy raising 9 children to try and publish.; [pers.] I dedicate this poem to my parents, both of whom are deceased, but who encouraged me to write since I was a child. Also to my husband John, and all my adorable children and grandchildren. Life is only a blink in time - So my advice is - Don't blink.; [a.] Redhill, Surrey

NIXON, MATTHEW
[b.] 8 March 1980, Sunderland; [p.] Angela Nixon and David Nixon; [ed.] St. Mary's Primary School, Sunderland. St. Aidans Comprehensive School, Sunderland; [oth. writ.] I started writing in May 1995 and have wrote over 200 poems. One pome is to be published in an Anthology for Anchor Books in January 1997 and several poems in a school anthology. I continue to enjoy and thrive on writing poetry.; [pers.] My poetry is straight from the heart, it speaks the truth about the way I felt and the way I feel now. My poetry is inspired by one person whom I adored and will always adore to my dying day.; [a.] Shadforth, Durham

NOBLE, OLIVE-JOYCE
[pen.] Olive-Joyce Noble; [b.] 24 July 1919, Birmingham; [p.] Mr. and Mrs. P. Dean; [m.] Stanley Noble, 22 March 1974; [ch.] One daughter; [ed.] Grammar, Commercial, Ministerial Colleges, Birmingham and Sheffield; [occ.] Retired Civil Servant; [memb.] W.A.A.F. 1942-1945 (Evangelist), Staff of the Air Ministry, Hallam St London, Mobile Stenographer/Secretary, Methodist Lay-Minister, United-Churches London and North West; [hon.] Literary Award for paper on John Wesley's Life. Cliff College Sheffield; [oth. writ.] Autobiography of War Services in Military War Museum London. Poems included within.; [pers.] Poetry was influenced by the works of Wordsworth and the style of Patience Strong.; [a.] Bolton, Lancashire

NOBLETT, DESMOND RONALD
[b.] 20 April 1925, Pentre, Rhondda; [p.] Albert Edward and Rose Noblett; [m.] Eileen (Deceased 1993), 5 April 1947; [ch.] Pat, Avril, Christine; [ed.] Tony Pandy Grammar School, Tony Pandy, Rhondda Valley, South Wales; [occ.] Retired; [memb.] Normandy Veterans Association; [hon.] None - only medals from my Army Service; [oth. writ.] Many, but none published.; [pers.] I try to portray poems that tug at the heart strings of people.; [a.] Treherbert, Rhondda, Cynon Taff

NOLAN, JOSEPH
[b.] 19 November 1923, Belfast; [p.] William John and Christina; [ed.] Secondary School 1937-1942; [occ.] Retired Oct. 1988 from Harland and Wolff Ltd (1944-68) and B.E.L.B. (1975-88); [memb.] Founder Member of Falls Community Council 1974, now life member. Founder Member Belfast writers group 1984 to date. Also member of Conway Mill writers and McCorley writers Groups; [hon.] Youth and Community (in service) Diploma ex Northern Ireland Polytechnic 1975; [oth. writ.] A poetry book "Down by the Slipway" published in 1991. Various poems published locally and articles in "Figments" magazine published Belfast.; [pers.] Worked as volunteer in various youth clubs since 1981 and as a full time

leader from 1968 to 1972, and Youth Welfare Dept Belfast Education and Library Board from 1976 to retirement.; [a.] Belfast, Northern Ireland

NOLAN, LAURA
[b.] 31 July 1981, Killarney; [p.] Frank and Mary Nolan; [ed.] Rockwell College, Chashel Co. Tipperary Ireland; [occ.] Student; [hon.] Gold Plaque for poetry recital at County Level. Piano Certificate to Grade 6. 'Distinction' in Speech and Drama.; [pers.] The single force that inspired me has "Ignited the spark of divinity in me and given meaning to my life".; [a.] Athea, Limerick

NORFLEET, PATRICIA ANN
[pen.] Patricia Ann Haines; [b.] 31 March 1942, Maidenhead, Berkshire; [p.] Mr. and Mrs. T. H. Haines; [m.] Bobby G. Norfleet, (Divorced 5 November 75), 28 December 1959; [ch.] Four: Karen, Curtis, Jeffrey, Tracy; [ed.] Secondary Modern School for Girls, Mercia Training Ltd. Tamworth, return to learn, Atherstone; [occ.] Housewife - Carer to partner, Mr. L. T. Conway; [hon.] Received a merit from Mensa, for participating in an intelligence test. I have also received from N.V.Q. Levels I-II, Typing, Word Processing, Spreadsheets and Data-Base; [oth. writ.] I have written other poems, but this is my first attempt to have any of my work looked at, I am so pleased you find my work worthy of publication; [pers.] I have always loved poetry, but made no attempt to write any. My mother died two years ago, and I believe she is the reason I've written the poem you are publishing for her, for me.; [a.] Tamworth, Staffordshire

NORRIS, LAUREN
[b.] 27 November 1980, Rochford; [p.] Nick Norris; [ed.] Currently attending Secondary School; [occ.] Pupil at school; [oth. writ.] Small selection of poems written in the past two years.; [pers.] The poem comes from a painful memory of my seeing my mum suffer from multiple Brain Tumors and eventually dying at the age of thirty three. These poems are dedicated to her memory.; [a.] Canvey Island, Essex

NORRISH, THELMA
[b.] Devon, England; [ed.] Educated in Devon; [oth. writ.] Slim-line books "Heaven and Earth" Book I, "Heaven and Earth" Book II (poem for local paper); [pers.] In much of my writing I try to convey the beauty and tranquility of "Nature's Garden.".; [a.] Devon

NOTTAGE, KENIA M.
[b.] 17 April 1974, Bahamas; [p.] Rubie and Kendal Nottage; [ed.] St. Elphin's School, University of Kent at Canterbury BPP Law School - London; [occ.] Student; [hon.] The Snowdon Awards - 1996, Various Drama and Music Certificates Awarded. Award for Classics - St. Elphev's School Derbyshire; [oth. writ.] Published poem via the International Library of Poets entitled "Crazed Tigers". Other works published in the University of Kent's magazine.; [pers.] To my parents - thank you for your support and love. I love you both.; [a.] London, London

NUNDY, JOHN
[pen.] John Nundy; [b.] 22 November 1933, Covenham St, Bartholomew, Nr Louth, Lincs; [p.] Mr. and Mrs. B. A. Nundy; [ed.] Lumley Secondary Skegness left 1948 to become a printers apprentice; [occ.] None, suffered 3 severe strokes 1961-1992-93 but am still mobile positive; [memb.] Used to belong to Skegness Art Club 1946 to 1971 when it was disbanded have played for several cricket teams.; [hon.] Lincolnshire Royal show certificate of Merit for an Oil Painting (1963) highly commended for water Col Painting at First Post War Exhibition at Embassy Skegness, in 1948 when 14 yrs old.; [oth. writ.] Unpublished "The Moonlight Fantasy", "The Half Cast Shadow" unpublished "The Bluestone Heath" unpublished various other pieces over the years 1950's to present date.; [pers.] Words paint a picture of the outside world bird's animals, and nature, particularly the thoughts and lifestyles of other people, their ways, and feelings and our own.; [a.] Skegness, Lincoln

NUNN, CLAIRE
[pen.] Claire Nunn; [b.] September 9, 1979, Greenwich, London; [p.] Mrs. Yvonne Bharaj, Mr. James Nunn; [ed.] Plumstead Manor Secondary School, Negus Sixth from Centie, Education A Levels: English Literature, French, Biology at NEGUS Sixth from Centie at Plumstead Manor School; [hon.] GCSE Awards, English language grade A, English literature - A, Mathematics - A, Drama - B, Science double award - AA, French - B, Design and Technology - A, Geography - C, Religious studies - C; [a.] London, Plumstead

NWODO, NKIRU GENEVIEVE
[pen.] Nky; [b.] 1 March 1980, Lagos, Nigeria; [p.] Dr. and Mrs. J. N. Nwodo; [ed.] Corona Primary School, Ikoyi, Lagos, Atlantic Hall, Ikeja, Lagos, St. Edmunds College, Herts; [occ.] Student, St. Edmund's College, Hertfordshire; [hon.] Valedictorian for the year 1996 at Atlantic Hall School Lagos, Nigeria; [oth. writ.] Poverty (unpublished).; [pers.] "Life is too short to be wasted. Make the best use of it in any way while you live. Do not be upset about the evil/harm other do unto you for they shall be paid back in their own coin."; [a.] Ware, Hertfordshire

O'BRIEN, LEAH
[pen.] Alia; [b.] 2 June 1980, California; [p.] Dad and Mom; [occ.] Student; [memb.] I am a chair person in the Society of Ladies against Gangs, I'm proud to say I am a S.L.A.G.; [hon.] Public Speaking Award; [oth. writ.] None published; [pers.] My writings depict the more unpleasant side of life. I was influenced at an early age by my parents, grandparents and the notorious Beverly Copland. But the pleasant side comes from the love of my best friend. Christina VanWert.

O'BRIEN, MARGARET R.
[b.] 5 February 1931, Plymouth, England; [p.] Annie Wilcox (Nee McConkey), George Wilcox; [m.] Dennis James O'Brien, 25 July 1953; [ch.] Three sons, two daughters; [ed.] Oxford St. Primary, Plymouth Public Secondary; [memb.] Australasian Performing Right Ass. The New Zealand Society of Authors, formerly Charter President I.T.C. (I.T.C. was International Toastmistress Training in Communication); [oth. writ.] Wow snippets (sense and nonsense) walking on Eggshells (Depowered parents 1965-85) Songs Ribbons of Love, Christmas Memories; [pers.] We see the world through stained - glass windows coloured by our own experience... As time passed, light and life moderate the view. Rigidity is rigor mortise!; [a.] Christchurch, New Zealand

O'CONNELL, JOYCE VIOLET
[b.] 29 December 1939, London; [p.] Joe Stevens, Louise Stevens; [m.] Divorced, 21 December 1957; [ch.] Michael, John, David, Iris; [ed.] Secondary Schools London, now attending computer course, English course; [occ.] Housekeeper; [hon.] City and Guilds, Word Power (1995); [oth. writ.] Poem to be printed in anthology (London Poetry Guild) very soon. And story printed in college magazine (1995).; [pers.] Nature is wonderful I try to reflect this through my poetry.; [a.] Bexhillow Sea, East Sussex

O'CONNELL, MAURICE
[pen.] Mossie; [b.] 10 February 1927, Kilmore, Kilduff, Tralee, Co. Kerry, Ireland; [m.] Noel O'Connell; [ch.] Five sons (2 deceased) and 1 daughter; [ed.] Secondary level; [occ.] Farmer; [memb.] Ballymacelligott Active Retirement Association, Ballymacelligott Drama Group; [hon.] RTE "Live at Three" award, 29 March 1993 for a poem entitled "The Sun"; [oth. writ.] "The Dump", "The Roscrea Cows" (both published in "CUM, an anthology of new writing from Kerry", published by the Kerry County Council and edited by Moya Cannon in December, 1996), and 14 other unpublished poems; [pers.] We live in a modern world where everything looks grand. The scare of war and poverty can be seen in many lands. We pray that the God who rules the sky may direct the powers that be and give to the world the lasting joy of peace and prosperity. (From my unpublished poem "The Changing Times"); [a.] Tralee, Kerry, Ireland

O'CONNOR, KYLE
[b.] 7 August 1978, Dublin; [p.] John O'Connor, Mary Gaffney; [ed.] Scoil Mhuire, Sutton Park School; [occ.] Student of Computer Applications, Dublin City University; [memb.] MENSA, Irish Council for Civil Liberties, Amnesty International, Alliance for Animal Rights, Irish Vegetarian Association; [pers.] My writing is an honest expression into words of universal feelings and emotions as they apply on a personal level. [a.] Howth, Co. Dublin, Ireland

O'CONNOR, SARAH E.
[b.] 10 June 1985, Southend; [p.] Alan O'Connor, Doreen O'Connor; [ed.] Belfairs Community College; [occ.] Student; [memb.] Blenheim Poetry Club; [oth. writ.] Just for personal pleasure; [pers.] I was inspired to write after I formed an interest in the history of World War II I will try and continue to find further inspirations.; [a.] Southend, Essex

O'DAOIRIN, PADRAIG
[pen.] Patrick O'Dea; [b.] 14 May 1940, Co. Wicklow, Ireland; [p.] Mark and Rosaleen Deering; [m.] Bernadette, 28 August 1972; [ch.] two boys: Adam and David; [ed.] 3 GCSE's. 'A' level and 4 'O's; [occ.] Hospital Administration (Medical Records' Officer or Archivist); [memb.] 'Fine Gael' political party, Lapsed Tenis Club; [oth. writ.] Poems, lampoons, limericks, but none of note or at least not sent for publication.; [pers.] 'Do unto others as they should do unto you.'

O'DONNELL, HUGH
[pen.] Hugh O'Donnell; [b.] 6 December 1970, Glasgow; [p.] Hugh and Margaret O'Donnell; [ed.] Notre Dame High School, University of Paisley, studying P Grad./Msc. Computing with O.U. at present; [occ.] Software Engineer, Kuaerner FSSL Ltd; [hon.] 1993 George Thompson award of Technology; [pers.] I lay down the deepness that comes from within.; [a.] Greenock, Renfrewshire

O'DWYER, LINDA
[pen.] Martha Rose; [b.] 31 May 1952, Brighton; [p.] Arnold Cliffe (D), Jean Cliffe; [m.] Tony O'Dwyer, 30 September 1972; [ch.] Anthony and Nicola; [ed.] Woodhouse Grammar School; [occ.] Doctor's Receptionist; [hon.] English Language Art; [pers.] I am blessed with the gift of words to give my feelings life but the greatest gift is to give of yourself.; [a.] London

O'GRADY, DERMOT
[pen.] Standish; [b.] 24 August 1926, Wicklow Town; [p.] Dermot O'Grady, Mary O'Grady; [m.] Pauline O'Grady, 23 June 1958; [ch.] John, Dermot, Anthony, Margaret, Paula, David; [ed.] "De La Salle", Christian Brothers, Primary and Secondary Schools, Wicklow Town, Rep. of Ireland; [occ.] Retired Engineering Technician University College Dublin; [memb.] National Library of Ireland, Amateur Musician Clubs, Local Art Club; [hon.] Award Winner 1993, 'Memory Make Comp.' 'Irish Times', Lit. Comp. Song Contest Winner; [memb.] Published book of poetry 1995 "Dublin, Wicklow, Songs, Poetry and the Craic." Many of my poems have been published in the newspaper and magazines. With some short storied in "Ireland's Eye", mag.; [pers.] My poetry has been mainly influenced by my early years in a seaside town with its magnificent sea and mountain scapes and colorful language of local characters.; [a.] Dublin, Rep. of Ireland

O'HARA, JENNY
[b.] 10 September 1982, Aylesbury; [p.] Yvonne O'Hara, James O'Hara; [ed.] I go to Buckingham Secondary; [occ.] At school; [memb.] (C.P.L.) Cats protection league; [oth. writ.] Written books, stories but I have not sent for publication.; [pers.] This is my first poetry competition. I have been taking up story writing but I thought I may be too young for publication at 14.; [a.] Buckinghamshire

O'NEILL, CAROLE
[pen.] Cass; [a.] Gateshead, Tyne and Wear

O'SHAUGHNESSY, CLAIRE
[b.] 7 November 1985, Dublin; [p.] Anne Marie and Joseph; [ed.] Primary School student Abbeylands, Navan Co Meath Ireland; [occ.] Student; [memb.] I am a member of Setarta Book club and Meath Co Library and I am poetry editor for school magazine; [hon.] I have won a couple of poetry competitions in my school and poems published in Local Library; [oth. writ.] Have written poetry as gifts for people I've written for school magazine also; [pers.] Teacher's rotary has achieved a very high standards in writing both in prose and poetry. From a very young age she has shown a flair and natural talent for language and writing; [a.] Navan, Co. Meath

OGUNSULIRE, MOJISOLA
[b.] 15/09/75, Lagos Island; [p.] Mr. & Dr.(Mrs.) Ogunsulire; [siblings} Oladipo, Oluwafemi, Oladunni, Ojuolape; [ed.] Corona Primary School, Gbagada Federal Gout Girls' College, Sagamu The University of Lagos (currently); [occ.] Student (undergraduate) Bsc. Accounting, University of Lagos; [memb.] AIESEC, University of Lagos; Amnesty International, University of Lagos; The Nigeria-Britain Association; [oth. writ.] Entry for the BBC 'African Performance' Radio Drama Writing Competition 1997; [a.] Lagos, Lagos State

OKOLO, COSMAS
[b.] 2 January 1971, Enugu; [p.] Mr. Simon Okolo and Mrs. Lydia Okolo; [ed.] final year undergraduate of the Faculty of Law, University of Nigeria; [occ.] student; [memb.] Law students Association, University of Nigeria; Christian Law Students Fellowship of Nigeria; The Student Christian Movement.; [oth. writ.] 'Letter to a Youth'—(an unpublished book), other poems/ plays/articles; [pers.] He who wants to get to the top, must learn to climb.; [a.] Enugu, Enugu State, Nigeria

OLIVER, JAMES HARRY
[pen.] James H. Oliver; [b.] 2 April 1942, NW London; [p.] Vera Oliver, James Oliver; [m.] Carol Oliver, 26 August 1978; [ch.] Christopher Anthony James, Diane Phyllis and Ivan James; [ed.] Lead Stone Hall Boarding School, Yorks Whitefields, Second yr NW London; [oth. writ.] I am at present compiling all my work into book form, entitled "My Anthology" The Window Of My Life.; [pers.] I find I can express myself more in writing what I feel, there for my works are a reflection of my life.; [a.] Milton Keynes, Bucks

OLIVER, JUNE
[pers.] Father son of an Austrian Musician, mother a Fothergill, family tree from 1066 includes eccentric John Fothergill, author of an Inn Keepers Diary. Family including self, travelled around the world. I am an inveterate reader and writer, including poetry. Trained as a graphologiar, giving psychological portraits of people.; [a.] Hurstpierpoint, W. Sussex

ORMROD, PETER
[pen.] William Story; [b.] 14 April 1956, Manchester; [m.] Joyce Ormrod; [ed.] De La Salle College Salford, Manchester; [occ.] Fund Raiser; [oth. writ.] Many poems, short stories, comedy T.V. scripts; [pers.] The enjoyment of any poem rests firmly on the shoulders of the reader - although some poems require weight training.; [a.] Wetherby, West Yorkshire

OSBORNE, EILEEN
[b.] 11 February 1949, Leytonstone; [p.] Douglas and Vera Moyler; [m.] Alan Osborne, 6 February, 1971; [ch.] Clare and Paul and David and Ian; [ed.] Leyton County Grammar School; [occ.] School Welfare Assistant; [hon.] 1st Dan Black Belt in Karate; [a.] Hornchurch, Essex

OSBORNE, JOAN RUTH
[b.] 21 July 1922, Dover, Kent; [p.] Ernest and Ethel Gasking; [m.] Ernest Stanley Osborne, 26 September 1986; [ed.] Convent School, French Order of Nuns - Des Ursulines - Dover; [occ.] Retired; [oth. writ.] "A Poem for Easter"; [pers.] I am deeply grateful for my parents who sincerely believed that education the best - illuminates the mind to lift it from the mundane to the rare.; [a.] Harrow, Middlesex

OSHOMAH, NICHOLAS O.
[pen.] Nick Adegwe-Oshomah; [b.] 28/04/59, Iyerekhu, via Auchi, Nigeria; [p.] Adegwe Oshomah, Mary Adegwe; [m.] Hilda Oshomah nee John, 19th September 1996; [ch.] Adonesi Don Oshomah; [ed.] Fatima College, Auchi; University of Benin, Benin City; [occ.] Customs Officer, Nigeria; Customs Service P/Harcourt, Nigeria; [memb.] Grail Movement of Nigeria; [oth. writ.] Assassins in Power (unpublished novel), The Deadly Assignment (unpublished novel) NB Both are manuscripts, several poems published in local magazines like Times International Mag. since 1980: "Furious Flood", "The Dry Season Bade Goodbye", "Scene of Transition - 1", "The Harmattan", "Nightmare of Night Noises", "Thirst for your Requiem", "Still in Chains", "Stillborn Vacation", "Rain Flakes", "The Wooer", etc.; [pers.] A well crafted, musically sounding poem gives me joy. I celebrate each beautiful poem I write with a sense of fulfillment. With my poems, I desire to consciously draw world attention to the sufferings of man, esp. in the third world. Thus, man's existence and nature generally are my main focus. So also the abstract. With my poetry, I hope to leave a lasting legacy in the sands of time - God willing.; [a.] Port Harcourt, Nigeria

OSUCH, PANEL
[pen.] Oliver Poley; [b.] 27 October 1970, Kielce, Poland; [ed.] Slowacki IV grammar, College of Foreign Languages, Lodz University; [occ.] English Teacher, Technical School No I, Kielce; [hon.] Award of Merit Certificate by World of Poetry, Sacramento, CA; [oth. writ.] Two poems published in "The World of English", Warsaw, lots unrecognized yet; [pers.] "Per aspera ad astra" I want to show that circumstances don't change people, they unmask them.; [a.] Kielce, Ul. H. Sawickiej, Poland

OTU, OBAL
[b.] 14 August 1979, Calabar, Nigeria; [p.] Akpan Otu, Obal Adiaha Otu; [ed.] University of Calabar Primary School, Federal Government Girls Secondary School, Calabar; [occ.] Just out of secondary school and waiting to enter university.; [memb.] Interact Club, Girls Power Initiative (GPI), Press Club.; [hon.] (award winner) Press Club of Federal Government School; [oth. writ.] Articles for School Magazines. Short stories and poems; [pers.] Poetry is a means of self-expression, and should convey both the positive and negative feelings of the author. "School Life" has resulted from jottings I made in 1991 in my first term in boarding school.; [a.] Calabar, Cross River State

OYEFUGA, MISS ODUNTAN
[B.] 21st Dec '76, Lagos, Nigeria; [p.] Rev. & Mrs. O. Oyefuga; [ed.] Queen's College, Lagos, University of Lagos, Lagos, Nigeria; [occ.] Student (third year Economics, University of Lagos); [memb.] AIESEC, Lagos, Nigeria; [oth. writ.] A Cry in the Night, My Wish, Rebirth of the World (All poems); [pers.] With God all things shall be possible.; [a.] Lagos, Nigeria

PAGE, TERRY
[pen.] Terry; [b.] 18 February 1957, Chatham; [p.] Fred Page and Dora Page; [m.] Teresa Page, 15 July 1983; [ch.] Emma and Christina; [ed.] Fort Luton Secondary Limited! But enjoyable; [occ.] Builder; [memb.] Gillingham South Road Flying Club; [hon.] City and Guilds, Advance City and Guilds; [oth. writ.] Many written. Few published; [pers.] I would rather participate is all of life vices, and "Live" life. Than to shun them all, and just exist.; [a.] Gillingham, Kent

PAGTANAC, MONIEN
[pen.] Monien; [b.] 25 February 1967, Philippines; [p.] Milagros Gimeno, Feliciano Pastanac; [ed.] A graduate of bossiness management; [occ.] domestic helper (Hong Kong); [oth. writ.] compiled several compositions of my own which weren't published yet, except for "Nowhere" (more than fifty, I think); [pers.] Poetry is every man's worlds from his soul—expressing one is more than enough to understand the nature of mankind.; [a.] San Jose, Antique

PANAYIOTOU, C.
[b.] 5 July 1976, Chelsea; [p.] Amin Badr and Mary Badr; [ed.] Hurlingham and Chelsea Secondary School, Westminster College; [occ.] Full time Student, studying Accounting at London Guildhall University; [hon.] I have attained various awards in arts and crafts, drama, first aid, swimming and sprinting. I have also achieved a BTEC (GNVQ) National Diploma in Business at Distinction Level.; [oth. writ.] None, although I am currently writing a series of poems which I hope to have published in the near future.; [pers.] My parents have always encouraged me to expand my creativity and it has always been an ambition to further my poetry by having some of my work published. My poems portray ideas, emotions and situations of love, life, hopes, and dreams.; [a.] Battersea, London

PARGETER, SHARON
[b.] 13 June 1970, Stirling, Scotland; [p.] Daniel Bridges McDonald, Jean McDonald; [m.] James Vincent Pargeter, 18 February 1995; [ch.] Cara Louise and Gordon Daniel; [occ.] Nursery School Teacher; [oth. writ.] Poetry, Children's Books Awaiting Recognition and publication; [pers.] I write about the ups and downs of reality that we endure as we travel along life's riddle-filled paths.; [a.] Grimsby, NE Lincolnshire

PARK, MAY
[pen.] May Park; [b.] 15 May 1942, Welling, Kent; [p.] Bill and Carrie Blowers; [m.] Divorced; [ch.] Michael and Jeffrey; [ed.] Secondary Modern Westwood School for Girls; [occ.] Warden Sheltered Housing.; [memb.] Speakers Club—two years, Spiritualist Church—nine years, belonged to a writers group for twelve years and edited annual magazine comedienne singer with Co. 80 Old Tyme Music Hall; [hon.] 'O' level English; [oth. writ.] Several poems and articles published in magazines and local papers 2nd prize in local writing comp. with story 'A need to belong' and several songs performed by local schools. National Winner 1997 Speech Contest; [pers.] I have 2 lovely grandsons Shaun and Ryan, for whom I have written prayers I am a working medium and get most of my writing through inspirations. I give talks using my own poems and stories to local clubs.; [a.] Dartford, Kent

PARKER, MARGARET MARY
[b.] 1 August, Widnes; [p.] William Colquitt and Mary Colquitt; [m.] Robert Parker, 5 April 1947; [ch.] Roberta Jennifer Ann; [ed.] Wade Deacon Grammar School Widnes; [occ.] Retired but weekend florist; [a.] Widnes, Cheshire

PARKER, SHIRLEY
[b.] 21 February 1953, Kelloe; [p.] Mathew Davison Cutty, Janette Cutty; [m.] Deceased; [ch.] Victoria Emma; [ed.] Bowburn Secondary Modern, Spennymoor West School; [occ.] Secretary; [pers.] My inspiration has always been Elizabeth Barrett Browning and feel very fortunate having the same birth place only half a mile away. I feel a very special affinity with this great lady.; [a.] Kelloe, Durham

PARRATT, MR. VICTOR
[pen.] Smith and Jones; [b.] 8 June 1946, Bowes; [p.] Deceased; [m.] Rosealeen Elizabeth, 10 July 1972; [ch.] Rachel Marie and Charles Edward; [ed.] Army Apprentices College Chepston, Gwent, Ryhope Secondary Modern; [occ.] Writer; [memb.] B.O.B.A. and R.E.A. and Anti Nazi League; [hon.] Freeman City of Winchester, I.Q. 154 British Army 1962, I.Q. 200 N.A.S.A. space research London, 1972; [oth. writ.] Letters to papers and poem in between laugh and a tear warning of the dangers of doing nothing about nazism.; [pers.] God exists, obey the ten commandments. Join the Anti Nazi League, 5 pounds life membership, inform on crime, God exists.; [a.] Sunderland, Tyne and Wear

PARRY, MRS. DORIS GERTRUDE
[pen.] (Yum-Yum) Lambeth Certificate; [b.] South London, Brixton; [p.] Mr. George Walter Eccles Hall, Jessie Caroline Gear; [ed.] My education was at Lyham Road School Brixton 5W2 London left school at (14) worked 15 yrs on London none transport (Piccadilly Circus); [occ.] Just a housewife; [memb.] Passed (2) exams (Pedestal - Bookkeeping and Lifts); [hon.] Certificate for writing from poets of Kent, 1 poem in "Passage To Time", 1 poem in "Mist of Time" another poem coming up in "Jewels of Imagination", "Mother"; [oth. writ.] Poems published (Love) have poems been read out on (Tele) and radio and letters also write short stories (Child's and Ghosts); [pers.] I just like writing I see or notice something interesting and I want to write it comes so easy to me won essay for writing about nature at school.; [a.] Amlweh, Anglesey

PARRY, RICHARD J.
[b.] 18 October 1974, Sunderland; [p.] Laura and John Parry; [m.] Sheri L. Parry, 29 April 1995; [ed.] Southmoor Comprehensive; [occ.] Radar operator in the Royal Navy; [memb.] I am a member off the fountain parts team in Northend Portsmouth; [hon.] 1 JSM for service in Northern Island; [oth. writ.] I am currently writing a mythical novel completely in rhyme; [pers.] Angels may guard over you but the only one who can save you is yourself.; [a.] Portsmouth, Hants

PARTRIDGE, EITHNE
[b.] 9 May 1925, Newbridge; [p.] Joseph and Evelyn Partridge; [m.] James Flanagan, 28 March 1951; [ch.] Three; [ed.] Teacher's Diploma in Domestic Science St Catherines, Dom. Sc. College, Blackrock Dublin 1947; [occ.] Retired; [hon.] Was awarded a place of John we Paherus writers workshop when he was writer in Residence at Trinity College - eight years ago.; [oth. writ.] One book "Without Reasonable Cause" not published! Various historical articles on local history.; [pers.] One of the hardest parts of writing is the ability to be totally honest.

PASZYN, HELEN
[b.] 25 February 1971, Barnet; [p.] Aleksander Paszyn, Zofia Kitzol; [ed.] Bishop Douglass School, Barnet College; [occ.] Independent Film Maker and Lifeguard, Dulwich Leisure Centre; [memb.] Institute of Amateur Cinematographers, Airborne Trampoline Club, Aquabatics Diving Club, Barnet Copthall Diving Club; [hon.] Top team '95 National Life Guarding Champion, Highly Commended Award at British Amateur Video Awards '96; [oth. writ.] Several poems published in various anthologies.; [pers.] Most inspiration comes from 'life' and people around me. Use this as a platform to understand the problems faced by young adults in the world today.; [a.] Finchley, London

PATCHING, BETTY
[b.] 4 January 1929, London; [p.] George Strickett, Louise Strickett; [m.] Stanley Patching, (Deceased 1991), 30 April 1955; [ed.] Elementary, Secondary Modern. Age 14 Commercial College, age 15 Employed by Coutts and Co. Bankers; [occ.] Retired; [memb.] Royal British Legion, briefly joined C.O.C.A. (Croydon Operatic and Dramatic Association); [oth. writ.] Approximately 35 other poems and one monologue. (Unpublished); [pers.] My late husband and I moved to Spain in 1977, where we lived in a Villa on a mountainside surrounded by Almond Orchards. Started writing poetry in 1983, but only when inspired by subject matter, not to order.; [a.] Reigate, Surrey

PATEL, JENNIFER
[pen.] Jennifer; [b.] 18 October 1982, London; [p.] Helen Apilado Arellano; [ed.] La Sainte Union Convent School; [occ.] Student; [hon.] High marks and certificates in Academic Achievements, came 1st Place in a Camden Drawing Competition; [pers.] I study hard to look forward to a successful life in the future.; [a.] Camden

PATEL, NEESHA
[b.] 6 February 1983; Warford; [p.] Jayanti C. Patel (deceased) and Gita Patel; [ed.] Bushey Meads School; [a.] Watford, Hertfordshire

PAUL, GORDON
[b.] 27 March 1922, Broxburn; [p.] David Fordyce Paul (Founder Member of College of Opticians); [m.] Elizabeth Mary Urquhart, 1920; [ch.] William James Nancy; [ed.] Kirkcaldy High School, Skerrys College; [occ.] Retired; [hon.] Honours in Chiropidy honoured for saving life by "Royal Humane Society". 1947 "Five Army Medals" plus army pension which is an honour.; [oth. writ.] As 'Monty' knew me chief scout of B.A. never had time to write my memoirs, of how I ordered the date of the Normandy landings.; [pers.] Trust in God, trust in her majesty you'll win! Then go and buy yourself a medal out of Woolworths! I told her that too when she never let me down! - Spy; [a.] Bilston, Midlothian

PAYNE, JIM
[b.] 30 January 1979, Hong Kong; [ed.] Frensham Heights School; [occ.] Student; [memb.] Su-Ha-Ri Karate School Rya Yachting Association; [oth. writ.] Various poems; [pers.] My ambition in life is to be a professional writer of poems, plays, short stories, novels and filmscripts. I find writing deeply fulfilling and derive great satisfaction from my poems.; [a.] Highgate, London

PEACOCK, PAMELA
[b.] 28 April 1934, Hayes, Middx; [p.] Enid and Laurie Taylor; [m.] Roy Peacock, 7 September 1957; [ch.] Marion, Christopher; [ed.] Teacher Training Coll Trent park taught art English drama laterly (of necessity) infants for 20 yrs.; [occ.] Retired; [memb.] Gemmological Association and Gem Testing Laboratory G.B.; [hon.] Distinction in diploma Gemmological finals 1971. Discovering emeralds to be quieter than infants spent the next 20 yrs working with gems.; [oth. writ.] None submitted (yet); [pers.] In order to find contentment. Realize you can change nothing. No-one else. You must change yourself.; [a.] Stourbridge, West Midlands

PEARCE, BELINDA
[b.] 16 March 1968, Hertfordshire; [p.] Averil Pearce and Stanley Pearce; [ed.] The Tendring High School, Frinton-on-Sea, Essex; [occ.] Casino Administrator; [pers.] I try to express, extremes of emotion and one's inner strength, which I admire and find a great source of inspiration and comfort.; [a.] Beckenham, Kent

PEARSON, COLLEEN
[b.] 19 November 1928, Mablethorpe; [p.] Gladys and Charles Jones; [m.] Ernest Pearson, 24 December 1946; [ch.] 3 sons, 2 daughters; [ed.] C of E Secondary Modern; [occ.] Retired; [memb.] Freelance; [hon.] "Merit"; [oth. writ.] Waltham Windmill International Library of Poetry, Newspaper Articles; [pers.] Enjoy writing in General, some people are born painters, my paintbrush is my pen.; [a.] Waltham, Grimsby, NE Lincolnshire

PEARSON, DEE
[b.] 20 July 1971, Wordsley; [ed.] Willingsworth High School, Tipton; [occ.] Waiter, cleaner!; [oth. writ.] 3 Poems, published by Anchor books; [pers.] Cherish the earth, for it is our mother! Just remove the blindfold of Society and look closer at reality!; [a.] Tipton, West Midlands

PEERS, MRS. VALERIE J. C.
[pen.] Valerie J. C. Peers; [b.] 27 February 1918, Cultra, Co Down; [p.] Doris and James Kemp; [m.] Roger E. Peers, 1 January 1966; [ch.] Dr. Nicholas Wagner and Philip Wagner; [ed.] Private Thornleigh, Tunbridge Wells, Boarding School, Green Banstead. Surrey; [occ.] Disabled, Paint, Draw Poetry; [memb.] Was Member Royal, Geographical Society, Swimming Coach; [hon.] Certificate for public speaking; [oth. writ.] The polders in Holland for entry to Roy: Geog. Society. (Land Reclamation); [pers.] Was member Kings fund "Emergency Bed Service". Did radar during war. Friendly - sense of humour. Creative. Sailing live in lovely nursing home.; [a.] Maidenhead, Berkshire

PEMBERTON, MR. CARL B.
[pen.] Carl B. Pemberton; [b.] 12 November 1957, Birmingham; [p.] Brian Pemberton, Margaret Pemberton; [m.] Susan Ann Pemberton; [ed.] Cherrywood Secondary Modern, Matthew Boulton Technical College; [hon.] Certificate in office studies - R.S.A.; [oth. writ.] None. This is the first time I have decided to enter a competition and put thought to paper.; [pers.] Poetry is true meaning, true thought, an expression, unlike a gift from within one's heart, is given.; [a.] Kidderminster, Worcs

PENDERS, MARSCHA
[b.] 4 June 1977, Bunde; [p.] John Penders, Netty Penders; [ed.] English Literature and Culture; [oth. writ.] Several poems, none of them have been published yet.; [pers.] Knowing that there are still many people who cannot express themselves freely, I hope that one day they will have the ability to find comfort and strength in my writings.; [a.] Bunde, Limburg, Holland

PENFOLD, CAROLINE MICHELE
[b.] 21 August 1970, Canterbury; [p.] Pamela Irene Smith; [m.] John Marc Filtness; [ch.] Bobby, Bonny, Billy, Cheyvonne, Cheyenne; [ed.] Woodlands High School; [occ.] Housewife and mother; [oth. writ.] Poem published in a book called "Welcome to the Jungle" by Anchor Books; [pers.] This poem is dedicated to the memory of my best friend Yvonne and to her parents Sheila and Graham, to my mum, sister Tarnya, Charlene, Bobby, Bonny, Billy, Cheyvonne and Cheyenne, and lastly to Paul whose constant perseverance made me take my poetry seriously which lead to getting my poetry published.; [a.] Gillingham, Kent

PENROSE, PAT
[b.] 3 October 1925, Swansea, Wales; [p.] Lily-May and Brinley-Charles Dorrell; [m.] Ray Penrose, 9 June 1949; [ch.] One daughter, Sue (now Dr. S. Owens Cambr. Uni.); [occ.] Retired Secretary/P.A.; [oth. writ.] Village Correspondent, Hitchin Gazette, Articles/Poems, school and staff magazines, North Herts; [pers.] The nursing of babies swathed in a traditional, fringes flannel shawl was a very old Welsh custom - handed down through generations. A form of bonding rarely seem today. After the sad death of my mother, when it became necessary to return to the silent, family hone to dispose of precious possessions, the shawl was retrieved. It evoked as hers, who gave so much and asked so little in return.; [a.] Swansea, Glamorgan

PERNER, MATTHIAS
[b.] 11 September 1971, Hannover, Germany; [p.] Karl-Heinz, Christel; [ed.] George-Buchner Gymnasium/Letter University of Hannover, University of Bristol; [occ.] Student of Modern Languages; [pers.] Words help to think without them, My poetry helped me through my troubled years. And I thank my family and friends for all I here care and help through those days.; [a.] Hannover, Germany/NDS

PERREN, LINDA EDITH
[b.] 28 February 1942, Eastleigh; [m.] 27 October 1962; [ch.] Two; [ed.] Secondary Modern, plus 3 yr. college course in Nursing; [occ.] Retired nurse due to injury at work; [hon.] SEN ENB Certificate; [oth. writ.] Only just started since bereavement, as very therapeutic; [pers.] My husband died suddenly in July 1996 and as a family we decided to scatter his ashes in a small fishing village "Beesands in South Devon, where we had spent all our free time over many years. This inspired me to write "Golden Man and brought some comfort as a lasting memorial.; [a.] Eastleigh, Hampshire

PERRY, CAROLINE
[b.] 8 May 1948, Surrey; [m.] John Perry; [ch.] Four children and Eight Grandchildren; [ed.] Left School at 15 to become a hairdresser always been a frustrated poet and writer; [occ.] Still a hairdresser; [oth. writ.] Several poems published in similar anthologies and local newspaper. A short story to be broadcast on radio Kent soon and another in women's weekly magazine.; [pers.] Although most of my work has a personal statement behind it and is often based on think of my poems as humorous. This I feel is very important for a healthy life.; [a.] Folkestone, Kent

PERRY, LOMSE
[b.] 17 July 1980, Cheltenham; [p.] Ian Robert Perry, Katherine Lindsay Perry; [ed.] (Currently at) Dean Close School Cheltenham; [a.] Cheltenham, Gloucestershire

PETERS, CHARMAINE
[b.] 22 November 1974, Saint Helena Island; [p.] Hazel Youde, Ishmael Stevens; [ed.] Longwood Junior, Secondary Selective, Prince Andrew School; [occ.]

Nanny; [hon.] Duke of Edinburgh Bronze and Silver, RSA, Computer Literacy GCSE, Keyboardng, English Literature and Language-History-Science-Maths St Helena Day 1983 - Poetry award, St Helena Childcare Award; [oth. writ.] St Helena Day 1983, poetry competition - poem entitled 'The Place I Like Best'.; [pers.] May those who read my poetry, understand it and enjoy it. I like to thank all my friends and relatives who has encouraged me in the past to write poetry. God bless.; [a.] London

PHILLIPS, SHARRON
[b.] 21 August 1939, London; [p.] Nathan and Dorothy Cashman; [m.] Norman Phillips, 8 June 1959; [ch.] Mark, Karen, David, Eli; [ed.] Henrietta Bamett School; [occ.] Company Director (Hairdressing Company); [memb.] Fine Arts NADFAS, MEA (Hairdressing Employees Association) WWF, RSPB; [oth. writ.] I have written only for family and friends to celebrate and comfort.; [pers.] I try to give comfort and pleasure to others, to share their joys and sorrows and to always give hope for tomorrow.; [a.] Beaconsfield, Bucks

PHIPPS, MRS. LORRAINE SUSAN
[b.] 20 November 1960, Weymouth; [p.] Robert Everest, Maureen Riggs; [m.] Ian Phipps, 27 June 1987; [ch.] Jade Cora Parsonage, Dawn Katie Parsonage; [ed.] Weymouth Grammar School; [occ.] I work at an animal sanctuary; [memb.] Legion of Dreams, Things That Should Not Be; [oth. writ.] Poem "Midnight Glory" published in "The Other Side of the Mirror" 1996; [pers.] This poem is dedicated to my late grandfather, Mr William Everest, and to my husbands mother, Mrs. Mary Phipps, who plays as loving a role in my children's lives.; [a.] Stadhampton, Oxfordshire

PICKLES, MARY
[b.] 25 April 1912, Denton; [p.] Fred and Edith Barlow; [m.] Samuel Pickles, 4 December 1978 (Divorced); [ed.] Duke Street Council School Denton, Denton Technical School; [occ.] Retired; [hon.] Certificates for Dressmaking and Millenery; [a.] Blackpool, Lancashire

PIKE, ROSALIE
[b.] 20 May 1979, Chertsey; [p.] Lionel Pike, Jennifer Pike; [ed.] St. Cuthbert's Upton House School, Sir William Perkins's School, Strode's College; [occ.] Student (6th Form); [memb.] Church Choir; [hon.] A.V.C.M. (Hons) in speech and drama; [oth. writ.] Two of my poems have been published as part of a song cycle, 'encircled by sea', music by Lionel Pike; [pers.] My writing is influenced mainly by my love of nature in all it's forms, and particularly by the sea. By which I have always been fascinated. I try to convey the beauty of nature, but also its less gentle side. As in "cold comfort".; [a.] Egham, Surrey

PILKINGTON, MRS. FLORENCE
[b.] 10 December 1906, Higher Walton; [p.] James and Florence Pilkington; [m.] William Pilkington; [ch.] Two daughter, greatgrandmother of seven, four boys and three girls; [ed.] Elementary in the Village School, All Saint Higher Walton; [occ.] I am 90 years old I was a Cotton Weaver in the local mill; [hon.] I am at present writing for an housing association, I do and quarterly poem for the Housing news. This is the new process housing association Leyland. Lancashire, this week I was presented with a Bouquet and had my photo tapes.; [oth. writ.] I have had success writing to papers such as the Lancashire evening past and in competitions in local papers.; [pers.] I have been content to write just for an hobby, I have written poems since I was seven years old I love the poems of Thomas Hood and wordswork.; [a.] Preston, Lancashire

PINDER, STEPHANIE
[b.] 23 February 1972, Chelmsford; [p.] Michael Pinder, Christine Pinder; [ed.] Boswells Comprehensive School; [occ.] Fingerprint Support Officer; [oth. writ.] I have a book full of unpublished work that I keep like a diary and until now I have never considered releasing any of them; [pers.] My writing of this poem and many others were greatly influenced by my

first long term serious relationship and the hurt and upset that goes with a final goodbye.; [a.] Chelmsford, Essex

PITTARD, MR. K. H.
[b.] 14 July 1933, Seven Sisters; [p.] William Pittard, Deborah Pittard; [m.] Lilian Pittard, 22 September 1956; [ch.] Karen, Wayne; [ed.] Neath Technical College; [occ.] Retired; [a.] Swansea, West Glamorgan

PLATT, MARGARET
[b.] 28 August 1934, London; [p.] Res Hale, Doris Hale; [m.] Ernie Platt, 22 November 1975 (2nd); [ch.] Carol and Ian, Granddaughter Amy; [memb.] Member of Cheshunt Chimes Handbell Ringers and Member of the Handbell Ringers of Great Britain; [hon.] In the past 4 1/2 yrs in Cheshunt Red Cross 3 Certificates Passed; [oth. writ.] Several poems published in separate books and one printed in local paper The Cheshunt and Waltham Mercury.; [pers.] I always loved poetry by William Lordsworth he put such feelings into his writings.; [a.] Cheshunt, Herts

PLAYLE, NORMA
[pen.] Norma Playle; [b.] 25 March 1938, London; [p.] Evelyn and George Wilson; [m.] 1st marriage 13 August 1960, 2nd marriage 5 May 1973; [ch.] Three, 2 daughters and 1 son; [ed.] Priestmead Primary Harrow, Belmont High School Harrow, moved to Croydon went to Tavistock High School; [occ.] Advice Bureau, Part Time - Advice Worker and Clerical; [memb.] Other than Riva Bingo (well who knows if it will be lucky) and the Library; [hon.] C.V. for Credit Union Management, C.V. for Counselling, Open University Award, working with the Elderly; [oth. writ.] A play entitled "Take Three Girls", for a competition for TV, made the finals. Poem for "C.A.B." also one for "Carer's Centre" and one about "Credit Unions". All accepted for their "AGM's; [pers.] Poetry is a thing I love and enjoy, I write a verse in all my cards (X'mas, birthdays, anniversaries and all special types. People and friends all wait for their card to see if they have a verse.; [a.] Wallsend, North Tyneside

POLAND, DEAN
[b.] 20 April 1973, Liverpool; [p.] Brian and Lynda Poland; [ed.] University of Greenwich; [hon.] BA (Hons) Theology; [pers.] To establish a church (culture) of imaginitive tradition, that both reveals and transforms.; [a.] Liverpool, Merseyside

POLAND, LORETTE
[pen.] Lorette Poland; [b.] 5 October 1944, South Africa; [p.] Dr. and Mrs. John Durr; [m.] P. Poland, 27 March 1969; [ch.] Daughter; [ed.] Matriculated in South Africa, attended St Cyprians and Rhenish School; [occ.] Housewife; [memb.] Kelvin Grove, Country Club, have lived in England for 20 year Royal Ocean Rock Club; [oth. writ.] Various articles for local magazines. I have always written poetry but privately, I write hundreds.; [pers.] Being fluent in appearance as well I like to prayed African feel in the English language I love John Ryamin.; [a.] Cape Town, South Africa

POLDRUGO, ELLEN
[b.] 16 July 1967, Germany; [p.] Irene and Luciano Poldrugo; [ed.] Comprehensive and Grammar School (A-Level)-Germany.; [occ.] Hotel Business since 1986, work experience in Germany, England and Switzerland, Floor housekeeper at Mandarin Oriental Hyde Park - Knightsbridge, London; [memb.] Member of the Roman Catholic Church; [pers.] Taking the courage to explore an unknown country on my own despite approaching it full of prejudice and fear was the main inspiration for "my visit to earth" being rather timid and reserved by nature the inviting warm welcome, the courtesy and respect as well as the countless opportunities offered to me there were a great motivation and gave me confidence we developing talents of mine such as painting or writing. The "Stranger" beside myself came to existence beyond the human race and meant no harm, just visited.; [a.] London, Borough of Ealing

POLLARD, MICHELLE
[b.] 3 September 1974, Eastbourne; [p.] Graham and Emelia Pollard; [ed.] Hailsham Community College studied to a level standard; [occ.] Nursery Nurse, Pooh's Nursery School; [memb.] MJ News International Care for the Wild (I adopted and orphan Rhino four years ago); [hon.] A levels in history and English Literature, City of Guilds (and NVQ) in Caring Stage 1 - British Sign Language; [oth. writ.] Four poems published in anthologies by "Poetry Now". Two entered in amateur competitions. Historical manuscript submitted for publication.; [pers.] It is better to find a way to express your innermost feelings rather than spend the same time convincing others those feelings do not exist.; [a.] Hailsham, East Sussex

POLLITT, BRENDAN CARLTON
[pen.] Raven; [b.] 22 October 1974, Hannover, Germany; [p.] Raymond Pollitt, Teresa Pollitt; [m.] Katherine Pollitt, 14 February 1996; [ch.] None; [ed.] Sir Frank Markham Secondary, Milton Keynes College Leadenhall; [occ.] Merchandiser, House of Fraser; [memb.] The poetry Society Wargames Society; [oth. writ.] In excess of over 100 other poems, as yet unpublished; [pers.] Good and evil, which groups do they cover, and can you easily recognize one from the other. Taken from its opposite, could what remains exist.; [a.] Milton Keynes, Buckinghamshire

POOLE, HEATHER
[b.] 23 September 1952, Bristol; [p.] John Harris, Janet Harris; [m.] David Poole, 20 March 1971; [ch.] Jo-Anne; [ed.] Hartcliffe Secondary School, Brunel College; [occ.] Slimming Consultant for Slimming World; [oth. writ.] Numerous poems. Me being the only poem I have ever entered.; [pers.] I read my poem to members of my class. I believe it makes them understand their feelings more, and to know that they are not alone, because I too feel the same.; [a.] Bristol, Avon

PORRITT, MARGARET ANNE
[b.] 19 February 1942, York; [p.] Margaret N. E. Hewson, Leonard Hewson; [m.] Lt. Col. (Retd) Anthony James Porritt, 24 March 1962; [ch.] James Ivan, Dawn Margaret; [ed.] Mill Mount Grammar, York; [occ.] House wife; [pers.] I am inspired by all aspects of the natural world, especially the flora and never cease to be amazed by the most minute 'patterns' of life. I also Abhor the destruction of this planet by mankind.; [a.] Westbury, Wiltshire

PORT, MRS. JOYCE EVELYN
[b.] 16 January 1928, Reigate, Surrey; [p.] Mrs. and Mr. F. G. Clark; [m.] Major (QM) Sandy Port (deceased 7 July 1990), married 26 July 1948; [ch.] Trevor and Barry Port; [ed.] St. John's School Redhill, Surrey; [occ.] Widow, Retired; [oth. writ.] The MayFlower - (Poem), 'Joyce's Jolly Jotting's In The Bunde, North Germany - Weekly Army Magazine; [pers.] 'Ode To Dalmatia'. Inspired by bird-song and beauty of the isle of Korcula-Yugoslavia, while walking with my beloved late husband Sandy.; [a.] Horley, Surrey

PORTER, SUSIE ROSE
[pen.] Susan Rose Porter; [b.] 3 October 1978, Aldershot, England; [p.] Sandy Porter, David Porter; [ed.] Presently attending Merrist Wood College for Land Based Industry.; [occ.] Student; [pers.] I love to write poems, they reflect how you feel and release emotions you are unable to express otherwise.; [a.] Farnham, Surrey

POSTLETHWAITE, MRS. ROSEMARY L.
[b.] 29 January 1930, Greenwich; [p.] Lilian and Stanley Jones; [m.] George Henry, October 1955; [ch.] Gaibria; [ed.] Secondary School, Sydenham County, Interference because of Evacuation during war; [occ.] Retired; [memb.] Spiritualist Church, Eltham, London; [oth. writ.] Other verses, spiritualist messages, which I regularly receive; [pers.] I lost my memory, when I was a young woman, one has to forever, with God's help so, I am still receiving my messages about God's Act of divinity, which will be preceded by God's Justice. Just a little more darkness of evil, to be out shore by God's light of Divinity.; [a.] Eltham, London

POTTER, JENNIFER M.
[b.] 3 January 1946, Nottingham; [m.] Tony, 1968; [ch.] Jeremy - 24, Elizabeth - 22; [ed.] Nottingham University; [occ.] Teacher/Business Woman; [hon.] B.Sc Hons Geog and Geology; [a.] Nafferton, East Yorkshire

POULTER, SHELLEY
[b.] 26 May 1972, Enfield; [p.] Prof. L. W. and Mrs. J. Poulter; [ed.] St. Albans Girls School, University of Westminster; [occ.] Immunologist, Royal Free Hospital School of Medicine; [pers.] I dedicate this poem to my Mother and Father, my Partner Dudley, my dear friends Caroline, Clare and Ian and most Especially my sister Lara - my greatest inspiration.; [a.] Saint Albans, Herts

POVEY, VINCE
[b.] 10 March 1973, Wolverhampton; [p.] Paul Povey, Christine Povey; [ed.] Bradon Forest School Purton Wilts; [occ.] Group Purchasing and Quality Administrator; [memb.] British Motorcycle Federation (BMF), British Unidentified Flying Object Research Association (BUFORA); [oth. writ.] Several poems for family and friends - mainly for amusement; [pers.] Do not be discouraged of being an individual by people who are not and do not become discouraged from taking risks by people who never do.; [a.] Cricklade, Wiltshire

POWELL, ERICA GEORGINA
[pen.] Erica Stanton-Powell; [b.] 15 January 1963, Swansea; [p.] Marlene and Peter Stanton; [m.] Geoffrey William John Powell, 30 March 1988; [ch.] One (Sarah Louise Powell); [ed.] Cefn Hengoed Comp., left school at sixteen to become a professional musician; [occ.] Training to become a horse riding instructor; [oth. writ.] "A Walk On The Light Side", short story, submitted for a Cambridge I.T. certificate in word processing.; [pers.] If only mankind were as noble, and loyal as a Welsh cob, or a golden retriever, then life would truly be heaven on earth.; [a.] Swansea, West Glamorgan

POWELL, MICHAEL E.
[b.] 12 July 1976, Swansea; [p.] Edward Powell, Irina Powell; [ed.] Penyrheol Comprehensive School, Gorseinon College; [occ.] Sales Assistant, Sports Division, Swansea; [memb.] Mountain Ash Poetry Club; [hon.] Chartered Poet with the New Atlantis University of Life; [oth. writ.] One poem published in the next Mountain Ash Poetry Club anthology entitled "And Here It Begins".; [pers.] An imagination is a set of wings which any person can use to fly.; [a.] Swansea, West Glamorgan

PRATT, KENNETH
[pen.] Blaze; [b.] 8 March 1969, London; [p.] Chrispin D. M. Pratt, Jasmin M. Pratt; [m.] Joanne Shand; [ed.] Colchester Boys' High School, Colchester Gilberd Grammar, Colchester Institute, London Guildhall University; [occ.] Freelance Computer Graphic Designer; [memb.] Book Club Associates, Writers' Society, Musicians' Union; [hon.] A.L.C.M. (Associate of London College of Music) - Diploma in Music, Duke of Edinburgh Gold Award; [oth. writ.] A collection of inspirational thoughts and quotations, several poems ranging from politics to romanticism; [pers.] I always endeavour to embrace the inspirational message of peace, love & harmony in my writings. [a.] West Norwood, London

PRESTON, IRIS L.
[b.] 30 September 1923, Cheshunt; [p.] Deceased; [m.] Jack O. Preston, 26 July 1947; [ch.] One Son; [ed.] Elementary; [occ.] Housewife; [hon.] 2 poems published; [a.] Cheshunt, Herts

PRINGLE, ELIZABETH
[b.] 7 June 1950, Newmains; [p.] James Donnelly, Lex Donnelly; [m.] John, 7 March 1975; [ch.] Karen, Darren, Lisa and Elaine; [ed.] Dalkeith High School, Telford College, Health studies, Lothian College of Nursing; [occ.] Support worker; [memb.] Midlothian Labour Party; [hon.] My honours are better than any letters I work with men and women who require my support, as in my Wee poem. It's an honour to have them in my life; [pers.] The lack of verbal communication shouldn't be the lack of holistic care; [a.] Dalkeith, Midlothian

PRIOR, MS. JILL
[b.] 24 June 1960; [p.] Geoffrey Walter Stephen and Amy Winifred Margaret Goodwin; [occ.] Project Leader for Abbey National PLC; [hon.] Certificate in Management Studies, ISO 9000 registered internal auditor, MAAT pt. one accountancy exams; [pers.] This is my first attempt at poetry. Adopted as a baby, I could not have wished for more loving and attentive parents. Following my father's death, this poem expresses my feelings, and I wish he could be here to read it.; [a.] Ruislip, Middlesex

PRITCHARD, LORRAINE
[pen.] Teresa Green; [b.] 1 November 1952, Hereford; [m.] James Barry Pritchard, 6 October 1973; [ch.] Caroline, Mary, David; [ed.] Kingstone Secondary Modern, Hereford; [occ.] Housewife; [memb.] Radnorshire Association for the Disabled; [oth. writ.] Unsuccessful story for the Brecon and Radnor Express.; [pers.] I am just an ordinary housewife, and I come from Knighton Mid Wales - and the countryside inspired me.; [a.] Knighton, Powys

PRITCHARD, TONIA ELIZABETH
[b.] 11 January 1980, Dudley; [p.] Mrs. Sharon Lesley Coffield; [ed.] Grace Mary Primary School, Warley High School; [pers.] I enjoy writing both songs and poetry. I long to build a career a songwriter or poet, though my work is yet to be discovered. I hope the public will gain as much pleasure reading my poem, as I did in writing it.; [a.] Trividale, Warley, West Mids

PULLEN, MRS. ENA FRANCES
[b.] 11 March 1932, Isle of Man; [p.] Mr. W. A. and Mrs. E. Hornbuckle; [m.] Deceased, 7 November 1951; [ch.] Two sons; [oth. writ.] Hidden Feelings (Published) by Anchor Books Apl. '96 (Inspirations from the Midlands)

QUINN, JEANNE
[pen.] Jennie Johns; [b.] 17 June 1932, London; [p.] Albert and Ellen Guinchard; [m.] John Anthony Quinn, 7 March 1953; [ch.] Glynis, John, Gary, Ian; [ed.] Very varied went to over 42 different schools. As my father was always moving from farm to farm.; [occ.] Sales Person; [hon.] Won The Brixton Festival for poems called "My Neighbour" which was dedicated to my dear friend Tom Goldsmith, my daughters father-in-law; [oth. writ.] Several poems published in magazines. Having started to write from age of 12 - I have written over 400 poems, plus short stories.; [pers.] I like to write poems with a meaning or a message. Poems that reflect beauty. I get inspiration from places and people and flowers. Byron is my favourite poet.; [a.] London

QUINN, MARY
[b.] 6 January 1916, West Clare; [p.] Ned Kennelly, Nona Frawley; [m.] Alfie Quinn, R.I.P.; [ch.] Michael, Gerard, Malachy; [ed.] Michael, U. C. Galway Gerard - Harvard U.S. Malachy - T. C. Dubblin and Language School - Peking; [occ.] "The Waiting Game"; [oth. writ.] Un-published poems; [pers.] I shall try to inspire before I expire; [a.] Galway, Galway, Ireland

QUINN, NICOLA
[b.] 12 December 1975, Ireland; [p.] Fons and Carmel Quinn; [occ.] Student; [pers.] Imagination and dreams are what find many people.; [a.] Claremorris, Mayo

RAI, MRS. DOROTHY
[b.] 17 January 1959, Trichur, Kerala, India; [p.] Late Kamal Krishna, Annie Chatterji; [m.] Mr. Vincent Rai, 5 April 1983; [ch.] Two sons Cyril (12 yrs), Clement (8 yrs); [ed.] M.A., B.Ed, M. Phil (English) School - Girls High School, Allahabad College - A.N.D. College, Kanpur University - Kanpur University; [occ.] Lecturer in English, Christ Church College - Kanpur; [memb.] 1) M.L.A. New York, 2) American Studies Research Center, Hyderabad, 3) Inner Wheel Club (Hon) Kanpur; [hon.] 1) Best Student - Rotary Club, 2) Best Teacher - Rotary Club, 3) Semi-Finalist - 1996 International Open Amateur Poetry Competition, 4) Prizes for highest marks in the University in a) M.A., b) B.Ed c) M. Phil., 5) Vice Chancellor's Gold Medal for 1st position in the University M.A. 1988; [oth. writ.] 1) Several Poems on Women, Faith Hymns, Scripture in Verse, published

in local and international magazines. 2) Articles on Christian Apologetics; [pers.] I have an unswerving faith in Jesus Christ and try through my writing and poems to help my readers lead joyous fulfilled lives inspite of the traumas inflicted on them by society; [a.] Kanpur, Uttar Pradesh, India

RAISON, MRS. JOSEPHINE
[b.] 5 September 1933, Mile End, London; [p.] Deceased; [occ.] Retired Nurse (OAP); [oth. writ.] Several Poems published in Church magazines.; [pers.] My aim is to uplift and sustain those finding their faith has grown weak, and to see the goodness of God in all things! Romans 8:28 "all things work together for good to them that love God"!; [a.] Plaistow, London

RALPH, MARIE
[b.] 7 May 1968, Rustington, W Sussex; [p.] Deceased; [ed.] St Margarets Convent Midhurst West Sussex. Royal Holloway University Egham; [occ.] Student (Theatre and Drama); [oth. writ.] Poetry Published in RSPCA Magazine. Article printed in horse and hound magazine; [pers.] I wish to dedicate this poem to P.T. my true love who taught me the joy of love of love and the misery and english of abandonment.; [a.] London

RAVENSCROFT, FRANK
[b.] 17 June 1922, Preston; [p.] William and Alice Ravenscroft; [m.] Olga Claire Ravenscroft (Deceased), 11 May 1946; [ch.] Five; [occ.] Retired; [oth. writ.] Numerous poems and works of prose. Novels and manuscripts. Illustrated children's books; [pers.] My writings reflect my environment and life in general. Sentiment and reality.; [a.] Leyland, Preston, Lancashire

RAWLINGS, JAYNE
[b.] 1 July 1964, Birmingham; [oth. writ.] Another poem published in a National anthology. Book to be published, mid 1997, about the reality of coping with 'cot death'.; [pers.] All my published writings have been dedicated to my daughter Louise, who died from cyst death at only nine weeks and four days old.; [a.] Belhelvie, Aberdeen

RAWLINGS, MRS. ROSE
[b.] 19 February 1935, Crookham, Hants; [p.] Mabel and George Wooldridge; [m.] Thomas Rawlings, 27 June 1959; [ch.] Paul and Michael Rawlings; [ed.] Comprehensive School, Fleet; [occ.] Housewife; [memb.] Guider for the Brownies; [hon.] A painting shown in a national art show for the Sunday People House Competition (1972); [oth. writ.] A poem in a book for Christians two more might be published.; [pers.] Two and a half years ago, I stood over my sons body he squeezed my hand and came back to life after a week. He is doing well now, I find life to any person, animal, or plant. Very special and how wonderful God's works are, so I have started to write.; [a.] Tadley, Hants

REASON, TONY
[pen.] T. Reason; [b.] 30 September 1961, Aylesbury, Bucks; [p.] Bill Reason, Ivy Reason; [m.] Carol Bleaney, 14 February 1987; [ch.] Christopher; [occ.] Freelance Writer; [oth. writ.] Several articles on various subjects for International Company.; [pers.] I believe that poetry should reflect experience. As experiences change so does my poetry. My preferred subjects are the passage of time and nature.; [a.] Dunstable, Beds

REDFORD, VICTORIA LOUISE
[b.] 2 December 1977, Lancaster; [p.] Mr. and Mrs. Redford (John, Jean); [ed.] Ripley St. Thomas C.E. School; [occ.] Professional Dancer; [hon.] International Dance Teachers Association (IDTA) Grade Awards For Ballet, Tap, Stage, Gym and Modern; [pers.] I write for me. The process of writing releases my feeling and helps me to see and helps me to see clearly what's happening in my life; [a.] Morecambe, Lancashire

REES, STEPHEN
[pen.] Stephen Rees; [b.] 8 October 1976, Morriston, S. Wales; [p.] Mrs. Sarah Christine Powell; [ch.] One son, Jacob Scott Rees; [ed.] Studied at Bryngwyn Comprehensive School and Graig Tertiary College;

[occ.] Laboratory Technician; [hon.] This is the first piece of work I have submitted for external review; [oth. writ.] Many poems and short stories; [pers.] I hope that through my writing I can stir some thoughts that would other wise have been ignored, and in doing so sharing a small part of my world with everyone who reads it.; [a.] Llanelli, Carmarthenshire

REEVE, TREVOR
[b.] 7 July 1947, Cambridge; [p.] Claude Reeve, Miriam Reeve; [m.] Christine Reeve, 16 October 1971; [ch.] Karen, Paul and Claire; [ed.] Keysoe Secondary Modern; [occ.] Sales/Purchasing Clerk; [oth. writ.] Other poems published by International Library of Poetry; [pers.] Always remember to step back and think before you speak out and regret.; [a.] Kempston, Beds

REID, CLIVE
[b.] 1 February 1958, Balham; [p.] Sylvia Reid and Ovan Reid; [ch.] Jamie, Chanel and Morgan; [ed.] Stepney Green Comprehensive School and East Ham Technical College; [occ.] Carpenter; [oth. writ.] I have other writings but as of yet I have not put them forward for publishing.; [pers.] It would be nice to be influenced by great writes, but I am not. What I am influenced with is the good in people and hopefully when I put pen to paper it comes from the sole.; [a.] Hornchurch, Essex

REID, ELIZABETH
[pen.] Silver Birch; [b.] 16/08/29, Crick; [p.] Mary & Jack Collinson; [ed.] Ordinary; [occ.] Retired; [hon.] Editor's Award for poem, in Voices on the Wind; [oth. writ.] Poem published, in the path of a poet (Motorway Madness by Silver Birch); [pers.] I think to be able to write poems, you must feel for people, nature, animals, and notice all things around.; [a.] Hinckley, Leics

REID, HELEN M.
[pen.] Aunt Nellie; [b.] 28 March 1911, Ayr; [p.] Helen Dickson and George Muir; [m.] Alexander Reid, 25 November 1933; [ed.] Ayr Grammer School 1916-1931, Hendon Technical College 29/6 Ct - 28 July 1953; [occ.] Housewife; [hon.] County Certificate in Crafts Botany pass 17th June 1960

REID, VALERIE
[b.] 28 July 1954, Kilmarnock; [p.] Alastair Irving and Patricia McCrone; [m.] William Reid (Deceased), 21 April 1976; [ch.] Alastair William and Lorna Patricia; [ed.] Grammar Primary, Kilmarnock Academy, Langside College, Glasgow; [occ.] Domestic Engineer; [pers.] 'Moving on' is dedicated to my family and friends who helped me during my late husband's illness and in my bereavement.; [a.] Kilmarnock, East Ayrshire

RHODES, JACQUELINE DEWAR
[pen.] Jacqueline D. Rhodes; [b.] 3 July 1942, Dundee; [p.] James Gordon Forbes, Flora Forbes; [m.] John Michael Rhodes, 12 December 1964; [ch.] Gillian, Susan and Jane; [ed.] Dundee - followed by RGN, SCM; [occ.] Housewife - formerly a Nursing Sister/Midwife; [memb.] Member of children 1st, (RSSPCC), Policy and Resources Committee and Chairman of the Local Group; [occ.] Hospital Medal - Mary Field Hospital, Dundee, Top Nursing Award on Competition of Training, presented 11/12/63; [oth. writ.] Have only been submitting poetry for publication in the past year and am delighted at the large number of my poems being published in poetry books and anthologies.; [pers.] Have love the poetry of Dylan Thomas since studying him for higher English many years ago. I think the best Poetry comes from the heart and is seasoned by life's experiences. You reap what you sow, do you sow wisely.; [a.] Perth, Perthshire

RHODES, VICTORIA
[b.] 6 May 1980, Bradford; [p.] Stanley and Catherine Rhodes; [ed.] Ripon City School; [occ.] Pupil at Ripon City School; [memb.] Y.M.C.A. Red Triangle Drama School; [oth. writ.] Poems published in Inspirations from Yorkshire; [pers.] My outlook on life seems very pessimistic through my poetry. But I am a very optimistic young woman. I am not influenced by other poets. But I am encouraged by the people I know. Especially Mrs. Anne Towse.; [a.] Ripon, North Yorks

RICHARDSON, PHYLLIS
[pen.] Belinda Boston, Felix S. Greaves; [b.] 24 December 1950, Canklow, Rotherham; [p.] Elsie (Nee Poskitt), Seth Greaves; [m.] Alan Richardson, 2 April 1968, David Pimperton, 5 September 1978; [ch.] Deborah Jayne, Stephan Alan, Garry, Julie Michala, Jeffrey David, Victoria Isabell and Vincent Weslie Seth; [ed.] South Grove Comprehensive Rotherham College of Further Education, Wentworth College, Stainborough; [occ.] Volunteer 'Tuck Shop' Manageress - Playscheme Organizer - Compiler of Local News Magazine 'Canklow C.A.N.'; [hon.] S.Y.O.C. Credits for Desk Top Publishing Money Management, Playscheme Organizing 'So you want to work with young persons'. Came 2nd in a P.G. Tips Painting Comp - at South Grove School in 1963/64; [oth. writ.] "The Oxwell Rescue". A short story for children, wrote for Jeffrey, whilst trying to set him to sleep! Essay's, Editorials, Stories, Poems in local C.A.N. Magazine anthology of small poems. Aladdin Pantomime for local drama group. 'Satan's Slave' - ongoing autobiography - ongoing.; [pers.] I have been married twice first to Alan Richardson, 2 April 1968 then to David Pimperton - 5 September 1978 both ended in divorce - writing poems helped me through these difficult times - now I can reflect and learn from my earlier attempts whilst showing others that there is hope and release from writing.; [a.] Rotherham, South Yorkshire

RISDALE, MRS. CAROL ANNE
[pen.] Mrs. Carol Anne Risdale; [b.] 19 December 1950, Bristol; [p.] Clifford and Ruby Hopes; [m.] Roger Risdale, 27 June 1968; [ch.] Roger and Michael; [ed.] Hanham RD for Girls; [occ.] Domestic and Housewife; [memb.] Kingswood Royal British Legion; [oth. writ.] 2 poems published in Arrival Press; [pers.] Poems are a joy to read they are inspiration of life.; [a.] Kingswood, Bristol

RISPOLI, MRS. DONNA RITA
[b.] 13 November 1966, Balham; [p.] Mr G. E. Hersey, Mrs. R. E. Fagence; [m.] Mr. Antony Rispoli, 27 July 1988; [ch.] Toni Rispolt and Danielle Rispoli; [ed.] English - CSE3 Maths - CSE4, RECSE4 Typing and office practice CSE3 Social Studies CSE? 3/4; [occ.] Civil staff for the Metropolitan Police; [oth. writ.] Dearest Barron (My Beloved Dog), Dearest Tina, Dearest Toni, When I'm Cleaning, To my Darling Husband Antony; [pers.] I express how I feel in my poems. Life is so short and when I'm old my book of poems will give me great pleasure on cold wintery nights. Memories that will be with me forever.; [a.] Croydon, Surrey

RIXON, JACQUELINE
[b.] 27 June 1966, London; [m.] Robert Rixon, 3 February 1996; [ch.] Jessica Catherine; [occ.] Student; [pers.] In memory of my mother, Patricia Mary Sumpter, who taught me that broken hearts, like broken bones, ultimately heal and there is life beyond hurting.; [a.] Southampton, Hampshire

ROBB, STUART
[b.] 18 August 1974, Alton, Hampshire; [p.] David James and Margaret Angela Robb; [ed.] The Grange School - Aylesbury, Aylesbury College; [occ.] I work in the Administration Department for the Thames Vally Police; [hon.] B.T.E.C. National Diploma in Business - Finance; [oth. writ.] Numerous poems plus song lyrics. My poem entitled "Never-Ending Flame" was published in the book "Between A Laugh and A Tear".; [pers.] Don't pretend to be something you're not. You need to be true to your family and friends and true to yourself. Be proud of who you are, believe in yourself and never give up.; [a.] Aylesbury, Buckinghamshire

ROBB, STUART CRAIG
[b.] 14 November 1969, Kirkcaldy; [p.] Cyril Robb, Isabella Gwen Adams; [ed.] Kirkcaldy High School, St. Andrews Theatre Training School; [memb.] International Tae Kwon Do Federation; [pers.] All that is around us lies within a Nexus of Infinite Diversity. By embracing this myriad of entire complexities, we realize it's all encompassing power to afford us pleasures that satiate our passion of long life, unrestrained love and the integrity of honor.; [a.] Kirkcaldy, Fife

ROBERTS, LINDA
[b.] 23 March 1947, Bangor, Gwynedd; [m.] John Morris Roberts, 4 September 1971; [ch.] 5 daughters; [ed.] Caernarfon Grammar School, 2 yrs. B.Ed. Course (Realized teaching was not my vocation) intend to complete A B.A. - English Literature course open University; [occ.] Housewife; [oth. writ.] I have several pieces of prose and poetry, but I have never sought publication. This competition is the first I have entered.; [pers.] My inspiration lies within my own experience of life, and my belief that human nature never changes. I relate to questions that great philosopher have asked through the ages.; [a.] Caernarfon, Gwynedd

ROBERTS, ROBERT WILLIAM
[pen.] Bob Roberts; [b.] 17 December 1926, Ludlow-Salop; [p.] William and Winefred Roberts; [m.] Barbara Nee Jones, 5 March 1949; [ch.] Olwen Mary-Evans; [ed.] Guest House Proprietor Ambleside, Friory School, Shrewsbury; [occ.] Retired (Previous Merchant Service 1943/50) Shropshire and West Mercia Police, Retired 1976 Sergeant - Education Office Powys County to 1991, Burma Star Association; [memb.] St. John Ambulance; [hon.] George Medal 1961, Commander Order of St. John 1991; [oth. writ.] None published. Except in St. John Magazines.; [pers.] Greatly influenced by the Great Rodyard Kipling.

ROBERTS, RON
[b.] 8 September 1947, Farnborough, Kent; [p.] Alfred (Jack) Roberts, Maude Roberts; [m.] Denise Cheeseman, 5 September 1992 (2nd marriage); [ch.] Lisa, Nicola, Prev (M.) Gemma-Rose; [ed.] Edgebury Sec. Modern, Chislehurst, Kent, no qualifications achieved; [occ.] Proprietor of a small 17th C Quest Mouse in Uttoxeter; [pers.] I draw inspiration from long country walks, I listen to and for the sights, sounds of my surroundings. I look forward to having more of my works published in the future.; [a.] Uttoxeter, Staffordshire

ROBERTSON, MABEL JANE ANN
[b.] 12 January 1940, Glasgow; [p.] Bert and Mabel MacRate; [m.] David, 4 April 1963; [ch.] Scott and Ashleigh; [ed.] North Kelvinside School Glasgow, Stow College, Angus College; [occ.] Housewife; [pers.] Life's experiences are man's ultimate wisdom.; [a.] Brechin, Angus

ROBERTSON, PAUL
[b.] 11 November 1959, Sydney; [ed.] Bachelor Arts, University of Adelaide, Bachelor Laws, Diploma of Laws (University of South Australia), MA (Univ of South Australia), BA LLB Dip Laws MA, T.E.F.L.; [occ.] "Foreign Language Lecturer"; [memb.] I lead the life of a loner gypsiing around the world!; [oth. writ.] A novel about International Terrorism, "A Minutes Silence For The Apocalypse" ISBM 960 226 552 3 release Greece (in English) Australia, U.K.; [pers.] My writing reflects my mystical experiences when living in Central Arabia, Middle Greece and the former Soviet Union.

ROBILLARD, BRIAN WILLIAM EDWARD
[b.] 15 May 1948, Canada; [p.] Larry and Judy Robillard; [ed.] Bachelor of Arts Middlesex University - Music and Science/Technology, City and Guilds Keyboard Instruments City of London Univ.; [occ.] Piano and guitar teacher and piano tuner; [memb.] Middlesex University Alumni Ass., Musicians Benevolent Fund Associate; [hon.] BA Hons. Middlesex University, City and Guilds/City of London University, grade eight music theory Trinity College of Music; [oth. writ.] "From Little Acorns" (Piano Pieces), "Une Peu De Comedies De Musicke" (Piano pieces) for piano impromptus eight little pieces for guitar and "The Guitarist" (A play); [pers.] "Take things in their natural order and try to express order and try to express your feelings whatever they may be and never take life too seriously".; [a.] London, Middlesex

ROBINSON, JACK
[pen.] The Teesdale Tyke; [b.] 28 January 1928, Otley, Wharfedale; [p.] Widower; [occ.] Retired Publican; [memb.] Yorkshire Riding Society; [oth. writ.] Poems written for special occasions Private Publication of "Reflections of a Teesdale Tyke" "Continued Reflections of a Teesdale Tyke" continuing the continued reflections of a Teesdale Tyke' all three editions in aid of charity Guide Dogs for Blind. Darlington Memorial Hospital.; [pers.] All my writings have been done for charity. 150 unpublished poems.; [a.] Mickleton Barnard Castle, Teesdale

ROBINSON, JAMES
[b.] 5 April 1920; [p.] Henry Austin Robinson and Alice Emma; [m.] Phyllis Dorothy, 18 July 1942; [ch.] Barry, Austin, Robinson, Carol, June, Robert Peter and David James; [ed.] Began on leaving school, safe from the cane-happy teachers; [occ.] Retired; [memb.] Towerlands Golf Club and Finchingfield Carpet Bowls Club; [hon.] Once won a medal as a pick nose champion from a school teacher who instead of resorting to pain for tears used humiliation; [oth. writ.] First time entry was included in the Anthology "Voices on the Wind".; [pers.] An inferiority complex should have denied me any recognition. But thanks to my daughter, my ego is now inflated; [a.] Finchingfield, Essex

ROBINSON, NORMAN
[pen.] Robbo; [b.] 3 September 1926, Doncaster; [m.] July 1948; [ch.] One; [ed.] Nil; [occ.] Retired; [hon.] Medal for outstanding services for the Community; [oth. writ.] I'm sending you my love can you please put this in the book a lasting calm with my ulther, little Ben hairdweck scargille's our saviour I've paid for the book.; [pers.] Please send me price attractive walnut plaques

ROBINSON, PATRICIA
[pen.] Pat; [b.] 8 March 1942, Willingham-by-Stow; [p.] Joe and Marjorie Rieran; [m.] Trevor Robinson, 12 August 1961; [ch.] Dean; [ed.] St. Marys Brigg; [occ.] Housewife, Part Time Cleaner; [memb.] Close Knit Knitting Club; [oth. writ.] Poets Corner, local papers; [pers.] I am greatly inspired by the wonders of nature all around us.; [a.] Scunthorpe, North Lincolnshire

ROBINSON, PETER
[b.] 30 July 1963, Bishops, Stortford; [p.] Gillian Burrell, M.W.E. Robinson; [m.] Vicki Bayford; [ch.] Harry and Thomas; [ed.] Leventhorpe Comprehensive; [occ.] Electrician; [pers.] I would like to thank my mom who was confident enough to send the work in love you.; [a.] Herts

RODDY, LORRAINE
[b.] 12 January 1952, Newcastle upon Tyne; [p.] Joseph and June Moore; [m.] Divorced; [ch.] Victoria Louise and Katie Louise; [ed.] Western Comprehensive; [occ.] None Teaching Assistant Whitgift School, Grimsby; [memb.] Royal Life saving society, Amateur Swimming Society; [hon.] RLSS Bronze Cross, RLSS Silver Cross, RLSS Award of Merit; [pers.] Life is so unpredictable. We should meet the challenges facing us with hope and determination; [a.] Grimsby, North East Lincolnshire

RODGERS, MICHELLE AIMEE
[b.] 31 May 1983, Derby; [p.] Julie Madden and Paul Rodgers; [ed.] I attend Murrypark School. Mickleover - Derby; [pers.] I have experienced friends and family around me who have been through bad times. I wrote this poem at school when my granddad died.; [a.] Derby

ROE, LARRY
[b.] 22 October 1947, Dublin; [p.] Patrick Roe, Mary Roe; [ed.] Christian Brothers, Eblana, Dun Laoghaire, University College Dublin (B.A. English and Maths); [occ.] Teacher, Secondary (Maths, English Literature); [memb.] Kilmacud Musical and Dramatic Society, Three Rock Orienteering Club, Amnesty International; [hon.] Ten musicals and eight plays (acting, directing, producing and set design), orienteering championship '88, several other sports awards; [oth. writ.] One act play "Someday" (produced and directed). Currently doing a children's writing course. Have completed a screenwriting for TV and film course.; [pers.] I have travelled widely and worked and lived for 3 years in a rural area of Lesotho, Africa. I am a lover of nature and am alarmed at the effect of modern technology on the human spirit.; [a.] Rathdrum, Wicklow, Rep. of Ireland

ROGERS, MRS. DANN
[b.] 22 August 1948, India; [p.] Charles Roberts, Agnes Roberts; [m.] David Rogers, 24 August 1968; [ch.] Emma, Christian, Sebastian; [ed.] Hewdon County Grammar, All Saints College, London, (B.Ed), Univ. of East Anglia (MA); [occ.] (Home Economics Teacher) currently self employed independent consultant (Business); [hon.] B.Ed degree (Home Economics and Education), MA - degree (Assertiveness Training and Management); [oth. writ.] Poems, short stories training material (Assertiveness Training and Management Skills); [pers.] Writing is a means of cleansing the soul and regenerating the spirit and hopefully feeds the soul and spirit of others.; [a.] Diss, Norfolk

ROMERO, ANNA GUIDA
[pen.] Anna Guida; [b.] 10 October 1950, Italy; [p.] Carmine and Giuseppina Guida; [m.] Jose Romero, 20 June 1970; [ch.] Angelina - Roberto - Ricardo; [ed.] Llanelli Coleshill Girls Secondary Modern Technical School; [occ.] Housewife; [oth. writ.] This is my first writing; [pers.] I have always had a great love for poetry, and found comfort in writing and expressing my feelings of love as a mother through my writing "sharing."; [a.] Llanelli, Dyfed

ROONEY, PATRICIA
[b.] 23 January 1984, Ennis Killen; [p.] Patricia and Jim Rooney; [ed.] St. Marys Primary School Killesher, Mount Lourdes Grammar School Enniskillen; [occ.] Student; [hon.] Grade A in 11 +; [pers.] A dream fulfilled.; [a.] Enniskillen, Fermanagh, Ireland

ROSAN, STEPHEN
[b.] 14 April 1977, Epsom; [pers.] Poetry became an anger release when my dad was diagnosed with cancer. For all that he has suffered and endured his will power has kept him fighting. For that and the thought that he is a major part in all our lives I wish to dedicate my poem to him.; [a.] Epsom, Surrey

ROSE, DEREK MICHAEL
[b.] 14 February 1950, Guildford; [p.] George (Deceased) and Rosetta; [m.] Janet Mary, 18 May 1974; [ch.] Charlotte and Teresa, Grandson Samuel; [ed.] Glebelands Secondary Modern School, Cranleigh, Surrey; [occ.] Milkman; [memb.] Chertsey Street Baptist Church, Guildford, Surrey, The Hebrew Christian Alliance of Great Britain, Ramsgate, Kent; [oth. writ.] Personal testimony of faith in Jesus Christ and 2 poems - published in the Messianic Jew and Hebrew Christian. The quarterly organ of the Hebrew Christian Alliance.; [pers.] I am greatly influenced by the Biblical poetry set out in the old testament. — I also admire the writings of Bob Dylan. My poems reflect my own personal experience and feeling, and I hope others can identify with that experience, and find enjoyment, from my poems.; [a.] Guildford, Surrey

ROSSI, HELEN L.
[b.] 10 August 1978, Portsmouth; [p.] Patricia Rossi; [ed.] College Student; [pers.] In May 1993 Helen had a brain virus called Encephilitis which nearly killed her, fortunately she pulled through but was left a severe Epileptic with long and short term memory loss. After a lot of hard work she has managed to relearn how to do all the normal things that people do. Helen now goes to college three times a week and to a day care centre once a week. Unfortunately Helen can not go out on her own because she doesn't remember how to get to places. Thanks to a new doctor and new tablets her Epilepsy is nearly under control, but I'm afraid her memory will never come back, infact she'd forgotten she'd entered your competition and was over the moon when she received your letter. Helen is very interested in all wildlife and belongs to the R.S.P.B. (Patricia M. Rossi, Helen's Mum); [a.] Gosport, Hants

ROYLE, PATRICIA
[pen.] Pat Royle; [b.] 14 April 1947, Crewe, Cheshire; [p.] Ronald Dodd, Millicent Dodd; [m.] Vivian Royle, 19 September 1970; [ch.] Tamsin, Philip, Vivien;

[ed.] Northwich Grammar School for Girls, Cheshire; [occ.] Project Administrator NSPCC, Wrexham; [memb.] Active member of the Scout Association; [oth. writ.] One other poem published "A Day In The Hills"; [pers.] A newspaper to the literary world, my ideas come from life around me and feelings about this.; [a.] Buckley, Flintshire

RUDGE, SAMANTHA
[b.] 17 November 1977; [p.] Marion and Alan Rudge; [pers.] I am an uncontrolled epileptic I had to forego most of my education because of my illness. I live with my grandparents "Albert and Margaret Guest" who gave me the inspiration to carry on writing, releasing feelings past and presents.; [a.] Warley, West Midlands

RUDKIN, ANNETTE
[b.] 8 May 1950, Billinghay; [p.] Albert King, Irene King; [m.] Trevor Rudkin, 22 November 1969; [ch.] Rhonda Lena, Natasha Naomi; [ed.] Kesteven and Sleaford High School; [occ.] Housewife; [pers.] My writing reflects my character, sometimes serious and often humorous.; [a.] Billinghay, Lincolnshire

RYLE, ZOE
[b.] 1931, Crawley, Sussex; [p.] A. J. Leppard and E. J. Leppard; [m.] Deceased; [ch.] Laura Ann; [ed.] Horsham High School, Bognor Regis T.T. College, University of London, Open University; [occ.] Retired Teacher; [memb.] National Al Trust Willesden and Brent Chess Club MENSA; [oth. writ.] Other poems; [a.] London

RYMER, ANDREW S.
[pen.] Eli Lyric; [b.] 18 April 1944, York; [p.] Joseph and Barbara Rymer (Deceased); [m.] Joy Rymer, 11 September 1991; [ed.] Lanceston Grammar School (Tasmania) Scarborough Courses; [occ.] Machine Operator in a Rope Making Factory Hansham; [hon.] City and Guilds for Security and House Maintenance Mensa Certificate with a grade of 140; [oth. writ.] Poems for 25th Wedding Anniversary and Golden Wedding Anniversary pretend in frames as gifts; [pers.] Due to my surname I thought that I would write poetry which was backed up by my wife and to self how it develops.; [a.] Eastbourne, East Sussex

SANDISON, PAUL C.
[b.] March 28, 1947, Durban, South Africa; [p.] George and Joan Sandison; [ed.] BA hons (Natal), M Cert Ed (UPPSALA), B Soc Sci, M Soc Sci, B Soc Sci (Stockholm), MA (Bath); [occ.] Educational author and consultant; [memb.] University of Natal Alumni Association; [hon.] Gabriel Massey Speech Prize 1962, M Certed 1983 (2 Distractions), B Soc Sci 1986 Distinction, M Soc Sci 1986 Distinction; [oth. writ.] Artilles for Newspapers, Journals Book Reviews, MS for School Radio Programmes and Magazines, Translations and the Book "A Key To A New Educational Strategy" Publ. by Shadow, Rivonia, South Africa, 1994 ISBN 0 620 186860; [pers.] A new threat of dictatorship is appearing in Europe in the form of the European Union - a huge European state run by a council of ministers supported by a monolithic bureaucracy! The court of Human Rights in Strasbourg is infiltrated by dictatorial Scandinavian lawyers who put appeals from victims of human rights in Fringemists in Sweden into the waste-paper basket!; [a.] Durban, South Africa

SARGANT, NOEL
[pen.] Nonie Sargant; [b.] 12 December 1925, Gloucester; [p.] Frank and Evelyn Arnold-Wallinger; [m.] Sir Edmund Sargant, 6 August 1981; formerly married to Anthony Montague Browne 1950-1970; [ch.] one daughter, one step-son; [ed.] day girl, Cheltenham Ladies College; St. Mary's Paddington; London School of Physiotherapy; [occ.] married woman; classes for pregnant women until 1985; [memb.] M.C.S.P., A.C.P.O.G., Malcolm Sergeants Choral Society (retired), United Oxford and Cambridge University Club, 71 Pall Mall; [hon.] London School Certificate, Member of the Chartered Society of Physiotherapist and also the Association of Physiotherapists, Obstetrics, and Gynaecology, Cheltenham

Horse Shows; [oth. writ.] Some poems and words for students songs; thank you letters, etc.; most of my poems were written between the age of 30 and 50 years and kept in an envelope.; [pers.] You have to make your own happiness. I come from a musical family on both sides—when I hear music the words come flowing out astonishing my friends. My first husband quoted poetry ad lib and we would love to play on words.; [a.] London

SARGENT, JULIET
[pen.] Juliet Sargent; [b.] 4 February 1957, Norwich; [p.] Julian Eve, Sheila Eve; [m.] David Sargent, 10 July 1982; [ch.] Tim David, William Toby, George Hugh; [ed.] Norwich High School for Girls, Newcollege of Speech and Drama, St. Mary's College; [occ.] Drama Teacher; [hon.] Diploma in Dramatic Art, Lram Mime, Certificate in Education; [oth. writ.] Librettos for 1 musicals, short stories, poetry - all unpublished; [pers.] I write with an ever growing fascination about the wonders, mysteries, frialties and strengths which make us up as human beings.; [a.] Norwich, Norfolk

SARPONG, JOHN KOFI ASIEDU
[pen.] Jason; [b.] 2 April 1948, Akim Asene, Ghana; [p.] Nana Kofi Sarpong, Madam Afua Darkoaa; [m.] Mrs. Comfort Asiedu Sarpong, 31 December 1983; [ch.] Fred Sarpong, Priscillia Sarpong; [ed.] St. Andrews College, Mampong-Ashanti, Ghana, Ahmadu Bello University, Institute of Education Zaria - Nigeria; [occ.] Primary Writing, Publisher Kaduna; [memb.] Association of Nigerian Authors African Network for Protection and Prevention of Child Abuse and Neglect (ANPPCAN), OMEP Nigerian Chapter; [oth. writ.] Jason Poems (Poetry for young ones), Jason Poems (Sweet Talking Drums), Jason Poems (On Child Abuse and Neglect)—all published. Several poems published in local magazines.; [pers.] Strive to instill discipline into children in my writing. The Child is the centre of every home, therefore in all ways of learning, discipline must go along.; [a.] Kaduna, Nigeria

SAUNDERS, JUNE
[pen.] June Saunders; [b.] 5 February 1940, Edmonton, London; [p.] Violet Grace Barrett and Dennis William Barrett; [m.] Eric Terry Saunders; [ch.] Two, four grandchildren; [ed.] Tottenham County Grammar, took opportunity to take exams and passed for Edmonton Technical School for fashion trades; [occ.] Proprietor of antique and period fireplace shop; [memb.] Middlesex University, retired members association, (I was secretary there for 18 years before taking an early retirement opportunity); [hon.] None, left school at 15 instead of the 16 agreed when passing entry exams, much to the disappointment of my parents at the time; [oth. writ.] As and when something inspires me I write down my thoughts and put them in a drawer. Have never thought any would be good enough to get published.; [pers.] I feel very fortunate to have grown up in a house where books played a large part of our leisure time. I believe the written word is an important way of teaching us compassion and understanding as the words are someone's thoughts and feelings; [a.] Edmonton

SAVAGE, LINDA-JANE
[b.] 12 March 1962, Chadwell, Heath; [p.] Arthur and Eileen Gulliver; [m.] Glen Savage, 12 September 1987; [ch.] Bradley Arthur, Amy Jo; [ed.] Warren Comprehensive; [occ.] Local Government Officer; [pers.] I endeavour to write what I feel not, what I think; [a.] Romford, Essex

SCALLAN, FRANCIS
[b.] 1 April 1946, Limerick City; [m.] 1980; [occ.] Art Teacher Secondary School Dublin

SCHLETTE, MRS. M. E. M.
[b.] 17 October 1908, London; [p.] Deceased; [m.] Deceased, 19 October 1928; [ch.] Wendy and Peter; [ed.] L.C.C. Elementary L.C.C. Trade School Shoreditch; [occ.] Retired Teacher Subjects Needle Work and Religions Instruction; [hon.] L.C.C. Trade Scholarship 1922; [oth. writ.] Laughter Published 1996 3 OL Village, Life (48 Lines. Earthly Angels

(58 lines A Lesson From The Daisies (56 lines, Our Planet (24 lines years 2000 (The 7th millennium 14 (This is a prophetic poems etc.; [pers.] I became a visionary soon after the death of my mother when I was 13. The best of my poems have been inspired by a higher power, an outlet for emotions both pleasure and pain.; [a.] Saffron Walden, Essex

SCOTT, JIM
[b.] 26 February 1953, London; [p.] Robert Scott, Eileen Scott; [m.] Esther-Ann Scherer Scott, 2 October 1991; [ch.] Nicholas, Courtney and Oliver; [ed.] Boundstone Secondary Sch Sompting, West Sussex; [occ.] Country Manager of International Shipping Line; [memb.] Virgin Island's Search and Rescue (former President); [hon.] Lloyd's of London for co-ordinating marine safety and rescue during hurricane hogo '89. Virgin Island's Search and Rescue for Dedication and Leadership '94; [oth. writ.] Articles in "Scandanavian" and European Shipping Review "Charter Magazine"; [pers.] Through years of travel and working close to nature I draw from born muck of my philosophy and inspiration.; [a.] Tortona, British Virgin Island

SCOTT-FLOUNDERS, DENISE
[b.] 21 September 1963, Gloucester; [p.] Arthur Thomas Scott and Helen Noelle Scott; [m.] Ian Flounders, 11 November 1989; [ch.] Daniel, Joshua, Gareth, Jack; [ed.] Linden Secondary School Gloucester; [occ.] Homemaker; [pers.] I have enjoyed writing poetry and stories for many years. Having a young family I have little time to spend on my pleasure. My writings are influenced by my own personal experiences and emotions from the past and for the future. I hope one day to achieve my ambition to have my own book published.; [a.] Gloucester, Glo'shire

SCREEN, DAVID ROBERT
[b.] 28 January 1934, Nottingham; [p.] The Late Arthur and Ethel Hilda Screen; [ed.] Trent Bridge Secondary School; [occ.] Warehouseman; [oth. writ.] "Averting The Elements", "An April Shower", I Would Like To Journey Through", ("The Ultimate"); [pers.] If you have a happy heart happy thoughts will follow. That's when I pick up my pen, putting my thoughts on a blank page becomes quite easy.; [a.] Nottingham

SEAMAN, DENNIS LEWIS
[b.] 24 May 1934, Chadwell St. Mary, Grays; [p.] George and Florence Seaman; [m.] Carole Maureen, 14 March 1964; [ch.] Peter, Jenny and Colin; [ed.] Wanstead Church of England, Fairlop High Ilford; [occ.] Foreman Toolmaker; [memb.] Hon. Secretary of Ilford and Dis. Aquarist and Pondkeepers Society, Life Member; [hon.] O.N.C. Engineering; [oth. writ.] Several poems.; [pers.] My poems tend to reflect times past.; [a.] Romford, Essex

SEELEY, JESSICA MARGUERITE
[b.] 25 August 1948, Eastbourne; [ch.] Two sons age 27 years and 30 years, and seven grandchildren; [ed.] Secondary School, left at the age of 14 years; [occ.] None as I have a Lung Desease. But nurses my daughter for her twelve years of life before she died. She died from spinal muscular atrophy, I looked after her at home with a tracheotomy until it was close up, and physio all through her life.; [oth.writ.] None I have never wrote anything before except the book I have just completed, which explains opposite, I am waiting to see if someone will sponsor the rest of the money I need to have it printed, I shall know in a few weeks time, I have just completed a book, "In memory of Lynette", and "The Heart She Touched," I have wrote about her twelve years of life plus my grief, the book also has extracts of Lynette's own work plush writings from her boyfriends and friends, who loved her very much. My promise to her, was to write about her. Watching my daughter cope with knowing she did not have long to live at the age of twelve, and listen to her planning my future without her, this gave me the strength and the love I have for her to do this.; [a.] Langwey, Eastbourne

SELL, NICOLA CAROL
[b.] 22 March 1964, Hammersmith; [p.] Ronald Sell, Gwendolen Sell; [m.] Philip Harpin; [ch.] Lee Darren; [ed.] Gumley House Isleworth; [occ.] Medical Computer Supervisor; [oth. writ.] Many poems written for personal pleasure and for friends and relatives.; [pers.] One life, one change - cherish each moment of your own and others.; [a.] Wallisdown, Dorset

SEMERARO, LARA
[pen.] Lara The Cat; [b.] 5 July 1974, England; [p.] Lynn and John Semeraro; [occ.] Hair Stylist part time and Poet part time; [memb.] Rauqes Sharki - Eygptian Dance School. Ponana, North African Theme Dancing Bar; [hon.] None until now, I am shy with my writing; [oth. writ.] Books full of poetry and short stories for children but nothing published.; [pers.] The whole world inspires me everything in and around it, especially the things that you can't see.

SEN, IAN
[b.] 12 May 1973, Bridlington; [p.] Jean Sen; [ed.] Headlands School, The East Yorkshire College, Bridlington; [occ.] Self Employed; [memb.] The Vampire Society; [hon.] Award of Excellence from The Poetry Institute of the British Isles; [oth. writ.] Several poems published in P.I.B.I. and Poetry now publications.; [pers.] I finally got sick of repeatedly turning on my T.V. only to see people resembling myself portrayed either as criminals or brainless drips. This poem was written in retaliation to such cultural prejudices.; [a.] Harrogate, North Yorkshire

SEWOKE, SAMMY VISHNU
[pen.] Lion Son; [b.] 27 December 1971, London; [p.] Anirood Sewoke, Jeeawantee Sewoke; [ed.] Grinling Gibbons Primary School, Deptford Green Comprehensive School, Lewisham College, Goldsmiths' College (University of London); [occ.] Gardener; [memb.] Dennis The Menace Fan Club; [hon.] BSc Mathematical Studies; [oth. writ.] School magazine, letters in Mask and Transformers comics; [pers.] "Always feed the birds in your garden"; [a.] London, Deptford

SEYMOUR, CHRISTOPHER DREWE
[pen.] Chris Drewe; [b.] 03/09/56, Newport, I.W.; [p.] Jean & Mervyn Seymour; [m.] Anne Seymour, 26/07/86; [ch.] Richard (8), Robert (3); [ed.] Totland County Primary School; Carisbrooke High; [occ.] Civil Servant, Department of Health; [oth. writ.] Nothing published; [pers.] I write to record my thoughts and moods, essentially to capture transient states of mind. It's a purely personal, reflective process; [a.] Dacre Banks, North Yorkshire

SHAFII, MEHDI
[pen.] Mehdi; [b.] 26 May 1950, Jiroft, Iran; [m.] Alex Shafii, 3 October 1979; [ch.] Darrioush Shafii; [ed.] B.A. Industrial Design Ealing, College of Higher Education; [occ.] Director; [memb.] S.I.A.D.; [oth. writ.] Unpublished poems; [pers.] I am greatly influence by Omar Khyam and believe we come from earth and return to it. In between every second, every breath is beautiful and that is absolute.; [a.] London

SHAHNAWAZ, JAHANGIR
[b.] 21 Oct 1932, Dacca; [m.] Afroza Begum; [oth. writ.] By way of checking homosexuality and prevent premature end of life in this world, I have been assigned by Allah to write a novel highlighting and glorifying heterosexual love. This I have been doing for 2 decades. A novel called PREM(Love) is being published in 12 volumes. It would be completed in the near future and would be the largest of its kind in the world of literature. So far published the first six volumes cover pages more than three thousand. It is all about love, and nothing but love.

SHAMSI, S. H.
[b.] 4 March 1914, Nairobi; [p.] Deceased; [m.] Darshi, 24 June 1971; [ed.] Secondary; [occ.] Retired; [hon.] Life Accomplishment award by the National Council of Culture and Arts, Pakistan; [oth. writ.] Several poems published locally, Kenya, India and Pakistan, Books of poems published: (1) IK Jungle Insano KA (Human Jungle, (2) Koh-Enida (Voices from the Mountain), (3) Inkishaf (Revelation), (4) Gathering Shadows in Urdu (Pub. in the USA) in English; [pers.] Write in four different languages: English, Persian, Urdu and Punjabi I have been influenced by the Persian mystic poets and my works depict the philosophy of life.; [a.] Isle Worth, Middlesex

SHANAHAN, FLORENCE KATHLEEN
[b.] 13 January 1960, Dublin, Ireland; [p.] William and Bernadette O'Reilly (Both Deceased); [m.] Divorced; [ch.] Iain, Ailbhe, Aaron, Krystal; [ed.] In Ireland and further education at Thames Valley University London C.F.P. Nursing; [occ.] Care of the elderly; [oth. writ.] I have been writing since I were eight years old and have a desire to have all my work published collectively at some stage "where there is life, there is love"; [pers.] I have been greatly influenced by my life experience, and being a romantic I use this to create a vision of reality in my writing and also a means to escape into a safe world.; [a.] Chiswick, London

SHANLEY, VERONICA
[b.] 30 October 1978, Longford; [p.] Thomas and Angela; [ed.] Primary School: Stonepark Co. Longford, Secondary: St. Josephs, Newtownforbes, Co. Longford; [occ.] Working and training horses and studying horses; [hon.] Got a poem published in local book on poets in Longford, won Certificate in Third World Competition for a poem on famine.; [oth. writ.] Now working on my second book of poetry. Wrote hundreds of poems over the years on experiences, feelings of all kinds, of losses and achievements.; [pers.] I love to write poetry as it is how I truly express myself. Instead of saying something I prefer to write it down. I believe if written right, you can reach inside a person with your words.; [a.] Longford, Longford

SHARMA, SHIV
[b.] 24 May 1937, India; [p.] Father Film Director; [m.] Dr. Swatantrata Chandiok, 27 September 1976; [ch.] Sachin Sharma; [ed.] MA in Philosophy (Punjab, India); [occ.] Columnist on the International Guardian Weekly; [memb.] National Union of Journalists; [hon.] A finalist in Channel Four URDU Poetry Competition Former Staff Journalist on The Daily Telegraph, Daily Mail, The Guardian and Daily Mirror; [oth. writ.] Dimly before dawn (novel), Weekly Column in the Guardian Weekly, URDU poems recited and sung all over Britain; [pers.] My poems, both in English and Urdu, deal with the human condition sympathetically.; [a.] Wilmslow, Cheshire

SHARMAN, ROBERT
[b.] 14 August 1964, Stoke-on-Trent; [m.] Divorced; [ch.] Kira (11), Declan (5); [ed.] Bradwell High School, Staffs; [memb.] Royal Society for the Protection of Birds (RSPB), Sustrans; [pers.] I write poetry and short stories as an occasional relaxation. This is the first time I have submitted anything for possible publication.; [a.] Newcastle, Staffordshire

SHARP, MARGARET ANN
[b.] 25 May 1935, Parkeston; [p.] Harold and Margaret Wilson; [m.] Bryan Trevor Sharp, 18 March 1963; [ch.] Belinda and Matthew; [ed.] Sir Anthoney Deane Comprehensive School Dovercourt Essex; [occ.] Housewife (Widow); [memb.] None except Cope Church; [oth. writ.] Only for personal use none sent for publishing.; [pers.] August 1990 Brain Tumour on right side of skull results of operation, scar tissue damage, gran mal Epileptsy, control by tablets plus, causes dyskexia. Fight mentally to control my life and become independent of others.; [a.] Louth, Lincolnshire

SHARPE, MR. DANNATT ROBERT
[b.] 6 April 1943, Portsmouth; [p.] Lt. Robert Sharpe, RN Winifred Dorothy nee Norton; [m.] Jennifer Ursula, 28 December 1978; [ch.] Son - Christopher James Alexander, daughter - Nadine Ursula May; [ed.] St. John's College Southsea, University of Leicester BSC, University of Southampton Dip Ed., Lady Spencer Churchill College, Oxford (Cert. Ed for Deaf); [occ.] Retired from Head of Unit for Hearing Impaired, present past time stock counter in Retail Trade.; [memb.] Chartered Biologist, member Institute of Biology, Fellow Zoological Society London, Royal Observer Corps Association No. 1 Group, Radio Society of Great Britain, Royal Naval Amateur Radio Society, Royal Air force Amateur Radio Society; [hon.] Long Service Medal Royal Observer Corps 1988, Lord Lieutenants Meritorious Service Certificate by Lord Lieutenant East Sussex (1989); [oth. writ.] University of Southampton Biological Bulletin 1964-65, School Science Review. Several poems local magazines, poetry now, up and running and some poems in The International Library of Poetry publication.; [pers.] Nature with it's humour and pathos. I have been influenced by writers like Gerald Derrell and Early Poets.; [a.] Uckfield, East Sussex

SHARPE, NICOLE MARTINE
[b.] 16 June 1968, Leeds; [p.] Roy Sharpe, Cherie Sharpe; [ed.] Church of England Middle School, Prince Henrys Grammar; [occ.] Purchasing manager; [memb.] The Manor Gym; [oth. writ.] Several poems but have never entered into my other competitions.

SHAW, ANGELA
[b.] 6 April 1975, Irvine; [p.] Dugald Shaw, Margaret Shaw; [ed.] Auchenharvie Academy; [pers.] I have never really thought of myself as a poet until now. And I can say I am proud of what I have achieved so far.; [a.] Stevenston, Ayrshire

SHEEHAN, DECLAN
[pen.] Osbourne Williams; [b.] 24 July 1979, Co. Cork, Eire; [p.] John and Peggy Sheehan; [ed.] Second Level, (Leaving Cert.), Scoil, Mhuire Gan Smal; [occ.] Student; [memb.] Grenagh G.A.A.; [oth. writ.] 15 other poems, not published; [pers.] Poetry should never come from the mind, always the heart.; [a.] Donoughmore, Co. Cork, Ireland

SHEPPARD, LINDA
[b.] April 2, 1957, Rhondda; [p.] Maureen and John; [m.] Partner George Lightfoot; [ch.] Michelle Gareth, Martin Jonathan; [ed.] Craig Er Eyos School, Penygraig, Tai School Penygraig; [occ.] Not working; [hon.] Have no honour or awards; [oth. writ.] I have a poem before published in a book called The Touch of Love, title of poem, Valentine's Day; [pers.] I want to say that my poems have been inspired by my partner whom I am living with Mr. George Lightfoot, he give me a lot of inspiration to write poems; [a.] Tonyrefail, Mid-Glam

SHERIF, SARA
[b.] 6 November 1980, London; [p.] Al Nadhir Sherif, Kate Sherif; [ed.] Secondary; [occ.] Student; [memb.] Chalfont Others Swimming Club, Festival Orchestra of Abu Dhabi; [hon.] The associated board of the royal schools of music. For the flute and theory. Numerous Swimming Awards.; [oth. writ.] Various poems for school bulletins, other unpublished works; [pers.] I find poetry a spiritual release from trials and tribulations of every day life. I particularly enjoy reading and writing war poetry.; [a.] Iver, Buckinghamshire

SHEVLANE, SUSAN
[b.] 1 June 1953, Melton; [p.] Adopted 1954, Richard and Lillian Lee; [m.] Hugh Shevlane, Deceased 1992, 7 October 1972; [ch.] Rachael, Theresa, Bridget, James, Maria, Kathleen; [ed.] Walton Girls High School, Grantham Lincolnshire; [occ.] Housewife; [memb.] World Vision Child Sponsership with a Sponsored child in Zambia, Africa; [hon.] Certificates of Distinction, Honours, and Commendation in Ballet, Latin American Tap Dancing and Acrobatics; [oth. writ.] A personal collection of poems and songs written since childhood. In the process of writing my Biography.; [pers.] To unite people in the similarities of mankind through words, to understand, and benefit from my philosophy is reward itself.; [a.] Nottingham, Nottinghamshire

SHISTON, ANDREW
[pen.] Andre Johann; [b.] 16 March 1943, Portland; [p.] Harry and Joan Shiston; [ch.] Mary-Jane Shiston; [ed.] Broadwey Modern Weymouth, College of Technology Southampton, Nautical College; [occ.] Engineer and Nautical Engineering Rigger; [memb.] Royal British Legion, British Mercantile Marine, Royal Humane Society; [hon.] Poems and short story's published in local rag, and also present company's (mine) monthly magazine.; [oth. writ.] At present writing a non fiction book title "4,000,000 miles at sea" (pen

name) also a complete book of nautical poems (pen name); [pers.] I write mostly of the sea, I believe from where man evolved, of the peace and tranquility of nature that the sea and oceans represent; [a.] London

SIER, EILEEN
[pen.] Ed or Edward Somers; [occ.] Musician; [oth. writ.] Poetry, songs and lyrics, short stories, sketches.; [a.] London

SIGMUNDSDOTTIR, SIGRIDUR
[pen.] Dagaz; [b.] 29 July 1959, Reykjavik; [p.] Kristin and Sigmundur-Gudbjarnason; [m.] D.V.; [ch.] Elia and Karlog Petur; [ed.] To School of fishing Industry Seafood Quality Technician; [occ.] Mother and writer; [hon.] One to mention (Award in the English Language in High School - this is just for fun! Seriously; [oth. writ.] A whole lot none published.; [pers.] The reason I write poems is to express my feelings, to relieve of my desires, my dreams and the sorrow that all to often me and with my heart.; [a.] Reykjavik, Iceland

SIMMONS, FREDERICK RONALD SEYMOUR
[pen.] Frederick Seymour; [b.] 24 August 1932, London; [p.] William & Florence Simmons; [m.] Rita, 9 August 1958; [ch.] Stewart Lisa; [ed.] Grove Lane Technical, Camberwell, London; [occ.] Semi-Retired; [memb.] St. Mary's Anglican Church, Green St., Green Orpington, Kent; [hon.] School Certificates, Poetry, English, Art, History; [oth. writ.] Several poems published in anthologies, researching for a book on Hatton Garden and Security; [pers.] I was influenced by my teacher at eleven years old. I have been writing poetry since then poetry to me is like a painting with beautiful lines and a picture of life.; [a.] Bromley, Kent

SIMMS, DAVID
[b.] 28 June 1943, England; [p.] Frank and Dorothy; [m.] Lorraine, 15 May 1971; [ch.] Diana, Alison and Lauren; [ed.] Grammar School; [occ.] Tele Communications; [pers.] Thanks to the inner child of JRW for the idea and ancient wisdom for the inspiration.; [a.] Southampton, Hants

SIMPSON, LOUISE
[pen.] Louise Simpson; [b.] 6 December 1982, Cuckfield; [p.] Glynis Simpson, Peter Simpson; [ed.] Sackville School; [occ.] Student; [oth. writ.] Poems and stories for my own pleasure and school work.; [pers.] I enjoy poetry a lot and writing stories I read more poetry that any other book. This is my first time I have entered a poem in a competition.; [a.] East Grinstead, West Sussex

SINCLAIR, LILY MERRILLA
[pen.] Rilla; [b.] 24 January 1916, Ashby De La Zouch; [hon.] Certificate of appreciation for service to the National Saving's Stamp, all most fourteen years, from, Sir John Anstey President and Chairman; [oth. writ.] To achieve something so late in life give's me great satisfaction.; [a.] Ashby De La Zouch, Leicestershire

SINGH-MARWA, JACQUELINE
[pen.] Claudia Flaxton; [b.] 21 January 1967, Wimbledon; [p.] Agnes and Patrick Doherty; [m.] Prince Singh-Marwa, 20 December 1989; [ch.] Jake-Elliott Marwa; [ed.] Holy Cross Convent School, New Malden, Surrey; [occ.] Company Director with Gerrard and Geaken Advertizing/Mother; [memb.] Member of the Inst of Trl and Kourism; [oth. writ.] Poems and short stories not published; [pers.] Poetry is for me, a way to express my feelings - on matters close to my heart!; [a.] Hampstead, London

SISK, BILL
[b.] 19 January 1938, Cloyne; [p.] Nellie Roche, Dick Sisk; [m.] Margaret Ahern, 23 April 1962; [ch.] John, Declan, Helen, Catherine; [ed.] Cloyne Nat. Sch., Midleton CBS., School of Commerce Cork; [occ.] Retired Army Sgt. (Irish Army); [memb.] Irish Un Veterans' Association, Organization of National Ex-Servicemen, Irish Amateur Swimming Assn.; [hon.] Long Service Medal and Bar, ONVC Medal (Congo), Unficyp Medal (Cyprus), Mid East Medal (Sinai), Un Peace Medal (Nobel); [oth. writ.] The Dream, (Sht

Story), Jockey Dan, (Sht Story), Brother, Dark Cynic, Padraig Pax, The Swift; [pers.] To see is to know.; [a.] Midleton, Cork

SKILLINGS-CALDWELL, SHELENE
[b.] 4 March 1968, Minneapolis, MN; [p.] Tom and Judy Skillings; [m.] Ian Caldwell, 3 May 1996; [oth. writ.] Poem published in: 'Poets At Large' and 'Poets In Scotland'; [pers.] The compositions of my heart are of those I love, and what I believe.; [a.] Kilcreggan, Helensburgh

SLATER, WINIFRED
[pen.] Win Slater; [b.] 20 June 1930, Preston, Lancashire; [p.] John and Annie Slater; [ed.] Talbot Primary School, Winckley Square Convent School - both these in Preston; [occ.] Retired High School Bursar; [oth. writ.] Several poems but nothing published.; [pers.] My poems tend to be related to felines. These have been my favourite life companions, my style of verse was once likened to Alexander Pope.; [a.] Preston, Lancashire

SMALL, JENNIFER
[pen.] J. R. Small; [m.] Sgt. Small L.S.G.C.; [ch.] Layne, Cassius, Gersoni; [occ.] Housewifely mother; [memb.] "Musician's Union"; [oth. writ.] Song writing-released.; [pers.] "Sail in the ship of success and anchor in the harbour of fame, fortune and goodwill.";[a.] Hounslow, Middlesex

SMITH, ANDREW
[b.] 3 June 1971, Salford; [p.] Derek Smith, Susan Smith; [m.] Samantha, 24 June 1995; [ed.] Leigh College, North Trafford College; [occ.] Civil Servant; [hon.] English, Economics, Management Skills; [oth. writ.] Writer/Performer in School plays; [pers.] As I believe poetry should be witty, accessible and salutary, not the exclusive property of intelligentsia, I write in an uncomplicated style. I share a movement I post-movement tradition after Larkin, Roy Fuller, Dunn, John Fuller.; [a.] Manchester

SMITH, BARBARA ANNE
[b.] 13 July 1940, London; [p.] George De Banks, Lilian De Banks; [m.] John Harding Smith, 12 August 1961; [ch.] Caroline Emma, Jennifer Anne; [memb.] Member of The Woodlands Trust; [pers.] This poem was written about my walks on Cranborne Chase with my husband and family. My poems are inspired by my love of nature and sadness for human suffering.; [a.] Wimborne, Dorset

SMITH, MISS DOROTHY
[b.] 6 December 1939, Liverpool; [p.] Lilian and Leonard G. Smith; [ed.] Secondary Modern School for Girls "Highfield. Alice Elliott School for Deaf Adults.; [occ.] Civil Servant; [memb.] National Trust, R.S.P.B. Ex Girl guide, Ex Leader Boys Brigade, Ex Sunday School Teacher; [hon.] 2x0 Levels and 2xA levels English and History; [oth. writ.] Poem "Nature" in Quiet Moments; [pers.] Being deaf I tend to use my eyes more and I love the mountains the country and the sea.; [a.] Hayton with Roby, Merseyside

SMITH, GRAEME
[b.] 26 February 1980, Beaford; [p.] Sandra Smith and Robert Smith; [occ.] Student; [a.] Waltham Abbey, Essex

SMITH, MRS. JEAN
[b.] 13 August 1922, Manchester; [p.] John Black; [m.] Margaret Black, 23 December 1944; [ch.] Two, boy and girl; [ed.] Due to prolonged illness. I never went to school.; [occ.] Retired; [hon.] 5 years Hospital Queen for Manchester and Salford; [oth. writ.] Two spiritual songs and many poems. I have started on an autobiography which my husband is writing due to my inability to continue using his word processor.; [pers.] Due to no use of both hands and parkinsons disease I am unable to write I used my husband w/p. With a pencil help in my teeth, (which now I cannot do owing to P.D).; [a.] Wymondham, Norfolk

SMITH, JOSEPHINE DOROTHY ANN
[pen.] Josie; [b.] 15 November 1943, Hammersmith; [p.] Violet May Shunn; [m.] Kenneth Smith, 16 March 1963; [ch.] Kenneth Edward, Trevor John; [ed.]

Shipton Bellinger Primary Tidworth Down Secondary Modern; [occ.] Vitacress, working on Hygiene; [memb.] Amesbury Baptist Church; [oth. writ.] Many poems, The King And I, Sloe Spring, Universes, Invisible Men, Thank You (All of these unpublished) Children's stories (all unpublished) believe, squiggle and peep, Ezra 1-2-3 series; [pers.] Since a young girl, I have always loved writing poems, Jesus Christ is my greatest love, since young. I find so much beauty in his work. When angry or concerned I write it down, sometimes in a prayer.; [a.] Shipton, Bellinger, Hampshire

SMITH, JUDITH
[b.] 5 January 1945, Hertfordshire; [ed.] Trained as a teacher at 'Trent Park' college, music as a main subject; [occ.] Infant school teacher, at fly county infant school; [memb.] A member of the fly of the Ely Choral Society; [a.] Ely, Cambridgeshire

SMITH, MR. MALCOLM
[b.] 15 November 1952, Prescot; [m.] Karen Smith, 29 March 1975; [ed.] Whiston Sec. Modern, Widnes Technical College; [occ.] Security; [memb.] St. Helens and District CHA and H.F. Rambling Club; [pers.] My greatest influence is life itself. Both good and bad, which I aim to reflect in my poetry.; [a.] Prescot, Merseyside

SMITH, MICHAEL
[pen.] Michael Smith; [b.] 3 February 1961, Blackpool; [occ.] Offshore Oil Industry; [pers.] To inspire other potential writers, to show their inner thoughts.; [a.] Fleetmont, Lancs

SMITH, REGINALD PETER
[b.] 30 October 1939, York; [p.] Reginald and Mary; [m.] Valerie, 25 March 1961; [ch.] Maria Jane; [ed.] Manor Cofe School York, University College Scarborough; [occ.] Retired School Teacher (English Literature); [memb.] Chairman Scouts/Guides (1st Scalby), Swimming Instructor at Scarborough Swimming Club; [hon.] Cert Ed. (College), B.A. (Open University); [oth. writ.] "Revolutions, The Second Coming." Anthology "Quiet Moments" (I.L.O.P), "Scarborough Sands", "My First Love", "The Beef Eater's Lament", "United We Stand", (Anchor Books); [pers.] Poetry is an art form in which one can express concise thoughts and feelings.; [a.] Scarborough, North Yorkshire

SMITH, RICHARD NIGEL
[b.] 25/01/65; Rotherham; [p.] Brenda and Geoff; [m.] Jayne; [ed.] Sheffield Hallam University; [occ.] Sheffield University computer instructor; [oth. writ.] Many poems; [pers.] Writing is fun. Reading is often more fun; [a.] Rotherham, South Yorkshire.

SMITH, ROY
[pen.] Rojoth; [b.] 5 January 1932, Birmingham; [p.] Frank and May Smith; [m.] Julia Helen Smith, 28 July 1951; [ed.] Royal Wolverhampton School, Penn., Wolverhampton; [occ.] Retired - Systems Analyst/ Programmer; [oth. writ.] Twenty poems which form the main part of an anthology by renal patients - to be published - for kidney research.; [pers.] I am kept alive by a kidney machine (three times a week) I have only started writing since I saw your advertisement last year.; [a.] Mablethorpe, Lincolnshire

SMYTER, BERYL
[b.] 2 January 1940, London; [p.] Phyllis Pateman, Fredrick Pateman; [m.] Phillip Smyter (Deceased); [occ.] Retired (early); [memb.] Sidmouth Poetry Circle, East Devon Organ Club; [oth. writ.] Several poems published with and without photograph's. Own published "Diary Of Thoughts"; [pers.] Only started writing ten years ago, find it very relaxing. Devon Countryside, a great influenced and inspiration to me.; [a.] Sidmouth, Devon

SNEDDON, JOHN (and SHANE JASON)
[pen.] Johnnie Rocco; [b.] 23 March 1944, Bainsford; [p.] Margaret Giffen, George Sneddon; [ed.] Bainsford Primary, Graeme High School; [pers.] Unemployed in invalidity; [oth. writ.] I am a providing lyricist write hundreds of lyrics, poetry love songs, science fiction in poetry future songs.; [a.] Falkirk

SNELL, KAREN
[b.] 26 March 1951, West Indies; [p.] Lt. Col. and Mrs. W. L. Farrow; [m.] Michael Snell, 6 December 1974, (Divorced - 1989); [ch.] David, Gavin, Camilla and Robbie; [ed.] Various Schools Abroad St. Nicholas School, Fleet, Hants; [occ.] Student - West Thames College (2nd year NNEB); [memb.] BUAV Federation of Holistic Therapists; [oth. writ.] Several poems as yet unpublished - mostly humorous.; [pers.] I have found my writing very therapeutic over the years.; [a.] Brentford, Middlesex

SOBIERALSKI, STELLA W. J.
[b.] 6 May 1930, Barnsley; [p.] John William and Florence Dumford; [m.] Kazimierz Sobieralski (Kaz), 26 December 1947; [ch.] Four, 2 sons and 2 daughters; [ed.] Woodhouse Sheffield Normal School, Elementary Council; [occ.] Disabled Housewife, Mother, Grandmother, soon Great Grandmother; [oth. writ.] Poems only for family and friends for birthdays anniversaries, births etc. But environmental disasters worry me, so I write down my thoughts because of all growing children's futures.; [pers.] Since the 1960's I have had ill health. I have a wonderful husband and a loving family. But my husband was diagnosed in Nov. 96. As terminally ill. I pray he will see 1997 out to celebrate our first great grandchild and our golden wedding.; [a.] Sheffield, South Yorkshire

SOHANTA, KAVITA
[b.] 19 November 1979; [p.] Ms. Devi Sohanta JP and Mr. Jazz Sohanta; [ed.] Coundon Court School and Community College; [occ.] Full time student; [hon.] Music Award; [pers.] "If life was death, and death was life - I would live a little everyday without dying." Influences, my family.; [a.] Coventry, Warwickshire

SOLDAT, SANJA
[b.] 29 January 1984, Zenica; [p.] Vlado Soldat, Ana Soldat; [ed.] Sutjeska Middle School, Haydon Abbey Combined School, Sir Henry Floyd Grammar School; [occ.] Student; [memb.] Radio Times Press Pack; [hon.] Regional and National Young Letter Writer of the Year - Year 1994; [oth. writ.] Letter of Peace published in a Book called 'Letters of Peace'; [pers.] I believe that the best and most moving poems are written out of personal experience. I also believe that in order to achieve your dream you've got to aim high.; [a.] Aylesbury, Bucks

SOMERSET, MARIE
[b.] 8 March, Buckingham; [p.] Charles Somerset and Esther Somerset; [m.] Divorced; [ch.] Nigel Milton and Joanne Bryony; [memb.] Royal Photographic Society; [hon.] L.R.P.S. (Royal Photographic Society) Distinction; [oth. writ.] Poems published in magazines and newspapers. 'Quiet Moments' anthology complete book of poems planned for release end of 1997 title yet undecided. Tape. The Sound Poetry.; [pers.] I spent my youth writing poems with a romantic or emotional theme to be seen by my eyes only. I feel my poem should now fun and be shared. With others I am concentrating on poems inspired by everyday incidents which hopefully induce a smile.; [a.] Bracknell, Berks

SOULSBY, BEN
[pen.] Abednego; [b.] 8 April 1929, Hull; [p.] Olive and Alfred Soulsby; [m.] Clarice Soulsby, 1 June 1946; [ch.] John Anthony (only child); [ed.] West Dock Ave Junior Boys Hull School from 5 years to 10 years then on evacuation during World War 2 to Dyke (Nr Bourne) Lincs (1939) School until Leaving at age 14 in 1943; [occ.] Retired; [memb.] Transport and General Workers Union USDAW (Shopworkers Section) Union; [hon.] Retail Management Award and appointed manager of Milletts Stores (1928) Ltd in 1966 at Hull, then Liverpool and Leeds; [oth. writ.] I have several poems unpublished at home, only waiting for approval.; [pers.] I have an unusual Christian name (Abednego) called after my grandfather but I prepare to be called Ben but would consider Abednego as a pen name for any future publications.; [a.] Hull, E. Yorkshire

SOUTHALL, DOREEN J.
[b.] 20 July 1926; [p.] Anne Samuel Allen; [m.] Bernard William, 14 February 1945; [ch.] Seven; [ed.] Secondary Modern; [occ.] Housewife; [oth. writ.] One poem published but have written eighty poems never sent any away, only the two published; [pers.] Do a bit of painting, love cooking, flower arranging, writing; [a.] Northfield, Birmingham

SPAVINS, ANDREW
[b.] 19 October 1986, Maidstone, Kent; [p.] Mark and Deborah Spavins; [ed.] Arnold Middle School; [memb.] The Whale and Dolphin Conservation Society; [oth. writ.] Two other poems published in Arnold Middle School 1996 Christmas Newsletter.; [pers.] I get great pleasure in writing poems and hope that others get pleasure in reading them.; [a.] Luton, Bedfordshire

SPEAKE, W. C.
[pen.] Gogia; [b.] 18 June 1925, Talgarth; [p.] Francis and Emily; [m.] Pearl Mary Towersey, 1 March 1952; [ch.] Carol, Vivienne, Russell, Paul; [occ.] Retired; [memb.] Royal College of Nursing British Horological Institute. Clacton- on-Sea British Legion Branch. Royal Regt of Wales Assoc.; [hon.] R.G.N. M.B.H.I.; [pers.] I have been greatly influenced by early romantic poets from my school days.; [a.] Little Clacton, Essex

SPEED, KATHLEEN
[b.] 3 December 1963, Burnley; [p.] W. E. Rockliffe, M. S. Rockliffe (Deceased); [m.] David Patrick Speed, 11 November 1995; [ch.] Rebecca Simons, Stacey Simons; [ed.] Lumley Secondary Modern School; [occ.] Quality Controller (Fashion - Industry); [oth. writ.] One poem in magazine. Twenty-four poems published in anthologies for five book companies - three of which I now do work for on a regular basis. Currently putting my own book together.; [pers.] Learn from your mistakes and go for it! You can't be a failure if you've given everything you have to give.; [a.] Skegness, Lincolnshire

SPENCER, JENNIE
[b.] 6 January 1963, Hertfordshire; [p.] Mary and Leslie Spencer; [m.] Separated, 7 May 1986; [ch.] Glenn, Gabrella, Bianca; [ed.] Primary School, Saint John, The Baptist Amwell, Herts John Warner Secondary School Hoddesdon Road Herts; [occ.] Housewife; [pers.] I just wrote what I felt when I was a young girl and my mother sent the poem to you out of interest. I also wrote a short story at school and 2 other poems.; [a.] Stanstead, Abbotts, Herts

SPICER, MRS. SYLVIA
[pen.] Sylvia Spicer; [b.] 23 April 1922, Hull; [p.] Annie and Theordo Wickholm; [m.] Widow, 16 November 1940; [ch.] One son Percy; [ed.] Comprehensive; [occ.] Housewife; [oth. writ.] One poem; [pers.] My writing is simple but from the heart. My thanks to Rita, for her help and encouragement.; [a.] Hull, East Yorkshire

SPILKA, CLARE
[b.] 7 December 1980, Chatham; [p.] Thelma Spilka and Matt Spilka; [ed.] St. Gregory's (Tun-wells) Home tuition due to illness (M.E.); [pers.] My inspiration is spontaneous but I am not influenced by one specific thing.; [a.] Rotherfield, East Sussex

SSENKUNGU, CHARLES
[b.] 12 February 1968, Mulajje, Uganda; [p.] Francis Xavier Lutaaya (R.I.P) and Dezidera N. Nabawanuka; [ed.] St. Bonaventure's Primary School Mulajje, St. Joseph's and St. Gabriel's Junior Seminary Nswanjere, St. Joseph's Minor Seminary Nyenga, Uganda Martyrs' National Major Seminary Alokolum, Urbaniana University, Rome; [occ.] currently, a B.TH. honours degree final year student at St. John's Seminary Wonersh and Southampton University; [memb.] The Carolines, Uganda Martyrs Christian Association, IUS, ISOP, ILP; [hon.] PLE certificate, UOCE, UACE, Diploma in Philosophical and Higher Religious Studies (Alokolum), Bachelor's degree in Philosophy (Urban University, Rome); [oth. writ.] 'Genocide in Luwero Triangle 1981-1986 and its Conse-

quences', 'African Politics', and several other poems and articles published in 'The Lily', 'The Star Herald' magazines and in 'The New Vision' newspaper; [pers.] I try to live every day as if it's my last, because some day it will certainly be! I value writing poems as an ideal way of conveying what I feel because the written word remains. I revolve greatly on nature, politics, religion, morality and humanity in general; [a.] Rotherhithe, London

STAINTON, SYLVIE
[b.] 29 December 1952, France; [p.] Claude Stainton, Marcel Stainton; [ed.] Applied arts - Paris Edinburgh University (BSC Honours Nursing), Moray House Edinburgh (ongoing studying Counselling); [occ.] Staff Nurse in a stroke Rehabilitation Unit; [hon.] BSC Honours in Nursing subjects studied Nursing as a Science and an Art, Psychology, Anthropology Social History; [oth. writ.] Unpublished poems and other writings; [pers.] I write about the human experience of suffering and vulnerability, of it's uniqueness and beauty for each individual. I use words, a painter uses Brush strokes and colour to create powerful images and impressions in the Realtor.; [a.] Edinburgh, Lothian, Scotland

STARR, JAMES MOLINEAUX
[b.] 28 August 1946, Manchester; [p.] Paul Starr, Florence Starr; [m.] Angela Mary Starr, 4 December 1971; [ch.] Marie Starr, Jean Starr; [ed.] Secondary School at Oldwood Secondary School Portway Wythenshawe; [occ.] Unemployed; [oth. writ.] Had other poems published in different books i.e. "All Over Again" in book the way it is "Golden Days" in book pleasure and pain; [pers.] I write for fun about anything and everything I keep my writings simple making them easy to read and understand

STEAD, JOANNE
[b.] I am over-60 and belong to the Chinese horoscope sign of the metal Monkey; [ed.] Life-long, latterly with the Open College of the Arts (England) and a local lively, Writers Circle; [occ.] Retired, from being Manager of a London Citizens Advice Bureau. (Also used to be Warden of a Seafarers Centre where I laughed all the time).; [memb.] 1. The World Peace Prayer Society (a non-profit, non-sectarian organization of New York, USA, Munich, Germany and Japan. 2. The Theosophical Society (England); [oth. writ.] One-act plays, non-fiction articles, radio-scripts, with humorous slant; [pers.] I meditate twice a day from ten minutes to 30 minutes after being initiated into a Hindu mantra in 1963. It changed my life for the better! Have lots of crystals reflecting the light on my windows and statues of Kuan Yin, the celestial Bodhisattva of Compassion around my rooms to remind me to be kinder of other people and to myself!; [a.] Leigh-on-Sea, Essex

STEPHENSON, MRS. WINIFRED
[b.] 24 March 1931, Liverpool; [p.] Hannah and Joseph Young; [m.] Thomas Stephenson, 2 December 1950; [ch.] Thomas, Alan, Susan, Mark; [ed.] St. Alphonsus Junior R.C. School, St. Bernard RC School; [occ.] Pensioner; [oth. writ.] Several poem as yet unpublished; [pers.] To the memory of my late parents, and beloved husband Thomas deceased. "All that I ask is you remember me"; [a.] Kirkby, Merseyside

STEVENS, CHARLOTTE
[b.] 8 April 1978, W'ton; [p.] Pam and Mike Stevens; [ed.] W'ton University after gaining 3 a levels at college; [occ.] University student; [oth. writ.] This is my first published poem as I have never considered them for publication before.; [pers.] I believe that communication and expression can create ultimate bonds between human beings.; [a.] W'ton, Staffs

STEVENSON, ROSALYN C.
[pen.] Rosalyn C. Ellis; [b.] 28 November 1916, Beckenham, Kent; [p.] Mr. and Mrs. A. E. Virgo; [m.] Arther Noel Stevenson, 19 August 1963; [ed.] Howard Secondary unable to learn, as I suffer from Dislexia self taught; [occ.] Retired; [memb.] The International Library of Poetry; [hon.] I won a small prize for art, age eight yrs. Later, I had an oil painting accepted for

hanging in gallery, for a while. Have good references.; [oth. writ.] 38 poems, and two prayers. Letters to politicians a royalty. Writing a book. But help up for the time being.; [pers.] I was a dance at school. But have taught myself. So am a late starter. I still have trouble with the dislexia I suffer from. I have a good ear for music.; [a.] Seaford, E. Sussex

STEWART, JOSEPHINE
[pen.] a private pseudonym which I use often as it has great meaning; [p.] "Of Good Stock"; [m.] Retired Professional Design Eng., 4 September 1961; [ch.] One; [ed.] Colleges in Gloucester area; [occ.] House Manager. Gardener. Hobbies are painting, music, poetry, photography, pictures, observing textiles; [memb.] Honorary mem: International Adoption Whale Soc, was frontline Greenpeace (supporter still) "Nature Conservation" RSPCA supporter, badger group, "Compassion World Farming", supporter painswich shows men.; [hon.] "Merit" in photography. At college, gained A/S pass and in painting and drawing an A pass. A remark at college was - we have a budding Shakespeare!! I was amused, flattered.; [oth. writ.] Poems of mine have been sent to important people around this planet. "Regency Press" have published my poems (in 1974). A short children's story is at fruition, but not published yet. I call all men to respect the "Jewel", "Mother Nature" the Children's "Noah's Ark of Compassion".; [pers.] I observe all around me and fell deeply unhappy about the way Nature, animals and children are treated. "The struggle for them is terribly intense." My poetry comes naturally for planet and all animals. "I try to make a point of great importance". Hoping people will see. I read a few at St. Andrews, Scotland. (All understood) and here sometime ago. "I want respect, dignity, protection."; [a.] Dursley, Gloucester

STONE, PAT
[pen.] Pat Stone; [b.] 7 February 1954, Bristol; [p.] June and Ivor Weaver; [m.] Robert Stone, 7 June 1975; [ch.] Richard and Robert; [ed.] Lockleaze Secondary School, Bristol; [occ.] School Secretary and School General Assistant (Juniors); [pers.] I began writing following the death of my daughter Leanne. I do not understand the source of my work - it just happens!; [a.] Bristol, Avon

STONEMAN, BRIAN
[b.] 4 May 1965, Walthamstow; [p.] Alan Stoneman, Gwen Stoneman; [m.] Kelly Stoneman, 12 March 1993; [ed.] Ertonwald Comprehensive School Dagenham Essex; [occ.] Mini cab driver; [pers.] This poem is dedicated to my mom and dad, for all the support and encouragement they have given me. I hope seeing my name in print will make them proud of their eldest son.; [a.] Romford, Essex

STORE, ROLAND
[b.] 26 May 1937, Dunfermline; [p.] Gordon Store, Elizabeth Store; [m.] Mairi Symon, 22 July 1967; [ch.] Christopher Gordon, Diana Mairi; [ed.] Mill Hill School; [occ.] Security Officer; [memb.] Subud Brotherhood; [pers.] Inspiration and the life within have been dominant influences.; [a.] Yateley, Hampshire

STRATFORD, SUSAN ROSE
[b.] 19 March 1955, Dorchester; [p.] Betty and Brian Gale; [m.] Paul Stratford, 29 July 1972; [ch.] Cara-Dawn and Zowie; [ed.] Dorchester Secondary Modern School; [occ.] School Dinner Lady; [pers.] This poem was written as a birthday gift to my mother. That is where I got my inspiration. Because I have always been surrounded by love.; [a.] Dorchester, Dorset

STRAUGHAN, MRS. P. A.
[pen.] Patricia Ann Straughan; [b.] 8 May 1943, Chipping, Norton, Oxon; [p.] Mr. J. Stowe, Mrs. E. Stowe (Deceased); [m.] James Leslie Straughan, 21 December 1966; [ch.] Colin Straughan, Iain Straughan; [ed.] Secondary Modern Mixed School; [occ.] Domestic Help; [hon.] Shorthand certificate Gow P.M., 6 School Leaving certificates, Domestic Science Needlework English, Maths, Science religious knowledge; [oth. writ.] I have 10-20 more poems here to submit if the need be.; [pers.]

I would like to publish all my poems and make them into an anthology; [a.] Cowley, Oxfordshire

STRAWBRIDGE, STANLEY
[b.] 25 October 1910; [p.] John Williams; [m.] Emma; [ch.] 1 Daughter, 1 Son; [ed.] Nottingham University 1929 to 1932, qualified as Mining Engineer and Geologist; [occ.] Retired; [memb.] Mimine FGS, Chairman of British Association of Colliery Management - South Wales Opencast Branch for twelve years 1961 to 1973; [pers.] Copy of Family Crest enclosed Motto Pee Ardua ad Sapientia I have an interest in the local good neighbors club (Free Masons) also member of local Old Age Pensioners Clubs, A Christian Believe in Helping others, Strawbridges were residents in the Moorland area of Devon and Cornwall and laid straw bales at the ends of clapper Bridges to facilitate crossing in times of flood.

STYLES, LESLEY
[pen.] Silver Underkoffler; [b.] Sunbury, PA; [oth. writ.] Poetry, children's stories; [a.] S. Devon

SURMAN, LINDA
[b.] 16 November 1961, Nelson, Lancs; [p.] Bill and May Surman; [m.] Alex, 1981; [ed.] Noadswood Secondary School, Waterside Adult Education Centre; [pers.] Personal interests: So newriting, poetry, playing the guitar and keyboard instruments; [a.] Southampton, Hampshire

SUTHERLAND, DONALD W.
[b.] 10 September 1936, Black-Isle; [p.] William Sutherland, Nina Sutherland; [m.] Brenda Sutherland, 17 March 1958; [ch.] Marcia, Lyn, Sutherland, Linda, Anne, Gordon; [ed.] Dingwall Academy, Invergordon Academy; [occ.] Retired (Funeral Director); [memb.] Writers North Invergordon Arts Centre; [pers.] I have an ear for all poetry of most types, when well read, the writings of the late Neil Gunn did wonders for my inspiration.; [a.] Alness, Ross-shire

SWABY, JOY
[pen.] Lunette Swaby; [b.] 10 November 1936, Jamaica, WI; [p.] Deceased; [m.] J. S. Swaby, 28 March 1959; [ch.] Howard, Richard, Paul, Pauline and Roger; [ed.] Jubilee Town Sch. Jamaica WI Community Education Lewisham; [occ.] Writing poems and short stories writers work shop CEL; [memb.] Holbeach Baptist Church SS Teacher, CEL Granville Park Swimming, CEL Morning Centre, Writers Work Shop, Storytelling Circle Lewisham; [hon.] English GCSE N.E.A. RSA Typewriting Skills WP skills; [oth. writ.] Short Stories and poem published in the mornington's cornucopia. Poem 'Anger' performed at Lewisham Theatre; [pers.] I am to express my feelings and others in my writing, I have been greatly encourage by my youngest son Roger, my poet grandson Damien and my Tutor Allison.; [a.] Catford, London

SWANSON, AVES
[b.] Dorset; [m.] David Swanson, 8 February 1963; [ch.] Two; [ed.] High School, Sturminsted, Newton Dorset; [occ.] Part time Nursing - Attendant (Retired Nurse); [oth. writ.] Poem published in a book of poetry in 1996 other poems written short stories.; [pers.] I like to bring in the beauty of nature and the natural things of life into my poems.; [a.] Sheringham, Norfolk

SWIDENBANK, PAUL ANTHONY
[pen.] Poet Swidenbank; [b.] 16 January 1974, Kendal; [p.] Mark Swidenbank, Glynis Jones; [ed.] Ghyllside Primary, Kirbie Kendal Lower, Kirbie Kendal Upper; [occ.] Waiter/Barman, Hotel Services; [oth. writ.] Poem published in an anthology called 'Sands Of Time' edited by Julie Bomber of poetry today; [pers.] My inspiration to write comes from seeing, hearing and feeling pain, happiness, sadness, joy, tragedy and love, my love for one very special woman Katy you know who you are! I feel that words are immortal, spoken or written, striving for world peace with a pen and paper.; [a.] Kendal, Cumbria

SYMES, BRADLEY BRUCE
[b.] 5 May 1958, Clacton-on-Sea, Essex; [p.] Harold Thomas Symes, Daisy Symes; [ch.] Robert Symes, Charlene Symes; [ed.] Colbayns High School; [occ.] Painter and Decorator; [oth. writ.] One other poem published in hardback.; [pers.] I come from a family of

8 brothers and 8 sisters of which I am the youngest brother. My hobbies are chess, which I find challenging, also anything artistic, e.g. painting in water colours and making decorative eggs from goose egg shells. I also enjoy country walks, this is frequently what inspires me to write poetry.; [a.] Clacton-on-Sea, Essex

SYMON, JUDITH EVELYN
[b.] 22 October 1935, Wimbledon; [p.] William Cran, Joan Cran; [m.] Alexander Symon, 7 March 1957; [ch.] Leslie Alexander Symon; [ed.] Sacred Heart Convent, Queens Cross, Aberdeen; [occ.] Housewife, Former Librarian and Teacher; [oth. writ.] Poems and short stories, this has been a hobby for many years - but I have not submitted any until now.; [pers.] I have enjoyed expressing my feelings upon life and it's situations, through poetry and landscape painting.; [a.] Aberchirder, Aberdeenshire

TAL, MICHAL
[pen.] Michal Tal; [b.] 12 May 1951, New York, USA; [p.] Rabbi Maurice and Mildred Aranor; [m.] Divorce (1990), 1971; [ch.] Four - Benji (21), Rami (18), Sarit (13 1/2), Edon (10 1/2); [ed.] Bachelor of Arts, Hebrew Literature (B.H.L.) Jewish Theological Seminary 1/2 M.A. (Teaneck) Fairleigh Dickenson U.; [occ.] Writer, writing 3rd novel, romance in ancient (Archarc) Greece; [memb.] Was student of the Artist and Internationally acclaimed Zohar (the Hague, e.g.) for 2 1/2 years, and model for 2 of his works. Inside me, "the writer", is an artist struggling to get out; [hon.] I have published several articles in Israel, the best, on mate dancers called "Guys Gotta Dance" in the Jerusalem Post. My book, "The Lion and the Cross" will be entered this spring in the "Jerusalem Prize for literature" contest fellow author, Naomi Gal, previous winner is pushing it for me.; [oth. writ.] 1st Novel Eastern Light (not yet pub. in English), 2 novel - The Won and Cross, Minerva in Jewish Boot Week, London, Press Mur. 10-17. I write a lot to the newspapers, t.v. etc. when something disturbs me morally lethically, justice is a big issue with me.; [pers.] Real feelings and real experiences, turned inside out and redecorated, make my characters "breathe". I like exotic themes (the Spanish Inquisition, Israel Archaic Greece) with characters that have universal empathy - potential.; [a.] Jerusalem, Israel

TALBOT, SAMANTHA
[b.] 15 August 1951, London, Dulwich; [p.] Harold Talbot, Vee Talbot; [m.] Divorced; [ed.] St. Johns (Private) Crawley Sx., Corona Academy of Dramatic Arts, London; [occ.] Female Vocalist (International Cabaret Artist); [oth. writ.] None published; [pers.] My writings are from my own experiences and deepest innermost feelings.; [a.] Crawley, West Sussex

TAYLOR, CLARE MICHELLE
[b.] 20 September 1979, Dewsbury; [p.] Michael and Gillian Taylor; [ed.] Ossett School 'A' Level Student; [occ.] 'A' Level Student; [oth. writ.] Poetry Anthology submitted for 'A' Level English course work; [pers.] In my writing I have tried to reflect the unfairness of society, the corruption of governments worldwide and the strength of "ordinary" people.; [a.] Wakefield, Yorkshire

TAYLOR, JANICE
[pen.] Janice Taylor; [b.] 23 September 1951, Birmingham; [p.] William and Elsie Taylor; [m.] Divorced; [ch.] Kerry, Claire; [ed.] Swanshurst Grammar School Bournville College of Further Education; [occ.] Shorthand/Audio Typist; [oth. writ.] Just for family and friends; [pers.] I like to write humorous anecdotes in verse on everyday life as I see it.; [a.] Birmingham, West Midlands

TAYLOR, JOANNE
[b.] 25 January 1970, Easington; [p.] Mr. Robert Kyle, Mrs. C. A. O'Connor; [m.] Paul Taylor, 29 October 1994; [ch.] Toni Michelle, Damien Aaryn Paul; [ed.] Shotton Hall Comprehensive, Co Durham; [occ.] Factory Worker, Housewife and Devoted Mother; [oth. writ.] I have my own person collection of poems and writings.; [pers.] If children were the light of life, the world be a much brighter place.; [a.] Chatteris, Cambs

575

TAYLOR, JULIE
[pen.] Julie Taylor; [b.] 15 September 1965, Birmingham; [p.] John Bennett, Marie Burbank; [m.] Lee Taylor, 21 February 1986; [ch.] James-Dean, Lisa-Marie, John Graham; [ed.] Waseley Hills High School; [occ.] House wife; [oth. writ.] Several poems published in anthologies.; [pers.] After receiving very little education through the fault of my own rebellion, I get a real thrill when I see my work in print.; [a.] King Norton, Birmingham

TAYLOR, MRS. KAY
[b.] 1909, Newport, Gwent; [p.] Mr. and Mrs. Burleigh; [m.] Mr. Sidney Taylor, 1946; [ch.] 3 step children; [ed.] Enville House Drayton High School, Newport, Gwent; [occ.] retired, was doctor's receptionist for years which I really loved, it was so interesting in those days; [oth. writ.] "As Time Goes Quickly By", published in Voices on the Wind; [pers.] I do lots of competitions, have won quite a few. I have only lately had poems published by you, but even in school days I loved writing poetry but never thought I'd have any published, now I am retired.; [a.] Newport, Gwent

TAYLOR, MR. LACHLAN
[pen.] Lachlan Taylor; [b.] 26 June 1922, Falkirk; [p.] William and Margaret Taylor (Deceased); [m.] Anne Henry Taylor (Deceased), 4 March 1967; [ed.] Comprehensive left at fourteen achieved day school lower certificate; [occ.] Retired Pensioner; [memb.] None today but previously had some; [hon.] Just Medals from the last war, being involved from 1939 until 1947; [oth. writ.] Have had numerous poems published in Anthology by different published firms.; [pers.] I have always been I interested in poetry but did not send in my work to poetry groups until 1993 and I have had more success than I expected. Words worth burns and shakespeare I enjoy.; [a.] Falkirk, Stirlingshire

TAYLOR, MALCOLM TAYLOR
[b.] 21 February 1950, York, England; [p.] George Thomas Taylor; [ed.] Chelsea School of Art (England) Saint Martins School of Art London. Royal College and Art. London, England; [occ.] Artist, Poet, Sculptor, Lecturer in Fine Art, drawing and sculpture; [memb.] Royal College of Art, Research Groups - Various, including Poetry, Film and Performance Group R.C.A. school of communication; [hon.] B.A. (Hons) 1st class, Guest Artist in Fine Art Drawing Glasgow School of Art, Guest Artist Musashino Art University, External Examiner Liverpool J.M. University, Ph.D. Supervisor Royal College of Art London; [oth. writ.] Several poems, published in hardback group compilations, Religious and Zen Metaphysical Type, Extensive fine art writing, currently compiling a book of reductive Zen Narrative Verses; [pers.] Large Scale Welded Steel, U.S.A. Type Sculpture produced as Resident Sculptor at Kvaener Cleveland Bridge LTD Darlington U.K., both find art and poetry endeavor to be accessive at all levels, dealing with both the spiritual and the everyday.; [a.] York, Yorkshire

TAYLOR, NICOLA SALLY
[pen.] Nicola Taylor; [b.] 6 May 1976, Wolverhampton; [p.] Ian Taylor, Bridget Clifford; [ed.] Red Hall Primary/Junior, Ellowes Hall Secondary, Halesowen College; [occ.] Student at Wolverhampton University; [pers.] I suffer with a disease called cystic fibrosis and have undergone a heart/lung transplant, currently awaiting a lung transplant. Through my poetry I can express myself without excursion or damage to my health.; [a.] Dudley, West Midlands

TAYLOR-KENT, APRIL LORRAINE
[pen.] April Raine; [b.] 18 October 1941, Barnsley; [p.] Myra and Bill Taylor; [m.] Bill Kent (Divorced), 29 October 1965; [ch.] Sarah, Alexander and Olivia; [ed.] Longcar Central School Barnsley, College of House craft, Ilkley W. Yorkshire, Open University Arts Course (Foundation); [occ.] Supply Teacher; [memb.] Barnsley Art Society/Committee Member of the Fan Circle International Member of St. Edward The Confessor Church Choir; [oth. writ.] For the Fan Circle International (F.C.I) Bulletin. For the Fan

Assoc. of North America (Fana) Quarterly and Freelance for variety and magazines.; [pers.] Poetry is one part of a creative force which includes many other discipline, all of which are exciting in themselves. It's often difficult to decide which one to take up any particular day, but they all have an influenced one on another. Poetry with strong visual qualities are especially enjoyable.; [a.] Barnsley, South Yorkshire

TEARE, WILLIAM
[b.] 21/01/1911, Sandygate, Isle of Man; [p.] Alfred Teare, Catherine Teare; [ed.] Sulby Primary School, Ramsey Grammar School, I obtained the only scholarship to Ramsey Grammar School (secondary school; [occ.] Retired Draper; [memb.] Have been a member and attended Sandygate Methodist Chapel for the past 78 years.; [hon.] As a Manx Gaelic Scholar I have conducted services at my local chapel in the Manx language which have been recorded and are held in the Manx Museum; [oth. writ.] Have had my own book of poems published entitled "The Manxland Muse". Most of my poems were composed whilst serving in the RAF out in Iraq during 1940-45; [pers.] I live for my faith and derive peace from it. My best work concerns itself with nature, death, war and "the ways of God with man".; [a.] Jurby, Isle of Man

TEEHAN, ANNMARIE
[pen.] Annmarie Teehan; [b.] 12 August 1984, London; [p.] Ann Teehan, John Hennessy; [ed.] Scoil Muire Lourdes Tullow, Co. Carlow, (Girls N.S.); [occ.] Student; [memb.] Foroige Exclamation Club; [hon.] Speech, Music, Poetry, Handwriting, Art, Football, Distinction in Music; [oth. writ.] Several other poems; [pers.] In personal poems I try to bring the character's personality in my writings.; [a.] Tullow, Carlow

TESTER-ELLIS, FREDA G.
[b.] 20 February 1920, Bognor Regis, West Sussex; [p.] Frederick and Gladys White; [m.] Philip Ellis (3rd), 22 March 1980; [ch.] David Grant Tester; [ed.] Chichester High School for girls; [occ.] Writer and Home Maker; [oth. writ.] Autobiography 'The Days Grow Short' published May '96 poems in many anthologies children's books yet to be published.; [pers.] My poems reflect the joy and pain of my life up to now.; [a.] Brighton, E. Sussex

THOM, IRENE
[pen.] Irini; [b.] 27 October, Accrington; [occ.] Retired; [oth. writ.] Personal poems for friends special occasions.

THOMAS, KATRINA MARIE
[b.] 5 November 1961, Sale Moor; [p.] Marie Elizabeth Maddick (Deceased), George Walter Maddick (Deceased); [m.] Martin Richard Thomas, 8 December 1990; [ch.] David Mark and Matthew Joseph; [ed.] Sale Grammar School for Girls; [occ.] Medical Social Worker; [hon.] (DIPSW) Diploma of Social Work; [pers.] My fathers death has deepened my belief in spiritual existence. I take heart that he will guide me along the right path during my life. The poem came from my inner soul.; [a.] Baguley, Manchester

THOMAS, NATALIE
[pen.] Ann Pageant; [b.] London; [p.] Charles Arnold and Minnie Arnold; [m.] Gil Thomas; [ch.] Debbie, Christopher; [ed.] Boarding School, Bexhill-on-Sea; [occ.] Retired (Foreign Office); [memb.] Wickwoods Country Club, West Sussex; [oth. writ.] Children's poem in Scottish Magazine. Short story, Woman's Own, short story My Weekly, articles, Kent Life.; [pers.] I am fascinated by science fiction and fantasy. Alternatively, I find the writings of Colette riveting and the early poets influential.; [a.] Rustington, W. Sussex

THOMAS, PHIL
[b.] 28 August 1968, Wakefield; [p.] Melvyn and Jackie Thomas; [ch.] Kyle Dominic Thomas - 2 yrs. old; [ed.] Wakefield City High, Eastmoor, Wakefield, West Yorkshire; [occ.] Retail Management; [memb.] Member of R.S.P.B., supporter of any other animal welfare charities or trusts; [oth. writ.] Various poems of different subjects and styles. None of which I've sent for possible publication - however I'm working on it!!; [pers.] Words cannot describe the tremendous feeling of

knowing I'd made print. But a second publication would prove to me that the first wasn't a fluke. We'll see!?; [a.] Wakefield, West Yorkshire

THOMAS, RHYS
[pen.] Donald David; [b.] 13 June 1918, Llandovery, Carmarthenshire; [p.] Thomas Thomas, Mary Thomas; [m.] Catherine Thomas nee Barret, 21 January 1945; [ch.] Son - Rhydian Thomas (Deceased); [ed.] Amman Valley Grammar (South Wales), Loughborough College, Dudley Art-School - Art Diploma, Birmingham University; [occ.] Retired Headmaster - Combe Down School, Bath 1962-1979; [memb.] Life Membership - National Association of Head Teachers; [hon.] Many and varied!; [oth. writ.] Poems, plays, Christmas Plays, part-time sport correspondent - "Donald David" - "Amman Valley Chronicle" Local press "The Welshman" - Welsh National Press; [pers.] Still interested in sporting activities. Regret that much of the fun, fellowship and sheer enjoyment of taking part, seems to have almost disappeared. Avid reader of the poetry of young students.; [a.] City of Bath, North Somerset

THOMASON-MACLEOD, MAGGI
[pen.] Maggi L. Thomason-MacLeod; [b.] 19 September 1945, Dudley, England; [p.] Ethel Hurst and Charles Leslie Thomason; [m.] Jim MacLeod, 1984; [ch.] Tessa, Jenny; [ed.] Dudley Girls High School, Wolverhampton Art School, University of Victoria in Canada; [occ.] Hotel Proprietor and Craftsperson; [hon.] B.F.A. University of Victoria B.C. Canada; [oth. writ.] Many poems, some published in "poetry now" anthology; [pers.] North West Sutherland has been my home and inspiration for the last 22 years. I hope some of the magic of this place reaches other people through my poems; [a.] Bettyhill, Sutherland

THOMPSON-HUGHES, JESS
[b.] 24 February 1944, Manchester; [p.] Frank Thompson-Hughes, Joan; [m.] Margaret Kathleen Lee, 18 December 1962; [ch.] Jess David, Denise Margaret; [ed.] Barrow-in-Furness Technical School, University College Salford.; [occ.] Business Liaison Consultant. Manchester College of Arts and Technology; [memb.] Institute of Supervisory Management. English Heritage; [oth. writ.] Several articles published in local news papers, and historical news letters.; [pers.] Inspired by the writings of Conan Doyle, I try to explore the richness of the past.; [a.] Mobberley, Cheshire

THORN, JOANNA
[b.] 20 September 1979; [p.] Shirley Thorn; [occ.] Student (College), BTEC National Diploma (Childhood Studies); [oth. writ.] Life As Love, 1. Garden Of Love, 2. Both As One, 3. Thoughts, 4. You Care, I Care, 5. Feelings, 6. Strong Love, 7. Sonnet Of Love; [a.] London

THORNE, BRENDA MAVIS
[b.] 19 September 1936, Chesterfield; [p.] Arthur Souter, Lilian Souter; [m.] Alan Thorne, 4 May 1981; [ch.] Carol Ann, Philip Arthur; [ed.] Hollingwood Girls Secondary Modern School (Chesterfield Area); [occ.] Retired Education Care Officer for Special Needs; [memb.] Chesterfield Mission Choir and involvement in local church work; [hon.] City and Guilds Initial Teaching Certificates for Literacy and Numeracy in Adult Basic Education; [oth. writ.] "Rhythm and Rhyme" Locally published compilation of religious poems and songs; [pers.] I have received much encouragement over the years, from family and friends and I am happy for this opportunity for my poetry to reach a wider audience.; [a.] Chesterfield, Derbyshire

THORNE, JACQUELYNE WENDY
[b.] 10 January 1945, Ryde, IOW; [p.] Arthur Nevett, Cynthia Nevett; [m.] Darryl Lee Thorne, 26 September 1992; [ch.] David-James Gary Lindsay; [ed.] Secondary Modern; [occ.] Electronics Assembler; [hon.] NVQ 2 Electronics; [oth. writ.] None published; [pers.] I get my inspiration from life, and the way of the world, the poems I write reflect if I am happy or sad, so they are written from the heart.; [a.] Havant, Hampshire

THORNTON, LESLEY
[b.] 22 October 1975, Kidderminster; [p.] Pauline Thornton, Brian Thornton; [ed.] Arnewood Comprehensive School, New Milton, Bournemouth and Poole College of Further Education, Eastleigh College; [occ.] Decorating Advisor-Assistant, New Milton, British Red Cross - Voluntary; [memb.] The National Asthma Campaign, British Red Cross - Lymington, Lymington Hospital Broadcasting Association, Hordle Church Choir, Highcliffe Infinity Camera Club; [hon.] The Royal School of Church Music - Amateur Athletic Association 5 Star Award Scheme; [oth. writ.] Several poems which are yet to be published.; [pers.] "To read a line gives us the basis of what is being said. To be able to read between the lines, explodes us into new depths of hidden thoughts and meanings."; [a.] Lymington, Hants

THRELFALL, JADE
[b.] 14 July 1981, Wolverhampton; [p.] Kevin Threlfall and Gillian Threlfall; [ed.] St. Dominic's School, Brewood; [pers.] I would like to dedicate this poem to the memory of my late grandfather, Arthur D'Arcy Thomas, who was a great lover of poetry.; [a.] Wolverhampton, West Midlands

TICA, MARLENE-ANN
[b.] 15 April 1952, Atherstone; [p.] Joyce and Vic Tica; [m.] Keith Tica, 20 September 1980; [ch.] Luke Simon; [ed.] Kingsbury High School and currently studying with the Open University - BA in Literature; [occ.] Mature Student; [oth. writ.] Poetry and short stories. One of my poems, 'A Carpet Red' was published in an anthology called 'Midland Poets'.; [pers.] To me prose is a house with many windows, the scenery changes from every view point. But poetry is a mirror, for no matter how we may tilt or turn it, it only reflects reality.; [a.] Atherstone, Warwickshire

TICKLE, ARTHUR JOSEPH
[b.] 20 July 1939, Moorthorpe; [p.] Arthur Tickle, Sally Tickle; [m.] Eileen Ellis (Deceased - 4 July 1995), 10 March 1962; [ch.] Andrea and Mandy; [ed.] Hemsworth Grammar School, Doncaster Technical College; [occ.] Retired - was a British Coal Colliery Undermanager; [memb.] Chartered Engineer, Member of British Association Colliery Management (BACM), R.S.P.B. member; [hon.] First class Certificate of Competency for mining, Associate member of Institute of Mining Engineers (A.M.J.Min. E.), Chartered Engineer (C. Eng.); [oth. writ.] Several poems published in local papers, and some accepted by arrival press publishing, Peterboro.; [pers.] I was spurred into writing poetry upon the death of my wife. Initially all was to her memory and was dedicated. Latterly passed onto sporting and humerus verse.; [a.] Hemsworth, Pontefract, West Yorks

TIERNEY, DAVID PATRICK
[pen.] Odd Job; [b.] 2 February 1954, Oldham ; [p.] James Tierney, Mabel Tierney; [m.] Josephine Tierney, 8 October 1972; [ch.] Four, James, Annamarie, Michael, Lee; [ed.] Count Hill Grammer School, Derker Secondary Modern, University of Life; [occ.] Engineer; [memb.] GSD (Gibraltar, Soisel Democrats); [hon.] Diploma, Import, Export; [oth. writ.] Songs thoughts and of course poetry; [pers.] Poetry is the true heart of mankind and the poet is the voice of all that is true in the spirit of man - Dr. Tierney.; [a.] Gibraltar

TILBURY, PAULINE HAZEL
[b.] 8 April 1936, Sunninghill, Berks; [p.] Tom and Kate, Laney Berks; [m.] Kenneth Bernard Tilbury, 17 April 1954; [ch.] Sylvia, Angela, June, Keith; [ed.] Sunninghill Berks, C.E. on to Windsor College Further Education. I am so thrilled I really cannot believe this, thank you all.; [occ.] Housewife; [memb.] Healer Practitioner Association International, Membership No. 1608, have qualified for this at AMIDA School of Healing; [hon.] Top at School for scripture and won a beautiful Bible. Many years ago. I also have been blessed with 4 beautiful children, 5 grandchildren, all boys.; [oth. writ.] I have written quite a lot of poems, and have been trying to write a book. On one of my children all the sad things that have happened in her life.; [pers.] I have been a spiritual healer for 5 years and love doing the healing, it

is so nice when you have it confirmed that the person, or animal, is much better or the pain gone.; [a.] Torquay, Devon

TINKLER, MRS. GLORIA
[b.] 22 November 1931, Peterborough; [p.] Arthur Steels, Lucy Steels; [m.] Leslie Gordon Tinkler, 3 July 1951; [ch.] Ann Susan; [ed.] Secondary School; [occ.] Housewife; [memb.] John Clare Society, The Poetry Club, Wales.; [hon.] 2 Commendations from the Poetry Club 1995 and 1996 editor's choice award from the International Library of Poetry.; [oth. writ.] Book published 1986 have written many other poems since 1953.; [pers.] I try to express my feelings and thoughts in poetry.; [a.] Peterboro, Cambs

TOLLEY, CONSTANCE MAY
[b.] 21 April 1936, Corley, Warwickshire; [ed.] Basic Education, self taught on most subjects; [occ.] Retired; [hon.] In younger life - commended Balerina (Certificate Stating this) 6th grade Classical Guitar Player. Extra material only.; [oth. writ.] "Svengali", Child In The Snow "Despair", ("The Face At The Window", "The Letter"), not entered into any competitions as yet; [pers.] Pain is more than a word one speaks it is a layer of skin that suddenly grows all over you. The root being inside. Making you want to tear your self apart from inside out. Writing my pain on paper helped to heal the huge space left inside this shell of a body.; [a.] Birmingham, West Midlands

TOLLEY, DOUG
[pen.] Doug Tolley; [b.] 10 May 1976, Duns, Scotland; [p.] Anita Tolley, Chris Tolley; [ed.] Sir Henry Floyd Grammar School Aylesbury, Guildhall University London (Classical Guitar Making Course); [occ.] Business Support Assistant Oxford Customs and Excise Office; [oth. writ.] Large selection of unpublished poetry and philosophical notes written over the last 2-3 years; [pers.] Influences and inspiration from Jim Morrison's poetry and that from Jason noble. I have also been affected by the music of June of 44, Rachel's, Slint, Rodan and Steve Albwi. I strive for respect from worthy contemporaries rather than compromise for mass, and often meaningless appeal.; [a.] Waddesdon, Bucks

TOMPKIN, TREVOR MICHAEL
[b.] 9 March 1957, Stafford; [p.] Cyril Tompkin, Ruth Tompkin; [m.] Susan Elizabeth Tompkin, 17 June 1978; [ch.] Sarah Louise Elizabeth, Jennifer Ann Marie; [ed.] The Leys High School; [occ.] Works Director T.T. Fasteners L.T.D.; [oth. writ.] None published; [pers.] I was attempting to portray an honest and true life experience of my feelings at the time.; [a.] Inkberrow, Worcestershire

TOPLISS, CAROL
[pen.] Carol Mashiter-Harrison, Carol Maud; [b.] 14 December 1948, Barrow-in-Furness; [p.] Ethel Mashiter, Len Mashiter; [m.] Alan Topliss, 24 May 1980; [ed.] Seymour Park Sec. Modern for girls: Stretford Technical College, Derby College of Art and Technology; [occ.] Retired Secretary; [oth. writ.] Poems in local newspapers and school magazines. Short stories in teenage and women's magazines. Articles for school magazine.; [pers.] I strive to use my experience of life by celebrating the highs and exercising the lows in my poetry and stories.; [a.] Swadlincole, Leicestershire

TORNEY, GAYE
[b.] 4 July 1955, Melbourne, Australia; [ed.] Lowther Hall Anglican Girls Grammar, Essendon, Australia; [occ.] Intensive Care Nurse, Redcliff Hospital, Queensland, Australia; [memb.] President-Peninsula Poets Society, Redcliff, Qld, Australia, member - Fellowship of Australian Writers, Qld, member - Queensland Writers Centre; [hon.] Justice of the Peace (Qual.) Bachelor of Health Science; [oth. writ.] Highly Commended in National Short Story Competition. Poems published in Anthology by Peninsula Poets.; [pers.] England is my second home and my ancestral home. I endeavour to visit every second year. My poetry is varied but generally reflects on our environment.; [a.] Hapton, Lancs

TRAINOR, JAMES D.
[b.] 22 April 1932, Manchester; [occ.] Retired; [a.] Huyton, Merseyside

TULLY, GORDON GILBERT
[pen.] G.G.T.; [b.] 27 July 1921, Cardiff; [p.] James Alan Tully, Mary Elizabeth Jane Tully; [m.] Sara Alice (Marshall) Tully, 23 August 1941; [ch.] (Seven) youngest Sally-Ann (Artist); [ed.] Kitchener Road School; [occ.] Retired Senior Section Manager British Steel; [memb.] S.I.M.A., R.O.A.B.; [oth. writ.] Several poems published; [pers.] To really know God is the only way to really live.; [a.] Drakewalls, Cornwall

TURNER, JOHN MARTIN
[pen.] John Martin Turner; [b.] 1 May 1938, Loughton, Essex; [p.] George Turner, Elenor Turner; [ed.] Secondary, Loughton, Essex; [occ.] Helping out in heaven; [pers.] John died on 29th Feb 1996 from lung cancer, he had been fighting it for quite sometime. Writing poems came to John late in his life but he said he loved it and enjoyed reading it - a surprise to himself.; [a.] Loughton, Essex

TURNER, RICHARD
[b.] 22 March 1970, Reading, Berks; [p.] Anthony Phillip, Brenda Joy Turner; [m.] Sarah-Jane Turner, 31 March 1990; [ch.] Laura-Leigh, Tarnya Jane, Chelsea Emica; [ed.] Theale Green School, Newbury College; [occ.] Storeman; [oth. writ.] Several personal "The Sighting" is first attempt at competition. Also some unpublished lyrics.; [pers.] "Enjoy what you have but reach for your dreams."; [a.] Thatcham, Berkshire

TURNER, SHAUN
[b.] 4 March 1979, Forest Gate; [p.] Mr. and Mrs. Haynes; [ed.] Business Gnuq Course, Qualification at St. Bonventures, St. Angecas College; [occ.] College Student; [oth. writ.] Myself as a car, poets life etc.; [pers.] I am grateful for this great opportunity I am duly inspired by my parents Mrs. and Mrs. Haynes, and I hope to continue writing.; [a.] London

TWOSE, ERIC
[pen.] Rohan Powell, H. M. Forester; [b.] 7 November 1957, Scarborough; [ed.] Scarborough Boys High School, Scarborough VIth form College, Newcastle-upon-Tyne Polytechnic; [occ.] Electronics Test Engineer; [oth. writ.] Lead article in a corn user magazine, collection of poetry entitled 'Heart To Heart' published (Istari Publishing); [pers.] Gratefully dedicated to Doris Lessing-and to the late Sufi Mystic Idries Shah, 'People Like Us'. Whose action-philosophy has profoundly influenced my life. May you stay forever young at heart. Baraka!; [a.] Scarborough, North Yorkshire

UDEH, GREGORY PATRICK
[pen.] Gregory Patricks; [b.] 15 August 1956, Nigeria; [p.] Mr. Udeh Akparike, Mrs. Margaret Williams; [ed.] Awgu High School, Nenwe, Nigeria, University of Nigeria, Nsukka, Enugu State, Nigeria; [occ.] Accountancy, Auditing; [memb.] The Chartered Association of Certified Accountants, Association of Nigerian Authors. Institute of Chartered Accountants of Nigeria. Amnesty International; [oth. writ.] Author: 'The Devil's Vineyard', an unpublished novel, of which the nominated poem is a prologue. Columnist: 'The Point' and 'The Daily Observer' newspapers in The Gambia. Writings included regular short stories, poems, philosophical essays and opinions articles.; [pers.] My writings are influenced by my keen sense of injustice around the world today. I strive to point out that people should stop hiding under the ignoble cloak of 'society' to cause suffering and death to others. A just social order can only evolve when people realize that 'society' is you and me, and that our individual actions can make or mar us all.; [a.] Mitcham, Surrey

UGBA, DAVID
I was born in my home town of Ogwashi-Uku, Delta State, Nigeria in October 22nd, 1965. I attended Ikelike Primary School and latter Nshiagu College all in the aforementioned town and country. My poetry has been published in various newspapers and jour-

nals in Nigeria. I am presently a final year Law Student (500L) in the University of Benin, Nigeria. My dream is to major in International Law as well as to settle in real business with poetry.

VAID, MONICA
[pen.] Mon; [b.] 14 September 1978, Harrow; [p.] Rani and Sardar Vaid; [ed.] Rooksheath High School - I did nine GCSE's and achieved 4A's, 2A's, 2B's and 1C. Now I'm at Greenhill College. After Uni, I want to go to National School of Drama in India; [memb.] I have attended in numerous drama classes. At the moment, I attend 'Kathak' and 'Bhangra' dance classes. I have done courses in cake decorating and flower-arranging; [hon.] I was awarded first prize for a poem I had written and short story of mine received a commendation by the Harrow Borough; [oth. writ.] Besides 'Art: The Lie That Reveals A Truth,' I have written many other poems and short stories.; [pers.] Words are so important, but only when said with feeling and emotion. I write, not for the sake of writing but only when I have something powerful, something compelling to write about. Words, to me, are ways of expression of my inner thoughts and dreams.; [a.] Harrow, Middlesex

VAIL, GEORGE
[b.] 6 December 1943, Bury; [p.] Marian and Sidney Vail; [m.] Edna, 13 August 1988; [ch.] Four; [ed.] Secondary Modern; [occ.] P.S.V. Driver; [memb.] Royal Naval Association; [hon.] 14 Yrs. Safe Driving Award; [pers.] I believe in enjoying life to the full, and if you can't do a good turn for someone don't do a bad one.; [a.] Bury, Lancs

VALE, ADRIAN
After Cambridge, where he was Footlights President in his last year, he joined M.C.A. (England) and T.V. & Radio script agent. Moved into Associated-Rediffusion as drama script editor, and later two other I.T.V. companies before being invited to Dublin to set up the drama script department of about-to-open R.T.E.
During his 18 years there he wrote his own T.V. and Radio plays, and devised two Dublin Theatre Festival productions, coming back after 18 years to work in B.B.C. T.V. Series & Serials, and to read for a play competition. Subsequently he ran a postal writing course, and is now a reader for a London literary agency.
Married to the actress, Angela Vale. They have five daughters, including twins who, almost inevitably, are in the business tool

VALENTINE, MISS CHARLEY
[pen.] Miss Charley Valentine; [ed.] Currently in final year studying English Lit. at University of Glamorgan, was previously training to be a Psychiatric Nurse; [occ.] Student, (also part-time nursing); [oth. writ.] Non-fiction, currently doing research for project on self-injury. Unpublished poetry and short fiction.; [pers.] 'Do not listen to a word I say, just listen to what I can keep silent'. The truth is always too dangerous to utter, and the true matter of my poetry is encoded into its structure. It is this dichotomy that reflects the duality of the mind.; [a.] Pontypridd, Mid-Glamorgan

VARA, MISS REKHA
[b.] 24 September 1971, Wansjalia, India; [p.] Mr. Sundarji Vara and Mrs. Bhanumati Vara; [ed.] 10 GCSE's, 3 'A' Levels currently doing 3 year BSC Psychology honours degree at University of East London; [occ.] Student; [hon.] Awarded 2nd prize for London schools poetry competition in 1987 when I was 15; [pers.] Being female, the Asian community aims to protect its daughter's from the evils of the outside world. Not realizing that the world they are protecting them from, is the one they have to live in. Being female and Asian, Western Society imposes enormous boundaries on achievements and enforces negative stereotypes to promote the status quo. Freedom seems far away to me.; [a.] Charlton, London

VARNHAM, SUSAN ALBERTA
[pen.] Berlie Varnham; [b.] 13/9/1915, Rothbury; [p.] deceased; [m.] married in 1934; [ch.] one son; [ed.] I was educated in a village school, at Embleton, Northumberland; [occ.] housewife; [oth. writ.] My birthday will be on the 13th Sept. This will be a special

moment as I will be 82.; [pers.] I have never won anything as great as this honour. I am just out of the hospital and this has certainly given my life a big lift; [a.] Alnwick, Northumberland

VEITCH, MRS. EDITH MAY
[b.] 19 May 1914, Chelmsford, Essex; [p.] Herbert and Louisa Whybrow; [m.] Gordon A. R. Veitch, 5 July 1947; [ch.] John R. Veitch, 25 July 1944; [ed.] St. John's School, Chelmsford, Essex; [occ.] Housewife, Mother, Retired School Meals Service Assistant Cook; [memb.] Local Flower Club (Floral Art for Church, etc.) and WI during lifetime; [oth. writ.] Many poems and personalized tributes (in poetry) for friends, relatives, birthday cards, etc.; [pers.] A "Natural" Amateur Poetess inspired by events throughout her life, many tragic, a kind but strong and humorous character, loved by all her friends and relatives village - Hatfield Peverel.; [a.] Chelmsford, Essex

VERNON, GWENDA
[pen.] Gwen Vernon; [b.] 14 April 1949, Richmond, N Yorks; [p.] Ronald Stanley and Dorothy Mary Gilligan; [m.] 8 March 1969, Divorced in 1983; [ch.] Stephanie, Cavern; [ed.] Richmond Cofe County Modern; [occ.] Factory worker in an Upmarket Lighting Company; [memb.] Peacehaven Machine Knitting Club; [pers.] I like to write poetry from personal experiences, of which I try to make humorous, to lighten the situations I inevidently find myself in this is the first poem I have ever sent off for any reason.; [a.] Seaford, East Sussex

VERRIER, JAMES L. G.
[b.] 29 December 1971; [p.] Carel Verrier, Leonard Verrier; [m.] Elaine Hardy; [ch.] Natalie A.B., Robin A.B., Maderine C.L.; [ed.] St. Edwards Cofe Comprehensive London Rd, Romford. Writte College Essex; [occ.] Propagator Writte College Essex; [pers.] I doubt everything, except that which I believe in and that is for all others to doubt for to believe would be foolish therefore to disbelieve would be believable.; [a.] Witham, Essex

VIAL, NOELLE
[b.] 25 December 1959, Donegal; [p.] Patrick and Peggy Sharkey; [m.] Charles E. Vial, 26 June 1976; [ch.] Four boys and one girl; [ed.] Left school at Sixteen to get married; [occ.] Poet/Housewife Part-time Creative Writing Instructor; [memb.] Killybegs Writer's Group of which I am The Founder and it's very first Chairperson (1982) and Donegal Endeavors an Intermediate Arts Organization (92); [hon.] Donegal Poet of the Year 1990, The William Allingham Award, The Patrick McGill Summer School Award, 2nd prize Gerard Manely Hopkins Award, Short-listed Poetry Ireland Award and "Best poetry by an Emerging Poet Hennessy Literary Award"; [oth. writ.] First book published in Dec. 1995 "Promiscuous Winds", poems by Noelle Vial, published by Story Line Press, Org. U.S.A. (only on sale in America, I am looking for a publisher this side of the Atlantic).; [pers.] Being a poet is my vocations in life - it's what I do - I do not see it as a hobby! My only female influence has been Carol Ann Duffy (The Poet) who work I admire greatly.; [a.] Killybegs, Donegal, Ireland

VINALL-BURNETT, MARGARET
[b.] 3 October 1913, Haslemere; [p.] Frances and Arthur Benneyworth; [m.] Albert Vinall - Robert Burnett, 1940 - 1945 (Widow Twice); [ch.] Naney, Albert, Carolina Rosalind, Robert, Dorothy, Jeff, Kenneth; [ed.] Cross in Hand Village School 1924-29; [occ.] Retired Cook; [memb.] Disabled Association Sussex Access; [oth. writ.] Sussex poems, magazines, poetry now Devin and Dorset P1B1; [pers.] All of my poem's are taken from real life incidents.; [a.] East Borne, Sussex

VINER, DEBBIE
[b.] 18 April 1968, Reading; [m.] Mike, 20 April 1996; [ch.] Liam, Step-children: Cathy, Tim and Chris; [ed.] Meadway Comprehensive, Reading; [occ.] Childcare; [memb.] Member of Mensa; [pers.] My poems are triggered by my emotions, and are about experiences I I have had.; [a.] Shrewsbury, Shropshire

VINEY, MARIE
[b.] 9 December 1936, Barrow in Furness; [p.] Victor and Mary Dempsey; [m.] Geoffrey J. Viney; [ed.] Victoria Secondary Modern School Barrow-in-Furness; [occ.] Housewife; [pers.] In a world influenced by quick change, the media, the thoughts and ideas others. Wisdom should be sought in the unfading beauty in our natural surroundings. In what we are, what we can be.; [a.] Leeds, W. Yorkshire, LS8 2NB

VONRANKEN, ANGELA
[b.] 4 June 1933, Eltham; [p.] Ena and Harry Quicke; [m.] Deceased, 10 May 1952; [ch.] Peter, Stephen, Christine, Beverley, Teresa and Debbie,; [ed.] St. Winifreds Grammar, N. Wales Municipal College, Southend-on-Sea; [occ.] Retired; [hon.] Commercial Art and Design, Athletics Awards; [oth. writ.] Poems short stories articles published.; [pers.] My originality derives from within and from my perception of life past Andi present. Works of Art, books poems etc.; [a.] Southend, Essex

WADDELL, CAROLINE
[b.] 9 June 1976, Glasgow; [p.] Jean and John Waddell; [ed.] Eastbank Academy, Glasgow; [occ.] I am currently unemployed; [oth. writ.] Amateur poems and personal poems for family and friends.; [pers.] My poem "The Window of Life" is the way I see life, living in a Glasgow Housing Scheme.; [a.] Glasgow

WADIKAR, MADHUKAR
[pen.] M. L.; [b.] 30 January 1937, Satara; [p.] Laxman Wadikar, Indira Wadikar; [m.] Vijaya Wadikar, 8 June 1963; [ch.] Sucharita, Suvarna, Animesh; [ed.] Fergusson College and Poona University, Kashi Vidyapeeth; [occ.] Professor of English, R.K.T. College, Bombay University; [memb.] All India English Teachers Association, International Association of Teachers of English, as a Foreign Language, Distinguished Member of The International Society of Poets; [hon.] Semi-final Round, International Poetry Competition, 1955, Poem 'Aufklarung' published in 'Voices on the Wind' by the International Society of Poets (Franz), Presenting a paper on Hopkins in April 97 at IATEFL Conference, Brighton, Sussex; [oth. writ.] Several poems written, articles written, published in 'New Quest' and 'Vikram University Journal'; [pers.] I always seek internal reality behind things. The idea of integrity and inner honor overwhelms me.; [a.] Bombay, Ulhasnagar, India

WAKEFIELD, R. E.
[b.] 8 February 1913, Islington.; [p.] Thomas George, Elizabeth Jane; [m.] Mary Ellen Wakefield, 17 November 1935.; [ch.] Ronald Eric, Peter John, David Michael; [ed.] Secondary: Islington Polytechnic, qualified Electrician, Radio Mechanic, Fireman, Pro Boxer; [occ.] retired.; [hon.] Editors choice award—International Society of Poets; [oth. writ.] Many small poems, essays and etc.; [pers.] I strive to assist folk in need in the interest of compassion and the understanding of human frailty; and to show, in my works, the importance of hope and a way out of the most trivial difficulties.; [a.] London

WAKEFIELD, REBECCA MARY
[pen.] Rebecca Wakefield; [b.] 15 June 1981, Saint Leonards; [p.] Keith and Mary Wakefield; [ed.] St. Pauls C of E Primary, St. Richards R.C. Comprehensive School; [occ.] Student; [hon.] 1066 Hastings Poetry Competition - highly commended 12/10/89; [oth. writ.] Other poems for local competitions; [pers.] I have always had an interest in poetry from an early age, I find it the best way to describe my thoughts, whether happy or sad.; [a.] Hastings, East Sussex

WAKEFORD, AILEEN
[b.] Suffolk; [p.] George Rivett-Carnac; [m.] Edward Wakeford, 1945; [memb.] Arvon Fountain; [hon.] Previously, I have had poems published in 'Smith Knolls' and other known publications. I have diploma in English Literature. [oth. writ.] I've had a poem and short stories on the radio. I have written two novels and I'm currently working on my autobiography. I have been several short stories published.; [pers.] I write for our conviction in life. My poems are both sad and humorous.; [a.] London

WALDRON, CARMEN LAMAS
[pen.] Carmen Lamas Waldron; [b.] 27 April 1945, Lima, Peru; [p.] Carlos Lamas and Dora Crespo; [m.] Luke Waldron, 18 December 1971; [ch.] Kathleen, William and Anthony; [ed.] Social Studies, Public Relations and Literature; [occ.] Social Worker, Poet; [hon.] 1st prize Women's Festival Poetry Competition, Tallaght, Co. Dublin, Ireland; [oth. writ.] Book of poems: "Comunicandonos" in Spanish.; [a.] Maynooth, Co. Kildare, Ireland

WALKER, GLEN
[b.] 27 June 1972, Southampton; [p.] Wendy, Mike Walker; [ed.] Millbrook Community School Life (School of); [occ.] Dog Handler for Lowes Guarding Services (Assistant Supv); [oth. writ.] I have written a book entitled "My Words, Your Interpretations" but as yet have not submitted it for publication.; [pers.] Look into your heart with your mind and then write about what you see. That is poetry! Thanks to my Nan `Mims', who is always my greatest inspiration.; [a.] Soton, Hampshire

WALKER, MRS. JEAN MARGARET
[pen.] "Rose Petal"; [b.] October 22, 1921, London; [p.] Rosina and Walter Bradstock; [m.] Thomas Leslie Walker, (Deceased) May 10, 1943; [ch.] Jill Rosina and Peter Graham Walker (deceased); [ed.] Carlton House School Brighton Regretfully closed as a school many years ago, and Evening Classes Brighton Technical College; [occ.] Retired Fully trained ABTA Travel Agent Manager.; [memb.] Was a member of travel agent's club, and was on the committee. And various connections with travel; [hon.] Received several certificates connected with travel; [oth. writ.] Just one small article in national magazine, not a poem; [pers.] I want to dedicate this poem in everlasting memory of my beloved son and also with fondest love and deep gratitude to my dearest daughter who has helped me so much, and her family, and my beloved husband, without whom none of this poem would have been possible; [a.] Brighton, East Sussex

WALKER, NICOLA NATASHA G.
[b.] 11 February 1976, Middlesex; [p.] Geraldine Walker, Roy Walker; [ed.] The Douay Martyr's School (R.C.) Ickenham, London Guildhall University; [occ.] Politics Student; [hon.] Academic Awards, Water Skiing certificate and Bronze and Silver medals for skiing; [oth. writ.] Several other poems as yet unpublished; [pers.] Poetry is a means whereby one can capture a certain mood, or period of history. I hope my poetry both reflects and provokes comment on our present society.; [a.] Northolt, Middlesex

WALKER, MISS NINA-MARIE
[b.] 7 April 1967, Guildford; [p.] Mrs. I. Andrews; [ed.] Broadwater County, Farncombe, Godalming Surrey; [occ.] Care Assistant; [memb.] The Red Cross Society; [hon.] None tho many certificates all to do with the red cross.; [oth. writ.] Nothing published, but I have written many poems on personal and private accounts and on things in life which have touched me.; [pers.] I am an optimist, unrepentant and militant. After all, in order not to be a fool, an optimist must know how sad a place the world can be. It is only the pessimist who finds this out a new every day.; [a.] Guildford, Surrey

WALL, EDGAR
[b.] 19 May 1916, Bristol; [p.] George and Florence; [m.] Edna Audrey Sowden (Deceased 1986), 9 April 1939; [ch.] Peter Richard and Jane Roberta; [ed.] School Bristol, East Bristol Central School, Full time Co-operative College, Business and Management Study; [occ.] Retired, Formerly Training Mgr.; [oth. writ.] Winner several national Essay Compts., Under pen-name "Ad Referendum"; [pers.] I attempt to write from heart in poems of a sentimental nature. If tears come to my eyes I know I am succeeding. Other poems I write from my head and general observation.; [a.] Bristol

WALTERS, OLIVE
[b.] 12 June 1915, Birmingham; [p.] William Ingram, Minnie Ingram; [m.] Reginald Evans, 27 March 1937, Gerald Walters, 6 May 1967, (twice married); [ch.] Patricia Ann, Reginald, Frank Arthur; [ed.] Primary and Secondary; [occ.] Retired; [memb.] BASCA; [oth. writ.] Poems published in local magazines and various anthologies and songwriting, which I have had many demonstrated by diamond studios of Bristol; [pers.] I have been writing poems and songs for many years trying to reflect, life's changes, from the sad to the humorous.; [a.] Solihull, Bentley Heath, West Midlands

WALTON, ELEANOR
[b.] 12 March 1968, Suffolk; [p.] Marlene and Bernard Walton; [occ.] H. M. Forces Royal Army Veterinary Corps Dog Handler; [oth. writ.] Unpublished; [pers.] Our memories are our strength, through harder times, in life.; [a.] Saxmundham, Suffolk

WALUSIMBI, OLGAR
[pen.] Audrey, Toma; [b.] 27 March 1977, Kampala; [p.] Y. Walusimbi, Solomy Naluwoza; [ed.] St. Teresa's School, Namasagali College School; [occ.] Student; [oth. writ.] 'Guy on Board', 'Fantasia', 'My World', 'Romance Flies In'; [pers.] You only live once, so make the best out of life. And whatever you do, remember to enjoy it!; [a.] Dorking, Surrey

WAMBUA, ESTHER KAVESU
[pen.] Kathy Mulala; [b.] 24 August 1956, Machakas; [p.] Steve Mangee and Susan Mangee; [m.] 24 January 1976; [ch.] Tinar, Judy, Mambo, Susan; [ed.] High School and Primary - Kilombwa, Secondary School - Mbaikini; [pers.] "Why", Hurt The Nature, that's my greatest, influence. I'm from Kenya born Machakos Dis. Now I'm living in one of the Swedish Institute Care. Hinseberg Frovi.; [a.] Nairobi, Kenya

WANDLESS, SHARON JOY
[b.] 16 October 1959, Castleford; [p.] Edward Wandless; [m.] Jean Wandless; [ed.] Castleford High School; [occ.] I don't work as I am disabled; [memb.] Woman's Center Castleford; [oth. writ.] Had one poem published; [pers.] I try and show love in my poems, and peace of life and to tell others that God is a one of love and hope.; [a.] Castleford, West Yorkshire

WANN, SHEILA IRVINE
[pen.] Sheila Irvine Fraser Wann; [b.] 5 September 1946, Perth; [p.] Constance and Irvine Fraser; [m.] John Wann, 7th August 1969; [ch.] Irvine, Fraser and Donald Wann; [ed.] Perth High School, Robert Gordons Domestic Science College, Aberdeen. Qualified in Institutional Management; [occ.] Catering Supervisor, Inchture Primary School; [memb.] Scottish Womans Rural Institute, Guild in Church of Scotland; [hon.] Institutional Management Association Certificate. For Matron Housekeepers; [oth. writ.] "The Countryside" in high Spots by Anchor books. "Country Freedom" Poets in Scotland by arrival press, and "The Old Lady" in inspirations from Scotland by Anchor Books.; [pers.] I win many prizes in the womans rural for art and crafts, cooking and baking, I won the trophy of Perth Agricultural Show 3 years in succession also win the trophy at Local Rural.; [a.] Glencarse, Perth

WANT, ELIZABETH (neé LAVERS)
[b.] 2 August 1939, Plumstead; [p.] Both deceased; [m.] Derek S. Want, 4 April 1959; [ch.] Sharon Hawkins, Raymond Want; [ed.] "Gypsy Hill", Comprehensive School, Upper Norwood, SE London; [occ.] Housewife; [memb.] Parish church choir "St Catherine of Sienna"; [oth. writ.] Several poems written for church magazine issued monthly; [pers.] I am a christian and I strongly feel that my writing is influenced by my faith. I developed cancer three years ago and I endeavour to bring words of true meaning into the lives of others.; [a.] Reading, Berkshire

WARD, JANICE ELIZABETH
[pen.] Elizabeth Ward; [b.] 3 August 1944, Rhondda; [m.] Peter Ward, 14 February 1981; [ch.] Julie Ann, Andrew Charles; [ed.] Eastwood Secondary Modern; [occ.] Bookkeeper Literacy and Computer Tutor; [hon.] English Language; [oth. writ.] I have compiled a book of my poetry; [pers.] My writings reflect my inner most feelings and the thoughts of others.; [a.] Ammanford, Carmarthenshire

WARD, KERRY
[pen.] Kerry Ward; [b.] 19 March 1979, Rotherham; [p.] Mr. and Mrs. Ward; [ed.] Wickerscey Compre-

hensive School - Rotherham - September '90 - May '95, Thomas Rotherham College; [occ.] Student - Thomas Rotherham College; [oth. writ.] "Child" - poem in "Awaken To A Dream" several articles in local newspaper.; [pers.] This poem - "Wise Old Woman" is dedicated to my late grandma Prescott, for her love and kindness that helped me to grow up. Always remembered.; [a.] Rotherham, South Yorkshire

WARD, MICHAEL JOHN
[b.] 20 August 1943, St. Annes-on-Sea, Lancs; [p.] Harold Owen and Eileen Ward; [m.] Muriel Betty Ward, 21 August 1971; [ch.] Stephen J. Ward, Matthew P. Ward; [ed.] King Edward VII Grammar School Lytham, qualified as Chartered Accountant 1966; [occ.] Chartered Accountant in Practice; [memb.] M.E.N.S.A, I.C.A.E.W.; [pers.] I have only recently taken an interest in poetry, having read little Hitherto. This is my first poem. I am interested in the power of words to express feelings and to describe both real and imaginary events.; [a.] Lytham, Lancs

WARREN, GEORGE
[b.] 12 April 1943; [p.] George A. Warren, Daisey Warren (Nee Kirby); [m.] Valerie Ann Warren (Nee Hughes), 3 February 1968; [ch.] Jamie and Daniel; [ed.] Glengall Rd., Secondary Modern School (Isle Of Dogs); [occ.] Civil Servant; [memb.] Millwall Youth Old Boys F.C.; [oth. writ.] The Isle Of Dogs, A Socialist Carol, A Docker's Plea plus several other's printed by Arrival Press; [pers.] My english is atrocious, my grammar even worse so what I have to say, I get away by writing it down in verse; [a.] Belvedere, Kent

WARREN, PAULINE
[pen.] Felicity Wells; [b.] 9 May 1947, Bromley, Kent; [p.] Percy Walker and Margaret Walker; [m.] Leslie Warren, 4 September 1971; [occ.] Housewife and Resting typist; [hon.] Editor's Choice Award for 'Fill It Full Lord' poem published in the ISoP book The Other Side Of The Mirror, 1996; [oth. writ.] Poems used by two previous employers as company Christmas card insert and recruitment advertisement, plus poem published in latter employer's internal magazine.; [pers.] I endeavour to write from the abundant wealth of experiences my senses and emotions are daily priviledge to absorb, creating from all the Creator creates.; [a.] Croydon, Surrey

WARRIER, DEBBIE
[b.] 6 March 1970, Kuching, Malaysia; [p.] Quin Warrier, Matthew Warrier; [ed.] Servite College 1983 to 1987 - High School Certificate, Curtin University (Western Australia) 1988 - 91 Bachelor of Social Work; [occ.] Hospital Social Worker; [memb.] The Poetry Society, 22 Betterton Street, Convent Garden, London; [oth. writ.] Presently attempting to publish book "Reflections" collection of poems written between 1985 to 1996 which I have dedicated to my family.; [pers.] Grew up on Australia and an presently on working holiday with my sister Daphne in London. Have been travelling around the world since 1995. I believe strongly in following your dreams.; [a.] Waterloo, London

WASSELL, BRIAN
[b.] 11 January 1939, Rotherham; [p.] Helen P. Kitelliner Wassell; [m.] Eileen Wassell, 27 August 1960; [ch.] Four; [ed.] Secondary Modern School, (Spurley Hey); [occ.] Care-Assistant; [oth. writ.] Several other poems written for own enjoyment.; [a.] Rotherham, Yorkshire

WATKIS, MRS. ADLIN
[pen.] Shirley May; [b.] 26 May 1938, Saint Ann, Jamaica; [p.] Osborne and Florence Williams; [occ.] Catering Assistant; [oth. writ.] Poem in "The Other Side Of The Mirror" and "Awaken To A dream", published by The International Society Of Poets; [pers.] Mixed Up Emotions affects the minds of almost all persons alive today, be it Kings or Subjects. There is regrets, loss, Love, Hate, Loneliness, jealousy what ever, no one is Free from its affect. This is why Mixed Up Emotions was written and especially for my Friend named below.; [a.] Ealing

WATSON, B.K.
[pen.] B. K. Watson; [b.] 29 December 1946, Kent; [m.] Herbert Watson, 11 September 1965; [ch.] Two sons; [ed.] Secondary School; [occ.] Farm Worker; [oth. writ.] Poetry not published as yet.; [pers.] I love writing of the beauty of nature. I particularly enjoy reading 'Patience Strong'.; [a.] Rainham, Kent

WATSON, MRS. LINDA
[b.] 10 July 1953, Carlisle; [p.] Norman George and Edith May Spooner; [m.] Divorced; [ch.] Kirsty Cherene, Philip Miles, Linsey Xaneta; [ed.] Danum Grammar School for Girls - Doncaster; [occ.] Mature student in Management Development and Training; [memb.] Active member of Local School Association and also Barnby Dun Players Amateur Dramatic Society; [oth. writ.] Nothing published; [pers.] Having been inspired for years with poetry I find my first submission to a competition being considered for prize very encouraging and hope that the inspiration will continue; [a.] Doncaster, South Yorkshire

WATSON, STANLEY
[b.] 21 June 1922, West Hartlepool; [p.] Deceased; [m.] Nora Watson, 24 August 1946; [ch.] 2 - Stephen and Anne; [ed.] Snapethorpe Secondary School; [occ.] Retired; [memb.] Burma Star Association; [hon.] (War Medals) 1939-1945 Star, War Medal, Defence Medal and Burma Star, ISTD International School Teaching Dancing (Tap) 1, 2 and 3 levels; [oth. writ.] I've wrote a book of mostly humorous poetry just 60 books for my friends.; [a.] Wakefield, Yorkshire

WATTS, AMY LOUISE
[b.] 19 December 1981, Kettering; [p.] Roger and Jane Watts; [ed.] The Rushden School; [occ.] Student; [oth. writ.] Short story published in "Once Upon A Celebration."; [pers.] I want to prove that poetry can be enjoyed by anyone of any age.; [a.] Rushden, Northants

WEBB, CHRISTINE
[p.]Christine Webb; [b.] 23 December 1938; Bognor Regis;[p.] Mr. and Mrs. McMillen;[m.] Derek E. Webb; 20 August 1958;[ch.] Stephen, Richard, Julie, Jo;[ed.] COmprehensive School "O" level English;[occ.] Poet and Writer; Housewife;[memb.] A.C.W. Rhyme Arrival;[hon.] Academy of Children's Writers Diploma, Editor's Award with the International Society of Poets(twice semi-finalist); [oth. writ.] Short story, "Empty Regrets," published by New Fiction; Several poems published by Arrival Press and two with International Society of Poets;[pers.] Most of my poetry has an element of humour and often includes a moral together with a profound sense of hope for humanity;[a.] Bognor Regis, West Sussex.

WEBSTER, SHARON
[pen.] Sharon Webster; [b.] 6 October 1976, Middlesbrough; [p.] Raymond Webster, Christine Webster; [ed.] Acklam Grange Secondary School, University of Northumbria at Newcastle; [occ.] Law Student; [memb.] Law Society, Student Union; [hon.] Won Cleveland Poetry and Art Competition, won Law Mooting Final 1996, currently studying for Law Honours Degree; [oth. writ.] A collection of private poems.; [pers.] Love to family and friends, especially my parents and their unconditional love which keeps me eternally strong. Live for today, and protect our tomorrow.; [a.] Middlesbrough, Cleveland

WEIR, KATHERINE
[pen.] Rose Marie Clare; [ed.] S.R.N. Sister, Diploma of Opthalmalgia (Dip. Opth.); [pers.] I have a great respect for the art of poetry and the poets especially those whose works are bordered on the scientific; [a.] Larne, Antrim

WELDS, MICHELLE MELINDA
[pen.] Sky Blue Purple; [b.] 14 June 1977, London; [p.] Cyprian Welds, Gloria Welds; [ed.] St. Martin in the Fields, St. Francis Xavier sixth form college, Nene College, High School for girls; [occ.] Student; [pers.] All glory to God special thanks to the artist and Jodeci.; [a.] Brixton, London

WELLINGS, JENNIFER
[b.] 29 December 1941, Yorks; [p.] John and Lily Simpson; [m.] David G. Wellings, 11 August 1962; [ch.] Two; [ed.] Manchester High School; [occ.] Housewife and Sunday School Teacher; [oth. writ.] Poetry - other some published; [a.] Peterboro, Cambs

WEST, DONNA
[b.] 26 February 1973, Iseriohn; [p.] George West, Sally West; [ed.] George Ward Comprehensive School, Chantmarle Police Training Centre; [occ.] Woman Police Constable - Wiltshire Constabulary; [pers.] 'Breath of Goodbye' was written as a tribute to my father George Henry West born 1950, who died in 1994 from leukemia. It reflects his life during his illness and the struggle.; [a.] Swindon, Wiltshire

WEST, HELEN E. M.
[b.] 3 January 1969, Williamstown, MA; [ed.] Sir Graham Balfour High School, Huddersfield University BSC (Hons); [occ.] Designer (Textiles); [oth. writ.] Currently working on first novel.; [pers.] Through my writing I wish to create a dream-like aura, for my reader to step into and become inspired to think, consider, and use their creative imagination to its fullest potential.; [a.] Stafford, Staffordshire

WEST, LINDA
[b.] 11 February 1946, Sheffield; [p.] Douglas Stephenson, Emily Stephenson; [m.] Esmond West, 6 July 1968; [ch.] Steven West; [ed.] Dronfield Henry Fanshawe Grammar School; [occ.] Food Production Operative; [memb.] Competitors Companion; [oth. writ.] Poem published in women and work an anthology of creative writing to celebrate international women's day 1996. Poem narrated on local radio at the time of Charles and Diana's Wedding.; [pers.] Part realist, part dreamer, I have the perfect excuse for writing poems which reflect my various mood swings! Illustrations of life and the complexities of human emotions which, for me, hold a particular fascination.; [a.] Rotherham, South Yorkshire

WESTON, PAULA
[b.] 24 November 1968, Bridgend, S. Wales; [p.] Jeffrey Weston, Gillian Weston; [m.] Divorced, 27 February 1988; [ch.] Charlotte Philippa Weston-Morgan; [ed.] Olchfa Comprehensive, Swansea College, Reading University (Correspondence); [occ.] Sales Negotiator for Barratt Homes South Wales; [hon.] Cert, R.E.A.; [oth. writ.] Many poems and lyrics which have not, as yet been submitted for publication anywhere.; [pers.] I have always been encouraged by the pleasure and solace that writing provides. It is an outlet for all kinds of emotions and thoughts.; [a.] Swansea, West Glamorgan

WHISKERD, BETH
[pen.] Beth Whiskerd; [b.] 31 March 1974, Norwich; [p.] Pat Whiskerd, David Flynn (Common Law Husband of Heidi Whiskerd - Sister); [ed.] Hellesdon High School; [occ.] Sales Assistant for British Home Stores; [hon.] Outstanding stage presence (whilst dancing) N.U. Volleyball 1st place (2 years running); [oth. writ.] A full compilation of my own poems (approx. 40 poems); [pers.] My writing reflects all that I am and all that I have seen. An empty page is but a tomorrow not yet remembered.; [a.] Norwich, Norfolk

WHITE, GEMMA
[b.] 2 December 1982, Wimbledon; [p.] Margaret and David White; [ed.] Nonsuch High School for Girls; [occ.] Student; [oth. writ.] Poem in Local Newspaper; [pers.] Never be afraid of achieving your dreams.; [a.] Sutton, Surrey

WHITE, JOHN GEORGE WILLIAM
[pen.] "Stagger The Bard", "The Benbow Bard" or "Bard Of Benbow"; [b.] 5 January 1926, Portsmouth; [p.] Hilda Clemett White (Nee Evans), George Thomas Albert White; [m.] Annie Patricia White (Nee Widdicombe), 20 March 1950 (Belfast); [ch.] Graham John White (43 yrs.), Trevor Michael White (38 yrs.); [ed.] Portsmouth Junior Technical School then Naval aircraft apprenticeship (Fleet Air Arm) also Borough Polytechnic (London); [occ.] Retired; [memb.] Society of friends of the Fleet Air Arm Museum (SoFFRAM) Civil Service Motoring Assoc. (C.S.M.A.); [hon.] Imperial Service Medal; [oth. writ.] 20 'Odes', eight of which were written for and about my ex Fleet Air Arm colleagues. One "A Benbow Gathering", published in SoFFRAM newsletter-magazine No 46 (April 1996) Other 'Odes' about various happenings in my life or of people I've met. All unpublished.; [pers.] Not given to writing poetry. - This is my first attempt. Write humorous and topical odes, because they are not bound by conventional restrictions, which apply to poetry and limericks.; [a.] Gillingham, Kent

WHITE, KATIE LOUISE
[pen.] Katie White; [b.] 7 March 1986, Leicester; [p.] Mark White and Anya White (nee Plucinski); [ed.] Holy Cross R.C. School Stonesby Ave, Leicester; [occ.] School girl; [memb.] Magpie Club; [hon.] 2 art competitions, 2 radio competitions; [pers.] Loves reading, writing and painting.; [a.] Leicester, Leics

WHITE, PATRICIA
[b.] 11 June 1947, London; [p.] Vera and Frederick Fuller; [m.] John White, 3 June 1967; [ch.] Darren and Stuart White; [ed.] Blackheath and Bluecoats C of E, London; [occ.] Housewife; [pers.] Through my writing my aim is to express the sights and sounds of life my work is influenced by the writings of patience strong.; [a.] Blackheath, London

WHITE, PATRICIA
[b.] September 1945; [pers.] I believe that, all creatures great and small are given a precious gift...life...; [a.] Blackpool, Lancashire

WHITE, SUSAN
[b.] 15 April 1947, Canvey Island; [p.] Iris White and George White; [ed.] Timberlog School Basildon Gray's Thurrock Technical Colleges Charlotte Mason Teachers Training College, Ambleside; [occ.] Teacher at Farley Hill Primary School Luton, and Stanford-Le-Hope, history and modern studies Gable Hall School, Gray's Essex interests local history, Proprietor book shop; [memb.] Canvey Island Sailing Club; [oth. writ.] Wrote and published book history of Canvey Island, five Generations; [a.] Canvey Island, Essex

WHITEHEAD, SHARON
[b.] 11 May 1961, Coventry; [p.] Richard and Gwendoline Stubbings; [m.] Keith Whitehead, 29 May 1993; [ch.] John, Michael, Andrew and Thomas; [ed.] Binley Park Comprehensive School, Coventry; [occ.] Nursing Auxiliary George Eliot Hospital, Nuneaton; [memb.] Hartshill Windscape Handbell Ringers; [a.] Atherstone, Warwickshire

WHITNALL, CAROL
[b.] 2 October 1947, Lambeth, London; [p.] Arthur and Rose Shepherd; [m.] Arthur Whitnall, 23 March 1968; [ch.] Karen and Sarah; [ed.] Comprehensive School, Southwark and Camberwell, Commercial College; [occ.] Housewife; [hon.] Music Piano Theory, grade 1-4 passed with distinction. Now studying for grade 5 typing and shorthand certificates; [oth. writ.] Other poems published; [pers.] I have been writing since young and most of my poems are based on people and events in my life.; [a.] Bromley, Kent

WHITTAKER, SHIRLEY
[pen.] Shirley E. Whittaker; [b.] 5 March 1941, Bolton, Lancs; [p.] Harry Bulpitt, Phyliss Bulpitt; [m.] Leonard Whittaker, 28 March 1959; [ch.] Russell Barry, Peter Henry; [ed.] Secondary and Bolton Tec College; [occ.] Retired nursing sister/midwife; [memb.] Private; [oth. writ.] Various poems and numerous prose written for special occasions, when commissioned.; [pers.] Greatly influenced by the great English poet and essayist, Leigh Hunt.; [a.] Saint Marys, Isles of Scilly

WHITTAKER, SUE
[b.] 5 January 1949; [m.] Robert Whittaker, 28 December 1968; [ch.] Daughter Samantha; [ed.] Comp School Tech College; [occ.] Housewife; [memb.] Rufford Park Gold Club; [oth. writ.] Poems on golf and 1914, 1918 war published in local paper; [pers.] Remember life is a gift, wrapped in laughter and love.; [a.] Newark, Notts

WIELAND, SUSAN MARY
[b.] 28 August 1960, Ramsgate, England; [p.] William Plumbridge, Maureen Plumbridge; [m.] Christian Wieland, 26 October 1984; [ch.] Steven Daniel, Sara Susan; [ed.] Charters Towers, England, Academie De Langues Et Commerce, Geneva; [occ.] Housewife; [oth. writ.] Several poems published in 1979, 1980 in an easter anthology, contemporary poets of 1979, treasury of modern poets 1980 and spring poets 1980. All books by Regency Press London and New York.; [pers.] Poetry touches the soul and heart of humankind, spreading joy and hope for all. I have always written and adored poetry since an early age.; [a.] Geneva, Switzerland

WIGGINS, SHARON MAY
[b.] 6 May 1968, Cheltenham; [pers.] I dedicate this poem to my own father Mr. Antony John Watts these words come from the heart and were written with love.; [a.] Tewkesbury, Gloucester

WILDING, TONY
[pen.] Gregg Wilde; [b.] 27 November 1941, Bridlington; [oth. writ.] Several Plays Loosely Tekmed Black Comedies of a Anarchic Nature; [pers.] I would say that though I enjoy the trappings of Bourgeois Society I am at heart a surrealist an aged one at that who has reached the age of his geriatric factor.; [a.] Hessle, Yorkshire

WILDY, ALEXANDRA
[b.] 15 September 1977, Burnley General; [p.] Alexandra Wildy and Joe Wildy; [ed.] SS J Fisher and T. More R.C. High School, Nelson and Colne College, A Levels Graphics and Fine Art; [occ.] Student; [pers.] I wish to dedicate this poem to my boyfriend Matthew Redwood, and tell Edward, Cindy, Jo-Ann, Samantha, Maria, Joseph, Poppy, and Bianca-Mercedes that I love them all.; [a.] Burnley, Lancashire

WILKINSON, ELAINE MARGARET
[b.] 9 May 1960, Hull; [p.] David Paris Davidson, Alice Mary Davidson; [m.] Kenneth Wilkinson, 28 May 1983; [ch.] Rachel Mary; [ed.] Greatfield High School and Hull College; [occ.] Housewife and Mum; [memb.] London Chamber of Commerce and Industry's, Institute of Qualified Private Secretaries Limited; [pers.] My grandmother developed Alzheimers when I was 14, she died when I was 21. This poem is dedicated to all victims, and their relatives.; [a.] Hull, East Yorkshire

WILLARD, JOHN
[b.] 16 November 1969, Sevenoaks, Kent; [p.] Harry Willard, Carol Willard; [occ.] Retail Sales Supervisor; [oth. writ.] Several, not yet published.; [pers.] True originality can only come from within ones heart and mind.; [a.] Hastings, East Sussex

WILLIAMS, CAROL ANN DAWN
[b.] 27 April 1961, Birmingham; [p.] Jean Hasty, Bernard Hasty (Deceased); [m.] Trevor Williams, 11 May 1979; [ch.] Brian John, Ian James, Beejay Trevor, Patricia Carol Jean, Stuart Jason; [ed.] Four Dwellings, Comprehensive Senior School, Birmingham; [occ.] Housewife, and Mother; [memb.] Darts Club (Team Captain); [hon.] Dart Trophies; [pers.] I have written my own personal poetry book but this poem was a extra special poem. Dedicated to my Mum. I was talked into sending it by my children. But I have read some poetry. It's my first publication.; [a.] Brentwood, Essex

WILLIAMS, ELWYN
[b.] 21 June 1929, Bangor, North Wales; [p.] John Williams, Elizabeth Williams; [m.] Mary Williams, 21 March 1959; [ch.] Clive Williams, Peter Williams; [ed.] Friars Grammar School, Bangor, North Wales, Liverpool College of Art; [occ.] Retired Head of Education Services, Manchester Art Galleries, Based at the Manchester Athenaeum; [memb.] Founder Member, Mountaineering Club of North Wales; [hon.] National diploma in Design, Art Teacher's Diploma, taught fine art at different secondary schools for many years ending eventually as head of one of the Largest Art Departments in secondary Education in the U.K. during my headship of Art studies at the David Hughes School, Anglesey, North Wales, My Art Department was visited by H.R.H. prin-

cess Margaret and Lord Snowdon C1963 because of their deep interest in the work displayed, they overran their schedule. In 1972 I left school teaching and moved into the art gallery service where I could work with children, Teachers, students, foreign visitors and the general public. It also gave me the rare privilege of working closely with the original works of great artists and craftsmen which helped greatly in my development. Appointed first ever chairman of moderators to Supervise Art examinations in Secondary School throughout Northern England. Responsible for 90,000 and candidates in 1987. This was an annual appointment which I held for twelve years. I was sent several times to Northern Ireland to help develop Art Examinations in the Province.; [oth. writ.] Practising artist, many works held in private collections throughout England and some held in private collections in Ireland, the U.S.A and Australia. I have lectured at several universities and Art Galleries in the United Kingdom including the National Gallery, London.; [a.] Tarleton, Lancashire

WILLIAMS, MRS. FLORENCE
[b.] 2 June 1931, Plymouth; [m.] Mr. R. Williams, 17 December 1966; [ch.] One son and 3 grandchildren; [occ.] Retired; [oth. writ.] Now writing life story.; [a.] Exminster, Devon

WILLIAMS, GILLIAN
[b.] 13 July 1953, Wolverhampton; [pers.] I have always liked to write but have never took part in any competition until now I felt proud when I received my letter to say my poem had been entered into the final.; [a.] Wolverhampton, West Midlands

WILLIAMS, JESSIE
[pen.] Jessie Williams; [b.] 19 June 1923, Manchester, Lancs; [p.] Joseph E. Siddall and Maggie Siddall; [m.] Raymond Smith, 1986; [ch.] Sylvia, Alison and Carter B. Smith; [ed.] General, Church School served in the W.R.N.s. during the war; [occ.] Retired; [hon.] Won for events for many charities; [oth. writ.] Faith, now published the gloom casters; [pers.] I have a scrap book with my poems in which have not been sent to be published because, I did not think they would be though fit my family talked me into sending, them in.; [a.] Manchester, Lancashire

WILLIAMS, KATE LAURA
[b.] 18 May 1978; Swansea [p.] Dr.and Mrs. Stuart Williams; [pers.] Through my writing, I strive to reflect the good and bad aspects of the world today and its people, through the eyes of a younger generation; [a.] Burry Port, Carmarthenshire.

WILLIAMS, MARGARETTA GRACE
[pen.] Greta Kinnear-Williams; [b.] 19 December 1945, Wales; [p.] Mr. Fred Kinnear and Mrs. Joyce Kinnear; [m.] Derek Gordon Williams, 17 August 1968; [ch.] Gary Robert Williams; [ed.] Patchway High School (Secondary); [occ.] Telesales; [hon.] Certificate of Hairdressing; [pers.] I have written many stories and poems, but this is the first article I have ever sent to a publisher.; [a.] Bristol, Avon

WILLIAMS, MARK
[b.] 31 August 1972, Birmingham; [p.] Marilyn and David Williams; [ed.] 1983-90 Exhall Grange, Coventry 1990-1992 Queen Alexandra College, B'Ham 1992-1996 Solihull College, Birmingham, 1996-1997 Coventry University; [occ.] Student; [memb.] Royal National Institute For The Blind, Guide Does For The Blind Association, Braille, Chess Association; [hon.] BTEC and Business and Finance, 2nd Prize National Poetry Competition 1989 (Agricultural Society/Partially Sighted Society); [oth. writ.] Global Suicide, Age, Redundant, Greed, Christmas Tree, Infantry Man, Darkness, Night Flight, Ghost Town; [pers.] I have seen writing poetry on and off since the age of 15. As a result of being partially blind, I need to pay more attention to what is going on around me and in current affairs, often reflecting personal beliefs and feelings in my poetry.; [a.] Coventry, Warwickshire

WILLIAMS, PETER ROBERT
[pen.] P. R. Williams; [b.] 17 August 1964, Port Talbot, South Wales; [p.] John Robert Williams, Anne Williams; [ed.] Glanakan Comprehensive in Port Talbot; [occ.] Semi-skilled Production Operator,

Ford Motor Co.; [memb.] C.C. International (Classic Cars Club), R.N.L.I. (Life Boat Institute Land-Based Member), Oxfam; [a.] Port Talbot, West Glamorgan

WILLIAMS, SHELLEY
[b.] 31 October 1982, Harrogate; [p.] Glynne V. Williams and Katherine M. Williams; [ed.] King James School Knaresborough; [occ.] Still in full time education; [oth. writ.] Poems, a heavenly place published in "The World of Horses." My pony dreams published in "World of Horses".; [pers.] I am inspired to write poetry because of the way I feel about aspects of life in the influenced by my true feelings also by the late writers and poets words worth and shakespere.; [a.] Harrogate, North Yorkshire, HG2 7RF

WILLIAMS, SUSAN MARGARET
[pen.] Sue Williams; [b.] 21 January 1949, Cinderford; [p.] Raymond Mills, Muriel Mills; [m.] Michael Stuart Alan Williams, 19 December 1970; [ch.] Jason Francis, Michelle S., Elizabeth Williams; [ed.] Ruardean Woodside Primary, Abenhall Secondary Modern, Royal Forest of Dean College, R.F.D.C.; [occ.] Housewife, Carer; [hon.] The International Society of Poets. Editors Choice Award - 'The Other Side of the Mirror'; [oth. writ.] Review/The Citizen. Anchor Books - various, Poetry Now - A Day In The Life Of..., Triumph House - Seek From Within, The International Society of Poets.; [pers.] 'Go for it', anyway, that's what my friends say.; [a.] Royal Forest of Dean, Glos

WILLIAMSON, PATRICK
[b.] 15 June 1961, Thornley; [p.] Thomas William - Ann; [m.] Jacqueline Williamson, 19 July 1986; [ed.] St. Bedes Comprehensive School Peterlee; [occ.] Occupational Therapy Assistant; [memb.] Hartlepool General Hospitals; [oth. writ.] An affair of conscience was published in my Hospital Magazine Comment November 1994 and was part of my English literature course work - summer 1994.; [pers.] My thoughts are expressed enabling everyone to relate - I dedicate this poem to my belated father who encouraged me to further my education after leaving the mining industry.; [a.] Durham

WILLIAMSON, PETER
[b.] 24 May 1937, Gutcher; [p.] John and Bella; [m.] Greta, 18 July 1968, (Deceased, 14 November 1985); [ch.] Ian Avril and Norman; [ed.] Mid Yell Jun High; [occ.] Ferry-Man; [pers.] The healing power of "Spring" after illness, or loss of a loved one; [a.] Shetland Isles

WILLIS, JENNY
[pen.] Hannah Grossick; [b.] 1950; [p.] Peripathetic Childhood with the R.A.F.; [ed.] Manchester University Bahons Trend/Russian, Brunel University M Phil (Education) Opow University M Phil (Management); [occ.] Lecturer, O.U.; [oth. writ.] As of 1/1/97: 1989 World Languages Project, Hodder and Stoughton, Nov/Dec 1995 Anthology of poetry, Minerva Press, First novel Minerva Press, Nov 1995 Kingston Poetry competition/Dillions: highly commended entry, resulting in inclusion in anthology: Dec. 1995 Hear My Voice, Napier Nationwide Ltd. ("The Snail Tree"), Jan. 1996 Contributor To Inspirations from the Home Counties, anthology of poetry, Anchor Books ("Gambolling"), Feb. 1996 Contributor to Heebie-Jeebies poetry anthology, Anchor Books ("Phobia"), Feb. 1996 Contribution to Winter Thoughts, poetry anthology, Anchor Books ("Rebirth"), March 1996 Contributor to Skool Daze, Poetry anthology, Anchor Books ("End of Term"), May 1996 Contributor to Young at Heart, poetry anthology, Anchor Books ("Spirit of the Sixties"), Feb. 1996 Semi-finalist International Society of Poets, leading to: 1996 Contributor to Voices on the Wind, International Society of Poets ("Rebirth"), June 1996 Contributor to Addictive Poetry, Anchor Books ("Defiance"), August 1996 Contributor to Our Psychic World, Anchor Books (Hypnotherapy), October 1996 Contributor to A Friendly Book, Anchor Books (My Golden Penny), Nov. 1996 Contributor to Loving Hearts, Anchor Books (April Love), Nov. 1996 Kingston-upon-Thames/Dillons Poetry competition: Highly commended, resulting in inclusion in: Dec. 1996 Hear My

Voice 1996, Napier Nationwide Ltd. (`An Existence'), Jan. 1997 Semi-finalist International Open Amateur Poetry Competition, leading to inclusion in: Summer '97 A Lasting Calm, (`Indian Summer'), Summer 1997 Losing Control (novel on anorexia nervosa), Minerva Press, To come: - Coming out, coming in (novel, changing sexuality), - All in the Mind (novel, boundaries of fantasy/reality), - Selection of short stories; [pers.] In my prose writings, I prove the psychological responses we make to the events and relationships of everyday life.; [a.] Surrey

WILLIS, MAUREEN
[b.] 22 July 1937, Pontnewydd; [p.] Ernest Pattimore, Lily Pattimore; [m.] Maxwell Karl Willis, 17 November 1950; [ch.] Douglas Wade Claire; [ed.] Church School Pontnewydd; [occ.] Housewife; [oth. writ.] Poem published in British Goat Society Magazine, several other poems written for members of my family and for my own pleasure.; [pers.] I dedicate "Memories of Africa" to my brother-in-law Melville S. Nunley M.Sc. O.B.E. and his wife Gabrielle, as they inspired me to write this poem. Melville worked in Africa and the Sudan for 25 years. Recognition for his work came in November 1992. When he was awarded the O.B.E., sadly just a few months later he passed away.; [a.] Cwmbran, Gwent, S. Wales

WILLSHER, LYNN
[pen.] Catherine Evans James-Thompson; [b.] 1955, Leeds; [p.] Margeret Thompson Nee Jones; [m.] Ronald Willsher; [ch.] Seven - Life span of 24 years; [ed.] Hillside Sec Modern, Beeston, Leeds, Outwood Sec Modern, Nr Wakefield, "Sight and Sound College", Leeds public servant and Transport; [occ.] Now Retired, Compiling Biography; [memb.] Coach Drivers Club; [oth. writ.] Logos for private companies and poems; [pers.] "With this picture from the mind. The powers within, will only be kind."; [a.] Leeds, Yorkshire

WILLSON, PERCY REGINALD
[pen.] Bob Robert - Reg; [b.] 11 March 1922, Nordelph; [p.] Fernley and Florence Willson; [m.] Clarice Mary Willson, 7 October 1942; [ch.] 1 Daughter 53 years; [ed.] Taught at the Nordelph small Elementary School Silt Road Nordelph from 1926 to 1935; [occ.] Retired to care for my wife; [memb.] Addenbrooks Hospital Community National Kidney Federation also Kidney Care Patients Association; [hon.] Layton Pearman's Award by the Federation of Kidney Patients Certificate from Accolade of Caring Gold Pins Solves Awards in Caring for the very sick patients raising thousands of pounds known as Bob (caring Bob) or Robert Wilson.; [oth. writ.] I write poems regarding what I see and watch like the early morning 'Daybreak' that you are about to print in your anthology.; [pers.] I have had poems printed by "Anchor Books" Peterborough and was awarded certificate for poems and raised, 1-363-64 to Animal Shelters. 11 July 1996 I love writing poetry in the early dawn.; [a.] Downham Mkt, Norfolk

WILSON, CHRISTINE H.
[b.] 20 February 1966, Bo'Ness; [p.] Walter and Isabella Wilson; [ed.] Forres Academy RAF Swinderby; [occ.] Officers Mess Catering Flt Royal Air Force; [memb.] Royal Air Force Association; [pers.] As a relative newcomer to poetry. I've found a new way to express and share my feelings about life.; [a.] Forres, Morayshire

WILSON, DOREEN
[b.] 15 August 1928, Shipley, W. Yorks; [m.] Kenneth Wilson, 6 June 1953; [ch.] Andrew Philip/David John; [ed.] Lilycroft Primary School Bradford, Belle Vue Girls Grammar School Bradford; [occ.] Retired; [memb.] Committee Member (Fairweather Greentowns Women's Guild) Bradford Committee Member (Bradford Photographic Society); [hon.] Winner of the 1995 National Children's Short Story Competition, Townswomen's Guild; [oth. writ.] Three Booklets of poems published several articles/letters published in local newspaper and magazines, regular poems printed in my church magazine.; [pers.] My poetry is simple, based on every day thoughts, on a multitude of topics.; [a.] Bradford, West Yorkshire

WILSON, JOSEPHINE
[b.] 6 January 1978, London North; [p.] George Francis and Mary Broughton-Wilson; [ed.] Rudolf Steiner School King Langley; [occ.] Optical Advisor; [pers.] The only way I can express my feelings is when I write them down, as poetry or prose.; [a.] Farnham, Surrey

WILSON, MRS. MONICA
[b.] 9 June 1930, Whitton, Rothbury; [p.] Joanna and William Foster; [m.] Jimmy Wilson, 14 August 1954; [ch.] Ann, Alan and Barbara; [ed.] C of E School "Thomlinsons", Rothbury, Morpeth, Northumberland; [occ.] Housewife; [oth. writ.] Just a poem or two; [pers.] We live in the lovely country side close to the cheviot hills. Hobbies, walking, cycling, gardening.; [a.] Alnwick, Northumberland

WILSON, NIVES
[b.] 12 November 1923, Trieste, Italy; [p.] Guido Franco and Emma Ciotar; [m.] Arthur Wilson (Deceased), 5 October 1946; [ch.] Frances, Christine, Diana, Brian, Patricia and Julie-Ann; [ed.] "Magistrali" (Grammar) Trieste Italy; [hon.] Sports Medals; [pers.] (If Suitable) I was going to come to London for the 1948 Olympics, for fencing, but met my future husband, a staffs sergeant in the army, and married him instead, and came in time for the new year of 1967, I have many interests in arts, history etc.; [a.] Merstham, Surrey

WILSON, SHEILA
[b.] 11 January 1961, Tharston, Norfolk; [p.] Harry Wilson and Rose Wilson; [ed.] Long Stratton Secondary, Hewett Comprehensive, Norwich City, York BA (Hons.); [occ.] Administrator; [memb.] Member of the Soka Gakkai International Buddhist Lay Movement for Peace, Education and Culture; [oth. writ.] Freelance blurbs (back cover copy of books) for Penguin Publishing; [pers.] The Kegon Sutra says. "The heart is like a skilled painter." Your heart is the designer, the painter, the sculptor, the architect of your being. The more specific and detailed the blueprint we have in our hearts, the better. The point is to continue vividly painting the target we have for ourselves in our hearts, and to advance towards that goal single mindedly. Then, at each instant, the reality of our lives will gradually approach the painting that is our aspiration.; [a.] Norwich, Norfolk

WILSON, YVONNE
[pen.] Yvonne Wilson-Hall; [b.] 7 June 1958, Hurley, Staffs; [p.] Beryl and Tom Wagstaff; [m.] Victor Harry Wilson, 25 February 1982; [ch.] 1. Stewart Harry and 2. Dean Victor; [ed.] Wilnecote High School, Nr Tamworth Staffs and Atherstone High School, Atherstone, Warks); [occ.] Telephonist-Receptionist; [oth. writ.] Small private collection of poems and children's stories written for and about my boys. None published.; [pers.] I write about life as I see it influenced by the emotions and thoughts that situations provoke.; [a.] Northfield, West Midlands

WILTON, MRS. P. I.
[b.] 22 September 1914, Wellow, Somerset; [p.] Edgar and Jane Bryan; [m.] Roderick A. V. Wilton, 8 October 1938 (Died November 1986); [ch.] Ann, June and Margaret; [ed.] Little Church-of-England School Near Bath, Somerset; [occ.] Retired - Reading Embroidery, Gardening when possible; [memb.] British Red Cross Member - many moons ago. Served in Conchill First Aid Post Belfast 1941. Member of the Heedlework Circle at Bristol Cathedral which included Embroidery for Alter Frontol and Repairing Bishops Vestments.; [oth. writ.] No claim to fame at all I am afraid - unless I count the occasion when as a child of 12-13 years I wrote the life of Jesus and actually won 51! During the years that we were parted during the war - my letters to my husband often included a verse or two. Otherwise most of my efforts have been to the family or friends in greeting cards or items in the Church Magazine.; [a.] Bristol, Avon

WIMALASEKERA, DULMINI
[b.] 11 October 1973, Croydon; [ed.] Bexley Technical High School for girls, Kent Institute of Art and Design (Canterbury); [hon.] BA Honours Architec-

ture (2:1); [pers.] I am ultimately attracted to art that is heartfelt and direct in its expression, and admire the work of Kate Bush, David Bowie, Madonna, Suede, Kraftwerk and the Auteurs for being both modern and hopelessly romantic.; [a.] Bexleyheath, Kent

WINGROVE, JOY
[b.] 10 February 1936, Sheffield; [p.] Ethel Leech, Percy Moor; [m.] Charles Wingrove, 2nd October 1982; [ch.] 1 son, 1 daughter; [ed.] Frecheville Infant and Junior School; Dronfield Grammar School, Derbyshire; [occ.] Occupational Health Nurse; [memb.] Royal College of Nursing, Motor Caravan Club, National Geographical Society; [hon.] Registered general nurse, registered mental nurse, occupational health nurse (RGN, RMN, OHNC); [oth. writ.] poetry, short stories, one hymn; [pers.] I write poetry for my pleasure but hope it gives others pleasure when they read it.; [a.] Lincoln, Lincolnshire

WINN, NICHOLAS
[pen.] Nick; [b.] 10 December 1949, Bristol, England; [p.] Mrs. Doris Joyce Winn; [occ.] Nurse; [hon.] Editors Choice Award, from the International Society of Poets, 1996; [oth. writ.] My own selection of poems entitled "Personal Poems." I am at present preparing another anthology for publication. Various poems published in other anthologies.; [pers.] I enjoy writing poetry because it is relaxing, creative, and I know it can be read in years to come. Most rewarding, and fulfilling!; [a.] Midsomer Norton, Somerset

WINTER, MARY PAULINE
[pen.] Mary Pauline Winter; [b.] 2 September 1939, Loughborough; [p.] Mary Elizabeth, George Harry Coleman; [m.] Ernest Charles Winter, 11 February 1956; [ch.] (4) Denise Pauline, Jeanette Shiralee, Roy Christopher and Robbie Paul; [ed.] "Rendall St", "Limehurst", "Loughborough", "East Leake" School, "The Stewart School," Sussex Rd., Brixton, and several colleges for evening classes; [occ.] Housewife and P/T Home Tutor; [memb.] Baptist Woman's League; [hon.] Ballroom, Latin, Jive, and Old Time Dancing; [oth. writ.] Working on my childhood memories: "Memories Of A Towpath Child." Over 300 poems - just stated getting a few published - in "Anchor Book", "Peace Freedom Press", local "College Presses," "Northamptonshire and Bedfordshire Life", and writing friction, songs, carols and hymns, children's stones - etc! for pleasure!; [pers.] My many hobbies include antiques, old dolls, a memorabilia of "Loughborough", Leicestershire collecting, "Ring Graft" and "Obedience Dog Training", "Tea-Dancing and Social Dancing." - All given up to devote my time to "Animal Welfare" and to my own rescued pets of many kinds.; [a.] Dunstable, Bedfordshire

WINTER, VIVIEN
[b.] 9 January 1943, Bristol; [p.] Ivy Flood; [m.] Geoffrey William Winter, 20 August 1960; [ch.] Sharon, David, Jackie, Niki, Debbie, Paul; [ed.] Wiveliscombe Secondary Modern; [occ.] Child Minder. Foster Parents.; [memb.] St. James Church, St. James Youth Club. Priors Wood Youth Club. I help run these clubs. I am also a Christian.; [hon.]; [oth. writ.] I have composed several other poems, and I have written a few stories, I am currently writing a book. I have never entered anything for publication.; [pers.] I started to write poems and short stories when I was a child. My own children have been very encouraging, especially when needing help with this subject for school homework. I like to look at something or someone and then I can write about it.; [a.] Taunton, Somerset

WINTON, LINZIE NICOLE
[b.] 18 May 1981, Aberdeen; [p.] Elizabeth and Lewis Winton; [ed.] St Machar Academy; [occ.] School Girl; [pers.] I find it easy to express the way I feel through my writing. I enjoy writing poetry and reading other people's work. I think of my poems as a hobby but I am hoping to develop it in the future. Having my poem in print has encouraged me to write more.; [a.] Aberdeen, Scotland

WISMER, SALLY J.
[pen.] Yvonne Barrie; [b.] 29 January 1980, Hamburg, Germany; [p.] Gerti Mantler, Peter Hoenow;

[ed.] Hill Primary School, Blairgowrie High School; [occ.] Student; [oth. writ.] Won an Oscar, for writing a novel, By The Sunday Post.; [pers.] I strive to find beauty in all I behold, and therefore write poetry to express my most inner feelings. Thanks to my best friend Yvonne, for everything.; [a.] Blairgowrie, Perthshire

WONG, MRS. LORNA
[ch.] Jason Wong (11), Jordan Wong (9), Jade Wong (7); [occ.] M/Wife; [memb.] W.R.V.S.; [oth. writ.] A collection of poems as yet unpublished.; [pers.] I enjoy trying to capture both the good and sides of life in my poems. Having my first accepted has given me the incentive to put more forward for consideration to other publications.; [a.] Peterculter, Aberdeen

WOOD, AGNES ELIZABETH
[pen.] Nessie; [b.] 9 May 1939, Dunfermline, Fife; [p.] Robert Cardiner Palmer and Elizabeth; [m.] Divorced, 14 December 1957; [ch.] Karena, Lynda, Mandy, Natalie, Larraine and David Andrew; [ed.] Milesmark Primary, then Dunfermline High School. Then further education at the Lauder Technical College Dunfermline; [occ.] Housewife; [memb.] Link Christian Fellowship; [oth. writ.] Several poems published in church newsletters of magazines also a local weekly free paper and one of my poems published in the book "Poets for Scotland by Anchor Published in November '95". And one to be published in February '97 "Faith Hoper Charity". in the book "Scottish Christian Messengers."; [pers.] I love reading and writing poetry and have done since I was a child. He certainly has made me genuinely proud of the talent my sweet Lord has given me for I suffered a nervous breakdown many years ago and lose all confidence. Thank for your faith in my writings.; [a.] Dunfermline, Fife

WOOD, KATHLEEN MARY
[pen.] Kath Wood; [b.] 12 April 1946, Hull; [p.] John Conyers, Ruby Kay; [m.] Peter Wood, 1 October 1977; [ch.] Hazel Wordsworth, Emma Wordsworth, Robert Wood; [ed.] Welton High Secondary Modern Hull, N. Humberside, University of Wales, Wrexham, N. Wales; [occ.] Seasonal work for the National Trust; [memb.] History Society; [hon.] English/History Degree; [oth. writ.] One poem published in 'Inspirations from Wales' 1996 achor books. One poem to be published in 'Anchor poets of 1997'.; [pers.] I have been writing poems most of my life but only writing serouisly for two years. My aim is to continue writing on the subjects that I feel passionate about.; [a.] Mold, Flintshire

WOOD, MONICA ELAINE
[b.] 26 March 1943, Gwent; [m.] Dennis Wood, 3 February 1972; [ch.] Gary Roy Brigden and Scott James Brigden; [ed.] Oatnall Comprehensive School, Hawyards Heath West Sussex; [occ.] Housewife; [memb.] Adventures' Art Club and Various Animal Protection Societies; [pers.] The poems I write are a form of self expression. I am inspired by many things. Happiness, sadness, fear, the beauty of Nature and many more. Really just the wonder of life.; [a.] Horsted Keynes, West Sussex

WOOLFREY, CAROLINE A.
[b.] 15 August 1984, Sidcup; [p.] Lesley Ann Woolfrey, John Peter Woolfrey; [ed.] Ringwood School; [occ.] Student; [pers.] My poem was inspired by a project at school and was encouraged by my English teacher.; [a.] Ringwood, Hampshire

WORTHINGTON, LORETTA
[b.] 9 June 1966, Liverpool; [p.] J. A. Watkins; [m.] Robert, 10 April 1992; [ch.] Seven; [ed.] Secondary Moden; [occ.] House wife; [memb.] Distinguished member of the Internationally Society of Poets; [hon.] I have been given the honour of writing poetry for Marie Curie appeal; [oth. writ.] "We The Lonely People" published in voices on the wind. "Why", "Play", "Helping Hand", "Eyes", "Dance". Published by Marie Curie to help raise money for charity.; [pers.] At the age of fifty one I returned to education, and I descoved a love for writing. This became a why for me to express all my hopes, fears, and decides. For Humankind.; [a.] Liverpool

WRIGHT, DEANA
[b.] 8 March 1959, Gretna Green; [p.] George Watson, Marion Watson; [m.] Nigel Wright, 14 August 1993; [ch.] Patricia, Charlotte, Sophie, Deborah; [ed.] Morton Secondary School; [occ.] Housewife; [pers.] I'm an ordinary housewife, but I found out, there's no such thing. As an ordinary person every body's special to someone, somewhere.; [a.] Chertsey, Surrey

WRIGHT, JESSICA
[oth. writ.] 2 books. One entitled, The Wealth Of Life And Spiritual Knowledge, and number 2 book entitled, Where Has Our World Gone. Also five volumes of Inspiration Poetry, plus new book entitled A Child's Prayer.; [pers.] In my writings I aim to let people be closer to God, and to feel the true love of His work for us all, now and forever.; [a.] Blackpool, Lancs

WRIGHT, R. D.
[p.] U. G. Burnett; [m.] 1961; [ch.] Six; [ed.] Primary School; [occ.] Ret. NA/Nurse; [oth. writ.] O. O. Wright (B) Jan. 1961 London, J. C. Wright (B) 28 June London, J. W. Wright (B) 16 Sept. 1964 London, Patsy and Precious (twins) B. Oct. 1995 Swindon, P. J. Wright (B) Aug. 1997, Swindon; [pers.] I was a nurse for Swindon Health Authority for 14 yrs. before, I worked for, Brent health authority in the London Borough. Those nursing days I did enjoyed.; [a.] Swindon, Wiltshire

WYNDER, SUZETTE VAILLIA
[b.] 11 August 1951, Pennsylvania; [p.] George James Schmidbauer (father), Assunta Peruzzi-Schmidbauer (mother); [m.] Don Wynder; [ch.] Georgina, Deana, Justin, Vaughn, Paul and Victoria; [ed.] Neshaminy High, Pennsylvania, USA; [hon.] International Academy of Lymphology; [pers.] Only a freed spirit can break the shackles of yesterday and open the doors of tomorrow.; [a.] Sudbury, Suffolk

WYNTER, TRICIA
[b.] 13 April 1972, London; [p.] Mable Harper - guardian; [ed.] Wembley High School East Lane - HAO, G.C.S.E. English, Art, Music, Science and Child-Development; [occ.] Catering Assistant; [memb.] I will be a member very shortly to The Writers Club, P.O. Box 269 - Redhill RH1 6BR; [hon.] R.S.A. - National Vocational Qualification Computer Cause Level (2) (Information Technology); [oth. writ.] I have done a lot of poems, which are of my inner feelings. I haven't get anything published yet, but I am working on it!; [pers.] My writing is directed towards reality experiences, that occur in everyday life. Not of just my own experiences, but also to my surroundings.; [a.] London

YARWOOD, ELIZABETH DELLA
[b.] 8 September 1940, Lanelley, S Wales; [p.] Ronald and Della Binning; [m.] David Yarwood, 11 July 1959; [ch.] Three sons, four grandchildren; [ed.] St. Winifriades Convent Swansea and Swansea College of Art; [occ.] Housewife and Artist; [memb.] Hereford, Conservation group; [hon.] An a Level in Art; [pers.] I live in a lonely cottage in the hereford countryside with my husband David my cocker Spaniel Nicky and our Cat 'Merlin' who inspired the poem.; [a.] Hereford, Herefordshire

YATES, JULIE MARIE
[b.] 20 July 1965, Davyhulme; [p.] James Yates, Blanche Yates; [m.] Martin John Bowyer (Partner); [ch.] Steven, Amy, Jenny, Joanathan Bowyer; [ed.] Saint Pauls Secondary School, G. Hare School of Dancing; [occ.] Dancing Teacher; [memb.] I.D.T.A. Association; [hon.] Dramatic Ability; [pers.] A once in a lifetime achievement for my family to look back on.; [a.] Urmston, Manchester

YATES, KEVIN
[pen.] The Body; [b.] 25 September 1968, Banbury; [p.] Derek Yates, Maureen Yates; [ed.] Drayton Secondary School Banbury, Oxon; [occ.] Senior Technician British Telecom; [pers.] I hope to influence younger past early works and that real people can relate to my own writings.; [a.] Banbury, Oxon

YEARSLEY, JULIA
[b.] 24 March 1937, England; [p.] Edward and Sheila Whitley; [m.] Karl Yearsley, 1964; [ch.] Tana, Ross; [ed.] Adcote School Art School; [occ.] Artist - exhibit at local galleries mixed media - animals; [oth. writ.] 6 Self published illustrated books of children's poetry.; [pers.] Trying to make a contribution by my writing to threatened Flora and Fauna.; [a.] Whitianga, New Zealand

YEOMANS, MRS. KAYE
[b.] 7 May 1940, Preston; [p.] Hilda and Charles Edmonds; [m.] Albert Leslie Yeomans, 16 June 1967; [ch.] Claire Susannah and Jason Leslie; [ed.] Larkhall Junior and Primary Schools and Bath Diocesan Girls School; [occ.] Government employee; [memb.] Various Luncheon/Lecture Clubs and University of the 3rd Age and Friend of Bath Theatre Royal; [hon.] Awards - 'Pitman' Typewriting Certificates and Shorthand Certificates 'Mid-Somerset' Festival Certificates for singing, 'Trinity' College Certificates for Theory of Music, 'Trinity' College Certificates for Pianoforte; [oth. writ.] School magazines and Letters in newspapers, etc.; [pers.] Discipline is an essential quality to our every day lives and helps us to sort problems. Regarding another quality, compassion, we must look after and protect the environment, birds animals and all living things for future generations.; [a.] Bath, North East Somerset

YIANNI, JOANNA
[b.] 10 March 1979, London; [p.] George and Afroditti Yiannj; [ed.] Queen Elizabeth's Girls School - Barnet Oaklands College, Borehamwood; [occ.] Student; [hon.] 5 GCSES and an A-Level in modern Greek. Taking Psychology, English Literature and Media Studies A-Levels in 1998; [oth. writ.] I have five of my poems published in anthologies by different agencies such as Anchor Books, Triumph House and Poetry Now.; [pers.] I have an intense passion for poetry, therefore I hope to convey my love for poetry to others in my work so they can understand my heart too.; [a.] London

YOUNG, CAROL
[b.] 21 April 1960, Leeds; [p.] Ronnie Jones and Doreen Jones; [ch.] Lee, Lindsey, Amanda and Luke; [ed.] West Leeds Girls High; [occ.] Pre-School Supervisor and Registered Child Minder; [oth. writ.] Up until now I have never sent any poems for competitions or publication but I have written poems for family and friends.; [pers.] I have worked with children for many years and also have four children of my own so the majority of my poems are about children and their antics.; [a.] Leeds, Yorkshire

YOUNG, DAPHNE WINIFRED
[b.] 15 February 1924, Freemantle, Western Australia; [p.] John William Hinson (Deceased), Bertha Hinson; [m.] Clifford Young (Deceased), 30 June 1945; [ch.] Clifford Douglas Young and Trevor John Young; [ed.] South Terrace School Freementle, Western Australia; [occ.] Housewife, Part Time Cleaner; [oth. writ.] What can't say Ef man could only pray for the children for the world.

YOUNG, DAWN
[pen.] Gabbey Copperstone; [b.] 16 March 1957, Bristol; [ch.] Micah, Stephen David, Rhyanna; [ed.] Southville Secondary but just returned to College South Bristol; [occ.] Mother; [pers.] My poems are statements on ordinary situations that people can relate to but are unable to express.; [a.] Bristol

YOUNG, KATHLEEN
[pen.] Malcolm Young; [b.] 2 April 1946, Salford; [p.] Albert, Violet; [m.] Kathleen; [ch.] Jane and Steven; [ed.] Trafford Rd Boy's School Salford; [occ.] Company Director; [pers.] I have written this poem to put on paper. How I personally feel about the world around me.; [a.] Radcliffe, Lancashire

YOUNG, STEPHEN
[m.] Brigitte Morellet of Le Verger, Busserolles, 28 May 1994; [pers.] As a token of love for Brigitte I try to echo her joie de vivre, and turn again to life. Having touched the lives of those who knew and loved her, she lives on in our thoughts and deeds.

ZAHAN, NASRIN
[pen.] Nasrin-Binte-Mohammad; [b.] 12 January 1997, Barisal; [p.] late Nur Mohammad Haolader and Renuara Begum; [ed.] B.Sc. Botany, Zoology, Psychology 1995. National University, Bangladesh. Currently studying M.Sc. in Zoology at N.U.B.; [occ.] university student; [oth. writ.] poems, novels. poem name: "Desh Mata" (Mother Land) published in Youth Society Magazine, Bangladesh.; [pers.] I write poems to reflect the reality of life.; [a.] Dhaka, Bangladesh.

ZUCKERMAN, NOMI
[b.] 22 July 1920, USA; [p.] Baruch and Nina Zuckerman; [ed.] 1945 BFA and BSC in Ed. Temple U. Philadelphia, USA, 1970 M.Ed. Temple U. Philadelphia and Rome, Italy; [occ.] Retired Artist, writer and translator; [memb.] 1946 to date Israel Ass. of University Women-various positions in Branch and National Board - 1962 to date INSEA (International Society of Education Through Art), 1969-75 Member of World Council of INSEA, 1962 Soroptimist International Positions in Branch and National Board, 1980 Voices Israel Group of Poets in English; [hon.] Various International, Prizes and Awards, the most recent judged by Danny Abse Publication of poems in US and Israeli magazines; [a.] Jerusalem, Israel

ZURLINDEN, HELEN
[pen.] Anna Zurlinden; [b.] Canton Aargau, Switzerland; [p.] Fritz Wespi, Helen Gertrude Wespi; [m.] Widowed in 1992; [ch.] Merryl, Shirley, Brenda, Brian; [ed.] Ursuline Convent in London Finishing School in Switzerland; [occ.] Retired. Attend Higher Education Colleges and Summer Schools; [memb.] Association of Historians, Welsh Academy, London Region Arts club connected with Open university.; [hon.] BA (Hons) Art History and Literature (English and European) Honours Art Certificate - Royal Drawing Society.; [oth. writ.] Articles in Parish magazine of Benedictine Church and Monastery of Christ the King, London. Have submitted poems to Welsh Academy.; [pers.] I strive to reflect in my writing my country of origin, Switzerland, and the attitude of people to care about and protect the land and flora and fauna. These characteristics are inherent in the Swiss. However I am content to live in London which offers so much. Poets with whom I feel a special affinity are Blake, Byron, Keats, Tennyson and Gerard Manley Hopkins.; [a.] London

Index
of
Poets